MW01514589

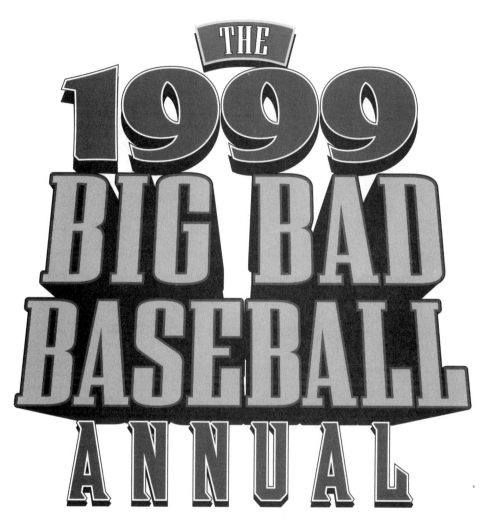

The 1999 BIG BAD BASEBALL ANNUAL

The Book Baseball Deserves

DON MALCOLM, BROCK J. HANKE, KEN ADAMS, AND G. JAY WALKER

FEATURING: SEAN FORMAN, DOUG DRINEN, TOM AUSTIN

MASTERS PRESS

NTC/Contemporary Publishing Group

Dedicated to the memory of two exemplary baseball men:
Dan Quisenberry and Ralph Horton

Cover design by Todd Petersen
Interior design by Mary-Anne King

Published by Masters Press
A division of NTC/Contemporary Publishing Group, Inc.
4255 West Touhy Avenue, Lincolnwood (Chicago), Illinois 60646-1975 U.S.A.
Copyright © 1999 by Don Malcolm
**All rights reserved. No part of this book may be reproduced, stored in a retrieval
system, or transmitted in any form or by any means, electronic, mechanical,
photocopying, recording, or otherwise, without the prior permission of
NTC/Contemporary Publishing Group, Inc.**
Printed in the United States of America
International Standard Book Number: 0-8092-2655-3
99 00 01 02 03 04 CU 19 18 17 16 15 14 13 12 11 10 9 8 7 6 5 4 3 2 1

CROSSING THE RUBICON:

A Conversation Between Don Malcolm and Brock J. Hanke

[EDITOR's NOTE: In the latter stages of development of BBBA 99, primary co-authors Don Malcolm (DM) and Brock J. Hanke (BJH) got together to discuss the current status of sabermetric methods, and other related topics. As usual, they got a little rambunctious. We join them in mid-conversation. . .]

BJH: Instead of a Socratic dialogue—

DM: Let's give 'em a knock-down drag-out FIGHT!!! (laughter)

BJH: (mock contentious tone) Take your best shot, big guy.

DM: How did we get into this, anyway?

BJH: You mean following in the footsteps of a leg end, right? Not how we ended up in the Matterhorn pool at Disneylan... *[editor's note: reference to Angels team essay, 1992 Baseball Sabermetric]*

DM: You've never forgiven me for writing that one, have you?

BJH: No, no, I liked it. But I think our audience went south on us. They fell overboard.

DM: Into the drowning pool of sabermetrics.

BJH: Yeah, ten long years of being underwater. That's what happened when Bill [James] decided to climb out of the pool. Now he's back, and the waters have been muddied up but good.

DM: Where would you like to begin?

BJH: At the end. We've got a new method, it takes the place of Runs Created, and it snaps back into the framework designed for this book back in 1988.

DM: So you don't think that the field has really changed much since then.

BJH: Not in any major way, no. That's because it's been mostly confined to its original precepts, and the tiny cults that have been trying to build on it were mostly re-inventing the wheel.

DM: What about trying to move these tools closer to the individual game level—the area where sabermetrics meets its brick wall?

BJH: Well, that's your dream, Don. And though I know that some may call you a dreamer, I also know that you're not the only one. [editor's note: smart-aleck reference to John Lennon's "Imagine"] And with the help of guys like Tom Ruane, you might just get there.

DM: OK, enough foreplay. Do you think we need to have a new run estimation tool to replace Runs Created?
Especially in light of Bill's recent changes to it?

BJH: Dammit, Malcolm, you know I want to dodge this one.

DM: And you know I'm not going to let you.

BJH: (sighs) Yeah. The answer is—yes, we do. What Bill has done is create a fine method that he then twists up with the addition of some new bells and whistles that look to be uncharacteristically arbitrary.

DM: I agree. (Hanke lets out an audible gasp.) But don't let it go to your head. (laughter) I'd say that it's a very inorganic method, and one that would be very hard to follow at home unless you were a card-carrying member of the sabermetric cargo cult. And notice that my finger is pointed at you, Dev, not me, when I say this.

BJH: Oh, no. You're not weaseling out of this one! (grabs Malcolm by the collar and shakes him) You're implicated! IMPLICATED!!!

continued on page 6

THE 1999 BIG BAD BASEBALL ANNUAL

TABLE OF CONTENTS

CROSSING THE RUBICON:

A Conversation Between Don Malcolm and Brock J. Hanke

continued from page 3

DM: OK, OK!! I was kidding when I said let's give 'em a fight, for Crissakes!!

BJH: All right, I'm calmed down now. Throttling you has a strangely soothing effect. But you're right, actually. Bill has clearly deviated from his position of sharing how his methods work. And your term for it—inorganic—is pretty much on the mark.

DM: It's almost as if he were more concerned with getting out new product than providing enlightenment.

BJH: That's probably a bit harsh, but I, too, am troubled by his movement away from open methods and research. My understanding is that Bill tried to shop those new books to every major sports publisher around, and was turned down by all of them.

DM: That shows how the market has constricted.

BJH: Sure. Macmillan has eighty-sixed the Baseball Encyclopedia, and Total Sports is spun off from major publishers and distributing its own books. It's a whole new world of increasingly direct competition, and it makes my throttling of you just a minute ago look like a gentle caress.

DM: That makes for a lot of repackaging, and in a sense Bill's latest Runs Created is nothing more than the New Coke, except that Bill Cosby hasn't been trotted out in a nationwide ad campaign to cram it down our throats.

BJH: The New Coke fizzled, and I think that the new RC will fizzle, too, in a sense, because it won't be possible for the people who care about such things to recreate it for themselves.

DM: Of course, what many in the field seem to be banking on is that the "dumbing down" trend that cropped up in the eighties and has been transformed into a mega-trend in the nineties will continue to prevail.

BJH: I don't see that going away for awhile, because I think people are going to want to draw in the reins on the amount of information that is readily available. Making the Internet into a commercial success is really just a new way, ultimately, to control the flow of information.

DM: Interesting, but let's not get too far afield. You've looked over the methods. What's your reaction to Bill's new RC versus, say, our Extrapolated Runs replacement for RC?

BJH: Well, it's not a particularly well-kept secret that the old RC had some glitches in it. We've covered a lot of that ground elsewhere in BBBA already, and based on what you tell me, Jay [Walker] and [Jim] Furtado are going to walk us through it one more time. The fact is that a linear method like Paul Johnson's does eliminate a lot of the top-end distortion from RC. The new method [Extrapolated Runs, or XR for short] further improves on Johnson's approach, and that's a worthwhile refinement.

Of course, I think there's going to be room for both methods, and while I hope that ours gets a lot of airplay, I doubt that Bill is going to bother to write about it with the same, uh—

DM: —same "generosity of spirit"??

BJH: Exactly. This really isn't a return to sabermetrics for Bill. There's no dialogue, or even an implied one.

DM: I was interested in the notion you put forth in an earlier conversation about the two versions of RC asking essentially different questions.

BJH: Interested in it, but as I recall you didn't agree with it.

DM: You don't have to convince me, it's the readers out there I'm giving you a chance with.

BJH: Well, when you put it that way. [in mock salesman voice] "Friends, there are two questions that RC can try to answer: the MVP Question and the Hall of Fame Question. The old RC tried to answer the Hall of Fame Question; the new RC is tilted toward the MVP Question. Which one you want to use depends upon which question you're trying to answer."
Still don't buy it, do you?

DM: No, because I don't think the questions are really all that removed from one another. And I don't see how any run estimation method is geared toward the long haul more than it is toward a single season.

BJH: So adding in a team context doesn't strike you as asking a fundamentally different question?

DM: Different, yes. But not fundamentally different. Correcting a bias isn't a paradigm shift. We're

continued on page 464

INTRODUCTION

SECTION ONE

THIS IS THE TALE OF OUR CASTAWAYS...

Inside the Book Baseball Deserves

DON MALCOLM

Baseball is a vast subject, and if you're reading these pages, you've probably been aware of that for some time. With thirty teams in the major leagues, the sheer amount of information that needs to be disseminated has reached critical mass. You are hereby forewarned: there is a lot of data and information contained herein--a good bit of which is available nowhere else.

What we do here at the Big Bad Baseball Annual is far more idiosyncratic than elsewhere. Rather than ask the same questions over and over again--as so often happens in a book like the STATS Baseball Scoreboard--or attempt to fashion a revisionist myth around the tools and precepts of so-called "advanced baseball analysis"--as so often mars the work of other baseball annuals, here at BBBA our writers develop new tools and actively question the old ones.

And that's one reason why we have "crossed the Rubicon" and developed a better alternative to the classic run estimation methods which have defined the field of "sabermetrics" for the past twenty years. The result of these efforts can be found in Section Six, where the most comprehensive presentation of the methods and issues to date can be found.

For many of you, however, such matters are not of paramount importance. That's why BBBA does more than simply throw a lot of numbers at you. As noted, baseball is a vast subject, and the aesthetic, human interest, and economic elements of the game are all deserving of a page count equivalent to the overall size of this book. We'd love to cover all of these elements in the same depth as we do for players and teams, but if we did so, the name of this book would have to be changed to The Big Bad Baseball Yellow Pages.

Let's take a quick tour of the contents of this year's book, during which I'll introduce the growing cast of characters who inhabit these pages. We're sorry not to have Gerry Myerson or David Nemec with us this year; we look forward to their return to these pages in BBBA 2000.

Starting at the beginning:

SECTION I--INTRODUCTION

If this book had one of those "You Are Here" diagrams, you'd be looking at it now. Rest easy, pardner, even that visual aid will not guarantee safe passage here. Before leaving this section, I hope you'll wade through "Stats to Die For (And Live With)", which provides an overview of the precepts in this book and introduces the major data formats provided with the team essays (found in section four).

SECTION II--AFTER THE FACTS

Our short-feature section is divided into three parts this year, with "Numbers Unnumbed" leading off with David Grabiner's look at the 1998 Yankees. David's "Frequently Asked Questions About the Strike" appeared in BBBA 95, and is still the definitive source for information concerning that labor dispute. Next is my look at "The Changing Face of Competition," which tries to dispel several myths about the issue of competitive balance. After that, David Grabiner does a masterful job in interpreting "Mixed Signals," and sorts out the near-term future of baseball in the wake of an historic, heavily-hyped 1998. Sean Lahman and I live up to the title of this subsection in "By God, It's ByCount, Too!", which revisits our unique, exclusive look at the pitcher/batter match-up.

Part two, "Blasts From the Past," is new, and in it we take a quick look back at some noteworthy occurrences from baseball yesteryear. In "1949", I pay homage to one of baseball's greatest seasons from a variety of perspectives. Ron Johnson then hones in on one of the greatest hitting performances in the last fifty years, "George Brett's White-Hot Summer" of 1980. If you've not seen the full-blown BBBA table and chart approach before, you'll get acquainted with it here (and, as you see, there's a lot more where that came from!).

The third and final subsection, "Other Voices, Other Places," is a far-flung potpourri of human interest stories ranging from homage to humor. First is Heather Henderson's tribute to the late Dan Quisenberry, which features a selection of the great Royals closer's poetry. We are especially thankful to Heather for all her efforts in developing this very special article.

Next, Jay Walker re-examines the ever-timely Pete Rose situation in "Give Pete A Break," a pungent look at Pete and the Hall of Fame. He's followed by two provocative examinations of Japanese baseball and culture: the first, "Mr. Giant," is supplied by new correpondent Mike Patrick, and examines the strange hold of the Yomiuri Giants on Japanese baseball and culture. Long-time contributor Jim Allen follows with "Dodging the Draft," a look at Japan's odd player draft and its (literally) fatal consequences.

We conclude with a trio of pieces from writers who have come to us via the Internet. The Usenet newsgroup rec.sport.baseball is one of the Internet's most literate and opinionated, and possesses an abundance of talented writers and historians. Home to both statistical presentations and off-beat humor, r.s.bb (as it's often abbreviated) is a truly unique meeting place, and we are honored to have some of its best talent here with us.

Randy St.Loup's "Virtual Hall of Fame" is one of the more intriguing attempts at using an informed fan base to recreate a hypothetical Cooperstown: you can examine this in-process effort here.

Humor is the focus of our final two selections. A unique talent is profiled in "Jeff Drummond's Greatest Hits": our resident wild man C.O. Jones provides a road map for Jeff's wide-ranging surrealist humor, all of which was first made available at r.s.bb. And revisiting the scene of his 1998 literary "crime and punishment" is deadpan Tom Austin, who takes us back to all this (and heaven, too!) in "The Old GM and the Sea." Never have so many been this sardonic per celestial square mile...

SECTTION III–GENERAL ESSAYS

There's no doubt that this is the strongest group of essays we've been privileged to present. I have seen the future of the new baseball historical analysis, and his name is Tom Ruane. Tom's "Empire Building in the First and Second Expansion Eras" is excerpted from a forthcoming book that examines the history of talent development in major league baseball, and it's an amazing synthesis of history and analysis.

Next, Charlie Saeger provides us with a roadmap for an entirely revised look at defensive proficiency in "Ready For The Defense." Charlie uses the defensive data from the 1941 American League to frame his "context-adjusted" method, which is a strong candidate to become BBBA's revamped defensive evaluation tool in the future.

Thanks to David Smith and Retrosheet, we're proud to take a detailed look at one of the game's epic figures in "Deconstructing Jackie Robinson." Thanks to Retrosheet's efforts, it may soon be possible to look at the complete careers of many other great players from the past. (Ron Johnson's look at new Hall of Famer George Brett's 1980 campaign is also courtesy of Retrosheet's efforts.) Charts and data are, of course, here in the typical BBBA profusion. Thanks again, Dave.

Up next is Doug Drinen's magisterial look at relief pitching ("The ABCs of Relief, Part Deux"). Last year in these pages, Doug presented a new method for evaluating relief pitcher performance--Win Probability Added (WPA). This year, Doug reports on a full season's worth of data that he collected, and the results are revelatory. You will never look at relief pitching in the same way.

And a similar statement can be made for starting pitching as treated in "QMAX To The Max," our third annual application of the Quality Matrix (QMAX) to the start-by-start performances of pitchers in both leagues. The fruits of our ongoing historical reconstruction of starting pitcher performance (spearheaded by the yeoman efforts of Sean Lahman--a big thanks to you, Sean) are represented in Tom Austin's engaging coda, "QMAX Presents: Bad Pitchers", which kicks off a feature that you'll find accompanying each and every team essay in section four.

Sixth in the general essay lineup is Ken Adams' "Inside Straight," which re-examines the evolutionary arguments of Stephen Jay Gould in his engaging book Full House. Gould used batting average as a way of measuring the "natural selection" inherent in all complex systems; Ken argues that batting average is not the standard of value that should be applied, and

replicates Professor Gould's work using more encompassing statistical measures.

Finally, my long-time colleague Tom Hull revamps his percentile ranking system and applies it to a series of interesting issues in "Percentiles: Past, Present and Future." This is a flat-out terrific method for getting a quick read on hitter performance that bypasses most of the difficulties inherent in cross-era comparisons, and you'll find it applied in several other places in the book, most notably in the player comments (section five).

SECTION IV–TEAM ESSAYS

As always, BBBA gives you a unique look at each and every major league team, accompanied by our exclusive data and charts:

--20-game run charts
--In-depth team breakouts
--Doug Drinen's WPA Bullpen Boxes
--Sean Forman's Prospectwatch
--Tom Austin's "QMAX Presents: Bad Pitchers"

You'll find a more detailed description of the first three items in our introduction to section four. Sean Forman also provides an introduction for his exhaustive look at young players.

A terrfic influx of new writing talent can be found in this year's section four. In addition to long-time collaborators Brock J. Hanke, Ken Adams, and Jay Walker, the team essay section has benefitted from the work of Sean Forman, Doug Drinen, Sean Lahman, Jim Furtado and Tom Austin. Just as important, however, is the addition of terrific local correspondents in various cities: Toronto (Stephen Tomlinson), Montreal (Ron Johnson and Scot Hughes), Seattle (Dave Paisley), and Minnesota (Jeff Drummond).

And, last but most, we're honored to have baseball's best beat writer, the Providence Journal-Bulletin's Art Martone, back with us to cover the Boston Red Sox.

Those of you who enjoyed Ken Adams' "Tales of Psycho" in BBBA 98 will be pleased to know that there's more Psycho interspersed throughout the team essay section. There are five installments this time: they can be found as segments in the Orioles, Tigers, Athletics, Mets and Brewers team essays.

SECTION V–PLAYER RANKINGS AND COMMENTS

Former BBBA editor Brock J. Hanke comes to the fore here, anchoring our wide-ranging and colorful commentary on more than 800 major league players. Brock's effort is beyond heroic, as he provides a framework for the rest of us, who only have to write about a small fraction of player. You'll find positional rankings, supplementary fielding statistics, and a whole lot more.

This year's player comments section is ordered by league and position:

AL: C, 1B, 2B, 3B, SS, LF, CF, RF, DH, relief pitchers, starting pitchers

NL: starting pitchers, relief pitchers, C, 1B, 2B, 3B, SS, LF, CF, RF

Kudos are also due to Doug Drinen for his yeoman work in the relief pitcher section. What's unique about BBBA's player comments, however, is a multiplicity of voices. We do not fear to disagree, and make those disagreements public knowledge.

SECTION VI–CROSSING THE RUBICON

BBBA's new Extrapolated Runs measure (henceforth referred to by its abbreviation, XR), which replaces Bill James' Runs Created as our run estimation tool of choice, is presented and placed into historical perspective by Jay Walker and Jim Furtado. As noted above, Crossing the Rubicon is the most exhaustive, comprehensive treatment of run estimation methods to appear anywhere, and will likely remain the standard in the field for many years to come. Jay and Jim worked hard to get both the big picture and the tiny details in sync, and we're proud to implement their method as part of BBBA.

Next year, Jim will use XR as the basis for developing a comprehensive 1990s player compendium which will appear in BBBA 2000. We can hardly wait.

SECTION VII–OTHER EARTHLY DELIGHTS

Here you will find a brief miscellany of materials which function as a shameless plug for the Big Bad Baseball Annual web site (http://www.backatcha.com). We hope you'll visit us during 1999, as we'll have a series of interesting materials in our premium area called BBBA Plus.

SPECIAL THANKS...

...go, as usual, to my very significant other, Louise Cook, for living through the chaotic, combative, and cacaphonic process that is BBBA.

And, as always, to book designer Mary-Anne King, for managing to capture a fast-moving target and creating a bulls-eye on the page despite all of the mayhem inherent in the process.

A very big thank you to Sean Forman, for his astonishing skills in developing data manipulation tools that effortlessly keep pace with just about every crazy idea that the BBBA team comes up with.

And to Jay Walker and Jim Furtado, for giving BBBA a truly independent voice in the world of baseball analysis.

And to Ken Samelson and Julia Anderson at Contemporary Books, for holding their breath.

And to the many contributors at rec.sport.baseball, whose informed companionship has rubbed off on our efforts here in countless ways.

STATS TO DIE FOR (AND LIVE WITH)

There's a glut of statistics being generated in the closing days of the fin de siecle; which ones should you pay attention to in the twenty-first century? BBBA has some answers, and introduces its new displays for hitter and pitcher data

Don Malcolm

INTRODUCTION

We might as well blame it on the Bossa Nova. In 1979, Bill James coined a statistic called Runs Created, and the floodgates opened. In the twenty years since then, there have been countless new stats developed in a blizzard of energy that can't help but remind you of the frenetic dance crazes of the early-to-mid sixties, when there was a new one every fortnight.

As you read this book, ten years after it took over for Bill (ten years after he introduced Runs Created), you will be virtually assaulted with statistics. Some of you will not have heard of any of them, which is mostly due to the media's unwillingness to assume that you are intelligent enough to grasp anything other than what is spoon-fed. If you're the inquisitive type, however, you may be quite familiar with some of what follows. If not, don't worry—despite our reputation, we'll be gentle.

My job here is to set out what statistics you should pay attention to as we move into the next century. There are a lot of voices out there in the bulrushes who've pumped up the volume with respect to this issue; each one seems to fancy himself a baby Moses, ordained by fate (and a vividly ambitious imagination) to return from the mountain with a set of tablets.

In short, the tug of war in the field has reached a new phase of frenetic activity that has all the earmarkings of St. Vitus' greatest hits. The effort to refine and re-cast the work of Bill James has been going on for most of the 1990s. Unresolved problems within his original Runs Created formulation have created a cottage industry that finally achieved sufficient critical mass (in both senses of that term) to bring Bill out of "retirement" last year; in his weightiest effort to date, Bill has revamp Runs Created in a manner that attempts to close the door on the field as one of ongoing inquiry.

A great deal of this year's book will deal with the ramifications of those efforts, and how they have not become the new set of tablets in the field. Most of that discussion can be found in Section Six, which is where we "banish" our more "advanced," technically-oriented essays. Here at BBBA, we've arrived at the Rubicon, and we have crossed it: after careful consideration, we've decided that there is a better way. Thanks to the efforts of G. Jay Walker, Jim Furtado, Brock J. Hanke, and a small army of peers, we're introducing a new and improved variant to Runs Created. It is the most accurate rendering of what we've taken to calling "run estimation " that can currently be found in the field. We call it Extrapolated Runs, or XR for short.

But before we delve further into XR (a suite of articles devoted to "run estimation" and hitter evaluation issues in general, and XR in particular, can be found in Section Six), we think it's both relevant and appropriate that we revisit the traditional statistical foundation of the game. Bill James covered this issue in the 1987 Baseball Abstract, and a dozen years later it's a topic whose time has come again.

REVISITING THE WOMB

Bill James' article "Meaningful and Meaningless Statistics" (1987 Baseball Abstract, pp. 9-27) was meant at the time to be a summation of what had been discovered and argued during the so-called "revolutionary phase" of advanced baseball analysis (1978-86). It didn't take long for the tenuous connection between Bill's approach and the interest/attention span of the mainstream audience (aka the media) to shrivel.

Once that happened, the field went underground, as Bill's idea for a research arm, Project Scoresheet, splintered into two entities, one of which was rechristened STATS, Inc. and found a niche in the expanding sports information market. The advanced analytical component of Bill's work was "dumbed down" (a phrase that has tremendous resonance for the entire decade of the 90s) and de-emphasized. It was left to the inheritors (that's us, folks: we took over the Baseball Abstract format from Bill in 1989) and the revisionists (more about them later) to try to reconnect the umbilical cord—which, in effect, had been snapped in Bill's 1987 essay.

There is a great deal of valuable context in "Meaningful and Meaningless Statistics," but the end result of the essay was clearly dissatisfying to most of those who've tried to follow in Bill's footsteps. Bill does little to integrate his own work into the world of statistics, choosing to rank only traditional (or, at best, neo-traditional) stats. His list of the ten most meaningful stats has not worn well with the passage of time, because the list doesn't tackle the relationships between the stats. It was also a mistake not to create separate ranking lists for the different areas of the game (hitting, pitching, fielding) measured by statistics; this would have permitted Bill to have shown that the same measures work equally well whether looking at hitting or pitching——a topic that is completely avoided. Lamentably, the entire essay reads like a rehearsal for the "dumbing down" that has proceeded apace in recent years.

For sake of reference, here is Bill's list:

1	Earned Run Average (ERA);
2	On-Base Percentage (OBP);
3	Total Bases/Slugging Percentage (TB/SLG);
4	Batting Average (BA);
5	Home Runs (HR);
6	Pitcher's Walks (BB);
7	Saves (SV);
8	Batter's Walks (BB);
9	Runs Batted In (RBI);
10	Runs Scored (R)

You can see that the list, which certainly contains many important stats, isn't focused around the notion of furthering understanding by synthesizing commonly-known data with more advanced concepts. It had a more complex agenda, part of which was to ensure Bill James' crossover into a more mainstream position within the baseball publishing world. It was a canny move on his part, but it turned the field of sabermetrics into the equivalent of a "blue baby." For more than a decade, the field——ripped prematurely from its womb——has been surviving in an incubator. And now it's time to revisit the womb, to recapture and redirect the original moment of conception and inspiration, and to give the baby its fullest chance to survive and grow into a fully-realized maturity.

The major advances in understanding that stem from Bill's work were inherited (as the revisionists are quick to point out) from efforts spearheaded in the early 50s by Branch Rickey and statistician Allan Roth. These efforts were almost exclusively confined to the realm of offense, and to this day the primary focus of advanced baseball analysis revolves around this area. To provide a more useful overview, we need to start with a diagram that puts traditional statistics and the more advanced concepts into the same continuum:Most everyone is well-acquainted with the three basic stats, and all of the component stats listed at the left. For purposes of reading the diagram, keep in mind that the component stats (Components) are used to derive a formula (Derived) which is divided by another measure (the "/" column) to produce the value stat (Stat). In the case of BA, it's about as simple as it can be: H/AB. For OBP and SLG, things are a little more complicated, but not insurmountably so.

What Bill James did was coin a term to represent run estimation using a somewhat more complicated relationship between the basic stats. The actual basic Runs Created (RC) formula is (H+BB)*(TB)/PA, but as you'll see, this is really equivalent to OBP*SLG. The later version of the formulas (and there are now enough of them to fill a volunteer army) incorporated stolen bases (as shown in RC2, the most rudimentary of his enhancements).

This has spawned a virtual cottage industry of tinkerers who have attempted to refine the method and reduce the discrepancies between the RC value and the actual team runs scored total. The most formidable alternative to the RC formulation, as we'll discuss in more detail a bit later, is the Linear Weight Runs (LWR) method devised by Pete Palmer, which

Components							Derived	/	Stat
BASIC STATS									
H								AB	**BA**
H						BB	H + BB	PA	**OBP**
H	D	T	HR				TB (H + D + 2*T+3*HR)	AB	**SLG**
JAMES' MEASURES									
H	D	T	HR			BB	OBP*SLG	PA	**RC**
H	D	T	HR	SB	CS	BB	OBP*SLG	PA	**RC2**
H	D	T	HR				TB-H	AB	**ISO**
H	D	T	HR	SB	CS	BB	(TB +SB)-(H+CS)+BB	AB	**SECA**
OTHER MEASURES									
H	D	T	HR	SB	CS	BB	weighted elements		**LWR**
H	D	T	HR			BB	OBP+SLG		**OPS**
H	D	T	HR	SB	CS	BB	OBP+SLG	3	**QEQA**
H	D	T	HR	SB	CS	BB	refined weighted elements		**XR**

forms the basis for a suite of other measures that are well-known to those who own one or more editions of the post-modern baseball encyclopedia Total Baseball.

Sticking with RC for the time being, however, we see that it represents a single numerical summary of the value of a players' performance expressed in runs. James later developed a way of representing this figure in terms of an individual game, in his "RC/27" measure, which expressed how many runs per 27 outs a player with a given RC total would generate.

It was a big step forward, but it wasn't perfect, and by 1987 Bill seemed more interested in soft-pedaling these measures. He made passing reference to a linear (meaning additive) version of RC called Estimated Runs Produced (ERP, an acronym that has been singled out as the major influence on yours truly's fascination with oddly evocative abbreviations). This method, developed by Paul Johnson, had the advantage of eliminating the distortion in the RC values at the top and bottom end of the spectrum. Keep this particular variant in mind (if not the acronym), because we will be returning to it later on.

What also happened when RC became well-known to the hard-core advanced analysts (who later were christened with the term "stathead," a putdown that this rebellious subculture soon was wearing proudly, as a sort of sabermetric "gay pride" gesture) was that batting average (BA) took a precipitous plunge in perceived value. One of the major ongoing areas of contention is over the place of BA, which continues to be applied as a standard of value by the casual fan. Bill's placement of BA on his list was, in the minds of many revisionists, a crime against his own insights.

Bill's other formulations, isolated power (ISO) and secondary average (SECA), are less sweeping innovations but are probably destined to have greater staying power. ISO is one of his earliest stats, developed during the Baseball Abstract's DIY days (1977-81; the first nationally published edition of the Abstract occurred in 1982). Its value is in separating SLG from BA while keeping the relationship scale constant. Other measures, such as Eric Walker's Power Factor (PF), which divides TB by hits, give a similar sense of a player's power but abandon the scale: for example, Babe Ruth and Rob Deer have similar PFs, but their ISO is significantly different. And the value of that ISO is far more descriptive of a player's abilities than is his PF.

SECA is probably Bill's best invention. It bundles all of the elements other than singles hitting (which, when you think of it, is all that batting average measures) and calculates the value of all those elements (extra bases on D, T, and HR; BB, and net stolen bases—-SB-CS) against the player's at-bat total. As becomes clear from examining a list of SECA for various players, there is a far wider variation in this stat than in BA, OBP, or SLG. This sense of separation is a valuable one, and it provides an immediate insight into the nature of a player's offensive contributions.

There are many other statistical measures that Bill generated that pertain to offense, but these are the most significant. Most of the others can be found in BBBA's Annotated Opinionated Glossary (in Section Seven) should you care to delve further. What you should take away with you from this brief discussion is that RC was a significant advance in our way of viewing run estimation issues, though it is no longer the most accurate of the tools which attempt to measure player and team performance. That, and the fact that ISO and SECA are valuable additions to neo-traditional statistics.

In addition to Pete Palmer's Linear Weights Runs, the Total Baseball toolkit features a knockoff of RC called On-Base Plus Slugging (OPS). Bill was not high on OPS for several legitimate reasons, though he did a rather limp job of elucidating those reasons in his 1987 essay. And what has happened is that OPS has taken the lead in the 90s as the statistic to replace BA as the best quick measure of a hitter's performance.

And this has led to several attempts to generate a new BA-based measure that incorporates all of a hitter's other production value into one statistic. The one you see above, with the odd name of QEQA, is our satirical knockoff of a statistic that has been proclaimed by its creator as having all of the advantages of advanced methods like RC and LWR but with the accessibility of BA (since it has been modeled onto the scale of BA). This stat, called Equivalent Average (EQA), is in reality little more than a park and league adjusted OPS with net stolen bases added in, and then divided by 3 in order to simulate a batting average. (There is a more complex set of formulas that have been developed, most likely as a kind of ingenious window-dressing for what is otherwise a very rudimentary refinement.) Our version, QEQA (which is short for "Quick EQA," akin to instant coffee) is a nice little diversion for those who feel more comfortable with a number that looks like BA, but it's no earth-shattering revelation.

So out of this, what are we taking forward for display purposes in the category of offensive statistics? Those of you

familiar with the BBBA format know that we've presented team hitting stats in a box with the following park adjusted basic data—

AB   R   H   D   T   HR   BB   SO   Outs

and these have been accompanied by the following rate/value stats:

BA OBP SLG RC RC27 OWP OG OWAR WAR TWAR

The first five of these stats you're either familiar with already or have at least seen mentioned in passing during the above discussion. The second five are part of the value/ranking method originally developed for the first edition of this book (the 1989 Baseball Abstract) by Dr. Richard Cramer, then of STATS, Inc, and Brock J. Hanke. The first two, OWP (Offensive Winning Percentage) and OG (Offensive Games), were inherited from Bill James' early toolkit. They have always been reference points, and not primary estimators of value. The last three stats are part of the Wins Above Replacement (WAR) system that Cramer and Hanke synthesized from several other Jamesian methods. They have formed the basis of the rankings, organized by position, that are included with the player commentaries (located in Section Five).

These measures are:
Offensive Wins Above Replacement (OWAR)
Defensive Wins Above Replacement (DWAR)
Total Wins Above Replacement (TWAR)

These will change to the following:
Offensive Extrapolated Wins (OXW)
Defensive Extrapolated Wins (DXW)
Total Extrapolated Wins (TXW)

Even though we are replacing the Jamesian version of Runs Created in this year's book, we will be retaining the general WAR methodology, which has undergone some additional refinement by G. Jay Walker. The new run estimation engine for the WAR method is, as noted in the introduction, a refinement on Paul Johnson's Estimated Runs Produced (ERP) formula called Extrapolated Runs (XR), developed by Jim Furtado. We're pleased to have Jim on board this year to provide a step-by-step description of his new method. After having examined every competing methodology, we firmly believe that Jim's approach represents the best organic solution to the difficulties inherent in run estimation methods; while it doesn't eliminate all of the discrepancies, it also doesn't force-fit a set of adjustments, as does the new RC method unveiled by Bill James in the STATS All-Time Major League Handbook.

BBBA'S NEW SABERMETRIC HITTING BOX AND ANCILLARY STATISTICS DISPLAY

With Jim Furtado's XR/XW firmly in place, then, we can unveil the new Sabermetric Hitting Box that will accompa-

13

ny each team essay. (We will discuss the new displays for pitching briefly in a subsequent section.) In addition, we will preview an Ancillary Stats breakout that will make its appearance in BBBA 2000 as part of a player compendium covering the entire decade of the 1990s. In short, BBBA 2000 will contain a complete "sabermetric encyclopedia" for 1990-99.

Here is what the new Sabermetric Hitting Box will contain:

	<———						Park Adjusted Statistics								———>					
																Adj	Raw			
Name	**AB**	**R**	**H**	**D**	**T**	**HR**	**RBI**	**BB**	**SO**	**SB**	**CS**	**BA**	**OBP**	**SLG**	**XR**	**XR/27**	**XR/27**	**OXW**	**DXW**	**TXW**
Bonds	539	129	181	38	4	46	123	126	79	29	12	.336	.462	.677	156	8.83	8.91	8.67	1.06	9.73
Williams	456	135	185	33	3	37	120	145	57	2	4	.406	.549	.735	160	10	10.1	9.74	0.32	10.06
Ruth	458	158	172	36	9	54	137	148	80	14	14	.376	.528	.847	173	10.7	10.8	10.18	0.48	10.66
Greenberg	573	129	195	50	8	41	150	83	75	6	3	.340	.424	.670	145	8.31	8.39	8.06	0.23	8.29
Cobb	591	147	248	47	24	6	127	44	—	83	—	.420	.460	.611	151	8.95	9.04	8.34	0.98	9.32
Lezcano	473	84	152	29	3	28	101	77	74	4	3	.321	.416	.573	107	7.31	7.38	6.49	0.84	7.33
Mueller	619	90	212	35	8	4	71	22	17	2	3	.342	.365	.444	92	5.41	5.47	3.44	0.04	3.48

Aside from the substitution of the XR values in place of old RC as the run estimation engine, we've also restored SB and CS data so that the park-adjusted data will provide all of the most significant traditional stats. Yes, we have gone ahead and park-adjusted SB and CS; you can read more about that in Jay Walker's "Park Effects Today and Tomorrow" article in Section Six. (Just in case you're wondering, the sample seasons used here are Barry Bonds 1993; Ted Williams 1941; Babe Ruth 1920; Hank Greenberg 1940; Ty Cobb 1911; Sixto Lezcano 1979; and Don Mueller 1954.)

We've also included the adjusted and raw XR/G figures so that you'll be able to compare the values and better gauge the extent of the park effect.

And here is what the new Ancillary Statistics display, scheduled for BBBA 2000, will look like:

ANCILLARY OFFENSIVE STATISTICS

	OFFENSIVE SHAPE			SPEED/LINEUP			OTHER GENERAL			
Name	**BBP**	**ISO**	**SECA**	**XBA**	**RER**	**SpSc**	**LOI**	**OWP**	**OPS**	**QEQA**
Bonds	18.9	.341	.607	.745	0.84	6.33	.421	.893	1.139	.382
Williams	24.1	.329	.643	.666	0.98	3.44	.394	.944	1.284	.418
Ruth	24.4	.472	.795	.812	0.75	5.31	.377	.953	1.375	.444
Greenberg	12.7	.330	.480	.750	0.47	3.37	.361	.867	1.094	.361
Cobb	6.9	.191	.406	.526	1.12	7.66	.411	.850	1.071	.400
Lezcano	14.0	.252	.416	.661	0.68	4.05	.349	.783	.989	.326
Mueller	3.4	.102	.136	.400	0.38	3.09	.243	.548	.809	.269

This is a veritable smorgasbord of specialized offensive stats that provide additional context. We've organized these into three categories to link together stats which provide information about related aspects of a player's performance. These are:

Offensive Shape Those stats that look at the internal relationships of a player's offensive performance.

BBP Base On Balls Percentage or Walking Percentage

The most rudimentary measure of a player's ability to draw walks, BBP is simply BB/PA*100. Jay Walker has developed several more specialized measures for bases on balls; they will emerge in the not-too-distant future in a full-length treatment of players who walk a lot (a category of players called "Walkmen" here at BBBA).

ISO Isolated Power

Basically, SLG-BA. Bill James championed this in his early, home-grown Baseball Abstracts, and it's still an extremely useful (and simple) measure of a player's power.

SECA Secondary Average

You should be familiar with this one from the above discussion. This is the ratio of a player's offensive contributions from everything other than BA. The formula is in the "basic stats" diagram. As noted, the value of this stat is that its range is wider, and hence more expressive of a player's overall offensive contributions. A player who hits .250 with a .400 SECA is often more valuable offensively than a player who hits .300 with a .200 SECA.

XBA   Extra Base Average

A variation on isolated power; whereas ISO merely subtracts hits from total bases, XBA takes the sum of total bases from extra-base hits and divides it by total bases, as in the formula (2*D)+(3*T)+(4*HR)/TB.

Speed/Lineup Stats-These measure a player's speed and/or elements in his offensive profile that indicate what end of the batting order might be the most appropriate location for him to occupy.

SpSc   Speed Scores

A Bill James invention, modified by G. Jay Walker in 1996, which uses seven different measures to generate an estimate of a player's speed; it's also interesting when applied to teams.

RER   Run Element Ratio

The ratio between the things a hitter does which are of use early in the inning (walks and stolen bases) and those which are more useful later in the inning (power). Derived from the formula (BB+SB)/(TB-H).

LOI   Leadoff Index

Jay Walker's measure of a player's ability to perform in the leadoff slot of the lineup, which will be introduced in greater detail next year in an article with the same name. While Jay advocates using LOI solely to evaluate players whose power profiles and speed scores correspond to a certain set of criteria, we've cajoled him into calculating LOIs for all players as part of this break-out. Since players other than leadoff hitters do often lead off innings, the LOI of power hitters may well be of some interest: for example, Barry Bonds is far more effective leading off an inning than Juan Gonzalez, and this is valuable additional information.

Other General-These are other "offensive overview" stats that give you a quick read on a player's offensive achievement. OPS and QEQA were covered above; OWP stands for Offensive Winning Percentage, and estimates what the value of the player's performance would be in terms of wins and losses in the context of average league performance.

In addition to these, we will be adding a new set of defensive statistics to round out the depiction of a player's overall performance. Some of the above may change a bit as we gear up for our "1990s Player Compendium," but this is basically what you can expect as part of the millennial edition of the Book Baseball Deserves.

PITCHING STATISTICS DISPLAY

We are breaking up our pitching data into two components in 1999, breaking with our old presentation. For starters, we will provide you a team-by-team listing of data dominated by our exclusive Quality Matrix (QMAX) method. Here is a sample of what that data looks like:

Pitcher	S	C	T	SS	ES	IC	HH	PP	TJ	S12	S35	S67	C1	C23	C45	C67	QWP
Chen	4.25	4.00	8.25	.50	.00	.25	.50	.00	.00	.25	.25	.50	.00	.25	.75	.00	.383
De Martinez	5.60	3.40	9.00	.20	.00	.40	.80	.00	.20	.20	.00	.80	.20	.20	.60	.00	.328
G Maddux	2.85	2.12	4.97	.85	.35	.74	.15	.00	.09	.53	.32	.15	.44	.44	.12	.00	.711
Glavine	3.45	2.82	6.27	.61	.27	.61	.27	.09	.09	.48	.24	.27	.15	.52	.33	.00	.606
Millwood	4.14	3.28	7.41	.48	.17	.31	.31	.03	.07	.24	.45	.31	.10	.48	.38	.03	.504
Neagle	3.68	2.87	6.55	.61	.16	.61	.19	.10	.19	.39	.42	.19	.10	.68	.19	.03	.591
Smoltz	3.35	2.81	6.15	.69	.23	.54	.15	.04	.08	.46	.38	.15	.19	.58	.19	.04	.625
ATL	3.56	2.81	6.37	.64	.23	.56	.24	.05	.10	.41	.35	.24	.20	.52	.27	.02	.596

QMAX "S" measures hit prevention, the MLB average in 1998 for that stat was 4.18. QMAX "C" measures walk prevention; the MLB average in 1998 for that was 3.35. QMAX "T" is, simply, S + C. The MLB average for QMAX "T" in 1998 was 4.18 + 3.35 = 7.53. Over at the right, you see the Quality Winning Percentage (QWP), which is a probabilistic rendering of the team's chances of winning based on the location of the pitcher's starts within the matrix. At the bottom is, of course, the bottom line: a summary for all Atlanta starting pitchers. Either measure you choose (QMAX "T" or QWP),you can see that the Braves had a tremendous starting staff in 1998.

The details of the other QMAX measures and stats (all those other columns of data—SS, ES, IC, HH, PP, etc.—that add shape to the starting pitcher performance) are described in the article "QMAX to the Max," which appears in Section Three. Read that, and by the time you get to the team essays, you'll either have the hang of it or will be bringing some rope to hang us with. We think it's the most complete look at starters around. For those who would also like to see some more traditional stats, they are available with the starting pitcher comments in Section Five. You'll also find Ken Adams' QmB rankings for starters, a very easy and useful thumbnail guide to quality.

For relievers, we are providing you with a set of data culled from Doug Drinen's WPA method, which appears as a separate box in each team essay. Doug describes this data in some detail as part of his "The ABCs of Relief, Part Deux" essay, found in

Section Three. While this method is elaborate and requires some time to get used to, the results are intuitive in nature and provide a more revealing measure of a reliever's true contribution than the traditional stats. For those who desire those type of stats, we've provided a listing of those in our Relief Pitcher comments in Section Five.

THE WIND-UP

So what are the stats that you should die for and live with as we go into the next century of baseball? All of them, of course. The basic stats are sometimes attacked for not providing the most logical display of a player's contribution, but even most "statheads" realize that the basic stats are here to stay. Our picks for the stats that will give you the most bang for your buck in the 21st century are as follows (and, yes, we're being a bit immodest here):

1	Extrapolated Runs (XR);
2	On-Base Percentage (OBP);
3	Slugging Percentage (SLG)
4	Runs Scored/Runs Allowed (Pythagorean Winning Percentage);
5	Adjusted Earned Run Average (ERA+);
6	Win Probability Added (WPA) for relief pitchers;
7	On-Base Plus Slugging (OPS);
8	an upgraded Defensive Extrapolated Wins (DXW+);
9	a revised and upgraded version of the Quality Matrix (QMAX+) for starting pitchers;
10 (tied)	Secondary Average (SECA) and Batting Average (BA).

Check back with us in twenty years and we'll see how good our predictions turned out to be.

AFTER THE FACTS

SECTIONTWO

AFTER THE FACTS:

NUMBERS UNNUMBED

THE 1998 YANKEES: HOW DO THEY STACK UP AGAINST THE GREATEST?

David Grabiner

There has been considerable discussion about the 1998 Yankees as a candidate for the greatest team ever. They did set a record for the most games won, and they have the best percentage (including playoffs) since the 1927 Yankees. However, the great teams are not identified by their numbers in one year, but by the players on the teams. If the 1998 Yankees took the field against the Big Red Machine, or the 1961 Yankees, who would be the favorite?

In the 1985 Baseball Abstract, Bill James compared the 1984 Tigers to the other great teams of the expansion era, position by position, and concluded that the Tigers were comparable in quality to the other great teams. We will extend James's method and use his rankings by adding the other recognized great teams since 1984, to see how this year's Yankees stack up.

The contenders:

1961	Yankees
1967	Cardinals
1970	Orioles
1973	A's
1976	Reds
1977	Yankees
1984	Tigers
1986	Mets
1989	A's
1995	Braves
1998	Yankees

The standard of comparison is the established ability of the players at the time in question, not their stats in any one year. This is particularly important because most of these great teams were great over a period of several years but only one year is chosen for comparison; the Big Red Machine included Johnny Bench's off year in 1976, but it also won the World Series when Bench was fourth in the MVP voting in 1975 and won the pennant when Bench was MVP in 1972. Bench was the top catcher of his time, arguably the best ever, and should be ranked above catchers who happened to have better stats in one year. Likewise, Andy Pettitte had an off year in 1998, but he was an excellent pitcher in the previous two years, and thus ranks above most of the other third starters.

However, some players may have unexpected ranks because the year in question is far from their peak year; Mark McGwire in 1998 would lead the first basemen, but in 1989, he wasn't as impressive. Also note the differences in offensive levels over time; the 1967 Cardinals do not need to hit as well as the 1998 Yankees to rate highly.

Remember that these are great teams, so the standards are fairly high. The top player at most positions is a Hall of Famer at his peak, followed by several All-Stars. Average players are usually eighth or ninth, with some decent players and a few major holes at the bottom.

As Bill James did, we will keep a scorecard; in each head-to-head comparison, the better player will be credited with a win, and the worse will be credited with a loss. This will create a 150-game "season" for our comparisons. We will follow the overall standings, and the Yankees' head-to-head matchups. At each position, we will pay most attention to the proper rank of the Yankees and to the leader.

CATCHER

Bench 1976, Carter 1986, Munson 1977, Howard/Blanchard 1961, Parrish 1984, McCarver 1967, Lopez 1995, Fosse 1973, Posada/Girardi 1998, Steinbach 1989, Hendricks/Etchebarren 1970.

This shows how tough the competition is. Posada could hit, but so could the pre-injury Ray Fosse, and Fosse was a better fielder.

Bench and Carter both had off years, but they deserve to lead this position as two of the all-time great catchers.

FIRST BASE

Cepeda 1967, Hernandez 1986, Powell 1970, Perez 1976, McGwire 1989, Martinez 1998, Skowron 1961, Tenace 1973, McGriff 1995, Chambliss 1977, Evans/Garbey 1984.

Skowron and Martinez are quite comparable. Both were sluggers who hit .280 regularly and had off years in their team's big year. Martinez's slugging averages were a little higher, thanks to his 44 HR in 1997. The league difference isn't that great; the 1961 AL had a 4.02 ERA with no DH, compared to this year's 4.65 with the DH.

Cepeda was the unanimous MVP, hit .325/.403/.524 in a pitchers' park and had many other seasons at that level before 1967; then he started to have knee problems and fell off.

Hernandez could also be rated first; he wasn't as good a hitter as Cepeda, but he defined defense at the position.

SECOND BASE

Morgan 1976, Whitaker 1984, Knoblauch 1998, Johnson 1970, Randolph 1977, Lemke 1995, Phillips 1989, Backman 1986, Richardson 1961, Javier 1967, Green 1973.

Johnson won some Gold Gloves, but he couldn't hit with Knoblauch except in 1973. Lou Whitaker could; the AL ERA in 1984 was 3.99 compared to this year's 4.65, and that covers the superficial difference.

Morgan at first is a clear choice; he is arguably the best second baseman ever, and the Big Red Machine's 1975-1976 peak was in his two best years.

THIRD BASE

Nettles 1977, Robinson 1970, Bando 1973, Jones 1995, Rose 1976, Boyer 1961, Brosius 1998, Shannon 1967, Evans/Johnson 1984, Lansford 1989, Knight 1986.

Brosius has been inconsistent, but he was good this year. That puts him behind everyone who was consistently good (Boyer was a great fielder), and ahead of everyone who wasn't.

Nettles over Brooks Robinson looks surprising, but this is a comparison between Nettles at his peak and Brooks at 33. Both were great fielders, and Robinson hit much better in 1964 than Nettles did in 1977, but by 1970, he was on the way down.

SHORTSTOP

Trammell 1984, Jeter 1998, Concepcion 1976, Kubek 1961, Campaneris 1973, Belanger 1970, Blauser 1995, Dent 1977, Maxvill 1967, Gallego 1989, Santana 1986.

Jeter is quite comparable to Trammell, who hit .314/.383/.468 to Jeter's .324/.384/.481. Trammell has a slight offensive edge because of the league difference, and his performance from 1983-1988 shows that this was his level of ability. Jeter was more durable but is unproven. Also, Trammell was probably the better fielder; he won Gold Gloves in 1983-1984, and even if those weren't deserved (Ripken set a record for assists in 1984 and didn't win), it is evidence that he was seen as a top fielder.

After 1/3 of the season, the standings have taken shape, and the 1976 Reds are off to the same runaway lead that the 1984 Tigers had in their championship season.

STANDINGS AFTER FIVE POSITIONS
Big Red Machine in High Gear;
Oakland Builds Second Cellar

Year	Team	W		Lvs. 98 Yankees
1976	Reds	41	9	4-1
1970	O's	29	21	2-3
1977	Yanks	28	22	2-3
1998	Yanks	28	22	—
1984	Tigers	27	23	3-2
1961	Yanks	25	25	2-3
1995	Braves	22	28	2-3
1967	Cards	21	29	2-3
1986	Mets	21	29	2-3
1973	A's	20	30	2-3
1989	A's	13	37	1-4

LEFT FIELD

Henderson 1989, Foster 1976, Brock 1967, Rudi 1973, Klesko 1995, Buford 1970, Wilson 1986, White 1977, Herndon/Jones 1984, Berra/Lopez 1961, Curtis 1998.

The new Yanks finish last, just behind the old ones. Berra was a great player in his prime, and he could still hit; he drops to tenth because he was not valuable as a slow left fielder. Lopez, like Curtis, had an off year, and his was worse but in only 243 AB.

This is the first position topped by a recent player. Rickey deserves the top spot even if he is only given credit for the part of 1989 he played with the A's; he was the greatest lead-off hitter ever, while nobody else on the list was a candidate for the all-time greats.

And look again at the Big Red Machine: six positions, and six players on the Reds who were good Hall of Fame candidates at the time, all near their peak. Bench and Morgan are in, Rose would be in based on what he did on the field, and Perez is likely to make it although he probably shouldn't. Foster stopped hitting in 1982, and Concepcion in 1983. That team looks like it will have a serious case as the greatest team ever.

CENTER FIELD

Mantle 1961, Williams 1998, Lemon 1984, Dykstra 1986, Flood 1967, Henderson 1989, Blair 1970, Grissom 1995, Rivers 1977, North 1973, Geronimo 1976.

Williams is a clear second here; he's no Mickey Mantle, but a batting title and non-fluke MVP candidacy put him well above everyone else.

Mickey in first place needs no comment.

RIGHT FIELD

Jackson 1973, Maris 1961, Strawberry 1986, Robinson 1970, Jackson 1977, Gibson 1984, O'Neill 1998, Justice 1995, Griffey 1976, Maris/Tolan 1967, Javier 1989.

Again, the Yankees are stopped by tough company. It seems hard to put O'Neill, who consistently slugs .500, in seventh place. However, Justice did just the same except for injuries, and Gibson was comparable at bat and was a better baserunner.

Reggie is taken over Maris based on established ability; Maris's 1961 was better than any of Reggie's seasons, but his 1960 MVP season isn't was good as Reggie's 1973-1974 in Oakland, and Maris has no other season close to that level. There really isn't that much difference between first and eighth here, as you can see from the fact that Reggie ranks first in 1973 and fifth in 1977.

We have now reached the All-Star break, with a complete starting lineup for all eleven teams after eighty games. The race has tightened up a bit, but the Big Red Machine still has a solid lead. and has a head-to-head edge over everyone except the 1970 O's. Joe Morgan said that only two of the current Yankees would crack the Reds' starting lineup; we have three with O'Neill over Griffey, and all but one of the other great teams have the same two or three. Is it really fair to compare them to the Big Red Machine?

STANDINGS AFTER EIGHT POSITIONS
Reds Slow Down, But Still Lead;
'98 Yanks Struggling to Stay at .500

Year	Team	W		Lvs. 98 Yankees
1976	Reds	52	28	5-3
1961	Yanks	45	35	5-3
1970	O's	45	35	4-4
1984	Tigers	42	38	5-3
1998	Yanks	41	39	—
1986	Mets	40	40	4-4
1977	Yanks	39	41	4-4
1973	A's	38	42	4-4
1967	Cards	36	44	3-5
1995	Braves	34	46	3-5
1989	A's	28	52	2-6

TOP RIGHT-HANDED STARTER
Maddux 1995, Gibson 1967, Gooden 1986, Cone 1998, Hunter 1973, Palmer 1970, Morris 1984, Stewart 1989, Figueroa 1977, Nolan 1976, Terry 1961.

Gooden over Cone is based on what he did as a young pitcher; Cone has had a better career, but Gooden was great in 1984-1987, and his 1985 is the only season other than Gibson's 1968 which would be a good year for Maddux.

Maddux tops this position easily, as he was in the middle of the greatest stretch ever for a starting pitcher, and it's not over yet. As great as Gibson was, he was only comparable to Maddux in 1968 and 1969.

TOP LEFT-HANDED STARTER
Ford 1961, Glavine 1995, Guidry 1977, Cuellar 1970, Blue 1973, Wells 1998, Ojeda 1986, Carlton 1967, Norman 1976, Young 1989, None 1984.

Wells is being compared not just to starters but to the aces of several great teams; average isn't a bad finish. The top four were consistently good or great, and Blue was inconsistently great. Ojeda was better in 1986 than Wells was this year, but he didn't have another great year. Carlton is rated low because this was his first full season; his first great years were 1969 and 1972.

First place goes to Ford without question.

The bottom three teams had several strong right-handed starters but no good lefties; they are hurt here, but will have the advantage comparing their second-best right-handers to everyone else's third starters.

THIRD STARTER
Smoltz 1995, Pettitte 1998, McNally 1970, Welch 1989, Petry 1984, Holtzman 1973, Darling 1986, Gullett 1977, Gullett 1976, Stafford 1961, Hughes 1967.

Pettitte wouldn't be second based on 1998 alone, which was only a little better than league average, but his 1997 suggests that he is a better pitcher than that. Given the difference in offense, McNally's 1.95 ERA in 1968 doesn't match Pettitte's 2.88 in 1997 in almost as many innings.

Smoltz wins here because he is the only pitcher on this list who has been consistently great. The Braves' big three, ranking 1/2/1, is clearly the class of the pitching rotations.

FOURTH STARTER
Torrez 1977, Moore 1989, Fernandez 1986, Wilcox 1984, Briles 1967, Avery 1995, Irabu 1998, Zachry 1976, Odom 1973, Phoebus 1970, Sheldon 1961.

The rating of Irabu here is a guess since he has no established ability; Briles and Zachry were two impressive young pitchers who didn't pan out, which suggests that Irabo should be ranked in that category. Avery was a great fourth starter in 1991-1993, average in 1994-1996, and then lost it; with a better established career, he should rate above Irabu.

Moore had the best season in the year in question, but his 2.63 ERA was a fluke. Torrez was an established above-average pitcher with a decent 1977 which was an off year; that entitles him to the top spot in a group of fourth starters.

As we head into the stretch drive, with all starting positions covered, can you say, "Miracle Braves?" The 1995 Braves were in tenth place but have jumped all the way to first with one of the best starting rotations in major-league history. The Big Red Machine, which looked invincible, has fallen all the way to .500. And we have a great pennant race as the benches and bullpens come in for the stretch run.

STANDINGS AFTER TWELVE POSITIONS
Braves, O's and '98 Yanks Make Their
Moves; Reds Fall to Sixth

Year	Team	W	L	vs. 98 Yankees
1995	Braves	68	52	7-5
1970	O's	66	54	5-7
1998	Yanks	66	54	—
1986	Mets	64	56	6-6
1977	Yanks	62	58	6-6
1976	Reds	60	60	5-7
1984	Tigers	59	61	6-6
1973	A's	57	63	5-7
1961	Yanks	56	64	6-6
1967	Cards	54	66	5-7
1989	A's	48	72	3-9

RELIEF ACE
Eckersley 1989, Fingers 1973, Rivera 1998, Lyle 1977, Orosco 1986, Hernandez 1984, Wohlers 1995, Arroyo 1961, Eastwick 1976, Hoerner 1967, Richert 1970.

Fingers was the greatest relief ace of his era, and Eckersley the greatest of his era; Rivera in 61 innings doesn't quite measure up.

All eleven teams had outstanding relief aces; this is the position at which the bottom is highest, but it's still fairly easy to rank. Eckersley, Fingers, and Rivera were truly outstanding for several years. Lyle and Orosco were also good relief aces over a long period. Hernandez, Wohlers, Arroyo, and Eastwick were great for one year; Hernandez won the MVP in 1984 based on that year, but he was no Lyle or Fingers. Hoerner and Richert were not true relief aces, merely the best pitcher in more shared bullpens.

SPOT STARTERS AND BULLPEN SUPPORT
Yankees 1998, A's 1989, Cardinals 1967, Braves 1995, A's 1973, Orioles 1970, Mets 1986, Tigers 1984, Reds 1976, Yankees 1977, Yankees 1961.

This is the only position that the Yankees win. Four solid starters do not include 21 starts by Orlando Hernandez and 14 by Ramiro Mendoza, with 3.13 and 3.25 ERA's better than any of the starters. Mendoza also helped in the bullpen. Graeme Lloyd was great as a spot left-hander in 37.2 innings, and even more effective against right-handers. Mike Stanton's numbers other than his 5.47 ERA don't look bad; Mike Buddie, in 41.2 innings, was the only ineffective pitcher on the staff.

The 1989 A's are also a contender. The rest of the bullpen included Todd Burns, Gene Nelson, and Rick Honeycutt, all in long stretches with ERA's near 3. The list of starters above didn't include Storm Davis, who pitched 169.1 innings of slightly below average ball; he didn't earn his 19-7 record. The A's may have had the better bullpen, but the Yankees win this position based on the quality of their fifth starters.

A quick look at the pennant race, with one position to go: 1998 Yankees 84-56, 1995 Braves 79-61, 1986 Mets 74-66. The 1989 A's returned to respectability with the best bullpen, but they were so far back that they haven't reached .500.

BENCH AND DH

Reds 1976, Mets 1986, Tigers 1984, Yankees 1998, A's 1989, Orioles 1970, Yankees 1977, A's 1973, Braves 1995, Yankees 1961, Cardinals 1967.

Tim Raines and Darryl Strawberry were great at DH; other than that, the Yankees didn't use their bench much. However, Shane Spencer had the best cup of coffee ever, slugging .910 in 67 AB, and that has to count. Luis Sojo, as a backup infielder, didn't hit at all. Chili Davis was the only other bench player with 100 AB, and he didn't hit well for a DH. Homer Bush was OK, and, until the World Series, Ricky Ledee was a disappointment.

The Mets and Tigers had benches which were deeper, and productive all around. The Mets had Tim Teufel at second, Kevin Mitchell at third and short, Howard Johnson at third, and George Foster in the outfield, all productive in semi-platoons. The Tigers had Dave Bergman at first, Tom Brookens at third (effective as a backup but didn't hit well as a regular), and Johnny Grubb in the outfield. Both teams must rate above the Yankees on the bench because they used their benches to get more production out of several positions than the starters rated above.

The Reds win on the bench because their lineup was so powerful it forced several good players to the bench. Dan Driessen, Bob Bailey, and Doug Flynn all hit very well on the bench but were blocked by Foster, Rose, and Morgan/Concepcion; all three had careers as regulars elsewhere. There were several other productive career bench players; Ed Armbrister was an excellent pinch-hitter, and Bill Plummer backed up Bench respectably.

FINAL STANDINGS (FIFTEEN POSITIONS)

Year	Team	W		Lvs. 98 Yankees
1998	Yanks	91	59	—
1986	Mets	83	67	7-8
1995	Braves	81	69	7-8
1970	O's	76	74	5-10
1973	A's	75	75	6-9
1984	Tigers	75	75	7-8
1976	Reds	74	76	6-9
1977	Yanks	74	76	6-9
1989	A's	73	77	4-11
1967	Cards	63	87	5-10
1961	Yanks	60	90	6-9

And here are the final standings. The 1998 Yankees came out handily on top, beating all other teams head to head. The 1989 A's also mounted an impressive comeback to return to the middle of the pack. A difference of a few games is not really signifcant, so these teams split into four groups of comparable teams.

It's surprising to see the 1961 Yankees at the bottom, but look at that team again. The pitching staff was Whitey Ford and a lot of nobodies, most of them with good years in 1961; even so, it was only a little better than the league average that year. The lineup had Mantle, easily the best at his position, and Maris at his peak, but nothing else remarkable; Elston Howard was the third-best regular with Berra playing left. Mantle and Ford did dominate their positions more than the normal difference between first and second or other adjacent pairs, so it would be reasonable to rank these Yankees above the 1967 Cardinals.

There's a large group of comparable great teams; the 1989 A's join the top five from James's article. The Big Red Machine may have had the greatest starting lineup ever, but its ERA was 0.01 worse than the league average in 1976 and was never significantly better, and in these ratings, pitching is 40% of the game. The 1973 and 1989 A's had better pitching even after park adjustments, but several weaknesses in their starting lineups.

Of the two runners-up, the 1995 Braves are probably the better team. Again, the straight scale of the rankings creates a bias when there is a larger gap between first and second, or tenth and last, than there is between other ranks. Maddux and Smoltz are far better than any of the other pitchers in their categories; Gibson, as great as he was, is not close to Maddux given the league difference. The team had no real weakness, with Fred McGriff the worst player and no position rated below ninth. The Mets do not lead any position, nor do they have a dominant second-place player, and Rafael Santana is by far the worst shortstop in the study; he hit .218 with no walks or power, and although he may have been a decent fielder, he was probably the worst regular in the league.

And the current Yankees are on top, with the best overall collection of talent of any team since 1961. The rating appears fair. The 1995 Braves' regulars, including their outstanding starting rotiation, are better than the 1998 Yankees' regulars, but the pitching staff has nobody to match Rivera, Hernandez, and Mendoza, who pitched 375.1 great innings, almost as much as two regular starters. The Braves played without a DH, which wouldn't be counted against them if the Yankees had only an average DH,

STANDINGS BY POSITION:

	61 Yanks	67 Cards	70 O's	73 A's	76 Reds	77 Yanks	84 Tigers	86 Mets	89 A's	95 Braves	98 Yanks
C	4	6	11	8	1	3	5	2	10	7	9
1B	7	1	3	8	4	10	11	2	5	9	6
2B	9	10	4	11	1	5	2	8	7	6	3
3B	6	8	2	3	5	1	9	11	10	4	7
SS	4	9	6	5	3	8	1	11	10	7	2
LF	10	3	6	4	2	8	9	7	1	5	11
CF	1	5	7	10	11	9	3	4	6	8	2
RF	2	10	4	1	9	5	6	3	11	8	7
RSP	11	2	6	5	10	9	7	3	8	1	4
LSP	1	8	4	5	9	3	11	7	10	2	6
3SP	10	11	3	6	9	8	5	7	4	1	2
4SP	11	5	10	9	8	1	4	3	2	6	7
RA	8	10	11	2	9	4	6	5	1	7	3
Pen	11	3	6	5	9	10	8	7	2	4	1
Bench	10	11	6	8	1	7	3	2	5	9	4

but the Yankees got excellent production from their DH's, who also backed up in the outfield.

I should close with James's cautionary comment. "I offer no proof of that; it is only a carefully worked out opinion, which is very different from anything which could be shown to be true."

THE CHANGING FACE OF COMPETITION

DON MALCOLM

A lot of ink is spilled in sports pages about the issue of "competitive balance" in baseball, and the ostensible threat to it that now looms ominously over the game as a result of ongoing economic inequities. Doomsayers of all stripes have surfaced as a sort of afterimage in the blinding corona of baseball's most celebrated season in more than fifty years, pointing to the extreme success of the Yankees as a sign that the overall economic situation of the game is fundamentally unsound.

While such an assessment may in fact be accurate, it seems clear that analysts, writers and other media commentators about the game have seized upon an issue whose relevance is not borne out when it is examined over the course of baseball history. For example, there has been a great deal of attention paid to the fact that the Yankees, Braves and Astros all won more than 100 games in 1998, and the purported ramifications of this fact for the "future of baseball." Little attention, however, has been paid to the fact that this amounts to only 10% of the league population, and that this percentage has been exceeded in eighteen seasons during the twentieth century.

As it turns out, no one appears to have done a systematic study of competition in baseball in the twentieth century based on the actual seasonal results. Without such a study, of course, we have no way of knowing how aberrant the results of a season such as 1998 really are, and whether a pattern of decreasing competitive balance--a charge that is increasingly being leveled at the game to the point where media sources refer to it as if it has been factually established--can be seen in the seasonal results of the 1990s.

So we did what we usually do here at BBBA--we gathered the data. We decided to use winning percentage instead of raw games won, as changes in schedule length and seasonal interruptions play havoc with the ability to use all of the available data. We broke the data into six thresholds of team winning percentages (WPCT). Above .500, we looked at so-called "dominating" teams, ones with a WPCT of .630 or higher (102 or more wins in a 162-games season); followed by "championship" teams, ones with a WPCT of .600 or higher (roughly 97 wins or more per 162 games); and "contending" teams, those with a WPCT of .570 or higher (roughly 92 wins or more). Below .500, the breakouts were .370 or lower (teams with 60 or fewer wins per 162 games); .400 or lower (roughly 65 or fewer wins per 162 games); and .430 or lower (roughly 70 wins or less per 162 games).

We looked at the six WPCT thresholds in 10-year summaries, and discovered some surprising facts. First, here is the data:

As can be seen, the effect of expansion has been to cut the incidence of "elite teams" (those with .600 or better WPCT) by more than half. The percentage of .600+ teams had stabilized at around 15% of the total population as early as the 1910s and had remained at that level

Distribution of Team WPCT

Decade	.630+	.600+	.570+	.370-	.400-	.430-
1900-09	9.7%	21.5%	32.6%	17.4%	23.6%	29.9%
1910-19	8.8%	14.4%	28.8%	10.0%	16.3%	23.1%
1920-29	5.6%	15.0%	24.4%	9.4%	15.6%	21.9%
1930-39	7.5%	15.6%	25.6%	12.5%	19.4%	27.5%
1940-49	9.4%	15.6%	24.4%	8.8%	13.1%	25.0%
1950-59	6.3%	15.0%	25.6%	8.1%	14.4%	24.4%
1960-69	3.0%	9.1%	18.2%	6.6%	12.6%	18.7%
1970-79	3.3%	10.6%	16.3%	5.3%	9.8%	16.7%
1980-89	1.5%	5.8%	11.5%	3.8%	8.1%	15.4%
1990-	3.2%	6.5%	14.5%	1.6%	4.4%	12.9%
1901-98	5.3%	12.0%	20.8%	7.5%	12.7%	20.5%
1901-60	7.8%	16.0%	26.8%	10.8%	17.0%	25.2%
1961-98	2.7%	7.8%	14.7%	4.2%	8.3%	15.6%

for the next four decades; expansion in the 1960s/1970s had caused that figure to drop by about one third, and the evolving effects of free agency have served to drive that average to historic lows in the 1980s/1990s.

Of particular interest is the fact that there have always been more "hapless teams" (.370 or lower) in the game than "top-rank teams" (.630 or higher). There are only two decades during the twentieth century which go against this trend: the 1940s and the 1990s. We'll return to the differing reasons for these anomalies a bit later.

Note that in the 1900s more than 60% of all teams played either .570+ or .430- ball. In the 1950s, that percentage was 50%. In the 1960s that figure dropped to 36%; by the 1980s, it had fallen to just 26%. Despite the presence of the Yankees, Braves, Astros and Padres at the top end during 1998, and the Marlins at the other end of the spectrum, the percentage of "extreme spectrum" teams rose only slightly in the 1990s, up just one point (27%).

In the entire history of baseball, a bit more than one-fifth of all teams have managed a .570 or better WPCT (20.8%). That figure was more than one-fourth of all teams in the period 1901-60 (27%); since baseball's first expansion, this percentage has dropped below one-sixth (15%). In 1998, there were only four teams who played at .570 or better (13.3%).

Of course, those four teams also played at .600 or better, and that same 13.3% applies at that level as well (compare to the historical average of 12%). However, there are two factors to keep in mind:

--First, it's only a single season. In the period 1901-98, there have been 35 seasons where the average percentage of teams playing .600 ball or better has exceeded the 1998 average.

--Second, 1998 was an expansion year. As the data below indicates, expansion years have generally produced a rise in .600+ teams:

Expansion Years

Year	.630+	.600+	.570+	.370-	.400-	.430-
1961	5.6%	16.7%	27.8%	5.6%	16.7%	22.2%
1962	0.0%	15.0%	25.0%	10.0%	15.0%	15.0%
1969	4.2%	8.3%	12.5%	8.3%	20.8%	29.2%
1977	3.8%	23.1%	30.8%	3.8%	19.2%	26.9%
1993	7.1%	7.1%	21.4%	3.6%	10.7%	21.4%
1998	10.0%	13.3%	13.3%	3.3%	6.7%	20.0%
Expansion	5.5%	13.7%	21.2%	5.5%	14.4%	22.6%
1901-98	5.3%	12.0%	20.8%	7.5%	12.7%	20.5%

There is no clear pattern in expansion seasons aside from the rise in teams playing .600+ and .400- ball. But as you can see, the raw percentage of teams playing .400- ball during a year of expansion has dropped dramatically in the two 1990s expansion years.

Only 1969 had a lower percentage of teams playing .570+ ball than 1998, despite the elite performances of the Yankees, Braves and Astros. In 1977, AL expansion produced a league in which five of the fourteen teams (36%) played .570+ ball; in 1998, the Yankees were the only AL team exceeding that percentage. All of the other AL franchises with large payrolls (Baltimore, Boston, Chicago, Cleveland, Seattle) did not play .570 ball--and in some cases, missed that figure by a wide margin.

All indications point to the 1998 results as being anomalous, and not somehow resulting from a deep-seated structural imbalance in competition. The data shows that the free agency period continues to produce WPCT distributions indicative of tighter competition than the historical average:

Even in the 1993-98 time frame, the WPCT distributions are well below the historical averages, and the incidence of "hapless teams" (.370-) is at its lowest point in baseball history. And at least one of those teams--last year's Marlins--were made that way on purpose.

Years	.630+	.600+	.570+	.370-	.400-	.430-
1961-76	3.1%	9.1%	15.7%	5.7%	10.3%	16.0%
1977-92	1.7%	6.7%	13.9%	3.8%	8.2%	15.6%
1993-98	4.1%	7.6%	14.7%	1.8%	4.7%	14.7%
1977-98	2.4%	7.0%	14.2%	3.2%	7.2%	15.4%
1901-98	5.3%	12.0%	20.8%	7.5%	12.7%	20.5%

MIXED SIGNALS   Economics, Sleight-of-Hand, and the Near-Term Future of Baseball

DAVID GRABINER

Baseball teams are losing money, tickets are too expensive, fans are losing interest, and many teams can't afford to compete. On the other hand, baseball teams are selling for ever-increasing prices, attendance this year set a record, the teams that couldn't afford to compete a few years ago are winning pennants now, and baseball finally has a commissioner. There is enough confusing information and deliberate deception that many fans believe either set of facts. It is possible to understand what is really going on with a bit of analysis, and discover that the doomsday scenario is mostly an illusion.

The reported losses are probably the biggest illusion. Owners make various claims about profits and losses, and sportswriters accept these claims without question and report the numbers. Owners have an incentive for the public to believe they are losing money, since it is easier to convince the public to support a new park, or concessions from the players, for a team which is losing money than for one which is making a large profit. As a result, any claim made by an owner about his own losses should be considered skeptically.

The owners' behavior is also inconsistent with the claims of large losses. Businesses which expect to lose money should not have high value, and an industry which loses money should see franchise values drop. The Marlins, following the fire sale which occurred because they could not compete, are in the process of being sold for $150 million. Team president Don Smiley, who knew the team's actual finances, was willing to put together a group to pay this much for the team. Two expansion teams paid similar amounts for the right to join an industry which claimed to be in financial trouble. The values of established franchises are going up.

23

Without open books, it isn't possible to tell how much profit or loss a team is actually making. When the owners opened their books to economist Roger Noll in the 1985 negotiations, he found enough hidden revenue and misleading accounting to turn the claimed $50 million loss for 1984 into a $9 million profit. Many of the same techniques are being used now, and it is possible to get some idea of the effects.

The outstanding example of a profit or loss created by accounting is a related-party transaction; that is, a transaction between two different entities with the same owner. For example, Wayne Huizenga owned both the Marlins and their stadium; as a result, his own profits did not depend on how much the Marlins kept from stadium revenue, or paid in rent to the stadium. In an article in the New York Times Magazine, Andrew Zimbalist concluded that the Marlins could show a book loss of about the $30 million Huizenga claimed because the stadium earned all the revenue for luxury boxes, club seats, and parking, and most of the revenue from concessions, while the Marlins paid $5 million in stadium expenses. After these and other corrections, Zimbalist estimated that the team's profit in 1997 was $13.8 million. Huizenga also claimed that the team would lose about $30 million late in the season, and continued to claim in 1998 that it had lost $34 million in 1997; this was only possible if his share of the playoff revenue was not credited to the team.

Sportswriters compound the problem by not questioning reported figures. The Marlins claimed to have lost $34 million in 1997. When they had cut their 1998 payroll by $30 million, they claimed to expect to break even in 1998; as they cut it further, they claimed to expect a profit equal to the additional cuts. However, these cuts clearly did not come without a cost in revenue. Attendance in 1998 was much less than in 1997, and there was no chance that the team would make the playoffs. The claimed losses were reported as facts. Likewise, reporters could question why many teams which claimed to be incapable of making a profit were selling for such large values.

Regardless of the reported profits, there is a clear inequality between rich and poor teams. Teams in large cities, or with good parks, earn a lot more revenue. However, this inequality is not an inequity; it is a return on the value of the franchise, which is something the owners paid. The Dodgers sold for $300 million, twice the price for the Marlins; they were able to command this price because they own their stadium, draw three million fans every year, and are in the Los Angeles TV market. Murdoch could have earned about as much by buying a less expensive team, with fewer fans in good years and bad, and then putting the price difference into the stock market.

It is often quoted that all of the teams in contention have high payrolls. It is true that high-payroll teams tend to do better than low-payroll teams, because good players are more expensive. This is not a problem by itself, since every team can choose to have a high or low payroll. Another part of the reason is that teams out of contention trade expensive players to teams in contention at mid-season in return for prospects. This raises the contenders' payrolls, but has no direct effect on the ability of specific teams to compete in the current economic situation.

Sportswriters have often talked about the inability of "small-market" teams to compete. However, the current definition of "small-market" tends to be any teams which are not in the largest cities and are not competitive in the current year.

The Pirates won their division from 1990-1992. The Expos had the best record in the majors when the strike hit in 1994. The Twins were World Champions in 1991. None of these teams was close to leading the league in attendance at the time, but all drew reasonably well, and only the Expos had a low payroll. These teams chose not to keep their stars, and are now seen as non-competitive.

Conversely, the 1993 Padres held a fire sale similar to the Marlins' sale this year, trading away almost all of their stars for prospects. With the NL's lowest payroll in 1993 and 1994, they were seen as a small-market team with no chance to compete. With help from those prospects, such as Trevor Hoffman and the trade return on Derek Bell, the Padres won the National League pennant and are no longer considered a small-market team which cannot compete, even though neither the city nor the stadium changed. Likewise, the Mariners were a small-market team until they won the division title; they chose to keep Ken Griffey Jr., Edgar Martinez, and (until this year) Randy Johnson, and became contenders.

Any team can choose not to compete in any year, trading for prospects and letting free agents go, or choose to sign or keep free agents and compete. Whether the team is in a small or a large market, it will get more revenue from improved attendance and (if successful) playoff money if it is a contender; the increased spending may be a good investment for a team in either a large or small market. This year's World Series teams provide a good illustration of the value of winning; the Yankees may be sold for a higher price because they won, while the Padres' pennant led to increased support for the ballot proposal to build a new stadium with tax money.

The money that is spent on these players should not be a direct concern to the fans. Owners are trying to make a profit, not to break even, and thus they set ticket prices at the level which maximizes revenue, since they are committed to paying the players regardless of attendance. This is why ticket prices in the same parks have gone up at the rate of inflation for years. Ticket prices in the new parks tend to be slightly higher, because the new parks provide better products, and many of them sell out even at the higher prices. The game has not been priced out of the reach of most fans; the fans themselves have proved this by turning out in increasing numbers.

Again, the reported figures are misleading. The published "Fan Cost Index" is the cost to take a family of four to a once-a-year game, not what a single fan pays. It includes four tickets and parking, but also several souvenirs, two beers, and food for everyone. Fans look at this $100 price, and compare it to the $3 they paid for a box seat thirty years ago. The correct comparison is between the $3 that one box seat used to cost and the $12 it now costs, which is the same in purchasing power.

While the prices have not driven away fans, the strike has had an effect, and in this case, the popular opinion is better than reality. Attendance in 1998 was at an all-time high, but it was really only second best. Attendance per game was higher in 1993, but nobody makes that comparison. And 1998's attendance includes a large number of fans drawn by the McGwire-Sosa home-run chase. Some of these fans may remain, improving baseball's potential fan base, but most will not. Per-game attendance in 1999 will probably remain about 5% below the peak. That isn't bad, but it does show that fan interest was hurt by something after 1994, and the strike is probably the cause.

In addition, attendance increased in 1993 partly because the NL changed its definition; prior to 1993, the NL counted only tickets used, rather than all tickets sold. (The AL made the same change in 1973, which is the main reason attendance jumped that year; the DH wasn't responsible for the whole effect.) Thus 1993 wasn't really an anomaly; this can be confirmed by noting that AL attendance wasn't up as much.

Another strike will hurt baseball again, and commissioner Bud Selig says that he wants to avoid one, but will he succeed? With and without a commissioner, every labor negotiation since there has been a strong union has involved a strike or a lockout. The 1994-1996 negotiations were particularly drawn out because of divisions among the owners. They could not even accept their own negotiator's proposal until Jerry Reinsdorf spoke against its inadequate controls on salaries and then tried to exploit the lack of a tax by signing Albert Belle to a record contract. In theory, a commissioner could help because he is an employee of all the owners, and can try to convince the owners to work in the best interests of the group; as an owner, Selig didn't have that position in 1994. However, the positions of the owners haven't changed, and there is no reason to believe Selig's perception of the situation has changed. If the owners are not willing to make a reasonable offer, there will be another strike or lockout.

The existence of a commissioner will not have much effect on anything else in the game. The commissioner is often viewed as impartial, but he is an employee of the owners, and as Bowie Kuhn and Fay Vincent discovered, he can be fired if he does not satisfy the owners. When there is a dispute under the labor agreement, it is resolved by a truly neutral arbitrator, not by the commissioner. This is the principle that prevented Bowie Kuhn from advising the owners, as their representative, that they were not risking free agency for Messersmith, and then ruling, as a judge, that Messersmith was not a free agent. Selig will be in the same position.

Regardless of any power or lack of power, the commissioner is seen as the leader of the game. Baseball is in a good position now, much better than the public perception. With the NBA lockout, baseball has a chance to win some fans. The 1994-1995 strike is passing into distant memory. Many of the other problems are not real. Bud Selig has a chance to be known as the commissioner who presided over baseball's 1998-2002 growth and the first peaceful labor negotiation in thirty years, or the commissioner who caused the 2001 lockout and disastrous decline. Either impression might be an exaggeration, but baseball does have an opportunity.

BY GOD, IT'S ByCOUNT, TOO!
Don Malcolm and Sean Lahman

Last year in these pages we introduced the world to a new type of situational breakout, which we gave the name ByCount. What is it? It's a compilation of hitter's count stages (0-0, 0-1, 0-2, 1-0, 1-1, 1-2, 2-0, 2-1, 2-2, 3-0, 3-1, and 3-2) organized into groups differentiated as "early," "middle," and "late." The location of the various stages in the count where a batter's plate appearance is decided are lumped into this formulation as follows:

Favors	Number of pitches						OPS
	1	**2**	**3**	**4**	**5**	**6+**	
Batter		1-0	2-0	3-0	2-1	3-1	1.059
Neutral	0-0		1-1		2-2	3-2	.767
Pitcher		0-1	0-2	1-2			.535
OPS	.896	.869	.699	.659	.690	.834	.767
	Early		.881 Middle		.683 Late		.751

The chart shows the count stages and number of pitchers which fall into each count grouping (early, middle, late) and what we last year called the "sagging middle" (the count stages in the middle produce a markedly lower level of performance as measured by on-base plus slugging—OPS).

How consistent is the overall count data from year to year? Here's a comparison for the past two years:

Year	Early	Middle	Late
1997	.863	.659	.741
1998	.001	.683	.751

As you can see, the "sagging middle" is another constant feature of the game. As you can see from the data, pitchers get a tremendous advantage when they have two strikes on a hitter. Even the supposedly "neutral" 2-2 count is seriously tilted in favor of the pitcher.

Our database of ByCount data has, among other things, an early, middle and late OPS value for all but a handful of batters and pitchers for the past two seasons. One of the things we were interested in seeing was how much variability there was in this data from year to year. Here are a few selected players and a quick analysis of their performance as seen through the ByCount lens:

Count	1998	1997
0-0	.896	.881
0-1	.814	.805
0-2	.388	.375
1-0	.921	.890
1-1	.848	.825
1-2	.441	.416
2-0	.999	.973
2-1	.907	.899
2-2	.497	.485
3-0	1.670	1.736
3-1	1.309	1.307
3-2	.834	.845

How do the individual count stages compare over the past two years? Let's take a look:

FRANK THOMAS

Year	Early	Middle	Late
1997	1.090	1.056	1.053
1998	.783	.880	.865

Let's start right at the top with the Big Hurt. Looks as though Frank took a hit in every phase of the count; his biggest drop was early, though. After a few years' worth of this data, we should be able to tell you if an across-the-board decline is more symptomatic of a permanent downturn than, say, a more localized drop in a particular count stage, but for now we just don't know. That's why we gather the data, however, so we can learn more.

Here are a couple of players whose ByCount profile turned completely around from 1997 to 1998:

GARY SHEFFIELD

Year	Early	Middle	Late
1997	.818	.718	1.075
1998	1.071	.980	.801

J.T. SNOW

Year	Early	Middle	Late
1997	.977	.890	.837
1998	.732	1.004	.591

Sheffield had a much better season in 1998 than in 1997, while the opposite was the case for Snow. There are very few hitters who put up big seasons without hitting well early in the count; the average hitter compiles a .331 BA and a .519 SLG in early-count situations.

Now let's look at several guys whose ByCount profile was eerily similar over those two years:

ERIC DAVIS

Year	Early	Middle	Late
1997	1.138	.847	.810
1998	1.287	.856	.861

JOSE CANSECO

Year	Early	Middle	Late
1997	.901	.653	.850
1998	.945	.692	.866

JAVY LOPEZ

Year	Early	Middle	Late
1997	1.140	.763	.690
1998	1.155	.706	.697

This is probably coincidence more than anything else, given the sample sizes involved. Still, there appears to be a subclass of hitters who post very consistent ByCount breakouts.

Who's the best hitter we found with a very poor showing in any particular count phase? Take a look:

Player	Year	Early	Middle	Late
Rickey Henderson	1997	.490	.405	.818
Reggie Sanders	1997	1.271	.499	.860
Rickey Henderson	1998	1.000	.765	.496

Just an interesting oddity that Henderson can be found on both ends of this list. Rickey didn't hit at all in the late count phase during 1998, but still drew a lot of walks and hit much more often in the early part of the count than he had previously. None of these seasons were particularly notable, and it's clear that good players having top-flight years have no holes in their game:

Player	Year	Early	Middle	Late
Albert Belle	1998	1.089	1.134	.973
Barry Bonds	1998	1.232	.921	.970
Barry Bonds	1997	1.032	1.018	1.040
David Justice	1997	1.110	1.035	.919
Edgar Martinez	1997	1.215	.947	.935
Edgar Martinez	1998	1.006	1.062	.917
Frank Thomas	1997	1.090	1.056	1.053
Jeff Bagwell	1998	1.046	.955	.920
Ken Griffey Jr.	1997	1.006	1.120	.946
Larry Walker	1998	1.162	1.000	1.001
Mark McGwire	1997	1.217	1.079	.958
Mike Piazza	1997	1.063	1.024	1.157

These are true superstar seasons, as you can see. The only one that might be considered a bit out of place is Justice's 1997. Everyone else on this list, with the possible exception of Larry Walker, has a helluva chance to make the Hall of Fame.

You might have noticed that Mark McGwire's 1997 season shows up on this elite list, but not his 1998. How is that possible? Let's take a look:

Player	Year	Early	Middle	Late
Mark McGwire	1998	1.681	.883	1.176
Sammy Sosa	1998	1.382	.898	.889

We couldn't resist printing Sammy's ByCount numbers here alongside Mac's. As you can see, Sosa did manage to outperform McGwire in mid-count situations, though if the truth be told, it's not enough to brag about. While Mac missed the top echelon of mid-count hitters, a look at his performance early and late in the count may well make you more than a little weak in the knees. Sammy's early count performance is nothing to sneeze at, either.

Here are some other lusty performers in early-county situations:

Player	Year	Early	Middle	Late
Ray Lankford	1997	1.549	.875	.830
Jim Thome	1998	1.527	.895	.766
Jim Thome	1997	1.390	1.113	.741
Mo Vaughn	1997	1.358	.928	.767
Juan Gonzalez	1998	1.348	.795	.842

Player	Year	Early	Middle	Late
Larry Walker	1997	1.296	1.194	.893
Andres Galarraga	1998	1.295	.827	.851
Eric Davis	1998	1.287	.856	.861
Ray Lankford	1998	1.276	.884	.771
Mo Vaughn	1998	1.272	.825	.910
Jeff Bagwell	1997	1.262	.820	1.035
Craig Biggio	1997	1.259	.857	.646
Tim Salmon	1997	1.254	.620	.893
Dean Palmer	1998	1.250	.626	.668
Vinny Castilla	1997	1.242	.757	.583
Bernie Williams	1998	1.240	.913	.848
Vladimir Guerrero	1998	1.232	.988	.685

As you can see, Ray Lankford, Jim Thome and Mo Vaughn are especially deadly in early-count situations. Further down the list, we see sharp dropoffs after the early count stages for lesser hitters such as Dean Palmer and Vinny Castilla.

Let's look at Vladimir Guerrero's breakout season in 1998 a bit more closely. Or, more precisely, let's compare it to his 1997 ByCount data:

VLADIMIR GUERRERO

Year	Early	Middle	Late
1997	.867	.783	.857
1998	1.232	.988	.685

A huge jump in early-count hitting, and a very sizable gain in the middle counts as well. Great hitters thrive early in the count, racking up their BA and SLG components. Who had the best season in the past two years with the lowest OPS in early count situations?

Player	Year	Early	Middle	Late
Rusty Greer	1997	.874	.902	1.010

As you can see, that's not a particularly low OPS (though it is a bit below the MLB average in early-count situations). The point is that it's just not possible to have a top-notch offensive season with a truly poor showing early in the count.

Let's look at another highly-touted young player, the Braves' Andruw Jones. Did Andruw show much movement in his ByCount data while he upped his HR output from 18 to 31 and gained almost fifty points in BA?

ANDRUW JONES

Year	Early	Middle	Late
1997	1.129	.542	.613
1998	1.125	.653	.676

This one pretty much belongs in that earlier "eerily similar" category. Andruw improved in mid and late count situations in 1998, but he is still below league average in both.

A player who also improved in 1998, but who did in it a completely different way than Jones, is Minnesota's Matt Lawton. Here are Matt's ByCount numbers for the past two years:

MATT LAWTON

Year	Early	Middle	Late
1997	1.008	.661	.676
1998	.882	.862	.810

This is a remarkably consistent performance across all count phases, but given the prevailing tendency for top-notch hitters to dominate early in the count, we can't get really excited about Matt's chances at a breakout season.

Let's shift gears and take a look at some of the worst hitters in the mid-count phase:

Player	Year	Early	Middle	Late
Brian Hunter	1998	.872	.316	.627
Juan Castro	1997	.494	.317	.657
Tyler Houston	1997	.811	.319	.803
Robert Perez	1998	.887	.321	.313
Ruben Amaro	1998	.641	.327	.455
Ron Karkovice	1997	.598	.328	.910
Adrian Brown	1998	.870	.329	.619
Ruben Rivera	1997	.750	.333	.717
Butch Huskey	1998	.968	.373	.698
Curtis Goodwin	1997	.784	.378	.705
Kirt Manwaring	1997	.741	.392	.601
John Vander Wal	1997	.786	.395	.313
Mariano Duncan	1997	.818	.400	.333
Darrin Jackson	1998	.795	.403	.586
Rickey Henderson	1997	.490	.405	.818
Bernard Gilkey	1998	1.005	.411	.523
Rey Ordonez	1997	.546	.415	.635
Chris Snopek	1997	.661	.415	.706

Not too many players you'd want to build a franchise around on this list. Often the best thing to do with a player with this kind of performance is to give him a job in the front office, as the Phillies did with Ruben Amaro, Jr. Now if only the Mets would consider the same step with Rey Ordonez. . .

Let's continue in this vein and examine the players who have trouble hitting late in the count:

Player	Year	Early	Middle	Late
John Vander Wal	1997	.786	.395	.313
Juan Castro	1998	.573	.698	.338
Juan Samuel	1998	.875	.452	.350
Melvin Nieves	1998	1.052	.864	.368
Felix Martinez	1998	.371	.234	.373
Greg Norton	1998	1.007	.791	.378
Geoff Jenkins	1998	.899	.747	.397
Troy Glaus	1998	.974	.508	.398
Jermaine Dye	1998	.748	.714	.400
Pokey Reese	1997	.871	.532	.418
John Jaha	1998	1.156	.655	.422
Marc Newfield	1998	.915	.584	.424
Ryan Christenson	1998	.950	.783	.427
Joe Oliver	1998	.738	.795	.433
Al Martin	1998	.843	.681	.434
Yamil Benitez	1998	.740	1.158	.435
Joe Girardi	1998	.938	.748	.436

A preponderance of young players can be found on this list, along with a legendary performance of colossal ineptness in the person of Felix (Sucker Punch) Martinez, a player whose "skills" as a batter are literally offensive. There are a large number of Royals and Brewers on this list, as well as some members of the Reds. Interestingly, most of this list comes from the 1998 season, and there are a couple of highly touted rookies who fall into this category (the Angels' Troy Glaus and the As' Ryan Christenson).

Let's close by taking a look at the most consistently average hitters in the game today. These are the players whose OPS in each count stage is between .700 and .800. It takes a lot of work to be this consistent—and this mediocre. Despite this fact, there are two likely future Hall of Famers on this list:

Name	Year	Early	Middle	Late
Tim Raines	1998	.782	.759	.754
Kevin Orie	1997	.797	.770	.762
Garret Anderson	1997	.729	.743	.776
Dave Martinez	1997	.755	.755	.789
Stan Javier	1997	.771	.730	.789
Wade Boggs	1997	.712	.780	.789

Our editor says that we have a little more room, so we'll wrap up (this time for sure!) with a little more detailed data on ByCount stages. Here is the E-M-L data shown with all of the standard offensive measures:

Count	BA	OBP	SLG	OPS	ISO
Early	.336	.347	.534	.881	.198
Middle	.251	.288	.395	.683	.144
Late	.222	.392	.359	.751	.137

As you can see, it's harder to hit late in the count, but if you can get there, you will benefit from a gargantuan increase in OBP. We added in isolated power (ISO, or SLG-BA) to show the decline in power from the early stages of the count on. As you can see, it's not so pronounced a drop between middle and late.

Finally, here is Don Malcolm's favorite breakout, a breakdown of how well hitters do with 0, 1, or 2 strikes on them:

Strikes	BA	OBP	SLG	OPS	Pct.
0 strikes	.343	.402	.562	.965	26.6
1 strike	.333	.399	.530	.929	27.8
2 strikes	.190	.263	.292	.554	45.6

It's just plain hard to hit with two strikes, and there really is no pitcher-hitter balance in the count when sliced this way—just a big dropoff from success at 0 strikes/1 strikes and failure at 2 strikes. What keeps the balance in the matchup is the fact that 2-strike situations account for close to half of all plate appearances. Next year we'll look at pitchers using ByCount, and examine if success might well be based on how often pitchers get two strikes on hitters.

BLASTS FROM THE PAST

1949 AND THE GREAT WALK SPIKE An Abbreviated Look Back at Baseball's Peak Year

DON MALCOLM

A BRIEF LOOK BACK AT 50 YEARS AGO

Space doesn't permit us to delve into the 1949 baseball season in the way that it deserves, but let's start by noting that the dynamic of post-war expansion reached its zenith in this year, with a record 59 minor leagues in operation across the entire span of America. The beginning of New York's golden age, as memorialized by partisans such as David Halberstam (Summer of '49) and Roger Kahn (The Era, 1947-57), can be seen in the swift transformation of the Yankees and Dodgers into perennial powerhouses. (The Yanks appeared in nine of ten World Series from 1949-58; the Dodgers joined them five times. The other team from Gotham, the New York Giants, reached the Fall Classic twice. All in all, New York teams won nine of the ten World Series from 1949-58.)

But that was later. The problems that this so-called "Golden Age" of baseball caused for the game in the 50s were on the horizon in 1949, but the signs weren't readily visible. Attendance was still riding a massive post-war crest that had begun in 1945 (the first year in which total attendance exceeded ten million) and peaked in 1948 (nearly 21 million). 1949 was the second consecutive year in which twenty million people would visit major league ballparks, but these post-war spoils proved illusory: MLB attendance didn't again exceed twenty million until 1962.

What makes 1949 so interesting in retrospect isn't simply the fact that there were two nailbiting pennant races that went down to the last day of the season. (Halberstam, in his paean to the Yankee-Red Sox rivalry, completely overlooks the equally intense competition between the Dodgers and the St. Louis Cardinals, who had dominated the NL for most of the 1940s.) 1949 was the year in which the balance of power in the NL shifted from St. Louis to Brooklyn: the Dodgers took over the lead in five-year win average in 1950, while the Cardinals fell from first in 1949 to fourth (behind the Dodgers, Giants and Braves) by 1955. It wasn't until 1958, when the Dodgers had packed up and moved to Los Angeles, that the Braves eclipsed them in the five-year win averages:

	Cards	Dodgers	Giants	Braves
1940s	96	89	72	72
1950s	78	91	82	85
40-44	99	87	71	64
45-49	93	92	74	80
50-54	80	96	89	81
55-59	75	87	76	90

But most interesting was a phenomenon that we at BBBA have taken to calling the Great Walk Spike. Before the DH made the two leagues distinct from the standpoint of the rulebook, the AL and NL had been divergent in more subtle ways. This difference in style of play was most pronounced in the two leagues' BBP (or walking percentage). The Great Walk Spike took place solely in the American League, and reached its peak in 1949, when the league as a whole drew 11.9 walks for every 100 plate appearances. As the chart below shows, this was a formidable spike, and it represents the highest such league BBP in the history of the game.

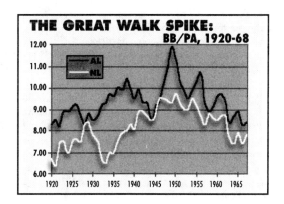

THE GREAT WALK SPIKE: BB/PA, 1920-68

As long-time readers of BBBA already know, the all-time team walk record (835) was set in 1949 by the Boston Red Sox. Ted Williams, the poster boy for the batter's base on balls, led the AL with 162. Two other Red Sox teammates, Johnny Pesky and Vern Stephens, also drew 100+ walks. Another team with a cluster of walkmen: the Philadelphia Athletics, who drew 783 walks in Connie Mack's penultimate season as manager. Eddie Joost (149 BBs), Ferris Fain (136) and Elmer Valo (119) were the patient trio, a group more remarkable for the fact that they hit just 31 HRs among them, 12 less than Ted Williams managed by himself.

Other members of the 100+ BB club in 1949: 42-year old Luke Appling (121) and his 23-year old keystone partner Cass Michaels (101) for the Chicago White Sox, who were one of five teams in the AL to exceed 700 walks. Two teams--the Tigers and the eventual World Series-winning Yankees--also had more than 700 walks without a single 100+ player on their squad. The Tigers, with 761 walks, could have challenged the all-time record had they kept first baseman Roy Cullenbine (whose last season had produced 137 walks, 40 more than the combined totals of the men who replaced him in the next two seasons), and if they had chosen to keep the fading Eddie Lake (120 walks in 1947) in the starting lineup.

Only the Washington Senators failed to exceed 600 walks, despite the presence of 22-year old third baseman Eddie Yost, who drew 91 walks as a second-year player. As walks began a slow fade in the AL over the next decade, Yost would become the poster boy for them, drawing 100+ in five straight seasons (1950-54) and seven times in the 1950s.

What caused the Great AL Walk Spike? Those historians of the game who have bothered to note its existence have not developed definitive answers to that question. Bill James speculated that the change was due to a "generational" shift in pitchers: he uses Bob Feller and Robin Roberts as the exemplars of this change, overlooking the fact that the walk phenomenon is strictly an AL phenomenon.

Another problem with the "generational shift" theory is that Feller's own team was the only AL franchise to buck the rising walk levels. Here are the walks allowed totals for the eight AL teams from 1946-49:

The numbers at the bottom represent the percentage change from 1946 walk levels as the AL moves closer to the actual 1949 walk spike. The 1946 average (551 walks per team) is baselined at 100; the Yankees, closest to league average in 1946, actually allowed the most walks in 1949 and registered close to a 50% increase over the period. Only the Indians walked fewer men in 1949 than they did in 1946. While some of this can be attributed to the fact that Bob Feller logged more than 160 fewer IP in 1949 than he did in 1946, a good bit of it is due to the emergence of pitchers such as Early Wynn and Mike Garcia on the Indians' staff. But to call these pitchers a new "generation" is misleading: Early Wynn was only a year younger than Feller and had been pitching in the big leagues since 1939.

Craig Wright theorized that AL pitchers were more

fearful of the rising homer totals that manifested themselves and refused to throw strikes. One problem with this theory is that the AL continued to trail the NL in homers allowed well into the 1950s when the walk spike subsided. The other is that such an approach, if it was in fact implemented by AL pitchers, was a failure: despite hitter fewer HRs, AL hitters scored more runs than their NL counterparts during the Great Walk Spike years.

A closer look at our Walk Spike diagram provides us with what might well be a better clue to what was going on. After 1930, the style of play in the AL and NL diverged radically, with one manifestation of this being in walk levels. The AL walk levels were rising throughout the 30s, and peak in 1938, when Bob Feller was 19 and in his second full season with the Indians. They dipped in 1939-40, but rose to a level close to that 1938 peak in 1941, the last year that was mostly unaffected by World War II.If you mentally draw a line from the 1938 AL walk levels to those of 1949, you'll see what can be interpreted as an linear progression. The AL had a completely different style of play which remained in effect from the 1930s through the walk spike, and only gradually decayed during the 50s, when the league styles began to merge. This reconvergence was pretty much complete by 1958, when the AL again drew fewer walks than the NL--for only the second time in thirty years.

Viewed in this light, 1949 can be seen as the pinnacle of a much longer process that had been institutionalized in the AL and was a distinctive signature of its separate style of play. It can be seen as early as the 20s, possibly as a result of Babe Ruth's emergence. By the time interleague trading was permitted in 1959, the two leagues had already converged, and they would remain so until the adoption of the DH rule.

MR. WALK SPIKE HIMSELF

As noted, 1949 deserves a far more exhaustive examination than is possible here: it is a watershed year in many ways. We'd be remiss, however, if we didn't try to provide a little more flavor for the unique offensive conditions in the AL during that season.

Yr	NY	Bos	Cle	Chi	Det	Phi	StL	Was	AL
46	552	501	649	508	497	577	573	547	551
47	628	575	628	603	531	597	604	579	593
48	641	592	628	673	589	639	737	734	654
49	812	681	611	693	628	758	685	779	706
46-47	114	115	97	119	107	103	105	106	108
46-48	116	118	97	132	119	111	129	134	119
46-49	147	136	94	136	126	131	120	142	128

We mentioned earlier that the Yankees, who won the first of five straight World Series in 1949, had a pitching staff that allowed the most walks in the AL that year (812). Only one team, the hapless 1915 Philadelphia A's, allowed more (827).

440 of these walks, or 54%, were concentrated in three pitchers--Vic Raschi, Allie Reynolds, and Tommy Byrne, whose won-loss record for the Yankees was a combined 53-23 (.697). Of these three, the chief perpetrator was undeniably Byrne, who

earned the title of Mr. Walk Spike by contributing 179 walks in 196 IP. Here at BBBA we have a tool called the Quality Matrix (QMAX) which we use to evaluate the value and shape of a starting pitcher's performance. While you can read a great deal more about it elsewhere in the book, the nickel tour is that QMAX uses each start (GS) in order to grade a pitcher's performance in terms of hit and walk prevention. Each start is then placed in a two-dimensional value matrix, and separate averages are computed for each dimension ("S", or stuff, measures hit prevention; "C", or command, measures walk prevention.)

One of the first discoveries made with the QMAX method was that hit prevention has more impact on starting pitcher success than walk prevention. This is not a lesson that major league managers have taken to heart, however; they are extremely skittish with wild pitchers, and have become increasingly so over the past fifty years. It would be virtually impossible for any pitcher in the current game to have a QMAX profile like that of Tommy Byrne in 1949:

TOMMY BYRNE, NYY, 1949

	1	2	3	4	5	6	7	S
1			3	6			3	12
2				2	1		4	7
3							3	3
4								0
5				1	2	1	2	6
6					1		1	2
7								0
C	0	0	3	9	4	1	13	30

It's a staggering performance. The "7C" column at the extreme right of the QMAX box indicates those starts in which Byrne allowed more walks than innings pitched. In 1949, Byrne had 13 such starts--more than the totals of 40% of major league TEAMS in 1998. Tommy had more 1,7 and 2,7 games in a single season than the total number of such games thrown in both leagues during 1997-98.

But Byrne had 63% of his starts in what we call the "dominating" hit prevention range (S12, as shown in the "range data" listing). That percentage is more than twice the league average in current times. And Tommy had 12 starts in the "1S" range, where pitchers allow at least four fewer hits than innings pitched. As you can see, 40% of the time Byrne was a .900 pitcher:

TOMMY BYRNE 1949

	W	L	TW	TL	IP	H	R	ER	BB	SO	ERA
1S	9	1	10	2	103.33	43	17	16	77	62	1.39
all others	6	5	10	8	88.66	79	63	61	98	67	6.19

Despite walking nearly seven batters per nine innings in his 12 "1S" outings, Byrne fashioned a 1.39 ERA. That's because in those dozen games, he allowed an average of just 3.75 hits per nine innings. A corollary to Byrne's success with such

backward-looking numbers is the fact that he was "hit hard" (the shaded region at the bottom of the chart encompassing the "6S" and "7S" rows) only twice, or just 7% of the time. The average pitcher gets "hit hard" about one-third of the time (33%).

To get an idea of the pitcher whose game patterns are more in line with the current view of acceptable performance, let's look at the fourth member of the Yankees' 1949 rotation, left-hander Ed Lopat. Lopat pitched 20 more innings than Byrne, and walked 110 fewer men. He also allowed more than a hit per inning, while Byrne allowed a little more than six-tenths of a hit per inning. Here is Lopat's QMAX box:

EDDIE LOPAT, NYY, 1949

	1	2	3	4	5	6	7	S
1	2			1				3
2	3		2	1				6
3	2	1						3
4	2			1				3
5		1	2				2	5
6	1	1	2	1				5
7				4	1			5
C	10	3	6	8	1	0	2	30

As even a casual comparison with Byrne's QMAX box indicates, Lopat is a completely different type of pitcher. He is titled toward the lower left of the QMAX box, while Byrne is pushed as far to the top right as anyone has ever been in the baseball history. Lopat brought top-notch control (as measured in the leftmost column, labeled "C1") to the mound in one-third of his games. The average in 1994-98 was 12%, and it was probably closer to 8% in 1949.

A similar breakout of Lopat's performance by QMAX categories shows that he was a master at minimizing damage. His three "1S" starts all resulted in shutouts, and his ten "hit hard" games produced an average of just under eighteen baserunners per nine innings. He still managed to strand almost two-thirds of these runners, which was just a little worse than he did in the rest of games. That is a rare achievement: the usual result of extra baserunners is a steep decline in the strand rate.

Lopat's 1949 is virtually indistinguishable from the profiles of current-day control pitchers. He went on to have a tremendous run with the Yankees over the next five years, going 77-30 in 1950-54 despite ongoing arm miseries. In 1955, his arm finally gave way, and he was replaced in the Yankee rotation by none other than Tommy Byrne, who had been banished in 1951 due to the fact that his wild style of pitching made Yankees' GM George Weiss extremely uncomfortable. In the hands of Casey Stengel, however, Byrne picked up where he left off in 1949-50: he went 16-5.

The overall QMAX "range data" for these two is instructive:

QMAX RANGE DATA

	GS	SS	ES	IC	HH	PP		TJ	S12	S35	S67	C1	C23	C45	C67
Lopat	30	14	5	16	10	2		5	9	11	10	10	9	8	3
Byrne	30	11	0	19	2	16		0	19	9	2	0	3	13	14

	SS	ES	IC	HH	PP	TJ	S12	S35	S67	C1	C23	C45	C67
Lopat	.47	.17	.53	.33	.07	.17	.30	.37	.33	.33	.30	.27	.10
Byrne	.37	.00	.63	.07	.53	.00	.63	.30	.07	.00	.10	.43	.47

The key stylistic comparisons here are the percentages shown in the "PP" and "TJ" regions. "PP" stands for "power precipice" and is the region highlighted by the lined box at the upper right of the QMAX box. Byrne lives in it; Lopat has only two starts at the extreme left edge of the region. "TJ" stands for "Tommy John" region and includes those starts where the pitcher gives up at least a hit an inning but has excellent control. Byrne never even gets close to this area, while one out of six Lopat starts wind up here.

We said stylistic comparisons, and we meant it. It's possible to live in these regions and be a very successful pitcher. Lopat's way is the accepted one; Byrne's way is one that drives managers to the nearest bar. Casey Stengel, in 1949, came up with the perfect solution for managers who cannot countenance the "power precipice" style of pitching exemplified by Tommy Byrne. The key, as Stengel related to Ralph Houk, was not to watch Byrne while he pitched. Sometimes the art of successful managing is knoweing when to turn your back on the action.

Byrne's 1949 is the most radical example of "power precipice" pitching in the history of baseball, and demonstrates the fact that pitchers who are good enough at hit prevention can often overcome extremely shaky control. Byrne never did master his control, but he was never less than an effective pitcher, even for teams other than the Yankees. He could not have had a career of such success or such length, however, at any other point in baseball history. For that, we must give thanks to 1949 and the Great AL Walk Spike.

GEORGE BRETT's WHITE-HOT SUMMER

RON JOHNSON

Before we get started, let me pay thanks to the folks at Retrosheet (http://www.retrosheet.org) without whom I couldn't have considered this article. The work being done there is of unbelievable value. I really can't do it justice here: check it out for yourself. Their goal is nothing short of having a full play by play of every game prior to 1984.

It's funny how things work. George Brett had the most amazing summer of my lifetime; yet I'm sure that more people remember his 1980 for the problem he had with hemorrhoids than anything else. A lot of people are aware that he made a serious run at .400 (he was at .400 as late as September 19) but I don't think anyone recalls the summer.

As you can see from the splits at the end of the article, Brett wasn't playing poorly through the end of May, but it's hard to imagine someone making a serious attempt at .400 when he's only hitting .301 through the end of May. At that, he'd been as low as .255 on May 23.

His first hot spell started in the last week of May. Between May 23th and June 10th, he raised his average 84 points. He had hits in all but one game in that stretch (Gaylord Perry and two relief pitchers shut him down.). And it wasn't just singles. He slugged over .900 in that stretch. The game log for Brett for this period, shown below, tells the story with even more punch:

Date	AB	H	D	T	HR	RBI	BB	TB
5/23	6	2	1	0	0	2	0	3
5/24	4	1	0	0	0	1	1	1
5/25	5	3	2	0	1	3	0	8
5/26	3	0	0	0	0	0	1	0
5/27	5	3	0	0	0	0	0	3
5/28	4	1	0	0	0	2	0	1
5/30	4	2	0	0	0	0	1	2
5/31	4	3	0	0	0	1	0	3
6/1	3	1	1	0	0	0	1	2
6/2	4	1	0	0	1	2	0	4
6/3	5	3	0	0	1	2	0	6
6/4	5	3	0	0	1	4	0	6
6/5	5	2	0	0	0	2	0	2
6/6	4	3	1	0	0	1	0	4
6/7	4	0	0	0	0	0	1	0
6/8	5	3	1	0	1	2	0	7
6/10	1	1	0	0	1	1	1	4
TOT	**71**	**32**	**6**	**0**	**6**	**23**	**6**	**56**

Then he got hurt. Not the more well-remembered hemorrhoids, but a more mundane ankle injury. It would keep him out until after the All Star game.

When he came back he wasn't quite as hot—but then that's asking an awful lot. He did have a hit in every game but one between July 10th and August 18th. In the 29th game of a 30 game hitting streak, he reached .400 for the first time on August 17th. And he continued to hit the ball hard.

The 30-game streak, as you would expect, featured some truly remarkable hitting. All told, Brett hit .467 and slugged .745 during this period. After game 30 of the streak, Brett's BA stood at .404. Here is the day-by-day log for the streak (left-hand column, top of next page):

I don't think anyone was really aware what a remarkable season Brett was having until late July. Even then, there was no serious talk about a run at .400 until the middle of August. And it was far from the only story. A 21 year old kid named Rickey Henderson was on his way to 100 stolen bases. Reggie Jackson was having his best year while the Yankees were winning the AL East with 103 wins—only 3 more than the Orioles. (This two-teams-in-the-same-division-with-100+-wins thing has only happened twice,

Date	AB	H	D	T	HR	RBI	BB	TB
7/18	5	4	0	0	1	4	1	7
7/19	5	2	1	0	0	2	0	3
7/20	4	1	1	0	0	3	1	2
7/21	3	2	0	0	0	0	1	2
7/22	4	1	0	0	0	0	0	1
7/23	5	2	1	0	1	1	0	6
7/24	4	2	0	0	0	2	0	2
7/25	3	1	0	1	0	1	1	3
7/26	4	1	1	0	0	2	0	2
7/27	5	1	0	1	0	2	0	3
7/29	5	4	2	0	1	1	0	9
7/30	2	2	0	0	0	1	1	2
7/31	3	2	0	0	0	1	2	2
8/1	4	1	0	0	0	1	0	1
8/2	5	2	0	0	0	0	0	2
8/3	4	1	0	0	0	0	0	1
8/4	4	1	0	0	1	1	0	4
8/5	3	1	0	0	1	3	0	4
8/6	4	2	0	0	0	1	0	2
8/8	4	2	0	0	0	2	1	2
8/8	3	2	1	0	0	0	2	3
8/9	5	1	0	0	0	1	1	1
8/10	5	3	1	0	0	1	0	4
8/11	4	1	0	0	0	0	0	1
8/12	4	2	0	1	0	1	1	4
8/13	4	2	0	0	0	1	0	2
8/15	4	1	0	0	1	3	0	4
8/16	4	3	0	0	0	2	0	3
8/17	4	4	2	0	0	5	1	6
8/18	5	3	0	0	0	0	0	3
TOT	**122**	**57**	**10**	**3**	**6**	**42**	**13**	**91**

by the way: the other time was in 1993). And in the NL, there were two great races. The Phillies won the East by a game and the Astros won the West in a playoff—after losing J. R. Richard to a stroke.

All of this meant that there wasn't the media circus that the McGwire/Sosa chase produced last year. Even so, Brett was getting a lot of attention by the end of August.

August hadn't been quite as remarkable as June and July. Even so, .430 with a few walks and some power is a month anyone would settle for. Especially as the team was winning.

He couldn't keep it up. Not that he played badly in September and October (though it was presented as a slump, that's silly—Mike Schmidt in his prime would take that month.). Still, as the running 20-game BA chart shows, the falloff was big—mainly because he had been so incredibly hot during the summer. Brett kept his BA above, at , or near .500 for a considerable spell, most of it (of course) in June and July.

His stats for the summer? .459/.511/.752 in 276 plate appearances. And remember, league offensive levels were lower in 1980 than today. The league as a whole hit .269/.334/.399.

A few more notes about Brett's September are in order. Brett entered the month hitting .403. Despite homering in consecutive games of 9/3 and 9/4, his BA had slipped to .396 before he missed 10 games—no, not due to those infamous hemorrhoids, but because of an injury to his right hand. Returning to the lineup on 9/17, he went 6-for-12 in the next three games to inch back up to .400 (actually, .3995 for you purists out there).

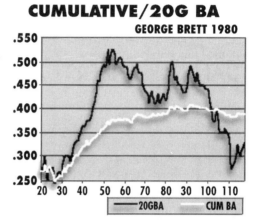

CUMULATIVE/20G BA
GEORGE BRETT 1980

— 20GBA — CUM BA

It was the 9/20-9/27 stretch that did in his .400 chances. During the seven games played in this time frame, Brett hit just .143 (4-for-28). At the end of this week, his BA had skidded all the way to .384. A final week flurry, including homers in three consecutive games from 9/28 through 10/1, got him back to .390.

Since the editor of this book is a known charthound, let's go for one more 20-game snapshot, this time using on-base plus slugging (OPS) as the measure:

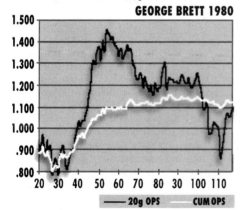

CUMULATIVE/20G OPS
GEORGE BRETT 1980

— 20g OPS — CUM OPS

For slightly more than four weeks (from July 11 to August 1)., Brett kept his OPS above 1.300. His peak 20-game OPS (1.449) occurred on July 18: in his past twenty games he'd hit .524/.571/.878. Now that is what can safely be called "white hot."

One final observation: I distinctly recall hearing about how there was no point in trying to get Brett out with lefties - that he was hitting everyone. As you can see, while he was far from ineffective against lefties, he had a massive platoon split. At least you hear less of this particular nonsense these days. (Of course the down side is that we get so much "information" that is meaningless. Ah well, I'll save that rant for another day.)

We'll leave you with a classic situational breakout of Brett's 1980 stats. Bill James had a lot of these in his 1981 Baseball Abstract (the one before he hit the big time). But he didn't have those RISP numbers—and they were worth the nearly twenty-year wait. They are otherworldly—I don't think I've ever seen anything close.

OTHER VOICES, OTHER PLACES

DAN QUISENBERRY IN HIS OWN WORDS

HEATHER HENDERSON

This summer the game lost its most distinguished poet. It was an unusual thing for a retired ballplayer to turn his hand to writing free verse, but Dan Quisenberry was an unusual man.

He had never expected to make the big leagues. He didn't have an impressive enough fastball and his record in the minors was less than electrifying. Frank White, who played second base behind him in Kansas City, says, "He had to beg the scouts to look at him." Quisenberry had no illusions. "I knew I had limited talent," he told a writer. "I was just happy I could play minor league baseball for two or three years and figure out what I wanted to do in life."

But he made it to the majors in 1979 as a mid-season callup for the Royals. In spring training the next year, manager Jim Frey had the idea of training Quisenberry to throw sidearm, like Pirates pitcher Kent Tekulve. When he changed his style, he found his groove. He went on to become one of the premier relief pitchers of the '80s, notching a major league record in 1983 with 45 saves. "The save meant something different then than it does now," says John Wathan, a friend who both played with and managed Quisenberry. "Now guys come in and throw to one batter. He'd pitch for three innings."

His eccentric delivery helped him fool hitters. No less quirky was his way of expressing himself. He was a naturally humorous man, with a disarming originality that endeared him to the press and to the fans. His pronouncement "I have seen the future, and it is much like the present, only longer" became famous. He enjoyed playing with words and poking fun at the conventions of baseball that demanded the post-game quote, no matter how trite. After coming out of a slump, he dryly informed reporters, "I found a delivery in my flaw."

In a world where immature bravado is commonplace, he seemed to have a humble sense of himself, and downplayed his prowess. His friend and teammate Paul Splittorff says, "He

didn't look like a professional athlete, and didn't carry himself like one. He was kind of wide-eyed every day about everything. He was always surprised, maybe even amused, by his success. He didn't think he was that good." Much of his understated wit was directed at himself. Other top relievers were intimidating fireballers who came in and "slammed the door." Quisenberry, as he put it, just "closed the door quietly."

"He'd joke about his abilities," says Wathan. "He didn't have a lot of athleticism, but he was a tremendous competitor. He could throw strikes at will, with a good sinking fastball, and get a lot of ground balls. Whenever we needed a ground ball for a big double play to end a game or finish off an inning, Dan could do it. Here's a guy who most people thought would never be a professional athlete, never pitch in the big leagues. He was used to hearing people say, 'you can't do that'. Yet he became one of the most dominant relievers of the era."

Quisenberry was careful to keep things in perspective in the face of his success. He told the writer Roger Angell, "I'm trying to be very good at baseball and to keep it from becoming too important in my life. I have to live on that border all the time." Some athletes isolate themselves, hiding within their own egos, but he reached out to others. With his wife Janie, he became involved with the Harvesters, a charity dedicated to feeding the hungry. "I can't save the world," he said, "but at least I can feed my neighbors." Among their projects were food drives and a fundraising golf tournament that raised over $100,000. This work was something that remained important to Quisenberry throughout the years, even during his final illness. "He stayed with it until the end," Splittorff says. "And he put time into it too. He didn't just put his name on it."

When Quisenberry signed a hefty contract with Kansas City at the peak of his fame, he faltered a bit. Every player feels pressure to live up to the big bucks, but his doubts extended beyond the baseball field. He seemed to have diffi-culty understanding why he was being paid that much. How did he and the game of baseball fit into the grand scheme of things? Splittorff talked with him at length about it. "I think he felt that there were a lot of people in the world that were overlooked, and had more important roles in terms of mankind than a baseball player did."

His teammates knew he was a thinker. White remem-bers, "He was a reader—astute and brainy. Judging by his intellect, he was the kind of guy who, if he hadn't been a ballplayer, would have been a teacher." But nobody saw him as a poet. "I don't think anybody knew, when Dan was playing, that he had that ambition," Wathan says. "We always consid-ered him a very intelligent guy—he had a tremendous vocab-ulary—but we never dreamed that he would be as talented as he was. About the only thing we did that had anything to do with writing was the crossword puzzle in the newspaper. We'd do that together in the bullpen early in the game, and maybe the Jumble. But as far as writing poetry, I don't think anybody had a clue that he would get into that. To be honest, I don't know if he knew."

After his career in baseball was over, Quisenberry began to attend writing groups. Eventually he enrolled in a poetry course taught by Gloria Vando Hickok, editor and pub-lisher of Helicon Nine Editions, a small press in Kansas City. "He was a wonderful, enthusiastic participant," she remem-bers. "He had good things to say." When she read his poems, she realized that he had talent too. "When you're dealing with students, people who have just started writing and have not published, very often they don't have their own voice. They sound like other people. But the thing I recognized right away with Dan was that he had his own voice. Even when we wrote something in class, it was him. It was Dan Quisenberry writ-ing as he was thinking and feeling. It wasn't pretentious and it wasn't distant. It was very real and straight from the heart. He was a natural writer. That doesn't mean that he couldn't have gotten better and better, and he probably would have. But he was just instinctively, naturally good. He asked questions. He was curious about everything. He had an open imagination and interest in people and everything that was happening. And he had brains. It helps to be intelligent and a quick thinker—to be able to absorb things, make connections and synthesize them so that they're relevant to whatever you're doing. He had the ability to set his mind to it and do so very gracefully. And, it seemed, effortlessly. But it wasn't effortless at all. He worked hard and he rewrote a lot."

His former teammates were startled by his new inter-est, but they saw how much he loved it. "We were all surprised when he started doing that but we were very happy for him," Wathan says. "The stuff he wrote was just really good." Says Splittorff, "He went to class and he enjoyed that. He thrived on it. I think he was very comfortable with the writing and really at peace with what he was doing. He talked about it some, but he was shy about it. That kind of fit the profile—he didn't talk about himself a lot."

Not everyone was ready for the notion of a "jock poet." Some observers reacted with derision and skepticism. Splittorff says, "I told them, 'you don't understand.' When you know him personally, he comes across more as a writer or a poet than he does as a relief pitcher—and a closer, at that. That's usually a big tough mean guy who'll take a bite out of the world and not think anything of it. But he was anything but that. That's where he was out of character—the way the pub-lic knew him."

In 1995, Hickok published a chapbook of Quisenberry's entitled Down and In, consisting of three baseball poems. Friends and teammates, including Wathan, make cameo appearances. "He mentions throwing to the catcher, 'Duke'. That's my nickname," Wathan says. "I felt honored that he thought enough of me to put me in there." In the poems "The Double Play" and "A Night in Cleveland", Quisenberry sketches the world of the bullpen and the mound in bold strokes, showing humor as well as action and offering insight into the real human being behind the "game face". The third poem, "Baseball Cards", is a bittersweet look back at his career and the price he paid for success.

Journals and poetry anthologies began to publish his work. He participated in poetry readings, obviously enjoying the interaction with the audience. Hickok says, "He was a wonderful reader of his own poems. He loved doing it, and he was so funny. He had a showman quality. He would stand up there and not be the slightest bit nervous. As far as he was con-cerned, it was a piece of cake."

Quisenberry's full-length collection, On Days Like This, was published this year by Helicon Nine Editions. Fans who expect to be charmed by his humor will not be disap-pointed, but they may be surprised by his contemplative tone. Many of the poems are philosophical, and some contain a sub-tle shadow of mortality. There are 22 baseball pieces in the book, including the three from the chapbook. Among them are small, heartfelt masterpieces that are among the best poems ever written about the game. In "Ode to Dick Howser", the Royals manager who died of brain cancer, Quisenberry writes:

> *this small man*
> *who fought big*
> *now looked us in the eyes*
> *just a man*
> *who no longer talked of winning*
> *but hinted at life beyond champagne*

And at the end of the wistful "A Day at the Park", a remembrance of a ball field, he concludes:

> *now old friend*
> *I walk on cement*
> *and carpet*
> *and sit in cars*
> *I miss dancing on*
> *turf*
> *dirt*
> *looking at sky*
> *for clouds*
> *to daydream with*
> *wind to judge*
> *friend or foe*
> *immense blue sky*

35

full
of the mind of God

The other 28 poems are about the rest of the world in all its variety: love, marriage, teenage kids, fathers, mountains, stars, potatoes, war, materialism, religious faith. The style is simple and fresh, giving the sense that each word was chosen with care—not to trumpet the poet's expertise, but to convey the essence of the subject. Whether funny or serious—and often both at the same time—Quisenberry's voice is full of feeling. When he turns ironic, as he sometimes does when he talks of controversial topics, there is nothing detached about his emotions: he cares deeply.

From "How I know the world as we know it is almost over":

> *in the newspaper I read*
> *they have a new vacuum*
> *so strong it can suck*
> *a baby's head off before it can breathe*
> *and some people are so mad*
> *they shoot the doctors who*
> *do that, in the name of god*
> *saying "thou shalt not kill"*
> *I wonder who will sorrow*
> *when other babies reach eighteen*
> *twenty-one or thirty-something*
> *and get sniped in bosnia*
> *somalia, iraq, okinawa, korea*

In "Antelope Wall Mount", a poem about an antelope he shot while hunting, he writes:

> *did he hear a death call?*
> *will i hear mine*
> *and stop all to stare at it*
> *widely pointing my way?*

When he wrote these poems he didn't know that, like his old manager, he had a brain tumor that would kill him. As the book was nearing completion, he experienced headaches and blurred vision. The diagnosis was a Grade IV astrocytoma, the worst kind of tumor. There was little chance of survival.

Despite this, he refused to give up hope. He continued his charity projects and even did a poetry reading. He took delight in the idea that he would soon have a book of his own. Hickok recalls, "When I told him this book was back from the printer and it was ready to go out, he bent down and got real small. He looked at me with this little-boyish, gleeful look and he said, 'I can't imagine that I deserve this!' He was just beaming. I'm sure if he had not gotten ill he would have kept writing and he would have had a full-blown career."

Throughout his months of treatment, Quisenberry retained his sense of perspective. Wathan recalls, "The thing that struck me the most during his sickness was that people asked him all the time, 'Do you ever say, why me?' And he'd say, 'No! Why not me? I've had a great life and a lot of blessings from God, but why am I any different from anyone else?'"

It was, indeed, a great life. Usually when a hero dies this young, we mourn for the things left undone. But Dan Quisenberry accomplished amazing things. He helped win the World Series, transformed himself from an athlete into a fine poet, and used his fame to help the hungry. We could hardly ask more of him. What we grieve for is his presence. He made a difference in the world with his caring. Hickok says, "I think he was born with 'sweet genes'. He was the sweetest, most thoughtful man. He had the ability to turn the conversation to you and make you feel as if you were the most important person in the entire world. And that's rare."

After reading aloud from his friend's book, John Wathan says quietly, "I was thinking about him today. I do often. I miss talking to him."

We will all miss his voice.

The Double Play

> *come into a one out, one on jam*
> *score three to one*
> *good guys ahead*
> *fans hootin, hollerin, and buzzin like hornets*
> *in the newer town of york*
>
> *Skipper says*
> *"get us a grounder and let's get the hell outta here"*
> *I check with duke, the catcher, and tell the wad in his cheek*
> *"we're throwin all sinkers"*
> *and he says "make em all inside"*
> *and pats his chest for emphasis*
> *cuz we both know Willie doesn't like em there*
> *Willie knows it too*
> *but he still doesn't like em there*
>
> *after eight tosses*
> *three dirt swipes with my toe*
> *two grabs at the resin bag*
> *six tugs of my cap*
> *three spits*
> *and one jock adjustment*
> *I go to a stretch and a pause*
> *fake a look at the runner I can't see at first*
> *then a wind and a whip*
> *the ball is loosed to the microspace*
> *between me, willie and duke*
> *in the flashes that make a second*
> *I hear the*
> *whhhrrrr*
> *as the ball spins to the zone of strikes*
> *and duke opens his fat glove*
> *to welcome and nestle its entry*
> *Willie begins the act of repelling*
> *my offering*
> *my hands go up involuntarily*
> *to protect my torso*
> *a God-given defense*
> *I hear the pop!*
> *of lumber hitting corked leather and string*
> *the ball snakes back in a one hop explosion*
> *half a lunge to my left, thigh high*
> *it goes 93 miles an hour*
> *but in my eyes*
> *it is a snowball, frozen in air*
> *snatched with my leathered left hand*

don't panic, I think
as my heart thumps with rabbit feet
I spin
see open air over second base
shortstop and base runner race to the bag
with cartoon legs spinning
I throw a 3/4-speed toss to the intersection of points
shortstop wins the race, catches the toss and throws to
first
in a bound he jumps over the sliding, grasping man

denied his right to property
a double play made

"good play" says the pressman
"that's what practice is for" says the pitching coach
"damn you're good" say the teammates

I panicked in the right direction
is what I think

Baseball Cards

that first baseball card I saw myself
in a triage of rookies
atop the bodies
that made the hill
we played king of
I am the older one
the one on the right
game-face sincere
long red hair unkempt
a symbol of the '70s
somehow a sign of manhood
you don't see
how my knees shook on my debut
or my desperation to make it

the second one I look boyish with a gap-toothed smile
the smile of a guy who has it his way
expects it
I rode the wave's crest
of pennant and trophies
I sat relaxed with one thought
"I can do this"
you don't see
me stay up till two
reining in nerves
or post-game hands that shook involuntarily

glory years catch action shots
arm whips and body contortions
a human catapult
the backs of those cards
cite numbers
that tell stories of saves, wins, flags, records
handshakes, butt slaps, celebration mobs
you can't see
the cost of winning
lines on my forehead under the hat
trench line between my eyes
you don't see my wife, daughter and son
left behind

the last few cards
I do not smile
I grim-face the camera
tight lipped
no more forced poses to win fans
eyes squint
scanning distance
crow's-feet turn into eagle's claws
you don't see
the quiver in my heart
knowledge that it is over
just playing out the end

I look back
at who I thought I was
or used to be
now, trying to be funny
I tell folks
I used to be famous
I used to be good
they say
we thought you were bigger
I say
I was

"Words," "The Double Play," "Baseball Cards" copyright © 1998 by the Estate of Dan Quisenberry. Reprinted from On Days Like This by permission of Helicon Nine Editions, Kansas City, MO.
Photo at left courtesy of The Topps Company, Inc.
Card at right provided courtesy of The Upper Deck Company, LLC. Upper Deck is a registered trademark of the Upper Deck Company, LLC. Major League Baseball trademarks and copyrights are used with permission of Major League Baseball Properties, Inc.

GIVE PETE A BREAK

G. JAY WALKER

Some years ago I worked for a small, privately-owned market research firm. Semi-annually, the president of the company would call the employees together to review the work of the past half year, touch upon the company's current financial situation and outline the key proposals we'd be gunning for in the months ahead. After signaling out a few employees whose recent performance was considered noteworthy, the president would always end the meeting the same way.

Pointing out that much of the company's success over 25-plus years rested on its reputation for data and reporting integrity, he made it clear that the one sure way to get fired was to fabricate data or otherwise compromise the company's reputation for integrity. He was not about to allow this reputation to be jeopardized by any one employee regardless of how well they performed otherwise. He made sure everyone understood that in this company, one rule stood above all, with dire consequences to those who violated it.

In chapter 3 of the Book of Genesis, we see this same principle being applied by another boss in the Garden of Eden. Adam and Eve were allowed to freely partake of the fruit of any tree except for one, and if they ate of that one tree, they would "surely die." The Lord allowed for much leeway, but He was adamant about obedience to one rule, again with dire consequences to those who violated it.

Just as both the president of the marketing firm and the Lord insisted upon adherence to one rule, so too does Major League Baseball. You can be a dope fiend, an adulterer, a crack head, a sexual deviant, engage in domestic violence or possibly even be a murderer (baseball has yet to have its version of OJ to test this out)—just do not bet on baseball games. Funny as this position may sound initially, there are actually good historical reasons why betting on games has become baseball's version of the tree in the garden. While stories of the Black Sox and the 1919 World Series might sometimes come across as an isolated incident, any serious student of baseball history knows it was the culmination of decades of problems baseball faced with betting scandals and players willing to give less than optimal performance in the name of dishonest gain.

The reason the climate changed so dramatically after the 1919 World Series was because of the lifetime bans handed down by newly-appointed commissioner Keneshaw Mountain Landis, along with a firm edict against betting on games and the promise of future bans for those caught violating this one rule. Suddenly the equation had changed from ethics versus money to ethics and loss of livelihood versus money. If the ethics part of it didn't whet your whistle, perhaps the loss of livelihood might. In 1955, noted author and sportswriter Lee Allen made the following remark on the long-term effects of Landis' action:

"The belief that big-league baseball is completely honest is not a myth; it is a fact. Anyone who has ever associated with professional players knows that they not only do not bet on games, they even avoid the company of persons who do. Although throughout the United States there is an enormous amount of money daily wagered on games, the players are disinterested. Their complete divorce from the gambling element cannot be traced to any superiority of character on their part, but it is a tradition of the game, a heritage from the stern administration of Kenesaw Mountain Landis."

Perhaps Allen was a bit presumptuous to assume no one has ever been on the take since Landis imposed his rule, but the threat of harsh retribution has kept such incidents minimal and isolated. Most of us would agree with the thrust of Allen's statement even today, some 43 years later.

The problem now is that its been so long since baseball's had any whiff of a betting scandal, that most fans assume this is the natural course of events, and that an honest game is something that happens automatically. Among some, there's almost a cavalier attitude that says you could remove the guards at the gate and things would go on the same because an honest game is now ingrained as part of baseball's culture, and besides, baseball players make too much these days to be on the take.

To those who site the escalation of player's salaries as sufficient deterrent, I would say you have half an argument. Yes, a comfortable living standard makes it less likely one would seek other "sources" of income. But there is still a big difference between the average salary of players today (the mean, which is over $1,000,000) and the salary of the average player (the median, which is under $400,000). True, you're not going to get to the Ken Griffeys and Tom Glavines, but what about the financially over-extended pitcher making $200,000 who finds himself pitching in key games as a 5th starter, and who's probable fate in a few weeks will be to accept a minor league assignment or become a free agent? When you tell the guards they're no longer needed and reduce the equation to a simple choice of ethics versus money, my experience is that money will always win out with a few of the people at least some of the time.

Lest you be naive enough to think that problems with baseball betting are relics of a bygone era, Baseball Weekly ran an interesting piece this past August about two Americans playing for the Mercury Tigers in the Taiwan professional league, who one day found themselves sitting in a hotel room across from a man brandishing a gun:

"For three hours, the gunman and an accomplice - believed to have been gamblers who had lost the Chinese equivalent of $1 million on the Tigers game the night before - browbeat and intimidated the players ... They slapped the larger Americans two or three times each in the face. The punched one of the Chinese players in the stomach and chest. They threatened to kill the players if they didn't recoup their losses in three future games. . . The two 28-year old Americans concluded it would be a good idea to leave Taiwan and return home. Before they did, they played one more game - in fear. 'I didn't know if I would be shot at in the outfield,' Gordon said. 'We couldn't trust anybody, not even our teammates'. . . Gordon and Tokheim apparently were caught up in a burgeoning gambling scandal that has rocked Taiwan's 8-year-old league like a tsunami. A total of 39 people, including 23 players, have been indicted so far and charged with fixing games."

So if you're saying it's a thing of the past, what you're really saying is it couldn't happen here. Yet with the impending globalization of baseball and the increasing cultural diversity in the major leagues, why would you assume here is somehow going to be different from anyplace else? And how many examples can we site from history of self-policing working over an extended period of time? The threat of harsh retribution is what has kept baseball an honest game over the past 79 years, and strict enforcement of the anti-betting policy is needed as much now as in the past. And finally, why do I get the feeling the Taiwanese league would have reinstated Pete Rose by now?

Rose's defenders argue that there was no proof that Rose bet on baseball. What they are really saying is that in a strictly guilty until proven innocent world, Giamatti couldn't produce the smoking gun. But this wasn't a formal legal proceeding with a courtroom venue and a potential jail term to anyone found guilty. (Note: the jail term that Rose served was for income tax evasion and unrelated to the question of whether he bet on baseball). Major League Baseball lacks subpoena power to even carry out this type of investigation or legal proceeding anyways. The bottom line is that it was really a workplace issue, and just as your boss can fire you if s/he feels there is sufficient reason to believe you've threatened the integrity of the company, Giamatti also had the right, given sufficient evidence, to make a decision that he felt was in the best interests of baseball—a mandate he was given upon accepting the job as commissioner.

Giamatti was new to the job and made some early tactical mistakes, which Rose's legal team exploited to make it seem that the commissioner was obligated to bring a legal case against Rose and prove in court that he was guilty. This largely contributed to the argument that lingers today that Rose should be reinstated because Giamatti didn't "prove" that he was guilty. Giamatti's job was to determine if there was sufficient evidence to believe Rose bet on baseball games, and if so, to act in the best interest of the game.

The circumstantial evidence gathered against Rose was overwhelming, including phone records of calls placed to bookies from Rose's home and betting slips on Reds games with Rose's handwriting and fingerprints. As Michael Sokolove, the author of the Rose biography Hustle, stated:

"Rose insists that he did not wager on baseball, and anyone who chooses to believe him with absolute certainty cannot be proved wrong. But if he did not, Rose was the victim of an elaborate, ingenious frame-up, a hoax of monumental proportions involving lies by witnesses who testified that Rose bet on baseball, forged betting sheets, fabricated betting notebooks and telephone toll records from Rose's home, hotel rooms, and baseball clubhouses."

But perhaps the most damning evidence against Rose is that when he was offered the choice of a full investigation to clear his name or to accept a lifetime ban and halt any further investigations, Rose bellied up to the table and made what was essentially a plea of no contest. Are we to believe Rose would have accepted such a deal if he only bet on football games? Charlie Hustle? As his lawyer Robert Stachler later remarked: "This was the best deal we could get. Believe me, we weren't looking at a lot of options."

To those who would like to believe that Rose's baseball betting was a temporary, isolated detour, the truth is it was a culmination of a lifestyle going back over a decade or more. For years, Rose had had a history of hanging around gamblers and bookies—and of not paying gambling debts. He had been under investigation by major league baseball security as early as the mid-1970's. Even Leo Durocher is reported to have once remarked that Rose should have been suspended long before the lifetime ban came down.

At the time Rose took the actions that brought about his downfall, he was no kid but in his mid-40s, with a 24-year playing career behind him. Moreover he was in a position of leadership as manager of the Reds. Any hazy notions he had about mixing baseball and gambling had to have been brought into sharper focus during the prior investigations by major league security. One is led to one of three conclusions about Rose:

> He didn't think he would be caught.
> He thought he might be caught, but felt he would get off since he was Pete Rose.
> He thought he might be caught, but if he was, he was willing to pay the price for his actions.

If it is one of the former two, Rose displayed an extreme arrogance and disregard for the game of baseball. And if it is the third conclusion, then he is really without complaint for what happened, isn't he?

Now if you let Rose back in, what kind of message does it send? That it is absolutely positively forbidden to bet on games, but we're not that serious about it if you do? Are you willing to trade off 79 years of honest baseball for the possibility of another Black Sox scandal some years down the road, or have a situation like the Taiwan league, possibly with players being shot at instead of merely roughed up? Just so Petie can have his little plaque in Cooperstown? As one writer commented: "Rose has to be where the game doesn't bend."

There's one other point that those advocating the induction Rose into the Hall of Fame might want to consider—even for Pete Rose, he's better off being outside the Hall of Fame than in.

When was the last time you read a book on the life of Zack Wheat? Caught a movie featuring actors playing Tris Speaker or Sam Crawford? Had a good discussion about Al

Simmons or Goose Goslin? But consider Joe Jackson.

Joe Jackson LIVES. Field of Dreams, Eight Men Out, Shoeless Joe Comes to Iowa, Shoeless Joe and Ragtime Baseball—Jackson has become one of the most noteworthy figures of early twentieth century baseball, while the others, all contemporaries or near-contemporaries of Jackson and all Hall of Fame outfielders, are largely forgotten.

Tris Speaker, born within a year of Jackson and clearly the superior player, would be lucky if he's received 2% of the media play that Jackson has in the past ten years. The reason of course is that Jackson was banned for throwing baseball games and never reinstated, making the question of his ultimate guilt, the punishment he received and the fairness of it all the product of endless debate. Over time, the debate has transformed Jackson into almost a mythic figure of baseball folklore. For the others, they were all enshrined into the Hall of Fame and, over time, quietly forgotten.

While Pete Rose's playing career is unquestionably of Hall of Fame caliber, let's face it, when it comes to being in baseball's pantheon, when it comes to hanging with the Ruths and Williams and Wagners and Mantles, Rose is still a few french fries short of a happy meal. Or as Mantle so succinctly put it after Rose set the all-time hit record: "Heck, if I had hit that many singles, I'd of worn a dress." A career .303 hitter who never hit more than 20 homers or stole more than 20 bases in a season, Rose was able to become baseball's Hit King with an additional 2,619 more at-bats than Ty Cobb, from which he produced 65 more hits than Cobb.

Internet correspondent Don Sibrel referred to Rose's 14,053 at-bats as his greatest achievement, and I concur. It symbolizes the characteristics most admired in Rose as a player: durability, longevity, tenacity. Rose was able to reach this magnificent number of at-bats through a fortunate confluence of events and circumstances:

Longevity - Rose played for 24 years.
For most of his career Rose batted leadoff.

Durability - Rose never suffered a major injury in his entire career. In fact, he spent a grand total of 6 weeks of his career on the disabled list, half of that when he was 45 years old.
Rose drew an average amount of walks, cer-

tainly less than what would be expected for a good hitting leadoff man.
Rose generally played for high-scoring teams, resulting in more turns of the batting order.

The point is that while Rose had some enduring and endearing characteristics as a player, he was simply good, perhaps very good, but not great. That he was able to get so many hits is a byproduct of his generating an enormous amount of at-bats. And if in the long-run he doesn't want to become this semi-obscure figure of baseball history and go the way of the Sam Crawfords and Al Simmons and Goose Goslins, he's going to have to pull a Joe Jackson and become a baseball folk hero, or at least a folk anti-hero. Like Jackson, he'll need to become something of a baseball outlaw. And the one way to kill off any chance of that will be to be inducted into the Hall of Fame.

The morning after his Hall of Fame induction ceremony, Pete Rose's life will be essentially over. No more of your name in the news, no more great debates about whether you should or should not go. No more mystique, no more bit of the outlaw aura. Sooner or later, even the hit record will be broken, and then what do you have to look forward to but answering "didn't you use to be Pete Rose?" inquiries at celebrity golf tournaments and pushing up daises in due time.

To the Rose-for-the-Hall advocates with their tireless diatribes of "How can you keep the Hit King out of the Hall?" or "He only bet on baseball games, it's not like he killed his mother," I say give Pete a break. Do you really prefer to give him some dusty plague in Cooperstown over having his case discussed and argued by fans for decades, possibly centuries? Rather than having sportswriters endlessly debating and fuming about the fairness of it all? It's the one assurance he won't be ignored or forgotten. If I were Pete Rose, I'd keep the mystique going by making frequent visits to casinos and racetracks, all the while moaning about the sheer injustice of it all. The only thing I'd ask of the Hall of Fame is a $5 million insurance policy to me or my heirs if they were ever so foolish enough to vote me in.

The simple truth is, Pete Rose is better off just where he's at. Keep him out of the Hall—for now and forever. Not only will you be preserving the integrity of the game, but in the long run you'll be doing old Pete a favor too.

MISTER GIANT

MIKE PATRICK

"There aren't any pro baseball fans in Japan, just people who love the Giants and people who love to see them lose." —Robert Whiting

"Winning isn't everything. Image is everything." —Andre Agassi

The main interest in Japanese pro baseball every season is largely what happens to the Yomiuri Giants. The team is always news, whether they are newsworthy or not. The Giants popularity stems from their history and the reach of the media empire that owns them.

While the team is expected to win, it is also expected to drive profits for its parent company, the Yomiuri Shimbun, Japan's largest newspaper. Since 1974, the story of the Giants is the story of an organization trying to strike a perfect balance between winning and good copy.

The story begins in 1974. The Giants have just lost a pennant race for the first time in 10 seasons. The Giants' so-called "V-9" era, when the team won nine straight Japan Series titles under manager Tetsuharu Kawakami has ended. Kawakami is set to retire. Third baseman Shigeo Nagashima, Mr. Giant, will quit playing and take over as the manager.

Nagashima was a Japanese baseball legend, not because he was the best player ever, but because he was the most charismatic star Japan had ever seen. Before Nagashima, the Japanese game had a dour, spartan image that derived from its development in Japan as a team sport that coopted traditional martial art concepts. Nagashima, who played the game with boundless joy and determination, energized the game. As a player, he had an intuitive feel for the game and a flair for the dramatic. Although Nagashima was a fighter and a winner, he never lost his cheerful demeanor and was adored by the fans. While the V-9 Giants were fashioned by Kawakami and would have been great champions without Nagashima, Nagashima was the one who gave the Giants their sparkle. Without him, it is very unlikely that fans would have taken to them the way they did.

With Nagashima at the helm, the Giants were assured of tons of good PR in season and out. It was a powerful veteran team, still loaded with stars in their prime including first baseman Sadaharu Oh and ace pitcher Tsuneo Horiuchi. It seemed to every Giants fan and everyone in the parent company like a match made in heaven a dream team led by the country's most popular star.

Nagashima proved as eccentric and intense a manager as he had been a player. He managed by his feel for the game. Very little seemed planned out in advance. He would occasionally bring in relief pitchers straight from the bench without having them warm up in the bullpen at all.

With no experience running a team, Nagashima's Giants fell apart at the seams in 1975, finishing last for the first time in the club's history. It was only the second time that the team had ever finished below .500.

The Giants rebounded with a vengeance in 1976 and 1977, winning Central League pennants both seasons, but falling in the Japan Series each time. When the next three seasons brought no pennants, an indignity the Giants hadn't suffered since the end of the war, Nagashima was fired.

Times had changed. A draft had been introduced in the fall of 1965, so that by the late 1970's teams access to talent was far more evenly distributed. Still, there was no question in anyone's mind that the Giants had the horses to win. A faction within the Giants organization pushed and pushed until Nagashima was dismissed.

Nagashima's firing sent shock waves through the country. The shock was most keenly felt by the Yomiuri Shimbun, Japan's largest daily newspaper and the Giants parent company. Fans canceled subscriptions en masse to protest the company's shabby handling of the beloved Nagashima.

To replace the legend, the Giants named former pitcher Motoshi Fujita as manager. Fujita was joined on the Giants bench by two new coaches: Shigeru Makino, one of Kawakami's lieutenants with the V-9 Giants and by the newly retired Sadaharu Oh. Fujita, Makino and Oh were referred to as the Giants Triumverate, a situation that led to occasional confusion with players not knowing who was in charge. The awkwardness of the situation apparently bothered few in the Giants organization, since it was clear from day one that Fujita's purpose was to give Oh the time he needed to mature into the Giants next great manager. Fujita and Makino were expected to be no more than caretakers.

Fujita, a terrific pitcher for a few years, was a relative unknown. The low key, bespectacled Fujita was the exact opposite of the intense Nagashima. As Bill James pointed out in his book on managers, switching intense managers with a low-key managers often provides instant rewards. The 1981 Giants proved to be no exception, winning the pennant and the Japan Series in Fujita's first season. In 1982, they finished a half game back, and in 1983, they won the league again although not the Series.

Fujita had returned the Giants to the top, but he was beaten in the Japan Series by the Seibu Lions and their abrasive manager Tatsuro Hirooka. Hirooka was a former Giant star who had coveted the Giants' manager position when it became vacant in 1980. As manager of the Lions, he vowed he would beat the Giants and made good on his word. Hirooka's revenge was an embarrassment to the organization and an opportunity to push Fujita aside and give the Giants' managing job to homerun champ Sadaharu Oh.

The Giants did not start off well under Oh's tenure, finishing third in both 1984 and 1985. However, the Giants lost the pennant by only half a game in 1986 and won the pennant in 1987, although they were beaten again in the Japan Series. In 1988, the Giants finished second, 12 games back of the Dragons and before the end of the season, Oh announced that he was leaving.

While it is hard to argue that Oh was a failure, the problem was that the Giants were still considered the class of the league. Except for his first season, the Giants were in first place at some point after the All-Star break every season during Oh's tenure. Yet in three of those four seasons the Giants faded. The team was always a contender, but one pennant in five years for the most ambitious organization in the world was another bitter let down.

For reasons that are not altogether clear, the Giants decided not to replace Oh with Nagashima. Perhaps Nagashima was still bitter about his being fired. Perhaps the Giants organization had had enough of legends and was looking for a winner. Motoshi Fujita, with two pennants and one near-miss in three seasons, was their choice, and for a second time, Fujita delivered the goods.

Fujita has two virtues as a manager. He knows pitching talent and is patient with young pitchers who he feels are good. He also makes sure to put a good defense on the field so his pitchers can succeed. When Fujita took over there were a couple of young pitchers on the Giants' staff that had been over-looked by Oh because of their control problems. Fujita took one of them, worked with him and made him a star.

The results were spectacular. In 1989, the Giants team ERA plummeted, and the Giants won the Central League by nine games, capping it off with a victory in the Japan Series after being down three games to none. The next year, the Giants won the pennant by 22 games but were swept in the Series.

Because Fujita wanted smart competent fielders, he put a high value on experience and completely ignored young players who were less than average fielders regardless of what they could do with the bat. While this policy created a pitchers paradise in his first two seasons, it also caused the Giants lineup to age and lose its punch as key hitters were injured.

The Giants fell to fourth in 1991 and tied for second in 1992. Fujita, one of the Giants most successful managers ever, had failed to win a pennant for two straight years. By the middle of the 1992 season, calls for Fujita's head were getting louder and louder, and the Yomiuri Shimbun was beginning to hear them.

While the Giants were floundering, a change had occurred in the structure of the amateur draft. In the fall of 1992, the draft rules changed to allow teams to negotiate directly with up to two college or industrial league players who would then join a team of their choosing as either a first or second-round draft pick.

Now the Giants could avoid the lottery that top amateur players had always been subject to when being selected by more than one team. Rather they could use their considerable influence and sizable capital to sway top amateur talent. By improving the Giants' access to amateur talent, perhaps the organization felt that they would soon return to their dominant position in the baseball world. And who better to lead the new generation of megaheroes but Mr. Giant, Shigeo Nagashima.

Nagashima's second coming was an amazing media event. Nagashima is a charmer. Although many who dislike the Giants are annoyed by the amount of press Nagashima gets, very few people hold it against him personally. However, Nagashima's first season back was a disappointment as the team finished under .500 for the fourth time since the end of the war, and for the third time under Nagashima.

Rather than panic, the Giants did what they've often done in times of crisis, change the rules. After the 1993 season, Giants owner Tsuneo Watanabe threatened to pull the Giants from the existing league structure if Japanese baseball didn't introduce a free agent system.

Watanabe got together with a few of the richer owners who could to flex their financial muscle to acquire other teams veteran talent and forced the weaker teams to go along. Since free agency was instituted, most of the big name free agents have signed with the Giants.

In 1994, Nagashima's Giants ushered in the free agent era by signing the biggest name available and going on to win the Japan Series, Nagashima's first, despite blowing an enormous lead in the Central League pennant race and having to win on the final day of the season. Since then, the Giants have

signed almost all of the big name free agents while continuing to skim off two of the top amateurs in every year's crop. Still, they have won only a single league championship in the last four seasons under Nagashima. Every year, it seems, the Giants have achieve the critical mass in talent they need to win with anyone as manager, but three years out of the last four have been bitter disappointments.

By the end of the 1997 season, only Nagashima's staunchest supporters were arguing that Nagashima was pushing the Giants any closer to a pennant. Still, few Giants fans want to see him go. When the powerful 1998 squad fell out of contention, both the Giants faithful and owner Watanabe blamed injuries rather than Nagashima for the Giants failure.

The Giants, even with the injuries, should have been in the pennant race in 1998. They are a collection of talented players that have been assembled with little forethought or planning. Every year, they are told that they are expected to win. Yet, under Nagashima, the team has been very vulnerable to exaggerated slumps. Seemingly, the only thing the team is missing is confidence and direction.

Still, when rumors spread that Nagashima was preparing to step down last summer, the Yomiuri Shimbun was besieged by fans who begged Nagashima to reconsider. It was said that the newspaper's department heads pleaded with president Watanabe to keep Nagashima in his rightful place. Watanabe, a smart poker player, saw the way the wind was blowing and emphasized what he had always said, that Nagashima had the job as long as he wanted it. Nagashima then announced that he would stay on for another season.

It turns out that Nagashima had become seriously disillusioned during the season when one of his pitchers, Dominican Balvino Galvez threw a ball at an umpire who had squeezed his strike zone. The event shook Nagashima and made him think whether the time had come for him to hang up his uniform for good.

So for better or worse, the Giants are stuck with Nagashima, hoping to amass so much talent that the team could win with anyone at the helm. Should the Giants win in 1999, you can bet the house on two things: Nagashima will be given most of the credit and the Yomiuri group will milk it for as much as its worth. Should the Giants collapse in 1999, the organization will hold El Nino more culpable than the manager.

If the public wants Nagashima as Giants manager, that's who the Yomiuri Shimbun wants. For the Giants, the name of the game is not only winning baseball games but selling newspapers. If Nagashima is a millstone in the win-loss column, so be it; he's good copy, and the Giants will eventually be strong enough to win with the owner's hamster making the decisions. Remember it's not whether you win or lose but the quality of the image you create.

Mike Patrick has been a systems analyst for an American Company in Japan for six years. An avid fan of the Yakult Swallows, he is very glad that Nagashima never became manager of his beloved birds. Despite being a native Californian, he was never much of a baseball fan until he moved to Japan and learned to sing the Tokyo Ondo and wave his green plastic umbrella after every Swallows' run.

DODGING THE DRAFT

JIM ALLEN

On Friday, Nov. 27, 1998, Katsutoshi Miwata took his life in Naha, Okinawa Prefecture. Miwata worked for the Orix BlueWave as the director of player personnel and was, at the time, trying unsuccessfully to sign the team's first-round draft choice, Nagisa Arakaki.

Arakaki, the star pitcher of Okinawa Suisan High School, had announced after the draft that he would only sign with the Fukuoka Daiei Hawks, and that he would go to college and reenter the draft in four years rather than sign with the BlueWave.

The current draft system allows any player with three years of college or industrial league ball under their belts to designate the team they want to play for, provided that team expends a first or second round pick to select him.

This system, known as gyaku shimei or reverse designation, was rammed down the throats of the baseball world by Tokyo Giants owner Tsuneo Watanabe in 1992. Despite the fact that the teams have agreed to limits on bonuses paid to amateur players of 100 million yen (~$830,000) for signing and 50 million yen (~$415,000) for first-year incentives, these limits are, according to one Japanese pro baseball insider, quietly and routinely exceeded.

The gyaku shimei system has accelerated the costs of signing all top amateur prospects and forced teams on tighter budgets to scrape and scramble to sign without throwing tons of yen under the table.

A BlueWave official who accompanied Miwata on the trip suggested that the outrageous cost of signing players is what drove Miwata to his death. Reportedly, Miwata's superiors ordered him not to return without Arakaki's signature on a contract. These two items suggest that either Arakaki was demanding excessive amounts of cash or Orix believed that it would require large sums of money to get him to change course and join the BlueWave.

While no one can ever know what other unrelated pressures bore on Miwata, the pressure to sign an 18-year-old high school pitcher may have been the last straw.

One critic in the Asahi Shimbun newspaper laid the blame for Miwata's death squarely at the door of Giants owner Watanabe for inaugurating the evil gyaku shimei system.

Another critic, Marty Kuehnert wrote, in a column apparently written before Miwata's death, that the reason for excessive amounts of under-the-table cash incentives was greed on the part of the players. He longed for the days when players played for the love of the game.

Of course, amateur players wouldn't be asking for outrageous sums of money if no one was willing to pay it. Expecting a baseball player to sign for less than market value is equivalent to asking a businessman, such as Mr. Kuehnert, to give away his valuable time and expertise—in order for someone else to turn a profit from it.

Teams shell out hundreds of millions of yen because they want to remain competitive. It has always been that way. The draft was originated in 1965 because signing bonuses were racing out of control. The draft was instituted to reduce amateur players' bargaining power.

Rather than drafting in reverse order of finish, as is done in the United States, a lottery was established for the first two rounds of the draft, allowing every team equal access to the biggest names in the draft. Presumably, this was done to get the more powerful teams to agree to the draft in the first place.

The draft forced players into a corner by requiring them to either sign with one team or remain an amateur. The draft slowed but did not stop the escalation of signing bonuses since players still had the option of maintaining their amateur status until they were free to enter the draft again. (Teams hold exclusive signing rights for one, two or three years for Industrial League, college and high school players respectively.)

Since Miwata's death, proponents of draft reform have begun clamoring for change. One group, who wants to see gyaku shimei rights extended to high school players. That way, all players will be free to negotiate in an open market. The other group wants to end both gyaku shimei rights and the draft lottery altogether and switch to an American-style draft, with teams drafting in the reverse order of finish.

Despite the hubbub surrounding Miwata's death, it appears unlikely that the reformers will make much headway. Essentially, the Giants hold most of the cards and most of the cash and they have no desire to see a system that does not allow them to throw their weight around.

If backed into a corner, Mr. Watanabe would likely waste no time in threatening to withdraw the Giants from the current system and form a new league. Should that happen, other teams would follow but only with Mr. Watanabe's consent, leaving the weaker teams and dissidents on the outside.

As a result, some modifications may be made to the draft, such as limiting the lottery and gyaku shimei to only the first pick in the draft. Unless there is an incredible public uproar to change the draft system, there will no motivation for the big money teams to budge more than an inch.

At press time, plans for Jim Allen's 1999 Guide to Japanese Baseball were still pending. Those interested in details concerning its avaiability may inquire by sending a post card to Jim Allen 1999, 2232 Harding Ave., Redwood City, CA 94062

THE VIRTUAL HALL OF FAME   A rec.sport.baseball Project

RANDY ST. LOUP*

EDITOR's NOTE: The Internet's home for informed and opinionated baseball discussion, rec.sport.baseball, has not only nurtured the work of Jeff Drummond, but has permitted several enterprising baseball historians to make use of the group in interestingly structured Hall of Fame simulations.

The most elegantly designed and evocative of these efforts has been spearheaded by writer and baseball historian Charles Blahous, who posts to rec.sport.baseball under the pseudonym Randy St. Loup. He calls it the Virtual Hall of Fame (VHOF), and it is a more exclusive version of the Hall than most other simulations of HoF voting.

The appealing historical fiction in Blahous/St. Loup's rendition of the Hall is its point of inception in 1921, a point in time when baseball was in the process of picking up the pieces of the Black Sox scandal. This permits the project to successfully implement its one inductee per year stratagem. And the rec.sport.baseball folks have rallied to the project: the early results of this effort are most impressive and interesting, as you will see. We look forward to seeing the complete results of the Virtual Hall of Fame as they unfold in 1999. <DM>

INTRODUCTION

Like many baseball fans, I have long viewed Baseball's Hall of Fame with mixed feelings. The predominant ones are extremely positive. I love the idea of honoring, evaluating, and ranking players, of arguing over who should be in, and who shouldn't. Most of all, however, I appreciate the link established by the HOF between baseball's past and its present, the way that the institution itself seems as much embedded in history as the game that it commemorates,

Amid these enthusiastic feelings are some frustrations as well. If only there were an election process that well defined the number and the caliber of the inductees. If only there weren't a separate veterans' committee, employing standards for enshrinement that were unrelated to those used by the BBWAA. If only baseball hadn't been segregated for so long, keeping out great African American players for decades. If only those who voted for HOF inductees were the students of baseball history that so are many of my friends.

I founded the Virtual Hall of Fame to fulfill a vision of what the Hall of Fame could be, without surrendering the wonderful things it already is. I didn't want yet another list of the 100 greatest players of all-time, assembled from the distant vantage point of the present. I wanted to roll back the tape of history and to re-create the HOF as I might have wished it were constituted. I still wanted an institution that one could roam through in something close to chronological order, starting first with the pioneers of baseball's early days, in their handle-bar mustaches and old-fashioned knickers, then proceeding, as the real HOF does, to honor more recent greats, with occasional bows to a long-ago player during a slow election year.

Indulging my taste for the highly exclusive, I set a pace of induction of one player per year. This would ensure that the players in the Virtual HOF were always at least of the caliber of the toughest standards in play for the real-world HOF. And the

voting process would be orderly and well-defined, something more like baseball's MVP voting than the methods used in Cooperstown. Instead of allowing voters to choose whatever number of candidates they wished, they would pick five each year, ranked in order of preference. The selections would be limited to players only, who had to have been retired by the "year" of the current election.

I chose 1921 as the first year for elections for a couple of reasons. One was that this would allow, through the present time, for 78 players to be selected, roughly the level of quality that I wished to establish. Plus it also seemed to provide a good fictional narrative explanation for the Virtual HOF. Baseball was rocked by scandal in 1920 — by the exposure of the Black Sox Scandal, and the death of Ray Chapman. A Commissioner was coming in to "clean up" and to revive interest in the sport. It seemed to me to be a good year to introduce a new HOF, to aggressively promote the game anew.

The Virtual HOF took a little while to get off the ground. Voting at first was spotty, with only a few participating. Only four ballots were received in the 1922 election. But those who did vote in the early elections made credible choices, and with each post of the results on rec.sport.baseball, interest in the elections grew.

THE RESULTS

Honus Wagner was the initial inductee in 1921, garnering every first-place vote but one. This feat was not matched until Walter Johnson in 1928, and was finally exceeded by Babe Ruth's unanimous selection in 1936.

The elections in 1925 and 1926 were each especially close. Dan Brouthers prevailed by only two points in 1925, and Kid Nichols by the same margin in 1926. This reflected considerable division of opinion over who among 19th century players should first be recognized.

Buck Ewing may have had the most interesting, certainly the most protracted, journey to VHOF induction. He was the man who blocked Wagner and Johnson from receiving unanimous support. At various times, he seemed to be on an orderly progression towards induction, only to be passed over by those who had been behind him. He finished 5th in 1921, 4th in 1922, 3rd in 1923, and 2nd in 1924, only to slip back to 4th place in 1925. Gradually moving up to 2nd place again in 1927, his candidacy was again postponed by the arrival of Walter Johnson, Ty Cobb, Tris Speaker, Eddie Collins, and Grover Alexander among the new eligibles. He finally broke through in 1933.

John Henry Lloyd in 1934 ensured that the VHOF would not duplicate baseball's color line, elected despite the scarcity of good statistical information about his Negro League career. Although his candidacy suffered from these institutional disadvantages, his election margin was quite comfortable by VHOF standards, signifying that the voters saw no reason to take issue with the reputation that Lloyd had left behind.

On a personal note, I have found that my own opinions have generally agreed with the majority opinions expressed by the voters. Only in a few years were my selections not those made by the group as a whole. In 1926 and 1927, I voted for Buck Ewing first. In 1935 and in 1937, I picked Fred Clarke. But in every other year, the voters' selection has also been my own.

ISSUES AND OBSERVATIONS

The VHOF has been generally free of divisive controversy, but a few issues are worth noting. Though not formally banned from VHOF induction, Joe Jackson has received almost no support. Cap Anson's reputation for having helped to establish baseball's color line has clearly hurt his candidacy, producing vote totals much lower than might have been expected solely on the basis of his on-the-field performance.

Certain players have been the subject of significant debate. George Davis is in neither the real HOF nor the virtual HOF, but his candidacy has been promoted by many voters who believe that his statistical record deserves a closer look than Cooperstown gave to him. After a lengthy public discussion of Davis's qualifications, support for Davis increased somewhat, though it has since faded again.

The candidacy of Home Run Baker was also given a boost by some electors who publicly opined that the VHOF should not be without a third baseman, and that Baker was the best that would be around for several decades. Enough voters found this persuasive to result in Baker's induction in 1937.

Other players of great popular reputation have moved in the opposite direction. George Sisler began his candidacy with significant support, which collapsed in between the 1933 and 1934 elections. Several voters who had included him prominently on their ballots dropped him from their subsequent ones, apparently giving up on his chances.

The average VHOF elector maintains a respectful but skeptical relationship with those who voted for the real HOF in Cooperstown. VHOF voters do not appear willing to wholly dismiss the opinons of the Cooperstown voters, but they are fully willing to challenge a decision that they deem to have been a mistake. George Sisler, in real life, outpolled Eddie Collins in the 1939

VHOF Inductees:
(Actual HOF Induction)

1921
HONUS WAGNER
ss, 1897-1917, (1936)

1922
CY YOUNG
rhp, 1890-1911 (1937)

1923
CHRISTY MATHEWSON
rhp, 1900-1916 (1936)

1924
NAPOLEON LAJOIE
2b, 1896-1916 (1937)

1925
DAN BROUTHERS
1b, 1879-1904 (1945)

1926
KID NICHOLS
rhp, 1890-1906 (1949)

1927
ED DELAHANTY
of, 1888-1903 (1945)

1928
WALTER JOHNSON
rhp, 1907-1927 (1936)

1929
TY COBB
cf, 1905-1928 (1936)

1930
TRIS SPEAKER
cf, 1907-1928 (1937)

1931
EDDIE COLLINS
2b, 1906-1930 (1939)

1932
GROVER ALEXANDER
rhp, 1911-1930 (1938)

1933
BUCK EWING
c, 1880-1897 (1939)

1934
JOHN HENRY LLOYD
ss, 1905-1931 (1977)

1935
MORDECAI BROWN
rhp, 1903-1916 (1949)

1936
BABE RUTH
rf, 1914-1935 (1936)

1937
FRANK BAKER
3b, 1908-1922 (1955)

HOF vote. VHOF voters installed Collins in 1931, whereas it is uncertain whether Sisler will ever make it.

Of the five original inductees to Cooperstown, each save one was selected in his first year of eligibility by VHOF voters, the exception being Christy Mathewson. Mathewson was up against another original inductee, Honus Wagner, in 1921. Mathewson waited one additional year, in which Cy Young was inducted, before himself being chosen in 1923.

The biggest discrepancy between the VHOF and HOF induction schedules occurred in the case of John Henry Lloyd, for the obvious reason of baseball's segregation. VHOF voters had no reason to wait to vote Lloyd in, and did so in 1934.

Frank Baker is another player who was elected well ahead of the HOF's schedule. Cooperstown waited until 1955 to elect Baker, choosing Jimmy Collins first among third basemen. VHOF electors gave only minimal support to Collins before turning to Baker.

Kid Nichols is one pitcher who seems to have been more highly thought of by VHOF electors than by Cooperstown voters. Nichols was inducted fully ten years after Old Hoss Radbourn into Cooperstown, but VHOF voters gave Nichols a decisive edge.

On the other side of the coin., VHOF voters looked skeptically at the candidacies of real-life HOF inductees such as Willie Keeler and Rube Waddell, in addition to the aforementioned cases of Sisler, Radbourn, Anson, and Jimmy Collins.

The VHOF will soon be presented with an impressive array of new credentials. The next ten years will bring forth claims to the honor by Gabby Hartnett, Mickey Cochrane, Bill Dickey, Lou Gehrig, Jimmie Foxx, Rogers Hornsby, Charlie Gehringer, Pie Traynor, Joe Cronin, Goose Goslin, Paul Waner, Lefty Grove, Carl Hubbell, Josh Gibson, Cool Papa Bell, and Judy Johnson. There will not be enough inductions to go around.

CONCLUSIONS

All told, the VHOF provides, for me, a much more credible record of enshrinement even than Cooperstown's. I have learned a lot in the course of conducting, and participating, in the elections, especially about 19th century players. I have developed renewed appreciation, not only for Dan Brouthers and Kid Nichols, but for George Davis and John Clarkson.

Few aspects of baseball are more fun than the annual arguments over MVP, Cy Young, and HOF selections. The VHOF provides a forum in which many of the most knowledgeable baseball fans can give voice to their opinions about the greatest ever, and provide a pleasant walk through history at the same time. It's been a pleasure to be the "curator," and I look forward to elections still to come.

Randy St. Loup is the pen name used at rec.sport.baseball by Charles Blahous

JEFF DRUMMOND's GREATEST HITS

Commentary by C.O. Jones

Occasionally that hard-ass editor of this tome, one Don Malcolm, manages to toss an assignment my way that doesn't resemble trench warfare, or a hand grenade sans pin. This is one of them. Though I don't participate in the high jinx at the Usenet newsgroup rec.sport.baseball (one of thousands of such forums where people with overly high opinions of their intellect and writing skills can engage in verbal mayhem), I am intimately aware of its existence thanks to Dandy Don, who has forwarded many of its missives my way in the past few years.

Invariably, I have found myself clamoring for more material from certain authors who frequent rec.sport.baseball (or rsb for short). Number one on that list is the inestimable Jeff Drummond, a mild-mannered technogeek by day but the Ubu Roi of Usenet by night. After harping at Don for months about Jeff's work, I was finally brought over to BBBA World Headquarters, chained in front of the computer, and quickly put through the paces of the DejaNews newsgroup archive.

I soon discovered an avalanche of Jeff Drummond material, and swiftly realized that this was more than a feeling, as the song goes. The nature of Jeff's achievement is unique even in a forum (rsb) that prides itself on a rebelliousness that occasionally borders on the cultish. He has made an art form out of the otherwise mundane concept of posting what is essentially public e-mail. There is a formal multi-dimensionality to Jeff's writings, an added element of his ability to use the medium itself as part of its content and meaning.

So I implored Don to let me put together a compendium of Jeff's "greatest hits," a selection of his unique contributions to rsb. Fortunately, Don was sympathetic to such a scheme, and Jeff himself proved amenable. What follows is but a small sampling of Jeff's work, but it should be sufficient to confirm why his posts are among the most eagerly anticipated at rsb.

1. COUNTERPUNCHER EXTRAORDINAIRE

A good portion of Jeff's posts consist of exemplary, deftly delivered one-liners. The keys to such a gift are brevity and an unerring sense of the perfect word.

In article <6qn1gnnaj1@nnrp1.dejanews.com>, mar-shad_786@my-dejanews.com writes:
|> Then you have come to the right place.

http://xxx.xxxxxxx.xxx hosts over
|> 450 pure and alcohol free perfumes and they last a long time unlike the
|> imitations in cheap store that evaporate 30 minutes later. We carry Boss,
|> Jazz, Brute and a lot more. Come and take a look. Mention
|> rec.sport.baseball and you will get a 20% discount.

I'm glad someone is finally doing something to improve the atmosphere in this newsgroup.

-Jeff   jjd@xxxx.com   Smells better than Ty Cobb

The other feature you'll notice here is the use of a tag line, as in "smells better than Ty Cobb." (A running gag at rsb is the evocation of the ornery Cobb, who has an equally ornery defender in rsb regular James Weisberg. As you can imagine, smelling better than Ty is no guarantee of a clean, fresh scent.)

Jeff is often at his best when encountering "spammers," people who post advertisements to non-commercial newsgroups (such as rsb). That type of exchange is represented above, but Jeff has a number of riffs on this. A more extended reply, and one that incorporates his own wary but affectionate interest in his hometown team (the Minnesota Twins), can be seen in the following:

In article
<1998061516425100.MAA14112@ladder01.news.aol.com>, skydivemik@aol.com (SkydiveMik) writes:
|> We are a team of dedicated Skydiving Instructors offering Skydiving Courses in
|> Florida.
|>
|> For more information check out our web site http://www.ffadventures.com
|>
|> Look forward to flying with you

Flying? Skydiving consists of falling very fast and then—if your chute opens—falling somewhat slower.

I suppose the ride up qualifies as flying; but I have to wonder about any skydiving instructor who would emphasize that part of it (kinda like a scuba instructor who says, 'looking

forward to boating with you.')
ObBaseball: *Twins outfielders this year have been competing in the 'skydiving batting average' department; with only Marty Cordova cracking the mythical 800 OPS ceiling.*

  Marty Cordova: bruised his heel on a hard landing; never quite the same since.
  Matt Lawton: gets dizzy in airplanes.
  Orlando Merced: jumps occasionally—usually remembers parachute.
  Otis Nixon: jumps whenever he gets the chance—usually forgets parachute.
  Alex Ochoa: frequently loses the ripcord in the lights.
  Torii Hunter: too young to believe in the law of gravity.
  Denny Hocking: can't seem to find a sport he's good at. Bounces nicely.
  Chris Latham: jumps too low for chute to deploy. . .

-Jeff jjd@xxxx.com   Prefers to remain inside perfectly good airplanes

This sensitivity to the proper use of phrasing and phraseology is often the subject matter of a Drummond post, and it might even take precedence over the original subject matter. That is the gently surreal art of subversion that Jeff practices in many of his posts. Of course, he's also capable of going for the broad effect, as this example demonstrates:

In article <6mtl3v$2k3$1@nnrp1.dejanews.com>,
nomos919@aol.com writes:
I> Not so long ago, baseball could lay claim to its exalted status. Natural
I> grass, quirky stadiums (not the homogenized, corporate-welfarist
I> monstrosities of today) and the pitcher's place in the batting order ensured
I> the game's integrity and continuity with the past.
I>
I> Not so long ago, undeclared war and diminishing civil liberties still sparked
I> controversy and dissent. As goes baseball, alas, so goes the Constitution.

Has Bud Selig gone and suspended the Constitution again?

Damn that man!

-Jeff jjd@xxxx.com

Fortunately for all of us, Bud's powers don't extend nearly that far, but Jeff's ability to give us a belly laugh certainly does. Those whose posts are overwrought or overreaching are prime targets for the elegant, economical yet devastating counterpunch. Our last example shows how rsb often wanders off its purported subject matter (baseball, remember?), and how Jeff is there to

bring baseball back into even the most far-flung topic, adding a wrenching twist to an already strained analogy:

I> Since when does lasting for a number of years make something good?
I> Communism hung on for 70+ years in Russia. Was it good?

No, which is probably why the Soviet Union wasn't breaking any attendance records.

2. ABERRANT ATTRIBUTIONS

I noted above that Jeff often adds a tag line to his signature, but there's often a more elaborate stylistic parting shot. Most email systems allow for a "signature file" to be created and attached to outgoing messages. Many users create a standard one with their name and email address; some even add some additional text in the form of a quote. Few rotate these quotes or use the signature file in anything remotely resembling a creative way.

And then there's Jeff. The most distinctive feature of Jeff's posts is an ongoing avalanche of new, novel, often side-splittingly surreal "codas" in the form of his "signature file." Many of these take the form of ersatz quotes from bowdlerized works, twisted into aberrant forms by Jeff's devious sense of satire. It is the eye for detail, and the ability to link completely unrelated subject matters with baseball, that make these fake quotes so much fun and of lasting pleasure:

"'Keep, yuppie ballparks, your storied pomp!'
cries she
  With silent dome. 'Give me your loyal, your poor,
  Your huddled fans yearning for no-frills glee,
  The wretched refuse of your teeming, overpriced outdoors.
  Send these, the domeless, over-taxed to me,
  I lift my lamp beside the puffed eyesore!'"
  Emma "Libby" Lazarus in The MetroMuffin: Engulfing The Twins

"A throw to first my heart afeard
But pitch my fears undid
How precious second base appeared
When 'neath the tag I slid."
John "Speedy" Newton in Amazing Base

"They that give up possible outs by intentionally walking batters to set-up double-plays deserve neither outs nor double-plays."
  Benjamin "Lightning" Franklin in "Poor Richard's Baseball Almanac"

BEN: *It is you and your money the Selig wants.*

47

That is why you fans are made to suffer.
LUKE: And that is why I have to go.
BEN: Luke, I don't want to lose you to the Selig the way I lost Vader.
LUKE: You won't.
THE SELIG STRIKES BACK

"Even the Umpire is bound by forces of balance and proportion which he does not see. The inches he squeezes from the strike zone when you are a petulant rookie on the mound are returned to you in full measure in the late innings of your no-hitter."
St. "Peewee" Augustine in Letter to a Young Hurler

"The genius of some general managers is that they never make clear-cut stupid moves. Only complicated stupid moves which make us wonder at the possibility that there may be something to them [which] we are missing."
Gamel Abdul "Pudge" Nasser in Meditations on the Arab League

"Out of Washington D.C. to Minnesota have I come. Here shall I abide, and my heirs, until the world ends. Or until I get a better offer."
Calvin "J. R. R." Griffith in Lord of the World Series Rings

"'When you face a new pitcher, Pooh,' said Piglet at last, 'What's the first thing you say to yourself?' 'I hope I get on base!' said Pooh. 'What do _you_ say Piglet?' 'I say, I hope I don't make an out,' said Piglet. Pooh nodded thoughtfully. 'It's the same thing,' he said."
A. A. "Ack-Ack" Milne in Now We Are in Little League

"There was Comte's crumpled body lying at the base of the fence; the ball perched precariously in his glove. Schopenhauer and I looked at each other in stunned silence, torn between our humanist desire to help Auguste and the moral imperative to stop that materialist Marx who, even now, was rounding second."
Soren "Kasey" Kierkegaard in Fear and Trembling in the Outfield

"Get two, Brutus."
Caesar's last words

"Don't cry for me DiSarcina
The truth is I never left you
All through my wild life
My mad existence
I kept my promise
Don't keep your distance."

Tim Rice and Andrew Lloyd Webber in Selig

"It is rather for us to be here dedicated to the great task remaining before us— that from this protested game we take increased devotion to that cause for which he here gave the last full measure of devotion— that we here highly resolve that this ejection shall not have been in vain; that this nation shall have a new birth of freedom; and that the liberal use of pine tar of the people, by the people, for the people, shall not perish from the earth."
Lincoln's "Pine Tar" Address

"Often it is easier to steal second than to explain how you missed the sign."
Benjamin "Lightning" Franklin in "Poor Richard's Baseball Almanac"

"...therefore, goest not into second with thy spikes held high, but neither canst thou fail to sunder the double play."
St. "Peewee" Augustine in The Moral Dilemma at Second Base

"He was a diminutive little gnome of a man. His beady eyes darted to and fro, and from his hunched stature one expected him to fall over at any moment. In short, he was the perfect shortstop."
Victor "Spanky" Hugo in L'Hunchback de Notre Stade

"I hear rookies whining,
I watch them look flaccid.
They'll make so much more,
Than I ever did.
And I think to myself:
'What a wonderful game.'"
Thomas "Louis B." Kelly in What A Wonderful Game

3. TECHNOCRATIC TALES OUT OF SCHOOL
We're not going to reveal where Jeff is currently employed, but suffice to say it's a very advanced computing firm whose name conjures up the utopian undercurrent of technocracy that Microsoft can only dream about. As a result, Jeff can spin technocratic tales out of school with the best of 'em. Several of these are bonafide rsb legends, and only Jeff really knows how much truth they actually contain.

In article <33142EB1.7117@erols.com>, "D.E.Nixon" <nixn@erols.com> writes:
|> To Any/All;
|>
|> There must be many of you baseball fans with extraordinary
|> technical expertise. Why don't you come up with a radar, sonar,
|> ,optical, or laser device that will take away all doubt about
|> whether or not the pitched ball went over the plate???

|> I could probably design a workable one myself in less than a
|> half day. !
|>
|> I suspect the reason for not doing so is that the arguments,
|> stares, spitting, petulant flouncing about the plate, etc. are
|> parts of the tradition of the game.
|>
|> Oh, well, it was a thought.   But, I still think it would
|> help the game.

I actually had such a system at one time, though you'd never know to look at me now. Perhaps an excerpt from my autobiography *(Bio of a Sabermatriculator)* will explain:

Early in 1982, I had a chance meeting with a VP of a large defense contractor to whom my company was selling a computer. They were looking to spin-off some Star Wars technology and I had the perfect application. We created a laser triangularization system that was able to track a baseball "on the fly" to within an inch. We presented the idea to then-Twins owner Calvin Griffith just before the '82 season opener. Griffith was enthusiastic, especially since it wasn't going to cost him anything (the defense contractor was willing to take a loss on the first unit, and I was just in it for access to the raw data). However, then-AL President Lee MacPhail and then-Commissioner Bowie Kuhn had serious reservations. They were concerned that such detailed knowledge of the game (especially concerning pitchers) would have given the Twins an unfair advantage in the American League (a remarkably prescient observation, in my opinion). Though, of course, the Twins of the early '80s arguably needed all the help they could get. It was only after we signed a bunch of documents and agreed to make all of the data the property of Major League Baseball, that we were given the go-ahead during the All-Star break. It looked like I would finally have plenty of data for my research and—even more importantly—I was making some inroads in the upper echelons of Major League Baseball. I could see the promised land.

We got the system up and operational in only two months and it worked even better than we'd expected. We were able to track every pitch, hit and throw in the Metrodome to within 11 millimeters (.43 inches).

My preliminary analysis of the data showed some incredible variations in the strike zone, not only between umpires but even between batters.

I remember one game when Kent Hrbek was riding plate-umpire Ken Kaiser.

We watched our screens in fascination as Hrbek's strike zone grew over the course of the game from about 20 inches wide to over 32 inches wide. Needless to say, Hrbek didn't have a very good day at the plate.

With such detailed data, the door was open to hundreds of studies of such diverse topics as: Quisenberry's pitch effectiveness as a function of arm angle; the tendency of Winfield's throws to the plate to tail away slightly towards third base; the phenomenon of Cal Ripken's opposite field hits not slicing as much in September; etc, etc, etc.

We generated mounds of data from late 1982 to June of 1983, when a laser malfunction accidentally blinded an umpire. Kuhn was afraid of adverse publicity and `blind umpire' jokes and ordered the whole affair hushed up. The defense company made an out-of-court settlement with the umpire and Kuhn impounded all of our data (one of those documents we signed apparently gave him the power to do that). My appeals went for naught. Griffith felt he'd been disgraced with the baseball community, and he initiated talks to sell the Twins. Both MacPhail and Kuhn took a lot of heat from the umpire's union and from the owners, and both were out of office within a year. Their successors, Dr. Bobby Brown and Peter Ueberroth, refused to return my calls. I had come this close.

I try not to think about it anymore. It's just one of those things.

While the topic of getting rid of the home plate umpire has apparently been a recurring discussion at rsb over the years, a more recent exchange between rsb gargoyle James Weisberg and Jeff took technocracy to new levels of surreal silliness:

Actually, [company name withheld] has had me semi-officially involved with a number of the design firms working on plans for a new Twins stadium.

Since the new stadium seems to be dead in the water, I guess I can share some of ideas that I (and my co-workers) developed in the field of ballpark design.

1) A revolving field. Put the entire field on a revolving turntable that keeps the field's orientation fixed relative to the sun.

Viola—no more 'sun field.' Not only would the players appreciate it, but the fans get to see different views of the action as the game progresses. Plus, the team can sell over an eighth of all seats at 'directly behind home plate' prices. I actually had Bud Selig talked into one of these for the now Miller Park in Milwaukee, but he backed out at the last minute. Apparently, he became worried that the "coriolis effect" would send too many fly balls into right field and that Jeromy Burnitz (who, at the time, had just been acquired from Cleveland) wouldn't be up to it. Idiot.

Once you can get past the notion that the spatial relationship between the field and the stands doesn't have to be permanently fixed, a whole bunch interesting "innovations" suddenly present themselves (which I won't go into at this time).

2) Reactive field surface. By placing 6 inch interlocking hexagonal plates under the playing field, each independently connected to an individual high-pressure, quick response cylinder, you can raise and lower any part of the field by as much as an inch.

This can be used to lower the field at the point of a runners leading foot and raising it for the trailing foot. In essence, this means that the runners are always running downhill! And while the resulting ~3% grade is small, the effect is noticable.

More importantly is the effect on a player's crucial first step, where the key movement is pushing off on the trailing foot. Now imagine that the field is, in effect, `pushing back.'

Our simulations showed that such a field would improve RonCoomer's range factor by a staggering 46% (though this is admittedly an extreme case). Of course, you need a lot of sensor and computer technology to monitor the players and their movements, but that's a tractable problem.

3) We did a lot of research on retractable roof (RR) technology. RRs are hideously expensive and, for reasons which are not fully understood, won't work in Quebec. It turns out that RRs are really an attempt to solve two independent problems: the temperature problem and the water problem. I felt that these problems might be solved separately—and for a lot less money—without resorting to a roof.

a The temperature problem is this—how do you control the temperature in an outdoor stadium (fans claim to prefer outdoor stadiums, but they nonetheless stay home in droves if it gets too uncomfortable)? Our solution was to develop a "radiator" stadium whereby we could pump a cooling (or heating) fluid through the superstructure of the stadium and, using the stadium itself as a thermal mass, we could generate microclimates that were as much as 10-15 degrees cooler (or warmer) than the ambient temperatures—depending on wind speed.

Utilizing VPA (very small aperture) misters and a giant sunscreen, we felt we could handle the hottest climates. Cold temperature abatement is a more difficult problem—our OSL (Orbiting Solar Lens) solution proved to be too expensive to implement. It's my understanding that at least some of our cooling technology is being utilized at Bank One stadium in Phoenix.

b The water problem is much more difficult because it covers not only protection from rain and snow (where applicable), but also excessive humidity. We had good success with a "laser blanket" that would operate high above the stadium and vaporize both rain and snow (up to all but the heaviest rates of precipitation).

The only problem was that it turned the precipitation problem into a humidity (and fog) problem in low wind conditions. And unfortunately, we ran out of funding before we could tackle the humidity problem.

4 We also considered a number of the more "mundane" problems of stadium design: parking, entrance/egress, etc. In particular, we tackled the infamous LLRR (Lack of Ladies Rest Rooms) problem that's been the fly in the ointment of so many stadium designs.

Unfortunately, we were completely stymied on that one.

We did, however, develop a synthetic nacho "cheese" product that didn't look like it came from an Alien sequel.

And here's the follow-up, where Jeff's replies to James Weisberg help us see the difference between sarcasm and wit:

In article <6h81th$i3d@tekka.wwa.com>,
chadbour@news.wwa.com (James Weisberg) writes:

I> Jeff Drummond <jjd@xxx.com> wrote:
I>
I> > Once you can get past the notion that the spatial relationship
I> > between the field and the stands doesn't have to be permanently
I> > fixed, a whole bunch interesting "innovations" suddenly present
I> > themselves (which I won't go into at this time).
I>
I> Heh. Finally something to drive scalpers bonkers! ;-)
I>
I> Just out of curiosity, do you have any figures on what
I> the angular velocity would be to accomplish this?

Well, assuming the field moves to track the sun, that's only 15 (360/24) degrees of arc per hour (or, of course, minutes of arc per minute or seconds of arc per second). Hardly noticable at all.

I> Also,
I> as long as an inning didn't last too long, you could simply
I> rotate the field in between innings; or perhaps for a moment
I> or two in between batters. Thus the field wouldn't have to
I> be moving while the ball was in play.

Do you know how much inertial mass we're talking about here? Sure, it could be done, but that's a good chunk of energy to get that puppy moving, especially if you're just going to shut it back down.

Do that 50 times a game and you're talking about a lot of energy and a lot of wear-and-tear. Of course, you can recover some of the breaking energy and store it in flywheels, but those aren't free either.

In any case, as I tried to explain to Mr. Selig, the rotational velocity wouldn't be anywhere large enough to effect the ball in play; but he kept babbling on about "coriolis effects", balls curving into right field, and Burnitz not being a good outfielder.

Proof, I suppose, that a little knowledge is a dangerous thing.

I> However, just as a side-bar to this, you see many stadiums
I> with the center field empty to provide a hitting backdrop for
I> the batter. If you rotate the field, that isn't really possible
I> and you might get a lot of complaints.

We were planning to have the outfield wall (with a hitting backdrop attached to it) part of the (rotating) field. It means that some fans in the OF bleachers have to move as the screen rotates in front of them (or not, if they're just working on their tans). Of course, as the backdrop rotated, as many seats are obscured as are unobscured, so the fans, in essence, just 'shift left.'

I> However, from the fan
I> perspective, it might be pretty cool. Those with season tickets
I> or luxury boxes might not be so keen on it, though. Now if
I> could have the expensive seats rotate along with the field,
I> *then* you might be on to something. ;-)

Actually, we thought about rotating the luxury suites in sync with the field (they would be suspended from an overhead track attached to the upper deck), but after some careful analysis we concluded that the rotation was so slow that many luxury suite patrons would never notice it (especially since their major point of reference would be the field which would move at the same rate).

However, when they left their suites and found themselves in a totally different section of the stadium, many of them would become completely disorientated and unable to find their cars.

I doubt any owner would want to risk alienating their highest-paying customers.

I> To add my own contribution to this thread, I've always
I> wanted a stadium that could bring the concessions right to
I> your seat, especially the beer. Imagine a huge network of
I> tubes running through the stadium filled with beer. And on
I> the back of the seat in front of you is a beer dispenser.
I> You just punch up what you want, pay with your credit card,
I> and stick your glass underneath one of the spigots. Wallah!
I> No more waiting in line, rustling up a vendor, or missing
I> the game.

We looked at that. The problem is that you have to have miles of tubing in the stadium (separate lines for each beverage).

That in itself isn't so bad, but what happens to the thousands of gallons of beverages sitting in uninsulated neoprene tubing for God knows how long? Sure, we can deliver warm beer or cold coffee that's lost what little taste it ever had, but that's no better than the current system.

You really want to go with insulated, recirculating lines. But then you're talking real money.

I> And at the arm rest, there's some air-tube like
I> thing which shoots hot dogs your way. And while their at
I> it, they could put a little lid at your feet which you
I> could pull up and drop your trash into.

The pneumatic tube approach actually had promise (used to deliver both food and drink). The problem there is to get a large enough tube to deliver enough food and drink per capsule. We figured a 3" diameter tube (using a 32 oz capsule) was the smallest practical size we go with (and even that cuts into beer and popcorn sales).

However, at 3", tubing to each seat consumes all available space in the structure (restrooms? Forget it).

So we backed off and looked at providing one tube for each 3-4 seats. But then fans are vying with each other for access to the tube. Finally, pneumatic tubes are noisy. You wouldn't want to be sitting next to one, especially if it's being used to deliver a steady stream of stuff for someone else.

I> If all this is too complicated, then how bout a little
I> hollow compartment underneath your seat where people can
I> scamper about underneath. You still keep the computerized
I> menu-thingy on the back of the seat in front of you and
I> it knows what seat is placing the order. So you place
I> your order and sometime later the space under your seat
I> opens up and out pops your stuff!

I can see you've never dealt with the unions representing the concession workers, James. I can hear them now...

`You want our workers to scurry about *under* the stands in dimly-lit corridors and pass food and drink up to the fat cat ubermenschen? Do you think we're troglodytes?'

No, of course we don't. But Jeff's view of Bud Selig is almost as derisive as that of BBBA's editor, and at his behest we include Jeff's techno-based satires of Budzilla's addled activities. The first is a send-up of how the issues of labor relations and league realignment might look if they could be handled as part of an on-line computer operating system:

bs% telnet mlb.org
Trying 204.91.134.2 ...
Connected to mlb442.org
Escape character is '^]'.

MLB-OS UNIX (mlb.org)

login: bselig
Password:
Login incorrect

```
login: bselig
Password:
login incorrect
login: root
Password:
Last login: Aug 25 1992 02:45:50 from faye.vincent.org
MLB-OS Release 2.1.1 (MLB422) #422: Nov 8 09:07:30
GMT 1993
Message of the day:
    Donald Fehr is Satan.
You have mail.
mlb442% lockout players
Lockout: preempted, players on strike
mlb442% realign -radical
Realign: insufficient resources, cancelled
mlb442% setenv INTERLEAGUE_PLAY ON
mlb442% make schedule
mlb442% expand -playoffs
Expand playoffs how?
 1) Add more playoff games
 2) Add more divisions
 3) Qualify second place finishers
 4) Add wild card
Enter option:
> 4
mlb442% expand -league
Enter expansion teams (even number of teams only,
please!!!):
> arizona
> tampa
^D
mlb442% make schedule
Make: don't know how to make arizona schedule.  Stop.
mlb442% mv arizona nl/arizona
mlb442% mv tampa al/tampa
mlb442% make schedule
Make: Odd number of teams.  Stop.
mlb442% mv al/brewers nl/brewers
mlb442% make schedule
mlb442% logout
Connection closed by foreign host.
bs%
```

Ah, if it were only this simple, as opposed to simple-minded. For a more scabrous piece of satire, check out Jeff at his most ferocious, blistering the bathetic Budzilla with a malevolent parody of baseball a la Selig dressed up as a mendacious computer simulation:

More Realism Than You Ever Thought Possible!

PLANTAGENET GAMES ANNOUNCES BUD SELIG BASEBALL

Most baseball simulation games put you in the role of a manager or general manager. Bud Selig Baseball allows you to be an owner AND acting Commissioner—the ultimate in macro level team and league management. BS Baseball puts whole leagues into the palm of your hand. Why settle for calling for pitchouts when you can be calling for lockouts?

Player strikes, rules changes, realignment, expansion, wild cards, interleague play, relocation, it's all here. BS Baseball allows you to adjust ALL of the parameters that conventional baseball sims simply assume are constants. Nothing is fixed in BS Baseball. Is your team stuck in a tough division? Not a problem in BS Baseball—just switch your team into another league!

In BS Baseball, YOU make the rules.

Realism and Accuracy

Conventional baseball sims are hung-up trying to "recreate" the on-field game, but that's not where it's happening. What baseball game can give you a season-long strike? A cancelled World Series?

Interleague Play? BS Baseball can—and will!

Statistics and Reports

BS Baseball utilizes all the latest statistics and can generate mounds of reports. Watch the offensive totals soar as you shrink the strike zone to the size of a postcard.

Flexibility

Play against other people

Allow other players to become owners. Sure, they can gang up and vote down your proposals; but you're the acting Commissioner—suspend them! Order them to sell their team! Threaten them with massive realignment!

Play against the computer

Normally, you wouldn't stand a chance against a computer AI designed to lead its team to dominance. But remember, in BS Baseball, the computer has to play by the rules that YOU make up.

Create a league

Create a league. Geographically realign leagues. Whatever. As acting Commissioner, you call the shots.

Ease of use

We have tried very hard to make it possible for any baseball fan to play BS Baseball, regardless of how little they know about the game.

There is no annoying "learning curve" in BS Baseball. The leagues will actually run themselves until you're ready to take over.

System Requirements

BS Baseball runs on any Windows 95 or MAC/OS computer. It requires surprisingly little memory. In fact, it actually works better with LESS memory.

Bud Selig Baseball - baseball the way it's never been played before!
Order your copy today from Plantagenet Games.

4. SURVIVING THE TWINS

Another of Jeff's identities is as a wise-cracking, long-suffering fan of the Minnesota Twins. For some reason, the Twins seem to bring out an especially macabre side of Jeff's humor. Here is a sample of his Twins' related material:

This is Tom Kelly's brain: "Hm, that Walker kid is really hitting the ball..."
This is Tom Kelly's brain on drugs: "...I think I'll bat him seventh!"
Any questions?

Q: What happens when Todd Walker, Pat Meares and Alex Ochoa collide on popup behind second base?
A: Marty Cordova goes on the DL. (representative Twins joke this year)

Dear Abby:
I have two second baseman and I can't decide which one to play. One, I'll call him Brent Gates, is a proven veteran. The other, call him Todd Walker, is a rookie who's still wet behind the ears. I'm leaning towards the proven veteran, but I just can't decide. Is there something I'm overlooking?
(signed) TK

Dear TK:
Yes; about 250 pts of batting average, 200 pts of on-base percentage, and 350 pts of slugging average. But don't feel bad—lots of managers would have missed that.
(signed) Abby

I> *Does anyone know the rest? In particular, my sister in law wants to know who*
I> *the Minnesota Twins mascot is.*

The Twins don't have a mascot. Anymore.
During the 1985 season, as new owner Carl Pohlad tried to dress up the team, the Twins debuted a pair of mascots (Twins, actually) named "Minnie" and "Paulie" (after the Twin Cities: Minneapolis and St. Paul).
The "Twins" were larger-than-life humanoid-like creatures with sickly smiles. Their highly-choreographed "act" consisted of walking around in foul territory and waving to the fans. They were widely disliked (although, to their credit, they eventually did learn to

stop frightening small children).
They lasted about half a season when one of them (no one could tell which was which) was kidnapped. Ransom demands were made but Pohlad refused to negotiate. Rumors floated around that the kidnappers were actually disgruntled fans; some even suggested that the mascots had staged the kidnapping in response to a salary dispute; even Pohlad was accused of kidnapping one of his own mascots in an attempt to boost their popularity.
In any event, by the end of the season, the ransom demands had stopped.
Most observers believed that the kidnapped mascot had been executed, though no "body" has ever been found. The surviving mascot—fearful for it's life—quit and moved out of the state. Last I heard, it was working in Shreveport, in the Texas League.

"I could while away the hours,
Conferrin' with the flowers
Consultin' with the rain
And my head, I'd be scratchin'
While my thoughts were busy hatchin'
If I only had a brain."
Terry "Scarecrow" Ryan in The Wizard of Minneapolis

Long-suffering? Yes. Silent? Not on your life. We are pleased to report that a more extended example of Jeff's eclectic mix of analysis and satire can be found in the Minnesota team essay (section four).

5. THE TAO OF BASEBALL

Not to be confused with a book of the same name (but inferior execution), Jeff's collection of maxims in the style of ancient Chinese sayings has been doled out over the years in snippets via his signature file. The full volume awaits final collation and assembly, but a few examples of it here will show that there is yet another dimension to Jeff's work, a work as multi-faceted as the Tao itself:

"If you want to shrink the strike zone,
you must first allow it to expand.
If you want to get rid of a base runner,
you must first allow him to get on base.
If you want the batter to take a pitch,
you must first allow him to swing away.
This is called the subtle perception
of the way things are."
Lao "Lefty" Tzu in The Tao of Baseball, Chapter 36.

"Wood is born soft and supple;
dead, it is rigid and hard.
Leather is born stiff and dry;
worn, it is tender and pliant.

Thus, whoever becomes hard and inflexible,
is a disciple of the bat.
Whoever becomes soft and yielding,
is a disciple of the glove.
The hard and rigid bat will soon be broken.
The pliant and tender glove will last many sea
sons."
Lao "Lefty" Tzu in The Tao of Baseball, Chapter 76.

"The Tao is like a rosin bag:
used but never used up.
It is like the knuckleball:
filled with infinite possibilities."
*Lao "Lefty" Tzu in The Tao of Baseball, Chapter
4.*

"The Tao is called the Great Slider:
just over the plate but unhittable,

it gives rise to infinite strikeouts.
It is always in your glove.
You can throw it any time you want."
Lao "Lefty" Tzu in The Tao of Baseball, Chapter 6

"There was something formless and perfect
before the first pitch was thrown.
It is serene. Empty.
Solitary. Unchanging.
Infinite. Eternally present.
It is the mother of baseball.
For lack of a better name,
I call it the Tao."
*Lao "Lefty" Tzu in The Tao of Baseball, Chapter
25.*

"Express yourself completely,
then keep quiet.

THE OLD GM AND THE SEA or: There's a Philosopher Born Every Minute

TOM AUSTIN

Things were downright slow in the Philosopher's Club—so clearly so that the statisticians who measured such things had been shipped back to purgatory. In other places, this would be a problem; but in heaven, you weren't allowed to go out of business—God would just send down some Monopoly money if you were short.

Things had been slow since the new rules had implemented, rules prompted by the cream-pie melee that had erupted the previous winter over an improbable discussion of baseball managers as they applied to philosophy—or perhaps it was the other way around. At any rate, God had sent his right-hand man, St. Peter, down to conference with some of the miscreants (God was always sending St. Peter on dirty little jobs like this, but Peter bore his cross like, well, a saint). The discussion was civilized, as it was in heaven most of the time, and the philosophers had agreed to steer their conversations toward more appropriate subject matter, such as the ontology of the logical positivists, or why it mattered how much pine tar was on a bat. The philosophers had dutifully complied, but in truth they had become a bit bored with such questions, and many of them eventually wandered off in search of women who had lived fast, died young, and left beautiful corpses. Most of whom, of course, were not to be found in the immediate environs: what had once been a boisterous melee was now little more than a muted murmur.

Plato and Aristotle still lingered, however, being not so interested in the aforementioned women. Plato looked around nervously before speaking, in spite of the sparse population. "Aristotle, this is a foolish and furtive conversation. Not only is it a trivial distinction, but it's against the rules!"

"I must disagree with you, my platonic friend, at least with regard to your first article. The distinction between field manager and general manager is a profound one. For although they share the common goal of winning baseball, they are cloven in twain by a profound difference in perspective: the field manager has as his tools the twenty five, of which nine to eleven are known as pitchers, and within those there are the categories of the long man, the spot starter, the lefty one-out specialist, the eighth-inning—"

"—Yes, Ari, we know, there are many categories to consider, right down to the 20 Mule Team Borax of the clubhouse boy. Can we please not get bogged down in details?" for once, Plato thought to himself.

"Harrumph! This is why I got the Alexander the Great gig and not you, my former mentor, for details are all. However, I will slum to your cave-enshrouded intellect and summarize: the manager is king to but a subset of the general manager's kingdom, to the top talent. The General Manager, by opposition, must needs be master of all the thousand details, from the Roster of Forty, to the Schmoozing of Agents, to the Avoidance of Arbitration. The position of General Manager, then, is far more appropriate a stage to demonstrate the superiority of the underlying philosophical—"

"—philosophy, schlimosofy. Where can a man get a stiff drink and a fight in this bar?" a white-bearded bear of a man was gesturing impatiently at the bartender. "And besides, any general manager who allowed himself to be emasculated by all this verbose rambling would surely lose a hundred games."

"Really, Ernest." The speaker was a trim brunette

woman, sitting at the center of a sophisticated-looking (read: slightly tipsy) group in the corner booth. "And what, in your esteemed opinion, would make a good General Manager? A hairy chest? A twelve-foot Marlin on the wall? Wait, I know: Dave Dombrowski." The woman's companions cackled archly at her jest.

Aristotle, looking befuddled, turned to Plato. The grey eminence rolled his eyes. "Algonquin Circle. They always commandeer that corner booth."

Another woman, also brown-haired but more severe-looking, looked up from her barstool, where she was nursing her fourth martini. "Dombrowski was unintentional genius on your part, Dorothy. What could be a better demonstration of the Virtue of Selfishness than the dismantling of the 1997 Marlins? Buy low, sell high, I always say. Speaking of buying— can I buy you a drink, big boy?" She slithered over to the stool next to Hemingway.

Hemingway, never one to refuse a drink, lifted his glass at the bartender. "It's much simpler than that. The best GM would be the one who ignored all of the petty details (here Plato shot a superior look at Aristotle) and reduced the game to its simplest, most manly elements: home runs, fastballs, and strikeouts. The one who gathered men's men, paid them their worth, and got out of the way. Ed Barrow, the man who made Ruth an outfielder and later put together the first Bronx Bombers was such a man." Hemingway eyed his whiskey for a split second, then downed it in a lightning-fast gesture, and belched. "Now, who's up for a bullfight?"

French literary critic and undead philosopher Jacques Derrida returned from the restroom. "Who keeps letting the riffraff in?" he sneered, with a sidelong long in Hemingway's direction.

Ayn Rand, so far unsuccessfully attaching herself to Hemingway's elbow, looked up with bleary eyes. "Ah, my dear Jacques. You will of course agree with me that Dombrowski was the greatest of general managers, due to his successful deconstruction of the World Champions!"

Derrida signaled for yet another double espresso and lit yet another Gauloise. "Your talent at missing the point is as predictable as that geyser in the Parque of the Yellow-colored Stone, how do you say, the 'Old Fidelity.' And I am not your 'dear.' It would seem that your American writer of monosyllabic he-man tales has earned that honor."

Ignoring Hemingway's grunted offer of fisticuffs, Derrida walked toward his booth, while an indignant Aristotle bustled past him on the way to the bar. "Mr. Bartender, I must ask how these mere writers have gained entrance to a club devoted to a discussion of the Natural Sciences!"

Bakunin, the bartender, kept his back to the pouting Greek and continued washing glasses. "The antinomies of expansion—it dilutes the talent level."

Aristotle rolled his eyes. "What is this otherworld coming to?"

"Can we talk about baseball, please?" Derrida, mugging for a non-existent camera, was doing his best Joan Rivers imitation. "Can we even make the claim that General Managers operate on some philosophic basis? Seems to me most of them

are just, how you say, Organization Men who got lucky."

A slightly slurred drawl, not heard from before: "And managers aren't? That's not very clear thinking on your part, frenchy. You must be part of the conspiracy. Buy my book."

Aristotle threw up his hands, miraculously refraining from a spit-take at the very last instant. "And who is THIS? I don't even know who you are, and I know EVERYthing."

"L. Ron Hubbard, at your service. And clearly you don't know everything, or you'd be able to explain to me how one general manager differs philosophically from another. I'll bet you can't even name a half dozen General Managers other than Branch Rickey and the current crop of bozos. Buy my set of tapes. Become clear in your mind."

"Easy. There was George Weiss, and Trader Lane, and Ed Barrow, and, um, Al Campanis, and, who was that guy who ruined the Giants in the 70's, Specs Richardson?"

Ayn Rand cackled dryly from her perch on the barstool, where she had returned after being rebuffed by Hemingway. "That's only five, Ari. Strange as it might seem, I agree with the "Battlefield Earth" boy. There's not a dime's worth of difference between most general managers, or should I say there is precisely a dime's worth of difference between genius and dolt in the General Manager game. George Weiss was a genius because he had Yankee money. Connie Mack alternated between sage guru and addled old coot precisely as his bank balance dictated. "

"So the pure well of baseball philosophy is again poisoned by filthy lucre. Life imitates art yet again. Too rich, too rich, no pun intended." Oscar Wilde had just emerged from the back room amidst a bevy of beautiful young men and women, and was grinning quite contentedly. Heaven had top-shelf booze, no jails, and no blue laws.

"I must yet again protest the profaning of our noble science, and our noble wood-grained club, by all of these dilettantes. Of course you would posit that General Managers possess no philosophy, for if they do not, the likes of yourself are free to 'wax philosophical,' knowing that you have already debased and debauched the term.!" Plato was on his feet, indignant and huffing.

"Debased and debauched, Plates old shoe?" Wilde was smiling broadly and simultaneously signaling the bartender for a another round. If I didn't take that as the grandest of compliments, I think I'd have to engage you in a battle of wits— bons mots at fifteen paces! But as it is, I'm feeling too cheerful, and I'll just ask you this. What possible philosophical stance can you discern in the career of Trader Frank Lane?" The young pre-Raphaelite Dionysians around Wilde giggled in anticipation.

"Very well, sir. I shall take your thrown-down gauntlet and make a pretty pincushion of it, you'll see." Plato looked to Aristotle for support, but his partner was making himself very busy counting the beer nuts.

"Ahem. Trader Frank Lane represented the philosophical principle of—of. . .". He trailed off, and there was uncomfortable silence in the bar. "With his, um, frenetic trading, often just for the sake of trading, Lane exemplified the principle of—OK, I got it. There's these three guys in a cave, see?

55

And they can only see the shadows on the wall, cast by the fire. . ." Plato was waving his arms and prancing about the floor in a King-Lear-on-crystal-meth kind of way.

"You're done, Plato. You can't do it. Nobody can. Now come to the bar and drink your medicine." Ernest Hemingway, having successfully thrown off the amorous advances of Ayn Rand, was offering a double bourbon as a consolation prize to the defeated philosopher. "After that, it's time to go fishing."

A bespectacled, gray-bearded man stood up from the corner booth where he had been sitting unnoticed, observing. "But it is not true that no one can explain the general manager. I can. Will you allow me?" There was a murmur of assent from the now-silent bar, and the bearded man relit his cigar, which was in this case just a cigar, puffed a leisurely puff and continued.

"Now, your Mr. Lane is clearly suffering from feelings of inadequacy, brought on by being handed off by his mother to a series uff baby-sitters, who zo ripe with sexual bounty brought feelings of fear und shame to young Frank as he struggled to avoid coming to terms with his Oedipal conflict—but I think you get ze idea. The same psychoanalysis could also explain the Smiling Python Dick Walsh, although I find ze symbolism of his nickname predictably rich."

"Ah, but what of Harry Dalton? Gabe Paul? Tom Haller? Al Rosen? Fred Claire? What is their psychosis, oh Sigmund the Great? Buy my book. Help me pay off my house-boat. Get 'clear'." L. Ron Hubbard whined in a cranky, yet slurred voice curiously reminiscent of a sedated Larry Flynt.

"Zey are boys whose Tinker Toys und Lincoln Logs vere taken from them too early. Ever since then they haff compensated by wheeling und dealing wit ze horsehide horseflesh. Zis gives them ze feeling of power zey require."

"Your analysis is as always strangely satisfying, Dr. Freud, but somehow just a touch too glib." Jacques Derrida spoke from his table. "Perhaps we could deconstru-"

Derrida was interrupted by a loud fit of coughing from the kitchen. "Don't worry, I'm not having an epileptic fit in here. I'm just working off some gambling debts by washing the dishes, and some soap got up my nose." The bearded, impossibly gaunt Russian writer Fyodor Dostoevsky stumbled into the bar, leaning on it through another coughing fit. After checking his handkerchief worriedly for signs of blood, Dostoevsky brightened. "What do I care? I'm already dead! So it's general managers, huh? What do you guys think of my favorite GM of all time, Brian Sabean? I wrote a book about him!"

GENERAL ESSAYS

SECTION THREE

EMPIRE BUILDING IN THE FIRST AND SECOND EXPANSION ERAS

Tom Ruane

Introduction

This effort began as an investigation into trades. In addition to identifying the biggest and most lopsided ones, I wanted to find out if certain teams and their general managers habitually did better than others, or if success in trading seemed randomly distributed. Finally, I wanted to find out if teams that traded well won more often than those that didn't. This last question had an obvious answer, but it wasn't the one I expected.

Before I could start, however, I needed some way of evaluating groups of players. For this, I borrowed and modified the Total Player Rating which appears in Thorn and Palmer's Total Baseball. I renamed it PV, short for Player Value, and it attempts to express the value of a player in wins over what a replacement (high minors) player would have done in the same number of plate appearances, innings pitched and so on.

Using this measurement, I looked at over 3000 trades involving nearly 8800 players before being forced to conclude that, for the most part, teams that traded poorly won more often than those that traded well. For example, the three worst trading teams in the American League from 1951 to 1960, the Yankees, Indians and White Sox, had the three highest winning percentages. The three best trading teams in the league over the same period, the Senators, Tigers and Athletics, lost 246, 112 and 279 more games than they won. Clearly, stronger forces were at work here, and rather than conclude that either trading didn't matter at all, or that doing it poorly was a sure path into the first division, I decided to enlarge the scope of my study and deal with the general subject of how teams have been built and dismantled in the twentieth century.

I started with the rookie season of every player who appeared in a major league game between 1901 and 1994.

This was the first year he either appeared in a game or was traded, sold or drafted by a major league team. I then determined the PV remaining in his career at the end of each year as well as at every point he changed teams. I broke down player transfers into the following categories:

- straight trades
- trades including cash
- straight sales (including waiver deals)
- league jumping (AL-NL to 1903 and the Federal League)
- minor league draft (since 1945)
- expansion draft
- free-agent signings
- anything else (called Lost+Found in this study).

In addition to the original questions, I added several more that I expected all this data to answer:

- How important a part has each type of transaction played in building teams? Has its importance changed over time?

- What teams have done the best and worst job of developing rookies? What team had the single greatest rookie class?

- What impact have the development of farm systems, the reintegration of baseball, the expansion from 16 to 28 teams, the creation of the amateur draft, and free agency had on the way teams are created? Have they increased or decreased the competitive balance? And what have they done to team stability?

- In terms of talent left in each player's career, what were the greatest teams of all time? What were the worst?

In the book-length version of this study, a five-year period from 1901 to 1990 (1901-05, 1926-30, etc.)

was chosen as the unit of measure. Our excerpt for BBBA covers the years 1961-75, or three consecutive chapters.

At the end of each five-year "chapter," I have included three pairs of tables and three lists. The first table pair (one for each league) looks at basic performance in terms of PV and winning percentage; we call it, for lack of a better term, the Basic Performance table. It contains the following columns for each team:

• the positive PV used during this period (labeled "+PV").
• the negative PV used (labeled "-PV"). In the categories above, I converted negative PVs to zero. This is where I added them back in.
• the total PV used (labeled "TPV"). The table is sorted by this column.
• the team's wins, losses and winning percentage.
• the team's expected winning percentage.

BASIC PERFORMANCE

AL 61-65	+PV	-PV	TPV	W	L	WPct	EPct
CHI A	193	20	173	458	352	.565	.561
NY A	204	32	171	485	324	.600	.581
MIN A	202	40	162	433	374	.537	.551
BAL A	186	34	152	449	361	.554	.537
DET A	174	31	143	439	370	.543	.537
CAL A	170	38	132	383	425	.474	.482
BOS A	158	38	120	362	445	.449	.464
CLE A	144	38	106	403	406	.498	.484
WAS A	109	55	55	309	499	.382	.394
KC A	104	57	47	322	487	.398	.406

The second pair of tables provides an expanded look at the amount of PV available to each team in the five-year period. These tables---again, one for each league-have the following columns:

• the PV left in the career of all the players on its roster at the start of the first year (labeled "Start").

Unlike a calendar year, the baseball year runs from October to October. As a result, the players on a roster at the start of 1901, for example, are those on the team as of October 1900.

• the PV gained and lost during the period through trades, purchases and so on (labeled "Got" and "Lost").
• the PV of all the players on its roster at the end of the last year (labeled "End").
• the positive PV used during this period (labeled "+PV"). The relationship between these five numbers, not surprisingly, is:

$$\text{"Start"} + \text{"Got"} - \text{"Lost"} - \text{"+PV"} = \text{"End"}$$

ORGANIZATION TALENT BALANCE SHEET

AL 61-65	Start	Got	Lost	+PV	End
BAL A	252	531	-245	186	352
DET A	246	326	-133	174	266
BOS A	94	457	-154	158	239
MIN A	284	327	-179	202	230
CHI A	172	402	-153	193	229
KC A	105	422	-208	104	216
NY A	197	289	-74	204	209
CLE A	139	447	-251	144	191
CAL A	0	403	-76	170	157
WAS A	0	373	-114	109	150

Note that the teams line up differently in this second table, which we're calling the Organization Talent Balance Sheet. That's because we've sorted the teams in order of the PV in their organization (all levels, not just the majors) at the end of the five year period (in this case, at the end of 1965). The PV value shown in the "End" column operates as a kind of predictor for the level of success a team will have in the next five-year period; as you can see, the Orioles are predicted to do rather well in the 1966-70 time frame, and so they did.

The third table, which we're calling the Detailed Talent Ledger, is an expansion of the "Got" and "Lost" columns, representing the talent shift in each of the eight categories mentioned above (rookies, trades...). If a column doesn't appear in a table, it simply means that there was none of that activity during the period (no expansion draft, no free-agents and so on).

Following the tables there are lists of:
• the players with the highest PV ("MPVs") for the period,
• the top rookies, and
• the most valuable players changing teams.

DETAILED TALENT LEDGER, AL 1961-65															
TEAM	**Rookie**	**Trading**		**Trades+$**		**Sales**		**Lost+Found**		**Draft**		**Exp-Draft**		**Total**
CHI A	119	237	-99	1	-4	7	-4	2	-4	36	-22	0	-20	249
NY A	245	27	-36	3	-1	1	-12	4	-2	9	-9	0	-14	215
MIN A	224	67	-30	0	-0	9	-5	17	-29	10	-99	0	-17	148
BAL A	350	109	-96	9	-14	22	-13	5	-26	36	-47	0	-49	286
DET A	220	52	-54	13	-17	29	-40	1	-4	10	-7	0	-11	194
CAL A	67	93	-26	19	-9	34	-23	37	-16	32	-1	120	0	327
BOS A	318	42	-21	0	0	0	-4	3	-40	93	-33	0	-56	303
CLE A	287	62	-164	23	-6	30	-36	29	-4	16	-20	0	-21	196
WAS A	47	51	-77	117	-32	30	-4	16	-1	37	0	76	0	259
KC A	269	89	-94	23	-32	20	-26	18	-32	4	-16	0	-8	214
Total	**2146**	**831**	**-697**	**209**	**-114**	**182**	**-167**	**132**	**-160**	**282**	**-252**	**196**	**-196**	**2392**

Most of the time, I'll be rounding PVs to the nearest whole number and this might occasionally cause what look like basic arithmetic errors. So whenever you see something like: "43 - 10 = 32", it's not that I've forgotten how to subtract. I've simply converted numbers like: "42.7 - 10.3 = 32.4" to integers.

1961 TO 1965: LEVELING THE PLAYING FIELD

The birth of the amateur free-agent draft

By the end of World War Two, every major league team had some form of a farm system and had discovered that they'd merely exchanged one expensive problem for another. Farm systems had originated to protect teams from having to pay huge sums of money to the minor leagues for players. But far from providing the majors with a steady supply of cheap talent, they simply shifted the problem down a level; now, instead of competing for minor league stars, big league teams found themselves in a bidding war for untested high-school players.

At the 1946 winter meetings, Organized Baseball made its first attempt to deal with this problem when they created the category of the bonus player. A bonus player was anyone who received a signing bonus greater than $6,000 from a major league team, $4,000 from a AAA team, $3,000 for a AA team, and so on. Once a man was designated a bonus player, he could not be demoted without first clearing irrevocable waivers; he could be drafted at the end of any year he was not protected on a big league roster and retained this designation for his entire career. This was basically the same rule that had been rejected earlier in the year when W. G. Brahman, the president of the National Association, complained that it was too complicated to be workable. His solution had been to prohibit all bonus payments but many in baseball felt that such a rule would be illegal, and so nothing was done until the end of the year, when Brahman resigned his position due to ill health, and Organized Baseball agreed to give the bonus rule a try.

It was a failure for a few reasons. First of all, while the rule provided some incentive for keeping bonuses under $6,000, it did nothing to reduce the money being thrown at the top players. For example, when Johnny Antonelli started accepting bids in 1948, it was clear that whoever signed him was going to have to shell out more than $6,000. Since he was going to be a bonus player anyway, it didn't matter whether he signed for $6,001 or for the $75,000 he eventually received from the Braves. The rule also had the unintended effect of hurting independent minor league teams. The bonus limit for a class D team, for example, was $800. A farm team in one of these leagues, however, could always have the player signed by their parent club, given a $5,999 bonus, and then assigned to them.

In 1947, Curt Simmons signed for $65,000. Antonelli got his $75,000 the next summer. Frank House received that much, plus two automobiles, to sign the same season with the Tigers. Two years later, Branch Rickey and the Pirates obtained pitcher Paul Pettit for a reported $100,000. Despite all the evidence that the rule wasn't working, it stayed on the books until 1950. When it was finally defeated that December, George Trautman, who had succeeded Brahman as president of the National Association, quipped: *"We got rid of quite a baby, didn't we?"* All affected players were released from their bonus status and Organized Baseball resumed its mad scramble for young talent.

In 1952, the Red Sox spent $700,000 in less than a month on 17 high-school players. Other organizations spent lavishly as well. The situation was a foreshadowing of what would happen twenty-five years later in the wake of the Messersmith decision. Ossie Bluege, the director of the Senators' farm system, offered this opinion shortly after the Red Sox' spending binge:

"The whole bonus procedure is suicidal. Even the rich teams can't afford the kind of money they've been paying out to the bonus babies. Not without taking all the practicability out of the game and reducing it to a rich man's hobby."

Hank Greenberg, urged a return to the old rule, stating: "We've got to put some shackles on the bonus situation or it will ruin all of us." And The Sporting News ran an editorial that summer that read, in part:

"The Sporting News refuses to believe that baseball lacks the brains or the courage to curb an evil that threatens its stability. We feel sure there are enough good businessmen among owners and club officials... to work out a sound solution."

In December 1952 the good businessmen of Organized Baseball instituted a revised version of the bonus rule. This time, a bonus player was any free agent with less than three months of professional experience who signed for more than one season or got more than a $4,000 bonus; he retained that designation for two years and could not be sent to the minor leagues during that time without first clearing irrevocable waivers. I'm not sure why anyone thought this form of the rule was going to succeed where the other had failed. A commentator at the time noted that the new rule wasn't really any better than the old one and that self-restraint by the owners was its only chance for success. Such restraint never materialized during the five years it remained in force and the only thing the rule managed to accomplish was to force young players like Sandy Koufax and Harmon Killebrew to sit on a major league bench instead of gaining valuable experience in the minors.

It was thrown out during the 1957 winter meetings and the major leagues spent $5,000,000 on bonuses the following summer. Once again, everyone agreed that something had to be done. *"Deep in our hearts,"* said one executive, *"I think we all know we can't go on like this.... But we can't go on changing the bonus rule every year."* Ford Frick, who had succeeded Happy Chandler as commissioner, favored giving the rule a third try and said:

"The other approach is a suggestion for an unrestricted draft of first-year players. I'd call it somewhat socialistic but don't doubt that it would be an effective curb."

Frank Lane had suggested a first-year draft of players as far back as 1953. It would permit organizations to give as much money as they wanted to young players, but these players would be subjected to the major league draft if not placed on their team's 40-man roster. Some influential men in baseball were opposed to such a draft. George Weiss, the general manager of the powerful Yankees, was against anything that got in the way of the rich teams:

"There is an effort by clubs which do not throw strong initiative and effort--yes, and money, too--into their operations to establish serious handicaps for organizations which are fighting to get somewhere, year after year."

Despite his objection and Frick's reservations, a first-year draft was adopted at the 1958 winter meetings. Each drafted player would cost $15,000 and had to remain on the team's roster for the following year. Initially, there wasn't much interest; only one first-year player was selected following that season. The price was reduced from $15,000 to $12,000 the next year and the restriction on farming out drafted players lifted. Six and then fifteen players were selected over the next two years. The price was further cut to $8,000 following 1962 and interest skyrocketed. The number of first-year players drafted and their career PV from 1960 to1967:

Year	#	CPV
1960	1	0.2
1961	6	0.0
1962	15	4.3
1963	45	127.6
1964	52	126.9
1965	59	87.4
1966	6	12.4
1967	9	1.4

The best of those drafted players:

Year	From	To	PV	Name
1964	MIN A	BOS A	56	Reggie Smith
1963	CIN N	HOU N	54	Jim Wynn
1965	BAL A	BOS A	36	Sparky Lyle
1964	MIN A	CHI A	23	Rudy May
1963	NY N	BAL A	20	Paul Blair
1963	CLE A	WAS A	20	Lou Piniella
1964	PIT N	STL N	12	Bobby Tolan

Despite helping some pretty bad teams, the first-year draft did little to curb the huge bonuses given to players coming out of high-school and college. Bob Bailey coaxed $175,000 from the Pirates in 1961. The Red Sox threw away $130,000 on someone named Bob Guindon and at least six other players received six-figure bonuses before that summer was over. After University of Wisconsin outfielder Rick Reichardt signed a bonus of $205,000 in June 1964, the owners were ready to try yet another approach: an amateur free agent draft.

Such a draft had been used in football for nearly thirty years. Back in 1952, Ford Frick appointed Branch Rickey to chair a committee to look into the bonus problem. At the time, both Rickey and Bob Carpenter, the owner of the Phillies, favored a football-style draft of amateur athletes. So why did it take another twelve years before a draft was attempted? There are probably several reasons for this. The one usually provided is that the owners were worried about the legal ramifications of a draft. Football hadn't experienced any difficulty with theirs, but there were these important differences:

1) Football didn't have the anti-trust exemption that baseball had.

2) Football was, for the most part, drafting adults. The vast majority of the baseball players drafted would be minors.

3) Football players had alternatives (the Canadian Football League and later, the American Football League) to the NFL. Baseball players did not.

Still, it's surprising that, considering the huge sums of money being lost every year, the owners wouldn't have at least attempted an amateur draft during the fifties. Or, as an unnamed AL official said in 1961:

"If it is illegal to put all these kids in a pool, let's find out why it is illegal. Let's find out from Washington what we can do to make it legal."

I suspect that the real reason behind Organized Baseball's reluctance to adopt the amateur draft was that the rich teams, and in particular Walter O'Malley, were against it. There were few things off the playing field that didn't go the Dodgers owner's way during these years. As it was, O'Malley and Buzzie Bavasi, his general manager and point man, did not go quietly. A week before the 1964 winter meetings, Gabe Paul, the general manager of the Indians and one of the draft's biggest supporters, blasted O'Malley and Bavasi for lobbying against it. He accused them of putting the interest of their team ahead of what was good for all of baseball. O'Malley replied: *"We've always believed that what's good for the Dodgers is good for baseball, and vice versa."*

But this was one battle the Dodgers owner lost. Even commissioner Ford Frick, a man who made a career out of siding with O'Malley, opposed him on this issue. When he realized that he didn't have the votes to kill the plan, O'Malley cast a *"yes"* vote, leaving Gussie Busch the only owner to vote against it. Paul called his victory *"one of the greatest things that's happened in baseball"* and predicted that even its opponents would come around once they saw how well it worked. He was right. The first draft took place on June 8, 1965, when Kansas City, selecting first as a result of its last-place finish the previous year, picked Rick Monday, an outfielder with Arizona State. At last, the owners had stumbled upon something that worked. Instead of making it inconvenient for teams to throw money at young players, the free agent draft made it unnecessary; players could either sign with the team that picked them or wait for the next draft (there was one in January as well as June.) The players picked in the free agent draft could not be selected in the first-year draft, a fact which explains the dramatic decrease in the number of those players drafted in 1966.

In addition to saving the owners money, this new draft was also intended to eliminate the disparity between the good and bad teams in the major leagues. Drafting in the reverse order of the previous year's finish, the worst teams got first crack at the top players. Buzzie Bavasi, the general manager of the Dodgers, didn't think the draft would help the poorer clubs *"...because clubs that were making personnel mistakes under the old system will make them under this one,"* but the general feeling today is that Buzzie was wrong. The hard part for the bad teams prior to the draft was not so much identifying blue-chip prospects as it was convincing them to come to Kansas City or Philadelphia instead of Yankee Stadium. Even Bavasi admitted as much. *"The tough job was not finding the prospects,"* he said, *"but sweet-talking them into signing."* With the free agent draft, the players no longer had much to say about where they played and that simply had to help the lousy teams.

The bottom falls out of the Yankee farm system

Another development in 1965 that had even more to do with improving the competitive balance than the free agent draft, at least in the American League, was the long-hoped-for collapse of the Yankees. Based upon the PV left in its players' careers, New York had started each season from 1951 to 1958 with the strongest roster in the league. Here's what happened next:

Year	Start	Got	Lost	End	+PV	-PV	=	TPV
1958	296	4	-6	249	46	-2	=	44
1959	249	23	-26	209	37	-7	=	30
1960	209	53	-25	197	40	-3	=	37
1961	197	58	-32	171	52	-5	=	46

Between 1958 and 1963, their rookies had a career PV of 124. Here's how that ranked with their competition:

I'm not sure why the Yankee farm system went dry in the late fifties; in 1958, Lee MacPhail left as their farm system boss and director of player personnel, but the timing is probably coincidental. For whatever reason, even the Houston Colt .45s, in their first two years of existence, had a much better group of rookies (PV of 210) than the Yankees did over that six-year span. Eventually, those poor rookie classes accomplished what the rest of the American League had been trying to do for decades, and by the mid-sixties the Yankees had tumbled into the second division.

Team	CPV	Team	CPV
BOS A	336	SF N	494
CLE A	288	CIN N	366
CHI A	264	CHI N	286
BAL A	236	LA N	268
MIN A	223	MIL N	242
DET A	216	PIT N	234
KC A	130	STL N	220
NY A	124	PHI N	139

As you can see from the chart above, the Giants spent their first six years in San Francisco gathering an impressive collection of young talent, and by the start of 1963, had one of the strongest rosters in history. Since we've seen nearly all of them by now, here are the top ten rosters from 1901 to 1994:

The key players on the 1963 Giants, along with how they came to San Francisco:

PV	Pos	Name	Obtained
71	P	Gaylord Perry	1962 Rookie
55	1O	Willie McCovey	1959 Rookie
50	OF	Willie Mays	1951 Rookie
48	P	Juan Marichal	1960 Rookie
24	P	Frank Linzy	1963 Rookie
24	1O	Orlando Cepeda	1958 Rookie
23	OF	Jose Cardenal	1963 Rookie
20	C	Tom Haller	1961 Rookie
16	P	Bobby Bolin	1961 Rookie
16	3O	Jim Hart	1963 Rookie
16	OF	Felipe Alou	1958 Rookie
13	OF	Matty Alou	1960 Rookie

Year	Team	TPV	Year	Team	TPV
1941	STL N	488	1943	STL N	423
1942	STL N	440	1925	PHI A	422
1951	NY A	434	1932	NY A	417
1954	MIL N	428	1962	SF N	415
1963	SF N	425	1974	LA N	410

Other than their reliance on home-grown talent, the other thing notable about the Giants was their lack of success. Every other team on the list above played in at least one World Series within six years, and they often played in several. After their pennant-winning season in 1962, the Giants would finish third, fourth, and then second for four straight years.

To explain what went wrong, let's look at the TPV for both the Giants and the teams that finished ahead of them in those pennant races from 1963 and 1966:

None of these other teams had better--or worse--players than the Giants did during these years. In short, they came close to winning each year because they had excellent pitching, catching, Willie Mays and a couple of top first-basemen. They didn't win, however, because they had almost no middle-infield talent and made some poor choices in the rest of the outfield. The players contributing the most to that negative PV during those years:

Team	+PV	-PV	TPV
LA N	151	- 21	= 131
PHI N	144	- 25	= 119
SF N	163	- 55	= 108
STL N	137	- 30	= 107

The Giants would have a winning percentage of .566 over this period. Of the 36 other teams that had a four-year negative PV of 55 or more, the next best winning percentage was 92 points lower, .474 for the 1989 to 1992 Houston Astros. In 1966, the Giants won 93 games with a negative PV of 16. No other team with a negative PV that high has had a winning record.

PV	Pos	Name	PV	Pos	Name
-5.1	S3	Jose Pagan	-2.5	2B	Chuck Hiller
-3.8	OF	Jesus Alou	-2.4	P	Billy O'Dell
-3.7	OF	Matty Alou	-2.1	SS	Dick Schofield
-3.2	3S	Jim Davenport	-2.1	OF	Len Gabrielson
-3.0	O3	Harvey Kuenn	-2.1	S2	Tito Fuentes
-2.5	OF	Cap Peterson	-2.1	OF	Ollie Brown

The First Round of Expansion

On October 17, 1960, the National League voted to expand to ten teams in 1962 with the addition of entries in New York and Houston. Beaten to the punch, the American League issued a surprise announcement nine days later. The surprise wasn't so much its decision to expand to ten teams, but to jump the gun on the NL by adding the new teams (in Los Angeles and Washington) in the spring of 1961.

So began the first wave of expansion in modern baseball history. For the AL entries, it looked like a recipe for disaster. An ownership group for the Washington franchise had been selected on November 17th, but the league went into the annual winter meetings with the Los Angeles franchise still up in the air. The Dodgers wanted to delay the move of another team into their area, while the AL countered with a proposal for both leagues to expand to nine teams in 1961 with inter-league play. The NL refused, saying that four months simply wasn't enough time to get a club ready to play. The AL disagreed and on December 6th, rejecting a proposal by Charlie Finley, selected a group of owners for Los Angeles headed by Gene Autry. They'd already missed the major-minor league draft and had only a week to prepare for the expansion draft.

Pushed back a day by a severe snowstorm, the expansion draft took place in Boston on December 14, 1960. Each of the eight existing clubs provided a list of 15 players, selected from their 40-man reserve list, who would be made available to the new teams. At least seven had to have been on their 25-man rosters as of September 1st. The Angels and Senators were required to pick 28 players from these lists, with at least three but no more than four coming from each club. In addition, each expansion team had to take at least ten pitchers, two catchers, six infielders and four outfielders. This was similar to the draft on October 10, 1961, to stock the National League teams. Most of the differences seemed to favor the NL entries. They'd had a year to scout and prepare for the draft instead of a week. There was no requirement that a team pick a certain number of players by position. In addition to the 15-man lists, each existing club also had to make available two additional players from their 25-man roster. Half of these so-called "premium" players would be doled out in a supplemental draft.

The disadvantages? One was that the talent pool had already been diluted by the previous expansion draft. But the largest potential disadvantage--and the one generating the most argument at the time--was that the NL teams had been able to formulate their expansion lists prior to the deadline for setting their 40-man winter rosters. Since a team will typically release marginal players at that time in order to protect minor league prospects, these fringe players could not be included on the AL lists of available players. Promising younger ones, or more valuable veterans, had to be added instead.

At the time, the feeling was that the National League teams were getting a raw deal. The owners of the Houston Colts threatened to give their franchise back to the league if the player pool wasn't improved. George Weiss, now with the Mets, and Paul Richards of the Colts made a special appeal to the league's other general managers at a meeting held during the World Series. Even AL officials joined in the criticism. Bing Devine, Cardinal general manager and one of the plan's architects, offered a weak defense, saying that the league had never promised the new clubs *"pennant contending teams or even first-division outfits,"* and that he was *"sure the Colts and Mets didn't enter the league with the expectation that we'd furnish them--at any price--with a sure-fire pennant winner."*

He wasn't kidding. No one was going to confuse either the Mets or the Colts with a first-division outfit for a long, long time. The Angels, on the other hand, would find themselves in first place on July 4, 1962, in the middle of only their second season, and would finish that year a solid third-place team. The comparative records of each league's expansion teams for their first five years:

Not only were the AL teams better each year, but only the best year for the Mets and Colts/Astros (1966) was better than the worst year for the Angels and Senators (1963). Things got so bad for the new National League teams that a special draft was held for them following the 1963 season. Part of this was due, no doubt, to the amount of talent each team got in the expansion draft. The

American League				National League			
Year	W	L	WPct	Year	W	L	WPct
1961	131	191	.407	1962	104	216	.325
1962	146	177	.452	1963	117	207	.361
1963	126	197	.390	1964	117	205	.363
1964	144	180	.445	1965	115	209	.355
1965	145	179	.448	1966	138	185	.427

Angels got as much talent (PV of 120) as both the Colts (65) and the Mets (54) combined. But was that because the players made available in the National League draft were significantly less talented than those made available in the American League? Or did the Angels and Senators just do a better job, even with almost no preparation time, than the Mets and Colts? We know the players the American League teams had to choose from and have a pretty good idea who was made available to the Mets and Colts Below is the talent each team made available in the draft, how much of that they lost, along with the key players (an asterisk before their name means they were selected).

Team	Key Players
BOS A	Wilbur Wood (41); *Jim Fregosi (40); *Fred Newman (8)
BAL A	*Dean Chance (27); *Chuck Hinton (10); *Albie Pearson (9)
KC A	Ken Sanders (16)
DET A	Pat Dobson (17)
CHI A	*Ken McBride(9); *Dick Donovan (8)
MIN A	*Hal Woodeshick (12)
NY A	*Bobby Shantz (9)
CLE A	*Johnny Klippstein (8); *Jim King (7)
PHI N	Dick Allen (53); Ray Culp (13); Robin Roberts (10)
SF N	Eddie Fisher (19); Dick Dietz (13); *Ed Bressoud (13)
CIN N	Orlando Pena (13); *Ken Johnson (12); Vic Davalillo (11)
MIL N	Don McMahon (21); *Felix Mantilla (7)
STL N	*Bob Miller (18); *Jim Hickman (8)
LA N	*Turk Farrell (12)
PIT N	*Al Jackson (8); *Bobby Shantz (7)
CHI N	Jim Brewer (21)

Team	Avail	Lost	Team	Avail	Lost
BOS A	101	56	PHI N	81	0
BAL A	56	49	SF N	57	18
KC A	35	8	CIN N	39	13
DET A	32	11	MIL N	32	11
CHI A	26	20	STL N	30	29
MIN A	22	17	LA N	26	23
NY A	22	14	PIT N	24	23
CLE A	21	21	CHI N	22	1
Total	**315**	**196**	**Total**	**311**	**119**

The quality of the two pools of talent were about the same. The Angels and the Senators simply did a much better job of finding it. The only top players they missed were late blooming pitchers. In 1971, Wilbur Wood and Pat Dobson would win 22 and 20 games, respectively, and Ken Sanders would be the best relief pitcher in baseball. But those seasons were a long way off in December, 1960:

Wood blossomed the soonest and he didn't have his first good year until 1967. The Mets and Colts, on the other hand, missed the 1963 Rookie Pitcher of the Year (Ray Culp) as well as the 1964 Rookie of the Year (Dick Allen).

So what happened after the draft? *Here's what each team did during their first five years:*

Most of the talent the Angels got, they got and

	Angels					Senators				
Year	Start	Got	Lost	End	TPV	Start	Got	Lost	End	TPV
1961	0	198	-20	145	25	0	156	-27	105	16
1962	145	37	-12	138	29	105	34	-14	102	16
1963	138	5	-8	102	24	102	55	-16	120	5
1964	102	84	-14	133	29	120	8	-25	80	11
1965	133	79	-22	157	25	80	121	-33	150	7

	Colt .45s					Mets				
Year	Start	Got	Lost	End	TPV	Start	Got	Lost	End	TPV
1962	0	136	-21	91	18	0	75	-2	60	2
1963	91	259	-37	297	0	60	68	-44	70	-4
1964	297	59	-9	328	9	70	24	-9	68	7
1965	328	53	-31	325	12	68	76	-3	131	-4
1966	325	66	-41	320	17	131	90	-12	189	7

Date	From	To	How	PV	Name
10-10-61	SF N		Exp-Draft	13	Ed Bressoud
10-10-61	CIN N		Exp-Draft	12	Ken Johnson
10-10-61	LA N		Exp-Draft	12	Turk Farrell
10-12-61	DET A		Bought	12	Hal Woodeshick
11-26-61		BOS A	Traded	-13	Ed Bressoud
1962			Rookie	19	Dave Giusti
5- 9-62	MIL N		Bought	21	Don McMahon
11-26-62	CIN N		Drafted	54	Jim Wynn
1963			Rookie	85	Joe Morgan
1963			Rookie	56	Rusty Staub
1963			Rookie	19	Jerry Grote
1963			Rookie	16	Joe Hoerner
9-30-63		CLE A	Sold	-17	Don McMahon
2-17-64	STL N		Traded	11	Carl Taylor
1964			Rookie	17	Larry Dierker
6-15-65	STL N		Traded	30	Mike Cuellar
6-15-65		STL N	Traded	-11	Carl Taylor
10-19-65	NY N		Trade+$	-19	Jerry Grote
11-29-65	STL N		Drafted	13	Nate Colbert
11-29-65		STL N	Drafted	-15	Joe Hoerner
1966			Rookie	30	Bob Watson
1966			Rookie	16	Don Wilson

spent early. It provided them with their early success, but if you're trying to determine which team had the best five-year plan, that honor clearly goes to the Astros (as Houston was renamed in 1965). The players moving to and from the Astros during those years:

Only the 1901 Athletics and the 1902 Indians got as much talent in a single season as the 1963 Colts. If I had counted Jimmy Wynn as being a Houston rookie in 1963 (instead of counting him as a Reds rookie coming to the Colts in the draft), the Colts' rookie class that year would have been the greatest of all time, eclipsing the mark of the 1925 Athletics.

So what happened? Why weren't the Astros able to take advantage of all the talent in their organization. Well, we'll talk more about this in the next chapter or so, but the answer has a lot to do with why they changed their nickname. In the meantime, consider that at the start of the 1968 season, the two National League teams with the most talent (in terms of future PV) on their roster were the Mets (courtesy of a great 1967 rookie class) and the Astros. The Mets would be World Champions one year later, while the Astros were still four years away from their first winning season.

PERIOD MPVS:

PV	Team(s)	Name
40	SF	N Willie Mays
36	MIL N	Hank Aaron
31	CIN N	Frank Robinson
28	PIT N	Bill Mazeroski

MOST VALUABLE PLAYERS TRANSFERRED

Date	From	To	How	PV	Name
1-20-65	CLE A	CHI A	Traded	58	Tommy John
12- 2-63	MIN A	BOS A	Draft	56	Reggie Smith
11-26-62	CIN N	HOU N	Draft	54	Jim Wynn
6-15-64	CHI N	STL N	Traded	44	Lou Brock
-1964	BOS A	PIT N	Found	40	Wilbur Wood
12-14-60	BOS A	LA A	Expans	40	Jim Fregosi
9-16-61	CIN N	WAS A	Traded$	36	Claude Osteen
11-30-64	BAL A	BOS A	Draft	36	Sparky Lyle

TOP ROOKIES:

Year	Team	PV	Name
1963	HOU N	85	Joe Morgan
1961	BOS A	84	Carl Yastrzemski
1964	MIL N	75	Phil Niekro
1965	STL N	73	Steve Carlton
1962	SF N	71	Gaylord Perry
1963	CIN N	64	Pete Rose
1965	BAL A	63	Jim Palmer
1965	PHI N	62	Ferguson Jenkins
1963	CLE A	59	Tommy John
1964	MIN A	56	Reggie Smith
1963	HOU N	56	Rusty Staub
1962	PIT N	55	Willie Stargell

ORGANIZATION TALENT BALANCE SHEET

AL 1961-65	Start	Got	Lost	+PV	End
CHI A	172	402	-153	193	229
NY A	197	289	-74	204	209
MIN A	284	327	-179	202	230
BAL A	252	531	-245	186	352
DET A	246	326	-133	174	266
CAL A	0	403	-76	170	157
BOS A	94	457	-154	158	239
CLE A	139	447	-251	144	191
WAS A	0	373	-114	109	150
KC A	105	422	-208	104	216

NL 1961-65	Start	Got	Lost	+PV	End
SF N	357	359	-179	188	349
HOU N	0	506	-98	84	325
STL N	338	357	-212	177	306
MIL N	314	423	-260	179	298
PHI N	170	363	-101	157	274
PIT N	245	327	-98	204	270
CIN N	296	414	-265	188	257
LA N	341	227	-154	183	231
CHI N	248	265	-128	157	228
NY N	0	243	-58	53	131

BASIC PERFORMANCE

AL 61-65	+PV	-PV	TPV	W	L	WPct	EPct
CHI A	193	20	173	458	352	.565	.561
NY A	204	32	171	485	324	.600	.581
MIN A	202	40	162	433	374	.537	.551
BAL A	186	34	152	449	361	.554	.537
DET A	174	31	143	439	370	.543	.537
CAL A	170	38	132	383	425	.474	.482
BOS A	158	38	120	362	445	.449	.464
CLE A	144	38	106	403	406	.498	.484
WAS A	109	55	55	309	499	.382	.394
KC A	104	57	47	322	407	.398	.406

NL 61-65	+PV	-PV	TPV	W	L	WPct	EPct
PIT N	204	26	178	412	389	.514	.529
CIN N	188	33	155	458	344	.571	.554
LA N	183	28	155	467	338	.580	.534
SF N	188	49	139	461	344	.573	.555
MIL N	179	40	139	427	375	.532	.532
STL N	177	43	134	430	371	.537	.538
PHI N	157	35	122	392	408	.490	.476
CHI N	157	44	113	353	449	.440	.447

DETAILED TALENT LEDGER

AL 61-65	Rookie	Trading		Trades+$		Sales		Lost+Found		Draft		Exp-Draft		Total
CHI A	119	237	-99	1	-4	7	-4	2	-4	36	-22	0	-20	249
NY A	245	27	-36	3	-1	1	-12	4	-2	9	-9	0	-14	215
MIN A	224	67	-30	0	-0	9	-5	17	-29	10	-99	0	-17	148
BAL A	350	109	-96	9	-14	22	-13	5	-26	36	-47	0	-49	286
DET A	220	52	-54	13	-17	29	-40	1	-4	10	-7	0	-11	194
CAL A	67	93	-26	19	-9	34	-23	37	-16	32	-1	120	0	327
BOS A	318	42	-21	0	0	0	-4	3	-40	93	-33	0	-56	303
CLE A	287	62	-164	23	-6	30	-36	29	-4	16	-20	0	-21	196
WAS A	47	51	-77	117	-32	30	-4	16	-1	37	0	76	0	259
KC A	269	89	-94	23	-32	20	-26	18	-32	4	-16	0	-8	214
Total	2146	831	-697	209	-114	182	-167	132	-160	282	-252	196	-196	2392

NL 61-65	Rookie	Trading		Trades+$		Sales		Lost+Found		Draft		Exp-Draft		Total
PIT N	225	47	-36	8	-5	2	-3	41	-7	5	-24	0	-23	229
CIN N	290	49	-77	2	-39	18	-24	22	-45	33	-68	0	-13	149
LA N	124	64	-31	39	-76	0	-6	0	-9	1	-8	0	-23	73
SF N	295	53	-128	0	0	0	-9	1	-3	10	-21	0	-18	180
MIL N	286	96	-125	1	-15	6	-38	26	-15	8	-55	0	-11	164
STL N	174	112	-140	2	-15	8	-19	49	-8	12	-1	0	-29	145
PHI N	247	82	-70	2	-7	14	-20	7	-2	11	-2	0	-0	261
CHI N	123	85	-120	5	-1	24	-4	11	-1	16	-2	0	-1	137
HOU N	235	77	-52	3	-10	50	-30	13	-5	64	0	65	0	409
NY N	141	12	-32	13	-2	17	-0	2	-1	3	-23	54	0	185
Total	2140	677	-810	75	-171	138	-153	171	-97	164	-204	119	-119	1932

1966 TO 1970: THE HOUSE OF CARDS

Bing Devine and his nine-year trading frenzy

Sometimes you don't know what you've got 'til it's gone; sometimes you don't even know then. In 1970, one of the strongest rosters in history passed through St. Louis without anyone ever noticing. Bing Devine had returned to the Cardinals for a second try as their general manager at the end of 1967. He was replacing St. Louis legend Stan Musial, who had seen his team win a championship in his first and only season as GM before stepping down amid rumors of front-office strife.

Strife was nothing new to the Cardinals front-office. As a matter of fact, Devine's first tenure as general manager had ended in August 1964, when he was ousted at the suggestion of Branch Rickey. Gussie Busch had brought back the legendary executive as a special personnel consultant following the 1962 season. It's not clear what the Cardinal owner expected from the 80 year-old Rickey, but if he was looking for controversy, Busch certainly got his money's worth. Rickey immediately started feuding with Bing Devine and upset more than a few St. Louis fans by suggesting that Stan Musial might want to consider retiring after his fine comeback season at the age of 41. Actually, he had complained about the Cardinal great *"...keeping a young player out of the lineup."*

When Devine was fired, the Cardinals were closer to the eighth-place Cubs than the first-place Phillies. He was replaced by Bob Howsam, a Rickey protege, and Branch decided it was time to start rebuilding for 1965. He circulated a memo outlining his plans for the rest of the season. They included sending rookie outfielder Mike Shannon back to the minors, unloading reliever Barney Schultz and recalling pitchers Steve Carlton, Dave Dowling and Nelson Briles. He also didn't see much of a Cardinal future for a host of their players, including Julian Javier and Dal Maxvill. It was a classic case of bad timing. The Cardinals rallied to win the pennant, the contents of the memo were leaked, and Rickey was fired shortly after being snubbed at the team's victory dinner. In retrospect, however, he was basically correct in most of his recommendations. Musial had been washed up by the end of 1962, and Carlton and Briles would be mainstays of the pitching staff during the late sixties.

Devine would be rewarded for the Cardinal resurgence by being named The Sporting News Executive of the Year. It was the second straight time he had won the award, having received it following the Cards surprising second-place finish the previous year. He had held his position since replacing Lane in 1958 and here's how he did during those seven years, along with the average of the other seven non-expansion teams:

	Start	Got	Lost	End
	232	541	-279	250
AVG	232	520	-231	285

68

	ROOKIE	TRADING	SALES	LOST+FOUND	DRAFTS	TOTAL
	239	224 -200	13 -25	53 -17	13 -38	262
AVG.	352	123 -144	8 -18	20 -27	17 -42	289

His slight advantage in heavy trading was not quite able to overcome a sluggish farm system. The Cardinals were average when he took over and a little below average when he left. If this seems a harsh appraisal of the Cards' 1964 talent in light of their World Series victory that year, consider that only five games separated the top half of the league that year and that they would follow up their championship with seventh and sixth-place finishes.

He was the busiest trader in the National League during his first term as GM, exchanging 138 players with a PV of 424, ahead of both the 110 players traded by vice-president John Holland of the Cubs and the PV of 350 swapped by the Reds, led during these years by first Gabe Paul and then Bill DeWitt. Still, there was nothing extraordinary about the amount of trading he did; three teams in the American League (Cleveland, Chicago and Kansas City) traded more talent than the Cards over the same period of time.

His first year back was a quiet one. He made four minor trades. The only player he picked up who contributed much in 1968 was Johnny Edwards, the backup catcher, and the only player of consequence he got rid of was Alex Johnson. Perhaps he was unwilling to tamper too much with a successful team and his reluctance paid off with a second straight World Series appearance. Unfortunately for St. Louis, Bing rolled up his sleeves after his team lost the World Series that year and went to work.

The day after dropping the seventh-game of the World Series to the Tigers, he traded Johnny Edwards to the Astros for Dave Giusti and a backup catcher. That same day he sent Wayne Granger and Bobby Tolan to the Reds for Vada Pinson. Three days later he lost the newly acquired Dave Giusti to the Padres in the expansion draft, which he remedied by sending four players to San Diego in December to reclaim him. The big deal of the off-season, however, was the one that sent Orlando Cepeda, the 1967 MVP and the player many considered to be the heart of the team, to Atlanta a few weeks before the start of the season for Joe Torre.

Much of his off-season activity stemmed from two factors: the loss of the regular right-fielder, Roger Maris, to retirement, and a large drop-off in run production from the previous year. Rather than trust the outfield job to Bobby Tolan, the best outfield prospect in the organization, he traded for a fading veteran. As it turned out, Bing had over-estimated the Cards' offensive slump; taking into account the overall decline in offense during 1968, the team's scoring had actually decreased by less then seven percent.

The Pinson deal turned out badly. Tolan was one of the more exciting outfielders in the league for a few years, at least until his career was side-tracked by injuries. Pinson, on the other hand, hit only .255 and was gone after the end of the season. The other big trade was more successful, with Torre having several excellent years, including an MVP season two years later. In 1969, however, his 101 RBIs were not enough to offset a genuine offensive slump, and the Cardinals fell to fourth in their division. Had the National League been a twelve-team league that year, St. Louis would have ended up in seventh place. If he hadn't been reluctant to tinker with a pennant-winner, Devine certainly wasn't going to keep his hands off of a fourth-place outfit and he once again dove into the trade market. His big move this time was a seven-player deal with the Phillies for Dick Allen, a trade that would have long-lasting repercussions when Curt Flood, one of the players Bing sent to Philadelphia, refused to report, deciding to challenge baseball's reserve clause instead.

Allen had a good year, but this time the pitching staff collapsed and the Cardinals went 76-86, good for another fourth-place finish. Despite its losing record, this team had a lot of talent. Three straight good rookie classes had driven up the cumulative PV left in its players' careers to 400, one of only 16 teams between 1901 and 1985 to hit that figure. Only the 1974 Dodgers would exceed that total in the following fifteen years. The key players on that team, along with how they came and left the Cardinals:

PV	Pos	Name	Obtained	Disposed
62	P	Steve Carlton	1965 Rookie	2-25-72 Trade PHI N
50	OF	Jose Cruz	1970 Rookie	10-24-74 Sold HOU N
44	C	Ted Simmons	1968 Rookie	12-12-80 Trade MIL A
33	P	Jerry Reuss	1969 Rookie	4-15-72 Trade HOU N
21	1B	Dick Allen	10- 7-69 Trade PHI N	10- 5-70 Trade LA N
21	OF	Lou Brock	6-15-64 Trade CHI N	1979 Retired
21	P	Bob Gibson	1959 Rookie	1975 Retired
20	P	Mike Torrez	1967 Rookie	6-15-71 Trade MON N
17	3B	Joe Torre	3-17-69 Trade ATL N	10-13-74 Trade NY N
17	P	Al Hrabosky	1970 Rookie	12- 8-77 Trade KC A
16	OF	Jose Cardenal	11-21-69 Trade CLE A	7-29-71 Trade MIL A
11	P	R. Cleveland	1969 Rookie	12- 7-73 Trade BOS A
10	SS	Dal Maxvill	1962 Rookie	8-30-72 Trade OAK A

Much of the talent, especially the pitching, was young and not much help that summer: Cleveland went 0-4 with a 7.62 ERA, Hrabosky was 2-1 in only 19 innings, and Reuss finished 7-8 with a 4.11 ERA. It would have been nice to see what this team could have accomplished if left alone. Of course, you could say the same about the 1969 team, as well as any of Devine's other teams in the seventies. All of them, unfortunately, ended up being broken apart not long after they were formed by a seemingly endless succession of trades.

The teams exchanging the most players in each league between 1969 and 1977:

Earlier, I showed a chart of the teams trading the most players in a season between 1901 and 1961. Here's a similar chart for the period from 1962 to 1994:

Year	Team	Players		Year	Team	Players
1977	STL N	53		1982	NY A	39
1979	TEX A	50		1993	SD N	39
1975	STL N	44		1972	STL N	38
1971	MIL A	40		1973	STL N	38
1989	NY A	40		1976	STL N	38

Year	Team	Players	Team	Players
1969	STL N	31	SEA A	28
1970	STL N	32	MIL A	30
1971	STL N	35	MIL A	40
1972	STL N	38	TEX A/OAK A	30
1973	STL N	38	CLE A	37
1974	STL N	34	CLE A	33
1975	STL N	44	CHI A/OAK A	23
1976	STL N	38	CHI A	29
1977	STL N	53	TEX A	31

How Devine did from 1969 to 1977, compared to the league average:

	Rookie	Trading		Sales		Lost+Found		Drafts		Free-Agent		Total		Start	Got	Lost	End
	435	470	-578	50	-80	23	-50	2	-48	0	0	224		303	981	-756	212
AVG	310	230	-263	30	-23	19	-16	28	-19	7	-4	299	AVG	218	624	-325	218

If Frank Lane and Bill Veeck had revolutionized trading in the early fifties, Bing Devine raised it to another level two decades later. In 1978, the Cardinals lost 93 games, their worst record in 54 years, and Bing Devine was replaced as their general manager by John Claiborne.

Charlie Finley in Kansas City

All in all, it was a short honeymoon and an awfully long divorce. Soon after purchasing the A's from the estate of Arnold Johnson before the 1961 season, Charlie O. Finley hired Frank Lane, ostensibly to run his team, and set about trying to win over the hearts and minds of his players and their fans. He said that he wanted to make the A's a "Happy Family." During spring training that year, he made a special visit to ensure that the segregated quarters of his three black players were acceptable and a few nights later even had dinner with them where "...the owner made it apparent he was thoroughly enjoying himself." When his team broke camp that year, he purchased expensive clock radios for his players and threw them a party costing four thousand dollars. He offered to pay for their wives to join them on a road trip during the season and promised the players bonuses if the team was able to finish in the first division.

He'd been trying to buy a team for at least six years and it seemed as if he was in a rush to make up for lost time. "Finley is impulsive," Ernest Mehl, the beat writer for The Sporting News wrote that spring. "He wants to discover as quickly as possible whether a scheme will work." He had a thousand ideas and, since he was the one paying the bills and throwing the parties, his team would end up having to try them all. Or almost all: he bought an old bus, painted "Shuttle Bus to Yankee Stadium" on its side and asked Frank Lane to douse it with gasoline and set it on fire. Frank refused.

He was certainly enthusiastic and dearly wanted that enthusiasm to be contagious. He also wanted to be obeyed. He readily admitted, at least in the early days, that he didn't know much about baseball, but that didn't keep him from overruling Lane on trades, roster moves and spring training facilities, or from dictating pitching changes and line-ups to Joe Gordon, his manager for the first part of 1961. In a lot of ways, Finley wasn't much different from any number of opinionated fans, except that people had to listen to him.

Reports of a feud between Finley and Lane first surfaced in May and things started to turn ugly soon afterwards. Where earlier reports were titled "Dynamo Finley Ace-High Guy to A's Fans, Players," they now started with sentences like: "Latest in a series of bizarre and sometimes alarming developments is the experiment attempted by Manager Joe Gordon to run his club during the games from a vantage point next to the press box." It must have been an easy club to write about. One week, Finley decided to install fluorescent lights in each dugout to help the fans see what was going on. The Yankees kept turning them off; Finley kept ordering his electrician into the dugout to turn them back on again. The next day, the switch had been removed from the dugout, eliciting a protest to the league from the Yankees (which they won.)

In June, Finley fired Joe Gordon. Lane was forced to hold a very uncomfortable press conference where he tried to make sense of a decision that hadn't been his. Soon after he admitted that Gordon hadn't been told of his dismissal yet, the phone rang in the hotel suite. It was Gordon.

"Joe," Lane began, "this is Frank. I guess, Joe, you can have the next year and one-half off at full pay."

"You mean I'm fired?"

"That's what it looks like."

At this point, Gordon asked to talk to Ernest Mehl, the sportswriter.

"What the hell is going on?" he asked.

It was a question the rest of the league would be asking by the time Finley got around to canning Lane in August. It was a messy affair. The owner blamed his ex-GM for undermining him: *"Wherever he went, Lane left his trail of poison and dirt."* Lane responded that:

"What Finley has not realized is that fans don't pay to see new paint on a ball park. They don't pay to see some machine pop out of the ground to bring baseballs to the umpire.... What brings the fans out is a good ball club and nothing else."

Lane also revealed that Finley had been secretly plotting to move his team to Dallas. This shouldn't have been a surprise to anyone. Every chance he got that year, Charlie had been denying that he had any intention of moving the A's anywhere. It didn't seem to matter what the interview was about, Finley somehow managed to mention how he wasn't going to move the team.

An editorial in The Sporting News at the end of August read:

"At this point, it appears that Finley is creating the impression that he is trying to tear down the ball club in Kansas City to the extent that he may use this as an excuse for moving elsewhere."

It was quite a rookie season. He would remain in Kansas City for another six extremely contentious years. In addition to Dallas, he would threaten to move his team to Atlanta, San Diego, Seattle and Oakland. He would sign an agreement to move it to Louisville in 1964, only to be turned down by the American League (only he voted in favor it). He would fire one manager after another. By the time of the player revolt in August 1967, Ken Harrelson wasn't exactly giving away any league secrets when he called Finley a menace to baseball.

In an interview in 1961, during the first few months of his reign, he said that he wanted his players to feel that they were working with him, not for him. But as time went on, it became more and more apparent that what really appealed to Charlie Finley about buying a baseball club was the prospect of actually owning his employees. Unlike the insurance business, his players didn't have the option of quitting and going to work for another organization. And once the free agent draft started in 1965, players didn't have much to say about what team they originally signed with either.

Not surprisingly, Finley's team was one of the big beneficiaries of the new draft. They picked first in 1965 and got Rick Monday, adding Sal Bando and Gene Tenace in later rounds. They picked second in 1966 and ended up with Reggie Jackson. They got Vida Blue in the second round of the 1967 draft. Perhaps Charlie's money could have convinced these players to sign with Kansas City under the old rules, but I doubt it. By the time he finally packed his bags and headed to Oakland, he took with him the youngest winning-team in baseball history. A list of them:

Year	Team	Age	W	L	WPct
1968	OAK A	25.0	82	80	.506
1911	BOS A	25.4	78	75	.510
1914	BOS A	25.6	91	62	.595
1914	WAS A	25.7	81	73	.526
1910	BOS A	25.7	81	72	.529

I've always wondered what would have happened if Finley had been easier to get along with. After all, he did have money and the willingness to spend it. Unfortunately, he had purchased a lousy team in a run-down stadium and expected to turn it around in a year. When that didn't happen, he became convinced that Kansas City couldn't support major league baseball and spent the rest of this stay there alienating the natives and trying to leave. From 1971 to 1975, his Oakland A's would win five-straight division titles, including three-straight World Series, and draw an average of less than a million fans a year. One of the teams with a higher attendance over that period was the expansion Kansas City Royals.

The Second Round of expansion and the KC miracle

Unlike the franchise shifts of the fifties, which were in response to gradual demographic changes, both the A's move to Oakland and the Braves relocation to Atlanta were caused by owners simply looking for a better deal elsewhere. Kansas City and Milwaukee were capable of supporting major-league baseball; Finley may not have realized this until he was stuck across the bay from the Giants, but the owners of the Braves left a town that had led the majors in attendance from 1953 to 1958 and finished second in 1959. The two abandoned cities would receive new teams within a few years. Kansas City would get its first, during the next wave of expansion in 1969, while Milwaukee fans would get their expansion team second-hand, when the financially-troubled Seattle Pilots moved to their city at the start of 1970.

This time, both leagues expanded at the same time, using the same set of rules. Each established team was allowed to protect fifteen players at the start of the draft, protecting an additional three players after each of the six rounds. During each round, the two expansion teams alternately selected five players, one from each club. Was this method better or worse for the new teams? While we don't know how much talent was made available to the new clubs (nearly thirty years later, these lists are still considered confidential by the leagues), we do know the players who were picked. Here's how the amount of talent each team got compared to the earlier ones:

Year	Team	PV	Year	Team	PV
1969	KC A	148	1961	LA A	120
1969	SEA A	146	1961	WAS A	76
1969	SD N	96	1962	HOU N	65
1969	MON N	76	1962	NY N	54
Total		**466**		**Total**	**315**

Once again, both American League teams got more talent than either of the NL clubs. Here's how their records for their first five seasons compare:

American League				**National League**			
Year	W	L	WPct	Year	W	L	WPct
1969	133	191	.410	1969	104	220	.321
1970	130	194	.401	1970	136	188	.420
1971	154	168	.478	1971	132	190	.410
1972	141	169	.455	1972	128	181	.414
1973	162	162	.500	1973	139	185	.429
Total	720	884	.449	Total	639	964	.399

The first year marks of both groups were extremely close to what their league's expansion clubs had done the first time around: 133-191 versus 131-191 for the American League and 104-220 versus 104-216 for the NL. Although both sets of teams won more often than the earlier squads, the American League's teams still did significantly better, which is not too surprising in light of the talent they got in the draft.

The record of the eight expansion teams during their first five years:

Years	Team	W	L	WPct
1969-73	KC A	383	418	.478
1961-65	LA A	383	425	.474
1969-73	MON N	345	458	.430
1969-73	MIL A	337	466	.420
1962-66	HOU N	333	475	.412
1961-65	WAS A	309	499	.382
1969-73	SD N	294	506	.368
1962-66	NY N	260	547	.322

The Royals had the greatest short-term success, but what about the talent left in their organization afterwards? Here's a comparison of the talent that moved in and out of each organization during those years:

This time, the team with the best short-term record also had the most successful five-year plan. The man calling the shots for the Royals during this period was their general manager, Cedric Tallis, and here's how he did during those years, compared to the league average:

		Royals					**Brewers**			
Year	Start	Got	Lost	End	TPV	Start	Got	Lost	End	TPV
1969	0	182	-9	146	12	0	182	-40	120	8
1970	146	89	-8	202	16	120	63	-70	91	2
1971	202	33	-23	172	33	91	97	-32	128	18
1972	172	54	-9	180	30	128	64	-39	136	4
1973	180	222	-54	318	19	136	67	-28	141	22

		Expos					**Padres**			
Year	Start	Got	Lost	End	TPV	Start	Got	Lost	End	TPV
1969	0	173	-34	118	10	0	130	-29	92	-5
1970	118	43	-7	129	11	92	25	-26	67	16
1971	129	26	-6	130	8	67	62	-20	80	20
1972	130	75	-25	156	13	80	35	-16	82	3
1973	156	73	-18	174	27	82	95	-15	144	8

	Rookie	Trading		Sales		Lost+Found		Drafts		Total
	180	225	-97	8	-1	17	-4	149	-1	477
AVG	158	126	-99	13	-15	8	-13	14	-35	157

The players moving to and from the Royals during those years:

It was an incredible record. Apart from that last trade with the Giants, Tallis did almost everything right. He didn't make a ton of meaningless trades, but he managed to get a future all-star from the National League during each winter meeting from 1969 to 1972. I think that if I had been an NL owner at the 1973 meeting, I might have just forgotten to return his phone calls.

In one of life's little mysteries, Ewing Kauffman, the popular owner of the Royals, fired Tallis in June 1974, and replaced him with the team's business manager. Ewing never adequately explained the reasoning behind his move and it was unpopular with both the fans and media. The talent Tallis had collected during his stay, however, would keep the Royals at or near the top of their division well into the next decade.

Date	From	To	How	PV	Name
10-15-68	CAL A		Exp-Draft	27	Tom Burgmeier
10-15-68	NY A		Exp-Draft	20	Jim Rooker
10-15-68	DET A		Exp-Draft	18	Dick Drago
10-15-68	CHI A		Exp-Draft	13	Al Fitzmorris
10-15-68	MIN A		Exp-Draft	13	Pat Kelly
4- 1-69	SEA A		Traded	20	Lou Piniella
12- 3-69	NY N		Traded	43	Amos Otis
1970			Rookie	22	Paul Splittorff
12- 2-70	PIT N		Traded	22	Fred Patek
12- 2-71	HOU N		Traded	20	John Mayberry
1972			Rookie	11	Steve Busby
10-25-72	PIT N		Traded	33	Gene Garber
10-25-72		PIT N	Traded	- 16	Jim Rooker
11-30-72	CIN N		Traded	33	Hal McRae
1973			Rookie	69	George Brett
1973			Rookie	26	Greg Minton
1973			Rookie	22	Frank White
1973			Rookie	12	Doug Bird
1973			Rookie	11	Mark Littell
4- 2-73		SF N	Traded	- 26	Greg Minton

MOST VALUABLE PLAYERS TRANSFERRED

Date	From	To	How	PV	Name
12- 2-68	OAK A	ATL N	Draft	63	Darrell Evans
4-21-66	PHI N	CHI N	Traded	62	Ferguson Jenkins
12-10-69	MIN A	CLE A	Traded	48	Graig Nettles
12- 9-65	CIN N	BAL A	Traded	44	Frank Robinson
12- 3-69	NY N	KC A	Traded	43	Amos Otis
1-22-69	HOU N	MON N	Traded	42	Rusty Staub
10-12-66	PIT N	CHI A	Traded	40	Wilbur Wood
10-15-68	DET A	SEA A	Expans	36	Mike Marshall
-1970	SEA A	HOU N	Found	36	Mike Marshall
-1970	HOU N	MON N	Found	36	Mike Marshall

PERIOD MPVS:

PV	Team(s)	Name
35	BOS A	Carl Yastrzemski
33	CHI N	Ron Santo
33	ATL N	Hank Aaron
31	STL N	Bob Gibson
31	SF N	Willie McCovey

TOP ROOKIES:

Year	Team	PV	Name
1967	NY N	83	Tom Seaver
1967	KC A	71	Reggie Jackson
1970	MIN A	68	Bert Blyleven
1970	BAL A	63	Bobby Grich
1969	OAK A	63	Darrell Evans
1966	NY N	59	Nolan Ryan
1967	MIN A	58	Rod Carew
1969	BOS A	52	Carlton Fisk
1968	SF N	51	Bobby Bonds
1970	STL N	50	Jose Cruz
1966	LA N	50	Don Sutton

ORGANIZATION TALENT BALANCE SHEET

1966-70 AL	Start	Got	Lost	+PV	End
BAL A	352	327	-144	226	309
OAK A	216	458	-225	143	305
BOS A	239	289	-76	179	273
MIN A	230	342	-134	203	235
KC A	0	271	-17	51	202
NY A	209	226	-102	169	164
CAL A	157	326	-186	134	164
WAS A	150	213	-70	144	149
DET A	266	181	-139	171	137
CHI A	229	205	-140	173	120
CLE A	191	257	-213	136	99
MIL A	0	245	-110	44	91

ORGANIZATION TALENT BALANCE SHEET

1966-70 NL	Start	Got	Lost	+PV	End
STL N	306	506	-254	188	370
NY N	131	490	-143	148	330
CIN N	257	370	-148	176	303
LA N	231	383	-165	164	286
HOU N	325	336	-232	145	284
PIT N	270	395	-175	209	281
ATL N	298	300	-185	166	248
PHI N	274	277	-177	147	227
SF N	349	198	-136	200	212
CHI N	228	326	-187	180	187
MON N	0	216	-41	46	129
SD N	0	155	-55	34	67

DETAILED TALENT LEDGER

AL 66-70	Rookie	Trading		Trades+$		Sales		Lost+Found		Draft		Exp-Draft		Total
BAL A	178	121	-108	0	-4	1	-3	8	-0	19	-7	0	-22	183
MIN A	242	92	-100	0	0	4	-4	1	-3	3	-6	0	-20	208
NY A	129	44	-30	7	-12	40	-11	4	-9	3	-9	0	-32	124
DET A	125	50	-41	0	0	3	-35	2	-3	1	-3	0	-56	42
BOS A	178	57	-63	13	-1	11	-3	13	-2	16	-2	0	-5	213
CHI A	81	106	-97	4	-2	11	-11	3	-4	0	0	0	-26	64
OAK A	325	91	-58	0	-6	36	-23	2	-16	4	-87	0	-34	233
CAL A	225	65	-91	1	-2	4	-5	4	-5	28	-25	0	-57	141
CLE A	91	117	-149	6	-1	8	-4	32	-10	3	-9	0	-40	44
WAS A	92	82	-55	25	-2	12	-10	2	-1	0	-2	0	-0	143
KC A	24	93	-13	0	0	3	0	2	-4	1	0	148	0	254
MIL A	6	69	-54	0	-2	17	-14	4	-40	3	0	146	0	135
Total	1697	987	-858	55	-33	149	-123	76	-97	80	-151	294	-294	1784

AL 66-70	Rookie	Trading		Trades+$		Sales		Lost+Found		Draft		Exp-Draft		Total
PIT N	313	58	-125	7	-3	2	-12	16	-2	0	0	0	-32	220
STL N	271	189	-151	0	-1	13	-14	17	-2	16	-57	0	-29	252
SF N	128	58	-111	0	0	6	-8	1	-0	6	-1	0	-16	63
LA N	252	94	-94	4	-1	4	-35	14	-5	15	-10	0	-19	219
CIN N	218	125	-130	0	-1	4	-7	0	-2	23	-1	0	-7	222
CHI N	118	148	-132	10	-11	34	-5	5	-27	11	0	0	-12	139
ATL N	155	60	-98	0	0	7	-20	4	-1	74	-42	0	-23	115
PHI N	107	148	-125	4	-36	11	-2	6	-4	0	-1	0	-9	100
HOU N	194	60	-66	15	-62	2	-32	42	-39	23	-19	0	-14	103
NY N	370	55	-106	23	-2	26	-18	1	-3	15	-3	0	-13	347
MON N	2	41	-27	42	-11	17	-0	37	-3	2	0	76	0	175
SD N	1	55	-55	0	0	3	0	1	0	0	0	96	0	101
Total	2128	1091	-1220	105	-128	128	-154	143	-89	185	-134	173	-173	2055

1971-1975: THE TRADE WINDS OF 1972

I mentioned in the introduction that this began as an investigation into trades. Well, that investigation began with a look at the winter of 1971-72. Years ago, I was looking through Joseph Reichler's book, The Baseball Trade Register, and noticed that an unusual number of big and lopsided trades took place between the 1971 and 1972 seasons. It started during the league championships and didn't stop until Opening Day (which had been delayed ten days by a player strike). The highlights:

Date	Team	PV	Key Players
10-11-71	MIL A	41	George Scott;Ken Brett
	BOS A	18	Marty Pattin
10-18-71	STL N	19	Jim Bibby
	NY N	7	Jim Beauchamp
11-29-71	CLE A	50	Gaylord Perry
	SF N	1	Sam McDowell
11-29-71	CIN N	77	Joe Morgan;Jack Billingham
	HOU N	16	Lee May;Tommy Helms
11-29-71	CHI N	16	Rick Monday
	OAK A	15	Ken Holtzman
11-30-71	MIN A	16	Dave LaRoche
	CAL A	3	Leo Cardenas
12- 2-71	BAL A	30	Doyle Alexander
	LA N	15	Frank Robinson
12- 2-71	LA N	36	Tommy John
	CHI A	15	Dick Allen
12- 2-71	KC A	20	John Mayberry
	HOU N	1	Jim York
12-10-71	CAL A	64	Nolan Ryan
	NY N	2	Jim Fregosi
2-25-72	PHI N	57	Steve Carlton
	STL N	15	Rick Wise
3-22-72	NY A	27	Sparky Lyle
	BOS A	1	Danny Cater
4- 5-72	MON N	61	Ken Singleton;Tim Foli
	NY N	25	Rusty Staub
4-15-72	HOU N	33	Jerry R

The expansion at the end of the decade also didn't have much of an impact. The amount of talent traded per team continued along at about half of 1960's level until 1972:

Year	Trad	Play	TPV	PV/T
1968	39	123	398	19.9
1969	62	173	462	19.3
1970	56	162	539	22.5
1971	64	194	466	19.4
1972	66	196	942	39.2

While the amount of trades and the players involved that year weren't much above the levels established since the second expansion, the quality of the traded players was twice what it had been the previous year.

The trading box for 1972:

This seems like a lot of activity, but was it really? How did the amount of trading compare to other years? This was the original question I set out trying to answer, and here's what I finally came up with: even taking into account the inflation caused by expansion, more talent was swapped during 1972 than in any previous year of the twentieth century. I mentioned earlier that for a long time the record for the highest PV traded in a year was the 383 that changed hands in 1918. That would stand until 1958, when the 36 trades, 115 players and 414 PV all set new highs. Two years later that would fall, a victim of the start of interleague trading as well as Bill Veeck and Frank Lane's efforts to rebuild the two best teams in the American League. The 50 trades that year would relocate players with a PV of 609.

For some reason, the first round of expansion would see a decline in trading. Perhaps it was the spectacular failures of both Veeck and Lane, but here's the trading activity from 1960 to 1964, including the PV traded per team:

Year	Trad	Play	TPV	PV/T
1960	50	147	609	38.1
1961	37	112	400	22.2
1962	40	108	211	10.6
1963	47	134	429	21.5
1964	36	102	299	15.0

Team	+PV	-PV	TPV	Team	+PV	-PV	TPV
CLE A	85	17	68	MON N	71	25	46
CAL A	81	32	49	CIN N	82	45	36
KC A	30	8	22	ATL N	29	2	26
BAL A	39	20	19	LA N	71	51	20
MIL A	55	37	18	PIT N	0	0	0
MIN A	23	6	17	CHI N	35	35	0
NY A	30	15	15	SD N	12	13	-1
TEX A	18	13	5	PHI N	63	70	-7
DET A	1	0	1	SF N	6	51	-46
OAK A	24	27	-3	HOU N	61	107	-46
CHI A	26	44	-18	STL N	48	105	-57
BOS A	19	68	-49	NY N	35	148	-113
Total	430	289	142	Total	512	653	-142

This year contained the following trades that ranked among each team's five best or worst between 1901 and 1985:

The World Champion Pirates sat out the 1972 trading season which, given the American League's dominance in trades during the year, was probably a good thing. Here's how the inter-league trading went during the first fourteen years:

Team	Rank	Date	Team	PV	Key gain/loss
CAL A	Best	12-10-71	NY N	+ 61.9	Nolan Ryan
CLE A	4th Best	11-29-71	SF N	+ 49.1	Gaylord Perry
MIL A	Best	10-11-71	BOS A	+ 22.8	George Scott
ATL N	Best	6-15-72	PHI N	+ 28.7	Andre Thornton
CIN N	Best	11-29-71	HOU N	+ 61.4	Joe Morgan
HOU N	Best	4-15-72	STL N	+ 31.2	Jerry Reuss
	Worst	11-29-71	CIN N	- 61.4	Joe Morgan
	5th Worst	12- 2-71	KC A	- 19.6	John Mayberry
MON N	Best	4- 5-72	NY N	+ 35.5	Ken Singleton
NY N	Worst	12-10-71	CAL A	- 61.9	Nolan Ryan
	3rd Worst	4- 5-72	MON N	- 35.5	Ken Singleton
PHI N	3rd Best	2-25-72	STL N	+ 41.8	Steve Carlton
STL N	Worst	2-25-72	PHI N	- 41.8	Steve Carlton
SF N	2nd Worst	11-29-71	CLE A	- 49.1	Gaylord Perry

Year	AL	NL	Diff
1960	59.3	81.5	-22.2
1961	131.7	33.3	98.4
1962	84.0	41.8	42.2
1963	76.7	37.1	39.6
1964	16.8	43.9	-27.1
1965	149.8	73.9	75.9
1966	62.7	74.2	-11.5
1967	84.3	39.6	44.7
1968	72.8	35.8	37.0
1969	58.4	18.6	39.8
1970	104.2	63.2	41.0
1971	109.9	43.8	66.1
1972	243.1	101.7	141.4
1973	277.1	161.3	115.8
Total	1530.8	849.7	681.1

The American League out-traded the National League in eleven out of the first fourteen years of interleague trading, getting almost twice as much talent as it lost. Part of this was due, no doubt, to the differences in the talent of the two leagues at the start of this period. Because of its owners' reluctance to promote black players, the American League started 1960 with a lot less talent than the National League and, in general, when two teams trade, the one with less talent is most likely to get the best of it.

M. Donald Grant Brings The Mets Back to Earth

For a decade that began with such promise, the seventies were a rough time to be a Mets fan. Bad things started to happen shortly after the end of the Miracle Mets 1969 season. That December, general manager Johnny Murphy traded Amos Otis to the Royals for Joe Foy. A few weeks later, Murphy suffered a heart attack and died following a brief illness. Team chairman of the board M. Donald Grant bypassed Whitey Herzog, assumed by many to be the obvious choice to succeed Murphy, in favor of special assignment scout Bob Scheffing. Grant's choice wasn't especially qualified to be general manager--Scheffing had no front-office experience--but he did have one quality the chairman admired: a willingness to listen to his boss. Or as Grant put it during the press conference announcing the appointment: *"...if either Scheffing or (farm director Joe) McDonald do encounter any difficulty, I will be close by to step in."* Grant teamed up with his GM during the 1972 trading season and the two of them made history. Earlier, I listed the worst trading seasons between 1901 and 1961. The ones from 1962 to 1994:

Their poor trading wasn't limited to a single season. Scheffing bowed out after 1974, but Grant simply replaced him with Joe McDonald, a man who needed the chairman's help at least as much as his predecessor, and the trading debacle continued. The teams with the worst trading record over two to ten years, along with the runner-up:

Year	Team	Got	Lost	Total
1972	NY N	35.2	-148.2	-113.0
1982	PHI N	29.7	-104.7	-75.0
1975	OAK A	18.5	-90.1	-71.6
1969	HOU N	25.3	-92.4	-67.0
1989	NY N	21.4	-84.7	-63.4
1965	CLE A	20.8	-83.7	-62.9
1976	PIT N	7.8	-70.4	-62.6
1974	CLE A	18.6	-80.0	-61.4
1971	STL N	29.4	-87.4	-58.1
1972	STL N	48.3	-105.4	-57.1

Years	Team	Total	Years	Team	Total
2-Years	1972-73 NY N	-118.2	1971-72	STL N	-115.2
3-Years	1970-72 NY N	-156.4	1970-72	STL N	-114.9
4-Years	1969-72 NY N	-171.6	1963-66	CLE A	-125.3
5-Years	1969-73 NY N	-176.8	1913-17	NY N	-130.0
6-Years	1969-74 NY N	-176.8	1949-54	NY A	-139.3
7-Years	1969-75 NY N	-179.9	1949-55	NY A	-158.9
8-Years	1970-77 NY N	-192.6	1949-56	NY A	-164.0
9-Years	1969-77 NY N	-207.7	1958-66	CLE A	-177.6
10-Years	1969-78 NY N	-218.5	1963-72	SF N	-192.1

While 5 different teams occupied second place, the Mets during these years had a lock on the top spot. Amos Otis and Nolan Ryan, two of the most valuable players traded away during these years, were lost in the Mets' on-going obsession with finding a third-baseman. Joe Foy and Jim Fregosi, the players obtained for Otis and Ryan, would play about a hundred games each at that position for the Mets. Wayne Garrett, the regular third-baseman before either of them showed up, would still be there long after both had gone. Ironically, prior to trading Rusty Staub to the Tigers for Mickey Lolich, the Mets turned down an Oriole offer of Doug DeCinces for Staub. DeCinces would play another dozen years at third base for the Orioles and Angels, finishing third in the 1982 MVP voting and starting the 1983 all-star game. Lolich would win ten more games over the rest of his career.

Once fans started to sour on the Fregosi deal, Grant, always a stand-up guy, blamed New York sportswriter Jack Lang for the trade. It seems that Lang had approached Grant during the 1971 winter meetings and told him that he needed to make a trade. With so many big deals being made, he reasoned, Mets fans were going to be upset if Grant came away from the meetings empty-handed.

"You've been knocking us all year for the Fregosi deal," Grant shouted at Lang in the press-box the following June. *"You're the one who told me we had to make a deal, and now you're ripping us."*

"I told you to make a deal," Lang shouted back. *"I didn't tell you to make that deal."*

Mets broadcaster Lindsey Nelson overhead the exchange and later told Lang that he had to start paying the writer more respect. *"I didn't know you had enough power with the club to make a deal."*

The New York Post ran a poll that summer on which of the Mets leaders should be fired--manager Yogi Berra, Scheffing or Grant. When Scheffing and Grant finished first and second in the poll, the chairman said he would *"...not make a change unless forced to by public opinion."*

In addition to Jack Lang's influence on their front-office, the Mets also lost Otis and Ryan because their executives thought they had talent to burn in the farm system. The press felt much the same way. Lang's reaction to the Otis deal was typical:

"Branch Rickey would have been proud of the Mets.... He would have been proud of the way they developed their own and then peddled off excess farmhands to fill the spots they needed.

"In the last six months of 1969, the Mets made three major deals and got three front-line major league players. And they did it without giving up a single regular on their own club. In fact, not even a single established major leaguer. Oh, how Branch would have loved that!"

The farm system had been extremely productive during the sixties. Only the Cards of the late thirties, the Yankees of the early fifties, and the A's of the mid-twenties produced a three-year collection of rookies better than what the Mets got from 1965 to 1967. The key players coming to the team during those years, their first and last year with New York, along with their career PV and how much of that they produced in a Mets uniform:

First	Last	CPV	MPV	Pos	Name
1967	1977	83	56	P	Tom Seaver
1966	1971	59	3	P	Nolan Ryan
1967	1969	43	0	OF	Amos Otis
1967	1978	41	29	P	Jerry Koosman
1965	1974	33	17	P	Tug McGraw
1965	1979	20	15	SS	Bud Harrelson
1965	1968	11	4	P	Dick Selma
1967	1972	10	7	P	Danny Frisella
		300	131		

They held onto enough of this talent to win a championship in 1969. They squandered enough of it to ensure that they were not much more than an average team after that. By comparison, here's a similar chart for the Orioles, the team with the second most rookie talent during these years:

First	Last	CPV	BPV	Pos	Name
1965	1984	63	63	P	Jim Palmer
1965	1981	32	31	SS	Mark Belanger
1965	1972	30	20	2B	Dave Johnson
1965	1965	25	0	P	Darold Knowles
1966	1973	14	13	P	Eddie Watt
1966	1967	13	0	1B	Mike Epstein
1965	1968	12	10	OC	Curt Blefary
		189	137		

The Mets farm system produced another group of fine players from 1969 to 1971, but the team got even less out of these:

First	Last	CPV	MPV	Pos	Name
1970	1971	42	1	OF	Ken Singleton
1971	1977	28	18	P	Jon Matlack
1969	1969	17	0	P	Steve Renko
1970	1971	13	1	SS	Tim Foli
1971	1977	11	8	1B	John Milne
		111	28		

Trading young talent isn't necessarily bad; it all depends upon who the team gets in return. For example, the Orioles were able to trade Curt Blefary after the 1968 season for Mike Cuellar. The Mets, however, got very little for their young players. Donn Clendenon (obtained in the trade involving Steve Renko) was a significant contributor during the 1969 championship season; Rusty Staub (picked up for Ken Singleton, Tim Foli and Mike Jorgensen in 1972) was a fine player during his first stay in New York. Unfortunately, Clendenon had almost nothing left after 1969, and Staub was thrown away after four productive years in that awful trade for Mickey Lolich.

Joan Payson, the owner of the Mets, died in 1975 and the control of the team fell to her daughter, Lorinda De Roulet, a woman who relied even more than her mother on the advice of Grant. The increase in his power eventually resulted in the infamous Wednesday Night Massacre of June 15, 1977, when the Mets unloaded Tom Seaver, the greatest player in the franchise's history, and Dave Kingman, their most exciting hitter, in pair of deals right before the trading deadline. It was the culmination of a bitter disagreement centered around contract disputes and the team's policy of not pursuing free-agents. Much of the argument was played out in the New York newspapers, as Grant used Dick Young, a columnist who had depended upon inside information from the Mets front office for years, to blast his disobedient players (as well as Seaver's wife) in the press. Grant resented Seaver's support for the player's union as well as his pitcher's stature in the game. Once, after a sportswriter had referred to Seaver as "The Franchise," Grant screamed back: *"Mrs. Payson and I are the franchise."* On another occasion, he put his job with the team in perspective this way: *"I'm the guy who did everything good for the Mets."*

The results of these deals were devastating for the Mets. After finishing third or better in seven out of the previous eight years, they dropped into the cellar in 1977 for a three-year stay. Attendance plummeted. Only 1,066,825 paid to see their games that year, down from 2,697,479 fans in 1970. Grant took to hiring a bodyguard, never a good sign for a chairman of the board, and was fired when the Mets trailed the field again the next year. His exit signaled the end of the worst trading decade in history, but it would take a new owner, a complete turnover in front-office personnel, and five more years for the franchise to recover from the damage done by Grant.

Judge Hofheinz and the Astros' Fizzled Blast-off

I mentioned earlier that the Mets and the Astros by the end of the sixties had the most talent left in their players' careers. Unfortunately, the Astros followed the Mets' lead in dealing away valuable players, and from 1969 to 1975 ran a trading deficit of 147 PV. At the same time, they had below average rookie classes--not a good combination and one that would turn one of the most promising teams in the National League into a mediocre outfit heading nowhere.

The tide really turned for the Astros in 1965, when three things happened that would negatively affect them for years to come. First, the Astrodome opened in April, dramatically decreasing Houston's offensive totals and presenting special challenges to any club official attempting to accurately gauge his team's strengths and weaknesses. Second, Judge Roy Hofheinz became the principal owner of the Astros, buying out his ex-partner Robert E. Smith in May. Hofheinz was described as having an *"intelligence quotient that would make eyeballs spin in Harvard,"* along with *"an infallible instinct for making people angry."* He was also a *"penny-wise, pound-foolish blowhard"* who knew little about baseball but had strong opinions about how he wanted to run his team. We've seen owners like him before (and will again). Finally, he finished off 1965 (as well as the hopes of his team), by firing Paul Richards as general manager on December 12th and putting his men in charge: Tal Smith, Grady Hatton and Spec Richardson.

At the time, the Judge expressed disappointment in Richards' progress in building the club. But in an editorial a few weeks later, C. C. Johnson Spink wrote in The Sporting News that:

"The game's professionals feel that Richards has built soundly and shrewdly in Houston and leaves them on the verge of a climb that could be rapid and dramatic. No National League team employed more promising young players last season than Houston with its crop of Joe Morgan, Jim Wynn, Rusty Staub and Larry Dierker."

He was right about the promising players, but their rise was neither rapid nor dramatic. After setting a franchise record with 72 wins in 1966, the Astros won only 69 and 72 games the next two years. Why didn't they do better? Well, here's their top players along with how they performed from 1966 to 1968:

Here's what their top players produced along with the others during those years:

	Top Players		Others		
Year	+PV	-PV	+PV	-PV	TPV
1966	14.6	-0.7	15.2	-12.0	17.1
1967	21.1	-0.8	4.9	-10.1	15.1
1968	16.0	-1.8	6.1	-8.8	11.5

Player	Start	1966	1967	1968	End
Joe Morgan	79.2	2.7	4.8	0.0	71.7
Rusty Staub	53.4	3.1	5.3	3.1	41.9
Jim Wynn	45.6	2.4	5.0	6.0	32.2
Mike Cuellar	30.1	4.5	2.6	1.9	21.2
Bob Watson	29.9	0.0	-0.1	-0.6	29.9
Doug Rader	24.0		0.8	1.8	21.4
John Mayberry	20.4			-0.3	20.4
Dave Giusti	18.3	-0.5	-0.7	1.6	16.7
Larry Dierker	16.6	1.8	0.7	0.0	14.1
Don Wilson	15.7	0.1	1.9	0.6	13.1
Nate Colbert	13.1	-0.2		-0.9	13.1
Dennis Menke	11.8			1.0	10.8

Two factors are at work: the top Astro players were still young and not at the most productive stage of their career, and the rest of the roster was extremely weak, especially in 1967 and 1968. The top nine players on the team at the start of 1966 had an aggregate PV of 300 left in their careers and produced only 14.6 of it during that year. Even the 1967 total is low considering their potential. Here's how their top players played over the next five years, both with Houston and elsewhere:

	With Astros		Elsewhere		
Year	+PV	-PV	+PV	-PV	TPV
1969	24.0	-0.1	15.5	0.0	39.4
1970	22.1	-0.3	10.4	0.0	32.2
1971	12.0	-1.5	12.0	0.0	22.5
1972	16.8	0.0	24.8	0.0	41.6
1973	7.3	0.0	27.2	0.0	34.5

In short, those young Astro players would really start to deliver in 1969. All Richardson had to do was fill out his roster with average to marginal players and Houston was looking at two or three divisional titles over the next five years. Unfortunately, by the end of 1968, the time for patience was over. The year before, Spec Richardson had been named general manager, a job he had previously shared with Smith and Hatton, so he could move aggressively to solve the Astro's problems in the trade market.

So what did he do? He started by trading Mike Cuellar, his best pitcher, to the Orioles for Curt Blefary, an outfielder and catcher who had averaged 20 home runs for the past four years, but had hit only .200 the year before. Cuellar would win 125 games over the next 6 years for Baltimore. Blefary would actually have a decent year in 1969, especially considering the dome-effect, hitting 12 home runs and raising his batting average to .253. This was not enough for Spec, however, and Blefary was gone at the end of the year. A month and a half later, he made another big trade, sending Rusty Staub, one of those promising young players Spink had mentioned, to the Expos for Donn Clendenon and Jesus Alou. Clendenon had tried to hit in the Dome before and refused to go, preferring Montreal's cozy Jarry Park instead. Rather than cancel the deal, Bowie Kuhn, the new commissioner, had the Expos send Houston two other players and cash in place of the reluctant slugger. This upset the Astros, but what did they seriously think Clendenon was going to be able to accomplish in Houston?

Of course, we could ask the same question about Lee May and Joe Pepitone, two other slow sluggers the Astros traded for during these years. It seems that Spec Richardson took an awfully long time to realize that the Astros actually had better hitting and worse pitching than it appeared. After the 1971 season, he swapped Joe Morgan and four others to the Reds for Lee May, Tommy Helms and Jimmy Stewart. Houston that year had hit only 71 home runs, the worst in the league, and this was the problem Richardson was trying to solve with the acquisition of May. Had they hit 153 home runs that year, like Atlanta, there would have been no reason for the trade. But Houston hit 53 of their home runs on the road that year while Atlanta hit 57. In reality, both teams had average power; their parks simply created the illusion of an Atlanta powerhouse on one hand, and a team in a need of unloading a future superstar on the other.

To be fair, many of the hitters Houston traded during these years would not have done as well had they stayed put. Even taking in account the effect the Astrodome had on offense, the departing players still improved once they left. Simply put, hitters didn't like trying to hit in the dome, they didn't like playing for an organization like the Astros, and it showed in their performance on the field. Teams that play in parks that strongly favor either pitching or hitting tend not to do as well as teams in more neutral stadiums. As I've mentioned before, one reason for this is that their parks make it more difficult to figure out their teams' needs. Another reason is that park effects are usually more pronounced on the home team than the visitors. Hitting in the Dome was a momentarily unpleasantness for the other teams; it was a depressing way of life for the Astro hitters. For example, in 1971, the Astros hit more home runs than the opposition on the road (53-48) and fewer in the dome (18-27). Normally, you'd expect to do better in your own park. Free agency will probably cause these effects to be exaggerated, especially in an extreme park like Mile High Stadium in Colorado, by far the greatest hitters' park of the twentieth century. Given the choice, no pitcher in his right mind would want to play there, while hitters would be smart to pay their way on to the team. If the park can make Dante Bichette look like an all-star, think what it could do for a good player.

Eventually it would all end: the years of lousy trades, Roy Hofheinz's ownership and Spec Richardson's term as GM, in an embarrassing mess of unpaid bills during 1975. Hofheinz, who always billed himself as a financial genius and wheeler-dealer, ended his stay in Houston being maneuvered out of power by his creditors as he fought to stave off bankruptcy.

The Arrival of Steinbrenner

George Steinbrenner arrived from Cleveland to take over ownership of the Yankees in April 1973. At the time, he said that he wasn't going to take an active part in running the team. "We plan absentee ownership," he said. "We're not going to pretend to be something we aren't. I'll stick to building ships." His arrival coincided with a return to prominence for the New York team brought about, at least initially, by a sustained period of excellent trading. Earlier, I listed the teams with the worst trading record over two to ten years. The best:

Years	Team	Total	Years	Team	Total
2-Years 1973-74	NY A	119.0	1901-02	NY N	101.5
3-Years 973-75	NY A	141.3	1949-51	CHI A	129.0
4-Years 1973-76	NY A	166.5	1949-52	CHI A	148.6
5-Years 1972-76	NY A	181.8	1932-36	BOS A	153.4
6-Years 1971-76	NY A	176.8	1932-37	BOS A	166.7
7-Years 1973-79	NY A	207.9	1931-37	BOS A	170.8
8-Years 1972-79	NY A	223.2	1961-68	CHI A	152.5
9-Years 1973-81	NY A	253.5	1931-39	BOS A	146.5
10-Years 1972-81	NY A	268.8	1962-71	CHI A	158.9

The primary deals during the start of the Yankee run:

Date	Team	PV	Key Player(s)
3-22-72	NY A	(27)	Sparky Lyle
	BOS A	(1)	Danny Cater
10-27-72	NY A	(19)	Rick Dempsey
	MIN A	(0)	Danny Walton
11-27-72	NY A	(35)	Graig Nettles
	CLE A	(4)	Johnny Ellis
12-7-73	NY A	(12)	Lou Piniella
	KC A	(2)	Lindy McDaniel
4-27-74	NY A	(34)	Chris Chambliss
	CLE A	(9)	Fritz Peterson
5-8-74	NY A	(22)	Larry Gura
	TEX A	(0)	Duke Sims
10-22-74	NY A	(19)	Bobby Bonds
	SF N	(8)	Bobby Murcer
11-22-75	NY A	(18)	Oscar Gamble
	CLE A	(1)	Pat Dobson
12-11-75	NY A	(25)	Mickey Rivers
	CAL A	(14)	Bobby Bonds
12-11-75	NY A	(58)	Willie Randolph
	PIT N	(7)	Doc Medich

Lee MacPhail was running the show at the start of this period. He assumed the American League presidency shortly after Steinbrenner bought the team in 1973 and was replaced by Gabe Paul. Cedric Tallis came to New York shortly after being dumped by Royals' owner Ewing Kauffman and in 1977, started a six-year stint as the Yankees' general manager. At times, they were more lucky than good. One proposed deal that never came off involved trading Ron Guidry to the Blue Jays early in 1977 for Bill Singer. Pat Gillick, Toronto's vice-president in charge of baseball operations, had agreed to the trade, before being overruled by club president Peter Bavasi. Singer, it turned out, was on the cover of the club's media guide and Bavasi didn't think it would look good for the club to trade him. A victim of a variety of shoulder and back ailments, their cover boy struggled to a 2-8 record with a 6.79 ERA in what turned out to be his last major league season.

Following the 1981 World Series loss to the Dodgers, George Steinbrenner decided to take a more active role running the team. His increased involvement would coincide with the end of his team's unprecedented run of good trading. In 1982 and 1983 the Yankees were the worst trading team in the American League, and in July 1983, Cedric Tallis was fired as general manager. In quick succession, he would be replaced by Gene Michael, Bill Bergesch, Murray Cook, Clyde King, Woody Woodward, Lou Piniella, Syd Thrift and Gene Michael (back for a second time). In other words, the fun was just beginning for Yankee fans.

ORGANIZATION TALENT BALANCE SHEET

AL 1971-75	Start	Got	Lost	+PV	End
BOS A	273	376	-178	160	311
BAL A	309	278	-100	212	274
CLE A	99	521	-219	130	273
KC A	202	404	-179	177	250
NY A	164	356	-72	203	244
CHI A	120	377	-102	170	225
MIL A	91	375	-127	119	220
OAK A	305	347	-242	205	205
TEX A	149	361	-209	121	180
CAL A	164	297	-135	149	177
MIN A	235	202	-96	166	174
DET A	137	176	-65	126	122

NL 1971-75	Start	Got	Lost	+PV	End
LA N	286	438	-156	202	366
PIT N	281	397	-112	218	348
PHI N	227	448	-233	147	295
STL N	370	492	-426	181	256
SF N	212	431	-231	162	250
CIN N	303	256	-122	206	231
HOU N	284	262	-194	149	203
CHI N	187	369	-195	159	202
MON N	129	336	-138	138	190
NY N	330	203	-200	162	170
ATL N	248	183	-120	154	157
SD N	67	257	-80	106	139

TOP ROOKIES:

Year	Team	PV	Name
1972	PHI N	105	Mike Schmidt
1974	MIL A	73	Robin Yount
1973	KC A	69	George Brett
1973	SD N	69	Dave Winfield
1972	BOS A	58	Dwight Evans
1974	STL N	56	Keith Hernandez
1975	CLE A	55	Dennis Eckersley
1974	MON N	53	Gary Carter
1974	BOS A	52	Jim Rice
1975	SF N	51	Jack Clark
1972	CHI A	51	Rich Gossage
1972	CHI N	50	Rick Reuschel
1973	PIT N	50	Dave Parker

Most valuable players transferred

Date	From	To	How	PV	Name
2-25-72	STL N	PHI N	Traded	57	Steve Carlton
11-29-71	HOU N	CIN N	Traded	57	Joe Morgan
12-10-71	NY N	CAL A	Traded	56	Nolan Ryan
10-24-74	STL N	HOU N	Sold	47	Jose Cruz
5-29-71	SF N	CIN N	Traded	44	George Foster
6-15-75	OAK A	CHI A	Traded	42	Chet Lemon
4- 5-72	NY N	MON N	Traded	41	Ken Singleton
11-29-71	SF N	CLE A	Traded	40	Gaylord Perry
12-2-71	CHI A	LA N	Traded	36	Tommy John

BASIC PERFORMANCE

AL 1971-75	+PV	-PV	TPV	W	L	WPct	EPct
BAL A	212	13	199	459	336	.577	.605
OAK A	205	32	173	476	326	.594	.585
NY A	203	30	173	413	388	.516	.534
KC A	177	40	137	417	384	.521	.520
CHI A	170	37	133	398	401	.498	.494
MIN A	166	34	132	390	407	.489	.512
BOS A	160	33	126	438	363	.547	.532
CAL A	149	40	108	370	432	.461	.451
DET A	126	37	89	391	410	.488	.462
MIL A	119	50	69	352	451	.438	.447
CLE A	130	61	69	359	442	.448	.432
EX A	121	54	67	337	460	.423	.418

NL 1971-75	+PV	-PV	TPV	W	L	WPct	EPct
PIT N	218	23	194	453	349	.565	.582
CIN N	206	29	176	479	323	.597	.584
LA N	202	26	176	459	343	.572	.590
STL N	181	42	139	414	389	.516	.514
SF N	162	36	126	399	403	.498	.503
CHI N	159	42	117	386	416	.481	.471
NY N	162	46	116	401	402	.499	.492
HOU N	149	36	113	390	410	.488	.498
PHI N	147	46	101	363	441	.451	.470
ATL N	154	61	93	383	417	.479	.484
MON N	138	45	92	374	428	.466	.454
SD N	106	60	46	310	490	.388	.375

PERIOD MPVS:

PV	Team(s)	Name
35	HOU N-CIN N	Joe Morgan
28	NY N	Tom Seaver
28	SFN-CLE A	Gaylord Perry
27	BAL A	Jim Palmer
26	MIN A	Rod Carew
26	PIT N	Willie Stargell

READY FOR THE DEFENSE

Adjusting for context gives new insight into the thorny problem of evaluating defense; our intrepid BBBA analyst time-travels back to 1941 to do just that.

Charlie Saeger

Evaluating baseball fielders is a murky, inexact science that lures few people. As a result, I like going to that science, since people are a noisy, opinionated lot. There's something fun about being able to look at Dick Stuart and saying, "That oaf must cost his team 40 runs with his glove every year!" It's even more fun to tell people that Stuart is probably only costing his team 12 runs, but hey, he stinks, so why do we really want to measure it?

We do want to measure. We want to find out if Bobby Doerr was really a better fielder than Joe Gordon or if everything we've been told is a lie, and that Doerr couldn't field his way out of a paper bag. However, we've often made serious errors in measuring this. Now, a trip down memory lane (not my memory, probably Bob Dole's) to the beginning of recorded time (in about 1871) when people first decided to note how many outs old Bob "Death to Flying Things" Ferguson recorded, or how many Cap Anson recorded, or how many Al Spalding recorded. Reporters, and Henry Chadwick (the "Father of Baseball Statistics," and no one has charged him with palimony), came up with the following scheme to figuring out how good a fielder a ballplayer was:

1 Number of outs he recorded.
2 Number of outs he helped someone else record.
3 Number of times he screwed up.

They added #1 and #2 together and divided the result by itself plus #3, and called is Fielding Percentage. It worked well, because good fielders didn't screw up. However, something came to disturb Fielding Percentage, something called a "glove." Players wore these "gloves" on their hands and they stopped making an error every game.

The end result of gloves is that the difference between the best and worst shortstop became about 25 plays a year. Since everyone knew that Rabbit Maranville was much more than 25 plays be than ge Grantham, people just ignored fielding statistics, since obviously the be-all, end-all result, Fielding Percentage, wasn't very good.

However, in the 1970s, Americans used many illicit drugs, and men started trying to make sense of 100 years of fielding statistics. One man, Bill James, came up with a measure of fielding performance called Range Factor. Range Factor was plays made per game, and James created this on the principle that good field-ers make more outs than bad ones make. He published this in Baseball Digest. I have never read this particular article, but I read the letters following it up a few months later. The readers wrote to tell James that he was on drugs.

However, James was not using PCP or LSD or some other narcotic acronym that could conceivably become a base-ball statistic someday (and very possibly in this book, for that matter). James was right: good fielders do make more outs than bad ones do. However, subsequent research revealed that every team records 27 outs each game, so that good defensive teams record the same number of outs as bad ones record. This led to much wailing and gnashing of teeth, and a big mistake.

The big mistake was eliminating strikeouts from the total number of team outs each game. People reasoned since the batter had struck out, he had not put the ball into play, and did not create a fielding opportunity for anyone. This is true, but it says that to Mike Schmidt, a failed opportunity could be a strikeout or a fly out to Bake McBride. Since Mike Schmidt had nothing to do with either play, it makes little sense to penalise him for either one, but many methods do penalise his fielding for Bake McBride catching the ball.

Pete Palmer, a justly renowned sabermetrician, is prob-ably the man who pushed this practice too far. In The Hidden Game of Baseball he showed everyone what the value of a sin-gle was, what the value of a walk was, what the value of a caught stealing was, and so on. He then combined these values into a number, and he called it Batting Runs. It says that Eddie Collins contributed 604 runs and that Rogers Hornsby contributed 844 runs, both more than an average non-pitcher would have con-tributed. This has become the method of choice for such mea-surements.

But Palmer couldn't just say that Hornsby was a better player than Collins based on this alone, since Collins was a won-derful second baseman and Hornsby was a clod. So he applied the principle of strikeouts not being an opportunity to players so he could come with how many runs each player saved. Within a few years of this method's appearance in The Hidden Game, everyone's fielding formulations took this principle into account. Other people at the same time, however, did note what was a real failed opportunity for a fielder—his team allowing a hit. Bill James created a Range Index in his 1984 Baseball Abstract, and that shows a player's range as a percentage of total balls in play for his team. I developed a similar method a decade later (posted to the Usenet group rec.sport.baseball in June 1994).

In last year's Baseball Prospectus, Clay Davenport devised a fielding method based on the same basic concept, that each ball in play should count as an opportunity. This is an improvement over Palmer's method, since it accounts for the number of hits a team allowed, and the hits are the bad thing. Teams shouldn't allow hits.

However, team strikeouts should not be used when evaluating fielders. Suppose a team allows an average number of hits, but strikes out 100 fewer batters than average. Also suppose that the left fielder recorded 40 of those extra outs and the second baseman recorded the other 60. Now, the shortstop recorded an average number of outs. Both the Palmer method and the Davenport method would show him to be a below-average fielder since each posits that he had 100 more chances to field a ball. This is silly, since the left fielder and the second baseman took those chances and made the outs.

Let's examine another big Palmer mistake, then an important positive contribution by Bill James. (I don't want to sound like I'm picking on Pete, but he makes just about every possible mistake other than believing in fielding percentage.) Palmer doubled assists in his method because, he argues, assists require greater skill to record than putouts. For infielders in particular, putouts are often easy pop-ups or recorded on the back end of a fielder's choice.

I have two problems with this. The first is that statisticians are in the business of evaluating performance, not skill. Scouts are often lousy judges of performance, but they're excellent measurers of skill. Statistics cannot measure skill, they can only measure performance, and so using them to measure skill will never work. My second problem is: why should one out count more than another? The same thing happens if you catch a fly ball as if you throw out a batter after fielding a ground ball: the batter is out. While the assist may require more skill (dubious, since infielders also handle many routine ground balls), the result is the same, and the value to the team is the same. An out is an out is an out is an out.

Now, back to Bill James. James devised a fielding method that tried to take everything into account and come up with a won-lost percentage for a result. Of course, he used a number of tables that had arbitrary values and couldn't be moved from its time and place, in this case the early 1980s. However, he did make several important observations. James counted double plays as a percentage of runners on base. He also noted if you removed some double plays recorded by other fielders from the team total, you would have the number of double plays of which a first baseman was not just on the back end. I've used these and other assumptions of his in this method. Anyhow, my method is based on a few specific principles, some of which come from other methods. They are:

1   A hit is a failed opportunity for a fielder.
2   The pitching staff can affect fielding totals.
3   An opportunity to remove a runner via a double play, an outfield assist or a caught stealing is a
     runner on base.

Now let's walk through the method by using Yankee sec-

ond baseman Joe Gordon's totals in 1941. Gordon is legendary for his fielding, and played for a great team even if they are (Oriole fan gut wrenching here) the Yankees. Gordon's basic defensive totals for 1941, as a second baseman, were 131 games, 332 putouts, 397 assists, 32 errors and 109 double plays. Just to get this out of the way, Gordon recorded a .958 Fielding Percentage, a 5.56 Range Factor and 7 Fielding Runs. American League second basemen had a fielding percentage of .967 and a Range Factor of 5.47.

This was not Gordon's best season, but it still wasn't bad, and the Yankees were a great team, allowing the fewest hits of any American League team. The Yankees led the league in double plays despite playing Gordon for a month at first base. (Actually, playing Gordon at first probably helped the Yankees defensively. Jerry Priddy, who replaced Gordon at second base, was also a good fielder and the best Yankee prospect at the time. Priddy still holds the AL record for double plays in a season with 150 in 1950 while playing for Detroit. Johnny Sturm became the regular Yankee first baseman after that first month of the season, and was terrible. As we'll see, it didn't really matter, not with an outfield of Henrich, DiMaggio and Keller.)

Let's evaluate Gordon's range first. I calculate that Gordon made 588 plays. I calculated this through this formula: PO+A-E-DP I subtract double plays since otherwise we count them twice. This is an important observation that Bill James made, one lost on Pete Palmer. I evaluate them separately. I also subtract errors. While errors are unimportant, we can't just ignore them. Pete Palmer makes an excellent case for this, noting that an error means a missed out AND a runner on base. Therefore, I let them cancel out one play made. I also count them against the player when counting opportunities, something I shall demonstrate in a moment.

I use that formula for all middle infielders, but I use different formulae for other fielders:

1b   PO-2bA-3bA-ssA+A-E
2b   PO+A-E-DP
3b   PO+A-E
ss   PO+A-E-DP
of   PO-E
c   PO-SO+A-E
p   PO+A-E

For third basemen and pitchers, I don't subtract double plays. These men are starting double plays, and therefore don't have the double-count problem. I don't count outfield assists for a similar reason, since outfield assists remove runners already on base. We're concerned here with the fielder's ability to keep runners off base. First basemen's opportunities come from an observation I made about a decade ago. If you subtract the assists of the other infielders from a first baseman's outs, you have about the number of plays he really made.

Catchers' fielding is a great murky area. I count all putouts that are not strikeouts, and I count all the assists. In our time, about half of a catcher's assists come from throwing out baserunners, while the rest come from other things like fielding bunts. Therefore, I count assists once on the range side of the equation, and once on the arm side of the equation. I don't claim a great level of accuracy for catchers, but the formula does work fairly well.

So, Gordon made 588 plays, how many opportunities did he have? He had 1422 chances, or 1421.947751 to be really precise. I calculated this as follows:

1 The Yankees allowed 1309 hits, and 81 home runs.
2 Based on league totals, I figure that the Yankees allowed about 934 singles. For an infielder, singles are all that matter.
3 Based on a couple of estimates, I figure that Gordon played 82.4 percent of the time at second base.
4 I then multiplied 934 by .824, and added Gordon's own PO+A+E-DP.

You figure chances for all infielders and catchers based on this, though obviously you tailor the chances slightly for each position (for example, first basemen are PO-ifA+A+E added to singles allowed). For outfielders, the number of failures is all hits allowed that are not home runs. For outfielders before 1920, you also count the home runs. Gordon's plays made as a percentage of total opportunities, a number I call Range Rating, is .414.

Is that good or is that bad? It's good. American League second basemen had a Range Rating of .399, but under the circumstances under which Gordon played, it would have been .401. The Yankees allowed a normal rate of ground balls (46.4% as a percentage of outs in play, as opposed to a league rate of 46.6%). However, they had less than a normal number of right-handed pitchers (the Yankees had only two left-handers, Lefty Gomez and Marius Russo, but both were in the starting rotation, so 74.3% of all balls in play were against right-handed pitchers as opposed to 77.5% for the league).

The Yankees played in a pitcher's park, therefore allowing fewer hits than normal. How did each affect Gordon? I calculated the following adjustments:

1 I found the number of ground ball and fly ball outs, and then calculated a ground ball percentage. The number of fly ball outs is PO-SO-A (every out that was not a strikeout or required help from another fielder). The number of ground ball outs is PO-SO-flyouts-DP-cA-ofA (every out that wasn't a strikeout, a flyout, a double play, a catcher's assist (aka caught stealing) or an outfield assist). This does have the wrong effect of having more fly balls than ground balls, but it does accurately show how much better or worse a team was than the league. I then compare this to the league average. I then make an assumption that this probably a bit extreme. A good fielder could run up this total, and we don't have the number of ground ball and fly ball hits. Therefore, I make the adjustment for this equal to the square root of team ground ball percentage over the league average.

2 I found the number of balls put into play (AB+SH-HR-SO) for each team's lefty and righty pitchers. I took the righties' total as a percentage of the team total (using lefties' data would be too extreme), and compared it to the league average. I then made the same assumption as I did with ground ball/fly ball data, that this was too extreme and a better adjustment would be the square root of this figure.

3 didn't have the number of hits allowed by park, but I had runs and home runs. I took R-HR and used that in

place of hits, an assumption that works well in our own time, and came up with a Palmer-style park adjustment. I further took the square root of this and applied this figure to infielders' totals, since parks do not have as an extreme effect on singles. Outfielders get the full adjustment. You need to make a park adjustment or else you unfairly penalize Dante Bichette and Larry Walker for playing in Colorado. It's the opposite of an adjustment to hitting, which keeps us from overrating Bichette (the poster boy for park adjustments) and Walker because they play in Colorado. I don't make lefty-righty adjustments for catchers, center fielders and pitchers.

The Yankees had a normal ground ball frequency. The Yankees were also a bit more reliant than the league was on left-handed pitching, so this would lower the expected percentage. As a side note, there were not many left-handers in the league at this time. Finally, Yankee Stadium was a pitcher's park, which would raise the expected percentage, a bit more than the amount of left-handed pitching would lower it. All in all, a typical second baseman could expect to have a Range Rating of .401 with the Yankees, as opposed to a .399 for the league as a whole. Since Gordon had a .414 Range Rating, he helped the Yankees.

How much did he help the Yankees? Well, a typical second baseman playing for the Yankees given Gordon's chances would have made 571 outs. Gordon made 588, so he added 17 outs more than a normal second baseman would have. Now, remember double plays? Remember how I lobbed them out of the range area of the formula since they represented something else? Well, now we evaluate them.

Joe Gordon turned 109 double plays. For second basemen, third basemen, shortstops and pitchers, I use the raw double play total to evaluate their arms. For outfielders and catchers, I use the assist total. In this case, I do double the value of outfielder's assists, as they show something not in the statistics, the ability to keep runners from advancing. For first basemen, I evaluate their double plays less second basemen's double plays. This keeps us from always looking at the first baseman on the receiving end of a double play, something that takes precious little skill. Thank you, Bill James, for that idea.

Another item I borrowed from James is placing arm skills (double plays, caught stealing and base runner kills) in the context of base runners. This reflects the fact that you cannot double off a runner who is not already on base. I did need to exclude some things, like base runners that someone else has already removed (for example, I subtracted outfielders' and catchers' assists from base runners for infielders).

I also needed to make sure that infielders and catchers did not have extra base hits counted, since their opportunity is on first base. I also removed sacrifice hits from catchers' and infielders' opportunities, since those compete with double plays and stolen base attempts. I then make the above adjustments, with a few differences. I do not adjust for lefty-righty totals for middle infielders, since it doesn't matter for double plays at all. While a left-handed pitcher will allow a shortstop to start more double plays, it allows a second baseman to turn more double plays. It all washes out. I do not make park adjustments here, since we are no longer talking about hits allowed.

Furthermore, I violate one of my own rules: I use strikeouts. I make an adjustment for balls in play, since teams that strikeout more batters will have fewer balls in play. I need to make this adjustment since I don't have everyone else's opportunities excluded as I do with range. The adjustment for all fielders except catchers is (AB-HR-SO+SH)/(AB+SH).

Anyhow, back to Joe Gordon. Just so it is out of the air, the 1941 Yankees did have fewer balls in play than a typical AL team, 87.5% to 88.2%. Therefore, a typical second baseman would turn 6.65% of all runners into double plays. Gordon turned 9.01% of 1210 runners into double plays. This gave the Yankees 28 more outs. In case you're wondering, both figures led the AL by a large margin. Gordon posted the league best double play rate while not having a spectacular defensive season by his standards. His reputation for having an excellent double play pivot is deserved.

So, how many runs did Gordon save the Yankees? I multiplied the total number of outs he saved (46, difference is in rounding) by this figure: (LgR-LgHR)/(LgPO-LgSO) This indicates that the run is the result of a fielder if it wasn't a home run, and that total opportunities is putouts less strikeouts. I then doubled this, since this alone represents outs. Doubling this adds hits back into the mix. (I'm not overly fond of this figure, so if you have a better suggestion, I'd love to hear it.) The calculated run value for the 1941 American League is .179. Therefore, I figure that Joe Gordon saved the Yankees 16.4 runs.

I've also calculated a winning percentage and a wins above a marginal (.350 winning percentage) player. I calculated runs for which a fielder was responsible by simply multiplying the league run value by his total outs (putouts and assists). I removed the other infielders' assists from first basemen, but I did keep strikeouts for catchers. I then add or subtract how man runs a fielder saved or botched, and work it through the Pythagorean Theorem to come up with a Defensive Winning Percentage. I also calculate how many runs a fielder with a .350 DWP would have allowed, and that gives me a Runs Saved/Marginal. Gordon had 16.4 Runs Saved, a .535 DWP and a 51.2 Runs Saved/Marginal.

Now lets do the same thing for Bobby Doerr. Doerr's overall defensive statistics for his career are better, in sheer range factor, double plays per game and fielding runs, but Gordon had a better defensive reputation while both men were active. Doerr recorded 290 putouts, 389 assists, 20 errors and 85 double plays in 132 games. Like Gordon, he did not have a good year by his own standards. He had a Range Factor of 5.14, a Fielding Percentage of .971 and -6 Fielding Runs.

Doerr played for Boston. The Red Sox had much more left-handed pitching than average (depreciating Doerr's totals), allowed more ground balls (inflating Doerr's totals), and played in a bit of a hitter's park (not extreme in 1941). Add them together, and you find that a typical second baseman has a .380 Range Rating; Doerr had a .390 Range Rating, and he had 1472 opportunities, so he saved the Red Sox 15 outs. The Red Sox allowed a bit fewer balls in play than average, depreciating Doerr's double play rate, and the ground balls would inflate that rate. Therefore, a typical second baseman would have an Arm Rating of .0681, as opposed to Doerr's .0650 Arm Rating. Therefore, Doerr cost the Red Sox 4 double plays. Overall, Doerr saved 4 runs for the Red Sox over an average second baseman and 36 over a marginal second baseman. That translates to a .516 DWP. In all, Doerr did not have as good a year as Gordon, but he didn't have a bad year, as Palmer's method claims.

Who was number one at second base? Why, Ray Mack of Cleveland. No doubt about it, Mack's numbers were flat-out good. His 5.17 Range Factor was nothing special, but the Indians had 5 left-handed pitchers, and two were in the rotation, so Mack didn't have many balls coming to him. The other adjustments were close to average but favored Mack. The Indians allowed 1366 hits, the league average was 1437, though the pitchers did have control problems. Add it all up, and Ray Mack's Range Rating was .394—but an average fielder would have recorded a .347 Range Rating under the same circumstances. Throw in an above-average double play rate, and Mack grades out at 30 Runs Saved, 66 over marginal and a .600 DWP. The first two figures are tops for anyone in the league at any position.

Let's look at the numbers for all of the AL second basemen in 1941, just to get our bearings with these new measures. First, the basic fielding stats:

Player	Team	G	PO	A	E	DP	Pct.	Range
Bobby Doerr	Bos	132	290	389	20	85	.971	5.14
Bill Knickerbocker	Chi	88	204	221	13	58	.970	4.80
Ray Mack	Cle	145	363	386	23	109	.970	5.19
Charlie Gehringer	Det	116	279	324	11	59	.982	5.20
Joe Gordon	NY	131	332	397	32	109	.958	5.56
Benny McCoy	Phi	135	285	423	27	87	.963	5.24
Don Heffner	StL	105	224	307	14	52	.974	5.06
Jimmy Bloodworth	Was	132	380	436	24	107	.971	6.18

At a glance, I would conclude that Jimmy Bloodworth was the best fielder, as Palmer's methods did. After him, I'd rank Joe Gordon, as he had a really good DP rate. Now let's look at the data that we generate when we adjust the defensive context. We'll explain these terms as we go:

DP you know. PM is the estimate of Plays Made, based on the formula for second basemen. Opp is the Opportunities to make plays, based on the formulas discussed above (opportunities for second basemen are calculated from the formula H-HR+PO+A-DP+E.). RR is, of course, Range Rating. RR/e is what I would expect the Range Rating to be, as modified by the defensive context (ballpark, pitchers' handedness and groundball/flyball tendencies).. The next

Player	Team	DP	PM	Opp	RR	RR/e	BR	AR	AR/e
Bobby Doerr	Bos	85	574	1472	.390	.380	1308	.065	.068
Bill Knickerbocker	Chi	58	354	907	.390	.366	765	.076	.067
Ray Mack	Cle	109	617	1567	.394	.347	1444	.075	.067
Charlie Gehringer	Det	59	533	1279	.417	.415	1133	.052	.066
Joe Gordon	NY	109	588	1422	.414	.401	1210	.090	.067
Benny McCoy	Phi	87	592	1562	.380	.418	1352	.064	.068
Don Heffner	StL	52	465	1189	.391	.435	1000	.052	.068
Jimmy Bloodworth	Was	107	685	1656	.413	.412	1362	.079	.068
League Totals		831			.399			.067	

column, BR, stands for Base Runners. We then calculate AR (Arm Rating) using DP/BR. AR/e is the Expected Arm Rating. (Note that this doesn't vary nearly as much from park to park as the expected Range Rating.)

Finally, the bottom line. Here are the results in several different methods of measure:

Player	Team	Runs	Marg.	DWP	DXW
Bobby Doerr	Bos	4	36	.516	1.1
Bill Knickerbocker	Chi	10	31	.563	0.9
Ray Mack	Cle	30	66	.601	1.8
Charlie Gehringer	Det	-5	24	.476	0.7
Joe Gordon	NY	16	51	.559	1.4
Benny McCoy	Phi	-23	11	.403	0.4
Don Heffner	StL	-24	1	.356	0
Jimmy Bloodworth	Was	6	45	.520	1.1

Use whichever measure you are most comfortable with. I prefer Runs, though some like to set the comparison level lower (Marg, which measures against a .350 player). Defensive Winning Percentage (DWP) is a more contextually accurate version of the Jamesian measure, and Defensive Extrapolated Wins (DXW, formerly DWAR) translates the Marg and DWP data into a win value, adjusted for playing time.

Another note on the Cleveland Indians' left-handed pitching. The team's high number of left-handers caused Pete Palmer's method to read everyone wrong. He pegged Mack at -5 FR but shortstop Lou Boudreau at 13 FR and third baseman Ken Keltner at 22 FR. I have Boudreau pegged at -20 RS, second worst in the league, and Keltner at -7. I think Boudreau's total might be a little extreme since I use the same lefty-righty adjustment for middle infielders as I do for corner infielders; still, he did not a good year defensively.. Keltner probably did have better years, as did Boudreau, but these aren't good marks.

Let's take a look around the league at other Hall of Famers, Hall of Fame candidates, and outstanding fielders, either good or bad. I've provided league summaries as we move from position to position.

CATCHERS

Mike Tresh,, Chicago: Tresh just had a damn fine year, with a RR of .192 (league best, average was .167), an AR of .084 (second best, behind Birdie Tebbetts of Detroit at .086, average was .061). He also had a Wild Pitch Rating of .029 and the White Sox pitchers had 90 Pitching Runs. What's that you say? What the heck are these terms? I'd best explain them before proceeding.

For catchers, I figure the number of Wild Pitches each catcher probably allowed and add it to the number of Passed Balls he allowed. I then divided it by the number of runners on base and called it his Wild Pitch Rating. (The league average was .026 for 1941, so I was exaggerating Tresh's defensive achievements. Low is good.) I then took the number saved and divided it by 10, half of Palmer's original calculated value for a stolen base, which has the same effect as a wild pitch or a passed ball, and distributes the responsibility equally between pitcher and catcher. I also did the same thing Pete Palmer did with Pitching Runs, which is divide them by 10 and proportion them between the catchers. Chicago's 90 led the league, which helped Tresh considerably (about 7 runs). This total, and throwing, are the two things that affect catchers' fielding the most, as expected.

Anyhow, Tresh could throw, catch and call the game. His minor problems blocking pitches not withstanding, he had a great year, saving 22 runs over average and 49 over marginal, a .594 DWP. Palmer also had him as the top catcher, but at 11 FR.

Bill Dickey, New York: Dickey had an average year. He had a .162 Range Rating, which is sub-par (expected was .171) and an Arm Rating .053 (nothing affects expected AR for catchers). However, he did catch the Yankees, at 63 PR, and had a .020 WPR, so his totals are at -1/21/.492 (average/marginal/DWP). Dickey is not in Cooperstown for his fielding , but this should dispel the notion that Dickey was the greatest catcher in Yankee history, because if you made the same checks for Yogi Berra, my guess is that he would be higher. Palmer had him about where I had him, at 0 FR.

Rick Ferrell, St. Louis: Ferrell might be the worst Hall of Famer around. The guy was a good fielder throughout the Thirties, but his .163 RR (expected) and his average .058 AR and .020 WPR don't make up for the fact that he caught for the Browns. The Browns were their usual selves with -64 PR. Anyhow, a guy in Cooperstown for his fielding should have good defensive stats even under these circumstances. Note I only looked at his totals with the Browns (this study uses only regular players). Palmer had him at -5 with them, and I had him at -5/14/462, same spot.

FIRST BASEMEN

Joe Kuhel, Chicago: He's a no-name with a great glove. He had a .248 RR (expected .191, average .209) and a .018 AR (expected .018, average .020). A key factor in his stats looking so good in context is that the White Sox had a left-handed staff, with their two left-handers combining for 563.2 innings. Anyhow, Kuhel really helped everyone, with final numbers of 26/41/.676. Palmer's -1 FR is way off base here,

Player	Team	Runs	Marg.	DWP	DXW
Mike Tresh	Chi	22	49	.594	2.1
Birdie Tebbetts	Det	11	37	.555	1.5
Bill Dickey	NY	-1	21	.492	1.1
Frankie Hayes	Phi	-2	20	.485	1.2
Rick Ferrell	StL	-5	14	.462	0.8
Frankie Pytlak	Bos	-6	16	.461	0.8
Rollie Helmsley	Cle	-7	4	.456	0.7
Jake Early	Was	-13	8	.411	0.4

as it ignores both pitchers' handedness and first basemens' putouts. Without adjustments, Kuhel led the league in putouts with 1444. The Sox infielders did record the second-most assists in the league, behind the Yankees, but even when you take that into account, Kuhel still comes out high in net putouts. As a team, the White Sox 1bPO-ifA was 224, second only to the Browns' 234, and the Browns allowed many more hits.

Kuhel's high DWP leads to a related point. Players at key defensive positions will have a lower spread of DWP than will players at non-key positions like first base. This is because managers will not play clods at shortstop to put their bats in the lineup; they'll play them in left field. However, there are legitimately good left fielders, resulting in a large spread in DWP. For this reason, I prefer the two runs saved measures, or at least a won-lost record, using the old Bill James Defensive Games as the spread.

Jimmie Foxx, Boston: Foxx wasn't a good first baseman, at .185 RR (.198 expected) and .016 AR (.019 expected). He did have his pitching staff handedness working against him, but we've already taken that into account in the expected. His final totals are -8/4/.409, but he's a first baseman with 534 home runs. Palmer missed on him, 7 FR, because he ignored the putouts.

Mickey Vernon, Washington: Vernon's 155 assists in 1949 is still one of the highest totals for a first baseman in history, but he was just flat-out awful in 1941. He had a .168 RR on a staff without many lefties, so his expected RR was .215. He led the league with 122 double plays, but his second basemen recorded 121, second best in the league behind the Yankees, so his AR is .014, .021 expected. He finished at -23/-13/.117, one of the worst showings in the league. Palmer thought he was bad, at -6 FR, but I think he's worse.

Player	Team	Runs	Marg.	DWP	DXW
Joe Kuhel	Chi	26	41	.676	0.9
George McQuinn	StL	13	27	.610	0.6
Rudy York	Det	1	16	.505	0.5
Dick Siebert	Phi	0	12	.502	0.4
Hal Trosky	Cle	-2	4	.458	0.2
Jimmie Foxx	Bos	-8	4	.407	0.1
Johnny Sturm	NY	-9	0	.343	0
Mickey Vernon	Was	-23	-13	.117	-0.6

SECOND BASEMEN

We've already examined Gordon and Doerr and presented the second base data above, but there's one other Hall of Famer here who ought to be discussed.

Charlie Gehringer, Detroit: He wasn't Mechanical Man anymore in his last season as a regular, though he did lead the league with a .982 Fielding Percentage. But he couldn't move around. His .417 RR looks good at a glance, but he had a lack of lefties and a bit of a ground ball staff working against him, with only a slight hitters' park offsetting that, expected RR of .415. And he couldn't turn the double play at all anymore, .052 AR (.066 expected), so he wound up at -5/24/.476, about where Palmer had him (-3 FR).

THIRD BASEMEN

Harlond Clift, St. Louis: I'm starting to wonder if he really does have a case for Cooperstown. I expected his outstanding defensive stats to wilt under scrutiny, since the Brownie pitchers were just awful, but he held his own. The Brownies had a group of right-handed fly ballers, helping his and shortstop Johnny Berardino's stats. He had a .307 RR, and the league average was .308, but the expected RR for him was .272. Similar story with his arm, he was at .018, the league at .019 and the expected at .017. He comes out as the top third sacker at 20/45/.600. Palmer had him at 1 FR.

Player	Team	Runs	Marg.	DWP	DXW
Harlond Clift	StL	20	45	.600	1.4
Pete Suder	Phi	18	39	.600	1.3
Pinky Higgins	Det	1	23	.507	0.9
Dario Lodigiani	Chi	0	15	.501	0.5
Red Rolfe	NY	-3	16	.478	0.6
Ken Keltner	Cle	-7	19	.464	0.6
George Archie	Was	-5	6	.433	0.2
Jim Tabor	Bos	-17	2	.367	0.1

SHORTSTOPS

Phil Rizzuto, New York: Rizzuto was the top shortstop in the AL, though his stats weren't as good as Gordon's overall. Scooter had a .386 RR, and the average was .361, but the Yankee lefties pushed the expected to .379. However, possibly as a result of Gordon, his double play stats were great, .092 AR, .066 league, .065 expected. His overall was 14/46/.558, right where Palmer had him at 16 FR.

Joe Cronin, Boston: Cronin was nearing the end of the line as a fielder. He had a .377 RR, but the lefties made his expected .388. He couldn't turn two anymore, as he had a .059 AR, the expected was .067. I have him at -8/18/.458, Palmer at -5 FR. Cronin seems to have been aware of his decline; acting as manager of the Sox, he took himself out of the lineup after that season.

Luke Appling, Chicago: The guy really was an offensive shortstop. His best years were in the 1930s, but he was 32 and already a defensive wreck. Palmer thinks Appling's OK (0 FR) because he led the league with 473 assists, but his .379 RR is inflated by the Chicago lefties and park (expected: .417). As noted earlier, Palmer's methods exaggerate the importance of assists. Overall, I have him pegged at -21/16/.418, one of the worst infielders in the league. Again, I think I might be a bit extreme.

Player	Team	Runs	Marg.	DWP	DXW
Phil Rizzuto	NY	14	46	.558	1.5
Johnny Berardino	StL	11	38	.552	1.4
Cecil Travis	Was	6	38	.525	1.4
Al Brancato	Phi	4	36	.518	1.3
Frank Croucher	Det	4	34	.517	1.2
Joe Cronin	Bos	-8	18	.458	0.7
Luke Appling	Chi	-21	16	.418	0.6
Lou Boudreau	Cle	-20	15	.418	0.6

LEFT FIELDERS

Bob Johnson, Philadelphia: This guy really was a good ballplayer. His .208 RR is better than average (.192) and much better than expected (.176). The Athletics had a right-handed ground ball staff, which kept him from having center fielder-like stats. He had a good arm, .012 AR against .008 average, .007 expected. In all, he was at 20/35/.652, much better than Pete Palmer's 8 FR.

I should make a few notes for outfielders in general. What I did was I plucked the Macmillan-listed center fielders out of the bin, set their stats aside, and then left the remaining averages for both left and right fielders. I then let the Macmillan listing chart direction. For assists, I compared all outfielders to each other. As a result of some moron deciding to lump all out-fielders together 100 years ago, it is hard to figure playing time.

Ted Williams, Boston: I'm sure Ted couldn't care less about my defensive evaluation of him, since all he really cared about was being the best hitter ever, which he is. Anyhow, I always figured that Williams was probably a better outfielder in his youth than for which most people gave him credit, and I was dead wrong, he was always a bad outfielder. My reading of his assist totals was way off base with reality, since the Red Sox had plenty of left-handers and plenty of runners, so his .007 AR was worse than the expected .008. His range was even worse, a .177 RR against a .198 expected. The final numbers for him are -12/1/.365 (Palmer has him at -5), which gives DiMaggio a better case for MVP. I still would have voted for Williams.

Tuck Stainback, lf, Detroit. Tuck comes out as being awful in my system, but here is a case where I think playing time is in error. Pete Palmer rated Stainback higher than the other Tiger left fielder, Rip Radcliff, despite the fact that Radcliff's Range Factor was much better than Stainback. Here is a case where I think we should listen to Pete Palmer, as he has access to much better playing time estimates than I do. Anyhow, Tuck is at -11/-5/.178, which is probably a bit low. He may have played some right field, but it was clear from the games played that he played mostly left.

Player	Team	Runs	Marg.	DWP	DXW
Bob Johnson	Phi	20	35	.652	1.2
George Case	Was	17	36	.610	1.3
Roy Cullenbine	StL	7	20	.564	0.8
Charlie Keller	NY	8	24	.560	0.9
Gee Walker	Cle	-1	11	.486	0.5
Rip Radcliff	Det	-1	6	.478	0.3
Ted Williams	Bos	-12	1	.365	0.1
Myril Hoag	Chi	-14	-3	.300	-0.2
Tuck Stainback	Det	-11	-5	.178	-0.4

CENTER FIELDERS

Joe DiMaggio, New York: The man was good. His RR was .255 (.233 average, .247 expected, as he played in a great pitchers' park). He pegged 16 runners, a .011 AR against a .008 expected. I have him at 8/27/.551, Palmer has him at 7 FR.

Doc Cramer, Washington: Please, pretty please, never make a Hall of Fame case for him again. The guy had a .203 RR, a normal .228 was expected. He nailed 9 baserunners, an average outfielder would have had 14; his AR was .005, expected was .008. Washington had plenty of baserunners. He was at -19/-1/.337, Palmer has him at -10.

Player	Team	Runs	Marg.	DWP	DXW
Soup Campbell	Cle	6	16	.570	0.6
Barney McCosky	Det	9	25	.567	1.0
Sam Chapman	Phi	10	31	.561	1.1
Joe DiMaggio	NY	8	27	.551	1.1
Dom DiMaggio	Bos	2	21	.515	0.9
Mike Kreevich	Chi	-3	12	.470	0.5
Wally Judnich	StL	-5	14	.462	0.6
Roy Weatherly	Cle	-9	1	.366	0.1
Doc Cramer	Was	-19	-1	.337	-0.1

RIGHT FIELDERS

Tommy Henrich, New York: The class of the bunch, and the best ranking in the stellar Yankee outfield as well. Top range and above-average arm add up to 11/25/.597. Palmer's method picks Buddy Lewis (11FR) and ranks Henrich at -3, which is almost certainly due to the lack of adjustment for left-ies.

Player	Team	Runs	Marg.	DWP	DXW
Tommy Henrich	NY	11	25	.597	0.9
Buddy Lewis	Was	5	17	.554	0.5
Taffy Wright	Chi	6	19	.551	0.6
Jeff Heath	Cle	3	17	.531	0.7
Wally Moses	Phi	1	14	.510	0.4
Joe Grace (OF)	StL	-1	7	.478	0.3
Lou Finney	Bos	-2	7	.476	0.4
Bruce Campbell	Det	-10	1	.370	0.1
Chet Laabs	StL	-13	-2	.317	-0.1

The two biggest differences between Palmer's method and my Context-Adjusted Defense ratings (CAD) are how many lefties a team has and how many hits a team allows. I think those both are big deals. The areas where I have best nailed is first baseman's fielding, until now a murky area, and the proper direction of how to evaluate fielders in terms of range and arm. I'm sure someone will use a cube root where I have used a square root, and I do plan to chart out fielders opportunities in our own time, where we have Zone Ratings and Defensive Averages to show us where the hits fell. And, of course, I have a wish list: outfielders broken down into left-center-right, innings played defensively, hits, doubles and triples allowed and broken down by park. But fielding stats looked worse just five years ago.

DECONSTRUCTING JACKIE ROBINSON

Retrosheet and the Future of Baseball Past

David W. Smith and Don Malcolm

Even before Ken Burns utilized him as the leitmotif and primary symbol of the constantly evolving National Pastime in his 1994 documentary Baseball, Jackie Robinson was one of the game's epic figures. Modern research and detailed historical reconstruction of Robinson's day-by-day major league playing career (spanning the years 1947 to 1956) now give us a completely new perspective on his celebrated career.

What follows is a detailed "deconstruction" of Jackie Robinson that focuses on his daily offensive log, compiled and verified by a group of researchers banded together under the collective name of Retrosheet, which is endeavoring to collect, input, and document the complete day-by-day history of major league baseball. (More information on this effort can be found in the post-script to this article, "A Few Words About Retrosheet.")

Those of you familiar with the statistical breakouts now commonly available in books such as STATS Player Profiles and the Elias Baseball Analyst will recognize many of the same categories as we conduct a detailed survey of Jackie Robinson's playing career. We hope, however, that you will be as astonished and amazed as we are at the prospect of seeing this amount of detail for a player whose career began more than fifty years ago. It is Retrosheet's goal to provide this same amount of detail for every player in the history of major league baseball. While that is a monumental and almost superhuman task, progress toward that goal has been steady and inexorable over the past ten years. And it is only fitting that the first example of such a reconstructed "deconstruction" should be one of baseball's most important personages.

But enough talk---let's get to the data!

BASIC SPLITS

The basic statistical splits now commonly available for players are Home/Away, Left/Right, Day/Night, and monthly totals (April, May, June, July, August, and September/October). Let's begin with Robinson's Home and Away data. Was Jackie helped a lot by Ebbets Field?

Where	G	AB	R	H	2B	3B	HR	RBI	SH	SF	BB	HP	SO	GDP	SB	CS	BA	OBP	SLG	OPS
Home	702	2445	489	767	143	29	78	380	48	4	368	35	149	75	109	39	.314	.403	.492	.895
Away	680	2432	458	751	130	25	59	354	56	5	374	37	141	72	87	37	.309	.400	.456	.856

As the data shows, Robinson hit a little better at home, but not a lot. Most of the difference was in terms of power (78 homers at home, 59 on the road). Another measure of this can be found in the Bill James statistic Isolated Power (ISO). Jackie's ISO at in home games (which, by the way, include six games he played for the Dodgers when they played seven home games at Roosevelt Stadium in Jersey City during the 1956 season) was .181. On the road, his ISO was .147.

In general, however, moving Robinson away from Ebbets Field would not have altered his career profile greatly. There are a couple of exceptions to this statement, however, that we will examine when we look at Jackie's performance in individual ballparks (further below).

How about Robinson versus left-handed or right-handed pitchers (Left/Right)? Are there any significant platoon differentials to be found in these splits? (Note that several statistical categories shown in the Home/Away data are not replicated below--- for example, baserunning data.)

Pitcher	BA	OBP	SLG	AB	H	2B	3B	HR	RBI	BB	SO
Left	.317	.406	.494	1232	390	96	12	33	158	175	67
Right	.309	.410	.467	3645	1128	177	42	104	576	567	223

This data shows us that Jackie hit lefties a little better than righties, but again, the differences were not great. However, since Robinson faced righties three times as often as lefties (and more about this a bit later), it's hard for us to really compare the raw stats. There's a way we can do that, however, and that is by normalizing each line to what the numbers would look like if each represented 600 plate appearances (roughly a season's worth). When we do that, this is how those numbers look:

600 PA	BA	OBP	SLG	AB	H	2B	3B	HR	RBI	BB	SO
Left	.317	.406	.494	525	166	41	5	14	67	75	29
Right	.309	.410	.467	519	161	25	6	15	82	81	32

Now we have a better sense of the shapes in these stats. Jackie hit a lot more doubles against left-handers (per 600 PA), had slightly more doubles and triples against righties, and drew a few more walks against righties as well. Aside from the discrepancy in doubles, however, there's really very little variation in his level of performance.

And this consistency continues to be a hallmark when we look at Jackie's performance broken out by time of day (Day/Night). One interesting feature of this data is actually unrelated to Jackie's performance: we will see that Robinson had almost two-thirds of his plate appearances during the day. The current ratio of Day/Night plate appearances in baseball is almost an exact mirror image of this percentage.

When	BA	OBP	SLG	AB	H	2B	3B	HR	RBI	BB	SO
Day	.317	.414	.489	3170	1004	183	39	95	485	486	181
Night	.301	.400	.445	1707	514	90	15	42	249	256	109

Jackie hits a bit better in the daytime, but not a lot. We'll look at this data again in our year-by-year examination of his career. Let's use that same 600 plate appearance rate to get a better look at the normalized differences in these stats:

600 PA	BA	OBP	SLG	AB	H	2B	3B	HR	RBI	BB	SO
Day	.317	.414	.489	520	165	30	6	16	80	80	30
Night	.301	.400	.445	522	157	28	5	13	76	78	33

There is only a little more variation here than in the Left/Right stats above. Let's summarize the differences in Jackie's basic splits using Total Baseball's convenient summary statistic, On-Base Plus Slugging (OPS):

Split	OPS
Home	.900
Away	.877
Left	.902
Right	.864
Day	.903
Night	.845

Jackie Robinson's statistics point to the same imperturbability that was the hallmark of his on-field demeanor during his mercurial rookie year of 1947. Let's conclude our look at Jackie's basic splits by examining his performance in the individual months of the season.

Month	BA	OBP	SLG	AB	H	2B	3B	HR	RBI	BB	SO
April	.312	.423	.471	401	125	19	3	13	61	71	28
May	.326	.427	.498	866	282	60	10	23	139	141	43
June	.346	.428	.531	889	308	56	12	28	134	119	46
July	.299	.399	.462	893	267	47	9	27	153	130	47
August	.289	.381	.433	1004	290	44	10	27	135	142	74
Sept/Oct	.299	.408	.449	824	246	47	10	19	112	139	52

Here we do see some sizable performance variation. Jackie appears to have been a first-half player, hitting a good bit better in April-June than in July-October:

WHEN	BA	OBP	SLG	AB	H	2B	3B	HR	RBI	BB	SO
April-June	.332	.421	.506	2156	715	135	25	64	334	331	117
July-October	.295	.388	.448	2721	803	138	29	73	400	411	173

Again, let's look at this data adjusted to the rate of 600 plate appearances:

600 PA	BA	OBP	SLG	AB	H	2B	3B	HR	RBI	BB	SO
April-June	.332	.421	.506	520	172	33	6	15	81	80	28
July-October	.295	.388	.448	521	154	26	6	14	77	79	33

The only big difference here is in batting average, actually; there are a few more doubles, but everything else is about the same. It looks as though Jackie, like many players, was just worn down a bit by the length of the season. The OPS difference here, however, is a good bit more sizable than in any of the other splits:

And as we'll see when we look at Jackie's career on a year-by-year basis (below), his cumulative batting average often exhibits this pattern of peaking in the first half of the year, and then fading toward its eventual resting place.

When	OPS
April-June	.927
July-October	.836

BEYOND THE BASICS

So far we've looked at the standard breakouts. Now we'll venture into the realm of situational statistics (ones that often get sliced to such small sample sizes that they almost become parodies of themselves). Since we're looking at a ten-year breakout for Robinson, however, these numbers are free from such a stigma, and should give us a good sense of Jackie's abilities in various game situations.

The stats we'll be presenting here are Robinson's plate appearances when the bases are empty (Bases Empty, Leadoff, and Not Leadoff) and when there are men on base (Runners On, First Base Only, Scoring Position, and Bases Loaded). After these breakouts, we'll look at what some analysts call "clutch performance": hitting in "Late and Close" situations. And finally, we'll examine Jackie's hitting in terms of what the ball-strike count was when the outcome of the plate appearance was decided (Ahead in Count, Behind in Count).

First, batting with the bases empty:

	BA	OBP	SLG	AB	H	2B	3B	HR	RBI	BB	SO
Bases Empty	.303	.407	.472	2464	747	138	28	74	74	396	169
Leadoff	.300	.399	.497	1025	308	71	11	36	36	160	72
Not Leadoff	.305	.412	.454	1439	439	67	17	38	38	236	97

What we see in this data is that like many great hitters, Jackie hit for more power when leading off an inning than in other bases-empty situations. This is again made more obvious by pro-rating the two "Bases Empty" categories (Leadoff, Not Leadoff) to 600 plate appearances:

600 PA	BA	OBP	SLG	AB	H	2B	3B	HR	RBI	BB	SO
Leadoff	.300	.399	.497	519	156	36	6	18	18	81	36
Not Leadoff	.305	.412	.454	515	157	24	6	14	14	85	35

As this view of the data makes clear, Jackie hit a lot more doubles and more HRs when leading off an inning than when batting later in an inning with the bases empty.

Now let's examine Jackie's batting with men on base:

	BA	OBP	SLG	AB	H	2B	3B	HR	RBI	BB	SO
Runners On	.320	.411	.475	2413	771	135	26	63	660	346	121
1st Base Only	.335	.398	.504	1031	345	64	9	31	96	97	53
Scoring Position	.308	.421	.454	1382	426	71	17	32	564	249	68
Bases Loaded	.268	.352	.366	123	33	6	0	2	107	14	7

As you can see, Jackie's best situational hitting came with runners on first base only. Again, however, to get a better sense of the shape of Robinson's performance, we need to use the 600 plate appearance notation:

600 PA	BA	OBP	SLG	AB	H	2B	3B	HR	RBI	BB	SO
Runners On	.320	.411	.475	525	168	29	6	14	144	75	26
1st Base Only	.335	.398	.504	548	184	34	5	16	51	52	28
Scoring Position	.308	.421	.454	508	157	26	6	12	207	92	25
Bases Loaded	.268	.352	.366	539	145	26	0	9	469	61	31

While the RBI extrapolations here are pretty wild, of course you should really ignore them, since no player will ever have 600 plate appearances in a year comprised of these particular situations. But what is interesting here is the fact that Jackie drew a lot fewer walks while batting with men on first than in any other batting situation---fewer, even, than with the bases loaded.

And, in fact, Robinson's worst overall performance comes with the bases loaded. His ISO actually drops below .100 (.098) in those situations. Interesting, and a bit odd, when we juxtapose that with his performance in "Late and Close" situations:

	BA	OBP	SLG	AB	H	2B	3B	HR	RBI	BB	SO
Late & Close	.341	.446	.545	694	237	39	6	30	131	123	44
600 PA	.341	.446	.545	510	174	29	4	22	96	90	32

In these "clutch" situations, Jackie is at his absolute best---best BA, best OBP, best SLG, best ISO of all his splits. His performance in these type of situations may help to explain some surprising revelations concerning the slot in the Dodger batting order that he most often occupied (discussed below).

Finally, let's look at Jackie's performance relative to the ball-strike count. Note that for about 5% of Robinson's plate appearances, we do not have count information. We've broken that out below as "unknown":

	BA	OBP	SLG	AB	H	2B	3B	HR	RBI	BB	SO
Ahead in Count	.327	.469	.507	2688	878	171	29	85	479	704	113
Behind in Count	.290	.305	.433	1891	549	92	20	46	231	0	162
Unknown Count	.305	.402	.433	298	91	10	5	6	24	38	15

In 1997, the characteristic split in the major leagues for ahead in the count/behind in the count was as follows:

Jackie did not hit as well as current major leagues do when they are ahead in the count, but he hit significantly better (as measured by OPS: .738 to .515) when behind in the count. Sandy Koufax, in his discussion of statistics in his eponymous 1966 autobiography, referred to Allan Roth's breakouts that indicated Jackie as the best Dodger hitter with two strikes on him. These numbers, while not an exact match for that breakout, do provide solid corroborative evidence for that assertion.

Count	BA	OBP	SLG
Ahead	.346	.470	.564
Behind	.204	.211	.304

JACKIE AND NL BALLPARKS

While we've looked at the basic Home/Road breakout already, there is more detail available in the form of individual ballparks. Were there any parks where Jackie performed especially well or poorly? How might these numbers have affected his career numbers had he come up with a different team? First, the basic breakouts:

Ballpark	G	AB	R	H	2B	3B	HR	RBI	BB	HP	SO	GDP	SB	CS	BA	OBP	SLG	OPS
Forbes Field (PIT)	102	383	91	131	19	2	18	71	59	8	19	10	14	8	.342	.438	.543	.981
Crosley Field (CIN)	89	313	63	102	23	5	7	55	49	1	12	7	5	8	.326	.418	.498	.916
Ebbets Field (BRO)	696	2428	487	762	143	29	77	377	368	35	147	75	109	39	.314	.411	.492	.903
Connie Mack Stadium (PHI)	98	360	76	114	18	3	11	49	39	8	26	18	19	5	.317	.395	.475	.870
Wrigley Field (CHN)	93	336	59	99	22	7	5	43	58	1	23	7	14	3	.295	.400	.446	.846
Busch Stadium (SLN)	94	328	52	100	22	3	5	52	49	3	19	9	7	5	.305	.400	.436	.836
Polo Grounds (NYG)	104	371	67	112	11	2	9	42	58	8	19	14	17	4	.302	.406	.415	.821
County Stadium (MIL)	34	105	13	26	6	1	3	15	20	1	6	3	2	0	.248	.373	.410	.783
Roosevelt Stadium (JC1)	6	17	2	5	0	0	1	3	0	0	2	0	0	0	.294	.294	.471	.765
Braves Field (BOS)	66	236	37	67	9	2	1	27	42	7	17	4	9	4	.284	.407	.352	.759

As you can see, we've sorted the ballpark data in descending order of OPS. And we've also included a couple of other statistics that are in the database that we haven't shown before, such as hit by pitch (HP) and grounded into double plays (GDP).

What leaps out, of course, is the tremendous hitting that Jackie did in Pittsburgh. It appears that the friendly left-center field dimensions from 1947 to 1953 (known as Kiner's Korner) had a salubrious effect on Jackie's HR totals as well. (We'll see that a bit more clearly when the data is broken out in 154-game notation below.) Jackie's worst performances came in the home park of the Braves, regardless of its location in Boston's Braves Field (1947-52) or Milwaukee's County Stadium (1953-56).

Here's the same data (minus the six games at Roosevelt Field) shown in 154-game notation (a slight variation on the 600 PA notation used previously):

BALLPARK/PER 154 GAMES	G	AB	R	H	2B	3B	HR	RBI	BB	HP	SO	GDP	SB	CS	BA	OBP	SLG	OPS
Forbes Field (PIT)	154	578	137	198	29	3	27	107	89	12	29	15	21	12	.342	.438	.543	.981
Crosley Field (CIN)	154	542	109	176	40	9	12	95	85	2	21	12	9	14	.326	.418	.498	.916
Ebbets Field (BRO)	154	537	108	169	32	6	17	83	81	8	33	17	24	9	.314	.411	.492	.903
Connie Mack Stadium (PHI)	154	566	119	179	28	5	17	77	61	13	41	28	30	8	.317	.395	.475	.870
Wrigley Field (CHN)	154	556	98	164	36	12	8	71	96	2	38	12	23	5	.295	.400	.446	.846
Busch Stadium (SLN)	154	537	85	164	36	5	8	85	80	5	31	15	11	8	.305	.400	.436	.836
Polo Grounds (NYG)	154	549	99	166	16	3	13	62	86	12	28	21	25	6	.302	.406	.415	.821
County Stadium (MIL)	154	476	59	118	27	5	14	68	91	5	27	14	9	0	.248	.373	.410	.783
Braves Field (BOS)	154	551	86	156	21	5	2	63	98	16	40	9	21	9	.284	.407	.352	.759

As you can see, Jackie got a big HR boost from Pittsburgh's Forbes Field, while his extra-base hit totals shriveled dramatically at Braves Field. There are other interesting variations here, such as Jackie's high triples totals in Wrigley Field, his low walk and high GDP totals in Philadelphia, and his poor percentage base-stealing in Cincinnati. Part of the reason, of course, that Robinson hit well in Forbes Field is due to the fact that the Pirates were at or near the bottom of the National League for most of this period.

ROBINSON AND THE BROOKLYN BATTING ORDER

Jackie Robinson's lingering memory as a on-field player, as opposed to the game's pioneer of integration, is centered around his re-introduction of speed to the game, in the form of stolen bases and aggressive baserunning.

These attributes have become synonymous with memorable leadoff batters, beginning in the 50s and 60s with Luis Aparicio and Maury Wills, continuing through the 70s with Lou Brock, and on to the present day with all-time SB king Rickey Henderson (all non-Caucasian players).

What's extremely surprising given the Robinson legacy in this regard is the discovery that Jackie batted leadoff for the Dodgers in only 20 games during his career. In fact, most of Jackie's plate appearances came as the Dodgers' cleanup hitter, as the data below displays:

BOP	G	AB	R	H	D	T	HR	RBI	SH	SF	HP	BB	SO	SB	CS	GDP	BA	OBP	SLG
1	20	80	15	25	6	1	1	14	0	0	0	10	7	0	1	3	.313	.389	.450
2	253	999	205	288	55	12	22	110	33	0	18	120	66	48	22	8	.288	.364	.433
3	176	645	130	207	32	4	20	90	12	0	12	110	41	26	9	14	.321	.422	.476
4	683	2483	496	818	157	32	79	439	49	2	35	382	139	106	37	68	.329	.419	.514
5	34	112	18	31	5	0	1	12	0	0	2	18	9	1	0	7	.277	.386	.348
6	93	290	47	84	12	5	7	45	4	5	3	58	12	10	5	7	.290	.403	.438
7	58	191	26	48	3	0	6	17	3	1	2	34	10	4	1	5	.251	.364	.361
8	25	49	7	12	1	0	1	5	1	1	0	6	2	1	0	1	.245	.316	.327
9	33	28	3	5	2	0	0	2	2	0	0	4	4	0	1	0	.179	.265	.250

And it's interesting to note that Robinson hit best in the cleanup slot, as an examination of his BA, OBP and SLG data will indicate. This appears to have been recognized early on by the Dodgers, as the following year-by-year log of Robinson's games by batting order position (BOP) indicates:

Year	1	2	3	4	5	6	7	8	9
1947		140	10	1					
1948	18	102	21					4	2
1949				156					
1950				137		1	2	1	1
1951	1		12	136		1		2	1
1952		3	108	34			1	2	1
1953			14	114	1	1	3		3
1954			3	61	9	26	15	2	4
1955	1	5		7	2	30	36	12	12
1956		3	7	37	22	35	1	2	10

And a sampling of Dodger post-season lineups from this period simply re-confirms Robinson's pre-eminent role as the cleanup man for the Boys of Summer:

BOP	1949 WS	1951 playoff	1952 WS	1953 WS
1	Reese ss	Furillo rf	Cox 3b	Gilliam 2b
2	Jorgensen 3b	Reese ss	Reese ss	Reese ss
3	Snider cf	Snider cf	Snider cf	Snider cf
4	Robinson 2b	Robinson 2b	Robinson 2b	Robinson lf
5	Hermanski lf	Campanella c	Campanella c	Campanella c
6	Furillo rf	Pafko lf	Pafko lf	Hodges 1b
7	Hodges 1b	Hodges 1b	Hodges 1b	Furillo rf
8	Campanella c	Cox 3b	Furillo rf	Cox 3b

As a cleanup hitter, Jackie had a .933 OPS, and averaged 99 RBI per 154 games played in the #4 slot. It's not part of history's collective memory, but Robinson may well have been the best cleanup hitter in baseball during what Roger Kahn calls "the Era" (1947-57).

A YEAR-BY YEAR TOUR

And now let's get into the serious detail of Robinson's career, from his first major league game on April 15, 1947 (in Ebbets Field against the Boston Braves) to his final regular season appearance (also at Ebbets, against the Pittsburgh Pirates). We will accompany our tour with some brief descriptive highlights on a year-by-year basis, but let's begin with the type of chart that BBBA has made famous in analogous contexts. Here is a display of Robinson's running 20-game OPS average over his entire career, beginning with games 1-20 in 1947 and concluding with games 1363-1382 in 1956. This is an epic chart, showing the ebb and flow of Jackie's offensive performance, describing all of his 20-game peaks and valleys:

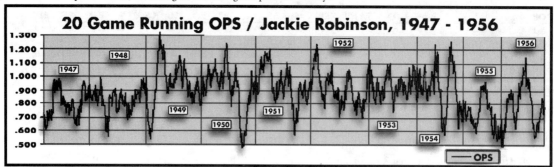

At 20 games, these charts resemble EKG charts as much as anything, but this one is a wonderful running snapshot of Jackie's ongoing offensive heartbeat. You can see the general level of offense that he establishes in 1947-48, with peaks that approach but do not exceed an OPS of 1.000. In 1949, however, that all changes early in the year; Jackie generates what is his greatest career 20-game peak in May, and establishes a new level of performance which carries him to the batting title (and the Dodgers back to the World Series).

He continues that level of performance, including another spike over 1.200, in 1950, until he enters a brief but dramatic tailspin in the second half of the year. From this point through 1952, he has a wider 20-game fluctuation than in previous years (wider than either the lower pre-1949 performance levels, or the 1949-50 year-and-a-half peak). In 1953, he is once again more consistent within a range of OPS performance, and this continues into mid-1954, when he then exhibits an extreme set of fluctuations that become pervasive for the rest of his career.

In 1955, Jackie is at his lowest ebb, but he rallies in 1956 and winds up with one more 20-game spike above 1.100. He finishes the season and his career batting cleanup for the Dodgers. In early 1957, the Dodgers trade him to the Giants, and he retires.

When we have concluded our year-by year tour of Jackie's career, we'll look at another version of this chart--one which displays Robinson's offensive data in much larger snapshots--that will provide a more stable picture of his overall offensive performance.

1947: BREAKING IN WITH A BANG

Jackie went 0-for-3 in his first major league game, but went 9-for-19 in his next five games to move his batting average over .400. He was 0-for-19 in his next five games, however, which is about where we pick him up on our "Cumulative Batting Average" chart (and there's one provided for each year in Robinson's career).

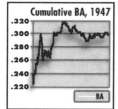

Jackie had a small flurry in mid-May that got his average close to .300, but he fell back over the next couple of weeks toward .260. Starting on June 5th, however, Jackie had a six-game skein where he went 14-for-29 (including a 4-for-4 day against the Reds in Ebbets Field on June 11th) that brought his average over .300.

From June 14th to July 4th, he had a 21-game hitting streak that pushed his average to .316. He hit less than .200 (8-for-41) over the next ten games, however, and fell to .299, and for the rest of the year he struggled to get back to .300, eventually winding up just short at .296. He established his Forbes Field home run connection early on, however, hitting two long balls there in late July, and two more in consecutive games in mid-September.

1947	BA	OBP	SLG	AB	H	2B	3B	HR	RBI	BB	SO
April	.225	.354	.325	40	9	1	0	1	1	7	3
May	.282	.373	.340	103	29	3	0	1	7	10	7
June	.381	.449	.496	113	43	5	1	2	9	13	4
July	.257	.344	.412	136	35	7	1	4	16	17	6
August	.306	.394	.460	124	38	10	3	1	6	17	11
Sept/Oct	.284	.369	.473	74	21	5	0	3	9	10	5

1948: STEADY AS SHE GOES

Actually, not quite so, as Jackie was hot early in the year, hitting .355 for the first 20 games in May to boost his season average to .333, but hitting just .200 over his next 20 to slump below .270. After that, however, he righted himself, got back to the .300 mark, and was exceptionally consistent for the rest of the season, as the Cumulative BA chart shows.

Jackie messed up in Forbes Field in early June, going 0-for-12, but he paid the Bucs back two weeks later at home when he went 9-for-14 with three doubles, a homer and eight RBI in a three-game series. He pushed his BA over .300 with a 5-for-9 day in a doubleheader against the Pirates on September 14th, and still had it there on September 29th, but he went 2-for-14 in his final four games and finished at .296.

1948	BA	OBP	SLG	AB	H	2B	3B	HR	RBI	BB	SO
April	.280	.308	.400	25	7	3	0	0	4	1	3
May	.304	.396	.481	79	24	6	1	2	13	12	5
June	.310	.362	.460	87	27	8	1	1	13	7	4
July	.301	.372	.414	133	40	7	1	2	23	12	9
August	.270	.350	.451	122	33	3	2	5	16	12	13
Sept/Oct	.305	.382	.484	128	39	11	3	2	16	15	3

1949: THE BIG BREAKOUT

The early going in 1949 did not provide even the slightest indication that Robinson was going to establish a new performance level: on May 7th, two weeks into the season, Jackie was hitting just .222. But when Robinson banged out three hits in successive games against the Cardinals on May 8-9, he began a skein that would rank as his greatest sustained hitting performance. Over the 70 games from May 8th through July 23rd, Jackie hit .394, had an OBP of .463, and slugged .602. Ten days later, his seventy-game BA topped .400, though his OBP and SLG had tailed off some (!). He had pushed his seasonal batting average to its peak of .368 as July came to a close, and coasted to the batting title, holding off a late-season challenge from two rather well-known members of the St. Louis Cardinals, Stan Musial and Enos Slaughter.

Cumulative BA, 1949

Jackie's skein from May to July was punctuated by an incredible number of multiple hit games. For the year, Robinson wound up with 65 multiple-hit games (47 two-hit games and 18 three-hit games); 44 of these came from May 1-July 31. Here is the May-July breakout:

Month	2-hit	3-hit
May	11	7
June	11	4
July	9	2

Jackie never had another month with as many multiple hit games as he amassed in either May or June 1949. He was at his peak, and his reward at the end of the season was the Most Valuable Player award in the National League.

1949	BA	OBP	SLG	AB	H	2B	3B	HR	RBI	BB	SO
April	.188	.264	.250	48	9	0	0	1	5	5	3
May	.431	.480	.741	116	50	12	3	6	34	9	5
June	.374	.427	.495	107	40	6	2	1	21	9	6
July	.360	.488	.540	100	36	5	2	3	20	23	6
August	.308	.394	.533	120	37	9	3	4	25	15	2
Sept/Oct	.304	.445	.431	102	31	6	2	1	19	25	4

1950: RIDING THE CREST

As 1950 began, Jackie was the most feared hitter in the National League; this was driven home by the a streak in the first three weeks of May where Robinson was walked 17 times in 16 games. By the end of May, he was hitting .378; early in July he peaked at .380.

However, August 1950 was one of the worst months of Jackie's career. He hit just .188, and his 20-game BA fell from .402 early in the month all the way to .149 on August 24th. By the time September rolled around, Jackie had lost 50 points off his batting average.

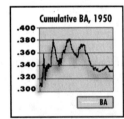

Cumulative BA, 1950

Jackie rallied in the early part of September, but he and the Dodgers, who were trying to make a run at the faltering Whiz Kids, were forced to play four doubleheaders in five days as the season came to an end. Jackie went 7-for-34 over these nine games and wound up second in the batting race at .328; the Dodgers also finished second.

1950	BA	OBP	SLG	AB	H	2B	3B	HR	RBI	BB	SO
April	.306	.375	.500	36	11	5	1	0	7	4	1
May	.398	.517	.634	93	37	11	1	3	17	23	3
June	.380	.432	.611	108	41	8	1	5	20	10	7
July	.363	.444	.500	102	37	8	0	2	18	13	5
August	.188	.311	.267	101	19	2	0	2	13	17	3
Sept/Oct	.321	.430	.487	78	25	5	1	2	6	13	5

1951: TRIPPED UP BY A MIRACLE

Jackie and the Dodgers were both determined to atone for having been also-rans in 1950; they came charging out of the gate at an incredible pace. In early June, Brooklyn was eight games in front of the Giants, and Robinson was hitting over .400. At the end of July, Jackie was down to .360 and in a dog fight for the batting crown with that Musial guy (who else?), but the Dodgers were even further in front.

Of course, we all know what happened next. The Giants got white hot, while the Dodgers (and Robinson) cooled off. Jackie's fourteenth-inning homer against the Phillies on the final day of the season kept Brooklyn alive, and they went into a best of three playoff with their cross-town rivals after squandering a 13 1/2 game lead. Jackie was now a distant third in the batting race, and his cumulative BA chart mirrored the Dodgers' fortunes.

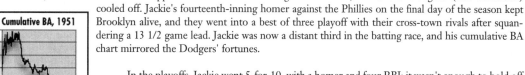

In the playoffs, Jackie went 5-for-10, with a homer and four RBI; it wasn't enough to hold off the Giants and Bobby Thomson.

1951	BA	OBP	SLG	AB	H	2B	3B	HR	RBI	BB	SO
April	.412	.474	.706	51	21	3	0	4	14	5	3
May	.404	.509	.574	94	38	8	1	2	15	19	3
June	.278	.386	.485	97	27	6	1	4	11	17	3
July	.375	.459	.562	96	36	7	1	3	19	12	3
August	.277	.354	.436	101	28	5	1	3	14	12	7
Sept/Oct	.321	.417	.495	109	35	4	3	3	15	14	8

1952-53: THE COAST IS CLEAR

For Jackie, the next two seasons turned out to be much calmer than anything he had experienced in the past. The Dodgers got better, and walked away with two pennants. Robinson rediscovered Forbes Field and the bottom-dwelling Pirate pitching staff, hitting four homers there in 1952, including two in consecutive games in early June. But Jackie had a tough July, and it wasn't a season where he was destined to challenge for the batting title. The rest of the Brooklyn juggernaut cut him some slack.

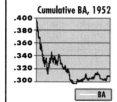

But Jackie did all right in August and September, though his power numbers had slipped some. Maybe it was due to the fact that he wasn't batting cleanup; manager Chuck Dressen had restructured the Dodger lineup, batting Jackie third.

1952	BA	OBP	SLG	AB	H	2B	3B	HR	RBI	BB	SO
April	.448	.652	.552	29	13	0	0	1	5	14	2
May	.296	.441	.444	81	24	6	0	2	10	17	4
June	.317	.469	.465	101	32	4	1	3	14	27	7
July	.218	.313	.460	87	19	1	1	6	17	11	7
August	.328	.429	.462	119	39	2	1	4	16	19	11
Sept/Oct	.323	.442	.462	93	30	4	0	3	13	18	9

The next season, Jackie was hitting under .300 early in June when he had another remarkable multiple-hit skein, posting at least two hits in seven straight games and eight out of nine. When the streak ended, Robinson had gone 21-for-36 and had raised his average to .349.

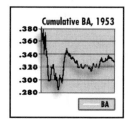

After tailing off in July, Jackie had 12 more multiple-hit games in August, and both he and the Dodgers coasted home to another magnificent season, only to come up short again in the Fall Classic against the Yankees, who had now beaten them in five straight World Series.

1953	BA	OBP	SLG	AB	H	2B	3B	HR	RBI	BB	SO
April	.375	.483	.479	48	18	3	1	0	5	10	3
May	.274	.367	.495	95	26	7	1	4	19	12	7
June	.392	.464	.541	74	29	7	2	0	16	8	5
July	.280	.408	.495	107	30	7	2	4	22	21	3
August	.362	.432	.505	105	38	6	0	3	20	13	10
Sept/Oct	.327	.439	.491	55	18	4	1	1	13	10	2

1954-55: THE LEFTIES DISAPPEAR

One of the phenomena often discussed about the Boys of Summer is the configuration of the offense; this was predominantly a right-handed hitting team, with Duke Snider often being the only left-handed batter in the lineup. Starting in 1953, switch-hitting Jim Gilliam became a fixture at the top of the lineup, but that just added another proficient bat against lefties, and someone else who could get on base a lot.

So what happened was that the rest of the league just stopped throwing lefties at the Dodgers at all. And thanks to the data we have on Jackie Robinson through this period, we can track the progress of this tactical change. Here is a list of Robinson's number of plate appearances against left-handed pitchers from 1947-56:

Year	PA	Year	PA
1947	253	1952	88
1948	220	1953	88
1949	262	1954	82
1950	206	1955	23
1951	147	1956	58

Of course, it didn't really make much difference: the Dodgers managed to finish second in 1954, but an almost exclusive diet of right-handed pitchers didn't prevent them from returning to the post-season in 1955 and 1956.

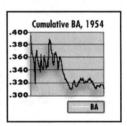

Cumulative BA, 1954

For Jackie, 1954 looked an awful lot like his standard pattern: hot start, followed by a cold stretch, and a long finish at a level close to his overall season average. His batting average peaked at .388 in early June thanks to back-to-back four hit games against the Cubs in Wrigley Field; ten days later, he had a third four-hit game, followed by a fourth on June 26th. There was, of course, the usual cold spell in July, including an eighteen-game stretch in which Jackie hit just .146. And September was a premonition of the season to come---Jackie's worst and the Dodgers' best.

1954	BA	OBP	SLG	AB	H	2B	3B	HR	RBI	BB	SO
April	.368	.520	.579	38	14	2	0	2	8	10	3
May	.345	.426	.483	58	20	4	2	0	6	9	3
June	.351	.413	.670	94	33	7	1	7	15	9	3
July	.211	.360	.310	71	15	2	1	1	10	14	2
August	.342	.422	.566	76	26	5	0	4	16	12	5
Sept/Oct	.245	.373	.347	49	12	2	0	1	4	9	4

In 1955, the Dodgers bolted to a 22-2 record and coasted to the pennant and an eventual World Series win--their first-ever. They did a great deal of that coasting without Jackie Robinson, who missed most of July with a series of nagging injuries. When he returned, he wasn't the same player: age and injury had taken their toll. He hit less than .200 in limited playing time over the last two months of the season, then hit .182 in the World Series as the Dodgers took advantage of an even more telling injury to Mickey Mantle, who managed only 10 at-bats in the seven games.

Cumulative BA, 1955

The only game in 1955 in which Jackie looked much like his old self at the plate was on June 12th, when in the second game of a doubleheader against the Cubs, he went 3-for-3 with two triples (his only two three-baggers all year). Later, in the midst of his second-half slump, he showed some of the fabled Robinson panache by stealing home for the 18th time on August 29th. A lot of people thought it might be the last time they'd see him do it.

1955	BA	OBP	SLG	AB	H	2B	3B	HR	RBI	BB	SO
April	.308	.431	.442	52	16	1	0	2	8	11	4
May	.211	.329	.254	71	15	0	0	1	5	13	2
June	.338	.436	.537	80	27	3	2	3	12	13	6
July	.217	.280	.304	23	5	2	0	0	2	1	3
August	.208	.356	.271	48	10	0	0	1	4	11	2
Sept/Oct	.186	.357	.256	43	8	0	0	1	5	12	1

1956: THE LAST HURRAH

The core of the Brooklyn team was growing older, and Jackie was the oldest member of that core. Early in 1956, it looked as though the Dodgers might be through, as they stumbled out of the gate, languishing near the .500 mark into June.

For Jackie, it looked even worse: in mid-June he was hitting just .224 and rumors were swirling that he was going to announce his retirement. But slowly, inexorably, Robinson mustered one last great effort. Late in July he rose to the occasion in a crucial series against the league-leading Braves, going 6-for-10 with a critical three-run homer in the opening game. On August 3rd, he had four hits and three RBIs to help beat St. Louis as the Dodgers moved back into second place and signaled to the Braves that the chase was on.

Almost in tribute to Jackie, manager Walt Alston re-inserted him into his old cleanup slot in the batting order in early September. Playing on fumes, Jackie hit .290 in September, and capped his regular season career with a homer in the final game against (who else?) the Pirates. The Dodgers won the pennant with their victory that day.

Cumulative BA, 1956

1956	BA	OBP	SLG	AB	H	2B	3B	HR	RBI	BB	SO
April	.206	.282	.471	34	7	1	1	2	4	4	3
May	.250	.387	.395	76	19	3	1	2	13	17	4
June	.321	.429	.607	28	9	2	0	2	3	6	1
July	.368	.467	.553	38	14	1	0	2	6	6	3
August	.250	.353	.273	88	22	2	0	0	5	14	10
Sept/Oct	.290	.389	.419	93	27	6	0	2	12	13	11

In the World Series, Jackie was the last batter in both Games 6 and 7, driving in the only run of Game 6 with a tenth-inning single, and ending his career by striking out to seal the Dodgers' doom in Game 7, a game they lost 9-0. Neither Jackie nor the Brooklyn Dodgers would ever return to the post-season.

GOING HOME

We suspect that even with the revelation that Jackie Robinson batted cleanup more often than anywhere else in the Brooklyn lineup during his career, he is still going to be remembered first and foremost for his daring baserunning. No single play in his career is more memorable than his steal of home against the Yankees in the Game 1 of the 1955 World Series. (To this day, Yogi Berra still insists that Robinson was out. The Dodgers won the game, 6-5.)

All told, Jackie Robinson made 32 attempts to steal home, and was successful on 20 of those occasions. Here is a complete list of his successful steals of home:

THE 70-GAME SNAPSHOT

Back at the beginning of this article, we displayed a chart with the running 20-game OPS for Jackie from 1947 to 1956; at that time, we promised to print a similar graphic showing Robinson's running 70-game OPS. And so we have. One of the reasons for doing it is to smooth out some of that EKG-like movement in the line, and to get a sense of what the peaks and valleys look like for a sample size that is close to half a season's worth of data.

Date	Opposing Pitcher	Team City	HA	Inn
6/24/47	Ostermueller. Fritz	PIT	a	5
7/19/47	Pollet. Howie	STL	h	1
8/29/47	Beggs. Joe	NYG	h	6
7/4/48	Hansen. Andy	NYG	h	7
7/25/48	Lombardi. Vic	PIT	a	8
8/4/48	Meyer. Russ	CHC	h	1
8/22/48	Voiselle. Bill	BOS	h	5
9/28/48	Spahn. Warren	BOS	h	5
6/2/49	Brecheen. Harry	STL	h	6
7/16/49	Wehmeier. Herm	CIN	h	2
7/18/49	Rush. Bob	CHC	h	6
8/9/49	Trinkle. Ken	PHI	a	5
9/20/49	Muncrief. Bob	CHC	a	8
7/2/50	Meyer. Russ	PHI	a	4
9/26/51	Burdette. Lew	BOS	a	8
5/18/52	Ramsdell. Willie	CHC	h	4
4/23/54	Friend. Bob	PIT	a	6
8/29/55	LaPalme. Paul	STL	h	6
9/28/55	Ford. Whitey	NYY	a	8
4/25/56	Hearn. Jim	NYG	a	2

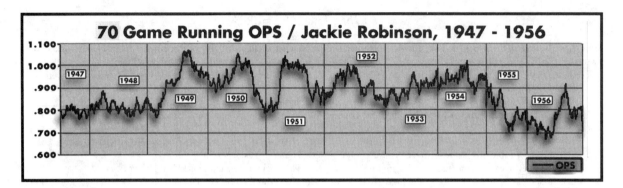

With this chart, we see more clearly the consistent offensive level established by Jackie in the 1947-48 period, and the 1949 peak is seen as a long climb with a small plateau in between the established level and the eventual high point, midway between 1.000 and 1.100.

Robinson then is able to maintain his 70-game OPS at a new level of at least .900, peaking over 1.000 again in mid-1950. This is followed by a severe dropoff all the way back to the .800 level at the end of 1950 and on into the early part of 1951, countered by a sustained plateau right at the 1.000 level for the middle of that year.

From that point on, Jackie is able to keep his 70-game OPS mostly in the .900 to 1.000 range for the next three years in an impressive display of consistency. Midway through 1955, however, injuries and aging take their toll and Jackie drops precipitously toward the .700 mark. He rallies toward .800 in the final month of 1955, but slumps badly in the early going of his final year, dipping below .700 for the first and only time in his career. One final rally ensures, however, and by August Jackie has edged his 70-game OPS back over the .900 mark as the Dodgers begin their stretch drive for their last Brooklyn pennant. Jackie levels off at around .800 the rest of the way; exit, stage left.

MORE, MORE, MORE

Yes, there is a sizable amount of additional data available from Retrosheet's complete Jackie Robinson career database. Space doesn't permit us to print more, but you'll eventually be able to view the complete dossier at the BBBA web site. Some of the items that will be included are:

- A complete log of Robinson's batting records against the pitchers he faced during the 1947-56 regular season
- Complete situational data for each season
- Listings of all the players who pinch-hit or pinch-ran for Robinson during his career

SOME WORDS ABOUT RETROSHEET

Don Malcolm here, thanking Dave Smith and Retrosheet for providing BBBA with access to the incredible Jackie Robinson database. In 1983, I attended a regional Society for American Baseball Research (SABR) meeting in Boston, where I had the opportunity to talk with the future editor of Total Baseball, John Thorn. I asked John if there was any chance that we would be able to reconstruct the details of box scores from the past to develop detailed statistical breakouts for past players similar to those that were just beginning to become commonly available for current players.

John thought about it for a moment, and replied that no, he didn't really think this was going to be possible, that too much had been lost. John, of course, had yet to make the acquaintance of Dave Smith. Six years later, Dave founded Retrosheet, and with a small but incredibly dedicated group of co-workers, he began what may be the most miraculous historical reconstruction since Heinrich Schliemann stumbled across Troy. Now, in 1999, Retrosheet has more than 40% of baseball history's play by play results in hand, either in their database or awaiting processing, and they are furiously beating the bushes for the rest.

Retrosheet's web site (http://www.retrosheet.org) has an incredible treasure trove of data, newsletters, facts, figures, and downloadable software in case you are bitten by the bug and want to dive into the details of baseball's past. And if you're interested in joining their most noble crusade, they're always looking for new recruits. If the Jackie Robinson data presented here has proven entrancing, imagine what else lies in store for baseball fans when the entire history of baseball is available in play-by-play format. There are a few ideas that truly change the world, and the world of baseball will be indebted forever to Retrosheet for bringing the past back to life in a way no one ever though possible.

THE ABCs OF RELIEF, PART DEUX

Doug Drinen

INTRODUCTION

It's April 1, 1999. Somehow you've managed to get the day off work and are at the local ball yard preparing to root for your favorite team. The park is mostly full but, as luck would have it, the row in front of you is empty, giving you plenty of space to prop up your feet and experiment with your sunflower-seed-spitting technique without infringing on the rights or hygiene of your fellow fans. Better make that two rows. All your projects at work are going swimmingly, all the bills are paid, and your kids are behaving. As the hurler for the hometown nine completes his last warm-up toss, some thoughts about the strife and political unrest at home and abroad creep into your mind, but you pledge to worry about them tomorrow. Right now, you want to think about the baseball, the whole baseball, and nothing but the baseball. The pitcher toes the rubber and starts his first windup of the season. The question is: what, exactly, is going through your mind?

a. *I hope he throws a good pitch here,*
b. *I hope he gets this batter out,*
c. *I hope he doesn't allow any runs this inning,*
d. *I hope the hometown nine wins this ballgame,*
e. *I hope the hometown nine wins the World Series this year,*
f. *I hope the hometown nine eventually wins 20 consecutive World Series and ultimately goes down in history as the greatest dynasty in the history of baseball.*

Your exact thoughts probably involve some combination of these aspirations for your team, as they are all related. Indeed, at every level, successfully meeting the goal significantly improves your chances of meeting the goal at the next level. Throwing good pitches generally leads to getting batters out. Getting batters out at a good overall rate improves your chances of allowing few runs, allowing few runs is a darn good way to help yourself win a lot of ballgames, and so on.

But what happens when one goal does not lead to the next? If, for instance, your pitcher throws a nearly-unhittable high-riding fastball but the hitter breaks his bat while dinking it into shallow left for a single, what is your reaction? Is it, "damn! A base hit" or do you take a broader view, something like, "if he keeps throwing pitches like that, he'll get a lot of hitters out in the future"? If your team loses its opener 3-2 despite out-hitting the opponent 10 to 3, are you ticked off at the bottom line, or optimistic about the future?

The way you answer these questions has a direct impact on what data you should look at when assessing the worth of a baseball player. Which of the following two lines indicates a more successful performance?

IP	H	R	ER	BB	K	HR
8	3	3	3	2	9	1
8	10	2	2	4	3	1

Again, it depends on how you define "successful." To someone who answered (c) above, 3 runs allowed in 8 innings is not as valuable as 2 runs allowed in 8 innings. But those who lean more toward (b) would make a case that allowing 5 baserunners in 8 innings is a more successful performance than allowing 14 in 8. The second pitcher helped you more yesterday, but the first one is likely to help you more tomorrow.

How about these two reliever outings?

IP	H	R	ER	BB	K	HR
1	1	0	0	0	1	0
1	1	0	0	0	1	0

Let's further assume that both relievers started and finished a complete inning, so we don't have to worry about inherited runner issues, and that the hit that each gave up was a single. Are these performances of equal quality? Are they of equal value? If you opted for (c), you can answer those questions right now, but if your choice was (d), you need more information. Suppose now that the first pitcher's inning was the 3rd. He came on in relief of an ineffective starter, his team trailing 8-0 at the time. Despite this reliever's effort, his team went on to lose by a count of 12-2. The second reliever, meanwhile, pitched a scoreless 8th inning with the score tied at 4-4, and his team went on to win it 5-4 in the ninth.

If you view winning games as the objective, you would have to say that the second reliever's performance was more valuable because it had more impact on whether or not that particular game was won or lost. By holding the opposing team scoreless in the 8th inning of a tie game, the second reliever significantly improved the probability that his team would win the game. The first reliever, though his performance was identical, changed his team's chances by only a tiny amount. To look at it another way, had reliever #1 given up a run in his inning, it would likely have changed the final outcome of the game. A run given up by reliever #2, however, has almost no impact. Who cares if you're down 8 going into the 4th or down 9? Either way, you're sunk.

Win Probability Added (WPA) is a tool that can be used to measure the value of any event that occurs during a baseball game, but we here at BBBA use it primarily to assess the value of relief pitchers. It starts from the premise that winning games is what matters. As far as WPA is concerned, giving up a run in the top of the first on an infield single, a sacrifice, a grounder, and an error is no different from giving up a run in the top of the first on a single and two sharply-hit doubles. Both effect your chances of winning the game in an identical way, so they are treated as identical. If you lead by 4 runs going into the bottom of the 9th, WPA cares not a whit whether you give up three towering home runs followed by three warning track fly outs, or mow down the side with three straight K's. In either case, the result is the same: you get to mark a tally in the W column.

Let's get into the nuts and bolts.

1. WHAT WPA IS

At any point in time, a team's probability of winning a ballgame depends on several factors, including:

The score: Obviously, a team with a 3-run lead is more likely to win than a team which trails by 2 runs.

The inning: A team which is leading by 1 in the 9th inning is more likely to win than a team which leads by 1 in the 2nd.

The base/out situation: Trailing by 2 with 2 outs

and no one on in the bottom of the 9th is a pretty bleak situation. Trailing by 2 in the bottom of the 9th with nobody out and the bases loaded is much different.

Many, many, many other things: Who the hitter is, who the pitcher is, the ballpark, the weather, the speed of the runner on first, the range of the left fielder, how wide the umpire's strike zone is, whether or not the bullpen is rested, etc.

The list goes on and on, of course. For the sake of making this a manageable task, we only consider the score, the inning, and the base/out situation. Actually, we consider the ballpark as well, but more on that later.

So to every base/out/inning/score situation, there is an associated win probability. For example, if it's the bottom of the 7th inning, there are two outs, men on first and third, and the home team trails by 2 runs, there is approximately a 22% chance that they will end up winning that game. Now, any event that changes the base/out/inning/score situation will also almost certainly change the win probability. A strikeout ends the rally and puts us into the top of the 8th, no one out, no one on, home team trailing by 2 situation. Killing that rally really took the air out of the home team's chances, and the win probability registers this. The home team's chance of winning is now more like 14%. It is reasonable to say that that strikeout was worth negative .08 wins (that's .14 - .22) to the home team. The batter who struck out will be charged with a WPA of -.08. Of course, this is a zero-sum game. The home team's chances of winning cannot go down without the visiting team's chances going up. In this case, the visiting team's win probability went from 78% to 86%. We credit the pitcher with +.08 WPA.

Suppose now that, instead of whiffing, the home team slugger lined one into center for a single, scoring the man from third and advancing the runner on first to second. We're still in the 7th inning, men on first and second, 2 out, home team down by 1; this situation carries a win probability of about 35%. In this case, we would credit the hitter with +.13 WPA, and the pitcher with -.13.

What makes WPA different from most other statistics is its sensitivity to context. In the example above, a strikeout was worth +.08 wins for the pitcher, and a single was worth -.13. If we change the context, we can dramatically change those values. For instance, had there been no runners on at the time (instead of runners at the corners - but still 2 outs in the 7th, and the home team down 2), the WP would've been 15%. The K pushes it down to 7%, hence is worth only +.01 WPA for the pitcher. The single only lifts the WP to 10%, so it costs the pitcher just -.04 WPA. If we leave the runners at the corners, but change the lead from 3 runs to 12 runs, both the strikeout and the single become virtually meaningless. The K, for instance, changes the WP from 'damn near zero' to 'damn, damn near zero.'

Generally, when we want to measure a player's value, we compute an estimate based on his overall season statistics. For example, Justin Thompson gave up 114 runs in 219 IP in 1998. An average hurler would have surrendered 125 runs in the same number of innings, so we would say that Thompson saved 11 runs compared to the average pitcher. How many wins is that worth? A general rule of thumb for translating runs to wins is to take the runs and divide by *2.2*(league average runs per game)*. That would be right at 11 for the '98 AL, so Thompson's 11 runs saved convert to one extra win on the dot.

The problem here is that that calculation treats all runs as having an equal impact on the outcome of the games in which they occurred, which may or may not be true. If Thompson were consistently giving up truckloads of runs when he had a comfortable lead, but was unhittable when the game was tight, his actual value would be greater than our estimate. Likewise, if he was perfect in blowouts but got hit hard when the games were close, our estimate of Thompson's value would be too high. Is it reasonable to assume that this evens out? Did Justin Thompson see a fairly typical distribution of important situations and meaningless ones, and did he pitch more or less equally well in both situations? Probably, but we cannot say for sure from just looking at his overall numbers. Did Andy Benes see a typical distribution of different contexts last year? Probably. Did Livan Hernandez? Probably. Did Tom Gordon? What about Todd Rizzo?

In the last two cases, the answer is definitely "no." Gordon entered 23 games in the 8th, 9th or extra innings with the score tied or with the Bosox up by just 1 run. In many of those cases, runners were aboard when Flash got the call. Giving up runs in those situations has a much more direct impact on the outcome of the game than a typical run does, and "saving" runs in those situations has a greater positive impact than saving typical runs. Treating all runs as typical runs underestimates Gordon's value. On the flip side, consider Rizzo. He was rarely pitching in important situations. 8 of his 9 appearances started while the White Sox were either leading or trailing by at least 3 runs. The runs he gives up are not as damaging as typical runs. Traditional methods tend to overestimate the damage he caused.

Gordon and Rizzo are, of course, not all that unusual. Lots of relievers do not see typical contexts. Closers like Gordon and setup men like, say, Paul Quantrill are systematically used in such a way that they see more than a typical amount of important situations. Meanwhile, mopup men like Rizzo are systematically used in situations which are not crucial. Because WPA takes context into account, it is an especially useful metric for gauging the value of relief pitchers, whose jobs are necessarily context-dependent.

Thus, we took it upon ourselves to calculate the WPA of every reliever who appeared during the 1998 season. One technical note about how the WPAs you'll see throughout the book are computed: WPAs are computed by considering the difference between the WP when the pitcher entered and the WP when he left for every inning in which he appeared. For example, on September 12th, Jay Witasick entered the game for the A's at the beginning of the 2nd inning. The A's were down 3-0 at the time. By the time Witasick left in the middle of the 7th, the A's were up 6-3. and their win probability was 88.7%, but we don't give Witasick .887 - .186 = .701 WPA. That would give him credit not only for pitching a few scoreless innings, but also for scoring the 6 runs.

As mentioned above, Oakland's WP when Witasick entered to start the bottom of the 2nd was 18.6%. Witasick held the Twins scoreless for that half inning, which boosted the Athletics' WP to 21.6%. So Jay gets credited with a WPA of .030. The A's then scored 3 in the top of the 3rd, which put their WP at 44.2%. The offense gets credit for that. When Witasick pitched a scoreless bottom of the 3rd, it pushed Oakland's WP up to 50.0%, so he gets another .500 - .442 = .058, and so on. Witasick ended up with a WPA of .319 for that contest.

WHAT'S CHANGED FROM LAST YEAR

Two things. More data and better data.

First, the "more" part. In the '98 BBBA, we tracked 44 relievers--most of the guys that were, at one time or another, considered closers. For this year, as we mentioned, we kept track of all the pitchers (starters as well as relievers--more on that later). To do this, of course, it was necessary to computerize the data-entry and record-keeping system (a big thanks to Sean Forman for helping make this less painful). Last year I did everything by hand.

In addition to simply tallying up WPA for more pitchers, computerizing the data means we'll be able to give you many more breakouts and lots of detailed information about usage. The avalanche of data will begin shortly, so prepare yourself.

Now for the "better" part: this year's data will be park- and league-adjusted, whereas last year's data for everyone in both leagues was calibrated to generic 1996 NL run-scoring distributions. Deriving park-adjusted win probabilities is a non-trivial issue, and would be impossible to do using "real" data. There are simply not enough games played in a given park in a given year to collect accurate run distributions, and even if there were, they would be irreparably skewed by the characteristics of the home team.

To get around this, we need to simulate. To get a set of park-adjusted WPs, we simply use the appropriate league averages and park factors to determine the probability of an average hitter getting a single, double, triple, etc. in the given park, then tell the simulator to simulate 20,000 innings starting from each of the 24 base/out situations, and record how many runs score each time. This gives the park-adjusted run distributions which, along with basic probability theory, are sufficient to calculate the WPs.

The simulator is not at all perfect at this point, and it's something that I'll probably continue to tinker with for years and years. At this point, the things that it doesn't take into account which would boost offense seem to be negating the things it doesn't take into account which would suppress offense, so it gives run distributions which match the actual distributions reasonably well.

As expected, the ballpark can have a major impact on your chances of winning a ballgame from a given situation. As an example, take a look at three randomly-selected situations, and the WP associated with each in Coors Field and Dodger Stadium:

Situation	Inn/Out	Base Sit.	Coors WP	Dodgers WP
Home team down 1	9th inning, 0 outs	empty	.220	.139
Home team up 1	7th inning, 2 out	1st/3rd	.747	.811
Visitors down 1	6th inning, 0 outs	man on 1st	.454	.413

Changing ballparks can alter win probabilities in counter-intuitive ways. For example, consider Jose Cabrera's August 1st, 1997 effort in the Astrodome. He entered the game in the top of the 10th inning with the bases loaded, nobody out, and the game tied. He allowed all three inherited runners to cross the plate, and added one more of his own for good measure before retiring the side. So he left his offense with a four-run deficit going into the bottom of the 10th.

Now pause for a minute and try to figure out which is more damaging, pulling a Cabrera in the Astrodome or pulling a Cabrera in a neutral park. My intuition reasoned as follows: Cabrera gave up more runs than expected in that situation, runs are more valuable in the Dome than they are in a neutral park, so his performance was more damaging in the Dome than it would have been in a neutral park. Wrong. It turns out the damage was already done before Jose even toed the rubber. Even if you're playing underwater, you're going to tally a few runs if you have the bases full and none out. The odds of the home team being able to overcome that in their half of the 10th, however, are significantly lower in Houston than they are elsewhere. Actual figures: in the Dome, Cabrera lowered Houston's WP by .082. In a neutral park, it would've been lowered by .150.

TECHNICAL NOTES

This is presented as reproducible research, so we have to tell you exactly how everything was done.

First of all, the WPs were based on 1997 scoring distributions and park factors from 1995-1997 where applicable, and as close to it as possible for new ballparks and altered parks. Overall levels of offense were very similar in '97 and '98, so this shouldn't cause too much problem. Before the season started, I made a wild guess that the Bank One Ballpark would behave similarly to Wrigley, and that does not seem too far off. I called Tropicana Field a completely neutral park.

For simplicity in some of the calculations, I've categorized the ballparks into 8 groups according to their level of offense. Group 1 is Coors. Group 2 is Texas and Minnesota. Group 3 is Boston, Oakland, Detroit, and Anaheim. Group 5 is Cincinnati, Atlanta, St. Louis, and San Francisco. Group 6 is Comiskey. Group 7 is Florida, San Diego, and Shea. Group 8 is Houston and Dodger Stadium. Group 4 is everyone else (it turns out some AL pitcher's parks have about the same level of offense as some NL hitter's parks). The park in boldface from each group is their representative, and pitchers' road appearances will be computed with respect to this park (their home appearances will always be computed with respect to their actual home park).

In other words, when computing Kerry Ligtenberg's WPA, his home appearances will be computed on the basis of Turner Field WPs, his appearances in Florida, San Diego, and New York will be computed on the basis of the Shea Stadium WPs, his Dodger Stadium appearances will refer to the Astrodome WPs, and so on.

Finally, a few words about P. P was originally intended to stand for "perfection," but it seems more appropriate to say it stands for "pressure." P is defined as the amount of win probability a "perfect" pitcher would have added in a given situation, and, like WPA, it is computed on a per-inning basis. Note that "perfect" does not mean "no baserunners," it means "added the maximum possible amount of win probability." Allowing 3 runs in a 9th inning that your team began with a 4-run lead, for example, constitutes perfection in this sense.

If you are interested in investigating issues such as which managers use their bullpens most efficiently or which relievers pitch the toughest innings (and who isn't?!?!), it is essential to have a good feel for P. With that in mind, here is some data, along with several examples of relief appearances and their P values:

Examples:

The Angels' Greg Cadaret enters in the 7th inning with 2 outs and men on 1st and 2nd, Angels up by 4 in Texas. He finishes just that inning. P: .023

Derek Lowe of the Bosox enters to start the 7th inning with the Sox down by 1 run in Toronto. He pitches just that inning. P: .046

Jose Mesa of Cleveland pitches a complete 7th and 8th inning with the Indians up by 3 at home. P: .072

Todd Jones throws a complete 10th with the Tigers up by 2 in Minnesota. P: .112

Scott Service of the Royals enters in the 7th with a man on first, 2 outs and the Royals up 1 in Cleveland. He finishes the 7th and pitches the 8th. P: .173

The Twins' Mike Trombley enters with men on 1st and 2nd, nobody out, and the Twins up 3 runs in the 7th. He pitches that inning, plus the 8th. P: .225

Mariano Rivera enters in the 8th with men on 1st and 2nd, one out, and a 2-run lead in Fenway. He finishes that one and the 9th. P: .303

P Value	% of Relief Apps
< .025	31.9
.025 - .050	14.9
.050 - .075	8.8
.075 - .100	8.6
.100 - .125	6.9
.125 - .150	6.5
.150 - .175	5.3
.175 - .200	3.7
.200 - .225	3.7
.225 - .250	1.7
> .250	8.0

One final note: last year, as a general gauge of the overall importance of a reliever's innings, we used PPI (P per inning - simply P divided by innings pitched). We made a slight change for this year and are now using PPPI (P per partial inning). This is intended to combat the Jesse Orosco effect. Suppose Jesse comes in to start the 8th with a 1-run lead. That earns him a P of around .160 or so (depending on the ballpark). If he gets yanked after facing two batters, retiring one of them, he's pitched 1/3 of an inning. If he does that exact same thing three times, he's got a total P of .480 and 1 IP, for a PPI of .480. Meanwhile, Doug Henry starts three 8th innings with a 1-run lead, and completes all three. He also has a total P of .480, but has 3 IP, for a PPI of .160. But it doesn't really make sense to say Orosco faced more pressure than Henry, and we'd like our measure to tell us that. PPPI says they both faced an "average P" of .160, so we'll go with that.

A TOUR THROUGH THE DATA VAULTS

Each of the team essays in this year's BBBA has a "Bullpen Box" which is brimming with information about the usage and effectiveness of that team's 'pen. We'll give you a guided tour here, so you'll be able to make sense of it. The Yankees will serve as our example.

First and foremost, you'll see each individual's overall WPA numbers.

Name	G	PI	WPA	P	PPPI	MI	ROB	T
Banks W	9	16	-.3	.8	.051	6	0	2
Borowski J	8	10	.4	.4	.039	2	0	1
Bradley R	4	8	.2	.6	.070	3	1	0
Bruske J	2	4	.1	.2	.053	1	0	0
Buddie M	22	41	.5	2.1	.050	12	13	2
Erdos T	2	2	.0	.0	.015	0	0	0
Holmes D	34	61	-.3	2.3	.038	17	14	4
Irabu H	1	2	.0	.0	.015	1	0	0
Jerzembeck M	1	1	.0	.0	.000	0	0	0
Lloyd G	50	63	.2	3.0	.047	12	25	4
Mendoza R	27	56	.4	3.5	.062	15	15	4
Nelson J	45	61	-.4	3.9	.063	16	15	4
Pettitte A	1	3	.1	.1	.020	1	0	0
Rivera M	54	69	4.6	6.6	.096	15	15	3
Stanton M	67	106	1.5	7.7	.073	35	29	10
Tessmer J	7	10	.2	.2	.021	2	2	1

MI stands for multiple-inning and denotes the number of a reliever's appearances which spanned more than one inning (technically, it should be called 'multiple partial inning.'). The T column tells you how many of the reliever's appearances started with the game tied. ROB lists how many times the reliever came into the game with one or more runners already on base. The numbers you see here only apply to an individual's relief appearances, not his starts (if any).

Next up is the overall team performance, broken down according to several categories. All the numbers you see here (except for the first set) pertain to the team's bullpen only.

	PI	WPA	P	PPPI
Starters	1109	8.4	55.8	0.050
Relievers	513	7.2	31.3	0.061
Road	252	1.3	15.7	0.062
Home	261	5.9	15.5	0.059
Mar/Apr	87	0.7	6.0	0.069
May	86	0.6	6.1	0.071
June	67	-0.2	3.4	0.051
July	80	3.1	5.7	0.071
August	92	1.1	5.4	0.058
September	101	1.9	4.7	0.046
Non S/H Sit.	363	3.5	15.1	0.042
S/H Sit.	150	3.7	16.2	0.108
Low Pressure	210	-0.1	2.7	0.013
Med. Pressure	146	1.7	9.0	0.062
High Pressure	157	5.6	19.5	0.124
Entered behind	180	1.0	5.1	0.028
Entered tied	60	2.4	7.0	0.116
Entered ahead	273	3.8	19.2	0.070

This next table, minus some of the data, appeared in BBBA 98. They tell you how many times each team was tied, up by one, and up by two when their turn to pitch came in the 7th, 8th, or 9th inning, and who the manager elected to have start that inning on the hill. At the bottom, you'll see the team's record in each situation, so this imparts some information about effectiveness as well as usage:

	7th inning			8th inning			9th inning		
	0	+1	+2	0	+1	+2	0	+1	+2
Bradley R	0	0	0	0	0	1	0	0	0
Bruske J	0	1	0	0	0	0	0	0	0
Buddie M	0	1	0	0	0	0	0	0	0
Holmes D	1	0	0	1	1	0	0	0	0
Lloyd G	0	1	1	0	0	2	0	0	0
Mendoza R	3	1	1	6	1	0	2	1	0
Nelson J	1	2	1	0	0	3	1	0	0
Rivera M	0	0	0	0	0	0	2	12	13
Stanton M	1	0	1	0	3	4	2	0	3
Starters	14	11	10	7	6	6	1	0	1
TOTAL	20	17	14	14	11	16	8	13	17
Record	12-8	16-1	13-1	9-5	11-0	16-0	6-2	12-1	17-0

Next up is a chart that gives a general overview of the usage and contribution of each member of each of the three bullpens. A complete explanation follows.

	|---------Quality----------|					|----Pressure----|			
	Dis.	Poor	Fair	Good	Her.	Lo	Med	Hi	
Buddie M	0	3	15	2	2	12	3	7	(4)
Holmes D	1	5	22	6	0	20	10	4	(1)
Lloyd G	1	6	34	9	0	32	12	6	(6)
Mendoza R	2	4	9	11	1	7	11	9	(8)
Nelson J	5	4	24	11	1	20	17	8	(4)
Rivera M	0	2	19	31	2	17	19	18	(15)
Stanton M	5	12	24	22	4	25	20	22	(15)
Others	0	5	22	7	1	24	4	7	(5)

In the "Quality" section, 'Dis.' stands for disastrous and it denotes an appearance which resulted in a WPA of -.25 or worse. A 'Poor' outing is one in which the WPA is between -.05 and -.25. 'Fair' means between -.05 and +.05, 'Good' denotes a WPA of between +.05 and +.25, and anything greater than +.25 means you get to mark a tally in the 'Her.' (for heroic) column. +.25 was chosen as the cutoff because it's nearly impossible to earn a WPA of +.25 without either pitching more than 1 inning or inheriting some runners (a 1-inning, 1-run lead save at Coors is the only heroic performance that doesn't involve pitching multiple innings or stranding runners).

Over on the "Pressure" side, you get a quick glance at the breakdown of how many high-pressure (over .15 P), medium-pressure (between .05 and .15 P), and low-pressure (below .05 P) appearances each hurler faced. In parentheses next to the number of high-pressure situations is the number of those appearances which resulted in positive WPA.

This next one simply summarizes a few of the ratios that could be deduced from the above table, and a few more interesting numbers. Reading left to right, we have:

S/H% - the percentage of a reliever's appearances which were a save/hold situation.
VLP% - "Very Low P %". This is the percentage of appearances that had a P of .01 or less.
+WPA% - the percentage of appearances in which the reliever had a positive WPA.
+HiP% - the percentage of high-pressure appearances in which the reliever added win probability.

That completes the bullpen box. Now for a few items that appear occasionally in the reliever comments portion of Section five:

Miscellaneous percentages

	S/H%	VLP%	+WPA%	+HiP%
Buddie M	0.0	40.9	59.1	57.1
Holmes D	8.8	38.2	70.6	25.0
Lloyd G	26.0	44.0	72.0	100.0
Mendoza R	22.2	14.8	74.1	88.9
Nelson J	37.8	20.0	71.1	50.0
Rivera M	75.9	14.8	94.4	83.3
Stanton M	37.3	20.9	67.2	68.2
Others	5.7	48.6	65.7	71.4
TOTAL	32.0	28.7	73.1	71.6

This chart does not tell us anything about effectiveness, only usage. You'll remember it from BBBA 98. It shows how often each pitcher (who has more than 10 relief appearances) appeared on each given number of days rest, and how many times he appeared on 3 consecutive days.

Finally, a detailed breakdown of all a team's pitching changes by inning/score situation. On the right, you can see what fraction of the team's changes in the given inning occurred during the middle of an inning as opposed to between innings.

	---------Days Rest---------						
Name	**0**	**1**	**2**	**3**	**4**	**5+**	**3str**
Buddie M	2	6	2	2	3	9	0
Holmes D	3	7	8	5	1	10	0
Lloyd G	10	11	10	8	4	7	0
Mendoza R	3	7	6	4	9	12	1
Nelson J	15	11	9	4	4	2	2
Rivera M	14	14	4	8	6	8	3
Stanton M	21	19	9	8	4	6	6

Pitching Change Matrix

Inn	-5	-4	-3	-2	-1	0	1	2	3	4	5	Tot	Pct
1												0	---
2												0	---
3	1	2	1	1				1				6	83.3
4	5	1				1	2		1			10	60.0
5	1		1						1		1	4	100.0
6	3		5	1	7	5	5	2	3	3	2	36	77.8
7	5	6	6	6	8	7	11	3	9	5	10	76	72.4
8	10	5	8	10	5	6	15	19	15	5	19	117	65.0
9	5	1	1	2	2	6	10	11	10	8	17	73	34.2
X						10	1		1			12	25.0
	30	**15**	**22**	**20**	**22**	**35**	**44**	**36**	**40**	**21**	**49**	**334**	

Behind: 32.6 **Tied:** 10.5 **Ahead:** 56.9
202 mid-inning pitching changes (60.5)

Where to go from here? If you want to check out your favorite team's bullpen box, now wouldn't be a bad time. If you read on, here's what you'll find: in the next section, a recap of some of the stellar bullpen performances of 1998. Section 3 contains an in-depth look at usage patterns and some attempts to figure out what made each team's bullpen tick. In section 4, we move beyond the bullpen to see what WPA has to say about starting pitchers, offenses, and those invisible wins and losses that sabermetricians so often refer to as "luck." We close in section 5 by tying up a few loose ends and making a few grandiose promises for the future.

2. 1998: THE YEAR IN RELIEF

Thanks to Big Mac and Sammy, 1998 will forever be remembered as the year of the tater. Overall levels of offense did not budge from their lofty heights, meaning that average pitchers were still taking a beating. The elite pitchers, however, appear to be immune to the trend, as the most outstanding pitching performances appear to be getting more and more outstanding.

What I look for in an ace reliever is the ability to dominate, to absolutely overmatch hitters. This shows up in a pitcher's line in the hits allowed column, and the strikeouts column. You want the strikeouts high and the hits low, of course, so let's just roll these two together into one number, called the Domination Factor. DF = Ks divided by Hits Allowed. Define a dominant season as one with a DF greater than 1.5. There have been 114 such seasons in major league history (using a minimum of 60 IP), 47 of which have occurred in the 90s.

Of course, we'd like the dominance to be tempered with some semblance of control, so let's get that old Roto standby, WHIP, into the mix. WHIP = (Walks allowed + Hits allowed) divided by (Innings Pitched). 1 is a fairly good benchmark of superb WHIP. It essentially means a pitcher allowed less than a baserunner per inning.

Now define an elite season as one with a DF above 1.5 and a WHIP below 1. Prior to last season only 32 seasons in major league history qualified as elite seasons, and 13 of them had occurred in the 90s. For the record, those 13 belong to Pedro Martinez (1997), Troy Percival (96 and 95), Trevor Hoffman (96), Mariano Rivera (96), John Wetteland (95), Bryan Harvey (93 and 91), Rod Beck (93), Roberto Hernandez (92), Dennis Eckersley (92 and 90), and Rob Dibble (90). It is not surprising that this list consists mostly of relievers, and Martinez' presence on it is another illustration of how amazing his 97 season was. The only other starters in history to post an elite season are Mike Scott (1986), J.R. Richard (80), Luis Tiant (68), and Sandy Koufax (65).

1998 saw three relievers post elite seasons, which matches an all-time high set in 1996 (Hoffman, Percival, Rivera):

	IP	H	BB	K	ERA
Hoffman	73.0	41	21	86	1.48
Nen	88.2	59	25	110	1.52
Wetteland	62.0	47	14	72	2.03

Two others narrowly missed:

	IP	H	BB	K	ERA
Urbina	69.1	37	33	94	1.30
Gordon	79.1	55	25	78	2.72

To get a context-neutral estimate of the value of these performances, we use pitching wins. PWins is a metric to which we'll refer frequently in this essay, so it's worth going through a complete explanation. First determine how many runs the pitcher gave up. That's easy, just look in the paper. Then adjust these to reflect the park where he plays his home games. Wetteland, for example, plays in a park which inflates offense by about 10%, so we adjust his runs downward by 5% (because he pitched roughly half his innings there). Next, compare this figure to the number of runs a league average pitcher would have surrendered in the same number of innings. The difference can be thought of as the number of runs the pitcher in question saved compared to an average pitcher. We need to translate these runs to wins, and research indicates that it takes about *[(league average runs per game)*2.2]* runs over the course of a season to add a win, so we divide our subject's runs saved by this constant. This gives an estimate of how many wins he was worth compared to the average Joe.

Here are the relevant data for our five aces:

	IP	R	RA	AdjR	AdjRA	RSaved	PWins
Hoffman	73	12	1.48	12.6	1.56	24.9	2.4
Urbina	69.1	11	1.43	10.8	1.40	24.9	2.4
Nen	88.2	21	2.13	21.5	2.19	24.1	2.4
Gordon	79.1	24	2.72	23.5	2.67	20.4	1.9
Wetteland	62	17	2.47	16.2	2.35	18.1	1.7

You know what IP is. R stands for runs allowed, and RA is run average—just like ERA, but it counts the unearned runs. AdjR is park-adjusted runs allowed, and AdjRA is park-adjusted run average. RSaved is the number of runs each reliever saved, and PWins is the bottom line, pitching wins.

PWins estimates, in as context-neutral a way as possible, the precise thing that WPA endeavors to estimate: wins above average. To keep the comparison as tight as possible, all league averages are from the 1997 AL or NL, and all park factors are for the three years 1995-1997 because these are the league averages and park factors that were fed into the simulator that creates the win probabilities. Also, the reason we use RA as opposed to ERA is because WPA makes no distinction between earned and unearned runs.

According to the above, there was not much difference — less than a game's worth — between the best of those five performances and the worst. WPA tells a different story.

Pitcher	WPA
Hoffman	6.5
Gordon	5.9
Urbina	3.4
Nen	3.1
Wetteland	2.5

So two seasons, Hoffman's and Nen's, that were virtually indistinguishable to pitching wins are nearly three and a half wins apart according to WPA. WPA claims Gordon's season was worth four wins more than pitching wins thinks it was worth. This needs investigating. As always, there are two factors involved here: context and timing. We'll first take a look at context.

Of the five, John Wetteland was used the least creatively, as is clearly seen from the matrix below, which shows how many of his appearances started with a given inning and relative score.

	-5	-4	-3	-2	-1	0	+1	+2	+3	+4	+5	T
5												
6												
7												
8							1	3	1			5
9						1	2	14	12	12	8	6	55
10+							1	1	1			3
TOT						1	4	18	14	12	8	6	63

Wetteland very rarely entered before the 9th and very rarely without a lead. As you know, this seems to be the default closer usage plan. He only had 4 multiple-inning appearances and he entered the game with runners on base 8 times. This all adds up to a total P of 6.7 and a PPPI of .100.

If you just take a quick glance, Trevor Hoffman's usage matrix looks similar to Wetteland's.

Hoffman

	-5	-4	-3	-2	-1	0	+1	+2	+3	+4	+5	T
5												
6												
7												
8						2	5	3	1			11
9						3	16	15	9	4	1	48
10+						5		2				7
TOT						10	21	20	10	4	1	66

Gordon

	-5	-4	-3	-2	-1	0	+1	+2	+3	+4	+5	T
5												
6												
7												
8						2	4	7	2	2		17
9			2	1	1	4	7	9	11	8	6	49
10+						5	1	1				7
TOT			2	1	1	11	12	17	13	10	6	73

Nen

	-5	-4	-3	-2	-1	0	+1	+2	+3	+4	+5	T
5												
6												
7												
8	1					1	2	5				9
9					2	11	11	15	10	7	4	60
10+						7	1	1				9
TOT	1				2	19	14	21	10	7	4	78

A closer inspection of Hoffman's appearances, however, reveals that Bruce Bochy was a bit more liberal with the use of his ace reliever than was Johnny Oates. Hoffman entered 10 tie games and 11 times before the 9th.

Also, 16 of his outings started with runners aboard and 15 spanned more than one inning. He picked up a large chunk of P because of his relatively high number of appearances (21) with a 1-run lead. Total P: 8.7. PPPI: .108.

Tom Gordon and Robb Nen had roles which scarcely fit the 90s closer stereotypes at all. Gordon entered far more games early (17 8th inning appearances) and came in with runners aboard far more often (25 times) than most closers. Nen, meanwhile entered 19 tie games, tying Dennis Cook for the highest total in the major leagues. Nen had a total P of 10.5 and a PPPI of .107 while Gordon had a total of 9.4 and a PPPI of .100. Here are their usage matrices:

Urbina's profile looks a little different. His matrix shows that he had more appearances with his team trailing than the other 4 combined.

Urbina

	-5	-4	-3	-2	-1	0	+1	+2	+3	+4	+5	T
5												
6												
7												
8	2	1			3	1	5	4	4			20
9	1	1		1	1	7	7	11	5	4	4	42
10+						1	1					2
TOT	3	2		1	4	9	13	15	9	4	4	64

One of Felipe Alou's alleged strengths is his ability to handle pitchers. Yet, despite having no other relievers who even remotely approach Urbina's quality, he was only able to give Ugueth a total P of 6.4 and a PPPI of .083, which ranked only 17th in the NL, behind guys like Antonio Alfonseca and Dan Miceli and just ahead of Lance Painter and Rich Rodriguez.

Even more curious is Urbina's PPPI by month:

	PPPI
April	.108
May	.094
June	.090
July	.072
August	.063
September	.062

Urbina certainly did not become less effective as the season progressed, so why did the importance of his innings decline so drastically? To what extent is Alou to blame for failing to maximize the value of his tremendous young closer?

As it turns out, the Expos just did not happen to be involved in very many games which were close late. As a result, all the Montreal relievers had relatively low PPPIs. Among those with 20 or more appearances, Urbina's PPPI was the highest at .083, followed by Mike Maddux (.059), Rick DeHart (.056), Steve Kline (.054), Anthony Telford (.049), Shayne Bennett (.042), and Miguel Batista (.035). The Expos' overall bullpen PPPI was .051, compared to a league average of .062.

After the all-star break, Montreal's bullpen PPPI was .048, and the save opportunities were few and far between. The Expos took a one-run lead into the 9th only 3 times in the last half of the year, and this is where the top closers typically pick up a large chunk of their P. So, at least in part, Urbina's lack of important innings seems to have been beyond Alou's control.

On the other hand, the Expos were tied going into the 9th a fair number of times late in the year (8 after the break). Alou could have used Urbina in the majority of those situations, but did not. Urbina got the call on 3 of the 8 occasions with Kline (3) and Telford (2), two clearly inferior hurlers, divvying up the other 5. In fact, Urbina entered only 9 tie games this year, which is not an embarrassing total, but is in sharp contrast to 1997, when he entered 18 tie games and had a PPPI of .102.

One wonders if Urbina's becoming a bona fide closer caused Alou to make his role more closer-like, i.e. conservative. One also might wonder whether Urbina would have had the same remarkable season had he been used in more stressful situations. Recall that he took a nosedive in the second half of the 97 season.

To sum up the contexts in which these five pitchers toiled, we offer the following table. MI stands for multiple-inning appearances. In the ROB column is the number of appearances which started with runners on base. T stands for tied, and Up1 is the number of appearances which began with a lead of one run.

PITCHER	PI	P	PPPI	MI	ROB	T	Up 1
Nen	98	10.5	.107	19	13	19	14
Gordon	94	9.4	.100	19	25	11	12
Hoffman	81	8.7	.108	15	16	10	21
Wetteland	67	6.7	.100	4	8	4	18
Urbina	77	6.4	.083	13	12	9	13

But context, it appears, does not play as big a role as timing does. Tom Gordon, for instance, had six appearances where he gave up 2 or more runs last year. His overall line from those six games:

IP	H	R	ER	BB	SO
4.2	13	16	16	7	3

You just cannot give up 16 runs in 4.2 innings without doing some damage to your team's record, particularly if you're pitching in crucial situations, as Gordon frequently was. PWins estimates the damage at about a game and a quarter, but Gordon's WPA for these 6 games is a not-so-disastrous -.8. Two of these 6 games were tied when Gordon entered them, but the other four were essentially over. In one, the Bosox were down 3, and the other three times they had leads of 4, 5, and 6 runs.

Contrast that with Urbina, who only had two outings in which he allowed more than a run, but those two outings cost him a full 1.0 WPA. Wetteland's five appearances where he gave up 2 or more runs added up to a WPA of -2.1, and Nen's numbers were identical: five games giving up two or more, WPA of -2.1 in those games. This table summarizes the WPA numbers of each pitcher when giving up 0, 1 or 2+ runs.

Pitcher	Giving up 0 runs		Giving up 1 run		Giving up 2+ runs	
	Apps	WPA	Apps	WPA	Apps	WPA
Gordon	59	6.7	8	-.0	6	-.8
Hoffman	57	7.4	6	-.3	3	-.6
Nen	62	6.6	11	-1.4	5	-2.1
Urbina	56	5.1	6	-.7	2	-1.0
Wetteland	52	5.0	6	-.4	5	-2.1

Given that Hoffman and Gordon were hit far less hard by their bad outings, it is not surprising that they ended up with the highest WPAs of the group. There seems to be more variation in the WPA resulting from bad appearances than there is in the number of bad appearances, which is evidence that timing is more important than context in determining the overall WPAs of relievers of similar quality with similar roles.

Question 1: Were Gordon and Hoffman simply lucky to have had their worst performances at times when it did not hurt their teams much, or did they somehow have some control over it? **Question 2:** Do we care? If we are interested in determining whether Gordon or Nen had more impact on his team's record during the 1998 season, then the answer to Question 2 is no. The fact is that Nen's disastrous outings cost the Giants more than Gordon's did the Red Sox. If, however, we want to know whether Gordon or Nen is more likely to have a positive impact in 1999, we need to investigate Question 1, for which I know of little evidence on either side.

On one hand, closing appears to be a job with a large mental component, and it is not difficult to imagine that some relievers might not bear down as hard when the game is not hanging in the balance. On the other hand, no study has ever found evidence that the ability to successfully coast at only the appropriate times exists in hitters or starting pitchers, so there is reason to believe it would not be found in relievers either. Several years worth of WPA data could go a long way toward settling this issue. Maybe BBBA 2001.

We would be remiss if we left the topic of sterling individual relief pitcher performances without mentioning several others in addition to these five. Here are the AL's Top 20 WPAs:

Name	s/r	TM	G	PI	WPA	P	PPPI	MI	ROB	T
Gordon T	r	bos	73	94	5.9	9.4	.100	19	25	11
Rivera M	r	nyy	54	69	4.6	6.6	.096	15	15	3
Jackson M	r	cle	69	76	2.9	7.6	.100	7	18	6
Brocail D	r	det	60	80	2.7	5.2	.065	19	25	10
Howry B	r	chw	44	63	2.7	5.8	.092	18	15	4
Wetteland J	r	tex	63	67	2.5	6.7	.100	4	8	4
Plesac D	r	tor	78	97	2.3	8.0	.083	19	52	16
Mills A	r	bal	72	102	2.2	6.7	.066	26	28	8
Mecir J	r	tbd	68	99	2.2	7.1	.072	25	28	9
Trombley M	r	min	76	130	2.0	9.9	.076	40	38	13
Orosco J	r	bal	69	90	1.9	6.4	.071	20	26	12
Hasegawa S	r	ana	61	122	1.8	7.2	.059	37	34	12
Jones T	r	det	65	71	1.7	6.5	.091	6	10	7
Whisenant M	r	kcr	70	90	1.7	6.9	.077	20	39	8
Timlin M	r	sea	70	97	1.7	7.5	.077	22	30	5
Swindell G	r	min	52	91	1.6	5.9	.064	26	22	6
Quantrill P	r	tor	82	114	1.6	10.2	.089	28	38	13
Harris P	r	ana	49	87	1.6	4.9	.056	27	32	3
Lowe D	r	bos	53	93	1.5	6.9	.074	27	24	8
Foulke K	r	chw	54	81	1.5	4.7	.058	23	24	8

This is an interesting group. It contains several well-known relievers that you are used to seeing at the top of various "firemen" lists, but it also contains obscure hurlers of all descriptions, from out-of-nowhere youngsters like Bobby Howry to old war horses like Dan Plesac and Jesse Orosco. Lefties and Righties are both well-represented, as are short, middle, and long relievers. Hell, there's even a Mariner, of all things, on there. (OK, he's not very high on the list, but given what the standard line on the Seatlte bullpen was like in the media during 1998, this is exactly the type of added context that WPA provides.)

Name	s/r	TM	G	PI	WPA	P	PPPI	MI	ROB	T
Hoffman T	r	sdp	66	81	6.5	8.7	.108	15	16	10
Urbina U	r	mon	64	77	3.4	6.4	.083	13	12	9
Nen R	r	sfg	78	98	3.1	10.5	.107	19	13	19
Veres D	r	col	63	89	3.0	6.4	.072	23	21	5
Ligtenberg K	r	atl	75	81	3.0	7.0	.086	6	12	6
Beck R	r	chc	81	91	2.4	9.1	.100	8	18	9
Olson G	r	azd	64	76	2.4	5.9	.078	10	9	8
Acevedo J	r	stl	41	53	2.3	4.2	.080	10	6	6
DeJean M	r	col	58	83	2.2	4.7	.056	22	17	5
White G	r	cin	66	104	2.0	7.8	.075	31	30	10
Graves D	r	cin	62	94	1.7	4.4	.046	23	20	5
Mantei M	r	fla	42	68	1.7	6.4	.093	23	17	9
Franco J	r	nym	61	71	1.6	8.5	.119	8	11	6
Miceli D	r	sdp	67	91	1.6	7.7	.085	22	18	14
Painter L	r	stl	65	84	1.6	6.8	.081	17	37	11
Wickman B	r	mil	72	96	1.5	9.7	.101	22	19	12
Fox C	r	mil	49	68	1.5	5.4	.079	17	16	8
Shaw J	r	cin	39	54	1.5	6.2	.115	14	14	6
Wendell T	r	nym	66	91	1.4	6.2	.068	25	19	10
Henry D	r	hou	59	87	1.4	6.5	.075	26	24	16

Now let's look at the National League's Top 20:

This list has roughly the same flavor as the AL list. There are a few more closers here, but not necessarily the same closers we would have expected before the season started.

We now turn our attention to the performances of entire bullpens. Here, in order of WPA, are the AL bullpens (top right on the following page):

So the Yankees pitched the least and yet accrued the most value. It's no mystery how that happened. All else equal, getting hitters out while your team is leading will increase your chances of winning more than getting hitters out while your team is trailing. No one had leads more often than did the Pinstripers last year, and in general their relief corps did a good job of holding onto those leads.

A notch below New York, we find the two AL teams whose closers were profiled earlier, Boston and Texas. Tom Gordon was substantially more valuable than John Wetteland, but the non-Wetteland Texas contingent soundly out-WPAed the rest of Boston's bullpen, leaving their overall team WPAs about even.

Team	PI	WPA	P	PPPI
New York	513	7.2	31.3	.061
Boston	649	5.2	41.0	.063
Texas	631	5.0	34.2	.054
Anaheim	670	4.1	41.8	.062
Cleveland	612	3.9	41.6	.068
Kansas City	587	2.5	31.5	.054
Toronto	571	2.4	38.9	.068
Baltimore	631	2.1	36.2	.057
Detroit	660	1.7	37.9	.057
Minnesota	693	1.6	43.3	.062
Tampa Bay	637	.9	35.9	.056
Chicago	654	-.9	34.3	.052
Oakland	630	-2.8	37.1	.059
Seattle	566	-5.9	31.5	.056

Anaheim got value across the board, with five members of their bullpen posting a WPA between +1 and +2, while Cleveland was paced primarily by the still-excellent Mike Jackson. The Royals got contributions from many, the Blue Jays rode one of the best righty-lefty tandems in the league (Paul Quantrill and Dan Plesac), and the Orioles, behind Alan Mills and Jesse Orosco, overcame the loss of Randy Myers and a disappointing season from Armando Benitez.

Detroit's Doug Brocail was outstanding and Todd Jones' WPA was surprisingly high for the second straight year. Rick Aguilera did his best to drag down the Twins' bullpen, but Mike Trombley and Greg Swindell wouldn't let it happen. Meanwhile, it was Jim Mecir and Albie Lopez bailing out Roberto Hernandez in Tampa. The Chisox got unexpectedly good performances from a couple of youngsters, Bobby Howry and Keith Foulke, but expectedly not-so-good performances from most everybody else. Art Howe never managed to find anything that worked in Oakland, and Seattle, well, you know all about Seattle. Or do you? Did you know that, due in large part to Mike Timlin, they had a positive WPA over the last four months of the season?

Now on to the National League team WPAs:

Bruce Bochy's bullpen management was reminiscent of that fictitious Texan Dale Gribble, who is so resourceful that he can build a bomb out of nothing but a roll of toilet paper and a stick of dynamite. When you have Hoffman, it doesn't take a lot of creativity to construct a valuable bullpen. The Rockies, meanwhile, got unexpected solid performances from literally everyone in their bullpen to post a WPA nearly as high as the Padres'.

It is then a huge drop down to the Reds, who were fueled by youngsters Danny Graves and Gabe White, at #3. Next came two teams whose bullpens started strong but staggered through August and September, San Francisco (-2.1 WPA after July) and Milwaukee (-2.6). Then we have Atlanta, whose mid-season decision to trust Kerry Ligtenberg proved to be a wise one. Houston, with no standout performances but several solid ones, followed the Braves.

Pittsburgh and Chicago are another pair of teams that took a nosedive in the second half of the year, Montreal's

Team	PI	WPA	P	PPPI
San Diego	524	8.9	35.7	.068
Colorado	537	8.2	36.6	.068
Cincinnati	607	4.4	35.5	.058
San Francisco	645	3.4	44.2	.068
Milwaukee	640	2.7	40.4	.063
Atlanta	436	2.6	26.6	.061
Houston	499	2.4	32.4	.065
Pittsburgh	569	1.3	34.0	.060
Chicago	643	.7	41.5	.065
Montreal	657	.4	33.8	.051
St. Louis	662	.2	44.1	.067
New York	527	-.6	38.0	.072
Arizona	517	-1.4	26.0	.050
Philadelphia	548	-1.6	32.2	.059
Los Angeles	496	-2.2	32.2	.065
Florida	667	-2.7	42.6	.064

bullpen would have been a complete disaster without Urbina, and St. Louis finished strong behind Juan Acevedo. The Mets were never able to put anything together and had some really bizarre splits (see their bullpen box). Arizona, Florida, and Philadelphia performed about as well as expected overall, but each got some pleasant surprises. In Los Angeles, meanwhile, Tommy Lasorda never found whatever it was he was looking for, as the post-trade Dodger bullpen turned out to be more destructive than the pre-trade bullpen.

That's a quick review of the value each bullpen amassed during the 1998 season. In the next section, we turn our attention to determining how that value came to be by looking at usage patterns and bullpen shape.

3. BULLPEN SHAPE AND USAGE
Who pitched the toughest innings?

This is really not a well-defined question. It could mean any number of things. If the question is, "who hits home runs the most often?", you could answer with the guy who actually had the most homers, or you could answer with the guy who had the best HR/AB ratio or the best HR/PA ratio. You could even park-adjust everyone's homers to account for the fact that some players have an unfair advantage when it comes to hitting the long ball. Which of these answers is most appropriate depends on your reason for asking the question in the first place.

It's the same here. Mariano Rivera compiled a total P of 6.6 last season in 69 partial innings for a PPPI of .096. Scott Service of the Royals ended up with a higher P at 7.1, but he needed 104 partial innings to get it done, meaning that his PPPI was .068, much lower than Rivera's. Which of them would you say pitched tougher innings in 1998? It depends. If you want to know who faced more total pressure over the course of the entire season, you'd probably say Service, but if are more interested in knowing whose typical appearance was more pressure-packed, Rivera's your man.

How about Gregg Olson of the Diamondbacks vs. the Cubs' Rod Beck? Olson had 76 PI and a P of 5.9, making a PPPI of .078. Beck pitched 91 partial innings and racked up a P of 9.1, for a PPPI of .100. It looks like Beck is the clear choice, but consider that the Cubs were involved in many more close games than the DBacks. In fact, Chicago's bullpen accumulated a total P of 41.5 and a PPPI of .065 compared to 26.0 and .050 for Arizona. If your primary interest is to determine whether Jim Riggleman or Buck Showalter relied more on his closer, a case could be made for Olson.

Looking at the above question from different angles can give widely varied answers. Of course, we'll consider all of them.

First let's take a look at each league's top 10 by PPPI (minimum 60 PI).

These listings consists mainly of 9th-inning guys, and that's no surprise. It is a little surprising to see John Franco and Rick Aguilera, two graybeards who did not have particularly successful seasons, topping the lists. And in fact their presence there is nothing more than coincidence. Both of them were used in traditional 90s closer roles. Here is Franco's appearance matrix.

American League

Pitcher	PI	P	PPPI	WPA
Aguilera	84	9.5	.113	-1.0
Percival	77	8.2	.107	1.5
Gordon	94	9.4	.100	5.9
Wetteland	67	6.7	.100	2.5
Jackson	76	7.6	.100	2.9
Rivera	69	6.6	.096	4.6
Assenmacher	85	8.0	.094	.1
Howry	63	5.8	.092	2.7
T Jones	71	6.5	.091	1.7
Quantrill	114	10.2	.089	1.6

National League

Pitcher	PI	P	PPPI	WPA
Franco	71	8.5	.119	1.6
Hoffman	81	8.7	.108	6.5
Nen	98	10.5	.107	3.1
Wickman	96	9.7	.101	1.5
Beck	91	9.1	.100	2.4
M Leiter	96	9.4	.098	.4
Radinsky	80	7.7	.097	-1.2
Wagner	67	6.5	.097	1.2
Cook	93	8.9	.095	1.2
Mantei	68	6.4	.093	1.7

Nothing the least bit creative going on here. Franco inherited runners on 11 of his appearances, which is a fair number, but not really out of the ordinary. Aguilera's matrix shows a bit more variety:

Franco	-5	-4	-3	-2	-1	0	+1	+2	+3	+4	+5	T
5												
6												
7												
8							5					5
9	1			1	1	2	16	10	9	4	4	48
10+						4	3		1			8
TOT	1			1	1	6	24	10	10	4	4	61

Aguilera	-5	-4	-3	-2	-1	0	+1	+2	+3	+4	+5	T
5												
6												
7												
8	1			1	2	1	3	1		1		10
9	1	1	1	1	2	1	18	13	10	2	2	52
10+					1	3	2					6
TOT	2	1	1	2	5	5	23	14	10	3	2	68

But it still doesn't scream league-leading PPPI. The common bond between these two is in the '+1' column. The Twins took a 1-run lead into their pitching half of the 9th inning 21 times last year, which led the American League. Rick Aguilera started all 21 of those 9th innings, which is why his PPPI was so high. For the record, the Twins went 16-5 in those games. Likewise, the Mets led the NL (tied with San Diego) in taking 1-run leads into the 9th inning with 24, 20 of which were started by Franco.

In short, looking at the league leaders in PPPI does not reveal too much about usage. Because of the nature of P, relievers who are pitching in the 9th inning with a lead (i.e. closers) are generally going to top the charts.

And among those, it seems that the variations in luck swamp the variations in managerial strategy. That is, Tom Kelly did not make appreciably different decisions with respect to Aguilera's use than, say, Larry Rothschild did with respect to Roberto Hernandez'. The difference in their PPPIs comes solely from the fact that the Twins were involved in more close games late.

Let's now look at the top 10 in total P:

American League

Pitcher	P	PPPI	WPA
Quantrill	10.2	.089	1.6
Trombley	9.9	.076	2.0
Aguilera	9.5	.113	-1.0
Gordon	9.4	.100	5.9
Percival	8.2	.107	1.5
Plesac	8.0	.083	2.3
Assenmacher	8.0	.094	.1
B Taylor	7.8	.086	.7
Stanton	7.7	.073	1.5
M Jackson	7.6	.100	2.9

National League

Pitcher	P	PPPI	WPA
Nen	10.5	.107	3.1
Wickman	9.7	.101	1.5
M Leiter	9.4	.098	.4
Beck	9.1	.100	2.4
D Cook	8.9	.095	1.2
Hoffman	8.7	.108	6.5
Franco	8.5	.119	1.6
McElroy	8.3	.088	.7
Alfonseca	7.8	.089	.7
G White	7.8	.075	2.0

We see some new names popping up here, most notably the Braves' Kerry Ligtenberg in the NL, and Seattle's Mike Timlin in the AL. The success of the Braves' bullpen (yes, national media, the Braves bullpen did succeed) was due in large part to the fact that Bobby Cox leaned heavily on Ligtenberg and Kerry did not disappoint him. Likewise, Lou Piniella's reliance on Timlin in the second half of the season helped the M's field a decent overall bullpen for the first time in two years.

One problem with the MRF is that it fails to notice guys like Bobby Howry who were not around for the whole season, but were leaned upon heavily when they were. With that in mind, we can look at another version of MRF, which is rather unimaginatively named MRF2 (I can't crank out the acronyms like Don can). MRF2 = 100 * (individual's PPPI / team PPPI).

So here we get a more diverse group. There are still some closers here, but the ones who did not pitch many innings, like Wagner and Wetteland, have been pushed aside by innings-eaters like Paul Quantrill and Mike Trombley and ubiquitous lefties like Dennis Cook and Dan Plesac.

Recall, though, that overall team Ps vary widely. All those close games the Twins played made it inevitable that a couple of Minnesotans would be near the top of the P list. The highest-ranking Diamondback reliever is Gregg Olson, whose P of 5.9 is 34th in the NL. Is that a sign of a balanced bullpen, or a season full of blowouts? In Arizona's case, it was the latter. In order to take out this bias, we introduce the MRF. That stands for Manager Reliance Factor and it is computed by dividing the individual's P by the overall team P and then multiplying by 100 to express it as a percent.

American League

Pitcher	P	TeamP	MRF	WPA
Quantrill	10.2	38.9	26.1	1.6
Stanton	7.7	31.2	24.7	1.5
Timlin	7.5	31.5	23.7	1.7
Gordon	9.4	41.0	22.9	5.9
Trombley	9.9	43.3	22.8	2.0
Service	7.1	31.5	22.6	.8
Aguilera	9.5	43.3	21.9	-1.0
Whisenant	6.9	31.5	21.9	1.7
Rivera	6.6	31.2	21.1	4.6
Ayala	6.7	31.5	21.1	-3.9

National League

Pitcher	P	TeamP	MRF	WPA
M Leiter	9.4	32.2	29.1	.4
Ligtenberg	7.0	26.6	26.3	3.0
Hoffman	8.7	35.7	24.4	6.5
Wickman	9.7	40.3	24.1	1.5
Radinsky	7.7	32.2	24.0	-1.2
Nen	10.5	44.2	23.7	3.1
D Cook	8.9	38.0	23.3	1.2
Gomes	7.4	32.2	23.0	.0
McElroy	8.3	36.6	22.7	.7
G Olson	5.9	26.0	22.7	2.4

American League				
Pitcher	**PPPI**	**TmPPPI**	**MRF2**	**WPA**
Wetteland	.100	.054	185.2	2.5
Aguilera	.113	.062	182.3	-1.0
Howry	.092	.052	176.9	2.7
Percival	.107	.062	172.6	1.5
Montgomery	.087	.054	161.1	.2
T Jones	.091	.057	159.6	1.7
Gordon	.100	.063	158.7	5.9
Rivera	.096	.061	157.4	4.6
M Jackson	.100	.068	147.1	2.9
B Taylor	.086	.059	145.8	.7

National League				
Pitcher	**PPPI**	**TmPPPI**	**MRF2**	**WPA**
M Leiter	.098	.059	166.1	.4
Franco	.119	.072	165.3	1.6
Urbina	.083	.051	162.7	3.4
Wickman	.101	.063	160.3	1.5
Hoffman	.108	.068	158.8	6.5
Nen	.107	.068	157.4	3.1
G Olson	.078	.050	156.0	2.4
Beck	.100	.065	153.8	2.4
Radinsky	.097	.065	149.2	-1.2
Wagner	.097	.065	149.2	1.2

This looks much the same as the first list (by straight PPPI), but shuffled a bit and with a few closers from low P teams, like Olson and Urbina, sneaking in.

So who pitched the toughest innings in 1998? Take your pick. A good case could be made for just about anyone that appears on the above lists. I'd probably narrow it down to, in no particular order, Nen, Wickman, and Leiter in the NL and Quantrill and Gordon in the AL.

We shouldn't leave this topic without taking note of the trailers in these categories. It really only makes sense to list the trailers in the rate stats, so here they are: the bottom 5 in each league in PPPI and MRF2 (with a minimum of 60 partial innings pitched).

PPPI

American League

Pitcher	PPPI	WPA
Pittsley	.014	-.4
Levine	.031	-.2
Bailes	.034	.2
R White	.035	.0
D Holmes	.038	-.3

National League

Pitcher	PPPI	WPA
Tre Miller	.030	-.1
Tabaka	.032	-.3
M Batista	.035	-.7
S Bennett	.042	-1.1
Guthrie	.044	.1

MRF2

American League

Pitcher	MRF2	WPA
Pittsley	25.9	-.4
Levine	57.4	-.2
Holmes	62.3	-.3
R White	62.5	.0
Bailes	63.0	.2

National League

Pitcher	MRF2	WPA
Tre Miller	46.2	-.1
Tabaka	53.3	-.3
Guthrie	67.7	.1
M Batista	68.6	-.7
Boehringer	72.1	.3

Pittsley absolutely lapped the field here. Check out his appearance matrix:

Pittsley												
	-5	**-4**	**-3**	**-2**	**-1**	**0**	**+1**	**+2**	**+3**	**+4**	**+5**	**T**
5	4		2									6
6	3	1	2	1							1	8
7	7		1	2				2			1	13
8	4	1	1		1						1	8
9			1								1	2
10+												
TOT	18	2	7	3	1			2			4	37

Others of note appearing in the bottom 20 for one of these two categories include John Johnstone of the Giants, Jose Mesa (in his Indians stint), and Graeme Lloyd of the Yankees. Finally, a quick note to all Roto players: the Reds' Danny Graves, thought of by many as a potential future closer, narrowly missed the bottom 5 with a PPPI of .046 and an MRF2 of 79.3. That strikes me as an indicator that there may not be a lot of saves in Graves' immediate future.

WHICH BULLPENS ARE CLOSER-DEPENDENT?

Most bullpens have one guy who is designated as the closer. It's generally accepted that he's the best reliever on the team, and he usually makes more money than any other member of the bullpen. Commentators and beat writers tend to give him the lion's share of the credit for the success of the bullpen, and tend not to trust any bullpen that does not have someone they deem worthy of the role. And just who is worthy of the role? Well, anyone who has a resume with a lot of saves on it. And how do you get a lot of saves on your resume? Be a closer, of course. Because closer literally means "he who gets to pitch whenever there is a save situation in the 9th (or sometimes the 8th) inning," all closers get saves whether they pitch particularly well or not.

Is it possible to put together a great bullpen without a great closer? Of course. Look at last year's Rockies, who were one of the best groups in baseball last year by any measure, but whose leader in saves, Jerry DiPoto, ranked only 25th. It's even possible to get good value from a bullpen despite a distinctly unsatisfactory performance out of

115

the closer. For evidence of this, check out Pittsburgh and Milwaukee, who were being dragged down by Rich Loiselle and Doug Jones respectively for the first half of the season.

On the other hand, a great performance by a closer can have a huge impact. Some of baseball's best bullpens in 1998. got net contributions near or below zero from the non-closing component of the pen. The Red Sox, for example, ended up with the AL's second-best WPA last year, and almost all that value came from Tom Gordon. Here's a graphical representation of Boston's overall cumulative bullpen WPA and Gordon's cumulative WPA.Note how closely linked they were throughout the season.

Likewise, a good season from a closer can turn an absolute disaster of a bullpen into a respectable one. Gregg Olson did this in Arizona and Ugueth Urbina in Montreal last year.

So which bullpens fell into which categories? To answer that, we look at what we call the CDF--Closer Dependence Factor. For now, define the closer for each team as the guy who had the most saves, then rank the closers (1 through 30) by WPA. Next, compute the WPA of the non-closer contingent (let's call this the EE Factor--for Everybody Else) for each team, and rank them. The EE rank subtracted from the closer rank is the CDF. A high (positive) CDF connotes a strongly closer-dependent team, a CDF near zero indicates a balanced bullpen, and a negative CDF indicates a team that overcame a poor closer effort. For example, Marlins save leader was Matt Mantei, whose WPA of 1.7 ranked 13th among the 30 closers. The rest of the Florida bullpen tallied a WPA of -4.5, which was #29 among the EE portions of the 30 bullpens. So the Marlins CDF is 29 - 13 = 16. Here are all 30 bullpens, ranked in order of closer-dependence.

Interestingly, this list rather pointedly indicates that there are very few teams who seem to have bullpens which produce a consistent performance across the various functions. Looking down the ranking lists, we see only the Yankees and the Padres (the 1998 World Series opponents) ranking in the top 25% of teams in both WPA and EE categories. The Rangers, with their indifferent starting pitching, were the only other team to get both rankings into the Top Ten. Consistently poor performances show up in Oakland, Philadelphia, and Los Angeles.

Of course, the original purpose of this breakout was not to rank the teams, but to look at the amount of reliance on the closer. The problem here is that several teams had different closers during different parts of the season. Therefore, we're not getting the complete value represented in the "closer" function as shown by this data.

Let's define closer a little more abstractly. Say the "closer" for each team is the aggregate of all the pitching performances which were a save situation and either (a) started in the 9th inning, or

Team	Closer	WPA	rank	EE	rank	CDF
MON	Urbina	3.4	4	-3.0	25	21
BOS	Gordon	5.9	2	-.7	21	19
AZ	Olson	2.4	9	-3.8	28	19
FLA	Mantei	1.7	13	-4.5	29	16
SEA	Timlin	1.7	14	-7.6	30	16
ATL	Ligtenberg	3.0	6	-.4	20	14
CHC	Beck	2.4	10	-1.7	22	12
SF	Nen	3.1	5	.3	16	11
NYM	Franco	1.6	15	-2.2	24	9
CLE	Jackson	2.9	7	1.0	15	8
SD	Hoffman	6.5	1	2.4	7	6
STL	Acevedo	2.3	11	.2	17	6
DET	T Jones	1.7	12	.1	18	6
OAK	Taylor	.7	21	-3.5	27	6
PHI	Leiter	.4	23	-3.0	26	3
NYY	Rivera	4.6	3	2.6	4	1
TEX	Wetteland	2.5	8	2.5	6	-2
LA	Shaw	-.1	26	-2.1	23	-3
ANA	Percival	1.5	16	1.6	12	-4
MIL	Wickman	1.5	18	1.2	13	-5
HOU	Wagner	1.2	20	1.2	14	-6
CHW	Simas	-.8	27	-.1	19	-8
CIN	Shaw	1.5	17	2.9	3	-14
TOR	Myers	.7	22	2.4	8	-14
BAL	Benitez	.0	25	2.1	11	-14
KC	Montgomery	.2	24	2.3	9	-15
COL	DiPoto	1.2	19	7.0	1	-18
TB	Hernandez	-1.4	29	2.3	10	-19
MIN	Aguilera	-1.0	28	2.6	5	-23
PIT	Loiselle	-1.8	30	3.1	2	-28

(b) started in the 8th inning and continued into the 9th.

The teams that stuck with a single closer throughout the entire season stayed put for the most part, but some multiple-closer squads changed their position significantly. Florida, for instance, moves way down because the pitchers that were closing before Mantei arrived and while he was hurt did not perform nearly as well as Mantei himself did. Similarly, the Brewers slide down the list because of Doug Jones' troubles as a closer early in the year. On the flip side, Baltimore moved all the way from -14 to +11. They got decent production from their closers in general, just not from Benitez in particular.

By making these modifications, we see that the Padres and Yankees still remain well-balanced between the functions as we've defined them, but the Rockies have joined the short list of "balanced bullpens," replacing the Rangers.

Let's now see which bullpens depended most upon their setup men for value. Define the "setup man" for each team as the aggregate of all that team's appearances which were not "closer" situations, but which were save situations and started in the 7th or 8th inning. Here are the teams ranked by SDF, Setup-man Dependence Factor:

	"Setup"				
Team	WPA	rank	EE	rank	SDF
MON	1.7	2	-1.3	27	25
CHW	1.0	4	-1.9	28	24
MIL	2.2	1	.5	22	21
MIN	1.6	3	.0	23	20
DET	.7	7	1.1	20	13
PIT	.7	8	.6	21	13
FLA	-.1	16	-2.7	29	13
SEA	-1.1	21	-4.8	30	9
AZ	-.3	17	-1.1	25	8
KC	.6	9	1.9	16	7
CLE	.8	6	3.1	10	4
TEX	1.0	5	4.0	7	2
PHI	-1.3	24	-1.3	26	2
ATL	.2	13	2.4	13	0
ANA	.4	12	2.7	11	-1
CHC	-.8	19	1.5	17	-2
HOU	-.1	15	2.5	12	-3
STL	-1.2	22	1.4	19	-3
BOS	.5	10	4.7	6	-4
OAK	-2.4	28	-.4	24	-4
TB	-1.0	20	1.9	15	-5
COL	.5	11	7.7	2	-9
NYY	.1	14	7.1	3	-11
LA	-3.7	30	1.5	18	-12
TOR	-1.3	23	3.7	8	-15
NYM	-2.8	29	2.2	14	-15
BAL	-1.4	25	3.5	9	-16
SD	-.3	18	9.2	1	-17
CIN	-1.5	26	5.9	4	-22

	"Closer"				
Team	WPA	rank	EE	rank	CDF2
MON	3.1	7	-2.7	25	18
NYM	2.9	11	-3.5	27	16
OAK	2.4	14	-5.2	30	16
BOS	5.1	2	.1	16	14
CLE	3.8	4	.1	15	11
ANA	3.3	6	-.2	17	11
BAL	3.1	8	-1.0	19	11
LA	1.3	17	-3.5	28	11
CHC	2.4	13	-1.7	23	10
AZ	1.5	16	-2.9	26	10
ATL	3.0	9	-.4	18	9
SD	6.7	1	2.2	6	5
NYY	4.5	3	2.8	4	1
CIN	2.9	10	1.5	11	1
STL	1.2	19	-1.0	20	1
SEA	-1.4	28	-4.5	29	1
CHW	.3	22	-1.2	21	-1
SF	2.4	15	1.0	13	-2
FLA	-.9	26	-1.9	24	-2
COL	3.6	5	4.6	1	-4
DET	1.2	18	.6	14	-4
TEX	2.8	12	2.2	7	-5
PHI	-1.0	27	-1.6	22	-5
TOR	1.1	20	1.3	12	-8
KC	.7	21	1.8	9	-12
MIN	-.2	23	1.8	10	-13
PIT	-.8	24	2.1	8	-16
HOU	-.9	25	3.3	3	-22
TB	-1.5	29	2.4	5	-24
MIL	-1.9	30	4.6	2	-28

Again, it's interesting to look at the value achieved by the "setup" function; the range here is more reflective of a wider set of game situations than generally encountered in the "closer" function. Some part of the Mets' failure in the 1998 NL wild card race should be ascribed to the abysmal performance of their setup men. (Only the Dodgers were worse.) In general, however, playoff teams did not rely heavily on this function in order to achieve success: the top ten teams in SDF had losing records in 1998.

Now would probably be a good time to examine which bullpens overachieved (in the sense that their WPA exceeded their PWins) and which underachieved. More importantly, we'd like to see how good the correlation between performing well in closing/setup situations and achieving maximum value. In this next table, you'll find the WPA of each team in "closer" and "set-up" situations (as defined above) combined, and the corresponding C/SDF, Closer/Setup Dependence Factor. Along with that, you'll see each team's overall WPA, their overall bullpen PWins, and the difference between the two:

TEAM	CWPA	SWPAC/SWPA		rank	EE	rank	C/SDF	WPA	PWins	Diff
MON	3.1	1.7	4.9	3	-4.5	30	27	.4	.5	-.1
CLE	3.8	.8	4.6	4	-.7	23	19	3.9	.8	3.1
BOS	5.1	.5	5.6	2	-.4	19	17	5.2	3.9	1.3
ANA	3.3	.4	3.7	7	-.6	21	14	3.1	3.9	-.8
CHC	2.4	-.8	1.6	12	-.9	24	12	.7	-.8	1.5
ATL	3.0	.2	3.2	9	-.6	20	11	2.6	.9	1.7
CHW	.3	1.0	1.4	15	-2.3	26	11	-.9	-5.2	4.3
AZ	1.5	-.3	1.3	17	-2.7	27	10	-1.4	-2.4	1.0
DET	1.2	.7	1.9	10	-.1	17	7	1.8	1.7	.1
OAK	2.4	-2.4	.0	21	-2.8	28	7	-2.8	-1.2	-1.6
SD	6.7	-.3	6.3	1	2.6	8	7	8.9	3.2	5.7
TEX	2.8	1.0	3.7	8	1.3	11	3	5.0	3.2	1.8
BAL	3.1	-1.4	1.7	11	.4	13	2	2.1	1.9	.2
NYM	2.9	-2.8	.0	20	-.6	22	2	-.6	1.2	-1.8
MIN	-.2	1.6	1.4	14	.2	15	1	1.6	2.1	-.5
NYY	4.5	.1	4.6	5	2.6	6	1	7.2	4.0	3.2
SEA	-1.4	-1.1	-2.5	29	-3.4	29	0	-5.9	-3.3	-2.6
FLA	-.9	-.1	-1.0	26	-1.8	25	-1	-2.8	-4.9	2.1
KC	.7	.6	1.3	16	1.2	12	-4	2.5	-2.9	5.4
COL	3.6	.5	4.1	6	4.1	1	-5	8.2	7.5	.7
CIN	2.9	-1.5	1.5	13	2.9	5	-8	4.4	.6	3.8
STL	1.2	-1.2	.0	22	.2	14	-8	.2	-.2	.4
MIL	-1.9	2.2	.4	18	2.3	9	-9	2.7	2.0	.7
PHI	-1.0	-1.3	-2.3	27	-.3	18	-9	-2.6	-.3	-2.3
LA	1.3	-3.7	-2.4	28	.2	16	-12	-2.2	-.6	-1.6
PIT	-.8	.7	-.1	23	1.4	10	-13	1.3	3.0	-1.7
SF	2.4	-2.2	.2	19	3.2	4	-15	3.4	5.7	-2.3
TOR	1.1	-1.3	-.2	24	2.6	7	-17	2.4	-.3	2.7
HOU	-.9	-.1	-1.0	25	3.4	3	-22	2.4	3.4	-1.0
TB	-1.5	-1.0	-2.5	30	3.4	2	-28	.9	4.2	-3.3

There does seem to be a relationship here, but not a particularly stong one. Montreal was the team whose setup men and closers performed best relative to the rest of their bullpen, yet their WPA was actually lower than PWins said it should have been. The Expos were simply horrible in low pressure situations and in tie games. The other Canadian team, Toronto, is peculiar for the opposite reason: their WPA was much higher than their PWins despite failing to get good value from their setup men and closers. The Blue Jays had a +2.5 WPA, the best in baseball, in appearances which began with the game tied.

TIE GAME THEORY

In general, managers like to use their closers primarily in 9th inning save situations, and this is why a great deal of sabermetrically-enlightened baseball fans feel that a closer's value is vastly overestimated by most baseball people and members of the mainstream media.

Personally, I think it's a good idea (or at least a defensible one) for a manager to have clearly-defined temoral roles for his relievers. That is, Relievers A and B need to be ready to go if the starter gets in trouble early, Relievers C and D should be prepared to pitch in the 6th or 7th if the need arises, Reliever E takes the 8th, and Reliever F, the closer, pitches the 9th if at all. These roles shouldn't be set in stone, obviously, but much of the relief game seems to be mental, and it's reasonable to believe that roles of this type might help relievers better prepare themselves to do their jobs. So the "only in the 9th" (or occasionally the 8th) portion of standard closer usage does not bother me.

The other aspect of it is "only in save situations." Now, with one major exception, every pressure situation that arises in the 9th is a save situation. 9th inning non-save opportunities include:

(a) situations where your team leads by a comfortable margin,
(b) situations where your team trails, and
(c) tie games.

There is simply not much to be gained by pitching well in situations (a) and (b), so using your best in those spots need not be a priority. On the other hand, (c) is crucial. The WPs say that pitching a scoreless 9th inning in a tie game is nearly as valuable as closing out a 1-run game, and significantly more valuable than closing out a 2-run game. Yet the default for many managers is not to pitch their best reliever in the 9th inning of tie games. Why is this? Maybe the answer lies in the brach of theoretical economics known as Game Theory.

Academicians (you gotta love 'em, otherwise you'd strangle 'em) define a game as "a contest wherein several players choose, according to a specified set of rules from among a number of permitted alternative actions, in an effort to win certain rewards" (that's from Studies in Game Theory and Mathematical Economics, by James Case). The idea of game theory is to determine the probable outcome of a game in which rational players are faced with certain decisions. Before we get back to relief pitching, let's look at a few examples of games.

The most widely-known game is called the prisoner's dilemma. Imagine that Rupert Murdoch has commissioned you to help him break into Ted Turner's office and swipe his free agent want list. Being the rabid Dodger fan you are, you agree to it, so you and Rupe don the ski masks, grab the grappling hook, and head for Turner Field. You break, and then you enter. You procure the list, and you head back to La-la land. Unfortunately for you and Rupert, though, Atlanta's finest turn out to be just that. They gather enough evidence to haul you and Murdoch in for questioning.

As it turns out, the DA does not have enough evidence to convict either one of you without a confession or a witness. So they offer you the following deal: if you confess to the crime, but agree to roll on Rupe, Rupert does 10 years hard time, and you go free in exchange for your testimony. Of course, you've watched enough Law and Order to know that they're offering Rupert the same deal in the next room. If you both confess, they'll go easy on the two of you and reduce your sentences to 6 years. If neither of you confesses, the best they can do is put you both away for 2 years on some trumped-up lesser charge.

Let's look at this from your perspective. Assume you know Rupert is going to confess. What's your best move in that situation? If he confesses and you don't, you get 10, whereas if he confesses and you do too, you only get 6. Easy choice: confess. Now assume you know that Murdoch won't talk. What do you do now? Confessing gets you off altogether, while silence gets you 2 years. Again, confessing is your best choice. If you're rational and pursuing your own self-interest, you must confess.

But the kicker, as you've probably figured out by now, is that Rupert is thinking the exact same thing. No matter what you do, his best move is to confess. So each of you making the only reasonable choice you can make leads to an outcome which is not optimal for either of you. If you both clam up, you're both better off.

Other simple examples of the same kind of paradox can be found in economics. Suppose Jon Torre and Brian Bochy each own a gas station in a small town. There's no other gas to be had in any direction for 200 miles.

So Jon and Brian can choose to compete or collude. If they compete, they each try to offer the better price, and thus get more than their share of the town's gas business. If they collude, they are agreeing that they'll both set the price high, but equal, thereby gouging the town and splitting the profits 50/50. Let's assume they opt for collusion.

Jon and Brian don't quite trust each other completely, as you might expect. Each and every day, Jon and Brian each have to reckon with this choice: stick to the deal, or cheat. There are major gains to be made by cheating. If Jon's charging a reasonable price and Brian is still setting his price at the collusion level, Jon will make scads of cash. If, on the other hand, Brian decides to cheat, then Jon has to cheat just to keep up. Just as in the prisoner's dilemma, if Jon is rational, he *must* cheat. It's his best move *no matter what Brian does*. But likewise, Brian's best move is to cheat *no matter what Jon does*. But again, if they both cheat, they both lose.

An interesting question to ponder is what factors impact the likelihood of two rational actors making choices that collectively benefit them most. If it's a one-shot deal (as with you and Rupert), you have more incentive to cheat, and make the move that's in your own self-interest. If the game is played repeatedly and each participant has the ability to retaliate when the other cheats (as with Jon Torre and Brian Bochy), there is more incentive to keep the agreement.

Maybe there is a collusive agreement in the 9th innings of tied baseball games. Suppose now that the Padres are playing the Yanks in a mid-June interleague game, and they're all tied up heading into the 9th. Bochy can go with the guy that gives him the best chance of winning, Trevor Hoffman, or he can choose Dan Miceli, a capable pitcher to be sure, but not even a reasonable facsimile of Hoffman. Torre's options are similar: the fairly solid Ramiro Mendoza, or the superlative Mariano Rivera.

If the Yankees are throwing Rivera and the Padres Miceli, the Yanks have a clear edge. Similarly, if San Diego goes with Hoffman, and Mendoza comes on for the Yankees, a Padre victory is likely. Let's assume for the sake of argument that a Hoffman/Rivera matchup is 50/50 and so is a Miceli/Mendoza. Maybe Bochy's thinking, "if I go with Hoffman, he'll answer with Rivera, and we both will have wasted our closers. I'd rather tire out Miceli and have a 50% of winning than tire out Hoffman and have a 50% chance of winning," just as his gas-station-owning cousin might have reasoned, "if I undercut Jon's price, he'll just respond by lowering his prices, and we'll both be making less profit."

Of course, this is not a perfect analogy. A major difference is that one team, the visiting team, can have full knowledge of the other team's choice before he makes his own. On the other hand, if the home team plays it straight (Miceli), then the visitors know that if they cheat (Rivera), the home team can retaliate (Hoffman) in the 10th.

Over the course of the season, we sometimes see Hoffman/Rivera, and we sometimes see Hoffman/Mendoza, but the most common result is Miceli/Mendoza. Is this collusion? It would be interesting to make a detailed examination of the circumstances of each instance of "cheating." For example, Dusty Baker cheated a lot in 1998 with Robb Nen. I wonder if other managers, after they figured out that Baker wasn't going to follow the agreement, chose to cheat when playing against the Giants. I wonder if managers cheated more often in the last game of a 3- or 4-game series (when retaliation the next day is not possible) than they did in series openers.

One question we *can* answer is which managers cheated and how often in 1998? First, let's gather up all the guys who were their team's closer, their whole closer, and nothing but their closer for the entire season. That list is as follows: Aguilera, Beck, Franco, Gordon, Hernandez, Hoffman, Jackson, T Jones, Montgomery, Nen, Rivera, Urbina, Wetteland. Here are those 13 sorted according to the number of tie games in which they appeared.

As was mentioned earlier, no reliever in baseball appeared in more tie games than Nen last year. The important thing to notice about this list is that, with a few exceptions, it's roughly in order of quality. Nen, Gordon, Hoffman, and Urbina were arguably the four best closers in baseball last year, and they also top this list. Todd Jones is a little out of place, and Wetteland and Rivera would be moved up if you were ordering these hurlers qualitatively, but the above is not a horrible estimate. The point is, managers deserve a bit more credit than we sometimes give them. The ones who had great closers used them in tie games. The ones who didn't, in general, did-n't. Dusty Baker, used Nen in nearly four times more tie games than was the case with Rod Beck in 97. I have to believe that's because he knows Nen is a fantastic pitcher, and Beck a fairly mediocre one.

Pitcher	Tie Games
Nen	19
Gordon	11
Hoffman	10
Urbina	9
Beck	9
T Jones	7
Jackson	6
Franco	6
Aguilera	5
Wetteland	4
Hernandez	4
Rivera	3
Montgomery	1

A lot of the tie games these closers appeared in were in extra innings, and that is sometimes more indicative of the fact that the team was out of other options rather than a desire on the part of the manager to use his closer. Also, some teams were involved in many more tie games than others. This next table orders the 13 closers based on how many times each of them started a tied 9th inning as a percentage of the number of times he theoretically could have (i.e. the number of times his team was tied going into their pitching half of the 9th). The last column is the team leader in starting tied 9ths or, if the closer is the team leader, the next-highest reliever.

Pitcher	tied 9th	Tm Tot tied 9th	Pct.	Other
Urbina	8	19	42.1	(Telford - 6)
Nen	10	25	40.0	(Johnstone - 5)
Hernandez	4	13	30.8	(Mecir - 5)
Gordon	4	14	28.6	(Eckersley - 4)
Wetteland	2	7	28.6	(Hernandez - 4)
Rivera	2	8	25.0	(Mendoza; Stanton - 2)
Hoffman	3	14	21.4	(Miceli - 4)
Jackson	2	16	12.5	(Shuey - 6)
Aguilera	2	16	12.5	(Trombley - 6)
Beck	2	19	10.5	(Adams - 7)
T Jones	1	11	9.1	(Anderson; Brocail - 3)
Montgomery	1	11	9.1	(Service - 3)
Franco	1	18	5.6	(Cook - 9)

Note that the number you see here is the number of times the reliever *started* a tied 9th inning. It does not count the appearances (if any) which began in the middle of a tied 9th, and it may include some which started in the 8th, so it may not match up with what you see in the 9,0 entry in his usage matrix.

It's interesting to note that the Dusty Baker had 18 more opportunities to bring Nen into a tie game than Oates had to bring Wetteland in. This indicates something important about the distribution of these opportunities: they can be very skewed, even among teams whose overall won-loss records are quite similar. A few more years' worth of data may show a more definitive pattern between a team's won-loss record and the number of "late-inning tied" situations--as you can see from the partial listing, the three teams in the hunt for the 1998 NL wild card race rank at or near the top in this category. Simliarly, Mariano Rivera's low tie game total also is partially explained by the fact that the Yanks simply were not tied going into the 9th very often.

Again, closers who were arguably not the best reliever on their team tend to appear low on the list, and the studs are at the top, with a few exceptions. Managers, it seems, can tell the difference between true ace closers and guys who get a lot of saves, and that's more than we sometimes give them credit for.

4. BEYOND RELIEF

Determining the value of a run is tricky business, and I'm convinced it cannot be done without running into a contradiction somewhere along the line.

One option is simply to assume that all runs have equal value, and this is the road most often taken by sabermetric analysis. It certainly simplifies matters, and is probably not an unrealistic assumption in most cases over the course of a season or several seasons. But on the game level, it goes strongly against intuition. If the goal is to win ballgames, it just does not make sense to claim that a run which changes the score from 12-0 to 12-1 is worth the same amount as one which turns a 2-1 game into a 2-2 game.

Once you've come to terms with the fact that all runs do not have the same value, you have a choice. You can assign value to a run (or any other event) based on:

(a) the impact it had on the game at the time it occurred, or
(b) the impact that it ended up having on the game using full hindsight.

Consider these four solo homeruns:

Solo HR #1: led off the top of the 1st. Team ends up winning 1-0.
Solo HR #2: led off the top of the 1st. Team ends up winning 15-2.
Solo HR #3: hit in the bottom of the 9th. Team wins 1-0.
Solo HR #4: hit in the bottom of the 9th. Team still loses 9-1.

If you prefer to assess value in an at-the-time fashion, you would order these homers, from most to least valuable, as follows: 3, 1 and 2 tied, 4. But this is not satisfactory. How can HR #3 be worth more than HR #1? It can't be. The equation 'shutout + solo HR = win' is always true and in no way depends upon the inning in which the homer was hit. In fact, if you assess value at the time, HR #3 will be *much* more valuable than HR #1, and that just can't be.

So you decide to use hindsight. Now you order the solo shots like this: 1 and 3 tied, 2 and 4 essentially tied. So far so good. But what about Solo HR #5, which led off the top of the 1st, giving the visitors a 1-0 lead which they would later relinquish, losing 2-1? If you're using hindsight to its fullest extent, you have to conclude that this HR was just as useless as HRs #2 and 4. Take away that HR, and you change a 1-run loss into a 2-run loss. But a loss is a loss, so that HR was worth nothing. Taking this thought process to its logical conclusion, you would be forced to conclude that nothing done in a loss has any positive value. 3-for-4 with 3 round-trippers and 8 RBIs? Worth zilch, if your team lost 9-8.

This relates to WPA, of course, because WPA is based on an at-the-time approach. If Greg Maddux pitches 8 scoreless innings, before giving way to Kerry Ligtenberg, who throws a perfect 9th to seal a 1-0 victory, WPA is going to estimate that Ligtenberg's contribution was roughly a third as valuable as Maddux's. But it took 9 scoreless innings to win that game and Ligtenberg only provided one of them to Maddux's 8. In retrospect, Maddux's scoreless 1st was just as important as Ligtenberg's scoreless 9th. WPA would seem to give Kerry too much credit and Greg not enough.

On the other hand, suppose the Padres, behind Kevin Brown, play 7 1/2 innings of scoreless ball before erupting for 8 runs in the bottom of the 8th. Donne Wall comes in and shuts down the opponent to ensure the 8-0 victory. With hindsight, Brown's performance looks meaningless. A AAA pitcher could have pitched 8 innings and given up fewer than 8 runs. WPA, valuing events at the time, gives Brown a huge chunk of the credit for this win, maybe too much.

So sometimes WPA tends to overestimate the value of a starter and sometimes it tends to underestimate it. What is the overall tendency? To answer this, I took the top 20 and bottom 20 starting pitchers in baseball according to PWins, and looked at their WPAs. Here they are:

If you're wondering about Kevin Brown, he had a relief appearance, so I left him out. For what it's worth, his PWins was 5.0 and he had a WPA of 5.5. The Astro version of Randy Johnson (3.0 PWins, 2.8 WPA) also fails to appear here because the study was limited to pitchers with 25 starts or more.

So PWins likes 12 of these pitchers, WPA likes 6, and they agree on 2. Overall, PWins says these 20 pitchers are worth 4.7 more wins above average than WPA says they are, or about a quarter of a win per pitcher. Every discrepancy of more than half a win is a case where PWins values the pitcher more highly than WPA does.

Here are the 20 starters who did the most damage (again, no relief appearances and a minimum of 25 starts):

The overall difference here is exactly the same as it was above: 4.7 wins, and the difference points in the same direction. That is, PWins believes these 20 pitchers harmed their teams more than WPA does.

So how do we interpret this? Is this evidence that WPA systematically undervalues the contributions of starting pitchers? Or is it evidence that treating all runs as equal systematically overvalues them? I do not believe either of these answers to be absolutely correct. This is simply evidence that, in general, a run given up (or a run saved) by a starting pitcher is, *as far as we know at the time*, very slightly less valuable than a typical run.

There are very few situations where I would claim that WPA adds something to our knowledge of how effective or how valuable a starting pitcher was. But the fact that, in general, WPA matches up reasonably well with other estimates is encouraging. WPA is not blindly robbing from starters and giving to relievers (much).

WHO ARE THE WPA HEROES: STARTERS OR RELIEVERS

With caveats in place concerning WPA and its use for starters, it's nonetheless of some interest to see which group of pitchers are considered most valuable as a whole. Is it the guys who pitch the most innings, or the ones who pitch in consistently more high-leverage innings? Starters or relievers? Candy mint or breath mint?

As we'll see, the answer pretty much comes down on the side of relievers. And the reason for this is simply structural, I think: there are just more chances for poor starting pitchers to irreparably damage their team's chances

Top 20 starters

Pitcher	PWins	WPA	Diff
Maddux	5.2	5.1	.1
Glavine	4.9	3.8	1.1
Clemens	4.7	4.2	.5
Martinez	4.5	5.0	-.5
A Leiter	4.1	3.7	.4
Schilling	3.8	3.4	.4
Rogers	3.4	3.5	-.1
Wells	2.9	2.9	.0
Harnisch	2.8	2.0	.8
Moyer	2.7	2.5	.2
Smoltz	2.7	3.2	-.5
Cordova	2.5	1.7	.8
Arrojo	2.5	2.5	.0
Mussina	2.5	2.0	.5
Finley	2.4	1.1	1.3
Cone	2.3	2.5	-.2
Ashby	2.2	2.6	-.4
Reed	2.0	1.8	.2
Wood	1.8	2.3	-.5
Colon	1.8	1.3	.5

Bottom 20 starters

Pitcher	PWins	WPA	Diff
Cloude	-2.8	-2.4	-.4
Sirotka	-2.5	-1.1	-1.4
Nagy	-2.3	-1.7	-.6
Meadows	-2.1	-2.1	.0
Mlicki (w/ LA)	-1.9	-1.1	-.8
L Hernandez	-1.8	-2.2	.4
Hawkins	-1.6	-2.1	.5
Burkett	-1.5	-.6	-.9
Estes	-1.4	-.9	-.5
Milton	-1.4	-1.4	.0
Haynes	-1.3	-1.5	.2
Green	-1.3	-2.2	.9
Rapp	-1.3	-1.0	-.3
Hentgen	-1.0	-.7	-.3
Candiotti	-1.0	-1.0	.0
Hamilton	-.7	-.4	-.3
Rueter	-.6	-.1	-.5
Wright Jam	-.5	-1.0	.5
Karl	-.5	.4	-.9
Wright Jar	-.4	-.3	-.1

Team	Starters	Relief	Total
New York (A)	8.4	7.2	15.6
Boston	4.5	5.2	9.7
Toronto	4.9	2.4	7.3
Cleveland	.8	3.9	4.7
Anaheim	-2.5	4.1	1.6
Texas	-5.2	5.0	-.2
Tampa Bay	-2.2	.9	-1.3
Baltimore	-3.8	2.1	-1.7
Minnesota	-4.3	1.6	-2.7
Kansas City	-7.1	2.5	-4.6
Detroit	-7.2	1.7	-5.5
Oakland	-3.8	-2.8	-6.6
Seattle	-3.0	-5.9	-8.9
Chicago (A)	-10.6.	-.9	-11.5

to win. There are only four teams out of fourteen in the AL with positive WPA from their starters, while eleven of fourteen have positive WPA from their relievers:

This situation is a little more balanced in the NL, where seven of sixteen teams have positive WPA from starters (and check out that Atlanta total), while eleven of sixteen have positive WPA from relievers.

Team	Starters	Relief	Total
Atlanta	13.4	2.6	16.0
San Diego	6.6	8.9	15.5
Colorado	-.3	8.2	7.9
Houston	2.6	2.4	5.0
New York (N)	4.6	-.6	4.0
Pittsburgh	2.1	1.3	3.4
Los Angeles	4.3	-2.2	2.1
Chicago (N)	.9	.7	1.6
Cincinnati	-2.9	4.4	1.5
San Francisco	-4.3	3.4	-.9
St. Louis	-2.1	.2	-1.9
Arizona	-.8	-1.4	-2.2
Milwaukee	-5.1	2.7	-2.4
Montreal	-4.8	.4	-4.4
Philadelphia	-3.4	-1.6	-5.0
Florida	-15.4	-2.7	-18.1

It's probably not completely a coincidence that the only two teams to show a great deal of balance in WPA totals from both starters and relievers (the Yankees and the Padres) wound up facing each other in the World Series.

WHERE DID THE LUCK COME FROM?

Last year the Tigers scored more runs than the Royals did, and allowed fewer. In spite of this, Detroit won 7 fewer games than Kansas City. Based on this alone, it's reasonable to say that the Royals' runs were more efficiently distributed than the Tigers' runs. The Royals had a better record in 1-run games than the Tigers, and had a better record in extra-inning contests. They were not a better team overall, but they were better when it counted most.

This type of situation is not all that uncommon, and in general sabermetricians are wont to write it off as "luck." And with good reason. Bill James, Pete Palmer and many others have derived formulae which predict a team's won-loss record based on how many runs it scored and allowed. The most popular of these is Bill James' Pythagorean formula, which states that a team's winning percentage is can be estimated by:

$$\text{Estimated winning percentage} = \frac{(runs\ scored)^2}{(runs\ scored)^2\ +\ (runs\ allowed)^2}$$

Some teams (like the Royals in 1998) win more games than this formula would predict. This may be due to shrewd managerial tactics, good clutch performance, or just dumb luck. Here's why most sabermetricians believe it's luck: because teams which exceed their Pythagorean projection in year n are no more and no less likely to exceed it in year n + 1 as teams which underperformed in year n. If some team really had a special ability to outperform its projection (for instance, a legitimate clutch ability), we would expect them to do so year in and year out, but this does not happen. KC was about 9.5 games better than their runs scored and allowed would suggest in 98 (which is a lot, by the way) and Detroit was a game or 2 worse, but next year that state of affairs is as likely to be reversed as it is to repeat itself.

In this section, we'll take a look at which teams got lucky in 1998 and, more importantly, we'll try to use WPA to figure out *why* they got lucky. In order to successfully separate bullpen and starter contributions, we'll use a different formula to estimate winning percentage. To see how it works, let's run through the process for the Royals.

Last season, the Royals scored 715 runs in 161 games. Taking into account their park, which depresses offense very slightly, we'll bump them up to 722 runs. An average team would have scored 794 runs in 161 games (using 1997 averages and park factors again -- the reason will be clear shortly), so the Royals were 72 runs below average on offense. Recall that we can convert runs to wins by dividing by 2.2*(league average runs per game). Doing so, we estimate that the Royals would've been about 6.6 wins better had they had an average offense. Thus, we credit KC with -6.6 batting wins (BWins).

Now to the mound. The Royals' starters pitched 961 innings and allowed 607 runs (which amounts to about 613 neutral-park runs). Those 961 innings were about 67% of Kansas City's total innings pitched, so we say the starters gave up 613 runs in 107.7 "games" (107.7 = .67 * 161). Again we compare to average. An average team would allow 531 runs in 107.7 games, so the Royals starters were roughly 82 runs worse than average, which converts to 7.5 wins. Thus the Royals racked up -7.5 starting pitcher wins (SPWins).

Relief pitcher wins (RPWins) are calculated similarly. KC's pen worked 53.3 "games" and allowed 295 neutral-park runs, which was 32 runs worse than average. That makes -3.0 RPWins.

To recap, the Royals' offense was about 6 and a half games worse than average, their starters were around 7 and a half games below average, and their bullpen cost them another 3 games. Altogether, the Royals appear to be roughly 17 wins worse than an average team. An average team wins 80.5 games out of 161, so the Royals' projected number of wins is approximately 80.5 - 17 = 63.5. They actually won 72, so they were about 8 and a half games lucky.

Here's where WPA comes into the picture. The above procedure obviously treats all runs as equal, so the fact that the Royals made out better than expected means that the runs they scored and prevented were more efficiently distributed than a random collection of runs. One strength of WPA is that it can distinguish between important runs and unimportant ones. It internalizes the luck.

Every game the Royals won last year resulted in a net WPA of +.5 (they started with a .500 WP and end with a 1.000 WP), and every game they lost was worth a WPA of -.5. They had 72 wins and 89 losses, so their overall season WPA was -8.5. We know how much WPA the starters and relievers accounted for (-7.1 and +2.5, respectively, for a total of -4.6), which means the Royals' bats must have accounted for the rest: -3.9.

We can summarize the above into this handy little chart (WAV stands for Wins Above Average, meaning BWins, SPWins, or RPWins):

	WPA	WAV	Diff
Offense	-3.9	-6.6	+2.7
Starters	-7.1	-7.5	+ .4
Bullpen	+2.5	-3.0	+5.5
"Luck"	----	+8.6	
Total	-8.5	-8.5	

The Royals had -6.6 BWins, but their offense's WPA was -3.9. In the 'Diff' column is the difference between the two, +2.7 wins. This can be interpreted as meaning that 2.7 of KC's 8.6 games worth of luck were attributable to their offense. About half a game came from the starters, and 5 and a half games worth of luck came from the bullpen.

Now the bullpen is a place where "luck" is not necessarily caused by luck. Go back to section 3 and remind yourself what kind of situations Jim Pittsley was pitching in. He had an absolutely atrocious year, giving up 56 runs in 68.1 innings, but because he only pitched in meaningless situations, he didn't do much damage to the Royals' record. He had -1.7 PWins, but his WPA was -.5. There's a game's worth of "luck" right there.

But that's not luck. That's just plain old common sense: pitch your worst pitchers when it matters least.

Because of this, we would expect most teams to have positive bullpen "luck." And indeed most do, though Kansas City's was much higher than normal, ranking second in baseball to San Diego. The following table (at the top of the next page) presents all the data necessary to answer the question "where did the luck come from?" for each team in baseball. There's a lot of information here. To get your bearings, read the Kansas City line first, since you're already familiar with it. The teams are sorted from lucky to unlucky.

Of course, as with our Closer Dependence and Setup Man Dependence tables earlier, it's possible to use this information in ways that exceed the scope of our inquiry. For example, using the TWins formulation, we can see that the 1998 World Series was clearly a mismatch: a Fall Classic featuring either Houston or Atlanta as the NL representive would likely have produced a far more interesting contest. The PWins method also suggests that the Giants and Padres were much more closely matched in the NL West than the final division standings indicate.

From the standpoint of "luck," however, it's interesting to note that it has little or no relationship to a team's actual won-loss record. Teams with mediocre and downright poor records can be found at either extreme of the specturm' this is also the case for teams bound for the post-season. This point is cemented by the two teams adjacent to one another right at the center of the chart--teams with the least amount of overall "luck." Those two teams? The Atlanta Braves (106-56) and the Florida Marlins (54-108).

Team	B Wins	SP Wins	RP Wins	T Wins	Proj Win	Luck	OWPA	SWPA	RWPA	OLuck	SLuck	RLuck
Kansas City	-6.6	-7.6	-3.0	-17.1	63.4	8.6	-3.9	-7.1	2.5	2.7	.5	5.5
Chicago (A)	9.9	-11.7	-5.0	-6.8	74.7	5.8	10.5	-10.6	-.9	.6	1.1	4.1
Chicago (N)	5.6	-.8	-1.1	3.7	85.2	5.8	7.9	.9	.7	2.3	1.7	1.8
San Diego	4.3	4.5	3.1	11.9	92.9	5.1	1.5	6.6	8.9	-2.8	2.1	5.8
New York (A)	16.2	8.7	3.9	28.8	109.8	4.2	17.4	8.4	7.2	1.2	-.3	3.3
Anaheim	-1.1	-2.5	3.9	.4	81.4	3.6	2.4	-2.5	4.1	3.5	.0	.2
Milwaukee	-3.8	-8.6	2.0	-10.4	70.6	3.4	-4.6	-5.1	2.7	-.8	3.5	.7
Philadelphia	-4.2	-4.5	-.6	-9.2	71.8	3.2	-1.0	-3.4	-1.6	3.2	1.1	-1.0
Los Angeles	-.6	.2	-.6	-1.0	80.0	3.0	-.1	4.3	-2.2	.5	4.1	-1.6
Toronto	1.5	3.4	-.5	4.4	85.9	2.1	-.8	4.9	2.4	-2.3	1.5	2.9
Cleveland	6.3	-.2	.5	6.7	87.7	1.3	3.3	.8	3.9	-3.0	1.0	3.4
Texas	8.9	-6.2	3.4	6.1	87.1	.9	7.2	-5.2	5.0	-1.7	1.0	1.6
New York (N)	-.2	5.5	1.1	6.3	87.3	.7	3.0	4.6	-.6	3.2	-.9	-1.7
Atlanta	9.2	14.3	1.1	24.6	105.6	.4	9.0	13.4	2.6	-.2	-.9	1.5
Florida	-4.6	-16.9	-5.0	-26.5	54.5	-.5	-8.9	-15.4	-2.7	-4.3	1.5	2.3
St. Louis	7.6	-4.3	-.4	2.8	84.3	-.8	3.9	-2.1	.2	-3.7	2.2	.6
Oakland	-.7	-3.9	-1.1	-5.7	75.3	-1.3	-.4	-3.8	-2.8	.3	.1	-1.7
Colorado	-9.9	-.2	7.8	-2.2	78.8	-1.8	-11.9	-.3	8.2	-2.0	-.1	.4
Arizona	-9.8	-2.1	-2.2	-14.1	66.9	-1.9	-13.8	-.8	-1.4	-4.0	1.3	.8
Boston	5.5	3.7	4.0	13.3	94.3	-2.3	1.3	4.5	5.2	-4.2	.8	1.2
Montreal	-11.2	-3.1	.9	-13.5	67.5	-2.5	-11.6	-4.8	.4	-.4	-1.7	-.5
Minnesota	-7.6	-2.0	2.0	-7.6	73.4	-2.9	-7.8	-4.3	1.6	-.2	-2.3	-.4
Cincinnati	.5	-2.2	.7	-1.0	80.0	-3.0	-5.5	-2.9	4.4	-6.0	-.7	3.7
Detroit	-7.4	-7.3	1.7	-12.9	68.1	-3.1	-10.5	-7.2	1.7	-3.1	.1	.0
San Francisco	11.5	-6.2	5.4	10.7	92.2	-3.2	8.4	-4.3	3.4	-3.1	1.9	-2.0
Seattle	6.8	-3.3	-3.1	.4	80.9	-4.9	4.4	-3.0	-5.9	-2.4	.3	-2.8
Baltimore	3.2	-2.4	2.1	3.0	84.0	-5.0	-.3	-3.8	2.1	-3.5	-1.4	.0
Pittsburgh	-12.3	2.7	3.2	-6.5	75.0	-5.5	-15.4	2.1	1.3	-3.1	-.6	-1.9
Tampa Bay	-16.5	.2	4.2	-12.1	68.9	-5.9	-16.7	-2.2	.9	-.2	-2.4	-3.3
Houston	20.8	3.6	3.1	27.4	108.4	-6.4	16.0	2.6	2.4	-4.8	-1.0	-.7

Those of you that broke out your calculators may have noticed that everything that should add to zero doesn't quite add to zero. One reason for this is the fact that we're using 1997 league averages (because these are the data the WPAs are based upon) rather than 1998 averages. Another is because of a few games which were rained out before 9 innings were completed, leading to some missing WPA. You'll also note that the RLuck (the difference between WPA and relief PWins) column here does not exactly match up with what you saw in the last section, although it is very close. That's because here the calculations were game-based, and in section 4 they were innings-based.

There are countless interesting stories hiding in this table, and I invite you to find them all. I'll just close by saying a few words about relief luck.

As was mentioned earlier, the Padres led the league in bullpen luck, and this is attributable to a combination of three factors:

(1) they were involved in a lot of close games late,
(2) they had one of the best relievers in the game pitching a lot of innings late in those close games, and
(3) he (and the others) pitched better in those situations than in other situations.

(1) is almost certainly luck, (2) is definitely not luck, and (3) may or may not be luck. The Padres' bullpen was worth 5.8 games more than we would expect, and it's an open question how much of that 5.8 games was due to random chance and how much of it was due to proper allocation of resources. Again, managed properly, an entire bullpen should be worth more than PWins would expect it to be worth.

Did San Diego, Kansas City, the White Sox, Cincinnati, and Cleveland (the teams with the most bullpen luck) get extra value out of their bullpens because of their bullpen management or their bullpen makeup? Or was it just a fluke? Next year, we'll revisit the issue and see if there's any meaningful year-to-year correlation in bullpen luck. And if so, we'll investigate what types of bullpens are best able to capitalize on it.

5. WRAPUP

Last year, all we had was non-park-adjusted WPA data for 44 relievers, plus 4 complete bullpens, and 2 team's worth of starters. If you go back and read the WPA article which appeared in BBBA 98, you'll find approximately 316 instances where we claimed that having a full year's worth of data for everyone would help us better understand this, or would help shed some light on that. Well here we are one year later, with complete data for everyone who strode to the mound in 1998. Are we better off because of it?

In section 2, we took an in-depth look at some of the fine relief performances of 1998, and WPA was able to make some distinctions that traditional stats could not. Tom Gordon's and Trevor Hoffman's seasons came out looking much more valuable than Nen's, Wetteland's, and Urbina's, despite very similar summary stats. Gordon's extra value came from good timing (his blowups occurred for the most part at opportune times), and Hoffman's came from circumstance and timing (his team was involved in lots of close games, and he pitched well in those games). It's interesting that the mainstream media chose Hoffman and Gordon as the relievers to champion as Cy Young candidates despite several comparable efforts by other closers (not only Nen, Wetteland, and Urbina, but also Mariano Rivera and Mike Jackson). Maybe the media is recognizing and informally giving credit for the same things WPA gives credit for. Maybe it's because those two played for unexpected playoff teams. Or maybe they just counted up saves.

Section 3 dealt with usage issues and dispelled a couple of myths. First, there's the media belief that a bullpen cannot be successful without a great closer. Most readers of this fine publication probably didn't put much stock in that one anyway, but section 3 contains plenty more evidence that it's not the case. And as usual, wherever you find a media myth, you find a radical faction of the stathead community which hyperextends its collective knee jerking it. Indeed, you'll find people who believe that closers are meaningless because they only pitch 60 innings a year, all 9th innings with a 3-run lead. That description roughly fits Jeff Montgomery, but it does not fit Tom Gordon or Robb Nen or many others. Utilized properly, a good closer can have a huge impact. In short, good bullpens (and bad ones) come in all shapes and sizes.

In section 4, we see what WPA has to say about starting pitchers and conclude that, while we would never claim it to be superior to the QMAX-based tools or even PWins, it is not an unreasonable way to assess their value. WPA's systematic bias against starters turns out to be fairly small.

SO WHERE DO WE GO FROM HERE?

Again in this year's article, we were not shy about claiming that more data would help us better understand this or that. Fortunately, thanks to the heroic efforts of David Smith and everyone else associated with Retrosheet, we have ways of getting more data other than simply waiting for the 1999 season to unfold. My goal for BBBA 2000 is to extract all the WPA and usage data that you see in this book for the 1998 season for each season that Retrosheet has made public. Such a database would undoubtedly answer some of our questions and raise many, many more.

QMAX TO THE MAX

Further Adventures with the Quality Matrix

Don Malcolm

THE VOICE FROM THE ALLEY

Suppose that you're one of those "private cops" in the movies, and you're on a case. Sooner or later there's going to be a point in your investigation where an off-stage voice will go "Psst. . ." and you'll end up following a shadowy figure down an alley in search of the real dope. Along the way you might get rapped over the head with a tire iron, or slugged by a man with a package of nickels in his hand.

That's the risk when you go snooping around. So most people don't listen to those voices from the alley. But sometimes the alley is the only place where the truth, or perhaps merely the path to the truth, resides. Back in the 1980s, the path to new insight about baseball was not forthcoming from within the game itself, but from a group of outsiders who beckoned to you from the alley. They became known as the "gnomes of baseball" and eventually moved up the ladder, from the alley to the bookstore to the board room.

Their precepts have formed the basis for an alternate view of the game, one that is at odds with much of the ongoing "traditional wisdom" in baseball. That view has become its own orthodoxy, and all of the former "gnomes" have pretty much eschewed the alley, where newer ideas continue to be formed.

The Quality Matrix is a voice from that alley. It calls to you with a strange, plaintive tone, already realizing that you're going to be incredulous, or at best skeptical. It knows that its claims seem odd, outrageous, and quite possibly unbelievable. But that voice has a haunting quality to it---on second thought, maybe that adjective should be "haunted," not "haunting." It has a different story to tell, and as you walk down the alley you have the strange feeling that things are never going to be the same again.

THE VOICE TALKS: WHAT IS QMAX?

OK, enough atmosphere. Just what is a Quality Matrix, anyway? What does it do and who does it do it to? How does it compare to other baseball analysis tools? What's different about it? What are its strengths and weaknesses?

The small room hidden off the alley is filled with books and papers, and---undercutting the 40s noir tone—several computers. The face of the neo-gnome is still not visible to you, but the voice begins to sound more like that of a human.

The Quality Matrix, it begins, is a probabilistic model of starting pitcher performance. It's built in the shape of a 7-by-7 value grid in which every start made by a pitcher is given two values on a 1-to-7 scale, with 1 being the best and 7 the worst. Each value measures a key aspect of the pitcher's performance; the first is hit prevention (called "stuff" and often abbreviated to just "S"), and the second is walk prevention, (called "command," and just as often abbreviated to "C"). The data generated for each start is stored, summed, averaged, and compared to the league average.

In other words, the "S" and "C" values generated from these value ranges are added together into a value called "T" (for "total"). The lower this "T" value is, the better---just as the lower a pitcher's ERA, the better.

Hold it, you say. This Quality Matrix measures hits and walks somehow, right? What about runs? ERA measures runs, and those are what decide ballgames. What good is a measure that doesn't use runs?

The voice gets softer. Runs, it explains, are the results of how hits, walks and outs intersect. But those results are not uniform: sometimes pitchers allow a lot of baserunners and strand all of them; sometimes they allow only a few baserunners and all of them will score. Hits and walks are the original building blocks of runs, and what the Quality Matrix does is to put those components into an equalized probabilistic continuum.

Nice phrase, you interject. Now what does that mean in English?

It means that each of the 49 categories, or "sectors" in the Quality Matrix show a different combination of hit and walk prevention relative to the number of innings pitched in an individual start. The actual results of those starts are also recorded, and we get a probabilistic winning percentage for each of these sectors. Other systems, using runs, measure based on what the pitcher actually allowed; the Quality Matrix, or QMAX for short, assumes that the run scoring associated with each sector should be made uniform, based on the actual average in the sector.

And not by the differences in actual runs allowed in each start?

Exactly! (The voice begins to betray something akin to human emotion.) ERA measures what the pitcher actually allowed; QMAX is measuring what the pitcher ought to have allowed based on the hits and walks he allowed relative to the number of innings pitched. Though I'm repeating myself, that is a probabilistic look at the pitchers' performance, not a deterministic one.

What are the won-loss ranges of these---how many?-- "sectors" that you mentioned?

They range from upwards of .900 in the best sectors, to .000 in the worst. We can generate an average winning percentage from the combination of individual winning percentages represented by each start that a pitcher has made, and by which of the 49 QMAX sectors it resides in. And there are a host of other statistical measures that become possible when we use individual games as discrete and equal units, not just items that are lost in the sum of the whole, as is the case with ERA.

What does a representative QMAX score look like, and how is it displayed?

The major league average QMAX score in 1998 was 7.53, which is made up of the components for hit prevention ("stuff" or "S"), which graded out at 4.18, and for walk prevention ("command" or "C") which graded out at 3.35. The standard notation is like this: S, C/ T (or 4.18,3.35/7.53). The best average QMAX score in MLB during 1998 belonged to Greg Maddux (2.85,2.12/4.97). QMAX "T" scores under five are exceptional years, and ones close to four are historic achievements.

So, you say slowly, as your eyes begin to widen a bit, this tool isn't like a lot of those nutty things that tries to convince you that Joe Schmoe was a greater player than Babe Ruth—

Or Greg Maddux, the voice softly interjects.

Yes, or Maddux. We are talking about pitchers here.

Only starting pitchers, the voice again breaks in.

All right, only starters. Tell me again why a probabilistic method makes for better understanding of a starter's performance. I gotta go in a minute; the missus has dinner on the table and she really squawks when I'm late.

The voice emits a long sigh. Here is the best I can do in such a short time span. ERA is the best determin-

istic tool available for evaluating pitcher performance. It is subject to some potential distortions, however. For example, runners left on base by a starter when he leaves the game. There are varying results with respect to these bequeathed runners, and they don't even out. The more general example is that a pitcher can allow ten baserunners and strand all ten, and another can allow just two and have them both score. Probabilistically, the latter pitcher is going to win more often, but a given season will not necessarily even those scenarios out, either.

So QMAX evens all that out as it goes.

Yes! (Once again, you can hear the Voice shed its tension.)

And that's a big deal because. . .

Because each start matters equally, and most if not all value tools can't take individual game results into account as part of their measurement. That's what makes QMAX different, and a bit difficult to grasp at first. We're not used to having a measurement tool work in this way; it goes against the grain, and it takes some time to assimilate it.

OK, fair enough. Now I r-e-e-ally gotta go!!

As you leave, some sheets of paper are thrust at you by an unseen hand. The top sheet contains a diagram entitled "The Skeleton Key to QMAX":

	SS	ES	HH	PP	TJ
	.44	.12	.32	.08	.08

S12	S35	S67	C1	C23	C45	C67
.26	.42	.32	.12	.44	.37	.08

The next sheets you unravel after that "dinner" the missus was holding for you---leftovers and cold cuts. Sheesh! Third time this week already! If you weren't a private cop, and hadn't tailed her off and on over the last few months, you'd think she was steppin' out on you or something. You look at the diagram again, and the funny acronyms, and suddenly there's a little flicker in your upstairs light bulb. You begin to read. . .

QMAX AND THE FALL OF 1998

You've heard about QMAX and the phrases "QMAX scores" and "QMAX averages." Here is a great way for you to get some practice in seeing how they're calculated. And while we're at it, we may find out some interesting things about the somewhat different nature of "autumn baseball" (as first differentiated by Thomas Boswell, before he became Just Another Big Name). The Fall of 1998, however, may herald a new understanding of some dynamics in post-season baseball, and QMAX may help us in discovering just what those dynamics are.

Ready? Here we go. Game One of the 1998 World Series, October 17th. San Diego at New York, Kevin Brown vs. David Wells. To get you started, let's look at the previous post-season performances of these two:

First, Kevin Brown:

Date	Opp	HA	QMAX	Log	Res
9/29	HOU	A	1,2	8.0 2 0 0 2 16	W
10/3	HOU	H	2,5	6.2 3 1 1 5 5	ND/W
10/8	ATL	A	1,2	9.0 3 0 0 3 11	W

As you can see, we've given you both the QMAX score and the game log to work with. Brown has been superb in the post-season (except for that relief appearance against the Braves in Game Five, but that doesn't get counted in QMAX: we're only evaluating starting pitchers here). That first game against the Astros was huge, beating Randy Johnson and setting the tone for the entire series. On the QMAX scale, it's a 1 "S" because the hits minus innings pitched (HIP) is minus 6, and anything equal or better to minus 4 is a "1". It's a 2 on the "C" scale because the walks minus innings pitched (WIP) is minus 6, and you need a minus seven for a 1 on the "C" scale; minus 6 is the range limit for a 2, and so there you have it: 1,2.

When we graph that on the QMAX matrix diagram, and keeping in mind that the closer to the upper left on the graph the game is, the better the performance, we can see that Brown's 9/29 game is close to as good as it gets. Pitchers win close to 90% of their 1,2 games.

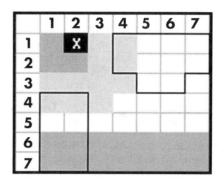

And we can see that Kevin had a second 1,2 game on October 8th, in Game Two of the NLCS against the Braves (in Atlanta). Again his HIP and WIP numbers are minus 6. But what about that game in between, the one where he had five walks? How does that game grade out?

Here's how. The "S" range limits (hits minus innings pitched, or HIP) are as follows:

"S"	1	2	3	4	5	6	7
HIP	-4*	-2	-0.33	0	+1.67	+3.67	+4**

*or lower
**or higher

Kevin's HIP for this game is -3.67, the closest you can get to a "1S" but not make it. Therefore it's a 2 on the "S" scale. Now let's look at his walks minus innings pitched (WIP).

The "C" range limits (walks minus innings pitched, or WIP) are as follows:

"C"	1	2	3	4	5	6	7
WIP	-7*	-6	-4	-2	-0.33	0	>0

*or lower

Kevin's HIP for this game is -1.67, again just short of the range limit for a 4. Therefore it's a 5 on the "C" scale, and his total QMAX score for this game is: 2,5. Think of it as excellent hit prevention (or "stuff"), but mediocre walk prevention ("command").

What we do, of course, is add up the "S" and "C" values for each start, and average them. When we do that for Kevin after his first three post-season starts, we get the following: 1.33 "S", 3.00 "C"/4.33 "T". The "T" score is the aggregate QMAX value, the sum of the "S" and "C" averages. The average "T" score for major league baseball over the past five years is almost exactly 7.50.

You'll often see QMAX scores written in that shorthand: S, C/T. When you see the expression 4.16,3.36/7.52 in the future (or some other set of values expressed in that format), you'll know that the first number is the "S" average, the second is the "C" average/and the third is the "T" (or total) average.

Now let's look at Kevin's Game One opponent, burly left-hander David Wells. After going 18-4 in the regular season, Boomer (as he's known) is also having a fine post-season. Here are his games to date:

Date	Opp	HA	QMAX	Log	Res
9/29	TEX	H	2,1	8.0 5 0 0 0 1 9	W
10/6	CLE	H	2,1	8.1 5 2 2 2 1 7	W
10/11	CLE	A	3,2	7.1 7 3 3 1 1 11	W

Let's run through these quickly. Boomer held the Rangers to five hits in eight innings in Game One of the ALDS; his HIP value is minus 3 (a 2 on the "S" scale) and his WIP value is minus 7 (a 1 on the "C" scale). A week later, he had an almost identical outing against the Indians in Game One of the ALCS. The HIP and WIP values are minus 3.3 and minus 7.3, which are just slightly better due to the fact that Wells pitched into the ninth inning, and got a man out (5 minus 8.3 is -3.3, and 1 minus 8.3 is -7.3). That's another 2,1.

Five days later, Wells survived some early inning uprisings by the Indians, found his strikeout pitch, and settled into a more workmanlike performance. At the end of his outing, he had given up seven hits in 7.3 IP, which works out to a -0.3 HIP, just good enough for a 3 on the "S" scale. (If Wells had departed without a man out in that eighth inning, his "S" value would have been 4---the exact center of the "S" scale, where hits and inning pitched are set to 0.) His walk prevention (WIP, remember?) is 1 minus 7.3, or -6.3, which is a bit short of qualifying for a 1 (-7 is needed for that) so it's a 2. The QMAX score for this game is 3,2---a good solid effort that pitchers win a bit more than 70% of the time.

So after three post-season starts, Wells' QMAX average is 2.33,1.67/4.00. Let's put Kevin and David's QMAX averages side-by-side (actually one on top of the other, but that's the curse of rationalized Western civilization):

Pitcher	GS	S	C	T
Brown	3	1.33	3.00	4.33
Wells	3	2.33	1.67	4.00

Remembering that the league average over the past five years is just about 7.50, it's safe to say that both these guys are on a roll. Brown has been more dominating in terms of hit prevention, but Wells has shown superb control. The QMAX "T" value puts Wells slightly ahead, but at this level of performance it's really a moot point.

We again get a sense of how good these guys have been doing by looking at where their games reside in the QMAX matrix diagram:

We've put the QMAX notation ("S" value first, "C" value second) into each square, or "sector," as we call them, to help you familiarize yourself with their location. Just so you get a sense of how good these games are in the scheme of things, here are the corresponding ERAs for 1994-96 for each of these sectors:

Sector	ERA	ERA98
1.2	1.13	0.80
2.1	1.44	1.57
2.5	2.92	2.95
3.2	2.62	2.43

We've added in the ERA data from 1998 to show that while the data does move around a bit, it's very consistent in how it's structured. QMAX sectors are tightly correlated to ERA. The best game (1,1) has an average ERA of less than one, while the worst (7,7--where a pitcher gives up at least four more hits than IP and has more walks than IP) has an average ERA of 25.44!

A great deal of this data has been presented in earlier editions of BBBA and is available at the BBBA web site, so we aren't going to run through all of that here. As we've developed QMAX over the past few years, we've been able to broaden its lexicon a great deal by examining the properties of related regions within the matrix diagram---areas with colorful names and acronyms, such as the "Hit Hard" zone, the "Power Precipice," the "Tommy John region," the "Success Square" and the "Elite Square" (only one of which is actually a square, but more on that later).

All of these areas of the QMAX matrix chart are quantifiable, and they are usually expressed in percentages of games started. We'll explore those as we delve further into the World Series, and the entire 1998 post-season---what we like to call "the Fall of 1998." That's not a Tragic Fall, but rather a most Fortunate Fall, one that is centered around baseball's Fall Classic.

Game 1 QMAX results

Pitcher	Opp	HA	QMAX	Log	Res
Kevin Brown	NYY	A	3,4	6.1 6 4 4 3 5	ND/L
David Wells	SD	H	4,3	7.0 7 5 5 2 4	W

It's hard to keep pitching as well as both Brown and Wells had been doing in their first three post-season starts. There have been a few pitchers who've gone entire seasons with QMAX "T" averages in the low 4's; Greg Maddux and Sandy Koufax are two of them. For most pitchers, though, it's hard to keep a QMAX "T" average in the low 4's for even four or five consecutive starts.

In this game, Wells allowed three homers, including two to Greg Vaughn, and was trailing 5-2 as the Yankees batted in the bottom of the seventh. Brown however, couldn't get through the inning, giving up a single and a walk after getting the first man out. Suffering from the flu, he was taken out at this point, and the Padres' bullpen (Donne Wall and Mark Langston) surrendered the lead and the game as the Yanks rolled a seven in the seventh.

The QMAX scores, of course, are based on hit and walk prevention only, and bypass runs (remember, QMAX is probabilistic, not deterministic: we're not interested in seeing the exact result, but the most probable result based on the gradations of HIP and WIP); as you can see, the scores aren't really bad. They are more in the middle of the spectrum. Wells and Brown pretty much duelled to a draw, and neither was close to his best. Boomer was the beneficiary of some late inning lightning from his teammates, and got a W out of it.

And that happens with QMAX about 20% of the time, actually, where the pitcher whose numbers are the lesser of the two starters will win the game. Sometimes that's because he's beaten the probabilities, and allowed fewer runs than his HIP and WIP indicate would be the case. And sometimes it's because he's lasted longer than his opponent, and (as in Game One here) his teammates have pulled the game out by putting the slug on his opponent's successor(s).

Let's quickly go over those QMAX scores, just so we stay in practice. Brown had 6.3 IP, 6 hits, and 3 walks.

That's a HIP of -0.3 and a WIP of -3.3. A 3 "S" and a "4" C. Wells had 7 IP, 7 hits, and 2 walks---a HIP of exactly 0, and a WIP of -5. That's a 4 "S" and a "3" C.

In this region of the QMAX chart, these two areas (3,4 and 4,3) result in wins for the pitcher's team about 55% of the time. We are at the outer reaches of what we call the "Success Square." A matchup between two pitchers in these regions is pretty much a toss-up, and the results of Game One certainly bear that out.

Game 2 QMAX results

Pitcher	Opp	HA	QMAX	Log	Res
Andy Ashby	NYY	A	7,5	2.2 10 7 4 1 1	L
Orlando Hernandez	SD	H	3,3	7.0 6 1 1 3 7	W

QMAX scores in the three previous games were as follows:

Date	Opp	HA	QMAX	Log	Res
10/1	HOU	A	6,4	4.06 3 3 1 4	ND/L
10/7	ATL	A	2,2	7.05 1 1 1 5	W
10/12	ATL	H	6,3	6.09 2 2 1 3	ND/L

This game was over early. Andy Ashby, the Padres' 17-game winner and #2 starter, had struggled in the past two months of the season, and in the post-season had been sharp in only one game. His

Even though Andy walked only one man in each game, he has three different "C" values in the games due to the number of innings pitched. While this may look a

131

bit arbitrary, in fact it's not: what we're doing is rewarding the pitcher for longevity in a game. Longevity has as much to do with winning games as any other factor, even in an age where pitchers supposedly go only six innings and turn the game over to the bullpen.

Andy's two 6 "S" games have different HIP values. Why? Because there are ranges in the QMAX sectors, they are not merely one-to-one assignments of value rankings to measures. Part of this is to ensure that we don't have 156 separate performance categories, which would make the system simply incomprehensible. At 49 sectors, we've ensured that there are discrete differences between "S" values, and we've created a qualitative relationship between sectors that we call "mirror pairs" (for example: 1,2 and 2,1; 4, 2 and 2,4; 1,7 and 7,1). These "mirror pairs" give similar results in won-loss and ERA, but are created from radically different H/9 and BB/9 averages. They demonstrate that, at the edges of the chart, sectors with lower "S" numbers than "C" numbers produce better results, while in the middle of the chart, the opposite is the case.

Andy's first game against Houston, the 6,4 game, is the most commonly reached QMAX sector. And it is an area mostly of failure: teams lose 73% of the time their starter has a 6,4 game. One sector to the left, the 6,3 game (like the one Andy had against the Braves on 10/12), the team winning percentage goes up from 27% to 37%. And if the pitcher can last one more inning than Andy did, with the same number of hits and walks allowed, he moves into the 6,2 region, part of the "Tommy John" area (TJ) where pitchers who get hit hard but have excellent control can actually win a bit more often than they lose (53%).

But none of that applied to Andy's start against the Yankees in Game Two. He had nothing, and was hit hard and consistently for 2.3 innings before Bruce Bochy lifted him from the game. He had allowed 10 hits in that time, for a HIP of +6.7, which is a 7 on the "S" scale. He walked one, and so had a WIP of -1.3, which is a 5 on the "C" scale. This 7,5 game is almost always a loss for the pitcher (.009), though the team comes back to win in almost 17% of these games.

Orlando Hernandez, the celebrated Cuban defector whose brother Livan had been the World Series MVP in 1997, had no such problems with the Padres, scattering six hits in his seven innings of work, walking three. That works out to a -1 HIP, or a 3 on the "S" scale, and a -4 WIP, for a 3 on the "C" scale. A 3,3 is a nice, solid outing that produces a win for the pitcher in 63% of his decisions, and produces an aggregate team winning percentage of .581. If your pitching staff averaged 3.00,3.00/6.00 for the entire year, and all the rest of your team's performance was dead average, QMAX posits that your team will win 94 games.

Game 3 QMAX results

Pitcher	Opp	HA	QMAX	Log	Res
David Cone	SD	A	1,4	6.0 2 3 2 3 4	ND/W
Sterling Hitchcock	NYY	H	5,3	6.0 7 2 1 1 7	ND/L

Game Three of the World Series demonstrates another point that QMAX illustrates---that hit prevention and high strikeout totals are not necessarily linked. David Cone struck out less men than Sterling Hitchcock in the same number of innings pitched, but was far better at hit prevention.

Two related studies using QMAX with standard data make this point. First, a breakout of games by "S" value shows that while there is a greater percentage of games with at least a strikeout an inning in the "1S" family of games (1,1; 1,2; 1,3 and so on), this percentage is not very dramatic. A "1S" game results in an outing where the pitcher has at least a strikeout an inning only a bit less than twice as often as a "7S" game, while the aggregate ERAs for these games differ by a factor of 12 (1.05 for the "1S" games, and 12.17 for the "7S" games). It's clearly not the power of the strikeout that is generating such a massive difference in performance level. Here is the complete table of high-K games as a percentage of starts in QMAX "S" families:

QMAX "S" >= 9 K/9 Pct.	
1	31.6
2	25.1
3	23.5
4	27.8
5	21.8
6	21.3
7	16.7

Second, a study of winning percentage using "1S" games and all high-K games (meaning more than a strikeout per inning) shows that the "1S" games produced a .772 winning percentage, while the big-K games produced a .680 percentage. When the common games were removed from each set---meaning the big-K games from the 1s population and the 1S games from the big-K population, both groups had their winning percentage fall, but the big-K games fell more:

Performance	All games	Common games removed
Big-K	.680	.612
Low-hit (1S)	.772	.752

In short, if you're going to predict the winner of a game, and you have a choice between a 1S game and a high-K, take the 1S game. In Game Three of the World Series, both men got a no-decision, but the team with the low-hit starting performance won. That 24% edge in winning percentage is no illusion.

Game 4 QMAX results

	1	2	3	4	5	6	7
1				1,4			
2							
3							
4							
5			5,3				
6							
7							

Pitcher	Opp	HA	QMAX	Log	Res
Andy Pettitte	SD	A	2,3	7.1 5 0 0 3 4	W
Kevin Brown	NYY	H	4,3	8.0 8 3 3 3 8	L

Another clear cut choice here, as Andy Pettitte had a sizable edge in hit prevention over Kevin Brown. Note again that Brown struck out more men than Pettitte, but came out on the losing end of the game.

Let's close by taking a look at the concepts of Sector and Range data. (We'll discuss them again in more detail after we look at the QMAX results for 1998.) Here is the QMAX matrix box for the World Series:

WORLD SERIES QMAX BOX

	1	2	3	4	5	6	7	S
1				1				1
2			1					1
3			1	1				2
4			2					2
5			1					1
6								0
7				1				1
C	0	0	5	2	1	0	0	

And here is the Sector and Range data that goes with that chart:

Percentages	SS	ES	HH	PP	TJ	S12	S35	S67	C1	C23	C45	C67
World Series	.75	.00	.13	.13	.00	.25	.63	.13	.00	.63	.38	.00
1998	.44	.12	.32	.08	.08	.26	.42	.32	.12	.44	.37	.07
PS starters in '98	.52	.17	.27	.07	.10	.31	.43	.27	.19	.45	.32	.04

Now there are only eight starts' worth of data here, and the results of those games won't necessarily match those of more than 5,000 starts made in an entire season, which is represented above by the row marked "1998." In the World Series, there were a lot of games in the "Success Square" (SS), that shaded group of fifteen sectors to the upper left of the matrix diagram. (As noted before, it's not really a square, but very little these days is what it seems.) That total of 75% is much higher than the overall average in MLB for 1998 (44%).

But note that second interior square within the Success Square (shaded in darker grey). This is the area called the Elite Square, which is where the best games of all occur---games in which a team wins more than 80% of the time. (Geometers and aesthetes will be relieved to discover that the Elite Square is, in fact, a square.) There are no games within that square in the World Series, corresponding to the .00 in the ES sector column. In MLB during 1998, pitchers reached the Elite Square 12% of the time. (Another comparison we've provided is the data pertaining to the 1998 data for those starters who appeared in the post-season. A somewhat better group than the overall MLB average, as might be expected for pitchers on winning teams, these starters reached the Elite Square 17% of the time.)

So while World Series starters reached the Success Square 75% of the time, these were games in the outer, "less successful" regions of the Success Square. The two regions below and to the right of the Success Square (and each sharing two of the SS' outlying sectors) are areas which also promote success despite elevated totals of hits or walks. The region where extra hits but few walks produce unexpected success levels outside the SS is called the Tommy John region (TJ). This includes the 4,1-7,2 sectors, and produces wins about 57% of the time. The region where few hits but extra walks also produce unusually high success levels is called the Power Precipice (PP). David Cone's Game Three performance falls in this category. Like the TJ region, the PP zone produces more wins than one would expect; in fact, it actually produces a somewhat higher winning percentage that the TJ zone, about 62%. There are almost an identical number of these games in any given season (about 8% each).

Next is the "Range Data," which measures adjacent regions of the QMAX matrix diagram in both dimensions. These are broken into three components for the "S" dimension, and four for the "C" dimension. These are as follows:

S dimension:

S12—he top two rows of the chart, representing the top hit prevention games;
S35—The next three rows, representing moderate to average hit prevention
S67—he bottom two rows, representing games where the pitcher is "hit hard"

The S67 region is identical with the "HH" (Hit Hard) region broken out as a separate entry. As you can see, almost one-third of all games over the past five years (32%) fall in this region.

C dimension:

C1—The very best walk prevention games;
C23—Good to very good walk prevention;
C45—Average to mediocre walk prevention;
C67—Downright poor walk prevention.

As the 1998 data indicates, C1 games (12%) are about as common as ES games. S12 games are a little less plentiful than HH (or S67) games (26% to 32%).

The 1998 World Series did not produce any particularly memorable pitching performances, unlike many in the past. Often, however, the World Series (and in recent years with the increasing size of the post-season) has been the focal point of a string of Elite Games. For example, here is the QMAX Matrix Diagram for the 1966 World Series, another four-game sweep of a southern California team:

1966 WORLD SERIES QMAX BOX								
	1	2	3	4	5	6	7	S
1	2	2						4
2	1							1
3						1	1	1
4		1						1
5								0
6					1			1
7								0
C	3	2	1	0	0	1	1	

We have the same number of games in the Success Square (75%), except that in 1966 five were also inside the Elite Square. After the first game, where both Dave McNally of the Orioles and the Dodgers' Don Drysdale struggled, starters reached the Elite Square in five of six outings.

We'll take a look at the phenomenon of accelerated pitching performance in the post-season by zeroing in on the 1998 post-season in the next section.

The Post-Season in a QMAX Nutshell: Flame Up and Fade Away

Pitchers have often taken charge in the post-season, especially in the pre-divisional days when there were far fewer post-season games. The recent history of post-season competition has uncovered an interesting trend in starting pitcher performance, which was epitomized by the 1998 post-season. This might be characterized by the phrase "flame up and fade away," which refers to the pronounced pattern for pitchers to reach a "hot" or heightened level of performance in the first round of the post-season, only to fall back to earth in the second round.

In 1998, MLB pitchers posted an average QMAX score of 4.15,3.38/7.53. Pitchers who participated in the post-season were, as you might expect, somewhat better: 3.89,3.03/6.92. Yet in the first round of the 1998 post-season, these pitchers "flamed up" to an average performance of 2.97,2.90/5.87. That average performance is in the realm of a #1-2 pitcher in a starting rotation, as defined by the following chart:

QMAX	Pitcher Ranking
< 6.00	#1-2 starter
6.00-6.50	#2-#3 starter
6.50-7.00	#3-#4 starter
7.00-7.50	#4-#5 starter
7.50-8.00	#5 starter-swing man
> 8.00	borderline major leagues

So a group of 28 different pitchers (Kevin Brown and Randy Johnson each pitched twice) with an aggregate QMAX "T" (6.92) that placed them as #3 starters in a rotation managed to generate an average performance over 30 games (5.87) that was about 18% better than their established season level. Astonishing? Frankly, yes. And even more so is the fact that most of this gain came from the "S", or hit prevention, element, as shown in the next table:

So virtually all post-season pitchers simply "flame up" to a heightened level of performance, at least in the first round, as shown in the Range and Sector data comparison:

QMAX Axis			
"S"	2.97	3.89	-0.92
"C"	2.90	3.03	-0.13

Percentages	SS	ES	IC	HH	PP	TJ	S12	S35	S67	C1	C23	C45	C67
First round	.57	.33	.73	.13	.13	.10	.60	.27	.13	.27	.43	.23	.07
1998	.44	.12	.38	.32	.08	.08	.26	.42	.32	.12	.44	.37	.07
PS starters in '98	.52	.17	.47	.27	.07	.10	.31	.43	.27	.19	.45	.32	.04

This heightened level is characterized by a virtual doubling of Elite Square (ES) games (17% for post-season pitchers during the 1998 season to 33% in round one of the post-season), and a halving of Hit Hard (HH) games (27% to 13%). Going hand-in-hand with the rise in ES games is a welling-up of top hit prevention games (S12), which also nearly doubles (31% to 60%).

You may have noticed an additional column in this display that hasn't been there before---the one marked by the acronym IC. What does this stand for? It is the most recent regional area defined as part of the QMAX matrix diagram, the Interior Corridor. This region looks at the S12 and C12 regions as a unit, focusing on the top hit prevention and walk prevention games regardless of whether they happen separately on in concert.

By contrast, the Success Square most looks at games where stuff and command are linked (1,1; 2,2; 3,3; 2,3, 4,3). The IC brings in all of the rarer games (1,5; 6,2; 7,1) as part of the diagram where it is possible to have success. As you can see, the IC is usually less populated than the SS, but look at the percentages in the first round of the 1998 post-season. Like an unexpected event of nature, the IC rose up in an incredible vortex and possessed the first week of the fall of 1998. The QMAX matrix diagram below defines the IC and shows the exact nature of its almost tectonic uplift:

FIRST ROUND QMAX BOX								
	1	2	3	4	5	6	7	S
1	2	2	1		1			6
2	3	3	3		3			12
3	1			1				2
4	1							1
5	1	1	1			2		5
6			2	2				4
7								0
C	8	6	7	3	4	0	2	

Power Precipice (PP) games nearly doubled in frequency during this period (13% as opposed to 7% for these starters during the regular season), and all of these PP games were concentrated in the S12 region.

It was an amazing performance, this "flame up." And it was followed by an even more interesting "fade away" by many of these same pitchers in the second round. Here are the two rounds of the post-season compared:

Round	S	C	T
One	2.97	2.90	5.87
Two	3.79	3.75	7.54

Though the shape relationship of the "S" and "C" averages is a good bit different, the overall average for Round Two of the post-season, with pitchers whose average 1998 "T" score is actually lower than the first round average (6.65 as opposed to 6.92), has actually risen to slightly above the MLB average for 1998 (4.15, 3.38/7.53). This is a performance decline of nearly 30%.

We can trace the nature of this decline by comparing the Range and Sector data for each round:

Percentages	SS	ES	IC	HH	PP		TJ	S12	S35	S67	C1	C23	C45	C67
First round	.57	.33	.73	.13	.13		.10	.60	.27	.13	.27	.43	.23	.07
Second round	.42	.13	.42	.29	.17		.00	.38	.33	.29	.00	.54	.29	.17
1998	.44	.12	.38	.32	.08		.08	.26	.42	.32	.12	.44	.37	.07
PS starters in '98	.52	.17	.47	.27	.07		.10	.31	.43	.27	.19	.45	.32	.04

Like the tectonic process known as uplift and subsidence, Round One and Round Two are possibly part of a volatile mixture of events that see pitchers ramp themselves up for a post-season that has become too long; like a supernova, they expend huge amounts of energy in a short burst, and then have little left. Both the ES and IC values dramatically subside, HH levels return toward normal; in keeping with this sense of burnout, we see that PP levels actually increase somewhat, while C1 levels simply disappear.

Let's look at the entire post-season through the prism of the teams involved. The following diagram summarizes QMAX performance by team according to rounds of the post-season, including the World Series:

	OVERALL			ROUND ONE			ROUND TWO			WORLD SERIES		
TEAM	S	C	T	S	C	T	S	C	T	S	C	T
ATL	3.67	3.11	6.78	2.33	1.33	3.67	4.33	4.00	8.33			
BOS	3.00	3.75	6.75	3.00	3.75	6.75						
CHC	2.25	3.50	5.75	2.25	3.50	5.75						
CLE	4.20	4.40	8.60	3.67	4.00	7.67	4.50	4.67	9.17			
HOU	2.50	2.25	4.75	2.50	2.25	4.75						
NYY	2.69	2.77	5.46	1.67	1.67	3.33	3.17	3.00	6.17	2.50	3.17	5.67
SD	3.43	3.43	6.86	2.75	3.25	6.00	3.00	3.17	6.17	4.75	3.75	8.50
SF	5.00	3.00	8.00	5.00	3.00	8.00						
TEX	4.67	3.00	7.67	4.67	3.00	7.67						
Total	3.35	3.32	6.67	2.97	2.90	5.87	3.79	3.75	7.54	3.63	3.50	7.13

Overall, the post-season performance of pitchers is still a bit better than their aggregate performance in the 1998 regular season (6.67 to 6.92 QMAX "T" average), but the means by which they get there is anything but uniform. We can see, however, that the "flame up" phenomenon in Round One is virtually uniform. By breaking out the data by team, we can also identify the culprits involved in the Round Two "fade away." These turn out to be the Indians (not surprising) and the Braves (very surprising). QMAX identifies that the primary reason for the Braves' failure to make it to the World Series rests upon the disastrous downturn of their starters' performance.

And by the time the Padres reached the World Series, they had pretty much used up all of their fuel as well. The Yankees' starters, as evidenced by their three-round "T" average of 5.46, were the group with the right stuff, and were able to hold on to it throughout the protracted post-season. That they did so, as QMAX points out, might properly be regarded as a miracle in its own right.

QMAX SNEAKS SALLY THROUGH THE ALLEY

Next day you're back on the case. Actually, it's another case, though just like in those mystery stories this one is really part of the other one, only you just don't know it yet. You're tracking a hooker named Sally who knows too much. You think she's a go-between and a courier, and she's taking a circuitous route to make her contact. She's a bit nervous, and looks over her shoulder a lot, and you've got to be careful so that she doesn't spot you.

Suddenly she turns into an alley and makes a break for it. You dash into the alley, but she's nowhere to be found. Then you realize that this alley looks awfully familiar. A door opens, and a hand with a gun points itself at you. That damn hooker was a decoy. And this is the damnedest way to indoctrinate someone into the nuances of some cockamamie statistical method. You feel like turning in your trench coat, except you remember that you aren't wearing one.

It's that same Voice again. How did the reading go, it asks, in that annoying, otherworldly tone.

It makes a lot more sense now. But why do we have to keep meeting this way?

Someone is testing the limits of your suspension of disbelief. What's important now is to keep going, and take a look at more information. There's five years of this data currently available, and more from past years is being generated all the time.

Got some unemployed elves stashed near the North Pole or something?

You're not far off, except the location is closer to upstate New York. Are you comfortable about how the basic diagram works, how the calculations are performed, and the various categories?

Well, yeah. But I'd like to see some of that seasonal data, and maybe a few more direct comparisons of pitchers. And I'd like to know more about those QWPs that were referred to.

You shall have it. Now that you've come this far, however, you won't be needing me any longer. The path to understanding is from this point onward a solitary one.

Getting a little preachy there, aren't you, pal? Why can't you just get a day job and publish this stuff in some academic journal somewhere? We have enough pseudo-cult groups already. Hey, you still there? Hel-lo???

But there's no answer. Suddenly the already dim light source is gone, and you're trying to remember which way leads back outside. As you grope in the darkness, you stumble over something and fall to the floor. It's Sally. She's not breathing. You crawl out of there on your hands and knees, vowing that you're going to fling your fedora into the ocean. Only you realize that you don't own a fedora: nobody has for the last forty years.

The next day a package arrives in the mail, a package you didn't know was coming but expected anyway. It's a big book---a big, bad book about baseball. And pretty soon in spite of yourself you're reading that book, and you've come to this point in the article about QMAX and you realize that you've been set up. You want to throw the book across the room, but it's so heavy you might hurt yourself, so you shrug your shoulders, pull that baseball cap down lower over your eyes, and keep on reading.

QMAX AND THE SUMMER OF 1998

The best starting pitcher in baseball during 1998 was Greg Maddux of the Atlanta Braves. His QMAX average was 2.85,2.12/4.97. Neither of Maddux' QMAX components (the "S" and "C" dimensions) were the best in baseball, but when taken together, Greg's total score (the "T" value) was the lowest, and hence the best.

QMAX ranks the following twenty pitchers (with 20 or more GS in 1998) as the best in baseball last year:

Pitcher Name	GS	S	C	T
Maddux. Greg	34	2.85	2.12	4.97
Schilling. Curt	35	3.46	2.06	5.51
Brown. Kevin	35	3.46	2.14	5.60
Wells. David	30	3.60	2.00	5.60
Martinez. Pedro	33	3.09	2.58	5.67
Clemens. Roger	33	2.82	3.00	5.82
Reed. Rick	31	3.77	2.06	5.84
Leiter. Al	28	2.86	3.04	5.89
Lima. Jose	33	3.91	2.09	6.00
Mussina. Mike	29	3.72	2.41	6.14
Johnson. Randy	34	3.29	2.85	6.15
Smoltz. John	26	3.35	2.81	6.15
Rogers. Kenny	34	3.53	2.74	6.26
Glavine. Tom	33	3.45	2.82	6.27
Hernandez. Orlando	21	3.05	3.24	6.29
Moyer. Jamie	34	3.97	2.32	6.29
Harnisch. Pete	32	3.28	3.03	6.31
Cone. David	31	3.48	2.84	6.32
Ashby. Andy	33	3.76	2.67	6.42
Daal. Omar	22	3.50	2.95	6.45

A complete list of pitchers and 1998 QMAX scores can be found in Section Five, accompanying the comments about starting pitchers. All QMAX scores back to 1994 are featured.

Note on this list that there are only a few pitchers whose "C" value is higher than their "S" value. These are the most extreme power pitchers in the game---and by power, we refer to hit prevention, not strikeouts. The three pitchers on the Top 20 list with higher "C" than "S" are Roger Clemens, Al Leiter, and Orlando Hernandez.

Conversely, pitchers whose "S" is furthest removed from their "C" are finesse pitchers. These pitchers rely on their walk prevention a great deal, quite possibly to a greater extent than their hit prevention. These pitchers will often have been K/BB ratios than average, even though they often strike out considerably less than the league average K/9. The three pitchers on the Top 20 list with the greatest distance between their "S" and "C" averages are Jose Lima, Rick Reed, and Jamie Moyer.

Let's look at each QMAX dimension separately for a moment. The MLB average for the QMAX "S" value in 1998 was 4.18. Here are the top ten pitchers in QMAX "S" (20 or more starts):

Pitcher	QMAX "S"
Wood, Kerry	2.69
Clemens, Roger	2.82
Maddux, Greg	2.85
Leiter, Al	2.86
Hernandez, Orlando	3.05
Martinez, Pedro	3.09
Harnisch, Pete	3.28
Irabu, Hideki	3.29
Johnson, Randy	3.29
Smoltz, John	3.35

As you can see, there are only four pitchers with sub-three "S" averages who had more than 20 starts in 1998. Let's look at the leaders over the past five years:

Pitcher Name	Year	QMAX "S"
Martinez, Pedro	1997	2.32
Johnson, Randy	1997	2.48
Nomo, Hideo	1995	2.50
Maddux, Greg	1995	2.57
Maddux, Greg	1994	2.60
Wood, Kerry	1998	2.69
Johnson, Randy	1995	2.80
Clemens, Roger	1998	2.82
Clemens, Roger	1997	2.82
Clemens, Roger	1994	2.83
Maddux, Greg	1998	2.85
Leiter, Al	1998	2.86
Brown, Kevin	1996	2.88
Johnson, Randy	1994	2.91
Leiter, Al	1996	2.94
Cone, David	1994	2.96

There are, as you can see, a number of repeating names on this five-year list (Maddux, Clemens, Johnson, Leiter). Will Pedro Martinez and Kerry Wood become fixtures on this list, or will they fall back toward the pack as has happened to Nomo, Cone, and Brown?

Let's look at the leaders in QMAX "C" for 1998:

Pitcher Name	QMAX "C"
Wells, David	2.00
Schilling, Curt	2.06
Reed, Rick	2.06
Lima, Jose	2.09
Maddux, Greg	2.12
Brown, Kevin	2.14
Anderson, Brian	2.22
Moyer, Jamie	2.32
Mussina, Mike	2.41
Reynolds, Shane	2.57

The average QMAX "C" in MLB during 1998 was 3.35. Only nine pitchers managed to have a "C" average below 2.50. Only Greg Maddux appears on both lists in 1998.

Here are the single-season leaders in QMAX "C" over the past five years:

Pitcher Name	Year	QMAX "C"
Saberhagen, Bret	1994	1.71
Maddux, Greg	1994	1.76
Maddux, Greg	1997	1.79
Maddux, Greg	1995	1.86
Brown, Kevin	1996	1.91
Maddux, Greg	1996	1.91
Wells, David	1998	2.00
Schilling, Curt	1998	2.06
Reed, Rick	1998	2.06
Lima, Jose	1998	2.09
Maddux, Greg	1998	2.12
Brown, Kevin	1998	2.14
Anderson, Brian	1998	2.22
Smoltz, John	1996	2.23
Mussina, Mike	1994	2.25

While 1998 was not a year that featured any sub-2 level "C" averages, it produced seven of the top fifteen QMAX "C" performances over the past five years. And there are far fewer repeaters on this list—only Maddux and Kevin Brown.

What this means is that it is easier for a pitcher to crack into the top level of the "C" list than the "S" list. This indicates that in the scheme of things, the "S" value is the more significant of the two values, and the lower a pitcher's "S" value is, the better his chances are for significant development.

In other words, when faced with the following two QMAX scores—

S	C	T
2.89	3.65	6.54
4.25	2.22	6.47

—bet on the one with the lower "S" score to show the greatest amount of career development. (The two pitchers represented in the above sample, by the way, are Kerry Wood and Brian Anderson.)

Let's move on to the QMAX regions, as represented in the diagram that our fictional gumshoe was given earlier. Just to refresh your memory, here are the definitions of those regions:

Success square--Term for fifteen of the forty-nine matrix sectors that produce the most team and pitcher wins. Pitchers reach this region about half the time. Abbreviated SS. Measured as a rate stat by SS%.

Elite square--Term for the four leftmost and topmost sectors within the Success Square, which produce aggregate team winning percentages above .800. Pitchers reach this region about 12% of the time. Abbreviated ES. Measured as a rate stat by ES%.

Hit Hard region--The portions of the "S" axis that include all sectors from 6,1 to 7,7. Games where the pitcher gives up many more hits than innings pitched. About one third of all games were found in this region from 1994-97, and 32% of games in 1998 . Abbreviated HH. Measured as a rate stat by HH%.

Soldier of fortune region--A small group of four sectors from 5,1-6,2 below the Success Square where pitchers with exceptional control can work effectively despite giving up more hits than innings pitched. Abbreviated SF. Measured as a rate stat by SF%.

Tommy John region--An expansion of the above region to include 4,1-4,2 and 7-1, 7-2 games. Abbreviated TJ. Measured as a rate stat by TJ%. About 8% of all starts fall in this region.

Power precipice--The region at the right edge and to the right of the Success Square where pitchers can pitch effectively despite giving up an average of more than six walks per nine innings, due to exceptional hit prevention. Abbreviated PP. Measured as a rate stat by PP%. As with the TJ region, about 8% of all starts fall in this region.

Now that we've reintroduced the regions, let's look at the leaders in each, beginning with he most basic measure of proficiency, the Success Square (SS). There were 18 starting pitchers in 1998 who had at least 60% of their starts within the SS. We'll list them in terms of three thresholds: 80% and higher, 70-79%, and 60-69%.

80%+ (1)
Greg Maddux (85)

70-79% (3)
Pedro Martinez (73), Al Leiter (71), Roger Clemens (70)

60-69 (14)
John Smoltz (69), David Wells (69), Andy Ashby (67), Dustin Hermanson (67), Orlando Hernandez (67), Curt Schlling (66), Kevin Brown (66), Bobby Jones (63), David Cone (61), Francisco Cordova (61), Tom Glavine (61), Hideki Irabu (61), Denny Neagle (61), Rick Reed (61).

This is not an exact list of the best 18 pitchers in baseball, but there are very few ringers here.

There have only been six single-season performances in the past five years in which a pitcher has had 80% or more of his starts in the SS. Here is the list:

Pitcher Name	Year	SS%
Maddux. Greg	1994	88%
Maddux. Greg	1998	85%
Martinez. Pedro	1997	84%
Clemens. Roger	1997	82%
Maddux. Greg	1995	82%
Schilling. Curt	1997	80%

At the other end of the spectrum, there are not very many pitchers who made 20 or more starts and entered the SS less than 30% of the time. The principle of replacement level comes into play here: when pitches are this ineffective, they are removed from the rotation. Here are the pitchers in 1998 with 20 or more starts who are at the low end of the SS:

And just to get a sense of what the dead average pitcher as ranked by SS looks like, let's run a list of the pitchers with 20 or more starts in 1994-98 whose SS% is exactly average (44%)

20-29% (8)

Mike Morgan (23), Darren Oliver (24), Sidney Ponson (25), Pat Hentgen (28), Shawn Estes (28), Javier Vazquez (28), Jim Parque (29), Brian Meadows (29).

Pitcher Name	Year	S	C	T	SS%
Appier. Kevin	1996	3.66	3.13	6.78	44%
Belcher. Tim	1998	4.26	2.76	7.03	44%
Blair. Willie	1997	4.26	2.96	7.22	44%
Hampton. Mike	1997	3.91	3.32	7.24	44%
Tapani. Kevin	1998	4.44	2.91	7.35	44%
Valdes. Ismael	1998	3.96	3.41	7.37	44%
Finley. Chuck	1998	3.68	3.74	7.41	44%
Burkett. John	1998	4.53	2.88	7.41	44%
Key. Jimmy	1997	3.97	3.47	7.44	44%
Finley. Chuck	1995	3.91	3.53	7.44	44%
Mercker. Kent	1997	3.80	3.68	7.48	44%
Hampton. Mike	1998	4.25	3.25	7.50	44%
Hershiser. Orel	1998	3.97	3.59	7.56	44%
Wakefield. Tim	1996	4.31	3.41	7.72	44%
Burba. Dave	1997	3.93	3.93	7.85	44%
Watson. Allen	1997	4.32	3.59	7.91	44%
Bullinger. Jim	1997	4.36	4.08	8.44	44%

On this list, however, we've retained the QMAX scores so we can get a feel for their range with respect to the Success Square. As you can see, eleven of the seventeen pitchers on this list are within 0.30 of each other in terms of QMAX "T". There are a few outliers, but most of the time, pitchers who reach the SS at the league average frequency get ranked as league average by QMAX.

Let's move on to the Elite Square, where the games are what the name says: the best of all. These are the top 12% of all starts, and they produce wins more than 80% of the time. In 1998 there were eleven pitchers who reached the ES at least one-fourth of the time (or about twice as often as the average pitcher). Here they are:

We've left in the QMAX "T" score and the SS% for added context. As you can see, there are no league average pitchers here. And they are not average in terms of the relationship between the number of starts in the ES and the SS, either. The ES/SS percentage is 12/44, or about .27. All of these pitchers are well above that average, which we call the Big Game Percentage.

At the bottom of this list are six pitchers who didn't make it into the ES even once during 1998. That usually means that they can't combine their best hit and walk prevention ("stuff" and "command") in the same game. It also usually means that they tend to get hit harder than average. Let's check them out:

Pitcher Name	QMAX "T"	SS	ES
Wells. David	5.60	67%	37%
Maddux. Greg	4.97	85%	35%
Schilling. Curt	5.51	66%	31%
Reed. Rick	5.84	61%	29%
Hernandez. Orlando	6.29	67%	29%
Martinez. Pedro	5.67	73%	27%
Glavine. Tom	6.27	61%	27%
Lima. Jose	6.00	52%	27%
Hermanson. Dustin	6.57	67%	27%
Johnson. Randy	6.15	59%	26%
Brown. Kevin	5.60	66%	26%

Pitcher Name	QMAX "T"	SS%	ES%	HH%
Saunders. Tony	8.03	39%	0%	23%
Cloude. Ken	8.83	33%	0%	40%
Ponson. Sidney	8.40	25%	0%	40%
Olivares. Omar	8.50	31%	0%	42%
Parque. Jim	8.67	29%	0%	57%
Navarro. Jaime	8.93	30%	0%	59%

Five of the six guys are hit significantly harder than the league average (32%). That sixth guy is an interesting exception: Tony Saunders, the first pick by the Tampa Bay Devil Rays in the expansion draft. Tony is a young pitcher with excellent stuff but command problems, and he is the pet project of Devil Rays manager Larry Rothschild, who was his pitching coach when both were affiliated with the Florida Marlins in 1997, Tony's rookie year. Saunders' HH% indicates that he is not really similar to these other pitchers, and there's a good chance that he'll soon make some real career headway.

Below are the best single-season ES percentages posted during 1994-98:

Greg Maddux' 1995 just leaps out at you, doesn't it? Not quite one pitcher per year will get to the 40% barrier, and only about four a year will make it to 33%. Only Maddux (four times) and Curt Schilling (twice) have made it more than once in the past five years.

Another sign of effectiveness is avoiding the Hit Hard (HH) zone. Pitchers with great stuff are rarely hit hard, and this contributes to overall success. The average pitcher will be hit hard just about one time in three (32%); take a look at the pitchers who were hit hard least often in 1998.

Pitcher Name	Year	ES%
Maddux. Greg	1995	61%
Martinez. Pedro	1997	42%
Brown. Kevin	1996	41%
Maddux. Greg	1994	40%
Schourek. Pete	1995	38%
Ashby. Andy	1994	38%
Avery. Steve	1994	38%
Guzman. Juan	1996	37%
Wells. David	1998	37%
Maddux. Greg	1997	36%
Maddux. Greg	1998	35%
Johnson. Randy	1994	35%
Schilling. Curt	1996	35%
Mussina. Mike	1995	34%
Schilling. Curt	1997	34%
Smoltz. John	1996	34%
Saberhagen. Bret	1994	33%

Pitcher Name	QMAX "T"	SS%	ES%	HH%
Leiter. Al	5.89	71%	21%	4%
Wood. Kerry	6.54	58%	12%	4%
Harnisch. Pete	6.31	59%	16%	6%
Clemens. Roger	5.82	70%	24%	12%
Brown. Kevin	5.60	66%	26%	14%
Maddux. Greg	4.97	85%	35%	15%
Wakefield. Tim	7.24	45%	6%	15%
Smoltz. John	6.15	69%	23%	15%

This is mostly a list of top pitchers, but it's interesting to see knuckleballer Tim Wakefield here. Do knuckleballers get hit hard less than league average? Here are the 1998 HH% of several other knuckleballers: Steve Sparks 20%, Tom Candiotti 33%, Dennis Springer 47%. The answer is: probably not.

We dropped the GS limit down to 15 or more to take a look at some of the pitchers who were hit the hardest in 1998. These are pitchers who were Hit Hard in at least half their starts.

Of this group, only Loaiza, Meadows, Morgan, and Rusch appear to have any kind of future in the big leagues.

Here are the pitchers with the lowest HH% over the past five years. We've brought the minimum number of starts back up to 20 for this list

Pitcher Name	GS	S	C	T	HH%
Winchester. Scott	16	4.94	3.81	8.75	69%
Navarro. Jaime	27	5.07	3.85	8.93	59%
Castillo. Frank	19	5.58	4.05	9.63	58%
Parque. Jim	21	4.76	3.90	8.67	57%
Meadows. Brian	31	5.00	3.16	8.16	55%
Loaiza. Esteban	28	4.68	3.29	7.96	54%
Dickson. Jason	18	5.33	3.61	8.94	50%
Langston. Mark	16	5.13	4.25	9.38	50%
Rusch. Glendon	24	4.83	3.38	8.21	50%
Morgan. Mike	22	4.64	3.55	8.18	50%
Loewer. Carlton	22	5.09	3.36	8.45	50%
Witt. Bobby	18	5.00	4.11	9.11	50%

141

Pitcher Name	Year	S	C	T	HH%
Leiter. Al	1998	2.86	3.04	5.89	4%
Wood. Kerry	1998	2.69	3.85	6.54	4%
Cone. David	1994	2.96	2.57	5.52	4%
Kile. Darryl	1995	3.43	4.14	7.57	5%
Harnisch. Pete	1998	3.28	3.03	6.31	6%
Johnson. Randy	1997	2.48	2.83	5.31	7%
Maddux. Greg	1995	2.57	1.86	4.43	7%
Martinez. Ramon	1996	3.56	3.89	7.44	7%
Drabek. Doug	1994	3.09	2.48	5.57	9%
Brown. Kevin	1996	2.88	1.91	4.78	9%

There are no repeaters in this Top Ten list, which shows how hard it is to avoid being Hit Hard during the current period of explosive offense. Note, though, that the range of overall performance as measured by the QMAX "T" average is much wider in this group. Merely avoiding the Hit Hard zone does not guarantee that a pitcher will be among the league's best.

Now let's move to the periphery of the QMAX diagram, and visit the Tommy John (TJ) and Power Precipice (PP) zones. These are areas which define an extreme style in a pitcher; the TJ region identifies pitchers who can be hit but remain successful via superb walk prevention. The Power Precipice is so named because pitchers who have dominating hit prevention games but who struggle with their control are probably the most demonized of all moundsmen, despite the fact that games in this region are won at more than a 60% rate. Each region accounts for about 8% of all games.

Pitcher Name	TJ%
Lima. Jose	30%
Schilling. Curt	29%
Wells. David	27%
Anderson. Brian	25%
Belcher. Tim	24%
Brown. Kevin	23%
Reynolds. Shane	23%
Reed. Rick	23%
Fassero. Jeff	22%
Carpenter. Chris	21%
Perez. Carlos	21%

First, the TJ zone, home of extreme finesse pitchers. Here are the 1998 leaders in TJ%:

The biggest surprise on this list, of course, is the appearance of Curt Schilling, but it makes sense if you think about it. Schilling has terrific control, but still throws a lot of pitches. It stands to reason that there are a number of games where he will surrender more hits due to the cumulative effect of his seasonal pitch counts.

The rest of the names, however, contain few if any anomalies from the "nibbler with great control" profile. Kevin Brown, despite his hit prevention skills, has been high on the TJ list in three of the last five seasons.

Pitchers who never venture into the TJ zone are usually of three types: 1) finesse pitchers who are too hittable and who are unable to pitch enough innings with few enough walks for their outings to land in the TJ sectors; 2) pitchers wild enough that they seldom if ever reach the two leftmost "C" sectors; and 3) pitchers who have both their stuff and command in their best outings and thus have the vast majority of their top control games wind up in the Elite Square. We present you with one example of each type of 0% TJ pitcher:

Pitcher Name	S	C	T	HH%	PP%	TJ%
Rusch. Glendon (1)	4.83	3.38	8.21	50%	4%	0%
Nomo. Hideo (2)	3.36	4.46	7.82	21%	18%	0%
Harnisch. Pete (3)	3.28	3.03	6.31	6%	9%	0%

Here are the pitchers with the highest single-season TJ% over the past five years:

Pitcher Name	Year	TJ%
Neagle. Denny	1995	35%
Burkett. John	1997	31%
Smiley. John	1997	31%
Lima. Jose	1998	30%
Schilling. Curt	1998	29%
Brown. Kevin	1994	28%
Wells. David	1998	27%
Nagy. Charles	1994	26%
Leiter. Mark	1997	26%
Anderson. Brian	1998	25%
Mussina. Mike	1994	25%
Saberhagen. Bret	1994	25%

Swinging to the opposite end of the spectrum (and the opposite side of the QMAX Matrix diagram), we have the Power Precipice. Pitchers with great stuff and shaky command often alight here, often on their way to greater glory or complete collapse. Last year we suggested that pitchers often move from the PP to the TJ region over the course of their careers, and while that does happen quite often, it is not a sufficient explanation for the general evolution of most pitchers. It is safe to say that there are very few old pitchers who frequent the PP region unless they have been doing so for many years already.

Young flamethrowers whose control often makes them miss not only the broad side of the barn, but the entire barn, are the order of the day here. And this will all come into focus when you see who is at the top of the 1998 PP% list.

Pitcher Name	PP%
Wood. Kerry	31%
Alvarez. Wilson	28%
Estes. Shawn	24%
Saunders. Tony	23%
Avery. Steve	22%
Dreifort. Darren	19%
Olivares. Omar	19%
Rapp. Pat	19%
Guzman. Juan	18%
Nomo. Hideo	18%

If you guessed Kerry Wood, you've gotten the hang of QMAX and are probably ready to take on Wall Street. (But remember what happened to Gordon Gekko in these pages last year.) Wood is the epitome of the Power Precipice pitcher, though he is not even in the same neighborhood as the archetypal PP guy, the Yankees' wild-ass lefty from the late 40s-early 50s, Tommy Byrne (whose QMAX chart, in all its radiant, implausible glory, can be found in our 1949 retrospective in Section Two).

What we're seeing this year is the fact that some pitchers never escape the Power Precipice, while others do so temporarily and then stumble back in. Many of these pitchers have had spectacularly successful seasons, but their Achilles heel is consistency. The younger pitchers (Wood, Saunders, Dreifort) are the ones with the best chance of pulling off an career-transforming escape, though Saunders has been high on the list two years in a row and a third year would not be a good sign.

There's really no point in showing you the pitchers who never venture into this area; they are precisely the pitchers who frequent the TJ zone, and there is very little instance of pitchers who have above average percentages

Pitcher Name	S	C	T	PP%	TJ%
Dreifort. Darren	3.96	3.19	7.15	19%	19%
Hampton. Mike	4.25	3.25	7.50	16%	13%
Green. Tyler	3.68	4.21	7.89	14%	11%
Williams. Woody	3.78	3.25	7.03	13%	13%
Wakefield. Tim	3.91	3.33	7.24	12%	12%
Belcher. Tim	4.26	2.76	7.03	12%	24%
Rogers. Kenny	3.53	2.74	6.26	12%	15%

in both zones. There are a few, however, and they're an interesting group, so here they are:

As you can see, there are very few pitchers with a really pronounced tendency to both edges of the QMAX diagram, and all this distension usually keeps them from being anything more than slightly above average pitchers. Occasionally one of them has a season as good as Rogers', but it's often part of a mid-season stylistic change that is occurring; it's very rare to pitch like this for an entire career. The only two pitches who are on this list more than once in the past five years are Williams and Wakefield.

Pitcher Name	Year	PP%
Wood. Kerry	1998	31%
Leiter. Al	1997	30%
Saunders. Tony	1997	29%
Alvarez. Wilson	1998	28%
Leiter. Al	1996	27%
Gonzalez. Jeremi	1997	26%
Van Poppel. Todd	1994	26%
Martinez. Ramon	1996	26%
Bere. Jason	1994	25%
Leiter. Al	1995	25%

Over the past five years, the poster boy for the PP zone has been Al Leiter, as the five-year Top Ten indicates:

Al had only a 11% PP in 1998, however, and it's possible that a three-year apprenticeship is what a potentially dominating power pitcher needs to get his act together. Of course, he just might be back in 1999. . .

QMAX RANGE DATA

The fabulously colorful QMAX regions above provide a great deal of descriptive and qualitative information, but the QMAX Range data might be even more valuable.

The Range Data is calculated for both QMAX dimensions, and each dimension is broken up into smaller segments. For the "S" dimension, there are three segments: S1 and S2 (S12), which represent the top hit prevention games; S3 through S5 (S35), which represent the medium hit prevention games, and S6 and S7 (S67), which is the HH zone we've seen earlier.

	1	2	3	4	5	6	7
1							
2	26						
3							
4			42				
5							
6					32		
7							

For the "C" dimension, there are four segments: C1, the very best walk prevention games; C2 and C3 (C23), the good to very good walk prevention games; C4 and C5 (C45), the fair to mediocre walk prevention games; and C6 and C7 (C67), games where walk prevention is simply a misnomer.

We can, of course, measure pitchers according to their percentages in each of these ranges, and compare them with each other and the league average. The numbers in the shaded range areas show the average percentages for each range.

For example, we can see how often Greg Maddux has a C1 game compared to the average MLB pitcher. As you might expect, any year that you pick for Maddux is going to be stellar in this category:

	1	2	3	4	5	6	7
1							
2	12						
3			44				
4							
5					37		
6							8
7							

Year	Maddux C1
1994	64%
1995	57%
1996	54%
1997	48%
1998	44%

Phenomenal when you consider that the MLB average is just 12%, n'est-ce pas? Interestingly, though, we can also see a declining trend in progress, though it appears that Greg has plenty of breathing room.

The leaders in the C1 category in 1998:

Name	T	C1
Brown. Kevin	5.60	49%
Wells. David	5.60	47%
Maddux. Greg	4.97	44%
Schilling. Curt	5.51	43%
Lima. Jose	6.00	39%
Reed. Rick	5.84	39%
Anderson. Brian	6.47	38%
Mussina. Mike	6.14	31%

We included the QMAX "T" scores to show that there are no real slouches in this group. Brian Anderson and Jose Lima are the two possible ringers here. Poor Maddux has fallen all the way to third place in a range that should probably be renamed the GM zone.

Let's turn our attention to the S12 range, where the top hit prevention games occur. The average pitcher will have a game in the S12 area just slightly more than one-fourth of the time (26%). The likely leaders in this range are probably culled from the list of pitchers with the lowest "S" ranking. We'll include the entire QMAX average for the S12 leaders.

Pitcher Name	S	C	T	S12%
Wood. Kerry	2.69	3.85	6.54	58%
Clemens. Roger	2.82	3.00	5.82	58%
Nomo. Hideo	3.36	4.46	7.82	54%
Maddux. Greg	2.85	2.12	4.97	53%
Martinez. Pedro	3.09	2.58	5.67	52%
Leiter. Al	2.86	3.04	5.89	50%
Glavine. Tom	3.45	2.82	6.27	48%
Hernandez. Orlando	3.05	3.24	6.29	48%
Johnson. Randy	3.29	2.85	6.15	47%
Smoltz. John	3.35	2.81	6.15	46%

With the exception of Hideo Nomo, whose command has spiraled up into the danger zone over the past two years, this is the other faction in the 1998 top pitcher group. The only pitcher on both lists? Who else but Greg Maddux.

The pitchers on the other end of the S12 list might be characterized as guys who are pitching on fumes. It's hard to be a successful pitcher when you're not bringing a lot of juice with you, though there is one interesting exceptions on this list. Here are the S12 trailers:

Pitcher Name	S	C	T	S12%
Loewer. Carlton	5.09	3.36	8.45	5%
Vazquez. Javier	4.59	3.91	8.50	9%
Navarro. Jaime	5.07	3.85	8.93	11%
Hawkins. LaTroy	4.64	3.42	8.06	12%
Darwin. Danny	4.52	3.52	8.04	12%
Swift. Bill	4.77	3.62	8.38	12%
Reynolds. Shane	4.51	2.57	7.09	14%
Drabek. Doug	4.81	3.48	8.29	14%
Oquist. Mike	4.48	3.34	7.83	14%
Oliver. Darren	4.90	3.69	8.59	14%

Other than Shane Reynolds, whose excellent command keeps him in the above league-average range, these are pretty much guys whose use is to be fed to the wolves. As you can see, a couple of fine pitchers (Bill Swift and Doug Drabek) are not being allowed to go gentle into that good night by opposing hitters.

The C1 and S12 regions are the showcase areas of range data, but it is also possible to combine ranges, or examine the patterns across ranges. We call this range configuration, and it's a shifting mass of patterns that are often best monitored over several seasons, in running snapshots, as is often done with the basic QMAX averages. There are many instances where range shift from Year 1 to Year 2 presages a more pronounced improvement in Year 3; a good example of this is the shift between C23 and C45 ranges that occurred in Jamie Moyer's performance from 1996 to 1997. Moyer's C23/C45 ratio went from 48/43 in 1996 to 72/21 in 1997, pointing to a strong improvement in command which continued in 1998. What really sold us on the idea that Moyer was making a genuine improvement, however, was the series of 15-game snapshots of this ratio that showed a continuous, unbroken upward movement in the C23% over those two years.

The data is not always so clear, and there are many conflicting trends. Pitchers are far more volatile in their performance patterns than are hitters; injuries, setbacks, crises, and hot streaks are all evident in data that operates at such a low sample size. On the whole, however, QMAX averages, and the supporting sector and range data is surprisingly consistent and less variable than ERA. Take, for example, the recent career of Mike Mussina. When we compare the standard deviation of Mike's QMAX "T" average from 1994-98 with his ERA for the same period, we see that his performance has fluctuated less as measured by QMAX.

Year	QMAX "T"	ERA
1994	5.88	3.06
1995	5.84	3.29
1996	7.00	4.81
1997	6.12	3.20
1998	6.14	3.49
STDEV	0.47	0.71

This can be explained by the probabilistic nature of the QMAX measurements. The QMAX model is based on aggregated ERA; ERA itself is simply the measurement of what happened to the individual pitcher, with all of the variables intact. The fact that each sector has a range of possible events within it helps to smooth out the edges of the distribution.

It is this interlocking relationship between sectors that provides QMAX with the ability to create a model of performance that reconciles run scoring without applying it as a direct factor in assigning value to performance. Hits minus IP (HIP) and Walks minus IP (WIP) are the direct value models, and they presume a uniform distribution of runs allowed based on the actual results in all the games within an individual sector. The model feeds reality, which in turn feeds the model.

And it is each sector which in turn lends its inherent QMAX win value (QWV)---the historical won-loss record of all the games within itself---to the ultimate QMAX value measurement, the QMAX Winning Percentage (QWP).

A QWP FOR ALL SEASONS

A pitcher's QMAX Winning Percentage (QWP) is nothing more than a sum of all the winning percentages (QMAX win values, or QWVs) associated with his starts in a given season. This QWP represents what a pitcher's winning percentage "ought to be," based on the combination of QMAX sectors and their winning percentages.

Or, more accurately, it tells you what his team's winning percentage should have been in the games he started. This is a twofold advantage over similar measures such as Support-Neutral Won-Loss percentage (SNWL), because it places the starter's won-loss percentage into the team context and applies those results to every start that the pitcher made. So a team QWP will represent a winning percentage that encompasses all of the games, showing what the modeled value of the starters' performance was worth over 162 games.

First, let's look at the 1998 QWP leaders. Here are all of the starters in 1998 whose QWP is .600 or higher:

Pitcher	QWP
Maddux. Greg	.711
Brown. Kevin	.666
Schilling. Curt	.663
Martinez. Pedro	.660
Leiter. Al	.657
Clemens. Roger	.654
Reed. Rick	.651
Wells. David	.646
Lima. Jose	.638
Smoltz. John	.625
Mussina. Mike	.616
Rogers. Kenny	.615
Wood. Kerry	.611
Harnisch. Pete	.609
Glavine. Tom	.606
Hernandez. Orlando	.605
Moyer. Jamie	.605

There is one name missing from this list who would appear if his 1998 stats were combined, and that is Randy Johnson (.561 QWP with Seattle in 22 starts, .722 QWP with Houston in 12 starts).

As you can see, the name Maddux is once again prominent here. If we were to decide the Cy Young Awards using QWP, Maddux would win in the NL, and Pedro Martinez in the AL. Those of you favoring Roger Clemens for the AL Cy should keep in mind that QWP doesn't consider runs, and the ballpark adjustments made by QMAX are done so by using hits and walks, which have a much smaller range of difference within ballparks. That being said, it is an exceptionally close choice between Martinez and Clemens in the AL, and either would be deserving of the award.

Moving to the opposite side of the spectrum, here are the pitchers with 20 or more starts whose QWP is below .400.

Not as many as you would think, perhaps, but remember that the cutoff here is 20 starts. There are a slew of pitchers below .400 who were not given 20 starts during 1998. If we drop the requirement down to 15 starts with a single team, we add six more pitchers below Ken Cloude, with the lowest being Frank Castillo (QWP of just .286). Lowering the bar to 10 starts, we add twelve more pitchers, with three names below Castillo's (two of them being young Florida pitchers Rafael Medina and Ryan Dempster, part of an unfortunate chorus line we've taken to calling the "Fish fillets" due to the battering that they received).

Pitcher Name	QWP
Rapp. Pat	.399
Vazquez. Javier	.397
Swift. Bill	.397
Haynes. Jimmy	.394
Rusch. Glendon	.387
Parque. Jim	.386
FLORIDA	.385
Navarro. Jaime	.374
Drabek. Doug	.372
Cloude. Ken	.371

And this is as good a time as any to mention that, yes, that is the entire Florida team listed at a .385 QWP. One of our favorite outputs from the QMAX database (and a big thank you to Sean Forman for automating that effort) is the month-by-month team snapshot. The Marlins' monthly QWP is gruesome but instructive. You may want to find some dark glasses when viewing this (forget about the fedora and trench coat, they're completely useless at this point).

FLA	Apr	May	Jun	Jul	Aug	Sep	Tot
A Larkin	.425	.229		.467	.218		.317
Dempster			.347	.139	.024		.242
F Heredia	.233						.233
Fontenot		.049	.452	.163			.315
Hammond		.236					.236
J Sanchez	.635	.537	.390	.378	.462	.468	.461
L Hernandez	.395	.502	.524	.544	.422	.369	.461
Ludwick	.399	.076		.207			.281
Meadows	.531	.399	.449	.354	.268	.365	.405
Medina	.126				.407	.327	.283
Ojala				.590	.415	.345	.420
Total	.396	.366	.430	.376	.368	.374	.385

This is what is called unrelenting AAA-level pitching at the major league level. The best pitchers here, Jesus Sanchez and Livan Hernandez, are still below league average, and there are only two other starters (Brian Meadows and Kirt Ojala, who spent half the year in the bullpen) over .400. The Marlins QWP of .385, when apportioned over a 162-game season, means that the Florida starting pitchers' base value in terms of a won-loss record in 1998 was 62-100.

Month-by-month QWP reports for each team can be found in the statistical material accompanying each essay in Section Four (Team Essays).

Our final list for this year's QMAX survey lists all of the team QWPs and also supplies the team's basic QMAX averages (the S, C, T values). As you'll see, there is an almost linear relationship between the QWP and the QMAX "T" value. In the several instances where this is not the case, the higher QWP in all but one case belongs to the team whose QMAX "S" value (hit prevention) is superior.

Team	S	C	T	QWP
ATL	3.56	2.81	6.37	.596
NYM	3.59	3.12	6.70	.579
NYY	3.65	3.04	6.70	.561
LA	3.58	3.41	6.99	.553
HOU	4.15	2.84	6.99	.548
TOR	3.84	3.29	7.13	.533
SD	3.92	3.08	7.00	.532
AZ	4.14	3.06	7.20	.526
BOS	3.94	3.31	7.25	.521
CHC	4.02	3.29	7.31	.516
PIT	4.09	3.19	7.27	.512
SFG	4.04	3.48	7.52	.493
SEA	4.26	3.25	7.51	.492
CIN	3.97	3.56	7.53	.489
PHI	4.15	3.33	7.48	.488
STL	4.18	3.56	7.74	.483
OAK	4.27	3.36	7.63	.476
MIN	4.44	3.25	7.69	.470
CLE	4.25	3.41	7.66	.469
MON	4.21	3.56	7.77	.461
TB	4.05	3.81	7.86	.459
KC	4.40	3.47	7.86	.456
MIL	4.31	3.58	7.90	.456
BAL	4.47	3.36	7.83	.453
DET	4.46	3.47	7.93	.443
COL	4.53	3.49	8.02	.442
ANA	4.34	3.75	8.09	.442
TEX	4.61	3.51	8.12	.425
CHW	4.52	3.73	8.25	.416
FLA	4.64	3.93	8.57	.385

Amazing to consider that the Texas Rangers managed to win a division with a starting staff that ranked 28th out of a possible 30, isn't it? It's a tribute to their hitting and their bullpen (and, just possibly, to their crusty manager Johnny Oates) that they did so. Of course, it helped that the other three teams in their division also had below-average pitching staffs.

Best team QMAX "S" scores:
Atlanta (3.56), Los Angeles (3.58), New York Mets (3.59), New York ,Yankees (3.65), Toronto (3.82)

Best team QMAX "C" scores:
Atlanta (2.81), Houston (2.84), New York Yankees (3.04), Arizona,(3.06), San Diego (3.08)

Worst team QMAX "S" scores:
Florida (4.64), Texas (4.61), Colorado (4.53), Chicago White Sox ,(4.52), Baltimore (4.47)

Worst team QMAX "C" scores:
Florida (3.93), Tampa Bay (3.81), Anaheim (3.75), Chicago White ,Sox (3.73), Milwaukee (3.58)

We could go on like this forever, but as the sign on the door says, check-out time is 11 a.m. Next year, QMAX will return with a look at a selection of Hall of Fame pitchers from all eras of baseball. Don't miss it---fedoras and trench coats optional.

QMAX Presents: "Bad" Pitchers

That's Right, We Baaad. . .

The thing that has always intrigued me about QMAX, beyond the welter of traditional and neo-traditional pitching statistics, is its ability to convey shape as well as value. I like "shape" statistics because they color in more of the picture for me than a "value" stat, which mainly tell me "who is the better player." I'm interested in that and all, but I want more.

My cohorts here at BBBA have spent a mind-blowing amount of time logging QMAX data, twisting and kneading it like pizza dough, tossing it in the air, and sprinkling a growing family of toppings on it: Soldier of Fortune regions, the Power Precipice, the "stuff" axis, transition quotient, the 5-start chart, and this year's special supreme combo topping, QWP (aka QMAX winning percentage). Like a great pizza joint's menu, it's a little dizzying, and takes some time to digest. Thus far I have mainly stood by the side, squinted my eyes, and looked askance at the whole thing, much like I do in Round Table most times. I've watched as Don and his Merry Men have done extended studies on some of the great careers and seasons of our times: Koufax, Maddux, Clemens, Hershiser '88, and much, much more.

As fascinating as that's been, though, greatness is only one corner of the pitching landscape, and I figure there must be some interesting nuggets out there where the great unwashed masses of pitchers toil. One day I hope to do an in-depth study of Paul Foytack, the most astonishingly mediocre pitcher ever, (you doubt me? look him up) but with the limited time available for this edition of BBBA I thought I would look at the far end of the beam in an attempt to balance the QMAX studies already presented. That's right: like Aykroyd's Leonard Pinth-Garnell, I studied Bad Pitching, with a big B and an uppercase P. To fit the QMAX format, I had to narrow the lens to study only starting pitchers, and only those with enough starts in a season to paper-weight the QMAX chart sufficiently to keep it from blowing out the window. Sorry to say, Todd Van Poppel's career didn't quite make the cut. Truly Bad Pitchers have an annoying habit of getting cut before they make their quota of starts, so what I ended up with are Bad Pitchers who, by dint of luck, fate, or marrying the GM's daughter, managed to hang in long enough to ring the bell while getting their bell rung. You might be surprised at the amount of varieties of Bad Pitcher there are: I was.

By way of introducing the series, and presenting a sampler of some the QMAX toppings, I present here two examples of that rare breed, the Bad 20-game winner. Just as it takes a pretty good pitcher to lose 20, sometimes it takes a pretty bad pitcher to win 20. First: "Hey Vern" Kennedy of the 1936 White Sox.

VERN KENNEDY			CHICAGO 1936				
	1	2	3	4	5	6	7	S
1	1	1	4	1				7
2	1		3				1	5
3	1		1	1	1			4
4	1		2	2				5
5		1						1
6	1			3			1	5
7	1			3	2		1	7
C	6	2	10	10	3	0	3	34

Vern Kennedy was reputed to be the best athlete in baseball during his playing days (and after: at age 70, he was a champion Senior Pentathlete). Further proof of what we might call the Bo Jackson syndrome, however, is given by Vern's career, and in particular the 1936 season. Vern pulled down a 4.63 ERA, which doesn't sound too impressive. A 21-9 record is impressive, however. One would be tempted to add "least deserving" to odder, but a closer examination puts that conclusion in some doubt.

Consider: 1) the AL ERA was 5.04 in 1936 (the highest in the twentieth century). 2) The White Sox, while a good team, were only fourth of eight teams in runs scored that year. Now, the issue is in some doubt. What does QMAX tell us about Vern Kennedy's 1936 season? It tells us that, most of the time, Vern was a pretty good pitcher. 17 of his 34 starts fell in the "success square," and if we adjust for league offense levels (which the QMAX scale does not—yet), that success square might well grow larger in years like 1936 and include more of Vern's starts, maybe some of his 5s starts. But wait: Vern only had one 5s start all year, a 5,2 performance on July 23 (he won it.)

What we do see are ten starts where Vern was terrible—6,4 or worse. The Pale Hose dutifully dropped nine of those ten, removing the idea that Vern was rescued by a thunderous offense. He did have two extreme Tommy John games (a 6,1 and a 7,1) and he got wins in both of those—11-hit and 15(!)-hit complete games.

Ouside of those ten terrible starts, Vern was a good pitcher. A VERY good pitcher: 24 starts, 3.03 ERA, 2.8s/2.8c/5.6t. The White Sox were 20-4 in those 24 starts, and Vern was 20-3. The terrible starts were oddly clustered: Bad starts at the end of April, end of May/beginning of June, end of June, end of July (Vern, buddy? How are things with the wife these days?); then, breaking the pattern, three in early/mid-August, and two lousy 7,5 starts at the end of September. Take a look at the chart showing Vern's 5-start "S" and "C" averages: every time he has one or two of "those days," you see his "S" line jump. A monthly pattern like that really makes a domestic explanation jump out at you, but I'm not gonna touch that—I've learned some things in this world.

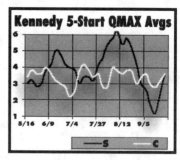

Kennedy 5-Start QMAX Avgs
—S — C

We move on to the anchovy-laden half of this Pitcher Pizza, to the incomparable Remy Kremer of the 1930 Pittsburgh Pirates. Remy turned in 276 innings for the Bucs, and came out with a 20-12 record. Oh yes, his ERA? A truly stupendous 5.02. Granted, 1930 was one of the big-time offensive years, but remember, Forbes Field was a pitcher's Valhalla. Can QMAX solve the mysterious case of the Pitcher Who Smelled? Let's check the QMAX chart and see what we find.

REY KREMER PITTSBURGH 1930

	1	2	3	4	5	6	7	S
1	1							1
2	1							1
3	3	1	1					5
4	2	1						3
5	1	4	4	1				10
6	1	2	1				1	6
7	4	1	3	1	2		1	12
C	13	9	9	3	2	0	2	38

Like all great mysteries, we found more than we expected. Those of you who have followed the QMAX story since the beginning know the Myth of the Finesse Pitcher, otherwise known as the Soldier of Fortune. We have honored Tommy John, the John Rambo of Soldier of Fortune pitchers, by naming the region after him. To recap, it is the QMAX conclusion that Soldier of Fortune type pitchers (those who soldier on grimly despite getting hit hard and often, and somehow survive by eating beetles and grubs—er, who survive by issuing walks as often as Rambo played the harpsichord) have been historically overrated by decades of managers who admire the true grit and who fudge the body count (wins and losses, if you're lost in the Fog of Bad Metaphor).

But back to Remy Kremer. What we found here was no less than the Original Gangsta, the guy who may have single-handedly started the Soldier of Fortune cult among managers. Look back at the QMAX chart again. Sixteen of Remy's 38 starts, or 42%, were in the Tommy John (TJ) region. That's an astoundingly high percentage compared to the 8% major league average we calculated from recent data. (There have been only four pitchers in the past five years who have broken 30%.) And look what happened? The guy won 20! So how did he do it? Well, run support, sure: he had Waner and Waner and Traynor behind him, scoring 6.4 runs a game for him. He had a big park: Forbes was where triples went to die. He had Pie Traynor and Dick Bartell and George Grantham in the infield, and those guys were pretty good. Uh, except for Grantham: he was known as "Boots" for a reason. . .

It's almost inconceivable, however, that someone could have 28 of 38 starts where he allowed more hits than IP and wind up with 20 wins. The distance between Kremer's "S" and "C" averages (5.26-2.47 = 2.79) might provide a clue, though, as might a look at his overall record in the TJ region. Let's take a look:

QMAX	W	L	TW	TL	IP	H	R	ER	BB	K	ERA
TJ	9	4	11	5	132	175	73	56	20	24	3.82
non-TJ	11	7	13	9	143	186	104	94	43	34	5.90

So the Pirates won 69% of Kremer's TJ region starts. Interestingly, the TJ region ERA for all of MLB in 1998 (covering the same definitions as used for Remy's 1930 season) was 3.80. Teams won only 55% of the time their pitchers were in this region during 1998, however. That's a couple of extra wins that Kremer was blessed with right there.

And then when we look at the games where Kremer allowed more hits than IP (5-7 "S"), we see that he also beat the odds:

QMAX	W	L	TW	TL	IP	H	R	ER	BB	K	ERA
5-7 S	11	10	15	13	186	283	151	126	46	36	6.09

There aren't too many guys posting a better-than-.500 record in these contests. In 1998, the average team won 33% of the time when its starter wound up in the 5-7 "S" range. "Winning ugly" has seldom been so systematically misshapen.

One can picture his manager, the unforgettable Jewel Ens (what? You forgot Jewel Ens? A lot easier to forget for some of you laddies than Jewel Kilcher, n'est-ce pas??) beaming broadly as Kremer finished another 16-hit, 8-run, 1-walk, zero-K complete game like the one he won on August 2 of that year against the Cubs. "Way to tough it out, Remy boy! You just make them put it in play, and Pie 'n' Boots 'n' Rowdy Richard will do the rest! We're going to the World Series, and you're going to Cooperstown, or my name's not Jewel Ens!"

With that, we'll take our leave, and allow you to linger over two starts which may possibly be the ugliest back-to-back wins in baseball history. You'll find thirty additional forays into the mottled universe of Bad Pitching in Section Four (Team Essays). In the meantime, check this out, and remember—don't try this at home.

Date	Opp	W	L	TW	TL	IP	H	R	ER	BB	SO
7/29/30	StL	1			1	9.00	14	5	4	1	1
8/2/30	ChC	1			1	9.00	16	8	5	1	0

Tom Austin

149

INSIDE STRAIGHT

Ken Adams

In his 1996 book Full House, Stephen Jay Gould seeks to prove the death of the .400 hitter is due to the raising level of play by Major League ballplayers. This book was an expansion of an earlier article in Vanity Fair that appeared in 1983. This goes against the grain for many 'Old Timers', who constantly rail against expansion and the general level of play in today's game. This steady drumbeat can be heard during any game broadcast as ex-ballplayers compare the current crop of players with those who played back in the 'good old days.' This has been going on for well over one hundred years.

While it is likely that 'Old Timers' will never be convinced of Gould's thesis, is Gould's thesis sound? Has he made his case so convincing that all objective observers go along with his thesis? As much as I agree with the his statement of general improvement I find his evidence lacking at least in how it is presented.

Before we get into Gould's study's shortcomings, we should look at how Gould's study is set up. His first study was done in the early 1980's while Gould was recovering from a serious illness and was done on the 'cheap'. Gould took the five highest and five lowest players by batting average from 1876 to 1980. Players qualified by having two at-bats per game over a full season. He then calculated the standard deviation of these players from the league (combined leagues actually) batting average. Several years later Gould extended the study to include all players who exceeded the two at-bats per season. 'The higher the value of the standard deviation, the more extensive, or spread out, the variation,' states Gould in Full House.

Gould's failure falls into three categories. 1) His use of batting average as a measuring device. 2) His mixing of leagues in gathering of data. 3) The advent of the DH in the AL in 1973 creates all sorts of problems with the data and is not addressed. Which also brings up the problem of mixing eras in baseball when looking at statistics.

Last summer Gould's study surfaced on rec.sport.baseball in the following post.

Date: Sun, 30 Aug 1998 14:56:46 -0500
From: danrl <danrl@IBM.NET>
Subject: Expansion and Gould Thesis

Paul Wendt commented in regards to Gould's thesis:

> Gould's thesis about competitive evolution and variation in baseball
> is true, I am sure. But I am sure only because I am sure that
> variation increases with each expansion. (Of course Rod Carew had

> that big year in '77, McCovey in '69, Killebrew in '61 . . . .)
> A few examples do not prove anything, but only because they do not
> measure league-wide variation. If Schell and others find no increase
> in league-wide variation in '61, '69, '77, and '93, then the Gould
> thesis is in big trouble as a principal explanation of an important
> phenomenon in baseball.

To recap: Gould hypothesized that the declining variation in batting averages over the course of baseball history evidenced an increase in the overall level of play. He noted that this declining variation plateaued around 1940.

While I intuitively believe in the merits of Gould thesis, I previously on this list raised two potential problem areas. Paul Wendt above notes a third area to investigate.

The table below calculates the standard deviation of batting average for all players with at least 300 at bats (the criteria Gould uses in his 1983 Vanity Fair article) over the past 45 years.

Year	StdDev	Year	StdDev	Year	StdDev
1953	.030	1968	.028	1983	.028
1954	.033	*1969	.029*	1984	.030
1955	.029	1970	.032	1985	.026
1956	.031	1971	.030	1986	.028
1957	.031	1972	.030	1987	.030
1958	.029	1973	.029	1988	.027
1959	.029	1974	.028	1989	.028
1960	.024	1975	.031	1990	.027
*1961	.028*	1976	.030	1991	.029
*1962	.027*	*1977	.029*	1992	.028
1963	.028	1978	.025	*1993	.030*
1964	.028	1979	.028	1994	.033
1965	.028	1980	.029	1995	.030
1966	.027	1981	.029	1996	.029
1967	.032	1982	.025	1997	.028

Average standard deviation 45 year period: .029
Average standard deviation 1961, 1962, 1969, 1977 & 1993: .029

In other words, no increase in league-wide variation exists in the expansion years.

--Dan Levitt

Lets look at Mr. Levitt's study using some other measures such as on-base percentage (OBP), slugging average (SLG), and on-base plus slugging (OPS). And see if the problem persists. We will turn our attention to OBP first.

Year	StdDev	Year	StdDev	Year	StdDev
1953	.038	1968	.039	1983	.035
1954	.043	*1969	.042*	1984	.035
1955	.043	1970	.044	1985	.035
1956	.043	1971	.040	1986	.035
1957	.043	1972	.040	1987	.040
1958	.041	1973	.039	1988	.036
1959	.037	1974	.038	1989	.036
1960	.036	1975	.040	1990	.036
*1961	.040*	1976	.035	1991	.036
*1962	.035*	*1977	.037*	1992	.038
1963	.034	1978	.033	*1993	.040*
1964	.037	1979	.037	1994	.042
1965	.037	1980	.037	1995	.037
1966	.035	1981	.039	1996	.041
1967	.040	1982	.035	1997	.040

Average standard deviation 45 year period: .039
Average standard deviation 1961, 1962, 1969, 1977 & 1993: .039

The results are the same as Levitt's calculations for Batting Average, but one should note that in every expansion year there is a bump upward from the previous year of 2-4 points other than 1962 which was the only time we had back to back expansion. Also note the standard deviation for OBP for the 1900-1997 period is .041. So lets move on to Slugging Average.

151

Year	StdDev	Year	StdDev	Year	StdDev
1953	.078	1968	.073	1983	.067
1954	.081	*1969	.085*	1984	.068
1955	.086	1970	.088	1985	.066
1956	.084	1971	.075	1986	.066
1957	.084	1972	.077	1987	.077
1958	.080	1973	.073	1988	.065
1959	.077	1974	.064	1989	.064
1960	.076	1975	.069	1990	.066
*1961	.088*	1976	.065	1991	.069
*1962	.074*	*1977	.075*	1992	.065
1963	.074	1978	.072	*1993	.075*
1964	.081	1979	.076	1994	.087
1965	.079	1980	.071	1995	.082
1966	.076	1981	.070	1996	.084
1967	.079	1982	.069	1997	.078

Average standard deviation 45 year period: .075
Average standard deviation 1961, 1962, 1969, 1977 & 1993: .079

Now we are looking in the right direction. We now have an upward swing of four points over the average standard deviation for this 45 year period (it should be noted that .075 is the standard deviation for the period 1900-1997 as well). And there is a bump upward from the previous year of 8-12 points with 10 points being the average if we throw out 1962. Now let's look at OPS:

Year	StdDev	Year	StdDev	Year	StdDev
1953	.110	1968	.107	1983	.093
1954	.117	*1969	.122*	1984	.094
1955	.118	1970	.125	1985	.091
1956	.117	1971	.108	1986	.090
1957	.120	1972	.110	1987	.107
1958	.112	1973	.104	1988	.093
1959	.105	1974	.094	1989	.091
1960	.104	1975	.102	1990	.093
*1961	.120*	1976	.092	1991	.096
*1962	.101*	*1977	.106*	1992	.094
1963	.102	1978	.097	*1993	.104*
1964	.111	1979	.105	1994	.119
1965	.110	1980	.098	1995	.111
1966	.106	1981	.101	1996	.115
1967	.115	1982	.097	1997	.109

Average standard deviation 45 year period: .105
Average standard deviation 1961, 1962, 1969, 1977 & 1993: .111

Again we see a net gain in expansion years, this time a six point gain. The bump upward is between 10-16 points with an average of 13.8 points. You have probably noticed some other trends going on. After the expansion of 61-62 and 77 the numbers return to their previous range the next year whereas in 1969 and 1993 the numbers go up again. In fact, 1970 marks the high point in both SLG and OPS for this period; if we look back to 1900, only the period of 1928-1930 ranks higher. After 1993, the numbers have not returned to their previous range (.093-.096) and have remained high. Part of the reason for this is that both 1994 and 1995 were strike shortened years. Another contributing factor is the addition of the Denver franchise, with the best offensive ballpark in all of baseball history.

When Gould first wrote in Vanity Fair, sabermetrics was in its infancy. The attack on batting average as a measure of a ballplayer's worth was evidently overlooked by Gould. This is a critical error. The reason is quite simple. The way you win a game is by scoring runs, not base hits; batting average only directly influences the latter, not the former. During the early years of baseball home runs were scarce. Batting Average was much more valuable up until 1920. Pitchers didn't issue a lot of walks in the early days because it was easier to throw the ball up and let the batter hit it. Batters would have to string together a series of hits before scoring runs, but with the end of the Deadball era in 1919 this changed. In the 20's a handful of hitters began to smack the ball out of the park on a regular basis which accelerated run scoring (see 1997 BBBA for more details). Gradually teams looked for more players who could hit the ball out of the park. The 1927 Yankees had three players hit homers in double figures; the 1998 Yankees had ten. It's no longer possible to pitch around one or two power hitters in a lineup--the whole batting order can take you deep. The result has been more walks as well as homers. Walks then take the place of hits and hence the relative little change in OBP.

This is the most critical shortcoming of Gould's study: he uses the wrong measuring stick, not taking into account that the game has changed. But there are other problems as well. Most of them revolve around the changing nature of the game. Between the mound moving back in 1893 and 1904 teams usually played 130-140 games with 154 games in 1898-1899. The fewer games played, the easier it is for a hot streak to lift a player over the .400 mark. It is not beyond belief that Rod Carew would have hit .400 in 1977 (an expansion year when he played 155 games and hit .388) in a 130-140 game season. Since Ted Williams last hit .400 in 1941 four players have exceeded .385 to come close to breaking the .400 mark. Tony Gwynn hit .394 in the strike shortened season of 1994 when he played in 110 games. George Brett hit .390 in 1980 in 117 games and Ted Williams himself hit .388 in 1957 while playing in 132 games.

Another offensive explosion occurred in 1929-1930 when the National League decided to join their junior partners in an slugfest. The standard deviation for those two years was .138 in OPS. Those two years were the two highest during the 20th Century. After the 1930 season the National League reverted to its previous style of play as the two leagues went their own way during the 30's (see Graphic Violence in the 1997 BBBA). They came back together in the 40's, 50's & 60's, but separated again during the 70's, 80's & 90's with the adoption of the DH in the American League. This is one reason why I think it would have been useful to separate the two leagues when making the study.

So is Gould off base? Not really: it's the way he put the data together that causes the problem. League averages fluctuate over time and the higher the offensive level the higher the variation, and the opposite is true as well. During periods of low offensive output the variation will shrink. How then do we determine if Gould's theory is right? The method I chose was to take matched occurrences and see if more recent years have less variation. We'll look at OBP first. Below are matched groups where the years are separated by more than five years.

Year	OBP	StdDev	Year	OBP	StdDev	Year	OBP	StdDev
1928	.344	.044	1945	.329	.040	1942	.323	.043
1939	.344	.042	1977	.329	.037	1943	.323	.037
1949	.344	.044				1978	.323	.033
			1946	.328	.044	1984	.323	.035
1935	.341	.040	1961	.328	.040	1985	.323	.035
1948	.341	.041				1991	.323	.036
			1901	.327	.051			
1900	.339	.048	1952	.327	.038	1902	.322	.047
1931	.339	.044	1975	.327	.040	1919	.322	.041
1994	.339	.042				1992	.322	.038
			1944	.326	.043			
1912	.337	.042	1962	.326	.035	1969	.320	.042
1932	.337	.041	1970	.326	.044	1976	.320	.035
1997	.337	.041	1980	.326	.037	1981	.320	.039
			1986	.326	.035	1989	.320	.036
1911	.336	.046						
1947	.336	.043	1913	.325	.043	1910	.318	.043
1951	.336	.040	1958	.325	.041	1915	.318	.042
1953	.336	.038	1973	.325	.039	1988	.318	.036
			1983	.325	.035			
1955	.332	.043	1990	.325	.036	1903	.317	.046
1993	.332	.040				1918	.317	.042
			1957	.324	.043	1971	.317	.040
1956	.331	.043	1959	.324	.037			
1987	.331	.040	1960	.324	.036	1917	.311	.038
			1974	.324	.038	1965	.311	.037
1933	.330	.042	1982	.324	.035	1972	.311	.040
1979	.330	.037						

So in the twenty groups above, 17 have a lower STD in the most recent year. In two exceptions there are only one or two points between them and both groups are at the ends of the spectrum as is the one with no difference. If you take the first year high and subtract the last year in each group, the average per group is .00485, or just under 5 points.

Now we'll turn our attention to SLG, and due to the increase in homers, we might expect this to be even more pronounced.

This time there were 22 groups and again two groups later years were higher than the first year and again one tie. This time the average group finished .00718 points lower in standard deviation. So again we have less variance as time goes on.

Year	SLG	StdDev	Year	SLG	StdDev	Year	SLG	StdDev
1929	.417	.093	1940	.392	.083	1933	.376	.080
1995	.417	.082	1959	.392	.077	1966	.376	.076
1921	.403	.078	1923	.391	.084	1941	.375	.083
1993	.403	.075	1931	.391	.085	1989	.375	.064
			1957	.391	.084			
1922	.401	.082	1985	.391	.066	1920	.372	.082
1977	.401	.075				1963	.372	.074
			1926	.389	.077	1965	.372	.079
1937	.399	.088	1982	.389	.069			
1961	.399	.088	1983	.389	.067	1969	.369	.085
						1974	.369	.064
1928	.397	.088	1960	.388	.076	1981	.369	.070
1934	.397	.081	1980	.388	.071			
1935	.397	.072				1901	.360	.075
1939	.397	.080	1970	.385	.088	1946	.360	.075
1953	.397	.078	1984	.385	.068			
1956	.397	.084	1990	.385	.066	1911	.357	.074
1979	.397	.076	1991	.385	.069	1967	.357	.079
1924	.394	.077	1964	.378	.081	1902	.344	.072
1955	.394	.086	1988	.378	.065	1943	.344	.064
1958	.394	.080						
			1947	.377	.073	1910	.326	.063
1927	.393	.085	1992	.377	.065	1916	.326	.060
1962	.393	.074						

Year	OPS	StdDev	Year	OPS	StdDev	Year	OPS	StdDev
1950	.748	.112	1979	.727	.105	1912	.695	.103
1987	.747	.107				1989	.695	.091
			1948	.723	.110			
1924	.742	.115	1951	.722	.105	1911	.693	.113
1937	.742	.125	1954	.723	.117	1974	.693	.094
			1986	.721	.090			
1923	.738	.125				1969	.689	.122
1927	.738	.124	1957	.715	.120	1981	.689	.101
1934	.738	.116	1980	.714	.098			
1935	.738	.105	1983	.714	.093	1901	.686	.121
			1985	.714	.091	1966	.686	.106
1926	.733	.112						
1953	.733	.110	1947	.713	.107	1944	.684	.115
			1960	.712	.104	1945	.684	.101
1931	.731	.124	1982	.713	.097	1965	.683	.110
1956	.729	.117						
1977	.730	.106	1941	.709	.124	1963	.681	.102
			1984	.708	.094	1976	.681	.092
1940	.726	.120	1991	.708	.096			
1955	.726	.118				1902	.665	.113
1961	.727	.120	1952	.696	.099	1903	.664	.108
			1988	.696	.083	1967	.664	.115
						1972	.664	.110

This time we turn our attention to OPS, but we are going to have to add years that may differ by a point to get enough groups.

This time there were only 18 groups and only one started off smaller than it finished with the average group coming in .01322 less than it started at. Overall we looked at 60 groups and only 5 groups ended up higher than they started, or only 8%. So evolution is out there if we group the data in a way that shows it.

But the nagging question remains: is this evolution really relevant to the actual nature of the game? Or is it just a feature of a "complex system" that is coincidental to actual "baseball evolution"? Let's begin by looking at the OPS STD's for the seasons in which there were .400 hitters:

.400 Seasons	
Year	**OPS StDev**
1901	.121
1911	.113
1912	.103
1920	.122
1922	.117
1923	.125
1924	.115
1925	.121
1930	.145
1941	.124
AVG	**.121**

The overall OPS STD over the 20th century (1900-97) is .108. Only one .400 season (Ty Cobb's .409 season in 1912) occurred in a year when the OPS STD was below the historical average. That average OPS STD for .400 seasons is pretty high; our plot of the STDs shows that the conditions which favor the presence of .400 hitters have occurred only intermittently since 1941, and are tied directly to offensive levels.

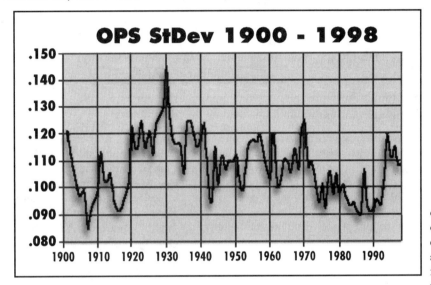

As for the evolution of the game itself (as opposed to its behavior as a complex system), we can see a consistent trend away from the importance of batting average in offense as we move through the twentieth century. We measure this by looking at the number of times the batter with the best BA also possesses the best OPS. Tracking this decade by decade, we see a dramatic and inexorable trend:

PERCENTAGE WHERE BEST BA AND BEST OPS ARE SAME PLAYER	
Decade	**Pct**
1900-09	80%
1910-19	50%
1920-29	40%
1930-39	40%
1940-49	45%
1950-59	45%
1960-69	20%
1970-79	20%
1980-89	15%
1990-	11%

(NL and AL data compiled separately)

The shifts in the game as measured in this fashion were sudden, but also contain rather long plateaus which make it harder to grasp the fundamental differences that have occurred in the game as the century has moved from front to back. The now common disconnection between high BA and high OPS is not only what brings about cult worship of extreme examples of this phenomenon (such as Rob Deer), but also causes people to denigrate the achievement of high-average performances (Carew in 1977, Brett in 1980, Gwynn in 1994) as being insignificant. It is the changing nature of the game that is most responsible for the extinction of the .400 hitter, not a continuing compression in the level of competition.

And finally, the notion that .400 hitters may in fact be permanently extinct is premature. Given the current rise in offensive levels, and with the possibility that baseball will embrace high offense as a way of building on its fan base, there is a good chance that we will see a .400 hitter in the next ten years. If that should occur, all of Gould's arguments concerning the evolution of complex systems will need some revision. We may well have the best measure of the ".400 hitter ambient conditions" in one final comparison (thanks to Don Malcolm for suggesting it), which is to overlay the five-year best BA average with the five-year ratio of best BA to best OPS. As the graph below demonstrates, this latter value happens to be in a similar numerical range as the best BA data, which makes it easy to grasp.

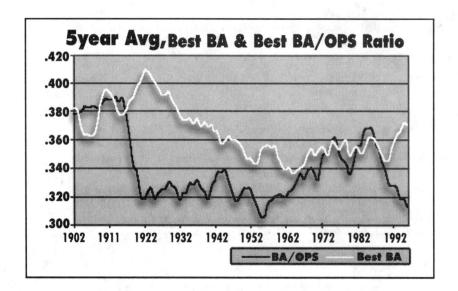

As you can see, the two measures are reasonably close during the deadball era (and you can see the effect of Ty Cobb on the BA line), but diverge sharply in 1920 as BA leads the offensive explosion. Over the course of the next forty years, these two lines slowly converge, as the various impacts on BA take their toll (the shift toward power hitting, night baseball, etc.) until they converge again in the sixties. What Gould does not take into account in his study is the fact that BA actually bottoms out (as measured by the five-year average) in the mid-sixties: as the chart shows, it has been making a steady comeback ever since. And with the recent offensive explosion, a gap between the five-year average best BA and the five-year best BA/best OPS ratio is re-emerging. If it continues in that direction, it may approach the 20s gap, which is the time period which produced eight of the twelve 20th-century .400 seasons.

PERCENTILES: PAST, PRESENT AND FUTURE

Tom Hull

INTRODUCTION

The percentile ranking system is a tool that we have been experimenting with for some time now as a means of making cross-era comparisons that don't get bogged down in major shifts between high scoring and low scoring eras, longer and shorter seasons, or similar discrepancies.

The main assumption behind the percentile rankings is that the best player for each year is a constant value. Whether this is true or not is highly debatable, but at least it gives us a lens through which we can view statistics in ways that reveal new insight and meaning.

We keep fiddling with the formulas, so this year's percentile rankings are different (in some ways improved) from the values that we used last year.

The percentile data was based on a Runs Created formula, which was calculated for each major league hitter from 1871 (the National Association) through 1998. The raw data came from Sean Lahman's www.baseball1.com database.

The same Runs Created formula was applied for each player/season:

$$(H + BB + HBP - CS) * (TB + (0.6 * SB) + SH + SF) /$$
$$(AB + BB + HBP + SF)$$

Any missing statistics were 0. The formula is a little arbitrary, but it seems unlikely that the more technical formulas would make much of a difference. The only distortion that seems likely is that early players with high SB totals and no CS data may be slightly inflated. On the other hand, in the dead ball (and relatively high error) era it would have been more distorting to ignore SB data.

The Runs Created totals were then sorted for each year (all leagues are combined), and the top N players were ranked with percentile values, ranging from 99 (the top score) down to 1. In this case, N is the number of non-pitcher hitters per team (8, or 9 for DH teams) times the number of teams. The N player limit was imposed because otherwise (if we rank everybody) the expansion of the bench and platooning and heavier use of the farm system causes regular players in more recent years to have inflated percentiles.

The main problem with using simple Runs Created totals is that they don't adequately take into account the number of outs made. In some ways it would be better to sort RC/O (especially once we made the cutoff at N). Maybe next year. Another problem is the lack of park adjustments. Again, maybe next year.

Once we have the percentile data, the most common way that we present it is to take the percentile scores and sort them, with the best year first, then the second best year, and so forth. This gives us listings like the following:

Rogers Hornsby	8447	99 99 99 98 98 97 97 95 95 92 92 90 83 75 69
Ryne Sandberg	5566	97 97 95 94 94 93 81 79 68 68 64 52 52 26
Hardy Richardson	4986	96 94 90 89 87 86 85 77 77 77 69 40 28
Jackie Robinson	4693	96 96 96 92 88 86 84 69 40 24
Frankie Frisch	4490	94 93 92 89 80 78 76 76 71 69 66 66 59 35 34 12
Roberto Alomar	4447	96 93 92 92 83 79 76 74 66 65 62
Lou Whitaker	3979	94 90 84 83 79 77 76 76 72 66 58 56 55 55 53 51 26 25
Chuck Knoblauch	3440	94 93 88 87 81 68 64 64
Nellie Fox	3322	89 82 82 82 79 76 76 73 71 66 50 44 29 27 12
Johnny Evers	2135	85 85 73 71 68 62 61 54 53 53 25 13
Davey Johnson	1652	94 76 61 59 59 58 50 34 22 3
Frank White	900	77 66 55 53 49 48 46 44 38 37 28 23 18 11

The (usually) 4-digit number is nothing more than an attempt to sort the percentile scores in a way that rates the more impressive careers above less impressive careers. This isn't totally successful, but seems to be "right" (i.e., it agrees with our subjective evaluations) more often than not. The algorithm for calculating this number is as follows (where L is the ordered list of percentile rankings):

```
Score = 0.0
K = 20
for I in L {Score = Score + ((I / 99.0) ** 3) * (K / 20) if (K > 1)K = K - 1 }
Score = Score / 0.09733
```

There are two main ideas embodied in this algorithm:

1. That the difference between high percentiles (e.g., 99 vs. 98) is more significant than an equivalent difference between low percentiles (e.g., 2 vs. 1). This is handled by converting the percentile into a ratio (99 becomes 1.0, 1 becomes 0.11), then taking the cube of the ratio.
2. That a player's best year should count more than lesser years. This is done by using 100% of the best year, 95% of the second best year, etc., down to a floor 5% of the 20th et seq. ranked years.

In other words, the algorithm tries to fold players with long careers in with players who had shorter careers but higher peak performances. Then there is the mysterious 0.09733 factor: the purpose of this magic number is to scale the Score result into a 4-digit number where the very top-rated player (turns out to be Ty Cobb) winds up with 9999.

One new thing that we did this year was to start analyzing the percentile data according to player ages. Player age was calculated as of June 30 for each year. We can then list players year-by-year, lined up by age, and slice the results for any age segment that we might like. The same list of second basemen from above would appear as follows:

Player	Pct	20	21	22	23	24	25	26	27	28	29	30	31	32	33	34	35	36	37	38
Rogers Hornsby	8447	92	95	75	90	95	98	99	92	98	99	83	97	97	99	69				
Ryne Sandberg	5566			64	68	97	94	81	68	79	94	97	93	95	52		52	26		
Hardy Richardson	4986				77	69	77	77	87	89	90	96	86	40	85	94	28			
Jackie Robinson	4693								92	84	96	86	96	96	88	69	24	40		
Frankie Frisch	4490		34	92	69	94	89	66	71	93	80	76	78	59	35	76	66	12		
Roberto Alomar	4447	66	83	74	92	93	96	76	79	92	62	65								
Lou Whitaker	3979		53	51	25	55	76	94	76	90	79	72	58	83	55	84	77	56	66	26
Chuck Knoblauch	3440			64	81	64	87	93	94	88	68									
Nellie Fox	3322			12	82	73	66	79	82	71	89	76	82	76	44	50	29	27		
Johnny Evers	2135		53	53	25	68	61	85	71	62	85	54	73	13						
Davey Johnson	1652				34	59	58	61	59	76	22	94	50		3					
Frank White	900						11	23	38	37	44	49	66	46	53	55	77	48	28	18

For instance, we could slice this to spotlight players from age 28-34, in which case Jackie Robinson ranks #3 all-time among second basemen:

We've only begun to scratch the surface of the interesting comparisons that are possible with percentile ranking data. You will find several more examples below, along with a Hall of Fame Watch for selected active players. We don't claim this as anything near the holy grail of baseball statistics, but it is a tool which makes it possible to bring otherwise incompatible data into much clearer focus.

Player	Pct	28	29	30	31	32	33	34
Joe Morgan	5012	96	97	98	99	99	93	48
Rogers Hornsby	4786	98	99	83	97	97	99	
Jackie Robinson	4519	92	84	96	86	96	96	88
Charlie Gehringer	4284	35	89	95	92	93	96	95
Eddie Collins	4253	97	95	93	66	95	95	72
Nap Lajoie	4236	92	99	20	98	88	92	87
Hardy Richardson	3569	87	89	90	96	86	40	85
Ryne Sandberg	3562	79	94	97	93	95	52	

PERCENTILES AND THE HALL OF FAME

Player	HOF?	Years	Pct
King Kelly	y	1878-91	6538
Deacon White	y	1871-90	5960
Ted Simmons		1971-85	5093
Cal McVey		1871-79	5092
Joe Torre		1961-76	4885
Johnny Bench	y	1968-83	4754
Gary Carter		1975-88	3916
Mike Piazza		1993-98	3879
Buck Ewing	y	1881-96	3694
Yogi Berra	y	1947-61	3658
Carlton Fisk		1972-91	3611
Mickey Cochrane	y	1925-35	2871
Roy Campanella	y	1948-57	2700
Bill Dickey	y	1929-43	2507
Charlie Bennett		1878-91	2492

What has always been a popular application for percentiles, of course, is to examine career achievements and compare the results with the list of players enshrined in the Hall of Fame. The best way to do this is to organize the players by position, but be warned that these percentile lists have the capability of generating heated arguments. Here are the top 15 catchers in baseball history according to the percentile system:

We can also look at this list organized by age, showing the career arc of each individual on the above list. As we'll see, it's rare for a catcher to dominate offensively in the manner that Mike Piazza has over the last few seasons:

Player/Age	20	21	22	23	24	25	26	27	28	29	30	31	32	33	34	35	36	37	38	39	40	41	42	43
King Kelly	58	95	86	95	91	69	98	89	98	93	92	88	67	47										
Deacon White				79	52	96	85	97	91	99	72	88	19	76	70	65	93	57	66	49	74		38	
Ted Simmons		71	89	89	84	95	75	87	91	74	87	44	63	87	12	64								
Cal McVey	96	81	79	99	99	86	94	78	79															
Joe Torre	29		67	89	83	94	70	51	84	94	99	82	71	73	12	25								
Johnny Bench	78	83	94	62	97	78	97	92	61	78	51	64	39	29	28	8								
Gary Carter		71		84	66	73	82	72	92	78	91	88	65	34	29									
Mike Piazza					92	86	89	90	98	90														
Buck Ewing		34	75	88	84	78	40	38	85	69	80		78	92		61	14							
Yogi Berra			12	66	51	92	79	82	78	89	77	88	59	56	63	36	43							
Carlton Fisk				88	61	12	38	65	94	92	13	67	57	54	83	31	77	9	46					
Mickey Cochrane			50	33	78	69	69	72	86	88	86	60	66						35	58	71	42		
Roy Campanella						7	69	67	95	65	95	14	85	28	12									
Bill Dickey			43	39	59	46	75	50	46	79	91	83	82	14	30	12	43							
Charlie Bennett				27		13	86	90	89	72	82	22		28		14	6							
AVG	65	73	66	71	79	74	71	73	81	85	82	68	58	57	36	35	38	67	38	48	55	58	55	42

The organization by age gives us a good sense of career patterns; as can be seen, these top catchers bloomed offensively a bit later than the canonical age-27 peak would indicate. (It's important to note, however, that several of these players were actually playing a position other than catcher in some of their peak seasons--Joe Torre and Deacon White come immediately to mind.)

It's also interesting to see how many of these players are still generating a percentile ranking after the age of 30. The precipitous decline that occurs even for top players at catcher is shown in the table below:

Age	28	29	30	31	32	33	34	35	36	37	38	39
# players	15	14	13	12	12	12	9	10	6	2	2	2
# over 50	14	14	13	9	9	7	3	4	1	2	1	0

Space doesn't permit us to provide a glimpse at every position in depth, or even to look at the entire Hall of Fame population in this year's BBBA; such an effort is likely a book unto itself. We will return with a more comprehensive look at the HoF in next year's installment. Some important things to keep in mind until then: the standards for HoF election as measured by percentiles are at significantly different levels according to position: the offensive careers of Johnny Bench, Buck Ewing, Mickey Cochrane, and Yogi Berra would be nowhere near the value needed for outfielders and first basemen to be considered seriously for induction.

Later in this article, we'll look at the Hall of Fame prospects for selected active players.

LOOKING INTO THE FUTURE

Another application of the percentile system is to project a young player's career into the future. One way that we do this is by looking for matching percentile scores at young ages. In this way, we can see what the general level of the past players was, and forecast the likely arc of a young player's career. This often produces interesting, though certainly not conclusive, results.

As an example of this process, let's look at two highly touted young outfielders, the Expos' Vladimir Guerrero (22) and the Braves' Andruw Jones (21). Guerrero broke out in 1998, posting a 93 percentile score; Jones made significant strides last year, but his percentile score was only 75---good, but not great.

By looking for matches or close near-misses with past players, we get a sense of what the development prospects are for the two players. Here are the matches for Vladimir Guerrero (93 percentile at age 22):

Name	Years	Pct	19	20	21	22	23	24	25	26	27	28
George Brett	1974-93	7785			34	93	97	91	77	98	99	86
Eddie Mathews	1952-67	6706		66	96	93	93	89	92	81	98	98
Ken Griffey	1989-98	6022	57	93	96	93	98	97	24	94	98	97
Jake Beckley	1888-06	5133		46	67	93	80	71	81	82	77	40
Cesar Cedeno	1970-85	4315	34	65	97	93	92	80	92	77	2	43
Vladimir Guerrero	1997-98	794			23	93						

As you can see, this is pretty fast company. The worst player on this list, and by a wide margin as measured by percentiles through the age of 28, is Cesar Cedeno. Two of the five are currently in the HoF (Mathews and Beckley), with Brett the likely inductee in 1999 and Griffey another certainty down the road a few years. There's always a chance that Guerrero might regress, or fall victim to injuries, but this is a very impressive list.

When we look at Andruw Jones, we don't see quite the same rosy picture that we were able to paint for Guerrero. This is in spite of the fact that Jones is a year younger. That 75 percentile score, even at 21, is not that compelling. Here are the percentile matches for Andruw:

Name	Years	Pct	19	20	21	22	23	24	25	26	27	28
Juan Gonzalez	1991-98	3786			75	84	95	72	53	90	87	96
Bill Dahlen	1891-08	3494			75	89	73	91	55	92	36	74
Ruben Sierra	1986-96	3439		34	75	75	97	81	97	80	58	68
Garry Templeton	1977-90	1374			75	65	87	59	45	36	19	30
Andruw Jones	1997-98	338		25	75							

The matches here aren't quite so scintillating. Check the average career score for these players, and then compare them to the average scores posted by the 22-year olds. While Andruw can always be an exception, his "matches player" set at age 21 doesn't show any strong indication of HoF level performance.

Another use for percentiles is to look at the probabilities of future performance. For example, Mo Vaughn (who posted a 97 percentile at age 30 for the Red Sox in 1998) was signed to a whopping $65 million contract by the Anaheim Angels over the off-season. What can the Angels expect to get for their money over the next five years? By looking at all of the 30-year old first basemen in baseball history with percentile scores of 90 or higher, and tracking their subsequent performance levels, we can use the past as a signpost for Mo's possible future:

Name	30	31	32	33	34	35	36	37	38
Jimmie Foxx	99	97	95	85	9				
Cap Anson	98	82	98	92	97	91	97	89	86
Cecil Cooper	98	96	95	95	64	86	47		
Lou Gehrig	97	99	96	99	97	93			
Rod Carew	97	99	95	55	87	78	73	73	21
Mo Vaughn	97								
Ripper Collins	97	89	22	46	52				
Rafael Palmeiro	96	92	80	93					
Fred McGriff	96	83	83	72	71				
Willie McCovey	96	99	97	53	8	81	63	54	
Ted Kluszewski	96	85		16					
Dan Brouthers	95	96	91	97	99	48	90		23
Harmon Killebrew	95	97	35	98	92	86	74		9
Gil Hodges	95	87	83	92	61	69			
Bob Watson	94	86	68	70	70				
Roger Connor	93	94	97	88	97	83	70	67	60
Steve Garvey	92	92	80	71	43	64	83	49	
Jeff Bagwell	92								
Mike Hargrove	92	82	64	52	17	4			
Donn Clendenon	91	40	76	20	55				
Dave Orr		90							
Nick Etten	90	90	13						
90+ PCT YEARS	21	11	8	7	5	2	1	0	0
80+ PCT YEARS	---	18	12	9	6	6	3	1	0
AVERAGE PCT	95	89	76	72	64	71	75	66	40

The decline phase, on average, is pronounced but not precipitous. One-third of all 90+-percentile first basemen were still in the 90+ range three years later. Many of the players above who fell off sharply from their 90+ year at age 30 (Clendenon, Hargrove, Collins, Etten) did not have a string of 90+ seasons prior to their age-30 year, as is the case with Mo. On the other hand, there is Fred McGriff, who had an even longer string of 90+ seasons, and has fallen off markedly since 30. The Angels might have been more prudent to offer Mo a three-year deal, but the current vogue for long-term "trophy contracts" did not make this a viable possibilty. They're going to have to hope that Mo can beat the odds.

HALL OF FAME WATCH

PAUL MOLITOR (41): With >3000 hits, Molitor is probably automatic. He is unusual in that while his best years were at DH, his primary fielding position is 3B, a relatively skilled position. He came up at SS, played a couple of years at 2B, and has one year in the OF. Consequently, there is no need to limit his closest comparisons to one position. Players with similar careers include:

George Brett	7785	99 99 98 97 97 95 93 91 91 90 86 77 77 72 71 64 61 58 50 34
Jim O'Rourke	7636	96 96 95 94 94 92 92 92 92 92 92 91 78 77 76 74 73 59 57 54 44 42
Nap Lajoie	7488	99 99 98 98 95 92 92 89 88 87 86 82 79 76 60 48 46 27 20 17
Rickey Henderson	7238	99 97 97 95 94 93 92 91 90 87 82 79 78 67 61 57 45 43 39 12
Paul Molitor	7229	97 97 96 95 95 95 93 93 88 87 84 78 70 69 66 57 51 44 42 26
Dave Winfield	7184	97 96 95 95 93 92 92 87 87 86 84 83 81 80 77 70 65 62 58 25
Reggie Jackson	6786	97 97 94 94 92 92 90 89 86 84 83 79 79 71 60 52 51 50 7 3
Roberto Clemente	6529	98 96 94 92 92 91 91 90 87 87 79 70 66 63 57 38 30 13
Al Kaline	6369	97 95 93 92 92 90 89 85 85 84 80 73 71 66 65 65 60 55 44 36 14
Robin Yount	6151	99 98 95 94 93 91 90 85 72 72 68 64 61 61 56 52 50 47 34

If Molitor's standing in this list seems surprisingly high, it is probably because his best years occurred in his mid-30s. For instance, his standing in the age 34-39 range is topped only by a couple of guys named Aaron and Ruth:

Player	Pct	34	35	36	37	38	39
Hank Aaron	4301	97	96	91	98	89	88
Babe Ruth	4217	93	95	99	96	96	68
Paul Molitor	4069	97	96	97	95	70	88
Pete Rose	3961	96	98	90	91	94	72
Honus Wagner	3937	99	97	95	90	93	42
Cap Anson	3851	97	91	97	89	86	81
Tris Speaker	3779	94	98	87	92	88	79
Ted Williams	3645	8	94	90	92	98	92
Ty Cobb	3455	95	96	86	92	90	17
Willie Mays	3074	99	93	73	91	48	80
Stan Musial	3042	95	93	95	91	34	39

WADE BOGGS (40): With a 36 percentile in 1998, Boggs is nearly done, but he's close enough to 3000 hits that another year is all-but-mandatory. Among 3B, he trails only Mike Schmidt, George Brett, and Paul Molitor:

Mike Schmidt	8295	99 99 98 98 96 96 95 94 94 93 93 91 89 78 42 23
George Brett	7785	99 99 98 97 97 95 93 91 91 90 86 77 77 72 71 64 61 58 50 34
Paul Molitor	7229	97 97 96 95 95 95 93 93 88 87 84 78 70 69 66 57 51 44 42 26
Wade Boggs	7186	99 98 98 98 98 96 92 91 91 86 71 67 58 51 43 36 21
Eddie Mathews	6706	98 98 96 93 93 92 90 89 87 83 81 77 66 57 53 51
Dick Allen	6337	98 98 97 96 93 93 92 91 84 80 45 38 37
Ron Santo	6230	97 97 95 95 91 90 89 87 84 82 79 72 45 16

RICKEY HENDERSON (39): Henderson shows up in Molitor's table, very comparable in terms of percentiles. Rickey will probably rank higher in voters' minds because of his SB records, plus his by-now-commonplace ranking as baseball's all-time best leadoff hitter.

GARY GAETTI (39): Is he still around? Few 3B have had longer careers, and all of them were much better players. Let's list a few rather loose comps:

Brooks Robinson	4524	95 91 85 84 82 81 80 79 78 75 68 63 60 60 50 14 7 7
Darrell Evans	4395	99 90 86 84 79 79 77 76 75 71 68 64 58 45 40 39 19 14
Ezra Sutton	4155	95 94 89 89 87 75 68 68 64 60 56 51 45 40 36 31 29
Buddy Bell	3663	87 87 84 83 83 79 78 70 69 62 62 60 50 46 45 28
Lave Cross	2704	92 84 82 79 64 63 61 59 57 54 54 48 45 34 24 14 7
Larry Parrish	2456	90 86 83 73 69 63 58 50 45 43 39 22 16 10
Gary Gaetti	2430	93 83 78 71 64 57 57 55 55 53 50 49 48 46 40 20 13
Terry Pendleton	2323	94 91 71 70 69 65 34 26 21 16 13 12 11
Richie Hebner	1925	85 83 76 69 61 54 52 52 50 43 40 39 11 9
Jimmy Dykes	1157	78 67 62 56 56 53 52 51 47 43 42 37 36 26 25 20

Gaetti is so clearly not a HOF candidate that this listing reflects poorly on Lave Cross. Not that the latter had much of a bandwagon.

HAROLD BAINES (39): Baines is seven years past his last 80+ percentile year (13 years past a 90+), so while he started quite young and keeps hanging on, he isn't really going anywhere. There are some marginal HOFs in his comps:

Kiki Cuyler	4739	98 93 92 90 88 85 84 77 73 43 26 15 14 11
Jimmy Sheckard	4655	99 96 86 85 85 82 79 78 76 63 63 47 46 42 39
Hal McRae	4576	97 95 93 91 89 83 73 72 71 43 24 23 20 15
Harold Baines	4535	94 91 85 83 83 82 81 80 73 73 71 65 59 57 56 55 54 37 19
Jack Clark	4533	97 91 86 85 83 79 78 77 76 75 74 72 28 26 1
Richie Ashburn	4470	95 93 88 86 81 80 79 74 73 72 71 68 47 43
Harry Hooper	4324	95 87 87 81 80 79 79 78 78 75 69 63 60 59 57 36 7
Jose Cruz	4322	93 93 92 90 87 79 77 74 64 62 53 30 29 25 13 10

OTIS NIXON (39): Only 82 players in baseball history have made the percentile list at age 39. Of those, if we throw out the catchers (Wilbert Robinson, Chief Zimmer, Bob Boone, Rick Ferrell--a couple of odd HOFs there, and perhaps one more coming in Boone) and the shortstops (Bones Ely, Dickey Pearce--the latter an aging star in 1871), the lowest all-time scores are:

Dave Philley	926	79 63 62 57 50 46 40 30 30 20 14
Harry Wright	614	73 62 56 53
Jimmy Austin	504	63 56 53 51 46 45 40 35 23 20 16 7
Otis Nixon	428	64 50 50 48 45 42 37 32
Johnny Cooney	47	44 24 24 19 14 2
Estel Crabtree	9	29 20 6 2

TONY GWYNN (38): Gwynn has 3 90+ years in his last 5, which makes him seem as solid as ever. But while he ranks #9 among outfielders in the 33-38 age grouping, he trails three non-HOFs (Minnie Minoso, Dwight Evans, and Dixie Walker). Careerwise, the following are quite similar:

Willie Keeler	6804	99 96 94 93 93 92 90 90 88 88 85 82 76 41 23 11
Paul Waner	6567	96 95 94 93 93 91 91 90 88 85 85 84 62 54 23 12 10
Roberto Clemente	6529	98 96 94 92 92 91 91 90 87 87 79 70 66 63 57 38 30 13
Tony Gwynn	6512	98 96 96 95 94 92 91 85 83 80 77 72 70 61 57 11
Al Simmons	6503	97 97 96 94 92 92 91 89 89 82 74 72 66 44 33 20
Paul Hines	6487	99 99 94 93 91 89 88 85 84 82 79 77 66 66 60 60 58 24 8

Gwynn will probably move up a bit on this list. Clemente is similar for his batting titles.

TIM RAINES (38): It's surprising how well Raines ranks, given that he was eclipsed by Rickey Henderson in his prime, and hasn't been a contender for quite a while. The comps here are mostly medium (not marginal) HOFs:

Duke Snider	6388	99 98 98 98 98 92 91 86 86 68 46 26 20 20
Kirby Puckett	6387	98 98 97 95 94 89 89 88 86 82 81 50
Sherry Magee	6325	97 96 96 96 93 92 88 85 84 82 81 70 46 37 36
Tim Raines	6320	97 96 96 96 96 90 86 85 83 76 73 69 67 64 62 22 18
Goose Goslin	6306	97 95 95 93 93 92 87 87 84 82 78 73 69 66 27
Fred Clarke	6290	97 92 92 92 90 90 89 88 87 86 81 80 74 66 55 50 30 11
Lou Brock	6196	95 94 93 92 91 90 89 87 86 86 86 73 70 54 32 26 23
Dwight Evans	6126	99 98 98 95 92 91 89 87 71 65 65 64 56 55 55 48 17 16 4

It's easy to forget how well Raines started out. Raines' age 21-26 stretch puts him in pretty exalted company:

Player	Pct	21	22	23	24	25	26
Ty Cobb	5157	98	99	99	99	98	95
Tris Speaker	4780	95	95	92	99	98	97
Hank Aaron	4740	92	95	96	96	99	97
Joe DiMaggio	4705	92	98	95	96	95	98
Mickey Mantle	4531	76	92	97	99	99	98
Frank Robinson	4473	94	84	95	95	97	99
Pete Browning	4457	96	89	93	99	89	98
Tim Raines	4298	90	83	96	96	96	97
Joe Jackson	4286	98	97	99	84	77	97
Rickey Henderson	4121	95	97	82	93	87	97
Stan Musial	4069	85	99	99	--	98	96
Ken Griffey	4015	96	93	98	97	24	94

JOE CARTER (38): Solid but overrated career, now over, puts him in range of some HOF marginals (Ashburn, Hooper, Doby), but doesn't really make him a candidate:

Frank Howard	4492	97 97 96 89 84 78 76 70 64 50 43 20 15
Amos Otis	4433	93 90 89 87 86 85 83 80 74 57 57 55 32 7
Brett Butler	4433	93 88 87 86 85 79 78 78 75 74 73 69 67 7
Bobby Murcer	4311	97 96 87 87 81 79 77 75 70 69 44 23
Joe Carter	4302	95 91 88 87 85 84 80 70 67 64 62 49 48 29
Dixie Walker	4297	97 94 93 89 82 80 79 66 59 54 50 36 25
Fred Lynn	4223	99 97 91 84 81 80 69 67 60 58 54 45 31 20 16
Larry Doby	4067	95 91 86 84 83 81 81 78 68 63 13

ANDRES GALARRAGA (37): Had a big year (very surprising to critics who thought his Denver sojurn was all park effects), so maybe he's not done. Careerwise, he rates with some marginal HOF candidates:

Steve Garvey	5783	97 96 96 93 92 92 89 83 80 71 64 49 43 27 18
Keith Hernandez	5727	97 97 95 91 89 89 87 86 82 80 67 54 27
Gil Hodges	5141	95 92 92 90 90 87 87 83 83 69 61 43
Don Mattingly	5435	99 98 98 94 92 90 80 72 70 65 51 12 6
Andres Galarraga	5120	95 94 94 92 92 91 85 80 70 66 15 6
Bill Terry	5081	95 94 94 90 90 90 89 85 64 63
Cecil Cooper	5066	98 96 95 95 93 86 83 64 60 57 47 42 35

However, Galarraga's real problem is his standing against his peers, many of whom have already passed him by. The following is in columns by age, up to Galarraga's age 37:

Player	Pct	21	22	23	24	25	26	27	28	29	30	31	32	33	34	35	36	37
Frank Thomas	6096		19	98	98	97	99	98	96	97	85							
Rafael Palmeiro	6056		4	82	70	92	98	83	96	94	96	92	80	93				
Fred McGriff	6013			26	95	96	96	90	95	94	96	83	83	72	71			
Mark McGwire	5548			96	85	76	89	49	92			87	95	96	99			
Will Clark	5276		46	86	96	98	91	92	86	66	89	78	47	58	83			
Andres Galarraga	5120				15	70	95	80	66		6	94	91	85	92	94	92	
Jeff Bagwell	5102			86	89	91	98	81	96	97	92							
Mark Grace	4607				67	87	86	71	91	93	66	94	73	86	85			
Mo Vaughn	4501				27	92	92	96	98	92	97							
Wally Joyner	3616				90	90	82	82	16	87	67	72	70	76	40	67	52	
Cecil Fielder	3293					98	93	80	82	79	70	75	24	26				
John Olerud	3206	40	63	74	98	79	68	45	84	95								
Tino Martinez	2222				54	40	52	90	75	94	75							

The fact that Galarraga is even close is due to his strong showing in the age 32-37 range. The top 1B in this age range are:

Player	Pct	32	33	34	35	36	37
Stan Musial	4595	99	97	95	93	95	91
Cap Anson	4434	98	92	97	91	97	89
Andres Galarraga	3935	94	91	85	92	94	92
Lou Gehrig	3390	96	99	97	93		
George Brett	3361	99	77	64	97	72	95
Willie Stargell	3202	95	98	96	85	62	6
Dan Brouthers	3196	91	97	99	48	90	
Roger Connor	3190	97	88	97	83	70	67

CAL RIPKEN (37): Ripken's so automatic he made the year-end highlight reels just for missing a game. He won't catch Honus Wagner, but that's his only limit. The all-time top shortstops are:

Honus Wagner	9019	99 99 99 98 98 97 97 96 96 95 95 93 90 89 80 75 57 54 **42** 21
Robin Yount	6151	99 98 95 94 93 91 90 85 72 72 68 64 61 61 56 52 50 47 34
Cal Ripken	6143	99 97 96 92 91 86 82 80 80 80 76 74 74 69 66 63 54
Ernie Banks	5784	97 96 95 93 92 84 81 80 77 77 76 71 68 67 62 31
Arky Vaughan	5023	97 93 92 92 90 89 84 83 65 58 53 52
Joe Cronin	4975	92 92 89 89 87 87 86 85 84 78 59 51 5
George Wright	4617	97 97 96 94 85 83 83 62 29
George Davis	4558	96 93 86 84 83 79 77 75 73 70 69 69 64 63 58 58 34 30

ERIC DAVIS (36): Davis has some pretty close comps. Subjectively, he seems like a much better player. One difference is that none of Davis' comps played past age 33.

Elmer Smith [1]	3071	94 88 86 84 79 74 58 39 28
Roy Cullenbine	2977	92 89 83 82 82 72 65 9
Irish Meusel	2960	89 88 81 78 77 75 74 69 43
Eric Davis	2950	93 88 86 81 77 73 61 41 20
Sam Mertes	2920	93 92 88 77 71 68 61 46 22
Von Hayes	2919	93 90 87 85 70 69 50 42 14

TONY FERNANDEZ (36): Fernandez has had the stigma of an unwanted man since Toronto dumped him, but he keeps showing up on pennant contenders (never with a secure job). His career comps put him in some pretty good company:

Herman Long	2993	93 88 82 76 71 70 65 61 60 59 58 45 23 17
Alvin Dark	2855	89 89 84 77 74 68 66 56 54 50 50 41 7
Tony Fernandez	2740	91 82 81 80 67 67 64 63 60 60 57 27 18
Bobby Wallace	2535	86 81 81 72 69 67 66 66 65 59 48 46 43 17 9 4
Dave Concepcion	2333	90 81 76 76 76 58 57 53 50 46 40 27 18 6 3
Dick Groat	2329	94 79 75 73 70 64 56 54 50 46 40 33 17

DARRYL STRAWBERRY (36) / PAUL O'NEILL (35): These two have turned out to be pretty evenly matched. They're in a thick crowd, which is a cut below the marginal HOFs.

Cy Seymour	3997	99 95 89 85 83 79 75 66 40 10
Roy White	3964	93 93 90 87 83 81 71 71 62 60 26
Jackie Jensen	3925	94 92 89 86 85 84 79 64 52
Ken Williams	3890	97 96 95 85 77 76 76 44 39 23
Gavvy Cravath	3879	96 96 94 89 85 67 63 61 25
Bill Nicholson	3862	98 98 94 77 76 75 71 71 11 10
Darryl Strawberry	3844	95 94 92 80 80 79 77 66 62 28
Paul O'Neill	3839	95 90 88 86 81 80 77 63 61 59 51
Chick Stahl	3745	95 95 85 84 83 80 76 62 50 23
Earle Combs	3736	95 88 88 85 81 78 78 77 54 14

EDGAR MARTINEZ (35): Martinez is probably too old to put together much in the way of a career score, though if you rank him as a 3B he isn't too shabby:

Frank Baker	5152	95 95 95 93 92 90 85 78 76 51 15
Ken Boyer	4892	94 91 91 91 89 89 88 86 65 57 53 53 12 2
Edgar Martinez	4817	99 96 95 94 93 87 76 66
Bob Elliott	4402	95 92 92 85 84 82 80 76 67 64 62 56 25 7
Darrell Evans	4395	99 90 86 84 79 79 77 76 75 71 68 64 58 45 40 39 19 14
Stan Hack	4258	95 92 92 88 88 80 76 68 67 60 40 33 28

However, his ranking in the 32-35 year group is not far from the top:

Player	Pct	32	33	34	35
Willie Mays	3535	98	99	99	93
Babe Ruth	3394	98	99	93	95
Lou Gehrig	3390	96	99	97	93
Stan Musial	3357	99	97	95	93
Sam Thompson	3274	94	97	94	97
Edgar Martinez	3253	99	93	95	94
Pete Rose	3231	96	90	96	98
Tris Speaker	3228	97	91	94	98
Billy Williams	3191	98	95	99	85
Cap Anson	3167	98	92	97	91

DEVON WHITE (35): My impression is that White is similar to, but not quite as good as, Garry Maddox. The comps to age 35 bear this out:

Charlie Jamieson	2254	93 90 76 68 65 54 51 37 34 20 18
Garry Maddox	2240	91 86 81 69 59 58 56 48 48 37 29 2
Mickey Rivers	2191	91 86 75 71 66 58 58 52 6
Cesar Tovar	2190	85 79 78 77 74 71 62 35 20 11
Dode Paskert	2167	89 87 79 72 64 58 55 36 24 18
Devon White	2165	89 81 76 71 66 63 61 59 49 37 24
Curt Walker	2061	91 85 72 70 60 59 56 49 42

KEN CAMINITI (35): Caminiti's MVP year was only a 94 percentile. His comps to age 35 include one HOF, but the list of 3B better than Freddy Lindstrom is lengthy.

Ken Keltner	2879	94 89 82 79 76 72 55 53 40 32
Pinky Higgins	2814	88 85 79 76 72 72 70 66 65 58 50 46
Heinie Zimmerman	2792	96 84 82 79 75 69 61 52 33 24
Kevin Seitzer	2693	92 84 81 80 75 73 61 53 30
Ken Caminiti	2680	94 88 80 75 73 65 58 57 47 31
Freddy Lindstrom	2637	94 92 79 76 72 65 50 23 19 14 1
Howard Johnson	2634	97 90 85 78 70 23 19 14 4
Art Devlin	2632	92 89 79 74 73 72 63 46 14

The difference is that if we look at the same data, organized by year, only Higgins lasted as long as Caminiti, and Caminiti probably has a couple of years left.

PLAYER	PCT	19	20	21	22	23	24	25	26	27	28	29	30	31	32	33	34	35
Ken Keltner	2879			72	89	55	79	76	40	82		32	53	94				
Pinky Higgins	2814						88	85	76	58	72	65	46	50	72	70	66	79
Heinie Zimmerman	2792					24	75	96	84	82	52	69	79	61	33			
Kevin Seitzer	2693							92	81	80	75		61	30	53	73	84	
Ken Caminiti	2680								65	31	57	73	47	75	88	94	80	58
Freddy Lindstrom	2637	14	72	79	94	65	92	19	50	76	23	1						
Howard Johnson	2634					23	14		85	70	97	78	90	19		4		
Art Devlin	2632						79	72	92	89	74	73	63	14	46			

BOBBY BONILLA (35): Bonilla is classified as an OF now, which seems OK given that his defensive reputation at 3B would be a liability. His comps are in the upper tier of non-HOFs. He should have a couple more respectable years, but is unlikely to make any real progress on this list.

Ken Singleton	5587	95 95 95 95 94 87 84 81 78 76 68 62 23
Greg Luzinski	5523	98 97 96 92 91 89 88 85 81 47 38 33 13
Joe Medwick	5518	96 95 94 92 90 88 86 85 76 76 75 54 12
George Gore	5486	99 94 93 93 92 91 84 82 81 71 48 43 10 4
Reggie Smith	5254	96 95 94 90 86 84 84 83 81 78 67 47 44 42 4
Joe Kelley	5161	97 96 94 92 89 88 82 73 68 66 66 65 39 22 4
Rocky Colavito	5061	95 95 95 91 91 87 87 74 71 68 50 17
Bobby Bonilla	5006	95 95 94 93 90 82 81 81 79 59 57 29 9
Mike Tiernan	4978	96 95 95 91 87 87 86 83 66 51 48 34
Chuck Klein	4905	99 98 98 97 95 80 66 55 54 33 30 19
George Foster	4879	98 98 97 96 83 81 79 68 62 57 45 38 11
Edd Roush	4801	94 92 91 89 88 88 85 78 75 66 59 50 32 10 4
Del Ennis	4798	95 93 92 90 89 85 83 76 68 64 63 61

MARK MCGWIRE (34): McGwire posted his first 99 percentile year in 1998, at age 34. The only other players to do that were: Dan Brouthers, Ed Delahanty, Honus Wagner, Willie Mays, and Billy Williams. However, McGwire is far behind those guys up through age 34:

Player	Pct	20	21	22	23	24	25	26	27	28	29	30	31	32	33	34
Willie Mays	8551	65			98	99	94	97	99	97	99	93	98	98	99	99
Dan Brouthers	8139		23		94	99	99	95	97	99	95	95	96	91	97	99
Ed Delahanty	7754	11	6	69	47	86	99	93	99	99	96	99	99	83	97	99
Honus Wagner	7478				21	75	89	99	95	96	98	98	97	96	99	99
Billy Williams	7187				75	89	92	95	98	91	92	95	88	98	95	99
Mark McGwire	5548				96	85	76	89	49	92			87	95	96	99

The obvious reason is the holes in his career, due to injuries, but it also appears that McGwire has simply become a better hitter. In his closest comps to age 34, only Johnny Mize (who missed three WWII years) approaches McGwire's closing level.

Player	Pct	20	21	22	23	24	25	26	27	28	29	30	31	32	33	34
Johnny Mize	5953				69	95	97	99	98	89	93				91	97
Keith Hernandez	5727			54	82	67	97	97	95	87	86	89	89	91	80	27
Mark McGwire	5548				96	85	76	89	49	92			87	95	96	99
Don Mattingly	5435			6	98	98	99	92	90	94	12	70	80	72	65	51
Steve Garvey	5381				18	27	93	96	96	89	97	92	92	80	71	43
Will Clark	5276			46	86	96	98	91	92	86	66	89	78	47	58	83
Hank Greenberg	5237			61	96	99		99	98	95	99					49
Willie McCovey	5208	37	11	32	22	95	30	93	94	87	96	99	97	53	8	

Player	Pct	32	33	34
Willie Mays	2862	98	99	99
Honus Wagner	2792	96	99	99
Billy Williams	2721	98	95	99
Lou Gehrig	2717	96	99	97
Stan Musial	2683	99	97	95
Babe Ruth	2657	98	99	93
Mark McGwire	2647	95	96	99
Willie Stargell	2607	95	98	96
Hank Aaron	2604	95	97	97
Dan Brouthers	2561	91	97	99
Cap Anson	2549	98	92	97
Edgar Martinez	2549	99	93	95
Harry Stovey	2540	98	95	94

If we just look at the three years from age 32-34, McGwire's performance is not unprecedented, but ranks very highly (conspicuously close to Babe Ruth):

BARRY LARKIN (34): Through age 34, Larkin is in the range of HOF shortstops, but not a sure bet. His age 34 comps:

George Davis	4475	96	93	86	84	83	79	77	75	73	70	69	64	63	58	58
Vern Stephens	4308	95	91	91	88	87	82	78	76	72	52	18	15			
Jack Glasscock	3994	95	90	90	89	89	74	69	63	62	57	55	46	37	27	19 12
Alan Trammell	3939	97	88	87	87	86	78	76	68	67	52	31	31	30	27	
Barry Larkin	3886	90	89	86	86	85	84	83	80	53	45	23	16			
Ed McKean	3865	91	87	86	84	84	80	78	75	72	69	48	47			
Joe Sewell	3804	95	87	86	86	83	83	76	66	63	55	46	44	14		
Lou Boudreau	3556	96	91	84	83	83	74	72	68	56	41	6				
Bill Dahlen	3333	92	91	89	75	74	73	67	63	59	57	56	55	49	36	

Larkin does a bit better with the age 29-34 comp list, so his prospects for improving his standing are good. After Honus Wagner and Joe Cronin:

Player	Pct	29	30	31	32	33	34
Cal Ripken	2474	80	99	69	74	82	66
Barry Larkin	2283	53	80	90	89	16	86
Ed McKean	2230	80	87	86	84	47	69
Alvin Dark	2180	89	84	89	77	41	54
Pee Wee Reese	2049	76	92	56	77	76	73
Luke Appling	2017	91	77	4	67	84	75
Jack Glasscock	1856	95	89	27	63	69	12
Alan Trammell	1844	97	76	31	87	27	

FRED MCGRIFF (34) / WILL CLARK (34) / MARK GRACE (34): There's a thick crowd of age 34 first basemen (including Mark McGwire). We've sorted them by age under Andres Galarraga, but let's list the age-34 cumulative comps here (leaving out some younger players, like Frank Thomas and Jeff Bagwell, and other players with higher peaks but holes in their careers, like Johnny Mize and Hank Greenberg):

Harmon Killebrew	6268	98	97	95	94	94	92	92	89	85	82	70	35	
Orlando Cepeda	6111	97	96	95	92	92	90	90	88	87	81	72	70	17
Rafael Palmeiro	6056	98	96	96	94	93	92	92	83	82	80	70	4	
Fred McGriff	6013	96	96	96	95	95	94	90	83	83	72	71	26	
Keith Hernandez	5727	97	97	95	91	89	89	87	86	82	80	67	54	27
Mark McGwire	5548	99	96	96	95	92	89	87	85	76	49			
Don Mattingly	5435	99	98	98	94	92	90	80	72	70	65	51	12	6
Steve Garvey	5381	97	96	96	93	92	92	89	80	71	43	27	18	
Will Clark	5276	98	96	92	91	89	86	86	83	78	66	58	47	46
Willie McCovey	5208	99	97	96	95	94	93	87	53	37	32	30	22	11 8

Gil Hodges	5018	95 92 92 90 90 87 87 83 83 61 43
Ed Konetchy	4660	97 92 90 88 88 82 78 77 73 67 65 56 42 27
Cecil Cooper	4657	98 96 95 95 93 83 64 60 57 42 35
Mark Grace	4607	94 93 91 87 86 86 85 73 71 67 66
Jake Beckley	4357	93 89 87 83 82 81 80 80 77 71 69 67 55 46 40
Kent Hrbek	4356	95 91 86 85 85 83 83 83 68 68 50 45 29
Rudy York	4344	97 96 88 85 84 79 79 79 69 53 50
George Scott	4326	94 93 90 85 83 82 82 79 68 61 60 27
Bill Terry	4269	95 94 94 90 90 89 64 63

Clark and Grace have essentially no HOF chances. Their problem is not so much that their paces are marginal (although they are), as that the competition among their peers is so stiff. (Rafael Palmeiro, Clark's college chum, is a year younger and already ahead of McGriff; Frank Thomas, Jeff Bagwell, and Mo Vaughn are younger still.) McGriff, on the other hand, looked for a while like he had a real HOF shot, but his immediate problem is that his last 4 year stretch has been well below his previous pace. For ages 31-34, McGriff's comps are:

PLAYER	PCT	31	32	33	34
Jake Daubert	1576	86	84	52	82
George Sisler	1555	74	89	64	82
Dan McGann	1487	64	86	90	55
Joe Start	1483	83	82	48	84
Fred McGriff	1464	83	83	72	71
Norm Cash	1453	89	72	65	78
Frank McCormick	1449	71	66	89	78
Steve Garvey	1443	92	80	71	43
Fred Tenney	1417	76	76	75	82

Sisler is the only HOF in this company, and McGriff doesn't have anything in his portfolio anywhere near as impressive as Sisler's .420 season and all-time base hit record.

CECIL FIELDER (34): Not listed with the trio above, because he is in another crowd, well back. His age 34 comps show him to be a very good match with John Mayberry:

Andres Galarraga	3449	95 94 91 85 80 70 66 15 6
Alvin Davis	3407	93 92 89 87 83 76 62 28
Cecil Fielder	3293	98 93 82 80 79 75 70 26 24
John Mayberry	3247	98 93 92 73 67 63 63 58 53 51
Frank Chance	3246	95 93 90 89 71 70 42 36 20 16
Jack Fournier	3228	95 95 89 89 77 52 42 30

BRADY ANDERSON (34): At this point in his career, Brady Anderson ranks pretty close to Cecil Fielder, sharing more than just a freak 50+ HR year. There aren't a lot of very good comps to Anderson: most players at his level got their careers started much younger. Some decent comps (with Fielder thrown in for good measure) include:

Augie Galan	3452	96 95 92 85 77 69 55 45 33
Dante Bichette	3402	96 90 89 87 83 79 36 29 16
Baby Doll Jacobson	3389	94 90 88 85 79 79 69 53
Brady Anderson	3372	95 95 87 85 81 75 53
Brett Butler	3353	93 88 85 79 78 75 74 73 67
Bob Allison	3348	93 92 81 80 80 79 69 67 62
Ken Williams	3322	97 96 95 85 76 23
Ed Swartwood	3299	97 95 90 82 82 63 25
Cecil Fielder	3293	98 93 82 80 79 75 70 26 24
George Stone	3289	99 95 94 91 57 24

STAN JAVIER (34): Stan has lasted longer than his father, but hasn't established himself as a better player--even ignoring the difference in defensive value, which got Julian many more at bats. By years:

Player	Pct	23	24	25	26	27	28	29	30	31	32	33	34
Julian Javier	578	22	24	51	64	37		13	63	53	56	22	
Stan Javier	367		19	1	25		10	3	67	52		48	41

BARRY BONDS (33): Bonds' age 33 comps (shown by year) are solid HOF:

Player		Pct	19	20	21	22	23	24	25	26	27	28	29	30	31	32	33
Ty Cobb		8997	53	98	98	99	99	99	98	95	85	99	99	99	99	97	69
Stan Musial		8486		85	99	99		98	96	99	98	99	99	99	99	99	97
Hank Aaron		8417		49	92	95	96	96	99	97	96	97	99	93	97	95	97
Tris Speaker		8261			95	95	92	99	98	97	93	98	98	96	92	97	91
Willie Mays		8068		65		98	99	94	97	99	97	99	93	98	98		99
Frank Robinson		8049		95	94	84	95	95	97	99	77	96	97	99	95	76	94
Mickey Mantle		7786	28	98	76	92	97	99	99	98	92	96	98	94	23	92	51
Barry Bonds		7595			46	73	87	84	98	95	99	99	96	97	97	96	97
Babe Ruth		7465				89	99	99	99	88	99	99	49	99	98	99	
Mel Ott		7451	75	95	89	87	95	85	95	94	95	88	96	86	82	91	96
Ted Williams		7369		98	97	99	99			99	99	98	99	77	97		

Bonds is one of 24 players with two 99 percentile seasons. One way to sort this data is to sort each ranked year from top to bottom. Again, we only consider data to age 34:

Player	Pct	Sorted percentiles
Ty Cobb	9298	99 99 99 99 99 99 99 98 98 98 97 95 95 85 69 53
Stan Musial	8847	99 99 99 99 99 99 99 98 98 97 96 95 85
Babe Ruth	7872	99 99 99 99 99 99 99 98 93 89 88 49
Ed Delahanty	7754	99 99 99 99 99 99 97 96 93 86 83 69 47 11 6
Willie Mays	8551	99 99 99 99 99 98 98 98 97 97 94 93 65
Ted Williams	7369	99 99 99 99 99 98 98 97 97 77 8
Dan Brouthers	8139	99 99 99 99 97 97 96 95 95 95 94 91 23
Lou Gehrig	8403	99 99 99 98 98 98 97 97 97 96 96 90 65
Rogers Hornsby	8375	99 99 99 98 98 97 97 95 95 92 92 90 83 75
Jimmie Foxx	8289	99 99 99 98 98 97 97 95 94 92 89 89 85 71 9
Honus Wagner	7478	99 99 99 98 98 97 96 96 95 89 75 21
Ross Barnes	4907	99 99 99 98 97 79 60 43
Hank Greenberg	5237	99 99 99 98 96 95 61 49
Carl Yastrzemski	6941	99 99 99 95 92 91 91 90 90 84 83 69 66 61
Mickey Mantle	7841	99 99 98 98 98 97 96 94 92 92 92 76 61 51 28 23
Mike Schmidt	7246	99 99 98 98 96 95 94 94 93 91 78 23
Barry Bonds	7595	99 99 98 97 97 97 96 96 95 87 84 73 46
Joe Morgan	6357	99 99 98 97 96 93 84 84 78 76 73 62 48
George Brett	6647	99 99 98 97 93 91 91 90 86 77 77 64 50 34
Nap Lajoie	6600	99 99 98 95 92 92 89 88 87 86 79 60 20
Hank Aaron	8771	99 99 97 97 97 97 97 96 96 96 95 95 93 92 49
Frank Robinson	8195	99 99 97 97 96 95 95 95 95 94 94 84 81 77 76
Cal McVey	5092	99 99 96 94 86 81 79 79 78
Paul Hines	6085	99 99 94 93 91 89 88 85 84 79 66 60 60 58

The non-HOFs are 1870's stars Barnes, McVey and Hines.

RAFAEL PALMEIRO (33): Palmeiro has pulled well ahead of Will Clark and Fred McGriff. He's on the cusp of a HOF pace. Comps through age 33:

Eddie Murray	7225	98 98 96 95 95 95 94 91 91 85 84 81 81
Orlando Cepeda	6111	97 96 95 92 92 90 90 88 87 81 72 70 17
Rafael Palmeiro	6056	98 96 96 94 93 92 92 83 82 80 70 4
George Sisler	6015	98 98 97 96 95 95 89 88 74 64 6
Fred McGriff	5879	96 96 96 95 95 94 90 83 83 72 26
Harmon Killebrew	5835	98 97 95 94 94 92 89 85 82 70 35
Keith Hernandez	5725	97 97 95 91 89 89 87 86 82 80 67 54

Murray isn't really a comp; he's just listed to give an indication of where this list fits. Murray and everyone above him (Foxx, Gehrig, Brouthers, Anson, Connor) are rock solid HOF. Cepeda isn't in the HoF, but has an active campaign. He started quite young, and was mostly done by this point (one more year at 77). Palmeiro is certain to eclipse Cepeda. Palmeiro's real problem is that Frank Thomas has already caught him, and Jeff Bagwell and Mo Vaughn are also likely to catch him, and Mark McGwire will outpoll him regardless of who has the most 90-94 percentile years.

CRAIG BIGGIO (32): His age 32 comps show HoF promise:

Ryne Sandberg	5498	97 97 95 94 94 93 81 79 68 68 64
Craig Biggio	4560	96 95 95 94 87 81 78 65 59 57
Roberto Alomar	4447	96 93 92 92 83 79 76 74 66 65 62
Charlie Gehringer	4440	95 93 92 89 89 87 85 72 36 35
Larry Doyle	4363	94 94 92 92 92 74 72 67 66 58 56 27
Bobby Doerr	4239	90 87 86 86 85 85 85 84 70 65 60 55
Frankie Frisch	4214	94 93 92 89 80 78 76 71 69 66 59 34

However, he's quite a ways behind Sandberg (not HOF yet, but very likely), and Alomar is 2 years younger.

GREG VAUGHN (32): Another freak 50 HR season, but no HOF chance. Rather than list his age 32 comps (the closest are Devon White and Joe Hornung), let's show where he stands (at age 32) in the world of 50+ HR hitters:

Jimmie Foxx	8082	99 99 99 98 98 97 97 95 94 92 89 89 71
Mickey Mantle	7758	99 99 98 98 98 97 96 94 92 92 92 76 28 23
Willie Mays	7534	99 99 99 98 98 98 97 97 94 93 65
Babe Ruth	6870	99 99 99 99 99 99 98 89 88 49
Ken Griffey	6022	98 98 97 97 96 94 93 93 57 24
Ralph Kiner	5808	98 98 97 97 93 92 92 84 73 33
Hank Greenberg	5198	99 99 99 98 96 95 61
Albert Belle	5157	98 98 98 97 95 83 82 71
Johnny Mize	4821	99 98 97 95 93 89 69
George Foster	4559	98 98 97 96 83 81 79 38 11
Mark McGwire	4152	96 95 92 89 87 85 76 49
Hack Wilson	4045	97 95 94 92 91 76 48 38
Cecil Fielder	3287	98 93 82 80 79 75 70
Brady Anderson	2834	95 95 85 81 75
Roger Maris	2821	96 93 84 76 69 60 53 48 30 12
Sammy Sosa	2761	98 87 84 76 73 67 46 2
Greg Vaughn	1932	90 84 76 69 63 55 31 24 11

Note that Sosa is only 29, so has 3 years left to pull ahead of Vaughn (or catch up to Cecil Fielder). Belle is 31, so give him another year, too. McGwire had 2 50+ HR season after age 32, so he's somewhat underrated here.

171

ALBERT BELLE (31): Belle's age 31 comps (shown by year) are pretty thick, but approximately half of them were destined for the HOF. Belle has a relatively late start, but generally has higher scores.

Player	Pct	20	21	22	23	24	25	26	27	28	29	30	31
Dale Murphy	5433			41	40	91	65	94	99	97	97	90	98
Vada Pinson	5362	95	92	89	86	97	78	94	83	88	59	40	73
Joe Medwick	5345		85	86	95	94	96	90	92	76	88	75	54
Kirby Puckett	5290				50	81	98	94	98	95	82	88	97
Reggie Jackson	5274			84	97	51	92	79	94	94	90	86	92
Bobby Bonds	5265			28	91	96	96	92	98	87	91	37	88
Greg Luzinski	5184		81	88	13	98	92	97	96	47	38	91	89
Paul Hines	5169		60	66	84	88	60	99	99	91	79	94	85
Albert Belle	5157				71	82	95	98	98	97	83	98	
Joe Kelley	5059		89	96	94	97	92	73	88	82	68	65	66
Mike Tiernan	4978	48	86	95	96	95	66	87	34	87	91	83	51
Rocky Colavito	4914			50	68	95	87	74	95	95	87	91	91
Dave Winfield	4886			58	70	80	83	95	97	86	93	87	92
Tony Oliva	4885				98	94	92	86	82	89	91	92	
Chuck Klein	4844				30	97	99	95	98	98	66	55	80

MOISES ALOU (31): Is Alou really this old? His age 31 comps (in age order), weeding out all those who didn't score a 90+ percentile from ages 29-31:

Player	Pct	23	24	25	26	27	28	29	30	31
Ron LeFlore	2527					40	84	92	95	84
Frank Howard	2498	50	15	76	64	43	78	70	84	97
Hal McRae	2470			20		15	89	73	93	95
Mike Mitchell	2437					90	27	95	91	73
Steve Evans	2432		68	59	72	62	4	98	94	
Moises Alou	2413			43	68	94	36	59	82	95
Dummy Hoy	2401				88	53	80	93	87	42
Roy Cullenbine	2400				9	89	65	82	83	92
Sam Rice	2357				1	86		92	91	81

Rice went on to the HOF after a late start.

KENNY LOFTON (31): Another guy who's older than he seems, which probably means he has no chance for a HOF career. Age 31 comps include:

Player	Pct	22	23	24	25	26	27	28	29	30	31
Ken Griffey	3225				67	95	87	85	49	88	89
Willie Stargell	3174		8	48	76	92	75	63	91	65	97
Roy Thomas	3172				87	85	71	70	87	85	92
Bobby Thomson	3171		85	36	94	60	92	91	82		23
Kip Selbach	3161	40	81	75	84	76	76	92	55	89	53
Mike Greenwell	3144		72	97	88	87	74		82	50	66
Ralph Garr	3128				94	86	84	97	71	63	60
Dusty Baker	3110		84	92	78	64	3	84	52	75	91
Kenny Lofton	3110				79	89	97	74	87	64	76
Bob Meusel	3084		76	92	73	55	85	89	52	85	62
Willie Wilson	3082		85	96	81	84	60	76	73	63	60
Elmer Smith	3055			79	94	86	58	88	74	84	28
Andy Pafko	2995		37	88	10	74	89	72	94	63	80
Frank Schulte	2989	63	87	40	30	69	92	96	76	68	43
Earle Combs	2963					88	78	95	88	78	77

That's Ken Griffey Sr. The two HOFs are Stargell and Combs. The best players from this list after age 31 were:

Player	Pct	32	33	34	35	36	37	38	39
Willie Stargell	3713	95	98	96	85	62	6	78	72
Dusty Baker	1475	91	85	69	4	31			
Earle Combs	1067	81	85	54	14				
Ken Griffey	611	50	60	30	47	76	38		3

MO VAUGHN (30): Vaughn at age 30 is still in the pack of near-HOF 1B.

Player	Pct										
Don Mattingly	4832	99	98	98	94	92	90	70	12	6	
Rafael Palmeiro	4827	98	96	96	94	92	83	82	70	4	
Johnny Mize	4821	99	98	97	95	93	89	69			
Will Clark	4661	98	96	92	91	89	86	86	66	46	
Harry Stovey	4644	97	96	95	92	89	87	79	69		
Keith Hernandez	4616	97	97	95	89	87	86	82	67	54	
Mo Vaughn	4501	98	97	96	92	92	92	27			
Steve Garvey	4384	97	96	96	93	92	89	27	18		
Ed Konetchy	4272	97	92	90	88	88	82	78	77	56	27
Jim Bottomley	4262	95	95	92	91	89	82	79	62		

However, his showing is largely damped by a late start. His last six years have been very consistent, and move him up a notch. Comps from age 25-30:

Player	Pct	25	26	27	28	29	30
Lou Gehrig	4785	98	90	96	98	97	97
Frank Thomas	4719	97	99	98	96	97	85
Eddie Murray	4551	95	96	98	98	95	85
Roger Connor	4529	98	92	98	95	92	93
Mo Vaughn	4497	92	92	96	98	92	97
Fred McGriff	4478	96	96	90	95	94	96
Steve Garvey	4379	93	96	96	89	97	92
Rafael Palmeiro	4326	92	98	83	96	94	96
Jeff Bagwell	4244	91	98	81	96	97	92

FRANK THOMAS (30): Thomas ranked among the best players ever for ages 24-29:

Player	Pct	24	25	26	27	28	29
Willie Mays	5065	99	94	97	99	97	99
Babe Ruth	5053	99	99	99	88	99	99
Frank Thomas	5045	98	97	99	98	96	97
Dan Brouthers	5032	99	99	95	97	99	95
Hank Aaron	5017	96	99	97	96	97	99
Tris Speaker	4998	99	98	97	93	98	98
Mickey Mantle	4981	99	99	98	92	96	98
Rogers Hornsby	4951	95	98	99	92	98	99
Jimmie Foxx	4940	99	99	98	98	97	89
Lou Gehrig	4861	99	98	90	96	98	97
Ty Cobb	4833	99	98	95	85	99	99

Despite a big dip in BA, Thomas only slipped to 85 in 1998. Such a slip is not common among players like this, but it is also not unprecedented: At age 30, Rogers Hornsby slipped to 83, and Babe Ruth dropped all the way to 49. Both bounced back (Hornsby posted 97, 97, and 99; Ruth did even better).

ROBERTO ALOMAR (30): Alomar started quite young, and has been piling up scores that are firmly in HOF territory. It is likely that he will keep a comfortable lead over Frankie Frisch, and will fend off Charlie Gehringer's late spurt. Comps to age 30:

Nap Lajoie	4749	99 99 95 92 89 86 79 60 20
Rod Carew	4477	98 97 97 96 79 78 73 66 49 9
Roberto Alomar	4447	96 93 92 92 83 79 76 74 66 65 62
Joe Morgan	4377	98 97 96 84 84 78 76 73 62
Ryne Sandberg	4360	97 97 94 94 81 79 68 68 64
Larry Doyle	4308	94 94 92 92 92 74 72 67 66 58
Frankie Frisch	3911	94 93 92 89 80 76 71 69 66 34

MIKE PIAZZA (29): Surprisingly, Piazza is not the top-rated catcher to age 29:

Johnny Bench	4616	97 97 94 92 83 78 78 78 62 61
Ted Simmons	4197	95 91 89 89 87 84 75 74 71
Deacon White	4140	99 97 96 91 85 79 52
Mike Piazza	3879	98 92 90 90 89 86
Joe Torre	3451	94 94 89 84 83 70 67 51 29
Gary Carter	2796	92 84 82 78 73 72 71 66
Yogi Berra	2685	92 89 82 79 78 66 51 12

This is due to a relatively late start. The age 24-29 group trails him:

Player	Pct	24	25	26	27	28	29
Mike Piazza	3879	92	86	89	90	98	90
Deacon White	3834	52	96	85	97	91	99
Johnny Bench	3267	97	78	97	92	61	78
Ted Simmons	3052	84	95	75	87	91	74
Joe Torre	2770	83	94	70	51	84	94
Yogi Berra	2538	51	92	79	82	78	89
Gary Carter	2200	66	73	82	72	92	78
Mickey Cochrane	2151	78	69	69	72	86	88

Deacon White ultimately played much longer at 3B, but had great years at C in the 1870s, and his best year ever at 1B.

BERNIE WILLIAMS (29): At this point Bernie Williams does not have comps that rank him among real HOFers. If we look for age 29 comps that were 80+ from ages 26-29, we get:

Player	Pct	21	22	23	24	25	26	27	28	29
Al Oliver	3000		57	60	70	86	87	95	83	74
Hack Wilson	2992				48		91	94	92	95
Zack Wheat	2953		86	61	68	79	93	60	96	50
Tommy Holmes	2915					69	81	92	99	89
Ralph Garr	2907					94	86	84	97	71
Roy White	2842				87	71	90	93	83	71
Bernie Williams	2826		13	8	57	77	91	87	89	88
Frank Schulte	2807		63	87	40	30	69	92	96	76
Bob Allison	2781				80	69	79	80	93	92
Roger Maris	2766		30	69	60	93	96	84	48	76
Sammy Sosa	2761	46		2	76	84	87	67	73	98

From age 30 on, Wheat and possibly Oliver made significant HOF progress:

Player	Pct	30	31	32	33	34	35	36	37	38	39
Zack Wheat	3802	69	83	88	80	90	53	96	94	27	2
Al Oliver	3605	79	85	73	94	84	98	81	37		
Roy White	1486	62	81	93	60	26					
Hack Wilson	1294	97	38	76	20						
Tommy Holmes	1024	86	81	31	25						

Williams could conceivably make that sort of progress, but there is that big gap between Roy White and Oliver where he seems mostt likely to inhabit.

CHUCK KNOBLAUCH (29): Knoblauch has some respectable age 29 comps, a notch below Alomar but still in mostly HOF territory:

Frankie Frisch	3682	94 93 92 89 80 71 69 66 34
Ryne Sandberg	3628	97 94 94 81 79 68 68 64
Joe Morgan	3605	97 96 84 84 78 76 73 62
Cupid Childs	3541	96 93 87 85 84 72 71 52
Chuck Knoblauch	3440	94 93 88 87 81 68 64 64
Bobby Doerr	3016	87 86 85 85 84 70 65 60 55
Craig Biggio	2906	95 94 87 81 65 59 57
Billy Herman	2874	92 90 85 82 80 60 58 40
Joe Gordon	2814	95 89 84 82 79 61

KEN GRIFFEY (28): To age 29, Griffey is just where he'd like to be:

Ty Cobb	6899	99 99 99 99 98 98 98 95 85 53
Mickey Mantle	6356	99 99 98 98 97 96 92 92 76 28
Hank Aaron	6043	99 97 97 96 96 96 95 92 49
Ken Griffey	6022	98 98 97 97 96 94 93 93 57 24
Tris Speaker	6005	99 98 98 97 95 95 93 92
Frank Robinson	5931	99 97 96 95 95 95 94 84 77
Mel Ott	5705	95 95 95 95 94 89 88 87 85 75
Stan Musial	5571	99 99 99 98 98 96 85
Joe DiMaggio	5314	98 98 96 95 95 95 92
Ted Williams	5247	99 99 99 99 98 97
Sherry Magee	5218	97 96 96 93 92 88 85 82 70 36
Willie Mays	5161	99 99 98 97 97 94 65

Magee didn't do much after age 29, and Mays did a lot. Griffey already has the prime years he needs to make the HOF. Now it's just a matter of rounding up the career totals.

JIM THOME (27): I'm surprised that he doesn't show up better among 3B, but his age 27 comps follow. The competition is even tougher at 1B.

Denny Lyons	3333	97 90 89 83 82 79 40
Harlond Clift	3017	95 93 90 74 70 69 64
John McGraw	3008	94 92 85 82 72 69 67 11
Bill Bradley	2757	97 95 91 70 58 46
Jim Ray Hart	2709	94 88 88 86 71
Jim Thome	2689	93 92 92 80 62
Gary Sheffield	2670	98 96 78 73 69 47 12
George Kell	2636	96 91 85 84 56 33 33
Freddy Lindstrom	2635	94 92 79 76 72 65 50 19 14
Davy Force	2630	96 93 84 74 71 37 27
Wade Boggs	2618	98 98 92 43

CHIPPER JONES (26): Jones' rookie year was at age 23, so he only has 4 years through age 26. That places him well back in terms of age 26 players. If we limit the comps to ages 23-26, he still places #10 among 3B. (Yes, Anson had only just moved from 3B to 1B at this tender age.) There are good players on this list (5 HOFs), but it's still pretty early to project Jones.

Player	Pct	23	24	25	26
Ron Santo	3221	91	97	95	97
Dick Allen	3188	96	98	93	92
George Brett	2837	97	91	77	98
Frank Baker	2727	93	78	95	95
Mike Schmidt	2691	23	99	94	98
Bill Bradley	2512	58	97	91	95
Eddie Mathews	2498	93	89	92	81
Cap Anson	2479	88	95	86	86
Harlond Clift	2456	90	93	95	70
Chipper Jones	2384	74	91	89	94
Jim Thome	2328	62	92	93	92
Jim Ray Hart	2230	88	88	94	71

IVAN RODRIGUEZ (26): Let's look at C who started at age 21 or less, up to age 26:

Player	Pct	19	20	21	22	23	24	25	26
Johnny Bench	3716		78	83	94	62	97	78	97
Ted Simmons	3009			71	89	89	84	95	75
Joe Torre	2302		29		67	89	83	94	70
Buck Ewing	1805			34	75	88	84	78	40
Ivan Rodriguez	1707		28	39	71	59	79	84	82
Gary Carter	1642			71		84	66	73	82
Bill Freehan	1557			12	75	23	31	86	90
Fred Carroll	1337	61	33	84	72	42	66	69	24
John Clapp	1288		38	52	42	72	72	76	76

The odds that Simmons, Torre and Carter will make the HOF are probably better than the odds that anyone other than David Nemec can tell you anything about Fred Carroll and John Clapp.

ALEX RODRIGUEZ (22): Too early to say much, but so far, so good. Among SS:

Player	Pct	20	21	22
Alex Rodriguez	2328	98	85	96
Rogers Hornsby	1884	92	95	75
Arky Vaughan	1587	58	92	92
Cal Ripken	1349		80	97

Among everyone:

Player	Pct	19	20	21	22
Ty Cobb	2895	53	98	98	99
Ted Williams	2788		98	97	99
Ken Griffey	2459	57	93	96	93
Sherry Magee	2451	36	96	92	96
Alex Rodriguez	2328		98	85	96
Al Kaline	2269	36	95	97	85
Cap Anson	2228	69	97	93	77
Vada Pinson	2181		95	92	89
Frank Robinson	2122		95	94	84
Orlando Cepeda	2043		90	92	90
Mickey Mantle	2020	28	98	76	92

TEAM ESSAYS

SECTION FOUR

INTRODUCTION TO TEAM ESSAYS

Don Malcolm

Thanks to the fourteen other writers who made their presence felt in this section of BBBA:

Ken Adams (Mets, Tigers, Orioles, A's); Tom Austin (Giants, Angels, Brewers); Doug Drinen (Diamondbacks, Devil Rays); Jeff Drummond (Twins); Sean Forman (Marlins, Phillies, Pirates, Astros); Jim Furtado (Rockies); Brock J. Hanke (Cardinals, Cubs); Scot Hughes/Ron Johnson (Expos); C.O. Jones (Padres); Sean Lahman (Reds); Art Martone (Red Sox); Dave Paisley (Mariners); Stephen Tomlinson (Blue Jays); G. Jay Walker (White Sox).

No editor has been so fortunate to have so many distinctive voices with which to blend. As usual, you'll find some of my additional commentary in the margins of their essays.

Long-time readers will note that our chart mania of the past has subsided a bit. We've retained only our 20-game run chart, which presents the ongoing 20-game snapshot of a team's runs scored and runs allowed. Our sample chart this year: the Toronto Blue Jays, who started playing really well only when they threw in the towel (as Stephen Tomlinson notes in his essay).

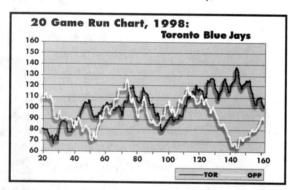

What's replaced the usual chart mania is Tom Austin's latest series, this one entitled "Bad Pitchers"-- the intro to which you've seen in section three, if you're reading this book in order. Using the Quality Matrix (QMAX) as a prism for viewing starting pitcher performance, Tom has fashioned a unique survey of baseball memories that are not so much waiting but lying in wait. You'll find Tom holding forth on page two of every team essay.

Across the way from him, you'll find the fruits of Doug Drinen's research into relief pitching, the team WPA Bullpen Box, which gives you new details using the Win Probability Added method. Doug's essay "The ABCs of Relief, Part Deux", a few pages back in section three, will walk you through the parameters of the methods and the terns used herein. One of the many fascinating pieces of info that Doug has compiled can be found at the bottom of the data set, where he shows what each team's record was when they faced certain score situations in the late innings. For example, the Yankees had 20 games in which they were tied going into the seventh inning, and went 12-8 in those games. The Marlins also had 20 such games, but went 5-15 in them. It's exciting to have a new wealth of data like this with the potential for groundbreaking insight--kudos to Doug for his yeoman efforts in this area.

NYY	7th inning			8th inning			9th inning		
	0	1	2	0	1	2	0	1	2
Bradley R	0	0	0	0	0	1	0	0	0
Bruske J	0	1	0	0	0	0	0	0	0
Buddie M	0	1	0	0	0	0	0	0	0
Holmes D	1	0	0	1	1	0	0	0	0
Lloyd G	0	1	1	0	0	2	0	0	0
Mendoza R	3	1	1	6	1	0	2	1	0
Nelson J	1	2	1	0	0	3	1	0	0
Rivera M	0	0	0	0	0	0	2	12	13
Stanton M	1	0	1	0	3	4	2	0	3
Starters	14	11	10	7	6	6	1	0	1
TOTAL	20	17	14	14	11	16	8	13	17
Record	12-8	16-1	13-1	9-5	11-0	16-0	6-2	12-1	17-0

FLA	7th inning			8th inning			9th inning		
	0	+1	+2	0	+1	+2	0	+1	+2
Alfonseca A	2	0	1	4	1	1	6	5	2
Darensbourg V	2	1	3	4	4	2	1	1	1
Edmondson B	0	0	4	1	3	1	1	0	0
Henriquez O	1	0	0	0	0	0	0	0	0
Heredia F	0	1	0	1	1	2	3	2	0
Mantei M	0	0	0	1	2	1	5	9	2
Pall D	0	0	0	0	0	1	0	0	0
Powell J	0	0	0	1	1	0	3	3	2
Speier J	0	0	0	1	0	0	2	0	0
Stanifer R	0	2	1	1	1	0	0	0	0
Starters	15	10	5	4	5	3	2	3	2
TOTAL	20	14	14	18	18	11	23	23	9
Record	5-15	7-7	9-5	5-13	11-7	8-3	8-15	19-4	8-1

Next you'll find another herculean effort--Sean Forman's Prospectwatch. (Sean will be along next in this space to give you a detailed description of his efforts.) This is the most succinct and best organized look at young players to be found anywhere.

Across from Prospectwatch is my favorite data set, the In-Depth Team Breakout. We've sorted close to thirty team performance categories by winning percentage, and added the league rank for that winning percentage to

TEAM BREAKOUT
PADRES 1998

Category	RS	RA	W	L	Pct.	Rk
5+ RUNS SCORED/HOME	207	93	30	0	1.000	1
CLOSE SLUGFESTS/HOME	24	21	3	0	1.000	1
5+ RUNS SCORED	523	312	60	9	.870	2
SLUGFESTS/HOME	69	65	7	2	.778	1
5+ RUNS SCORED/ROAD	316	219	30	9	.769	6
4- RUNS ALLOWED/ROAD	174	86	29	10	.744	4
4- RUNS ALLOWED	427	222	76	27	.738	5
4- RUNS ALLOWED/HOME	253	136	47	17	.734	10
CLOSE SLUGFESTS/ROAD	111	103	10	4	.714	4
RECORD IN SLUGFESTS	328	284	27	13	.675	2
SLUGFESTS/ROAD	259	219	20	11	.645	3
LOW SCORING GAMES/HOME	111	86	27	16	.628	5
CLOSE LOW SCORING GAMES	67	57	18	11	.621	8
RECORD IN CLOSE GAMES/HOME	142	128	27	17	.614	5
RECORD IN LOW SCORING GAMES	171	140	42	27	.609	2
SEASON TOTALS	749	635	98	64	.605	3
RECORD IN CLOSE GAMES	334	308	51	34	.600	1
CLOSE LOW SCORING GAMES/ROAD	38	32	10	7	.588	1
RECORD IN BLOWOUTS/ROAD	134	101	10	7	.588	4
RECORD IN CLOSE GAMES/ROAD	192	180	24	17	.585	1
RECORD IN BLOWOUTS	206	164	18	13	.581	5
LOW SCORING GAMES/ROAD	60	54	15	11	.577	1
RECORD IN BLOWOUTS/ROAD	72	63	8	6	.571	7
4- RUNS SCORED/HOME	125	160	24	27	.471	2
5+ RUNS ALLOWED/HOME	79	117	7	10	.412	2
4- RUNS SCORED	226	323	38	55	.409	2
5+ RUNS ALLOWED	322	413	22	37	.373	1
5+ RUNS ALLOWED/ROAD	243	296	15	27	.357	1
4- RUNS SCORED/ROAD	101	163	14	28	.333	3

give you some kind of context for the performance. It's not enough to tell you that a team has a .609 record in low-scoring games: you need to know where that ranks in the league. (In this case, it's the Padres, and their record in such games ranked second in the 1998 NL). And that's what gives these breakouts their added value.

Some quick notes about the category definitions. LOW SCORING GAMES are those in which the two teams combined to score six runs or less. SLUGFESTS are games in which both teams combine to score twelve runs or more. CLOSE GAMES are those in which the game is decided by one or two runs. BLOWOUTS are those in which the game is decided by five or more runs. CLOSE LOW-SCORING GAMES and CLOSE BLOWOUTS are high and low-scoring games where the outcome is by one or two runs. We've broken most of these categories out by HOME and ROAD, and we predict you'll spend a lot of time comparing the results.

Finally, our revamped "sabermetric hitter data" features the new Extrapolated Runs (XR) as developed by Jim Furtado, and starting pitcher performance is summarized in BBBA's exclusive QMAX data. Samples of these can be found in "Stats To Die For (And Live With)", in Section One.

Sean Forman's

PROSPECT WATCH

Minor league Quality Matrix averages for the past two seasons:

League	1998 S/C—T	1997 S/C—T
International	4.20/3.62—7.82	4.08/3.56—7.64
Pacific Coast	4.32/3.56—7.88	4.63/3.76—8.39
American Assn		4.05/3.47—7.51
Eastern	4.05/3.51—7.56	4.06/3.68—7.74
Texas	4.35/3.61—7.96	4.27/3.50—7.77
Southern	4.15/3.81—7.96	4.31/3.78—8.09
Carolina	3.72/3.32—7.03	
California	4.14/3.64—7.78	
Florida State	4.19/3.62—7.81	
Midwest	3.89/3.55—7.44	
South Atlantic	3.98/3.46—7.44	

Introduction

THE DATABASE

It is now year three of the Prospectwatch in BBBA. After tweaking the formulas for BBBA '98, they have remained the same for BBBA '99. Please don't take that as a sign that the grades are perfect. They quite clearly are not. Rather, we have come to realize that the lack of readily available minor league statistics is damping our ability to determine what sorts of players develop, which ones don't and how the shape of a player's statistics might change over the course of their development. For instance, a colleague was interested in looking at what type of players hold their value as they advance: high average free-swingers or more patient hitters. Unfortunately, data prior to 1994 is readily available digitally for only current major leaguers or players in the high minors, so without an extreme amount of data entry it is not possible to put together a listing of, say, all the players in AA in 1988 together with their ages and defensive position.

That is why we have started putting together a database of minor league statistics. The goal is to have complete team and player stats (back at least to the 1970's), accurate dates of birth, draft pick information and make it all compatible with the major league database put together by Sean Lahman (at www.baseball1.com). It's slow going as data must generally be hand-entered and there are a lot more (five to six times more) minor leaguers than major leaguers, but we hope to be back to 1992 by the start of the season and perhaps highlight some much older seasons as well in future editions of BBBA. Eventually, it will be available somewhere on the web, but the specifics need to be worked out. If you would like to make a contribution of statistics already entered or would like to help, let us know (bbba@backatcha.com).

THE GRADES

Now, about the grading system used to evaluate minor league prospects. In developing the grading system, we expressly wished to look beyond a player's tools and judge directly what his SKILLS are. Three skills are considered: the ability to reach base (OBP), power, and baserunning. Each player's skills are compared to those of the other players in his league. This prevents players from the highly offensive California and Pacific Coast Leagues from dominating the ratings. We're not quite done. A players' age needs to be taken into account. An age factor calculated, which considers both the player's age and the level at which he played. This factor increases as a player's level becomes higher and decreases as a player's age increases. Players at higher levels receive a boost, since they are closer to the majors. For instance, a 19-year-old in high-A would have a lower age factor than a 20-year-old in AA. Combine these two factors and you have a player's grade.

The grades are roughly on the scale of 0-100, though some particularly old players may turn in negative grades and some great prospects will earn grades in excess of 100. Grades over 80 are very good and generally indicate a player who will be a good major leaguer while a string of grades higher than 50-60 is needed to crack the major leagues. Naturally, a player's position is important as a grade of 70 indicates a top-notch catching prospect, but for first base that would be mediocre.

What has been included in Prospectwatch? Each team's prospects are separated into two groups: those who have considerable playing time in AA and above and those who have played primarily below AA. For a cutoff, a player is listed at the highest level they have attained 100 plate appearances. The columns are as follows:

AGE: This is the player's age at midnight on June 30, 1998. This is the date that baseball people use to determine a player's age for the season.

POS: This is the position played primarily in 1998. It often changes as teams attempt to find a defensive home for the player (see Hermanson, Chad).

LEVEL: This is the highest level at which the player earned a grade. The plate appearance cutoff used was 90 for the majors, 125 for the full season minor leagues and 75 for the short season leagues.
MAJ - Major Leagues
AAA - Triple A
AA - Double A
HIGH A - Low A
SS - Short Season
ROOK - Rookie

GR98, GR97, AND GR96: These are the player's grades from 98, 97 and 96. Some players either were injured or were in college, so they may not have grades for certain years. These seasons are noted with a "-". If a player appeared at several levels, the weighted average of those performances, based on the number of at bats he had at each level, was used.

AVG: This is the weighted average of the player's three seasons. The '98 season accounts for half and the '97 season a third and '96 season a sixth.

For the low minors, just the players' grade from 1998 is included. A word of warning: don't place too much importance on the grades for rookie leagues, and just a bit more importance on the short season grades.

After the player's comment, a "Comp:" blurb is sometimes added which utilizes another tool. A database with over 9,000 minor league seasons is searched, and the prospect's minor league career to those of current and previous minor leaguers. Let's compare a former Oriole with a current Oriole prospect.

NAME	AGE	YRLG-TEAM	R	H	2B	3B	HR	RBI	BB	SO	BA	OBP	SLG
Glenn Davis	21	82FS-DAYTONA	100	169	40	4	27	112	63	109	.315	.387	.555
Cal Pickering	20	97SA-DELMARVA	106	167	37	1	30	95	64	168	.312	.385	.552
Glenn Davis	22	83EL-COLUMBUS	84	165	24	4	31	105	49	108	.299	.357	.526
Cal Pickering	21	98EL-BOWIE	95	152	28	2	32	115	99	123	.303	.418	.559

Davis and Pickering's seasons in A-ball were nearly identical matches. Then in AA, their seasons remain similar, but Pickering's patience takes a big step forward. Pickering also has a slight age advantage on Davis. These comparisons are useful as they give you some historical perspective for a prospect's accomplishments. Another reason for an expanded minor league database is to determine just how reliable these comparisons are.

ON THE MOUND

For the last two years, only batters have been reviewed in the Prospectwatch, and that was all fine and good, but it is really only half the story. Since we are always pressing for innovation here at BBBA Plaza, we are now including starting pitcher information in our compendium of major leaguers-to-be. Evaluating major league hurlers is hard enough, but picking out which minor leaguers will be future aces is even more difficult. Typically, full-season statistics like K/9, WHIP, ERA, and K/BB have been used to identify up and coming prospects, but now with the maturation of the Internet and the development of QMAX we can do better. Over the last two summers, we have tracked down each and every (well, 98% of them) start made in AA and AAA. This has allowed us to compute minor league QMAX values and point to pitchers who have dominated the competition, but may have suffered from inconsistency. In the past, the season totals for these pitchers may have been skewed by a handful of bad starts. The difference in offensive levels between the various minor leagues is fairly well known, but what about the difference between starting pitching?

The folding of the American Association into (mostly) the Pacific Coast League and the International League had an interesting effect on the starting pitching numbers in AAA. Once the park factors become available, it will make for an interesting study. In AA, the Eastern League is by far the easiest league to pitch in, and the Carolina League was by far the best pitchers' league in all of baseball. Whether these are typical values for these leagues, we don't really know, but rest assured, we will continue to track these numbers.

For Prospectwatch, we have included all pitchers with 20+ starts in AA or AAA and a handful of low minors pitchers with exceptional numbers (unfortunately, start-by-start data for pitchers in the low minors is sporadically available, so we haven't included it for them). For each pitcher, their age, ERA, S/C and T numbers are included as is their won-loss record and the ratio of strikeouts to hits (K/H). Generally, a ratio above one indicates a potential power pitcher. Check out Orioles' prospect Matt Riley.

Those of you who have been checking out the BBBA web site know that Don Malcolm has been producing comprehensive looks at all the Atlanta Braves starters from when they first arrived in the majors to the present. It provided an in depth look at how the progression they took from young starters to the best starters in the game. Not much work has been done on how young pitchers develop, who tends to avoid injury, what sorts of pitchers develop, and whether there are signs showing which pitchers will develop. Now that start-by-start data is available we hope to change that. Starting in 1998, we will begin tracking a pool of 40-50 young starters as they attempt to progress from the minors to the major leagues. We will look at first round picks, late-round picks; collegians, high schoolers and Latin pitchers; power and finesse pitchers; and everything in between. This is a long term project, but we should update you every year as the study progresses, perhaps someday it will culminate in a publicly-available database of starts. We aren't really sure what the data will show, but up until now no one has attempted to look at minor league pitching at this level of detail.

INFO

For a much more thorough treatment of the players found in Prospectwatch and other treats (including reports from previous seasons and expanded pitcher listings), please peruse my web site, which will be moving to the BBBA site this off-season (www.backatcha.com).

Please e-mail any comments to me at sean-forman@uiowa.edu.

AMERICAN LEAGUE EAST

NEW YORK YANKEES

DON MALCOLM

THE KILLERS

If you haven't seen The Killers (1946, dir. Robert Siodmak), rent it just as soon as you can. That way, you'll see two menacing, inexorable thugs (played to perfection by Charles McGraw and William Conrad) who personify the unstoppable forces of human nature.

And like Burt Lancaster, the Oakland A's were helpless to prevent the onslaught of such a force as represented by the New York Yankees. Last August 4th, more than 23,000 in attendance at the Oakland Coliseum saw not a pair of thugs, but twenty-five focused, implacable, quietly ferocious athletes seize a game by the throat at the very last possible moment, waiting until the top of the ninth inning to deliver their fatal blows.

It was the second game of a doubleheader, and the Yankees had already won the opener 10-4 behind unsung swing man Ramiro Mendoza. Chuck Knoblauch had homered to lead off the game, and Darryl Strawberry added a two-run blast in the fifth. Emergency starter Mike Buddie, however, had not fared so well in the nightcap, giving up six hits, a walk, and five runs in the first inning to the A's.

Though Buddie settled down after that, things looked well in hand for Oakland as their ace, ex-Yankee Kenny Rogers, kept the Yankees bottled up on six hits through eight innings; the A's led 5-1 as the ninth inning began. Here is a transcript of that fateful ninth inning:

Rogers pitching for Oakland. (1-5)
Tino Martinez singled to center.
Tim Raines singled to center, Martinez to second.
Bill Taylor replaced Rogers.
Chad Curtis hit a grounder to third that Mike Bordick let go through his legs for an error, loading the bases.
Darryl Strawberry pinch-hit for Joe Girardi and hit a grand-slam home run to right field. (5-5).
Jorge Posada batted for Luis Sojo and grounded to the pitcher (1 out).
Chuck Knoblauch singled to center.
Taylor balked, Knoblauch to second.

Derek Jeter grounded to second, colliding with first baseman Giambi as the throw arrived; Jeter was declared out, but the ball eluded Giambi and Knoblauch scored. (6-5)
Mike Blowers replaced Giambi at first base. Ed Sprague took over at third base for Blowers.
Paul O'Neill homered to right. (7-5)
Tim Worrell replaced Taylor.
Bernie Williams singled to center.
Tino Martinez homered to right. (9-5)
Tim Raines singled to center.
Chad Curtis doubled to left, Raines scoring. (10-5)
Buddy Groom replaced Worrell.
Darryl Strawberry struck out.

For those of you scoring at home, that's nine runs, nine hits, one error, one left on base. There were a number of such innings for the Yankees in 1998, but none was a more dramatic indicator of their dominance. This inning typifies the exceptional relentlessness that characterized this team, and goes a long way in explaining how they ended up the 1998 season with 125 wins.

THE KILLING

Assembling such a team is not a casual enterprise, but it's been clear since early 1996 that the Yankees were headed for a serious level of achievement. The talent acquisition for this team is summarized in the list below:

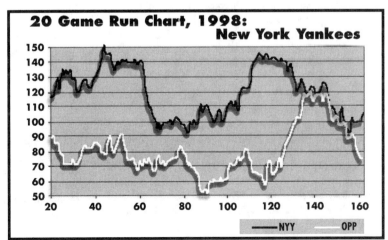

QMAX PRESENTS: "BAD" PITCHERS

REQUIEM FOR A JUNKBALLER

And we're not talking just any junkballer; Tommy John was such a quintessential Avatar of the Nibble that Bill James named an entire genre of pitchers after him: A guy with less than overpowering stuff who nevertheless survives and thrives in the major leagues courtesy of pinpoint control, lots of ground balls, and, to paraphrase Lefty Gomez, "clean living and a fast infield." At BBBA, this type of pitcher has been honored with his own QMAX region, the "Soldier of Fortune" section of the QMAX chart: a pitcher in this region gives up plenty of hits but, by clinging for dear life to the left side of the QMAX chart (that is, the "very few walks" region), manages to squeeze out the wins for his team.

TOMMY JOHN/NYY 1988

	1	2	3	4	5	6	7	S
1	1							1
2	1		2	1				4
3	1	1	3					5
4		1						1
5	2	1	1	1	1			6
6		1	1	2	2	1		7
7			1		2	4	1	8
C	5	5	7	6	7	1	1	32

Tommy John's 1988 season shows a-no, THE-control pitcher going the way of all flesh. As you can see from the chart, Tommy lost his grip on the QMAX 1,2 "C" region he needs so desperately to survive. Through June, he makes a valiant attempt at it, as his 5-start QMAX "C" averages nosed under 3.0. This relatively fine control, even in Tommy's golden years, worked pretty well for a while: as of July 5, Tommy was riding on a 6-2, 3.50 ERA. This coincided with the low point in his 5-start QMAX "C" average at a stingy 2.4. After that, though, it got ugly. Tommy lost his tenuous grip on the strike zone, started getting behind the batter, and started serving up gourmet room-temperature cheese to the hungry hitters. From July 5 to the end of the season, Tommy

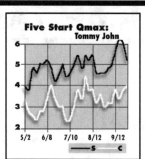

pleased AL hitters to the tune of a 3-6 record and a Big Six ERA.

One of the great things about QMAX is how it allows the reader to interpolate from the data and imagine the change in the typical at-bat vs. a pitcher like Tommy. Two factors are at work here: as the pitcher loses his stuff, he needs to live almost exclusively on the black, and a simultaneous loss of control makes it harder for him to get in there (Watch Danny Darwin of the Giants making faces on the mound as the umpire squeezes him to a two-foot wide strike zone for a current example). It's not a pretty sight, somewhat akin to Robert Shaw getting swallowed by the big shark in "Jaws."

When you think about it, though, it's a fitting end for a Soldier of Fortune.

Tom Austin

Year	Players
1991	Bernie Williams (min)
1993	Paul O'Neill (tr-CIN)
1995	David Cone (tr-TOR), Mariano Rivera (min) , Derek Jeter (min) , Andy Pettitte (min), Darryl Strawberry (FA)
1996	Tino Martinez (tr-SEA), Joe Girardi (FA), Tim Raines (FA) , Jeff Nelson (tr-SEA), Ramiro Mendoza (min), Graeme Lloyd (tr-MIL)
1997	David Wells (FA), Mike Stanton (FA), Hideki Irabu (tr-SD), Jorge Posada (min), Chad Curtis (tr-CLE), Luis Sojo (FA), Homer Bush (tr-SD)
1998	Chuck Knoblauch (tr-MIN), Orlando Hernandez (FA), Scott Brosius (tr-OAK), Chili Davis (FA), Shane Spencer (min), Ricky Ledee (min) , Darren Holmes (FA)

legend: (min)-minors; (tr-TEAM)-trade

The 1994 Yankees, under the management of Buck Showalter, played .619 baseball (70-43) in that strike-shortened year; in 1998, the Yankees won 125 games with exactly two players who were regulars on that 1994 squad.

The players dealt away in the trades who played in the majors subsequently were:

Year	Players
1993	Roberto Kelly
1995	Marty Janzen
1996	Sterling Hitchcock, Russ Davis, Gerald Williams
1997	Ruben Rivera, Stan Spencer
1998	Kenny Rogers, Eric Milton

As you can see, only Rogers has turned in a top-notch season, while the Yankees have had at least one very good year (and often a good bit more) from O'Neill, Cone, Martinez, Knoblauch, Brosius, Curtis, Lloyd and Irabu. Our old mentor Bill James and new collaborator Tom Ruane would be able to quantify the extra amount of value that the Yankees gleaned from their trading, but that isn't really necessary: it's mortally obvious that the Yankees made a fortune in these deals, a bigger one than Sterling Hayden et al were after in The Killing (1956, dir. Stanley Kubrick).

THE LINEUP

Yes, film fans, this is another noir reference (1958, dir. Don Siegel), and the results (for the AL at least) were just as harrowing. The Yankees' lineup was heavily tilted toward on-base percentage, and its most lethal weapons were actually found in the bottom half of the batting order:

BOP	NYY	Lg Best	Rank
#1	.370	.380	4
#2	.366	.376	2
#3	.382	.402	4
#4	.381	.401	5
#5	.398	--	1
#6	.371	--	1
#7	.365	--	1
#8	.342	--	1
#9	.290	.331	11

New York's front four (and we're not talking football here, either) were just fine, but their back four made the Yanks' batting order into the longest offensive sequence in recent memory.

In fact, no other team was close to the Yankees in the number of BOPs with OBPs at .360 or higher:

7 New York
5 Texas
4 Seattle
3 Boston, Cleveland, Oakland, Toronto
2 Anaheim, Baltimore, Chicago
1 Kansas City, Tampa Bay
0 Detroit, Minnesota

High OBP, like high blood pressure, transformed the nickname of this team from Murderer's Row to The Silent Killers.

THE SECRET WEAPON

Yes, yes, it was a fine collection of talent, all right, you say. But how the heck did this team win 114 games in the regular season? We're not looking at a truckload of Hall of Famers on this team.

We'll look at the Hall of Fame question a bit further below, but let's direct our attention to some benchmarks before we make any generalizations as to how this team played .700+ baseball. First, Tom Ruane compiled position-by-position PRO+ data for us, just like the big boys in Total Baseball; unlike those guys, though, Tom created it by position, and he organized it by team and year. (You'll find that data supplied for all 30 teams in one of the data boxes accompanying our team essays.)

What that data shows us is the following. There have only been two teams during the 90s to have all positions produce at above league average. (That's a 100 PRO+ or higher.) As it turns out, those two teams met in the 1998 World Series. That's right, the 1998 Yankees and 1998 San Diego Padres are the only two teams to do this during the 90s. Of course, the Yankees did it with nine positions to the Padres' eight, and that depth was clearly in evidence during the post-season.

WPA BULLPEN BOX—NEW YORK YANKEES

	PI	WPA	P	PPPI
Starters	1109	8.4	55.8	0.05
Relievers	513	7.2	31.3	0.061
Road	252	1.3	15.7	0.062
Home	261	5.9	15.5	0.059
Mar/Apr	87	0.7	6	0.069
May	86	0.6	6.1	0.071
June	67	-0.2	3.4	0.051
July	80	3.1	5.7	0.071
August	92	1.1	5.4	0.058
September	101	1.9	4.7	0.046
Non S/H Sit.	363	3.5	15.1	0.042
S/H Sit.	150	3.7	16.2	0.108
Low Pressure	210	-0.1	2.7	0.013
Med. Pressure	146	1.7	9	0.062
High Pressure	157	5.6	19.5	0.124

Name	G	PI	WPA	P	PPPI	MI	ROB	T
Banks W	9	16	-0.3	0.8	0.051	6	0	2
Borowski J	8	10	0.4	0.4	0.039	2	0	1
Bradley R	4	8	0.2	0.6	0.07	3	1	0
Bruske J	2	4	0.1	0.2	0.053	1	0	0
Buddie M	22	41	0.5	2.1	0.05	12	13	2
Holmes D	34	61	-0.3	2.3	0.038	17	14	4
Lloyd G	50	63	0.2	3	0.047	12	25	4
Mendoza R	27	56	0.4	3.5	0.062	15	15	4
Nelson J	45	61	-0.4	3.9	0.063	16	15	4
Rivera M	54	69	4.6	6.6	0.096	15	15	3
Stanton M	67	106	1.5	7.7	0.073	35	29	10
Tessmer J	7	10	0.2	0.2	0.021	2	2	1
Total		513	7.2	31.2	0.061			

		--------- Quality ----------					--- Pressure -------			
	Dis.	Poor	Fair	Good	Her.	Lo	Med	Hi	
Buddie M	0	3	15	2	2	12	3	7	(4)
Holmes D	1	5	22	6	0	20	10	4	(1)
Lloyd G	1	6	34	9	0	32	12	6	(6)
Mendoza R	2	4	9	11	1	7	11	9	(8)
Nelson J	5	4	24	11	1	20	17	8	(4)
Rivera M	0	2	19	31	2	17	19	18	(15)
Stanton M	5	12	24	22	4	25	20	22	(15)
Others	0	5	22	7	1	24	4	7	(5)
TOTAL	14	41	169	99	11	157	96	81	(58)

	7th inning			8th inning			9th inning		
	0	1	2	0	1	2	0	1	2
Bradley R	0	0	0	0	0	1	0	0	0
Bruske J	0	1	0	0	0	0	0	0	0
Buddie M	0	1	0	0	0	0	0	0	0
Holmes D	1	0	0	1	1	0	0	0	0
Lloyd G	0	1	1	0	0	2	0	0	0
Mendoza R	3	1	1	6	1	0	2	1	0
Nelson J	1	2	1	0	0	3	1	0	0
Rivera M	0	0	0	0	0	0	2	12	13
Stanton M	1	0	1	0	3	4	2	0	3
Starters	14	11	10	7	6	6	1	0	1
TOTAL	20	17	14	14	11	16	8	13	17
Record	12-8	16-1	13-1	9-5	11-0	16-0	6-2	12-1	17-0

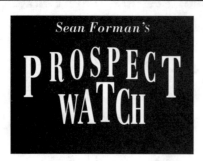

Sean Forman's
PROSPECT WATCH

NAME	AGE	POS	LEVEL	GR98	GR97	GR96	AVG
Ricky Ledee	24	OF	AAA	64	75	88	72
D'Angelo Jimenez	20	SS	AAA	83	63	53	71
Mike Lowell	24	3B	AAA	61	71	31	59
Chris Ashby	23	C	AAA	50	59	58	54
Shane Spencer	26	OF	AAA	53	57	49	54
Donzell McDonald	23	OF	AA	42	62	46	49

NAME	AGE	POS	LEVEL	GRADE
Nick Johnson	19	1B	High A	83
Richard Brown	21	OF	High A	56
Jackson Melian	18	OF	Low A	49
Omar Fuentes	18	C	Rookie	48
Teuris Olivares	19	2B	Rookie	46

NAME	AGE	GS	S	C	T	W-L	ERA	K/H	LEVEL
Jim Baron	24	20	4.40	3.05	7.45	7-9	3.38	0.65	High
Mike Jerzembeck	25	23	4.22	3.35	7.57	4-8	4.85	0.68	High
Frank Lankford	26	15	4.47	3.33	7.80	4-10	5.07	0.53	High
Wilson Heredia	25	20	4.00	3.85	7.85	6-10	6.55	0.71	High
Brett Schlomann	23	17	4.65	3.47	8.12	7-6	5.61	0.47	High
Marty Janzen	25	19	4.26	4.37	8.63	6-10	5.14	0.77	High
Brian Reith	20	20				6-7	2.28	1.35	Low

Sorry folks, those of you looking for parity in the American League, should look elsewhere. The Yankees have enough talent and enough wherewithal to remain competitive and perhaps dominant for some time to come. I'm not fired up about the Scott Brosius or Joe Girardi contracts, but they've got some guys who will be able to step in and keep them from getting too old.

TOP DOG: Nick Johnson

Johnson went nuclear on the Florida State League last year batting .317/.466/.538. Johnson was named the third best prospect in the league and was second in the minors in OBP behind the Royals' Jeremy Giambi. He has always had good patience, but he upped the batting average and power in what is generally a tough league to hit in. As with all Yankees' prospects, there is a good shot he will end up playing somewhere else, but with the Yankees' emphasis on plate discipline he could become an extreme walker in the major leagues.

YOUNG 'UN: Jackson Melian

I always get a few questions about Jackson Melian from Yankees fans. Except for maybe Glenn Williams, no other 16 year old has caused as much of a stir when he signed. Like Williams, Melian isn't exactly tearing through the minor leagues. He hit just .255/.322/.353 in low A this year, which is essentially the same as his previous year in the Gulf Coast League. His base-stealing is mediocre (15 of 27 last year), and he strikes out quite a bit. He was one of the younger players in the league, but you need to see a little more offense before you get excited about a player.

1999 COLUMBUS CLIPPERS' MVP: Mike Lowell

Lowell has turned it on the last two years after a fairly lackluster early career. He posted a .304/.355/.535 line, while putting up his second straight 25+ home run season. Due to the long-term signing of Scott Brosius, it appears that Lowell will continue to play in Columbus for a year or more unless he is traded, a distinct possibility. Lowell's MLE was .273/.312/.457, while Brosius hit .300/.371/.472. Of course, the year before Brosius hit .203/.259/.317.

Lowell is not as good defensively as Brosius, but he's about as good offensively and $5m cheaper. Comp: Russ Davis.

GO! SPEED RACER, GO!: Donzell McDonald

McDonald isn't as well known as his little brother, Orioles' prospect Darnell McDonald. Donzell was on the fast track until he hit AA this year. He struggled to a .253/.330/.358 line after batting .296/.400/.458 in the Florida State League in 1997. His basestealing also regressed as he stole 35 bases but with just a 61% success rate. He has historically been an outstanding basestealer, 104 steals out of 128 attempts. I'm guessing he'll be given another opportunity in AA, where he should be able to right himself. Still he's not going to make Yanks fans forget Bernie anytime soon. Comp: John Shelby, with some more patience.

ON THE MOUND: Brian Reith

Reith is another good-looking young player. He is not nearly as well-known as Ryan Bradley, frankly because he isn't as good. Reith pitched very well in the Sally, striking out 116 while allowing just 86 hits. He did pitch three complete games, but totaled just 118 innings. His control was likewise excellent as he allowed just 32 walks, about a baserunner an inning overall. He was prone to unearned runs as 12 of his 42 runs allowed were unearned.

Where the Yankees' depth may really have come into play, however, was in starting pitching. Beginning with Cone and Wells, New York had the best 1-2 punch in the American League. They were then able to follow that up with Pettitte, Irabu, Mendoza and their secret weapon, Orlando Hernandez. Just weeks after having barely survived an escape from Cuba via raft, El Duque became the Yankees' third best starter. In the post-season, Hernandez was the winner in two exceptionally important contests: Game Four of the ALCS, where the Yankees entered trailing the Indians two games to one; and Game Two of the World Series, where the Yankees needed a win to establish complete control (winning gave them a 2-0 going to San Diego).

El Duque is the kind of thing that happens to teams who set records for team wins. Not that the teams weren't excellent; it's just that it takes something extra special to create a special season. The 1906 Cubs traded for two pitchers in mid-season—Orval Overall and Jack Taylor—who were 12-14 for the teams they'd been on. The two of them went 24-6 for the Cubs, creating what is possibly the deepest six-man starting rotation of all time. The result: 116 wins. The 1954 Indians, already loaded with pitching, were able to pluck Vic Wertz away from the freshly-arrived-in-Baltimore Orioles for a chimp named Bob Chakeles (lifetime record: 15-25, 4.54 ERA). The Tribe was 38-21 when they acquired Wertz, and they went 73-22 afterwards en route to their 111 win season.

THE HALL OF FAME

A lot of air was passed on the subject of the 1998 Yankees and the Hall of Fame—specifically, the contention that a team this great should have more guys who seem like obvious choices for Cooperstown. Looking at the list of top win teams in history, we have the following Hall of Fame membership:

1906 Cubs Frank Chance, Johnny Evers, Joe Tinker, Three-Finger Brown
1927 Yankees Babe Ruth, Lou Gehrig, Earle Combs, Waite Hoyt
1931 A's Jimmie Foxx, Al Simmons, Mickey Cochrane, Lefty Grove
1954 Indians Bob Feller, Early Wynn, Bob Lemon, Hal Newhouser, Larry Doby
1969 Orioles Frank Robinson, Brooks Robinson, Jim Palmer
1975 Reds Joe Morgan, Johnny Bench, (Pete Rose)

None of these teams were overloaded with Hall members; the 1954 Indians had the most, but Newhouser was not much of a factor in their success that year and Feller was limited to 19 starts. The Yankees may well end up with three players from their 1998 team in the Hall of Fame.

Who are these guys, you ask? There are five players whose careers might pan out, and we'll list them in order of likelihood.

1 Tim Raines
2 David Cone
3 Derek Jeter
4 Chuck Knoblauch
5 Bernie Williams

Despite what many seem to think, Raines is already qualified for the Hall, and while he's likely to wind up as a Veteran's Committee pick, it's a safe bet that he'll get in. Tom Hull's percentile system, which you can read about in greater detail back in the General Essay section, shows that Tim has had a career that matches up to many of the mid-level Hall of Fame outfielders.

Cone's chances rest on his being able to reach 200 wins and keep his lifetime winning percentage above .600. There is only one pitcher in baseball history with that combination of achievements who is not in the Hall of Fame—Carl Mays, who is ostracized primarily for one fatal pitch thrown on August 16, 1920. David's lifetime record is currently 168-93 (.644). He may have enough finishing kick to make it.

Jeter, Knoblauch and Williams are all projections, and to my eye Jeter might be the best bet of the three. If his power surge holds up, he could put together enough peak seasons over the next five years to pull it off. Knoblauch is already on a Hall of Fame pace per the Hull percentile system, though

1999 will be important in that he needs to bounce back from an off-year.

Williams is probably the longest shot, though he was clearly the Yankees' best player over the past three years. He's going to need to win a few more batting titles and have a fairly long peak if he's going to have a chance.

When all is said and done, however, I suspect that we'll find three of these five individuals in the Hall of Fame somewhere in the 2015-2020 time frame.

THE YEAR AFTER

So what happens next year? Technically, that's this year, but you know what I mean. It's probably the safest bet in the history of wagering that the Yankees will win fewer games in 1999 than they did in 1998. There have been ten teams that have won 107 or more games in a season prior to the 1998 Yankees, and none of those teams won more games the following season (though, as you'll see below, the 1969 Orioles came close):

Team	Yr	Wins	Yr. +1	Diff
CHC	1906	116	107	-9
CHC	1907	107	99	-8
NYY	1927	110	101	-9
PHI	1931	107	94	-13

IN-DEPTH TEAM BREAKOUT YANKEES 1998

Category	RS	RA	W	L	WPct	Rk
4- RUNS ALLOWED/HOME	299	113	49	4	.925	2
5+ RUNS SCORED/HOME	390	215	47	5	.904	1
4- RUNS ALLOWED	592	212	90	12	.882	1
5+ RUNS SCORED	814	419	90	12	.882	1
5+ RUNS SCORED/ROAD	424	204	43	7	.860	2
LOW SCORING GAMES/HOME	56	24	16	3	.842	1
4- RUNS ALLOWED/ROAD	293	99	41	8	.837	1
CLOSE LOW-SCORING GAMES/HOME	29	16	10	2	.833	2
RECORD IN BLOWOUTS/ROAD	272	135	26	8	.765	1
RECORD IN BLOWOUTS	442	226	42	13	.764	1
RECORD IN BLOWOUTS/HOME	170	91	16	5	.762	1
SLUGFESTS/HOME	226	167	19	7	.731	1
RECORD IN LOW SCORING GAMES	100	52	27	10	.730	1
RECORD IN SLUGFESTS	515	357	41	16	.719	1
RECORD IN CLOSE GAMES/HOME	155	135	25	10	.714	2
SLUGFESTS/ROAD	289	190	22	9	.710	2
SEASON TOTALS	965	656	114	48	.704	1
CLOSE SLUGFESTS/ROAD	53	49	4	2	.667	3
RECORD IN CLOSE GAMES	274	247	41	22	.651	1
CLOSE SLUGFESTS/HOME	57	54	5	3	.625	2
LOW SCORING GAMES/ROAD	44	28	11	7	.611	2
RECORD IN CLOSE GAMES/ROAD	119	112	16	12	.571	2
CLOSE LOW SCORING GAMES/ROAD	19	19	6	5	.545	3
4- RUNS SCORED/HOME	82	99	15	14	.517	1
5+ RUNS ALLOWED/HOME	173	201	13	15	.464	1
4- RUNS SCORED	151	237	24	36	.400	1
5+ RUNS ALLOWED	373	444	24	36	.400	1
5+ RUNS ALLOWED/ROAD	200	243	11	21	.344	2
4- RUNS SCORED/ROAD	69	138	9	22	.290	2

Team	Yr	Wins	Yr. +1	Diff
NYY	1932	107	91	-16
CLE	1954	111	93	-18
BAL	1969	109	108	-1
BAL	1970	108	101	-7
CIN	1975	108	102	-6
NYM	1986	108	92	-16
AVG				-10

The average decline for these teams was 10 games. As you can see from the list, however, that decline is by no means uniform. A good bit of what happens to the Yankees in 1999 depends on how well the back end of their pitching rotation fares, because it's hard to believe that Cone and Wells, as good as they are, will both equal their 1998 performances. If Pettitte returns to his 1997 form, Irabu and Hernandez hold their 1998 levels, and Mendoza can remain in his role of the unsung swing man, the Yankees could become the first team since the 1969-70 Orioles to repeat on this list. (It's only happened twice: the 1906-07 Cubs are the other team to do it.)

More likely, however, is that the starters will give ground, and some of the veteran hitters will decline, and the Yankees could challenge the Mets and Indians for biggest dropoff. Of course, even winning 100 games in 1999 would put them in that category, so take all of this with a grain of salt. If the Yankees continue to be aggressive and either maintain or replenish the talent they've so assiduously acquired over the past three years, they have a reasonable shot at being the first team since the 1969-71 Orioles to win 100 or more games three years in a row.

Team		Years	Yr 1	Yr 2	Yr 3
PHI	A	1929-31	104	102	107
STL	N	1942-44	106	105	105
BAL	A	1969-71	109	108	101

As you can see, it's a short list. The only other teams who came close were the 1936-38 Yankees (99 wins in 1938, followed by 106 in 1939) and the 1988-90 A's (99 in 1989).

Name	AB	R	H	D	T	HR	RBI	BB	SO	SB	CS	BA	OBP	SLG	XR	Adj XR/27	Raw XR/27	OXW	DXW	TXW
Brosius S	528	88	160	33	0	20	100	54	96	11	8	.302	.375	.479	93	6.41	6.24	3.88	1.14	5.02
Bush H	71	17	27	3	0	1	5	5	19	5	3	.383	.425	.471	13	6.88	6.76	0.57	0.06	0.63
Curtis C	453	81	111	21	1	11	57	78	79	20	5	.246	.361	.367	68	5.06	4.87	1.95	1.10	3.05
Davis C	103	11	30	7	0	3	9	14	18	0	1	.292	.376	.451	15	5.15	5.05	0.44	0.00	0.44
Girardi J	253	32	70	11	4	3	32	15	38	2	4	.276	.320	.388	27	3.57	3.52	-0.02	1.53	1.51
Jeter D	624	130	204	25	8	20	85	59	118	28	6	.327	.388	.489	113	6.86	6.69	5.10	2.66	7.76
Knoblauch C	600	120	160	24	4	18	65	79	69	30	12	.266	.365	.408	96	5.47	5.36	3.17	1.56	4.73
Ledee R	79	13	19	5	2	1	12	7	29	3	1	.240	.301	.391	10	4.12	4.11	0.12	0.19	0.31
Martinez T	529	94	150	32	1	30	125	63	82	2	1	.284	.361	.517	96	6.36	6.12	3.91	0.42	4.33
O'Neill P	600	97	192	39	2	25	118	59	102	14	1	.320	.377	.519	111	6.77	6.57	4.86	1.29	6.15
Posada J	356	57	96	22	0	18	64	49	91	0	1	.270	.355	.483	58	5.58	5.39	1.94	2.02	3.96
Raines T	319	54	93	13	1	5	48	57	48	8	3	.291	.401	.387	54	6.16	5.99	2.22	0.15	2.37
Sojo L	147	16	34	3	1	0	14	4	15	1	0	.232	.252	.266	8	1.84	1.80	-0.73	0.37	-0.36
Spencer S	67	19	26	6	0	11	28	5	12	0	1	.388	.425	.969	23	14.21	12.94	1.54	0.14	1.68
Strawberry D	293	45	75	11	2	26	58	48	89	7	7	.254	.363	.568	61	7.18	6.70	2.80	-0.02	2.78
Sveum D	58	6	9	0	0	0	3	4	16	0	0	.156	.205	.156	1	0.70	0.67	-0.53	-0.02	-0.55
Williams B	496	104	170	29	5	28	99	77	80	14	9	.343	.430	.591	110	8.32	7.97	5.83	0.95	6.78
NY	5617	990	1632	284	31	220	922	679	1014	143	63	.291	.369	.470	957	6.03	5.84	37.06	13.54	50.60

Pitcher	S	C	T	SS	ES	IC	HH	PP	TJ	S12	S35	S67	C1	C23	C45	C67	QWP
Bradley	6.00	4.00	10.00	0%	0%	0%	100%	0%	0%	0%	0%	100%	0%	0%	100%	0%	.163
Bruske	3.00	3.00	6.00	100%	0%	0%	0%	0%	0%	0%	100%	0%	0%	100%	0%	0%	.633
Buddie	6.00	3.50	9.50	0%	0%	0%	100%	0%	0%	0%	0%	100%	0%	50%	50%	0%	.277
Cone	3.48	2.84	6.32	61%	23%	61%	19%	10%	13%	42%	39%	19%	19%	45%	35%	0%	.590
Irabu	3.29	3.68	6.96	61%	14%	54%	21%	11%	4%	43%	36%	21%	0%	50%	39%	11%	.555
Jerzembeck	5.50	5.00	10.50	0%	0%	0%	50%	0%	0%	0%	50%	50%	0%	0%	100%	0%	.140
Mendoza	3.71	2.93	6.64	50%	14%	43%	21%	7%	7%	36%	43%	21%	14%	57%	29%	0%	.583
O Hernandez	3.05	3.24	6.29	67%	29%	48%	19%	14%	0%	48%	33%	19%	24%	38%	24%	14%	.605
Pettitte	4.25	3.41	7.66	38%	13%	31%	28%	13%	9%	22%	50%	28%	13%	44%	38%	6%	.475
Wells	3.60	2.00	5.60	67%	37%	73%	23%	0%	27%	37%	40%	23%	47%	37%	17%	0%	.646

AMERICAN LEAGUE EAST

BOSTON RED SOX

Art Martone

IF YOU THINK there's polarization in Washington on the subject of Bill Clinton, mention the name "Dan Duquette" in Red Sox Nation. You're guaranteed to draw one of two responses:

Brilliant talent evaluator and organization builder who cleared away the Lou Gorman rubble and laid the foundation for long-range success, or

People-phobic, rotisserie-nerd GM who understands everything about statistics but nothing about the human beings responsible for them.

Duquette's supporters point proudly to the heavy lifting he's done to haul the Red Sox from the bottom of the talent spectrum to where they are today. Since his hiring in January, 1994, the Sox have twice qualified for the playoffs (as division champion in 1995 and the wild-card entry in 1998); only 10 major-league franchises have been to the postseason twice in that time. More significantly, he's helped turn the Red Sox farm system from a wasteland to—well, if not the land of milk and honey, at least the horn of plenty. Baseball America annually places the Sox in the top five in its yearly evaluation of minor-league organizations, and in the five years since Duquette's hiring the team has produced one superstar (Nomar Garciaparra), enough top-level prospects to trade for another (Pedro Martinez), and the quantity to net job-specific veterans like Mike Stanley and Greg Swindell. The Duke's skillful trolling of the waiver wire and low-level free-agent lists yielded no less than three regulars (Darren Lewis, Mike Benjamin and Troy O'Leary) for a team that finished 1998 with the second-best record in the American League.

Duquette's detractors turn the farm-system argument on its head: they point out that Garciaparra is the ONLY regular the Sox have produced from their organization since 1994 and that no other position players seem ready to contribute. When Duquette dismissed, without explanation, several of his top minor-league lieutenants last summer, it was taken not as a normal shakeup but as further proof that things aren't as rosy as they've been described. Duquette stressed pitching was his number-one minor-league priority when he took command, but pitchers developed in The Duquette Era have won a grand total of two games for Boston. (One by Brian

Rose in 1998, the other by Robinson Checo in 1997.) Nor do the Sox have any single prospect whose skills scream "can't-miss."

But that's just part of it, add the Duke-bashers. In the span of 23 months, the Red Sox lost two men—Roger Clemens and Mo Vaughn—who are, arguably, among the six best and/or most important players in franchise history (with Babe Ruth, Ted Williams, Carl Yastrzemski and Jim Rice). Clemens directly blames Duquette for his departure; Vaughn points his finger at The Duke more indirectly but just as strongly.

Those losses stem from a bigger problem that Peter Gammons articulated in a Boston Globe column in March, 1997. "Sorry," Gammons wrote, "but it's part of baseball's current landscape to get players to want to play for your team." Duquette's Red Sox, Gammons continued, have fallen down abysmally on that count. Not all of it is The Duke's fault, he stressed; he blamed reclusive owner John Harrington for calling at least some of the shots from his invisible bunker and letting Duquette take all the heat. (Gammons also cited other factors that make the Red Sox a difficult sell: a vicious, out-of-control, talk-show driven media; a negative, self-indulgent fandom that can't stop fixating on 1918; antiquated facilities that hold no sentimental value for professional athletes.)

But Duquette, he stressed, shoulders some of the responsibility with his detached, emotionless approach that alienates players and invites bashing from the press. Last offseason the Red Sox pursued Bernie Williams, Albert Belle, Rafael Palmeiro, Robin Ventura and Will Clark. All of them signed

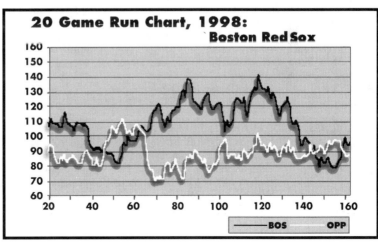

20 Game Run Chart, 1998:
Boston Red Sox

BOS — OPP

QMAX PRESENTS: "BAD" PITCHERS

HE COULD WALK THE WALK

I had a little bit of a hard time choosing the subject for the Red Sox' Bad Pitcher essay. The first pitcher to jump out at me was Jolted Jack Lamabe of the bedraggled 1964 club. He posted a 5.89 ERA in 177 innings in 1964. That was a pitcher's year, and Jack's adjusted ERA figure of 65 might just be the worst in history for anyone with enough innings to qualify for the ERA title. However, we found another Red Sox pitcher whose numbers, while on the whole not nearly as bad as Lamabe's, scatter across the QMAX palate in such an intriguing way that we here at BBBA just couldn't resist, suckers that we are for the cruel and unusual.

The 1950 Red Sox were a powerful club, a truly vintage year for the Red Sox fan who enjoys the lumbered arts, and virtually all of them do, being Red Sox fans. The team batting average was .302, and no regular batted under Bobby Doerr's .294. And yet, they finished third, four games behind (of course) the Yankees. Why? In a word, pitching. In two words, Bad Pitching. And no hurler on that 1950 squad was Badder than Slick Mickey McDermott. McDermott was hugely popular with Red Sox fans; he enjoyed the night life, and his sweet Irish tenor was heard in the wee hours in more than a few Boston pubs. He had a deserved reputation as a wild man.

Mickey started only 15 games for the Sox that year (although I included an 8 2/3 inning relief stint as a "start" to beef up the numbers a bit). In those 16 "starts", McDermott's QMAX "stuff" rating was 3.94, quite good, and probably under the league average for that year. His "command" rating, however, was an unbelievable 5.58, so far the worst "command" average ever found for any decent number of starts. A full nine of his 16 starts pegged the C meter at seven, and

MICKEY McDERMOTT/BOS 1950							
	1	2	3	4	5	6	7	S
1			2		1			3
2			1					3
3		1					2	3
4							1	1
5							2	2
6							2	2
7			2				1	3
C	0	0	3	3	1	0	9	16

only three of the 16 starts even got below 4. All three of those happened in his first five starts, before he completely lost sight of the strike zone. Mickey walked 93 men in 85 innings in his starting stints, including an amazing 10 walks in 3 1/3 innings on May 7, 1950. As it is wont to do, this kind of sustained performance landed Mickey in the bullpen most of the time after mid-June, denying us the chance to see what he really was capable of.

However, there is a happy ending: Mickey found control the next year, and eventually turned in a fine 18-10, 3.01 season for the Sox in 1953. He ended his career with a 69-69, 3.91 record after 12 years in the bigs. The QMAX moral once again asserts itself: let your young men sow their wild oats.

--Tom Austin

---

elsewhere. If you're inclined to believe that players—at least those with viable options—turn a deaf ear when The Duke begins warbling "Please Come To Boston," this would seem to fit into the category of evidence.

By early last December, Duquette seemed flattened. Gammons wrote that the offseason "fiasco" of Vaughn's loss and the failure to lure a big-name replacement could prove to be "Dan Duquette's Waterloo" as Red Sox general manager.

Will it? And should it?

THIS WAS THE NUCLEUS of the team Duquette inherited when he took command on Jan. 27, 1994:

ROTATION	Roger Clemens (age 31); Aaron Sele (24); Frank Viola (34); Danny Darwin (38); Joe Hesketh (35).
KEY RELIEVERS	Jeff Russell (33); Ken Ryan (25).
CATCHERS	Damon Berryhill (31); Dave Valle (33); Bob Melvin (32); John Flaherty (26).
INFIELDERS	Mo Vaughn (26); Scott Fletcher (35); John Valentin (27); Scott Cooper (26); Tim Naehring (26).
OUTFIELDERS	Mike Greenwell (30); Billy Hatcher (33); Otis Nixon (35); Greg Blosser (22); Carlos Quintana (28); Bob Zupcic (27).
DESIGNATED HITTER	Andre Dawson (39).

It would have been quite a powerhouse around about 1987. But this was 1994, and Duquette was repulsed by what he saw. Of the handful of twentysomethings, the only ones with any future were Vaughn, Valentin, Naehring, Sele and (arguably) Flaherty. The majority of the starters were over 30. The bulk of them were WELL over 30.

In hindsight, it's clear that sometime around 1989 it was decided in the executive suite to make an all-out effort to win the World Series before general partner Jean Yawkey died. The Sox, with Hall of Famers Roger Clemens and Wade Boggs in tow, had a strong team that had won the pennant in 1986 and the AL East in 1988. Mrs. Yawkey was then in her early 80s, and the Sox apparently felt the pressure to win a World Series championship with a Yawkey at the helm, having failed to do so during the 43 years her late husband, Tom, owned the team—or in the 13 years after his death.

And thus was instituted an unannounced, 180-degree change in organizational philosophy. Gorman, the GM at the time, received new marching orders. A team that, after early dabbling, had almost completely rejected free agency in favor of its traditional building from within, embraced the open market. It blew up on them.

There would be no titles before Mrs. Yawkey's death in 1992, not with the powerhouse A's straddling the West and the soon-to-be-powerhouse Blue Jays rising in the East. There were a series of sacrifice-the-future-for-the-present moves, which led to one for-the-ages blunder—Bagwell for Andersen—and resulted in the loss of precious draft picks, forfeited in pursuit of free agents such as Tony Pena, Jeff Reardon, Danny Darwin, Matt Young, Jack Clark, Frank Viola, Andre Dawson, Otis Nixon and Dave Valle. The end result was a farm system whose "prospects," once you got past Sele, Frank Rodriguez and Scott Hatteberg, were names that only an obsessive student of minor-league baseball would recognize.

By 1993, with nothing to trade and their farm system a dust bowl, the team was reduced to signing in-their-30s free agents as virtually its only means of player procurement. They had completely lost sight of what it takes to build a successful organization.

In came Duquette, to restore that vision.

FAST FORWARD to 1998.

ROTATION	Pedro Martinez (age 26); Bret Saberhagen (34); Tim Wakefield (31); Steve Avery (28); Pete Schourek (29).
KEY RELIEVERS	Tom Gordon (30); Jim Corsi (36), Dennis Eckersley (43).
CATCHERS	Scott Hatteberg (28); Jason Varitek (26).
INFIELDERS	Mo Vaughn (30); Mike Benjamin (32); Nomar Garciaparra (25); John Valentin (31).
OUTFIELDERS	Troy O'Leary (28); Darren Lewis (30); Damon Buford (28); Darren Bragg (28).
DESIGNATED HITTERS	Mike Stanley (35); Reggie Jefferson (29).

The '98 Sox showed age in only two places—relief pitching and designated hitting—places where experience is valued and athleticism isn't.

Still, it wasn't quite what everyone expected. Over the course of their history, the Red Sox' strongest teams have emerged only after a volcanic eruption of farm-system talent that had been bubbling for years under the surface. The 1998 Sox didn't follow in those footsteps. Of the key players, the only farm products were Vaughn, Valentin, Garciaparra and Hatteberg. And of those, only Garciaparra was drafted in the Duquette Era.

But waiting for the farm system to regenerate itself would have meant a half-decade (or more) of losing. Only now are the products of Duquette's first draft, in 1994, beginning to break through. Garciaparra is a regular; Brian Rose, Brian Barkley and Donnie Sadler all saw action with the big-league team in '98; Carl Pavano, sent to Montreal as part of the Martinez trade, pitched regularly for the Expos. (The Sox still hold out hope for two other members of the Class of '94:

WPA BULLPEN BOX—BOSTON RED SOX

	Pl	WPA	P	PPPI
Starters	981	4.5	51.5	0.053
Relievers	649	5.2	41.0	0.063
Road	301	2.3	16.9	0.056
Home	348	2.9	24.1	0.069
Mar/Apr	104	0.1	8.1	0.078
May	122	2.2	5.7	0.046
June	97	1.2	5.6	0.058
July	100	-0.2	5.3	0.053
August	111	1.6	7.7	0.070
September	115	0.3	8.6	0.075
Non S/H Sit.	471	-1.3	22.4	0.047
S/H Sit.	178	6.5	18.7	0.105
Low Pressure	252	-1.0	4.0	0.016
Med. Pressure	209	-0.5	13.3	0.064
High Pressure	188	6.6	23.7	0.126
Entered behind	267	0.1	8.1	0.030
Entered tied	92	-0.7	11.5	0.125
Entered ahead	290	5.8	21.5	0.074

Name	G	Pl	WPA	P	PPPI	MI	ROB	T
Avery S	11	12	-.5	.8	.063	1	5	1
Corsi J	59	86	.5	5.8	.067	25	24	10
Eckersley D	50	55	-.3	3.7	.067	5	15	9
Garces R	30	53	.2	5.0	.038	17	9	0
Gordon T	73	94	5.9	9.4	.100	19	25	11
Lowe D	53	93	1.5	6.9	.074	27	24	8
Mahay R	29	42	-.5	2.5	.058	9	14	4
Reyes C	24	47	.2	1.9	.040	14	11	3
Swindell G	29	39	.4	3.3	.085	9	12	8
Wasdin J	39	71	-.7	3.0	.043	19	20	6
TOTAL		649	5.2	41.0	.063			

	I--------- Quality ----------I					I--- Pressure -------I			
	Dis.	Poor	Fair	Good	Her.	Lo	Med	Hi	
Avery S	0	5	4	2	0	5	4	2	(0)
Corsi J	2	11	26	19	1	21	21	17	(11)
Eckersley D	4	7	28	11	0	27	17	6	(4)
Garces R	1	3	19	6	1	18	7	5	(5)
Gordon T	3	3	28	33	6	28	17	28	(23)
Lowe D	3	8	21	16	5	14	19	20	(13)
Mahay R	3	5	14	7	0	14	9	6	(5)
Reyes C	0	5	13	6	0	11	11	2	(1)
Swindell G	0	8	12	9	0	8	15	6	(3)
Wasdin J	2	6	20	11	0	19	12	8	(4)
Others	2	8	25	1	0	23	10	3	(2)
TOTAL	20	69	210	121	13	188	142	103	(71)

	7th inning			8th inning			9th inning		
	0	+1	+2	0	+1	+2	0	+1	+2
Avery S	0	0	0	1	0	0	0	0	0
Corsi J	3	1	5	4	3	6	0	0	0
Eckersley D	1	0	0	2	1	4	4	0	0
Garces R	0	2	1	0	2	1	1	0	0
Gordon T	0	0	0	1	0	0	4	13	13
Lowe D	4	5	3	5	2	2	0	0	0
Mahay R	0	0	1	1	1	1	1	0	0
Reyes C	1	1	0	0	0	0	0	0	0
Schourek P	0	0	0	0	1	0	0	0	0
Shouse B	1	0	0	0	0	0	0	0	0
Swindell G	1	0	1	3	2	3	3	0	0
Wasdin J	0	1	2	0	0	0	1	0	0
Starters	9	8	5	3	2	2	0	1	0
TOTAL	20	18	18	20	14	19	14	14	13
Record	8-12	13-5	16-2	8-12	12-2	19-0	6-8	14-0	13-0

Sean Forman's

PROSPECT WATCH

NAME	AGE	POS	LEVEL	GR98	GR97	GR96	AVG
Michael Coleman	22	OF	AAA	66	83	47	69
Cole Liniak	21	3B	AAA	79	62	47	68
Dernell Stenson	20	OF	AA	76	63	43	66
Trot Nixon	24	OF	AAA	70	61	49	64
Arquimedez Pozo	24	3B	AAA	55	71	-	61
Donnie Sadler	23	SS	AAA	60	59	68	61
Andy Abad	25	1B	AAA	57	54	51	55
Wilton Veras	20	3B	AA	72	41	29	55
Damian Sapp	22	C	AA	46	-	64	51
Jimmy Hurst	26	OF	AAA	47	50	36	46
Lou Merloni	27	3B	AAA	62	26	24	44
James Chambelee	23	SS	AA	46	40	8	38

NAME	AGE	POS	LEVEL	GRADE
Steve Lomasney	20	C	High A	56
Rontrez Johnson	21	OF	Low A	48
Carlos Leon	18	2B	Low A	47
Derek Rix	20	1B	Rookie	46
Shea Hillenbrand	22	C	Low A	42
David Eckstein	23	2B	High A	38

NAME	AGE	GS	S	C	T	W-L	ERA	K/H	LEVEL
Robert Ramsay	24	26	3.46	3.19	6.65	11-6	3.54	1.18	High
Jim Farrell	24	26	4.00	3.23	7.23	13-9	5.51	0.81	High
Juan Pena	21	22	4.05	3.41	7.45	8-9	4.38	1.04	High
Paxton Crawford	20	21	3.81	3.71	7.52	6-5	4.17	0.79	High
Brian Barkley	22	23	4.48	3.39	7.87	7-9	4.91	0.55	High
Jason Sekany	22	26	4.23	4.00	8.23	9-10	5.21	0.75	High
Jack Cressend	23	30	4.53	3.80	8.33	9-11	4.34	0.77	High

The Red Sox have taken their place among the big market teams, but they haven't abandoned their farm system. The Red Sox have a lot of depth all over the diamond and their top twenty prospects are probably better than anybody else's. Well, except maybe for the Marlins. They also have had some success in the pitching department, though it hasn't shown up on the big league squad yet. I suspect some of those pitchers will hit the bigs by late 1999 or 2000.

TOP DOG: Dernell Stenson

Dernell Stenson was the youngest player in the Eastern League for much of the year. He handled himself well hitting .257/.376/.446. He'll be just 21 next year and will likely be the starting left fielder in Pawtucket, where he could put up some big numbers. In addition to being young, he also jumped from low A ball to AA. He is a bit of a plodder, so he is not going to win any gold gloves or steal many bases, but he can swing a mean bat and should be helping the Red Sox in 2000. Comp: Chili Davis.

HOT CORNER HEIR: Cole Liniak

Liniak is another quick-mover. He played primarily in High A ball last year, but ended up in AAA despite being just 21. He improved his power dramatically as he doubled his career home run total and posted his highest isolated power of .196. His batting average was down at .261, and his walk numbers are a little low. It's hard to say how he will develop as he ages, but he may get another year or two in AAA as John Valentin and Jose Offerman are signed to long-term deals. I foresee him being a .300 hitter with 15-20 homer power. Comp: Dave Hansen with more power.

LATE-BLOOMER: Trot Nixon

Nixon has busted his hump the last three years and has finally re-established himself as a prospect. His first few seasons were marred by a back injury, that he appears to have moved past as he has put up three healthy seasons. He was repeating AAA after scuffling there last year, and he certainly got it right hitting .310/.400/.513, to go along with 26 steals in 39 tries. He generally walks about as much as he strikes out, and plays solid defense. Looking at his record one might think that this season was a fluke, but I think he has reached a new level of production. He's not going to be a star corner outfielder, but I think he'll be productive. Comp: Mark Whiten.

Backstops:

Damian Sapp - Sapp's 1997 season was lost to back surgery, which was unfortunate for the Sox as he was coming off a .965 OPS in low-A. Back injuries are a cause of concern for a catcher, and he played just 63 games this year. His bat is a big plus if he can get healthy.

Steve Lomasney - Lomasney is another good looking young catcher. He managed just a .239 batting average, but he has good power (22 home runs in 443 ABs) and good patience (59 walks) and has some speed (13 stolen bases). He whiffs just lot (145 Ks), but he's still young and will be moving into a much better park next year. He is also the best defensive catcher in the organization.

Shea Hillenbrand - Hillenbrand is a third base to catcher conversion project which explains why he is a 22-year-old playing in low A ball. Still anytime a catcher hits .349/.383/.546 you have to take notice.

ON THE MOUND: Robert Ramsay

Ramsay is a big, 6-5, lefty, who came into his own in his third pro season. As you can see by his 3.46/3.19 line he showed both good hit prevention and control He walked just 50 batters versus 166 strikeouts in 163 innings pitched. He also did an exceptional job of keeping the ball in the park as he allowed just 10 home runs. This was his best season by far, so he may regress. If he can keep his pitching at this level he'll be helping out in the majors quite quickly.

Damian Sapp, who is coming back from an injury, and Michael Coleman, who needs an attitude transplant.) A couple of 1995 draftees—Cole Liniak and Juan Pena—are inching closer to Boston. But many of the best prospects, like John Curtice, Dernell Stenson, Steve Lomasney and Shea Hillebrand, are two levels (or more) away.

What Duquette has been forced to do in the interim is turn to the trade and free-agent markets. His reputation was defined, in some circles, by two separate incidents:

In the post-strike chaos of April 1995, he tripled the team's talent base by quickly casting a net over many of the available veteran free agents: Jefferson, Mike Macfarlane, Stan Belinda, Erik Hanson, Alejandro Pena, Derek Lilliquist, Zane Smith. Not all of them made it and none, save for Jefferson, would prove to be long-term Sox. But

that fishing expedition brought in two starting pitchers, a valuable reliever, a starting catcher and a productive platoon bat, all of whom were crucial to the division championship that followed.

Almost exactly a year later, during spring training of 1996, he signed Kevin Mitchell—who then resembled a weather balloon more than a baseball player—and put him in right field. This move didn't work, as the Sox' 6-19 start and Mitchell's injury-riddled 27-game tenure in Boston would attest.

A tag was thus slapped on Duquette by many in the media: Short Term Dan, the free agent's best friend. He was accused by one national reporter of thinking that was the only road to success. "And," the reporter added sagely, "everyone knows it can't be done."

Like most generalizations, a germ of truth (Duquette

signs a bunch of veteran free agents) developed into an epidemic of misinformation (that's the way Duquette builds his teams).

OUTSIDE OF THE veteran pitchers signed as rehab projects (Bret Saberhagen, Butch Henry), the only free agents Dan Duquette signed as long-term acquisitions were Tom Gordon and Steve Avery. The rest—Mike Stanley, Jamie Moyer, Shane Mack, Chris Hammond, Dennis Eckersley, even Darren Lewis—were, at the time, fill-a-need signings; each of the players received short-term deals to plug a hole that couldn't otherwise be plugged. Prior to last off-season, when they felt pressure to do SOMEthing to cushion the public-relations blow of Vaughn's departure, the Sox never bid for high-price, high-profile free agents. Their modus operandi has always been youth over age, long-term building over short-term gains.

The fingerprints of that philosophy are all over Duquette's trading record:

1/10/96: Infielder Wil Cordero and pitcher Brian Eversgerd from Montreal for pitchers Rheal Cormier and Shayne Bennett and first baseman Ryan McGuire.

1/29/96: Pitchers Heathcliff Slocumb and Larry Wimberly and outfielder Rick Holifield from Philadelphia for pitcher Ken Ryan and outfielders Lee Tinsley and Glenn Murray.

7/30/96: Outfielder Darren Bragg from Seattle for pitcher Jamie Moyer.

1/27/97: Pitcher John Wasdin from Oakland for designated hitter Jose Canseco.

7/31/97: Pitcher Derek Lowe and catcher Jason Varitek from Seattle for pitcher Heathcliff Slocumb.

8/13/97: Pitcher Tony Armas Jr. and a player to be named later (pitcher Jim Mecir) from New York Yankees for designated hitter Mike Stanley and shortstop Randy Brown.

11/18/97: Pitcher Pedro Martinez from Montreal for pitchers Carl Pavano and Tony Armas Jr.

Duquette—except for last year, when he was attempting to strengthen the team for the playoffs—has always sought long-range solutions to chronic problems. Sometimes he fails. Cordero was a young All-Star at the time of his acquisition; the Sox thought he would be their second baseman for years. They hoped Slocumb would be their closer until the millenium. More often, he succeeds. He traded veterans for Lowe, Varitek and Bragg. Once the farm system got chugging, he traded prospects for Martinez. All except Bragg should be playing key roles in Boston for the foreseeable future; Martinez, of course, is one of the cornerstones of the franchise.

When it comes to judging talent, Dan Duquette hits more than he misses. How he treats that talent is another matter.

IN THE YEARS TO COME, Dan Duquette's legacy may be defined by two, and only two, things:

Roger Clemens leaving the Sox to sign with Toronto, Mo Vaughn leaving to sign with Anaheim.

No team of means has ever suffered two such devastating losses in the free-agent era. A case could have been made against signing Clemens—he had gone 40-39 in the years 1993-96, and, as they would soon discover in Blue Jay Land, can be rather insufferable even in the best of times—but your judgment has to be challenged when he subsequently wins back-to-back Cy Young Awards. It's difficult to make any case against signing Vaughn, who averages 40 homers and 120 RBI a season and is one of the most respected leaders in the game.

It's impossible to know who made the decisions to not re-sign Vaughn and Clemens, or why they made it. Harrington will give occasional interviews to friendly, non-threatening television reporters, but otherwise he refuses to speak to the media except for one veteran Boston columnist. This columnist has attacked both Clemens and Vaughn constantly in print over the last two years, accusing both of being greedy, selfish and duplicitous; he has dubbed Clemens "The Texas Con Man" and Vaughn "Mo Money". This, naturally, has led to a belief that the columnist is carrying Harrington's water, that this is the official line. There's no way of knowing: the Sox are such a secretive, almost paranoid organization that no one can crack the inner circle. But if Duquette is simply being the good soldier, he's following his commands to the letter. Never has he even hinted he disagrees with—or didn't formulate—either decision.

Category	RS	RA	W	L	Pct.	Rk
TEAM BREAKOUT						
RED SOX 1998						
4- RUNS ALLOWED/HOME	239	110	40	8	.833	5
5+ RUNS SCORED/HOME	360	228	40	10	.800	2
5+ RUNS SCORED	696	429	70	19	.787	3
5+ RUNS SCORED/ROAD	336	201	30	9	.769	6
4- RUNS ALLOWED	462	220	69	24	.742	10
RECORD IN BLOWOUTS/HOME	111	57	11	4	.733	2
RECORD IN BLOWOUTS	324	185	30	11	.732	2
RECORD IN BLOWOUTS/ROAD	213	128	19	7	.731	2
SLUGFESTS/ROAD	293	197	24	9	.727	1
RECORD IN CLOSE GAMES/HOME	203	186	26	13	.667	5
4- RUNS ALLOWED/ROAD	223	110	29	16	.644	13
LOW SCORING GAMES/HOME	56	35	13	8	.619	5
RECORD IN SLUGFESTS	509	397	37	23	.617	2
CLOSE LOW-SCORING GAMES/HOME	26	22	7	5	.583	8
CLOSE SLUGFESTS/ROAD	51	48	4	3	.571	6
SEASON TOTALS	876	729	92	70	.568	2
RECORD IN LOW SCORING GAMES	104	82	24	20	.545	6
RECORD IN CLOSE GAMES	331	322	40	36	.526	6
SLUGFESTS/HOME	216	200	13	14	.481	8
LOW SCORING GAMES/ROAD	48	47	11	12	.478	9
CLOSE LOW SCORING GAMES/ROAD	38	37	9	10	.474	6
CLOSE SLUGFESTS/HOME	117	120	7	8	.467	11
RECORD IN CLOSE GAMES/ROAD	128	136	14	23	.378	11
4- RUNS SCORED/HOME	79	136	11	20	.355	3
5+ RUNS ALLOWED	414	509	23	46	.333	2
5+ RUNS ALLOWED/HOME	200	254	11	22	.333	3
5+ RUNS ALLOWED/ROAD	214	255	12	24	.333	3
4- RUNS SCORED	180	300	22	51	.301	3
4- RUNS SCORED/ROAD	101	164	11	31	.262	3

If the Sox let Clemens and Vaughn go because they didn't think they were worth the money, that calls into question their professional competency. If they let them go because they didn't like them, because Clemens can be an overbearing tyrant and Vaughn is strong-willed and eager to speak his mind, that calls into question their ability to handle people (and their ability to put aside personal feelings and do what's best for the team). Either way, it reflects poorly on the organization—and on Duquette.

Everything else Duquette has done in Boston may be buried in the nuclear fallout of these back-to-back explosions. Suppose there had been free agency in the 1960s, and the San Francisco Giants had lost Willie Mays and Juan Marichal in the span of 23 months? Today, 30 years later, would you remember that the Giants were a strong team with a good farm system? Or would you remember that they were the dolts who couldn't hold onto Mays and Marichal?

LIKE EVERYTHING IN LIFE, the truth—as defined by the warring camps of Red Sox Nation—lies not in either extreme but somewhere in the middle. Duquette IS a good organizational builder. And he HAS demonstrated interpersonal problems in dealing with the media (with whom he is curt and often unavailable) and some of this players. The question is, which is more important?

No reasonable person can argue that the Red Sox are in worse shape today than they were the day Dan Duquette was hired. When he arrived, the Sox seemed headed into a period of decline that would rival the early '60s, when they averaged about 75 wins a year.

Conversely, no reasonable person can argue the Sox are better served without Roger Clemens and Mo Vaughn; you don't get better by exchanging Hall of Famers for draft choices. And no reasonable person can argue that such a team may have trouble attracting quality free agents in the future, if the free agents believe that how Vaughn and Clemens were treated is an indication of how things are run in Boston.

This subjective argument, however, has been placed on the most objective plane of all: the playing field. Duquette's place in history—and perhaps his fate with the organization—now depends almost solely on how well the Brave New Sox perform in 1999 and beyond.

If they win, he's vindicated. His faith in his development system and trading ability will have been rewarded, and all else will be forgotten. It'll be Mo Who? And Roger What?

If they lose . . .

Name	AB	R	H	D	T	HR	RBI	BB	SO	SB	CS	BA	OBP	SLG	XR	Adj XR/27	Raw XR/27	OXW	DXW	TXW
Benjamin M	349	46	91	22	0	4	39	15	70	3	0	.262	.303	.362	36	3.41	3.63	-0.17	1.43	1.26
Bragg D	408	51	110	27	3	8	57	43	95	7	3	.270	.345	.411	55	4.61	4.79	1.21	0.97	2.18
Buford D	216	37	59	13	4	10	42	22	41	6	5	.275	.344	.517	36	5.82	5.94	1.31	0.74	2.05
Cummings M	120	20	33	7	0	6	15	17	18	4	3	.277	.378	.479	21	6.16	6.14	0.85	-0.02	0.83
Garciaparra N	603	112	190	35	7	37	123	34	59	14	6	.316	.356	.582	114	6.90	7.01	5.10	1.42	6.52
Hatteberg S	358	46	96	22	1	12	43	44	56	0	0	.267	.353	.439	54	5.30	5.48	1.73	1.86	3.59
Jefferson R	196	24	58	15	1	8	31	21	39	0	0	.296	.367	.510	33	6.14	6.39	1.33	0.01	1.34
Lemke M	91	10	16	4	0	0	7	6	14	0	1	.181	.229	.222	5	1.65	1.77	-0.54	0.18	-0.36
Lewis D	583	95	152	23	3	9	63	72	90	34	12	.260	.346	.354	78	4.54	4.66	1.64	1.63	3.27
Leyritz J	129	17	37	6	0	9	24	21	32	0	0	.288	.387	.537	27	7.43	7.16	1.36	0.12	1.48
Merloni L	96	10	26	6	0	1	15	7	19	1	0	.274	.338	.368	12	4.52	4.64	0.26	0.06	0.32
Mitchell K	33	4	8	2	0	0	6	7	5	1	0	.253	.389	.305	5	5.33	5.86	0.17	0.01	0.18
O'Leary T	610	96	159	33	7	25	83	37	104	2	2	.260	.306	.459	81	4.61	4.82	1.69	0.99	2.68
Sadler D	124	21	27	4	4	3	15	6	26	5	0	.218	.270	.382	14	3.76	3.93	0.05	0.16	0.21
Stanley M	155	25	44	11	0	7	32	27	41	1	0	.281	.385	.489	30	6.56	6.73	1.30	0.14	1.44
Valentin J	586	114	141	40	1	24	73	79	79	5	5	.240	.336	.437	89	5.17	5.27	2.68	1.20	3.88
Varitek J	221	31	54	12	0	7	33	17	44	2	2	.244	.301	.394	25	3.71	3.95	0.07	0.85	0.92
Vaughn M	608	108	202	29	2	42	115	62	138	0	0	.332	.399	.596	130	8.29	8.30	6.98	0.38	7.36
BOS	**5588**	**880**	**1521**	**315**	**33**	**217**	**830**	**554**	**1008**	**85**	**40**	**.272**	**.342**	**.457**	**856**	**5.33**	**5.46**	**27.00**	**12.13**	**39.13**

Pitcher	S	C	T	SS	ES	IC	HH	PP	TJ	S12	S35	S67	C1	C23	C45	C67	QWP
Avery	3.78	4.26	8.04	39%	9%	39%	30%	22%	4%	35%	35%	30%	0%	35%	43%	22%	.446
B Henry	3.50	4.00	7.50	50%	0%	0%	0%	0%	0%	0%	100%	0%	0%	0%	100%	0%	.514
Checo	5.50	4.50	10.00	0%	0%	0%	50%	0%	0%	0%	50%	50%	0%	0%	100%	0%	.219
Cho	5.50	3.50	9.00	25%	0%	0%	50%	0%	0%	0%	50%	50%	0%	50%	50%	0%	.356
J Wasdin	5.25	3.25	8.50	13%	0%	13%	38%	0%	13%	0%	63%	38%	13%	38%	50%	0%	.416
Lowe	4.70	4.00	8.70	40%	0%	20%	30%	0%	10%	10%	60%	30%	0%	40%	50%	10%	.383
P Martinez	3.09	2.58	5.67	73%	27%	64%	18%	6%	6%	52%	30%	18%	27%	52%	21%	0%	.660
Rose	4.38	4.00	8.38	38%	13%	13%	38%	13%	0%	13%	50%	38%	13%	25%	50%	13%	.419
Saberhagen	4.06	2.81	6.87	52%	10%	42%	26%	6%	13%	23%	52%	26%	16%	65%	19%	0%	.556
Schourek	3.88	3.38	7.25	50%	13%	25%	25%	13%	0%	25%	50%	25%	13%	50%	38%	0%	.510
Wakefield	3.91	3.33	7.24	45%	6%	42%	15%	12%	12%	24%	61%	15%	6%	55%	33%	6%	.532
BOS	**3.94**	**3.31**	**7.25**	**48%**	**11%**	**39%**	**25%**	**9%**	**8%**	**27%**	**48%**	**25%**	**12%**	**48%**	**35%**	**6%**	**.521**

TORONTO BLUE JAYS

Stephen Tomlinson

LOOK WHAT HAPPENS WHEN YOU THROW IN THE TOWEL

On July 26, 1998, the Blue Jays gave up. They had a losing record, had just lost 3 of 4 in a crucial Fenway series, and were 9 1/2 games out of a playoff spot.

To cut payroll, DH Mike Stanley, SP Juan Guzman, LF Tony Phillips, 3B Ed Sprague and closer Randy Myers were traded for prospects. Inexpensive replacements Shawn Green and Shannon Stewart moved from platooning in centre to everyday-work in right and left; SP Kelvim Escobar, CF Jose Cruz and LHP Steve Sinclair were recalled from Syracuse; and utility-man Craig Grebeck took over at second. Tony Fernandez moved from second to third, and Jose Canseco from outfield to DH.

The result? In the last two months, the low-priced Jays had the best record in the league. They swept the Red Sox, swept the Orioles and took 3 of 4 from the Yankees. The Jays finished with the same record as AL West winner Texas, just one win behind AL Central winner Cleveland, and just 4 wins behind the wildcard Red Sox.

Despite that, Roger Clemens, who would never have joined the Jays in '97 if he knew sabermetrics, now wants to leave a team brimming with talent, ostensibly to find a contender, and the honorable Gord Ash will reluctantly comply. The Rocket was 7 wins better than replacement level in '98. Without him, the '98 Jays were just an averageteam. Can the young Jays contend in '99?

It's a secret, but the Jays hitting in the 2nd-half was just as good as the Jays pitching, and better-than-average forthe first time since '93. 1B Carlos Delgado (age 27 in '99) is the new Fred McGriff. The outfield of Green (26), Stewart (25), Cruz (25) is reminiscent of Barfield, Moseby and Bell. 3B Tom Evans (24) should be the next Kelly Gruber. That's 5 spots in the lineup with good players on the rise. Delgado and Evans are also excellent fielders, and there is evidence that the outfield is solid too (see study below).

The biggest hole in the lineup is at second-base, where Craig Grebeck (34), an excellent fielder, isn't a good bet to repeat his outstanding clutch hitting of '98. The Clemens trade is an opportunity to plug this hole. A substantial gain is also possible at shortstop, where Alex Gonzalez (26) appears uninterested in improving his anemic on-base percentage. More modest gains can be made at catcher and DH. Acquiring another outfielder or first-baseman would be a waste.

The starting pitching, even without Clemens, has lots of promise. Chris Carpenter (24), Kelvim Escobar (23), and Roy Halladay (22) are the same ages as Jim Clancy (24), Luis Leal (23) and Dave Stieb (22) of 1980 (Clancy and Stieb pitched well, rookie Leal did not). Pat Hentgen (30) hopes to catch a 2nd wind as Stieb did at the same age in 1988. Woody Williams (32) slumped in the 2nd-half but may still be average in '99. Nerio Rodriguez (26) is the backup starter. LHP Clayton Andrews (21) might be ready to help part way through the year.

The pen, if Paul Quantrill (30) and Dan Plesac (37) don't collapse from their '98 workload, should be fine.

Carlos Almanzar (25) may be ready to handle the "protected closer" role if Robert Person (29) can't improve his 75% success rate (6 saves in 8 tries). Lefties Steve Sinclair (27) and Ben VanRyn (27), and the great Dave Stieb (41), are candidates

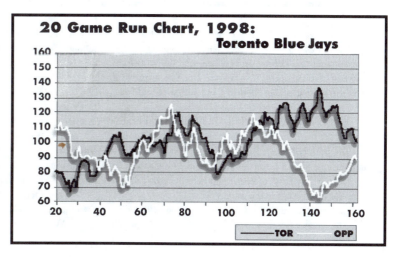

20 Game Run Chart, 1998: Toronto Blue Jays

QMAX PRESENTS: "BAD" PITCHERS

JUST LIKE TOM THUMB'S BLUES, OR PERHAPS LENNON'S "LOST WEEKEND"

Juan Guzman can be a frighteningly hard-to-hit pitcher when he's on his game. In 1992, he gave up a measly 6.75 hits per nine innings, and in 1996, he won the ERA title. He's not always on his game, however: he struggles with his command fairly constantly, and in some years he is incredibly hittable. 1995 was one of those years, as Juan turned in a horrific 4-14, 6.32 year for the Blue Jays, in the second year of their post-championship hangover period.

What was the cause behind Juan's miserable year? And how did he rebound so quickly to win the ERA title in 1996? (fantasy players, pull out your note-books!). Let's see if QMAX can crack the case. What we see is the familiar struggle with control: Guzman's 5-start "command" average hovered right at 4 all year, and he averaged 4.08 for the entire year. That's not good. However, it was the hits allowed that were unusual: Guzman allowed about 10 hits per nine innings, compared to around 8 for his career.

A look at the QMAX chart shows that Guzman fell neatly in the newly coined "Grand Avenue" QMAX category: a pitcher who studiously avoids both the "power precipice" (great stuff, poor command) and the "Tommy John" (great command, poor stuff) regions. A Grand Avenue pitcher is either all the way on or all the way off, usually the latter.

Is there any pattern we can spot that points to Guzman's resurgence in 1996? Not that I can see. The Grand Avenue pattern we see here more often leads to a job driving trucks than it does to an ERA title. My theory, backed by staring at columns of numbers and not by watching Guzman pitch, is that he had some severe problem with his mechanics in 1994 and 1995 that was corrected in 1996. The other likely theory, perhaps more likely, is that he was struggling through injuries all through those two years and, when finally healthy, returned to his prior form. Often, poor mechanics and injuries are related, though the cause-and-effect is sometimes reversed: think of Kelly Downs' nightmarish mechanics, with his pitching arm coming to a crash-dummy slam-stop against his body as an example of poor mechanics causing injury, and think of Dizzy Dean's favoring his sore toe and ruining his arm as an example of, well sort of both: injury ruins mechanics, which causes further injury.

The pitcher is a fragile machine.

--Tom Austin

JUAN GUZMAN/ TOR 1995							
1	2	3	4	5	6	7	S
	1		1				2
1		2	1				4
1							1
		1					2
	1	1	1	2		1	6
		2	1			2	5
	1	1		1		1	4
2	3	5	5	4	0	5	24

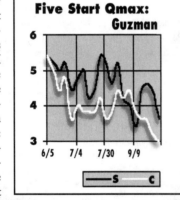

Five Start Qmax: Guzman

6 — 5 — 4 — 3

6/5   7/4   7/30   9/9

—— S   C

---

to fill out the pen.

Gord Ash has built an exciting young Jays team like those of the 1980's. The Jays have a contender's lineup, a contender's rotation, and a contender's bullpen, plus the booty from trading one of the greatest pitchers ever. Don't be surprised if the Jays win more games in '99 than Clemens' new team.

II. HOW BAD WAS THE OUTFIELD DEFENSE?

On July 17/98, the Jays' starting outfield was Tony Phillips in left, Shawn Green in centre and Jose Canseco in right. The next day it was the same, and Felipe Crespo relieved Canseco for defense late in the game.

Let's compare the '98 outfield to the '97 outfield (led by Nixon, Merced and Green) which was reasonably good, played in the same park, and had a similar pitching staff.

The '97 outfield made 6.73 plays per 9 innings (that's putouts plus assists minus double plays per 9 innings), out of 26.8 balls in play. The '98 outfield made 6.70 plays per 9 innings out of 27.1 balls in play. So the outfield range index was .251 in '97, .247 in '98. So the '98 outfield likely made 0.11 fewer plays per 9 innings ((.251-.247)*27.1), or allowed 9 more runs over the season if we assume all the extra hits were singles.

The '97 Jays allowed 2.04 extra bases on doubles and triples per 9 innings (9*(D+2T)/IP), and the '98 Jays allowed 2.46. Normalizing for balls in play, the '98 outfield allowed 0.40 more extra bases per 9 innings, about 21 more runs over a season.

Together, it appears the '98 outfield was 30 runs worse than the '97 outfield, or about 3 wins worse.

What about the '98 Jays' best defensive outfield of

Stewart, Cruz and Green?

Reviewing the boxscores, I found 64 games featuring just the elite 3 in the outfield, and in those games the Jays allowed 2.27 extra bases on doubles and triples per game. In the other 99 games, the Jays allowed 2.55 extra bases per game. So if the Jays' best trio had played every game, they'd probably have saved 9 runs, or 1 win.

The elite trio looked tentative in the outfield until after a memorable game August 4 in Texas in which Cruz failed to catch an routine fly ball to centre. In their 17 games together to that point, the elite trio allowed an awful 3.53 extra bases per game. But in their remaining 47 games, they allowed just 1.81 extra bases per game. If they can continue that pace in '99, the outfield defense will be 35 runs better than '98, an improvement of 3-4 wins.

An assumption made in this study is the measured differences are because of the outfielders. Of course, some of the differences may be from differing quality of pitching or opponent hitting.

HIGH PITCH-COUNT GAMES

On May 13/98, Tim Johnson let Roger Clemens throw 149 pitches.In his next start, the Rocket had his worst game of the year, allowing 9 runs in 5 innings. Coincidence?

I searched the '98 regular-season boxscores for high pitch-count games, and found 8 in which a pitcher threw more than 145 pitches. All 8 made another start within the next week: four of them were poor starts (game scores of 13, 18, 25 and 35), and the other four were about average (game scores of 46, 47, 48 and 53).

Clemens' game was the worst one. If you subtract Clemens' game, the ERA was 5.93 after the 146-pitch outings. None of the pitchers involved had an ERA over 5 for the season.

At 145 pitches and below, there wasn't the same effect.I found 45 times in which a pitcher threw between 135 and 145 pitches inclusive, and pitched both in the previous week and following week (it's possible I missed a few cases; I'm missing a few boxscores):

	W-L	ERA	IP/G	Pit/G
Previous Starts	22-18	4.26	6.9	112
Hi-Pitch Starts	23-16	2.85	8.1	139
Next Starts	22-12	2.83	7.2	113

These pitchers, as a group, performed better after their 135-pitch game than in their previous outings.

So if a starter is doing well, the '98 data suggests you can let him throw as many as 145 pitches before you're taking away from his next start. I was expecting a lower threshold. But beware, there may be a longer-term negative effect, especially for young pitchers (see next study).

WPA BULLPEN BOX—TORONTO BLUE JAYS

	PI	WPA	P	PPPI
Starters	1101	4.9	57.8	0.053
Relievers	571	2.4	38.9	0.068
Road	296	0.4	19.9	0.067
Home	275	2.0	19.0	0.069
Mar/Apr	113	0.2	6.6	0.058
May	94	1.1	4.9	0.052
June	96	0.2	8.3	0.087
July	76	-0.5	4.6	0.061
August	95	0.0	5.6	0.059
September	97	1.3	8.9	0.092
Non S/H Sit.	409	2.4	21.5	0.053
S/H Sit.	162	0.1	17.4	0.108
Low Pressure	231	0.0	3.1	0.013
Med. Pressure	170	-2.4	12.5	0.073
High Pressure	170	4.8	23.4	0.137
Entered behind	217	-0.3	5.3	0.024
Entered tied	108	2.5	14.2	0.131
Entered ahead	246	0.2	19.5	0.079

Name	G	PI	WPA	P	PPPI	MI	ROB	T
Almanzar C	25	44	-1.0	2.7	.061	14	11	5
Carpenter C	9	25	.4	.7	.028	9	4	1
Escobar K	12	17	-.5	1.0	.061	5	6	1
Myers R	41	49	.7	5.0	.102	7	8	6
Person R	27	46	.5	3.6	.078	12	5	7
Plesac D	78	97	2.3	8.0	.082	19	52	16
Quantrill P	82	114	1.6	10.2	.089	28	38	13
Risley B	44	71	-.3	3.3	.047	18	16	9
Sinclair S	24	32	-.1	2.0	.063	8	14	4
Stieb D	16	40	-.3	.9	.022	12	3	0
TOTAL		571	2.4	38.9	.068			

	|-------- Quality ----------|				|--- Pressure -------|			
	Dis.	Poor	Fair	Good	Her.	Lo	Med	Hi	
Almanzar C	4	0	17	3	1	13	6	6	(4)
Escobar K	1	4	4	3	0	3	7	2	(1)
Myers R	5	1	10	23	2	10	17	14	(11)
Person R	2	3	11	9	2	12	3	12	(9)
Plesac D	3	10	30	34	1	24	34	20	(15)
Quantrill P	4	11	37	27	3	28	28	26	(18)
Risley B	4	6	24	9	1	23	15	6	(5)
Sinclair S	1	2	16	4	1	13	7	4	(2)
Stieb D	0	2	13	1	0	10	5	1	(1)
Others	3	4	23	4	1	23	7	5	(2)
TOTAL	27	43	185	117	12	159	129	96	(68)

	7th inning			8th inning			9th inning		
	0	+1	+2	0	+1	+2	0	+1	+2
Almanzar C	0	2	0	0	0	0	1	0	0
Escobar K	0	0	0	0	1	4	0	0	0
Myers R	0	0	0	0	0	0	1	6	12
Person R	2	0	0	3	0	0	1	5	2
Plesac D	1	1	0	5	2	5	1	0	1
Quantrill P	0	1	1	2	5	4	10	4	2
Risley B	2	1	0	1	1	0	2	1	0
Rodriguez N	1	0	0	0	0	0	0	0	0
Sinclair S	0	1	0	0	1	0	0	0	0
Stieb D	0	0	1	0	0	1	0	0	0
Starters	20	13	17	6	5	9	1	1	1
TOTAL	26	19	19	17	15	23	17	17	18
Record	11-15	13-6	16-3	6-11	13-2	18-5	8-9	15-2	15-3

Sean Forman's PROSPECT WATCH

NAME	AGE	POS	LEVEL	GR98	GR97	GR96	AVG
Tom Evans	23	3B	AAA	75	70	83	75
Kevin Witt	22	1B	AAA	75	70	54	70
Andy Thompson	22	3B	AA	55	64	66	60
Ryan Freel	22	OF	AAA	64	59	51	60
Ben Candelaria	23	OF	AAA	55	55	45	53
Michael Peeples	21	1B	AA	51	49	51	50
Peter Tucci	22	OF	AA	63	31	40	49
Jonathan Rivers	23	OF	AA	51	39	39	45
Casey Blake	24	3B	AA	48	16	21	33

NAME	AGE	POS	LEVEL	GRADE
Brent Abernathy	20	2B	High A	63
Joe Lawrence	21	SS	High A	63
Domingo Estevez	20	2B	Rookie	56
Vernon Wells	19	OF	Low A	54
Jay Gibbons	21	DH	Rookie	53
Orlando Hudson	18	2B	Rookie	44

You have to give Tim Johnson some credit for giving the kids a chance to play. It definitely paid off as Carlos Delgado, Shannon Stewart and Shawn Green all had solid campaigns. With Ed Sprague's departure, Tom Evans should finally get a shot to play at third. Beyond that the Blue Jays are running a bit short of top prospects. They also have a stable of pitchers on the way up. The pitchers' development will go a long way in determining the Jays' future success.

Top Dog: Kevin Witt

Witt has played all over the infield as the Blue Jays have tried to figure out somewhere to get his bat into the lineup. He has settled at first base, but with Carlos Delgado hitting his stride on the big league squad there isn't much room for advancement there. He has fair power and hits for a decent average. His strikeout to walk ratio is above 2 to 1, though improving. He doesn't really have enough bat right now to hit in the majors, so I suspect he'll be back in Syracuse next year. Comp: Ryan Klesko with less patience.

Patience, Grasshopper: Ryan Freel

Freel has exceptional plate discipline, but he has had trouble getting hits. Over the last two years, he has drawn 124 walks versus 89 strikeouts, but he has managed just 45 extra base hits over that time. He will probably never manage to hit for much power. He does however have some speed and if he can get on base, he could become a decent leadoff batter. Freel needs to put together a solid season in AAA before he can be considered a potential major leaguer.

Young 'un: Brent Abernathy

Abernathy is a middle infielder with a nice package of offensive tools. He hit .328/.381/.425 in the Florida State League, while stealing 35 bases in 48 attempts. He puts the ball in play, just 38 strikeouts in 485 at bats. Right now, he has just gap power, but as he moves to the smaller AA parks, he may add some home run power. This is his second straight solid year, so he could move quickly.

NAME	AGE	GS	S	C	T	W-L	ERA	K/H	Level
Shannon Withem	24	27	3.56	2.93	6.48	16-5	3.27	0.64	High
Chris McBride	24	21	4.52	3.05	7.57	9-4	4.40	0.49	High
Beiker Graterol	23	28	4.32	3.32	7.64	14-8	4.86	0.64	High
Jay Yennaco	22	26	4.62	3.15	7.77	6-8	5.36	0.46	High
Jason Stevenson	23	22	4.27	3.55	7.82	6-10	5.43	0.62	High
Roy Halladay	20	20	3.90	4.00	7.90	8-5	3.79	0.66	High
Peter Munro	23	24	4.46	3.54	8.00	5-9	5.06	0.69	High
Mark Sievert	25	18	3.83	4.67	8.50	7-6	4.13	0.40	High
Tyson Hartshorn	23	19	4.89	3.79	8.68	7-6	5.18	0.41	High

Power Supply: Peter Tucci

Peter Gammons loves to talk about New Englanders in the minor leagues, and he was certain to mention Tucci's 30 home run season. Tucci nearly tripled his career home runs as his previous best was 10. Tucci is a free-swinger with 126 strikeouts versus 42 walks. If he makes it to the big leagues it will be because of his power bat. Comp: a step behind Rickey Ledee

On the Mound: Roy Halladay

Halladay is a weird case. He oscillated pretty wildly between good hit prevention (25% power precipice) and poor hit prevention (25% hit hard). He struggled some with his control and averaged 4.1 walks per 9 IP. International League managers were pretty high on Halladay as they named him the third best prospect in the league. He is still just 20, so he has a lot of time to develop, but I'm a bit skeptical of his ability to pitch in the majors next year, even if he did flirt with a no-hitter at the end of the season.

WORKLOAD OF JAYS' YOUNG PITCHERS

A famous study in Craig Wright's hard-to-find Diamond Appraised (I'm still trying to get my copy) found that pitchers under age 25 who averaged 31 or more batters faced per start over a season normally broke down soon afterward. That was about 109 pitches per start back in 1989.

In batters faced per start, none of the Jays' young trio were over 30: Escobar (age 22) was 28.8 in the majors, less than 25 in the minors; Carpenter (age 23) was 28.4 in the second-half, and Halladay (age 21) was 24.2 in Syracuse.

But in pitches per start, Escobar (114 in the majors) was over the threshold of 109, and Carpenter (108 in his last 15 starts) was very close. Fortunately, neither of these pitchers had a full season as starters, so Wright's system doesn't predict a breakdown for them.

The Jays expect full seasons as starters from these pitchers in '99 and so must be more cautious. Escobar threw 137 pitches on August 27. Carpenter threw 134 on June 2. Halladay threw 121 in an AAA game August 16, and I don't know if that was his highest. Such games aren't worth the risk.

TIM JOHNSON IN A BOX

"There is one indispensable quality of a baseball manager: The manager *must* be able to to command the respect of his players. This is absolute; everything else is negotiable."
The Bill James Guide To Baseball Managers, page 7

"Of the twenty-five greatest managers of all time, at least eighteen were alcoholics." — James, page 8

TJ's Age? He'll turn 50 in July of '99.

TJ's Record? He's won in the majors (88-74). He's won in the minors (304-285). He's made the playoffs twice in winter ball (in five tries).

TJ's Managers? As a player, 3 years for all-star catcher Del Crandall, then 2 years for utility shortstop Alex Grammas, then 2 years for expansion manager Roy Hartsfield. As a bench coach, 2 years each for Felipe Alou and Kevin Kennedy.

TJ's Other Influences? 8 years with the Dodgers as a scout and minor league manager. Instructed marines in mortar technology for the Vietnam War, but haunted by guilt for not serving in Vietnam himself.

TJ as a Player? No-hit shortstop and second-baseman for 7 years.

What He Brings To A Ball Club

TJ Easy-To-Get-Along-With? According to the local media, TJ criticized Stewart's toughness, tried to force Cruz to be a contact hitter, feuded with his pitching coach, and called his top bullpen lefty a quitter. Gord Ash said he was looking for the fiery type.

Is TJ More of an Emotional Leader or a Decision Maker? He's a motivator. Reportedly has used false Vietnam war stories for inspiration.

Is He More of an Optimist or More of a Problem Solver? He's an optimist with veterans; he stuck with Fletcher and Fernandez despite slow starts and was rewarded.

How He Uses His Personnel

TJ Favors a Set Lineup? Yes.

TJ Likes To Platoon? Not with his hitters. But he tries hard to get the platoon advantage with his relievers.

TJ Prefers Proven or Young Players? Brought in Jose Canseco when Delgado appeared to be out for 2 months, instead of trying Lennon or Witt. Brought in Tony Phillips when Cruz and Stewart got off to slow starts.

Did TJ Make any New Regulars? Some say Green, but he'd been close to a regular the past 3 years. Could have made Tom Evans a regular but went with Sprague. Made Escobar a starter and Person a closer.

TJ Prefers Hitters or Glove Men? Before August, willingly sacrificed defense for (perceived) offense. After that, an all-defense lineup was put together and not only did the staff ERA improve, but the team scored a bunch of runs and won a bunch of games. He'll probably prefer glove men from now on.

TJ Prefers Power, Speed or Averages? The Jays ranked 2nd in Home Runs, 1st in Stolen Bases, but just 9th in batting average and on-base percentage. He brought in Maury Wills to teach base stealing.

Does TJ Use His Entire Roster? No. Ask Juan Samuel.

TJ's Bench? This year he went for guys who could hit (Crespo, Dalesandro, Samuel) instead of defense (Brumfield was released).

Game Managing And Use Of Strategies

Does TJ Go For Big Innings or One-Run Strategies? One-run, particularly stealing bases and the contact play (more below). Drills his team in situational hitting (man on 3rd, get him home).

When Does TJ Pinch-Hit? Just late in the wildcard race with lots of extra players around. He would pinch-field for Canseco and pinch-run for Stanley.

TEAM BREAKOUT BLUEJAYS 1998						
Category	RS	RA	W	L	Pct.	Rk
4- RUNS ALLOWED/HOME	254	96	42	3	.933	1
4- RUNS ALLOWED	425	183	69	15	.821	4
5+ RUNS SCORED/HOME	328	187	33	9	.786	3
5+ RUNS SCORED	603	374	63	18	.778	4
LOW SCORING GAMES/HOME	51	29	14	4	.778	2
5+ RUNS SCORED/ROAD	275	187	30	9	.769	7
CLOSE LOW-SCORING GAMES/HOME	33	23	10	3	.769	5
RECORD IN CLOSE GAMES/HOME	139	123	24	9	.727	1
4- RUNS ALLOWED/ROAD	171	87	27	12	.692	10
RECORD IN LOW SCORING GAMES	96	63	24	13	.649	3
RECORD IN BLOWOUTS	191	126	17	10	.630	3
RECORD IN CLOSE GAMES	314	301	42	30	.583	3
SLUGFESTS/HOME	207	163	14	11	.560	3
RECORD IN BLOWOUTS	302	256	27	22	.551	4
SEASON TOTALS	811	763	88	74	.543	5
LOW SCORING GAMES/ROAD	45	34	10	9	.526	6
CLOSE SLUGFESTS/ROAD	93	94	6	6	.500	9
RECORD IN SLUGFESTS	386	376	25	26	.490	7
4- RUNS SCORED/HOME	108	174	18	21	.462	2
RECORD IN CLOSE GAMES/ROAD	175	178	18	21	.462	4
RECORD IN BLOWOUTS/ROAD	111	130	10	12	.455	8
CLOSE SLUGFESTS/HOME	47	50	3	4	.429	13
SLUGFESTS/ROAD	179	213	11	15	.423	11
CLOSE LOW SCORING GAMES/ROAD	19	22	5	7	.417	9
4- RUNS SCORED	208	389	25	56	.309	2
5+ RUNS ALLOWED/HOME	182	265	9	27	.250	8
5+ RUNS ALLOWED	386	580	19	59	.244	8
5+ RUNS ALLOWED/ROAD	204	315	10	32	.238	7
4- RUNS SCORED/ROAD	100	215	7	35	.167	12

Anything Unusual About TJ's Lineup? Batted Canseco ahead of higher-OBP guys like Delgado and Stanley, but that may be speed-over-OBP thinking, which isn't unusual.

Does TJ Sac Bunt Often? Not with his 2-hitter (Green).

Does TJ Like To Use the Running Game? Absolutely.

TJ's Idiosyncratic Strategies? The contact play. Runner at 3rd would break for home on any contact, even a ground ball back to the pitcher, in order to force the defense to make a play at home. Major league fieldersusually did.

Handling The Pitching Staff

TJ Prefers Power Pitchers? He seemed happy with the power staff he inherited, and showed lots of confidence in the hard-throwing Almanzar and Person. The put-the-ball-in-play types may be at a disadvantage on a turf field.

TJ Goes To His Bullpen Quickly? No. Allowed among the highest pitch counts in the league.

TJ Uses a Five-Man Rotation? Tended to stick with 5 starters even when there were off days, but sometimes kept Clemens on regular rest, most notably when the 5-man rotation would have had Clemens start a pivotal July series in Fenway,

but he missed the 4 games instead.

TJ Uses the Entire Staff? No. Nerio Rodriguez didn't appear the final month. Randy Myers wasn't given work between sparse save opportunities. Meanwhile, Quantrill and Plesac were 2nd and 4th in the league in appearances.

Anything Unique About TJ's Handling of Pitchers? I don't know. Is it unique to work both your starters (pitches) and relievers (appearances) hard?

TJ's Strongest Point as a Manager? His winning records.

If There Was No Professional Baseball, What Would TJ Probably Be Doing? It's been clarified that he wouldn't be playing basketball. Probably he would be a military officer turned politician, hounded by scandal in office.

A SHAMELESS PLUG FOR STEPHEN's WEB SITE

Check out http://www.stephent.com/jays/ for a sabermetric review of every Blue Jays team (1977-1998).

Name	AB	R	H	D	T	HR	RBI	BB	SO	SB	CS	BA	OBP	SLG	XR	Adj XR/27	Raw XR/27	OXW	DXW	TXW
Brown K	110	17	30	7	1	2	15	9	31	0	0	.267	.321	.399	16	4.84	4.82	0.40	0.28	0.68
Canseco J	585	97	142	25	0	48	106	63	158	24	18	.242	.320	.529	101	5.76	5.65	3.50	0.17	3.67
Crespo F	131	11	35	8	1	1	15	14	27	3	3	.270	.346	.369	18	4.52	4.42	0.36	0.24	0.60
Cruz J	354	55	92	14	3	11	42	55	98	10	4	.261	.357	.410	57	5.74	5.62	2.12	0.76	2.88
Dalesandro M	67	8	20	5	0	2	14	1	6	0	0	.305	.310	.468	9	4.56	4.40	0.17	0.01	0.18
Delgado C	532	93	158	41	1	39	114	71	138	2	0	.296	.386	.598	117	8.12	8.02	6.16	0.39	6.55
Fernandez T	487	70	161	35	2	9	71	44	53	11	8	.330	.393	.465	84	6.36	6.18	3.55	0.15	3.70
Fletcher D	407	37	118	22	1	9	52	25	39	0	0	.290	.334	.417	52	4.45	4.27	0.98	1.47	2.45
Gonzalez A	569	70	141	27	1	13	50	27	120	17	6	.247	.287	.368	59	3.43	3.31	-0.30	2.32	2.02
Grebeck C	302	33	80	16	2	2	27	28	42	2	2	.263	.332	.351	35	3.86	3.73	0.28	0.51	0.79
Green S	632	105	178	31	4	36	99	48	141	29	12	.282	.336	.516	108	6.16	6.09	4.24	1.09	5.33
Phillips T	48	9	17	5	0	1	7	9	6	0	0	.354	.463	.513	11	9.13	9.29	0.67	-0.04	0.63
Samuel J	50	14	9	2	0	1	2	7	13	11	8	.188	.296	.292	4	2.39	2.50	-0.23	0.02	-0.21
Sprague E	383	49	93	19	0	17	51	23	73	0	2	.244	.304	.429	46	4.07	3.96	0.50	-0.32	0.18
Stanley M	343	49	85	13	0	23	47	54	85	1	1	.249	.358	.485	62	6.24	6.02	2.52	0.09	2.61
Stewart S	519	90	149	28	3	12	55	64	77	43	19	.287	.381	.424	87	5.89	5.85	3.32	0.60	3.92
TOR	**5599**	**810**	**1524**	**302**	**18**	**228**	**770**	**545**	**1124**	**153**	**83**	**.272**	**.343**	**.455**	**869**	**5.39**	**5.28**	**28.23**	**7.74**	**35.97**

Pitcher	S	C	T	SS	ES	IC	HH	PP	TJ	S12	S35	S67	C1	C23	C45	C67	QWP
C Carpenter	4.13	3.13	7.25	42%	13%	50%	29%	4%	21%	29%	42%	29%	29%	33%	29%	8%	.522
Clemens	2.82	3.00	5.82	70%	24%	64%	12%	12%	3%	58%	30%	12%	18%	52%	27%	3%	.654
Escobar	2.80	3.20	6.00	70%	10%	70%	10%	10%	10%	50%	40%	10%	20%	40%	30%	10%	.682
Halladay	3.50	2.50	6.00	50%	50%	50%	50%	0%	0%	50%	0%	50%	50%	0%	50%	0%	.548
Hanson	5.75	4.38	10.13	13%	0%	0%	75%	0%	0%	0%	25%	75%	0%	38%	38%	25%	.234
Hentgen	4.66	3.45	8.10	28%	10%	24%	31%	7%	7%	17%	52%	31%	3%	48%	45%	3%	.440
Ju Guzman	3.59	3.45	7.05	55%	14%	45%	27%	18%	5%	41%	32%	27%	9%	41%	45%	5%	.551
Stieb	6.00	3.67	9.67	0%	0%	0%	67%	0%	0%	0%	33%	67%	0%	33%	67%	0%	.249
W Williams	3.78	3.25	7.03	41%	9%	47%	22%	13%	13%	34%	44%	22%	13%	34%	53%	0%	.542
TOR	**3.84**	**3.29**	**7.13**	**46%**	**13%**	**45%**	**26%**	**10%**	**9%**	**35%**	**39%**	**26%**	**14%**	**41%**	**40%**	**5%**	**.533**

BALTIMORE ORIOLES

Ken Adams

WINNING AT WHAT COST??

Life on the streets wasn't pretty in Baltimore last year, as we had predicted in our tribute to Homicide. The Orioles have been making moves all right, but not necessarily all the right moves. Last season the Orioles led the majors in the new statistical category, Cost of Victory (CoV). It is a rather simple calculation (especially for BBBA): you take the total team salary and divide by the number of wins. This gives you a dollar figure to see how effective your team is with the money they spent on player salaries.

In 1998 the Orioles spent $937,000 per victory which was over $200,000 more per victory than the next highest team, the Dodgers, and over $400,000 more than the average CoV. Of course the Dodgers seem to have secured a challenge to the Orioles for years to come in CoV by the signing of Kevin Brown for seven years at $105M. I'm sure that Dandy Don will have something to say about this in his Dodger essay, but being a Giant fan I couldn't help myself from rubbing it in. Here is a look at the AL East.

Team	Wins	Salary	CoV
Bal	79	74.0	$937,000
Bos	92	59.6	$648,000
NYY	114	73.8	$647,000
TB	63	27.6	$438,000
Tor	88	37.3	$424,000

The next time someone comes up and tells you that some teams just can't compete, remember the above. It didn't help the Orioles that they outspent the Yankees by $200K per win, as they finished with 35 fewer victories. And notice that the Blue Jays were outspent by almost 100% by the Orioles and Yankees and managed to finish ahead of the Orioles—and came close to the Red Sox, who outspent them by 22M.

So let's look at the data in a different view and expand it to all of the major league teams. The first breakout will be of the 15 teams that spent more than the ML average for team salary. The rank number is for how they ranked in team salary, so the Orioles would be number one followed by the Yankees, Rangers, Braves and Dodgers and would make up the top echelon. The Yankees won the Series while the Rangers and Braves made the playoffs, but were eliminated before the Series. The Orioles and Dodgers were a combined .500.

Rank	Wins	Avg$
1-5	94.0	66.48M
6-10	87.4	57.98M
11-15	91.0	49.58M

This breakout certainly doesn't show a gap between the "haves" and "have nots." This next breakout would tend to yield to this conclusion. Here we break out the teams by the range of team salary. The first column has the number of teams within a certain range followed by the range and then the average number of wins.

# of Teams	$$$	Wins
5	>60M	94.0
6	50-60M	90.2
5	40-50M	85.4
5	30-40M	75.8
9	<30M	68.4

Obviously nine teams have decided to cut salary to the bone. The best that any of these teams did was the Reds, with 77 wins. The next breakout shows how the various divisions look. We list both the average and the median salaries

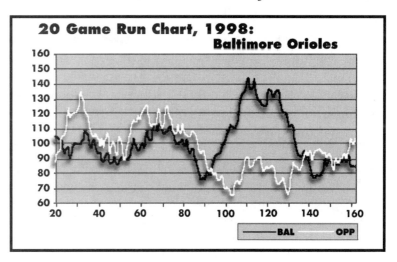

20 Game Run Chart, 1998: Baltimore Orioles

QMAX PRESENTS: "BAD" PITCHERS

JACK KNOCKED-OUT-OF-THE-BOX

I've been fighting this off for a while, but I might as well come clean: these Bad Pitchers are starting to run together in my mind, especially all these 30's guys pitching in front of tiny crowd for eternally lousy teams, belittled by managers paying more attention to the Racing Form than the lineup card (that's you, Hornsby) underpaid by skinflint owners for a few years before they dig out the phone number of that truck-driving school from the matchbook underneath the couch cushions. And for those of you pining and whining for the good old days, I ain't even hardly scratched the surface of lousy baseball in the 30's.

All right. Let's look at the woebegone 1936 season of Jack Knott. Jack toiled for the Browns through most of the 30's before moving on to the White Sox, and he was decent most of those years, with an ERA above the league average. Not so 1936, however; Jack posted a 7.29 ERA, and he earned it: AL batters declared Knott starts "fatten your batting average day" to the tune of a .330 batting average against him, to go with a .400 on-base percentage.

In Knott's defense, however, the defense calls to the stand the defense. Of the Browns, that is, and it wasn't much. Harlond Clift was a fine fielder, but the rest of them...Knott managed to strand only 53% of the baserunners he allowed that year. You can blame that on Knott's inability to pitch his way out of jams, but a more logical explanation might be that he got tired of trying to get four outs an inning. I have some sympathy for Jack Knott and the other Browns pitchers (if you have it, read the Ned Garver comment in Boyd and Harris' classic "The Great American Baseball Card Flipping, Trading, and Bubble Gum Book"; unfortunately, space prevents me printing the entire quote here.) A cruelly condensed version:

"now when a good hitter is with a bad ballclub he is basically all right...but a good pitcher with a bad ballclub is just plain screwed.. Nobody scores any runs for him...the outfielders kill him with errors and the infielders lack any kind of range. The management is often bitter and insulting. The crowds are sparse and often hostile...discourtesy and discouragement fill his days...he is like Sviatoslav Richter playing with a Salvation Army Band."

I know, I know: Sviatoslav who?

Suffice to say it was no picnic pitching for the Browns in the 30's. It beat truck driving, but not by as much as you would think.

--Tom Austin

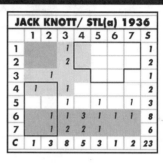

JACK KNOTT/ STL(a) 1936								
	1	2	3	4	5	6	7	S
1			1					1
2			2					2
3		1						1
4	1							2
5			1		1		1	3
6		1	1	3	1	1	1	8
7		1	2	2	1			6
C	1	3	8	5	3	1	2	23

Five Start Qmax: Knott

(chart with axis labels 7, 6, 5, 4, 3, 2 and dates 5/23, 6/16, 7/19, 8/6, 9/10; legend S — C)

---

for each division.

A couple of years ago I pointed out how the Tigers needed to get out of the AL East and into the Central. This last breakout explains why. The average and median is about the same as only the Indians spend over the ML average in the AL Central. Our last breakout will show how each team is doing in CoV (in thousands of dollars) by division.

Div.	98$$	Avg.	Med.
ALE	272.3	54.5	59.6
ALC	175.3	35.1	35.6
ALW	179.6	44.9	49.5
NLE	177.7	35.5	29.9
NLC	217.9	36.3	42.3
NLW	242.6	48.5	48.0

So the overall best use of money in the majors by a team award goes to the Montreal Expos at $128,000 per victory. The AL winner is the Oakland A's, checking in at $251,000. The most inept use of money goes to the O's, with the Dodgers the NL champ.

ALE	CoV		ALC	CoV		ALW	CoV
Tor	424		Min	314		Oak	251
TB	438		Det	358		Sea	588
NYY	647		ChW	473		Ana	638
Bos	648		KC	494		Tex	706
Bal	937		Cle	636			

NLE	CoV		NLC	CoV		NLW	CoV
Mon	128		Pit	199		Ari	506
Fla	354		Cin	269		SF	539
Phi	399		Hou	474		SD	541
Atl	582		Mil	499		Col	622
NYM	667		ChC	570		LA	733
			StL	573			

A NEO-RADICAL ECONOMIC DIGRESSION

At BBBA we have avoided talking about salaries in general so as not to fall into the popular refrain that ballplayers are paid too much. My answer is always, 'What, you would rather pay the owners?' Which is the real option if you are a baseball fan.

Of course we could all take it as our civic duty to call our congressman, or congresswoman, and tell them that we don't want businesses to be able to write off the ticket prices to a sporting event as a business expense and don't forget to include those luxury boxes. Because when those 'business expenses' are claimed the rest of us that pay taxes have to make up the difference.

I would think that it is real galling to know that the "suits" get to write off the cost of a ticket and you get a part of the bill. On top of that every time you turn around a franchise is threatening to take the beloved home team to some far off site unless the locals pay for a brand new stadium (with those luxury boxes). Why in the world would we want to reward an extortionist?

Why indeed? The reason is quite simple; Baseball is a monopoly that restricts the number of franchises. Cities without franchises dangle enticements to existing franchises while cities with franchises are forced to grant subsidies to keep theirs. By limiting the number of franchises, teams in a large market have an advantage over the smaller market franchises. Then the smaller market teams claim they need a subsidy to compete. The large market teams then insist that the smaller market teams get the money from the players by having a salary cap and then we have another labor strike.

But for an example of how this works: the Yankees generated more than $28 million in income more than the the next best franchise. However, the Yankees are now claiming that they need the city to build them a new stadium. Last year the owner of the Chicago White Sox, Jerry Reinsdorf, commented that baseball shouldn't have expanded because it gave the Montreal Expos no place to move to, or threaten to move to. The White Sox owner had used Tampa Bay for years as a device for getting a new stadium and other concessions; I guess Jerry is still upset about losing that leverage for any future franchise extortion racket.

What does this have to do with the Orioles? Their original corporatization, new stadium construction, and aggressive expenditures have been instrumental in defining the prevailing economic climate. As a matter of fact, most of baseball's economic lexicon has been borrowed from the Orioles. As we'll see, the Orioles' commitment to spending not wisely but too well is not going gentle into that good night.

REPLACING THE BIRD WITH $$ SIGNS

The Orioles lost Roberto Alomar (2B), Eric Davis (RF), and Rafael Palmeiro (1B) as free agents after the 1998 season. Were the Birds prepared for this eventuality by readying a new

WPA BULLPEN BOX—BALTIMORE ORIOLES

	PI	WPA	P	PPPI
Starters	1010	-3.8	50.3	0.050
Relievers	631	2.1	36.2	0.057
Road	320	1.2	17.8	0.056
Home	311	0.8	18.4	0.059
Mar/Apr	113	0.9	5.8	0.051
May	107	-2.9	6.4	0.060
June	122	1.7	6.5	0.054
July	95	2.2	6.1	0.065
August	100	1.4	6.2	0.062
September	94	-1.2	5.2	0.055
Non S/H Sit.	493	0.1	21.0	0.042
S/H Sit.	138	2.0	15.3	0.111
Low Pressure	260	-0.2	3.3	0.013
Med. Pressure	207	-3.3	12.7	0.061
High Pressure	164	5.6	20.1	0.123
Entered behind	338	-0.6	8.9	0.026
Entered tied	72	0.5	8.9	0.124
Entered ahead	221	2.1	18.4	0.083

Name	G	PI	WPA	P	PPPI	MI	ROB	T
Benitez A	71	88	.0	6.7	.076	14	29	9
Charlton N	36	51	-.7	2.2	.044	12	15	4
Coppinger R	5	12	-.1	.1	.008	4	0	0
Johns D	21	48	-.8	1.5	.032	12	13	2
Kamieniecki S	1	4	.0	.0	.008	1	1	0
Key J	14	19	.2	1.1	.059	5	8	1
Mathews Te	17	29	-.8	1.5	.052	11	11	2
Mills A	72	102	2.2	6.7	.066	26	28	8
Orosco J	69	90	1.9	6.4	.071	20	26	12
Ponson S	11	25	-.5	1.1	.044	6	2	1
Rhodes A	45	96	.9	6.0	.063	33	19	5
Smith P	23	36	.0	2.3	.064	8	12	2
Total		631	2.1	36.2	.057			

	Quality					Pressure		
	Dis.	Poor	FairGood	Her.	Lo	Med	Hi	
Benitez A	6	6	35 22	2	34	20	17	(13)
Charlton N	1	8	24 3	0	21	11	4	(2)
Johns D	2	4	13 2	0	10	8	3	(1)
Key J	0	4	4 6	0	5	9	0	(0)
Mathews Te	2	2	10 3	0	6	7	4	(2)
Mills A	3	6	36 25	2	27	27	18	(13)
Orosco J	0	9	45 12	3	38	14	17	(9)
Ponson S	1	2	7 1	0	5	3	3	(1)
Rhodes A	2	9	17 14	3	11	20	14	(12)
Smith P	0	5	13 5	0	9	9	5	(3)
Others	0	5	18 0	0	20	2	1	(0)
TOTAL	17	60	222 93	10	186	130	86	(56)

	7th inning			8th inning			9th inning		
	0	+1	+2	0	+1	+2	0	+1	+2
Benitez A	0	0	0	0	0	0	6	5	5
Charlton N	0	0	0	0	3	0	0	0	0
Johns D	0	0	1	0	0	1	0	0	0
Key J	0	0	1	0	1	0	0	0	0
Mathews Te	0	0	1	0	1	0	0	0	0
Mills A	2	3	1	3	4	2	2	0	0
Orosco J	0	0	0	7	1	1	1	5	1
Ponson S	0	0	0	0	1	1	0	0	0
Rhodes A	3	8	2	3	1	5	0	1	3
Smith P	1	1	0	0	0	0	0	0	0
Starters	10	11	13	3	1	4	1	1	1
TOTAL	16	23	19	16	13	14	10	12	10
Record	7-9	16-7	17-2	9-7	8-5	13-1	6-4	10-2	10-0

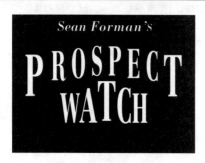

Sean Forman's

PROSPECT WATCH

NAME	AGE	POS	LEVEL	GR98	GR97	GR96	AVG
Calvin Pickering	21	1B	AA	86	64	79	78
Eugene Kingsale	21	OF	AAA	55	87	67	68
Danny Clyburn	24	OF	AAA	61	74	55	64
Julio Vinas	25	C	AAA	57	42	57	52
Willis Otanez	25	3B	AAA	47	41	52	46
Ricky Otero	26	OF	AAA	30	51	68	43
Jerry Hairston	22	SS	AA	50	29	-	42
Ryan Minor	24	3B	AA	22	37	15	26

NAME	AGE	POS	LEVEL	GRADE
Rick Elder	18	OF	Rookie	66
Timothy Raines	18	OF	Rookie	60
Richard Paz	20	3B	High A	58
Luis Matos	19	OF	Low A	53
Jayson Werth	19	C	Low A	52
Ntema Ndungidi	19	OF	Rookie	51
Eddy Garavito	19	2B	Low A	46
Maikell Diaz	19	SS	Low A	45
Darnell McDonald	19	OF	Low A	44
Ivanon Coffie	21	3B	High A	43

NAME	AGE	GS	S	C	T	W-L	ERA	K/H	LEVEL
Terry Burrows	29	15	3.00	2.53	5.53	8-6	2.92	1.08	High
Richie Lewis	32	21	3.43	3.38	6.81	5-7	5.01	1.22	High
Matt Snyder	23	20	3.75	3.10	6.85	9-6	4.25	0.90	High
Joel Bennett	28	23	3.83	3.13	6.96	11-2	4.17	0.89	High
Jason McCommon	26	19	3.89	3.26	7.16	6-8	4.24	0.66	High
Darin Blood	23	26	4.35	3.23	7.58	3-3	4.17	0.48	High
Rocky Coppinger	24	19	3.68	4.05	7.74	8-5	3.76	0.87	High
Rich Kelley	28	16	3.88	3.94	7.81	7-2	4.09	0.71	High
Chris Fussell	22	28	3.71	4.21	7.93	8-9	4.15	0.99	High
Matthew Riley	18	14				5-4	1.19	3.24	Low

It has been awhile since the Orioles have produced a position player of consequence. Jeffrey Hammonds washed out, and Alex Ochoa hasn't done much since he was traded. Still, Peter Angelos has to keep up with George Steinbrenner and now that the Boss has a farm system, the Orioles appear willing to pony up the bucks to develop their own. They broke the bank to sign Darnell McDonald and actually played some of the young kids at the end of the year. However, it is tough to teach an old dog new tricks, so when I see Calvin Pickering and Jerry Hairston in the lineup next year, I'll become a believer.

Top Dog: Calvin Pickering
Pickering's presence has muddled the Rafael Palmeiro situation. Pickering a big man, 290 pounds, who hits the ball a ton. He has never slugged below .550 in a minor league season, and last year he hit 31 dingers in AA. He is not just a masher though as he hit .309 and drew 98 walks, good for a .434 OBP. He has done this each of the last three seasons. It will take him a year or two to surpass Palmeiro's numbers, but I would let Palmeiro walk anyway. Pickering struggles a bit against lefties, so it would be worth it to pick up a lefty-killer to platoon some with him. Comp: Glenn Davis.

Take a seat Rip: Ryan Minor
Cal Ripken deserved a little better, in my opinion. Ryan Minor really isn't a good prospect, and the Orioles have been pushing him as the next big thing. Minor tried his hand in the NBA for a year, but then signed with the Orioles, so he was old when he began his pro career. He is now 24 and hasn't played a season above AA. His AA season wasn't all that hot at .250/.311/.397, with 152 strikeouts vs. 34 walks. He might become an average player, but I don't expect it.

Ken Phelps All-Star: Danny Clyburn
I guess Clyburn is a bit young for this moniker as he will be just 25 next year. He has put up two solid AAA seasons (.300/.372/.498 and .286/.358/.488), he runs fairly well, and he doesn't put up huge strikeout numbers. Still, you don't hear much about him. Clyburn had a pretty serious reverse platoon split last year, but it was a rather small sample size and that wasn't the case in 1997. This is the sort of guy who can help out a bench. He has good power and can get on-base some. I think too often managers go strictly for defensive bench players, while not giving chances to good hitters, who could help you out when a team is behind. Comp: Dante Bichette.

Rock Solid: Timothy Raines
There's a chance, not a good one mind you, but a chance that Tim Raines Sr. and Jr. could end up in the league together at some point. Senior will probably stick around for two or three more years, and if he can keep playing like he did this year, Junior might make it to the bigs in three years or so. The younger Raines has many of the same tools as his dad. He stole 37 bases in 41 attempts (197 at bats), and managed a .377 OBP. He didn't show much power batting .244 and slugging just .335. He will probably end up in Delmarva (South Atlantic League) next year. If he can continue to get on base, he could put up some gaudy stolen base numbers.

On the Mound: Matt Riley
No, I didn't reverse the K/H and ERA columns for Riley. He really did post a 3.2 K/H ratio, 136 strikeouts to 42 hits in 83 innings. He was a tad wild as he walked 44 batters, but who really cares with this level of hit prevention. And it gets better. He is a left-hander, as well. I would be curious where 3.2 K/H ranks all-time in the minors. I'm sure there are some even more audacious numbers, but Riley's is the best I have seen. He will only be 19 next year, and it will be tempting to pitch him for a lot of innings and move him quickly, but there doesn't need to be that much of a hurry.

nest of youngsters? Not hardly.

To get themselves back into competition for 1999, they went out and signed free agents Will Clark (1B), Delino DeShields (2B), Albert Belle (LF) and Mike Timlin (closer), re-signed free agent B.J. Surhoff (RF) and traded for Charles Johnson (C) with last year's closer, Armando Benitez. They join holdovers Brady Anderson (CF), Cal Ripken (3B), Mike Bordick (SS), and Harold Baines (DH). Sudden spare parts Chris Hoiles, Willie Greene and Rich Becker will try to look busy on the bench.

None of the free agents the Orioles signed were hot properties this winter; only Belle was a truly marquee player, but his contract situation limited his options. The end result of all this is that the O's bid against themselves, further driving up the CoV for this coming season.

Orioles' owner, Peter Angelos, uses money to buy his way out of problems. This principle has been disproven by his division rival, the New York Yankees, and by several other franchises. George Steinbrenner thought it was just a matter of going out and signing Free Agents and the championships would come to him. It took him several years to be disabused of this notion.

There's a name for this principle, and it was coined by Bill James some years ago: the treadmill effect. You have a hole at a position and fill it with a free agent that is coming off a career year who may be able to solve the problem for 2-3 years. In the meantime, you have several other similar problems that you solve in the same way, and the cycle just keeps repeating. What you want to do is take care of the position for 7-10 years by either signing a young free agent, a la the Giants with Barry Bonds, or acquiring a young veteran via trade, or—heaven forbid-by giving a young player from your own organization a chance to play. Getting on the treadmill will virtually assure the Orioles of a high CoV with no way off. Actually, there is a way off, but not many egotistical owners can just step off—they eventually jump or get pushed.

A DIFFERENT SHADE OF GREEN

I guess we can't finish talking about the O's without mentioning the end of the streak. Cal Ripken is a hero to many for showing up every day and playing the game. My hero in the area of streaks is Julia Butterfly, who has been perched in a redwood tree for one year (as of December 10, 1998) 180 feet off the ground in an effort to save the tree and the forest. Think about the effort of living in a tree during drenching rains and 90+ mile per hour winds (better known as El Nino). Cal gets the day off in such conditions.

A MIDSUMMER NIGHT's DRAFT (1)
(continued from last year's "Tales of Psycho")

—I was going to have to talk to Bear when I got back, but the immediate problem was to replace the water hose in the Blazer. The tape job would only work for so long. I did some mental calculations and concluded that I could probably make Mojave. Anything further, like Barstow was asking for it. Fortunately, it was almost all downhill to Mojave. I tried not to think about the brakes.

And, mirabiile dictu, the Blazer proved to be up to the task, rolling into Mojave without incident. It was probably trying to lull me into a false sense of security while planning its next demise. While I was waiting for the water temperature to cool down some before replacing the hose, I found myself musing over my early experiences with Tom "Psycho" Collins.

After that first Treestock my boss, Pat O'Doul, asked me to help him draft his fantasy baseball team. Unlike other fantasy leagues, they re-drafted at the All-Star break—which gave them two seasons a year and kept everyone interested for most of the season.

Pat told me that he had always been a middle of the pack kind of guy in the eight-team league, and he wanted to break out of the middle and start winning some money. Most of the money went to the first place team, but the second and third place teams got a cut. He was willing to front all the money if I would

make the picks. I usually had to work while Pat went to the draft, so I would give him a list and tell him to strictly adhere to it. This hadn't worked too well, as inevitably Pat would come home with Walt Terrell—even though Walt wasn't on my list. And somewhere around the middle of the draft all of the picks would suddenly become erratic. This happened in both that first draft and the following spring draft of the next season. After Pat came back with Terrell for the second time, I decided that I'd take a vacation day and be at the draft in person to make sure nothing went awry.

Prior to the spring draft, Psycho had called up one day at work to talk to Pat, but it was too soon after Treestock for Pat to talk to him, even if Tom was the commissioner of the fantasy league. I told Psycho that Pat had gone to lunch and wouldn't be back for awhile. He then proceeded to talk as if we were old friends. Explaining how he had been made "Commish" due to a work injury that kept him flat on his back most of the time, but this gave him time to watch his "Cubbies" on TV.

"Say by the way, what do you think of this kid the Cards brought up as a closer? I think his name is Worrell or something," he dropped into the middle of the conversation.

Did he know I was Pat's silent partner? Or was he just fishing? I felt like a deer in the headlights, not knowing what to do, frozen to the spot as the headlights got bigger and bigger.

"You're a baseball fan, aren't ya," he trolled.

TEAM BREAKOUT ORIOLES 1998						
Category	RS	RA	W	L	Pct.	Rk
4- RUNS ALLOWED/HOME	213	117	36	12	.750	9
4- RUNS ALLOWED	429	205	66	23	.742	9
4- RUNS ALLOWED/ROAD	216	88	30	11	.732	7
5+ RUNS SCORED/HOME	287	206	29	12	.707	10
5+ RUNS SCORED	619	442	58	26	.690	11
5+ RUNS SCORED/ROAD	332	236	29	14	.674	12
RECORD IN BLOWOUTS/HOME	137	116	13	8	.619	4
RECORD IN BLOWOUTS	319	262	27	18	.600	3
CLOSE LOW-SCORING GAMES/HOME	36	34	10	7	.588	7
RECORD IN BLOWOUTS/ROAD	182	146	14	10	.583	3
LOW SCORING GAMES/HOME	49	50	12	11	.522	9
RECORD IN LOW SCORING GAMES	80	75	20	19	.513	7
CLOSE SLUGFESTS/ROAD	33	32	2	2	.500	8
LOW SCORING GAMES/ROAD	31	25	8	8	.500	7
RECORD IN CLOSE GAMES/HOME	151	152	19	19	.500	10
SEASON TOTALS	817	785	79	83	.488	8
CLOSE SLUGFESTS/HOME	54	56	3	4	.429	12
SLUGFESTS/HOME	143	158	8	11	.421	10
RECORD IN CLOSE GAMES	250	268	27	39	.409	12
RECORD IN SLUGFESTS	348	377	18	27	.400	12
SLUGFESTS/ROAD	205	219	10	16	.385	12
CLOSE LOW SCORING GAMES/ROAD	16	23	4	8	.333	11
4- RUNS SCORED/HOME	97	166	13	27	.325	6
RECORD IN CLOSE GAMES/ROAD	99	116	8	20	.286	12
4- RUNS SCORED	198	343	21	57	.269	5
4- RUNS SCORED/ROAD	101	177	8	30	.211	7
5+ RUNS ALLOWED/HOME	171	255	6	27	.182	10
5+ RUNS ALLOWED	388	580	13	60	.178	11
5+ RUNS ALLOWED/ROAD	217	325	7	33	.175	12

"Well, yes." I stammered.

He then took the conversation off in a different direction altogether, or at least I thought so at the time. He started talking about how to make beer. He made beer in his kitchen and was interested in what kind of beer I liked. I told him that I preferred Pilsners in the spring and summer and then switched to the darker beers and stout in the fall and winter. He then meandered through many experiences in his current life in a torrent of what I later determined to be semi-consciousness. Until he came back to the subject he wanted to talk about.

"Do you think the Cards can win with that kid as a closer?"

"Well, he was a starter in the minors until the beginning of this year. I guess the Cards didn't like his lack of control as a starter, and figured they would see what happened in the pen."

I stopped, and then realized that I had slipped up. Now he knew I paid attention to the game, and probably was Pat's

mysterious silent partner. He meandered a bit more and then wanted to know if Worrell was good enough to get the Cards into the playoffs. What could I do? Us being such "buddies" and all. I gave it up.

"He throws hard enough to be effective and teams won't see him enough between now and the end of the season to probably figure him out that well."

He thanked me and continued the conversation some more to be polite before getting off the line to put his claim in on the new closer for the Cardinals.

Worrell put him into the money as he finished second in the fantasy league. I didn't mention to Pat about my giving Psycho the tip, and vowed to myself to be more careful in the future. <continued in DETROIT>

Name	AB	R	H	D	T	HR	RBI	BB	SO	SB	CS	BA	OBP	SLG	XR	Adj XR/27	Raw XR/27	OXW	DXW	TXW
Alomar R	584	90	170	39	1	14	59	63	70	20	5	.291	.360	.435	92	5.66	5.21	3.28	1.42	4.70
Anderson B	474	87	115	30	3	18	54	80	78	24	7	.244	.370	.436	83	5.92	5.44	3.18	0.04	3.22
Baines H	290	42	89	18	0	9	60	35	40	0	0	.308	.382	.464	45	5.54	5.15	1.55	0.00	1.55
Becker R	112	22	23	1	0	3	12	23	34	2	0	.206	.352	.298	13	3.69	3.46	0.06	0.39	0.45
Bordick M	462	62	124	31	1	13	54	42	65	6	7	.267	.339	.425	64	4.61	4.30	1.38	2.90	4.28
Carter J	281	38	72	16	1	11	36	20	48	4	1	.255	.309	.438	36	4.46	4.12	0.67	0.27	0.94
Davis E	449	85	152	32	1	28	95	47	109	8	6	.338	.401	.604	97	8.14	7.59	5.15	0.43	5.58
Greene W	39	9	6	1	0	1	5	14	10	1	0	.157	.385	.265	6	4.31	3.66	0.11	0.05	0.16
Hammonds J	169	37	46	13	1	6	29	28	38	8	2	.274	.381	.467	32	6.72	6.35	1.46	0.44	1.90
Hoiles C	265	37	70	12	0	15	57	40	50	0	1	.266	.366	.484	49	6.28	6.04	2.02	-0.35	1.67
Mouton L	39	5	12	2	0	2	7	4	8	0	0	.315	.384	.526	7	7.61	7.19	0.38	-0.04	0.34
Palmeiro R	613	103	185	37	1	44	128	85	91	12	7	.302	.391	.580	130	7.76	7.32	6.61	0.77	7.38
Reboulet J	125	21	31	6	0	1	8	20	34	0	1	.250	.358	.325	16	4.03	3.86	0.20	0.25	0.45
Ripken C	597	68	166	29	1	14	64	55	68	0	2	.278	.342	.401	80	4.86	4.55	2.11	0.67	2.78
Surhoff B	569	83	163	37	1	22	96	53	81	9	7	.287	.344	.473	90	5.57	5.19	3.06	0.76	3.82
Webster L	308	39	90	17	0	10	49	16	38	0	0	.293	.328	.449	41	4.78	4.44	0.98	0.30	1.28
BAL	5521	854	1547	325	12	216	822	637	908	95	49	.280	.358	.461	892	5.67	5.31	32.20	8.30	40.50

Pitcher	S	C	T	SS	ES	IC	HH	PP	TJ	S12	S35	S67	C1	C23	C45	C67	QWP
Coppinger	4.00	4.00	8.00	0%	0%	0%	0%	0%	0%	0%	100%	0%	0%	0%	100%	0%	.469
Drabek	4.81	3.48	8.29	33%	10%	24%	48%	0%	5%	14%	38%	48%	14%	24%	57%	5%	.372
Erickson	4.56	2.67	7.22	42%	17%	44%	42%	0%	19%	25%	33%	42%	25%	56%	17%	3%	.518
Fussell	4.00	6.00	10.00	0%	0%	0%	0%	50%	0%	0%	100%	0%	0%	0%	50%	50%	.223
Johns	5.50	3.80	9.30	10%	10%	20%	60%	0%	10%	10%	30%	60%	10%	10%	70%	10%	.284
Ju Guzman	4.00	4.36	8.36	45%	9%	36%	27%	18%	0%	36%	36%	27%	0%	36%	45%	18%	.404
Kamieniecki	4.55	4.36	8.91	36%	0%	27%	36%	18%	0%	18%	45%	36%	0%	27%	55%	18%	.372
Key	3.91	3.18	7.09	55%	18%	45%	27%	0%	9%	27%	45%	27%	18%	45%	27%	9%	.528
Lewis	5.00	7.00	12.00	0%	0%	0%	0%	0%	0%	0%	100%	0%	0%	0%	0%	100%	.024
Munoz	5.00	5.00	10.00	0%	0%	0%	0%	0%	0%	0%	100%	0%	0%	0%	100%	0%	.204
Mussina	3.72	2.41	6.14	55%	24%	59%	24%	3%	14%	34%	41%	24%	31%	48%	21%	0%	.616
N Rodriguez	4.50	4.75	9.25	25%	0%	25%	50%	0%	0%	25%	25%	50%	0%	25%	50%	25%	.323
P Smith	5.50	4.50	10.00	0%	0%	0%	25%	0%	0%	0%	75%	25%	0%	25%	50%	25%	.309
Ponson	4.85	3.55	8.40	25%	0%	20%	40%	0%	10%	10%	50%	40%	0%	60%	35%	5%	.409
BAL	4.47	3.36	7.83	37%	12%	35%	36%	4%	10%	22%	42%	36%	15%	41%	36%	8%	.453

AMERICAN LEAGUE EAST

TAMPA BAY DEVIL RAYS

DOUG DRINEN

DILUTE IT SOME MORE

Sabermetrics is now an old enough and rich enough field that its practitioners can (and do) feel very confident in our ability to understand the dynamics of baseball, sometimes better than many individuals whose job description requires an understanding of same. We know roughly what the value of a stolen base is, and the cost of a failed attempt. We know at what age hitters tend to peak. We know that ballparks can create huge illusions in the raw statistics. We know that a 21-year-old rookie is likely to have a much more productive career than a 24-year-old rookie who posts identical numbers. We know that properly-interpreted minor league hitting statistics have as much predictive value as major league stats. Baseball insiders, from GMS to managers to scouts to players to reporters, often betray, through their words and their deeds, an astounding degree of ignorance of these empirical verifiable facts.

Many in the sabermetric community believe that the first organization which decides to commit fully to practicing what James, Palmer, et al have preached will run roughshod through the league. And with a low payroll to boot. Well, that may or may not be true, and I have no doubt that a sabermetrically-run squad would be able to put together a pretty solid offense. When it comes to pitching, though, we're all still seeking enlightenment.

We know a few things. Letting young (under 25) pitchers throw a truckload of innings probably isn't a good idea in general, and power pitchers as a group have longer careers than finessers, to name two. Don, Ken, and others here tirelessly examine reams of QMAX range data in search of insights into how young pitchers develop. But it still seems to be largely a guessing game. The human arm is just too tenuous a structure to be predictable. Where did Todd Van Poppel's velocity go? Is it conceivable that he could get it back? Will Tom Glavine still be a top pitcher when he's 39? Will Shawn Estes ever have a season as good

as 1997 again?

These are questions that sabermetrics cannot answer with anywhere near the certainty with which it answers questions about offense. And it's not clear that we'll ever be able to do a better job tackling these questions than insiders can do (here I'm talking about scouts and pitching coaches, not journalists). It stands to reason, then, that the teams which have a special insight into pitching are way ahead of the game. The obvious example is the Braves, who seem not only to be able to develop an endless stream of talent and keep them healthy, but also know exactly when to hold 'em (Maddux, Smoltz, Glavine) and when to fold 'em (Mercker, Avery, etc).

It's way too early to tell, but based on one expansion draft and one year, the Rays look like an organization that may know things others don't. Manager Larry Rothschild, a former Reds' and Marlins' pitching coach with no prior managerial experience, was presumably hired with this in mind.

Open up any newspaper or turn on any talk-radio show and you'll be bombarded with woe-are-us sermons about the sorry state of major league pitching these days. And that was long before the 1997 expansion, which was to dilute the talent pool further. The expansion draft essentially gave the Snakes and Stingers (Don makes us call them that) a chance to sort out the replacement level pitchers no one else wanted.

Let's divide Tampa's expansion-draftees into two cate-

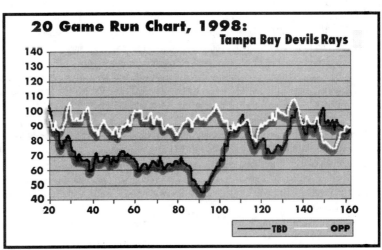

20 Game Run Chart, 1998:
Tampa Bay Devils Rays

QMAX PRESENTS: "BAD" PITCHERS

LOWERED EXPECTATIONS

One of the silver linings of suffering through an expansion team's first season is the lack of pressure to win right away. The grandiose expectations of bloated-ego buffoons like Colangelo aside, that's still pretty much true. It's a rule of thumb that expansion teams that try to win too quickly end up overpaying for mid-level stars on the downside of their careers, and the initial burst of pride from sudden success soon gives way to years--or possibly decades--of futility, as the chance to start with a clean slate never comes again, and old mistakes continue to drag the club into the second division. For examples of this, one need look no further than the Angels of the 1960's and (though this may yet be premature) the Rockies of this decade. On the other side of the coin are the teams that take their lumps early, get a base of talented youth in place, and turn into consistent winners when the youth matures. The prime example of this approach is the Kansas City Royals. The fact that I can't name

another one without hedging the qualifications shows how hard it really is to build a winner this way, or any way.

It's much too early to tell which way the Devil Rays will go (they have more than their share of superannuated sludge among the position players), but at least in the area of pitching, there seems to be a refreshing tendency to put young, live arms into the rotation and let them learn their craft.

As a consequence, the QMAX performance of the Devil Rays last year looks like anything but the usual expansion suspects. Missing are the cagey veteran junkballers who make their living in the Tommy John zone. In their place, the D-Rays have a collection of Young Guns who wind up and let 'er rip. Okay, so they're not exactly all young (Alvarez is certainly in the fat part of his career) and they're not all flamethrowers (Dennis Springer), but they do all share a definite preference for hit prevention over walk prevention; as a staff, they teeter on the power precipice much more than most.

With the exception of finesser Bryan Rekar, everyone who had more than five starts for the D-Rays was above the major league average of 8% of starts in the "power precipice." Alvarez led the way at 28%, followed by Jason Johnson and Tony Saunders at 23% and Dennis Springer at 18%. Springer demonstrates the QMAX conundrum of knuckleballers: you don't have to be a flamethrower to prevent hits. Springer's less-than-scintillating overall numbers in hit prevention, when examined through QMAX, show us that his problem was the eight starts out of seventeen where the butterfly ball failed to flutter. Springer had exactly one start in the (4,5) midrange of hit prevention--all other starts were either very good (3 or better) or very bad (six or worse.)

At any rate, it's good to see a major league team give pitchers with good stuff and control problems a shot in the rotation rather than prematurely shunting them to the bullpen, if only to give us QMAX wonks a few more data points to test our theories on.

--Tom Austin

gories, those with major league experience (75 IP was the cutoff I used), and prospects. Here are the experienced hurlers Tampa selected (I'm throwing out anyone that was involved in a draft-day trade, figuring they were only drafted with the trade in mind): Tony Saunders, Dennis Springer, Jim Mecir, Bryan Rekar, Albie Lopez, Terrell Wade, and Vaughn Eshelman.

Everyone here with the exception of Springer, who was obtained to eat up innings, was considered a prospect, and all but Saunders were considered failed prospects. I spilled a lot of ink in BBBA 97 explaining why I thought Saunders was a good first pick, and nothing happened in 98 to change my mind. A 24-year-old with better-than-average hit prevention and strikeout rates and a 4.12 ERA in an apparent hitters park doesn't leave much to complain about, despite an ugly 6-15 record. Of the 5 failed prospects, 3 got an extended look in Tampa. Of those, 2 (Mecir and Lopez) turned in truly outstanding seasons, and Rekar was not bad.

The draftees with little or no major league experience

were: Jason Johnson, Esteban Yan, Dan Carlson, Jose Paniagua, Mike Duvall, John LeRoy, Ryan Karp, Rick Gorecki, Ramon Tatis, and Santos Hernandez. Only 2 of these (Johnson and Yan) got a significant amount of time with the big club this year. Yan had a fine season. (Gorecki made the starting rotation in the spring, but was lost to injury after just three starts).

So the expansion-draft summary is as follows:
- ▼ the only good prospect the Rays took still looks like a good prospect,
- ▼ of 5 talent-pool-diluters that got time with Tampa last season, 3 had very good seasons, and only one was really awful.

You could also give Tampa credit for snapping up failed Ranger prospect Julio Santana, who turned in some quality innings for the Rays, and Scott Aldred, who had the best season of his very undistinguished career. Add Rick White to the list as well.

So how does this compare with other teams? To get a quick estimate, I looked at all the guys in the AL who could be considered talent-pool-diluters. This shouldn't be considered a serious study, as I essentially just eyeballed everyone and decided subjectively who was a talent-pool-diluter and who wasn't. Basically, I was looking for relatively young guys who aren't considered top prospects, had experienced little or no big-league success prior to 98, and got 30 or more innings in 1998. For example, the suspects from the other AL East clubs are: Carlos Almanzar, Robert Person, Nerio Rodriguez, Doug Johns, Rich Garces, John Wasdin, Carlos Reyes, Derek Lowe, Ron Mahay, and Mike Buddie. Here's a table showing how the 1998 ERAs of these folks were distributed:

	ERA			
	< 3	3-4	4-5	> 5
Devil Rays	1	4	2	1
Rest of AL	0	8	6	20

This shouldn't be taken as conclusive evidence of anything, but it does suggest that Tampa may have done a slightly better job of identifying and developing obscure pitching talent than their AL brethren. An expansion team in a hitters' park that finishes with the league's 4th-best ERA must be doing something right.

LITTLE BALL, LITTLE HELP

Funny thing, though. All that pitching, and somehow the Tampa hurlers were only credited with 63 wins while being saddled with 99 losses. That's what happens when an entire organization is as misguided with respect to offense as this north Florida bunch appears to be. This team has a solid case as the worst offensive team of the 90s. Here are some random facts to put it into perspective (keep in mind all of this is taking place in a park that boosted offense by about 8%). The Rays were last in the AL in OBP (.321), and last in SLG (.385). They were last in the entire major leagues in runs scored, with 620. The last time an AL team accomplished this feat was in 1991 (Cleveland). They were 24 runs behind the next-worst-scoring team in the majors, the Expos, and trailed the AL's 2nd-most-inept offensive squad, Kansas City, by an astounding 96 runs.

After park and league adjustments, they scored fewer runs than the Braves allowed. Think about that. This offense was so feeble it could have turned Atlanta's pitching staff into a below-.500 unit. Or, to put it another way, the Devil Rays could make an average staff pitch like the Braves.

Now, should we just chock this up to the fact that the Rays are an expansion team? After all, we know that expansion teams are going to be weak overall, and since this particular expansion team seems intent on developing pitching first and foremost, it's only natural that their bats are going to take awhile to come around.

However, I'm not sure the Tampa brass sees the offense as a major problem. In fact, it's not at all clear to me what, if

WPA BULLPEN BOX—TAMPA BAY DEVILS

	PI	WPA	P	PPPI
Starters	995	-2.2	49.6	0.050
Relievers	637	0.9	35.9	0.056
Road	294	-0.0	16.3	0.055
Home	343	1.0	19.6	0.057
Mar/Apr	102	0.5	4.6	0.045
May	113	0.5	6.0	0.054
June	117	1.8	8.9	0.076
July	93	-1.5	5.7	0.062
August	103	0.6	5.7	0.055
September	109	-1.0	5.0	0.046
Non S/H Sit.	527	2.8	22.9	0.044
S/H Sit.	110	-1.9	12.9	0.118
Low Pressure	295	-0.1	3.8	0.013
Med. Pressure	166	-0.3	9.5	0.057
High Pressure	176	1.4	22.7	0.129
Entered behind	359	0.5	8.8	0.024
Entered tied	86	2.0	11.5	0.134

Name	G	PI	WPA	P	PPPI	MI	ROB	T
Aldred S	48	56	-.1	3.3	.059	6	23	7
Hernandez R	67	80	-1.4	6.3	.079	13	12	4
Lopez A	54	98	1.0	6.7	.068	33	25	10
Mecir J	68	99	2.2	7.1	.072	25	28	9
Santana J	13	28	.0	.8	.027	8	6	1
Springer D	12	25	-.3	.3	.012	6	2	0
Tatis R	22	24	-.4	.5	.021	2	8	0
White R	35	69	.0	2.4	.035	20	19	4
Yan E	64	108	-.1	6.8	.063	32	24	10
Total		637	.9	35.9	.056			

	Quality					Pressure			
	Dis.	Poor	Fair	Good	Her.	Lo	Med	Hi	
Aldred S	0	10	29	9	0	25	18	5	(4)
Hernandez R	7	5	34	17	4	34	14	19	(10)
Lopez A	5	7	19	19	4	17	20	14	(14)
Mecir J	3	9	32	17	7	34	17	17	(11)
Santana J	0	1	11	1	0	10	1	2	(1)
Springer D	0	1	11	0	0	11	0	1	(0)
Tatis R	1	1	19	4	0	16	6	0	(0)
White R	1	6	20	8	0	20	11	4	(3)
Yan E	5	9	36	13	1	32	14	18	(10)
Others	0	4	21	2	0	19	5	3	(1)
TOTAL	22	53	232	87	16	218	103	89	(54)

	7th inning			8th inning			9th inning		
	0	+1	+2	0	+1	+2	0	+1	+2
Aldred S	1	0	0	3	1	0	1	0	0
Hernandez R	0	0	0	0	0	0	4	11	8
Lopez A	2	5	0	3	0	3	3	0	0
Mecir J	1	3	0	2	6	1	5	1	0
White R	0	0	0	1	0	0	0	0	0
Yan E	3	1	2	2	2	3	0	0	1
Starters	6	3	10	3	1	4	0	0	1
TOTAL	13	12	12	14	10	11	13	12	10
Record	6-7	7-5	10-2	7-7	7-3	9-2	6-7	8-4	9-1

Sean Forman's

PROSPECT WATCH

NAME	AGE	POS	LEVEL	GR98	GR97	GR96	AVG
Steve Cox	23	1B	AAA	57	77	65	65
Rich Butler	25	OF	AAA	59	68	-	63
Scott McClain	26	3B	AAA	55	54	56	55

NAME	AGE	POS	LEVEL	GRADE
Ramon Soler	16	SS	Rookie	65
Humberto Cota	19	C	Rookie	59
John Jacobs	18	3B	Rookie	56
Kenneth Kelly	19	OF	Low A	54
Aubrey Huff	21	3B	Low A	51
Isrrael Osorio	17	DH	Rookie	51
Alex Sanchez	21	OF	High A	50
Josh Pressley	18	1B	Rookie	47
Steven Goodson	19	1B	Rookie	47
Brian Martin	18	OF	Rookie	45
Jared Sandberg	20	3B	Low A	41

NAME	AGE	GS	S	C	T	W-L	ERA	K/H	LEVEL
Dave Eiland	30	28	4.04	2.64	6.68	13-5	2.99	0.63	High
Josias Manzanillo	30	27	3.93	3.44	7.37	11-8	3.98	0.78	High
Matt Ruebel	28	23	4.17	3.52	7.70	9-6	4.74	0.62	High
Michael Callaway	23	24	4.21	3.92	8.13	10-8	4.35	0.50	High
Bobby Seay	20	15				1-7	4.3	1.25	Low
Matt White	19	29				8-11	4.73	0.68	Low

The Devil Rays are experiencing the normal growing pains an expansion team goes through. They don't get a AA team until next year, so they are naturally short on high level prospects. In the lower levels the Devil Rays have drafted mostly athletes hoping that they will turn into baseball players.

HOT CORNER HOPING: Scott McClain

McClain produced what was probably his career year in Durham hitting .299/.385/.589 with 34 home runs. It was his fourth season in AAA, so he has received some opportunities in the past, but has never made serious case for himself. He deserves a bench job somewhere as a right-handed pinch-hitter/utility player. He is only two years older than third baseman-in-waiting Bobby Smith, but I doubt he will ever receive any chance as a starter. Comp: Craig Paquette with patience.

QUARTERBACK: Kenneth Kelly

Kelly is a quarterback for the Miami Hurricanes when he's not tracking fly balls for the Devil Rays. Because of his school and football commitments he managed just 211 at bats last year, but he showed some skills in that time. He hit .280/.347/.399, which isn't outstanding, but for a part-time 19-year-old in low-ball he's holding his own. His baserunning was excellent (19 of 23), and he can only get better as he gains experience. I'm not sure if he will get it done playing part time, but it sure has to be fun doing both.

FAMOUS NAME: Jared Sandberg

Sandberg is indeed a relative of Ryne Sandberg, his nephew in fact. Sandberg is a free-swinging third baseman. He struggled badly in low-A hitting .183/.293/.288. He was demoted to short-season ball and regained his stroke batting .288/.388/.491. The patience and power are promising, but he struck out 162 times in 462 at bats. If he can start making consistent contact, he could become a plus player, but the strikeout rate must decrease.

GO! SPEED RACER, GO!: Alex Sanchez

Sanchez is one of the more prolific basestealers in the minors. He stole 92 bases in 1997 and moved up to fast A ball where he stole 66. He is not particularly successful as he was caught 40 times in 1997 and 33 times in 1998. He is also the epitome of a punch-and-judy hitter, mostly reaching on singles. He has started using his speed to good effect batting .330 last year, but his patience is substandard (just 31 walks in 545 at bats). The Devil Rays don't appear to have a problem with low OBP players, so he will continue to more up the ladder.

ON THE MOUND: Matt White

Scouts continue to drool over him and the Devil Rays continue to say big things about him, but I'm a bit skeptical. He split time between the Sally and the Florida State League, and he was pretty young for those levels, but he wasn't all that dominant. He allowed 179 hits in 176 IP's and struck out 123. Those are respectable numbers, but not worthy of $10M. The Devil Rays are also overusing him. He made 29 starts (tops in the organization) and averaged 26 batters faced in those starts.

If I were a GM, I think I would leave high school pitchers alone in the first two or three rounds and use five of my 4-10 picks on high school pitchers. I would also concentrate on Latin pitching talent.

anything, the Tampa brass does see. There seems to be some evidence that the Devil Rays have no plan whatsoever for how to put together their offense. Note that they attempted to sign Dean Palmer over the offseason despite the fact that 3rd base is one of the few positions at Tropicana Field which is not currently emitting a foul odor.

And then there's evidence that the Devil Rays do in fact have a plan, but unfortunately it's a plan that is doomed to failure. In the expansion draft, Tampa went hunting primarily for a certain species of hitter: the slappin' swifty. Hoping to put the ball in play, make things happen, disrupt the opposing pitcher, manufacture runs, do the little things, put pressure on the defense, and every other conceivable thing that announcers love, but has never been shown to put any runs on the scoreboard, Tampa bagged its quota of McCrackens and Winns and Cairos.

Having done so, the Rays followed through by leading the league in little ball. They were second in the AL in sacrifice hits, and 4th in stolen base attempts. But this understates Tampa's love of one-run strategies. Since the Devil Rays had fewer runners on base than any other team, they had fewer opportunities to sacrifice and steal. Looking at stolen base attempts as a percentage of runners on first (singles + walks + HBP), the Rays trailed only Toronto in stolen base attempt frequency. Oh, by the way, they were dead last in the league in stolen base efficiency at 62%.

Here's a paradox for you. Before the season, the Rays expected their McCrackens, Winns, and Cairos to be decent offensive players. Statheads the world over expected them to stink. Well, it turns out they performed just the way the Rays expected them to. Oddly enough, they performed just the way statheads expected them to, as well. How'd that happen? It happened because Tampa Bay labors under the impression that batting average and stolen bases (that's stolen base totals, mind you, rates apparently don't matter) are sufficient to generate offense. McCracken's OBP was .335 and Winn's was .337. Cairo, who, to be fair, is viewed as more of a glove man, sported a .307. Together, they managed to swipe 64 bags and get caught 30 times, amassing a net gain of virtually nil.

So if in fact Devil Ray management has a plan, that plan is as follows: collect hitters that make outs at a high rate, then give away as many outs as possible on the bases. All in the name of putting pressure on the defense.

The Devil Rays also have a hard time distinguishing between "young" and "doesn't have much major-league experience." McCracken is not young (29) and is likely on the downside of his career. Winn, 25, figures to have 1 to 3 years of improvement left, which, with typical progress, will bring him about up to average for a centerfielder (but well below if he ends up at one of the corners). Cairo, also 25, doesn't ever figure to be average offensively. I get the impression that the Devil Ray organization thinks this is going to be the core of the first Tampa Bay playoff team.

Meanwhile, they're not quite ready to accept that McGriff is on a steep decline and Flaherty and Stocker simply can't play. Just bad luck. All the veterans except Boggs just had off years. "The worst mistake we can make is to not be patient," claims GM Chuck LaMar. So what we've got here is an organization that acknowledges its offense was terrible in 1998, but thinks:

1 Its youngsters are already good, and likely to improve, and

2 Its veterans are going to bounce back and provide some respectable offense until the youngsters are ready to take over.

Given that, and the fact that Tampa won't be competing for a playoff spot in 1999, it makes sense that the Devil Rays didn't make any significant changes to their offense this offseason (as I write this, it's late November and the Rays look to be taking exactly the same offense into 99 that they took into 98). Let's put on the rose-coloreds for a spin around the diamond, and see if the Rays can climb out of the AL run-scoring cellar in 99.

Behind the plate, Mike Difelice and John Flaherty teamed up to create a massive offensive sinkhole in 98. Both are past prime and decline is reasonable, but Flaherty's ineptitude (207/261/273) really was a bit greater than expected. It's possible that he rebounds by posting something closer to his career numbers, which would add maybe 15 runs or so.

At first base, Fred McGriff's decline is right on schedule and should continue. To expect a better season

in 99 is unreasonable. Second base will apparently be manned by Cairo again, who, if he displays typical development for a 25-year-old, might add an extra 5 or 10 runs to the scoreboard. Third base was the home of Wade Boggs and a mild surprise, Bobby Smith, a 25-year-old who developed nicely last year and hit 276/343/422 (nearly league average!). Continued progress and more playing time for Smith, who may also see time at short or second, could yield up to 20 additional runs (remember, these are heavy-duty rose-colored goggles: it's equally likely that Smith reverts to something more in line with his less-than-stellar minor league record). Kevin Stocker's stick, like Flaherty's, is bad, but not this bad. He might be 10 runs better in 99.

In the outfield, McCracken figures to play everyday. He had his best year last year at the age of 28, and I refuse to expect any improvement. The other outfield spots will probably be manned by some combination of Winn, Rich Butler, Mike Kelly, Bubba Trammell (who may DH some as well), and possibly Kerry Robinson. A lot of bodies, so there's a chance someone will pan out (though it won't be Kelly), but Tampa will likely spend 99 the same way they spent 98, giving each of these guys 300-400 plate appearances and getting very little production. Trammell's the only real hitter here, and more playing

**TEAM BREAKOUT
DEVIL RAYS 1998**

Category	RS	RA	W	L	Pct.	Rk
RUNS SCORED/ROAD	202	108	24	5	.828	3
5+ RUNS SCORED	429	273	47	15	.758	6
5+ RUNS SCORED/HOME	227	165	23	10	.697	11
4- RUNS ALLOWED/HOME	133	86	23	15	.605	14
4- RUNS ALLOWED	301	196	48	35	.578	14
4- RUNS ALLOWED/ROAD	168	110	25	20	.556	14
CLOSE SLUGFESTS/HOME	69	70	5	5	.500	10
RECORD IN CLOSE GAMES/HOME	138	142	17	18	.486	12
RECORD IN SLUGFESTS	233	249	15	18	.455	9
SLUGFESTS/HOME	149	167	10	12	.455	9
SLUGFESTS/ROAD	84	82	5	6	.455	9
RECORD IN BLOWOUTS/ROAD	99	124	10	14	.417	10
SEASON TOTALS	620	751	63	99	.389	14
LOW SCORING GAMES/ROAD	50	63	10	16	.385	13
RECORD IN BLOWOUTS	218	294	20	32	.385	13
CLOSE LOW-SCORING GAMES/HOME	27	34	6	10	.375	13
RECORD IN CLOSE GAMES	247	278	24	42	.364	14
RECORD IN BLOWOUTS/HOME	119	170	10	18	.357	13
RECORD IN LOW SCORING GAMES	111	146	19	38	.333	14
LOW SCORING GAMES/ROAD	61	83	9	22	.290	14
5+ RUNS ALLOWED/HOME	185	311	10	33	.233	9
RECORD IN CLOSE GAMES/ROAD	109	136	7	24	.226	14
4- RUNS SCORED/HOME	91	232	10	38	.208	13
CLOSE SLUGFESTS/ROAD	38	43	1	4	.200	13
5+ RUNS ALLOWED	319	555	15	64	.190	10
4- RUNS SCORED	191	478	16	84	.160	14
5+ RUNS ALLOWED/ROAD	134	244	5	31	.139	13
CLOSE LOW SCORING GAMES/ROAD	24	41	2	13	.133	14
4-.RUNS SCORED/ROAD	100	246	6	46	.115	14

time for him would help. At best, I can see a 20-run improvement in the outfield.

The DH will evidently be Paul Sorrento (and/or the aforementioned Trammell). Sorrento had a genuine off-year last year and should be better in 99. Figure 15 runs here.

Adding it up, we find an improvement of 90 runs, which would nearly get them out of last place. If we take off the glasses and look at things more realistically, that might shrink to 20 or 30 runs. If we wanted to take the half-empty view and look at worst-case scenarios, we'd see an offense so grotesque that even Royals' fans wouldn't be able to stomach it.

And this is the way it's going to be for the foreseeable future in Tampa Bay. There's no shame in an expansion team having the worst offense in baseball, but there's absolutely no help on the way and little chance of significant improvement. The first step is admitting you have a problem, and until the Rays do that, they're going to see many a fine pitching performance squandered, and many a 3-2 loss. Funny, those are exactly the kind of games that teams that "make things happen" are supposed to win.

Name	AB	R	H	D	T	HR	RBI	BB	SO	SB	CS	BA	OBP	SLG	XR	Adj XR/27	Raw XR/27	OXW	DXW	TXW
Boggs W	433	50	122	23	4	5	51	48	56	3	2	.282	.353	.392	57	4.68	4.67	1.38	0.42	1.80
Butler R	216	24	48	3	3	6	19	16	38	4	2	.223	.279	.344	22	3.36	3.57	-0.16	0.60	0.44
Cairo M	514	48	140	27	5	4	45	25	46	21	9	.272	.313	.370	58	3.88	3.76	0.44	2.03	2.47
Difelice M	247	16	58	12	3	3	22	16	57	0	0	.233	.281	.342	21	2.69	2.57	-0.69	1.61	0.92
Flaherty J	304	21	64	11	0	3	23	22	47	0	6	.211	.265	.276	19	2.00	1.94	-1.52	1.83	0.31
Kelly M	278	38	67	11	2	9	32	23	82	14	7	.240	.296	.394	31	3.72	3.78	0.08	0.63	0.71
Ledesma A	299	29	99	16	3	0	29	9	52	10	9	.330	.350	.405	37	4.46	4.32	0.72	1.71	2.43
Martinez D	307	30	80	11	0	3	20	37	53	9	8	.259	.341	.321	34	3.77	3.67	0.22	0.92	1.14
McCracken Q	612	75	181	39	7	6	57	43	110	20	12	.296	.341	.412	83	4.77	4.68	2.07	1.76	3.83
McGriff F	561	71	159	33	0	16	79	82	121	8	2	.283	.375	.428	90	5.73	5.82	3.41	0.51	3.92
Smith B	369	43	102	15	3	10	54	35	113	6	3	.276	.346	.416	53	5.00	5.01	1.50	0.64	2.14
Sorrento P	433	39	97	27	0	15	56	56	136	2	3	.223	.315	.389	54	4.19	4.34	0.81	0.31	1.12
Stocker K	335	36	70	11	3	5	24	28	82	6	3	.209	.286	.307	30	2.86	2.86	-0.74	2.55	1.81
Trammell B	198	27	56	18	1	11	34	17	46	0	2	.284	.339	.549	34	6.08	6.31	1.33	0.27	1.60
Winn R	337	50	95	9	9	1	17	30	71	28	13	.282	.342	.371	44	4.45	4.32	0.86	0.55	1.41
TB	5535	604	1455	272	44	96	565	493	1135	131	84	.263	.325	.380	669	4.12	4.12	9.70	16.34	26.04

Pitcher	S	C	T	SS	ES	IC	HH	PP	TJ	S12	S35	S67	C1	C23	C45	C67	QWP
Alvarez	3.68	4.12	7.80	56%	4%	40%	32%	28%	0%	40%	28%	32%	4%	28%	52%	16%	.478
Arrojo	3.75	3.13	6.88	56%	19%	53%	34%	9%	9%	34%	31%	34%	9%	56%	28%	6%	.539
D Springer	4.35	4.18	8.53	47%	0%	24%	47%	18%	0%	18%	35%	47%	0%	29%	59%	12%	.393
Eiland	6.00	7.00	13.00	0%	0%	0%	100%	0%	0%	0%	0%	100%	0%	0%	0%	100%	.021
Gorecki	3.33	4.00	7.33	67%	0%	33%	33%	0%	0%	33%	33%	33%	0%	33%	67%	0%	.490
J Johnson	4.62	4.23	8.85	23%	0%	31%	46%	23%	8%	23%	31%	46%	0%	23%	69%	8%	.348
R White	4.33	5.00	9.33	0%	0%	33%	67%	33%	0%	33%	0%	67%	0%	0%	67%	33%	.346
Rekar	4.47	3.13	7.60	33%	7%	33%	33%	0%	13%	20%	47%	33%	13%	53%	33%	0%	.493
Ruebel	5.00	5.00	10.00	0%	0%	0%	0%	0%	0%	0%	100%	0%	0%	0%	100%	0%	.204
Santana	4.11	3.58	7.68	37%	11%	37%	26%	11%	11%	26%	47%	26%	11%	21%	68%	0%	.466
Saunders	3.90	4.13	8.03	39%	0%	29%	23%	23%	10%	19%	58%	23%	3%	29%	52%	16%	.454
Wade	5.00	3.50	8.50	0%	0%	0%	50%	0%	0%	0%	50%	50%	0%	50%	50%	0%	.430
TBD	4.05	3.81	7.86	43%	6%	36%	34%	16%	7%	27%	40%	34%	6%	35%	50%	10%	.459

AMERICAN LEAGUE CENTRAL

CLEVELAND INDIANS

DON MALCOLM

HART OF DARKNESS

I have come to the conclusion that there is a deep-seated reason why John Hart is so often seen in dark clothing. Such a choice is more than a fashion decision, as John Harvey has documented in his definitive study of the roots of modernism, Men In Black. In the middle of the nineteenth century an element of mourning entered into Western culture, a kind of premonition of doom that was a response to the strident onrush of nationalism and imperialism. It has been with us ever since, and it has been institutionalized into the literal fabric of our lives. Even though we all profess to ignore such large-scale ambient conditions and get on with the business of our individual lives, we are all nonetheless subject to these forces.

As for John Hart, he is clearly something of the Black Prince type. His develop, divide and conquer strategy would have fit Prince Edward and his raiders to a tee. But remember that the Black Prince never became King, and the Cleveland Indians, for all of their achievements in the nineties, have yet to be World Champions.

Post-modernism meets medievalism: there's a prism for baseball that might provide an odd sliver of illumination, like those Burgundian manuscript paintings that ushered in the Renaissance and its enveloping nationalism. Thirty fiefdoms and a Grail, with an oddly in-bred insiders' network that struggles for power and glory. The late medieval era was one of plague and fear and accelerating economic ferment; the fin-de-siecle world of baseball has similar self-induced cultural traumas.

In those times as well as now, radical innovators are first imitated, then discarded and reviled. The renaissance of fortune, financial and otherwise, in Cleveland has been a model for imitators across the feudal terrain of baseball, but the revisionists are lining up take their licks at Hart and his approach to player development. Many have already realized that much of what passes for development

has been--like the warring dukes in the illuminated age--acquisition both desperate and calculated.

John Hart's homegrown approach to franchise development has been highly touted, but it is far more shallow in execution. The 1995 Indians contained three major home-grown players: Albert Belle, Jim Thome, and Manny Ramirez. Players that developed once acquired from other teams: Carlos Baerga, Kenny Lofton, Omar Vizquel. (Sandy Alomar was an extremely belated addition to this list in 1997.) The 1997 Indians added Brian Giles, Jaret Wright, and Bartolo Colon to the homegrown list, and subtracted Belle. (Richie Sexson will replace Giles on this list in 1999.) Let's compare the Indians' 1998 home-grown list of major players to the New York Yankees, a team considered to be the epitome of the "buy as you go" team building:

Indians	Yankees
Jim Thome	Bernie Williams
Manny Ramirez	Derek Jeter
Bartolo Colon	Andy Pettitte
Jaret Wright	Mariano Rivera

It's the exact same number of players, and overall the Yankees' achievement level is higher (thus far, at least). Hart built a great offense, but did not retain Albert Belle and has continually made major revisions to his personnal ever since. The

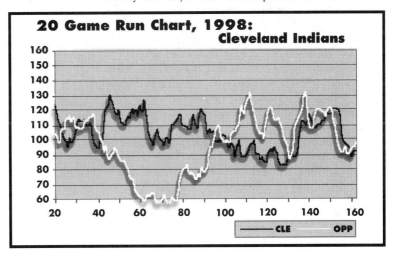

20 Game Run Chart, 1998:
Cleveland Indians

QMAX PRESENTS: "BAD" PITCHERS

THE SOFTER THEY COME

Some of you young folks mebbe could use a little remindin', but the Indians used to be a bad team. Every year. They made that movie "Major League" about 'em, that was no joke. Well, the movie was a joke, but that's another story. Our man Rick "They also serve those who only stand and" Waits was the quintessential tribester (and how's that for the worst Bermanism of all time? I try.). Rick's best year was 1978, the year he went 13-15 with a 3.20 ERA for a Tribe called Suck. Oh, that's a little harsh: they only lost 90, and in 1979 and 1981 the Indians actually had winning records (albeit one game over .500 each time, and with their 80-82 record in 1980 posted a dead-even .500 record over the span).

Now, Rick Waits was never a man blessed with great stuff; even in his better years he was sort of a poor man's Catfish Hunter, giving up around a hit an inning, many of those leaving the yard. In 1981, however, he went from poor man to beggar-man, as the American League batted a hefty .330 against him. A typical Waits start in 1981 was six innings, 8.3 hits, 3.5 runs, 3 walks, 2 strikeouts. Not that far from a minimum Quality Start, actually, and hence a prime argument against that flawed stat.

Waits pitched a 10-hit, one-run complete game victory in his first start of the year, followed it with two more complete-game victories, and after three starts had a 3-0 record and a 1.33 ERA. After that, my guess is the 228 innings he had averaged the

RICK WAITS/CLE 1981							
	1	2	3	4	5	6	7	S
1								0
2	2							2
3			1					1
4			1					1
5	2	1		1	2	1		7
6				1	1			2
7			1	1	2	2	2	8
C	4	1	3	5	4	2	2	21

previous three years came home to roost. Waits pitched seven straight poor starts (over a hit an inning every time out) before being pulled from the rotation (again, I'm guessing injury; he didn't appear in relief) until early August, where he picked up where he left off with eight more lousy starts (six of eight in the "7s" region). In all, Waits waited nearly five months between decent starts, from a 4,3 win on 4/30 to a 2,1 win on 9/21. I'm grasping for a numerology joke here, and failing. Some things just aren't funny.

--Tom Austin

initial impression of a nurturer has given way to a man who sets course via upheaval. He has not simply added value to his team in any season since 1995 without also making a significant subtraction as well.

Like the Black Prince, he appears to have an aversion to abundance, especially in the outfield, where he has relinquished major talent on an yearly basis. Restless and relentless, he is uneasy with the trappings of power and now approaches it with a uniquely intricate evasion. Like the man who invented the concept of the border skirmish, Hart has changed the terms of the game without actually winning anything, and in some odd, dark, deep-seated way, this condition may suit him just as much as the dark hues in his wardrobe.

Looking at such a formulation, one is reminded of the idea that someone's greatest skill--the "instrument of genius," so to speak--could also prove to be his tragic flaw (the Elizabethan twist on tragedy that is steeped in the medieval concept of de casibus--translated roughly as "the fall of great men"). Both on and off-field, baseball has entered into its own version of an Elizabethan age, where the darkness at its center allows a brilliant, blinding corona to stream out, dazzling us in its intensity as it decenters and disorients. An empire of misdirection is something that only the final decade of the twentieth century could produce, and John Hart is the prodigious symbol of baseball's newly-fashioned, dark-hewn prodigality. Should his half-decade in the spotlight as the game's great architect conclude without a World Series win, his demeanor and aura will come to be seen as poignantly prophetic.

ALOMAR FOR GILES

In terms of the 1999 Indians' lineup, Cleveland has in effect swapped left fielder Brian Giles (traded to Pittsburgh for relief pitcher Ricardo Rincon) for second baseman Roberto Alomar (signed as a free agent, costing the Indians a draft pick). What is the impact of this move on the Indians' lineup, and how might it affect the team's chances?

While there are a lot of independent variables at work here (the makeup of the Indians' starting rotation being the most prominent), we can make a few direct comparisons. First, it's almost certain that Alomar, who is 31 this year, will improve the Indians' offensive output at second base and in the #2 slot in their batting order. The amount of that improvement, based on looking at past performance, looks to be anywhere from 13-23 runs created.

Using the admittedly crude scale of 10 runs per win, and giving Alomar some credit for his defensive abilities, we can surmise that his addition to the team should account for about two more wins.

But what about losing Giles? How will that affect the Tribes' batting order? While Brian was only a platoon player for the Indians in 1997-98, his particular mix of hitting skills is not one that the Indians are featuring with the personnel they have retained. Replacing Giles in the mix will most likely be Richie Sexson, the 6'7" first baseman who had a hot streak of hitting in his first month in the majors and finished with some wvery gaudy looking numbers.

Sexson, however, does not have the plate discipline that Giles has, and there is more than a little chance that he was performing over his head last year. And then there is the overall declining offensive output of the Tribe's batting order in 1998. Here are the batting order position (BOP) comparisons for 1997 vs. 1998 (expressed in raw XR):

BOP	97	98	Diff
1	92	101	9
2	79	77	-2
3	134	113	-21
4	113	135	22
5	140	120	-20
6	109	88	-21
7	89	99	10
8	91	68	-23
9	86	74	-12
TOT	933	875	-58

Looking at the 1999 team with the 1997 offense as the benchmark, we see a team coming off a season where the lineup declined in six of nine slots. Four of these six, moreover, were drops of more than twenty runs. Roberto Alomar addresses one of these four slots, and there is a more than an even chance that Sexson's 1999 won't match Giles' 1998 (which itself was a downturn from 1997). The Indians' projected lineup in 1999 is as follows:

Lofton	cf (93)
R. Alomar	2b (100)
Thome	dh (124)
Ramirez	rf (123)
Justice	lf (98)
Fryman	3b (83)
Sexson	1b (79)
S. Alomar	c (70)
Vizquel	ss (73)

The numbers in parentheses represent the projected XR estimates for these players in 1999 once we've prorated their performances to a full 162 games. The XR estimate for the Indians is 842 runs, or a downturn of another ~30 runs from their XR in 1998.

A factor to take into account in such projections, however, is whether or not the lineup structure is likelier to exceed or come in below the XR projection. The Indians actually scored 850 runs in 1998, or ~25 less than they were expected to score given the sum of the XR for their individual lineup slots. Anywhere from 40% to 60% of teams in a given year will project to score more runs with XR than they actually manage to score; it's rare, however, for any individual team to do so year in and year out. The Indians are such a team, and it's possible that some of the reason for this has been due to lineup construction.

We await a definitive empirical study of such matters, despite the pronouncements of Bill James and others, who cite simulation studies as evidence to minimize the potential impact

WPA BULLPEN BOX—CLEVELAND INDIANS

	PI	WPA	P	PPPI
Starters	1048	0.8	53.9	0.051
Relievers	612	3.9	41.6	0.068
Road	292	3.8	22.7	0.078
Home	320	0.1	18.9	0.059
Mar/Apr	116	0.0	8.8	0.076
May	96	1.4	5.6	0.058
June	82	-0.3	6.0	0.073
July	108	2.8	7.7	0.071
August	116	-1.4	7.7	0.066
September	94	1.4	5.8	0.062
Non S/H Sit.	422	-0.3	20.2	0.048
S/H Sit.	190	4.2	21.4	0.112
Low Pressure	233	0.9	3.5	0.015
Med. Pressure	195	-1.1	13.9	0.071
High Pressure	184	4.1	24.2	0.132
Entered behind	238	-0.2	6.5	0.027
Entered tied	94	-0.5	11.0	0.117
Entered ahead	280	4.6	24.1	0.086

Name	G	PI	WPA	P	PPPI	MI	ROB	T
Assenmacher P	69	85	.1	8.0	.094	15	27	11
Jackson M	69	76	2.9	7.6	.100	7	18	6
Jones D	23	39	.2	2.3	.059	13	12	3
Martin T	14	22	-.5	.8	.037	6	8	1
Mesa J	44	68	-1.2	4.0	.059	21	17	8
Morman A	31	42	.6	2.5	.059	11	18	2
Plunk E	37	56	-.9	3.2	.056	17	16	5
Poole J	12	13	.0	.7	.050	1	3	1
Reed S	20	31	.9	2.9	.093	11	6	5
Shuey P	43	62	.8	5.1	.082	16	12	10
Villone R	25	35	.6	1.2	.035	9	8	4
Total		612	3.9	41.6	.068			

	I--------- Quality ----------I					I--- Pressure -------I		
	Dis.	Poor	Fair	Good	Her.	Lo	Med	Hi
Assenmacher P	5	10	35	17	2	29	23	17	(12)
Jackson M	5	3	28	33	0	26	19	24	(18)
Jones D	1	4	11	6	1	8	9	6	(3)
Martin T	1	2	7	4	0	7	6	1	(1)
Mesa J	4	7	23	10	0	18	17	9	(5)
Morman A	1	1	22	7	0	13	11	7	(5)
Plunk E	3	11	16	6	1	18	10	9	(3)
Poole J	0	2	8	2	0	7	4	1	(1)
Reed S	2	2	5	7	4	5	7	8	(6)
Shuey P	4	3	21	13	2	16	14	13	(7)
Villone R	0	3	18	3	1	19	4	2	(2)
Others	1	6	19	9	2	16	13	8	(6)
TOTAL	27	54	213	117	13	182	137	105	(69)

	7th inning			8th inning			9th inning		
	0	+1	+2	0	+1	+2	0	+1	+2
Assenmacher P	0	0	0	3	2	5	2	4	5
Jackson M	0	0	0	0	0	0	2	13	6
Jones D	1	0	1	1	1	1	0	0	0
Martin T	0	0	1	0	0	0	0	0	0
Mesa J	0	2	0	1	5	2	2	1	0
Morman A	1	2	1	0	0	1	0	0	0
Plunk E	0	2	0	0	1	0	0	0	0
Poole J	0	0	0	1	1	1	0	0	0
Reed S	1	1	1	0	1	2	3	0	0
Shuey P	2	0	1	3	4	2	6	0	0
Villone R	0	0	2	0	0	0	0	0	0
Starters	14	9	5	5	3	4	1	0	2
TOTAL	20	19	13	14	19	19	16	18	15
Record	7-13	15-4	12-1	7-7	14-5	16-3	7-9	17-1	13-2

213

Sean Forman's

PROSPECT WATCH

NAME	AGE	POS	LEVEL	GR98	GR97	GR96	AVG
Russ Branyan	22	3B	AA	93	76	64	83
Richie Sexson	23	1B	AAA	77	80	68	77
Enrique Wilson	22	3B	AAA	67	84	74	74
Alex Ramirez	23	OF	AAA	70	72	77	72
Jacob Cruz	25	OF	AAA	59	74	63	65
Marcos Scutaro	22	2B	AA	68	50	43	58
Scott Morgan	24	OF	AA	51	47	61	51
Daniel Peoples	23	OF	AA	53	54	33	50

NAME	AGE	POS	LEVEL	GRADE
Dennis Malave	18	OF	Rookie	58
Scott Pratt	21	2B	Rookie	54
Maicer Isturiz	17	SS	Rookie	52
Jonathan Hamilton	20	OF	Low A	51
Edgar Cruz	19	C	Low A	49
Zach Sorenson	21	SS	Rookie	43

NAME	AGE	GS	S	C	T	W-L	ERA	K/H	LEVEL
Jim Brower	25	23	3.61	2.78	6.39	13-5	3.01	0.64	High
Huck Flener	28	18	3.89	3.00	6.89	8-5	4.11	0.67	High
Jason Jacome	27	24	4.25	2.83	7.08	14-2	3.26	0.68	High
Frankie Sanders	22	29	3.90	3.31	7.21	11-8	3.48	0.62	High
Jason Rakers	25	27	4.11	3.11	7.22	12-7	4.18	0.69	High
Willie Martinez	20	25	4.36	3.20	7.56	8-7	4.26	0.68	High
Jared Camp	23	15	4.13	3.87	8.00	5-2	3.84	0.48	High
Mike Matthews	24	23	4.22	4.17	8.39	9-6	4.63	0.63	High
Marcus Moore	27	19	3.84	4.84	8.68	4-9	4.93	1.12	High

There are two ways to look at John Hart. He has become a bit chicken over the last few years, and no longer trusts young players with full-time jobs. Or, he and Mike Hargrove are to positional players what Earl Weaver was to pitchers. They prefer to break a hitter in slowly in low pressure situations.

After breaking in a number of young players like Kenny Lofton, Carlos Baerga, Manny Ramirez, Jim Thome and others, Hart has become more cautious with the utilization of his young talent. Brian Giles waited forever before being given a shot, Enrique Wilson is going to end up behind Robbie Alomar (a better, but far more expensive player), and even Jim Thome was handled with kid gloves at first. Of course, most of these players have become outstanding players, so it's hard to fault the success that Indians have had.

COMMONWEALTH EDISON: Russ Branyan
What the White Sox' Mark Johnson is to walks, this guy is to power. He has hit a home run every eleven at bats over the last three years. He certainly brings to mind Jim Thome: a left-handed batting third baseman with big-time power, good patience, a propensity for strikeouts, and some questions about his glove. He still hasn't played above AA, so a year in Buffalo probably wouldn't kill him, but I think he could probably outhit a dozen or so major league third basemen right now.

FREE SWINGER: Alex Ramirez
The Indians consistently have more big seasons from their minor league batters than any other organization. This year it was Alex Ramirez's turn to step up. He slugged 34 home runs, which nearly doubled his previous best. It was his second year in AAA, so that may have played some part. He was also an out machine managing just 16 walks in 521 at bats. He's played centerfield, so it's not beyond the realm of possibility that if the Gammonesque rumors of Kenny Lofton's availability are true, he could get some at bats in the bigs this year. I'm not a big fan of his, given his generally awful plate discipline, but he just might be able to hit enough to support his lack of walks. Comp: A better Nigel Wilson.

HAVE BAT WILL TRAVEL: Jacob Cruz
Last year, I proffered Cruz as an example of a player not really good enough to be a major league regular, but perhaps good enough to be a bench player. Well, Jacob didn't really do much to change my opinion of him. He was 25 this year and hit the ball pretty well going .309/.381/.560 between Fresno and Buffalo (both AAA). I still don't think he'll hit enough to be an average or better corner outfielder, and he really doesn't have a platoon split to recommend him for platooning. In fact, he might almost be better off if he were hitting .350 vs. right-handers and .260 vs. lefties. Then he could have a well-defined role.

Comp: between Darrell Whitmore and Keith Mitchell.

POWER SUPPLY: Scott Morgan
If the Indians were to sign Randy Johnson, they would have one heck of a front-court for the winter MLB basketball league. The Big Unit could man the middle while 6-7 forwards Richie Sexson and Scott Morgan handle the forward spots, and of course ex-Arizona Wildcat Kenny Lofton could run the point. Maybe Brian Giles or David Justice could handle the #2-guard spot.

Like the more advanced and younger (by a year) Sexson, Morgan uses his large frame to generate big-time power, a .567 SLG% the last three years. He has always been old for his level, so that has to take some of the air out of his numbers. He is patient and can hit for power and average. Unfortunately for him, he's in an organization without a whole lot of opportunity.

ON THE MOUND: Willie Martinez
Martinez or Frankie Sanders are usually mentioned as top starter prospects in the Indians' system since Jaret Wright and Bartolo Colon have established themselves in the majors. As you can see by the K/H levels, the Indians starters aren't exactly soft-tossers, but they also don't have any big horses on the way up either. Martinez's numbers look like that of a control pitcher, but he actually has shown some power in the past, striking out 120 vs. 125 hits in 137 innings last year. While his hit prevention regressed, his control improved as his walk rate dropped to 2.6/9IP. He'll be just 21, and he threw two complete games and faced 25.5 batters/start last year, so I'm a bit concerned about workload.

of lineup effects on scoring. I remain unconvinced that these studies can satisfactorily represent the various factors inherent in lineup construction. As run estimation tools improve, we should get a better sense of the true range of deviation between actual run scoring and the estimate based on modeling. As James noted in his article for the 1989 Baseball Abstract, there is a great deal of possible deviation in a team's won-loss performance as determined by simulation; it seems likely that there is an analogous amount of variation possible in run scoring. One major factor in this is lineup construction. While the Indians' inability to maximize an already powerful offense might be represented as a consistent failure in various aspects of situational hitting, but such an explanation founders on the notion that a team with so many different hitters in its lineup over the past four years could produce the same consistent underachievement.

The likeliest culprit in all this has been the placement of a sub-par hitter in the #2 slot of the lineup, a distinguishing characteristic of the Indians' batting order for most of 1995-98. That may in fact be what John Hart is hoping to alleviate in his acquisition of Roberto Alomar. The Indians' #2 lineup slot ranked 106th in OPS out of 126 lineup slots in the 1998 AL, and had a .346 SLG (tied with Oakland at the bottom of the AL #2 slots).

By contrast, the Orioles #2 slot, which was split in 1998 between Alomar and Brady Anderson, ranked 43rd amongst all AL lineup slots. So the Indians will very likely make a significant gain in the top of their lineup, and it is quite possible that this will narrow the gap between their actual run scoring and the projections from run estimation modeling.

But what about the loss of Giles? How do we factor this in at the back end of the lineup? With Giles and Mark Whiten as part of a platoon system in 1998, the Indians had a serviceable #6 slot, finishing with a .765 OPS. That finished 67th in the league. This was counterbalanced by a much stronger #7 slot, occupied for the most part in 1998 by Travis Fryman, which finshed 34th in the league. The likelihood is that Fryman will move up into the #6 slot in 1999, which may add to a "bunching effect" in the Indians' lineup. (Fryman's 1998 season, however, was significantly better than his performance in recent years, and there is some question as to whether he will hold that level in 1999.)

Sexson would appear to be the man to replace Giles in the lineup, and a comparison of their projected rates of production for 1999 tends to indicate that he will generate somewhere between 10-15 fewer runs. Sexson did not have a particularly good OBP in the minors, and should that continue to be the case in the big leagues, the results for the bottom third of the Indians' lineup will not be positive. While Vizquel's presence in the #9 slot will raise the OBP there, there is a great possibility that the Tribe will have a collective OBP of around .315 in the 7-9 slots in their batting order.

Most of Sexson's ability to contribute to the Indians' offense rests in his isolated power; for him to be a useful replacement for Giles, he will have to hit 30-35 HRs in 1999. If he does that, the Indians may well exceed their run scoring projection by more than 10%, given the synergistic elements that they will be gaining with Alomar in the #2 slot. But Sexson's range of potential contribution to the Indians' lineup is much narrower than Giles, and his chance of a serious setback is proportionately greater. Mark Whiten has been retained to forestall total disaster, but he won't provide any career upside for the Tribe, and Mark's performance level has been highly variable over the past five years--which is precisely why he's been mostly in a backup role during that time frame.

The bottom line? The Indians are going for it all in 1999, but they're doing it by gambling on top-of-the-lineup synergy and the ability of Mike Hargrove to rise to even greater heights of intricate bullpen overmanagement. The lineup is likely to decay a bit more, and has only about a 20% chance of achieving what its assembler is hoping it will.

WILL THE KID PITCHERS SURVIVE?

But it is the manager of the Indians who may well determine how far his team will go in 1999, and the answer to that question might turn out to have been given during the 1998 season. Mike Hargrove has captured a lot of attention for his flamboyant use of the bullpen, but he has also been the focus of intense scrutiny for the way he has handled two young right-handers in his starting rotation--Bartolo Colon and Jaret Wright.

Both pitchers have been given a medium-to-heavy workload--Wright in the second half of the 1997 season and into the post-season, and Colon during the first half of 1998. Both were subjected to high single-game pitch counts, while Colon had several series of consecutive high-pitch outings.

And both pitchers experienced a significant falloff in

TEAM BREAKOUT
INDIANS 1998

Category	RS	RA	W	L	Pct.	Rk
5+ RUNS SCORED/ROAD	292	164	34	5	.872	1
5+ RUNS SCORED	664	416	71	16	.816	2
CLOSE SLUGFESTS/ROAD	41	38	4	1	.800	1
4- RUNS ALLOWED/HOME	220	96	31	8	.795	8
5+ RUNS SCORED/HOME	372	252	37	11	.771	5
4- RUNS ALLOWED	448	211	65	22	.747	8
4- RUNS ALLOWED/ROAD	228	115	34	14	.708	8
CLOSE SLUGFESTS/HOME	73	67	6	4	.600	3
RECORD IN CLOSE GAMES/HOME	165	151	21	14	.600	7
RECORD IN BLOWOUTS/ROAD	147	131	12	9	.571	4
SLUGFESTS/ROAD	140	146	10	8	.556	5
SEASON TOTALS	850	779	89	73	.549	3
RECORD IN BLOWOUTS	356	323	27	23	.540	5
LOW SCORING GAMES/HOME	37	32	8	7	.533	7
RECORD IN SLUGFESTS	384	398	26	24	.520	5
RECORD IN BLOWOUTS/HOME	209	192	15	14	.517	6
RECORD IN CLOSE GAMES	312	310	38	37	.507	8
CLOSE LOW-SCORING GAMES/HOME	24	21	5	5	.500	10
SLUGFESTS/HOME	244	252	16	16	.500	6
RECORD IN LOW SCORING GAMES	83	82	17	21	.447	9
RECORD IN CLOSE GAMES/ROAD	147	159	17	23	.425	6
LOW SCORING GAMES/ROAD	46	50	9	14	.391	11
5+ RUNS ALLOWED/HOME	239	323	15	27	.357	2
5+ RUNS ALLOWED	402	568	24	51	.320	3
CLOSE LOW SCORING GAMES/ROAD	28	41	5	13	.278	13
4- RUNS SCORED/HOME	87	167	9	24	.273	8
5+ RUNS ALLOWED/ROAD	163	245	9	24	.273	5
4- RUNS SCORED	186	363	18	57	.240	8
4- RUNS SCORED/ROAD	99	196	9	33	.214	6

performance level after this workload--Wright for virtually the entire 1998 season, and Colon during the second half of the year after a blistering start. There are many baseball observers who have expressed extreme concern over the fate of the Indians' two young potential aces.

What all the hue (and most of the cry) stems from is the recent practice of examining single-game pitch counts. While these are more specific in nature than Craig Wright's BFS formulation (as introduced in his book, The Diamond Appraised), they are no more conclusive. What Wright's study showed was a tendency for young pitchers who were worked hard to suffer injury and/or premature decline. That tendency has been raised to the level of natural law by those who have inherited Wright's methods: single-game pitch counts are being used as a basis for direct or indirect predictions of future arm miseries, and the results of such predictions are mixed.

What is abundantly clear from such studies is that pitchers' arms are far more varied and individualistic in nature than is often espoused; we simply don't know if a pitcher's arm will withstand any level of work. Also clear is the fact that workload abuse is far less prevalent in the 1990s than at any other time in baseball history. The workloads given Colon and Wright, while high in the context of the immediate present, and mild in comparison with the workloads of even ten years ago.

My suspicion is that both will survive their workloads and pitch for a number of years without serious career interruptions. That is not to say that they will be exempt from such problems: few pitchers are, even if they have been given light workloads at an early age. But the doomsday scenarios envisioned by some analysts may simply be overstated. I would be surprised if at least one of these pitchers proved to be one of the games' best during the first decade of the next century.

| | | | | | | | | | | | | | | | | Adj | Raw | | | |
Name	AB	R	H	D	T	HR	RBI	BB	SO	SB	CS	BA	OBP	SLG	XR	XR/27	XR/27	OXW	DXW	TXW
Alomar S	409	42	92	26	2	6	41	18	47	0	3	.224	.259	.341	31	2.44	2.70	-1.44	2.04	0.60
Bell Da	340	36	85	21	2	10	39	22	56	0	4	.249	.294	.410	39	3.87	4.22	0.26	0.94	1.20
Berroa G	65	5	12	3	1	0	3	7	18	1	0	.182	.260	.257	4	1.92	2.35	-0.32	0.13	-0.19
Borders P	160	11	35	6	0	0	6	10	42	0	2	.220	.272	.256	10	2.04	2.45	-0.71	0.49	-0.22
Branson J	100	6	19	4	1	1	8	3	22	0	0	.187	.208	.276	5	1.68	1.97	-0.57	0.11	-0.46
Cora J	83	15	18	4	0	0	5	11	9	2	1	.212	.310	.259	7	2.54	2.95	-0.25	-0.22	-0.47
Diaz E	48	8	10	1	0	2	8	3	2	0	0	.217	.275	.365	6	3.81	4.07	0.02	0.01	0.03
Dunston S	156	24	35	11	3	3	11	6	19	9	2	.225	.253	.390	17	3.47	3.80	-0.08	0.04	-0.04
Fryman T	558	70	152	32	2	29	90	43	130	10	8	.273	.327	.492	85	5.37	5.78	2.65	0.24	2.89
Giles B	351	52	90	19	0	16	62	72	78	10	5	.256	.384	.449	64	6.20	6.60	2.61	0.52	3.13
Justice D	541	89	145	38	2	21	83	75	102	9	3	.267	.351	.463	91	5.86	6.25	3.37	0.10	3.47
Lofton K	601	95	161	30	6	12	61	86	83	52	11	.268	.358	.399	97	5.62	6.08	3.39	0.92	4.31
Ramirez M	572	101	163	34	2	46	136	75	126	5	3	.285	.368	.593	119	7.32	7.60	5.64	0.72	6.36
Sexson R	174	25	51	14	1	11	32	6	43	1	1	.295	.329	.580	30	6.44	6.89	1.24	0.13	1.37
Thome J	441	83	125	33	2	31	79	88	146	1	0	.282	.403	.575	99	8.19	8.56	5.29	0.40	5.69
Vizquel O	577	81	157	30	6	2	48	61	66	36	13	.273	.343	.355	75	4.42	4.89	1.41	2.78	4.19
Whiten M	226	29	60	14	0	6	27	29	62	2	1	.265	.355	.406	31	4.84	5.37	0.81	0.40	1.21
Wilson E	90	12	28	6	0	2	12	4	8	2	4	.313	.346	.447	12	4.88	5.15	0.31	0.23	0.54
CLE	**5626**	**799**	**1460**	**328**	**29**	**202**	**763**	**620**	**1101**	**138**	**63**	**.259**	**.334**	**.436**	**828**	**5.03**	**5.41**	**23.62**	**9.98**	**33.60**

Park Adjusted Statistics

Pitcher	S	C	T	SS	ES	IC	HH	PP	TJ	S12	S35	S67	C1	C23	C45	C67	QWP
Burba	3.90	3.16	7.06	55%	16%	35%	26%	10%	6%	23%	52%	26%	6%	55%	39%	0%	.534
Colon	4.10	3.32	7.42	42%	19%	39%	35%	3%	0%	32%	32%	35%	13%	39%	45%	3%	.473
Gooden	4.00	3.61	7.61	52%	9%	35%	26%	13%	0%	26%	48%	26%	4%	48%	39%	9%	.487
J Jacome	7.00	4.00	11.00	0%	0%	0%	100%	0%	0%	0%	0%	100%	0%	0%	100%	0%	.062
Karsay	5.00	3.00	8.00	0%	0%	0%	0%	0%	0%	0%	100%	0%	0%	100%	0%	0%	.522
Krivda	4.00	5.00	9.00	0%	0%	0%	0%	0%	0%	0%	100%	0%	0%	0%	100%	0%	.240
Nagy	4.67	3.00	7.67	33%	15%	33%	45%	3%	12%	18%	36%	45%	18%	39%	42%	0%	.471
Ogea	4.33	4.00	8.33	44%	0%	22%	33%	0%	11%	11%	56%	33%	0%	56%	22%	22%	.420
Wright Jaret	4.38	3.78	8.16	41%	13%	28%	34%	9%	6%	22%	44%	34%	0%	44%	47%	9%	.420
CLE	**4.25**	**3.41**	**7.66**	**43%**	**14%**	**33%**	**34%**	**7%**	**6%**	**23%**	**43%**	**34%**	**8%**	**45%**	**42%**	**5%**	**.469**

AMERICAN LEAGUE CENTRAL

CHICAGO WHITE SOX

G. JAY WALKER

WINNING THE BATTLE, BUT LOSING THE WAR

The date: November 1996. After four years of labor strife, negotiators representing baseball owners and players finally reach an agreement. However the owners, led by the backstage maneuverings of White Sox's owner Jerry Reinsdorf vote down the settlement bargained by their own negotiator. Two weeks later in the midst of an impasse, Reinsdorf preempts his fellow owners and blows the salary structure wide-open by signing slugger Albert Belle to a 5-year, $55 million dollar contract. It was something on the order of about 35% more than the going rate at the time for a top-notch player.

Let the record reflect that Albert Belle kept his end of the bargain. He finished third in the American League in average, second in homers and second in RBIs. He led the league in total bases and slugging. He led the league in Extrapolated Runs and Extrapolated Wins. He set the all-time White Sox records for homers, RBIs and total bases. He swept the Triple Crown stats for the second half of the season. If his name wasn't Albert Belle, he would have been MVP.

Belle did just about everything an owner could want except for the two things that were the most important to Reinsdorf—leading his team to a winning record and putting fannies in the seats. With a $38 million payroll, the Sox finished 80-82, and only a 24-9 record allowed them to come that close. Attendance was under 1.4 million, the third lowest in the league (in one of the biggest markets) and was down from 2.5 million as recently as 1993.

With the departure of Belle and Ventura, the Sox are probably going to be relying more on their youngsters than any team in baseball. As I write this in mid-December, the presently constituted supporting cast for Frank Thomas looks to be Mark Johnson catching, Paul Konerko, Ray Durham, Mike Caruso and Greg Norton in the infield, Jeff Abbott, Brian Simmons and Magglio Ordonez in the outfield with a rotation of James Baldwin, Mike Sirotka, Jim Parque, John Snyder and Scott Eyre. Certainly changes will be made by Opening Day, but the White Sox now truly have become a small market team in

a big market town, and it's hard to imagine a couple of trades or second-tier free agent signings changing that. Last year with Belle and Ventura on board, Thomas was quoted as saying: "You have to have some guys that have played at this level ... If not, you'll be the laughingstock of the league." Frank, you ain't seen nothing yet.

As a side note, there is an interesting site on the web that awards weekly "jerk" points to worthy actors on the baseball scene (www.jerkoftheweek.com). What makes this site better than most of this type is that it's comprehensive and well-written. At mid-December, members of the Kansas City Royals were leading the AL Central with 24 jerk points, followed by the White Sox with 21. The catch is that all 21 of the Sox points were earned by Albert Belle. Even Jerry Reinsdorf, who probably clinched jerk-of-the-decade a few years ago, was shut out of jerk points for 1998. While I personally feel Belle is overrated as a jerk, nevertheless he racks up the points on a consistent basis. With Belle packed off to Baltimore, the Sox are left with nary a jerk point earner, (though we may yet hear from the unusually quiet Jerry Reinsdorf). Do nice guys still finish last?

AND YOU THOUGHT YOUR TEAM HAD BAD PITCHING

The principal cause of the Sox malaise was not hard to pinpoint. The Sox had the worst pitching in the majors (ERA = 5.22), and this in one of the better pitching parks in the busi-

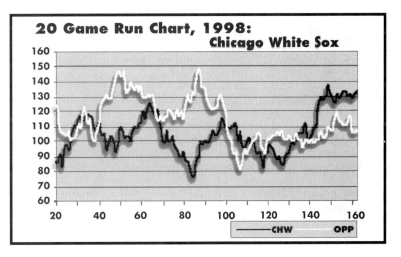

20 Game Run Chart, 1998: Chicago White Sox

QMAX PRESENTS: "BAD" PITCHERS

SURRENDERING WITH DIGNITY TO THE INEVITABLE

Sloppy Thurston got the nickname as a child for his propensity to spill soup in his father's restaurant. As an adult, he was anything but sloppy. He was considered one of the finest dandies of the Jazz age, and on the mound he was equally sharp, winning 20 games for the last-place White Sox (still feeling the hangover from the Black Sox scandal) in 1924. In 1925, Sloppy had a hangover of his own as his ERA shot up from 3.80 to 6.17, and his win total cut in half from 20-14 to 10-14. It wasn't Thurston's control that deserted him; his 2.88 QMAX "C" for 1925 probably put him in the upper echelon of control pitchers. A 5.04 QMAX "S" average, however, shows us that he was being lit up like a Chicago speakeasy on half price night. The league batted .335 against Thurston that year, which means that the better hitters, like Heilmann and Speaker and Simmons and Cobb, were probably batting .600 against him.

Through it all, Thurston remained unruffled, continuing to throw strikes, thin ones and fat ones alike. 14 of his 25 starts that year were in the "hit hard" region, and 7 were in the "Tommy John" region. Of the games where Thurston's QMAX "C" rating crept above 3, it was generally because he was knocked out of the game before he could log the number of innings required for a low "C" score; walking zero men in zero innings, or one in three innings, will get you a deceptively high "C" score. In Sloppy's ten starts with a "C" of four or higher, he averaged 3.1 IP, 6.3 hits, 1.5 walks, 4.1 earned runs, and 0.7 strikeouts.

It's a little bit of a stretch, but a certain picture is evoked for me: here's this jazz age dandy, the pride of Chicago's nightlife, getting hammered on a regular basis, but never losing his dignity, like some foppish Gatsbyite aristocrat whose stuff has been frittered away like the family fortune on stock market speculation and conspicuous consumption but who still insists on serving his dinner guests the very best that easy credit can buy. Hey, I said it was a stretch.

Thurston the pitcher, as opposed to the elegantly wasted socialite half-imagined above, did have a kind of genteel decline, posting a series of seasons that would merit a gentleman's C grade for the White Sox and, appropriately enough, for the Wilbert Robinson's Brooklyn Daffiness Boys before he hung up the spats in 1933. And I'll bet he still looks good smoking a cigar.

--TOM AUSTIN

SLOPPY THURSTON/CHW 1925								
	1	2	3	4	5	6	7	S
1								0
2	4							4
3	1		1	1				3
4				1				1
5	2						1	3
6	2	2			1	2	1	8
7		1	2	2	1			6
C	9	3	3	5	3	1	1	25

---

ness. The first half was particularly brutal, as no starter managed an ERA of under 5.00. It was only four years ago that the staff, anchored by a rotation of Jack McDowell, Alex Fernandez, Wilson Alvarez and a promising Jason Bere, had the league's best ERA. Of the five starters in the rotation in April, only one (Mike Sirotka) wouldn't be ostracized to the bullpen or waived out at some point during the season. No major injuries, no trades, just plain bad pitching. In case you weren't scoring at home, here's how the merry-go-round went:

April Rotation: Jaime Navarro, Mike Sirotka, James Baldwin, Jason Bere, Scott Eyre

Switch 1—mid-May:	Jim Parque replaces Baldwin
Switch 2—late June :	Tom Fordham replaces Eyre
Switch 3—late June:	Baldwin brought back from the bullpen to replace Bere
Switch 4—early July:	John Snyder replaces Fordham
Switch 5—mid-August:	Eyre returns from the bullpen to replace Navarro
Switch 6—early September:	im Abbott replaces Eyre

At times, we track pitchers using a stat we call Revised Game Scores. This is quite similar to Bill James' original Game Scores, we just give less credit for strikeouts and juggle a few of the weights to give more spread between a good and mediocre performance. Both the original and Revised Game Scores are designed so that 0 represents a horrible performance, 100 a superb one and 50 an average one (actual AL average 1995-97 was 46.1).

A Revised Game Score (RGS) of less than 30 is the point where a starter comes close to taking his team out of the game, while a score over 70 is the point where the starter puts his team in a solid position to win (depending on what the opposing starter's RGS is, of course). The Sox starters had an RGS of under 30 in 30% of their starts in 1998 (49 of 163 starts). Typical team percentages are in the low-to-mid twenties. Here are both the average RGS scores for the Sox starters, and the percent of starts with an RGS under 30 for the Sox starters:

Pitcher (Age)	Average	RGS < 30
John Snyder (23)	49.1	15% (2 of 14)
James Baldwin (26)	47.7	21% (5 of 24)
Mike Sirotka (27)	45.3	36% (12 of 33)
Jim Parque (22)	41.9	33% (7 of 21)
Scott Eyre (26)	39.8	29% (5 of 17)
Jaime Navarro (30)	38.7	41% (11 of 27)
Jason Bere (27)	36.5	33% (5 of 15)

Mike Sirotka had the second highest percent of starts with an RGS under 30 at 36%. Sirotka was one of those pitchers with little middle ground. The stuff he brought to the mound was either downright good or flat-out bad. Of the 21 other starts where his RGS was over 30, he had 16 with an RGS over 50 and 7 with an RGS of 79 or greater. Sirotka was 13-1 when his RGS was over 40, and 1-14 when it was under 40. (BBBA's QMAX matrix box for Sirotka, in its focus on hit and walk prevention, reaches a similar conclusion from a different vantage point.)

John Snyder was something of a pleasant surprise, as least as much as a pitcher with a 4.80 ERA can be. Not a hard thrower, he should do okay as long as his expected role is that of a #4 or #5 starter.

There was a time when Jason Bere was regarded as an up-and-comer on the White Sox pitching staff. Then major surgery at the end of the '96 season led to a loss of velocity. By June of last year, he was 3-7 with a 6.34 ERA and leading the league in walks. He was waived in June. The team regarded Scott Eyre as something of a lefty prospect, but he was also demoted in June after a 1-7 start and a 5.61 ERA.

Jaime Navarro was no more effective than Bere or Eyre, the only difference was that he was being paid $5 million for this trouble. In the first year of his $5 million per contract in 1997, Navarro had a 5.79 ERA and led the league in hits allowed, runs allowed and opposition batting average. He topped that in 1998. By the time he was pulled from the rotation in late August, he had a 6.24 ERA and was averaging over 15 runners and only 3 1/2 strikeouts per 9 innings pitched. Opponents were hitting .315 against him. With 2 years and $10 million still owed on his contract, Navarro is shaping up as one of the great free-agent busts of all time.

James Baldwin was the one guy to make it back from his bullpen banishment. He had an average RGS of 33.3 in his seven starts in April and May. There were implications that his banishment was for mental attitude as well as for his poor performance. After returning to the rotation in late June, his average RGS was 53.6. He finished with a 13-6 record, and while his 5.32 ERA is hardly a plus, consider that at one point in May it stood at 9.14.

The team went through three closers during the course of 1998, although there the news is a little better. Matt Karchner was the projected closer, but he was hurt in May, ineffective when he came back in July and sent packing cross-town to the Cubs before the trade deadline. His replacement, hard-throwing Bill Simas, was up to the task, and saved 14 of 15 games in August after Karchner departed. He was sidelined with a sprained rib cage in September, and Bob Howry took over closer duties and also did well. The club is considering using Simas and Howry in a dual closer role in 1999, especially since there are questions of Howry's effectiveness when he pitches on consecutive days. By the way, Howry along with Mike Caruso was part of the "surrender" trade when the Sox shipped Wilson Alvarez, Roberto Hernandez and Danny Darwin off to the Giants at the trade deadline on 1997 for six minor leaguers. Perhaps the book isn't closed on that deal yet.

READING THE MANUEL

Here is a list of games started for the 1998 White Sox:

Starts by Position (20 or more)

C	Chad Kreuter 71, Charlie Machado 54, Robert Machado 33
1B	Wil Cordero 81, Greg Norton 67
2B	Ray Durham 156
SS	Mike Caruso 129, Chris Snopek 26
3B	Robin Ventura 158

WPA BULLPEN BOX—CHICAGO WHITE SOX

	PI	WPA	P	PPPI
Starters	980	-10.6	49.3	0.050
Relievers	654	-0.9	34.3	0.052
Road	308	-1.2	18.3	0.060
Home	346	0.3	16.0	0.046
Mar/Apr	102	0.0	3.9	0.038
May	119	-2.5	5.5	0.046
June	125	0.5	7.1	0.057
July	89	-0.0	4.7	0.053
August	125	1.9	7.0	0.056
September	94	-0.9	6.1	0.065
Non S/H Sit.	506	-1.6	19.0	0.038
S/H Sit.	148	0.6	15.3	0.103
Low Pressure	288	-1.4	3.3	0.011
Med. Pressure	207	-3.4	11.6	0.056
High Pressure	159	3.8	19.5	0.123
Entered behind	328	-0.8	6.8	0.021
Entered tied	82	-0.3	9.5	0.116
Entered ahead	244	0.2	18.0	0.074

Name	G	PI	WPA	P	PPPI	MI	ROB	T
Baldwin J	13	26	-.7	.5	.019	8	5	1
Bradford C	29	42	-.1	2.3	.054	11	12	3
Castillo C	52	109	-.7	4.7	.043	32	28	4
Castillo T	25	38	-.7	1.6	.041	10	11	4
Eyre S	16	26	.0	.9	.035	7	6	2
Fordham T	24	45	-.1	.9	.021	13	13	2
Foulke K	54	81	1.5	4.7	.058	23	24	8
Howry B	44	63	2.7	5.8	.092	18	15	4
Karchner M	32	44	-.9	4.0	.090	10	8	7
Simas B	60	86	-.8	5.9	.069	24	20	7
Ward B	28	38	-.5	1.7	.044	9	12	1
Total		654	-.9	34.3	.052			

	|------- Quality ----------|				|--- Pressure -------|		
	Dis.	Poor	Fair	Good	Her.	Lo	Med	Hi	
Baldwin J	1	3	9	0	0	10	2	1	(0)
Bradford C	3	4	13	8	1	14	12	3	(3)
Castillo C	2	12	30	7	1	30	11	11	(7)
Castillo T	1	5	17	2	0	16	6	3	(1)
Eyre S	0	2	13	0	1	12	2	2	(1)
Fordham T	0	3	20	1	0	17	6	1	(1)
Foulke K	2	5	26	19	2	24	20	10	(8)
Howry B	5	2	12	21	4	10	19	15	(13)
Karchner M	6	2	11	9	4	10	10	12	(7)
Simas B	7	4	27	19	3	26	21	13	(6)
Ward B	1	6	18	3	0	19	6	3	(1)
Others	1	3	22	3	0	19	8	2	(1)
TOTAL	29	51	218	92	16	207	123	76	(49)

	7th inning			8th inning			9th inning		
	0	+1	+2	0	+1	+2	0	+1	+2
Bradford C	0	0	0	1	1	3	1	0	2
Castillo C	1	0	2	1	1	0	0	0	0
Castillo T	3	1	0	1	1	0	0	0	0
Fordham T	1	0	1	0	0	0	0	0	0
Foulke K	3	0	3	3	3	4	1	0	0
Howry B	2	4	2	1	8	5	0	5	1
Karchner M	0	0	0	2	0	0	3	6	4
Navarro J	0	0	0	0	0	1	0	0	0
Simas B	0	1	1	2	2	2	2	5	9
Ward B	0	0	1	1	0	0	0	0	1
Starters	6	12	4	2	4	3	1	1	2
TOTAL	16	18	15	14	20	18	8	17	19
Record	8-8	13-5	14-1	2-12	14-6	18-0	1-7	14-3	19-0

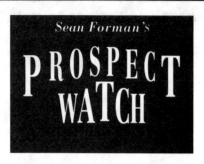

Sean Forman's

PROSPECT WATCH

NAME	AGE	POS	LEVEL	GR98	GR97	GR96	AVG
Mario Valdez	23	1B	AAA	76	88	68	79
Carlos Lee	22	3B	AA	56	56	47	55
Mark Johnson	22	C	AA	60	51	45	55
Jeff Inglin	22	OF	AA	54	54	45	53
Brian Simmons	24	OF	AAA	55	46	42	50

NAME	AGE	POS	LEVEL	GRADE
Junior Roman	17	SS	Rookie	70
Joe Crede	20	3B	High A	69
Aaron Rowand	20	OF	Low A	57
Rolando Garza	18	SS	Rookie	57
Jim Terrell	20	3B	Low A	55
Jonathan Acevas	20	C	Rookie	50
Eric Battersby	22	OF	Rookie	49

NAME	AGE	GS	S	C	T	W-L	ERA	K/H	LEVEL
Kevin Beirne	24	28	3.57	4.04	7.61	13-9	3.49	1.03	High
Jason Olsen	23	29	4.48	3.31	7.79	8-10	4.69	0.71	High
John Snyder	23	15	4.60	3.40	8.00	7-3	4.36	0.56	High
Ken Vining	23	27	4.11	3.96	8.07	8-12	4.07	0.71	High
Russ Herbert	26	26	4.38	3.85	8.23	7-9	4.99	0.83	High
Nelson Cruz	24	18	4.72	3.61	8.33	8-6	5.33	0.64	High
John Ambrose	23	21	4.57	3.81	8.38	7-11	5.18	0.66	High
Rich Pratt	26	22	5.55	3.55	9.09	6-10	6.29	0.40	High

The White Sox have some significant young talent, both in the minors and already on the team. Trading Robin Ventura or Albert Belle would have been good moves last year rather than letting them play out their contracts. For instance, Ventura for Fernando Tatis and Albert Belle for Bruce Chen would have bolstered the White Sox for this year.

HAVE BAT, WILL TRAVEL: Mario Valdez

The White Sox could have won themselves a game or two more last year if they had let Valdez play first instead of Wil Cordero. Cordero posted a .267/.314/.446 last year, while Valdez' MLE (of course, adjusted for new-Comiskey) was .291/.359/.447. Valdez' raw numbers are a more impressive .330/.420/.536, though he was playing in Calgary, so that takes a lot of the air out of those numbers. He doesn't appear to be a flash in the pan, as he put up essentially the same season the year before in Nashville. He is not as good as the newly-acquired Paul Konerko, but he could help in a back-up role. It's quite likely that he'll end up with a Roberto Petagine-type career. Comp: Mike Simms.

PATIENCE, GRASSHOPPER: Mark Johnson

One of my gripes with the usually outstanding STATS handbooks is that if you play at all in the major leagues your profile only appears in the Major League Handbook even if it is just 23 at bats like Johnson. Would it hurt them to put the ROY-eligible players in the Green Book as well, or at least include their career minor league numbers in the red book. Here are a couple of numbers that sum up Johnson's career thus far: 336 walks in just 1435 at bats, including a mammoth 211 walks in his last 757 at bats. His line the last two years has been .268/.428/.396. He's about the most extreme walker I've ever season. Not surprisingly his strikeout rate is a bit high, but not too bad and he even seems to be developing a little power (9 homers last year). If it's my team, I give him a little time in AAA and then say, "Kid, just get on base. If you hit .200 that's fine. Just get on base."

HOT CORNER HEIRS:

Carlos Lee - Lee is still fairly young, just 23 next year, and he is a career .304 hitter. Last year, he put up a .302/.350/.485 line for Birmingham of the Southern League. He doesn't have the best plate disci-

pline, but he doesn't strike out much and is starting to hit for more home run power. I haven't really studied it that closely yet (BBBA 2000?), but it seems to me that the hard to strike out, hard to walk players tend to hold their value a little better as they move up levels; players like Raul Mondesi, Mike Caruso and Jose Guillen come to mind. Their value is less than that of more disciplined hitters, but they seem to acclimate quicker. Comp: Scott Spezio, with some walks traded for singles.

Joe Crede - Crede was just two home runs short of the first Carolina League Triple Crown since Ray Jablonski hit .363 drove in 127 runs and smacked 28 home runs for the then Winston-Salem Cardinals. Crede played for the renamed Warthogs and finished with 20 home runs, 88 RBI, and a .315/.387/.514 line. He was named the top defensive third baseman in the Carolina League and the second-best prospect overall. He had struggled in his earlier pro experience, so he needs to solidify his gains in AA next year, but I don't see any reason why he won't continue to hit.

ON THE MOUND: Kevin Beirne

This was Beirne's second exposure to AA, and he improved considerably on his performance of a year ago. He struck out 153 in 167 innings and allowed just 142 hits. His control is a bit suspect as he's been above 4.5 walks/9IP each of the last two years. Still, his hit prevention has been quite good, and he may develop into a nice power pitcher if he can get the walk rates under control.

LF	Albert Belle 159
CF	Mike Cameron 104, Jeff Abbott 34, Magglio Ordonez 20
RF	Magglio Ordonez 118, Jeff Abbott 27
DH	Frank Thomas 146

Starts by Batting Order Position (20 or more)

1st	Ray Durham 149
2nd	Mike Caruso 90, Mike Cameron 20
3rd	Frank Thomas 158
4th	Albert Belle 160
5th	Robin Ventura 158
6th	Wil Cordero 62, Magglio Ordonez 46, Greg Norton 35
7th	Magglio Ordonez 59, Greg Norton 34, Jeff Abbott 26, Wil Cordero 24
8th	Mike Cameron 50, Chad Kreuter 33, Charlie O'Brien 31
9th	Chad Kreuter 38, Mike Caruso 34, Robert Machado 30, Charlie O'Brien 23

Manager Jerry Manuel proved to be not much of a lineup tinkerer. Lineup positions were set as much as reasonably could be expected, and he ranked second from the bottom among the league's managers in the use of pinch hitters. He decided to go with Mike Caruso over Benji Gil at short out of spring training, and once late signee Wil Cordero was in shape, Frank Thomas saw but one start at first except for interleague games at NL parks. Four of the top five slots in the order were on automatic pilot. Manuel went with a two-catcher system, first Kreuter and O'Brien and then Kreuter and Machado after O'Brien was traded. Otherwise, his only real platoon was Cordero and Norton at first, although Jeff Abbott had pretty much taken over center for the disappointing Cameron by season end. Manuel's most significant lineup move was to elevate 20-year old rookie Mike Caruso from 9th to 2nd in the lineup in late May. Caruso thrived in the #2 hole, the same place he hit in the minors, batting .397 in his first month there, and finishing the year at .306 for a 21-year old rookie shortstop. Thomas, Belle and Ventura were ironmen in the heart of the order, starting 476 of a possible 489 games among them (one game was suspended). He also issued the fewest intentional walks among the league's managers.

Manuel appears entrenched as the White Sox manager for the short term. Originally allowed to hire only one of his own coaches, he was allowed to fire pitching coach Mike Pazik and hitting coach Ron Jackson in late May in favor of Nardi Contreras and Von Joshua. There was some question as to whether the team was one of these clock-punching groups, and Jaime Navarro once referred to the clubhouse as a "cemetery" and his teammates as "a bunch of dead dogs." However, the team obviously didn't quit on Manuel, finishing the season with a 24-9 spurt that almost brought the team to the .500 level. Manuel was given a 2-year contract extension in the off-season.

UP THE MIDDLE

Next to Albert Belle, the development of middle infielders Ray Durham and Mike Caruso were the best news for the Sox in 1998. At 26, Durham became the type of leadoff hitter the Sox had hoped for—decent on-base average (.364) with good speed.

Caruso is a work in progress, but that's not really a knock when you're a 21-year old shortstop. He had mental lapses and was prone to throwing errors, but he did hit .306 for the year, most of it spent at the #2 slot in the order. Did we mention plate discipline? Caruso walked in whooping 14 times in 523 at-bats. Of course with Ozzie Guillen never drawing more than 26 walks in 13 years as the Sox shortstop, Chicago fans barely noticed.

A HURTIN' BIG HURT

With the departure of Albert Belle and Robin Ventura, more than ever the franchise is Frank Thomas. Several team officials have referred to Thomas the same way the Orioles might talk about Cal Ripken, or the Padres about Tony Gwynn.

Q Through the first 86 years of the Sox's existence, who held the franchise record for career homers?
A Bill Melton with 154.

Thomas is the first long-term big-time slugger in White Sox history. Unlike most teams, when you talk about all-time White Sox greats, you talk about pitchers, catchers and middle infielders—Ted Lyons, Red Faber, Billy Pierce, Ray Schalk, Eddie Collins, Luke Appling, Nellie Fox and Luis Aparicio. There simply aren't any power-hitting corner men or outfielders that have stayed around very long except for Thomas.

So how does one of baseball's premier hitters slump the way Thomas did last year? Speculation is rampant, but two reasons stand out. The first was his marital problems and impending divorce proceedings. Who among us hasn't had off-days and off-weeks at work because of depression of sadness? Maybe Frank just had a particularly hard time dealing with his situation.

The second was his inability to handle inside pitches. At first he blamed it on the umpires and league officials ("The strike zone is ridiculous"), and later admitted having problems ("I haven't been able to make adjustments so far") and finally confessed to something you'd rarely hear from a player of his skill ("It's gotten to the point where I've dreaded going to the plate, and that's something I never thought would happen"). Nevertheless, he vowed that "this is never going to happen again as long as I play this game".

Category	RS	RA	W	L	Pct.	Rk
TEAM BREAKOUT WHITE SOX 1998						
4- RUNS ALLOWED	334	167	54	13	.806	6
4- RUNS ALLOWED/HOME	182	96	29	7	.806	7
4- RUNS ALLOWED/ROAD	152	71	25	6	.806	3
5+ RUNS SCORED/HOME	360	271	36	12	.750	8
5+ RUNS SCORED	665	494	62	23	.729	10
5+ RUNS SCORED/ROAD	305	223	26	11	.703	10
CLOSE SLUGFESTS/HOME	92	86	8	4	.667	1
RECORD IN CLOSE GAMES/HOME	185	170	22	13	.629	6
CLOSE LOW-SCORING GAMES/HOME	11	9	3	2	.600	6
SLUGFESTS/HOME	267	276	19	16	.543	5
RECORD IN CLOSE GAMES	374	366	37	34	.521	7
RECORD IN SLUGFESTS	502	542	32	32	.500	6
SEASON TOTALS	856	926	80	82	.494	7
LOW SCORING GAMES/ROAD	27	39	7	8	.467	10
SLUGFESTS/ROAD	235	266	13	16	.448	10
RECORD IN LOW SCORING GAMES	50	70	12	15	.444	10
CLOSE LOW SCORING GAMES/ROAD	13	16	3	4	.429	8
RECORD IN BLOWOUTS/HOME	161	194	11	15	.423	11
LOW SCORING GAMES/HOME	23	31	5	7	.417	10
RECORD IN CLOSE GAMES/ROAD	189	196	15	21	.417	8
RECORD IN BLOWOUTS	322	413	23	33	.411	11
RECORD IN BLOWOUTS/ROAD	161	219	12	18	.400	12
CLOSE SLUGFESTS/ROAD	98	100	4	7	.364	11
5+ RUNS ALLOWED/HOME	255	356	15	30	.333	4
5+ RUNS ALLOWED	522	759	26	69	.274	5
4- RUNS SCORED/HOME	77	181	8	25	.242	9
4- RUNS SCORED	191	432	18	59	.234	9
4- RUNS SCORED/ROAD	114	251	10	34	.227	5
5+ RUNS ALLOWED/ROAD	267	403	11	39	.220	10

Can Thomas come back? In all likelihood yes, for it would be unprecedented for a player who's put up his kind of numbers to suddenly become an ordinary hitter at 30. Then again, one man's slump is another man's career year—in spite of his problems, Thomas still managed to finish 16th in Extrapolated Wins for the AL in 1998.

The prognosis for the Sox of '99 is simply that they'll only do as well as their youngsters. Most of their best prospects were with the team at some point last year, so what you see coming out of spring training is pretty much going to be what you get. If Thomas' slump last year was due to his personal problems, let's hope he's over the worst of it by now, because it's going to take a lot of fortitude to survive this next campaign.

Name	AB	R	H	D	T	HR	RBI	BB	SO	SB	CS	BA	OBP	SLG	XR	Adj XR/27	Raw XR/27	OXW	DXW	TXW
Abbott J	244	33	68	14	1	12	41	9	29	3	3	.278	.297	.494	37	5.26	5.25	1.08	-0.01	1.07
Belle A	611	112	201	47	2	51	152	79	88	6	4	.329	.399	.665	148	8.98	8.87	8.29	0.64	8.93
Cameron M	397	53	82	16	5	8	43	36	107	25	11	.206	.280	.334	40	3.20	3.33	-0.49	0.77	0.28
Caruso M	523	81	160	17	6	5	55	14	39	21	6	.305	.330	.390	66	4.55	4.58	1.37	1.10	2.47
Cordero W	341	58	91	18	2	13	49	22	69	2	1	.265	.311	.446	47	4.81	4.85	1.14	0.33	1.47
Durham R	637	125	180	34	8	20	67	71	111	35	9	.283	.359	.455	107	6.04	6.13	4.24	0.97	5.21
Kreuter C	246	26	62	9	1	2	33	31	48	1	0	.250	.341	.321	28	3.78	3.86	0.19	0.14	0.33
Machado R	111	14	23	6	0	3	15	7	23	0	0	.207	.253	.345	9	2.57	2.57	-0.35	0.21	-0.14
Norton G	300	38	70	17	2	9	36	25	81	3	3	.234	.296	.398	33	3.60	3.68	0.00	0.21	0.21
O'Brien C	164	12	42	9	0	4	18	9	33	0	0	.258	.299	.384	19	4.00	4.15	0.20	0.01	0.21
Ordonez M	536	70	151	25	2	15	65	27	55	9	7	.282	.326	.417	67	4.34	4.33	1.11	1.10	2.21
Sierra R	74	7	16	4	1	4	11	3	11	2	0	.214	.244	.454	8	3.72	3.83	0.01	0.03	0.04
Snopek C	125	17	26	2	0	1	4	14	26	3	0	.205	.286	.245	9	2.42	2.55	-0.42	0.38	-0.04
Thomas F	588	108	155	35	2	30	109	107	97	7	0	.264	.377	.484	113	6.70	6.74	5.12	0.00	5.12
Ventura R	592	84	155	31	4	22	91	77	116	1	1	.262	.347	.440	90	5.39	5.39	2.99	1.08	4.07
Wilson C	47	14	22	5	0	3	10	3	6	1	0	.467	.488	.766	14	13.70	13.76	1.01	0.08	1.09
CHI	**5598**	**857**	**1513**	**287**	**37**	**206**	**805**	**538**	**961**	**121**	**46**	**.270**	**.336**	**.445**	**840**	**5.22**	**5.25**	**25.48**	**7.04**	**32.52**

Pitcher	S	C	T	SS	ES	IC	HH	PP	TJ	S12	S35	S67	C1	C23	C45	C67	QWP
Baldwin	3.83	3.67	7.50	50%	4%	38%	21%	8%	4%	21%	58%	21%	13%	46%	25%	17%	.479
Bere	4.67	4.93	9.60	13%	0%	7%	33%	7%	0%	7%	60%	33%	0%	13%	53%	33%	.290
C Castillo	5.50	3.00	8.50	0%	0%	50%	50%	0%	50%	0%	50%	50%	0%	50%	50%	0%	.370
Eyre	3.94	4.59	8.53	47%	0%	29%	29%	18%	0%	29%	41%	29%	0%	24%	53%	24%	.399
Fordham	4.20	5.60	9.80	0%	0%	0%	0%	0%	0%	0%	100%	0%	0%	20%	20%	60%	.233
Ji Abbott	4.20	3.40	7.60	60%	0%	40%	20%	20%	0%	20%	60%	20%	0%	40%	60%	0%	.496
Navarro	5.07	3.85	8.93	30%	0%	26%	59%	11%	11%	11%	30%	59%	7%	41%	37%	15%	.374
Parque	4.76	3.90	8.67	29%	0%	33%	57%	10%	5%	29%	14%	57%	0%	52%	33%	14%	.386
Sirotka	4.79	2.67	7.45	36%	21%	42%	48%	0%	12%	21%	30%	48%	18%	61%	21%	0%	.467
Snyder	4.29	3.07	7.36	43%	21%	29%	29%	0%	7%	21%	50%	29%	7%	57%	36%	0%	.517
CHW	**4.52**	**3.73**	**8.25**	**35%**	**7%**	**31%**	**40%**	**7%**	**7%**	**19%**	**41%**	**40%**	**7%**	**44%**	**35%**	**14%**	**.416**

AMERICAN LEAGUE CENTRAL
KANSAS CITY ROYALS

DON MALCOLM

BOPPIN' THE BLUES

Why is it possible for us to claim that the Royals have hit bottom, even though they won a respectably bad total of 72 games in 1998? A look at their hitting by lineup is a good place to start:

BOP	BA	OBP	SLG	OPS	Rk
#1	.273	.339	.434	.773	5
#2	.275	.342	.396	.738	9
#3	.335	.403	.435	.838	9
#4	.260	.315	.470	.785	13
#5	.247	.309	.390	.699	14
#6	.265	.318	.438	.756	8
#7	.251	.305	.357	.662	13
#8	.218	.290	.335	.625	12
#9	.231	.282	.318	.600	12

Only the Twins and the first-year expansion Devil Rays were at this level of offensive torpor; Minnesota managed to avoid having any lineup slots with an OPS of .800 or higher, but had only three BOPs under .700, while Tampa Bay matched the Royals with four.

The best thing you can say for this lineup is that manager Tony Muser did manage to identify his best hitters and get them in the right slots in the batting order. (Well, all except for that #5 slot.) That .335 BA in the #3 slot looks good until you note that the isolated power (.100) ranks thirteenth out of fourteen #3 hitters in the AL last year. All that BA did not push the Royals' #3 hitters any higher than ninth overall (as represented in the Rk column).

What's worse is the fact that the man who was primarily responsible for the numbers belonging to that #3 slot--Jose Offerman--is no longer a Royal. Jose is a good #2 hitter who was forced into an inappropriate lineup slot, as was the case for years with Tony Gwynn in San Diego.

What will happen in 1999? It's likely that the Royals will move Johnny Damon into the #3 slot. Johnny batted leadoff for a good bit of 1998. While he has a good bit more power than Offerman, his overall numbers still project to be worse. The Royals don't even have someone to take over the RBI role that Dean Palmer fulfilled in 1998: their #4 hitter could be rookie Jeremy Giambi, retread Joe Vitiello, or resident flop Jermaine Dye. One senses that KC will be forced to gamble on an injured slugger like John Jaha in order to even get in position to crack the 100 barrier in homers during 1999.

And then there is that bottom of the order. As a look at the bottom ten BOPs for the 1998 AL will show, only the Tigers managed to match the Royals in landing two lineup slots in the league basement:

Team	BOP	BA	OBP	SLG	OPS
DET	#8	.255	.303	.352	.655
BOS	#9	.239	.297	.354	.651
NYY	#9	.245	.290	.346	.636
KC	#8	.218	.290	.335	.625
TB	#8	.233	.287	.327	.614
KC	#9	.231	.282	.318	.600
OAK	#7	.205	.256	.338	.594
CHW	#9	.213	.276	.317	.593
DET	#9	.227	.257	.303	.560
ANA	#8	.200	.242	.280	.522

The Royals were the only AL team with three lineup slots in the bottom fifteen. Given those numbers from the #7-9 BOPs in their lineup, it's not surprising to discover that the KC leadoff slot, which produced 294 total bases--second highest on the team--could only drive in 62 runs.

Conversely, the yeoman RBI work turned in by the Royals' #4 hitters (a .453 RBI/TB ratio, easily the highest in the

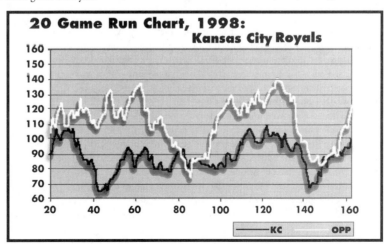

20 Game Run Chart, 1998: Kansas City Royals

QMAX PRESENTS: "BAD" PITCHERS

RUSCHING DOWN GRAND AVENUE

Glendon Rusch just finished his second year in the bigs in a noticeably undistinguished fashion, pulling down a 6-15, 6.26 record to go with 6-9, 5.50 in 1997. It's an interesting name, though, giving political overtones faintly reminiscent of Lyndon LaRouche (it's the euphony: try saying the two names in succession and see how smoothly they blend together) and former Kansas City Royals employee Rush Limbaugh. Other than that, it's an unpromising start for a major league career.

Our young Glendon illustrates a type of pitcher I saw frequently in my tour through the halls of Bad Pitching. My monicker for this type of pitcher is "Grand Avenue," referring to the broad swath of starts ranging from the upper left to the lower right of the QMAX box (and, metaphorically, to the "grand avenue" down the center of the plate also known as "main street"). The

QMAX chart shows that Rusch had only one start in the "power precipice" and none in the "Tommy John" region. In other words, all but one of Glendon's 1998 outings were either in the golden "success square," low in walks and hits, or in the nether regions of "hit hard," giving up hits and walks in bunches. I didn't put the term "Grand Avenue" on any other pitchers in this series, but I could have: Waits, Maddux, Fleming, and Mulholland all had less than 10% of their starts combined in the "power precipice"/"Tommy John" regions, and Weathers, McDermott, Knott, Drabek, and Abbott were knocking on the door (10-13% combined).

What is the essence of the "Grand Avenue" pitcher? Well, he's struggling, to be sure: his best starts cluster in the "outer rings" of the success square, the 3,3-3,4-4,3 area. More often, however, neither his stuff nor his

GLENDON RUSCH/KC 1998							
	1	2	3	4	5	6	7	S
1								0
2	1	2	1	1				5
3	1	1	1	2				5
4				1				1
5					1			1
6			1	1				2
7			2	7	1			10
C	2	3	5	12	2	0	0	24

command is that good, and he turns in the 6,4 or 7,4 start, lifted in the fifth inning with his team comfortably behind and a mop-up man sent in for garbage time. Amidst the muddled masters of mediocrity run rampant down the Avenue, Glendon's staggering seven starts in the 7,4 region stand out. I didn't get scientific about it, but I tended to notice that Grand Avenue pitchers tend to accumulate 7,4 games. I did take a look at Glendon's set of seven, and found some interesting things: all seven of his 7,4 starts lasted between four and five innings, featured between 9-13 hits and 2-3 walks. That type of consistency does not get you a good table at a fine restaurant, but a berth in the bullpen instead.

--Tom Austin

AL last season) is going to be exceptionally hard to duplicate. Kansas City may well have bunched its runs more effectively in 1998 than usual, which may have been a major reason why the team won 72 games instead of the 63 its Pythagorean won-loss record indicated it should. All of the warning signals for a 56-106 season are in place and blinking as insistently as a neon sign in the Vegas night air.

RABBIT PUNCH

Zeal and zest were words from an alien dictionary ever since the little well-dressed rabbit had packed up his wardrobe and disappeared into the shadows of a sunlit New Year's Day. It was the last such day I remember, even though long-time San Francisco residents spent most of the year marveling at the mild, sunny weather Bunsey had left behind.

There was no word from the little tyke, and no reports of any dramatic changes in the fortunes of his adopted team, the Kansas City Royals. After Bunsey had left, many of the appliances in the apartment I shared with the Girl and the rest of our menagerie began to fail one by one. Late in April, as I watched a satellite-transmitted game featuring the Royals, the picture on the TV set disappeared, accompanied by a strange metallic sucking sound. Try as I might, I could not make the set work again.

I could still hear the audio feed, however, and the disjointed ramblings of announcers who were not trying to describe the action made me realize the importance of context: it suddenly became clear to me how easily things could get out of sync. There was experience, and there were the things that defined experience. Life without Bunsey was like a TV set with sound and no picture.

I never got around to having the set repaired; all of the other rabbits and the fuzzy, slightly forlorn-looking spider (named Webster) kept quiet and pretended not to miss the flickering images they had shared with me on countless late-night forays into the world of baseball. What once had been a flurry of activity centered around the mercurial little rabbit settled into a passive, motionless charade. The rest of the menagerie spent endless hours exchanging glances, wishing they could close their eyes.

The Girl and I had also sensed the rift that Bunsey's absence had caused: both of us had thrown ourselves into our work so that we might avoid a confrontation. It was worse for her, of course: Bunsey had been her special companion, and she felt both abandoned and betrayed. The summer stretched out endlessly, accompanied by the echoes of paranoia and furtive glances behind one's back while sleepwalking down uncharacteristically sunny San Francisco streets. Crises real, imagined, and manufactured came into being, but no amount of such overwrought conspiracy could fill up the echoing empty space that grew between all of us in Bunsey's wake.

Another baseball season came and went: I listened to it from a distance, and took comfort in holding it at arm's length. There were no exploits in Kansas City for a little rabbit--or anyone else, for that matter--to celebrate. Young pitchers were treted rudely by their American League opponents; a young shortstop clearly overmatched at the plate created a controversy by striking a clearly uncalled-for blow in a beanball scuffle. At season's end, the team's three best performers (second baseman Jose Offerman, third baseman Dean Palmer, and pitcher Tim Belcher) would all leave for greener pastures.

One report clipped from a local newspaper gave us pause, however. On September 22nd, during a game the Royals would eventually lose to the Tigers by a score of 14-4, the late innings of the contest were disrupted twice by the appearance of a rabbit on the playing field. The animal was described as "exceptionally long-eared" in the account, and it led groundskeepers on a pair of wild-goose chases--first in the seventh inning while the Tigers were in the middle of a six-run rally, and again in the bottom of the ninth when the Royals were down to their last strike. The Royals ground crew proved to be as inept as their ballclub, for the little creature eluded capture on both occasions, making a spectacular disappearance in the ninth by wriggling under second base. When the crew pulled up the base, they found neither a rabbit nor a rabbit hole.

I assembled everyone in the living room--including the Girl--and read them the newspaper account that had been forwarded to me. The animals all exchanged knowing glances, and the Girl was certain that the rabbit described in the newspaper account had to be Bunsey. She pointed out that Bunsey had earlier been smitten with a tiny cape he had been given, and had taken up the art of magic, planning a career as a prestidigitator named the Great Bunzini. His specialty: making things disappear. What better added twist could he have devised than to make himself vanish in front of an otherwise somnolent home town crowd?

Before I knew it, I was packed onto an airplane headed for Kansas City, accompanied by the unlikely combination of a trench coat and an apricot pie. The former was considered de rigeur by the animals for a sleuthing assignment, and Bunsey had always wanted a trench coat after having seen The Big Sleep. (That fashion envy would somehow assist in having our paths cross seemed as farfetched to me as a Royals team over the .500 mark after the first week in May, but you don't argue with desperate men--or animals, in this case.) The latter was the Girl's idea: Bunsey was a known sucker for pie--especially apricot pie from the Madonna Inn--and the "reasoning" was that a guy in a trench coat carrying a trademark hot-pink Madonna Inn pie box would make it impossible for Bunsey to miss me (or resist me: never underestimate the power, isolated or otherwise, of pie.)

Once in Kansas City, I took myself, the coat, and the pie to Arrowhead Stadium (now named Kauffman Stadium in honor of the Royals' first owner) and after a considerable amount of effort, found a way to sneak in. I slipped in behind the bleachers, empty and silent, and picked my way carefully

WPA BULLPEN BOX—KANSAS CITY ROYALS

	PI	WPA	P	PPPI
Starters	1007	-7.1	51.2	0.051
Relievers	587	2.5	31.5	0.054
Road	271	2.9	17.8	0.066
Home	316	-0.4	13.7	0.043
Mar/Apr	105	-0.2	5.2	0.050
May	86	-1.2	3.6	0.042
June	96	0.7	6.1	0.064
July	96	2.0	4.7	0.049
August	116	2.0	7.8	0.067
September	88	-0.7	4.1	0.046
Non S/H Sit.	456	0.7	18.1	0.040
S/H Sit.	131	1.8	13.4	0.102
Low Pressure	292	-1.7	3.6	0.012
Med. Pressure	157	0.2	10.2	0.065
High Pressure	138	3.9	17.7	0.129
Entered behind	312	-0.9	6.8	0.022
Entered tied	70	0.9	9.1	0.131
Entered ahead	205	2.4	15.6	0.076

Name	G	PI	WPA	P	PPPI	MI	ROB	T
Bevil B	39	52	-.1	2.7	.052	12	13	4
Bones R	32	62	.8	3.1	.050	21	13	6
Evans B	8	11	.4	.6	.050	3	2	2
Haney C	21	47	.2	1.2	.026	14	8	3
Montgomery J	56	60	.2	5.2	.087	4	3	1
Pichardo H	9	14	-.8	1.1	.078	4	3	3
Pittsley J	37	70	-.4	1.0	.014	23	9	0
Rosado J	13	25	.3	1.2	.048	8	5	3
Service S	73	104	.8	7.1	.068	24	25	12
Walker J	4	8	-.4	.4	.045	1	3	1
Whisenant M	70	90	1.7	6.9	.077	20	39	8
Total		587	2.5	31.5	.054			

	Quality					Pressure		
	Dis.	Poor	Fair	Good	Her.	Lo	Med	Hi
Bevil B	1	7	22	7	2	22	11	6 (4)
Bones R	1	4	16	11	0	14	8	10 (9)
Haney C	0	1	17	3	0	14	5	2 (1)
Montgomery J	6	0	23	27	0	25	17	14 (11)
Pittsley J	0	5	31	1	0	32	4	1 (0)
Rosado J	0	2	6	5	0	5	6	2 (1)
Service S	4	9	37	20	3	33	27	13 (9)
Whisenant M	1	13	33	21	2	32	20	18 (11)
Others	3	8	28	8	0	29	11	7 (4)
TOTAL	16	49	213	103	7	206	109	73 (50)

	7th inning			8th inning			9th inning		
	0	+1	+2	0	+1	+2	0	+1	+2
Bevil B	1	1	3	1	0	1	1	0	0
Bones R	4	2	0	2	0	0	0	0	0
Evans B	0	0	0	0	0	0	1	0	0
Haney C	1	0	1	0	0	1	0	0	0
Montgomery J	0	0	0	0	0	0	1	9	12
Pichardo H	0	0	0	1	0	0	2	0	0
Pittsley J	0	1	1	0	0	0	0	0	0
Rosado J	0	0	0	2	0	0	0	0	0
Service S	1	3	0	4	6	6	3	0	1
Whisenant M	1	0	0	2	2	2	2	1	1
Starters	9	7	11	4	2	4	1	0	2
TOTAL	17	14	16	16	10	14	11	10	16
Record	5-12	11-3	14-2	6-10	9-1	12-2	6-5	9-1	14-2

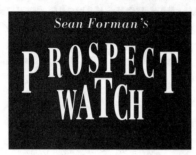

Sean Forman's PROSPECT WATCH

NAME	AGE	POS	LEVEL	GR98	GR97	GR96	AVG
Jeremy Giambi	23	OF	AAA	95	64	48	77
Jermaine Dye	24	OF	AAA	70	74	61	70
Carlos Febles	22	2B	AA	82	45	61	66
Carlos Beltran	21	OF	AA	76	43	49	61
Felix Martinez	24	SS	AAA	41	51	63	48
Mark Quinn	24	OF	AA	52	52	29	48
Jed Hansen	25	2B	AAA	47	51	39	47
Ray Brown	25	1B	AAA	41	48	60	47
Raul Gonzalez	24	OF	AA	45	45	-	45

NAME	AGE	POS	LEVEL	GRADE
Dermal Brown	20	OF	High A	60
Carlos Beltran	21	OF	High A	56
Goefrey Tomlinson	21	OF	High A	47
Henry Calderon	20	3B	Rookie	47
Juan Lebron	21	OF	Low A	44
Rafael Torres	19	OF	Low A	44

NAME	AGE	GS	S	C	T	W-L	ERA	K/H	LEVEL
Brian Barber	24	22	3.32	3.36	6.68	8-4	3.75	0.88	High
Kevin Rawitzer	27	24	4.33	3.33	7.67	10-9	4.96	0.55	High
Brian Harrison	28	25	4.64	3.16	7.80	9-10	6.41	0.38	High
Roland DeLaMaza	25	15	5.27	2.93	8.20	5-6	5.36	0.50	High
Matt Saier	25	29	5.00	3.28	8.28	12-11	6.17	0.53	High
Danny Rios	25	18	5.28	3.17	8.44	6-5	5.63	0.32	High
Ken Ray	22	22	4.91	3.64	8.55	10-5	5.20	0.48	High
Jason Gooding	23	22	5.23	3.36	8.59	5-6	5.00	0.40	High
Phil Grundy	25	29	4.79	4.07	8.86	7-12	6.67	0.58	High
Daron Kirkreit	25	19	5.37	4.11	9.47	2-9	6.29	0.35	High

Throughout the 70's and 80's, the Royals were known for their farm system, and it served them well developing much of their talent. They have continued to develop talent, unfortunately much of it is playing in other organizations or has been frittered away by the whims of managerial indiscretion. There is some talent on the way up, but whether it will be utilized any better than recent history is anyone's guess. Let's hope Miles Prentice holds people accountable where the Trust failed to do so in the past.

Top Dog: Jeremy Giambi

Giambi is a hitter, plain and simple. He hit .273/.440/.424 in Spokane in 1996. Then two years ago he hit .336/.451/.578 in the Midwest League and .321/.422/.507 in the Texas League. Last year, he upped the ante, batting .372/.469/.634 in the Pacific Coast League for the Omaha Royals. He was fair in a 58 at bat cup of joe batting .224/.343/.397. You have to love the fact that he pads his gaudy batting average with another 100 points of OBP. There are questions about his defense and power, but I don't see any reason his bat isn't good enough for a corner outfield position. He's a decent candidate for Rookie of the Year if the Royals choose to play him.

Young 'uns:

Dermal Brown - Brown struggled some in high-A ball after being named the top prospect in the Rookie Northwest League last year. He hit just .258/.347/.403 in 442 at bats. His main problem was an inability to make contact as he struck out 115 times. Still his power was decent and he drew a fair number of walks (53). He is also a plus basestealer as he has stolen 43 bases the last two years and been caught just 14 times. He's still two or three years off, but I think his batting average will rebound and he will retain his top prospect status.

Carlos Beltran - Beltran started off the year with a ho-hum 192 at bats in the Carolina League (.276/.364/.427), and then exploded in 182 at bats in the Texas League (.352/.427/.687). Before he knew it, he was in Kansas City for a September call up. I wouldn't get too excited about the Texas League line as he's never hit over .280 before and never slugged more than .450. Still he's a tools player and these guys sometimes just click. I'm sure he'll get plenty of opportunity to prove that it wasn't a fluke.

So Long Jose: Carlos Febles

With Jose Offerman moving onto the Olde Towne Team, Carlos Febles is an appealing option for the Royals up the middle. I touted Febles back in the 1997

BBBA and he proceeded to hit .237, but I stuck with him and he rebounded quite nicely last year, thank you very much. He could become a very similar player to Offerman with perhaps better defense. He hit .326/.441/.530 last year, and added 51 stolen bases in 67 attempts. His MLE worked out to .285/.358/.445, so he might be ready to contribute at the big league level. He gets on base and is an excellent basestealer. What more can you ask for a leadoff hitter? Comp: an improved and hopefully more durable Geronimo Pena

On the mound: Brian Barber

This is why Todd Van Poppel gets shot after shot at making a major league team. You never know when a youngster might put it together. Barber had used up every chance the Cardinals were going to give him and found a home with the Royals. He was excellent in AAA posting a 6.68 T-score for the Omaha Royals. He was exceptionally prone to the long ball however giving up 24 home runs in just 22 starts. More than a fifth of all hits he allowed were home runs. The Big League Royals gave him eight starts and he proceeded to struggle again with a 6.00 ERA. His stretch in Omaha was the best he had pitched in 6 years, so maybe it was a fluke. He will be just 26 years old and scouts have always loved his arm, so more opportunities are in the offing.

past the fountains, which for some reason were still in operation even though the season was nearly three months into the history books. The late fall day was windless and mild, and the blue sky was unblemished by clouds--in other words, perfect baseball weather. I placed the suddenly cumbersome coat and the pie box in the first row of the bleachers and lowered myself onto the field, looking for a tiny tan rabbit in the midst of a vast green ocean.

I had taken only a dozen steps toward second base--the location where the rabbit had last been seen--when it became all too clear that I was not alone. It wasn't Bunsey who came into

view, however, but a half-dozen rent-a-cops who were emerging from several vantage points as I trespassed onto the playing field. Sensing that I had only a fleeting opportunity to check out the location where the rabbit had disappeared, I broke into a sprint for second base.

But I wasn't quite fast enough. The rent-a-cops intercepted me at the edge of the outfield grass, still in short center field, a good thirty feet away from second. (My fadeaway slide had proven a bit premature.) No rabbit would emerge from his hole to witness this scene. Frantically, I tried to elude the security guards, but they gang-tackled me and wrestled me to the ground. I became a wild man, flailing, roaring, cursing--in short, a representative Royals fan of the nineties.

I resisted so fiercely that I angered one of the cops--an ex-lineman gone to seed--who decided that an object lesson in what happens to trespassers was what I had coming to me. While several other men held me down, Mister Mastodon began to jump up and down on my stomach, delivering crushing blows--pow! pow! pow!--in a rhythmic pounding that left me gasping for breath. I lost consciousness as the bludgeoning continued, but as I blacked out the blows seemed to lighten, as if the tummy-for-hire was shedding weight with every trampoline move on my body. Even though I was being mugged in Kauffman Stadium, I suddenly began to see stars...

◆◆◆◆◆

I opened my eyes. I was in my bed, and the grey light of an overcast San Francisco morning barely brought me sight. But something was still pounding on my stmoach. I looked up and saw two rabbit ears flailing in the semi-darkness.

It was Bunsey! I sat up, overjoyed, and quickly plucked him from mid-air. "You're really here!" I shouted.

Bunsey looked bewildered for an instant, and quickly zoomed into his usual point-blank position in front of my face. "Where'd you think I was, Bub?" he asked.

"In Kansas City," I replied groggily--not so out of it, though, to overlook the fact that he was sticking to that William Frawley/My Three Sons reference. Glancing to my right, I saw the Girl still asleep beside me.

Bunsey snorted. "Bub," he scoffed. "You're having that dream again. That'll teach you to eat that day-old pizza just before you go to bed. People have been warning you about that--it always gives you weird dreams."

"So you've never been in Kansas City?"

"Sheesh--that old yarn again?" Bunsey looked disgusted. "No way, Bub. Those guys are bad--and I don't root for any losers. You're starting to believe your own stories. Better lay off the pepperoni!"

He resumed jumping up and down on my stomach, just as he had done on each and every morning since I had started living with the Girl. The fuzzy, slightly forlorn-looking spider named Webster scampered over from the other side of the Girl's pillow to watch Bunsey's favorite morning ritual.

Just then the phone rang. As it was still quite early, I reached across the bed and quickly snatched up the receiver after the first ring so as to not disturb the Girl.

"Hello?"

Long distance. A woman's voice. "This is Miles Prentice's office calling."

I was still a little groggy. "Miles Prentice?" I repeated.

"Yes. Mr. Prentice just became principal owner of

the Kansas City Royals. Are you Mister Bunzini?"

"Am I--who??"

"Mr. Bunzini. Mr. Prentice is holding to speak with him."

"Please hold a minute." I turned back toward my side of the bed, but Bunsey and Webster had disappeared--their magical powers the Girl and I had joked about so often had managed to materialize at just the right moment.

"I'm sorry, but Mr. Bunzini has stepped out," I replied. "Is there a message?"

"Mr. Prentice would like to discuss the matter of Mr. Bunzini becoming the Royals' mascot."

I could see Bunsey poking his head out from under my blankets. I motioned in his direction, but he shook his head vigorously. I turned back to the phone.

"I'm afraid that Mr. Bunzini is interested only in the general manager's job, and he told me to have you tell Mr. Prentice that he's not cute and cuddly, and neither is Mr. Prentice's baseball team."

There was some spluttering on the other end of the line, but I cut it off. "Please make sure Mr. Prentice gets that message, won't you? Mr. Bunzini suggests that he give his current general manager the mascot position."

I hung up with a flourish, and turned back to go nose-

Category	RS	RA	W	L	Pct.	Rk
TEAM BREAKOUT ROYALS 1998						
5+ RUNS SCORED/ROAD	255	187	29	7	.806	4
4- RUNS ALLOWED/ROAD	214	118	35	10	.778	4
4- RUNS ALLOWED	368	207	58	19	.753	7
5+ RUNS SCORED	522	413	54	20	.730	9
4- RUNS ALLOWED/HOME	154	89	23	9	.719	11
5+ RUNS SCORED/HOME	267	226	25	13	.658	12
RECORD IN CLOSE GAMES/ROAD	148	134	21	12	.636	1
CLOSE SLUGFESTS/ROAD	35	34	3	2	.600	4
CLOSE LOW SCORING GAMES/ROAD	16	15	4	3	.571	2
LOW SCORING GAMES/ROAD	48	43	12	9	.571	3
RECORD IN CLOSE GAMES	251	236	33	25	.569	4
RECORD IN CLOSE GAMES/HOME	103	102	12	13	.480	13
SLUGFESTS/ROAD	149	182	10	12	.455	8
SEASON TOTALS	714	899	72	89	.447	11
RECORD IN LOW SCORING GAMES	65	93	14	23	.378	12
RECORD IN SLUGFESTS	349	463	20	33	.377	13
CLOSE SLUGFESTS/HOME	41	45	2	4	.333	14
SLUGFESTS/HOME	200	281	10	21	.323	13
RECORD IN BLOWOUTS/ROAD	111	193	8	17	.320	14
4- RUNS SCORED/ROAD	106	220	14	31	.311	1
RECORD IN BLOWOUTS	248	456	15	41	.268	14
RECORD IN BLOWOUTS/HOME	137	263	7	24	.226	14
5+ RUNS ALLOWED/ROAD	147	289	8	28	.222	8
CLOSE LOW-SCORING GAMES/HOME	14	19	2	7	.222	14
4- RUNS SCORED	192	486	18	69	.207	11
5+ RUNS ALLOWED	346	692	14	70	.167	14
5+ RUNS ALLOWED/HOME	199	403	6	42	.125	12
LOW SCORING GAMES/HOME	17	50	2	14	.125	14
4- RUNS SCORED/HOME	86	266	4	38	.095	14

to-nose with that rabbit, who had some explaining to do. But he had disappeared again, and given the virtually limitless hiding places available in our apartment for a eight-inch tall furry dynamo, I decided to wait him out--just as Royals fans were waiting out the long, cold interregum in Kansas City. Sooner or later, one or the other would surface.

Name	AB	R	H	D	T	HR	RBI	BB	SO	SB	CS	BA	OBP	SLG	XR	Adj XR/27	Raw XR/27	OXW	DXW	TXW
Allensworth J	73	15	15	5	0	0	3	9	18	7	0	.205	.326	.274	9	3.95	3.91	0.10	0.12	0.22
Beltran C	58	11	17	5	3	0	7	3	12	3	0	.285	.326	.491	9	5.46	5.02	0.29	-0.02	0.27
Conine J	309	29	79	27	0	7	42	26	69	3	0	.255	.311	.411	40	4.42	4.51	0.74	0.43	1.17
Damon J	642	101	177	31	11	16	64	58	86	27	14	.276	.339	.432	95	5.26	5.38	2.99	1.23	4.22
Dye J	214	23	50	6	1	4	22	11	47	2	2	.234	.270	.332	18	2.73	2.78	-0.57	0.56	-0.01
Fasano S	216	21	48	10	0	7	30	10	57	1	0	.224	.305	.373	26	3.99	4.15	0.27	1.23	1.50
Giambi J	58	6	13	4	0	2	8	11	9	0	1	.226	.346	.402	8	4.32	4.22	0.13	0.07	0.20
Halter S	204	17	45	12	0	2	13	12	39	2	5	.222	.266	.313	16	2.43	2.38	-0.75	0.66	-0.09
King J	486	80	126	18	1	22	90	42	75	11	2	.260	.315	.434	71	5.03	5.26	1.98	0.00	1.98
Leius S	46	2	8	0	0	0	4	1	6	0	0	.174	.192	.174	0	0.10	0.09	-0.51	0.57	0.06
Lopez M	206	17	50	10	2	1	15	12	41	6	3	.242	.286	.324	18	2.80	2.84	-0.48	1.08	0.60
Mack S	207	29	58	16	1	5	28	15	37	8	3	.281	.346	.446	30	5.21	5.28	0.93	0.05	0.98
Martinez F	85	7	11	1	1	0	5	5	21	3	1	.131	.189	.170	2	0.57	0.50	-0.88	0.09	-0.79
Morris H	472	49	148	29	2	1	39	32	53	1	0	.313	.353	.388	61	4.67	4.55	1.45	0.24	1.69
Offerman J	607	99	193	30	14	6	64	89	98	49	13	.317	.406	.443	114	7.00	6.88	5.55	0.73	6.28
Palmer D	572	81	155	28	2	30	115	48	137	8	2	.272	.328	.485	92	5.51	5.89	3.07	-0.82	2.25
Pendleton T	237	17	61	10	0	3	28	15	50	1	0	.256	.298	.332	24	3.60	3.67	0.04	0.01	0.05
Rivera L	89	14	22	4	0	0	7	7	17	1	1	.245	.300	.290	7	2.83	2.91	-0.18	0.03	-0.15
Sutton L	310	28	76	15	2	4	41	29	47	3	3	.246	.312	.351	36	3.85	3.85	0.26	0.43	0.69
Sweeney M	282	31	73	19	0	7	34	24	39	2	3	.258	.319	.398	34	4.10	4.24	0.42	0.58	1.00
Young E	53	2	10	3	0	1	3	2	9	2	1	.188	.232	.301	2	1.43	1.50	-0.38	0.24	-0.14
KC	5545	691	1455	285	43	120	664	476	1005	144	56	.262	.324	.394	721	4.45	4.53	14.48	7.51	21.99

Pitcher	S	C	T	SS	ES	IC	HH	PP	TJ	S12	S35	S67	C1	C23	C45	C67	QWP
Appier	5.33	3.67	9.00	0%	0%	0%	33%	0%	0%	0%	67%	33%	0%	33%	67%	0%	.351
Barber	4.25	3.63	7.88	50%	0%	38%	25%	0%	13%	25%	50%	25%	13%	50%	25%	13%	.480
C Haney	5.00	3.75	8.75	33%	0%	8%	50%	0%	0%	8%	42%	50%	0%	33%	67%	0%	.358
J Walker	5.50	3.00	8.50	50%	0%	0%	50%	0%	0%	0%	50%	50%	0%	100%	0%	0%	.418
Pichardo	4.00	3.56	7.56	39%	0%	22%	17%	22%	0%	22%	61%	17%	0%	56%	44%	0%	.520
Pittsley	5.50	4.50	10.00	0%	0%	0%	50%	0%	0%	0%	50%	50%	0%	0%	100%	0%	.219
Rapp	4.25	4.25	8.50	38%	3%	25%	34%	19%	0%	22%	44%	34%	3%	28%	53%	16%	.399
Rosado	4.20	3.20	7.40	40%	16%	44%	44%	8%	8%	32%	24%	44%	16%	44%	36%	4%	.505
Rusch	4.83	3.38	8.21	42%	13%	29%	50%	4%	0%	21%	29%	50%	8%	33%	58%	0%	.387
Suppan	2.00	3.00	5.00	100%	0%	100%	0%	0%	0%	100%	0%	0%	0%	100%	0%	0%	.753
T Belcher	4.26	2.76	7.03	44%	12%	56%	44%	12%	24%	24%	32%	44%	24%	38%	38%	0%	.537
KC	4.40	3.47	7.86	40%	7%	34%	39%	11%	7%	22%	39%	39%	10%	39%	47%	4%	.456

MINNESOTA TWINS

Jeff "The Fan" Drummond

A WORLD OF HURT

It's been another strange year in Minnesota. I could probably say that every year, but this year I really mean it. No, really. The election of former pro wrestler Jesse "The Body" Ventura as state governor doesn't even begin to scratch the surreal surface of our local landscape. In the baseball arena, there's plenty for a first-generation Twins fan such as myself to talk about (OK, complain about). First, let's start with the stadium.

THE STADIUM

This time last year (Thanksgiving), the Minnesota Twins had notified the Metropolitan Sports Facilities Commission that they were exercising the "escape clause" in the their lease. Twins owner Carl "The Penurious" Pohlad had signed a letter of intent to sell the team to a group of North Carolina investors headed by Don "The Shill" Beaver, contingent only on the failure to obtain funding for a new stadium in Minnesota by the end of November. Meanwhile, in a special session, the Minnesota Legislature had firmly rejected a number of proposals to build a new baseball stadium and had adjourned. It looked like all that remained for the Twins was to head down to the post office and fill out their change-of-address cards.

A lot has happened since then.

Carl and Don's self-imposed March 31st deadline for completing the deal came and went. The owners declined to consider approving the sale; reportedly because there was there was no stadium "plan" in place in North Carolina. And in May, the voters of the Triad area rejected a tax hike to pay for a major league stadium. Since then, no one talks much about Mr. Beaver anymore and with little fanfare, the Twins signed a two-year lease at the Metrodome.

Meanwhile, Clark "The Hopeful" Griffith (son of former Twins owner Calvin "The Frugal" Griffith) has been

trying to buy the team. His latest $110 million offer was rejected. Carl is reportedly seeking $140 million for the team (he bought the Twins from Calvin for $38 million in 1984).

It would be no small irony if the Griffith family reacquired the franchise. Under Calvin's frugal ownership, Twins fans prayed for rich buyer to deliver them from bondage. Unfortunately, we ended up with an owner who could easily afford to improve the team but was simply too miserly to so so—preferring instead to make demands and threats on the taxpayers for a new stadium. I guess this proves you really do need to be careful about what you wish for.

THE LEADERSHIP

With the Twins firmly ensconced in the Metrodome for the next few years, let's turn our attention to the Twins General Manager: Terry "The Bewildered" Ryan. Terry's secret fantasy is to get the Twins to a .500 record—a goal which thus far has eluded him. His primary strategy has been a continuation of his predecessor's (Andy "The Younger" MacPhail) practice of hiring old ballplayers born in Minnesota and bringing them home for a final curtain call (or two). Like the mythical elephant's graveyard, Minnesota born ballplayers, when they sense their careers nearing an end, slowly wend their way back to Minneapolis. The theory, apparently, is that fans will flock to the dome to watch the local-kid-who-made-good get his N-

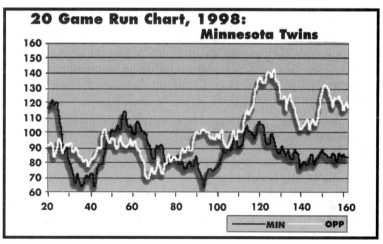

QMAX PRESENTS: "BAD" PITCHERS

TRUST ME, SKIP, I KNOW WHAT I'M DOING.

One of the emerging themes of this series might be "if you 've seen one Bad Pitcher, you haven't seen them all. In the many variations of QMAX charts and boxes sometimes lurk clues, indicators that the pitcher in question's stock is undervalued and may rise in the future. At least, that's the hope: forecasting pitcher futures is a black art even with the best of tools.

Let's take a hindsight-aided look at one such pattern, Frank Viola's 1983 season with the Twins. His overall numbers were pretty bad, to be sure: the 23-year old lefty went 7-15, 5.49 for a Twins club that lost 92 games. Looking at Viola's QMAX box, we see an unusual consistency in his starts: 24 of 34 starts were in the 3,4 "command" range, and 19 of 34 were in the 5,6 "stuff" range. Six starts were in the 5,4 box alone. When Billy Gardner sent Viola to the mound in 1983, he knew what he was getting: 6+ innings, seven hits, four walks, four runs. That's not enough to win most games, but it's within a walk and a hit or two of being a winning effort.

The unusual consistency, to me, shows a pitcher who is working within his limitations. Knowing he couldn't blow major league hitters away with his fastball, Viola kept it away from them; if they didn't bite, he wasn't averse to walking a few guys. Meanwhile, he's learning his craft: in 1984,

FRANK VIOLA / MIN 1983							
	1	2	3	4	5	6	7	S
1			1					1
2			1	2				3
3	1		3				1	5
4	1			1	6			2
5	1		3	3	1			11
6		1	2	1	2			8
7			1		2			4
C	3	1	12	12	5	0	1	34

Viola applied his 1983 "lessons learned" to a fine 18-12, 3.21 season and the start of a fine 15-year career.

The prototype of the QMAX "undervalued pitcher" is usually a young guy with great stuff and shaky control. These are the ones you find in the "power precipice", the ones who harness their stuff (like, say, Sandy Koufax once did) and go on to sit in the first chair of the baseball orchestra. Harder to spot, but no less valuable to a team's overall sound, are the less glamorous, workmanlike #2 starters, the finessing lefties, the Violas.

--Tom Austin

thousandth hit and won't notice that the team isn't actually winning many ballgames. Well, not many Twins fans are buying that theory, or—more to the point—tickets.

Terry Ryan's other infuriating habit is signing "veteran" free agents like Otis "The Face" Nixon. These are players a rational GM (forgive me, an oxymoron) might acquire to fill out a bench or as an emergency replacement for a September pennant drive; but who have no business being anywhere near an impoverished, small-market franchise that's in desperate need of a major rebuilding effort.

Like most GMs, Terry Ryan has had more money to spend than the sense to spend it wisely. However, Carl has cut his budget to the point where Terry has an outside chance to start looking like a genius. Unfortunately for Terry, the organization has been ominously quiet about his future.

Twins manager Tom "The Silent" Kelly isn't saying much these days. You might think that, after six consecutive losing seasons, he'd be worried about losing his job; but that's not the case. Kelly is regarded as a local hero for managing the team to two World Series championships. With the traditional scapegoat in protected status, most of criticism that would otherwise be directed towards Kelly ends up on pitching coach Dick "The Sorry" Such or Terry Ryan.

Kelly is being quiet because Terry Ryan keeps handing him rosters full of untested rookies (with whom he seems to have little patience) and over-the-hill veterans who frequently don't seem to live up to their billing. That's not to suggest that Kelly is purely an innocent victim. His strange obsession with giving lots of playing time to players who are struggling at the plate (Brent "The Feeble" Gates was his 1998 project) is particularly painful to watch.

THE SEASON

1998 started out with only modest expectations. Manager Tom Kelly stated early on that a .500 season was not out of the realm of possibility, if everyone stayed healthy. Unfortunately, everyone didn't stay healthy. The Twins played .500 over an 80-game stretch from May to July, but they couldn't sustain it and finished the season with a 70-92 record (only two wins better than their 1997 record). The intriguing aspect of that stretch was that the Twins did it mostly with pitching.

As an team, the biggest problem the Twins face is hitting; or more accurately, lack of hitting. In 1998, the Twins had the fourth lowest on-base percentage and second lowest slugging percentage in the league. When you consider that the Twins play in one of most hitter-friendly parks in the league, this power outage becomes even more acute.

THE INFIELD

Terry "The Prodigal" Steinbach was the primary catcher for the Twins in 1998. Solid and still marginally productive at the plate (although his hitting, especially against lefties, has started to head south). Steinbach's only major drawback for the Twins was his salary (second highest on the team). The Twins declined to pick up his option for 1999, but have hinted that they might be interested in signing him for less money.

Javier "The Proverbial" Valentin was utterly unremarkable as the backup catcher. A. J. "The Initials" Pierzynski will probably be behind the plate next year if Steinbach does not return.

Paul "The Eyes" Molitor was the more-or-less full-time DH for the Twins last year. He represents another of Terry Ryan's "native son" projects. He was remarkably productive for a 39-year-old when the Twins acquired him in 1996, but his production has declined steadily since then—leaving the Twins with the mere husk of a great ballplayer. And unfortunately, an expensive husk, as Molitor was the highest paid player on the team.

	AB	BA	OBP	SLG	SB
Molitor '96	660	.341	.390	.468	18
Molitor '97	538	.305	.351	.435	11
Molitor '98	502	.281	.335	.382	9

Molitor has announced that he will not be back in 1999 (at least, not on the field), so the Twins will be looking for someone to fill the DH slot.

First base remains something of a Bermuda Triangle for the Twins: players get sent there and then disappear. David "The Name" Ortiz spent the most time there in 1998 and showed some respectable power, at least until an injury put him on the DL for a couple of months. With Molitor gone, he may move to DH next year. Orlando "The Unhappy" Merced also played some first base for the Twins last year, but he was traded to Boston. Doug "The Mouthful" Mientkiewicz will probably get a look-see at first in 1999.

The brightest spot of the year for the Twins was over at second base. In February of 1997, the Twins finally acceded to Chuck "The Petulant" Knoblauch's request to be traded and sent him to the Yankees for a gaggle of prospects. The Twins and their apologists lost no time pointing out how the Knoblauch trade was proof that the Twins couldn't possibly compete against the large-market teams (unless, just maybe, they got a new stadium).

While nearly everyone was bemoaning the Knoblauch trade, his replacement Todd "The Kid" Walker quietly went out and had an excellent year. In fact, if you look at the numbers, Walker outperformed Knoblauch in nearly every offensive category last year. And of course, he did it for a lot less money.

	AB	BA	OBP	SLG	SB%
Walker '98	528	.316	.372	.473	.731
Knoblauch '98	603	.265	.361	.405	.721

Knoblauch may regain some of his offensive form and Walker may lose some of his, but when you consider that Walker is nearly five years younger than Knoblauch and add in the value of the prospects, the deal looks positively inspired. A cynic would counter that Terry Ryan shouldn't get any credit for doing something that he was essentially forced to do, but the lesson of the Knoblauch trade is one that every small-market

WPA BULLPEN BOX—MINNESOTA TWINS

	PI	WPA	P	PPPI
Starters	1002	-4.3	51.4	0.051
Relievers	693	1.6	43.3	0.062
Road	340	-0.6	20.8	0.061
Home	353	2.2	22.5	0.064
Mar/Apr	112	-1.4	7.6	0.067
May	101	1.4	6.3	0.062
June	115	1.4	7.0	0.061
July	95	0.1	7.2	0.076
August	146	-0.4	6.5	0.045
September	124	0.4	8.7	0.070
Non S/H Sit.	523	0.6	25.0	0.048
S/H Sit.	170	1.0	18.3	0.107
Low Pressure	280	-1.7	3.9	0.014
Med. Pressure	200	-0.2	12.7	0.063
High Pressure	213	3.5	26.7	0.125
Entered behind	354	-0.2	11.0	0.031
Entered tied	87	-0.0	11.4	0.131

Name	G	PI	WPA	P	PPPI	MI	ROB	T
Aguilera R	68	84	-1.0	9.5	.113	14	12	5
Baptist T	13	33	.1	1.0	.030	9	6	1
Carrasco H	63	92	-.3	4.7	.051	21	44	8
Guardado E	79	106	.4	7.3	.069	25	49	11
Miller Trav	14	32	-.2	1.1	.034	10	8	1
Naulty D	19	30	-.4	1.0	.033	8	1	2
Ritchie T	15	30	-.6	.5	.015	8	4	1
Serafini D	19	37	.3	1.7	.045	11	10	2
Swindell G	52	91	1.6	5.9	.065	26	22	6
Trombley M	76	130	2.0	9.9	.076	40	38	13
Total		693	1.6	43.3	.062			

	I-------- Quality ----------I					I--- Pressure ------I			
	Dis.	Poor	Fair	Good	Her.	Lo	Med	Hi	
Aguilera R	10	3	19	34	2	19	23	26	(16)
Baptist T	0	1	10	1	1	10	0	3	(2)
Carrasco H	2	14	37	9	1	35	19	9	(6)
Guardado E	5	9	43	20	2	38	23	18	(13)
Miller Trav	0	3	9	2	0	5	7	2	(2)
Naulty D	1	2	14	1	1	15	2	2	(2)
Ritchie T	1	1	13	0	0	12	2	1	(0)
Serafini D	0	2	11	6	0	10	5	4	(4)
Swindell G	4	5	19	21	3	16	21	15	(12)
Trombley M	3	11	33	27	2	25	27	24	(19)
Others	1	3	9	2	0	10	3	2	(1)
TOTAL	27	54	217	123	12	195	132	106	(77)

	7th inning			8th inning			9th inning		
	0	+1	+2	0	+1	+2	0	+1	+2
Aguilera R	0	0	0	0	1	0	2	21	13
Baptist T	1	0	1	0	0	1	0	0	0
Carrasco H	0	1	0	1	1	0	2	0	0
Guardado E	2	0	1	3	3	3	1	0	0
Miller Trav	1	0	0	1	0	0	0	0	0
Naulty D	0	0	0	0	0	0	2	0	0
Sampson B	0	0	0	1	0	0	0	0	0
Serafini D	0	0	0	0	1	0	0	0	0
Swindell G	4	2	2	4	5	1	3	0	0
Trombley M	1	3	5	5	6	7	6	0	0
Starters	14	8	7	1	5	1	0	0	0
TOTAL	23	14	16	16	22	13	16	21	13
Record	9-14	11-3	12-4	5-11	19-3	10-3	4-12	16-5	12-1

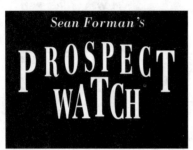

Sean Forman's
PROSPECT WATCH

The Twins have seen some recent returns from the farm system and they look like keepers. Matt Lawton was one of the better outfielders in the AL last year and Todd Walker was among the best second basemen. Once David Ortiz gets healthy he could be something, and they have a bunch of young catchers with potential. They need to get the pitching heading in the right direction, but if they do, they can hang around .500 for a number of years and lurch into contention every once and awhile.

HOT CORNER HEIR: Corey Koskie

Koskie is a left-handed hitting third baseman. He hasn't been a fast mover, though, so he's a bit old for a prospect at 25. He has now put up a decent year in AA (.286/.414/.531) and AAA (.301/.368/.539). His 1997 season in AA was actually quite a bit better when you consider park effects. He's had some problem hitting lefthanders, but what do you know? The Twins have Ron Coomer who murders lefties. A Koskie/Coomer platoon would provide pretty good production at the hot corner. Comp: a less patient Leo Gomez.

DAN SZYMBORSKI'S FAVORITE PLAYER: Doug Mientkiewicz

I wonder if the last names have something to do with his fascination with Mientkiewicz. I'm sure that the .328 batting average and .432 OBP have something to do with it as well. I doubt that Mientkiewicz get much of a shot as most will find his power lacking for a first baseman, but he can hit you some doubles and get on base like Wade Boggs. He is also one of the better basestealing first basemen out there. He must have a Shane Mack arm because he looks like he ought to be able to play another position. I wonder if he could turn the pivot? Comp: A speedy Gene Larkin.

KNOBLAUCH RETURNS:

Brian Buchanan - You can find out what happened with Eric Milton in other sections of the book, but I will look at the other two players in the Knoblauch trade here. Buchanan is a 24-year-old outfielder without one outstanding skill. He has some patience, hits for so-so average and could go 15-10 if given a full-season in the bigs. He's probably not going to provide much of a return. Comp: Stan Royer with more speed.

Cristian Guzman - Guzman put up essentially the same season as the last two batting .277/.304/.352. He added 23 steals, but was caught 14 times. He's still young, is good in the field and can switch-hit, so he might blossom. I doubt that his bat will ever be any kind of a bonus. Comp: Neifi Perez with more speed and strikeouts.

YOUNG AND UP THE MIDDLE:

Michael Cuddyer - Cuddyer was a first round pick in 1997 and signed too late to play that year, so he debuted in the Midwest League this year. His fielding was atrocious as he committed 61 errors, second in A ball only to Braves' prospect Troy Cameron (66). His bat though was pretty good (.276/.364/.451). There are already rumblings that the Twins will move him 60 feet over to third base. If his bat develops as expected, he should be able to handle it.

Luis Rivas - Rivas brings a different set of talents to the table. He's more of a defensive whiz and basestealer (34 bases in 42 attempts). He is just a slap hitter at the present moment (.281/.302/.374). I don't believe there is going to be much difference between Guzman and Rivas in the long run, though the Twins seem to be higher on Guzman.

ON THE MOUND: Jason Bell

Bell has consistently shown the typical power pitcher indicators throughout his career. He has 525 career strikeouts vs. 491 hits in 553 innings, and he continued that in AA this year striking out 166 in 170 innings. He was repeating AA, and inexplicably his ERA jumped 1.3 points despite the fact he improved in every category except home runs (19 up to 21). He did allow 18 earned runs between two July starts, and he does seem to allow an abnormally high percentage of baserunners to score. One of the nice things about QMAX is that it damps out some of the more horrific performances. I don't know if the Twins will move him to AAA or not, but he could help them in a year or two.

NAME	AGE	POS	LEVEL	GR98	GR97	GR96	AVG
Torii Hunter	22	OF	AAA	62	46	71	58
Marc Lewis	23	OF	AAA	62	44	54	55
Doug Mientkiewicz	24	1B	AA	58	53	43	54
A.J. Pierzynski	21	C	AAA	59	44	-	53
Cristian Guzman	20	SS	AA	59	40	-	51
Jacque Jones	23	OF	AA	57	42	-	51
Corey Koskie	25	3B	AAA	56	53	27	50
Chad Rupp	26	DH	AAA	44	54	40	47
Brian Buchanan	24	OF	AAA	51	45	31	46
J.J. Johnson	22	OF	AAA	48	42	-	46
Chad Allen	23	OF	AA	44	42	46	44
Chad Moeller	23	C	AA	40	27	-	35

NAME	AGE	POS	LEVEL	GRADE
Michael Restovich	19	OF	Rookie	73
Eric Sandberg	18	1B	Rookie	63
Luis Rivas	18	SS	High A	63
Michael Cuddyer	19	SS	Low A	61
Brian McMillin	21	OF	Rookie	58
Mike Ryan	20	3B	Low A	52
Dave Orndorff	20	2B	Low A	47
Allen Shrum	22	C	Rookie	46
Jamal Harrison	20	OF	Low A	44
Papo Bolivar	19	OF	High A	44
Matthew LeCroy	22	C	High A	41

NAME	AGE	GS	S	C	T	W-L	ERA	K/H	LEVEL
Rob Radlosky	24	19	3.68	2.79	6.47	9-3	4.00	0.97	High
Mike Lincoln	23	26	4.08	2.58	6.65	15-7	3.22	0.61	High
Travis Baptist	26	21	3.62	3.05	6.67	8-5	3.12	0.77	High
Jason Bell	23	28	3.46	3.43	6.89	8-10	4.67	1.12	High
Mark Redman	23	25	3.92	3.64	7.56	10-8	4.09	0.95	High
Frank Rodriguez	25	15	4.20	3.47	7.67	5-6	4.67	0.81	High
Dan Perkins	23	26	4.46	3.23	7.69	18-5	4.22	0.60	High
Shane Bowers	26	16	4.56	3.44	8.00	9-2	5.97	0.74	High
Benj Sampson	23	28	4.86	3.32	8.18	10-7	5.14	0.67	High
Trevor Cobb	24	24	4.75	3.63	8.38	6-9	5.06	0.54	High

franchise should learn: buy low, sell high. Sign players to long-term contracts while they're young (and while they're still relatively cheap), get the "sweet spot" of their careers, and when they get too expensive trade them for more prospects.

At shortstop, we find Pat "The Glove" Meares. Meares has never been much of an offensive threat and it's questionable whether his defense justifies his spot on a team starved for offense. As the fourth-highest paid player on the roster last year, it's also questionable whether he represents the best use of such a large chunk of Terry Ryan's ever-shrinking budget. The Twins almost certainly could find a shortstop that could hit as well as Meares, and for a lot less money.

Third base has been another problem spot for the Twins. Ron "The Happy" Coomer has been more-or-less the regular third baseman, though he filled in at first when Ortiz was on the DL with Gates backfilling at third. Coomer is reasonably effective at the plate against lefties, but probably should be parked on the bench against right-handed pitching. Corey "The Fox" Koskie and/or Jon "The Stubble" Shave may get an opportunity at third next year.

THE OUTFIELD

In left field we find Marty "The Foot" Cordova. He illustrates a downside to signing young ballplayers to long-term contracts. After winning AL Rookie of Year honors in 1995 and having an even better sophomore season, he looked to be another Knoblauch. But he suffered a foot injury in 1997 and hasn't really been the same since.

	AB	BA	OBP	SLG	SB
Cordova '95	512	.277	.352	.486	20
Cordova '96	569	.309	.371	.478	11
Cordova '97	378	.246	.305	.434	5
Cordova '98	438	.253	.333	.377	3

The Twins are praying that Cordova will regain his earlier form.

The Twins center fielder of choice for 1998 was Otis Nixon. Nixon is proof that a high, but empty, batting average and some stolen bases are all that's needed to be a desirable commodity in today's free agent market. The reality is that he's a mediocrity and, at least for the Twins, a relatively expensive one. Fortunately, he won't be back with the Twins in 1999. Torii "The Possible" Hunter may get a shot in center field.

Matt "The Dizzy" Lawton showed some promising offense last year, mostly playing right field, and certainly warrants a starting spot in 1999. Alex "The Lights" Ochoa also wandered around out there for a number of games. Ochoa was basically Otis Nixon Lite—about the same hitting but without the walks and stolen bases.

THE PITCHING

In spite of the many problems facing the Twins, their pitching isn't half bad. It isn't exactly great either, but for a team that aspires to .500, a middle-of-the-league team ERA of 4.76 (in the hitter-friendly Metrodome) is certainly up to the task.

Brad "The Free" Radke is the ace of the staff (W12-L14, 4.30 ERA, 213.2 IP). Radke was outstanding in the first half of the 1998 season, but fell back to earth with a resounding clunk in the second half. If he can put together a full season, he'd have a shot at a Cy Young award.

LaTroy "The Attitude" Hawkins (7-14, 5.25, 190.1) showed only slight improvement over the previous year. The Twins have been frustrated with his lack of progress and it's not clear how much longer they're going to wait.

Eric "The Garden" Milton (8-14, 5.64, 172.1). Milton was the top prospect in the Knoblauch trade and shows a bit of promise.

Mike "The Hand" Morgan (4-2, 3.49, 98) pitched well in the first half of the season and then spent some time on the DL. He was traded to the Cubs on August 1st.

Bob "The Veteran" Tewksbury (7-13, 4.79, 147.1) had a bit of an off year with the Twins in 1998. He spent some time on the DL and didn't get a lot of run support. Still, he pitched

```
┌─────────────────────────────────────┐
│          TEAM BREAKOUT              │
│          TWINS 1998                 │
```

Category	RS	RA	W	L	Pct.	Rk
4- RUNS ALLOWED/HOME	206	113	31	13	.705	12
4- RUNS ALLOWED	350	194	56	24	.700	11
4- RUNS ALLOWED/ROAD	144	81	25	11	.694	9
5+ RUNS SCORED/ROAD	260	200	23	12	.657	13
5+ RUNS SCORED	542	413	49	26	.653	14
5+ RUNS SCORED/HOME	282	213	26	14	.650	13
CLOSE SLUGFESTS/HOME	49	49	3	3	.500	8
LOW SCORING GAMES/ROAD	52	56	12	12	.500	8
RECORD IN CLOSE GAMES/HOME	161	162	20	20	.500	11
CLOSE LOW-SCORING GAMES/HOME	34	36	8	9	.471	11
CLOSE LOW SCORING GAMES/ROAD	29	31	6	7	.462	7
RECORD IN CLOSE GAMES	339	347	35	41	.461	9
RECORD IN LOW SCORING GAMES	100	116	22	26	.458	8
RECORD IN BLOWOUTS/HOME	140	144	10	13	.435	10
SEASON TOTALS	734	818	70	92	.432	12
RECORD IN BLOWOUTS	234	280	19	26	.422	10
LOW SCORING GAMES/HOME	48	60	10	14	.417	11
RECORD IN CLOSE GAMES/ROAD	178	185	15	21	.417	9
RECORD IN BLOWOUTS/ROAD	94	136	9	13	.409	11
SLUGFESTS/HOME	164	177	8	14	.364	12
RECORD IN SLUGFESTS	339	386	17	30	.362	14
SLUGFESTS/ROAD	175	209	9	16	.360	13
CLOSE SLUGFESTS/ROAD	103	110	4	9	.308	12
4- RUNS SCORED/ROAD	102	215	12	34	.261	4
4- RUNS SCORED	192	405	21	66	.241	7
5+ RUNS ALLOWED/ROAD	218	334	10	35	.222	9
4- RUNS SCORED/HOME	90	190	9	32	.220	12
5+ RUNS ALLOWED	384	624	14	68	.171	12
5+ RUNS ALLOWED/HOME	166	290	4	33	.108	14

a lot better than his record might suggest and I was surprised that the Twins did not want to pick up his option. Like Steinbach, they may be hoping to sign him at a discount.

Travis "The Prospect" Baptist had an excellent year in Salt Lake and ought to make the team next year.

The Twins bullpen also pitched well, led by Mike Trombley, Greg Swindell, Travis Miller and Hector Carrasco. The departures of Dan Naulty and—especially—Greg Swindell will make life a bit harder for the 1999 bullpen.

Rick "The Loyal" Aguilera (4-9, 4.24, 74.1 with 39 saves) continues to be the closer for the Twins. A thoughtful person might wonder why a team which aspires to win 80 games (but can only manage 70) needs a good (and expensive) closer.

THE FUTURE

1999 looks to be another year with modest expectations. Given the apparent uncertainty with the team's future, the severe budget constraints, and the fact that many Twins fans are already staying away in droves; the organization would appear to have little to lose by undertaking a whole-scale rebuilding effort. Lose the Minnesota native swan-songs, eschew the veteran free-agent retreads, and instead run the kids out there everyday and see what they can do. There'll never be a better time.

Could such a team break the mythical .500 barrier? Maybe, and maybe not. But it's certainly an affordable team, a team with some upside potential, and team that just might be fun to watch.

Name	AB	R	H	D	T	HR	RBI	BB	SO	SB	CS	BA	OBP	SLG	XR	Adj XR/27	Raw XR/27	OXW	DXW	TXW
Coomer R	530	55	145	21	1	15	72	17	71	2	1	.274	.292	.404	58	3.73	3.77	0.16	0.39	0.55
Cordova M	440	53	111	19	2	10	69	48	101	3	4	.252	.329	.376	54	4.11	4.15	0.70	0.43	1.13
Gates B	335	31	82	14	0	3	42	34	45	3	2	.246	.318	.317	35	3.59	3.69	0.05	0.02	0.07
Hocking D	199	32	40	6	1	3	15	15	43	2	1	.201	.255	.286	15	2.45	2.54	-0.68	0.21	-0.47
Latham C	95	14	15	1	0	1	5	12	35	4	2	.161	.258	.205	6	1.90	1.91	-0.49	0.10	-0.39
Lawton M	560	92	154	34	6	22	77	83	63	15	5	.275	.380	.473	103	6.47	6.60	4.47	1.49	5.96
Meares P	544	57	139	24	3	9	70	23	84	7	2	.255	.290	.361	55	3.49	3.62	-0.15	1.72	1.57
Merced O	204	22	58	11	0	5	33	17	28	1	3	.286	.341	.419	27	4.74	4.77	0.65	0.20	0.85
Molitor P	504	76	139	28	5	4	69	43	40	8	1	.276	.328	.373	61	4.16	4.36	0.84	0.06	0.90
Nixon O	450	72	132	6	6	1	20	42	55	36	5	.294	.356	.339	58	4.55	4.66	1.25	0.61	1.86
Ochoa A	250	36	63	13	2	2	25	9	34	6	2	.253	.283	.346	22	3.00	3.10	-0.42	0.28	-0.14
Ortiz D	280	48	76	19	0	9	46	37	71	1	0	.272	.363	.438	45	5.60	5.84	1.60	0.17	1.77
Shave J	40	7	10	3	0	1	5	3	10	1	2	.248	.299	.395	4	3.57	3.70	0.00	-0.04	-0.04
Steinbach T	423	46	101	24	2	14	54	37	87	0	1	.239	.305	.407	49	3.87	3.97	0.34	1.38	1.72
Valentin J	162	11	32	7	1	3	18	11	29	0	0	.194	.242	.304	10	1.92	2.01	-0.87	0.19	-0.68
Walker T	530	87	165	39	3	13	62	45	64	18	5	.311	.365	.466	85	5.91	6.08	3.26	-0.26	3.00
MIN	**5662**	**746**	**1486**	**271**	**30**	**119**	**695**	**485**	**898**	**107**	**38**	**.262**	**.323**	**.384**	**696**	**4.23**	**4.32**	**10.70**	**6.95**	**17.65**

Pitcher	S	C	T	SS	ES	IC	HH	PP	TJ	S12	S35	S67	C1	C23	C45	C67	QWP
B Radke	4.28	2.63	6.91	50%	13%	44%	34%	0%	9%	19%	47%	34%	16%	75%	6%	3%	.556
Fr Rodriguez	4.27	3.82	8.09	45%	18%	45%	45%	9%	9%	36%	18%	45%	0%	45%	36%	18%	.440
Hawkins	4.64	3.42	8.06	42%	3%	24%	45%	3%	6%	12%	42%	45%	6%	55%	36%	3%	.432
M Morgan	4.59	3.24	7.82	24%	12%	41%	47%	6%	12%	24%	29%	47%	12%	47%	35%	6%	.450
Milton	4.41	3.78	8.19	38%	6%	31%	38%	9%	6%	22%	41%	38%	3%	34%	53%	9%	.420
Sampson	2.00	3.00	5.00	100%	50%	100%	0%	50%	0%	100%	0%	0%	0%	50%	50%	0%	.761
Serafini	4.89	4.11	9.00	33%	0%	0%	33%	0%	0%	0%	67%	33%	0%	44%	44%	11%	.363
Tewksbury	4.40	2.60	7.00	52%	20%	44%	40%	0%	16%	24%	36%	40%	24%	56%	20%	0%	.525
Trombley	5.00	4.00	9.00	0%	0%	0%	0%	0%	0%	0%	100%	0%	0%	0%	100%	0%	.362
MIN	**4.44**	**3.25**	**7.69**	**43%**	**10%**	**35%**	**40%**	**4%**	**9%**	**20%**	**40%**	**40%**	**10%**	**52%**	**32%**	**6%**	**.470**

DETROIT TIGERS

KEN ADAMS

Last year we speculated that a move to the Central would be beneficial for the Tigers. And it may be in the long run, but in their maiden year they trailed the field. But they had some bad luck. If you look at their runs scored compared to runs allowed, you will see that it was no fluke and a team effort finishing 12th in runs scored and 10th in runs allowed.

Team	RA	RS	Dif	W-L
Indians	850	779	+71	89-73
White Sox	861	931	-70	80-82
Royals	714	899	-185	72-89
Twins	734	818	-84	70-92
Tigers	722	863	-141	65-97

This was quite a fall off from 1997 when they scored 784 runs and allowed 790 and went 79-83. The Tigers for their part have decided to sign the core of their young team to long term contracts in hopes of imitating the success of the AL Central leader, the Cleveland Indians. The Tigers will be moving into their new stadium in 2000 and have signed Tony Clark, Damion Easley, Dean Palmer, Bobby Higginson, Todd Jones, Willie Blair, Doug Brocail Brian Moehler and newcomer Maso Kida to long term contracts. Is this a winning strategy for the Tigers, how do they stack up against the 1994 Indians? Let's look at how the teams stack up against each other, keep in mind that this is not an exact comparison since the 1994 Indians were already in their new stadium while the Tigers are a year away.

Catcher: The Indians had 28 year old Sandy Alomar. Sandy set career highs in OBP (.347), SLG (.490) and OPS (.837) in the 1994 season. Keep in mind when drawing comparisons that Alomar had his first full season at the age of 24 in 1990 and had a .744 OPS. The Tigers do not have a settled situation behind the plate. The suspects are Paul Bako, Raul Casanova and Robert Fick. Bako did the majority of catching last season and had a OPS of .671 last season as a 26 year old rookie. Bako certainly is not as good as Alomar, but it isn't a large advantage. Casanova was injured and didn't play a great deal at the major league level last season and while he is only 26 he has roughly the same amount

of PA's that Alomar had in his 1990 season. While Alomar put up the following .290/.326/.418 in 472 PA's, Casanova has career numbers of .223/.290/.327 in 472 PA's. Casanvoa's .617 OPS doesn't compare well at all to Alomar's .744. Robert Fick, the youngest of the Tiger trio at 25, is the best bet to take over the job. He came up for a cup of coffee in September and had a positive review. He was promoted from AA where he produced a .939 OPS and is projected by STATS to produce a .805 OPS for the coming season. Fick should be better than Alomar, but he needs to prove it. The advantage would go to the Indians unless Fick slightly exceeds expectations.

First Base: The Indians in 1994 used Paul Sorrento at 1B (.754 OPS at 28, in his sixth year). The 94 season was about at the same level as his previous two season. The Tigers have a young veteran, Tony Clark, who produced a .880 OPS in the 1998 season at the age of 26. A clear advantage to the Tigers.

Second Base: The Indians sported one of the best 2B in baseball in 1994 with Carlos Baerga. Carlos has fallen on hard times since, but at the time he was considered the best or second best, and in 1994 he produced a .858 OPS in his 5th season at the age of 25. The Tigers also have a power hitting 2B with Damion Easley. Easley produced a .810 OPS in his 7th season at the age of 28. The advantage here would go to the Indians, with a slightly superior player who is also three years younger.

Third Base: The Indians had the young Jim Thome at third in 1994 who produced a .883 OPS at the age of

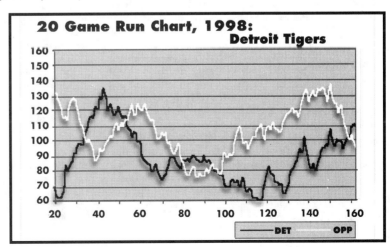

20 Game Run Chart, 1998: Detroit Tigers

QMAX PRESENTS: "BAD" PITCHERS

When the Detroit Tigers signed Tim Belcher for the 1994 season, they certain didn't think they were buying a Bad Pitcher. The man with the frat-boy's name averaged 215 IP, 12 wins, and a 3.68 ERA in the three seasons prior to joining the Motor City madmen. Something happened over the winter, though, and terrible Timmy started the new season like an outhouse on fire, reaching the seventh inning exactly once in his first seven starts. The burpmeister's QMAX data for these starts was, if anything, even more horrifying than his 9.91 ERA: a gaudy 6.17 on the "stuff" scale, and a relatively pedestrian 5.30 on the "command" scale. On May 8, Belcher found what he was looking for with an 8-inning, 8-hit performance that, while resulting in another loss, at least looked more like a major league pitcher than a beer-league softball player. For the next two months, Belcher seemed like the pitcher los Tigres had paid for, going 7-3 with a 4.17 ERA. His QMAX for that period: 3.79 stuff, 2.93 control. After that, though, the deluge: his last five starts before the strike mercifully cut things short were the very definition of "mailing it in": QMAX "stuff" score of 5.80, and a more tolerable 3.40 on the command scale.

It's hard to say what happens when a good pitcher has stretches like these. The first thought is usually

TIM BELCHER/DET 1994							
	1	2	3	4	5	6	7	S
1	1		1					2
2		1		1				2
3								1
4	1		1		1			3
5			4		3		1	8
6	1	1	1	1			1	5
7					4			4
C	3	2	8	2	8	0	2	25

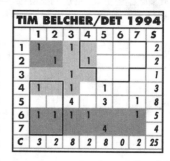

Five Start Qmax: Belcher

injury, but if that was the case this time we're looking for something really subtle, because Tim didn't miss a turn all year. In the beginning he was horrible on all counts, walking the ballpark and giving up Big Flies when he did find the plate. He found his control in May and more or less kept it all year, but around the all-star break he started getting beat like a drum again, giving up hits like a Pontiac Fiero leaks oil. Maybe he was the Detroit player rep and his mind wasn't on the game. Maybe it was Detroit Iron-poor blood: Belcher returned to his usual middling form with a change in scenery to Seattle the next year and continues to get major-league jobs to this day, although he's in no danger of winning the Cy. Whatever the cause was, 1994 was a season Tim would like to forget.

--Tom Austin

23. The Tigers signed Free Agent Dean Palmer in the off season. Palmer played with the Royals last season and managed to do well in a pitcher's park and came in at .843 OPS which should go up in Detroit. But Palmer is 30 years of age which is two years older than Thome is today, and Thome produced a .997 OPS in 1998. So while Palmer is certainly an upgrade at third base for the Tigers he is not going to beat out Thome, so the advantage goes to the Indians.

Shortstop: The Indians in 1994 had just acquired the slick fielding 27 year old Omar Vizquel and his .650 OPS from the Mariners. The Tigers also have a slick fielding SS, Deivi Cruz, who at 23 produced a .639 OPS. Deivi has a little bit more power but gives up onbase average. Due to the age difference we have to give the Tigers the nod.

Left Field: The big gun of the 1994 Indians was Albert Belle and his1.152 OPS which proceeded his plus 100 extra basehit 1995 season. Albert was only 27 years of age in his fourth season as a regular. The Tigers have no match here, as Luis Gonzalez is only a few months younger than Belle today. In 1998 Gonzalez managed to hit .815 in OPS which is only a little better than his year 27 Ops of .803. Gonzalez has

since been traded to Arizona for struggling ex-Dodger phenom Karim Garcia. Big advantage to the Indians.

Center Field The 1994 Indians had one of the best leadoff hitters his side of Ricky Henderson. Kenny Lofton had a .948 OPS that season as a 27 year old in his 4th season. The Tigers 1998 CF was the worst leadoff hitter in the league last season and one of the worst full time performers in the majors last season with a .629 OPS. In seven seasons as a fulltime player Lofton has never produced a OPS lower than .727 while Hunter has never produced anything over .687 and at 28 it looks like he will never get much higher. Another big advantage to the Indians.

Right Field: Manny Ramirez was a 22 year old rookie in 1994 when he produced a .878 OPS for the Indians. The Tigers played the 28 year old veteran, Bobby Higginson in RF in 1998. Bobby had his second consecutive season in which he posted a decline in OPS. In 1996 his OPS was .981 followed up with a .899 in 1997 and a .835 in 1998. The Tigers have a young OF, Juan Encarnacion who at 23 has less than 200 ML AB's. Juan's best minor league season came in 1997 at AA where he produced .323/.394/.560 at the age of 21.

Ramirez at the age of 21 split his season between AA and AAA in which he produced .323/.423/.613 (80 points higher in OPS, and a run per game higer in XR/27 at 10.54 to Encarnacion's 9.46). It should also be pointed out that Juan was hit 19 times to get his OBP up to the near .400 level while Ramirez was only hit four times which could signal injury problems ahead for the Tiger youngster. The Tigers occasionally played Juan in CF last year. He would be much better offensively for Detroit than Hunter (and much closer to Lofton). But his range was microscopic at 1.09 when compared to the ML average of 2.59 or Hunter's 2.95 so it is unlikely he will play there. Another young possibility is Gabe Kapler, but at 21 he was still in A ball with a .872 OPS and 7.19 RC/G which is far below Encarnacion's level. So again the advantage goes to the Indians whichever player the Tigers put in RF.

DH: The Indians only old-timer in their lineup in 1994 was Eddie Murray who was nearing the end of his career at 39. He only produced a .727 OPS. The Tigers will probably play some combination of young OF's Encarnacion and Kapler and maybe young third baseman Gabe Alvarez. Last year the trio combined for a .762 OPS and should do better in 1999 so here we will give the advantage to the Tigers.

Overall lineup: The Indians have a 6-3 lead by position, and here is another way of looking at the two.

Team	BAVG	OBP	SLG	OPS	XR/27
Indians-94	.298	.361	.509	.870	7.52
Tigers-98	.275	.327	.450	.778	5.70

That works out to a rather large advantage for the Indians regulars who averaged a year older. This doesn't bode well for the Tigers, who will be another year older by the time they move in and are nowhere near the Indians everyday lineup of 1994.

The team are much harder to compare when you look at pitching staffs, because the Indians used older veterans for the most part while the Tigers rely mainly on younger pitchers. The 1994 Indians had a top four rotation of Dennis Martinez (39), Jack Morris (39), Charles Nagy (27) and Mark Clark (26). The Tigers 1998 top four rotation was made up of Frank Castillo (29), Brian Moehler (26), Jason Thompson (25) and Seth Greisinger (22). It is not hard to see that Moehler and Thompson should be as good as Nagy and Clark and perhaps better there is no way to compare Castillo and Greisinger to Martinez and Morris even in the latter's dotage. Even with the return of Willie Blair (33) for the 1999 season this would not change. No one would mistake Blair for either Martinez or Morris. In 1994 the four Indian starters had a 4.04 ERA with 1.36 WHIP while striking out 5.3 batters per nine inning pitched. The four Tigers produced an ERA of 4.67 with a 1.40 WHIP while striking out 5.5 batters per nine. Another advantage then goes to the Indians starting rotation.

The bullpen of the Indians in 1994 was a mess as they searched for a closer and tried out Steve Farr and John Russell, neither of which was effective and they combined for only nine saves. Middle relievers Eric Plunk and closer to be Jose Mesa pitched better than either of the closers. The 1998 Tigers didn't have a good closer either with Todd Jones and his 4.97 ERA, but he did have 28 saves. The Tigers also have a closer to be in

WPA BULLPEN BOX—DETROIT TIGERS

	PI	WPA	P	PPPI
Starters	1010	-7.2	51.6	0.051
Relievers	660	1.7	37.9	0.057
Road	313	3.9	16.6	0.053
Home	347	-2.1	21.3	0.061
Mar/Apr	109	-1.8	4.8	0.044
May	108	0.3	4.8	0.045
June	112	-0.2	6.1	0.055
July	106	3.0	8.1	0.076
August	106	-0.3	5.9	0.056
September	119	0.6	8.1	0.068
Non S/H Sit.	557	-0.2	25.7	0.046
S/H Sit.	103	1.9	12.1	0.118
Low Pressure	307	-1.4	4.4	0.014
Med. Pressure	178	-1.2	10.4	0.059
High Pressure	175	4.3	23.1	0.132
Entered behind	390	-0.1	10.6	0.027
Entered tied	100	-0.0	13.4	0.134
Entered ahead	170	1.9	13.8	0.081

Name	G	PI	WPA	P	PPPI	MI	ROB	T
Anderson M	42	55	.5	4.4	.081	13	17	13
Bochtler D	51	85	-1.3	3.3	.039	25	28	4
Brocail D	60	80	2.7	5.2	.065	19	25	10
Crow D	32	56	.0	1.9	.034	22	10	4
Duran R	18	23	-.1	.4	.017	5	6	0
Florie B	26	54	.2	3.1	.057	15	16	4
Jones T	65	71	1.7	6.5	.091	6	10	7
Runyan S	88	105	-1.0	7.1	.067	17	45	13
Sager A	28	59	-.6	2.6	.044	19	14	5
Santana M	7	12	-.5	.8	.063	4	4	2
Worrell T	6	16	.0	.8	.049	5	3	0
Total		660	1.8	37.9	.057			

	Quality					Pressure			
	Dis.	Poor	Fair	Good	Her.	Lo	Med	Hi	
Anderson M	2	7	15	18	0	14	15	13	(8)
Bochtler D	3	9	34	4	1	33	12	6	(4)
Brocail D	1	7	32	16	4	34	15	11	(10)
Crow D	1	4	23	2	2	23	4	5	(2)
Duran R	0	1	17	0	0	16	1	1	(0)
Florie B	2	4	13	6	1	11	8	7	(5)
Jones T	5	2	28	29	1	29	12	24	(18)
Runyan S	2	19	52	14	1	45	25	18	(10)
Sager A	2	7	14	4	1	9	14	5	(2)
Others	4	2	22	7	1	18	8	10	(6)
TOTAL	22	62	250	100	12	232	114	100	(65)

	7th inning			8th inning			9th inning		
	0	1	2	0	1	2	0	1	2
Anderson M	3	1	2	4	2	2	3	0	0
Bochtler D	0	2	1	0	0	0	0	0	0
Brocail D	0	0	0	3	4	2	3	0	0
Crow D	0	0	0	1	1	0	0	0	0
Florie B	1	1	1	1	0	1	1	0	0
Jones T	0	0	0	0	0	0	1	13	8
Runyan S	3	1	0	3	2	0	1	0	0
Sager A	1	1	1	0	0	0	0	0	0
Santana M	0	1	0	0	1	0	1	0	0
Starters	12	6	8	3	3	2	1	1	3
TOTAL	21	13	13	15	13	7	11	14	11
Record	11-10	11-2	9-4	7-8	10-3	5-2	5-6	10-4	10-1

Sean Forman's
PROSPECT WATCH

NAME	AGE	POS	LEVEL	GR98	GR97	GR96	AVG
Juan Encarnacion	22	OF	AAA	70	79	48	69
Gabe Kapler	22	OF	AA	74	57	67	67
Gabe Alvarez	24	3B	AAA	70	47	51	59
Javaier Cardona	22	C	AAA	52	41	38	46
Alejandro Freire	23	OF	AA	37	55	44	44
Rob Fick	24	C	AA	52	46	4	42

NAME	AGE	POS	LEVEL	GRADE
Richard Gomez	20	OF	Rookie	66
Maxim St.Pierre	18	C	Rookie	65
Darrell Pender	19	OF	Rookie	50
Rodney Lindsey	22	OF	Low A	49
Matthew Boone	18	3B	Rookie	48
Chris Parker	18	C	Rookie	47

NAME	AGE	GS	S	C	T	W-L	ERA	K/H	LEVEL
Brian Powell	24	15	3.40	2.60	6.00	10-2	2.86	0.65	High
Denny Harriger	27	22	4.05	3.23	7.27	5-12	4.55	0.58	High
David Borkowski	21	28	4.43	3.00	7.43	16-7	4.63	0.48	High
Clay Bruner	21	27	4.04	3.56	7.59	9-6	3.79	0.53	High
David Darwin	24	25	4.16	3.48	7.64	12-6	5.15	0.52	High
Dave Melendez	22	24	4.46	3.38	7.83	9-6	5.06	0.50	High
Matt Drews	23	27	4.48	4.04	8.52	5-17	6.57	0.49	High
Kerry Taylor	26	17	4.71	4.00	8.71	7-10	5.77	0.66	High
Mike Drumright	23	27	4.63	4.37	9.00	4-19	6.96	0.48	High
Brandon Reed	23	15	5.20	4.07	9.27	4-6	5.88	0.47	High
Alan Webb	18	27				10-7	2.93	1.84	Low

The Tigers took a big step backwards from the perceived progress they were making after the 1997 season. If the Tigers can endure one more so-so season without panicking, they might be able to put together a solid young team when they enter their new ballpark. Signing Dean Palmer to a mega-deal doesn't exactly assure me that this will happen.

TOP DOG: Gabe Kapler

There is a picture of Kapler in the October 25, 1998 Baseball America, and I'm not sure I've ever seen a baseball player with the biceps that he has. Kapler is well-known for his weightlifting fanaticism, largely because Baseball America prefaces any comments about him with that fact. Due to this, he has been bypassed when you find lists of top prospects. In fact, he was only named Detroit's 11th best prospect after a .295/.361/.505 season in the Florida State League. This year, in the Southern League, he hit .322/.393/.583 with 113 runs scored and 146 RBI's!!! and yet he was still just considered the 7th best prospect in the league. He has 40 double, 20 home run power, and draws a fair number of walks without an inordinate number of strikeouts. Not bad for a 57th round draft pick. Comp: Jermaine Dye with patience.

HANDY MAN: Juan Encarnacion

Reading me sometimes, I'm sure I come across as an anti-tool talent evaluator. That's not the case. Too often tools prospects just don't play the game very well or can't learn the strike zone and no amount of talent is going to change that. Encarnacion is a tools prospect galore. He can hit for power, hit for average, run, throw and field, but I'm not entirely sold on him. He hit a ton in his 164 at bat major league debut, but he has been exceptionally erratic all of his career. He won't draw many walks, and he will strike out too much, but his talent will keep managers and GM's enchanted for years to come. Comp: Derek Bell.

BACKSTOP: Rob Fick

Fick also did a little hitting during his major league debut clubbing three home runs in 22 at bats. Fick has 20 home run power, and augments that with 50 double potential and a .300 batting stroke. For good measure he added 21 steals in 29 attempts. Not bad for a catcher. However, he is old (he'll be 25 next year) and he has yet to play above AA, excluding his cup of coffee. He is still a work in progress behind the plate, but if he can manage the tools of ignorance, he can be a plus offensive player for several years to come.

YOUNG 'UN: Maxim St.Pierre

I didn't pick St.Pierre for any real reason other than his name as the Tigers' low minors group isn't all that distinguished. Pierre is a Quebec native and was selected by the Tigers in the 26th round of the 1997 draft. He didn't get off to much of a start in 1997 managing just 41 at bats, but he returned to the Gulf Coast League with a vengeance in 1998 batting .385/.467/.471 in 104 at bats. Since he's just 18 and in rookie ball, he has a long way to go to the majors. I imagine he'll see time in the Midwest League for West Michigan next year.

ON THE MOUND: Alan Webb

Jeff Weaver is probably their best pitching prospect, but he signed late and managed just five low-A starts (14 hits and 33 strikeouts in 25 innings). Webb however spent the whole year in the Midwest League and was named the ninth best prospect in the league. He allowed just 168 baserunners in 172 innings while racking up 202 k's. That is a whole lot of innings for an 18-year-old and when you consider he is 5-10 and 165 pounds it is downright obscene. If he can make his way through the injury maze, he could be pretty good, but I fear there may be surgery in his not so distant future.

young Matt Anderson, but he wasn't able to convert any of his save opportunities to saves. The Tigers middle relievers, Sean Runyan and Doug Brocail were equal to the Indians 1994 middlemen. So the bullpens would have to be called a draw.

To sum up, the Tigers are trailing the Indians in both the atarting lineup and the atarting rotation, and are even (at best) in the bullpen. Their apparent commitment to two extremely inefficient hitters (Brian L. Hunter and Deivi Cruz) limits their latitude in developing a credible batting order. There is a nagging suspicion amongst analysts that several of the players they count on to anchor the middle of their lineup (Tony Clark, Bobby Higginson, Damion Easley) have performed over their true levels in the past couple of seasons. Signing Gregg Jefferies is little more than a replacement for Gonzalez. Garcia's major league upside appears dubious at best.

Bottom line: Tigers are going to have to stumble across a lot of good young ballplayers if they are going to come anywhere close to the 1994 Indians when they open up their new ballyard in Detroit.

A MIDSUMMER NIGHT's DRAFT (2)

–continued from BAL–

Pat agreed that I should attend the mid-summer draft and make the selections, but he denied he had wavered from my draft instructions. This defect in this memory made me suspect that it might be alcohol that had its effect in the later rounds. I decided to protect myself by putting some water in some empty brown beer bottles and placing the caps back on them. This way I could look like everyone else and not draw attention to myself, nor worry about the beer making choices for me. I had created some player listings on the computer for the draft. I then copied the information by hand onto sheets of paper and arranged them so that anyone looking at them couldn't figure out the order.

Psycho called me at work several days before the draft. After my first experience with him, I kept my conversations short. After all, I was supposed to be working. But this time I relented, I was curious about meeting him. Evidently he had heard that Pat's mysterious silent partner was going to be at the draft and was wondering if I knew who that was going to be.

"It's me," I confessed.

"Great," he said without missing a beat.

He continued to complain about his back and how much trouble it was giving him in his new job. He allowed as how he might have gone back to work too soon after the surgery he'd had. He meandered awhile longer and then asked whom I would pick if I had first choice in the draft.

"Geez Tom, you don't think I'm going to tell you," I laughed.

"Well what would it hurt? If you get the first pick, you got your guy and it doesn't matter. And what are the odds that you'll be picking behind me?"

I guessed that it would be about 100% if I told him, and then claimed that I hadn't made up my mind between a pitcher and a hitter yet, it would probably depend on how the drafting went. He persisted awhile bringing up this player and that trying to get me to comment on them. After exhausting most of the name players and a good portion of the sleepers, he got the message that I wasn't going to produce any Worrells this time. I thought I had been sufficiently vague and noncommittal enough that he wouldn't have any idea how I was drafting.

--The hose was easy; I even found a screwdriver and wrench in the back of the Blazer. I decided to check the truck over a little more carefully, but could find nothing seriously amiss. It still bothered me why the Blazer had been deserted. I got in line behind a group of semis heading east toward Barstow. I was never fond of the desert, preferring the shady woods and marveling at how I had found myself living in a dry oak and savanna valley in the heart of California instead of New England. The one thing about the desert was that you could see forever, no surprises, no coming around a curve in the road to find a picturesque little town nestled in a little valley, a beautiful lake, or fall foliage painted on a hillside. The Blazer didn't have enough power to pass the long line of semi trucks heading east; at least I thought I shouldn't push it. So I just stayed in line and watched the far off mountains slowly move forward. At least when I reached the highway going to Las Vegas there would be four lanes and I could make up some time. After Vegas, there wouldn't be much traffic. I then drifted back to that first draft that I attended many years ago.

The draft was being held at the home of Dan Wicznevski; everyone took the easy way out and called him "Wish." It was at least four miles to his house and Pat said he would pick me up about 5 in the afternoon and the draft would start at 6. The draft usually went on to 9 pm as they watched the All-Star game. What's distinctive about the Sacramento summer is that the hottest time of the day is usually 5 pm; it doesn't let up until 9 pm or so, unless a breeze comes in from the delta. The day of the draft was well over 100 degrees and rising like a Roger Clemens fastball. The best thing to do in a situation like that is to fan yourself and grab some pine in a nice cool spot in the dugout.

Pat picked me up in his Jeep Cherokee, which certainly ran better than my old Hornet wagon, except for the air-conditioner. He drove with the windows down as I kept a tight grip on my paperwork. On the way he kept making the point of how much he wanted to win. It seemed so important to him, but I

TEAM BREAKOUT TIGERS 1998

Category	RS	RA	W	L	Pct.	Rk
CLOSE SLUGFESTS/ROAD	67	60	7	2	.778	2
5+ RUNS SCORED/ROAD	260	172	25	9	.735	9
4- RUNS ALLOWED/HOME	164	93	27	10	.730	10
4- RUNS ALLOWED	326	179	50	22	.694	12
5+ RUNS SCORED	498	358	46	21	.687	12
4- RUNS ALLOWED/ROAD	162	86	23	12	.657	12
5+ RUNS SCORED/HOME	238	186	21	12	.636	14
CLOSE LOW-SCORING GAMES/HOME	28	25	8	6	.571	9
SLUGFESTS/ROAD	183	187	14	11	.560	4
LOW SCORING GAMES/HOME	35	32	9	8	.529	8
CLOSE SLUGFESTS/HOME	53	55	3	3	.500	7
RECORD IN CLOSE GAMES/HOME	162	168	18	21	.462	14
RECORD IN CLOSE GAMES	297	310	32	39	.451	10
RECORD IN CLOSE GAMES/ROAD	135	142	14	18	.438	5
RECORD IN LOW SCORING GAMES	76	91	17	22	.436	11
RECORD IN BLOWOUTS/ROAD	127	145	10	13	.435	9
RECORD IN SLUGFESTS	339	412	21	29	.420	11
RECORD IN BLOWOUTS	241	311	19	28	.404	12
SEASON TOTALS	722	863	65	97	.401	13
RECORD IN BLOWOUTS/HOME	114	166	9	15	.375	12
LOW SCORING GAMES/ROAD	41	59	8	14	.364	12
CLOSE LOW SCORING GAMES/ROAD	21	29	4	8	.333	12
SLUGFESTS/HOME	156	225	7	18	.280	14
4- RUNS SCORED/HOME	122	259	11	37	.229	10
5+ RUNS ALLOWED/ROAD	200	332	10	36	.217	11
4- RUNS SCORED	224	505	19	76	.200	12
4- RUNS SCORED/ROAD	102	246	8	39	.170	11
5+ RUNS ALLOWED	396	684	15	75	.167	13
5+ RUNS ALLOWED/HOME	196	352	5	39	.114	13

didn't get the impression that it was the money that he was after. I would find out shortly.

Wish greeted us at the door and instructed us to put our beer in the refrigerator out in the garage, not the house. I'm certain that hell itself is not hotter that Wish's garage was on that day, and the house itself was no cooler. I opened my first "beer" and downed it rapidly. Pat was nervous about my downing a beer so quickly and so early.

"Hey, I thought you wanted to be on your toes for the draft. Take it easy with that stuff."

"Don"t worry, it"s not beer, it"s missing some key ingredients," I whispered.

A smile came over his face and he relaxed. He then took a big swig from the can he was carrying. [continued in Oakland]

Name	AB	R	H	D	T	HR	RBI	BB	SO	SB	CS	BA	OBP	SLG	XR	Adj XR/27	Raw XR/27	OXW	DXW	TXW
Alvarez G	200	16	47	12	0	4	29	17	64	1	3	.233	.299	.355	21	3.58	3.67	0.01	-0.23	-0.22
Bako P	306	23	85	14	1	2	30	22	81	1	1	.279	.324	.354	36	4.24	4.10	0.59	0.57	1.16
Bartee K	98	20	20	6	1	2	15	6	35	8	5	.199	.240	.346	8	2.60	2.71	-0.33	0.16	-0.17
Beamon T	42	4	12	5	0	0	2	5	13	1	0	.279	.353	.388	5	3.76	3.31	0.02	0.02	0.04
Berroa G	126	17	31	5	1	1	10	17	27	0	1	.249	.345	.322	14	3.87	3.63	0.13	0.01	0.14
Casanova R	42	4	6	2	0	1	3	5	10	0	0	.138	.243	.234	3	1.95	2.33	-0.21	-0.01	-0.22
Catalanotto F	213	23	62	14	2	5	25	12	38	3	2	.290	.331	.451	32	5.28	5.12	0.98	0.22	1.20
Clark T	604	84	176	41	0	29	102	61	126	3	3	.292	.357	.504	102	6.14	6.36	4.12	0.43	4.55
Cruz D	454	52	121	24	4	4	44	13	54	3	4	.266	.289	.357	42	3.17	3.10	-0.54	2.72	2.18
Easley D	595	83	161	42	2	22	99	38	111	14	4	.271	.331	.456	88	5.31	5.60	2.79	2.44	5.23
Encarnacion J	164	30	55	10	4	6	21	7	31	7	4	.332	.357	.552	30	6.86	6.95	1.37	0.20	1.57
Gonzalez L	549	83	146	38	6	19	70	55	61	12	6	.267	.338	.458	86	5.45	5.68	2.85	0.56	3.41
Higginson B	614	91	179	41	5	22	84	61	100	3	3	.291	.359	.484	101	5.94	5.83	3.89	1.24	5.13
Hunter B	596	67	157	32	3	4	36	35	93	40	12	.262	.305	.346	64	3.71	3.51	0.22	1.50	1.72
Oliver J	155	8	36	9	0	3	22	7	33	0	1	.231	.257	.356	14	2.87	2.83	-0.35	0.21	-0.14
Randa J	461	56	120	23	2	8	50	40	69	8	7	.261	.327	.373	56	4.15	4.04	0.77	0.78	1.55
Ripken B	74	8	21	3	0	0	5	5	10	3	2	.278	.327	.322	8	3.54	3.34	-0.01	0.04	0.03
Roberts B	114	17	28	6	0	0	9	15	14	6	1	.249	.349	.301	13	3.95	4.01	0.15	-0.06	0.09
Siddall J	65	3	12	4	0	1	6	7	24	0	0	.191	.268	.279	5	2.31	2.28	-0.25	0.01	-0.24
Tomberlin A	69	8	15	2	0	2	12	3	25	1	0	.213	.275	.316	5	2.51	2.74	-0.22	0.00	-0.22
DET	5677	718	1524	337	32	140	683	442	1058	116	59	.268	.326	.413	751	4.63	4.63	16.01	10.81	26.82

Park Adjusted Statistics

Pitcher	S	C	T	SS	ES	IC	HH	PP	TJ	S12	S35	S67	C1	C23	C45	C67	QWP
B Powell	4.81	3.69	8.50	25%	13%	13%	50%	0%	6%	19%	31%	50%	6%	31%	50%	13%	.355
F Castillo	5.58	4.05	9.63	11%	0%	21%	58%	0%	16%	5%	37%	58%	5%	26%	53%	16%	.286
Florie	4.50	3.75	8.25	38%	13%	19%	31%	6%	0%	19%	50%	31%	13%	19%	63%	6%	.424
Greisinger	4.24	3.38	7.62	43%	14%	33%	33%	5%	10%	24%	43%	33%	10%	48%	33%	10%	.498
Harriger	5.50	4.00	9.50	0%	0%	0%	50%	0%	0%	0%	50%	50%	0%	0%	100%	0%	.263
J Thompson	4.03	3.24	7.26	47%	15%	47%	29%	9%	12%	35%	35%	29%	9%	50%	35%	6%	.513
Keagle	4.57	4.00	8.57	29%	14%	14%	29%	0%	0%	14%	57%	29%	14%	14%	57%	14%	.340
Moehler	3.85	2.76	6.61	55%	18%	45%	21%	3%	9%	27%	52%	21%	27%	42%	30%	0%	.563
Sager	5.67	4.00	9.67	33%	0%	0%	67%	0%	0%	0%	33%	67%	0%	33%	67%	0%	.233
Sanders	6.50	5.00	11.50	0%	0%	0%	100%	0%	0%	0%	0%	100%	0%	0%	100%	0%	.040
Worrell	4.56	3.44	8.00	33%	0%	33%	33%	0%	0%	22%	44%	33%	0%	67%	33%	0%	.440
DET	4.46	3.47	7.93	38%	12%	33%	36%	4%	8%	22%	42%	36%	12%	38%	43%	7%	.443

TEXAS RANGERS

DON MALCOLM

THAT GUY AGAIN

A couple of years ago in these pages we discussed how sabermetrics has had an impact on the baseball writers despite the loud claims of the stathead community that MVP = RBI, a formulation first brought to our attention by Bill James back in the early 1980s.

The evidence still points away from this thesis in the past twenty years, despite the AL writers' efforts over the past several seasons. But for those who persist in living the myth, let's examine the RBI rankings of the MVPs over the past ten years.

1989: Robin Yount wins in the AL, and doesn't finish in the top five in RBI. He does lead in the Jamesian category of Runs Created (RC), however, and finishes second in TB, third in SLG, fourth in BA, and fifth in doubles. Ruben Sierra, the RBI leader, finishes second in the balloting.

Over in the NL, say hello to Kevin Mitchell, who led the Giants to the World Series, and led the NL in HR, RBI, SLG, on-base plus slugging (OPS), TB, and RC.

1990: Rickey Henderson is AL MVP, leading in on-base percentage (OBP), RC, OPS, runs scored and stolen bases. He finishes second in SLG.

In the NL, meet Barry Bonds (you'll be seeing him again). Barry leads the NL in SLG, OPS and RC. He finishes second in BB, third in SB, fourth in OBP and RBI, and fifth in HR.

1991: Cal Ripken wins the AL MVP trophy, leading in TB (thanks in part to that streak). He finishes second in doubles, hits, RC, and SLG; third in HR and OPS, and fourth in RBI.

The NL MVP is the third baseman of that flash-in-the-pan 90s franchise, the Atlanta Braves. (Yes, that is sarcasm.) Oh, yes, the name: Terry Pendleton. He leads in three categories: BA, hits, and TB; he finishes third in SLG.

1992: Dennis Eckersley is awarded the AL MVP, which leaves us offensive types out of the loop. Eck probably won based on his cumulative perfor-

mance for the A's from 1990-92, which was at historic levels for a relief pitcher.

The NL BBWAA writers honored Barry Bonds again (and they weren't quite done, either). Barry led in runs, RC, OBP, SLG, OPS, and BB; he finished second in HR, and fourth in RBI.

1993: Frank Thomas wins the MVP, possibly as a result of missing out in the two previous years. Frank doesn't lead the league in a single offensive category, but finishes second in RC, OPS and RBI; third in HR, TB, and SLG; fourth in BB and OBP. John Olerud has a better profile, and a batting title to boot, but finishes third in the voting.

Back in the NL, its Bonds Uber Alles one more time, as Barry moves to San Francisco and explodes (no, not literally). He leads the league in HR, RBI, OBP, SLG, OPS, TB, and RC; he finishes second in runs scored and BB.

1994: In the abbreviated season, Frank Thomas and Jeff Bagwell win consolation MVPs. Thomas leads the AL in runs, BB, OBP, SLG, OPS and RC; finishes second in HR, third in BA, doubles, TB, and RBI; fourth in hits. Bagwell, injured just before the season is suspended, still leads in runs, RC, OBP, SLG, OPS, TB and RBI; he finishes second in BA and HR, third in hits, and fifth in BB.

1995: The first of the recent controversies: bypassing the notoriously nasty Albert Belle, the AL BBWAA chooses instead

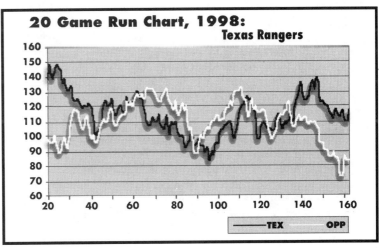

20 Game Run Chart, 1998: Texas Rangers

— TEX   OPP

QMAX PRESENTS: "BAD" PITCHERS

YOUNG MAN BLUES

Submitted for your approval (as Rod Serling was fond of intoning): a young Cuban right-hander named Camilo Pascual, getting lit up regularly (6-18, 5.87) for the woebegone Washington Senators (59-95). An ordinary case of a pitcher lacking the stuff to compete in the major leagues? Not so, for things are not always what they seem. . .in the QMAX zone.

Yes, it's true that the overall numbers here are very similar to other Bad Pitchers profiled, from old guys hanging on past their time to guys who just plain could never pitch in the first place. A closer look, however, shows the free bonus prize a "shape stat" like QMAX gives over more conventional "value stats" like ERA, OBA, OOPS, and the like. It takes a jeweler's loupe to spot it sometime, but Pascual's 1956 numbers glitter like a rough diamond, evidence of the fine pitcher he later grew to be.

Look at the QMAX summary chart. Look at those five starts in the "power precipice". Look at the 12 "success square" starts. Look at the eleven starts in the "4c" column. All of these are evidence of a pitcher with real stuff, struggling with control. This is a pitcher who will try a manager's soul: tantalizing glimpses of brilliance, offset way too many times by a struggle with control: a walk, another walk, a 2-0 pitch grooved because the young Nuke Laloosh on the mound had to come in with the heat after missing with the deuce. It's not easy to watch that kind of performance from the bench, and it's not easy to watch it from the shortstop's position either.

The grizzled veteran skipper and his sidekick, the star shortstop, should take heed, however: there's gold in them thar power precipices. Very often a pitcher with this kind of stuff learns to master it and goes on to a successful career. Pascual did: he won 20 games twice for the none-too-dominating Washington Senators (and the Twins they became) and ended his career with 174 wins. Credit Chuck Dressen and his successor Cookie Lavagetto with having the guts, patience and/or dumb luck to stick with this young gun until he learned to shoot straight. If Kerry Wood, Russ Ortiz, or some other touted rookie struggles this year (like, say, Shawn Estes did last year), the hometown fans should keep this in mind. It's not guaranteed, however: their wild young gunslinger could also turn into another Bobby Witt.

--Tom Austin

CAMILO PASQUAL/WAS 1956

	1	2	3	4	5	6	7	S
1	1			1				2
2	1			4				5
3		1	2	1			1	5
4	1					1		2
5		1		3				4
6	2		1	1			1	5
7				1	2		1	4
C	5	2	3	11	2	1	3	27

Five Start Qmax: Pascual

S   C

Mo Vaughn of the Boston Red Sox. Mo leads the league in RBI (tied, actually, with Belle), and finishes fourth in HR, and fifth in TB.

In the NL, another "intangible" MVP pick comes in the form of Reds' SS Barry Larkin. Barry is second in SB and fifth in runs scored. Dante Bichette, fueled by Coors Field gas, leads in many of the raw stat categories, but finishes fifth. Again, the cumulative MVP award scenario makes the most sense with respect to this selection.

1996: Out of the frying pan and into the fire, the AL over looks brilliant young SS Alex Rodriguez in favor of the Rangers' Juan Gonzalez in a very close vote. The RBI = MVP folks may be shocked to discover, however, that Juan did not lead the league in RBIs this season (how soon we forget). Juan was second in RBI and SLG, and fifth in HR and TB. Rodriguez was clearly the choice, leading in BA, TB, runs scored and doubles; finishing second in RC and hits; fourth in SLG, and fifth in OPS.

The NL award went to Padres' third baseman Ken Caminiti. NL BBWAA successfully resisted a Colorado choice for a second straight year. Caminiti finished third in SLG and RBI, fourth in OPS (and in the adjusted version, lest statheads overstate the park factor issue); fifth in HR, RC, and TB.

1997: Ken Griffey Jr. wins in the AL, finishing first in HRs, SLG, TB, runs scored, and RBI; second in RC; and fifth in OPS.

In the NL, Larry Walker's monster year finally overwhelms the brain cells of the BBWAA, and they choose him over Mike Piazza, despite park adjustments that indicate otherwise. Walker leads in HR, TB, OBP, SLG, RC and OPS (but not in the adjusted version); he finishes second in BA, hits and runs scored; third in RBI and doubles. Many statheads feel that this is a terrible pick, but it really isn't any stranger than some of the previous ones we've seen.

1998: That guy again. Juan Gonzalez was, possibly in the collective thinking of the AL BBWAA, the last man standing in a overcrowded field of MVP candidates. Unable to bring themselves to vote for Albert Belle yet again, the writers opted for power stats and, yes, RBIs. Juan finished first in RBI and doubles; second in SLG; fourth in HR, TB and OPS.

And the NL, there is Sammy, not Mac. McGwire, of course, led in HR, BB, OBP, SLG, OPS and RC, and was second in TB. Sammy got the trophy, and his rankings look like this: first in RBI, R, and TB; second in HR and SLG; third in RC; fourth in OPS; fifth in hits.

So there you have it. Now let's look at the results in terms of the RBI = MVP thing once again. We award five points to every MVP category with a league leading total, four points for a second place finish, 3 for third, etc. We add the numbers up for each league, and voila! The MVP offensive element weighting factors as they have influenced the voting in the last decade:

Yr	Lg	BB	RBI	R	BA	TB	SLG	OBP	OPS	RC	D	HR	SB	H
89-98	A	7	30	10	5	24	32	12	20	22	13	20	5	6
89-98	N	19	30	19	13	31	40	22	34	34	3	29	7	11
MLB		26	60	29	18	55	72	34	54	56	16	49	12	17

And the most important element is: SLG. It's very close in the AL as you can see, but RBI do not carry the greatest weight in MVP voting, even with the string of RBI-dominated awards in the AL over the past four years.

There is, as you can see, a significant difference in the order of MVP element importance in the two leagues. In the AL, that order is: SLG, RBI, TB, RC, OPS, HR. In the NL, the order is: SLG, RC, OPS, TB, RBI, HR. Perversely, doubles rank higher than OBP in the AL. OBP, which sabermetric types keep touting as the single most important stat, still isn't registering with the MVP voters: it ranks only sixth on the NL element list.

The MVP offensive element importance over the past ten years for both leagues is: SLG, RBI, RC, OPS, TB, HR, OBP, R, BB, BA, H, D, SB. Although RC still may not be particularly well-known amongst the writers, it is running a very strong third overall, and is ahead of RBI in the NL (as is also the case with OPS, another recent composite measure).

Possibly the most interesting breakout, and one that provides an explanation for all this odd voting behavior over the past four years, is one where we look at these numbers in two five-year groups: First, the NL:

Yr	Lg	BB	RBI	R	BA	TB	SLG	OBP	OPS	RC	D	HR	SB	H
89-93	N	13	14	9	5	15	23	12	20	20	0	15	3	5
94-98	N	6	16	10	8	16	17	10	14	14	3	14	4	6

Thanks in part to the Coors Field effect, most offensive categories have fallen off, with only RBI and TB making gains

WPA BULLPEN BOX—TEXAS RANGERS

	PI	WPA	P	PPPI
Starters	1034	-5.2	52.6	0.051
Relievers	631	5.0	34.2	0.054
Road	294	3.6	16.9	0.057
Home	337	1.4	17.3	0.051
Mar/Apr	88	2.1	4.3	0.049
May	127	1.5	7.0	0.055
June	110	0.9	6.3	0.057
July	88	-0.0	4.3	0.049
August	104	0.8	7.2	0.069
September	114	-0.2	5.2	0.046
Non S/H Sit.	482	0.9	19.3	0.040
S/H Sit.	149	4.2	14.9	0.100
Low Pressure	258	0.3	3.3	0.013
Med. Pressure	224	-1.6	12.6	0.056
High Pressure	149	6.3	18.3	0.123
Entered behind	318	0.6	8.4	0.027
Entered tied	63	-0.6	7.7	0.122
Entered ahead	250	5.0	18.1	0.072

Name	G	PI	WPA	P	PPPI	MI	ROB	T
Bailes S	46	63	.2	2.2	.034	14	25	2
Cadaret G	11	14	.0	.6	.041	3	7	1
Crabtree T	64	114	.8	5.5	.049	38	37	7
Fossas T	10	13	.2	.4	.034	3	7	0
Gunderson E	67	107	-.3	5.1	.048	29	42	7
Hernandez X	46	77	.9	5.5	.072	22	30	6
Levine A	30	73	-.2	2.2	.031	20	21	3
Patterson D	56	79	.7	4.6	.058	22	22	9
Pavlik R	5	16	.2	1.1	.068	4	4	1
Wetteland J	63	67	2.5	6.7	.100	4	8	4
Total		631	5.0	34.2	.054			

	I-------- Quality ----------I					I--- Pressure -------I			
	Dis.	Poor	Fair	Good	Her.	Lo	Med	Hi	
Bailes S	0	2	40	3	1	32	11	3	(2)
Cadaret G	0	3	7	1	0	6	5	0	(0)
Crabtree T	2	9	39	12	2	30	21	13	(9)
Gunderson E	2	7	44	14	0	32	26	9	(5)
Hernandez X	3	5	21	14	3	18	13	15	(11)
Levine A	0	6	20	4	0	16	10	4	(1)
Patterson D	3	6	28	18	1	21	24	11	(9)
Wetteland J	6	2	22	32	1	23	19	21	(16)
Others	0	1	13	4	1	10	5	4	(3)
TOTAL	16	41	234	102	9	188	134	80	(56)

	7th inning			8th inning			9th inning		
	0	+1	+2	0	+1	+2	0	+1	+2
Bailes S	0	0	0	1	1	1	0	0	0
Crabtree T	3	0	1	2	1	1	1	0	0
Gunderson E	1	2	2	2	0	0	0	0	0
Hernandez X	2	1	1	4	5	1	4	0	0
Levine A	1	0	0	0	0	0	0	0	0
Patterson D	1	0	0	3	1	2	0	0	0
Pavlik R	1	0	2	1	0	1	0	0	0
Wetteland J	0	0	0	0	0	0	2	16	12
Starters	11	9	11	4	4	10	0	0	0
TOTAL	20	12	17	17	12	16	7	16	12
Record	8-12	11-1	15-2	8-9	10-2	14-2	4-3	14-2	12-0

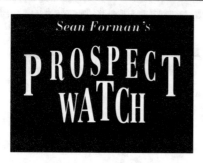

Sean Forman's

PROSPECT WATCH

NAME	AGE	POS	LEVEL	GR98	GR97	GR96	AVG
Ruben Mateo	20	OF	AA	82	76	62	77
Andy Barkett	23	1B	AAA	56	56	48	55
Cesar King	20	C	AA	47	67	53	55
Michael Zywica	22	OF	AA	65	46	32	53
Junior Spivey	23	2B	AA	51	-	-	51
Jason Conti	23	OF	AA	54	34	39	45
Kelly Dransfeldt	23	SS	AA	49	25	23	37

NAME	AGE	POS	LEVEL	GRADE
Carlos Pena	20	1B	Low A	72
Corey Wright	18	OF	Rookie	70
Shawn Gallagher	21	1B	High A	64
Juan Piniella	20	OF	High A	63
Craig Monroe	21	OF	High A	57
Danny Solano	19	SS	High A	56
Kelly Dransfeldt	23	SS	High A	54
Pedro Guerrero	18	2B	Rookie	52
Cody Nowlin	18	OF	Rookie	50
Jason Romano	19	2B	Low A	48

NAME	AGE	GS	S	C	T	W-L	ERA	K/H	LEVEL
Terry Clark	37	23	3.30	2.61	5.91	11-4	3.09	0.61	High
Ryan Glynn	23	25	3.52	3.36	6.88	10-6	3.44	0.79	High
Johathon Johnson	23	23	4.26	3.35	7.61	6-10	4.90	0.86	High
Corey Lee	23	25	3.00	4.68	7.68	9-9	4.51	1.26	High
Dan Smith	28	26	4.19	3.50	7.69	12-10	5.82	0.64	High
Matt Perisho	23	16	4.06	4.13	8.19	8-5	3.95	0.65	High
Dan Kolb	24	28	4.57	3.79	8.36	12-11	4.82	0.44	High
Jeff Granger	25	19	5.21	3.42	8.63	4-6	4.60	0.62	High
Brandon Knight	22	26	5.08	3.85	8.92	6-12	7.09	0.72	High
Doug Davis	22	27				11-7	3.24	1.34	Low

The Rangers tend to take a lot of grief about their farm system, but they have produced some good players: Juan Gonzalez, Ivan Rodriguez and Rusty Greer. Their pitching prospects haven't worked out quite as well, and it shows as their pitching staff is generally weak and mostly acquired by trade or free agency. Much of the Rangers' success has come from Latin signings and their top prospects Cesar King and Ruben Mateo were signed from Latin America as well.

Top Dog: Ruben Mateo
Mateo is well-known for his tools. He runs well, has a good arm and can hit for power and average. The Rangers turned down any and all trade offers for him and they appear set on using him in the not too distant future. His 1998 was nearly a carbon copy of his 1997 as he hit .309/.371/.522 while stealing 18 bases. He has 20-20 potential in the majors, and hasn't had any problem with strikeouts. I like this kid. He might be one of the top 10 prospects in all of baseball.

Up the Middle: Kelly Dransfeldt
Dransfeldt is one of those new breed shortstops who has pretty good power. He hit 27 home runs last year, eighteen of them for Charlotte of the Florida State League. Working against him though were the facts that he was repeating the league and that he was a 23-year-old playing in high-A ball. Once he was promoted at mid-season to the Texas League, his OPS dropped 220 points, and he wasn't nearly as impressive. Thus far, he only has those 245 at bats in the FSL that say he is a top prospect. The other 800 at bats say that he is a good power, low BA, low OBP middle infielder with some speed. Still 20-15 shortstops aren't falling out of trees, so I'm sure he'll get plenty of opportunity to prove me wrong. Comp: Scott Leius with pop.

Backstop: Cesar King
King is in an organization and at a position that isn't exactly conducive to career advancement. King is considered strong defensively and hit quite well in 1997. Last year, he struggled badly managing just a .222/.288/.313 line in AA. He has yet to hit for much power and his walk rates are essentially average, but as a good defensive catcher he won't have to hit a lot to have a long career. Just look at Joe Girardi. Comp: Jim Tatum.

Young 'un: Carlos Pena
Pena was the Rangers' number one pick in the 1998 draft. He was a collegiate first baseman and as such you want him to come in and hit a bunch. Pena obliged and hit .325/.385/.598 in low-A Savannah. Since he was a little late in signing, he managed just 144 at bats. He will probably end up in AA next year as the Rangers hope he can make the big leagues in a year or two. I think his bat will be big enough to get him to the majors, and he very well could move to the head of the Rangers' prospect class by this time next year.

On the Mound: Corey Lee
Lee is a hard-throwing lefthander. Lee was dominant at times allowing just 105 hits in 144 innings, but his control was atrocious as he walked 102 batters, nearly 6.3/9IP. Lee had the highest Power Precipice percentage in the high minors at 52%. He didn't pitch that many innings but with all the baserunners he faced 25 batters per start and I'm guessing he tossed a large number of pitches in those outings. Clearly, his control needs to improve before he can help out in the bigs, but I think he's got a shot.

among the top five elements. The Sosa-McGwire voting is, of course, more than an anomaly: it's more like what Churchill said about Russia.

Now, the AL:

Yr	Lg	BB	RBI	R	BA	TB	SLG	OBP	OPS	RC	D	HR	SB	H
89-93	A	2	8	0	2	12	14	7	12	13	5	6	5	4
94-98	A	5	22	10	3	12	18	5	8	9	8	14	0	2

Remember that the AL 89-93 totals are lower because Eckersley won the MVP in 1992. RBI have clearly shot into the foreground in the AL, though two other power categories—SLG and HR—are also on the rise.

Let's put the two leagues together in this formulation and see what we have:

Yr	Lg	BB	RBI	R	BA	TB	SLG	OBP	OPS	RC	D	HR	SB	H
89-93	MLB	15	22	9	7	27	37	19	32	33	5	21	8	9
94-98	MLB	11	38	20	11	28	35	15	22	23	11	28	4	8

Bingo. RBI have taken the lead in the last five years, at the expense of the four categories (SLG, RC, OPS, and TB) that it trailed in 1989-93. And now here's the explanation for why it's happened.

No, the BBWAA writers aren't stupid. But they are confused. The offensive explosion has made most of the available offensive numbers look out of whack, especially with respect to the previous five years, when there was a lot more separation in the statistics. The strong surge in two of the three triple crown stats (RBI and HR) shows us a crucial distinction in diagnosing what's going on. A key lesson in sabermetrics is that BA is an overrated stat, that OBP and SLG are more important in evaluating offensive performance. It's clear that the voters had absorbed that precept when you look at the 1989-93 results. They might have it backwards in the eyes of sabermetricians, who value OBP more, but they made BA a distant third in that element grouping prior to the offensive explosion taking hold.

Since then, I think their eyes are just glazing over at the numbers, and since they're not being handed park-adjusted data as a regular feature during the course of the season, they haven't got the frame of reference that they had when OBP and SLG showed more separation. The field is clogged with great hitters and great numbers, and so the writers are falling back on traditional stats and other contextual issues to pick their way through the minefield.

This isn't to condone their choices, but merely to explain why they have been happening over the past four years. I suspect that this phenomenon will subside along with the offensive explosion. Of course, if the explosion becomes a permanent feature of the landscape, then MVP voting is likely to remain as out of whack with sabermetric principles as it's become of late, especially in the AL.

It's also impossible to separate these trends from one other anomaly in the AL voting: the anti-Albert Belle trend. Make no mistake, Albert Belle was the best player in the AL in both 1995 and 1998, but his chances of winning an MVP award are nil. Just to emphasize the point, let's look at BBBA's Extrapolated Wins method for ranking offensive performance for the 1998 AL:

OVERALL RANKING (TXW), AL HITTERS 1998

Player	OXW	DXW	TXW
Belle A	8.29	0.64	8.93
Rodriguez A	5.97	1.89	7.86
Griffey K	6.40	1.44	7.84
Jeter D	5.10	2.66	7.76
Palmeiro R	6.61	0.77	7.38
Vaughn M	6.98	0.38	7.36
Rodriguez I	3.46	3.37	6.83
Martinez E	6.79	0.03	6.82
Williams B	5.83	0.95	6.78
Delgado C	6.16	0.39	6.55
Garciaparra N	5.10	1.42	6.52
Ramirez M	5.64	0.72	6.36
Salmon T	6.23	0.10	6.33
Gonzalez J	5.79	0.45	6.24
O'Neill P	4.86	1.29	6.15

That's right. Albert is the best, and by a not inconsiderable margin. Juan Gonzalez, the MVP winner, winds up at 14th on this list. Which is why you'll be reading some vintage ranting and raving by Brock

Hanke when you get to the player comments section.

It doesn't really get a lot better when we restrict the ranking to the offensive component of Extrapolated Wins, either. Gonzalez moves up the list, but he is still tenth:

OFFENSIVE RANKING (OXW), AL HITTERS 1998

Player	OXW
Belle A	8.29
Vaughn M	6.98
Martinez E	6.79
Palmeiro R	6.61
Griffey K	6.40
Salmon T	6.23
Delgado C	6.16
Rodriguez A	5.97
Williams B	5.83
Gonzalez J	5.79
Ramirez M	5.64
Offerman J	5.55
Giambi J	5.31
Thome J	5.29
Davis E	5.15

Albert Belle was the best hitter in the AL in 1998, and even factoring in his defensive position (far less demanding than Alex Rodriguez at SS, for example, or Juan's teammate, catcher Ivan Rodriguez), he's still the best player overall. But the AL voters will not give him the award, not even when faced with

TEAM BREAKOUT RANGERS 1998

Category	RS	RA	W	L	Pct.	Rk
4- RUNS ALLOWED/HOME	243	94	35	3	.921	3
4- RUNS ALLOWED	423	167	62	11	.849	2
CLOSE LOW-SCORING GAMES/HOME	18	10	5	1	.833	3
4- RUNS ALLOWED/ROAD	180	73	27	8	.771	5
5+ RUNS SCORED/ROAD	343	207	32	10	.762	8
5+ RUNS SCORED	771	519	70	24	.745	7
5+ RUNS SCORED/HOME	428	312	38	14	.731	9
RECORD IN CLOSE GAMES/HOME	189	171	21	9	.700	3
CLOSE SLUGFESTS/HOME	127	125	9	6	.600	5
LOW SCORING GAMES/HOME	34	34	8	6	.571	6
RECORD IN BLOWOUTS/ROAD	199	162	16	12	.571	6
RECORD IN CLOSE GAMES	323	311	35	28	.556	5
SLUGFESTS/ROAD	240	213	16	13	.552	6
RECORD IN LOW SCORING GAMES	68	62	17	14	.548	5
SEASON TOTALS	940	871	88	74	.543	4
LOW SCORING GAMES/ROAD	34	28	9	8	.529	5
RECORD IN SLUGFESTS	534	522	34	31	.523	4
RECORD IN BLOWOUTS	391	357	30	28	.517	7
CLOSE LOW SCORING GAMES/ROAD	19	18	6	6	.500	5
SLUGFESTS/HOME	294	309	18	18	.500	7
RECORD IN BLOWOUTS/HOME	192	195	14	16	.467	9
RECORD IN CLOSE GAMES/ROAD	134	140	14	19	.424	7
CLOSE SLUGFESTS/ROAD	56	58	3	5	.375	10
4- RUNS SCORED/HOME	74	156	10	19	.345	4
5+ RUNS ALLOWED/HOME	259	374	13	30	.302	5
5+ RUNS ALLOWED	517	704	26	63	.292	4
5+ RUNS ALLOWED/ROAD	258	330	13	33	.283	4
4- RUNS SCORED	169	352	18	50	.265	6
4- RUNS SCORED/ROAD	95	196	8	31	.205	8

impending natural disasters of Biblical proportions. And this, as much as anything, is skewing the results in the AL MVP voting.

And here's a look at how this distorts the offensive element rankings. Make Belle the 1995 and 1998 AL MVP, substitute his league rankings at the thirteen MVP offensive elements for Mo Vaughn's and Juan Gonzalez', and look at what the element importance list would look like for the AL in 1989-98 and for the last five years:

Yr	Lg	BB	RBI	R	BA	TB	SLG	OBP	OPS	RC	D	HR	SB	H
89-98	A	7	29	14	8	31	38	12	27	27	16	25	5	6
94-98	A	5	21	14	6	19	24	5	15	14	11	19	0	2
act 94-98	A	5	22	10	3	12	18	5	8	9	8	14	0	2

SLG for 1994-98, as in the previous five years, would be the pre-eminent offensive element in determining the MVP, and TB would move ahead of RBI for the ten-year period. Thus the AL voters would look a lot more reasonable were it not for their bias against Belle.

Finally, let's look at how these 10-year AL totals with two Belle MVPs would compare to the actual results in the National League from 1989-98:

Yr	Lg	BB	RBI	R	BA	TB	SLG	OBP	OPS	RC	D	HR	SB	H
89-98	A	7	29	14	8	31	38	12	27	27	16	25	5	6
89-98	N	19	30	19	13	31	40	22	34	34	3	29	7	11

The top five elements in the AL would be: SLG, TB, RBI, OPS, RC. The top five elements in the NL would be: SLG, OPS, RC, TB, RBI. In both cases, it'd be very clear that SLG, not RBI, equals MVP.

And you Ranger fans thought that this essay was gonna be about Juan Gonzalez, didn't you? Just as Juan was the "surrogate" MVP winner in 1998, he was the decoy here. The big question in the AL this year is: will Albert get mad enough to hit 60 HRs and still not get the MVP award? As we like to say in these situations: stay tuned.

| | | | | | | | Park Adjusted Statistics | | | | | | | | | Adj | Raw | | | |
Name	AB	R	H	D	T	HR	RBI	BB	SO	SB	CS	BA	OBP	SLG	XR	XR/27	XR/27	OXW	DXW	TXW
Alicea L	257	48	68	14	3	6	32	39	41	4	3	.265	.367	.411	42	5.69	5.94	1.53	0.11	1.64
Cedeno D	141	18	36	9	1	2	20	10	33	2	1	.253	.303	.369	15	3.58	3.81	0.00	-0.04	-0.04
Clark W	551	92	162	36	1	23	96	75	100	1	0	.294	.378	.491	99	6.51	6.80	4.25	0.24	4.49
Clayton R	186	28	51	11	1	5	23	13	33	5	5	.275	.322	.424	24	4.23	4.54	0.33	1.39	1.72
Elster K	295	31	66	9	1	8	35	35	68	0	2	.223	.307	.340	32	3.52	3.72	-0.03	0.67	0.64
Gonzalez J	603	104	186	45	2	46	149	49	129	2	1	.308	.360	.618	123	7.38	7.66	5.79	0.45	6.24
Goodwin T	518	96	146	12	3	2	31	75	93	39	22	.281	.373	.327	71	4.74	4.99	1.76	1.04	2.80
Greer R	594	99	176	28	4	16	103	84	96	2	4	.296	.382	.440	99	5.99	6.22	3.86	0.58	4.44
Haselman B	105	10	32	5	0	6	16	3	17	0	0	.305	.319	.533	17	6.09	6.35	0.66	0.21	0.87
Kelly R	257	45	80	6	3	16	44	8	48	0	3	.313	.340	.546	44	6.39	6.78	1.78	0.40	2.18
McLemore M	456	74	109	13	1	5	50	94	66	12	4	.239	.369	.306	60	4.28	4.36	1.05	0.17	1.22
Rodriguez I	578	83	180	37	4	22	86	33	91	9	0	.312	.351	.502	92	5.96	6.21	3.46	3.37	6.83
Simms M	185	33	53	9	0	16	44	25	48	0	1	.286	.376	.602	40	7.78	8.00	2.02	0.15	2.17
Stevens L	343	48	87	15	4	21	55	32	96	0	2	.254	.317	.499	52	5.35	5.60	1.61	0.15	1.76
Tatis F	330	38	85	16	2	3	30	12	68	6	2	.258	.293	.343	29	3.04	3.37	-0.49	0.22	-0.27
Zeile T	179	25	45	13	1	6	27	29	33	1	0	.252	.356	.438	30	5.74	5.90	1.08	-0.34	0.74
TEX	5645	882	1575	285	29	205	849	622	1078	83	52	.279	.351	.449	875	5.43	5.67	28.66	8.77	37.43

Pitcher	S	C	T	SS	ES	IC	HH	PP	TJ	S12	S35	S67	C1	C23	C45	C67	QWP
Burkett	4.53	2.88	7.41	44%	19%	38%	47%	0%	13%	19%	34%	47%	25%	41%	31%	3%	.486
D Oliver	5.32	3.74	9.05	16%	11%	21%	58%	0%	11%	11%	32%	58%	16%	21%	53%	11%	.330
Gunderson	5.00	5.00	10.00	0%	0%	0%	0%	0%	0%	0%	100%	0%	0%	0%	100%	0%	.204
Helling	3.97	3.21	7.18	45%	18%	36%	27%	3%	6%	27%	45%	27%	21%	42%	30%	6%	.526
Johnson	5.00	7.00	12.00	0%	0%	0%	0%	0%	0%	0%	100%	0%	0%	0%	0%	100%	.024
Loaiza	4.93	3.36	8.29	29%	14%	36%	57%	0%	7%	21%	21%	57%	7%	57%	29%	7%	.422
Perisho	6.50	7.00	13.50	0%	0%	0%	100%	0%	0%	0%	0%	100%	0%	0%	0%	100%	.011
Sele	4.42	3.55	7.97	39%	15%	36%	45%	3%	6%	21%	33%	45%	12%	42%	36%	9%	.432
Stottlemyre	4.50	3.90	8.40	30%	10%	30%	30%	0%	10%	20%	50%	30%	20%	10%	50%	20%	.389
Van Poppel	5.25	4.25	9.50	25%	25%	25%	75%	0%	0%	25%	0%	75%	0%	50%	25%	25%	.307
Witt	5.08	4.08	9.15	31%	8%	8%	46%	0%	0%	8%	46%	46%	0%	23%	69%	8%	.313
TEX	**4.61**	**3.51**	**8.12**	**35%**	**15%**	**31%**	**44%**	**1%**	**7%**	**19%**	**36%**	**44%**	**15%**	**36%**	**38%**	**10%**	**.425**

AMERICAN LEAGUE WEST

ANAHEIM ANGELS

TOM AUSTIN

A TALE OF TWO BALLCLUBS

I promise not to rag on Disney for the entire article this time. For better or worse, Disney is in charge of the team now, and my bitching about it would be a lot less entertaining than watching "Aladdin" for the fourteenth time..

Another classic Angels season, wasn't it? They surprised many by being pretty good, and just when the bandwagon got to standing-room only, they blew a tire in classic Angel fashion. A 9-15 September doesn't begin to tell the story of those three horrific losses to the Rangers. It reminded me of a high school team making the playoffs after nine losing seasons in a row facing—and getting mauled by—the team that goes 38-2 every year by recruiting from half the state.

It didn't have to be that way. The Rangers put their jocks on one, er, leg at a time, just like everyone else, and 88 wins does not a juggernaut make. The Rangers did, however, make big moves midseason, picking up Zeile, Clayton, and Stottlemyre, while the Disney boys opened the checkbook for—Jeff Juden? I have to think that the Matterhorn of cash the Angels threw at Mo Vaughn during the off-season was prompted in part by the audible growling emanating from a million suburban TV rooms.

The September Swoon was nothing new for this team. A study I did for the Giants essay has proven within a shadow of a doubt (soon to be a Disney remake) that the Angels have been the most heartbreaking team to follow in the American League in the last forty years, trailing only the Montreal Expos for the major league honor. If you factor in the Angels' extra eight years of existence, there has been greater total heartbreak in Orange County (235 "heartbreak points") than in Quebec (205).

Within the trove of data piled up for that essay was another measure of a team's tease tendency, the Close But No Cigar Index (CBNCI). This is determined by taking the number of "Hurts So Good" finishes (where, to review, a team misses the postseason by five or fewer games) and subtracting a weighted average of successful finishes, to wit: $CBNCI = (HSG-WWRY-0.5FWON-0.2ITATI)$.

1	**WWRY:**	We Will Rock You (wins it all)
2	**SCAYSF:**	So Close and Yet So Far (wins pennant, loses series)
3	**ITATI:**	Is That All There Is? (makes postseason, loses)
4	**HSG:**	Hurts So Good (just misses postseason)
5	**OSFTSB:**	One Step Forward, Two Steps back (muddles around .500)
6	**LS:**	Love Stinks (loses at least 90 games)
7	**DNE:**	Did Not Exist (no penalty yet devised)

The usual suspects are at the top of the leader boards, of course:

CLOSE BUT NO CIGAR INDEX, 1958-98

Team	1	2	3	4	5	6	7	CBNCI
Montreal	0	0	1	6	17	6	11	5.85
San Francisco	0	2	3	7	22	7	0	5.55
Anaheim	0	0	3	5	20	10	3	4.55
Milwaukee	0	1	0	3	20	9	8	2.50
New York Mets	2	1	1	5	15	16	1	2.35
Kansas City	1	1	3	4	17	4	11	2.05
Boston	0	3	4	4	27	3	0	1.90
Chicago Cubs	0	0	3	2	26	10	0	1.55
Toronto	2	0	3	4	7	6	19	1.55

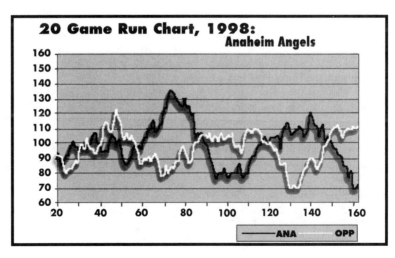

20 Game Run Chart, 1998:
Anaheim Angels

— ANA   OPP

QMAX PRESENTS: "BAD" PITCHERS

HE'S ALWAYS BEEN WELL-LIKED

Everyone likes Jim Abbott. I like Jim Abbott. He overcomes adversity, shows up in the Show without a day in the minors, and has killer stuff. The post-1986 Angels and their fans needed something to cheer for, and Jimmy was the ticket. This is why Angel fans and front office brass were so happy when he donned the Halo hat again midway through the tragic 1995 season. This human-interest angle also has to be why he got 23 chances in 1996 to try to recover what was lost, suddenly and mysteriously, in the 1996 off-season.

Gentleman Jim started the season with a rough April six start, but four of his first seven starts looked like the Abbott of old. After that, the deluge; the left-hander on the mound thereafter looked more like Bud "who's on first" Abbott than a major-league starter. The control problems hinted at in the April 21 and May 12 starts (pegging the meter in the 7c QMAX scale) came home to roost and settled in on the couch

for a permanent stay. Abbott's 5-game C running average popped up above 5, a (lack of) command level only tolerated in the likes of Nolan Ryan and other unhittable wonders. Unfortunately, sports fans, Lord Jim was anything but unhittable, as his QMAX "stuff" average was also above 5; on June 15, Abbot's QMAX "T" score was above eleven, or almost three times as high as, say, vintage Greg Maddux.

At this point in the season, a pitcher with a 1-6, 5.57 record would be grabbing pine, even on a losing team such as the 1996 Angels. Perhaps dazed a little by memories of The Way He Was only recently, skipper Marcel Lachemann kept running him out there to get pounded. July and August saw Abbott struggle manfully but vainly to get either his stuff or control averages below the QMAX "4" level, and his won-lost record (more precisely, his "lost" record) stood at 1-15 with an 8.38 ERA. Jim finally got his "com-

JIM ABBOTT/ CAL 1996							
	1	2	3	4	5	6	7	S
1								0
2			1					2
3			2			2		4
4	2					1		3
5			1	2		1		4
6		1	2	1	1	1		6
7			1	1	1	1		4
C	2	1	7	5	2	1	5	23

mand" running average below 4 on his last start of the season, mainly by tossing meatballs across the heart of the plate for hitters to feast on (his QMAX "stuff" running total was between 5.50 and 6 throughout September.)

Jim's final total of 2-18, 7.48 was bad enough, finally, for the Angels to give up on him. Happily, we hope, Jim has adjusted to his loss of stuff (I wonder, guiltily, if perhaps his lack of a right hand placed unusual stress on his left arm during delivery and contributed to his sudden loss of stuff) and showed up in the White Sox rotation at the end of last year, and he pitched well enough to get a shot at the rotation next year. I am, hopefully, already filling in his name on my Comeback Player of the year ballot. Because you just gotta root for the guy.

–Tom Austin

All of the teams here have earned to right to cry, although the Mets, the Royals and the Blue Jays have at least given their fans the brass ring once or twice. Not included in this is the incredibly painful way the Angels have managed to miss the boat: In 1982, 1986, 1995, and 1998, the Angels could reasonably be said to "have it in the bag" being either one strike, one game, or one month of .500 baseball away from reaching the goal, and in all cases they fell short.

Clearly the Angel brass looked at this history, particularly last fall, and saw "lack of leadership" writ large on the Clubhouse wall. For this, even more than for his big bat (wags might be tempted here to spell "bat" with a "u" and an extra "t", but I'll resist halfheartedly), the Disney coffers were sprung loose, and $80 million of "Little Mermaid" profits rained down on the Sergeant, Mighty Mo Vaughn. All concerned seem to think it's a good move, and it is indeed hard to argue with the numbers Mo has put up over the last five years: .319, 37 HR, 112 RBI, and a .986 OPS. This might be a little too much to

expect over the life of Mo's contract, though: Mo's road numbers over the last five years average out a little smaller: .301, 35 homers, 111 RBI, .929 OPS. That's still pretty good: he'll lose about seven doubles, two homers, and three singles a year from not having the Monster to shoot at.

But wait, there's more: Mo is 31 and livin' large (and I'm not talking about his nightlife.) He's already a defensive liability, and big boys like him tend to decline pretty rapidly relative to other major leaguers. I think he's still post 30+ homers and probably drive in 100 (assuming the offensive tone of the era holds a few more years), but he'll likely miss .300 more often than not, and a plus 1.000 OPS would surprise the hell out of me. (That being said, there are other takes on this, and you'll find one in Tom Hull's article on "Percentiles: Past, Present and Future" which paints a somewhat rosier depiction of this deal than what issues from my ochre-tinged palette.)

But I digress, or rather get ahead of myself, talking about Mo and next year. What of last year's club? Was the September collapse random, or was there a cause? While I certainly would hesitate before jumping to the typical "choke" conclusions, there is some weird numerology at work here.

There's the aforementioned history of heartbreak. There is Terry Collins' bizarre managerial record; his clubs have finished second for umpteen years in a row. Now, second place is a queer place to get stuck—neither fish nor fowl. (And we should note that Terry has always managed a club sans identification with beasties and birdies as well, though he's made a clean sweep of the available aerial imagery: Astros and Angels. Possibly a switch in media might be advised. Perhaps a sea voyage: Pirates or Mariners. Or possibly some skirt-chasing: Phillies or Twins. Terry needs a change of pace about as much as I need to wrap up this meta-digression.)

Second place can be the heavy favorite that fell apart due to complacence and internal dissension, or it can be the scrappy bunch of no-names who defy the low expectations of the nattering nabobs of negativism and soar almost, but not quite, to the clouds of the postseason. Terry's clubs look like that latter on first glance, but the AL West and the NL Central have not been the toughest of divisions, and Terry's Astros and Angels keep losing teams that themselves do not win even 91 games, let alone 100. And while we're on the subject of twos and twins (oh, no, you're saying, here he goes again!!), there is the split personality manifested by the Angels' pitching staff. Let's take a look at some numbers.

First, here are the Angels of April, June, and August:

	G	IP	H	W	L	ERA	Qs	Qc	Qt	QWP
March/April	26	233	245	15	11	4.08	4.38	3.15	7.54	.485
June	28	249	247	22	6	3.75	3.93	3.29	7.21	.526
August	30	270	259	18	12	4.17	4.10	3.30	7.40	.504
Total	84	752	751	55	29	4.00	4.14	3.25	7.38	.505

Not bad. In seasonal notation, 18-10, 4.00 would be a great record for most pitchers, let alone a whole staff. But take a look at the other three months:

	G	IP	H	W	L	ERA	Qs	Qc	Qt	QWP
May	27	238	266	12	15	5.35	4.56	4.26	8.81	.379
July	27	241	239	9	18	4.78	4.41	4.15	8.56	.404
Sept/Oct	24	211	225	9	15	4.90	4.75	4.46	9.21	.331
Total	78	690	730	30	48	5.01	4.57	4.29	8.86	.371

Urgh. 10-16 5.01. What caused the Angel pitchers to be good in the odd months of the season, and horrific in the even ones? How did the Angels go 55-29 (that's .655 or +.150) with a QWP of only .505 in the Jekyll months and only .385 in the Hyde months with a QWP of .371 (+.014)? The Angels averaged 5 runs a game (with a team OPS of .789) in the good months, and only 4 in the bad months (team OPS .708). So the whole team seemed to rise and fall on a monthly cycle, horrible following good following lousy following spectacular.

If I had to grope for an explanation (and I do), I'd cheat and look for a psychological one. Terry Collins is an intense rah-rah guy, and the players (so far) seem to respond to it.

WPA BULLPEN BOX—ANAHEIM ANGELS

	PI	WPA	P	PPPI
Starters	1015	-2.5	51.8	0.051
Relievers	670	4.1	41.8	0.062
Road	347	3.2	23.0	0.066
Home	323	0.9	18.9	0.058
Mar/Apr	92	1.1	4.7	0.051
May	124	-0.7	6.5	0.052
June	92	1.8	6.0	0.065
July	123	0.5	6.6	0.054
August	118	2.0	9.5	0.081
September	121	-0.5	8.5	0.070
Non S/H Sit.	495	-0.4	22.9	0.046
S/H Sit.	175	4.5	18.9	0.108
Low Pressure	263	-0.7	3.1	0.012
Med. Pressure	209	-0.5	14.2	0.068
High Pressure	198	5.3	24.5	0.124
Entered behind	303	0.3	7.8	0.026
Entered tied	109	-1.1	12.8	0.117
Entered ahead	258	4.9	21.2	0.082

Name	G	PI	WPA	P	PPPI	MI	ROB	T
Cadaret G	39	61	-1.3	2.7	.044	13	27	8
Delucia R	61	100	1.1	6.7	.066	28	27	13
Fetters M	12	17	-.9	1.0	.058	3	6	2
Harris P	49	87	1.6	4.9	.056	27	32	3
Hasegawa S	61	122	1.8	7.2	.059	37	34	12
Holtz M	53	62	-.2	4.5	.073	9	32	8
James M	11	18	-.2	.8	.041	5	3	2
Olivares O	11	27	.2	1.1	.039	8	4	3
Percival T	67	77	1.5	8.2	.107	10	16	8
Watson A	14	28	.0	.8	.028	8	7	1
Wilson T	15	16	-.3	1.7	.106	1	8	1
Total		670	4.1	41.8	.062			

	I-------- Quality ----------I					I--- Pressure -------I		
	Dis.	Poor	Fair	Good	Her.	Lo	Med	Hi	
Cadaret G	3	9	22	5	0	17	19	3	(2)
Delucia R	5	6	28	19	3	29	14	18	(14)
Fetters M	2	3	5	2	0	6	4	2	(0)
Harris P	0	5	32	10	2	25	11	13	(9)
Hasegawa S	3	7	28	19	4	21	19	21	(14)
Holtz M	1	14	25	13	0	23	23	7	(2)
James M	0	2	8	1	0	6	3	2	(0)
Olivares O	0	1	8	1	1	7	2	2	(1)
Percival T	9	2	14	38	4	15	31	21	(16)
Watson A	0	3	9	2	0	9	3	2	(1)
Wilson T	0	4	8	3	0	4	6	5	(2)
Others	1	2	12	5	2	9	7	6	(4)
TOTAL	24	58	199	118	16	171	142	102	(65)

	7th inning			8th inning			9th inning		
	0	+1	+2	0	+1	+2	0	+1	+2
Cadaret G	1	0	0	0	1	0	1	0	0
Delucia R	0	3	1	4	2	3	6	2	0
Dickson J	2	1	0	2	0	0	0	0	0
Fetters M	0	0	0	0	0	1	1	0	0
Harris P	2	2	1	2	3	6	0	0	1
Hasegawa S	0	1	5	4	1	5	3	0	1
Holtz M	1	0	0	1	1	1	2	1	1
Olivares O	1	1	0	0	0	0	0	0	0
Percival T	0	0	0	0	0	1	4	13	21
Washburn J	1	0	0	0	0	0	0	0	0
Wilson T	0	0	0	0	2	1	0	0	0
Starters	11	14	10	5	7	4	1	0	1
TOTAL	19	22	17	18	18	22	18	16	25
Record	6-13	15-7	13-4	8-10	12-6	20-2	5-13	14-2	24-1

Sean Forman's

PROSPECT WATCH

NAME	AGE	POS	LEVEL	GR98	GR97	GR96	AVG
Troy Glaus	21	3B	AAA	100	-	-	100
Keith Luuloa	23	2B	AAA	64	49	38	55
Norm Hutchins	22	OF	AAA	59	46	26	49
Ben Molina	23	C	AAA	51	45	42	48
Justin Baughman	23	SS	AAA	64	31	34	48
Jason Herrick	24	OF	AAA	46	45	40	45
Trent Durrington	22	2B	AA	34	43	67	43
Matt Curtis	23	DH	AA	28	54	45	40

NAME	AGE	POS	LEVEL	GRADE
Michael Colangelo	21	OF	High A	68
Jason Dewey	21	C	High A	59
Jose Santos	20	DH	Low A	55
Elpidio Guzman	19	OF	Rookie	53
Eric Gillespie	23	3B	High A	48
Jeff Guiel	24	OF	High A	46

NAME	AGE	GS	S	C	T	W-L	ERA	K/H	LEVEL
Rob Bonanno	27	17	4.47	2.35	6.82	7-7	4.49	0.47	High
Rich Robertson	29	27	3.67	3.33	7.00	11-12	3.81	0.72	High
Trevor Wilson	32	21	3.76	3.38	7.14	5-9	3.62	0.72	High
Scott Schoeneweis	24	27	4.07	3.11	7.19	11-8	4.50	0.71	High
Lou Pote	26	19	4.95	2.74	7.68	6-8	5.31	0.60	High
Matt Wise	22	27	4.74	2.96	7.70	9-10	5.42	0.67	High
Matt Beaumont	25	17	3.94	3.94	7.88	7-9	3.90	0.88	High
Brian Cooper	23	24	5.08	3.42	8.50	8-9	7.13	0.66	High

The Angels have quite a bit of home team talent on the big league squad. All four of the outfielders came up through the system, along with shortstop Gary DiSarcina. Not many teams can boast five homegrown starters. That number will likely remain constant as Troy Glaus will be the man at third and one of the outfielders will likely depart. If Todd Greene could ever get healthy he would be another one.

TOP DOG: Troy Glaus
Glaus absolutely ripped up the minors the half season he was there. When a player makes it to the majors in his first professional season like Glaus and Drew did, it is usually a pretty good indicator of future stardom. Glaus spent 50 games in Midland (Texas League) batting .309/.430/.691. Then he was promoted to the Pacific Coast League for 59 games and hit .306/.374/.598 for the Vancouver Canadians. Glaus is considered a good defensive player, and he actually played some shortstop in college, though at 6-5 and 225 pounds it's unlikely the Angels will play him there. He struggled in his 48 game call-up, but I expect him to hit the ground running this year. If he'd seen 25 fewer at bats he would be my hands down favorite for Rookie of the Year.

HANDY MAN: Norm Hutchins
The Angels can't stop drooling over Hutchins' tools and he finally repaid that adoration with a pretty good season. He managed to hit .312/.341/.490 in the Texas League, while stealing 32 bases in 42 attempts. He's a definite center fielder, and if he can keep this up he will be a pretty valuable one. I have been skeptical of his future potential for a couple of reasons. First, he's had his two good years in very good hitters' parks. Second, he has zero plate discipline. He has drawn 39 walks and struck out 240 times in the last two years. I have a feeling he'll be eaten alive in higher levels, but I've been wrong before.

BACKSTOP: Ben Molina
Getting Molina some positive publicity is one of my new pet projects. This guy has bounced around the Angels organization quite a bit the last four years, usually to replace Todd Greene whenever he got injured. He's logged time with eight teams in four seasons, which leads me to believe that the Angels aren't all that serious about him as a prospect, despite some pretty good numbers. He is an extreme contact hitter, who has tallied just 102 walks and 97 strikeouts in 1441 pro at bats. Despite that he's not really a slap hitter. He has slugged over .500 the last few years. His MLE this year was .280/.304/.368, which isn't so hot, but I think he could become a good cheap backup in the majors. Comp: Greg Colbrunn.

YOUNG 'UN: Jason Dewey
Dewey is another decent catcher prospect. He has pretty good power, slugging over .500 each of the last two years. His patience is all right and he managed a .394 OBP. He does have some trouble making contact as he struck out 118 times in just 391 at bats. Lake Elsinore is a pretty good hitters' park, so you always have to take those numbers with a grain of salt, but still, he's young enough that he can still improve with the bat and behind the plate. Check him out in Midland around June next year.

ON THE MOUND: Rob Bonanno
Bonanno is a Tommy John (35%) pitcher if there ever was one. He is pretty much the definitive crafty soft-tosser. He threw 114 innings and struck out just 62, but walked only 21 (1.65 BB/9). He is prone to the long ball, which is tough in the Pacific Coast League. Still, he has a career ERA of 4.07 and the Angels' affiliates play in some big-time hitters' parks.

However, the "win one for the gipper" stuff can backfire if players hear it too much. Could it be that the team got so fired up in April, June and August that they just went flat the following months? Adrenaline seems a good explanation for the way the Angels played in the good months (over their collective heads); and tired, aching, and sugar-crashed pretty well describes the other months. Being manic can be very productive, but those depressive periods can be murder.

Now it's time to talk about next year. The Angel/Disney brass clearly believes that the talent base is there to win, if a couple of high-dollar superstars can be thrown into the mix. They also seem to believe that more clubhouse leadership (in the form of Vaughn) will flatten out the mood swings. I'm a little dubious. It's more likely that the mood swings are the result of too much leadership, too many "blood, sweat and tears" speeches from Collins. Of course, I'm just guessing here. However, judging from the local press, it would seem that Vaughn's "drill sergeant" persona was a big factor in the Angels' signing him, and that spells Collins to me again.

All right, let's talk about Vaughn's "leadership" Clearly, he was the big man in Boston, at least on the field. And he did speak out about the directions he thought the team should or should not go in. This last let to very public friction with Dan Duquette, and Mo has emerged as the public relations winner of that contest. (Though winning a PR contest with Dan Duquette seems about as hard as beating the 1906 "Hitless Wonder" White Sox in Home Run Derby). Still, I don't quite get it.

How does Vaughn come out smelling like a rose for doing things not that different from , say, Barry Bonds or (lately) Jerry Rice? All of them are essentially bitching about the management of their team in public, and Mo gets the cloak of leadership while the other two (to name the first two I could think of) get called all sorts of "crybaby" names and worse. To my relief, it's not a race issue. Seems to me that Mo has figured out the local press in a way that Bonds can't and Rice has forgotten how to.

Where this pops up for me is imagining Mo doing the same thing in Anaheim. If the team makes personnel moves he doesn't agree to and he pops off about it, how is that going to play in the Orange County Register? How are Michael's minions (and when it comes to control-freakiness, Disney makes the Marquis De Sade look like Leo Buscaglia) going to react when their management of the Baseball Division, Entertainment Group is questioned in the local papers? I think Mo will ride it out - as long as he's hitting .310 with 40 homers. If he falls off to .260 with 18 homers, he turns into a pumpkin faster than you can say "Cecil Fielder."

BUT THEN AGAIN. . .

. . .you said you weren't going to rag on Disney, Tom. But who can blame you? The Mo Vaughn signing adds a big bat to the Angels' lineup, but it doesn't stop the bleeding in the bottom part of their lineup. The #2, #7, #8, and #9 slots of the Halo batting order were in the bottom third of the AL in terms of OPS last year, and the addition of Mo doesn't address that situation.

Just so you know, here are the number of lineup slots in the bottom third of the league (as measured by OPS) for the AL teams in 1998:

6	Tampa Bay;
5	Detroit, Minnesota, and Oakland;
4	Anaheim and Kansas City;
3	Cleveland, Seattle and Toronto;
2	Baltimore, Chicago, and Texas;
1	Boston and New York.

For the Halos, it's second base, shortstop, catcher, and third base that dragged down their offense last year, and while the hope is that Troy Glaus will turn it on in his next exposure to big league pitching, signing Mo really takes the place of Cecil Fielder in the Angel lineup. That's a big upgrade, but it doesn't provide any synergy in the form of a longer potential sequence. What kept the Angels earthbound in 1998

was, as always, a combination of ingredients, but these numbers stand out as ones that can stop things in their tracks:

AB	R	H	D	T	HR	RBI	BB	SO	BA	OBP	SLG	OPS
590	61	118	14	3	9	59	34	125	.200	.242	.280	.522

That's what the Angels' #8 slot coughed up in the form of offense in 1998. Disney veterans may find this reminiscent of one of their early forays into high-tech filmmaking, a commercial bomb known as "The Black Hole."

This was the 126th rated lineup slot in the American League last year. How many lineup slots are there in the American League. You guessed it: 126. This was a lineup slot that had it all: no BA, no OBP, no SLG. It scored 61 runs by virtue of the fact that Terry Collins led off Darin Erstad for much of the year, who front-loaded the Angels' offense spectacularly well (their leadoff slot was the best #1 BOP in the AL, and ranked 14th overall in the league).

But—then Terry put a weak #2 hitter into the mix between Erstad and Jim Edmonds, and diluted his offense. The #2 slot, as noted above, was one of the four Angel BOPs that ranked in the bottom third of the league. Only four of 14 #2 slots fell this low. The Angels were just sub-par enough in the

TEAM BREAKOUT ANGELS 1998						
Category	RS	RA	W	L	Pct.	Rk
CLOSE LOW-SCORING GAMES/HOME	31	15	11	0	1.000	1
4- RUNS ALLOWED/HOME	192	85	35	4	.897	4
4- RUNS ALLOWED	370	172	61	13	.824	3
5+ RUNS SCORED/ROAD	336	213	36	10	.783	5
5+ RUNS SCORED	583	363	62	18	.775	5
5+ RUNS SCORED/HOME	247	150	26	8	.765	6
LOW SCORING GAMES/HOME	54	39	16	5	.762	3
4- RUNS ALLOWED/ROAD	178	87	26	9	.743	6
RECORD IN LOW SCORING GAMES	88	69	24	10	.706	2
RECORD IN CLOSE GAMES/HOME	162	145	24	12	.667	4
CLOSE LOW SCORING GAMES/ROAD	28	24	7	4	.636	1
LOW SCORING GAMES/ROAD	34	30	8	5	.615	1
RECORD IN CLOSE GAMES	354	329	46	31	.597	2
CLOSE SLUGFESTS/ROAD	83	78	7	5	.583	5
SLUGFESTS/ROAD	212	183	16	12	.571	3
RECORD IN SLUGFESTS	356	308	26	20	.565	3
SLUGFESTS/HOME	144	125	10	8	.556	4
RECORD IN BLOWOUTS/ROAD	143	119	12	10	.545	7
RECORD IN CLOSE GAMES/ROAD	192	184	22	19	.537	3
SEASON TOTALS	787	783	85	77	.525	6
CLOSE SLUGFESTS/HOME	35	35	2	2	.500	6
RECORD IN BLOWOUTS	291	288	26	26	.500	8
RECORD IN BLOWOUTS/HOME	148	169	14	16	.467	8
5+ RUNS ALLOWED/ROAD	246	303	17	29	.370	1
4- RUNS SCORED/HOME	116	243	16	31	.340	5
4- RUNS SCORED	204	420	23	59	.280	4
5+ RUNS ALLOWED	417	611	24	64	.273	6
4- RUNS SCORED/ROAD	88	177	7	28	.200	9
5+ RUNS ALLOWED/HOME	171	308	7	35	.167	11

#2 slot to throw off their offense; Collins juggled the lineup so much that only the #1 and #4 slots wound up with better than an .800 OPS.

Here is the breakdown of AL lineup slots with an .800 OPS or higher in 1998:

6	New York;
5	Seattle and Texas;
4	Cleveland and Toronto;
3	Baltimore, Boston, Detroit, and Oakland;
2	Anaheim and Chicago;
1	Kansas City and Tampa Bay;
0	Minnesota.

The Angels should get to three such slots in 1999, with Vaughn, Salmon, and Erstad in place all year, and possibly four, if they don't trade Jim Edmonds, a long-whispered-about roster move which is about to attain permanent rumor status. Terry would be advised to bat these guys in order (Erstad, Edmonds, Vaughn, Salmon) and live off what these four give him.

More likely, though, he'll try to put someone into the #2 hole again, giving up outs when he could maximize his offense. Garret Anderson, a barely above-average hitter, might turn into an RBI machine in the #5 slot with the Big Four in front of him, but that's kind of like batting Willie McGee #5, isn't it? (Now go see how many RBI Willie McGee had in 1987, when he batted #5 for the Cardinals.) Rubbing shoulders with greatness doesn't rub off, but it gives the illusion of quality: if Garret Anderson drove in 120 runs for the Angels in 1999, they could then trade him for a lot more than they can now, and possibly beat the jinx Tom Austin has surveyed above. For Orange County troglodytes everywhere, that's a consummation devoutly to be wished. <DM>

Name	AB	R	H	D	T	HR	RBI	BB	SO	SB	CS	BA	OBP	SLG	XR	Adj XR/27	Raw XR/27	OXW	DXW	TXW
Anderson G	622	64	187	42	7	16	81	29	79	8	3	.300	.331	.467	88	5.19	4.96	2.63	1.15	3.78
Baughman J	196	25	51	9	1	1	20	6	35	10	4	.259	.280	.332	18	3.07	2.96	-0.31	0.17	-0.14
Bolick F	45	3	7	2	0	1	2	11	8	0	0	.160	.324	.272	5	3.39	3.30	-0.01	-0.01	-0.02
Disarcina G	551	76	160	40	3	3	58	21	50	11	7	.291	.325	.391	65	4.15	4.02	0.88	2.48	3.36
Edmonds J	599	118	189	44	1	27	94	57	112	7	5	.315	.375	.525	105	6.54	6.18	4.57	1.35	5.92
Erstad D	537	87	163	40	3	21	85	43	76	20	6	.304	.361	.507	96	6.71	6.30	4.30	0.57	4.87
Fielder C	381	49	95	17	1	18	70	52	96	0	1	.248	.341	.442	55	4.86	4.56	1.41	0.27	1.68
Glaus T	165	20	37	9	0	1	24	15	50	1	0	.222	.284	.297	14	2.89	2.78	-0.31	0.03	-0.28
Greene T	71	3	18	4	0	1	7	2	20	0	0	.257	.278	.356	7	3.45	3.35	-0.02	-0.03	-0.05
Hollins D	363	62	91	17	2	12	40	44	67	11	3	.249	.340	.404	53	5.04	4.78	1.52	-0.05	1.47
Jefferies G	72	7	25	6	0	1	10	0	5	1	0	.350	.350	.476	10	5.58	5.47	0.35	-0.08	0.27
Martin N	195	20	42	2	0	1	13	6	29	3	1	.217	.238	.243	8	1.35	1.31	-1.36	0.54	-0.82
Mashore D	98	13	24	6	0	2	11	9	22	1	0	.240	.323	.365	11	3.89	3.75	0.10	0.06	0.16
Nevin P	237	28	55	8	1	9	28	17	66	0	0	.234	.296	.386	27	3.88	3.65	0.20	0.42	0.62
Palmeiro O	165	29	54	7	2	0	22	20	11	5	4	.325	.398	.394	25	5.51	5.36	0.89	0.30	1.19
Pritchett C	80	12	23	2	1	2	8	4	16	2	0	.291	.325	.416	10	4.46	4.37	0.19	0.01	0.20
Salmon T	463	87	144	29	1	29	91	90	98	0	1	.310	.418	.562	109	8.80	8.26	6.23	0.10	6.33
Shipley C	147	18	38	7	1	2	17	5	22	0	4	.261	.307	.364	15	3.33	3.24	-0.11	0.26	0.15
Velarde R	188	30	50	13	1	4	27	34	41	7	2	.266	.379	.415	30	5.37	5.17	0.98	0.10	1.08
Walbeck M	338	42	89	15	2	7	48	30	67	1	1	.263	.322	.379	42	4.18	3.97	0.59	0.68	1.27
Williams R	36	7	13	1	0	1	5	7	11	3	3	.367	.482	.480	8	8.08	7.84	0.44	0.01	0.45
ANA	5631	812	1564	325	28	157	762	509	1009	94	43	.278	.341	.429	804	5.02	4.78	23.14	8.33	31.47

Pitcher	S	C	T	SS	ES	IC	HH	PP	TJ	S12	S35	S67	C1	C23	C45	C67	QWP
C Finley	3.68	3.74	7.41	44%	15%	44%	21%	12%	3%	35%	44%	21%	9%	29%	50%	12%	.495
Dickson	5.33	3.61	8.94	11%	0%	17%	50%	6%	11%	6%	44%	50%	6%	39%	50%	6%	.341
Juden	3.67	3.50	7.17	33%	17%	50%	17%	17%	0%	50%	33%	17%	0%	50%	50%	0%	.568
K Hill	4.68	3.95	8.63	32%	11%	21%	47%	11%	0%	21%	32%	47%	5%	32%	47%	16%	.376
Mcdowell	4.86	3.07	7.93	29%	7%	36%	36%	0%	7%	7%	57%	36%	14%	57%	21%	7%	.453
Olivares	4.35	4.15	8.50	31%	0%	23%	42%	19%	0%	15%	42%	42%	8%	19%	62%	12%	.401
Sparks	3.90	3.85	7.75	45%	5%	40%	20%	15%	5%	25%	55%	20%	5%	35%	50%	10%	.510
Washburn	3.82	3.27	7.09	36%	0%	45%	27%	27%	18%	27%	45%	27%	9%	55%	36%	0%	.586
Watson	5.00	3.93	8.93	29%	0%	14%	57%	14%	0%	7%	36%	57%	7%	21%	64%	7%	.327
ANA	4.34	3.75	8.09	33%	6%	31%	35%	13%	4%	21%	44%	35%	7%	34%	49%	9%	.442

AMERICAN LEAGUE WEST

SEATTLE MARINERS

DAVE PAISLEY

A LOOK BACK

For the 1998 Seattle Mariners, the whole was distinctly less than the sum of the parts. On the surface, the season looked promising. Opening night saw the second of two AL West championship banners hung from the dirty gray Kingdome roof and there was a heady air of more to come.

Storm clouds had been gathering for some time, however. In classic Mariner fashion, the front office had managed to completely botch negotiations with Randy. Unwilling or unable to sign him to the kind of long term deal he was looking for, the Mariners publicly decided not to offer him anything at all, but keep him and ride him to a World Series. If they had pitched even a lowball, two-year, $20M offer, they would have garnered some sympathy, but they conceded the PR battle to Johnson without a fight

The other major storm cloud was the continuing disgruntlement of the fans over the Jose Cruz Jr. trade and the continuing lack of a quality bullpen. It was going to be imperative that the bullpen collectively demonstrate an ability to close games out early in the season, as the fans weren't going to be patient. The defense was also suspect, with the ever-entertaining Glenallen Hill in left compounding the dubious defense of Russ Davis and Joey Cora at third and second respectively.

THE SHAPE OF THINGS TO COME

Opening night, Johnson pitched poorly, but still left in the sixth with a 9-6 lead. Bobby Ayala, the goat of the bullpen for the past three years, replaced him, and was able to get safely to the eighth inning without further damage. Unfortunately for him, Lou left him in, a classic Piniella mistake. After a walk, a run-scoring triple, an out and another walk, Ayala left with the tying runs on base. With David Justice up, Piniella went to his newly acquired lefty specialist, Tony Fossas, who promptly loaded

the bases with a walk. That didn't go over well, so in came Mike Timlin.

Bases loaded, one out, game on the line. Timlin's never been good with pressure, and so it proved again. A double to Manny Ramirez tied the game and an intentional walk to pinch-hitter Brian Giles loaded them up once more. With the bases loaded and the game tied, Timlin committed the unforgivable sin by walking in the go-ahead run. It was the ultimate crime to a city that has put up with all kinds of bullpen ineptitude over the years. An inning-ending double play was hardly any consolation.

The Mariner offense had two more innings to get that run back and more, but after two strikeouts, two groundouts, a flyball and a foul pop, it was all over. Little did we know then, but that was the Mariner season in microcosm. A shaky Randy Johnson, a shell-shocked bullpen, and an offense that just couldn't produce one more run when the team needed it.

During the month of April, the bullpen continued to rip the heart out of the team. Opening night wasn't even the worst example. Opening day in Fenway Park, Johnson was again on the mound, sporting a 0-1 record and a 9.26 ERA. With something to prove, he turned in a masterful eight innings and left after fifteen strikeouts in eight innings with a 7-2 lead, requiring only that the bullpen get three outs without giving up more than four runs.

In came Heathcliff Slocumb. He gave up a single, walk, and a run-scoring double. So in came Fossas, who again coughed up a walk to load the bases. Then came Timlin, who

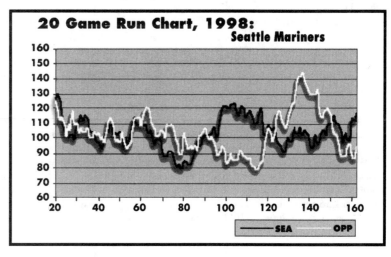

20 Game Run Chart, 1998:
Seattle Mariners

SEA — OPP

QMAX PRESENTS: "BAD" PITCHERS

THE WALKING MAN

The Aborigines (at least as explained to us in "Crocodile Dundee") have this tradition called the Walkabout. Without going into boring detail, Mariner pitcher Dave Fleming had his own walkabout in 1994. He would walkabout....a man an inning (biddabump/*crash* thangyouverymush...). All right, so I exaggerate. Dave Fleming only walked five or six per nine innings in 1994. More accurately, he walked around three in a typical five-inning start. These, along with the six or seven hits he also gave up, assured Dave of an early exit from the game, and ultimately his career. Opposing batters got on base at a staggering .394 clip against Gentleman Dave, leading to a 7-11 record and a 6.31 ERA. Fleming's flameout was so spectacular that just about any statistic you choose will tell you what Mariner management figured out-- that Fleming needed to take a walk.

Fleming's QMAX line bears all the signs of unquiet desperation, as his running five-start QMAX stuff and control averages dance a deadly dance, with one line dipping as the other shoots into the stratosphere. Fleming's April starts show respectable hit prevention, but the walk totals start looking really ugly, especially after the April 27 start, as Fleming is yanked in the third inning after walking his sixth man of the new day. No doubt with a stern admonishment to "throw strikes, Meat!" ringing in his ear, Dave brings the walk totals down, by the usual method of tossing dead fish into the hitter's wheelhouse. The results stink predictably, as six of the next eight starts fall heavily into the QMAX "hit hard" region. Then follows the Period of Nibbling, when Dave aims tremulous darts at the black borders of

DAVE FLEMING/ SEA 1994							
	1	2	3	4	5	6	7	S
1								0
2		1		1				2
3			2			1		3
4			1	1				2
5			2	1	1			4
6			3	1	2	1	2	9
7				2		1		3
C	0	1	6	8	3	2	3	23

the strike zone and achieves ephemeral success with two successive starts (2,4 and 4,4) near the now-elusive "success square". After this, the deluge of a June 27 start (the 27th of the month just didn't agree with Dave this year) featuring 3 1/3 innings, five hits, and six more free passes. The remainder of the season is a matter of Playing Out the String while Pulling the String (on his once-effective changeup, silly) as he does neither hit prevention or walk prevention terribly well, with a typical July-August start being 5 1/3 innings, seven hits, and three walks. And, of course, a loss. Ma, make up my bed, they're starting to squeeze the strike zone on me.

--Tom Austin

gave up a run-scoring single and a hit batter to force in another run. With the score at 7-5 Mariners with the bases still loaded and nobody out, lefty Paul Spoljaric was tagged to face Mo Vaughn. One grand slam home run later, the most infamous inning of relief in Mariner history finally came to an end.

During the first month of the season, the bullpen had an ERA of 7.11, a 2-7 record and blew five of eleven save opportunities. Despite all that, the team was 12-15, and in the mild, mild AL west, that was hardly a problem at all.

I'M GLAD THAT'S BEHIND US

May promised to be better. On the offensive side, David Segui and Glenallen Hill, both scorching hot in April, cooled off, but Edgar Martinez finally kicked into gear. However, bullpen ineptitude continued unabated (5.78 ERA, 3-4, six blown saves in nine tries) and Cloude and Swift, the #4 and #5 starters, staggered in May with a 7.01 ERA and a 2-5 record, disappointing after a combined 4.30 ERA and 5-1 record in April. All this resulted in a mediocre 14-14 record for the month, 26-29 overall, but only seven games back from the Rangers.

June started badly with a 10-9 loss to the Orioles, featuring two more errors from the unraveling Russ Davis. The next day, utility man Jeff Huson replaced Davis at third and also committed two errors in a 9-8 loss. The rot had set in.

With the team dropping out of sight of the division lead, Johnson trade talks with the Dodgers heated up, but fizzled, leaving the team and he fans more frustrated than ever.

The rest of the team finally began to crack from the constant pressure of bullpen failure and bad defense. The offense began to press, never knowing how many runs would be enough. Through June, they averaged more than a run per game less than the first two months. The starters pitched nervously, trying to be perfect, afraid of simple ground balls to third, and afraid to leave a close game in the hands of their friends from the pen.

By mid-June, the Mariners were 3-14 for the month and effectively out of the race, fourteen games back of the surging Angels, whose fortunes were the mirror image of Seattle's. The Mariners would never again climb higher than eight games below .500 the rest of the season.

The Johnson situation was finally resolved at the treading deadline. After a high-stakes game of chicken between the Yankees and Indians, Johnson surprisingly went to the Astros for three decent prospects. No doubt John Hart is still kicking himself.

The season trailed off to a 76-85 record, barely out of the AL West cellar and about twenty games worse than most pre-season predictions.

MARINER PERFORMANCE BY MONTH

Team Area	Apr	May	June	July	Aug	Sep
Top 3 starters	111%	117%	105%	120%	99%	132%
4&5 starters	96%	72%	100%	78%	80%	57%
Bullpen	73%	96%	93%	118%	88%	121%
Offense	113%	110%	98%	105%	95%	110%

Performance for the offense; OPS relative to the league season value.

For all pitching, the criterion is walks plus hits per inning pitched (WHIP), relative to the league season value

LOOKING AHEAD

Management

Nobody loves a GM, and Woody Woodward is no exception. He was roundly castigated for the Jose Cruz Jr. trade and the Randy Johnson situation, to name just two recent debacles, but to be fair, his hands are usually tied by ownership and manager Lou Piniella.

Piniella is an interesting study. Seen by the vast majority of Seattle fans as the man who finally brought a winner to Seattle, he has a couple of fatal flaws. The worst is his complete and utter lack of ability to handle a pitching staff. Young starters and relievers suffer incredibly under his impatient eye. He also seems unable to prepare a team for the season. Every year, no matter how good the team is, they stumble out of the gate and end up playing catch up all year. Sometimes it works, usually it doesn't.

Another debacle like 1998 and no doubt both Woodward and Piniella will be seeking alternate employment.

Offense

Dan Wilson will continue at catcher, providing good defense and tolerable offense, while John Marzano will probably back him up again. Piniella loves these two guys.

The situation at first base and DH will depend on Jay Buhner's recovery from elbow surgery. If he is able to play at all, it won't be in the outfield, so he will either displace David Segui at first, bumping him to left field or he'll displace Edgar Martinez at DH, moving Martinez to first, and again bumping Segui to left. Neither of these scenarios bodes well. Segui's outfield defense and either Buhner or Martinez' defense at first will be significant liabilities, and the distractions of fielding unfamiliar (and quite possibly unsuitable) positions will likely hurt their offensive output.

At second, Carlos Guillen will likely be given the opportunity to start, provided the Mariners don't panic and trade for a proven stiff like Tony Womack. However, Guillen showed in limited action last season that he can handle the job defensively, and his offense should be equivalent to Cora's. David Bell should provide adequate insurance if Guillen falters.

At third, Russ Davis is a man lost. Leaving him at third

WPA BULLPEN BOX—SEATTLE MARINERS

	PI	WPA	P	PPPI
Starters	1041	-3.0	53.2	0.051
Relievers	566	-5.9	31.5	0.056
Road	285	-5.9	17.2	0.060
Home	281	0.0	14.3	0.051
Mar/Apr	116	-3.0	9.2	0.079
May	102	-2.8	4.7	0.046
June	81	-2.0	4.8	0.060
July	72	0.6	4.3	0.060
August	99	0.4	4.4	0.044
September	96	0.9	4.1	0.042
Non S/H Sit.	438	-2.9	16.4	0.037
S/H Sit.	128	-3.0	15.1	0.118
Low Pressure	265	-0.5	3.2	0.012
Med. Pressure	153	-2.8	9.0	0.059
High Pressure	148	-2.6	19.3	0.130
Entered behind	260	-0.8	6.5	0.025
Entered tied	70	-1.8	7.9	0.113
Entered ahead	236	-3.3	17.1	0.073

Name	G	PI	WPA	P	PPPI	MI	ROB	T
Ayala B	62	94	-3.9	6.7	.071	25	18	5
Fossas T	23	25	-1.1	1.9	.076	2	15	4
Holdridge D	7	12	.0	.0	.003	4	3	0
Lira F	7	20	-.2	.4	.019	6	4	0
McCarthy G	29	38	-.6	2.2	.057	7	12	7
Paniagua J	18	26	1.0	1.5	.058	7	8	3
Slocumb H	57	84	-.3	4.4	.053	23	20	11
Spoljaric P	47	82	-1.3	4.3	.052	23	23	3
Timlin M	70	97	1.7	7.5	.077	22	30	5
Wells B	30	59	-.6	2.2	.037	16	11	3
Total		566	-5.9	31.5	.056			

Name	Dis.	Poor	Fair	Good	Her.	Lo	Med	Hi	
Ayala B	8	11	33	8	0	31	15	16	(6)
Fossas T	2	6	13	2	0	10	7	6	(2)
McCarthy G	2	3	21	3	0	19	6	4	(1)
Paniagua J	1	0	9	8	0	9	5	4	(4)
Slocumb H	3	7	36	10	1	35	12	10	(6)
Spoljaric P	3	9	23	12	0	18	19	10	(6)
Timlin M	5	6	36	18	5	32	18	20	(13)
Wells B	2	2	21	5	0	18	7	5	(0)
Others	1	5	24	2	0	26	5	1	(0)
TOTAL	27	49	216	68	8	198	94	76	(38)

	7th inning			8th inning			9th inning		
	0	+1	+2	0	+1	+2	0	+1	+2
Ayala B	1	1	2	2	2	1	2	4	3
Fossas T	0	0	1	1	0	0	0	0	0
Lira F	0	0	0	0	1	0	0	0	0
McCarthy G	1	0	1	1	0	0	1	0	0
Paniagua J	1	0	2	3	0	1	0	1	0
Slocumb H	1	0	0	5	0	0	5	1	0
Spoljaric P	1	1	2	1	2	1	0	0	1
Timlin M	0	1	0	3	2	3	2	3	5
Wells B	0	0	1	0	0	0	0	0	0
Starters	9	16	9	3	2	7	0	0	3
TOTAL	14	19	18	19	9	13	10	9	12
Record	5-9	10-9	12-6	6-13	6-3	12-1	3-7	5-4	11-1

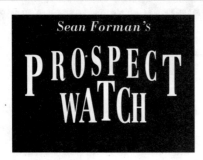

Sean Forman's

PROSPECT WATCH

NAME	AGE	POS	LEVEL	GR98	GR97	GR96	AVG
Carlos Guillen	22	SS	AAA	65	50	72	61
Adonis Harrison	21	2B	AA	61	58	49	58
Ryan Radmanovich	26	OF	AAA	43	50	52	47
Shane Monahan	23	OF	AAA	43	59	36	47

NAME	AGE	POS	LEVEL	GRADE
Alexander Fernandez	17	OF	Rookie	69
Jason Regan	22	3B	High A	57
Jermaine Clark	21	2B	Low A	55

NAME	AGE	GS	S	C	T	W-L	ERA	K/H	LEVEL
John Halama	25	17	3.94	1.94	5.88	12-3	3.20	0.73	High
Tim Harikkala	25	19	4.16	2.26	6.42	7-8	4.66	0.53	High
Freddy Garcia	21	25	3.40	3.64	7.04	10-8	3.35	1.14	High
Ryan Franklin	24	16	4.25	3.00	7.25	4-5	4.56	0.61	High
Chris Seelbach	25	21	3.52	3.81	7.33	7-3	4.23	1.00	High
Brett Hinchliffe	23	24	3.33	4.04	7.38	9-8	4.00	0.76	High
Felipe Lira	26	20	4.45	3.05	7.50	6-8	4.26	0.62	High
Mac Suzuki	22	20	3.70	3.95	7.65	7-8	4.38	0.90	High
Damaso Marte	23	20	4.20	3.55	7.75	6-6	5.27	0.73	High
Robert Luce	23	25	4.76	3.04	7.80	12-7	5.09	0.33	High
Jim Bullinger	32	16	4.13	4.25	8.38	5-7	5.05	0.69	High
Jarod Juelsgaard	30	21	4.43	4.43	8.86	5-5	5.57	0.70	High
Ryan Anderson	18	22				6-5	3.23	1.77	Low
Gil Meche	19	26				8-7	3.44	1.24	Low

The Mariners do a remarkable job of scouting amateur talent. Very rarely have they missed on a draft and after they trade away all of their prospects some more come up through the system. Unfortunately, most of their talent is now producing for other teams. (For a partial list, check out last year's book.) The pickings are currently slim, so they are going to have to go through the free agent route to improve their team much, but with two players like A-Rod and Junior they are never very far from contention.

Top Dog: Carlos Guillen
Guillen was one of the players, along with Freddy Garcia, picked up in the Big Unit trade. The Mariners probably could have used an outfielder or catcher more (Mitch Meluskey?) as they have some infield depth. Guillen isn't half bad and should help the Mariners next year. Guillen hit much better before the trade (.291/.350/.457) than after (.228/.297/.293), and he was injured upon his call up to Seattle. He is injury-prone and a bit inconsistent with the bat, but I think he can put up a .750 OPS in the majors and perhaps crack .850 once in awhile.

Middle of the infield: Adonis Harrison
Harrison started out like gangbusters in the California League batting .337/.444/.473 in 258 at bats. He then moved up to the Southern League and lost a hundred pointer across the board. Harrison has stolen 20+ bases each of the last two years, though not with great success. His career numbers are excellent at .298/.397/.425 and he will only be 22 next year, so keep your eye on him. I expect that he'll be in AA again next year. Comp: Jason Hardtke with speed.

Young 'un: Jason Regan
There have been some questions about Regan's defense, and he has moved from second base over to third. He has consistently produced a lot of secondary average over the last three years, and the past two he has bumped the batting average up as well. He was repeating time in the California League despite hitting 22 home runs there last year, so there has to be some air taken out of his .298/.447/.526 numbers. The Mariners don't have anybody at third above him blocking him, so he could move rather quickly.

On the Mound: Ryan Anderson
I'm missing four of Anderson's starts, but if I extrapolate them from his stats, his QMAX line is 3.00/4.40, 7.40. While this isn't spectacular, he shows the traditional budding power pitcher profile. Anderson is known as the Little Unit, for one because he is in the Mariners' system, but more specifically because he is a 6-10 lefthander. Anderson had nearly half of his starts in the Power Precipice area and was hit hard just twice in his 22 starts. Not surprisingly, control is problem area, as he walked 67 in 111 innings, though he had just four wild pitches, which suggests he may not be too far off. The comparisons to Randy Johnson look right on to me.

On the Mound: John Halama
From one extreme, we approach the other. Halama's control is Tewksburyesque. In his last two minor league seasons he has walked just 48 batters in 292 innings and this year walked just 1.2 batters/9IP. He allows about a hit an inning and does all the little things well. The Mariners acquired him as the player to be named in the Randy Johnson deal. He struggled with the Astros in his 6 starts with them, but that was largely because he started nibbling. I think he can have some success in the majors as long as he keeps it over the plate and gives up just solo home runs.

would be cruel and unusual punishment, both for him and the fans, yet his trade value is minimal and there are no immediately obvious alternatives. He may remain purely for lack of any other option. If he can maintain his batting focus, learn to take a walk, and improve his defense to merely atrocious, the team can probably live with him there.

Alex Rodriguez continues at short, naturally, while in the outfield, Griffey continues at center. The key to the Mariners future is to lock up both Griffey and Rodriguez for as long as they possibly can. Both are signed through the 2000 season, but it will never be too early to sign them up for the next decade. Given their ability, charisma, and star appeal, they may be the only players worth signing to ten-year deals. They will unleash a tandem assault on all kinds of career home run records, and their drawing power will be enormous. Given baseball salary inflation, it may take around $500M to sign both, but it should be worth it.

In the much cheaper parts of the outfield, if Segui moves to left, only right field remains open. There are numerous lackluster outfield prospects in the Seattle system (Monahan, Ibanez, and Gipson), but given Piniella's obsession with veterans, the team will probably be on the lookout for a proven major-leaguer to fill the slot. If Segui is traded or remains at first because Buhner can't play, then maybe one of the young guys gets a shot.

Starting Pitching

The obvious hole for next year is starting pitching. Johnson is impossible to replace directly, but the Mariners desperately need another starter of Jeff Fassero/Jamie Moyer caliber to fill out the top three rotation slots.

For the remaining two slots, Ken Cloude started last season well, but spent most of the season regressing to scrub form. That happens a lot to young pitchers under Piniella, and it remains to be seen if Cloude can survive. Billy Swift was truly terrible, but great run support obscured the fact all season. If the Mariners do pick him up again, it will be as a middle reliever.

Other options are Mark Leiter, obtained from the Phillies for Paul Spoljaric, and John Halama. Leiter has been a starter most of his career, and with the acquisition of Jose Mesa and the emergence of Jose Paniagua, the Mariners may have him in mind for the rotation if they can't sign another quality starter. The only good thing about getting Leiter is that he's flexible. Halama was acquired from the Astros in the Johnson trade and will get a chance to win a rotation spot in the spring, otherwise he'll probably end up in middle relief.

Bullpen

The bullpen, once again, will be a big question mark. Timlin and Spoljaric, the fruits of the Cruz Jr. trade, are gone. Timlin for too much money to Baltimore, and Spoljaric because he was perpetually camped in Piniella's doghouse. Slocumb is a free agent, leaving only Bobby Ayala from last year as a key bullpen figure. Ayala has surely worn out his welcome in Seattle, and it would be cruel to keep him there again next year.

The acquisition of closer Jose Mesa is a gamble, but not a terribly expensive one, and Jose Paniagua's emergence last year does provide an alternative. Mark Leiter could also be pressed into the closer role if necessary. It does seem that the remainder of the bullpen will have to be assembled from the leftovers from the rotation.

FINGERING THE CULPRITS

In July, the Mariners will move into Safeco Field, their new ballpark. With the core of talent they have, it's quite possible they could be in first place when they do. However, the team is shakier than last year, and it's equally likely they could be in last place instead. The difference will be how good a job Mariner management does in the off-season.

Ouch! I wish I hadn't said that.

. BOTTOMING OUT

For a team that rode the crest of the XBH tsunami in baseball from 1995-98, the Mariners are starting to break up ahead of the wave. Their #2-#6

slots (Rodriguez-Griffey-Martinez-Segui and a cast of stand-ins for Jay Buhner) make for a potent lineup, but the bottom of their order is filled with a particularly deadly type of hitter: the pseudo-slugger.

These are the guys the old incarnation of the Mariners used to glom onto from the scrap heap, get one season of production from, and then try to build an offense around, with results that you may remember from a certain overly-hyped movie. These guys swing from the heels but aren't really very good at it, and they have about as much discipline at the plate as a lemming in plain view of the ocean.

Here are the Mariners' pseudo-sluggers, as represented in the #7-#9 slots in their batting order:

BOP	AB	R	H	D	T	HR	RBI	BB	SO	BA	OBP	SLG	OPS
#7	613	70	153	36	2	18	84	39	140	.250	.296	.403	.699
#8	592	64	145	33	1	17	77	34	121	.245	.293	.390	.683
#9	557	60	124	27	1	16	63	50	119	.223	.297	.361	.658

Throw a blanket over these guys, and set it on fire—please. As Moon Unit Zappa would have said if she hadn't gotten too old to be a Valley Girl anymore, clone me with a spoon. Is it any wonder that the guys in the #1 slot in the Mariners' order, who hit just about at league average (.767 OPS) could

TEAM BREAKOUT MARINERS 1998

Category	RS	RA	W	L	Pct.	Rk
4- RUNS ALLOWED/HOME	178	72	28	6	.824	6
4- RUNS ALLOWED	389	168	58	13	.817	5
4- RUNS ALLOWED/ROAD	211	96	30	7	.811	2
CLOSE LOW-SCORING GAMES/HOME	22	12	7	2	.778	4
5+ RUNS SCORED/HOME	338	225	31	10	.756	7
LOW SCORING GAMES/HOME	39	27	11	5	.688	4
5+ RUNS SCORED	668	465	59	27	.686	13
5+ RUNS SCORED/ROAD	330	240	28	17	.622	14
RECORD IN LOW SCORING GAMES	78	66	19	12	.613	4
SLUGFESTS/HOME	265	234	18	13	.581	2
RECORD IN BLOWOUTS/ROAD	194	172	16	12	.571	5
RECORD IN BLOWOUTS	383	361	30	26	.536	6
LOW SCORING GAMES/ROAD	39	39	8	7	.533	4
RECORD IN CLOSE GAMES/HOME	146	143	16	14	.533	8
CLOSE LOW SCORING GAMES/ROAD	20	20	4	4	.500	4
CLOSE SLUGFESTS/HOME	81	81	5	5	.500	9
RECORD IN BLOWOUTS/HOME	189	189	14	14	.500	7
SEASON TOTALS	859	855	76	85	.472	9
RECORD IN SLUGFESTS	494	479	28	34	.452	10
RECORD IN CLOSE GAMES	278	290	24	35	.407	13
SLUGFESTS/ROAD	229	245	10	21	.323	14
5+ RUNS ALLOWED/HOME	256	355	14	33	.298	6
RECORD IN CLOSE GAMES/ROAD	132	147	8	21	.276	13
4- RUNS SCORED/HOME	96	202	11	29	.275	7
4- RUNS SCORED	191	390	17	58	.227	10
5+ RUNS ALLOWED	470	687	18	72	.200	9
4- RUNS SCORED/ROAD	95	188	6	29	.171	10
5+ RUNS ALLOWED/ROAD	214	332	4	39	.093	14
CLOSE SLUGFESTS/ROAD	65	76	0	9	.000	14

manage to drive in only 39 runs all season? Put another way, that's an RBI/TB ratio of .144, which is the lowest reading measured since the invention of the sundial.

Unfortunately for Dave Paisley and his Seattle cohorts at strikethree.com (check out their web site, it's a refreshing change from the commonplace take on baseball), the M's seem to have become fatally fascinated with this type of player again. One of their off-season moves was to trade for Butch Huskey, whose numbers last year for the Mets were:

BA	OBP	SLG	OPS
.252	.300	.407	.707

Looks familiar, doesn't it? Now, Butch is probably going to do a little better than this in Seattle, but it's just a milder version of the same flaw. This kind of creeping mediocrity is slowly going to work its way up the Seattle batting order, until the M's wake up with Alex and Junior and the seven dwarfs—assuming, of course, that Alex and Junior don't take a look at the 72-point type on the wall and put on their sailin' shoes. Then Seattle will be down to Bill Gates and the corpse of Kurt Cobain as cultural landmarks—unless David Foster Wallace decides to move his footnote collection to Puget Sound, of course.

Meanwhile, kiddies, the Mariners' ship is slowing down, scoffing at reports that the iceberg dead ahead could possibly be as large as it looks. But Leo and Kate know better (and James Cameron, too—of course, he knows everything): after all, they've already read the script. <DM>

Name	AB	R	H	D	T	HR	RBI	BB	SO	SB	CS	BA	OBP	SLG	XR	Adj XR/27	Raw XR/27	OXW	DXW	TXW
Amaral R	136	25	38	6	0	1	4	11	23	10	1	.279	.337	.345	18	4.80	4.93	0.45	0.24	0.69
Bell Da	81	11	26	8	0	0	8	4	8	0	0	.324	.359	.422	10	4.79	4.94	0.26	0.43	0.69
Buhner J	248	34	61	7	1	15	46	34	69	0	0	.244	.336	.462	41	5.75	5.93	1.49	0.41	1.90
Cora J	524	97	149	23	6	6	26	57	48	12	6	.285	.358	.386	76	5.21	5.34	2.39	-0.67	1.72
Davis R	504	69	132	30	1	20	83	32	131	4	4	.261	.304	.443	68	4.64	4.66	1.45	-0.44	1.01
Ducey R	219	30	53	18	2	5	23	21	60	4	4	.241	.332	.410	29	4.54	4.64	0.61	0.30	0.91
Gipson C	51	11	12	1	0	0	2	5	9	2	1	.241	.315	.261	4	2.83	2.80	-0.10	0.06	-0.04
Griffey K	639	122	182	33	3	56	149	70	118	20	7	.284	.359	.607	133	7.46	7.68	6.40	1.44	7.84
Guillen C	39	9	13	1	1	0	5	3	9	2	0	.341	.386	.419	6	6.66	6.47	0.29	0.03	0.32
Hill G	260	38	76	20	2	12	34	13	44	1	1	.291	.329	.521	38	5.17	5.22	1.08	0.22	1.30
Huson J	49	8	8	1	0	1	4	5	6	1	1	.163	.232	.243	3	1.77	1.92	-0.27	0.05	-0.22
Ibanez R	98	12	25	7	1	2	12	5	22	0	0	.257	.293	.410	10	3.52	3.48	-0.02	0.06	0.04
Martinez E	567	88	183	48	1	29	104	95	94	1	1	.322	.418	.563	125	8.32	8.62	6.79	0.03	6.82
Marzano J	133	13	31	7	1	4	12	9	24	0	0	.233	.323	.389	17	4.23	4.28	0.26	0.50	0.76
Monahan S	212	17	52	8	1	4	28	7	51	1	3	.245	.270	.348	19	3.11	3.12	-0.27	0.31	0.04
Oliver J	86	12	19	3	0	2	10	9	15	1	0	.224	.298	.329	8	3.11	3.24	-0.12	0.05	-0.07
Radmanovich R	70	5	15	4	0	2	10	3	24	1	2	.220	.258	.365	6	2.94	3.04	-0.13	-0.02	-0.15
Rodriguez A	689	125	215	35	5	42	126	42	118	44	16	.312	.358	.560	131	7.01	7.10	5.97	1.89	7.86
Rossy R	82	12	16	6	0	1	4	5	12	0	0	.198	.245	.307	6	2.46	2.59	-0.27	0.16	-0.11
Segui D	527	81	161	36	1	19	85	44	78	3	1	.306	.355	.486	87	6.08	6.17	3.43	0.89	4.32
Wilkins R	42	5	8	1	1	1	4	3	13	0	0	.202	.258	.347	4	3.06	3.07	-0.07	-0.01	-0.08
Wilson D	328	40	83	17	1	9	45	21	55	2	1	.255	.305	.395	41	4.21	4.26	0.58	0.55	1.13
SEA	**5678**	**875**	**1576**	**322**	**28**	**233**	**836**	**508**	**1054**	**110**	**46**	**.278**	**.340**	**.467**	**890**	**5.54**	**5.65**	**30.18**	**6.48**	**36.66**

Pitcher	S	C	T	SS	ES	IC	HH	PP	TJ	S12	S35	S67	C1	C23	C45	C67	QWP
Bullinger	7.00	4.00	11.00	0%	0%	0%	100%	0%	0%	0%	0%	100%	0%	0%	100%	0%	.062
Cloude	4.57	4.27	8.83	33%	0%	23%	40%	3%	3%	20%	40%	40%	0%	40%	40%	20%	.371
Fassero	4.06	2.63	6.69	53%	16%	56%	25%	3%	22%	25%	50%	25%	25%	53%	19%	3%	.581
Moyer	3.97	2.32	6.29	53%	24%	56%	29%	0%	18%	26%	44%	29%	29%	62%	6%	3%	.605
P Abbott	4.00	3.75	7.75	50%	0%	25%	25%	0%	0%	25%	50%	25%	0%	25%	75%	0%	.459
R Johnson	3.78	3.00	6.78	48%	22%	52%	26%	13%	17%	35%	39%	26%	22%	30%	48%	0%	.561
Spoljaric	4.33	4.67	9.00	17%	17%	17%	33%	33%	0%	17%	50%	33%	17%	0%	67%	17%	.331
Suzuki	4.80	4.40	9.20	40%	0%	20%	60%	20%	0%	20%	20%	60%	0%	20%	60%	20%	.364
Swift	4.77	3.62	8.38	31%	8%	15%	42%	4%	4%	12%	46%	42%	4%	42%	46%	8%	.397
SEA	**4.26**	**3.25**	**7.51**	**43%**	**13%**	**39%**	**34%**	**6%**	**12%**	**23%**	**43%**	**34%**	**16%**	**43%**	**34%**	**7%**	**.492**

OAKLAND ATHLETICS

KEN ADAMS

CHICKEN SALAD

The A's did the most amazing thing during Spring Training. They fired their pitching coach, Bob 'Foghorn Leghorn' Cluck on March 26th. In all my years following baseball, I cannot recall a similar occurrence.

Here at BBBA we were ecstatic. Last season's essay on the A's was a tag team event (yours truly and Don Malcolm) in which we roasted the A's pitching and their pitching coach in particular. The A's youthful GM, Billy Beane, denied that the firing had anything to do with a loud argument the day before with Cluck about the direction of the young staff, but we suspect that he was forced to contend with the obvious lack of results. Rick Peterson was named pitching coach in Cluck's place. Peterson had joined the A's six months before as the minor league pitching coach. What was interesting also was the ability of Art Howe to maintain his job. Despite being Cluck's sponsor and good friend, he agreed that there had not been enough progress with the young pitching.

First question in our post-mortem: did the A's pitching improve in 1998? Last year I produced a chart that showed the A's starting pitching was the worst in the league with a 5.95 ERA; in 1998 their starting pitchers came in with a 4.92 ERA. However, in 1998 the A's had two experienced starters in their rotation, Kenny Rogers and Tom Candiotti. Remove their performance, and we have a 5.72 ERA for the rest of the starters.

Not much of an improvement: note, though, that the A's relied much less on younger pitchers than they have over the previous two years. In fact the A's only had three pitchers under 26 that pitched very much at all, Jimmy Haynes (194 IP), Blake Stein (117 IP) and Jay Witasick (27 IP). (The other starters (Gil Heredia, Mike Oquist) have a great deal of tread wear from years of minor-league highway miles.) How did Peterson do with the three young pitchers?

Haynes (25) went 11-9 but with a 5.09 ERA. At the end of June, Haynes, was 6-3 with a 3.84 ERA and then fell off with a 5-6 record with a 6.39 ERA for the rest of the season and totally collapsed in September with a 1-3 record with a 9.27 ERA in five starts. He did not overcome his pervasive control problems, and regressed as the year dragged on.

Stein was called up in early May, started promisingly but was buried by his control problems. The final numbers: 5-8 with a 6.36 ERA (as a starter). He was removed from the rotation in late August.

Jay Witasick spent most of the year in AAA and only pitched 27 big-league innings. He allowed 36 hits and walked 15 batters with an ERA of 6.33.

Bottom line: Rick Peterson is not going to part the Red Sea any time soon. Bob Cluck left a lot of damage to be undone, but Peterson didn't undo any of it. Divine intervention may not be sufficient. The A's have left themselves in the postion where they will have to sift through little but their own slag heap of failed prospects (Ariel Prieto, Willie Adams, Brad Rigby) while toying with the potentially disastrous idea of force feeding #1 draft choice Mark Mulder at the major league level.

Unfathomable as it may seem, the bullpen is in even worse shape. The bullpen ERA (4.62) ranked 9th in the league, but the A's were thirteenth in allowing inherited runners to score (37%, 13% below the league average). Art Howe's over-managing doesn't help, either. The A's had a Hold/Win ratio of .86 compared to the league average of .68, which means Art is juggling his relievers too much. Howe's attempt to find a back-up closer in 1998 was a disaster of nuclear proportions: Bill Taylor saved 33 of 37, but the rest of the relievers went 6 for 22

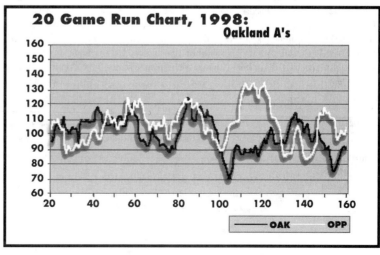

20 Game Run Chart, 1998: Oakland A's

QMAX PRESENTS: "BAD" PITCHERS

A LITTLE DAB'LL DO YA

Nelson Potter joined Connie Mack's Philadelphia A's in 1938 as a 25-year old rookie after a one-inning cup of java with the Browns the year before. He showed his gratitude at escaping the frying pan for the greasier frying pan by pulling down a 2-12 record with a 6.47 ERA. This season of great promise was duly rewarded by a spot in the starting rotation in 1939. Nelson showed the gentlemanly Mr. Mack that 1938 was no fluke, as he thrilled opposing batters into a .321 batting average. The accommodating Mr. Potter stayed in the game long enough to allow double figures in hits in 8 of his 25 starts. There is no truth to the cruel rumor, however, that Connie Mack faked his extended illness in 1939 to avoid being subjected to the sorry spectacle of Potter's putrid pitching.

Within the 1939 season there are several phases. An excellent 2,4 "power precipice" start (3 hits, 3 walks in 5 1/3 innings) leads to a no-decision loss, followed by three poor starts (in one of which he got the win). Then comes the best 5-start stretch of the season (3.6s, 3.4c/7.0t) leaves Nelson with a 5-1 record and a 4.97 ERA. The next phase begins with a 7,2 start , but Potter's luck held as he "earned" his sixth win. Luck ran out after that: seven straight losses as Potter found a groove, or, if you will, a rut: 5.8s, 3.6c/9.4t QMAX average after the all-star break.

Never let it be said, however, that Potter failed to learn from his struggles. He scuffled along at this level until 1943, when he went 10-5 with a 2.78 ERA for the Browns, and

NELS POTTER/PHI (a) 1939

	1	2	3	4	5	6	7	5
1		1						1
2	1			1				2
3			1		1			2
4	1	2						3
5						1		1
6	1		2	3		2		9
7		2	2	2	1			7
C	3	3	7	4	5	0	3	25

improved to 19-7, 2.83 for the 1944 pennant winners.

To what could we attribute this sudden and dramatic improvement in performance? Well, wartime baseball, sure. Look a little closer at a bit of trivia. For the first 24 years after the spitter was disallowed, no one was thrown out of a game for it. You guessed it: Potter was the first, on July 20, 1944. Umpire Cal Hubbard tossed him for going to his mouth during a game, and he was later fined and suspended ten days.

What a bad boy, huh? Here's what I'm thinking, though: no regrets for Nelson. He who laughs last and all.

Ha Ha!

--Tom Austin

(27%), well below the league average for non-closer save attempts (42%).

IS THERE ANYTHING TO CROW ABOUT?

A number of "experts" have claimed that the A's are sitting on a lot of good offensive prospects and young veterans. The most talked about youngsters are Ben Grieve (23), Eric Chavez (21), Miguel Tejada (23), A.J. Hinch (25), Ryan Christenson (25) and Scott Spiezio (26). Other than Grieve, these players have shown far less plate discipline once reaching the majors. As a result, they may fall short of expectations. Let's look at these players' BBP in 1998 (Chavez' totals include minor league play):

Player	BBP
Grieve	13%
Spiezio	10%
Chavez	9%
Christenson	9%
Hinch	8%
Tejada	7%

While Grieve's rate is fine, the others leave something to be desired. With virtually all of these players underperforming their minor league BBP rates, one senses a discontinuity between minor league instruction and follow-through at the major league level. Young players in the A's organization don't appear to get any encouragement to continue with the pattern of plate discipline they learn in the minors.

Ryan Christenson was a major disappointment in terms of BBP: his minor league numbers were more than twice as high (19%). Without some movement upwards this year to the 12-14% range, don't count on Ryan having a long career, as he's short on power. Hinch also suffered a greater than expected decline in walk rate from the high minors to the majors, going from 14% to 8%.

Tejada is what baseball announcers often refer to as a "free swinger." This isn't quite Mariano Duncan we're talking about here, but the effects of Rickey Henderson taking Tejada under his wing appear to have been minimal. His OBP so far is still on the wrong side of .300.

To sum up: the A's may generate higher than average walk totals in the minors, but the new wave of prospects do not appear to be translating those to the majors. While that is not fatal to the young A's chances, the expectation that they will evolve into a league-leading offense has a very rosy tint in its lenses.

THE WEAK GIVE UP AND STAY

That's the back half of a couplet from an old Hall and Oates song whose title eludes me at the moment. (Trust me, it's very late here as I type this.) The first half goes like this: "The strong give up and move on." And that's exactly what Sandy Alderson did with respect to the Oakland A's.

Alderson, who is the very definition of a successful baseball executive, left an indelible legacy behind him when he accepted Bud Selig's offer to be baseball's chief administrator. He also left what is clearly a ticking time bomb in Oakland, where his vision for the team has been undercut even as massive lip service was being paid to it.

It's pretty clear that the A's management was of two minds in how it perceived its next set of actions to rebuild its sagging fortunes. Alderson had readied a young manager named Gary Jones (chronicled as a player in a series on "Walkmen" that ran in these pages six years ago), who had been extremely successful in implementing a franchise-wide emphasis on plate discipline and had managed nothing but winning teams during a seven-year minor league career.

When Art Howe was hired as the A's manager in 1996, Alderson viewed him as a transitional figure whose people skills would be useful in moving from the remnants of the A's previous teams to the next geneation. He would facilitate the transition, and Jones would take over when the time was right.

Reports are that Alderson wanted to make this change after the 1997 season, a year in which the reuniting of Mark McGwire and Jose Canseco proved stillborn, with both men leaving the building well before the year limped to a conclusion. But he was overruled by his ownership group, who liked the folksy Howe and were oblivious to his deficiencies. Jones was brought to the big leagues as a coach, where he would get experience in major league situations and possibly take over the reins in the middle of the season.

That didn't happen, and the reason for it is not completely clear, but reports are that it stems from the fact that Alderson's protege, Billy Beane, sided with ownership on behalf of Howe. It was no coincidence that the announcement of Howe's return for 1999 was accompanied by the news that Alderson was leaving the A's. It was also no coincidence that Gary Jones was not retained in the A's organization after Alderson's departure. (Jones has since been hired, in another canny move by Dan Duquette, to manage the Boston Red Sox' AAA affiliate.)

So when Ken Adams alludes to the idea that there has been precious little "major league follow-through" for the minor league development efforts conceived by Alderson and implemented by Jones, he has scratched the surface of the A's internicine unravelment. Billy Beane is now in control of the A's, and he has decided that Art Howe is the man to execute his plan. Apparently that is less threatening than working with a man with real brains and definite opinions.

It will also be, as will soon become evident, a whole hell of a lot less successful. Billy Beane may mouth Sandy Alderson's precepts, but he is not truly capable of embracing those ideas,

WPA BULLPEN BOX—OAKLAND A'S

	PI	WPA	P	PPPI
Starters	1049	-3.8	55.6	0.053
Relievers	630	-2.8	37.1	0.059
Road	326	0.3	20.7	0.064
Home	304	-3.1	16.4	0.054
Mar/Apr	104	-1.0	8.9	0.085
May	97	-1.3	5.5	0.057
June	128	-0.1	6.0	0.047
July	95	-1.6	4.9	0.051
August	113	-0.3	7.1	0.063
September	93	1.5	4.7	0.051
Non S/H Sit.	458	-2.9	21.0	0.046
S/H Sit.	172	0.1	16.2	0.094
Low Pressure	242	-0.4	3.4	0.014
Med. Pressure	237	-5.8	15.1	0.064
High Pressure	151	3.4	18.6	0.123
Entered behind	294	0.5	7.9	0.027
Entered tied	90	-4.0	10.5	0.116
Entered ahead	246	0.7	18.8	0.076

Name	G	PI	WPA	P	PPPI	MI	ROB	T
Dougherty J	9	16	-.8	.8	.049	6	4	1
Fetters M	48	67	-1.4	4.3	.064	16	26	7
Groom B	75	104	-.5	6.2	.059	23	49	6
Holzemer M	13	16	.2	.7	.041	2	7	2
Mathews TJ	66	100	.4	6.3	.063	27	29	7
Mohler M	57	89	-.5	5.3	.060	23	30	11
Small A	24	47	-.9	1.7	.035	16	16	2
Taylor B	70	91	.7	7.8	.086	21	23	13
Witasick J	4	13	.1	.6	.042	3	2	1
Worrell T	25	50	.0	3.0	.060	17	11	3
Total		630	-2.8	37.2	.059			

	I---------- Quality ----------I					I--- Pressure -------I		
	Dis.	Poor	Fair	Good	Her.	Lo	Med	Hi
Fetters M	6	6	24	10	2	20	16	12 (8)
Groom B	5	10	42	17	1	36	25	14 (10)
Holzemer M	0	2	8	3	0	8	4	1 (1)
Mathews TJ	1	12	32	21	0	26	28	12 (8)
Mohler M	2	10	33	11	1	24	24	9 (6)
Small A	2	7	11	4	0	12	11	1 (1)
Taylor B	11	2	25	27	5	23	32	15 (10)
Worrell T	1	5	10	8	1	8	8	9 (6)
Others	4	2	21	2	1	18	9	3 (1)
TOTAL	32	56	206	103	11	175	157	76 (51)

	7th inning			8th inning			9th inning		
	0	+1	+2	0	+1	+2	0	+1	+2
Fetters M	0	0	0	3	1	3	6	0	2
Groom B	1	1	1	2	1	1	0	2	0
Heredia G	0	0	0	0	0	0	1	0	0
Mathews TJ	2	2	0	1	4	3	2	0	1
Mohler M	2	4	1	2	2	1	1	0	0
Taylor B	1	0	0	1	1	1	7	7	6
Worrell T	1	2	1	2	2	1	0	0	1
Starters	17	7	11	10	3	4	0	1	1
TOTAL	24	16	14	21	14	14	17	10	11
Record	10-14	9-7	11-3	9-12	9-5	11-3	5-12	10-0	10-1

Sean Forman's PROSPECT WATCH

NAME	AGE	POS	LEVEL	GR98	GR97	GR96	AVG
Eric Chavez	20	3B	AAA	103	57	-	85
Mark Bellhorn	23	2B	AAA	68	100	63	78
Mario Encarnacion	20	OF	AA	78	75	53	73
Santos Ortiz	21	SS	AA	67	50	62	61
Jorge Velandia	23	SS	AAA	55	54	48	54
Ramon Hernandez	22	C	AA	53	51	43	51

NAME	AGE	POS	LEVEL	GRADE
Esteban German	19	2B	Rookie	60
Nathan Haynes	18	OF	High A	60
Monty Davis	20	DH	High A	59
Tim Jones	20	OF	High A	56
Adam Piatt	22	3B	High A	52
Caonabo Cosme	19	2B	High A	51
Eric Byrnes	22	OF	High A	50
Dionys Cesar	21	3B	High A	49
Juan Camilo	20	OF	High A	47
Rodney Clifton	21	OF	High A	46

NAME	AGE	GS	S	C	T	W-L	ERA	K/H	LEVEL
Gil Heredia	32	18	4.50	2.33	6.83	8-6	3.67	0.64	High
Jay Witasick	25	26	3.58	3.54	7.12	10-7	3.87	1.23	High
Brett Laxton	24	27	3.37	4.11	7.48	11-8	4.28	0.66	High
Chris Enochs	22	26	4.08	3.77	7.85	9-10	4.74	0.63	High
Tim Hudson	27	22	3.82	4.05	7.86	10-9	4.55	0.76	High
Bill King	25	22	4.95	3.77	8.73	6-13	6.56	0.35	High
Benito Baez	21	16	4.44	4.38	8.81	3-6	5.80	0.52	High

Oakland has made an organizational commitment to promoting plate discipline among their prospects, which you know is a popular move here at BBBA Plaza. As evidence of this emphasis, every one of their affiliates led the league in walks drawn except for the two California League affiliates, who were second and third respectively. It will be interesting to see how all this plays out over the next five years. With the success the Yankees and Indians have had with similar approaches, I suspect that this will become a new trend.

Top Dog: Eric Chavez

Chavez was Baseball America's Minor League Player of the Year for 1998. It certainly came as somewhat of a surprise as he was coming off a good but not great year (.271/.321/.444) in the California League. He picked it up in a big way in the Southern League and Pacific Coast League batting .328/.402/.612 and .325/.364/.588, totaling 45 doubles and 33 home runs to go along with 14 stolen bases. He will probably have some rough moments in the field, but his bat is his ticket to the show. I wouldn't be surprised to see him regress a little bit next year in the majors, but he should become a very good third baseman. I think I would rather have Glaus, but you could do well with either one.

Young 'un: Nathan Haynes

Haynes was one of the younger players in the California League all year, at just 18. Consistent with the A's emphasis on plate discipline, he drew 54 walks in under 500 at bats. He was definitely overmatched as his OPS hovered above .600, but he was so young and is such a good base stealer (66 steals in 88 attempts in the last two years) that I think he'll bounce back with a good year as he matures. He can become a prototypical major league leadoff hitter/center fielder in three to four years.

Backstop: Ramon Hernandez

The A's aren't in a hurry to move Hernandez up the ladder with A.J. Hinch already on the big league squad. Hernandez is a .294/.389/.457 career hitter and has a pair of batting titles under his belt as well. He has 15-20 home run power and has walked more than he has struck out during his career. He's battled some injury problems, which have slowed him down, but he is considered solid behind the plate and his bat should continue to be an asset.

Top Dog II: Mario Encarnacion

Encarnacion may be one of the better prospects you haven't heard about. He was just 20 last year and played quite well in AA-Huntsville, posting a .272/.382/.451 line. This is a slight step down from his California League numbers the year before, but again he is young for the level and managed to hold his own. He has struck out a third of his at bats the last two years, which is a cause for concern, but so long as he can keep the walks up he should be OK. His basestealing is currently subpar (11 of 19 last year), but he has good speed and it should improve.

On the Mound: Jay Witasick

Witasick is another ex-Cardinal pitching for the A's. It is odd how trading patterns develop. A's-Cardinals, Padres-Tigers-Astros, Marlins-Mets. Witasick has never pitched well in his three call-ups, but he has only pitched 51 innings in the majors thus far, not enough to write him off. He needs to start showing that his minor league success can carry over. He allowed just 126 hits in 149 innings, which is outstanding for the PCL (Edmonton is old PCL, not new PCL like Nashville). This was his first season over 100 innings in the last three years, so he may just now be getting healthy. He has a live arm, and heaven knows the A's aren't brimming with top pitchers.

or seeing them through. He is as committed to those ideas as he was as a player, when, as an outfielder who played for the Mets, Twins, Tigers and A's, he drew a grand total of 11 walks in 320 lifetime plate appearances. That's a walk percentage (BBP) of around 3%. Gary Jones, who never made the majors as a player, walked in upwards of 20% of his plate appearances. Which one do you think is more committed to the concept of plate discipline?

No matter what the exact sequence of events inside the A's front office might have been, it's clear that something has gone terribly awry in the A's rebuilding efforts. The departure of Alderson and Jones is a significant—possibly fateful—point of demarcation. "The strong give up and move on." Beane and Howe have given up—but they're still here. Because of that, the A's chances for recovery have been significantly weakened. <DM>

A MIDSUMMER NIGHT's DRAFT (3)
—continued from DET—

Wish was in charge—and I don't think it would have mattered if it was his house or not: a total control freak. The draft was to be held in the family room, "cooled" by a room a/c unit. The only cool spot I could find was at the bar across from the a/c unit. The couch below the unit didn't catch any of the breeze, but did gather some condensation. The rest of the seating left much to be desired temperature-wise. The bar was risky, since anyone could come up and sit next to me and look at my listings, but I felt confident enough that no one could decipher them. I staked out my spot by putting the empty "beer" bottle in the one place that wasn't too hot. It did provide me with a view of the guests as they arrived, so I decided to amuse myself by trying to guess which one was Psycho.

A couple of guys were already there when Pat and I had arrived, but I'd concluded that neither of them were Psycho. It turned out that they were brothers, Stan and Chuck, who both held some sort of state job down at the Capitol and were co-owners. They were calm and didn't look like they were well prepared as they chatted about various players trying to decide who they would pick first, none of whom I would have wasted a third round pick on.

The next to arrive was a short friendly guy named Dave, whose jokes had a sharp edge. Next were a couple of Norwegian looking and sounding guys named Sven and Bernard. Turned out when they wanted to talk strategy they talked in Norwegian. They had several magazines, marked up and ready for the draft. Almost at the same time a dweeby looking guy with a note book and reams of computer listings appeared; he immediately sat in Wish's chair and started going over his notes. I was amused at Wish's reaction when this newcomer took his chair. The newcomer had just picked up Wish's paperwork and deposited it on the coffee table. I couldn't imagine that this would be Psycho—it just didn't fit—but we were running out of owners. I went over to introduce myself, but he took my intrusion as an opportunity to spy on him. This couldn't be him! I wondered over to Pat and asked him who the dweeb was, but he had never met him before. A murmur arose as the next guest arrived. "Hey, it's Pete," went the refrain. Pete was the winner from the first half, and had quite often won in the past. Pat told me that he was some sort of investment broker. It was a few minutes before 6 pm, but no Psycho.

I talked to Pat about who he wanted in the first round, but he wasn't particular as long as it was a Dodger.

"Pat, the only Dodger worth taking is Valenzuela."

"OK, so get him in the first round."

Now I knew I was in hell. A Dodger fan, not that there was anything wrong with taking Fernando in the first round, but after that there really wasn't much on the Dodger team. Especially considering the rules that the league ran under. The only advantage was picking Dodger starting pitchers, since Manager Tommy Lasorda was loath to take out his starters since he could never figure out how to set up a bullpen. In this league you got points from your starters in three categories: Wins, Complete Games and Shutouts. Ten points for a win, another ten for a

shutout and six more for a complete game. Relievers got ten points for a win and six for a save. Hitters got a point for every hit, stolen base, run and RBI, plus one extra point for a double, two for a triple and four for a HR, and if they got three, or more hits, in a game you got to double the players hit score.

The draft consisted of 20 rounds. You had to draft five infielders (which included catchers, not that anyone usually drafted one), five outfielders, six starting pitchers and four relievers. Each week you would give the Commissioner your line up which consisted of three infielders, three outfielders, two starting pitchers and two relievers. Which ever owner got the most points got eight wins followed by the second place team who would get seven wins and a loss and so on down the line. I didn't like the idea of not counting batter walks and pitcher ERA, but they weren't my rules. None of the guys had heard of Bill James, and had a traditional way of looking at the game. Great emphasis was put on batting average—low average hitters were looked down on even if they walked a lot and hit homers..

—Barstow had come up and I decided to get something to eat before getting on the road to Vegas. The Blazer was behaving so well it was scary. After I stopped in a little Mexican restaurant I popped the hood, nary a sign of a problem. The meal was good and the price reasonable. I hesitated getting back in the car. I really hated driving in the desert and it was still a long way to Vegas and many more

		TEAM BREAKOUT					
		A's 1998					
Category	**RS**	**RA**	**W**	**L**	**Pct.**	**Rk**
5+ RUNS SCORED/HOME	273	181	29	8	.784	4
5+ RUNS SCORED	611	446	59	21	.738	8
5+ RUNS SCORED/ROAD	338	265	30	13	.698	11
4- RUNS ALLOWED/HOME	178	102	29	13	.690	13
4- RUNS ALLOWED	351	194	51	24	.680	13
4- RUNS ALLOWED/ROAD	173	92	22	11	.667	11
CLOSE SLUGFESTS/HOME	40	37	3	2	.600	4
CLOSE SLUGFESTS/ROAD	96	95	7	6	.538	7
RECORD IN BLOWOUTS/HOME	150	156	13	12	.520	5
RECORD IN CLOSE GAMES/HOME	120	119	16	15	.516	9
SLUGFESTS/ROAD	272	278	18	17	.514	7
RECORD IN SLUGFESTS	433	466	27	30	.474	8
CLOSE LOW-SCORING GAMES/HOME	32	35	7	8	.467	12
SEASON TOTALS	804	866	74	88	.457	10
RECORD IN CLOSE GAMES	291	302	31	38	.449	11
RECORD IN BLOWOUTS	314	361	23	29	.442	9
LOW SCORING GAMES/HOME	45	57	9	13	.409	12
SLUGFESTS/HOME	161	188	9	13	.409	11
RECORD IN CLOSE GAMES/ROAD	171	183	15	23	.395	10
RECORD IN LOW SCORING GAMES	65	92	13	22	.371	13
RECORD IN BLOWOUTS/ROAD	164	205	10	17	.370	13
CLOSE LOW SCORING GAMES/ROAD	19	24	4	7	.364	10
LOW SCORING GAMES/ROAD	20	35	4	9	.308	13
5+ RUNS ALLOWED/ROAD	258	378	13	35	.271	6
5+ RUNS ALLOWED	453	672	23	64	.264	7
5+ RUNS ALLOWED/HOME	195	294	10	29	.256	7
4- RUNS SCORED/HOME	100	215	10	34	.227	11
4- RUNS SCORED	193	420	15	67	.183	13
4- RUNS SCORED/ROAD	93	205	5	33	.132	13

hours to Walker Lake, but I wasn't sure how many since I had never been there before. Ah, the hell with it. I'd never get there if I didn't get started again. <continued in NY METS>

Name	AB	R	H	D	T	HR	RBI	BB	SO	SB	CS	BA	OBP	SLG	XR	Adj XR/27	Raw XR/27	OXW	DXW	TXW
Abbott K	122	19	34	8	1	2	10	11	34	2	1	.278	.338	.411	16	4.72	4.27	0.39	0.07	0.46
Blowers M	407	59	99	25	2	11	76	41	116	1	0	.243	.311	.397	49	4.05	3.80	0.55	-0.35	0.20
Bournigal R	209	24	48	12	0	1	21	10	11	6	1	.230	.270	.303	17	2.59	2.40	-0.63	0.69	0.06
Chavez E	45	6	14	4	1	0	7	3	5	1	1	.323	.367	.468	6	5.42	4.92	0.21	-0.04	0.17
Christenson R	368	59	96	22	2	5	42	38	106	5	6	.261	.329	.377	48	4.40	4.16	0.89	0.65	1.54
Giambi J	558	98	170	30	0	29	118	85	102	2	1	.305	.396	.512	110	7.16	6.63	5.31	0.23	5.54
Grieve B	580	99	171	43	2	18	93	88	123	2	2	.296	.396	.472	102	6.41	6.06	4.44	0.75	5.19
Henderson R	536	107	130	17	1	15	61	124	114	72	11	.242	.387	.359	98	6.16	5.68	4.05	0.63	4.68
Hinch A	336	36	80	11	0	10	37	31	89	3	0	.237	.304	.355	41	3.92	3.66	0.34	0.45	0.79
Macfarlane M	206	30	54	13	0	8	38	13	34	1	0	.262	.314	.439	29	4.97	4.44	0.78	0.21	0.99
Magadan D	108	13	36	8	0	1	14	14	12	0	1	.330	.403	.435	17	5.76	5.32	0.64	0.10	0.74
McDonald J	174	27	45	10	0	1	17	28	33	11	4	.260	.371	.335	25	4.84	4.40	0.67	0.33	1.00
Mitchell K	127	15	30	7	1	2	23	9	26	0	0	.237	.290	.364	12	3.24	2.91	-0.12	0.02	-0.10
Roberts B	181	30	52	11	0	1	16	16	24	11	3	.285	.348	.364	24	4.60	4.33	0.52	0.05	0.57
Spiezio S	404	59	108	20	1	10	54	46	56	1	2	.268	.344	.397	54	4.61	4.18	1.21	0.17	1.38
Sprague E	87	9	14	5	0	4	8	2	17	1	0	.160	.197	.343	6	2.12	1.69	-0.40	0.31	-0.09
Stairs M	520	96	159	35	1	28	115	62	93	8	3	.307	.385	.543	102	7.21	6.52	4.90	0.16	5.06
Tejada M	364	57	87	21	1	12	48	29	86	6	5	.239	.306	.399	44	4.00	3.69	0.43	1.17	1.60
Voigt J	72	8	10	4	0	1	11	6	19	5	1	.145	.215	.253	4	1.73	1.40	-0.43	0.16	-0.27
OAK	**5459**	**860**	**1447**	**311**	**14**	**159**	**810**	**664**	**1124**	**142**	**40**	**.265**	**.348**	**.415**	**809**	**5.11**	**4.71**	**23.75**	**5.76**	**29.51**

Pitcher	S	C	T	SS	ES	IC	HH	PP	TJ	S12	S35	S67	C1	C23	C45	C67	QWP
Candiotti	4.33	3.15	7.48	45%	6%	39%	33%	9%	12%	18%	48%	33%	27%	42%	18%	12%	.480
G Heredia	4.17	1.83	6.00	50%	17%	67%	33%	0%	33%	17%	50%	33%	50%	50%	0%	0%	.646
J Haynes	4.70	3.76	8.45	30%	6%	21%	45%	9%	6%	15%	39%	45%	3%	39%	52%	6%	.394
Oquist	4.48	3.34	7.83	41%	3%	28%	34%	10%	10%	14%	52%	34%	14%	34%	48%	3%	.462
Prieto	6.50	5.00	11.50	0%	0%	0%	100%	0%	0%	0%	0%	100%	0%	50%	0%	50%	.123
Rogers	3.53	2.74	6.26	59%	15%	62%	21%	12%	15%	44%	35%	21%	21%	59%	21%	0%	.615
Stein	4.05	4.20	8.25	40%	5%	40%	40%	10%	5%	35%	25%	40%	5%	30%	50%	15%	.418
Telgheder	3.00	4.50	7.50	50%	0%	0%	0%	50%	0%	0%	100%	0%	0%	0%	100%	0%	.490
Witasick	6.00	4.33	10.33	0%	0%	33%	67%	0%	33%	0%	33%	67%	0%	33%	33%	33%	.198
OAK	**4.27**	**3.36**	**7.63**	**43%**	**7%**	**38%**	**35%**	**10%**	**11%**	**23%**	**41%**	**35%**	**15%**	**42%**	**35%**	**7%**	**.476**

ATLANTA BRAVES

DON MALCOLM

ARMADA

For some reason the year 1588 keeps cycling to my frontal lobes, beckoning to me with a strange insistence, whispering that there is a bizarre, out-of-left-field (where else?) analogy between the epic battle between Spain and England and the confrontation building between two baseball and media powerhouses, New York and Atlanta.

The question: who's who?

The answer: more and more, Atlanta is looking like Spain. They've had the jump on everyone in the race for the New World, piling on with a slew of homegrown talent, the epochal signing of Greg Maddux in 1993, and their shadow looms over the game in a way that only the Yankees did in the 30s and 50s. (And, of course, the World Series shadow looms over them.)

Pos	1996 Lineup	1999 Lineup
C	Javy Lopez (25)	Javy Lopez (28)
1B	Fred McGriff (32)	Andres Galarraga (38)
2B	Mark Lemke (30)	Bret Boone (30)
SS	Jeff Blauser (30)	Walt Weiss (35)
3B	Chipper Jones (24)	Chipper Jones (27)
LF	Ryan Klesko (25)	Ryan Klesko (28)
CF	Marquis Grissom (29)	Andruw Jones (22)
RF	David Justice (30)	Brian Jordan (32)

But for the second year in a row, the Braves have replaced talent from their existing team with with new talent that is older. This goes against the grain of how Atlanta has practiced roster turnover during the 90s, as the above comparison of the Braves' lineup in 1996 and the likely lineup in 1999 demonstrates.

What keeps the Braves from falling over a cliff in these maneuvers, of course, is Andruw Jones, who by himself compensates for the other ten years of extra age that the Braves have shouldered in their starting eight over the past three seasons. With Andruw in one of the Atlanta galleons, they are still holding the line on age, if you ignore the fact that six of the eight positions are older now than they were three years ago.

What has also happened is that the Braves have brought in two players (Boone and Jordan) who add to the variability quotient in their lineup (see below). While there is no question that if you take the peak years of the players in the 1999 lineup you will have better stats, the problem is that you are far less likely to get a representative season from half of that lineup in any given year than you would have from the 1996 lineup.

Still, this probably doesn't matter much in 1999. But those Anglicans up north, those round-headed Mets, have gone out and glommed onto a bushel of talent in their own right. They have narrowed the gap via some aggressive interventionism, and there is a showdown looming. While the Braves still have an edge in front-line talent, the Mets are a far deeper and more versatile club, and that is exactly what happened to Spain when they sailed on England in 1588.

Too many eggs in one basket.

The Mets have a number of people they can move around in case anything goes wrong, or anyone gets hurt. The Braves don't. The Mets' hitters will have a higher secondary average than the Braves, and this will close up the run gap a little bit more. All of the subtle little indicators are turning away from the Braves, and while both of these teams should make the post-season in 1999, only one of them will be back in 2000.

I don't think it will be the Braves. Here's what's happened to their starting rotation, using the same three-year snapshot:

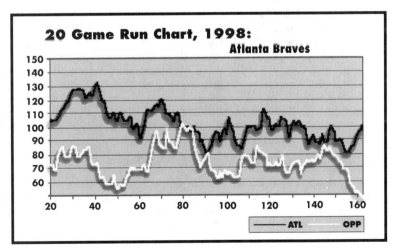

QMAX PRESENTS: "BAD" PITCHERS

HEY SKIP, EVER HEAR OF A PITCH COUNT?

When Tom Oeschger told me in Algebra class way back then that his grandfather had thrown the longest game in major league history, I laughed at him. Then I went home and looked it up. The son-of-a-gun was right, of course; Joe Oeschger and Leon Cadore hooked up to pitch a 26-inning 1-1 tie on May first of 1920 (maybe they were paying tribute to the workers of the world?).

One would be tempted to connect that marathon game to the horrible season Joe turned in 1923, but it would be pitching from the stretch, so to speak; the marathon game lasted less than four hours, and ol' Joe was no doubt pacing himself the way pitchers were wont to do back then.

Another thing pitchers and managers were wont to do back then was to shuttle between start and relief willy-nilly (to say nothing of Billy and Tilly), a practice Don Malcolm has coined the term "slap-dashing" to describe. Back then it was the usual practice, and Joe Oeschger did a lot of it in 1923. Of his 44 appearances, only 19 were starts (finishing 5-15, 5.68), and he never went longer than four appearances either starting or in the pen without an appearance in the other role.

The 1923 Boston Braves had three reasonable starters (Marquard, Genewich, Barnes) and then trouble. Fred Mitchell traded off between Oeschger and Tim McNamara (who went 3-13, 4.91 in 16 starts and 16

JOE OESCHGER/BOS(n) 1923							
1	2	3	4	5	6	7	S
1							1
1							1
		1					1
1							1
	1		1				2
	1	3	1	2			7
		1	3	1			5
C	3	1	5	4	5	0	0	18

relief appearances) in the #4 rotation spot. One suspects that Mitchell alternated between the right-handers based on whoever had the hottest hand, "hot" being a decidedly relative term here. If that's true, however, one wonders how Oeschger got any starts at all, because he didn't get any of his starts even into the "4" QMAX stuff region until a 4,1 start on August 4th. After that, though, Joe found the groove: four of his next five starts were at three or lower on the QMAX "stuff" scale, including a sparkling 1,1 5-hit shutout on August 11. What do you suppose happened then, after Joe showed that he was on track as a starter with his second straight complete game (QMAX 2,1)? You guessed it: banished to the 'pen for the rest of the season. I don't know about you, but I'm still scratching my head over that one.

--Tom Austin

Five Start Qmax: Oeschger

6/13 6/30 7/17 8/11 8/28

S   C

1996 Rotation	1999 Rotation
Greg Maddux (30)	Greg Maddux (33)
Tom Glavine (30)	Tom Glavine (33)
John Smoltz (29)	John Smoltz (32)
Steve Avery (26)	Kevin Millwood (24)
Denny Neagle (27)	Mike Remlinger (33)

This staff is a net seven years old going into 1999 and while that is not always a sign of difficulty, it is a significantly bigger age risk than any the Braves have taken with this part of their personnel base in quite some time. Swapping Neagle for Mike Remlinger may work out—and there is no bigger fan of Remlinger than yours truly—but it's not going to be a big pay-off, since the best that can really happen is that Mike surprises everyone, steps up a notch, and gets within 50 points of Neagle's 1998 ERA.

Likewise, Kevin Millwood was not much more than an average starter in 1998 despite his 17 wins, and there's more than a chance that he will backslide. One unorthodox thing that the Braves ought to consider doing in 1999 is to bring Steve Avery back: his QMAX "S" score was lower than either Remlinger's or Millwood's (3.78 vs. 3.89/4.14, and in a better hitting league in a tougher park to pitch in). In a sense, they have brought Avery back by acquiring Remlinger, but Mike does have the ability to work effectively out of the bullpen, and he might be most valuable to the Braves as a swing man.

Of course, the Braves do have a hot young pitching prospect in 21-year-old lefty Bruce Chen, and it's possible that they will opt to develop him more quickly than usual. The Braves have often nursed young pitchers into their rotation, but many of these were prospects whose upside was far more marginal than Chen's. Last year, Bobby Cos quit tinkering with his #5 slot and gave Millwood a shot in the rotation; this year, in order to have a homogeneous offense, the Braves are gambling that the back end of their starting staff will not undo a sufficient amount of what the Big Theee will achieve.

But the Big Three are starting to get long in the tooth. They are also starting their seventh year together, and there is only one other Big Three since World War II to do that. (No, it's not Larry, Moe and Curly.) That threesome: Early Wynn, Bob Lemon, and Mike Garcia. (Gerry Myerson, our expatriate analyst who presented us with a study on historic pitching trios in these pages last year, would want you to know that several trios were on the same team for this length of time or longer, but none since WWII have had six straight seasons with at least 20 starts.) Let's look at their record together from 1949-54 (the same six-year span that the Braves' Big Three has had) and afterward:

BIG THREE	SIX YEARS	RECORD	NEXT THREE YRS.
Lemon-Wynn-Garcia	1949-54	349-182 (.657)	129-105 (.551)
Maddux-Glavine-Smoltz	1993-98	296-139 (.680)	—??—

The Braves' trio is clearly zeroed in on immortality, but those Tribe pitchers weren't very far behind, and the Braves weren't in an eight-team league with the Yankees and their five straight World Series titles, either.

The seventh year was when the great Cleveland trio began its descent. They were a bit older than the Braves' trio: Wynn was 36, Lemon 35, and Garcia 32 in 1955, so we shouldn't rush into a prediction that Maddux et al are going to lose 100 points off their winning percentages in 1999. The great likelihood, however, is that they're not going to duplicate either their phenomenal 1998 winning percentage (55-18, .753) or their overall mark (.680, as shown above).

On the other hand: the Indians' Big Three had a .714 WPCT in 1954, a .575 WPCT in 1955. If the Braves' Big Three drop to .625 (50-32), and the rest of the Braves' pitchers come in at what they did in 1998 (51-38, or .573; prorated to the number of remaining decisions, that's 46-34), Atlanta will win 96 games. But the great likelihood is that without Neagle, and with Millwood probably also losing some of his WPCT luster, the Braves will come up 2-4 wins lower than that. They'll come in at 92-94, and that's enough to give the Mets a chance to slip by them to a division crown if things break right.

How likely is such a scenario? Higher than you might think. I'd give it close to 40%. I'd say it's upwards of 95% that Maddux-Glavine-Smoltz will turn in a worse performance as a unit in 1999 (it'd be hard for them not to, if you think about it), and about 60% that they get a net loss from the guys at the back end of the rotation and the bullpen. That's about a 55% chance that the overall pitching performance will decline significantly. Their hitting will probably improve, at least for 1999, and so that removes another ~15% off the chances that they will experience a major downturn in wins. That brings it down to around 40%, using (as you would expect herein) some of DM's home-brew "geometric logic" borrowed from our old pal Captain Queeg—a guy who never saw an Armada he didn't like.

LAST YEAR's MODEL

The not-so-hidden theme here, of course, is "too much reliance on yesterday." For the second year in a row, the Braves

WPA BULLPEN BOX—ATLANTA BRAVES

	PI	WPA	P	PPPI
Starters	1102	13.4	54.7	0.050
Relievers	436	2.6	26.6	0.061
Road	198	0.5	12.9	0.065
Home	238	2.1	13.7	0.058
Mar/Apr	79	0.5	6.5	0.082
May	86	-0.5	4.4	0.052
June	59	-1.0	1.7	0.029
July	72	1.9	4.0	0.055
August	65	0.7	5.2	0.081
September	75	0.9	4.7	0.063
Non S/H Sit.	298	-0.9	10.8	0.036
S/H Sit.	138	3.5	15.8	0.114
Low Pressure	227	0.4	3.4	0.015
Med. Pressure	136	-1.9	11.1	0.082
High Pressure	73	4.1	12.1	0.166
Entered behind	142	0.1	3.0	0.021
Entered tied	46	-1.5	5.9	0.129
Entered ahead	248	3.9	17.7	0.071

Name	G	PI	WPA	P	PP	PI	MI	ROB	T
Cather M	36	48	-1.5	2.0	.041	11	10	5	
Charlton N	13	16	.1	.2	.013	3	3	0	
Edmondson B	10	18	-.9	.7	.038	7	3	2	
Embree A	20	27	-.3	1.7	.062	5	8	2	
Ligtenberg K	75	81	3.0	7.0	.086	6	12	6	
Martinez D	48	72	.3	3.8	.053	21	9	4	
Rocker J	47	52	.5	3.8	.074	5	20	5	
Seanez R	34	39	1.3	2.4	.061	5	5	2	
Springer R	22	25	-.3	1.2	.046	5	5	2	
Wohlers M	27	28	.4	1.7	.061	1	1	3	
TOTAL		436	2.6	26.6	.061				

	|-------- Quality ----------|				|--- Pressure -------|		
	Dis.	Poor	Fair	Good	Her.	Lo	Med	Hi	
Cather M	3	6	24	3	0	23	11	2	(1)
Charlton N	0	0	13	0	0	13	0	0	(0)
Embree A	0	5	11	4	0	11	6	3	(2)
Ligtenberg K	5	3	33	32	2	34	25	16	(14)
Martinez D	3	5	24	16	0	21	19	8	(7)
Rocker J	2	5	23	17	0	24	16	7	(5)
Seanez R	1	0	20	12	1	19	12	3	(3)
Springer R	2	1	13	6	0	14	7	1	(1)
Wohlers M	2	0	17	8	0	16	6	5	(4)
Others	4	4	16	7	1	15	10	7	(4)
TOTAL	22	29	194	105	4	190	112	52	(41)

	7th inning			8th inning			9th inning		
	0	+1	+2	0	+1	+2	0	+1	+2
Cather M	0	0	1	2	1	0	2	0	0
Embree A	0	1	0	1	0	2	0	0	0
Ligtenberg K	0	0	2	0	1	4	5	9	14
Martinez D	1	3	3	2	0	2	0	0	2
Perez O	1	3	1	1	0	0	0	0	0
Rocker J	0	2	0	0	5	1	1	0	0
Seanez R	0	0	0	0	4	4	1	1	0
Springer R	0	0	1	1	2	0	1	0	0
Wohlers M	0	0	0	0	0	0	2	3	5
Starters	11	11	12	5	6	1	1	1	0
TOTAL	17	17	15	16	15	12	12	12	14
Record	4-13	10-7	10-5	5-11	11-4	11-1	4-8	10-2	13-1

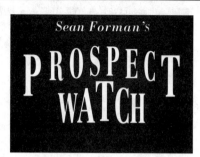

Sean Forman's PROSPECT WATCH

NAME	AGE	POS	LEVEL	GR98	GR97	GR96	AVG
George Lombard	22	OF	AA	79	54	45	65
Wes Helms	22	3B	AAA	67	60	62	64
Randall Simon	23	1B	AAA	45	75	60	58
Ricky Magdaleno	23	SS	AAA	54	62	57	57
Adam Johnson	22	OF	AA	51	59	41	52
Damon Hollins	24	OF	AAA	51	64	19	50

NAME	AGE	POS	LEVEL	GRADE
Rafael Furcal	17	2B	Rookie	85
Marcus Giles	20	2B	Low A	77
Asdrubal Oropeza	17	3B	Rookie	60
Ryan Lehr	19	1B	Low A	54
Ryan Langerhans	18	OF	Rookie	52
Travis Wilson	20	3B	Rookie	52
Wilson Betemit	17	SS	Rookie	52
Cory Aldridge	19	OF	Rookie	49
Troy Cameron	19	SS	Low A	48
Steve Torrealba	20	C	Low A	45
Tyrone Pendergrass	21	OF	High A	45
Glenn Williams	20	2B	High A	36

NAME	AGE	GS	S	C	T	W-L	ERA	K/H	LEVEL
Bruce Chen	21	27	3.11	3.50	6.61	14-9	3.09	1.57	High
Paul Byrd	27	17	3.71	3.29	7.00	5-5	3.69	0.91	High
Micah Bowie	23	30	3.27	3.77	7.03	11-6	3.48	1.21	High
Odaliz Perez	20	21	3.90	3.52	7.43	6-5	3.86	1.08	High
Derrin Ebert	21	28	4.61	3.14	7.75	8-9	4.51	0.45	High
Jon Ratliff	29	29	4.24	3.69	7.93	12-13	4.94	0.86	High
Ismael Villegas	21	18	3.94	4.22	8.17	3-5	5.28	0.90	High
Ken Carlyle	27	30	4.93	3.43	8.37	6-12	5.17	0.37	High
Anthony Briggs	24	20	4.45	4.10	8.55	5-9	5.36	0.74	High
Ryan Jacobs	24	15	3.93	4.87	8.80	4-5	5.90	0.66	High
Luis Rivera	20	20				5-5	3.98	1.51	Low

The Braves have a good farm system, especially in the pitching department, but I'm not really sure if they are utilizing it properly. Kevin Millwood, Odalis Perez, Kerry Ligtenberg and John Rocker have all played big roles in their current success, but do the Braves really need a big-time fifth starter. I think they would be better off going after some trade deadline pickups better than Greg Colbrunn.

TOP DOG: George Lombard
Lombard turned down a football scholarship with the Georgia Bulldogs in order to play baseball. At first, he appeared to be one of those normal athlete washouts as he struggled badly his first two professional seasons (140/260/155 and 206/325/300). In 1996, he showed some good power, and after improving his plate discipline in 1997 he became the Braves top prospect with a torrid first half. He went 20-20 in AA last year, and could become a 25-40 type player. His basestealing is excellent (70 of 83 in 97-98), and his plate discipline has improved each year. He's probably a 2000 arrival at one of the corner outfield positions. www.sportsjones.com did an excellent interview with Lombard last summer, and may still have it archived. Check it out. Comp: Moises Alou.

YOUNG GUN: Rafael Furcal
Furcal shot up the prospect charts with a tremendous 1998. He was younger than most of the competition in the Appalachian League, but still managed to be named the circuit's top prospect. He is above average defensively and may be moved to shortstop in the future. His baserunning is excellent as he stole 60 bases in just 304 plate appearances. Thus far he has mostly gap power, but that should improve given he'll just be 18 next year.

YOUNG GUN 2: Marcus Giles
What does a guy have to do to get some respect? Giles (the younger brother of Brian) has mashed the ball the last two years (.348/.435/.556 in 97 and .329/.425/.636 in 98), and yet after being named the league MVP, he still just merited mention as the 10th best prospect in the league?! Giles is considered a bit stiff as a middle infielder, but he'd have to certifiably stink before I'd move him. I'm guessing he'll move up to the Carolina League and rip the cover off the ball there as well.

BENCH PLAYER: Rickey Magdaleno
After acquiring every prospect ever to appear on these pages, the Reds cut Magdaleno loose and the Braves picked him up to play in Richmond. I'm sure they don't have much use for him as a major leaguer, but I think Magdaleno could serve many teams well as a backup/spot starter. He hits righties well, can get on base and has some pop for the middle of the infield. He'll struggle to hit for a high average, but he could help you with a 250/325/400 line. I think he would have been a better choice than Marty Malloy. Comp: Jose Valentin.

ON THE MOUND: Bruce Chen
Chen was a late-season call up for the Braves and if the Denny Neagle trade was any indication, he will probably spend some time in the rotation this year. He was excellent at all levels, as he struck out 210 versus 146 hits in 184 innings across three levels. His control was at times shaky as his walk rate was 3.7/9IP. However, working under Leo Mazzone I like his chances of becoming a star. One concern was his workload. 184 innings is quite a bit for a 21-year-old. When a pitcher advances across level, I think teams may lose track of just how many innings he is putting up. He averaged just 24.7 batters faced per start and had just one complete game, so it probably isn't a huge matter of concern. Still, it wouldn't surprise me if he had some fatigue-type problems.

have brought in talent coming off years where their production was close to their personal peak. In the case of Andres Galarraga, there was an established five-year pattern in place, and even though many people fixated on the Coors Field factor, it did not have much impact on the Big Cat's 1998 performance.

In the cases of Brian Jordan and Bret Boone, however, you have instances where both players are coming off their best performances in the past five years (in Boone's case, second-best: few if any baseball analysts out there have much of an idea what to do with Bret's 1994 season in the context of what has followed). While the Braves projected Galarraga's past performance correctly (at least as far as 1998 was concerned), there's probably more of a question as to whether they've done so in the cases of Boone and Jordan.

Just for point of comparison, here are the OPS numbers for these three, broken down into three categories—the year prior to coming to the Braves, the five-year average before coming to the Braves, and the first year with the Braves. We've added a fourth column, which is the standard deviation (STD) for the individual past five seasons of OPS.

Player	Prev. Yr.	Prev. 5	First Yr	STD
Galarraga	.974	.944	.992	.062
Boone	.782	.724		.097
Jordan	.902	.815		.132

Now this is merely an indicator of potential performance and a measure of how much deviation there is in it; it is not a predictive tool for telling us what anyone will do in a subsequent season. Other factors can enter into it—age, injury, personal problems, etc. Many analysts expected Galaragga to lose close to 200 points of OPS when he left Colorado. As you can see, he remained inside his STD range in 1998, increasing by .048.

Possibly the raw STD doesn't convey the true amount of possible deviation that this method projects for these players. Let's look at that STD as a percentage of the player's Prev 5 (previous five year OPS):

Galarraga	6.57%
Boone	13.40%
Jordan	16.20%

So measuring in this fashion, we can see that the Braves have signed two players whose performance deviation over the past five years is more than twice that of Galarraga's. That's a lot more uncertainty than they have normally opted for, and hence the chances are greater that these signings could produce less than the desired results. Add in the fact that Galarraga is a year older, and the odds are strong that somewhere in the midst of his tenure with the Braves he's going to evidence a sizable performance downturn, and Atlanta is pushing the limit on potential catastrophe.

TAKING A WHACK OUT OF THE OFFENSIVE SEQUENCE

And then there's the matter of the lineup paradox. The Braves will be using a lineup that features its oldest players batting #1 and #4, and have no really good OBP-driven hitter to bat #2 unless Cox decides to change this sequence around. (Bill James and others like to insist that lineup structure doesn't make much difference, but I'm of the opinion that their simulations of this issue are flawed, and don't reflect reality: I think the difference can be anywhere from 6-12%, and that's enough to make a big difference in game outcome.)

Here's the problem. Only Walt Weiss actually has a good enough OBP to bat leadoff. (Chipper Jones and Galarraga do so as well, but not even Ken Adams is going to suggest this as a serious alternative.) Once you pencil him in there, you then have a choice of Jordan, Andruw Jones, and Boone in the #2 slot. The problem with those choices has to do with OBP, as noted above. Here are the lifetime OBPs for those three:

Jordan	.339
A. Jones	.319
Boone	.311

Based on that, you pick Jordan, and the rest of the Braves' batting order pretty much falls into place from there:

Weiss	ss
Jordan	rf
C. Jones	3b
Galarraga	1b
Lopez	c
Klesko	lf
A. Jones	cf
Boone	2b

Now that's a solid lineup, but it's not likely to be particularly synergistic. Andruw Jones will have to regain some of the selectivity he showed prior to 1998 before the bottom part of this order produces enough OBP to make long offensive sequences very likely.. What the Braves are banking on, I think, is that Andruw is going to break out, and this is what they hope will resolve these lingering dilemmas. There is also some chance that they will decide to go against the OBP data and bat Andruw in the #2 slot. That's the only slot (aside from #4) that he didn't get used in to some extent last year, as the breakout of his ABs by lineup slot (next page) shows.

TEAM BREAKOUT
BRAVES 1998

Category	RS	RA	W	L	Pct.	Rk
5+ RUNS SCORED/ROAD	335	141	37	6	.860	1
4- RUNS ALLOWED/HOME	245	103	47	8	.855	2
RECORD IN BLOWOUTS/ROAD	203	78	21	4	.840	1
RECORD IN BLOWOUTS	322	139	35	8	.814	1
4- RUNS ALLOWED	537	212	90	21	.811	1
5+ RUNS SCORED	640	343	71	17	.807	4
RECORD IN BLOWOUTS/HOME	119	61	14	4	.778	3
4- RUNS ALLOWED/ROAD	292	109	43	13	.768	2
LOW SCORING GAMES/HOME	102	49	25	8	.758	1
5+ RUNS SCORED/HOME	305	202	34	11	.756	9
CLOSE LOW SCORING GAMES/HOME	50	34	14	6	.700	3
RECORD IN CLOSE GAMES/HOME	152	128	27	12	.692	2
RECORD IN LOW SCORING GAMES	183	107	42	22	.656	1
SEASON TOTALS	826	581	106	56	.654	1
SLUGFESTS/ROAD	171	116	12	7	.632	4
4- RUNS SCORED/HOME	98	100	22	14	.611	1
RECORD IN CLOSE GAMES	291	271	44	33	.571	3
LOW SCORING GAMES/ROAD	81	58	17	14	.548	2
RECORD IN SLUGFESTS	332	284	22	19	.537	5
CLOSE SLUGFESTS/HOME	40	40	3	3	.500	8
4- RUNS SCORED	186	238	35	39	.473	1
SLUGFESTS/HOME	161	168	10	12	.455	12
RECORD IN CLOSE GAMES/ROAD	139	143	17	21	.447	7
CLOSE LOW SCORING GAMES/ROAD	32	37	7	10	.412	9
CLOSE SLUGFESTS/ROAD	36	35	2	3	.400	11
5+ RUNS ALLOWED/HOME	158	199	9	17	.346	5
4- RUNS SCORED/ROAD	88	138	13	25	.342	1
5+ RUNS ALLOWED	289	369	16	35	.314	4
5+ RUNS ALLOWED/ROAD	131	170	7	18	.280	6

269

BOP	AB	R	H	D	T	HR	RBI	BB	SB	BA	OBP	SLG
#1	18	2	4	1	0	0	1	0	1	.222	.222	.278
#3	3	1	1	0	0	0	0	0	0	.333	.333	.333
#5	54	13	18	1	1	8	17	6	2	.333	.393	.833
#6	107	17	30	8	2	6	16	5	11	.280	.310	.561
#7	91	15	31	7	1	8	16	6	6	.341	.388	.703
#8	307	39	74	16	4	9	40	21	7	.241	.294	.407

Name	OPS
Javy Lopez	.919
Andres Galarraga	.767
Ryan Klesko	.747
Brian Jordan	.732
Gerald Williams	.713
Chipper Jones	.682
Otis Nixon	.653
Andruw Jones	.648
Bret Boone	.645
Walt Weiss	.584

Andruw's OPS after the All-Star Break last year was .885, figures that are best approximated by what he hit while batting in the #6 slot last year. As you've seen if you've read Tom Hull's essay "Percentiles: Past, Present and Future" (in Section Three), there is some question as to whether Andruw is really going to jump up to the "super-elite" level based on how he compares to other 21-year olds in history. It's clear, though, that batting him eighth doesn't agree with him, and I'll be shocked if Bobby Cox continues that.

I think a #2 hitter should be reasonably skilled at "taking a pitch" in order to allow for the running game (though in the Braves' case, the top of their lineup, with Weiss leading off, is not going to emphasize this).

Still, we now have some ways to quantify the above skill. Here's a list of the Braves' hitters and their OPS after taking a first pitch strike:

The MLB average OPS for all hitters in this situation is .637, so everyone is above average; you want someone who is a good bit better than average, however, and that lets out both Andruw and Bret Boone. Every way you slice it, the numbers indicate that Jordan is the best bet for the #2 slot.

We'll see what Bobby Cox decides; this time, it might actually make a difference what he does.

Name	AB	R	H	D	T	HR	RBI	BB	SO	SB	CS	BA	OBP	SLG	XR	Adj XR/27	Raw XR/27	OXW	DXW	TXW
Bautista D	144	17	36	11	0	3	17	7	21	1	0	.247	.278	.384	15	3.44	3.53	0.06	-0.09	-0.03
Colbrunn G	44	6	13	3	0	1	10	2	11	1	0	.289	.361	.423	7	5.96	6.19	0.33	0.17	0.50
Galarraga A	555	102	166	26	1	45	120	63	147	7	5	.299	.391	.589	122	8.06	8.24	7.39	0.37	7.76
Graffanino T	289	32	60	13	1	5	22	24	68	1	4	.206	.271	.312	23	2.51	2.61	-0.75	1.01	0.26
Guillen O	264	35	72	15	1	1	22	24	25	1	4	.272	.333	.346	31	4.05	4.18	0.64	0.69	1.33
Jones A	582	88	154	32	8	32	89	40	130	26	4	.265	.315	.509	94	5.69	5.86	4.02	2.77	6.79
Jones C	601	122	184	28	5	35	106	96	93	15	5	.306	.398	.541	125	7.54	7.75	7.28	1.33	8.61
Klesko R	427	69	113	28	1	18	69	56	66	4	3	.265	.352	.463	69	5.68	5.93	3.06	1.24	4.30
Lockhart K	366	50	91	20	0	9	37	29	37	2	2	.249	.303	.378	44	4.17	4.39	0.98	0.01	0.99
Lopez J	489	73	137	20	1	35	105	30	85	5	3	.280	.324	.537	80	5.62	5.72	3.35	2.92	6.27
Perez E	149	18	49	11	0	6	32	15	28	1	1	.327	.396	.527	28	7.16	7.46	1.58	0.85	2.43
Pride C	107	19	26	6	1	3	9	9	29	4	0	.246	.319	.403	15	4.69	4.89	0.46	0.18	0.64
Tucker M	414	54	98	26	3	13	45	49	112	7	3	.238	.321	.410	56	4.65	4.83	1.74	0.79	2.53
Weiss W	347	64	94	17	2	0	27	59	53	6	1	.270	.378	.330	50	4.98	5.27	1.90	1.49	3.39
Williams G	266	46	79	18	2	10	43	17	48	10	5	.296	.344	.493	42	5.72	5.97	1.85	0.39	2.24
ATL	5485	821	1454	284	25	219	786	547	1066	92	40	.265	.336	.446	826	5.19	5.36	33.90	14.12	48.02

Park Adjusted Statistics

Pitcher	S	C	T	SS	ES	IC	HH	PP	TJ	S12	S35	S67	C1	C23	C45	C67	QWP
Chen	4.25	4.00	8.25	50%	0%	25%	50%	0%	0%	25%	25%	50%	0%	25%	75%	0%	.383
De Martinez	5.60	3.40	9.00	20%	0%	40%	80%	0%	20%	20%	0%	80%	20%	20%	60%	0%	.328
G Maddux	2.85	2.12	4.97	85%	35%	74%	15%	0%	9%	53%	32%	15%	44%	44%	12%	0%	.711
Glavine	3.45	2.82	6.27	61%	27%	61%	27%	9%	9%	48%	24%	27%	15%	52%	33%	0%	.606
Millwood	4.14	3.28	7.41	48%	17%	31%	31%	3%	7%	24%	45%	31%	10%	48%	38%	3%	.504
Neagle	3.68	2.87	6.55	61%	16%	61%	19%	10%	19%	39%	42%	19%	10%	68%	19%	3%	.591
Smoltz	3.35	2.81	6.15	69%	23%	54%	15%	4%	8%	46%	38%	15%	19%	58%	19%	4%	.625
ATL	3.56	2.81	6.37	64%	23%	56%	24%	5%	10%	41%	35%	24%	20%	52%	27%	2%	.596

NEW YORK METS

KEN ADAMS

A WISHIN' & HOPIN' AN' HOPIN' & PRAYIN'...

The Mets just missed the playoffs in 1998 and they don't plan on repeating that mistake. They spent $91 million over seven years to keep Mike Piazza, and another $64 million over four years to sign Robin Ventura and Al Leiter. They've signed Rickey Henderson to come play LF and bat leadoff. They traded off the disappointing Mel Rojas and the surplus question mark named Todd Hundley and acquired Bobby Bonilla, Roger Cedeno and Charles Johnson from those new look Dodgers. Before exhaling, they traded Johnson to the Orioles for reliever Armando Benitez.

So what's the result of all this? A team headed to the playoffs? Or an overpriced collection of mercenaries? Let's look at the lineup first.

Rickey Henderson	LF
Edgardo Alfonzo	2B
John Olerud	1B
Mike Piazza	C
Robin Ventura	3B
Bobby Bonilla	RF
Brian McRae	CF
Rey Ordonez	SS

If the Mets don't sign Rickey they will go after another leadoff hitter, though eventually they may realize that they have one on their bench in Roger Cedeno. While this lineup doesn't have as much power as the revamped Braves lineup, it will be better at getting on base. Here are how the Mets and Braves lineups compare to each other (data refined

	BA	OBP	SLG	OPS	RC	RC/G
Mets	.275	.363	.435	.798	663	6.04
Braves	.275	.345	.470	.815	701	6.28

and manipulated from STATS' 1999 player projections):

It would be a big help if the Mets could find another SS to add some offense to the lineup rather than giving away two outs at the bottom of their order. Almost any other SS could produce more offense than Ordonez—even our old friend Ozzie Guillen (or, as Dandy Don refers to him, the Ozzard of Whizz) produced almost a hundred points more in OPS (.661 vs .577) than the Mets SS. In fact Rey was the lowest in OPS for all MLB players with 400+ ABs.. Here are the bottom five from 1998:

Name	TM	OPS
Rey Ordonez	Nyn	.577
Sandy Alomar	Cle	.622
Brian L. Hunter	Det	.631
Desi Relaford	Phi	.631
Deivi Cruz	Det	.639

That's bad enough, but Ordonez is also at the bottom in secondary average (TB-H+SB+BB/AB) as well. Here are the bottom five in SECA for 1998:

Name	TM	SECA
Rey Ordonez	Nyn	.105
Deivi Cruz	Det	.130
Hal Morris	Kc	.142
Carlos Baerga	Nyn	.145
Wilton Guerrero	LA-Mon	.149

Note that the Mets have jettisoned Ordonez' keystone partner, Carlos Baerga, who was fourth worst.

Can Rey go for the hat trick? Could he have the lowest

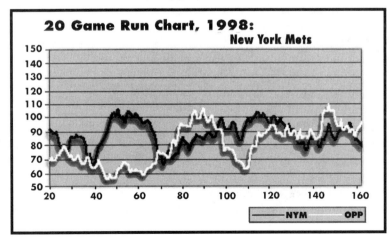

20 Game Run Chart, 1998: New York Mets

QMAX PRESENTS: "BAD" PITCHERS

CAN'T ANYBODY HERE PLAY THIS GAME?

No discussion of Bad Pitching would be complete without a discussion of the 1962 Mets, now would it? If you really want to stay up nights, consider that Jay Hook, the aptly named hurler of this piece, could arguably (all right, it wouldn't necessarily be a winning argument) be called the ace of the Mets' 1962 staff. I was tempted to "honor" the entire starting rotation of the Amazin's for this piece, but decided after all to take our man Jay as the quintessential member of that staff. He was an engineering student (as I once was) who once wrote an article for Sport magazine explaining why a curveball curves. (To paraphrase Brendan Boyd, "too bad he couldn't get the message through to his arm.")

JAY HOOK/NYM 1962								
	1	2	3	4	5	6	7	S
1	2							2
2	3		3	1				7
3		2	2					4
4	1	1	1	1				4
5	1		1			1		3
6	1		2	3		2	2	10
7			2		1	1		4
C	8	3	9	7	1	4	2	34

The interesting thing about that staff was that, because they were all so bad, there was no point in dumping anyone from the rotation for merely losing six or seven games in a row. Roger Craig (yes, the humm-baby one), Al Jackson, and Hook all logged more than 200 innings and 35 starts, so it could be said that They Still Had Their Health.

The strange thing about the staff is, they didn't pitch that badly. Look at Hook's QMAX totals: half (17 of 34) of his starts were in the "success square," meaning he gave the Mets a good chance to win every other time out of the box. This compares favorably with the ~25% most of the Bad Pitchers in this series are getting, and is

Five Start Qmax: Hook

6
5
4
3
2

5/8 5/30 6/23 7/19 8/11 9/3

S — C

actually pretty close to the league average. So how did he end up with such terrible numbers? A couple of things jump out at one: the defense behind him let in 22 unearned runs in his 34 starts, and no doubt many of the 229 hits Jay gave up were, well, catchable.

The other thing that jumps out is that when Jay wasn't pitching his team into the success square, he was pretty well horrible. In his bad games, he was really bad: the average ERA for games in "6S" games (top row of the "hit hard" region) is 7.47; Jay's was 11.46. And then there's the fact that losing is just plain tough, especially when you're actually pitching well: from August 6th to the end of the year, Jay's QMAX average was 6.18, and his ERA was 3.36. He went 1-8 in this stretch, and was thus ready for his time in the toaster oven the following season.

--Tom Austin

OPS, the lowest SECA, and the lowest isolated power (SLG-BA) all in one season? We might call this the Triple Crown of Thorns. St. Rey, as he's known to the Gen X contingent of statheads, is clearly a triple threat, but the crucifixion will have to wait for another year, as he managed to finish third from the bottom in ISO:

Name	TM	ISO
Otis Nixon	Min	.047
Tom Goodwin	Tex	.048
Rey Ordonez	Nyn	.053
Edgar Renteria	Fla	.060
Mark McLemore	Tex	.070

The Mets do have other options on their roster. Edgardo Alfonzo was a SS in the minors and played some at the major league level before moving to 3B. With the addition of Robin Ventura to the lineup the plan is to move Edgardo to 2B, but it might make more sense to move him to SS. They should give some consideration to ex-Marlin Ralph Milliard, who produced a .829 OPS at Norfolk last season and can play both 2B and SS.

Some argue that this would sacrifice defense, but these claims appear to be illusory. Both zone ratings and range factor put Ordonez below the league average. BBBA's Defensive Extrapolated Wins (DXW) is more charitable to St. Rey, putting him third in the league, but some of that is based on playing time. There were five NL shortstops with 500 or more defensive innings who had higher defensive winning percentages than Ordonez. Most of his reputation stems from his highlight film plays, not what he produces. So the Mets need to at least explore some other possibilities.

That being said, the Mets will have a deep bench. Allensworth, Huskey and Cedeno are a solid backup OF; Matt Franco and Mike Kinkade will be solid bats off the bench. Luis Lopez is the jack of all trades infielder, and Todd Pratt will spell Piazza once every lunar cycle. This is a good indication that the

Mets are serious about challenging the Braves this year.

But if you're really going to dethrone the Braves, you'll have to punch up the pitching side of the ledger. The Braves Big Three—Greg Maddux, Tom Glavine and John Smoltz—are better than the Mets' troika of Al Leiter, Rick Reed and Bobby Jones. The Mets 4-5 starters, Masato Yoshii and Hideo Nomo have more experience than the Braves' counterparts (Kevin Millwood and Bruce Chen), but experience doesn't always mean performance. The Mets will need Nomo to take a step or two back toward his initial performance level.

Big bullpen acquisition Benitez will be groomed to be the closer, but that job still belongs to John Franco, at least as we go into 1999. In last year's team essay we ran a paean to the diminutive left-hander. We based this on the fact that Little John had given up the fewest earned runs and had the most wins per 225 IP. In 1998 he managed to lose eight times without a single win and his ERA escalated to 3.62, the second highest of his career and a run higher than his career ERA before the 1998 season (2.57), but he still maintained his rank in both categories:

Name	IP	H	R	ER	HR	BB	SO	W	L
John Franco	225	207	79	66	12	87	171	17	15
John Wettleland	225	170	78	68	19	74	243	13	13
Trevor Hoffman	225	161	73	69	21	76	258	17	13
Dennis Eckersley	225	192	80	74	22	32	221	13	12
Rod Beck	225	203	82	75	26	47	196	10	13
Roberto Hernandez	225	187	83	75	17	93	222	16	14
Jeff Montgomery	225	196	85	76	20	76	194	12	13
Rick Aguilera	225	200	85	77	22	62	206	13	17
Robb Nen	225	195	89	79	16	91	238	15	13
Randy Myers	225	193	86	80	18	101	225	11	16
Mike Jackson	225	176	89	80	21	92	202	12	13
Doug Jones	225	228	92	81	17	49	187	14	17
Jeff Shaw	225	220	98	89	24	64	141	9	14

As you can see, Trevor Hoffman vaulted into 3rd place (he had been 7th last year). The listing below has been expanded to thirteen with some new additions such as Robb Nen, Rick Aguilera (relief appearances only), Mike Jackson and Jeff Shaw. (Lee Smith and Todd Worrell retired after 1997, and so they're off the list; this will also be Dennis Eckersely's last appearance.)

The rest of the Met bullpen is experienced and effective with Turk Wendell, Greg McMichael and Dennis Cook. The results might not be as good as last year as both Cook and Wendell are coming off career years and all three, plus Franco are over 30. This explains the Mets interest in Benitez, who is only 26.

One of the problems the Mets may need to address is on the bench, but we are not talking about a player. Manager Bobby Valentine has a history of coming up short when it comes to getting into the playoffs even with a good supporting cast. He never took the Rangers to the post season although Johnny Oates was able to do it twice with similarly flawed Rangers teams.

The Todd Hundley Fiasco shows how Valentine creates problems for himself and his team. Bobby clashed with Todd during the 1997 season due to Valentine's perception that

WPA BULLPEN BOX—NEW YORK METS

	PI	WPA	P	PPPI
Starters	1052	4.6	52.7	0.050
Relievers	527	-0.6	38.0	0.072
Road	273	2.1	19.8	0.073
Home	254	-2.7	18.1	0.071
Mar/Apr	91	1.7	6.6	0.072
May	72	-0.9	5.0	0.070
June	87	-0.4	6.4	0.074
July	97	-3.3	6.3	0.064
August	95	2.3	8.0	0.084
September	85	-0.0	5.7	0.067
Non S/H Sit.	383	-0.6	20.0	0.052
S/H Sit.	144	0.0	18.0	0.125
Low Pressure	206	-1.0	3.2	0.016
Med. Pressure	163	-5.9	11.9	0.073
High Pressure	158	6.4	22.8	0.145
Entered behind	218	-0.0	6.0	0.027
Entered tied	100	0.9	12.6	0.126
Entered ahead	209	-1.5	19.4	0.093

Name	G	PI	WPA	P	PPPI	MI	ROB	T
Beltran R	7	10	.2	.5	.046	2	2	1
Blair W	9	17	-.3	.5	.026	6	4	0
Bohannon B	21	40	-.6	2.5	.061	13	9	5
Cook D	73	93	1.2	8.9	.095	19	36	19
Franco J	61	71	1.6	8.5	.119	8	11	6
Hudek J	28	34	-1.3	1.2	.035	6	4	3
McMichael G	52	63	-.9	3.8	.060	10	12	9
Pulsipher B	14	16	-.3	.7	.041	2	7	0
Rojas M	50	66	-1.0	4.4	.066	16	9	7
Tam J	15	19	-.7	1.0	.053	4	2	4
Wendell T	66	91	1.4	6.2	.068	25	19	10
Total		527	-.6	38.0	.072			

	Quality					Pressure		
	Dis.	Poor	Fair	Good	Her.	Lo	Med	Hi
Bohannon B	3	2	8	8	0	6	7	8 (4)
Cook D	6	9	29	25	4	22	30	21 (15)
Franco J	9	1	20	25	6	19	14	28 (23)
Hudek J	3	4	21	0	0	22	5	1 (0)
McMichael G	5	6	29	11	1	30	13	9 (5)
Pulsipher B	1	3	8	2	0	8	6	0 (0)
Rojas M	4	8	26	10	2	27	13	10 (5)
Tam J	2	2	7	4	0	7	7	1 (1)
Wendell T	3	7	29	23	4	26	25	15 (14)
Others	0	4	13	2	0	12	6	1 (1)
TOTAL	36	46	190	110	17	179	126	94 (68)

	7th inning			8th inning			9th inning		
	0	+1	+2	0	+1	+2	0	+1	+2
Beltran R	0	0	0	0	0	0	1	0	0
Blair W	1	0	0	0	0	0	0	0	0
Bohannon B	3	0	0	1	1	0	1	0	0
Cook D	0	2	0	6	3	5	9	1	0
Franco J	0	0	0	0	0	0	1	20	10
Hudek J	0	0	1	0	1	0	1	0	0
McMichael G	4	2	0	3	2	1	1	0	0
Pulsipher B	0	0	0	0	1	0	0	0	0
Rojas M	0	1	0	5	6	2	2	0	2
Tam J	1	1	2	0	0	0	0	0	0
Wendell T	2	1	4	0	4	1	1	2	0
Starters	12	11	10	4	5	3	1	1	1
TOTAL	23	18	17	19	23	12	18	24	13
Record	10-13	14-4	11-6	11-8	19-4	10-2	8-10	23-1	9-4

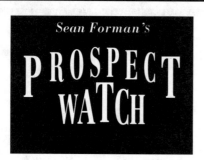

Sean Forman's PROSPECT WATCH

NAME	AGE	POS	LEVEL	GR98	GR97	GR96	AVG
Scott Hunter	22	OF	AAA	66	64	50	63
Ralph Milliard	24	2B	AAA	61	48	77	59
Terrence Long	22	OF	AA	68	43	55	58
Benny Agbayani	26	OF	AAA	46	54	51	50
Mike Kinkade	25	3B	AAA	48	61	29	49
Jay Payton	25		AAA	35	-	74	45
Jose Lopez	22	3B	AAA	33	32	60	37
Matt Raleigh	27	3B	AA	2	23	-	10

NAME	AGE	POS	LEVEL	GRADE
Alex Escobar	19	OF	Low A	87
Cesar Crespo	19	2B	Low A	53
Yorkis Guzman	19	C	Rookie	49
Alfredo Garcia	20	OF	Rookie	48
Brian Cole	19	OF	Rookie	46

NAME	AGE	GS	S	C	T	W-L	ERA	K/H	LEVEL
Mark Mimbs	28	15	2.87	2.53	5.40	9-2	2.08	1.24	High
Octavio Dotel	22	25	2.56	3.32	5.88	12-6	2.84	1.63	High
Dan Murray	24	27	3.63	3.30	6.93	11-6	3.18	1.04	High
Juan Arteaga	23	21	4.00	2.95	6.95	9-7	2.80	0.80	High
Arnold Gooch	21	28	4.07	3.29	7.36	11-15	3.87	0.71	High
Rick Steed	27	16	3.56	3.88	7.44	5-8	3.61	0.70	High
Scott Sauerbeck	26	27	4.30	3.59	7.89	7-13	3.93	0.67	High
Scott Stewart	22	22	4.32	3.68	8.00	7-10	4.76	0.64	High
Mike Fyhrie	28	16	4.31	3.81	8.13	3-7	6.64	0.52	High

The Mets' minor league system is to that of the 1980's Yankees. Minor leaguers are traded to fill holes on the big league squad and major league free agents are used to fill holes. In addition, the Mets' ability to injure their players is nearly legendary. When coupled with their emphasis on projectable high schoolers, this explains their horrible draft record in the 90's.

TOP DOG: Alex Escobar
Escobar was named the top prospect in the South Atlantic League, and could move up the ladder very quickly. He produced a monster year in Columbia hitting .310/.389/.584. Columbia is a pretty good hitters' park, but the Sally is generally a low-offense league and Escobar's 87 grade is very high for a full-season low-A performance. He has a strong power-speed combination (27 homers and 49 of 56 stolen bases) and his walk rates have been strong as well. He ran up 133 strikeouts in 416 at bats, so watch for that next year.

MR. SECONDARY AVERAGE: Matt Raleigh
Matt Raleigh turns 28 next year, so the odds of seeing him in a major league ballpark any time soon are approximately slim and none. Raleigh played college ball at Western Carolina and was drafted by the Expos in the 14th round of the 1992 draft. Because of organizational disinterest and probably some injuries (he's listed at 5-11, 235 lbs.) he's managed just 1792 at bats and 559 games in seven seasons. Only twice has he ever managed to hit over .270 in a league, but his career line is .229/.356/.473. In his seven seasons he has amassed 113 home runs, 348 walks and 692 strikeouts. Based on a 162 game season, that works out to 38 home runs, 100 walks, and 200 strikeouts in 520 at bats—dare I say, Rob Deer-like numbers.

YOUNG 'UN: Cesar Crespo
Since the draft was expanded to include Puerto Rico, Crespo is one of the higher draft picks from there. Crespo, a nineteen-year old shortstop, was a third round pick in the 1997 draft. He signed too late to play until this year. His main tools are his speed (47 stolen bases in 61 attempts) and his arm (voted best infield arm by league managers). Lest you assume he is the new Rey Ordonez, Crespo draws some walks and has so-so power, rather than draws no walks and has no power.

DR. STRANGEGLOVE: Mike Kinkade
There is little reason to question Mike Kinkade's offensive abilities. Through four minor league seasons the third baseman has hit .333/.399/.502. However, his travails with the glove have been legendary as he committed over 60 errors last year with El Paso. His defense did improve this year, but he's still considered a hitter. He's getting a bit long in the tooth to be a prospect, but in the right organization he might manage a career as a lefty-killer as he hit .357 against them last year. Comp: Matt Franco.

ON THE MOUND: Octavio Dotel
Like Seinfeld's parents, the top Mets' pitching prospects headed to Florida. Dotel, however, stayed put and established himself as a top prospect. Dotel is a smallish right-handed pitcher, who has a plus fastball and breaking ball, which he has used to great effect throughout his career. He has a career ERA of 3.28 and has allowed just 7.3 H/9IP and struck out 9.8/9IP. Dotel began the season dominating AA and was soon promoted to AAA where he continued to pitch well. The Mets have a ton of starters in the majors already, so there may not yet be room for Dotel there. I would utilize him in the bullpen and let him accumulate 90 innings there. He doesn't have much of a platoon differential, so he could have success in middle relief for a year or two.

Hundley's lack of sleep was affecting his play. Keep in mind that this was a season in which Hundley hit .273/.394/.549—his best year to date. Todd missed the first half of 1998 due to elbow surgery; when he cane back, Valentine moved him to the outfield, a position the slow-footed Hundley had never played before.

Met fans are still trying to block out the results of this experiment in terror. Hundley cost the team several wins due to his tentative play in the OF (and his .527 OPS didn't help). Hundley spent 34 games in the OF before the experiment was mercifully called off. Keep in mind that Bobby's mentor is Tommy Lasorda, the man who gave us Pedro Guerrero at third. If anything, Bobby is even more voluble than the leather-lunged

Lasorda, and his public feuds are a 180-degree contrast from the low-key style employed by Bobby Cox and cross-town rival Joe Torre. Despite the gains in talent, Valentine has the potential to push all the wrong buttons, just as he did in the last week of 1998.

A MIDSUMMER NIGHT's DRAFT (4)
<continued from OAK>

A rumbling started around 6:20 pm when Psycho still had not turned up. This was bad form, since it was delaying the draft—and, as Commissioner, he was to distribute the prize money for the season just completed. At 6:30 the door opened: a young woman came in and began talking to Wish. She was attractive in a pixyish way. Evidently she was Wish's girlfriend and she wanted to use the pool to cool off. Wish pointed out that her apartment complex had a pool, but she was insistent. It seemed she wanted some attention, but Wish was not receptive to this forward pass and it fell incomplete. She drifted out into the kitchen. A series of phone calls were placed to try to locate the tardy Commissioner, but Psycho couldn't be found.

The order of the draft was decided by placing numbers in a hat and each team could pick from the hat in inverse order of the finish from the previous season. It was suggested that we go ahead and pick our draft order and allow Pete to pick seventh and Psycho would have to pick last since he had held up the proceedings. Wish explained that one of the owners had dropped out and was being replaced by Mr. Dweeb (better known as Greg).

Just after we'd chosen the draft order, Psycho made his entrance. I thought the SWAT team was crashing in the front door. He was like a tornado, constantly in movement, talking without stopping to listen for a response. He asked what draft number was left and was told #6 which was right after Pat and I with our #5 pick in the first round, but we would be right after Psycho as we snaked back in the even rounds. He leapt around the room, glad-handing everyone—even Mr. Dweeb. I studied him from my perch at the bar. The first thing you noticed besides the perpetual movement was his height—easily 6'6" with dark brown hair and eyes. He was in his late twenties, maybe early thirties. Despite his back problems, he still moved like an athlete. He spotted me on my perch and made his way over.

"You must be Pat's partner. Hey, whatcha got there?"—as he spied the sports section of the Sunday paper with all the stats for the first half. "Mind if I barrow this for awhile"—as he grabbed it and began to read and lit up a cigarette.

"Not at all," I said, glad that he hadn't snatched up my hand-written listings as well.

Wish announced the beginning of the draft with Dave going first. Dave immediately picked Don Mattingly, a good pick. The next pick belonged to Mr. Dweeb, who looked at his printouts and announced Von Hayes. Stunned silence was the first reaction, followed by Dave laughing and saying, "That's a good one, now who's your first pick?"

But Greg was insistent that was his choice. Pat and I had picked Von in the 18th round during the previous draft, and he had worked out real well as a sleeper. But to take him with the second pick of the draft seemed ludicrous.

"Looks like you lost your number one pick," Psycho whispered to me.

I laughed and told him, "Yeah, might as well throw away any hope that we have to win."

Pete was next up and took George Brett. The next pick belonged to Wish who I had overheard

telling Stan that he felt that pitching was the key to winning. So I suspected that he would go in that direction. Which he did by taking Jack Morris. Pat made a beeline over to me. I could tell he would want Valenzuela, and I didn't want to discuss it in front of Psycho, nor did I want Fernando this early—next round, maybe. So before Pat made it to me I announced Mike Schmidt. Well at least no one laughed, but it was quiet. Pat approached me, but I motioned him not to talk. Psycho seemed involved with scanning the stats, but I didn't want him announcing our next pick to a guy that had two picks before we chose again. I motioned for him to go outside and we went out the sliding door at the end of the bar.

"I thought you would take Valenzuela?" Pat said in a hurt tone.

"We'll get him next round if he's available. The Dodgers aren't going anywhere—at least the Phillies will be in the race."

Pat decided it was time for another beer and headed back to the house, but called out when he was almost to the door, "Make sure you get him next round!"

Wish's pixie girl friend was swimming laps in the pool. She looked up at me and asked, "How's the draft going?"

"Just started really, it won't be over for quite some time. You going to swim all evening?"

"Well at least until it cools off," she laughed.

I could tell she wanted some company, but I really need-

TEAM BREAKOUT METS 1998						
Category	RS	RA	W	L	Pct.	Rk
5+ RUNS SCORED/ROAD	238	140	27	6	.818	4
5+ RUNS SCORED	492	301	56	15	.789	6
5+ RUNS SCORED/HOME	254	161	29	9	.763	8
4- RUNS ALLOWED/HOME	222	121	41	15	.732	11
4- RUNS ALLOWED	445	253	76	31	.710	8
RECORD IN BLOWOUTS/HOME	100	59	12	5	.706	5
4- RUNS ALLOWED/ROAD	223	132	35	16	.686	5
LOW SCORING GAMES/HOME	72	63	20	13	.606	6
RECORD IN BLOWOUTS	205	155	21	14	.600	4
CLOSE LOW SCORING GAMES/HOME	41	45	13	9	.591	9
CLOSE SLUGFESTS/ROAD	51	47	4	3	.571	6
SEASON TOTALS	706	645	88	74	.543	6
RECORD IN LOW SCORING GAMES	122	122	31	27	.534	6
RECORD IN CLOSE GAMES/HOME	155	165	22	21	.512	10
CLOSE SLUGFESTS/HOME	70	72	5	5	.500	10
RECORD IN BLOWOUTS/ROAD	105	96	9	9	.500	7
RECORD IN CLOSE GAMES	331	340	44	44	.500	8
SLUGFESTS/ROAD	104	110	7	7	.500	9
RECORD IN CLOSE GAMES/ROAD	176	175	22	23	.489	2
RECORD IN SLUGFESTS	234	255	16	18	.471	11
SLUGFESTS/HOME	130	145	9	11	.450	13
LOW SCORING GAMES/ROAD	50	59	11	14	.440	5
CLOSE LOW SCORING GAMES/ROAD	31	35	7	9	.438	5
4- RUNS SCORED/HOME	96	144	18	25	.419	6
4- RUNS SCORED	214	344	32	59	.352	5
4- RUNS SCORED/ROAD	118	200	14	34	.292	4
5+ RUNS ALLOWED/HOME	128	184	6	19	.240	8
5+ RUNS ALLOWED	261	392	12	43	.218	11
5+ RUNS ALLOWED/ROAD	133	208	6	24	.200	11

ed to get back inside, so I excused myself and went back inside. I assumed my position at the bar. I took a swig of my "beer," but it was the real thing, and tasty too. Psycho ha^d a smile on his face.

"Hey, I got you some real beer. That stuff you"re drinking was pretty weak looking, looked more like water."

"Thanks, good stuff," I replied.

"Made it myself, none of that namby-pamby stuff—I used champagne yeast."

"Champagne yeast? What does that do for beer?"

"Regular beer yeast will top out at 4.5 or so. Normal beer is in the 3 to 3.2 range. This baby is off the scale!"

"What do you mean—off the scale?"

"By my calculation it is in the 7.0 range give or take two tenths of a point. But the important thing is how good it tastes. I used honey instead of malt—that's why the alcohol rate is so high that it doesn't take much to get a good buzz going."

I took another swig. It was tasted good, and he was right about the buzz. I tried to put the bottle down, but that taste was something else and you just had to keep taking more. By the time I finished the bottle the buzz was growing louder by the minute. I slipped off the barstool with a step that was too light for my own good, and glided toward the bathroom. < *continued in BREWERS essay*>

Name	AB	R	H	D	T	HR	RBI	BB	SO	SB	CS	BA	OBP	SLG	XR	Adj XR/27	Raw XR/27	OXW	DXW	TXW
Alfonzo E	558	97	158	28	2	18	80	64	76	9	3	.283	.359	.439	87	5.64	5.42	3.83	1.01	4.84
Allensworth J	54	9	11	2	0	2	4	2	16	0	2	.208	.250	.360	4	2.65	2.52	-0.12	0.10	-0.02
Baerga C	511	47	139	28	1	7	54	24	55	0	1	.271	.308	.373	53	3.55	3.39	0.41	1.98	2.39
Becker R	100	16	20	4	2	3	10	21	42	3	1	.198	.336	.379	14	4.68	4.38	0.45	0.17	0.62
Castillo A	83	13	17	4	0	2	7	9	17	0	2	.210	.295	.333	8	2.94	2.81	-0.10	0.62	0.52
Franco M	161	20	45	7	2	1	13	23	26	0	1	.279	.370	.370	20	4.30	4.13	0.52	0.14	0.66
Gilkey B	264	34	61	15	0	4	29	32	65	6	6	.233	.321	.338	31	3.91	3.73	0.54	0.26	0.80
Harris L	168	18	40	7	0	6	17	9	12	6	2	.237	.277	.392	19	3.54	3.35	0.11	0.22	0.33
Hundley T	124	8	21	4	0	3·	12	16	55	1	1	.167	.264	.276	10	2.67	2.52	-0.24	-0.13	-0.37
Huskey B	369	44	95	18	0	14	60	26	65	8	6	.258	.305	.418	44	4.01	3.80	0.79	0.63	1.42
Lopez L	266	38	68	13	2	2	23	20	60	2	2	.256	.315	.345	27	3.33	3.21	0.05	0.69	0.74
McRae B	552	81	150	37	5	23	81	80	89	24	11	.271	.365	.478	99	6.28	5.96	4.89	0.59	5.48
Olerud J	558	93	202	36	4	24	95	95	72	2	2	.362	.453	.569	130	9.23	8.84	8.64	0.83	9.47
Ordonez R	505	47	126	20	2	1	43	23	59	3	6	.249	.281	.304	39	2.57	2.48	-1.16	2.63	1.47
Phillips T	188	26	43	11	0	3	14	38	44	1	1	.229	.356	.343	27	4.87	4.64	0.96	0.11	1.07
Piazza M	394	69	140	34	0	24	78	47	53	1	0	.355	.423	.625	89	8.97	8.58	5.80	1.14	6.94
Pratt T	69	9	19	9	1	2	18	2	20	0	0	.281	.301	.535	10	5.61	5.36	0.43	0.09	0.52
Spehr T	51	3	7	1	0	0	3	7	16	1	0	.141	.269	.162	3	1.82	1.71	-0.23	0.10	-0.13
Tatum J	50	4	9	1	2	2	13	3	19	0	0	.187	.217	.422	7	4.10	3.80	0.12	-0.03	0.09
NY	5514	726	1457	294	24	145	688	568	1040	71	46	.264	.334	.405	743	4.60	4.39	25.68	11.15	36.83

Park Adjusted Statistics

Pitcher	S	C	T	SS	ES	IC	HH	PP	TJ	S12	S35	S67	C1	C23	C45	C67	QWP
A Leiter	2.86	3.04	5.89	71%	21%	57%	4%	11%	4%	50%	46%	4%	14%	46%	39%	0%	.657
B Jones	3.70	2.83	6.53	63%	17%	47%	17%	7%	13%	33%	50%	17%	17%	57%	27%	0%	.589
Blair	1.00	2.00	3.00	100%	50%	100%	0%	0%	0%	100%	0%	0%	50%	50%	0%	0%	.884
Bohanon	3.25	4.00	7.25	75%	0%	50%	25%	25%	0%	50%	25%	25%	0%	25%	75%	0%	.525
Mlicki	4.90	3.70	8.60	20%	10%	10%	40%	0%	0%	10%	50%	40%	10%	20%	70%	0%	.362
Nomo	3.31	4.63	7.94	44%	13%	56%	19%	25%	0%	56%	25%	19%	6%	25%	31%	38%	.472
Pulsipher	7.00	4.00	11.00	0%	0%	0%	100%	0%	0%	0%	0%	100%	0%	0%	100%	0%	.062
R Reed	3.77	2.06	5.84	61%	29%	74%	32%	0%	23%	39%	29%	32%	39%	52%	10%	0%	.651
Reynoso	3.64	3.82	7.45	55%	18%	45%	36%	18%	0%	45%	18%	36%	9%	45%	27%	18%	.560
Yoshii	3.76	3.24	7.00	52%	3%	45%	21%	10%	10%	24%	55%	21%	0%	62%	38%	0%	.560
NYM	3.59	3.12	6.70	57%	17%	52%	22%	9%	9%	38%	40%	22%	15%	48%	32%	5%	.579

PHILADELPHIA PHILLIES

SEAN FORMAN

W(H)ITHER THE DRAFT?

Ever since the 1999 schedule came out in October, there have probably been Philadelphia Phillies fans with August 9, 1999, marked on their calendar with a big red circle. No later than the top of the second inning, the public address announcer will report, "Batting fifth for the St. Louis Cardinals: right fielder, J.D. Drew." Boos will rain down upon this, by most accounts, mild-mannered and very talented 23-year-old.

Curt Schilling won't even need to take a sign, as he will almost certainly stick it in Drew's ear on the very first pitch, unless the message was already delivered in their earlier May series. As dangerous as standing at home plate may be, Drew will want to wear a hard hat while patrolling the right field foul area in Veterans' Stadium.

When Travis Lee, Matt White and others were declared free agents following some clerical errors by several major league clubs, teams fell all over themselves to sign them. The two best prospects, Lee and White, signed for more than $10 million apiece. These signings, along with the $4.5 million given to Livan Hernandez, showed quite clearly what a quality amateur player was worth on the open market. Except, of course, it wasn't an open market. The talent available to teams was limited to four or five players. There were no fallback players available if a team was unable to sign one of the bonus babies. The presence of two well-funded and very publicity-conscious expansion franchises drove the prices even higher. As the top player in the draft, Drew felt he deserved a similar amount of money. On the open market, he would probably get it.

In 1997, Drew won every player of the year award in college baseball and was the first collegiate 30-30 man. He is considered by some to be the most complete college player ever. He is a true five-tool talent; speed, power, throwing arm, he has it all. He also led college baseball with 84 walks his final year at Florida State. A very strong case could be made that Drew was a better player than Travis Lee, and since Lee was worth $10 million, that is what Drew wanted as well.

Drew's agent, Scott Boras, had very publicly declared his client's

demands prior to the draft. He and Drew wanted $11 million over four years, guaranteed. The record bonus for a drafted player was at that time the Pirates' $2.0 million given to Kris Benson, a Clemson pitcher and the #1 pick in the 1996 draft. Well aware of his demands, the Phillies selected Drew with the second pick of the 1997 draft, following Detroit's selection of Matt Anderson. When the Phillies offered a $2.7 million signing bonus, a new record, Boras rebuffed them standing pat at their original demands. The Phillies clearly underestimated Drew's resolve.

When the contract talks with the Phillies went nowhere, Drew signed with the St. Paul Saints, the team of Daryl Strawberry and Jack Morris fame, in the independent Northern League. Part of this gambit was to keep his skills sharp and part of it was an attempt to circumvent the draft, as Scott Boras argued that Drew was no longer eligible for the amateur players' draft. Drew was playing for pay in St. Paul, and hence was no longer an amateur. All this time, the Phillies, other major leaguers, and journalists vilified his agent (and oftentimes Drew) for his "greed." The impasse continued throughout the year and as the 1998 draft approached the Phillies finally upped their offer to $6 million. Rather than agree to terms with the Phillies, Drew re-entered the draft and was selected by the St. Louis Cardinals.

It didn't take long for the Cardinals to get down to business as GM Walt Jocketty and Scott Boras settled on a contract less than a month after the draft. Drew received a $3 million bonus, a guaranteed salary of $4 million over four years and easily reachable incentives of $1.5 million. The effect on Drew's

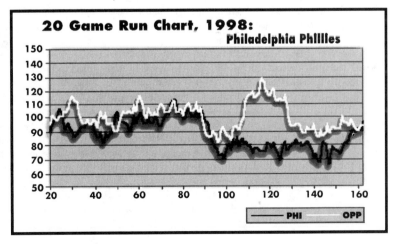

QMAX PRESENTS: "BAD" PITCHERS

SWEET LEO SWEETLAND'S BAADAASSSS SONG

Take this down, trivia mavens: Leo Sweetland is the Baddest Bad Pitcher of them all, the holder of the all-time record for highest ERA by anyone with enough innings to qualify for the title. Bad, Bad Leroy philed a 7.71 ERA in 1930 for the Bodacious Baker Bowl Bombers, a team that finished last despite a .315 team batting average, courtesy a 6.71 team ERA. This sky-high ERA and the lack of pitching choices implied therein explains why a smoking gun of Leo's caliber was given 25 starts to establish his deed of dubious distinction.

Let's tarry no further in dumping this heroic season into the QMAX barrel and shaking it a bit. Only horror fans should look inside, though, at some truly eye-popping numbers. Fully 20 of Leo's 25 starts were in the macabre "hit hard" region, while exactly two of the twenty-five made it to the fair-haired success square. One of those two entries, though, provides approximately 1,000 percent of the Minimum Daily Re-quirement for irony: on his first start on April 15, 1930, Sweet Leo marched out to the mound and shut out the Dodgers on three hits and one walk, a sparkler of a pitching performance in any era, though he only managed to whiff two batters on the day. Think of the high hopes he must have had! Think of the vertigo induced by the 24 (OK, fine, 23) horrible performances that followed!

Those two strikeouts (Leo averaged a mere 1.8 strikeouts per nine innings), the 20 "hit hard" outings, and his quite-reasonable

LES SWEETLAND/PHI 1930								
	1	2	3	4	5	6	7	S
1	1							1
2								0
3	1							1
4								0
5	1		1				1	3
6	2	1		1	2	2	1	9
7	1	2	3	1	3		1	11
C	6	3	5	3	5	0	3	25

control (3.60 "command" average for the season), and you get a picture of a man born without stuff, a veritable chocolate Èclair for the hit-starved batter's sweet tooth.

One imagines, however, that Leo's walk totals were held down by the fact that he usually served up a cream puff to hit long before a walk became a possibility. Imagine you're an NL hitter in 1930, carrying your gaudy .350+ batting average into Baker Bowl on a Sunday afternoon with Sweet Leo Sweetland on the opposing lineup card. It just couldn't get any better than that.

--Tom Austin

---

future arbitrated salaries will likely push the deal up to the $11 million that he and his agent were originally asking for.

Drew quickly proved he was worth the money, as he blitzed through AA and AAA, and then hit five home runs in 36 major league at bats. He will start for the Cardinals next year, and when compared to the $40 million/5-year contract signed by Brian Jordan, he is a tremendous bargain.

Once Travis Lee and the other bonus babies received multi-million dollar signing bonuses, scouting directors and media personnel alike have been awaiting the death of baseball's amateur draft. The draft was instituted in 1965, and has served its purpose well. It restricted the growth of signing bonuses and distributed talent in a relatively fair manner.

Some argue that an end to the draft will benefit the wealthier teams. Recent signings in the international market seem to reinforce this contention. Over the last two years, the Yankees have tossed over $8 million at players like El Duque, Hideki Irabu, Alfonso Soriano and Jackson Melian. If amateur players were in effect made free agents, then only the wealthiest pro teams would be able to sign the top talents. Draft bonuses would sky-rocket and small revenue teams would be squeezed out of the market. To a small extent, this is happening already. Teams like Pittsburgh, Kansas City and Montreal have recently become less ambitious in drafting top talent. Rather, they have chosen to consider a player's signability as an important consid-

eration bypassing some of the top players and instead drafting players willing to sign for less.

Some teams seem more willing to pay players what it takes than others. In this regard, I wonder if any change needs to be made, as the teams able to make smart, aggressive decisions are rewarded, and the lazier organizations are punished. The business of major league baseball is not unlike other businesses. If you fail to invest in your business, you will not be able to compete for very long. The successful teams view scouting budgets and signing bonuses as investments, while the weaker teams view them as necessary evils. Studies have shown that it usually takes about a $1 million investment to get a player to the majors. This is a small cost especially when these players will make less in their first four years than what Mo Vaughn will make in a single year. Investment in the farm system is the only guarantee of continued success.

There has been a lot of talk about the draft, so it appears certain the draft rules will be changed in some way. The question is how?

A complete abolition of the draft would have some interesting consequences. Contrary to popular belief, money would not be a guarantee of success in such a system. Plenty of high-priced first rounders, such as Brien Taylor, Todd Van Poppel, Mark Farris, have failed to make it to the major leagues. Such a free-market system would likely drive up the bonuses given to top players, not as high as some might think, but these new bonuses would necessarily preclude the teams paying them from going after other players. Perhaps a small revenue team, like Montreal, with a high-quality scouting department would be able to sign six would-be second rounders, rather than the one they would have signed previously. This might even be a better policy than breaking the bank on a top five pick. None of these questions are easily answered.

Teams are currently not able to trade draft picks, which can be done in other sports. This is another route to reward teams with a high pick, but an unwillingness to spend big bucks on a single player.

Another system that might have some appeal, would be similar to the current draft system, but would also give players the opportunity to negotiate with several organizations. Rather than an extended draft, teams would name five to ten players they wish to sign. Any player listed by one or more teams could negotiate only with those teams. Players not appearing on any list would be free to sign with any team they choose. At worst, a listed player could negotiate with only one team, which would put them in the same boat as before. However, in most cases, players would have several opportunities presented to them, and the teams would have more options as well. This would also prevent a more aggressive team from signing an inordinate number of the top prospects.

THE PHILS ON THE PHIELD

On July 29, the Phillies stood at 55-50, and just a handful of games behind the Chicago Cubs in the wild card race. It was an amazing comeback for the Phillies, who the year before were 68-94. They had finished remarkably well in 1997 going 35-22 over the final two months. In other words, over their previous 162 games they had gone 90-72. Ed Wade, the Phillies' GM, was discussing deadline acquisitions and the Phillies were acting like they were all the way back. Then following a loss to the Dodgers, San Francisco came to town and swept a four game set. It was all downhill from there as the Phillies finished out the season with 20-37 run. So which team are the Phillies, the group with a 90-72 162 game stretch or the team that went 53-109 over the other 162 games?

The pitching staff wasn't the reason for the dramatic fall off. The Phillies allowed 4.77 runs/game prior to the collapse, and allowed a slight increase to 4.95 runs/game over the final 57 games. The offense, however, lost all of its punch dropping from 5.00 runs/game to 3.91 runs/game. The Phillies also stopped winning close games. In the first four months, they were 23-18 in one-run games, but over the last two months they dropped ten of sixteen. The Phillies despite being in the middle of the pack overall in offense were producing in the clutch. For much of the season, they had the second best batting average and the most runs scored in late and close situations. Their relievers benefitted greatly as they posted a 25-26 record versus 50-61 for the starters.

The Phillies lineup revolved around two young and very good players. Scott Rolen was expected to lead the Phillies after winning the 1997 Rookie of the Year award. He didn't disap-

WPA BULLPEN BOX—PHILADELPHIA PHILLIES

	PI	WPA	P	PPPI
Starters	1040	-3.4	54.5	0.052
Relievers	548	-1.6	32.2	0.059
Road	268	-0.3	18.3	0.068
Home	280	-1.3	13.9	0.050
Mar/Apr	97	-0.6	5.9	0.061
May	100	0.9	6.5	0.065
June	79	-0.1	4.3	0.054
July	89	0.4	5.4	0.061
August	101	-1.6	5.3	0.052
September	82	-0.6	4.8	0.059
Non S/H Sit.	426	0.8	18.7	0.044
S/H Sit.	122	-2.4	13.5	0.110
Low Pressure	270	0.1	3.9	0.015
Med. Pressure	140	-1.6	10.3	0.073
High Pressure	138	-0.1	18.0	0.130
Entered behind	267	1.0	6.1	0.023
Entered tied	85	-0.2	10.5	0.124
Entered ahead	196	-2.4	15.5	0.079

Name	G	PI	WPA	P	PPPI	MI	ROB	T
Borland T	6	11	.0	.3	.024	3	6	0
Bottalico R	39	47	-.9	2.7	.056	7	3	5
Brewer B	2	2	-.5	.2	.090	0	0	1
Dodd R	4	5	-.1	.1	.010	1	0	0
Gomes W	71	110	.0	7.4	.067	36	15	17
Grace M	6	8	.1	.2	.020	2	0	0
Leiter M	69	96	.4	9.4	.098	26	10	10
Nye R	1	1	-.1	.0	.010	0	0	0
Perez Y	57	73	.3	3.7	.051	15	28	8
Ryan K	16	22	.0	.2	.009	6	3	0
Spradlin J	69	98	.3	5.1	.052	27	16	8
Welch M	8	16	.3	.4	.023	6	3	0
Whiteside M	10	22	-.4	.7	.031	9	7	1
Winston D	27	37	-1.0	2.0	.053	8	10	3
Total		548	-1.6	32.2	.059			

	I--------- Quality ----------I				I--- Pressure -------I			
	Dis.	Poor	Fair	Good	Her.	Lo	Med	Hi
Bottalico R	3	4	24	7	1	24	9	6	(2)
Gomes W	5	10	33	21	2	29	20	22	(13)
Leiter M	9	6	28	19	7	27	15	27	(18)
Perez Y	2	6	37	11	1	34	18	5	(4)
Ryan K	0	1	15	0	0	16	0	0	(0)
Spradlin J	4	9	37	16	3	38	23	8	(5)
Winston D	2	5	16	4	0	13	9	5	(2)
Others	2	6	23	6	0	26	10	1	(0)
TOTAL	27	47	213	84	14	207	104	74	(44)

	7th inning			8th inning			9th inning		
	0	+1	+2	0	+1	+2	0	+1	+2
Bottalico R	0	0	2	0	0	0	2	1	0
Gomes W	4	7	1	8	7	4	5	2	1
Grace M	0	1	0	0	0	0	0	0	0
Leiter M	0	1	0	1	4	3	7	11	4
Perez Y	1	1	1	1	1	0	1	0	1
Spradlin J	1	0	0	1	2	0	3	0	0
Winston D	0	0	1	1	0	0	0	0	0
Starters	17	12	9	7	8	9	3	5	4
TOTAL	23	22	14	19	22	16	21	19	10
Record	14-9	10-12	11-3	9-10	14-8	14-2	10-11	15-4	10-0

Sean Forman's
PROSPECT WATCH

NAME	AGE	POS	LEVEL	GR98	GR97	GR96	AVG
Bobby Estalella	23	C	AAA	85	71	78	79
Wendell Magee	25	OF	AAA	51	50	64	53
Billy McMillon	26	OF	AAA	38	60	80	52
Darren Burton	25	OF	AAA	48	46	70	51
Reggie Taylor	21	OF	AA	58	45	44	51
Marlon Anderson	24	2B	AAA	58	34	45	48
Manuel Amador	22	3B	AAA	36	59	55	47

NAME	AGE	POS	LEVEL	GRADE
Nate Espy	20	1B	Rookie	66
Pat Burrell	21	1B	High A	64
Jimmy Rollins	19	SS	High A	50
Shomari Beverly	20		Rookie	41
Ricky Williams	21	OF	Rookie	10
Eric Valent	21	OF	High A	69

NAME	AGE	GS	S	C	T	W-L	ERA	K/H	LEVEL
Anthony Shumaker	25	21	3.43	2.76	6.19	5-7	3.35	0.85	High
Randy Wolf	21	29	4.17	3.03	7.21	12-7	4.16	0.83	High
Ryan Nye	24	21	4.00	3.24	7.24	8-5	4.05	0.85	High
Evan Thomas	24	25	4.60	3.00	7.60	8-6	3.60	0.74	High
Calvin Maduro	22	27	4.67	3.33	8.00	11-9	5.98	0.57	High
Kris Stevens	20	24	4.29	3.96	8.25	8-11	5.77	0.69	High
David Coggin	21	19	3.95	4.32	8.26	4-8	4.25	0.59	High

Not to belabor the point, but wouldn't J.D. Drew and Pat Burrell be an impressive tandem at the top of this list? The Phillies do have some talent, but they block many of them with lesser talent. Also problematic for the Phillies has been the lack of a rookie league team, which forces their raw toolsy players to jump into leagues they aren't ready for.

TOP DOG: Pat Burrell
hit'ter n. 1. Pat Burrell. Burrell was the first overall selection of the 1998 draft. He played third base for the University of Miami, but with Scott Rolen filling that position for the foreseeable future he has been moved to first base. Burrell hit .303/.421/.530 in the minors last year, so the conversion to ash doesn't appear to have caused much of a problem. Burrell is the type of hitter who will be undervalued through much of his career largely due to his remarkable plate discipline. In college, he posted season OPS's of 1.557, 1.383, and 1.466, with OBP's over .530 each season. I wouldn't be surprised for him to be a hitter along the lines of John Olerud.

RECEIVER: Bobby Estalella
Estalella is a poster boy for secondary average. He struggles to hit over .250, but his plate discipline and power are so good that he is still a plus offensive player, not unlike previous Phillie backstop Darren Daulton. Unfortunately, he hasn't shown much ability to make contact in the majors yet. Given that the Phillies are enamored with Mike Lieberthal, he will need to hit a little better or risk getting sent back to AAA again. There is also the distinct possibility that they will trade one or the other for a pitcher.

NO RESPECT: Billy McMillon
For Billy McMillon, it has to seem like forever since he was considered a contender for the Marlins' left field job. When Moises Alou came in, there were hoots and hollers that McMillon was capable of playing equally well. Part of that reasoning was McMillon's .352/.412/.605 season. Since that time, his numbers have dropped across the board, down to .258/.342/.472 this season. That is still a better season than Ruben Amaro put up, but he's clearly heading down the Ray Montgomery career minor leaguer path. Comp: Ernie Young.

HEISMAN WATCH: Rickey Williams
Williams is a truly gifted athlete. He is a better football player than Bo Jackson, but he needs to stay on the football field. Williams is an avowed baseball fan and is said to like baseball better than football, but he will never be much of a baseball player. His grades have gone from 29 to 23 to 10, and this year he posted his career-best OPS, .592. Bo doesn't know hitting like that. In one of his more unusual rumors last fall, Peter Gammons reported that the Rangers wanted to trade for Williams and were then going to throw "J.D. Drew money" at him. Of course, Gammons' sources are usually fickle, so the chances of this actually happening are probably slim and none. Comp: Earl Campbell.

ON THE MOUND: Anthony Shumaker
Shumaker is a big, 6-5, left-hander. Up until this year he was almost exclusively a reliever. Around the end of May, the Phillies decided to use him as a starter and after a rough couple of starts he proceeded to pitch exceptionally well including three 1S games in August. Shumaker relies on exceptionally good control (2.3 BB/9IP), but he does have good hit prevention and has historically struck out a large number of batters. His career ERA is 3.01, so this season doesn't appear to be a fluke. I imagine that he will pitch in AAA next year, and he might end up surprising a large number of people.

point as he slugged .532 and managed a .391 OBP. A big surprise was the play of right fielder Bob Abreu. Abreu had been selected early in the expansion draft by the Tampa Bay Devil Rays. In what was not an inspired move, the Devil Rays traded Abreu to the Phillies for shortstop Kevin Stocker. Abreu posted a .908 OPS, while Stocker limped in at .595.

Beyond Abreu and Rolen, the Phillies received very little production at the plate. Rico Brogna had the next highest OPS among starters at .765. Brogna is among the worst offensive first basemen in the league, and would be merely good if he could play shortstop. If this is your clean-up hitter, your team will have problems. The Phillies also had problems finding proficient table-setters. Doug Glanville, the Phillies' big off-season acquisition, started off strong during the first half, but by the

end of the season he had slumped to a .325 OBP. Gregg Jefferies, who batted second for much of the year, was little better at .331. Abreu and his .409 OBP batted sixth for most of the year despite out-slugging cleanup hitter Rico Brogna and posting the top on-base percentage on the team.

Brogna's troubles point out another weakness of the Phillies' offense. They struggled against left-handed pitching, going 15-25 against southpaws. Rolen bats right-handed, but the only other batters with more than ten home runs, Abreu and Brogna, are both left-handed. Brogna especially struggles against left-handers (.627 OPS). Pat Burrell, the first pick in the 1998 draft and a right-handed batter, is the Phillies' first baseman-in-waiting. I have little doubt that he could handle major league left-handers better than Brogna already. The Phillies acknowledged this platoon problem during the off-season as they acquired Ron Gant from the St. Louis Cardinals. Gant will be an improvement over Jefferies at the plate and, unbelievable as it may seem, in the field as well.

Rookie Marlon Anderson appears to be the new second baseman as Mark Lewis was a major disappointment last year. Shortstop Desi Relaford should improve and catchers Bobby Estalella and Mike Lieberthal are both solid, though Estalella may spend some time on the disabled list with a shoulder injury. Glanville, Relaford and Anderson are all impatient hitters and will most likely batters to appear at the top of the order. Rolen, Abreu and eventually Burrell will have to drive each other in as the Phillies' table-setters will be subpar for some time to come.

THE PHILS ON THE HILL

On the mound, the Phillies were essentially a one-trick pony. Curt Schilling continued a remarkable run tallying 300 strikeouts once more. Schilling is a horse in every sense of the word as he has totalled 523 innings and 22 complete games over the last two years. Given the current contracts offered to Kevin Brown and Randy Johnson, Schilling is a remarkable bargain and as such is a hot commodity in trade talks. Unless somebody offered a sure-fire future all-star prospect, I would hang onto him as the Phillies have no one near ready to replace him. Beyond Schilling, their next best starter was Mark Portugal, who has departed through free agency.

Any injury to Schilling would be beyond catastrophic. The starting pitching behind him is poor, and the absence of his 270 innings and 15 complete games would severely tax an already shaky bullpen. The Phillies were already near the bottom of the league in innings pitched by starters, and Schilling accounted for nearly 27% of those innings. Schilling and the departed Mark Portugal pitched through the seventh inning 44 times in 71 starts, while the rest of the staff managed just 18 long outings in their 91 starts, including just three complete games.

Of the rest, Paul Byrd (eight starts) was the only pitcher with a sub-5.00 ERA. The Phillies have made some moves to patch these holes. Chad Ogea was acquired from the Indians, and should enter the rotation immediately. The rest of the rotation will probably include Byrd, Tyler Green and Carlton Loewer. Both Green and Loewer have potential, but Green needs to dramatically improve his control and Loewer needs to dramatically improve his hit prevention. Some darkhorses for the staff include minor leaguers Anthony Shumaker, Cliff Politte (acquired in Ron Gant-Ricky Botallico trade), Randy Wolf and Ryan Nye.

The Phillies traded away their three of their best relievers: Mark Leiter, Jerry Spradlin and Ricky Bottalico during this off-season. The remaining bullpen will include Jeff Brantley, Wayne Gomes, Paul

Splojaric and whoever they don't put in the rotation. If Brantley can't get healthy and Gomes and Splojaric don't progress, this could be an appallingly bad unit. The plan is to let Brantley close until Gomes is ready. Gomes has a live arm, but hasn't been particularly impressive in the major leagues yet, allowing 139 hits in 135 innings.

THE BOTTOM LINE

The main danger for the Phillies is the belief that the rebuilding is essentially over and they are ready to compete. Sometimes half-assed rebuilding is worse than not rebuilding at all. Brogna clearly needs to go, and the young players in the middle of the infield are shaky at best. Gant and Glanville are not long-term options in the outfield, though the Phillies seem to think Glanville is the best thing since sliced bread, and a good season from Gant might similarly enamor the Phils. The farm system is quite weak beyond one or two top prospects, and anyone following the Phillies for any length of time would not expect that to change soon.

Until the Phillies can acquire or develop another outstanding hitter (or two or three good ones) and about three more pitchers, expect them to oscillate between a .430 and .500 record. They are finally out from under the outrageous Gregg Jefferies and Lenny Dykstra contracts, so they will have some

Category	RS	RA	W	L	Pct.	Rk
TEAM BREAKOUT						
PHILLIES 1998						
4- RUNS ALLOWED/HOME	183	91	30	9	.769	8
CLOSE SLUGFESTS/ROAD	93	85	9	3	.750	2
5+ RUNS SCORED/ROAD	218	178	23	8	.742	10
5+ RUNS SCORED	504	403	49	20	.710	13
5+ RUNS SCORED/HOME	286	225	26	12	.684	14
4- RUNS ALLOWED	309	192	52	28	.650	13
LOW SCORING GAMES/HOME	41	32	11	8	.579	9
SLUGFESTS/ROAD	166	187	13	11	.542	6
CLOSE LOW SCORING GAMES/HOME	23	21	7	6	.538	12
4- RUNS ALLOWED/ROAD	126	101	22	19	.537	15
RECORD IN CLOSE GAMES/HOME	176	177	21	19	.525	9
RECORD IN CLOSE GAMES	368	369	44	44	.500	9
RECORD IN SLUGFESTS	383	422	26	27	.491	9
RECORD IN CLOSE GAMES/ROAD	192	192	23	25	.479	4
SEASON TOTALS	713	808	75	87	.463	11
SLUGFESTS/HOME	217	235	13	16	.448	14
RECORD IN LOW SCORING GAMES	99	119	22	30	.423	12
CLOSE SLUGFESTS/HOME	86	93	5	7	.417	13
RECORD IN BLOWOUTS/HOME	100	138	7	12	.368	14
CLOSE LOW SCORING GAMES/ROAD	49	58	9	16	.360	13
LOW SCORING GAMES/ROAD	58	87	11	22	.333	14
4- RUNS SCORED/HOME	103	195	14	29	.326	9
5+ RUNS ALLOWED/ROAD	198	287	13	27	.325	2
RECORD IN BLOWOUTS	151	249	10	23	.303	15
4- RUNS SCORED	209	405	26	67	.280	8
5+ RUNS ALLOWED	404	616	23	59	.280	7
4- RUNS SCORED/ROAD	106	210	12	38	.240	6
5+ RUNS ALLOWED/HOME	206	329	10	32	.238	9
RECORD IN BLOWOUTS/ROAD	51	111	3	11	.214	15

money to spend in the not so distant future. They are letting the young guys play and it is paying off, but they also need to invest in their team. Adding some more scouts and more aggressively drafting and signing amateur talent would significantly improve their future chances.

	<——Park Adjusted Statistics													——>	Adj	Raw			
Name	**AB**	**R**	**H**	**D**	**T**	**HR**	**RBI**	**BB**	**SO**	**SB**	**CS**	**BA**	**OBP**	**SLG**	**XR**	**XR/27**	**XR/27**	**OXW**	**DXW**	**TXW**
Abreu B	500	64	151	27	5	16	70	81	130	16	10	.302	.397	.476	93	6.72	7.24	4.92	1.12	6.04
Amaro R	107	6	19	5	0	1	10	6	15	0	0	.181	.218	.249	6	1.83	2.03	-0.52	0.13	-0.39
Anderson M	43	4	13	3	0	1	3	1	6	2	0	.313	.321	.439	7	5.77	6.31	0.29	0.10	0.39
Arias A	133	16	38	7	0	1	15	13	18	2	0	.283	.347	.358	17	4.74	5.15	0.57	0.27	0.84
Brogna R	566	72	145	33	3	19	98	48	123	6	7	.256	.309	.426	74	4.44	4.82	1.94	0.94	2.88
Estalella B	166	15	30	6	1	8	19	12	48	0	0	.182	.239	.370	16	3.00	3.22	-0.19	0.38	0.19
Glanville D	680	98	184	26	6	8	46	40	87	19	7	.270	.315	.362	79	4.12	4.48	1.71	1.73	3.44
Hudler R	41	2	5	1	0	0	2	4	12	0	0	.117	.193	.137	0	0.12	0.27	-0.45	-0.03	-0.48
Jefferies G	484	60	137	20	3	8	45	28	26	10	3	.283	.320	.384	56	4.08	4.47	1.13	0.63	1.76
Jordan K	250	21	67	12	0	2	26	8	29	0	0	.268	.294	.338	23	3.27	3.54	0.00	0.35	0.35
Lewis M	519	49	126	20	2	9	51	47	109	3	3	.242	.304	.338	53	3.38	3.62	0.17	1.42	1.59
Lieberthal M	314	37	78	14	3	8	41	16	43	2	1	.247	.295	.382	37	4.06	4.40	0.73	1.45	2.18
Magee W	75	9	22	6	1	1	11	7	11	0	0	.291	.350	.437	10	4.57	4.66	0.28	0.11	0.39
Parent M	113	7	24	4	0	1	12	10	29	1	1	.214	.270	.273	10	2.74	2.95	-0.19	0.43	0.24
Relaford D	495	41	117	23	3	5	38	32	85	8	5	.236	.283	.322	46	3.03	3.33	-0.41	1.17	0.76
Rolen S	604	112	168	42	4	30	101	90	138	12	7	.279	.379	.508	115	6.78	7.34	6.08	1.40	7.48
Sefcik K	170	25	52	7	2	3	19	24	31	4	2	.306	.412	.419	30	6.46	6.82	1.58	0.25	1.83
Zuber J	45	6	11	3	1	2	6	6	9	0	0	.242	.343	.490	7	5.71	5.75	0.32	0.02	0.34
PHI	**5634**	**666**	**1439**	**265**	**32**	**122**	**628**	**491**	**1059**	**85**	**47**	**.255**	**.317**	**.379**	**689**	**4.15**	**4.49**	**17.96**	**11.87**	**29.83**

Pitcher	S	C	T	SS	ES	IC	HH	PP	TJ	S12	S35	S67	C1	C23	C45	C67	QWP
Beech	4.29	4.10	8.38	38%	5%	19%	33%	14%	0%	19%	48%	33%	0%	29%	62%	10%	.414
Byrd	2.63	2.88	5.50	75%	25%	63%	25%	13%	0%	63%	13%	25%	25%	38%	38%	0%	.670
C Schilling	3.46	2.06	5.51	66%	31%	77%	23%	3%	29%	43%	34%	23%	43%	46%	11%	0%	.663
Loewer	5.09	3.36	8.45	32%	5%	23%	50%	0%	14%	5%	45%	50%	9%	50%	36%	5%	.404
Mi Grace	5.07	3.53	8.60	27%	13%	27%	60%	7%	7%	13%	27%	60%	13%	27%	53%	7%	.361
Portugal	4.31	2.65	6.96	58%	12%	50%	38%	8%	12%	27%	35%	38%	27%	46%	27%	0%	.521
Ryan	3.00	7.00	10.00	0%	0%	0%	0%	0%	0%	0%	100%	0%	0%	0%	0%	100%	.171
Stephenson	4.83	5.33	10.17	0%	0%	0%	33%	17%	0%	0%	67%	33%	0%	0%	50%	50%	.241
Ty Green	3.68	4.21	7.89	39%	4%	36%	18%	14%	11%	25%	57%	18%	4%	29%	43%	25%	.475
Welch	6.50	6.00	12.50	0%	0%	0%	100%	0%	0%	0%	0%	100%	0%	0%	50%	50%	.013
PHI	**4.15**	**3.33**	**7.48**	**45%**	**13%**	**41%**	**34%**	**8%**	**12%**	**25%**	**41%**	**34%**	**18%**	**37%**	**36%**	**10%**	**.488**

NATIONAL LEAGUE EAST

MONTREAL EXPOS

RON JOHNSON & SCOT HUGHES

THE EXPO ECONOMIC MYTH DISPELLED

It's an article of faith to most baseball observers that the Expos just aren't viable in Montreal. The perception: they can't afford the payroll required to compete and they're losing money hand over fist.

The reality: the Expos always make money and could readily afford a much larger payroll. (The longish answer follows. The really long answer will have to wait for Scot to write a book on the subject.)

The playing field isn't precisely level for the Expos. When people say Montreal is a hockey town, they're not kidding. Sean Lahman did a fascinating study and found that a Canadien's game (home or away) reduces Expos attendance by roughly 20%.

Most of their other problems are self-inflicted. They have a poor local TV contract in no small part because of departing team president Claude Brochu. (Space limitations prevent us from including the whole sorry saga). They almost literally don't promote the team at all. And their whining about how they can't afford to retain free agents (rather than focusing on the exciting new talent) carries the message to the casual fan that there's no hope.

Ironic aside: Don Malcolm wanted to recruit writers who live close to the team they will be writing about. It's not more than two hours from my home (Ron Johnson speaking) to the stadium; yet as far as Expos' marketing department is concerned, I might as well be on Mars. The Blue Jays find it worthwhile to advertise here, even though Ottawa is a natural and potentially very important part of the Expos market. Ottawa used to be an Expos town—period. Even now, in spite of the fact that the Jays dominate the TV news and local newspaper coverage, there are still thousands of Expos fans here. In addition, there's a natural tie-in with the AAA team.

While Montreal is plenty big enough to support a major league team, the city has gone through some pretty rocky times. Still, this isn't new: the Expos used to draw just fine. Even the most cursory examination of attendance records will show that Montreal responds as all cities do to successful teams.

Claude Brochu stated that the Expos took in about $25M US from US sources, and that US sources accounted for 50% of the team's revenues. He may have some reason to understate this, but it will do as a starting point. He was testifying before a government commission.

The Expos payroll for the 1998 season was about $9M US. In 1995, the Expos claimed $20M CAN (~$16M US at the time) in non-payroll expenses. Give them the benefit of the doubt, and bump that figure up to $20M US for 1998.

We can approach this another way. Assume total expenses are the same as in the preceding paragraph, or just under $30M US. What revenue streams did the Expos have?

Attendance and concessions: At a talk at Concordia University in 1995, Expos' Marketing Vice-President Richard Morency said the Expos take in $15 CAN for every ticket sold. Even with the current highly unfavorable exchange rate and assuming no increase in ticket prices, that still gives $10 US per ticket sold (which is almost certainly on the low side for 1998). In any event, assuming ~$10 US per fan, the Expos still took in ~$10M.

Local broadcast rights: Around $4M US (and will go up starting next year).

In-stadium advertising: Projected at $2M US a year when the Expos bought the rights to that.

Licensing revenue: Roughly $5M for each team.

US TV deal: $14M US.

Revenue sharing: At least $10M US. Probably closer to $15M.

This comes pretty close to the $50M that Brochu claimed. And these revenues are as low as is at all probable to project.

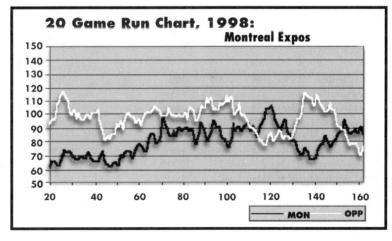

QMAX PRESENTS: "BAD" PITCHERS

WHEN YOU SAID HASH-SLINGER, I THOUGHT.

I must avoid the temptation to fill this space with pithy quotes and side-splitting anecdotes from the Spaceman's career, because I easily could. Suffice to say that the man was the first to refer to Don Zimmer as The Gerbil, and the first (that I know of) to suggest the sprinkling of marijuana on breakfast cereal (Weedies?).

What was often missed when discussing the Spaceman was that he could really pitch, and that there was often a method behind his madness (he claimed, with some justification, that some of his odder quotes had the ulterior motive of distracting the Boston media from harping on the Curse of the Bambino during a Bosox pennant race).

But there I go. We are here to bury the Spaceman, not to praise him. By 1980, injuries and age had robbed Bill of what fastball

he had; he had been making a living on junk (that's right, a "junkie") for several years. The evidence of 1980 shows that there was still a method to the madness. It's true that NL batters were fattening their batting averages on a diet of Lee's junk food, but precious few were getting free rides to first. Lee's QMAX box tells the story: 14 of 18 starts in the "hit hard" region, and 22% of them in the heart of the "soldier of fortune" region (6,1-6,2). This was a man who could still put the ball right where he wanted it, although he couldn't quite get it there as soon as he might have liked.

And here the (mezcal) worm turns, yet again: one of the findings of the original QMAX article by Ken and Don found that the typical "soldier of fortune" (which the

BILL LEE/MON 1980								
	1	2	3	4	5	6	7	S
1								0
2								0
3	2							2
4								0
5			2					2
6	1	3	3	2			1	10
7			3	1				4
C	3	3	8	3	0	0	1	18

1980 Bill Lee most certainly is) is held in rather too high of esteem by his manager, who admires his ability to "gut out" a tough game or a tough inning, even while giving up base hits with alarming regularity. Lee, even while playing the soldier of fortune part perfectly while on the mound, was too outspoken and too much a lefty on the political mound to play the good soldier on level ground. As a result of this, it is widely believed that his career ended via an informal blacklist among major league GM's. He may be the only case in the last several decades of a left-handed pitcher with a pulse who could not find work. He coulda been a contendah, you know.

--Tom Austin

It's certainly possible that the current ownership could choose to sell the team if the proposed new stadium is not built - and we really won't know for sure for months. Just because they make a healthy profit each year doesn't mean that the franchise would not be more valuable in another location. In which case, shed no tears for the ownership. The minimum they'll get is double (probably more like triple) their investment.

Assuming they do stay in Montreal and get a new stadium, the Expos are in great shape. A reasonable estimate of the financial picture follows.

(all figures US dollars)

REVENUES:	1998	1999	2000	2001
Attendance	$10M	$13M	$15M	$15M
Local Broadcast	$4M	$5M	$5M	$5M
Misc. Stadium	$2M	$2M	$2M	$2M
Licensing	$5M	$5M	$5M	$5M
US Broadcast	$14M	$14M	$14M	$14M
Revenue Sharing	$15M	$17M	$20M	$20M?
TOTAL REVENUE	**$50M**	**$56M**	**$61M**	**$61M**

EXPENSES

Misc. non-payroll	$20M	$22M	$25M	$27M
Payroll	$10M	$24M	$26M	$24M
Profit	$20M	$10M	$10M	$10M
TOTAL EXPENSES	**$50M**	**$56M**	**$61M**	**$61M**

All numbers projected, of course. We've tried to be conservative and underestimate revenues, and overestimate expenses.

A new stadium should have any number of positive effects. Best guess is a huge increase in attendance revenue. After all, all of the luxury boxes are sold and the proposed location is excellent. 35-40M in direct attendance revenue hardly seems unreasonable. In addition, miscellaneous stadium revenue will increase—and do so significantly.

Revenue sharing money will drop, but that should be offset by the new US TV deal. MLB has yet to sign a new US TV deal that paid less per team per season than the preceding deal, and it's extremely unlikely, given the current "buzz" about the game, that it will happen now. It's probably safe to predict that the new deal will average $20M+ per team per season).

Just in terms of local revenues, it's possible to project the Expos going from this year's low of ~$16M US to ~$20-25M US at the Big O over the next few seasons, to $75M+ US when they move into the new park.

Even without the new stadium, the Expos can afford to triple the 1998 payroll and still make a profit. The owners could very likely afford a $40M payroll for each of the next three years. Given the core of young players signed inexpensively, this could be enough to plug a few holes and turn the team into legitimate contenders in 2000 or 2001.

They could also keep the payroll below $10M and make $10M US in profits per season without selling a single ticket.

PLAY OF THE DECADE

The opportunity for a 53271 double play doesn't happen every day. That it would have happened in the 11th inning makes the play particularly interesting.

Mike Kelly drew a one out walk. With Kelly running on the play, third-baseman Shane Andrews charged a slow ground ball and threw Dave Martinez out at first. Kelly never even broke stride and Ryan McGuire threw to third. Just one hitch, nobody was covering the bag.

Catcher Chris Widger sized up the situation early and lit out for third at the same time Kelly did. He was almost in time, but was only able to get the tip of his glove on the ball which deflected into left field.

Again Kelly was alert and raced for home, just beating left fielder Robert Perez's throw to Steve Kline (the pitcher) who was covering the plate.

The initial thought was that McGuire was at fault—certainly he felt that he should have held the ball. Steve Kline said that he could have covered third. Felipe Alou was having none of it.

He pointed out that McGuire is trained to throw in that situation. He didn't have time to size it up and any hesitation would ensure that Kelly was safe. All bases are supposed to be covered—though in this case the pitcher has other responsibilities.

Chris Widger declined to press blame—directly. When I saw his interview he was still seething. All he would say directly was that on this play his job was to cover the plate. "Draw your own conclusions" he said.

What had happened was that Mark Grudzielanek had loafed through a critical play and the wheels had come off for the Expos. More revealing, perhaps, was the fact that everyone on the field expected this. As Scot Hughes pointed out, this wasn't the first time in the series that the Devil Rays had gone first to third on a groundball. The only reason for Widger to notice nobody was covering third as early as he did was that he'd been expecting it from past experience.

While Widger wouldn't comment directly on this, he did take the time to comment on Grudzielanek's contract situation. Grudzielanek has a pretty high opinion of his abilities and has always resented the Expos hardball negotiations with him. Widger said (a direct quote): "Let him play somewhere else."

Just over a month later everyone got their wish. Normally when the Expos trade a veteran there's much moaning. "The Expos just can't keep their good players." Not this time. More like "Don't let the door hit you on your way out" (and that's the polite version).

And acquiring two top-notch prospects (Peter Bergeron

WPA BULLPEN BOX—MONTREAL EXPOS

	PI	WPA	P	PPPI
Starters	946	-4.8	50.2	0.053
Relievers	657	0.4	33.8	0.051
Road	322	-3.3	15.9	0.049
Home	335	3.7	17.9	0.053
Mar/Apr	117	0.5	6.4	0.054
May	110	-0.6	6.9	0.062
June	100	1.2	5.1	0.051
July	110	0.0	4.7	0.043
August	116	-0.5	4.9	0.043
September	104	-0.3	5.8	0.056
Non S/H Sit.	528	-3.6	21.6	0.041
S/H Sit.	129	4.0	12.2	0.095
Low Pressure	299	-1.2	4.5	0.015
Med. Pressure	236	0.4	14.9	0.063
High Pressure	122	1.2	14.4	0.118
Entered behind	374	-0.4	9.5	0.025
Entered tied	90	-2.7	10.4	0.115
Entered ahead	193	3.5	14.0	0.072

Name	G	PI	WPA	P	PPPI	MI	ROB	T
Batista M	43	77	-.7	2.7	.035	18	17	6
Bennett S	62	113	-1.1	4.8	.042	35	23	9
Bullinger K	8	11	-.4	.5	.041	2	5	1
DeHart R	26	37	.0	2.1	.056	11	13	2
Kline S	78	105	.3	5.7	.054	26	36	16
Maddux M	51	70	.1	4.2	.059	18	19	10
Telford A	77	114	-1.2	5.6	.049	33	23	12
Urbina U	64	77	3.4	6.4	.083	13	12	9
Valdes M	16	27	.3	.7	.027	9	6	2
Young T	10	12	-.1	.8	.069	2	6	0
Total		657	.4	33.8	.051			

	I--------- Quality ----------I					I--- Pressure -------I			
	Dis.	Poor	Fair	Good	Her.	Lo	Med	Hi	
Batista M	2	9	23	9	0	23	16	4	(1)
Bennett S	5	11	33	13	0	32	19	11	(7)
DeHart R	0	5	14	7	0	11	4	2	(2)
Kline S	3	13	39	23	0	38	32	8	(4)
Maddux M	4	5	26	15	1	24	22	5	(3)
Telford A	6	6	53	12	0	42	22	13	(5)
Urbina U	3	3	23	33	2	24	25	15	(13)
Valdes M	0	2	12	2	0	12	4	0	(0)
Others	2	6	13	5	0	16	5	5	(3)
TOTAL	25	60	236	119	3	222	156	65	(38)

	7th inning			8th inning			9th inning		
	0	+1	+2	0	+1	+2	0	+1	+2
Batista M	1	1	0	2	0	0	1	0	0
Bennett S	0	0	0	2	0	0	0	0	0
DeHart R	0	0	0	0	0	0	0	1	0
Hermanson D	0	0	1	0	0	1	0	0	0
Kline S	3	1	0	3	2	6	3	0	0
Maddux M	1	1	1	5	1	2	1	0	0
Pavano C	1	0	0	0	0	0	0	0	0
Telford A	2	2	2	8	2	2	6	0	0
Urbina U	0	0	0	1	1	0	8	10	14
Valdes M	0	0	0	1	1	0	0	0	0
Young T	0	0	0	0	0	2	0	0	0
Starters	12	11	7	2	3	4	0	1	1
TOTAL	20	16	11	24	10	17	19	12	15
Record	4-16	10-6	9-2	9-15	9-1	16-1	8-11	11-1	14-1

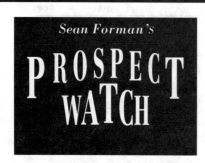

Sean Forman's PROSPECT WATCH

NAME	AGE	POS	LEVEL	GR98	GR97	GR96	AVG
Jose Vidro	23	3B	AAA	57	83	65	67
Peter Bergeron	20	OF	AA	79	54	47	65
Michael Barrett	21	C	AA	75	52	36	61
Jose Fernandez	23	3B	AAA	61	48	46	54
Fernando Seguignol	23	OF	AAA	66	34	28	49
Dave Post	24	2B	AAA	51	44	46	48
Trace Coquillette	24	2B	AAA	47	48	32	45

NAME	AGE	POS	LEVEL	GRADE	
Milton Bradley	20	OF		High A	55
Josh McKinley	18	SS		Rookie	49
Noah Hall	21	OF		Low A	49
Tomas Delarosa	20	SS		High A	46
Felix Lugo	17	3B		Rookie	45

NAME	AGE	GS	S	C	T	W-L	ERA	K/H	LEVEL
J.D. Smart	24	16	3.44	3.00	6.44	5-7	3.21	0.62	High
Jeremy Powell	22	22	3.55	3.14	6.68	9-7	3.01	0.67	High
Scott Mitchell	25	17	3.88	2.88	6.76	9-2	3.80	0.60	High
Mike Johnson	22	23	3.65	3.43	7.09	7-11	4.77	0.94	High
Keith Evans	22	20	4.30	2.90	7.20	8-9	3.56	0.57	High
Ted Lilly	22	29	4.33	3.17	7.50	12-9	3.91	0.86	High
Mike Thurman	24	19	4.00	3.89	7.89	7-7	3.41	0.71	High
Christian Parker	22	18	4.17	3.78	7.94	5-6	3.48	0.59	High
Mel Bunch	25	19	4.00	4.16	8.16	6-6	4.59	0.98	High
Jason Baker	23	20	3.65	5.05	8.70	4-10	5.64	0.93	High

Not surprisingly, the Expos' minor league system has the same problems as the major league team. They are unwilling to pay out large bonuses, so they are forced to take the second cut of prospects. That said, they are doing a good job of taking what they have and shaping them into fair major league talent. Recent trades have gone a long way to improving their pitching base and they should have some new arms for Felipe Alou to mold in the near future.

Top Dog: Michael Barrett

Barrett was a shortstop in high school and was quickly switched to catcher after being selected in the first round of the 1995 draft. He has progressed nicely through the Expos system and earned a late call up to the big league squad. Eastern League managers liked him enough to name him the top prospect in the league. Barrett has great power, but his patience is atrocious, as he has managed just 95 walks in 1566 professional at bats. Unfortunately, he is not in an organization that works to improve that. His strikeout rates are equally low, so he and Brad Fullmer will be mirror images of the same sort of player: some power, high average, and lots of outs.

Barrett also played quite a bit of third base at the end of last year, so it appears that he will be on the major league squad at one position or the other or both. Comp: Javy Lopez.

First Rounder: Josh McKinley

McKinley was the Expos first-round pick in the 1998 draft. Many suspected that he was chosen for his easy signability rather than his talent. True to form, he signed easily and then reported to the Gulf Coast League. For a middle of the infield player, he showed some promise. All of his skills look average (.269/.354/.385), but the Expos are good at developing this sort of player.

Trade Bait: Peter Bergeron

Bergeron, along with Ted Lilly, were the prizes in the Carlos Perez-Mark Grudzielanek deal with the Dodgers. Bergeron brings something to the Expos that they are sorely lacking, plate discipline. He drew 78 walks last year and 67 the year before. He has good speed with 75 steals over the last two years, and is considered a strong center fielder. If the rumored trade of Rondell White goes

through, Bergeron might see some action this year. He is not ready, and I don't think he'll rise much above average due to his lack of power, but he would just be keeping Milton Bradley's spot warm. Comp: Between Shannon Stewart and Milt Cuyler.

Handy Man: Milton Bradley

Bradley split his time between the Sally and the Florida State League. He didn't really miss a beat after the mid-season callup going from .302/.355/.470 to .287/.361/.406. He has shown sporadic patience and the strikeout levels are at an acceptable level, so he might be due for a step up in AA next year. He is also a switch-hitter who can play center field and hit with power, not something you see everyday. He will need a good year in AA, but I think he could start pushing Bergeron next year and become a good player for years to come.

On the Mound: Ted Lilly

Lilly was one of the players acquired in the Carlos Perez deal. Lilly made a name for himself his first two professional years striking out 233 in 188 innings and allowing just 187 baserunners. His 1998 wasn't quite as good as his hit rates and walk rates both increased. He was pitching in some tough leagues and he really didn't struggle badly until he was promoted to AAA. He's a hard-throwing lefty, so I'm sure the Expos will give him a shot at a starting job at the beginning of the year, but I think a bit more time in AAA would benefit him.

and Ted Lilly) in the deal might well turn this episode into the Play of the Decade for the Expos.

PLUCKING FELIPE FROM THE FIRE

So what happened that left Felipe Alou minutes from becoming the manager of the Dodgers?

Basically, it was a communications screw-up of the first order. There was a fair amount of uncertainty about the Expos

situation. There was a deadline for various governments to sign on for support of a new stadium and if this fell through, the team might well be sold (in fact the deadline passed, new negotiations have started, and team president Claude Brochu is leaving).

Jim Beattie (Expos GM) as a gesture of courtesy told Alou that he was free to listen to offers from other organizations. His feeling was that the Expos owed an enormous amount to Alou and he might not wish to stay in whatever the new situation was. (North Carolina? A lame-duck year and then a franchise move? A new owner? A plague of locusts?)

Alou was utterly furious. He took this to mean that the Expos were planning to replace him. He announced that he'd managed his last game for the Expos.

Beattie was horrified and the Expos had a public relations disaster on their hands. Further, it seems that Beattie hadn't cleared his gesture with his bosses. They felt that Alou was needed to add credibility to their stadium bid.

Beattie and all of the Expos senior management started damage control. Many "we love you Felipe, you're the best interviews" followed. A clearly anguished Beattie publicly offered his resignation in a television interview if that was Alou's price for returning. Claude Brochu (who was acting as the point man for the Expos ownership group) accepted on the same terms. Sorry to lose Beattie but willing to pay the price if required.

Alou was mollified by the gestures but still leaning towards signing with the Dodgers. What convinced him to stay with the Expos was a last-ditch personal appeal. Jim Beattie and Mark Routtenberg (now representing the Expos ownership group) flew down to Florida. They made sure he understood just how highly valued he was. In a highly symbolic move, they did it with the checkbook. Two million dollars a year with escape clauses if the Expos are sold or moved.

Let's be clear. This was never about money. To Alou it was all about loyalty and respect. But how else could Montreal make clear the high esteem they held him in? The Expos have a well-earned reputation for being cheap. Two million a year speaks volumes for the regard they hold him in.

ACHILLES' HEEL REDUX

For all of his many virtues, Felipe Alou has one truly dangerous failing. He quite literally does not understand the value of OBP. Don Malcolm made the case for this a bit more flamboyantly in these pages last year, and the 1998 did little to damage his thesis.

Vlad Guerrero and Rondell White are wonderful players, but they drew a grand total of 57 unintentional walks in 980 at-bats. Wilton Guerrero drew 14 in 402 and Brad Fullmer had 35 in 505. Robert Perez's choice as a bench player speaks volumes. He's not a horrible player but he is absurdly undisciplined. 10 career walks in 477 at-bats.

I'm not sure how much was bad luck but it is worth noting that the Expos had two players who had shown pretty decent plate discipline in the past, Ryan McGuire (before you say anything, check his minor league record) and F. P. Santangelo. Both were utterly terrible. Far worse than normal bad luck can explain. Maybe I shouldn't be trying to read minds, but it certainly looks to me like coaching.

With the Rondell White situation still up in the air as of this writing, it's not clear exactly what the Expos lineup will look like next year. Still it's a safe bet that the OBP will be under .320. None of the Expos potential new blood is very disciplined either.

The Expos are looking to get good players with little or no service time who can play in the majors next year. If pressed, I'd expect the Yankees to make the best offer. Neither Ricky Ledee or Mike Lowell figure very prominently in their plans.

It's far from clear that the Expos will in fact choose to deal White. They don't have to, he's merely requested a trade and Beattie has made it very clear that he wants quality in return. Seems like a mighty sensible attitude to me. Sure he'll deal White if the price is right. If not, never underestimate Felipe Alou's man management skills.

TEAM BREAKOUT
EXPOS 1998

Category	RS	RA	W	L	Pct.	Rk
5+ RUNS SCORED/HOME	183	96	24	3	.889	3
5+ RUNS SCORED	401	280	42	15	.737	11
4- RUNS ALLOWED/HOME	204	127	35	16	.686	16
4- RUNS ALLOWED	324	202	52	30	.634	15
5+ RUNS SCORED/ROAD	218	184	18	12	.600	15
4- RUNS ALLOWED/ROAD	120	75	17	14	.548	14
SLUGFESTS/HOME	96	103	8	7	.533	7
CLOSE LOW SCORING GAMES/HOME	42	40	10	9	.526	13
LOW SCORING GAMES/HOME	78	77	17	16	.515	12
CLOSE SLUGFESTS/ROAD	75	74	5	5	.500	9
RECORD IN BLOWOUTS/HOME	78	95	8	8	.500	11
RECORD IN LOW SCORING GAMES	110	111	24	25	.490	9
RECORD IN CLOSE GAMES/HOME	140	144	20	21	.488	11
LOW SCORING GAMES/ROAD	32	34	7	9	.438	6
RECORD IN CLOSE GAMES	298	314	34	45	.430	12
RECORD IN SLUGFESTS	273	333	18	24	.429	14
SEASON TOTALS	644	783	65	97	.401	15
CLOSE SLUGFESTS/HOME	30	32	2	3	.400	14
CLOSE LOW SCORING GAMES/ROAD	24	28	5	8	.385	12
RECORD IN BLOWOUTS	167	248	14	23	.378	12
SLUGFESTS/ROAD	177	230	10	17	.370	14
RECORD IN CLOSE GAMES/ROAD	158	170	14	24	.368	15
RECORD IN BLOWOUTS/ROAD	89	153	6	15	.286	13
4- RUNS SCORED/HOME	122	237	15	39	.278	11
4- RUNS SCORED	243	503	23	82	.219	12
5+ RUNS ALLOWED/ROAD	219	375	9	41	.180	12
5+ RUNS ALLOWED	320	581	13	67	.162	15
4- RUNS SCORED/ROAD	121	266	8	43	.157	14
5+ RUNS ALLOWED/HOME	101	206	4	26	.133	15

Park Adjusted Statistics

Name	AB	R	H	D	T	HR	RBI	BB	SO	SB	CS	BA	OBP	SLG	XR	Adj XR/27	Raw XR/27	OXW	DXW	TXW
Andrews S	491	53	124	32	1	29	79	59	136	1	5	.252	.328	.498	80	5.49	4.79	3.37	1.06	4.43
Cabrera O	261	48	75	16	6	4	24	18	27	6	2	.287	.333	.435	36	4.82	4.44	1.21	0.63	1.84
Fullmer B	504	63	143	47	2	14	82	40	70	6	5	.283	.337	.467	72	5.11	4.69	2.75	0.16	2.91
Grudzielanek M	396	57	112	16	1	9	46	21	50	12	5	.283	.331	.396	51	4.45	4.13	1.43	0.77	2.20
Guerrero V	622	121	213	40	7	44	123	43	95	12	8	.342	.388	.641	134	8.27	7.25	8.38	0.51	8.89
Guerrero W	222	32	64	11	6	2	22	10	30	3	0	.290	.319	.421	29	4.89	4.66	1.04	0.18	1.22
Henley B	115	17	36	8	1	3	20	11	26	3	0	.313	.385	.490	20	6.44	6.05	1.08	0.13	1.21
Hubbard M	55	4	9	1	0	1	3	0	17	0	0	.156	.171	.249	1	0.82	0.43	-0.48	0.61	0.13
Jones T	212	33	47	7	2	1	18	21	46	17	4	.223	.294	.296	21	3.10	2.85	-0.15	0.61	0.46
Livingstone S	110	1	24	6	0	0	14	5	15	1	1	.214	.243	.273	7	2.07	1.92	-0.45	0.02	-0.43
May D	180	14	44	9	0	5	16	11	24	0	0	.247	.290	.385	19	3.64	3.32	0.19	0.13	0.32
McGuire R	209	19	40	9	0	1	11	33	55	0	0	.191	.299	.255	16	2.37	2.16	-0.64	0.10	-0.54
Mordecai M	119	14	25	4	2	3	12	9	20	1	0	.211	.267	.366	12	3.25	2.90	-0.02	-0.02	-0.04
Perez R	106	10	26	1	0	1	9	2	23	0	0	.241	.260	.288	7	2.14	1.91	-0.39	0.09	-0.30
Santangelo F	382	60	85	19	0	5	26	45	72	7	3	.222	.338	.309	46	3.87	3.57	0.82	0.52	1.34
Seguignol F	42	7	12	4	0	3	4	3	15	0	0	.286	.327	.577	8	6.47	5.21	0.39	-0.04	0.35
Stovall D	78	12	16	2	1	2	6	6	29	1	0	.211	.268	.344	7	3.15	2.96	-0.03	0.10	0.07
Vidro J	204	27	46	13	0	0	21	28	33	2	2	.227	.326	.290	22	3.35	3.10	0.07	-0.03	0.04
White R	356	62	112	22	2	20	65	31	57	17	6	.314	.377	.555	70	7.27	6.45	4.06	1.15	5.21
Widger C	416	40	101	19	1	17	59	30	85	6	1	.243	.292	.417	52	4.34	3.86	1.33	-0.14	1.19
MON	5410	717	1399	298	34	167	677	447	1054	95	40	.259	.320	.419	721	4.54	4.10	23.97	6.54	30.51

Pitcher	S	C	T	SS	ES	IC	HH	PP	TJ	S12	S35	S67	C1	C23	C45	C67	QWP
Boskie	6.00	4.00	10.00	20%	0%	20%	80%	0%	0%	0%	20%	80%	0%	20%	80%	0%	.194
C Perez	4.35	2.35	6.70	48%	13%	61%	35%	0%	26%	17%	48%	35%	30%	52%	17%	0%	.557
Hermanson	3.47	3.10	6.57	67%	27%	50%	27%	3%	3%	43%	30%	27%	13%	53%	27%	7%	.575
Je Powell	4.17	4.33	8.50	33%	0%	33%	50%	0%	0%	33%	17%	50%	0%	33%	50%	17%	.362
M Batista	3.77	4.31	8.08	23%	0%	23%	8%	23%	0%	15%	77%	8%	0%	31%	54%	15%	.456
M Johnson	6.50	4.00	10.50	0%	0%	0%	100%	0%	0%	0%	0%	100%	0%	0%	100%	0%	.113
M Valdes	4.75	6.25	11.00	25%	0%	0%	25%	0%	0%	0%	75%	25%	0%	0%	25%	75%	.157
Pavano	3.82	3.32	7.14	59%	9%	36%	23%	5%	0%	27%	50%	23%	9%	41%	45%	5%	.514
T Moore	5.09	3.45	8.55	27%	9%	27%	45%	0%	0%	9%	45%	45%	0%	64%	27%	9%	.379
Thurman	3.62	3.92	7.54	46%	0%	31%	15%	23%	8%	23%	62%	15%	0%	46%	46%	8%	.513
Vazquez	4.59	3.91	8.50	28%	3%	13%	31%	3%	3%	9%	59%	31%	0%	44%	50%	6%	.397
MON	4.21	3.56	7.77	42%	9%	34%	31%	6%	6%	21%	48%	31%	8%	43%	40%	9%	.461

NATIONAL LEAGUE EAST

FLORIDA MARLINS

SEAN FORMAN

FISH FRY

It is finally over. The roller coaster that Marlins' fans have been on has pulled up to the little building decorated with fish market regalia and overly perky theme park workers, and, frankly, I think we are all a bit sickened. For those of you returning from a Turkish prison, H. Wayne Huizenga opened his deep pockets during the 1997 offseason and gave wunderkind GM Dave Dombrowski carte blanche. Dapper Dave wasted little time signing free agents Bobby Bonilla, Alex Fernandez, Moises Alou, Jim Eisenreich and John Cangelosi, re-signing Gary Sheffield, and then luring Jim Leyland to Miami. This talented crew won the World Series, and then just as quickly as he had signed them during the previous off-season, Dombrowski sent them all packing.

HURRICANE WAYNE

I don't begrudge owners the opportunity to make money. I understand that they need a return on their sizeable investment. I just want them to be baseball fans. For all the stunts that George Steinbrenner has pulled, he appears to actually like baseball; same goes for Bud Selig. However, when Wayne Huizenga's eyes lit up after the Marlins' World Series victory, I think it was from an owner's profit and not a fan's excitement.

Huizenga had been angling for a municipally built baseball stadium for several years. The quickest route to that goal appeared to be a contender. So Huizenga signed a number of free agents and wouldn't you know it they had a contender; so successful a contender that they won the World Series. I'm not implying that Huizenga bought a World Series title. They had a quality minor league system and coupled with some very successful free agent signings they put together a high quality team. Unfortunately, the World Series title didn't seem to sway the South Florida powers-that-be. The next tact involved monumental losses in the balance sheet. The more the merrier. Huizenga plead poverty and to prove his point slashed his payroll to 1985 levels.

Unfortunately, the cries of poverty just weren't true. John Helyar's book

Lords of the Realm (a must read for anyone with any interest in the economics of baseball) describes how teams are consistently able to hide revenue streams in holding companies and undervalued television rights. Huizenga utilized all of these tricks.

Andrew Zimbalist, a noted expert on baseball economics, wrote a piece that appeared in the New York Times titled "A Miami Fish Story." In the story, Zimbalist refutes any notion that the Marlins lost $34 million in 1997 and another sizable chunk in 1998. Zimbalist outlines how nearly all of the luxury and club seating revenues along with stadium naming, parking and concessions revenue went directly to Pro Player Stadium's balance sheet and not to the Marlins'. Despite this, the Marlins were still charged a $5 million stadium maintenance expense. In addition, an independent appraiser estimated the Marlins' television contract with Sportschannel to be $2.1 million below market value. Who owns Pro Player Stadium and Sportschannel? The one and only Wayne Huizenga. Zimbalist estimates that the Marlins actually turned a profit of $14 million dollars in 1997, and even more in 1998.

After posting his "losses", Huizenga discovered that Miami-Dade County didn't appear any more interested in building a stadium for their wealthiest citizen, so in a temper tantrum that would make any eight-year-old proud, Hurricane Wayne slashed and burned. Everyone making anything was traded away. General Manager Dave Dombrowski did well to get the value he did in the trades, but irreparable damage was done. Some Huizenga apologists might argue that the young talent the Marlins acquired will only speed their return to the

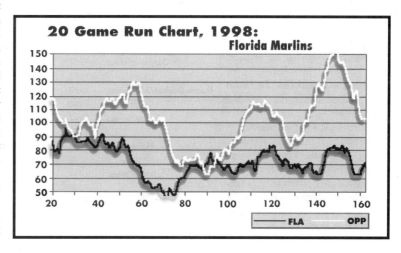

QMAX PRESENTS: "BAD" PITCHERS

STORMY WEATHERS

I'm scratching my head here. I've been looking at a variety of bad pitchers, and each one tells a story. We have the guys who were once good hanging on for one last year, the guys who are gonna be good still learning their trade, the guys who had an arm problem or a head problem or who knows, a wife problem and for some reason or reasons, they pitch badly. Somewhere in years prior to or following the Bad year, you'll find some decent pitching.

But help me out here with this Weathers guy. I just don't get it. I've looked over his entire career stats, and I can't find even a scintilla of evidence that this guy knows how to pitch. Nada. Bupkis. You think I'm exaggerating to make a point? C'mon, would I do that? All right, I would. But hear me now and believe me later: this guy sucks. The best this guy has EVER done was his rookie year, when he pulled down a 4.91 ERA. In FIFTEEN innings. He has NEVER, as a major leaguer, finished with fewer hits allowed than innings. He's not even a control pitcher; he's very consistent at walking four or five per nine innings, throughout his career. Fer crissakes, he's not even a damn lefty!

All right, let's take a look at 1994, the one and only year a major-league team was desperate to put this Really Bad Pitcher in the starting rotation. And lo and behold, he goes 4-1 with a 2.10 ERA in April of 1994. Fantasy players, as Ken Adams noted in the 1995 BBBA, were jumping all over themselves to grab this pheenom at a bargain price.

Think again, roti players; the hurricane warning was already there in the QMAX, telling you the Weathers was going to turn for the worse. (You didn't really think

DAVID WEATHERS/FLA 1994							
	1	2	3	4	5	6	7	S
1								0
2	1		1					2
3			4	2				6
4			1	1				2
5	2	1					1	4
6		1	2	1		2		6
7			2	2				4
C	0	3	7	8	3	0	3	24

I would be able to pass up the "weather" pun, did you?). For those five April starts, Weathers' QMAX averages were 4.2 stuff, 3.0 control. Not bad, but not remotely indicative of a 2.10 ERA either. Weathers was still getting hit, albeit not quite at his usual rate, and he had cut down on the walks a bit. What roti players were missing in the morning boxscores was pure dumb luck, either that or some great fielding: Weathers allowed 47 baserunners in those five starts, and allowed only 11 to score, three on unearned runs. That's a 77% strand rate, far higher than the approximately 60% strand rate a 4,3 pitcher usually gets.

QMAX: don't leave home without it.

--Tom Austin

World Series.

Erroneously, this assumes that this was a team at the end of its run. That wasn't the case with the Marlins. Their pitching staff was just 28.2 years old and their batters were only 29. They were the ninth youngest team in the majors. This was a team in its prime; a team, with a good farm system, immediately capable of making two or three more World Series runs. The most recent examples of other "fire sales" were the 1996 Pittsburgh Pirates and the 1993 San Diego Padres. While those moves did improve both teams in the long run, neither team was close to contending prior to trading their veterans. The San Diego teams had been third the two years previous and the Pirates weren't even that good. Another famous fire sale was the 1914 Philadelphia A's who went from first to worst as well. That team was also a young team, but the circumstances were somewhat different as the Federal League had given players an opportunity to significantly improve their salaries. Manager/Owner Connie Mack may actually have faced a fiscal loss if he had attempted to keep all of his star players.

WHAT MIGHT HAVE BEEN?

The 1997 Marlins were a pretty good baseball team, which often goes unnoticed. They went 92-70, which would have won any division except for the AL and NL Easts. Let's assume for a paragraph or two that the Marlins had been kept together. One of the striking things was just how good their ex-players performed. Moises Alou, Kevin Brown, Robb Nen, Devon White, Al Leiter and Rick Helling all had fantastic seasons, and if not for a late injury Gary Sheffield would have as well. From a 92-70 starting point, the improved performances of the above players may have pushed the Marlins near 100 wins. Sprinkling in Cliff Floyd at first base and Mark Kotsay off the bench would have added some youth and improved the team as well.

Player	Year	BA/OBP/SLG
Charles Johnson	1997	.250/.347/.454
	1998	.218/.289/.381
Darren Daulton/Jeff Conine	1997	.246/.344/.410
Cliff Floyd	1998	.282/.337/.481
Bobby Bonilla	1997	.297/.378/.468
	1998	.237/.315/.360
Moises Alou	1997	.292/.373/.493
	1998	.312/.399/.582
Devon White	1997	.245/.338/.370
	1998	.279/.335/.456
Gary Sheffield	1997	.250/.424/.446
	1998	.302/.428/.524

Unlike Sheffield; Bonilla and Johnson did not respond well to Southern California, but over

all it's clear the Marlins' offense would have been improved this year. How about on the mound?

Pitcher	Year	ERA	
Kevin Brown	1997	2.69	
	1998	2.38	
Alex Fernandez	1997	3.59	
	1998	injured	
Tony Saunders	1997	4.61	
	1998	4.12	
Al Leiter	1997	4.34	
	1998	2.47	
Rick Helling	1997	4.47	
	1998	4.41	
Livian Hernandez	1997	3.18	
	1998	4.72	
Robb Nen	1997	3.89	35 of 42 sv
	1998	1.52	40 of 45 sv

Even without Alex Fernandez this would have been an improved staff, and without the "ace" label, Livan Hernandez would have avoided having his arm slagged and probably would have pitched better.

This team also would not have finished 22nd in attendance like the actual 1998 version did. Florida was 18th in attendance in 1996 and had improved to 11th in 1997. The non-destroyed Marlins would have, at worst, been in the wild card race last year. Since 1980, there have been twelve teams that made consecutive playoff appearances after a non-playoff year. On average, those teams have improved two and a half places in attendance from their first playoff year to their second. Teams that at first ranked in the teens in attendance (8 teams) account for nearly all of the second year improvement, so the Marlins may have actually moved up three to five spots putting them 6th to 8th in attendance. Using the more conservative estimate, the Marlins likely would have drawn 600,000 more fans in 1998 than in 1997 raising nearly $10 million more than in 1997. Enough to pick up a pitcher to replace Alex Fernandez for a year.

FISHHEADS

Jim Leyland has become one of the more admired managers in all of baseball. His quiet toiling under difficult circumstances in Pittsburgh have produced a cadre of fans and backers. Leyland was the man who single-handedly took the Pirates to the playoffs three years in a row, but then due to forces entirely out of his control went 259-323 the four years hence. The mad scramble to woo Felipe Alou and Jim Leyland, a combined 119-205 last year, was one of the more surreal scenes this offseason. Alou and Leyland have had success, but they seem to have no culpability for their teams' play, while Davey Johnson, successful nearly everywhere, was hired as an afterthought.

WPA BULLPEN BOX—FLORIDA MARLINS

	PI	WPA	P	PPPI
Starters	972	-15.4	49.0	0.050
Relievers	667	-2.7	42.6	0.064
Road	324	-1.6	22.8	0.070
Home	343	-1.2	19.8	0.058
Mar/Apr	114	-1.5	7.1	0.062
May	111	-1.8	6.1	0.055
June	105	3.0	7.3	0.070
July	126	-0.8	10.1	0.080
August	128	-1.3	6.7	0.052
September	83	-0.3	5.3	0.064
Non S/H Sit.	546	-1.1	26.7	0.049
S/H Sit.	121	-1.6	15.8	0.131
Low Pressure	283	-0.7	3.7	0.013
Med. Pressure	184	-5.0	11.8	0.064
High Pressure	200	3.0	27.1	0.136
Entered behind	369	0.0	9.8	0.027
Entered tied	116	-0.8	14.5	0.125
Entered ahead	182	-1.9	18.2	0.100

Name	G	PI	WPA	P	PPPI	MI	ROB	T
Alfonseca A	58	87	.7	7.8	.089	27	18	13
Darensbourg V	59	96	-.1	6.8	.071	27	23	14
Edmondson B	43	79	-.8	5.2	.066	27	23	8
Henriquez O	15	24	-.3	.6	.025	6	4	1
Heredia F	39	48	1.2	3.7	.076	9	20	5
Mantei M	42	68	1.7	6.4	.093	23	17	9
Ojala K	28	59	-.6	1.4	.024	17	6	1
Pall D	23	38	-.3	.7	.019	10	5	1
Powell J	33	46	.2	4.1	.089	13	13	8
Speier J	18	25	-1.2	1.5	.061	6	7	3
Stanifer R	38	60	-1.7	2.9	.048	17	17	6
Total		667	-2.8	42.6	.064			

	I---------- Quality ----------I					I--- Pressure -------I		
	Dis.	Poor	Fair	Good	Her.	Lo	Med	Hi
Alfonseca A	6	10	18	18	6	18	20	20 (15)
Darensbourg V	4	7	31	15	2	22	23	14 (10)
Edmondson B	4	7	20	10	2	17	11	15 (8)
Henriquez O	0	3	11	1	0	12	3	0 (0)
Heredia F	2	4	17	15	1	16	16	7 (6)
Mantei M	3	4	17	14	4	13	8	21 (16)
Ojala K	1	5	20	2	0	21	5	2 (1)
Pall D	0	3	19	1	0	19	3	1 (0)
Powell J	2	7	15	6	3	16	5	12 (7)
Speier J	2	4	11	1	0	10	5	3 (1)
Stanifer R	4	8	19	7	0	17	15	6 (1)
Others	3	4	16	1	0	15	6	3 (1)
TOTAL	31	66	214	91	18	196	120	104 (66)

	7th inning			8th inning			9th inning		
	0	+1	+2	0	+1	+2	0	+1	+2
Alfonseca A	2	0	1	4	1	1	6	5	2
Darensbourg V	2	1	3	4	4	2	1	1	1
Edmondson B	0	0	4	1	3	1	1	0	0
Henriquez O	1	0	0	0	0	0	0	0	0
Heredia F	0	1	0	1	1	2	3	2	0
Mantei M	0	0	0	1	2	1	5	9	2
Pall D	0	0	0	0	0	1	0	0	0
Powell J	0	0	0	1	1	0	3	3	2
Speier J	0	0	0	1	0	0	2	0	0
Stanifer R	0	2	1	1	1	0	0	0	0
Starters	15	10	5	4	5	3	2	3	2
TOTAL	20	14	14	18	18	11	23	23	9
Record	5-15	7-7	9-5	5-13	11-7	8-3	8-15	19-4	8-1

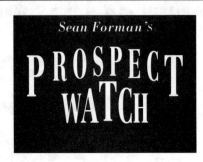

Sean Forman's
PROSPECT WATCH

NAME	AGE	POS	LEVEL	GR98	GR97	GR96	AVG
Luis Castillo	22	2B	AAA	76	88	94	83
Alex Gonzalez	21	SS	AAA	76	63	-	71
Preston Wilson	23	OF	AAA	76	48	-	65
John Roskos	23	1B	AAA	57	68	75	64
Brian Daubach	26	1B	AAA	64	56	56	60
Jaime Jones	21	OF	AA	63	59	53	60
Nate Rolison	21	1B	AA	70	46	50	59
Victor Rodriguez	21	SS	AA	56	61	52	57
Ramon Castro	22	C	AA	42	42	32	40
Josh Booty	23	3B	AAA	25	36	25	29

NAME	AGE	POS	LEVEL	GRADE
David Callahan	18	1B	Rookie	66
Julio Ramirez	20	OF	High A	63
Jesus Medrano	19	2B	Rookie	55
Jeff Bailey	19		Rookie	52
Brian Reed	20	OF	Rookie	47
Chris Aguila	19	3B	Rookie	45

The Marlins fire sale actually depleted the farm system of its hitting prospects as the top prospects (Kotsay, Dunwoody, and others) were pressed into major league duty rather than gain some more experience in the minors. The pitching side did receive a sizeable talent infusion in the fire sale and should provide some major league pitchers assuming John Boles can sort through them all.

COMMONWEALTH EDISON: Preston Wilson
He's part of the booty for Mike Piazza, and quite frankly the Marlins could have done better. Wilson's one skill is his home run power and that is a pretty good skill to have. Over his last 700 at bats, he has slugged 45 homers. His strike zone judgment however is practically non-existent (36 BB vs. 143 SO). He might be better off if he had a big platoon split as then you could use him that way. Unless his plate discipline turns a full 180, he is not going to be a good major leaguer. Comp: Billy Ashley.

HANDY MAN: Alex Gonzalez
Gonzalez was named the top prospect in the International League. He is an above average defender and has good pop for a middle infielder. He has never had a large number of extra base hits in a season, which concerns me. He also has drawn just 55 walks in the last two seasons and is a poor basestealer, 8 of 22 in that same span. He might become a great player, but he needs at least another year in the minors. Comp: Mark Lewis.

Go! SPEED RACER, Go!: Luis Castillo
I got embroiled in a mini-debate last fall as to whether Rickey Henderson could remain a starter for three more years. Basically, it boiled down to whether there is a minimum level of isolated power a player must maintain before he loses effectiveness. Luis Castillo is, essentially, a similar case. He is good for at most fifty to seventy points of isolated power, a huge number of walks and some high quality baserunning. If Boles can get Edgar Renteria straightened out and then morph Castillo into Brett Butler, the Marlins will be on a solid footing for the next few years.

YOUNG 'UN: Julio Ramirez
Ramirez has "tools coming out of ears" according to an opposing manager, and he has used those tools to hit .279/.333/.428 in 1998 and .255/.322/.452 in 1997. However, that is only part of the story as he also had 71 steals last year. He is a switch-hitting center fielder and could be a good major league center

NAME	AGE	GS	S	C	T	W-L	ERA	K/H	LEVEL
Brandon Leese	22	20	4.15	3.15	7.30	4-7	4.13	0.69	High
Ed Yarnall	22	23	3.52	4.04	7.57	12-6	3.76	1.06	High
Michael Tejera	21	18	4.28	3.39	7.67	9-5	4.11	0.86	High
Brent Billingsley	23	28	4.07	3.61	7.68	6-13	3.74	1.06	High
Ryan Hawblitzel	26	18	4.89	3.00	7.89	7-5	5.59	0.54	High
Mark Johnson	23	25	4.04	3.88	7.92	5-13	4.62	0.82	High
Reynol Mendoza	27	17	5.06	3.94	9.00	3-8	6.19	0.36	High
A.J. Burnett	21	20				10-4	1.97	2.51	Low

fielder in two years. The drop in power is not surprising for a player entering the Florida State League. The power should rebound in hitter-friendly Portland. I consider Ramirez the best prospect in the Marlins' system right now.

ON THE MOUND: Ed Yarnall
The Marlins received about eight of the better pitching prospects in all of baseball during their fire sale and not many of them did much last year. The Marlins picked off four pitching prospects from just the Mets: Jesus Sanchez, Ed Yarnall, Geoff Goetz and A.J. Burnett. Yarnall and Goetz were acquired in the Mike Piazza trade. At the time of the trade, Yarnall was the hottest pitcher in the minors. Once traded, he appeared for two more games in the Eastern League and was then promoted to the International League. While in the Eastern League, his QMAX line was 1.67/3.11, 4.78 and he allowed just 29 hits in 62 innings. Once promoted, though, he struggled badly with a 4.71/4.64, 9.36 line, and his numbers worsened across the board. The Mets weren't cavalier with Yarnall's pitch counts, so it isn't necessarily an injury, but that is a pretty dramatic change.

Given more recent evidence, one has to wonder if the Marlins won it all because of Leyland or despite him. The razed Pirate squad that finished 73-89 for him rebounded to 79-83 under Gene Lamont with half the payroll and the youngest roster in baseball. Nearly every one of the ex-Marlins improved after leaving the Marlins. Many of the pre-Leyland Marlins like Gary Sheffield, Kevin Brown, Edgar Renteria, Luis Castillo, Jeff Conine, Devon White and Robb Nen had much better seasons prior to his arrival as well. If Leyland can win in Planet Coors, I'll sing a different tune, but he certainly appears to me to be one of the more over-rated managers in the game today.

FISH KABOB

It might have been better for all involved if Leyland had left town with his players. He was the wrong man for what went on in Florida. After having spent four years dying on the vine as the Pirates went down once, twice, thrice, he was not exactly well equipped to relive the experience as one big sped-up flashback.

That said, he was clearly clockwatching this year. Oftentimes, he couldn't even be bothered to travel to the mound to make pitching changes. Starters would labor on through the seventh, eighth, ninth innings with pitch counts hitting 130 pitches or more, while Leyland was pulling a drag in the corner of the dugout, stealing glances at the scoreboard as Moises Alou or Kevin Brown were leading their teams to victory. Finally, he'd notice Livian Hernandez or Jesus Sanchez (who had just thrown more pitches than he weighed), huffing and puffing out on the mound and he would stroll out to the mound and signal for Vic Darensbourg or whatever rookie was in the bullpen that month.

The average age of the Marlins' staff was 24.9 years old with just 1.2 years of major league experience, but Leyland managed them as a staff of Nolan Ryans. The Marlins led the National League with 25 starts of more than 120 pitches, 6 of more than 140, and 5 starts on three days rest, and no other team was particularly close. Livian Hernandez, whose listed age was 23, had starts of 153, 150, and 148 pitches to go along with 15 more starts over 120 pitches. Jesus Sanchez, another 23-year-old, but just 5-10 153 pounds, tallied four starts over 120 pitches including a 146 pitch outing. The Marlins have a lot of talented pitchers, but the damage may have already been done.

SMALL FRY

Fortunately for the Marlins, they will no longer be under the gaze of Jim Leyland this year. Old/New manager John Boles should be a much kinder hand for this rebuilding operation. Boles was the surprise replacement for canned skipper Rene Lachemann during the second half of 1996. He moved in from a front office player development position and that background should be helpful next year.

While 75 games is certainly a small sample, the results from the 1996 season do point towards some optimism in 1999. Boles took over a team that was sputtering along at 40-47. The team continued to waver as they won just 18 of the next 41 games. From that point on, the Fish went 22-12 and nearly cracked the .500 barrier. Especially encouraging was the play of Edgar Renteria. Renteria came up early in the year and hit just .248 during the first half, but after the managerial change, he went on a tear hitting .334. Since that season, Renteria has stagnated and doesn't appear the same promising player he was two years ago. If Boles can return Renteria to the upper echelon of National League shortstops and turn keystone-mate Luis Castillo into an average second baseman, he will have solved many of the Marlins' problems.

Elsewhere, Jorge Fabregas was acquired to handle the young pitching staff, which makes you wonder if the Marlins are just spending money because they can. Fabregas is a .255 career hitter with almost no secondary offensive skills to recommend him. The

Marlins are probably in the market for a young catcher, or they may let Fabregas catch until youngster Ramon Castro is ready. Former top prospects Derrek Lee, Castillo, Renteria and Kevin Orie will man the infield, and could become a top group in two or three years. Cliff Floyd finally showed he could stay healthy for a full year, and could be a top two or three left fielder next year. The improving Mark Kotsay and Todd Dunwoody will man the other two outfield spots.

On the mound, the top three of Livan Hernandez, Jesus Sanchez and Brian Meadows appears set. Beyond that the Marlins have about thirteen choices most of them former Mets' farmhands. The bullpen likewise is set at the top with Matt Mantei, Vic Darensbourg and Antonio Alfonseca. After them only questions remain.

With the team's sale, the cost cutting appears over and the Marlins can start their return to respectability. John Boles will have to do some handholding with this team, but I think he and the Marlins will surprise a lot of people. There is enough talent to win 70-80 games next year and finish third in the top-heavy National League East.

Marlins' fans should also be happy if for no other reason than Wayne Huizenga is no longer the team owner. Huizenga had claimed to be ready to sell the team in October of 1997. He even had a suitor, team president Don Smiley. Smiley's bid never materialized, at least not to Huizenga's liking, and it does-

Category	RS	RA	W	L	Pct.	Rk
TEAM BREAKOUT MARLINS 1998						
4- RUNS ALLOWED/HOME	141	91	25	10	.714	12
4- RUNS ALLOWED	244	186	42	24	.636	14
CLOSE LOW SCORING GAMES/HOME	22	18	7	4	.636	7
5+ RUNS SCORED/HOME	207	164	19	11	.633	16
LOW SCORING GAMES/HOME	47	39	11	8	.579	7
4- RUNS ALLOWED/ROAD	103	95	17	14	.548	13
5+ RUNS SCORED	418	386	32	29	.525	16
RECORD IN CLOSE GAMES/HOME	160	167	19	21	.475	12
RECORD IN LOW SCORING GAMES	87	105	18	22	.450	11
CLOSE LOW SCORING GAMES/ROAD	36	43	7	9	.438	4
RECORD IN CLOSE GAMES	382	410	38	51	.427	13
5+ RUNS SCORED/ROAD	211	222	13	18	.419	16
RECORD IN CLOSE GAMES/ROAD	222	243	19	30	.388	14
LOW SCORING GAMES/ROAD	40	66	7	14	.333	13
SEASON TOTALS	667	923	54	108	.333	16
SLUGFESTS/HOME	156	174	7	15	.318	16
CLOSE SLUGFESTS/ROAD	120	129	5	12	.294	15
RECORD IN BLOWOUTS/HOME	93	154	6	15	.286	15
4- RUNS SCORED/HOME	125	263	12	39	.235	13
RECORD IN SLUGFESTS	337	442	12	39	.235	16
4- RUNS SCORED	249	537	22	79	.218	13
RECORD IN BLOWOUTS	150	308	8	29	.216	16
4- RUNS SCORED/ROAD	124	274	10	40	.200	11
SLUGFESTS/ROAD	181	268	5	24	.172	16
CLOSE SLUGFESTS/HOME	49	56	1	6	.143	16
5+ RUNS ALLOWED/HOME	191	336	6	40	.130	16
5+ RUNS ALLOWED	423	737	12	84	.125	16
RECORD IN BLOWOUTS/ROAD	57	154	2	14	.125	16
5+ RUNS ALLOWED/ROAD	232	401	6	44	.120	15

n't take a cynic to wonder if Smiley's bid was merely a bargaining chip to drive up the price. Huizenga's only serious offer came from a securities broker named John Henry. Henry's first formal offer came during the summer, and Huizenga continued to play bidders off each other in an attempt to drive up the $150 million asking price, a surprisingly high price for a team losing $34 million a year.

Eventually, Henry and Huizenga came to an apparent agreement. However, Huizenga failed to mention to Henry that he would require the Marlins to sign a twenty-year contract with Huizenga's Sportschannel for the same sweetheart deal

currently in place. Henry wisely backed out and the deal appeared dead in the water. The two sides later made up and a shortened television contract was signed. There was no word if the deal required Henry and his relatives to rent a weekly allotment of Blockbuster videos as well.

In a press conference just prior to the sale of the team, Huizenga blamed his lack of public appeal on the media. "You guys have turned all the fans against me," he said at the news conference. Clearly, none of Huizenga's underhanded tactics nor his dismantling of a popular championship team had anything to do it. Not used to being a public relations piÒata,

Name	AB	R	H	D	T	HR	RBI	BB	SO	SB	CS	BA	OBP	SLG	XR	Adj XR/27	Raw XR/27	OXW	DXW	TXW
Berg D	182	19	59	11	0	2	22	26	45	3	0	.325	.404	.421	33	6.77	6.37	1.81	0.34	2.15
Bonilla B	97	12	28	5	0	4	16	12	22	0	1	.288	.364	.472	15	5.09	4.74	0.53	-0.06	0.47
Cangelosi J	171	20	44	8	0	1	11	30	23	2	3	.259	.372	.324	22	4.23	4.02	0.55	0.02	0.57
Castillo L	153	22	31	3	2	1	10	22	33	3	0	.206	.310	.271	15	3.36	3.26	0.07	0.44	0.51
Counsell C	335	45	87	19	5	4	43	51	46	3	0	.259	.364	.386	49	5.09	4.80	1.89	1.22	3.11
Dunwoody T	434	56	113	27	7	5	29	21	111	6	1	.260	.301	.393	49	3.96	3.69	0.88	1.01	1.89
Eisenreich J	64	10	17	1	0	1	8	4	14	2	0	.262	.306	.330	7	3.72	3.30	0.09	0.02	0.11
Floyd C	588	89	171	46	3	23	95	47	110	29	15	.291	.345	.497	95	5.77	5.44	4.18	0.31	4.49
Gonzalez A	86	12	13	2	0	3	7	9	30	0	0	.154	.243	.285	6	2.10	2.00	-0.36	0.20	-0.16
Jackson R	260	28	67	15	1	5	34	20	72	1	1	.259	.314	.387	31	4.21	3.91	0.73	0.05	0.78
Johnson C	113	14	26	5	0	7	25	16	29	0	1	.231	.325	.474	18	5.16	4.76	0.65	0.41	1.06
Knorr R	49	4	10	4	1	2	11	1	10	0	0	.201	.213	.443	5	3.56	3.66	0.03	0.09	0.12
Kotsay M	578	76	165	26	7	11	71	34	60	11	5	.286	.325	.413	72	4.39	4.16	1.89	1.55	3.44
Lee D	454	64	109	30	1	17	77	47	118	5	2	.239	.324	.424	62	4.61	4.41	1.85	0.60	2.45
Orie K	175	23	47	8	1	6	18	14	24	1	0	.269	.341	.430	25	5.05	4.87	0.91	0.21	1.12
Redmond M	118	10	40	9	0	2	13	5	16	0	0	.340	.377	.471	17	5.25	4.93	0.67	0.23	0.90
Renteria E	517	84	151	18	2	3	34	48	77	46	23	.292	.356	.354	65	4.25	3.95	1.54	1.19	2.73
Sheffield G	136	23	39	11	1	7	31	26	16	5	2	.285	.404	.529	29	7.55	6.93	1.71	0.22	1.93
Wehner J	88	11	21	2	0	0	5	7	12	1	0	.233	.287	.256	6	2.42	2.27	-0.23	-0.01	-0.24
Zaun G	298	20	57	12	2	5	31	35	51	5	2	.193	.279	.301	26	2.77	2.62	-0.50	0.05	-0.45
Zeile T	234	39	70	12	1	6	41	31	34	2	3	.300	.382	.440	39	6.08	5.78	1.91	-0.18	1.73
FLA	**5554**	**703**	**1424**	**283**	**37**	**118**	**657**	**529**	**1100**	**126**	**60**	**.256**	**.325**	**.384**	**690**	**4.22**	**3.97**	**20.80**	**7.91**	**28.71**

(Park Adjusted Statistics)

Pitcher	S	C	T	SS	ES	IC	HH	PP	TJ	S12	S35	S67	C1	C23	C45	C67	QWP
A Larkin	5.00	4.43	9.43	29%	14%	21%	50%	7%	0%	21%	29%	50%	7%	21%	43%	29%	.317
Dempster	4.73	5.09	9.82	27%	0%	9%	36%	0%	0%	9%	55%	36%	0%	9%	55%	36%	.242
F Heredia	6.00	4.00	10.00	0%	0%	0%	100%	0%	0%	0%	0%	100%	0%	50%	50%	0%	.233
Fontenot	5.13	4.38	9.50	13%	0%	13%	50%	0%	0%	13%	38%	50%	0%	38%	38%	25%	.315
Hammond	5.33	4.33	9.67	0%	0%	0%	67%	0%	0%	0%	33%	67%	0%	0%	100%	0%	.236
J Sanchez	4.03	3.90	7.93	45%	10%	31%	31%	14%	3%	28%	41%	31%	14%	24%	45%	17%	.461
L Hernandez	4.48	3.30	7.79	42%	6%	30%	39%	3%	6%	15%	45%	39%	15%	48%	27%	9%	.461
Ludwick	4.83	4.67	9.50	17%	17%	17%	33%	0%	0%	17%	50%	33%	0%	33%	33%	33%	.281
Meadows	5.00	3.16	8.16	29%	10%	32%	55%	0%	13%	16%	29%	55%	13%	45%	42%	0%	.405
Medina	4.69	4.92	9.62	8%	0%	31%	62%	23%	0%	31%	8%	62%	0%	15%	46%	38%	.283
Ojala	4.31	4.15	8.46	31%	8%	38%	46%	23%	0%	38%	15%	46%	0%	31%	54%	15%	.420
FLA	**4.64**	**3.93**	**8.57**	**31%**	**7%**	**27%**	**45%**	**7%**	**4%**	**20%**	**34%**	**45%**	**9%**	**33%**	**42%**	**17%**	**.385**

HOUSTON ASTROS

SEAN FORMAN

NOT YOUR FATHER'S ASTROS

Did I miss something? Did Houston's new ball-park open two years early? Did the Astros play all of 1998 in Colt Field? Was the climate control re-configured to support Astros' bats?

Never have Houstonians seen such an offensive onslaught. Houston wasn't supposed to win this way. Astros had to hit singles, bunt the runner over, and then hit timely sac flies, maybe with a few stolen bases mixed in. Then the pitching staff would shut the opposition down, and the Astros would win 2-1. That is Houston baseball, not 6-3 wins.

The Astros led the National League in runs scored and were fourth in the entire major leagues. The Astros 874 runs were ahead of Seattle, Cleveland, and Baltimore. Houston's previous team record had been 777 runs, set just last year—a remarkable 12% improvement. The Astros also broke team records in hits, at bats, doubles, home runs, etc., etc. Signs are that the Astrodome is becoming a bit less of a pitchers' park as it had a 99 (100 is neutral) park factor this year. That may just be a fluke, as the two previous years were at 88 and 85.

How did they do it? Well, they were on base more that anybody else in the National League, with a .356 OBP. They weren't just waiting for three run homers though, as they stole 155 bases (in 206 attempts), which was second only to the little-ball Pirates.

The offense was led, as it has been for eight years, by Jeff Bagwell and Craig Biggio. Both fell off slightly from 1997 losing a few points of OPS, but a huge upswing in the outfield offense allowed the Astros to increase their offensive output. In last year's essay, we pointed out how mediocre the Astros' outfield was. Houston acknowledged this during the off-season and made two big moves. They picked up Moises Alou, for a package of minor league prospects, and Carl Everett, for one-time closer John Hudek. The data above and to the right shows what a difference a year can make,

Moises Alou probably won't be able to keep this up in left field, and Carl Everett may not to be able to either in center field, but anything other than a gentle dropoff from the above numbers would surprise me.

LF		
Year	BA / OBP/ SLG	
1997	.263/.352/.387	
1998	.310/.403/.574	

CF		
Year	BA / OBP/ SLG	
1997	.235/.305/.362	
1998	.293/.365/.485	

RF		
Year	BA / OBP/ SLG	
1997	.266/.332/.403	
1998	.312/.352/.471	

In an effort to bolster their playoff chances, the Astros signed prodigal son Ken Caminiti. Caminiti's playing time will likely decrease as the Astros will attempt to keep him healthy throughout the season. I would expect Caminiti and Bill Spiers to outperform Sean Berry and Bill Spiers in 1998, but I doubt they will outperform Berry and Spiers circa 1997. Behind the plate, Mitch Meluskey will likely replace Tony Eusebio as the backup catcher. If Meluskey hits anything like he did in AAA, he could end up with the majority of the at bats by July (check the Astros' Prospectwatch).

Meluskey and Caminiti, both switch-hitters, should help balance out the Astros lineup, which has been primarily right-handed. The Astros sent just 20% left-handers to the plate against right-handed starters and 96% right-handers to the plate against lefties. Montreal was the next most right-handed team with 40% left-handers versus right-handed starters. Last year, the Astros posted a reverse platoon split and this year wasn't any different, as their winning percentage against right-han-

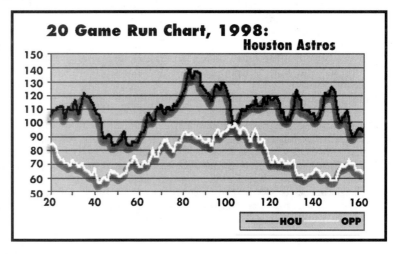

QMAX PRESENTS: "BAD" PITCHERS

IT'S HARD TO BE A SAINT...IN THE CITY

And it's hard to be a Bad Pitcher...in the Astrodome. Or so it seems. We had to look hard to find anyone with the kind of glaringly bad year we were looking for on the Houston team, and it's not hard to figure out why. Houston pitchers often find that Lefty Gomez' proverbial "clean living and a fast outfield" will absolve a multitude of pitching sins, and so found wayward control pitcher Doug Drabek in 1995. Doug came from the Pittsburgh Pirates with several years of Good Works behind him, and he may have thought he had entered pitcher's Valhalla in the ethereal, yet murky, Astrodome. It was not to be in 1993, as he fashioned a not-terrible 3.79 ERA in 237 yeoman innings, yet found himself banished to 9-18 won-lost purgatory due to poor run support. He did bounce back with a 12-6, 2.84 year in 1994,

looking like the Buccaneer of old.

That was it, though; the chickens came home to roost in the Astrodome rafters, a good vantage point to watch the 18 Big Flies Drabek surrendered (though only seven in 16 Astrodome outings) in 1995. 1995 was the first year of several, as it turned out, vintage Bad Pitcher years Drabek has turned in since then. It was not spectacularly bad; in fact there is sort of a pleasant, hazy ennui induced by looking at Doug's 1995 starts. He really only got murdered three times in 31 starts; the other starts were more of the "banality of evil" variety (your typical Drabek start: six innings, seven hits, three walks, a homer and three or four runs allowed, for a 4.3s, 3.3c QMAX), as Drabek's fastball was at times guilty of a lit-

DOUG DRABEK/HOU 1995

	1	2	3	4	5	6	7	S
1	3		1					4
2			2	1				3
3		2	1					3
4		1	2					3
5		2	3	1	1			7
6			1	3			1	6
7				2	1	1		4
C	3	5	10	7	3	1	1	30

tle slothfulness coming up to the plate, and opposing hitters greedily and gluttonously fattened their batting average and emerged with hit-lust temporarily sated. The fans, on the other hand, accused Drabek of a form of avarice as he pocketed some hefty wages of sin for putting up a 4.77 ERA with half of his games in the Astrodome. Fire and Brimstone followers could be forgiven for wondering if a deal had been struck, as Doug managed a 10-9 record for his trouble, and has consistently posted winning records (until this past year, when his demons seemed to catch up with him) despite hellishly high ERA's.
--Tom Austin

ders was .644 and .585 against lefties. This may have been a fluke though as the all the right-handed Astros except for Moises Alou hit lefties better.

Barring an injury to Bagwell or Biggio, the offense should be just as good as last year.

ON THE MOUND

Darryl who? During the off-season, you couldn't read a preview of the Astros without a discussion of the dearly departed Darryl Kile. Kile's departure had blown an irreparable hole in the Astros' rotation and hence their playoff chances as well. Injuries to pleasant surprises Chris Holt and Ramon Garcia didn't help either. Larry Dierker, however, continued to weave his magic with unknown pitchers. This year, Jose Lima and Sean Bergman were Dierker's reclamation projects. Lima pitched out of the bullpen in 1997 and had 228 major league innings with a career ERA of 5.92. Bergman was acquired from the Padres for backup outfielder James Mouton. Bergman had 577 career innings with a 4.77 ERA. In 1998, Bergman pitched 172 innings with a 3.71 ERA and Lima threw up a 3.70 ERA in 233 innings..

The small-market label is a difficult one to pin down. Pittsburgh, Minnesota, Oakland and Cincinnati were among the most successful franchises of the late 80's and early 90's. Now they are given little chance of ever winning again.

Houston was supposed to be a baseball ghost town during that same time, with the normal threats that the team would be leaving town. Imagine the surprise then when the Astros won the Randy Johnson sweepstakes. The Cubs were just three and a half games behind the Astros at the time of the trade, but the Astros went 37-16 the rest of the season and ended with a 12.5 game lead. Randy Johnson made a big difference going 10-1, but Houston was still 27-15 in other starts. Because of their deep pitching staff, the Astros were almost never blown out. They went 35-9 in blowouts (winning margins of 5+ runs), second best in the majors (Atlanta was 35-8).

Johnson has left for greener pastures in Arizona, and the Astros again have some questions about the top of the pitching staff. Four of the starters appear set. Mike Hampton, Shane Reynolds, Jose Lima and Sean Bergman should remain in the rotation. The fifth starter should and probably will be Scott Elarton. Elarton was the Astros' top prospect in 1997. The 6-7 right-hander began the season starting for New Orleans and was called up in June. He had a couple of rocky starts, and then was moved to long relief. Pitching 44 innings in relief, Elarton posted a 2.42 ERA, struck out 41, and allowed just a .185 batting average against. He might rise to the top of this staff in a very short period of time.

The other weakness that the Astros were facing at the start of 1998 was their bullpen. They patched this hole with a combination of minor leaguers, Scott Elarton and C.J. Nitkowski, a free-agent, Doug Henry, and a trade acquisition, Jay Powell. Powell's acquisition, along with Elarton's call-up, gave the Astros a strong right-handed presence to go along with lefty closer Billy Wagner. Despite a severe lack of bullpen arms, the Marlins let Powell go for a minor league catcher. Powell has always been considered one of the better young relievers in the game and was very strong after the trade posting a 2.38 ERA and striking out 38 in 34 innings. This bullpen depth allowed the Astros to continue rolling after Billy Wagner's frightening July injury.

In running his bullpen, Dierker may be the Anti-LaRussa. His relievers had the lowest number of appearances in the National League (340 vs. Jim Riggleman's leading 449), and he also had the lowest percentage of relievers enjoying the platoon advantage (48% vs. Jim Leyland's 68%)

LARRY DIERKER

There is little doubt that Larry Dierker is on his way to becoming the best manager in baseball, if he isn't there already. Dierker is a literate, introspective man, who dabbles in art and is keeping a journal of his managerial experience. He's also a no-nonsense, cigar-chomping leader. He understands what makes an offense go, and how to develop a pitching staff. It is very rare manager who can combine the considerable leadership skills, the situational management skills, talent development skills and analytical skills needed to succeed. Dierker appears to have most of these skills in abundance.

Since Dierker took over as manager, the Astros have developed unexpected starters Chris Holt, Jose Lima, Ramon Garcia, and Sean Bergman. Billy Wagner has developed his considerable potential. Middle relievers like Tom Martin, Mike Magnante, Doug Henry, Russ Springer and C.J. Nitkowski have all pitched better than expected.

On offense, the star players have continued to excel, and the role players have improved. Dierker has utilized platoons effectively, and has exploited the running game with exceptional efficiency.

Dierker isn't solely responsible for this run of success. The Astros had finished second three years in a row under Terry Collins, and had a very good core of players. Dierker, however, has had remarkable success with a previously lackluster bullpen, and has developed successful starters from pitchers with little or no success was evident before. He even appears to have the ability to develop young players as the success of Richard Hidalgo and Scott Elarton indicate.

The Astros haven't had much post-season success, and Dierker never pitched in the post-season as the Astros finished just second once in Dierker's tenure as a pitcher. There is no indignity in losing two short series, and I'm sure the Astros' management will address any team problems particular to playoff baseball.

FACE THE ACE

I have always found interleague play bothersome. In a league, where teams from different divisions are competing for the same wild card spot, an unbalanced schedule confers certain advantages to certain teams. For instance, the National League

WPA BULLPEN BOX—HOUSTON ASTROS

	Pl	WPA	P	PPPI
Starters	1091	2.6	51.1	0.047
Relievers	499	2.4	32.4	0.065
Road	261	1.7	17.7	0.068
Home	238	0.7	14.7	0.062
Mar/Apr	86	0.1	5.8	0.067
May	86	0.6	4.6	0.053
June	91	0.5	5.0	0.055
July	89	1.0	6.6	0.074
August	73	0.8	4.3	0.059
September	74	-0.6	6.1	0.083
Non S/H Sit.	373	3.4	19.3	0.052
S/H Sit.	126	-1.0	13.1	0.104
Low Pressure	199	0.6	2.8	0.014
Med. Pressure	158	-0.3	10.3	0.065
High Pressure	142	2.1	19.3	0.136
Entered behind	188	1.4	5.7	0.030
Entered tied	100	1.7	12.6	0.126
Entered ahead	211	-0.7	14.1	0.067

Name	G	Pl	WPA	P	PPPI	MI	ROB	T
Elarton S	26	47	.6	2.6	.055	17	5	4
Harris R	6	8	-.2	.6	.071	2	2	0
Henry D	59	87	1.4	6.5	.075	26	24	16
Magnante M	48	68	-1.4	4.7	.068	18	14	16
Miller T	36	61	-.1	1.8	.030	19	13	2
Nitkowski C	43	77	.7	4.6	.059	27	20	6
Powell J	29	42	1.2	3.8	.090	11	13	9
Scanlan B	27	32	-.5	1.2	.038	5	6	3
Wagner B	58	67	1.2	6.5	.097	9	5	8
Total		499	2.4	32.4	.065			

	I-------- Quality ---------I				I--- Pressure -------I			
	Dis.	Poor	Fair	Good	Her.	Lo	Med	Hi	
Elarton S	2	1	13	10	0	11	10	5	(3)
Henry D	4	9	22	20	4	23	22	14	(10)
Magnante M	4	11	24	9	0	22	13	13	(7)
Miller T	2	3	26	5	0	24	10	2	(2)
Nitkowski C	1	6	22	13	1	19	12	12	(8)
Powell J	1	5	8	13	2	7	13	9	(6)
Scanlan B	1	5	18	3	0	17	9	1	(0)
Wagner B	5	2	24	24	3	24	15	19	(13)
Others	1	4	7	2	0	9	4	1	(0)
TOTAL	21	46	164	99	10	156	108	76	(49)

	7th inning			8th inning			9th inning		
	0	+1	+2	0	+1	+2	0	+1	+2
Elarton S	1	0	0	1	3	0	0	0	1
Harris R	0	1	0	0	0	0	0	0	0
Henry D	0	0	0	4	2	2	12	0	0
Magnante M	3	1	0	6	0	0	1	1	0
Miller T	1	0	2	0	0	1	0	0	1
Nitkowski C	1	3	1	3	2	2	1	0	2
Powell J	2	0	0	2	2	1	0	0	0
Scanlan B	0	0	0	0	1	0	0	0	0
Wagner B	0	0	0	0	0	0	4	14	9
Starters	14	11	12	7	8	5	0	3	1
TOTAL	22	16	15	23	18	11	19	18	14
Record	13-9	11-5	12-3	13-10	12-6	9-2	9-10	15-3	12-2

Sean Forman's
PROSPECT WATCH

NAME	AGE	POS	LEVEL	GR98	GR97	GR96	AVG
Lance Berkman	22	OF	AAA	77	66	-	73
Mitch Meluskey	24	C	AAA	83	60	44	69
Daryle Ward	23	1B	AAA	70	67	50	66
Jhonny Perez	21	SS	AA	58	49	72	57
Carlos Hernandez2	22	2B	AAA	60	53	40	54
Russ Johnson	25	SS	AAA	50	48	40	48

NAME	AGE	POS	LEVEL	GRADE
John Buck	17	C	Rookie	58
David Matranga	21	SS	Rookie	56
Michael Rose	21	C	Low A	48
Alejandro Vasquez	20	OF	Rookie	47
Keith Ginter	22	2B	Rookie	46
Julio Lugo	22	SS	High A	45
Modesto DeAza	19	2B	Rookie	43
Nelson Samboy	21	2B	High A	42

NAME	AGE	GS	S	C	T	W-L	ERA	K/H	LEVEL
Bob Milacki	33	28	4.18	2.71	6.89	10-8	3.82	0.53	High
Brian Sikorski	24	29	3.62	3.62	7.24	11-12	4.86	0.85	High
Edgar Ramos	23	17	4.24	3.65	7.88	4-4	5.72	0.69	High
Scott Taylor	31	20	4.60	3.30	7.90	8-5	6.24	0.55	High
Kevin Hodges	25	15	4.40	3.67	8.07	4-5	3.61	0.65	High
Tony Mounce	23	17	4.53	3.65	8.18	5-5	5.09	0.64	High
Paul O'Malley	25	28	4.39	4.00	8.39	11-10	5.45	0.55	High

The Astros made a serious miscalculation when they allowed Bob Abreu to leave in the expansion draft. Despite this, they still had enough talent to go out and get Randy Johnson and Moises Alou. There is still some more talent in the pipeline, but given the age of their stars,I don't think there is anything wrong with dealing some kids in order to make some strong championship bids over the next two or three years.

TOP DOG: Lance Berkman
Berkman is a switch-hitting power prospect who managed 30 home runs between AA and AAA last year. He's sort of like Chipper Jones in that he has been much stronger from the left side than his right side. Unlike Chipper, his average suffers rather than his power. He also has tremendous patience for a power hitter as displayed by his 97 walks vs. 98 strikeouts in 479 at bats. He will never be a gold glover in the outfield,but given that the Astros could use some help from the left side, I expect him to make the big club at some point next year.

BACKSTOP: Mitch Meluskey
Witch-hitting catchers who have hit over .300 for the last three years don't grow on trees. Meluskey's .353 average last year is actually a bit depressed as New Orleans is a good pitchers' park (he hit .377 on the road). Not surprisingly, his MLE's are an extraordinary .316/.415/.505. If the Astros decide they can live with his defense, he would improve an already impressive offense and might sneak into Rookie of the Year consideration.

HAVE BAT   WILL TRAVEL: Daryle Ward
Ward probably will be traveling eventually, as nobody is moving Jeff Bagwell anytime soon. Ward has showed over the last two years that he can hit with the best of them. After a .922 OPS in AA during 1997, he slipped a bit to an .886 OPS this year. As I said above   New Orleans is a terrible hitters' park, and Ward did hit better on the road. His patience was off a bit also last year, but I suspect that may be just normal fluctuation. He could help a number of teams either as a starter or off the bench, and a decent pitching prospect is probably all it would cost you. Comp: Roberto

Petagine, trading a little bit of patience for pop.

UP THE MIDDLE: Jhonny Perez
After two and a half years at Kissimmee (high-A), Perez has spent the last year and a half at Jackson (AA). He hit a respectable .285/.353/.399 in Jackson and also stole 22 bases. He has always been in Carlos Guillen's shadow,but with Guillen gone, Perez has a chance at some playing time. Perez isn't going to be a star, but he could become a 10-10 middle infielder with a little patience. One thing Dierker hasn't shown he can do is utilize and develop a young positional player. He's going to have the talent to prove that he can do it, and I'm not going to put anything past him.

ON THE MOUND: Tony Mounce
The Astros have raided their farm system in order to get players like Moises Alou and Randy Johnson. Most of the players they have parted ways with have been pitchers: Oscar Henriquez, Mark Johnson, Freddy Garcia,and John Halama. They might have been trading away pitchers under the assumption that Dierker could make Jose Lima and Sean Bergman into stars, which thus far has been true.
With regards to Mounce, he is a subtle example of what a lack of strict pitch counts. In 1996, Mounce was in the Florida State League and he posted a 2.25 ERA in 25 starts. However,he faced on average 27 batters per start and was just 21. Since that time, he hasn't managed an ERA below 5.00 and his hit prevention has gone in the tank. He hasn't been injured   but he clearly has lost effectiveness.

Central had the advantage of playing the exceptionally weak American League Central. Of course, the Cubs were 5-8 against the AL, while the Mets were 9-7, so that lets some of the air out of that theory.

Another area where a team can gain an advantage is the quality of the opposition's pitching. Following their early post-season departure, the Astros' GM Gerry Hunsicker commented that while Houston beat up end of the rotation pitchers, they struggled against team aces. This is somewhat obvious as aces are aces for a reason, but there may actually be something to Hunsicker's comments. Through fortuitous scheduling, some teams could face a much smaller number of top pitchers. Logic would state that this will even out over the course of a 162-game season, but since when has logic stopped us here at BBBA.

Here is the average pitcher faced by each National League team:

Team	IP	WL%	ERA	BR/9	K/9
Florida	155	.537	4.08	11.89	6.76
Philadelphia	161	.533	4.10	12.03	6.59
Montreal	166	.535	4.12	11.92	6.65
Milwaukee	167	.524	4.16	12.15	6.56
St. Louis	162	.516	4.17	12.21	6.47
Chicago	155	.517	4.19	12.16	6.49
Pittsburgh	158	.527	4.20	12.06	6.51
Colorado	155	.522	4.20	12.18	6.50
Arizona	164	.536	4.21	12.19	6.75
Cincinnati	164	.514	4.23	12.23	6.56
New York	157	.523	4.23	12.22	6.52
Atlanta	163	.503	4.24	12.24	6.55
San Francisco	159	.519	4.27	12.23	6.53
Los Angeles	159	.518	4.28	12.22	6.49
San Diego	159	.517	4.28	12.25	6.46
Houston	150	.502	4.32	12.30	6.46

Some of this is intuitive. The Astros had the best offense in the league, so pitchers facing them would have higher ERA's, while Florida's offense was less than effective, so a reasonable baseball observer would expect pitchers facing them to be more effective. However, there is not a strong correlation between this list and run scoring. This method has some flaws, so let's look at this another way.

We have ranked all the starters from Greg Maddux to Pedro Astacio by pitching runs. The chart at the top of the next page breaks out the starters faced by each team according to their rankings. It's sorted in descending order of the number of times each team faced a top ten starter.

As you can see from the chart, the Astros managed to escape the top ten pitcher just about as often as it could be managed by a team during 1998. (Only the Rockies faced fewer top ten starters.) No playoff-bound team managed to face more than 20 top ten starters during the regular season.

Not only were the Marlins playing with half a deck, but they also were facing aces more than any other team. The Marlins faced Maddux, Schilling, Dustin Hermansen and Smoltz three times; Kevin Brown, Tom Glavine and Al Leiter twice; and Pete Harnisch, Pedro Martinez, David Cone, Rolando Arrojo, and Roger Clemens once.

We went a step further, and ranked the starters of each team in terms of innings pitched for that team. Also, we treated anyone worse than fifth as a #5 starter. There are some issues to deal with, such as traded players like Randy Johnson. We've

Team	Top 10	Top 20	50-166
Florida	23	40	90
Arizona	22	39	91
Philadelphia	21	35	91
Montreal	20	34	87
Milwaukee	20	34	91
San Francisco	18	30	98
San Diego	18	34	95
Pittsburgh	17	37	96
New York	17	33	100
St. Louis	16	31	97
Atlanta	16	31	89
Chicago	15	33	96
Cincinnati	13	29	94
Los Angeles	13	28	100
Houston	12	30	104
Colorado	11	26	97

TEAM BREAKOUT ASTROS 1998

Category	RS	RA	W	L	Pct.	Rk
5+ RUNS SCORED/HOME	335	143	40	2	.952	2
5+ RUNS SCORED	664	307	74	10	.881	1
5+ RUNS SCORED/ROAD	329	164	34	8	.810	5
RECORD IN BLOWOUTS/ROAD	175	73	17	4	.810	2
4- RUNS ALLOWED/HOME	300	121	44	11	.800	5
CLOSE SLUGFESTS/HOME	39	36	4	1	.800	2
4- RUNS ALLOWED	557	240	82	21	.796	2
RECORD IN BLOWOUTS	366	148	35	9	.795	2
4- RUNS ALLOWED/ROAD	257	119	38	10	.792	1
RECORD IN BLOWOUTS/HOME	191	75	18	5	.783	2
SLUGFESTS/HOME	180	111	14	5	.737	2
RECORD IN SLUGFESTS	373	224	29	11	.725	1
SLUGFESTS/ROAD	193	113	15	6	.714	4
CLOSE LOW SCORING GAMES/HOME	32	25	9	5	.643	6
RECORD IN CLOSE GAMES/HOME	151	140	24	14	.632	3
SEASON TOTALS	874	620	102	60	.630	2
LOW SCORING GAMES/HOME	41	37	11	8	.579	8
CLOSE LOW SCORING GAMES/ROAD	23	23	6	5	.545	2
RECORD IN CLOSE GAMES	301	301	41	35	.539	6
RECORD IN LOW SCORING GAMES	83	82	20	18	.526	7
LOW SCORING GAMES/ROAD	42	45	9	10	.474	3
RECORD IN CLOSE GAMES/ROAD	150	161	17	21	.447	8
5+ RUNS ALLOWED/HOME	142	173	11	15	.423	1
4- RUNS SCORED/HOME	107	151	15	24	.385	7
4- RUNS SCORED	210	313	28	50	.359	4
5+ RUNS ALLOWED	317	380	20	39	.339	2
4- RUNS SCORED/ROAD	103	162	13	26	.333	2
CLOSE SLUGFESTS/ROAD	40	43	2	4	.333	13
5+ RUNS ALLOWED/ROAD	175	207	9	24	.273	8

included starts against #1 starters, starts against the bottom of the rotation (#4 and #5) and the weighted average.

Team	#1	W-L	Bottom	W-L	Avg
Milwaukee	36	18-18	60	27-34	2.94
Arizona	36	12-24	61	26-35	2.96
Cincinnati	31	19-12	63	28-36	3.04
Montreal	36	14-22	69	27-42	3.04
Atlanta	33	16-17	65	52-14	3.06
Pittsburgh	38	13-25	72	36-39	3.07
St. Louis	36	16-20	69	42-28	3.07
Philadelphia	35	13-22	66	34-34	3.08
San Diego	35	19-16	67	42-24	3.10
Chicago	33	19-14	70	43-28	3.12
San Francisco	34	16-18	72	41-30	3.14
Los Angeles	33	16-17	70	36-34	3.16
Florida	34	15-19	79	25-54	3.24
New York	25	9-16	73	41-32	3.26
Colorado	27	13-14	77	40-36	3.27
Houston	30	22-8	79	52-27	3.27

Note the Marlins drop down the list here. They faced more of the top aces, but missed many of the lesser ones. Milwaukee faced a higher percentage of front of the rotation pitchers than any other team. The difference between the Astros 3.27 average and the Brewers 2.94 is nearly 13 starts against a number one starter rather than a number five. That is a pretty large difference when you consider the numbers at top right. In thirteen games against an ace a team would win 4 games, while

Starter	WL%	IP/GS	ERA	BR/9	K/9	S	C	T
1	.577	6.7	3.74	11.53	7.05	3.86	2.92	6.78
2	.525	6.3	4.23	12.08	6.17	4.06	3.12	7.18
3	.514	6.0	4.38	12.50	6.29	4.04	3.43	7.47
4	.481	6.0	4.62	12.71	6.24	4.14	3.48	7.62
5	.419	5.3	5.37	13.88	6.02	4.41	3.86	8.27

they would win 7.5 games against a number five starter. The Astros finished near the bottom of each of these indicators.

But these results also point out that Gerry Hunsicker needs one of those "improve your memory while sleeping" tapes; his take on the Astros' fortunes vs. top of the line pitchers was 180 degrees off. Let's re-run those Houston numbers:

Team	#1	W-L	Bottom	W-L
Houston	30	22-8	79	52-27

The Astros ate up #1 starters in 1998, in direct contrast to Hunsicker's recollection. Of course, there are #1s and there are the absolute top pitchers in the league. So we looked at all the pitchers Houston faced in 1998 whose seasonal QMAX "T" score was < 7, which focuses on all of the top pitchers (such as the #2-#4 guys in Atlanta, who would be #1s on many other teams). The Astros had 35 such games in 1998, and won 21 of them, for a .600 winning percentage.

Sorry, Gerry, but that memory is still going to need an upgrade. Of course, he may just be remembering Kevin Brown in the playoffs. And that's the irony of the Astros' 1998 season: after handling the top pitchers extremely well during the regular season, the team came up empty in the playoffs. It happens.

																Adj	Raw		
Name	AB	R	H	D	T	HR	RBI	BB	SO	SB	CS	BA	OBP	SLG	XR	XR/27	XR/27	OXW	DXW	TXW
Alou M	584	105	181	31	4	38	126	84	84	11	3	.309	.397	.573	126	7.95	8.09	7.30	0.43	7.73
Ausmus B	412	63	112	9	3	6	46	53	58	10	3	.271	.357	.352	50	4.14	4.15	1.09	2.46	3.55
Bagwell J	541	126	163	30	1	34	113	108	88	19	7	.302	.422	.550	123	8.21	8.31	7.34	0.84	8.18
Bell De	630	112	199	38	2	22	110	51	122	13	3	.316	.365	.486	108	6.38	6.38	5.26	0.55	5.81
Berry S	299	49	94	15	1	13	53	31	47	3	1	.315	.388	.503	56	6.88	6.91	2.94	0.51	3.45
Biggio C	646	124	212	48	2	20	89	64	109	51	8	.328	.405	.501	130	7.66	7.60	7.41	1.73	9.14
Bogar T	156	12	24	3	1	1	8	9	34	2	1	.156	.210	.210	4	0.85	0.84	-1.29	0.78	-0.51
Clark D	131	12	27	7	0	0	4	14	44	1	1	.210	.290	.261	10	2.44	2.38	-0.32	-0.01	-0.33
Eusebio T	182	13	46	6	1	1	36	18	31	1	0	.255	.322	.313	18	3.28	3.25	0.02	1.01	1.03
Everett C	467	73	137	31	4	15	77	44	98	14	12	.294	.357	.473	72	5.47	5.57	2.89	1.25	4.14
Gutierrez R	491	56	129	22	3	2	47	54	81	13	7	.262	.338	.331	55	3.70	3.70	0.66	2.77	3.43
Hidalgo R	211	31	64	14	0	7	36	17	36	3	3	.305	.356	.471	34	5.79	5.78	1.48	0.45	1.93
Howell J	38	4	10	4	0	1	7	4	12	0	0	.275	.344	.469	6	5.24	5.79	0.21	0.00	0.21
Phillips J	58	4	11	0	0	2	9	7	21	0	0	.197	.283	.300	5	2.92	2.75	-0.06	0.01	-0.05
Spiers B	384	67	104	25	4	4	44	45	59	12	2	.271	.353	.385	53	4.91	5.03	1.83	0.47	2.30
HOU	5644	884	1582	298	26	167	832	618	1080	159	52	.280	.356	.431	861	5.32	5.35	36.75	13.25	50.00

Table title: <----- Park Adjusted Statistics ----->

Pitcher	S	C	T	SS	ES	IC	HH	PP	TJ	S12	S35	S67	C1	C23	C45	C67	QWP
Bergman	4.48	2.93	7.41	33%	7%	37%	33%	0%	15%	19%	48%	33%	15%	67%	15%	4%	.516
Elarton	4.50	3.00	7.50	50%	0%	0%	50%	0%	0%	0%	50%	50%	0%	100%	0%	0%	.512
Halama	4.50	3.67	8.17	33%	17%	17%	33%	0%	0%	17%	50%	33%	0%	33%	67%	0%	.417
Hampton	4.25	3.25	7.50	44%	3%	34%	31%	16%	13%	16%	53%	31%	6%	63%	25%	6%	.526
Lima	3.91	2.09	6.00	52%	27%	70%	24%	0%	30%	36%	39%	24%	39%	52%	9%	0%	.638
R Johnson	2.27	2.55	4.82	82%	36%	82%	0%	0%	0%	73%	27%	0%	36%	45%	18%	0%	.722
Reynolds	4.51	2.57	7.09	46%	11%	54%	34%	0%	23%	14%	51%	34%	26%	51%	23%	0%	.523
Schourek	4.20	3.80	8.00	40%	13%	27%	33%	13%	0%	27%	40%	33%	13%	13%	60%	13%	.461
T Miller	4.00	5.00	9.00	0%	0%	0%	0%	0%	0%	0%	100%	0%	0%	0%	100%	0%	.240
HOU	4.15	2.84	6.99	46%	14%	48%	29%	4%	16%	25%	46%	29%	21%	52%	24%	3%	.548

NATIONAL LEAGUE CENTRAL

CHICAGO CUBS

BROCK J. HANKE

Okay. All you guys who bought last year's book, dig it out and read the Chicago Cubbie essay I wrote last year. Have yourselves a good chuckle—I sure did—and then settle back and read this one.

The gist of last year's essay, for those of you who (shame!) didn't buy the 1998 Big Bad Baseball Annual, exemplar of perfect journalism that it was, amounts to the following. The Cubs had brought in a raft of new players, and I noted that several of these players addressed Cubbie needs very well. I thought that they had a pretty good team there, except for their cleanup hitter. After comparing said cleanup hitter to the other lineup anchors in the league, I concluded that the Cubbie guy was the absolute worst of the lot. I then speculated that, except for this horrid weakness, the Cubs might be able to contend, but that this horrid lineup anchor would surely keep them out of contention for 1998.

As you are no doubt giggling over even now, the cleanup man in question is one Sammy Sosa, currently sporting his brand spanking new MVP award. And the Cubbies did, indeed, get into the playoffs, albeit by the scantiest of margins. (It's hard to get scantier than having to win a one-game playoff.) But how miserable an analysis was that? Are some of you, fully aware of Sosa's previous weaknesses, just a bit skeptical about that MVP award? Didn't the BBWAA spend almost the entire month of September warning everyone that it didn't matter how many homers Mark McGwire hit, if the Cubs got into the playoffs, Sammy would be the MVP?

Well, let's check the data in the same form as last year. Above and at the right is a list of the best full-time hitter on each National League club, except for Arizona, where you can claim with success that full-time utility man Andy Fox hit better than Devon White. I used White because he had a starting job all year.

You can quickly see a few things from this chart. First, not every team bats their best hitter cleanup. It's not just the Diamondbacks, who don't really have a big hitter. It's all those teams, including the one with Mark McGwire, who hit the best guy third. It's not fair, therefore, to compare Sammy Sosa just to other

Name	Team	XR/27
Mark McGwire	STL	11.94
John Olerud	NYN	9.23
Gary Sheffield	LA	8.98
Barry Bonds	SF	8.67
Greg Vaughn	SD	8.51
Vladimir Guerrero	MON	8.27
Jeff Bagwell	HOU	8.21
Larry Walker	COL	8.15
Andres Galarraga	ATL	8.06
Sammy Sosa	CHN	7.85
Jason Kendall	PIT	7.47
Barry Larkin	CIN	7.20
Scott Rolen	PHI	6.78
Jeromy Burnitz	MIL	6.05
Cliff Floyd	FLA	5.77
Devon White	ARI	5.44

cleanup men. Sammy is, and was going into the season, the Cubbies idea of their lineup anchor. They'd have thought that of him if they had batted him cleanup, third, leadoff, or ninth. The people to compare him to are the other teams' lineup men. I don't care that the Diamondbacks' lineup anchor bats leadoff because they don't actually have any big hitters; Devon White is the guy to compare to Sammy.

And, as you can see, Sammy Sosa finishes tenth in this rarefied company. Sixty-six homers or no 66 homers, he finishes tenth and no higher. The main reason is pretty much the one you'd expect. Although Sammy's 73 walks were a career high, and were the only time he's taken more than the average, they are very few for a top home run hitter. Without his 14 intentional walks, he'd be below the league average, even with the intimidation value of those 66 taters. Almost all of the guys

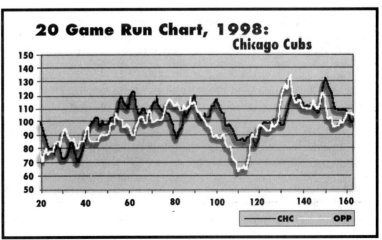

20 Game Run Chart, 1998:
Chicago Cubs

CHC · OPP

QMAX PRESENTS: "BAD" PITCHERS

PORTRAIT OF THE ARTIST AS A YOUNG MAN

Boy, here's one name I bet you weren't expecting in the Bad Pitchers series. The man recently dubbed "The Monet of the Mound" by Don Malcolm had a rough season in 1987, his first full season in the bigs. Let's look at these preliminary sketches and see what we can find.

Well, this isn't exactly what I expected. In April and May, Maddux looked a lot like many rookie pitchers: some really excellent starts sprinkled in with a few shellings. His 5 start QMAX stuff and control averages both hovered right around 4, and he was winning as many as he was losing. In June and July, you can see the beginnings of a style emerge, as the 5-start QMAX command average works its way down from 4 to a quite good 2.80 by the end of July. Meanwhile, the 5-start stuff average is holding steady around 4.

After that, it gets ugly: starting on July 29, Maddux turned in six horrible starts and one really good one. Except for a 2,3 performance on September 24, Maddux never got below 5 on the stuff scale and had three 7c starts on the command scale. It is this seven-start meatball run (5.43, 5.43/10.86 in QMAX notation) that sent Maddux' season numbers into the tank and onto this page.

What the

GREG MADDUX/CHC 1987							
	1	2	3	4	5	6	7	S
1	1		1					2
2		2						2
3			3	1	1			5
4		2						2
5				2	1		1	4
6	1			4	1		2	8
7				1	3			4
C	2	0	8	8	6	0	3	27

heck happened? The word "injury" leaps to mind, at least for me, and indeed Greg only took the mound once in a six-week period between his miserable August 3 start and September 15. A three-start refresher course at AAA was also included; Maddux did well at Iowa (1.00 ERA) but the recharge failed to hold when he returned to the majors. The whole problem might be seen as one of pacing: Greg may simply have not been ready for the rigors of the long season. In 1988, he blossomed in the first half until a tired arm again sent his numbers southward (or northward, if we're talking QMAX).

The rest, as they (and we, probably too many times) say, is history.

--Tom Austin

Five Start Qmax: Maddux

5/4 5/25 6/15 7/7 7/29 9/20

S   C

---

ranked above Sammy have more walks, and often many more. As a consequence, they all have higher on-base percentages except for Vladimir Guerrero and Greg Vaughn, who need ballpark adjustment help to generate higher PRC/27 that Sammy anyway.

Sammy's power numbers, before ballpark adjustment, do stand out. He can't match Mark McGwire's slugging percentage, but then Big Mac is out there in territory previously occupied only by Babe Ruth. The trouble is that power only counts once, in the slugging percentage itself. On-base percentage counts twice. It counts as getting on base, which contributes to scoring runs, and it also counts as lessening the number of outs made, which is the divisor for RC/27. So Sammy's strong point doesn't help his team produce runs as much as the strengths of the other top hitters do, because it's a one-trick pony, and getting on base is a double-barreled shotgun by comparison.

But this isn't simply the Sammy Sosa player comment. What does this all mean for the Chicago Cub team? Can they actually win a division title with Sammy as their lineup anchor? If so, how? Since there is no doubt that Sammy is far better than nothing, is there anyone else on the roster whom they could replace with an extra lineup anchor, if the Tribune would pony up the bucks?

First, check out the ranking list above. Note that no one lower on the list than Sammy comes from a contending team. Milwaukee is probably the best of the teams down there, and they aren't exactly printing World Series tickets. In general, it takes a better lineup anchor than Sammy Sosa to contend. And it gets worse. On some of the contending teams, not only does the lineup anchor rank higher than Sammy, but there is some confusion as to who the lineup anchor should be, and there are more players than just the one who outrank Sammy. Houston has people like Craig Biggio as well as Jeff Bagwell. Greg Vaughn was somebody the Padres were hoping could hit a solid sixth when the season started. Is Andres Galarraga the Braves' lineup anchor or is it Chipper Jones?

On top of that, do you really think Sammy Sosa is going to hit 50 homers again in 1999, much less 60? His previous high was an even 40. He was not 27 years old in 1998, or 26 or 28. He was 29. The Age-27 Career Year was the one when he hit the 40. Mark McGwire, on the other hand, hit 58 homers in 1997, and 52 the year before that. He hit almost all of those homers in one of the worst homer ballparks in the game, in

Oakland. In other words, if you were managing the Cardinals, you had a right to build your lineup around the expectation that Mark McGwire would hit somewhere in the vicinity of 50 taters, unless he got hurt. With Sammy, you figure the vicinity to be about 35. With very few walks. And a batting average that, as lineup anchors go, isn't exactly dominant.

In short, for the Cubs to get into the playoffs again with Sammy Sosa as their lineup anchor, either Sammy has to go on another out-of-nowhere rampage, or they have to do it with pitching. Those of you who have been reading these here books for several years may have your ears pricked up about now. And yes, it is true that I wrote a Cubbie essay once that showed that most winning teams in Wrigley Field have dominated in pitching rather than hitting. It's a ballpark-contrarian effect. The teams that won in Chicago in old Comiskey Park were built around dominant offenses. Old Comiskey was a notorious pitchers' park. In short, if you have a park with a bias, you build against the bias. There are several reasons for this, one of which is that the people favored by the ballpark always look better than they are, so it's hard to keep a fire lit under them. Hitters in Wrigley think they're doing fine when they're just average. It's pitchers that you can keep scared and completely focused.

The Cubbies didn't really do that. Their team ERA of 4.47 was only 11th in the league. That's OK, given the ballpark, but it's not dominant, even in Wrigley Field. So, the first thing the Cubbies could do to return to the postseason would be to focus on getting some more pitching. A couple of top starters would do it, but who isn't looking for top starters? The Trib didn't pony up for Randy Johnson or Kevin Brown, and the Cubs don't have a reservoir of highly-regarded talent to trade for Roger Clemens. So, right there, it's unlikely that the Cubs will enter the playoffs in 1999. To do so, they'd almost have to get another 60-homer season out of Sammy.

Or maybe they could get Sammy some help. That is, after all, what they tried last year. True, they concentrated on second-echelon talents like Henry Rodriguez, but at least they tried. And, hard as it might be for the Cubs to win with offense, they're closer to a top offense than they are to a top pitching staff. Let's take a look at the Cubbie position players, and see who might be jettisoned for a superstar with the most resulting gain. Here's a list of last year's Cubbie starters, again ranked by PRC/27.

Name	Pos	XR/27
Sammy Sosa	RF	7.85
Mark Grace	1B	6.39
Henry Rodriguez	LF	5.94
Gary Gaetti	3B	5.92
Mickey Morandini	2B	5.33
Jose Hernandez	UT	4.56
Lance Johnson	CF	4.08
Jeff Blauser	SS	3.84
Scott Servais	C	2.85

Can you spot the weakness? Yes, that's right, it's those up-the-middle positions that emphasize defense. Mickey Morandini is all right at second base, but shortstop features an

WPA BULLPEN BOX—CHICAGO CUBS

	PI	WPA	P	PPPI
Starters	1056	0.9	54.5	0.052
Relievers	643	0.7	41.5	0.065
Road	307	-0.7	19.5	0.064
Home	336	1.4	22.0	0.066
Mar/Apr	116	2.4	5.5	0.047
May	107	-0.6	8.8	0.082
June	102	0.5	7.3	0.072
July	82	0.4	4.6	0.056
August	131	-0.6	9.2	0.070
September	105	-1.4	6.2	0.059
Non S/H Sit.	462	-1.2	22.3	0.048
S/H Sit.	181	1.9	19.2	0.106
Low Pressure	274	-0.1	4.0	0.015
Med. Pressure	215	-3.9	15.0	0.070
High Pressure	154	4.8	22.5	0.146
Entered behind	271	-1.9	6.6	0.025
Entered tied	110	1.3	14.0	0.128
Entered ahead	262	1.3	20.9	0.080

Name	G	PI	WPA	P	PPPI	MI	ROB	T
Adams T	63	94	-.4	7.6	.081	26	25	16
Beck R	81	91	2.4	9.1	.100	8	18	9
Fossas T	8	9	-.7	.6	.069	1	5	2
Heredia F	30	34	-.1	2.2	.066	4	18	3
Karchner M	29	42	-.1	3.6	.086	13	12	4
Mulholland T	64	100	.4	6.5	.065	28	32	12
Myers Ro	12	22	-.1	.9	.039	9	2	0
Patterson B	33	42	.4	3.7	.087	7	17	7
Pisciotta M	43	65	-.3	3.2	.049	18	24	6
Stevens D	31	48	-.6	1.6	.033	10	16	4
Telemaco A	14	33	-.7	.9	.026	10	5	2
Wengert D	15	26	.3	.9	.035	7	5	2
Total		643	.7	41.5	.065			

	Quality					Pressure			
	Dis.	Poor	Fair	Good	Her.	Lo	Med	Hi	
Adams T	8	14	20	14	7	19	29	15	(11)
Beck R	6	5	29	38	3	28	27	26	(18)
Heredia F	1	5	15	9	0	12	15	3	(2)
Karchner M	2	8	8	11	0	7	12	10	(5)
Mulholland T	3	12	29	18	2	28	23	13	(7)
Myers Ro	0	3	6	3	0	6	4	2	(1)
Patterson B	0	7	19	4	3	17	7	9	(6)
Pisciotta M	1	12	22	8	0	21	18	4	(3)
Stevens D	2	1	27	1	0	23	6	2	(1)
Telemaco A	2	0	11	1	0	9	4	1	(0)
Wengert D	0	0	12	3	0	10	3	2	(1)
Others	2	5	21	6	0	21	11	2	(1)
TOTAL	27	72	219	116	15	201	159	89	(57)

	7th inning			8th inning			9th inning		
	0	+1	+2	0	+1	+2	0	+1	+2
Adams T	3	1	0	7	6	3	7	0	0
Beck R	0	0	0	0	0	0	2	15	15
Fossas T	1	0	0	0	0	0	0	0	0
Haney C	1	0	0	0	0	0	0	0	0
Heredia F	0	0	1	0	1	0	0	1	0
Karchner M	1	1	0	3	5	1	3	0	0
Mulholland T	2	4	1	0	3	0	3	0	0
Myers Ro	1	0	0	0	0	0	0	0	0
Patterson B	1	0	1	1	0	0	1	0	0
Pisciotta M	2	1	0	0	1	0	1	0	0
Telemaco A	0	0	1	0	0	0	0	0	0
Wengert D	0	0	0	0	0	0	1	0	0
Starters	16	10	12	6	5	6	1	0	1
TOTAL	28	17	16	18	20	10	19	16	16
Record	14-14	10-7	12-4	12-6	14-6	8-2	9-10	14-2	14-2

Sean Forman's

PROSPECT WATCH

NAME	AGE	POS	LEVEL	GR98	GR97	GR96	AVG
Pedro Valdes	25	OF	AAA	60	57	68	60
Micah Franklin	26	OF	AAA	64	38	61	55
Chad Meyers	22	2B	AA	57	53	40	53
Pat Cline	23	C	AAA	56	47	58	53
Rod McCall	26		AAA	45	51	59	49
Robin Jennings	26	OF	AAA	38	50	64	46
Roosevelt Brown	22	3B	AA	51	22	52	42
Jose Nieves	23	SS	AAA	49	30	25	39

NAME	AGE	POS	LEVEL	GRADE
Tydus Meadows	20	OF	Low A	59
Eric Hinske	20	1B	Rookie	56
Jeff Goldbach	17	C	Rookie	56
David Kelton	18	3B	Rookie	53
Ron Walker	22	3B	High A	51
Tony Schrager	21	2B	Low A	50
Jaisen Randolph	19	OF	Low A	49
Brad Ramsey	21	C	High A	46
Quincy Carter	20	OF	Low A	46

NAME	AGE	GS	S	C	T	W-L	ERA	K/H	LEVEL
Brian McNichol	24	26	4.00	3.00	7.00	11-8	3.95	0.92	High
Kyle Farnsworth	22	32	3.97	3.16	7.13	15-10	4.82	0.78	High
Kennie Steenstra	26	23	4.22	2.91	7.13	11-5	4.38	0.61	High
Kurt Miller	25	28	3.82	3.64	7.46	14-3	3.81	0.95	High
Phillip Norton	22	20	4.00	3.60	7.60	6-5	3.49	0.98	High
Jason Ryan	22	24	4.25	3.63	7.88	3-12	4.74	0.72	High
Earl Byrne	25	24	3.88	4.04	7.92	8-8	5.39	0.96	High
Courtney Duncan	23	28	3.57	4.64	8.21	6-9	4.28	1.12	High

Oy! This is not looking good for the Cubs. They are an aging team with not a whole lot of help on the way. If you look at the ages of the players in the high minors, notice how many of them were younger than 22 last year: zero. Also notice how many were over 24: four. The Cubs did pull out the pocketbook to sign first rounder Corey Patterson, a high schooler from Georgia, but they clearly need to spend a bit more attention to the farm system, or it will be a long time before they reach the World Series.

KEN PHELPS ALL-STARS: Pedro Valdes and Micah Franklin
Franklin went ballistic for Iowa in the PCL hitting .329/.437/.655, while Valdes was a tad more subdued at .314/.384/.590. These were probably their career seasons, but I think they each have something to offer major league teams. When I see somebody like John Vanderwaal or Marty Malloy come in to pinch hit in a playoff game, I wonder why people don't give a chance on players like these two. Franklin has a career OPS of .875 in the minors. I have a feeling that a Franklin/Valdes platoon would give the Cubs more offense than Henry Rodriguez next year. Comp: Franklin - Chito Martinez, Valdes - a bit below Brian Giles.

TOP DOG: Chad Meyers
Meyers is essentially the Cubs' top prospect by default. He is a converted outfielder, who is still getting his bearings in the pivot. He provides something the Cubs need more of, which is OBP. He has a career OBP of .398 in pro ball and 165 walks in the last two years. Thus far his OBP is higher than his slugging percentage, but he spent part of the year in the Florida State League, which is generally a poor power league. He is also a talented basestealer, who was 60 out of 72 in stolen base attempts last year. I imagine that he will be in AAA next year, and then playing for the big league club the following year. Comp: Quilvio Veras.

BACKSTOP: Pat Cline
It seems like Cline has been around forever, and I believe that I wrote him up in each of the last two books as well. He hasn't progressed from the 17 homer year he had in the Florida State League. One thing about young catchers is the defensive side of the game plays a huge role in their development, and Cline has had some defensive problems in the past few years. He can outhit Scott Servais (.627 OPS vs. .672 OPS MLE), but if I had a shot at Todd Hundley for not too much, I would go get him. Comp: Jorge Posada

QUARTERBACK: Quincy Carter
You may know more about Carter from his exploits on the football field with the Georgia Bulldogs. Carter was originally just a baseball player after the Cubs lured him away from a football scholarship. However, he started yearning for the gridiron and enrolled in Georgia this fall, where he has been electric. Baseball teams love football athletes, specifically quarterbacks, and it's not hard to see why. They have tremendous arms (usually) and if they are from some sort of an option attack they usually have tremendous athletic ability.
Carter hasn't shown nearly the same ability on the baseball diamond that he has on the football field, so I rate the chances of him making the show as 15% or so. Still with all that talent, teams will continue to give chances to quarterbacks.

ON THE MOUND: Brian McNichol
McNichol is a 6-6 lefthander who hasn't done much up until this year. For someone who has historically given up a large number of hits (9.7 H/9 career) he has also had a large number of strikeouts (7.8 K/9 career). His QMAX numbers point to a control pitcher (24% Hit Hard), but his strikeout numbers are pretty high. Quite frankly, I have no idea what this means.

aging Jeff Blauser, and third base featured an ancient Gary Gaetti. The catchers are universally poor, and the center fielder posted a poor season. You might expect Lance Johnson to bounce back, but he's not going to join Sammy as lineup-anchor hitters. The Cubs simply don't have a hitter anywhere you'd expect them not to.

Compare to the Braves. Bobby Cox is a notoriou Earl Weaver manager, which means he emphasizes offense down the lines and defense up the middle. But his center fielder was Andruw Jones, and his catcher is Javy Lopez. He just traded for Bret Boone to play second base. Only at shortstop is he playing

a punchless glove. The Astros? They have Craig Biggio at second and Carl Everett's emergence in center field is arguably the one thing that turned the corner for them. The Padres had Quilvio Veras at second, and Steve Finley in center, although he played poorly for him. But their shortstop and catcher played over their heads, and they were the team with the hot pitching. Even the Giants, who only tied the Cubs, had Jeff Kent at second to go along with Barry Bonds, and traded for Ellis Burks.

So, the ticket to the Cubbie World Series is apparent. They need to replace at least one pitcher with a top man, and at least one infielder. That would be possible, given Tribune money, and it would be enough. It won't be easy; the defense-first positions are the ones where it is hardest to find top hitters. But, short of that, I'm afraid they ain't goin' anywhere unless Sammy hits Sixty again.

BOP MANIA

Looking at offensive production by batting order position (BOP), as we at BBBA are always doing when there isn't a Barbara Steele retrospective going on, produces several interesting facts with respect to the Cubs' batting order in 1998.

First, there were five lineup slots in baseball last year that produced a SLG of higher than .600. Despite Sammy's fabulous 66, none of these slots belonged to the Cubs. Here they are:

Team	Lg	BOP	SLG
STL	N	#3	.718
CHW	A	#4	.646
TEX	A	#4	.617
COL	N	#5	.612
SEA	A	#3	.605

You can figure out the inhabitants of these lineup slots pretty easily. That's McGwire, Belle, Gonzalez in the top three, and Junior at .605: who's the Rox hitter at #5 in their order? Vinny Castilla.

These guys were pretty much put into their lineup slots and left there the entire year. Cubs manager Jim Riggleman moved his hitters around, and produced a blurring of the BOP statistics as a result.

BOP	AB	R	H	D	T	HR	RBI	BB	SO	BA	OBP	SLG	OPS
#3	671	124	190	22	0	52	125	70	149	.283	.351	.548	.899
#4	626	113	208	39	3	33	128	98	96	.332	.420	.562	.982

You can recognize the distinctive shape of Sammy's statistics in the #3 slot, even though the HR total is down. Note also that the rate stats are lower here, too. What gives?

Early in the year, Jim Riggleman had his batting order designed with Mark Grace batting third and Sammy Sosa batting fourth. In terms of hitter types, this would appear to make sense. Grace has the OBP element, and Sosa the SLG component. But in June, after about forty games with his lineup designed in this fashion, he flip-flopped them. Why? Because, for whatever reason, the logical lineup construction concept wasn't working. Grace just wasn't hitting in the #3 slot, while Sammy was red-hot at cleanup. Most managers would have left Sosa alone, figuring that you don't mess with success, but Riggleman made the flip-flop. You can see what they did in their ass-backward BOPs at the top of the next column.

For reasons known only to Riggleman's palm reader (does Madame Rosinka have a satellite office in Chicago?), Grace turned it around and put up his

usual numbers in the #4 slot. Sammy cooled off, but kept hitting those taters.

Who	BOP	G	AB	R	H	D	T	HR	RBI	BB	SO	BA	OBP	SLG
Sammy	#3	121	487	99	142	14	0	49	114	48	123	.292	.353	.622
Mark	#4	114	421	71	137	29	3	15	78	69	36	.325	.417	.515

The result of this switch was to give the Cubs RBI figures that look like a classic distribution. The #3 slot gets less opportunities, and thus drives in fewer runs. Despite McGwire's massive OBP, his #3 slot for the Cardinals produced the most RBI in their lineup. The Sosa/Grace flip-flop meant that the Cubs got a few more RBI out their #4 slot (128) than the #3 slot (125). 24 of 30 teams were aligned in such a way, and the average gain in RBI from #3 to #4 was 15. The six exceptions were as follows:

Team	#3	#4	Diff
NYY	127	121	-6
BOS	128	121	-7
LA	106	99	-7
BAL	133	115	-18
SEA	147	111	-36
STL	154	118	-36

TEAM BREAKOUT CUBS 1998

Category	RS	RA	W	L	Pct.	Rk
4- RUNS ALLOWED/HOME	181	88	36	5	.878	1
CLOSE LOW SCORING GAMES/HOME	45	28	14	3	.824	1
5+ RUNS SCORED/HOME	324	237	35	10	.778	7
5+ RUNS SCORED	637	444	65	20	.765	7
4- RUNS ALLOWED	392	207	65	21	.756	4
5+ RUNS SCORED/ROAD	313	207	30	10	.750	9
RECORD IN CLOSE GAMES/HOME	211	184	32	12	.727	1
LOW SCORING GAMES/HOME	67	47	18	7	.720	2
4- RUNS ALLOWED/ROAD	211	119	29	16	.644	7
RECORD IN BLOWOUTS/ROAD	114	94	10	7	.588	3
SLUGFESTS/ROAD	232	208	17	12	.586	5
RECORD IN CLOSE GAMES	382	359	47	34	.580	2
CLOSE SLUGFESTS/HOME	74	75	5	4	.556	6
RECORD IN LOW SCORING GAMES	101	99	25	20	.556	4
SEASON TOTALS	831	792	90	73	.552	4
RECORD IN SLUGFESTS	419	412	29	24	.547	4
RECORD IN BLOWOUTS	229	213	20	17	.541	6
CLOSE SLUGFESTS/ROAD	94	93	6	6	.500	7
RECORD IN BLOWOUTS/HOME	115	119	10	10	.500	10
SLUGFESTS/HOME	187	204	12	12	.500	9
4- RUNS SCORED/HOME	97	161	16	21	.432	5
CLOSE LOW SCORING GAMES/ROAD	26	26	5	7	.417	8
RECORD IN CLOSE GAMES/ROAD	171	175	15	22	.405	13
5+ RUNS ALLOWED/HOME	240	310	15	26	.366	4
LOW SCORING GAMES/ROAD	34	52	7	13	.350	11
5+ RUNS ALLOWED	439	585	25	52	.325	3
4- RUNS SCORED	194	348	25	53	.321	6
5+ RUNS ALLOWED/ROAD	199	275	10	26	.278	7
4- RUNS SCORED/ROAD	97	187	9	32	.220	9

The interesting thing is that if you look at the teams under the average Diff here, 6 of the 14 teams (Cubs, Astros, Yankees, Red Sox, Padres and Indians) can be found here, while the "standard" lineup construction produces only two playoff teams (Braves at +20, and Rangers at a whopping +49). Makes you think that, despite all of the throat-clearing from the batting order simulators, that there might be something in this front-loading concept after all. <COJ>

Name	AB	R	H	D	T	HR	RBI	BB	SO	SB	CS	BA	OBP	SLG	XR	Adj XR/27	Raw XR/27	OXW	DXW	TXW
Alexander M	264	34	59	10	1	5	25	18	67	4	1	.224	.274	.323	23	2.83	2.95	-0.38	0.35	-0.03
Blauser J	362	49	78	11	3	4	26	59	94	2	2	.215	.336	.293	42	3.84	3.96	0.70	-0.13	0.57
Brown B	347	56	99	16	7	14	48	30	96	4	5	.286	.343	.492	57	5.96	6.14	2.56	0.06	2.62
Gaetti G	128	21	41	11	0	8	27	12	23	0	0	.317	.394	.587	27	8.08	8.24	1.64	0.24	1.88
Grace M	596	91	182	38	3	17	89	92	57	4	6	.305	.396	.463	105	6.39	6.56	5.26	0.72	5.98
Hernandez J	489	75	122	22	7	23	75	39	142	4	5	.250	.306	.462	66	4.56	4.72	1.80	1.05	2.85
Hill G	131	26	46	5	0	8	23	14	34	0	0	.348	.410	.566	27	8.19	8.36	1.63	-0.05	1.58
Houston T	255	26	64	7	1	9	33	13	54	2	2	.252	.287	.391	27	3.65	3.75	0.25	0.26	0.51
Johnson L	304	51	84	8	4	2	21	26	22	10	6	.277	.332	.348	35	4.08	4.14	0.72	0.16	0.88
Martinez S	87	7	23	9	1	0	7	13	21	1	0	.259	.356	.381	12	4.67	4.88	0.37	0.10	0.47
Mieske M	97	16	29	7	0	1	12	11	17	0	0	.294	.368	.395	15	5.65	5.83	0.65	0.02	0.67
Morandini M	583	92	170	20	4	8	53	71	85	14	1	.292	.376	.379	86	5.33	5.48	3.47	0.79	4.26
Orie K	204	24	37	14	0	2	21	18	36	1	1	.179	.250	.276	15	2.25	2.32	-0.70	0.34	-0.36
Rodriguez H	416	56	102	20	1	31	85	53	114	1	3	.246	.329	.520	72	5.94	6.13	3.20	0.79	3.99
Servais S	325	35	71	15	1	7	36	26	52	1	0	.218	.285	.333	29	2.85	2.96	-0.45	0.72	0.27
Sosa S	644	133	195	19	0	65	158	72	173	19	8	.304	.372	.637	140	7.85	8.05	7.93	1.10	9.03
CHI	5657	825	1474	244	33	209	786	593	1237	68	40	.261	.333	.426	799	4.85	4.99	28.66	6.52	35.18

Pitcher	S	C	T	SS	ES	IC	HH	PP	TJ	S12	S35	S67	C1	C23	C45	C67	QWP
J Gonzalez	4.20	3.55	7.75	35%	15%	30%	45%	10%	5%	25%	30%	45%	0%	55%	40%	5%	.465
M Clark	4.48	2.67	7.15	39%	21%	45%	36%	3%	12%	27%	36%	36%	27%	48%	24%	0%	.530
M Morgan	4.80	4.60	9.40	20%	0%	20%	60%	20%	0%	20%	20%	60%	0%	0%	80%	20%	.265
Mulholland	3.17	2.67	5.83	83%	17%	33%	0%	0%	0%	17%	83%	0%	33%	33%	33%	0%	.645
Tapani	4.44	2.91	7.35	44%	18%	41%	41%	3%	15%	21%	38%	41%	21%	44%	32%	3%	.498
Trachsel	4.03	3.48	7.52	39%	9%	39%	30%	12%	9%	27%	42%	30%	15%	39%	36%	9%	.514
Wengert	4.33	4.00	8.33	33%	0%	0%	33%	17%	0%	0%	67%	33%	0%	33%	67%	0%	.395
Wood	2.69	3.85	6.54	58%	12%	62%	4%	31%	4%	58%	38%	4%	4%	42%	46%	8%	.611
CHC	4.02	3.29	7.31	44%	14%	41%	31%	11%	9%	29%	40%	31%	15%	43%	37%	5%	.516

NATIONAL LEAGUE CENTRAL

ST. LOUIS CARDINALS

BROCK J. HANKE

As you know, teams will, over time, acquire the characteristics that their manager is used to. Some managers force the issue immediately upon assuming the job. Whitey Herzog, for instance, is famous for either having his team in place within a year, or howling loudly about ownership interference. Tony LaRussa, on the other hand, is much more patient, and it shows in the results.

Tony's first major league team was the Chicago White Sox, which he took over in the middle of the 1979 season. The Sox were pretty awful; their only real asset was Chet Lemon. Tony brought them slow but steady progress, first by improving the pitching, and then by developing the offense from the outfield. In 1983, the team had a fine outfield full of hitters, a good middle infield defense, although none of the infielders hit much, a star catcher in Carlton Fisk, and a couple of overworked star pitchers named Hoyt and Dotson. Tony had already toasted the arm of his first good pitcher, Britt Burns. That was the team that won 99 games, which seemed a miracle for the Chisox at the time.

Hoyt and Dotson fell apart in 1984, and the team floundered, staying close to the division title, but unable to repeat. Finally, the pitching staff completely collapsed, and the team was in trouble when Tony left in 1986. He moved to Oakland, and immediately turned around a team that had been playing truly lousy baseball. This team, though, had talent, and Tony was able to win in his third year by getting the starting pitching together, converting Dennis Eckersley to a closer, moving power hitters into the outfield and good gloves into the infield, and developing Terry Steinbach at catcher.

The team won three more times, riding the arms of Dave Stewart, Bob Welch, and Mike Moore. Each year, one of the three would be off, but the other two, along with the fine power offense, would carry Tony to victory. Finally, though, the three big arms all began to suffer from overwork and age, and the team started to lose, and the ownership sold off the stars, and Tony moved to St. Louis.

In St. Louis, Tony slipped in a quickie division title in a weak division, and then has floundered, due to a large number of injuries, an often-weak offense with little power, and a pitching staff that has trouble getting two good seasons in a row out of its starters, who do pitch a lot of innings, although not the most in the league.

All along, Tony has move the team closer and closer to the type of team he is used to. The outfield and first base spots now have power, and the team focuses obsessively on starting pitching. The infield, meanwhile, has become very weak compared to the magnificent outfits of the Whitey Herzog days. This process has accelerated as the new ownership has become more confident in its role, and more confident in Tony. After this last off-season of player movement, the team has really started to resemble the winning outfits in Chicago and Oakland. What follows is a look at the St. Louis Cardinals as then enter the year of 1999, seen in the light of the configuration of Tony's best teams.

Let's start at catcher, because it's t this position that we can best see the biggest trap that awaited Tony when he changed leagues. As I said, Tony's basic idea on offense was to get it out of his outfield, first baseman, DH, and catcher. Part of this, no doubt, was the luck of having Terry Steinbach and Carlton Fisk available behind the plate, but you should be aware that Tony is trying to lure Steinbach out of retirement as insurance against hot kid Eli Marrero failing to develop. Most managers would just go with the kid, especially at catcher, where most managers don't expect offense.

Anyway, in the AL, Tony's formula produces a six-man

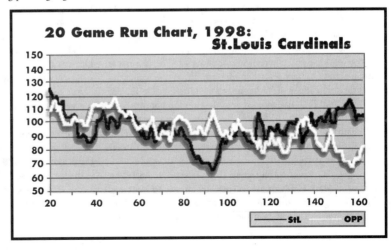

20 Game Run Chart, 1998: St.Louis Cardinals

QMAX PRESENTS: "BAD" PITCHERS

SOMETIMES THEY COME BACK...RIGHT UP THE MIDDLE

Wee Willie Sherdel was a pretty good pitcher for a while for the pre-Gas House Cardinals of the 1920's, usually logging 200-plus innings and double figures in wins. His best year was 1928, when he won 21 games with a 2.86 ERA. In the World Series, he quick-pitched a strike three past Babe Ruth. Unfortunately, the Yankees and the Cards had agreed not to use quick-pitches, so the Babe got another shot and used it, seconds later, to take Sherdel out of the yard. Nowadays I find it hard to picture either a quick-pitch or a Gentleman's Agreement not to use one. Wee Willie's other claim to fame was once entering the game with the bases loaded and no outs, throwing one pitch, and getting a triple play. Wow.

Not so famous was Willie's 1929 season. Perhaps fighting a dead arm, Sherdel started the season by giving up 12, 15,15,4 (yay!), 13, and 11 hits in his first six starts. If he was hurting, Sherdel must have kept quiet and rubbed tobacco juice on the owie, because he still took the ball roughly every fifth day (including a couple of three-week stints in the bullpen, and a number of relief appearances between starts) and got his team into the eighth inning before giving up the ball. Unfortunately for the Cards, the opposition generally had ten or eleven hits and five runs by that time.

The inspi-

BILL SHERDEL/STL(n) 1929							
	1	2	3	4	5	6	7	S
1	1	1						2
2								0
3			1					1
4	2							2
5				2				2
6	3		1					4
7	2	1	2	4	1		1	11
C	8	2	4	6	1	0	1	22

Five Start Qmax: Sherdel

7
6
5
4
3
2
1

5/12   6/14   7/16   7/29   9/2

S   C

rational part of Sherdel's season came in four starts from June 19-July 6. Four straight 7's would have been great in a floating casino, but in QMAX terms it meant that Wee Willie had sunk. The most incredible of these four games came on July 3rd, when the Pirates declared independence a day early: in eight innings, Sherdel allowed 21 hits (!) and 13 runs, all earned.

If you want to see something really strange, compare the season Willie had with the one Terry Mulholland (profiled in this space in the Giants essay) had in 1995. Examine their running 5-start QMAX averages in the chart shown and try not to whistle. In the Mulholland piece I advance the hypothesis, only partly for comic effect, that the pattern represented a control pitcher who has lost his fastball but doesn't know it yet. Now that we've seen it twice, I think I might be on to something.

--Tom Austin

offensive sequence, which is more than adequate. If you have that, you can afford to emphasize defense in the infield. But, in the National League, there is no DH. That's one man less in the sequence. And then, if your catcher doesn't hit—and Eli Marrero at his best won't hit like Steinbach and Fisk did—you're down to four hitters in your lineup. That won't do. You need at least five and you really do want the six. Therefore, it is vital for Tony to have a catcher who can hit. Without that, he runs the real danger of having only four hitters in the lineup. The solution Tony has adopted is to develop the hot prospect, but try to back him up with bench bats. Even before the wooing of Steinbach, Tony used Tom Lampkin as a backup catcher because he hits left handed, and so provides some sort of platoon relief for the starter.

At the power hitting spots, Tony is set. Of course, he starts with Mark McGwire at first base. Acquiring McGwire was the really big step in developing this team. He's a lineup anchor, and he's the top power man the Cardinals previously lacked.

The old outfield of Ray Lankford, Ron Gant, and Brian Jordan had some power, but Jordan kept getting hurt because he plays like a football guy, which he is, and Ron Gant has either had his career go under from earlier injuries or just can't hit in St. Louis for some reason. That happens. But the new outfield of Lankford, Eric Davis, and J. D. Drew is very likely a big step up. Davis is no less injury prone than Jordan, but is much better when he can play. Drew, based on his very short professional career to date, can hardly be worse than Gant, and is also a power type. Importantly, both Drew and Davis switch-hit. The 1998 Cardinals were low on lefty bats; they had two of any quality. This was probably the main reason that the Cardinals made no real effort to re-sign Jordan. They didn't expect to find Eric Davis available, but they needed someone who could hit lefty or switch.

The big key to the 1999 Cardinal infield is the most recent (as I write this) acquisition of all, Edgar Renteria. Remember that Tony wants an extra bat somewhere, to make up for the loss of the Designated Hitter. He tried, in 1998, to convert John Mabry to third base. Mabry had hit .300 a couple of times, and was a lefty. He couldn't beat out any of the incumbent outfielders, but he had a strong arm, and throws righty. Mabry, however, failed miserably to learn to play the hot corner, and so the Cards traded for Fernando Tatis. Tatis is more a "kid" than a "bat", though, so the team needed one more hitter from the two remaining spots around the keystone.

The 1998 team had one of those in second baseman Delino DeShields. De Shields had two things Tony desperately needed. He could lead off, and he hit lefty. But he also played poor defense, and Tony won't put up with that. His history is one of shuttling kids with hot gloves through is middle infield, rather than trying to develop incumbents. This was partially a matter of salary. You can always find a good-field-no-hit kid at second and short, and if that's all you want there, why pay a veteran? In Tony's 13 full seasons in Chicago and Oakland, he used ten second basemen and nine shortstops. That's astonishing, especially considering that these were usually good teams, not desperate ones. And, as a group, the 19 of them were clearly great gloves but generally poor bats.

This is where the push for Roberto Alomar began. Tony needed a bat from either second or short, and he also needed a fine glove, preferably Gold. Alomar fit the bill, as do precious few others. But the price for Roberto became too rich for a team that was, at the time, in hopes of landing Kevin Brown. When Brown also went elsewhere, the Cards were truly in need. When Renteria became available for prospects, the Cards' front office probably heaved a collective sigh of relief. Edgar has the makings of a fine leadoff man. He hits righty, but the Davis pickup made that no big deal. His defense hasn't been the best, but he's young, and Tony NEEDS that bat. The second baseman will be Placido Polanco, who had the second-highest Defensive Winning Percentage in the league at shortstop, and an even higher one at second base. The backup plan is Luis Ordaz, who also has very good defensive numbers.

All this produces at least a five-man offensive sequence of (probable batting order) Renteria, Davis, McGwire, Lankford, and Drew. If either Tatis or Marrero hits, that's six, with Terry Steinbach possibly available in an emergency situation.

On the pitching mound, Tony is trying to develop a trio or quartet of reliable and durable quality arms, but who isn't? So far, this staff resembles the ones in Chicago more than the Oakland ones. In Oakland, the starting rotation relied heavily on the three veterans Stewart, Welch, and Moore. The closer was also a veteran, although not a veteran closer. In Chicago, though, Tony developed a lot of kids, and his rotation was built around them.

In St. Louis, what he has is kids. The Cards have spent most of the last decade drafting pitchers in the first round, and their minor league system is loaded. The ace is Matt Morris, who looks like a decent #1 starter to me. Then there's Alan Benes, if he can ever get healthy, and Donovan Osborne, if he can ever stay healthy. Darren Oliver is the young lefty starter the Cards' got in the Tatis deal. That's nothing like the quality of rotation that Tony has had, and the Cardinals are blatantly in the market for a free agent pitcher. They probably did make the

WPA BULLPEN BOX—ST. LOUIS CARDINALS

	PI	WPA	P	PPPI
Starters	981	-2.1	51.1	0.052
Relievers	662	0.2	44.1	0.067
Road	305	0.9	19.4	0.064
Home	357	-0.7	24.6	0.069
Mar/Apr	111	-0.4	6.9	0.063
May	120	-0.3	7.9	0.065
June	112	-1.4	7.2	0.064
July	114	-0.3	8.3	0.073
August	112	0.6	8.4	0.075
September	93	2.0	5.4	0.059
Non S/H Sit.	488	0.2	24.6	0.050
S/H Sit.	174	-0.0	19.5	0.112
Low Pressure	242	-2.7	3.9	0.016
Med. Pressure	221	-7.0	14.4	0.065
High Pressure	199	9.9	25.8	0.130
Entered behind	268	1.7	7.3	0.027
Entered tied	104	-0.4	13.5	0.129
Entered ahead	290	-1.2	23.3	0.080

Name	G	PI	WPA	P	PPPI	MI	ROB	T
Acevedo J	41	53	2.3	4.2	.080	10	6	6
Bottenfield K	27	41	.3	2.6	.063	10	3	4
Brantley J	48	59	-1.4	4.5	.075	11	8	6
Busby M	24	41	.1	2.3	.055	14	11	4
Croushore R	41	65	-.1	5.1	.078	20	14	7
Frascatore J	69	117	-.1	7.1	.060	37	21	11
King C	36	62	-2.3	3.8	.061	19	15	4
Looper B	4	4	-1.0	.3	.063	0	2	0
Mercker K	1	1	-.5	.1	.140	0	0	1
Painter L	65	84	1.6	6.8	.081	17	37	11
Petkovsek M	38	67	1.3	4.5	.068	21	15	6
Witt B	12	25	.1	.8	.032	8	0	2
Total		662	.2	44.1	.067			

		--------- Quality ----------					--- Pressure -------		
	Dis.	Poor	Fair	Good	Her.	Lo	Med	Hi	
Acevedo J	2	2	22	14	1	20	11	10	(9)
Bottenfield K	1	6	12	6	2	14	8	5	(4)
Brantley J	9	2	20	16	1	20	16	12	(10)
Busby M	1	7	7	8	1	8	11	5	(3)
Croushore R	5	3	16	13	4	15	14	12	(10)
Frascatore J	7	7	33	19	3	29	23	17	(13)
King C	7	4	16	7	2	15	13	8	(3)
Painter L	3	9	26	23	4	24	27	14	(11)
Petkovsek M	2	5	15	14	2	13	14	11	(9)
Witt B	0	1	9	2	0	9	2	1	(0)
Others	5	3	12	8	0	12	10	6	(3)
TOTAL	42	49	188	130	20	179	149	101	(75)

	7th inning			8th inning			9th inning		
	0	+1	+2	0	+1	+2	0	+1	+2
Acevedo J	0	1	0	1	0	4	2	5	3
Bottenfield K	0	0	2	1	0	4	1	0	3
Brantley J	0	1	0	1	1	3	2	4	5
Busby M	1	2	0	1	0	2	2	0	0
Croushore R	0	0	0	3	1	2	3	2	5
Frascatore J	2	5	1	1	5	0	1	0	0
King C	0	3	0	0	4	0	0	1	1
Looper B	0	0	0	0	0	0	0	0	1
Painter L	1	2	2	1	1	0	0	0	0
Petkovsek M	0	2	1	1	2	1	2	0	0
Raggio B	0	0	0	1	0	0	0	0	0
Starters	12	11	7	1	6	3	0	3	2
TOTAL	16	27	13	12	20	19	13	15	20
Record	6-10	16-11	11-2	4-8	13-7	17-2	3-10	15-0	17-3

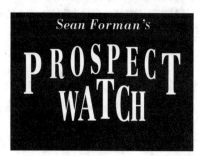

Sean Forman's

PROSPECT WATCH

NAME	AGE	POS	LEVEL	GR98	GR97	GR96	AVG
J.D. Drew	22	OF	AAA	90	-	-	90
Jason Woolf	21	SS	AA	69	64	52	65
Chris Haas	21	3B	AA	68	49	47	58
Luis Ordaz	22	SS	AAA	66	53	41	58
Placido Polanco	22	2B	AAA	61	46	42	53
Adam Kennedy	22	SS	AAA	59	40	-	51
Mark Little	25	OF	AAA	44	59	42	49
Nate Dishington	23	1B	AAA	57	50	24	49

Name	Age	Pos	Level	Grade
Pablo Ozuna	20	SS	Low A	66
Jose Leon	21	3B	High A	60
Jack Wilson	20	SS	Rookie	56
Luis Saturria	21	OF	High A	53
Brent Butler	20	SS	High A	52
Gabe Johnson	18	C	Rookie	52
Ramon Carvajal	17	2B	Rookie	46

Name	AGE	GS	S	C	T	W-L	ERA	K/H	Level
Jose Jimenez	24	26	3.46	3.08	6.54	15-6	3.11	0.56	High
Brady Raggio	24	22	4.14	2.59	6.73	8-9	3.10	0.63	High
Sean Lowe	26	20	3.60	3.30	6.90	9-7	3.15	0.79	High
Brian Barnes	30	21	3.76	3.24	7.00	7-4	3.58	1.12	High
Larry Luebbers	27	30	4.07	3.07	7.13	11-12	4.10	0.60	High
Cliff Politte	24	20	4.20	3.40	7.60	6-7	4.97	0.81	High
Steve Ontiveros	37	17	4.18	3.53	7.71	5-2	4.18	0.81	High
Clint Weibl	23	24	4.75	3.50	8.25	10-11	5.41	0.52	High
Kris Detmers	24	24	4.46	3.88	8.33	9-9	4.92	0.50	High
Steve Reed	22	16	5.44	3.50	8.94	3-6	6.03	0.33	High
Marcus Logan	26	20	5.15	3.85	9.00	7-5	5.52	0.41	High
Rich Ankiel	18	28				9-6	2.79	1.99	Low

The Cardinals have taken aggressiveness to a new level when it comes to acquiring amateur talent. They have paid record bonuses to J.D. Drew, Rick Ankiel and Chad Hutchison. Thus far, the strategy has worked wonders as they are stocking up quality talent. Beyond Drew, they are lacking non-middle infield prospects, so a couple of trades might serve them well.

TOP DOG: J.D. Drew

Well, I guess he was worth the money. The Cardinals expertly called him up during the Mark McGwire home run chase and incidentally his first game was the same one in which McGwire hit #62. The Cardinals have pretty much named him a starting outfielder as they have decided to let Brian Jordan go and traded Ron Gant. Drew hit 12 home runs and walked 39 times in 192 pro at bats. STATS projects a .305/.406/.531 line next year, which would pretty much make him a shoo-in for Rookie of the Year.

UP THE MIDDLE:

Luis Ordaz - Ordaz is known as slick fielder. He has some pop, though he's mostly a low walk, glove type player.
Placido Polanco - Polanco and Ordaz look fairly interchangeable to me. Ordaz has shown a tad more power and Polanco a tad more speed.
Adam Kennedy - Kennedy moved from high-A to AAA this year and hit better at each level along the way. He has the most power of this group and is a fair basestealer. He has an outside shot at a middle infield job for the big league club next year. Comp: Andujar Cedeno.
Jason Woolf - Woolf is a switch-hitter, who has been moving up the ladder a level per year. His main assets are very good patience and tremendous basestealing (82 of 104 the last three years). His average (.259 career) will have to improve if he wants to distinguish himself in this group. Comp: Speedier Jeff Blauser.
Brent Butler - Butler's numbers have been dropping from an outstanding debut season. He's the most balanced hitter of the group and the one I liked the most at the start of last season. He needs to improve his numbers in AA next season, but he's still just 21, so there isn't a great rush.
Pablo Ozuna - Ozuna was named the top prospect in the Midwest League after batting .357 and stealing 62 bases. For good measure, he also slugged .494. He may have the highest upside of the group and has made some of the guys above him expendable.

ON THE MOUND: Rick Ankiel

The Cardinals have proven that they aren't afraid to break the bank for a big-time amateur player. Ankiel was one of those amateurs. His signing bonus was a record for a second round pick and he hasn't disappointed yet. Ankiel split time between the Midwest League and the Carolina League and was named a top prospect in each. He is a hard throwing left-hander with a very good curveball. He pitched 161 innings, but faced just 23 batters per start, so the Cardinals appear to handling him with kid gloves. In those 161 innings, he allowed just 106 hits and 50 walks vs. 222 strikeouts. He is going to move quickly, and if the Cardinals' staff struggles again I wouldn't be surprised to see him with the big league squad at some point this year. LaRussa will have to go against his overuse tendencies and protect this very valuable asset.

highest six-year offer to Kevin Brown, but the Dodgers went seven. They may still make a trade, and are in the Roger Clemens hunt, though I doubt they can afford the trade material. In any case, they clearly perceive their main need right now as a solid, reliable, veteran starter, preferably a staff ace.

At closer, Tony has made clear the effect that Dennis Eckersley has had in his development as a manager. The Cardinals will try their very best out-of-nowhere discovery, Juan Acevedo, even though almost all his prior record is as a starter. They also traded for Rickey Bottalico, who was a closer at Philly, in order to make him Acevedo's backup. That's a sign of the importance Tony puts on the closer. He doesn't want to get caught short again, like he did this time.

To sum up, the 1999 Cardinals look a lot like a typical Tony LaRussa team, adjusting for the switch in leagues. If the catcher hits, and Tony is working at that, the team will have a six-man offensive sequence based on power and getting on base. The infield defense will be strong. The closer will be strong. The starting rotation is the only unusual item, being one completely solid starter short, and the team is working even now to try to fill that need for Tony.

For Cardinal fans, this is good news. It's the sort of team that Tony has won with before. And it only took four years, just like in Chicago. I don't know that I want to predict the Cardinals to win their division without that ace starter, but they are set up to be only the one pitcher away.

THE BATTING ORDER SWITCHOLA

As many of you doubtless recall, late in July Tony LaRussa began batting his pitcher eighth. He explained the move at the time as being away to ensure that there would be more men on base in the offensive sequence for Mark McGwire to drive in.

It didn't work. McGwire had driven in 32 runs in each of the first two months of the 1998 campaign, but the top two slots in the batting order quit producing in June and July. To be more precise, Royce Clayton didn't hit in the leadoff slot, and was moved to #7, while Delino DeShields, who had been hitting like there was no tomorrow at #2 in the early going, moved into the leadoff slot and promptly stopped hitting.

Eventually LaRussa settled on a flip-flop of Brian Jordan and Ray Lankford in the #2-#4 slots, and that kept the #2 slot productive down the stretch. It also siphoned off some of the RBIs that would have been McGwire's, because it became a power slot and not an on-base slot. Mac drove in 13 runs in July, just 19 in August, and made it to 28 in September only because he hit 15 HRs.

Here's the back and front ends of the Cardinal lineup. These slots represent the most likely players to be on base when McGwire stepped to the plate:

BOP	AB	R	H	D	T	HR	RBI	BB	SO	SB	CS	BA	OBP	SLG	OPS
#8	581	50	108	19	4	14	70	56	153	5	1	.186	.262	.305	.567
#9	569	56	121	22	0	5	37	47	147	4	2	.213	.273	.278	.551
#1	697	105	155	28	3	14	55	65	123	25	9	.222	.293	.331	.624
#2	671	131	208	49	10	26	99	75	122	30	12	.310	.382	.529	.911

As you can see, all three of the 8-9-1 slots are dismal in terms of OBP. (Actually, they're dismal in most every other way, too.) Later in the year, the #2 slot, with either Lankford or Jordan in it, began soaking up most of the available RBIs from these BOPs anyway—20 of the 26 HRs hit by Cardinals' #2 hitters came after the All-Star Break.

Just for a little context on the levels of production in these BOPs, the Cards ranked second in OPS in the #9 slot. That sounds good until you realize that most everyone else was batting pitchers and various pinch-hitters and some smattering of double-switched guys #9. The Cards batted real live ostensible hitters there for almost half a season, and could not dominate the BOP. Here are the rankings in the #8-#9-#1 BOPs in the 1998 NL:

Team	BOP	OPS
COL	#8	.748
SD	#8	.748
SF	#8	.686
MIL	#8	.684
AZ	#8	.682
MON	#8	.677
PHI	#8	.677
CIN	#8	.675
HOU	#8	.672
ATL	#8	.670
CHC	#8	.669
LA	#8	.657
PIT	#8	.650
FLA	#8	.640
NYM	#8	.592
STL	#8	.567

TEAM BREAKOUT
CARDINALS 1998

Category	RS	RA	W	L	Pct.	Rk
5+ RUNS SCORED/ROAD	260	157	28	5	.848	2
4- RUNS ALLOWED/HOME	206	102	35	8	.814	3
5+ RUNS SCORED	589	387	62	16	.795	5
5+ RUNS SCORED/HOME	329	230	34	11	.756	10
CLOSE SLUGFESTS/ROAD	66	61	6	2	.750	3
4- RUNS ALLOWED	373	201	58	23	.716	7
LOW SCORING GAMES/HOME	61	33	14	6	.700	3
SLUGFESTS/ROAD	186	166	16	7	.696	2
RECORD IN SLUGFESTS	385	334	29	17	.630	3
4- RUNS ALLOWED/ROAD	167	99	23	15	.605	11
SLUGFESTS/HOME	199	168	13	10	.565	5
RECORD IN BLOWOUTS/HOME	126	101	11	9	.550	9
RECORD IN CLOSE GAMES/HOME	204	203	23	19	.548	8
CLOSE LOW SCORING GAMES/HOME	26	26	6	5	.545	11
RECORD IN LOW SCORING GAMES	101	84	22	19	.537	5
RECORD IN BLOWOUTS	254	235	22	20	.524	7
SEASON TOTALS	805	777	83	79	.512	8
RECORD IN BLOWOUTS/ROAD	128	134	11	11	.500	9
RECORD IN CLOSE GAMES	355	355	39	40	.494	10
CLOSE SLUGFESTS/HOME	84	86	5	6	.455	11
CLOSE LOW SCORING GAMES/ROAD	32	32	7	9	.438	6
RECORD IN CLOSE GAMES/ROAD	151	152	16	21	.432	11
LOW SCORING GAMES/ROAD	40	51	8	13	.381	9
4- RUNS SCORED/HOME	103	151	14	23	.378	8
5+ RUNS ALLOWED/HOME	226	279	13	26	.333	6
5+ RUNS ALLOWED	432	576	25	56	.309	5
5+ RUNS ALLOWED/ROAD	206	297	12	30	.286	5
4- RUNS SCORED	216	390	21	63	.250	10
4- RUNS SCORED/ROAD	113	239	7	40	.149	15

Team	BOP	OPS		Team	BOP	OPS
CHC	#9	.598		HOU	#1	.893
STL	#9	.551		MIL	#1	.809
COL	#9	.549		SF	#1	.778
ATL	#9	.542		COL	#1	.769
SF	#9	.531		CIN	#1	.743
LA	#9	.511		AZ	#1	.739
PHI	#9	.498		LA	#1	.732
MIL	#9	.494		SD	#1	.727
MON	#9	.492		PHI	#1	.726
NYM	#9	.491		FLA	#1	.718
HOU	#9	.454		CHC	#1	.712
CIN	#9	.451		NYM	#1	.697
FLA	#9	.443		PIT	#1	.683
PIT	#9	.431		ATL	#1	.682
SD	#9	.424		STL	#1	.624
AZ	#9	.416		MON	#1	.613

Finishing second in the #9 slot hardly outweighs finishing 16th in the #8 slot and 15th in the #1 slot, so essentially what LaRussa did was create a bigger trough in front of McGwire. He'd have been better off pulling an old Billy Martin trick and using a front-loaded lineup, especially when DeShields got hurt. A first three of Lankford-Jordan-McGwire might well have gotten the results Tony was in search of. <DM>

Park Adjusted Statistics

Name	AB	R	H	D	T	HR	RBI	BB	SO	SB	CS	BA	OBP	SLG	XR	Adj XR/27	Raw XR/27	OXW	DXW	TXW
Clayton R	356	59	85	19	1	4	29	39	52	19	7	.238	.315	.331	38	3.54	3.50	0.29	1.22	1.51
Deshields D	421	75	124	21	8	7	44	55	62	27	12	.296	.374	.434	70	5.86	5.78	3.11	1.13	4.24
Drew J	36	9	15	3	1	5	13	4	10	0	0	.424	.469	.972	12	12.30	12.13	0.84	0.08	0.92
Gaetti G	307	39	82	23	1	11	43	30	39	1	1	.267	.340	.456	46	5.16	5.12	1.67	0.48	2.15
Gant R	384	60	93	17	1	25	67	50	93	8	0	.241	.330	.490	65	5.88	5.92	2.87	0.07	2.94
Howard D	102	15	25	1	1	2	12	12	22	0	0	.248	.323	.334	12	3.85	3.83	0.19	0.12	0.31
Hunter B	112	11	23	9	1	4	13	7	23	1	2	.208	.260	.414	11	3.01	3.01	-0.13	0.07	-0.06
Jordan B	565	101	182	35	7	25	92	39	67	18	6	.321	.373	.540	103	6.78	6.63	5.27	0.70	5.97
Kelly P	153	18	34	5	0	4	14	13	48	5	1	.219	.286	.328	15	3.28	3.25	0.00	0.25	0.25
Lampkin T	216	25	51	12	1	6	28	24	32	3	2	.234	.329	.381	27	4.19	4.16	0.61	0.40	1.01
Lankford R	535	95	158	38	1	30	106	84	153	27	5	.295	.392	.539	113	7.86	7.86	6.61	0.65	7.26
Mabry J	378	41	95	22	0	9	46	29	77	0	3	.253	.307	.382	43	3.90	3.85	0.69	0.18	0.87
Marrero E	254	28	63	19	1	4	20	28	43	6	3	.249	.321	.375	30	4.03	3.99	0.58	1.39	1.97
Mcgee W	269	27	69	10	1	3	34	14	50	7	3	.257	.290	.335	25	3.24	3.17	-0.03	0.19	0.16
Mcgwire M	512	131	153	21	0	69	148	159	157	1	0	.298	.467	.742	164	11.94	12.17	11.63	0.44	12.07
Ordaz L	153	9	32	5	0	0	8	12	18	2	0	.208	.264	.241	9	1.96	1.86	-0.63	0.67	0.04
Pagnozzi T	160	7	36	9	0	1	10	14	38	0	0	.224	.284	.301	13	2.69	2.57	-0.29	0.21	-0.08
Polanco P	114	10	30	3	2	1	11	5	9	2	0	.260	.296	.347	12	3.67	3.55	0.13	0.68	0.81
Tatis F	202	28	58	16	2	8	26	24	58	7	3	.289	.367	.505	35	6.08	6.12	1.60	0.18	1.78
STL	5605	816	1465	297	31	218	785	664	1194	137	49	.261	.342	.442	852	5.22	5.21	35.01	9.11	44.12

Pitcher	S	C	T	SS	ES	IC	HH	PP	TJ	S12	S35	S67	C1	C23	C45	C67	QWP
Acevedo	3.89	2.89	6.78	56%	0%	56%	22%	11%	11%	33%	44%	22%	11%	67%	22%	0%	.607
Aybar	4.69	4.38	9.08	31%	0%	23%	38%	8%	8%	15%	46%	38%	0%	46%	31%	23%	.356
Bottenfield	3.47	3.94	7.41	59%	0%	35%	12%	18%	0%	35%	53%	12%	0%	53%	29%	18%	.534
Busby	4.50	3.50	8.00	50%	0%	0%	0%	0%	0%	0%	100%	0%	0%	50%	50%	0%	.486
D Oliver	4.10	3.60	7.70	40%	0%	30%	30%	10%	10%	20%	50%	30%	0%	40%	60%	0%	.480
Jimenez	4.67	3.33	8.00	33%	0%	33%	67%	33%	0%	33%	0%	67%	0%	67%	33%	0%	.497
Lowe	7.00	7.00	14.00	0%	0%	0%	100%	0%	0%	0%	0%	100%	0%	0%	0%	100%	.000
M Morris	3.47	3.24	6.71	59%	18%	47%	24%	18%	6%	41%	35%	24%	6%	59%	35%	0%	.586
Mercker	4.77	3.57	8.33	37%	3%	30%	40%	3%	10%	20%	40%	40%	10%	43%	37%	10%	.416
Osborne	4.00	3.00	7.00	50%	21%	50%	43%	7%	14%	36%	21%	43%	14%	50%	36%	0%	.541
Petkovsek	4.50	4.00	8.50	40%	20%	40%	60%	10%	0%	40%	0%	60%	10%	40%	30%	20%	.401
Politte	4.75	4.25	9.00	25%	0%	13%	50%	25%	0%	13%	38%	50%	0%	38%	50%	13%	.354
Raggio	7.00	7.00	14.00	0%	0%	0%	100%	0%	0%	0%	0%	100%	0%	0%	0%	100%	.000
Stottlemyre	3.61	2.78	6.39	61%	17%	61%	26%	9%	17%	39%	35%	26%	26%	43%	30%	0%	.597
Witt	4.80	4.20	9.00	40%	0%	20%	60%	0%	0%	20%	20%	60%	0%	20%	60%	20%	.328
STL	4.18	3.56	7.74	46%	8%	38%	35%	10%	8%	29%	36%	35%	9%	47%	36%	9%	.483

CINCINNATI REDS

SEAN LAHMAN

At first glance it doesn't appear that much changed down at Cinergy Field in 1998. The Reds finished the season with one fewer loss than in 1997 and entered the off-season with just as many questions about young players. When you look more closely though, it's clear that the Reds are an organization that has made significant progress. The NL Central may be baseball's largest division, but none of those teams have the large payroll that separates them from the rest of the pack. There's every reason to suspect that the Reds can compete in this division, and if their key players stay healthy they can win the division title.

1998 VS. 1997: WHAT WAS DIFFERENT?

Look at some of the statistical categories, and the '98 Reds don't look much different than the '97 team:

	1998	1997
Record	77-85	76-86
ERA	4.44	4.42
Home Runs	138	142

Not much difference, right? But look at these statistics and you'll get a better idea of what happened to their offense:

	1998	1997
Runs	750	651
Stolen Bases	95	190

Stolen bases were down by exactly 50%, and the Reds scored 99 more runs. What's that all about? Two words: "Ray Knight".

Knight was one of those baseball guys convinced that a lineup needs a speedy center fielder leading off. Before he was fired, he clogged the top of the lineup with Deion Sanders and Curtis Goodwin. Sanders had 500 plate appearances in 1997, Goodwin nearly 300. They were arguably the fastest two players in baseball, but their combined on-base percentage of .320 meant they weren't on base often enough for their speed to matter. Because he was so focused on having base-stealers at the top of the lineup, Knight couldn't see that the number of outs they were making doomed them. A comparison of the Reds' performance in the leadoff slot in 1997 and 1998 shows this clearly:

Year	AB	R	H	D	T	HR	RBI	BB	SO	SB	CS	BA	OBP	SLG	OPS
1997	689	81	172	23	8	8	37	52	104	61	17	.250	.308	.341	.649
1998	675	116	180	25	4	19	62	73	144	33	11	.267	.343	.400	.743

When Jack McKeon took over as manager, he dumped Goodwin and convinced Sanders he ought to be playing football full-time. And the difference was a hundred runs.

It would be an over-simplification to suggest that shedding those two guys was the sole cause of the improved offense, but it illustrates the underlying difference in strategy between Knight and McKeon that does account for those 99 runs. Just look at a comparison of the two offenses:

	1998	1997
BA	.262	.253
OBP	.337	.321
SLG	.402	.389

That sixteen-point increase in on-base percentage translates to about one hundred more batters reaching base over the course of a season.

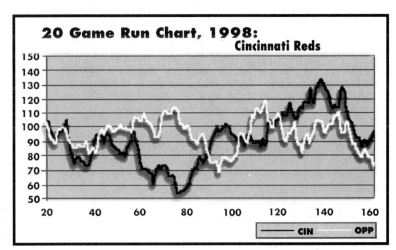

20 Game Run Chart, 1998: Cincinnati Reds

QMAX PRESENTS: "BAD" PITCHERS

THE OLD WARHORSE RIDES OFF INTO THE SUNSET

I've always thought the 1919 Reds, wherever they might be, have got to be mighty pissed off at history. The 1919 Black Sox both before and after they threw the Series, were considered to be mortal locks to beat the Reds, who actually won more games and had a better pitching staff than the Sox. Even John Sayles' otherwise fine movie "Eight Men Out" treated the Reds as sort of the Washington Generals of their time, trotted out to lose to the Globetrotters for the 493rd time in a row.

The Reds kept that fine staff into the 1920's, and contended every year. Every year, the Redleg rotation included names like Eppa Rixey, Dolf Luque, Dutch Ruether, Red Lucas, Rube Marquard, (I won't cheat and include Mathewson, who ended his career there) and Pete Donohue. Rixey and Luque and the others are fairly well known these days but Donohue was a fine pitcher in his own right, winning 20 three times in the 20's. He pitched 286 innings in his last 20-win season, and the Reds finished second, two games behind the Cardinals. Donohue was only 26 that year, and seemed to have the world by the tail.

As modern-day students of pitch counts and pitcher wear know, it was not to be. Pete scuffled through 1927 and 1928 with mid-4 ERAs, and the Reds inexorably declined from second to fifth, and their pitching did too, from near the league lead to league average. By 1929, the Reds were

PETE DONOHUE/CIN 1929							
	1	2	3	4	5	6	7	S
1	2							2
2				1				1
3	2		1	0				3
4	1		0					1
5	2		0	1				3
6	1			1		1		3
7		1	4	4	1	1		11
C	8	1	5	7	1	2	0	24

three years past contention, but their pitching staff still included stalwarts Rixey, Lucas, Luque, and Donohue. All were past their best days, none more so than Donohue. He seemingly never recovered from his 286-inning stint in 1926, as the QMAX chart shows. No doubt vowing to win comeback player of the year, Donohue started slowly and never recovered. He had a few fine starts, but could not string together three good starts in a row. By the end of the season, he had been demoted to spot start and relief duty as the Reds belatedly tried out new talent.

I don't really have a pithy comment or sharp analytical insight here; I just think it's only fair to shine a little light on the fine pitching staff of the 1920's Reds, even if it is a bit backhanded (coming as it does in a series on Bad Pitching). The Reds had some great arms, and they rode them until there was nothing left. That's loyalty of a sort, I guess.

--Tom Austin

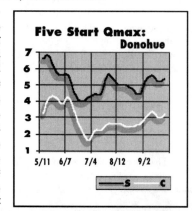

Five Start Qmax: Donohue

JIM BOWDEN: MAN OR MYTH

Reds manager Jack McKeon earned the nickname "Trader Jack" during his tenure as the Padres GM. Perhaps that title really belongs to Jim Bowden. During his six years as the Reds GM Bowden has developed a reputation for being able to acquire a lot of talent without giving much of anything in exchange.

The key has really been the low-budget free agent strategy. Every spring the Reds sign a half-dozen or more veterans who are a step away from the scrap heap due to injuries, slumps, or age. They come pretty cheaply, and if just one of those guys proves useful each year Bowden has been successful. Some of the surprise contributors were Ron Gant, Eric Davis, Pete Schourek, and Jeff Shaw. The losers have been players like Vince Coleman, Ruben Sierra, Ricky Bones, and Eric Anthony. After Bowden made several big trades in 1998, the con-

sensus among many observers is that he's the master of the trade, fleecing his colleagues at every turn. Is that a reputation he deserves? Let's take a look at the sixteen major trades he's made and see how he has done.

1993: Traded P Norm Charlton to Seattle for OF Kevin Mitchell - This deal allowed Rob Dibble to become the full-time closer, and Mitchell added some much-needed punch to the lineup. Dibble saved 19 games for the Reds in 1993 before arm troubles ended his career. The Reds could have really used Norm over the next few years. Mitchell hit well, but was to become a tremendous problem in the Reds clubhouse. We'll call this one **EVEN**.

1993: Traded OF Paul O'Neill to the Yankees for OF Roberto Kelly - If I were Bowden, this one would still be keeping me up at night. **BAD TRADE**

1993: Traded P Tim Belcher to Chicago for P Johnny Ruffin and P Jeff Pierce - Belcher was fading, but he was one of the top pitchers available for the pennant-stretch. Neither Ruffin nor Pierce panned out, and if you're going to trade a veteran starting pitcher for a bag of beans, you'd better end up with a beanstalk. **BAD TRADE**

1994: Traded C Dan Wilson and P Bobby Ayala to Seattle for 2B Bret Boone and P Erik Hanson - Wilson and Ayala were good prospects but essentially unknown quantities. Boone had played a half-season in the majors. Boone turned into a slightly player than Wilson. Ayala had two slightly effective seasons. Hanson left the Reds as a free-agent after one year. **EVEN**

1994: Traded OF Roberto Kelly to Atlanta for OF Deion Sanders - Sanders brought a lot of excitement to Cincinnati, but he was mostly ineffective. **EVEN**

1995: Traded OF Deion Sanders to San Francisco for OF Darren Lewis, P Mark Portugal, and P Dave Burba - There were some other fringe players involved in this deal, but any way you look at it this was Bowden's first big heist. Deion played 52 games for the Giants, then quit baseball to play a full season in the NFL. Portugal and Burba helped solidify the Reds rotation over the final two months, as the Reds advanced to the NL Championship Series. **GOOD TRADE**

1995: Traded P C.J. Nitkowski and 2B Mark Lewis to Detroit for David Wells - Wells was OK down the stretch and helped the Reds in the post-season, but he only started 11 games for the Reds. Nitkowski never developed. **GOOD TRADE**

1995: Traded P David Wells to Baltimore for OF Curtis Goodwin - Bowden had to cut payroll, but that's still no excuse for this one. Mere words can't describe how lopsided this trade was. **BAD TRADE**

1996: Traded P John Smiley to Cleveland for P Danny Graves and IF Damian Jackson - Smiley was pretty much washed up. Graves appears poised to become the Reds closer in 1999, and Jackson's two years at AAA were good enough that he may get a chance to start in 1999. **GOOD TRADE**

1997: Traded P Hector Carrasco and P Scott Service to Kansas City for IF Chris Stynes and OF Jon Nunnally - In the months after the trade, Stynes and Nunnally both looked like they could be starters. In 1998, those first impressions appeared to be premature. If the two can be competent backups, this is a net gain because Carrasco and Service were scrubs. **GOOD TRADE**

1997: Traded P Jeff Brantley to St. Louis for 1B Dmitri Young - Brantley was damaged goods and had lost his job as Reds closer, plus he had a hefty contract. The Reds moved Young to left field, where he posted an OPS of .856 and banged out 48 doubles. **GOOD TRADE**

1998: Traded P Dave Burba to Cleveland for 1B Sean Casey - The Indians were desperate for starting pitching and Casey was a top prospect with no place to play in Cleveland. Burba is a competent starter, but he'll turn 33 in 1999. Casey will be 25 and has given every indication that he'll be a significant offensive contributor. **GOOD TRADE**

1998: Traded P Jeff Shaw to Los Angeles for P Dennis Reyes and 1B Paul Konerko - The Reds converted Shaw from a journeyman middle reliever into the top NL closer. They were able to get two of the Dodgers' top prospects in an exchange during the All-Star break. But Konerko was a dis-

WPA BULLPEN BOX—CINCINNATI REDS

	PI	WPA	P	PPPI
Starters	977	-2.9	51.3	0.052
Relievers	607	4.4	35.5	0.058
Road	297	2.2	20.3	0.068
Home	310	2.2	15.2	0.049
Mar/Apr	86	-1.2	5.6	0.065
May	121	2.0	8.2	0.067
June	104	0.8	5.8	0.055
July	116	2.9	7.5	0.065
August	102	0.4	4.4	0.043
September	78	-0.5	4.1	0.053
Non S/H Sit.	482	2.5	22.1	0.046
S/H Sit.	125	1.9	13.4	0.107
Low Pressure	242	0.4	3.3	0.014
Med. Pressure	183	-3.1	10.2	0.056
High Pressure	182	7.1	22.0	0.121
Entered behind	317	1.7	9.3	0.029
Entered tied	92	0.8	10.6	0.115
Entered ahead	198	1.9	15.6	0.079

Name	G	PI	WPA	P	PPPI	MI	ROB	T
Graves D	62	94	1.7	4.4	.046	23	20	5
Hudek J	30	46	.1	2.7	.060	16	16	8
Hutton M	8	17	.1	.5	.030	6	3	0
Krivda R	15	30	-.5	1.4	.047	11	7	2
Remlinger M	7	13	-.2	.5	.035	3	4	0
Shaw J	39	54	1.5	6.2	.115	14	14	6
Sullivan S	67	119	.2	5.9	.050	35	20	9
Weathers D	7	15	.0	.3	.022	4	3	0
White G	66	104	2.0	7.8	.075	31	30	10
Williams T	6	12	-.6	.3	.024	5	3	1
Total		607	4.4	35.5	.058			

	I--------- Quality ----------I					I--- Pressure -------I			
	Dis.	Poor	Fair	Good	Her.	Lo	Med	Hi	
Belinda S	5	4	17	13	1	17	12	11	(6)
Graves D	1	9	36	13	3	39	12	11	(8)
Hudek J	2	7	11	9	1	12	11	7	(5)
Krivda R	1	3	8	3	0	7	3	5	(3)
Shaw J	4	3	11	15	6	11	13	15	(11)
Sullivan S	3	10	37	15	2	32	21	14	(11)
White G	4	7	34	13	8	26	19	21	(16)
Others	1	7	33	7	0	29	16	3	(2)
TOTAL	21	50	187	88	21	173	107	87	(62)

	7th inning			8th inning			9th inning		
	0	+1	+2	0	+1	+2	0	+1	+2
Belinda S	2	0	1	5	1	3	7	0	0
Graves D	1	2	1	1	4	1	3	1	1
Hudek J	0	1	0	4	0	1	0	0	1
Krivda R	1	1	0	1	1	0	1	0	0
Shaw J	0	0	0	1	0	0	2	4	7
Sullivan S	5	4	0	3	2	2	0	0	0
Weathers D	1	0	0	0	0	0	0	0	0
White G	2	1	3	2	4	1	3	3	2
Starters	14	9	7	2	5	4	1	2	1
TOTAL	26	18	12	19	17	12	17	10	12
Record	11-15	13-5	10-2	8-11	11-6	11-1	10-7	9-1	10-2

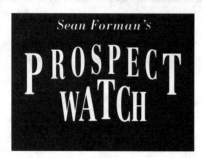

Sean Forman's
PROSPECT WATCH

NAME	AGE	POS	LEVEL	GR98	GR97	GR96	AVG
Paul Konerko	22	1B	AAA	96	105	76	96
Damian Jackson	24	SS	AAA	53	69	70	61
Roberto Petagine	27	1B	AAA	53	61	61	57
Pat Watkins	25	OF	AAA	57	56	38	54
Jon Nunnally	26		AAA	37	63	78	53
Mike Frank	23	OF	AAA	57	44	-	52
Justin Towle	24	C	AA	41	55	52	48
Aaron Boone	25	3B	AAA	34	64	53	47
Jason Larue	24	C	AAA	59	33	14	43
Jason Williams	24	SS	AAA	46	35	-	42

Name	Age	Pos	Level	Grade
Andy Burress	20	OF	Low A	54
Serafin Rodriguez	19	OF	Low A	49
Austin Kearns	18	OF	Rookie	48
Travis Dawkins	19	SS	Low A	47
Adam Dunn	18	OF	Rookie	41
Fernando Rios	19	OF	Low A	41
Dewayne Wise	20	OF	Low A	27

As I said in some of the player comments, the Reds appear to want a major league and AAA line up consisting of fourth outfielders and utility players. Depth is usually a good thing, but in the Reds case I think they could trade four or five of their outfielders for a big talent and come out ahead. The Indianapolis team featured a list of former phenoms including: Steve Gibralter, Mark Johnson, Glenn Murray, Melvin Nieves, Jon Nunnally, Jayhawk Owens, Roberto Petagine, Tony Tarasco, Ozzie Timmons and Pat Watkins.

KEN PHELPS ALL-STAR: Roberto Petagine
Petagine put in another phenomenal season in AAA hitting .331/.436/.617. He also hit well in his brief major league call-up batting .258/.405/.468. He clearly deserves some sort of a major league job and could start for a number of teams right now including San Francisco and Philadelphia. Will he ever get a shot? I suspect somewhere along the way he'll be manage 250+ major league at bats in a season, but Cincinnati is not the place for it to happen given the presence of Dmitri Young and Sean Casey.

UP THE MIDDLE: Damian Jackson
Jackson came over in the John Smiley trade last year, and he has fallen behind of his former double-play mate Enrique Wilson. Jackson committed 44 errors this year, well ahead of number two, Benji Gil at 30. His power did improve this year, largely due to a career high 36 doubles and 10 triples, and he continued to top the 20 steal mark. He has some patience and might put in a couple of major league average seasons if given a shot. Comp: Alex Arias.

YOUNG 'UN: Andy Burress
Burress split time in 1997 between the Pioneer League and the Sally. Not surprisingly, he hit well in the lower league and struggled once he was called up. This year he stayed in low-A ball, and he produced a .281/.368/.441 season. He has some line drive power to go along with 20 stolen base speed. He's too old to be an outstanding prospect, but I wouldn't be surprised to see him crack a major league roster at some point.

BACKSTOPS:
Jason LaRue - LaRue was named the 10th best prospect in the Southern League this year, despite a lack of defensive polish. Of course, a .365/.429/.617 line

Name	AGE	GS	S	C	T	W-L	ERA	K/H	Level
Rod Bolton	29	28	3.64	3.29	6.93	12-11	3.81	0.70	High
Scott Klingenbeck	26	15	4.13	2.93	7.07	7-4	3.90	0.64	High
Scott Williamson	22	23	3.48	4.04	7.52	4-5	3.73	1.16	High
Eddie Priest	24	25	4.16	3.40	7.56	7-8	4.32	0.61	High
Mark Hutton	28	17	4.12	3.94	8.06	5-6	4.43	0.52	High
Ted Rose	24	28	4.64	3.57	8.21	11-10	4.60	0.57	High
John Riedling	22	20	4.50	4.30	8.80	3-10	5.00	0.77	High
Jesus Martinez	23	18	4.83	4.39	9.22	7-6	6.85	0.33	High

makes it more understandable. This is a continuation of his previous performance in low-A ball the year before. He's already 25, the same age as Jason Kendall, so he is not going to be a top player, but he might see time as a major league regular.

Justin Towle - Like LaRue, Towle turns 25 next year, so his clock is ticking. Towle has excellent plate discipline to go along with fair gap power. Right now, he needs to show he can play at a higher level and continue to make contact. Comp: Hector Villanueva.

ON THE MOUND: Scott Williamson
Williamson is the first non-journeyman on the list, so let's look at him. He was a 1997 draft pick and has moved fairly quickly appearing in 18 AA games and 5 AAA games last year. Of course, some of this has to do with the setup of the Reds' farm system, but he has pitched fairly well. In 1997, he pitched 86 innings in the Pioneer League (he was named the 7th best prospect there), and was outstanding with a 1.78 ERA (the league batted .281). This year, Williamson tallied 122 strikeouts in 121 innings and allowed just 105 hits. He had some control problems as he walked 55 batters, but he's still fairly young. However, I'm not predicting anything more than a back of the rotation guy.

appointment, and Reyes has control problems may keep him at AAA for at least another year. **EVEN**

1998: Traded 3B Willie Greene to Baltimore for OF Jeffrey Hammonds - Both players have been huge disappointments; Hammonds because of injuries and Greene because of expectations that were too lofty. The Reds had tired of Greene and he wouldn't have come back for 1999. It's unclear if having Hammonds will be noticeably better than just waiving Greene. **EVEN**

1998: Traded 2B Bret Boone and P Mike Remlinger to Atlanta for P Denny Neagle and OF Michael Tucker - Boone's coming off a career year and Neagle's the kind of starter that wasn't available anywhere else. The Braves could

spare the pitching, but the Reds may have trouble filling the gap in the middle of the infield. **GOOD TRADE**

1998: Traded 1B Paul Konerko to White Sox for OF Mike Cameron - Both were considered top prospects in April and disappointments in September. Too soon to tell if either will pan out. **EVEN**

The tally on those sixteen deals is:

GOOD TRADES	7
BAD TRADES	3
EVEN	6

It started out shaky, but the deals have been getting better and better. He hasn't mad a "Bad Trade" since the

Commissioner removed Marge Schott, and it's hard to tell how much impact she had on those decisions. I think it's really exaggerating to say that all of his trades have been steals, but his savvy in working the phones is giving the Reds a source of acquiring talent that helps make up for their lack of participation in the free-agent market.

The Reds are extremely fortunate that Bowden agreed to come back despite offers from the Orioles and Dodgers. Nobody would blame him if he had left.

HOW BALLPARKS SAVE CITIES, AND OTHER FAIRYTALES

Cincinnati voters approved a half-cent sales tax increase in March 1996 to build new stadiums for the Cincinnati Bengals and the Reds, who have shared Riverfront Stadium/Cinergy Field since it opened in 1970. Each team would get their own single-purpose stadium. The Bengals got to work right away, and Paul Brown Stadium is under construction, set to open in August 2000. So when is the Reds new ballpark opening? Good question.

Cincinnati has always been a great baseball town, but it's a sign of how bad things have gotten that for three years, the citizens have been fighting about where to build the new facility. The Reds, Hamilton County, and the majority of the taxpayers wanted to keep the ball park on the river in a location called the Wedge, right next to the current ballpark. Another group, small but very vocal, lobbied for another site called Broadway Commons. It was in a downtown neighborhood that the residents wanted to revitalize. The debate raged for three years, and the issue was finally brought to a vote in November of 1998. The voters overwhelmingly rejected the Broadway site. Now they can finally start thinking about thinks like an architectural design, negotiating a lease, etc.

The urban resurgence that occurred in Baltimore and Cleveland has convinced everyone that building a new ballpark will solve all of their problems. It will save the local economy, revitalize downtown, turn the ball club into a powerhouse. If they'd look closer, they'd see that the new ballpark was just one part of a larger plan that made those things happen, not the sole cause. Neither the Orioles' nor the Rockies new ballparks have propelled them into postseason dominance. The White Sox' new ballpark dragged its neighborhood down, more than anything else. And the domed stadium built in St. Petersburg helped to land a major league team (the Devil Rays), but once that had been accomplished, Tropicana Field was an albatross in a bad location.

The Reds, like a half-dozen other teams on the low end of the revenue scale, are preaching about the glory days to come when they move into their new stadiums. Their rebuilding plans are all based on being competitive when the new ballpark opens, and the increased cash flow that will inevitably follow. These teams are all basing their future on this course of events, and most will be disappointed.

FINAL THOUGHTS ON MARGE SCHOTT

The Marge Schott era is coming to a close. Baseball has made it clear that her suspension will continue as long as she owns the team, and she finally put the team up for sale in October 1998.

The Reds majority owner was suspended for one year in 1993 for making racial comments. She was suspended again in 1996 for additional insensitive comments, a suspension that was essentially permanent. Those comments came in an ESPN interview when she argued that Adolf Hitler "was good at the beginning but he just went too far."

It would be unfortunate if those fateful words were also used to describe Schott. She brought Pete Rose back to town, the Reds were competitive for most of her tenure, they even won a World Series with her at the helm. But such a description would be just as inaccurate about Schott as it is about Hitler. There was nothing positive about Schott's twelve-year reign. She wreaked havoc on the Reds organization, on the city of Cincinnati, and on Baseball.

Marge Schott was an alcoholic, lonely, bitter women, cruel to everyone she came in contact with and interested in nothing but herself. Her pettiness drove away most long time employees, many of whom were never replaced. She cheated her employees and her partners, and committed fraud with her car dealership. She hired and fired people on a whim; not just secretaries-managers and general managers.

TEAM BREAKOUT
CINCINNATI 1998

Category	RS	RA	W	L	Pct.	Rk
5+ RUNS SCORED/ROAD	261	163	29	6	.829	3
5+ RUNS SCORED	541	326	56	13	.812	3
5+ RUNS SCORED/HOME	280	163	27	7	.794	6
4- RUNS ALLOWED/HOME	212	95	31	14	.689	15
CLOSE SLUGFESTS/ROAD	48	43	4	2	.667	5
4- RUNS ALLOWED	392	207	58	30	.659	11
4- RUNS ALLOWED/ROAD	180	112	27	16	.628	9
CLOSE SLUGFESTS/HOME	72	69	5	4	.556	7
SLUGFESTS/HOME	210	195	14	12	.538	6
RECORD IN SLUGFESTS	354	351	24	21	.533	6
SLUGFESTS/ROAD	144	156	10	9	.526	7
RECORD IN BLOWOUTS/ROAD	97	100	8	8	.500	5
SEASON TOTALS	750	760	77	85	.475	9
RECORD IN BLOWOUTS	230	251	18	21	.462	10
LOW SCORING GAMES/HOME	61	62	13	16	.448	15
RECORD IN BLOWOUTS/HOME	133	151	10	13	.435	12
RECORD IN CLOSE GAMES/ROAD	171	179	19	25	.432	10
RECORD IN CLOSE GAMES	302	318	32	45	.416	15
RECORD IN CLOSE GAMES/HOME	131	139	13	20	.394	16
RECORD IN LOW SCORING GAMES	114	129	21	33	.389	15
LOW SCORING GAMES/ROAD	53	67	8	17	.320	15
CLOSE LOW SCORING GAMES/HOME	25	34	5	11	.312	15
5+ RUNS ALLOWED/ROAD	191	266	11	27	.289	4
5+ RUNS ALLOWED	358	553	19	55	.257	8
4- RUNS SCORED/HOME	99	219	12	35	.255	12
CLOSE LOW SCORING GAMES/ROAD	39	55	5	15	.250	16
4- RUNS SCORED	209	434	21	72	.226	11
5+ RUNS ALLOWED/HOME	167	287	8	28	.222	10
4- RUNS SCORED/ROAD	110	215	9	37	.196	12

Everyone's heard some of the stories. She refused to reimburse a scout who submitted an expense account that included $2 for admission to a college game. When umpire John McSherry died on the field, she complained that the game wasn't resumed. She withheld post-season and All-Star tickets that were supposed to go to players, employees, and sponsors. She refused to play for Eric Davis to fly home from Oakland after he ruptured his spleen diving for a ball during the final game of the 1990 World Series. When Ken Griffey asked the Reds to rescind his retirement and waive him so he could join his son in Seattle, Schott asked "what's in it for me?"

Schott forged player's names on frequent-flyer vouchers so the team could get the mileage. She stole employee's lunches from the office refrigerator to feed her dog. She made a GM use two vacation days to attend the All-Star game. During pregame ceremonies at the 1990 World Series, she rushed onto the field and launched into a drunken monologue on national TV. She discontinued the service to show out-of-town scores in the ball-

park to save the $350 per month fee. She insisted that the newly hired trainer work in the ticket office during the off-season.

All of these stories that help to illustrate that she was not a very nice person, but the important thing to remember about Schott was that she nearly destroyed the Reds. She decimated the scouting department and minor league system. She ignored and offended Reds alumni like Tony Perez and Joe Morgan. She alienated the other major shareholders. She infuriated the city and the county. She drove away dozens of good players, two very good managers, and countless front-office employees, whose behind the scene efforts are vital to a successful organization.

That's how she should be remembered. Not as an owner who did some good things but had to go when she made some insensitive comments. Not as someone who was "good at the beginning but just went too far." But as truly the single worst thing that happened in the 130 year history of professional baseball in Cincinnati.

Thank God it's over.

Name	AB	R	H	D	T	HR	RBI	BB	SO	SB	CS	BA	OBP	SLG	XR	Adj XR/27	Raw XR/27	OXW	DXW	TXW
Boone A	182	24	53	12	2	2	28	14	36	5	1	.290	.352	.413	27	5.19	5.16	1.03	0.28	1.31
Boone B	587	75	159	36	1	24	95	44	104	5	5	.271	.324	.461	81	4.65	4.62	2.38	2.01	4.39
Casey S	305	43	86	21	1	7	52	40	45	1	1	.282	.367	.426	46	5.28	5.15	1.83	0.22	2.05
Fordyce B	147	8	39	9	0	3	14	10	28	0	1	.263	.311	.385	16	3.90	3.76	0.27	0.45	0.72
Frank M	89	14	20	6	0	0	7	7	12	0	0	.228	.280	.292	7	2.47	2.44	-0.23	0.29	0.06
Greene W	361	56	100	18	1	14	49	51	80	5	4	.276	.369	.450	60	5.91	5.93	2.78	0.50	3.28
Hammonds J	87	14	27	4	1	0	11	12	18	1	1	.310	.386	.373	14	5.61	5.67	0.60	0.11	0.71
Harris L	123	12	36	8	0	0	10	7	9	1	3	.297	.337	.361	12	3.20	3.23	-0.04	0.20	0.16
Jackson D	39	4	12	5	0	0	7	5	4	1	0	.319	.388	.435	7	6.38	6.87	0.34	0.08	0.42
Konerko P	73	7	16	3	0	3	13	6	10	0	0	.218	.278	.375	7	2.92	3.07	-0.10	0.28	0.18
Larkin B	544	92	172	33	10	17	72	73	69	22	3	.316	.396	.506	105	7.20	7.23	5.90	1.68	7.58
Nieves M	121	8	32	4	0	2	17	24	42	0	0	.265	.380	.348	18	5.19	5.11	0.73	0.16	0.89
Nunnally J	177	29	37	9	0	7	20	31	38	2	4	.210	.328	.378	24	4.22	4.39	0.54	0.50	1.04
Perez E	174	20	44	4	0	4	30	19	45	0	1	.251	.327	.342	21	4.15	4.01	0.48	0.16	0.64
Petagine R	64	14	17	2	1	3	7	14	11	1	0	.265	.392	.467	13	7.07	7.42	0.72	0.14	0.86
Reese P	134	20	36	2	2	1	16	13	28	3	2	.268	.327	.333	15	3.78	3.65	0.22	0.29	0.51
Sanders R	487	82	135	17	6	14	59	45	137	16	11	.277	.345	.423	69	4.94	4.98	2.40	0.46	2.86
Stynes C	349	52	92	9	1	6	27	30	36	13	1	.264	.329	.349	43	4.36	4.20	1.14	0.80	1.94
Taubensee E	436	60	126	26	0	11	72	47	93	1	0	.289	.354	.427	67	5.65	5.49	2.97	0.61	3.58
Watkins P	148	11	41	7	1	2	15	7	26	1	3	.276	.306	.380	17	3.83	3.71	0.24	0.18	0.42
Young D	540	80	170	46	1	14	83	43	94	2	5	.315	.365	.482	84	5.78	5.78	3.78	0.01	3.79
CIN	5550	741	1496	286	27	140	722	554	1110	79	47	.270	.337	.406	752	4.66	4.64	28.00	9.41	37.41

Park Adjusted Statistics

Pitcher	S	C	T	SS	ES	IC	HH	PP	TJ	S12	S35	S67	C1	C23	C45	C67	QWP
Bere	3.29	3.71	7.00	71%	14%	57%	29%	14%	0%	57%	14%	29%	0%	57%	29%	14%	.568
Cooke	2.00	2.00	4.00	100%	100%	100%	0%	0%	0%	100%	0%	0%	0%	100%	0%	0%	.811
D Reyes	3.86	4.43	8.29	29%	0%	43%	29%	43%	0%	43%	29%	29%	0%	0%	100%	0%	.455
G White	6.00	3.33	9.33	0%	0%	33%	67%	0%	33%	0%	33%	67%	0%	33%	67%	0%	.267
Harnisch	3.28	3.03	6.31	59%	16%	38%	6%	9%	0%	31%	63%	6%	13%	59%	28%	0%	.609
Hutton	5.00	6.00	11.00	0%	0%	0%	50%	0%	0%	0%	50%	50%	0%	0%	50%	50%	.065
Klingenbeck	4.25	3.50	7.75	50%	0%	25%	25%	25%	0%	0%	75%	25%	0%	50%	50%	0%	.458
Krivda	4.00	7.00	11.00	0%	0%	0%	0%	0%	0%	0%	100%	0%	0%	0%	0%	100%	.053
Parris	3.81	3.25	7.06	56%	19%	25%	25%	0%	0%	25%	50%	25%	6%	69%	19%	6%	.551
Priest	6.00	4.00	10.00	0%	0%	0%	100%	0%	0%	0%	0%	100%	0%	50%	50%	0%	.233
Remlinger	3.89	4.07	7.96	50%	7%	36%	21%	14%	4%	29%	50%	21%	0%	39%	43%	18%	.446
Tomko	3.82	3.18	7.00	53%	18%	41%	18%	0%	12%	26%	56%	18%	9%	56%	29%	6%	.537
Weathers	5.11	3.89	9.00	22%	11%	11%	56%	0%	0%	11%	33%	56%	0%	44%	44%	11%	.306

NATIONAL LEAGUE CENTRAL

MILWAUKEE BREWERS

TOM AUSTIN

PLEASANTVILLE UBER ALLES

You know, Wisconsin's got to be ticked at those California "It's the Cheese" ads. I mean, California's got the sun, the waves, the movie stars, and Baywatch. Wisconsin, the dairy state, has. . . cheese. Lots of it. And now those fingernails-on-skateboards surfer dudes are elbowing in on the muenster mash. What nerve!

Wisconsinites seem to be taking it with that wonderful midwestern good humor, however; you've got to give them that. It's dpwnright admirable the way they support their sports teams through thin and thick and thin again, too. Win or lose, they seem to be saying, they're our boys: apple-cheeked, 4% milkfat farm boys who just might have shucked their overalls for a quick game of country hardball. Never mind that those farm boys are tucking down more for an afternoon in the sun than Joe Farmer makes for this year's dairy harvest—we love 'em anyway.

And as you know if you're reading this book (or possibly vice-versa), Milwaukee's a great baseball town, reaching all the way back to the original (National League) Brewers of 1901. Oh, wait a minute: the 1901 Brewers were a junior league club; the storied Milwaukee NL tradition covered those short years from 1953-65 when the Braves called County Stadium home. All that history is downright inconvenient, not to mention confusing—but no matter. Brewers fans took to their new league with a heaping helpin' of corn-fed good graces, and sat cheerfully through another 74-88 season, although at the beginning it looked like the AL transplants were going to show the senior circuit a thing or two. Things reverted to normal in the second half, though, as a 31-46 record washed away the traces of a 16-8 start like a federally subsidized milk dump.

All that aside, it's a tricky thing to find an angle on such a team. They're certainly not an elite team, or a team on the rise, or a team on the decline; they don't have Hall-of-Famers at four positions, and they don't have clubhouse punch-ups, so far as we know. They don't really have any pitching to speak of,

although they're not horrible. They're just sort of, you know, In The Middle.

They have a few good young players: Jeff Cirillo looks like a player (although what's the deal with the Berry signing? I suppose he's going to play first, but as a hitter, Berry's no great shakes as a third baseman—actually, he's no great shakes as a third baseman with the glove, either). There's Jeromy Burnitz, rescued from the slag heap to pound out an astounding 38 homers (and only 32 off the pace, too!), a couple of almost-weres in Grissom and Nilsson, a couple of nice-to-know-yas in John Jaha and Fernando Vina, a crusty yet lovable manager (though Garner is showing alarming signs of learning on the job, which reduces his copy potential greatly), an old stadium, a baseball commissioner. . .

Hold on there. Is that an angle? Is it noteworthy that Bud Selig, the most famous used-car salesman in the universe after Cal Worthington and his dog Spot, is now the OFFICIAL high poobah of all things horsehide? Is this something we should stay awake nights pondering the ramifications thereof? Will the Brewers become the new Yankees, with Buddy ruling by fiat that free agents A-Rod and Junior must sign with the Brewers "for the good of baseball"? Will garlic fries be outlawed by major league baseball due to a sweetheart deal signed in the back room by the bratwurst lobby? Will Miller High Life cease being the Breakfast of Carpenters and become the official Beer of Major League Baseball? The Mind boggles—

—I tried, I really did. I tried to get all lathered up about

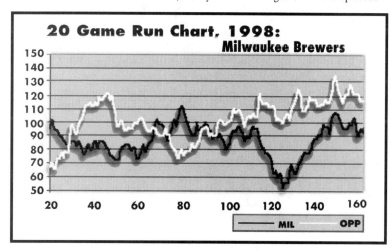

QMAX PRESENTS: "BAD" PITCHERS

SOME DAYS YOU GET THE BEAR...SOME DAYS THE BEAR GETS YOU.

The Bear must have been fat and happy in 1980, then, because Lary Sorensen gave him a few juicy meals on the way to a 12-10, 3.67 season for the Brew Crew in 1980. Hold on a minute! I can hear you saying. 12-10, 3.67? that's pretty darn...mediocre! what's THIS guy doing in a series on Bad Pitchers?

A good question. Lary Sorensen's 1980 was not nearly as bad a performance as some of the classic seasons we've covered here. It did, however, contain some interesting oddities, so we thought we'd include it as a way of shining a little light on different varieties of pitchers. Lary is a successful example of the "soldier of fortune" pitcher, the guy who gives up lots and lots of hits (235 in 188 innings as a starter) but manages, through gutty jam-pitching and the more-

than-occasional double play, to leave most of them on the bases. Lary managed to strand 68% of the baserunners he allowed, noticeably better than the 60% average strand rate for all pitchers, and the 63% average for a pitcher with a 5.0s/2.66c QMAX score(which Lary had in 1980). Given an average strand rate, Lary would have allowed 13 more earned runs in 1980, driving his ERA up from 3.67 to 4.27(an ERA which, in 1980, was not generally good enough to guarantee keeping your job).

So was Lary lucky, or was there something in his method which allowed him to strand more than the usual number of baserunners? It could have been skill: some pitchers induce more double plays than average, year after year. I don't have the numbers handy,

LARY SORENSEN/MIL 1980							
	1	2	3	4	5	6	7	S
1	1	1						2
2	3	1						4
3		1		1				2
4	1	1						2
5	2		1					3
6	1	2	3					6
7			2	6	2			10
C	8	5	7	7	2	0	0	29

but Lary didn't appear to be one of those pitchers: his lifetime strand rate was only 54%, worse than average.

One last item stands out in Lary's QMAX chart: Six starts in the 7,4 box out of a total of 29 starts. What is a typical 7,4 start? In Lary's case, in those six starts he averaged 4 innings, 9 hits, one walk, one strikeout, four runs. That's pretty terrible, but it's only 24 innings. That's another big reason why his ERA wasn't worse than it was, and probably why his strand rate was so good: those six starts torpedoed his QMAX scores (and his hits per inning) but had a much smaller effect on his ERA.

--Tom Austin

conflict-of-interest, apparent or otherwise, in a team owner becoming the stewed -er, the Steward of the Best Interests of the Game. The raw materials are all there: Bud's picture is in your Funkin' Wagnalls right next to "smarmy," and he did have as big a hand in the 1994 debacle as anyone not named Jerry Reinsdorf. But c'mon, take a breath or two before you light your oily rags for the peasants' torchlight march on the castle. The Commissioner is the owners' man—thus it is, thus it has been, thus shall it always be. Sure, go ahead and get mad as hell, and tell us you're not going to take it anymore. It'll be good for your blood pressure. Just don't pretend that it matters.

But still, appearances are important, and Bud will don the Cloak of Objectivity and lift the Sceptre of All-Knowing, Beneficent Fairness. We, the fans, will demand it of him: we're quite forgiving with reference to hard reality, but mess with our treasured illusions, and we'll hurt you but good. As such, Bud is relinquishing control of the team to his daughter, the fashionably hyphenated Wendy Selig-Prieb, so that he might utilize the Good Offices of the Commissioner in an Even-Handed and Broad-Minded fashion. (My spell-checker is frowning primly at my overuse of capitals, and as much as I fear the Wrath of Microsoft, I'm going to Courageously Persevere, so as to truly convey to the reader the Grand and Serious Mystery of the Commissioner's Office). After all, by God, Kenesaw Mountain

Landis swatted flies in that office in between banning Black Sox and Black Players, and let's not forget—no matter how hard we might want to—Happy Chandler, Ford Frick, and Meister Eckhart. (You know, the guy they buried in Grant's Tomb.) As you can see, Bud has a lot to live up to.

Of course, not everyone here at BBBA agrees with me. Just the other day Don Malcolm, Ken Adams and I were sitting around in BBBA's plush mid-town Manhattan offices after an extended, but intense, four-martini lunch—each! we're no lightweights!—groping for some clarity on the matter. We were discussing a proposed conference call to the Brewers' new ownership, and what strategies we might employ to get to the truth of Who's Running the Brewers Now. The following transcript was not acquired legally, but in the spirit of injustice we have donated it to the Richard M. Nixon Library, hoping for both a tax deduction and a suspended sentence.

DM: Ken, it's not going to work! No WAY she'll fall for that! We don't even know if it's true!

KA: Of course it'll work! And so what if it isn't true? If it's not that, she'll have some other skeleton in the closet close enough to it that she'll talk to us!

DM: Sure, she'll talk. She'll lie her little tush off, is what she'll do. And then she'll sic her lawyers on us.

TA: So let 'er! We've got three law firms on retainer in this building alone to take her on!

DM: Time for your pill, Tom. Are you getting all this down?

TA: yeah. Hold on. Yes! Sixteen seconds in Minesweeper! Beat THAT! Yess, I'm getting it. How do you spell "skeleton"?

KA: I get to be the Bad Cop, OK?! I like shakin' em down and grabbing people by the collar and growling quietly, "you can talk to us now, or we'll have to beat it out of you, Buck-o."

TA: And I'll be the good cop. I like saying "I'm going to the coke machine for a while. Don't do anything I wouldn't do, partner."

DM: So what does that leave for me? The apoplectic captain shouting "you're on suspension for this, Callahan!" Besides, that stuff only works when you have an interrogation room to lock 'em in. One false move and she's hanging up on us! No, we have to use stealth and guile, I'm afraid.

TA: (tries unsuccessfully to roll his eyes) What are we trying to find out again?

KA: We're trying to get her to 'fess up that Daddy's still running the team, that his giving up control was a sham.

TA: Perhaps the Socratic method would yield results...

DM: Yes, there you go! I will play the wise fool!

KA: I pity da fool...

DM: Just for that, wiseguy, you get to write the Brewers piece next year!

TA: Twelve seconds! I am the King!

DM & KA (in unison): You seriously need a life, Tom...

TA: Speaking of get a life, Bud Selig! Does he expect people to believe anything is going to change now that he's not running the Brewers? It wasn't like he helped small-market teams any more than Jack Kevorkian has.

DM: Enough Tom-foolery! I'm dialing the phone. Keep the roar as dull as usual, you two! (dials) Hi, Milwaukee Brewers? Could I speak to—I'm fine, how are you? Yes, this is Don Malcolm from the Big Bad Baseball—what? It's a bit cloudy here, not too bad. Really? Her lumbago is acting up? And she can tell when it's going to rain? Gee, that's something, Ma'am. If it's not too much trouble, could I speak to—no, I don't think I can make it to a picnic this Sunday, You see, I'm calling from—sweet corn? Mashed potatoes? Pearl onions? Why, that does sound nice. . .

TA: (to KA) DO something! It's Pleasantville uber alles!!

KA: Let me try. (taking phone from DM) Uh, Ma'am, this is Detective Axel Foley of the Detroit Police. We're looking for—uh-heh heh, aren't you sweet! You saw through that one right away, didn't you? No, I guess you didn't just fall off that turnip truck! Well, I'll come clean then: we here at the Big Bad Baseball Annual are trying to find out who's really running the Brewers now. See, we think that, even though he gave up the reins, that Bud is still running the show from behin—no, I don't think I can make it to that picnic either. Linda who? Linda Sue's going to be there?

WPA BULLPEN BOX—MILWAUKEE BREWERS

	PI	WPA	P	PPPI
Starters	987	-5.1	50.6	0.051
Relievers	640	2.7	40.4	0.063
Road	300	-0.9	20.4	0.068
Home	340	3.6	20.0	0.059
Mar/Apr	101	1.8	8.2	0.081
May	101	1.1	5.6	0.055
June	112	1.8	7.8	0.069
July	104	0.4	6.6	0.063
August	109	-1.4	6.4	0.059
September	113	-0.9	5.8	0.051
Non S/H Sit.	464	2.8	22.0	0.047
S/H Sit.	176	-0.1	18.4	0.104
Low Pressure	244	0.4	3.5	0.014
Med. Pressure	174	-1.6	11.9	0.069
High Pressure	222	4.0	24.9	0.112
Entered behind	292	0.6	7.4	0.025
Entered tied	102	1.8	11.6	0.114
Entered ahead	246	0.3	21.3	0.087

Name	G	PI	WPA	P	PPPI	MI	ROB	T
DeLosSantos V	13	24	.0	.2	.009	7	5	0
Fox C	49	68	1.5	5.4	.079	17	16	8
Jones D	46	59	-2.4	3.3	.056	10	7	3
Myers M	70	82	.4	5.6	.068	12	32	8
Patrick B	29	68	.6	4.0	.059	22	16	6
Plunk E	26	41	-.5	2.6	.064	13	11	3
Reyes A	50	78	.6	4.7	.060	25	25	7
Weathers D	28	56	.1	2.5	.044	17	9	3
Wickman B	72	96	1.5	9.7	.101	22	19	12
Woodall B	11	23	.5	1.0	.045	7	3	2
Woodard S	8	16	.7	.8	.052	4	2	2
Total		**640**	**2.7**	**40.3**	**.063**			

	|--------- Quality ----------|				|--- Pressure -------|		
	Dis.	Poor	Fair	Good	Her.	Lo	Med	Hi
DeLosSantos V	0	1	12	0	0	13	0	0	(0)
Fox C	5	4	17	21	2	14	21	14	(9)
Jones D	5	8	24	9	0	24	13	9	(3)
Myers M	3	6	43	17	1	35	24	11	(8)
Patrick B	0	7	15	5	2	12	5	12	(6)
Plunk E	3	4	12	5	2	9	12	5	(4)
Reyes A	1	10	24	13	2	22	17	11	(7)
Weathers D	2	2	16	8	0	14	6	8	(5)
Wickman B	8	2	23	33	6	20	26	26	(20)
Woodall B	0	0	8	3	0	6	2	3	(3)
Others	0	2	16	3	1	17	1	4	(3)
TOTAL	**27**	**46**	**210**	**117**	**16**	**186**	**127**	**103**	**(68)**

	7th inning			8th inning			9th inning		
	0	+1	+2	0	+1	+2	0	+1	+2
Fox C	4	5	2	5	3	5	2	0	0
Jones D	1	0	0	1	0	0	1	5	8
Mercedes J	0	0	1	0	0	1	0	0	0
Myers M	1	1	0	2	4	2	2	1	0
Patrick B	1	1	0	0	0	0	0	0	0
Plunk E	0	0	2	0	3	0	0	0	1
Reyes A	0	1	3	2	4	3	0	0	1
Weathers D	1	1	2	0	1	2	0	0	0
Wickman B	0	0	0	3	2	5	6	15	8
Woodall B	2	0	1	1	0	1	0	0	0
Woodard S	1	1	0	1	0	0	0	0	0
Starters	10	10	8	4	2	2	1	0	0
TOTAL	**21**	**20**	**19**	**19**	**19**	**21**	**12**	**21**	**18**
Record	**10-11**	**11-9**	**17-2**	**9-10**	**12-7**	**19-2**	**5-7**	**16-5**	**16-2**

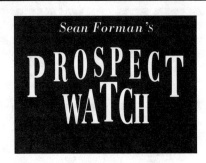

Sean Forman's PROSPECT WATCH

NAME	AGE	POS	LEVEL	GR98	GR97	GR96	AVG
Ron Belliard	23	2B	AAA	81	72	55	74
Geoff Jenkins	23	OF	AAA	67	62	57	64
Kevin Barker	22	1B	AAA	73	64	32	63
Scott Krause	24	OF	AAA	71	61	41	63
Antone Williamson	24	1B	AAA	40	64	68	53
Mike Rennhack	23	OF	AA	48	55	53	51
Santiago Perez	22	SS	AAA	57	38	33	47
Brian Banks	27	OF	AAA	48	34	53	44
Eric Owens	27	SS	AAA	38	39	61	42
Todd Dunn	27	OF	AAA	19	53	41	34

Name	Age	Pos	Level	Grade
Chad Green	23	OF	High A	50
Obispo Brito	18	C	Rookie	50
Jeff Deardorff	19	3B	Low A	47
Ramy Beatriz	19	OF	Low A	44
Bucky Jacobsen	22	OF	Low A	43
Frank Candela	19	OF	Rookie	41

Name	AGE	GS	S	C	T	W-L	ERA	K/H	Level
Rod Henderson	27	19	3.42	3.26	6.68	11-5	3.47	0.65	High
Tim VanEgmond	29	21	4.05	3.38	7.43	6-10	4.44	0.75	High
Rafael Roque	26	25	4.32	3.32	7.64	11-8	4.02	0.75	High
Bill Pulsipher	24	14	4.21	3.79	8.00	7-5	3.96	0.64	High
Kelly Wunsch	25	25	4.80	3.24	8.04	8-7	5.24	0.59	High
Greg Beck	25	22	5.05	3.55	8.59	8-10	6.38	0.61	High
Robert Ellis	26	28	4.36	4.25	8.61	10-9	5.63	0.46	High

Like their manager, much of the Brewers minor league system is scrap iron. The Brewers have concentrated almost exclusively on college players, which isn't a terrible strategy, but none of them have turned out to be much of anything prospect-wise. When you draft almost exclusively college players you end up with a lot of 25-year-olds milling around AAA hoping for a shot.

TOP DOG: Ronnie Belliard

Belliard is one player who isn't too old for his level. He is an above average second baseman and a good top of the order hitter. Has is above average numbers across the board, he has good power, speed, patience, and can hit for average. The Brewers have been actively shopping Fernando Vina, so starting Belliard at second base seems like a distinct possibility. The Brewers will not drop off much making that move. In fact, I'd rate Belliard as a darkhorse Rookie of the Year candidate. Comp: Tom Herr.

HAVE BAT, WILL TRAVEL: Geoff Jenkins

Jenkins has always been lauded for his big bat, but he has been so injury-prone that he hasn't had much time to show it off before this, his age-23, season. He is not going to be the most adept outfielder, but he has shown enough flashes with the bat (.330 average in AAA last year), that he'll probably do all right once he gets at bats under his belt. I suspect Jenkins will need a 500 at bat adjustment period before he turns it on. He has got 260 thus far, so I think he's a candidate for a strong second half. Also, I should mention that Jenkins really struggles against lefties (he bats left), so he needs to figure something out there, or he may become only a platoon player, not that there is anything wrong with that.

GO! SPEED RACER, GO!: Chad Green

Green's .344/.394/.457 line in the California League has all the trappings of a fluke. It was in a small number at bats (just 151), he was repeating the level, he was in a hitters' league, and he was a 23-year-old in a high-A league. The Brewers drafted Green in the first round for his speed (22 steals in 27 attempts). Unfortunately, he stikes out a lot and doesn't walk all that much. If you are drafting college players in the first round, you want them in the majors after three years, and Green is still two years away from sticking in the big leagues.

YOUNG 'UN: Bucky Jacobsen

Jacobson nearly grabbed the Midwest League triple crown, batting .293 to go along with 27 HR and 100 RBI. Again, his age is a problem. He was 22 putting up this season in low-A, so it's difficult to say how much was actual talent and how much was maturity beyond that of his opponents. He draws a fair number of walks, but his strikeout rates are near the rate where he may start to encounter problems. Still, he might put it together and shoot through the system in a year and half, but he needs to start moving quickly.

ON THE MOUND: Bill Pulsipher

I'm sure Don has some good comments on Pulsipher, but I'll weigh in with some thoughts here, as the rest of the Brew Crew is a pretty boring bunch.

AGE	GS	CG	IP	BF	BFS	
19	19	4	139.7	549	28.9	
20	28	5	201	849	30.3	(plus some post-season work)
21	30	6	218.3	907	30.3	
22			out for season			
23	14	0	82	393	~21	(15 relief appearances)
24	25	1	158.7	696	~24	(13 relief appearances)

Craig Wright showed that going above 27 batters per start is dangerous for young pitchers. That was nothing for Pulsipher, Wilson and Isringhausen. I doubt that Pulsipher will ever be more than a shell of his former self. It is a shame and the Mets are wholly responsible.

Oh, I'm sure she is cute as a button, ma'am, but I'm married, see, and we're trying to get an answer to this question about the ownership picture there in Milwaukee, and—yes, I'll bet Linda does bake a mean apple pie. But I'm married, see...

TA: I think you'd better let me handle this. This is no job for amateurs! Hi ma'am, this is To-yes, I'm single, why? Linda Sue, hmmm? Does she know who's running the Brewers now? Why yes, I do love peach cobbler. . .

(KA and DM can be heard groaning)

This Sunday? I'm kind of—well, I could take a plane out there, I suppose, if the cobbler is as good as you say. Say, Don, can you front me a couple hundred until my ship comes in? I've got a picnic to go to. . .

(eighteen and a half minutes of static)

Well, I'd love to fill you in on the sharp-talking BBBA investigative team ferreting out the dirty secrets of the Milwaukee baseball club, but the fact of the matter is that it just didn't happen. We were completely outfoxed and smothered in niceness by the nice lady answering the phone for the Brewers. We can only conclude that either they're just the darn nicest people in the whole gosh-forsaken world, or they're hiding something REALLY big.

Oh, and Linda Sue's Peach cobbler is every bit as good as advertised. This one's for you, Linda Sue, you sweet thing, you.

A MIDSUMMER NIGHT's DRAFT (5)
—continued from NYM—

By the time I got back, Psycho had found a replacement for my first Psycho Ale. This was going to be tougher than I thought. Psycho just smiled and went back to his beer, cig and my paper. As I tried to figure out how I was going to avoid drinking Psycho's potent beer, Pixie came in from the pool in just her swimsuit. She made her way into the kitchen and shortly reappeared carrying a bag of chips. She was headed to the back door, but seeing me, she stopped and brought her suntan over to the bar.

"Do you need any help drafting?" she asked.

"Well sure, if you don't mind sharing your chips," Psycho replied before I could say anything. He immediately started helping himself.

He showed her the Sunday paper and the stats and then started explaining the scoring system. She acted interested and began asking questions. Psycho just kept feeding her information and every once in awhile he would sneak a peek at me to see if I was paying attention. But it didn't stop him from chattering away about who he liked to draft and why. My head was a little cloudy from the Psycho Ale, but I couldn't believe he was sitting there giving away all of his strategy.

Actually, it wasn't really strategy. Basically he would psychoanalyze the player in question based on his own understanding of the science and interpret how the player would perform in the future. I thought flipping coins would be more effective. While all the discussion was going on Pixie grabbed my Psycho Ale and started drinking. I immediately brightened up: now I didn't have to worry about how not to drink it.

After her first sip, she looked at me and said, "Boy this is good beer, is it yours?"

"No, he made it and was kind enough to share it with me," I pointed to Psycho.

"Help yourself, I'll go get us some more." He got up rather abruptly and headed outside, only to return with an entire case of Psycho Ale.

The party was on now as Pat and others made their way over for some of the tasty brew. I now knew the source of Pat's erratic picks and would have to be

careful about drinking any more Psycho Ale. In fact I hadn't been keeping good track of the draft and went over to get a closer look at the board on which the picks were listed. I could feel a pair of eyes on my back and turned around to see Wish glaring at me. "What's up?" I inquired.

"You making a move on Chris?" he challenged.

"Who's Chris?"

"You know who she is, she's over talking to you and Tom at the bar."

"Well, I wasn't sure if we were talking about a girl, or not. And it's not like you introduced everyone. She's nice enough, but I think its Tom that's putting on the moves."

He looked over to the two, who happened to be laughing about something at the time. Good timing I thought, as he strode over to the bar. Well she had his attention now.

"Get away from my girlfriend," he demanded. The two were laughing so hard it took a few seconds for it to register.

"Your what?" he demanded.

"Girlfriend, you heard me."

Psycho turned to the girl in question and asked, "Do you belong to this, er, gentleman?"

She giggled, "Did you want to look for a brand?"

Psycho eyed her carefully, "Don't see one", he said cheerfully.

Too bad Wish didn't have a blood pressure monitor

Category	RS	RA	W	L	Pct.	Rk
4- RUNS ALLOWED/HOME	146	95	28	8	.778	7
5+ RUNS SCORED/HOME	239	208	24	11	.686	13
5+ RUNS SCORED	524	425	50	24	.676	15
5+ RUNS SCORED/ROAD	285	217	26	13	.667	12
4- RUNS ALLOWED	303	204	53	27	.663	10
CLOSE LOW SCORING GAMES/HOME	40	36	11	6	.647	5
RECORD IN CLOSE GAMES/HOME	159	151	24	14	.632	4
LOW SCORING GAMES/HOME	46	49	12	9	.571	10
4- RUNS ALLOWED/ROAD	157	109	25	19	.568	12
RECORD IN CLOSE GAMES	329	315	42	35	.545	4
CLOSE LOW SCORING GAMES/ROAD	32	29	8	8	.500	3
CLOSE SLUGFESTS/HOME	45	46	3	3	.500	9
RECORD IN BLOWOUTS/ROAD	84	91	8	8	.500	6
SLUGFESTS/ROAD	162	167	10	10	.500	8
RECORD IN SLUGFESTS	322	359	20	23	.465	12
RECORD IN CLOSE GAMES/ROAD	170	164	18	21	.462	5
RECORD IN LOW SCORING GAMES	86	109	21	25	.457	10
SEASON TOTALS	707	812	74	88	.457	12
CLOSE SLUGFESTS/ROAD	74	72	4	5	.444	10
SLUGFESTS/HOME	160	192	10	13	.435	15
LOW SCORING GAMES/ROAD	40	60	9	16	.360	10
4- RUNS SCORED/HOME	106	219	14	32	.304	10
RECORD IN BLOWOUTS	143	237	10	23	.303	14
5+ RUNS ALLOWED/ROAD	205	276	11	26	.297	3
4- RUNS SCORED	183	387	24	64	.273	9
5+ RUNS ALLOWED	404	608	21	61	.256	9
4- RUNS SCORED/ROAD	77	168	10	32	.238	7
5+ RUNS ALLOWED/HOME	199	332	10	35	.222	11
RECORD IN BLOWOUTS/HOME	59	146	2	15	.118	16

TEAM BREAKOUT BREWERS 1998

strapped on. You could tell he wanted to do something, but he wasn't sure what. He started to make a move toward Psycho.

"Do you want to go for a swim?"

Wish wasn't sure for an instant if the comment was aimed for him or his pixie girlfriend. But when Psycho stood up, he instinctively moved back. I wondered if Psycho's back would be up to the challenge.

Someone called out, "Tom it's your turn."

"OK, just a minute," he then sat down and started going over my paper.

I whispered to Wish, "Why don't you ask her to help you make your next pick? She needs some attention. Do you want to give her the attention, or do you want someone else to?"

He started to object but I cut him off, "Don't be a jerk, this draft is just a game. It's not that important."

Awkwardly he went behind the bar to make his amends. At first she put him off, but he was persistent. Finally they went into the kitchen. Psycho glanced up at me and winked.

"We make a pretty good team. The girl took your beer, better grab another."

The rest of the draft was a little blurry and my picks weren't much better than Pat's had been before, but I had made a friend—for better or worse. <KA>

Name	AB	R	H	D	T	HR	RBI	BB	SO	SB	CS	BA	OBP	SLG	XR	Adj XR/27	Raw XR/27	OXW	DXW	TXW
Burnitz J	609	91	158	28	1	41	123	70	169	7	4	.259	.336	.509	106	6.05	6.01	4.94	0.63	5.57
Cirillo J	604	96	191	31	1	15	67	79	94	9	4	.316	.397	.446	98	5.90	6.02	4.63	1.77	6.40
Grissom M	542	56	144	29	1	10	59	24	83	13	9	.267	.299	.380	57	3.63	3.75	0.54	0.91	1.45
Hamelin B	146	15	32	6	0	8	22	16	32	0	1	.219	.295	.421	18	3.88	3.71	0.26	0.02	0.28
Hughes B	218	28	49	7	2	10	29	16	57	1	2	.226	.281	.409	25	3.86	3.87	0.37	0.46	0.83
Jackson D	204	20	48	13	1	4	20	9	41	1	1	.237	.272	.377	19	3.13	3.16	-0.11	0.30	0.19
Jaha J	216	29	44	6	1	7	37	49	70	1	3	.205	.363	.343	31	4.65	4.71	1.01	0.15	1.16
Jenkins G	262	33	59	12	1	10	28	20	65	1	3	.227	.286	.392	27	3.45	3.43	0.11	0.18	0.29
Levis J	37	4	13	0	0	0	4	7	6	1	0	.342	.461	.342	6	5.94	6.19	0.32	0.05	0.37
Loretta M	434	54	135	30	0	7	53	42	51	8	7	.311	.378	.425	65	5.40	5.50	2.72	1.48	4.20
Matheny M	320	24	75	13	0	7	27	11	68	1	0	.234	.274	.338	28	2.99	3.01	-0.29	0.49	0.20
Newfield M	186	15	44	7	0	3	25	19	31	0	1	.235	.305	.328	18	3.24	3.22	-0.03	0.08	0.05
Nilsson D	309	38	82	14	1	13	55	33	52	2	2	.266	.337	.445	44	4.81	4.79	1.42	0.07	1.49
Owens E	40	5	5	2	0	1	4	2	6	0	0	.124	.166	.252	0	0.20	0.20	-0.48	0.07	-0.41
Valentin J	428	64	95	24	0	17	48	63	113	9	7	.222	.321	.398	59	4.57	4.58	1.73	1.12	2.85
Vina F	637	100	196	40	7	7	44	54	49	21	17	.308	.384	.428	101	5.78	5.86	4.61	3.26	7.87
MIL	**5541**	**697**	**1418**	**271**	**17**	**163**	**664**	**532**	**1113**	**76**	**64**	**.256**	**.327**	**.399**	**709**	**4.34**	**4.38**	**21.74**	**11.04**	**32.78**

Pitcher	S	C	T	SS	ES	IC	HH	PP	TJ	S12	S35	S67	C1	C23	C45	C67	QWP
B Woodall	4.35	3.50	7.85	40%	10%	30%	35%	0%	5%	25%	40%	35%	10%	40%	45%	5%	.442
Eldred	4.57	3.74	8.30	35%	4%	22%	35%	9%	4%	17%	48%	35%	4%	39%	48%	9%	.424
J Mercedes	4.40	3.40	7.80	40%	0%	40%	20%	20%	20%	20%	60%	20%	0%	60%	40%	0%	.489
Juden	4.29	3.88	8.17	29%	4%	38%	33%	17%	13%	21%	46%	33%	13%	29%	46%	13%	.437
Karl	4.27	3.52	7.79	48%	9%	33%	27%	9%	3%	27%	45%	27%	0%	52%	45%	3%	.466
P Wagner	4.56	4.22	8.78	33%	0%	11%	44%	11%	0%	11%	44%	44%	0%	44%	44%	11%	.334
Patrick	5.33	2.67	8.00	33%	0%	33%	67%	0%	33%	0%	33%	67%	0%	100%	0%	0%	.447
Pulsipher	4.10	3.90	8.00	40%	0%	10%	20%	0%	0%	10%	70%	20%	0%	40%	60%	0%	.423
Roque	3.56	4.11	7.67	22%	0%	44%	11%	22%	0%	33%	56%	11%	0%	33%	56%	11%	.525
S Woodard	4.27	2.92	7.19	50%	15%	35%	31%	4%	4%	23%	46%	31%	12%	58%	31%	0%	.524
MIL	**4.31**	**3.58**	**7.90**	**40%**	**7%**	**30%**	**31%**	**9%**	**6%**	**22%**	**48%**	**31%**	**6%**	**45%**	**44%**	**6%**	**.456**

PITTSBURGH PIRATES

SEAN FORMAN

ARE YOU EXPERIENCED?

Birthdays elicit different emotions. Some people dread them, others deny them, some celebrate them and Hallmark profits from them. Professional athletes are more acutely aware of age than anyone, except perhaps actresses. The professional athlete has a very, very short window of productivity. The most elite athletes stay at the pinnacle of their sport for fifteen years, while the lesser athlete may have only three to seven years in the spotlight. Teams are also sensitive to the ravages of time. As Ken Adams pointed out dramatically in BBBA 98, the Orioles were flirting with disaster putting their fate in the hands of golden oldies. And no one should have expected the 1998 Marlins to compete with their lack of experienced players.

TEAM AGES

It was a pretty safe bet that the Florida Marlins would be the youngest and least experienced team in the majors in 1998. It was

Youngest Teams			Oldest Teams		
	Age	Experience		Age	Experience
Florida	25.4	2.2	Baltimore	32.3	9.3
Montreal	26.1	2.7	San Francisco	31.7	7.8
Pittsburgh	26.8	3.1	Seattle	31.2	7.4
Chi. White Sox	27.3	4.0	San Diego	31.0	7.4
Detroit	27.3	3.3	NY Yankees	30.8	6.6

an equally safe bet that the Baltimore Orioles would be the most experienced and oldest. Just how old and how young are teams in the major leagues? Here is how teams stacked up for 1998 (above).

Baltimore's batters were nearly two years older than the nearest competitor's at 33.8 years of age, while San Francisco's pitching staff age was 32.4, just edging the surprisingly old Seattle Mariners' staff. The Marlins were the youngest in the league across the board. Their pitching staff averaged a remarkably immature 1.2 years of experience, which was among the top five lowest of all-time. Montreal's batters were slightly older, but less experienced than Florida's batters.

What about contending teams? Who are the least and most experienced teams to win pennants (or more recently divisions)?

		Wins	Age	Experience
Least Experienced				
1994	Montreal	74	27.1	3.2
1944	St. Louis (NL)	105	28.4	3.4
1912	Boston (AL)	105	26.1	3.6
1943	St. Louis (NL)	105	27.6	3.7
1947	Brooklyn	94	27.2	3.7
Most Experienced				
1982	California	93	32.8	9.6
1983	Philadelphia	90	32.0	9.5
1980	New York (AL)	103	31.3	9.3
1925	Washington	96	31.5	9.0
1992	Oakland	96	31.7	8.8

LEAGUES AS A WHOLE

As salaries have moved ever upward, pundits and fans alike have bemoaned the expected premature depature of star players. The premise is that players, financially secure by age 30, will buy a tropical island, name themselves king, and spend the rest of their days sipping pina coladas on the beach. "I am

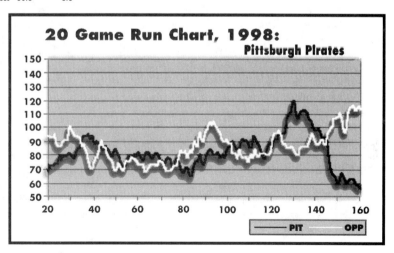

20 Game Run Chart, 1998: Pittsburgh Pirates

QMAX PRESENTS: "BAD" PITCHERS

IT'S ALRIGHT MA, I'M ONLY BLEEDING.

Bad pitching comes in many varieties, and inspires many emotions on the losing side, from frustration and impotent rage to quiet despair. The case of Steve Blass inspires more of an inner sadness, a kind of existential angst for those prone to phrase things that way.

Steve was a fine pitcher for the fine Pirates teams of the late 60's and early 70's, winning 18 games in 1968, 15 games for the 1971 World Champions, and a career-high 19 games with a 2.49 ERA in 1972. Then Roberto Clemente went down with the plane on New Year's Eve, and Steve was never the same. That's one theory, anyway, for why Steve suddenly and totally lost the ability to get the ball over the plate. Oh sure, he

threw strikes once in a while, sometimes two or three times in a row. Sooner or later in every start, though, the infielders would be kicking dirt impatiently as another batsman tossed his weapon aside and trotted down to first.

For most of April and May, Blass was merely struggling with a severe control problem, walking four or five or six in a six-inning start. In June, however, the wheels came off: one pictures Steve desperately aiming the ball at the middle of the plate, with a line drive his reward if he succeeded. Blass didn't see the fourth inning in any of his June starts, and he was mercifully dispatched to the bullpen through July.

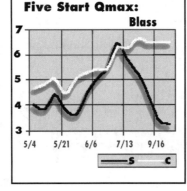

Five Start Qmax: Blass

He got the mopup work for a while, coming in with the Bucs on the short end of a lop-sided score to try to work out the kinks with nothing at stake. An August first start reached tragicomic proportions (five outs, five walks, one hit batsman) and it was down to the minors for more mopup work. Through all of this, many physical and mental examinations ensued, and nothing definite was found to be torn in either body or mind.

Steve returned in September for three more starts, and by this time the batters were keeping their bats on their shoulders for at least two called strikes a lot of the time. In the off-season, everything from shrinks to leeches was tried in vain; Steve walked seven in five innings in his first start of 1974, and he never pitched in the majors again.

The mysterious Blass collapse of 1973 is unsolved to this day.

--Tom Austin

A-Rod, ruler of the Isle of Alex. I declare all shall have two paper umbrellas per drink." Is this true? Not really. The major leagues are in fact turning into a geriatric ward, relatively speaking. The geezers have to be removed forcibly, usually kicking and screaming.

Before we divulge the numbers, some details. The values for age and experience are weighted by at bat and innings pitched, team age = (Sum for each player (at bats x Age))/Sum (at bats). For pitchers, substitute innings pitched for at bats. The two totals are then averaged for a team or league's age. Also, for the players' age we used their age on December 31. Baseball traditionally uses June 30, but month of birth is not always available. As for experience, we used the year minus the year of the player's debut, and used the same equation as above with experience substituted for age. In this method, Turner Ward is considered twice as experienced as Quilvio Veras, despite 400 fewer career at bats, but that effect is probably minor. There is also the matter of relief pitchers throwing fewer innings of greater import. Perhaps in future studies, we will attempt to mitigate these factors.

Here is a chart of league-wide player ages and experience from 1903 to the present.

Age & Experience in the 20th Century

There are several interesting trends in the chart above. I didn't include the Federal League in my study, but its existence is clearly shown here as the league age dropped precipitously in 1914 and 1915 when the Federal League was in operation. When that league folded, the league age returned to more established levels. During the Second World War, the age changed again, this time an upward surge as young players enlisted in the armed forces and older players took their place.

From 1960 to 1980, there is a long valley in the league age line where the baby boomers moved through baseball. First, they drove the league age downward as they arrived on the scene, but then as they got older, so did the league age. The rapid expansion of this time might also have had something to do with the initial drop in age. Now, we are at what appears to be a fairly standard age (29). There is a slight upward trend at the end of the chart, but it will take four or five more years until we know for certain if that is an actual trend or normal fluctuation.

The league experience line tells a slightly different story. Through the first fifty years of the 20th century, the lines follow essentially the same path. Then in the sixties as league ages are dropping, league experience is actually remaining fairly constant, then rises to historically high levels in the early 80s. Since that time, league experience has been dropping. Perhaps players are retiring sooner, but if that were the case, one would expect to see league ages dropping as well. It's likely that the drop in league experience is a result of the rise of college baseball. Players now enter the minor leagues at age 21 or 22 and reach the majors at a later age as well.

CHAMPIONSHIP TEAMS

Championship teams generally run through a cycle of ebb and flow. A kernel of young players is brought together. At first, these players are talented, but are likely to do little more than hold their own in the major leagues. The majority of them continue to improve building toward contention. A team with monetary resources (they should have been saving their pennies for a sunny day. . .) then adds a few more players, usually veterans, and the team is now in full bloom. If the core is good enough, they will make the playoffs several years in a row. If the core isn't all that great, you hang around .500 like the current Milwaukee Brewers. As this core passes through its prime, the team starts plugging holes with older available players.

Sometimes this works and sometimes it doesn't. Eventually, the team experiences a championship hangover and must lose, often catastrophically, before they realize the necessity to again rebuild with youth. Older players are either traded or allowed to leave and young kids are once again given playing time.

The Pirates are a good example of this cycle. Pittsburgh has experienced three periods of success since 1970. Starting in 1970, the Danny Murtaugh-led Pirates five of six division titles.

As you can see in the chart, the Pirates lowered their team age during the early 70s and achieved

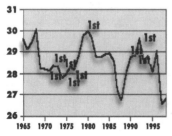

WPA BULLPEN BOX—PITTSBURGH PIRATES

	Pl	WPA	P	PPPI
Starters	1035	2.1	52.9	0.051
Relievers	569	1.3	34.0	0.060
Road	294	-0.9	18.2	0.062
Home	275	2.2	15.9	0.058
Mar/Apr	106	0.0	7.4	0.070
May	93	0.3	5.4	0.058
June	88	2.8	5.5	0.062
July	89	-0.6	5.1	0.058
August	96	-1.2	6.4	0.066
September	97	-0.1	4.2	0.044
Non S/H Sit.	417	1.0	18.2	0.044
S/H Sit.	152	0.2	15.8	0.104
Low Pressure	263	0.8	3.7	0.014
Med. Pressure	158	-3.2	10.1	0.064
High Pressure	148	3.7	20.2	0.137
Entered behind	259	1.9	5.5	0.021
Entered tied	82	-1.0	10.7	0.130
Entered ahead	228	0.3	17.8	0.078

Name	G	Pl	WPA	P	PPPI	MI	ROB	T
Christiansen J	60	86	1.1	6.7	.078	22	31	7
Dessens E	38	60	.3	3.4	.057	16	8	7
Loiselle R	54	65	-1.8	5.5	.084	11	12	7
Martinez J	37	48	-.5	1.1	.023	10	9	1
McCurry J	16	22	-.4	1.2	.055	5	3	4
Peters C	18	29	.3	1.7	.060	8	5	3
Rincon R	60	84	1.2	6.2	.074	22	22	7
Tabaka J	37	60	-.3	1.9	.032	18	12	6
VanPoppel T	11	13	-.1	.3	.022	2	5	1
Wilkins M	16	20	.1	1.3	.067	4	6	2
Williams M	36	58	1.3	3.6	.062	18	17	4
Total		569	1.3	34.0	.060			

		-------- Quality ----------					--- Pressure -------		
	Dis.	Poor	Fair	Good	Her.	Lo	Med	Hi
Christiansen J	5	1	30	21	3	26	19	15	(12)
Dessens E	3	4	19	9	3	17	16	5	(5)
Loiselle R	7	3	30	12	2	27	7	20	(12)
Martinez J	1	3	32	1	0	30	6	1	(0)
McCurry J	0	3	11	2	0	12	1	3	(2)
Peters C	0	3	10	4	1	7	8	3	(2)
Rincon R	3	11	24	18	4	27	14	19	(13)
Tabaka J	2	3	27	5	0	23	11	3	(3)
VanPoppel T	0	3	8	0	0	10	1	0	(0)
Wilkins M	2	0	10	3	1	8	6	2	(2)
Williams M	0	3	20	13	0	15	13	8	(6)
Others	1	1	7	3	0	7	3	2	(0)
TOTAL	24	38	228	91	14	209	105	81	(57)

	7th inning			8th inning			9th inning		
	0	+1	+2	0	+1	+2	0	+1	+2
Christiansen J	1	0	1	1	6	2	1	2	0
Dessens E	1	1	1	1	2	0	0	0	0
Loiselle R	0	0	0	2	1	0	1	8	3
Martinez J	0	1	0	0	1	0	0	0	0
Peters C	0	1	1	0	1	1	1	0	0
Rincon R	1	0	0	0	4	5	2	6	3
Tabaka J	0	1	0	0	0	0	0	0	0
VanPoppel T	1	0	0	0	0	0	0	0	0
Wilkins M	0	0	0	0	1	0	1	0	1
Williams M	0	1	1	3	2	0	1	1	0
Starters	8	15	11	2	4	3	0	1	0
TOTAL	12	20	16	9	21	11	7	18	8
Record	2-10	14-6	13-3	3-6	12-9	10-1	3-4	11-7	8-0

Sean Forman's
PROSPECT WATCH

NAME	AGE	POS	LEVEL	GR98	GR97	GR96	AVG
Chad Hermansen	20	SS	AAA	103	90	78	95
Aramis Ramirez	20	3B	AAA	89	75	67	81
Craig Wilson	21	C	AA	62	57	50	58
Emil Brown	23	OF	AA	57	-	56	57
T.J. Staton	23	OF	AAA	51	54	82	57
Adrian Brown	24	OF	AAA	51	56	48	52
Jeff Patzke	24	2B	AAA	41	64	61	52
Garrett Long	21	1B	AA	55	53	35	51
Alexander Hernandez	21	OF	AA	53	47	48	50
Abraham Nunez	22	SS	AAA	55	45	40	49
Kevin Haverbusch	22	SS	AA	55	36	-	47
Warren Morris	24	2B	AAA	47	37	-	43

Name	Age	Pos	Level	Grade
Jovanny Sosa	17	OF	Rookie	74
Eddy Furniss	22	1B	High A	57
Korwin Dehaan	21	OF	Low A	55
Jeremy Harts	18	OF	Rookie	52
Jonathan Prieto	18	2B	Rookie	52
Victor Araujo	17	SS	Rookie	51
Rico Washington	20	3B	Rookie	46
Corey Pointer	22	OF	High A	43
Jerry Davis	19	OF	Low A	43

Name	AGE	GS	S	C	T	W-L	ERA	K/H	Level
Kevin Pickford	23	19	3.89	2.95	6.84	8-2	3.66	0.77	High
Kris Benson	23	27	4.04	3.52	7.56	7-10	5.37	0.80	High
Sean Lawrence	26	26	3.96	3.62	7.58	12-8	5.02	0.82	High
Jason Phillips	24	29	4.48	3.31	7.79	9-13	4.34	0.68	High
Jason Haynie	24	18	4.33	3.67	8.00	4-5	4.44	0.47	High
Bronson Arroyo	21	22	4.95	3.55	8.50	9-8	5.46	0.57	High
Jimmy Anderson	21	17	4.59	4.35	8.94	5-7	5.02	0.44	High
Kane Davis	23	16	5.06	4.50	9.56	1-11	9.24	0.38	High

This is probably the longest list of any team. The Pirates have been accruing talent like crazy and it should be paying off here very shortly. They may have a problem sorting through all of it as they have several options at nearly every position.

TOP DOG: Chad Hermansen

I'm a huge Chad Hermansen fan, but I was very surprised when he ended up topping 100 in my ratings this year. If he doesn't become a top 10 left fielder in three years, I will consider it nothing less than an upset. Here is a kid who slugged .520 in AAA, stole 21 bases in 25 attempts and he wasn't legal till the end of this year. Somehow Baseball America managed to leave him off the Baseball America Pacific Coast League's top 10 prospect list. Critics will dwell on his .258 batting average and the fact he struck out once every three at bats. Those are both big negatives, but I have a couple of responses to that. He's been changing positions almost weekly as the Pirates have tried him in no less than four positions in the last two years. He also has been the youngest player in the league almost every one of his four seasons. I suspect that he will get a chance to catch his breath this year in AAA and he'll explode with a big season. Comp: Between Willie Greene and Juan Gonzalez.

RULE V'ER: Emil Brown

If I were running the Pirates, meet my new center fielder. Brown was snagged from the A's two years back and finally played some ball after sitting on the bench all of 1997. He has good gap power, can hit for average, is patient at the plate, and can steal bases at a high rate. The Pirates have some good looking players in here, but can Gene Lamont do anything with them?

UP THE MIDDLE:

Abraham Nunez - Nunez was one of the pickups in the lopsided Merced/Garcia/Plesac deals. His ticket to the majors is his slick glove. He's never going to be much of a hitter, but his patience has been improving and if he could get up to .260/.330/.350 with some steals, the Pirates would probably be happy, but that appears to be his ceiling. Comp: Carlos Garcia trading doubles for walks.

Kevin Haverbusch - Haverbusch has been a nice surprise for the Pirates. He has played himself off the shortstop spot, but a .352/.391/.516 line can play about anywhere. He's not the player Aramis Ramirez is, but he should be worth something in trade.

Warren Morris - Morris was picked up in the Loaiza/Van Poppel trade. I suspect the Pirates accepted Van Poppel as well only because Southwest had a "Friends

Fly Free" promotion that week. Morris has hit .316/.395/.492 over the last two years, and could be a real bonus offensively at second base. Comp: Bret Boone.

YOUNG 'UN: Korwin DeHaan

DeHaan is Dutch through and through as he hails from Pella, Iowa, home to Central College, my brother's alma mater. He struggled in his first pro year, but he turned it up a notch hitting .314/.404/.480 with 33 stolen bases in low A. He's still mostly a doubles hitter, but if he shows he can handle centerfield and if he can skip a level somewhere, he might stick in the majors.

ON THE MOUND: Kris Benson

The Pirates' pitching prospects all had something in common this year; they stunk. Each of the high level affiliates was near the bottom in ERA. Benson is the foremost of the Pirates' prospects. He was the first pick overall in the 1996 draft, but he has been a bit of a disappointment thus far. His career ERA is 4.69, and he's allowed more than a hit per inning each of the last two years. His strikeout rates (8.5 K/9) and walk rates (3.0 BB/9) have been good, but he is allowing entirely too many hits including nearly a home run per start this year. He was in the Elite Square four times, which is one of the higher amounts in the PCL, so perhaps he can put it together. I'm not hopeful for him becoming an ace.

their first extended success since the 20s. This faith in the youngsters was rewarded in 1979 as the "We Are Family" Pirates won the World Series. The Pirates experienced a hangover as they struggled and hit bottom in 1985 with a 57-104 record. They continued to get younger until 1987, when they began to win again and made three straight appearances in the NLCS. Once Barry Bonds left, the Pirates weren't the same as they struggled throughout the middle of this decade. In 1997, the Pirates featured the youngest team in the majors, and with a new ballpark on the way, they may be poised for another series of title runs in two or three years as the young kids gain experience.

Many other teams have exhibited this pattern. The Houston Astros, Oakland A's, and even the Philadelphia Phillies come to mind. This is why the small-market/large-market arguments are such a red herring. Teams have cycled through success and failure throughout baseball history. It is exceedingly difficult for a team to enjoy extended success, especially in the era of free agency. The relationship with quality of management and success appears to be much stronger than the relationship between success and market size.

LITTLE BALL

In 1998, the Pirates dropped ten games from their solid 79-83 1997 record. The pitching staff actually improved as their ERA went from 4.28 to 3.91. The defense, which was already poor, committed nine more errors, but that at worst canceled out the improvement in the pitching. The offense was the offending party on this team, and it was a real stinker.

Those of you who have made a habit of visiting the BBBA website (www.backatcha.com) know that much was made of the race to crack the 400-walk barrier. This is a rare "achievement," as in the last twenty years only the '83 Royals, '93 Rockies, and the '80 White Sox have been held below 400 walks in a full season. Even in the strike shortened 1995 season, every team drew at least 400 walks. Don Malcolm is a gambling man, and his money was riding on the Montreal Expos to earn this dubious honor. Montreal had established a clear pattern of playing low on-base percentage players. However, a darkhorse candidate appeared around the All-Star break and with a strong finish the Pirates amassed just 393 walks, well behind the Expos who drew 439.

It was a complete team effort. Jason Kendall led the team with 51 walks, and Kevin Young was the only other player to draw more than forty.

Pittsburgh's offense beat out the Expos by six runs, so they weren't officially the worst offense in the league. However, Olympic Stadium was a severe pitchers' park last year and the Three Rivers was a hitters' park, so the Pirates were actually the worst offense in the National League.

In the power department, the Pirates played the Washington Senators to Mark McGwire's Babe Ruth. Not only did the Pirates not draw many walks, but they were also last in the league with 107 home runs. Kevin Young led with 27; no one else exceeded 15 home runs. Rather than rely on boring things like home runs and walks, the go-go Pirates led the league in stolen bases with 159. In his Tampa Bay essay, Doug Drinen labeled this player the "slappin' swifty," a term for which Tony Womack may be the canonical form. The Pirates also utilized the black-and-blue offense as they dominated the majors with 91 HBPs.

Pittsburgh did bat .254 (middle of the league), but they managed just a .685 OPS, the worst in the league. The offense really went in the tank in September when the Pirates suffered through a 5-22 month. Pirates' batters hit just .219/.274/.320 in September and scored just 2.8 runs per game.

The pitching staff should be the real source of optimism for Pirates fans. Despite sporting the third youngest staff in the majors, the Pirates were solidly in the top half of the National League in ERA. This staff is still younger than the early Atlanta staffs, but they also are much less experienced and not quite as good as those staffs were. What would turn this from a good to a great staff is the development of a top ten pitcher. Jason Schmidt has been bandied about as the most likely candidate, but Francisco Cordova may already be there. Cordova showed that he could hold up thru a full season and posted a terrific 3.31 ERA in 220 innings. A lack of run support torpedoed his won-loss record (13-14), but he is a potential 20-game winner.. With Jason Christiansen's reemergence, lefty reliever Roberto Rincon became expendable, and he was traded for Brian Giles. Pittsburgh has had a knack at getting good middle relief performances out of some iffy talent: Mike Williams, Jeff Tabaka, and Marc Wilkins, so they should be all right in middle relief.

The Pirates have some terrific players on the way. Jason Kendall is already a star and the acquisition of Giles significantly improves the outfield and adds a much-needed left-handed bat. Aramis Ramirez was the youngest player in the majors at the time of his callup and should become a very good third baseman. Jose Guillen in right field is still quite young, and the Bucs have a plethora of options in the outfield, including top prospects Emil Brown and Chad Hermansen. The pitching staff is deep and could be one of the best groups in the league as early as next year.

That said, I am not convinced that GM Cam Bonifay

TEAM BREAKOUT PIRATES 1998

Category	RS	RA	W	L	Pct.	Rk
5+ RUNS SCORED/HOME	238	135	30	5	.857	5
5+ RUNS SCORED	433	278	48	15	.762	8
4- RUNS ALLOWED/HOME	208	103	33	14	.702	14
5+ RUNS SCORED/ROAD	195	143	18	10	.643	14
4- RUNS ALLOWED	369	220	58	37	.611	16
CLOSE SLUGFESTS/HOME	47	48	4	3	.571	5
RECORD IN BLOWOUTS/HOME	130	105	12	9	.571	6
4- RUNS ALLOWED/ROAD	161	117	25	23	.521	16
SLUGFESTS/HOME	119	116	8	8	.500	10
RECORD IN CLOSE GAMES/HOME	131	136	15	18	.455	13
RECORD IN BLOWOUTS	230	261	20	25	.444	11
SEASON TOTALS	645	713	69	93	.426	13
RECORD IN SLUGFESTS	256	278	15	21	.417	15
LOW SCORING GAMES/HOME	40	36	8	12	.400	16
RECORD IN CLOSE GAMES	251	268	28	42	.400	16
RECORD IN CLOSE GAMES/ROAD	120	132	13	24	.351	16
SLUGFESTS/ROAD	137	162	7	13	.350	15
RECORD IN LOW SCORING GAMES	96	113	18	34	.346	16
RECORD IN BLOWOUTS/ROAD	100	156	8	16	.333	12
LOW SCORING GAMES/ROAD	56	77	10	22	.312	16
CLOSE LOW SCORING GAMES/ROAD	33	45	6	15	.286	14
CLOSE SLUGFESTS/ROAD	49	51	2	5	.286	16
4- RUNS SCORED/HOME	111	196	10	35	.222	14
4- RUNS SCORED	212	435	21	78	.212	15
5+ RUNS ALLOWED/HOME	141	228	7	26	.212	12
4- RUNS SCORED/ROAD	101	239	11	43	.204	10
5+ RUNS ALLOWED	276	493	11	56	.164	14
5+ RUNS ALLOWED/ROAD	135	265	4	30	.118	16
CLOSE LOW SCORING GAMES/HOME	10	19	1	8	.111	16

and manager Gene Lamont know what it takes to score runs. Bonifay's recent acquisitions show a decided fascination with utility infielders and fourth outfielders. Over the last four years, the Pirates have picked up such luminaries as Dale Sveum, Turner Ward, Doug Strange, Charlie Hayes and Mike Kingery. The Pirates tight purse strings have tied Bonifay's hands, but few would expect those players to be of much help at all.

This off-season Bonifay signed journeyman infielder Mike Benjamin to a two-year contract and has promised Benjamin a chance to win the starting job at second base. Boston fans aren't exactly sad to see Benjamin and his .275 career OBP leave town. The Pirates would be far better off playing some of the many young kids coming up through the farm system. A few won't make it, but many of them will, and the Pirates need those players to develop into stars if they want to compete again.

After losing a 1997 ballot initiative, the Pirates have finally secured a combination of public and private financing for a new baseball facility. The state of Pennsylvania and Governor Tom Ridge have dragged their feet in allocating the $75 million they had promised for the project, so the ballpark has hit a temporary snag. Owner Kevin McClatchey has trotted out the usual threats and innuendoes, so expect the details to be ironed out and construction to eventually move forward. The new facility will be a riverfront retro park, and by the looks of the design may become one of the better venues in all of baseball. The Pirates have enough talent in the system that they could put an exciting young team on the field when the new park opens. However, they need to reduce the reliance on low OBP, low power batters and pick up some guys who can actually score runs.

Name	AB	R	H	D	T	HR	RBI	BB	SO	SB	CS	BA	OBP	SLG	XR	Adj XR/27	Raw XR/27	OXW	DXW	TXW
Allensworth J	233	29	71	11	2	3	23	17	42	8	4	.305	.368	.415	36	5.66	5.86	1.62	0.19	1.81
Brown A	152	20	44	4	1	0	5	9	17	4	0	.287	.326	.324	16	3.77	3.68	0.24	0.26	0.50
Brown E	39	2	10	1	0	0	3	1	11	0	0	.256	.292	.278	3	2.94	2.98	-0.03	0.01	-0.02
Collier L	334	29	82	12	6	2	33	31	68	2	2	.245	.316	.332	36	3.58	3.65	0.34	1.04	1.38
Garcia F	172	27	44	10	1	9	26	18	44	0	2	.254	.329	.481	26	5.26	5.38	1.03	0.33	1.36
Guillen J	573	59	152	34	2	14	83	21	98	3	6	.264	.295	.404	66	4.04	4.17	1.28	0.97	2.25
Kendall J	535	93	174	33	3	12	74	51	50	27	5	.325	.409	.465	106	7.47	7.58	6.33	2.41	8.74
Martin A	440	56	105	14	2	12	47	32	89	21	3	.239	.296	.360	48	3.67	3.69	0.52	0.43	0.95
Martinez M	180	21	45	10	2	6	23	9	43	0	3	.251	.290	.432	22	3.99	4.01	0.38	0.08	0.46
Nunez A	52	6	10	2	0	1	2	12	14	4	2	.195	.345	.291	6	3.62	3.60	0.07	0.25	0.32
Osik K	98	8	21	4	0	0	7	13	16	1	2	.213	.315	.251	8	2.36	2.43	-0.30	0.59	0.29
Polcovich K	212	18	39	10	0	0	14	15	32	4	3	.185	.252	.235	11	1.57	1.71	-1.29	0.80	-0.49
Ramirez A	251	23	60	8	1	6	24	18	70	0	1	.237	.297	.349	26	3.60	3.58	0.26	-0.05	0.21
Smith M	128	18	25	5	0	2	13	10	25	7	0	.194	.262	.283	12	3.14	3.19	-0.07	0.11	0.04
Strange D	185	9	32	8	0	0	14	10	38	1	0	.175	.218	.215	7	1.09	1.08	-1.42	0.11	-1.31
Ward T	282	32	73	11	2	9	45	27	39	5	4	.258	.324	.412	41	4.82	5.02	1.37	0.70	2.07
Womack T	655	84	185	24	6	3	44	38	92	60	9	.283	.320	.352	82	4.52	4.55	2.43	1.95	4.38
Young K	592	86	158	36	2	27	106	44	125	16	8	.267	.325	.472	88	5.07	5.21	3.22	0.50	3.72
PIT	5495	639	1390	247	31	108	604	391	1037	165	56	.253	.310	.368	650	3.99	4.07	15.97	10.68	26.65

Pitcher	S	C	T	SS	ES	IC	HH	PP	TJ	S12	S35	S67	C1	C23	C45	C67	QWP
C Peters	3.90	3.20	7.10	40%	20%	45%	20%	5%	10%	30%	50%	20%	5%	60%	35%	0%	.521
Dessens	4.60	4.00	8.60	40%	20%	20%	40%	0%	0%	20%	40%	40%	0%	40%	40%	20%	.387
F Cordova	3.64	3.06	6.70	61%	21%	42%	21%	3%	6%	30%	48%	21%	15%	48%	33%	3%	.552
Jo Silva	4.06	3.28	7.33	50%	22%	39%	28%	6%	6%	28%	44%	28%	22%	28%	44%	6%	.486
Lawrence	4.67	4.33	9.00	33%	0%	0%	33%	0%	0%	0%	67%	33%	0%	0%	100%	0%	.309
Lieber	4.15	2.93	7.07	41%	19%	44%	30%	7%	11%	33%	37%	30%	15%	63%	19%	4%	.543
Loaiza	4.43	3.21	7.64	43%	14%	36%	50%	0%	0%	29%	21%	50%	14%	43%	43%	0%	.451
Mi Williams	4.00	3.00	7.00	100%	0%	0%	0%	0%	0%	0%	100%	0%	0%	100%	0%	0%	.610
Schmidt	4.21	3.09	7.30	45%	15%	42%	27%	3%	12%	27%	45%	27%	9%	64%	21%	6%	.529
Van Poppel	4.71	3.86	8.57	14%	0%	43%	29%	0%	29%	14%	57%	29%	0%	57%	14%	29%	.457
PIT	4.09	3.19	7.27	46%	17%	40%	28%	4%	9%	28%	44%	28%	12%	52%	31%	5%	.512

NATIONAL LEAGUE WEST

SAN DIEGO PADRES

C.O JONES

THE LAST DOMINO

The efforts of the local San Diego press to portray Padres owner John Moores as a conniving new-age capitalist eager to build up a sports empire on the order of The Two Jerrys (Reinsdorf and Colangelo) did not translate into defeat of Proposition C at the ballot box on November 3, so tourists and the tourism industry will spend several decades subsidizing much of the cost of a new stadium.

The irony here is that, for once, the newspaper reports were correct, and yet it didn't matter. In a brilliant stroke of fortune, the 1998 Padres parlayed the acquisition of Kevin Brown into a pennant, squeezing one final spurt of juice from a gaggle of creaky veterans, until the team turned into a lemon in the World Series. Moores, his financial hatchet man Larry Lucchino, and head baseball maven Kevin Towers—the left coast's answer to Andy Hardy—reaped massive benefit from this storybook scenario, which managed to retain enough glitter despite being handed its lunch in the World Series. (That phrase might best be amended to four-course dinner.)

This inspiring display of Teflon is most appropriate for a region whose politics remain staunchly Reaganite, and it may have a lot to do with the appeal of the rumpled Moores, who is a master of aura. Like Bill Clinton, Moores has an ability to make people believe in some of the most incredible baloney, and he carries it off with a low-key panache that is a trademark of the nineties. Underneath it all, he is as aggressive as they come, however, and there is little doubt that he will attempt to corner the market on as many sports franchises that will heading San Diego's way over the next 3-5 years. (It's a good sign that such is the case when your key advisor—in this case "Lucky" Larry Lucchino—downplays such notions.)

So the Padres' victory in 1998 (as far as it went) was sufficient to get the voters to pony up close to $200 million of public money to give the Padres a new home. This will be the fifteenth new ballpark in the latest sequence of stadium building—the twelfth undertaken for a non-expansion team. And of all these new parks, the as-yet unnamed new San Diego Stadium may be the least necessary. Let's look at some factors that pertain to ballpark development, and see what we discover.

First, we're going to bypass the issue of economic revitalization, since it is so clearly prominent in the rhetoric of ballpark divination, and is so prominently a bogey. There is so much "corporate welfare" in these developments that the notion of a substantial benefit to local revenue is clearly misguided—or, perhaps, misdirected, since we should be looking at who will make the most from the development (the developers, initially, and the team owners, over the course of operation and from their ability to sell the team at a handsome profit).

Here is a list of the seventeen existing or proposed new ballparks of the nineties. They are ranked on three categories: age and condition of the previous facility, the need to boost the viability of the franchise at the point in time when the new park is built, and what we'll call the "domino effect," or the incentive to the current ownership to use new infrastructure as a way to move into different spheres of business. We'll abbreviate these (the most important thing to learn here in the waning hours of the nineties) as Facility, Franchise, and $$. We'll rank each category from 1 to 10, because Don Malcolm wouldn't want it any other way. The $$ ranking, by the way, is subtracted from the other two to create the final Total.

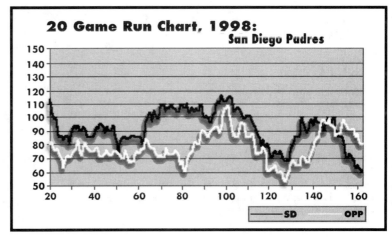

20 Game Run Chart, 1998: San Diego Padres

QMAX PRESENTS: "BAD" PITCHERS

SHOW, AS IN "POW!"

Eric Show was an interesting guy. He is most remembered now as the pitcher who gave up hit number 4,192 to Pete Rose (and who set in immortal example of sportsmanship for the kiddies by sitting on the mound and sulking through the ensuing celebration). He was also notable for being a devout and voluble member of the John Birch Society. My first inkling of the Birchers came around 1969, when I put ketchup on my burger in the shape of a peace sign and my father warned "the Birchers will get you for that." Well, they didn't, although possibly they're still after me for that; there is an American Opinion Bookstore on 4th street where I live.

But enough politics. Let's get back to Bad Pitching. Eric Show had reached the end of the road in 1990, perhaps from his butt getting stiff from sitting on the mound all that time the summer before. He started the year decently enough, with two Quality Starts in his first three attempts (true, they were kind of "slink over the bar" quality starts, with three runs in six innings each time), but starts 4,5, and 6 were unambiguously horrid, with Show failing to see the fifth inning each time. The Pads pulled the plug on Show at this point, and he didn't get another start until July. He fared a little better this time, although he was in the QMAX "success square" just once in five July/August starts. He got one last start in October garbage time, and finished out the string with the A's the next year.

ERIC SHOW/SD 1990								
	1	2	3	4	5	6	7	S
1								0
2								0
3			1					1
4		1	1					2
5					1			1
6			2	2	3			7
7		1						1
C	0	2	3	4	3	0	0	12

From a first glance I sort of wondered why Eric seemed to get the hook so much sooner than the other Bad Pitchers I've looked at, and I idly wondered if his Birchiness was rubbing people the wrong way in San Diego. It's possible, I suppose, but San Diego is more receptive country than most to the Birch ideology, and 1990 was also a simpler time, a time when a five-plus ERA was actually enough to cause a pitcher to lose his job. Be sure to tell your grandkids about that, huh?

--Tom Austin

Stadium	Team	Facility	Franchise	$$	Total
Bank One	AZ	10	10	-8	13
Turner Field	ATL	7	4	-7	4
Oriole Park	BAL	8	9	-8	9
Comiskey	CHI	10	5	-8	7
TBA	CIN	8	8	-5	11
Jacobs	CLE	10	8	-7	11
Coors	COL	8	9	-7	11
New Tiger	DET	9	8	-5	12
TBA	HOU	7	7	-7	7
Miller	MIL	9	9	-6	12
TBA	MON	9	8	-4	13
TBA	NY Mets	8	5	-6	7
PNC Park	PIT	8	9	-6	11
TBA	SD	4	7	-9	2
Pacific Bell	SF	9	6	-7	8
Safeco	SEA	8	6	-6	8
Tropicana	TB	10	10	-6	14
Ballpark	TEX	9	6	-6	9

Diego's current home is clearly in the best shape. (By the way, you'll notice that two of the three expansion teams with new parks during the nineties have 10s under Facility, while one—Colorado—has only an "8". That is because their original home, Mile High Stadium, is still under use by their old co-tenants.)

Sorting the Facility List in descending order, we have:

10-Arizona, Chicago, Cleveland, Tampa

9-Texas, San Francisco, Montreal, Milwaukee, Detroit

8-Baltimore, Cincinnati, Colorado, New York, Seattle

7-Atlanta, Houston

4-San Diego

Fatally flawed parks (White Sox and Indians) or new start-up parks where none are currently available (Arizona, Tampa) rate 10s. Seriously flawed parks (for whatever reason, and the five in this category cover the waterfront) rate 9s. Moderately flawed parks rate 8s, while modestly flawed parks rate 7s.

Only one facility falls well under this scale. Take a wild guess which one..

Now I've heard a lot of counterarguments (actually, a set of variations on the same counterargument) that there are serious flaws with Qualcomm Stadium, but most of these have to do with competing economic interests and a feud between the Padres and the Chargers. The genius of John Moores has been

Now there were several factors used in generating each category ranking, but space doesn't permit us to delve into all of them. I will admit that a good amount of subjectivity is exhibited herein. However, it's clear that or all the existing stadia being left behind in order to construct the new parks on the list, San to not take an overtly petulant, I'll-take-my-marbles-and-go-home-approach; he has managed to sell people on the ludicrous idea that the improvements to the stadium made for the Chargers have somehow turned it into a living hell for baseball. This, of course, is nonsense of the highest order, but like much of what has gone on in this decade, it seems to have been swallowed whole by a gullible populace too easily swayed by its Sports Inferiority Complex (or SIC, an acronym that will make Dandy Don exceedingly proud of me even as he groans long and loud into the night).

Let's go on to the Franchise ranking, and sort these in descending order for ease of viewing.

10-Arizona, Tampa

9-Baltimore, Colorado, Milwaukee, Pittsburgh

8-Cincinnati, Cleveland, Detroit, Montreal

7-San Diego

6-Texas, Seattle, Houston,

5-New York

4-Atlanta

For the most part this ranking is based upon market size, but as you can see the start-up costs of a new franchise are heavily weighted here, which is why the two newest teams rate 10s. Market size and lack of regional competition caused me to drop Colorado down a notch. (Florida isn't on the list because they do not have a new stadium, despite the elaborate efforts of outgoing owner and blackmailer/contortionist Wayne Huizenga.)

Baltimore is ranked highly due to the particular circumstances that the franchise found itself in during the five years before its transformation into a "large market" franchise, and the fact that they were unable to tap most of their unusually-distributed market area without a new facility. Similar problems and challenges exist in Milwaukee and Pittsburgh—and, for that matter, in all of the Midwest belt of teams: those problems are more acute in those two cities than in Cincinnati, Cleveland and Detroit, with larger market sizes. Montreal is a special case: clearly in need of image reconstruction, but not nearly as bad off as is so often claimed.

When you get to the Padres, you see that they are the top of a tier of teams that are in the Sun Belt or the Rain Belt, but areas where economic growth and population influx is still humming along at a good clip. And finally, you have the Mets, whose need to compete with the Yankees adds a notch or two to get them over Atlanta, where Ted's ego is a significant factor in the development of the new park, and is largely irrelevant to the needs of the franchise. For the Braves, the new park was a perk.

And now we get to the $$, or the "Domino Effect"—or the business motivation element. Abbreviating this to the "greed quotient" would be tempting, but there's a bit more to it than that. Simply put, baseball has changed more behind the scenes than it has on the field over the past thirty years. The motivations for being an owner are completely different, even if the class behavior and ruling class attitudes seem similar (and all-too-familiar). I don't necessarily object to the idea that rich folk should be allowed to play with expensive toys, even if they are things like sports franchises; that is the prerogative of

WPA BULLPEN BOX—SAN DIEGO PADRES

	PI	WPA	P	PPPI
Starters	1069	6.6	56.4	0.053
Relievers	524	8.9	35.7	0.068
Road	284	2.1	19.2	0.068
Home	240	6.8	16.5	0.069
Mar/Apr	100	3.3	6.6	0.066
May	87	-0.1	5.3	0.061
June	81	0.8	5.1	0.063
July	78	1.8	5.3	0.069
August	84	2.9	5.9	0.070
September	94	0.3	7.4	0.079
Non S/H Sit.	357	2.9	17.5	0.049
S/H Sit.	167	6.0	18.2	0.109
Low Pressure	200	0.8	3.0	0.015
Med. Pressure	162	-1.3	12.1	0.075
High Pressure	162	9.4	20.6	0.127
Entered behind	179	0.5	4.9	0.027
Entered tied	92	2.3	10.2	0.111
Entered ahead	253	6.1	20.6	0.082

Name	G	PI	WPA	P	PPPI	MI	ROB	T
Boehringer B	55	90	.3	4.4	.049	28	21	11
Bruske J	4	8	-.2	.2	.026	3	1	0
Hitchcock S	12	15	.1	.8	.056	3	6	1
Hoffman T	66	81	6.5	8.7	.108	15	16	10
Langston M	6	6	-.1	.6	.098	0	3	1
Miceli D	67	91	1.6	7.7	.085	22	18	14
Myers R	21	23	-.2	2.4	.106	2	6	4
Ramirez R	21	29	.7	1.4	.048	8	11	2
Reyes C	22	35	-.3	1.9	.055	10	10	2
Sanders S	23	37	.3	1.5	.042	11	10	1
Wall D	45	71	.6	4.9	.068	22	7	7
Wengert D	10	16	.1	.4	.028	4	1	1
Total		524	8.9	35.7	.068			

	|-------- Quality ----------|				|--- Pressure -------|		
	Dis.	Poor	Fair	Good	Her.	Lo	Med	Hi	
Boehringer B	2	7	34	11	1	27	16	12	(8)
Hitchcock S	0	2	8	2	0	6	5	1	(0)
Hoffman T	3	2	13	41	7	13	23	30	(26)
Miceli D	6	5	25	28	3	21	28	18	(13)
Myers R	3	2	9	7	0	6	12	3	(2)
Ramirez R	0	2	13	5	1	15	2	4	(4)
Reyes C	3	1	14	3	1	13	4	5	(3)
Sanders S	0	4	14	4	1	15	4	4	(3)
Wall D	4	7	17	17	0	13	20	12	(9)
Others	2	5	26	3	1	26	8	3	(3)
TOTAL	23	37	173	121	15	155	122	92	(71)

	7th inning			8th inning			9th inning		
	0	+1	+2	0	+1	+2	0	+1	+2
Boehringer B	3	2	1	5	1	3	0	0	0
Bruske J	0	0	1	0	0	0	0	0	0
Hitchcock S	0	0	0	1	0	2	0	0	0
Hoffman T	0	0	0	0	0	0	3	18	18
Langston M	0	0	0	0	1	0	0	0	0
Miceli D	2	0	0	3	12	5	4	1	0
Myers R	0	1	0	1	3	2	2	1	0
Ramirez R	1	0	0	1	0	1	0	1	0
Reyes C	0	1	2	0	0	0	1	0	0
Sanders S	0	2	0	0	0	0	0	0	0
Wall D	3	6	3	2	5	1	1	0	0
Starters	17	13	12	6	7	5	3	3	0
TOTAL	26	25	19	19	29	19	14	24	18
Record	12-14	21-4	18-1	11-8	25-4	19-0	7-7	24-0	18-0

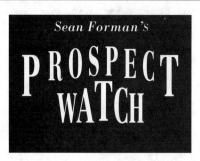

Sean Forman's

PROSPECT WATCH

NAME	AGE	POS	LEVEL	GR98	GR97	GR96	AVG
Mike Darr	22	OF	AA	61	60	-	61
Aaron Guiel	25	3B	AAA	61	63	35	57
Gary Matthews	23	OF	AA	60	47	-	55
George Arias	26	3B	AAA	56	43	71	54
Ben Davis	21	C	AA	63	47	28	52
Juan Melo	22	SS	AAA	56	52	41	52
Creighton Gubanich	26	C	AAA	46	51	47	48

NAME	AGE	POS	LEVEL	GRADE
Kevin Eberwein	21	3B	Low A	50
Alex Garcia	19	2B	Rookie	46
Kevin Burford	20	OF	Low A	43
Peter Paciorek	22	1B	High A	40

NAME	AGE	GS	S	C	T	W-L	ERA	K/H	LEVEL
Buddy Carlyle	20	28	3.79	2.68	6.46	14-7	3.44	0.54	High
Brian Tollberg	25	21	4.05	2.62	6.67	8-7	5.30	0.91	High
Matt Clement	23	26	3.46	3.54	7.00	10-9	3.92	1.05	High
Kevin Lomon	26	17	4.00	3.71	7.71	2-9	5.15	0.92	High
Ray Ricken	23	21	4.29	3.67	7.95	5-8	5.65	0.97	High
Eric Estes	25	26	4.73	3.38	8.12	12-6	4.97	0.59	High
Heath Murray	24	27	4.74	3.44	8.19	9-11	4.99	0.63	High
Eric Newman	25	24	4.38	4.13	8.50	9-11	5.59	0.79	High
Brad Kaufman	26	28	4.54	4.21	8.75	10-11	5.72	0.64	High
Stan Spencer	28	21	3.43	2.95	6.38	12-6	3.93	1.13	High

The Padres haven't produced very many top prospects in the last few years and it shows in the advanced age of their team. They are certainly happy with the results they have managed the last few years, but it now appears that they will need to rebuild some. That said the Padres don't have much talent on the way either. Ruben Rivera will become a good player and Ben Davis will hold his own as well, but there aren't any other plus players on the way.

CANNON ARM: Ben Davis

The Padres picked Davis second overall in the 1995 draft after the Angels picked Darin Erstad. Doing so they passed on college players like Jose Cruz, Todd Helton, and Matt Morris, and high schoolers like Chad Hermansen, Michael Barrett, and a Texan named Kerry Wood. A Baseball America study of first round draft picks showed that high school catchers are riskier picks than high school pitchers.

After his first few years, Davis appeared a potential draft bust as well, but that can't be said anymore. Davis has improved enough with the bat that he it is no longer a liability. He is a switch-hitter, which is unusual for a catcher and is considered a major league caliber receiver already. He is a thrower on the order of Ivan Rodriguez as he's thrown out nearly 50% of all opposing basestealers. I still have questions about his bat. His plate discipline has been acceptable just once, but he has slugged over .450 the last two years and was just a 21-year-old in AA. I suspect he will be with the big league squad some time this year and a starter for good by the beginning of next year. Comp: Greg Myers, at the plate only.

HOT CORNER: George Arias

Arias appears to be the new third baseman as San Diego let Ken Caminiti depart. Arias is no spring chicken as he will be 27 next year, but the Padres should be able to skim off the cream of his career the next two or three years. With little room on the big league squad, Arias went crazy in Las Vegas totalling 36 home runs in just 435 at bats. I think he'll be solid in his new role, probably around a .750 OPS. Comp: Mike Blowers.

WIMPY II: Pete Paciorek

For all of Hawk and Wimpy's blather about Ozzie Guillen, it didn't seem to wear off on Wimpy's progeny. Pete draws a good number of walks (63), strikes out a lot (135) and has some fairly good power (.466 SLG%). However he is a 22 year old first baseman in Fast A ball, so his numbers aren't extraordinary. If he takes some sort of a step up, he'll be an all right ballplayer.

YOUNG 'UN: Kevin Burford

Last year I waxed poetic about a certain Padre farmhand named Brandon Pernell. I mentioned how he was moving to the California League, how he was due for a big upturn, and how he was error-free, blah, blah, blah. Well, Brandon hit .200/.275/.376, and needless to say he's not making the Violent Phlegm's (my Ultra team) keeper list. Forget Pernell—Burford is the man this year. He stole 15 bases in 19 attempts this year and walked 62 times in 446 at bats. So what if he hit just .258 and slugged .374, he's going to a high offense league. He'll be on everyone's tongues by the end of next year, just you watch.

ON THE MOUND: Matt Clement

Clement's numbers don't look outstanding, but with respect to his park and league they are quite good. Clement is a right-hander, who is tremendously hard on right-handed batter (just .214 BA against), but he can be hurt by lefties (.281). Clement faded as the season went along, which causes me to wonder if his 1997 workload was catching up with him. He pitched 189 innings in 1997 and faced 29 batters per start in 1997 and 28 per start in 1998. That is way too high. Bruce Bochy if you are reading, let Clement throw about two innings in middle relief every fourth game, and I suspect you will be rewarded with an ace starter in a couple of years. Clement is also a bit of a headhunter as he hit 30 batters last year. Rolando Arrojo led the majors with 19.

wealth. What I object to is the idea of people using franchises as a means to empire. Most of the owners in baseball are not really doing this: they've made their money elsewhere, and are content to have a plaything. Very few owners are trying to create a sports empire: the Reinsdorfs, Huizengas and Colangelos are still the exception to the rule.

And this, I submit, is where the Wrath of Jones needs to be shrink-wrapped around the nerdy aggression of John Moores, who is following in the footsteps of the Reinsdorfians. The fact that he is far more adept at it and has managed to conceal the hard edge of what his project is about is not a point in his favor; in fact, it is a reason to be far more concerned about what may follow.

And that is why I've bestowed an extra negative point on Moores over and above the rankings given to Reinsdorf and Colangelo. That gives us "Domino Effect" scale as follows:

One of the factors used here the amount of public financing provided for the construction of the new stadium, and the

-9-San Diego
-8-Chicago, Arizona, Baltimore
-7-San Francisco, Colorado, Cleveland, Atlanta
-6-Milwaukee, New York, Pittsburgh, Seattle, Tampa Bay, Texas
-5-Cincinnati, Detroit
-4-Montreal

334

other benefits granted to the teams. That's factored in with the motivation of the owners for acquiring a new stadium. For franchises·such as Cincinnati or Montreal, where there is uncertainty concerning the ownership group itself, I'm more generous in my grading (no matter how uncharacteristic that may seem).

Adding all this up—and that is assuming that we should weight these elements equally—we have the following rankings, organized by subjective category:

11+Totally Necessary New Parks
Tampa, Arizona, Cincinnati, Cleveland, Detroit, Milwaukee, Montreal, Pittsburgh

8-10 Moderately Necessary New Parks
Baltimore, San Francisco, Seattle, Texas

5-7 Marginally Necessary New Parks
Chicago, Houston, New York

below 5 Totally Unnecessary New Parks
Atlanta, San Diego

Though there's some room for quibbling about the placement of a few teams at the top of the list, the method does do a good job of separating out the legitimate projects from the ones that should have been left on the drawing board. And for those who question whether the White Sox belong in the "marginal" list, consider this: another owner could have renovated the existing ballpark a la the effort undertaken in Anaheim, thus preserving historical continuity. That would have been very costly, but also had a very high chance of long-term payoff. Reinsdorf chose instead to extort a new park as part of a plan to consolidate his sports empire, and gave the city of Chicago a new facility that is distinctly inferior to the one it replaced.

Likewise, one wonders whether John Moores will cut and run at the first sign of setback for his new meal ticket. (As in sell out, not threaten to move: part of the terms of Prop C is to keep the Padres in town for the next 30 years. Such long-term guarantees, however, often turn into chokeholds of one form or another.) Such setback could take a number of forms, but the most likely in the short-term is a disastrous falloff in the team's fortunes as its new stadium launch date approaches. The next three years may not be particularly kind to the Padres: they have mortgaged their team around veterans and have traded away most of their top-notch prospects in earlier deals. Their projected lineup in 1999, as this is written is:

Quilvio Veras	2b
Chris Gomez	ss
Tony Gwynn	rf
Greg Vaughn	lf
Wally Joyne	1b
Jim Leyritz	c
Ruben Rivera	cf
George Arias	3b

If this is in fact the lineup that the Padres go with, they have an excellent chance of scoring the fewest runs in the NL. Fewer even than Tampa Bay over in the AL , which has trouble scoring even with four outs. With With Kevin Brown now ensconced 120 miles further north, the Padres aɪe looking at a starting rotation of Andy Ashby, Sterling Hitchcock, Woody Williams (just acquired from Toronto for Joey Hamilton) and two rookies, Stan Spencer and Matt Clement. Ashby is fragile; Hamilton has been declining every year since his rookie season; Hitchcock has yet to show any consistency. There is a nightmare worst-case scenario here:

Year	RS	RA	W-L
1998	749	635	98-64
1999?	660	745	72-90

Sans Brown, there will be a heavy burden on four inexperienced players (Arias, Rivera, Spencer, Clement) to stem the tide of advancing age (Gwynn, Joyner, Leyritz), inconsistency (Vaughn, Veras, Hitchcock), fragility (Ashby), unpredictability

TEAM BREAKOUT
PADRES 1998

Category	RS	RA	W	L	Pct.	Rk
5+ RUNS SCORED/HOME	207	93	30	0	1.000	1
CLOSE SLUGFESTS/HOME	24	21	3	0	1.000	1
5+ RUNS SCORED	523	312	60	9	.870	2
SLUGFESTS/HOME	69	65	7	2	.778	1
5+ RUNS SCORED/ROAD	316	219	30	9	.769	6
4- RUNS ALLOWED/ROAD	174	86	29	10	.744	4
4- RUNS ALLOWED	427	222	76	27	.738	5
4- RUNS ALLOWED/HOME	253	136	47	17	.734	10
CLOSE SLUGFESTS/ROAD	111	103	10	4	.714	4
RECORD IN SLUGFESTS	328	284	27	13	.675	2
SLUGFESTS/ROAD	259	219	20	11	.645	3
LOW SCORING GAMES/HOME	111	86	27	16	.628	5
CLOSE LOW SCORING GAMES/HOME	67	57	18	11	.621	8
RECORD IN CLOSE GAMES/HOME	142	128	27	17	.614	5
RECORD IN LOW SCORING GAMES	171	140	42	27	.609	2
SEASON TOTALS	749	635	98	64	.605	3
RECORD IN CLOSE GAMES	334	308	51	34	.600	1
CLOSE LOW SCORING GAMES/ROAD	38	32	10	7	.588	1
RECORD IN BLOWOUTS/ROAD	134	101	10	7	.588	4
RECORD IN CLOSE GAMES/ROAD	192	180	24	17	.585	1
RECORD IN BLOWOUTS	206	164	18	13	.581	5
LOW SCORING GAMES/ROAD	60	54	15	11	.577	1
RECORD IN BLOWOUTS/HOME	72	63	8	6	.571	7
4- RUNS SCORED/HOME	125	160	24	27	.471	2
5+ RUNS ALLOWED/HOME	79	117	7	10	.412	2
4- RUNS SCORED	226	323	38	55	.409	2
5+ RUNS ALLOWED	322	413	22	37	.373	1
5+ RUNS ALLOWED/ROAD	243	296	15	27	.357	1
4- RUNS SCORED/ROAD	101	163	14	28	.333	3

(Williams), and mediocrity (Gomez, backup catcher Carlos Hernandez). The one rock-solid feature of this team, closer Trevor Hoffman, can be neutralized by a collision of the contrarities currently circulating in Mission Valley. (After all, having Ugueth Urbina did not transform the Expos into contenders.)

Nor is there much additional help on the farm, either. What the San Diego sports fans with their SIC have ponied up for is the proverbial pig in a poke, and John Moores is betting that he can ride out three or four years of drought on a wave of golden memories. If he can't, he'll wait until the stadium comes on line, and sell. He's played the game like a high-stakes gambler, and he's been on a hot streak. The problem is that neither he, "Lucky" Larry, nor the citizens of San Diego have any backup plan in case the dice suddenly go cold. The first domino that falls here is also going to be the last.

																Adj	Raw			
Name	AB	R	H	D	T	HR	RBI	BB	SO	SB	CS	BA	OBP	SLG	XR	XR/27	XR/27	OXW	DXW	TXW
Caminiti K	448	100	122	35	0	30	93	75	98	6	2	.273	.376	.550	94	7.47	6.53	5.43	-0.09	5.34
Cianfrocco A	72	4	10	4	0	1	6	5	20	1	0	.141	.208	.243	2	1.00	0.57	-0.60	0.09	-0.51
Finley S	617	103	165	49	6	14	77	47	92	11	3	.268	.322	.438	86	4.91	4.20	2.95	1.04	3.99
Giovanola E	138	20	33	3	3	1	9	23	20	1	2	.235	.342	.322	16	3.87	3.70	0.28	0.56	0.84
Gomez C	447	64	129	38	3	4	44	53	80	1	3	.289	.369	.418	65	5.15	4.36	2.53	2.61	5.14
Gwynn T	460	71	156	42	0	16	78	36	16	3	1	.340	.383	.538	85	7.07	6.28	4.71	0.31	5.02
Hernandez C	389	40	108	18	0	9	61	17	48	2	2	.277	.320	.395	43	3.80	3.31	0.60	2.12	2.72
Joyner W	437	64	139	36	1	12	89	53	39	1	2	.318	.390	.488	76	6.56	5.78	4.00	0.42	4.42
Leyritz J	142	18	41	11	0	4	20	22	35	0	0	.285	.403	.447	26	6.83	6.09	1.46	0.38	1.84
Mouton J	63	10	13	2	2	0	8	7	10	4	3	.213	.289	.300	5	2.37	1.68	-0.21	0.11	-0.10
Myers G	170	22	44	11	0	4	21	18	32	0	1	.260	.328	.396	20	4.13	3.66	0.44	0.74	1.18
Rivera R	171	36	40	9	3	6	31	29	46	5	1	.233	.351	.421	28	5.62	4.71	1.23	0.23	1.46
Sheets A	193	34	51	6	5	7	34	22	57	6	2	.264	.341	.453	30	5.45	4.57	1.24	0.62	1.86
Sweeney M	190	19	47	9	3	2	17	28	34	1	2	.246	.340	.358	24	4.27	3.82	0.61	0.15	0.76
Vaughn G	569	127	165	33	5	51	133	83	109	10	4	.290	.383	.634	132	8.51	7.65	8.16	0.68	8.84
Veras Q	513	93	147	30	2	6	53	88	70	23	8	.286	.395	.389	86	6.02	5.24	4.19	2.53	6.72
SD	**5461**	**849**	**1485**	**350**	**34**	**171**	**806**	**633**	**967**	**74**	**34**	**.272**	**.350**	**.442**	**841**	**5.38**	**4.68**	**37.03**	**12.50**	**49.53**

Pitcher	S	C	T	SS	ES	IC	HH	PP	TJ	S12	S35	S67	C1	C23	C45	C67	QWP
Ashby	3.76	2.67	6.42	67%	18%	48%	18%	3%	18%	24%	58%	18%	27%	48%	21%	3%	.578
Boehringer	6.00	4.00	10.00	0%	0%	0%	100%	0%	0%	0%	0%	100%	0%	0%	100%	0%	.163
Clement	4.00	4.50	8.50	50%	0%	0%	0%	0%	0%	0%	100%	0%	0%	0%	100%	0%	.382
Hitchcock	3.81	3.04	6.85	52%	15%	41%	19%	7%	7%	30%	52%	19%	15%	52%	33%	0%	.557
J Hamilton	3.94	3.68	7.62	50%	6%	32%	26%	12%	0%	26%	47%	26%	9%	32%	50%	9%	.485
K Brown	3.46	2.14	5.60	66%	26%	69%	14%	3%	23%	31%	54%	14%	49%	37%	11%	3%	.666
Langston	5.13	4.25	9.38	19%	0%	19%	50%	6%	6%	13%	38%	50%	0%	19%	63%	19%	.288
P Smith	4.38	3.88	8.25	38%	0%	25%	50%	13%	0%	25%	25%	50%	0%	38%	63%	0%	.434
Spencer	3.80	2.80	6.60	80%	0%	20%	20%	0%	0%	0%	80%	20%	20%	60%	20%	0%	.535
Wall	3.00	3.00	6.00	100%	0%	0%	0%	0%	0%	0%	100%	0%	0%	100%	0%	0%	.633
SDP	**3.92**	**3.08**	**7.00**	**54%**	**13%**	**42%**	**24%**	**6%**	**10%**	**25%**	**51%**	**24%**	**21%**	**40%**	**35%**	**5%**	**.532**

NATIONAL LEAGUE WEST

SAN FRANCISCO GIANTS

TOM AUSTIN

CLOSE, BUT NO CIGAR

They did it again. The Giants cranked up the hurdy-gurdy, taking their fans on another funhouse ride through the Hall of Low Expectations, the steep slope of unexpected success, the stomach-pitching July Free-fall, the August muddle, and the September of rough magic and near misses. Get your hopes up, get 'em up right here, folks. See the Giants do battle with the $60 million Payroll Monsters! See the Pitching staff in their magnificent Geritol machine! Boo the petulant superstar! Count the days to the new stadium, count 'em right here on our fabulous foul-pole display! And don't forget to buy that PSL, they're going fast my friend, only a dozen good seats left going fast, step right up, a measly five large buys you three chances to knock over the milk bottles! Why, a mere child could do it!

Life for Giants fans is never easy; they are either bemoaning their team's horrid play or anxiously chewing on their hats when the boys are winning, afraid lest the merest hiccup upset the Baseball Gods, who will then vindictively wreak vengeance on the team. While fans elsewhere may dismiss this as low-grade X-files paranoia worthy of a place known as Babylon by the Bay, Giants fans have a point. The team has never won a World Series in San Francisco, and while there is no voodoo hex akin to the Curse of the Bambino, Jim Mutrie's Big Men have specialized in the art of the setback. It's gotten so bad that Giants fans have taken a rueful pride in it.

More accurately, though, they are taking pride (perverse and unintentional though it be) in the operatic style in which the Giants disappoint their fans. For the Giants have perfected the art of the Near Miss and the frantic, game-tooshort comeback. No team since 1958, when the Giants moved west, has compiled such a record of heartbreak.

Or so they say. And so I ask, is it true? Let's take a look.

As with all questions of this type, we need to invent a measuring stick on the fly. Just how do you measure a team's propensity to break hearts? After all,

every year, every team but one ends its season on a losing note. Which hurts more, to finish 29 games in the cellar or to lose in the seventh game of the World Series? Let's put that question on hold for a minute while I lay down some categories, bins into which I will sort team's performances:

1 We Will (we will) Rock You: your team wins it all. Nothing less will do.

2 So Close and Yet So Far: You get to the World Series and lose. Four-game sweep or seventh-game nailbiter, a Series loss is a series loss. But at least you got there. Lots of happy memories to ease the sting.

3 Is That All There Is? You reach the post-season and lose, either in the "Division Series" or whatever they're calling it, or in the LCS. You get to hang a banner in center field, but you don't remember watching the series on TV because you were either drinking or crying too much to watch it. You watched "Hogan's Heroes" reruns instead

4 Hurts So Good: Your team was in the hunt until the last week or the last day, until you lost the series you had to sweep because your cleanup hitter went 1-for 14 or your stopper, pitching with an inflamed bunion on his big toe, got knocked out of the box in the third inning.

5 One Step forward, Two Steps Back: your team muddles around the .500 mark all year, never really threatening the leaders (wild card, division, or otherwise) after the all-star break.

6 Love Stinks: Your team screws the pooch from day one,

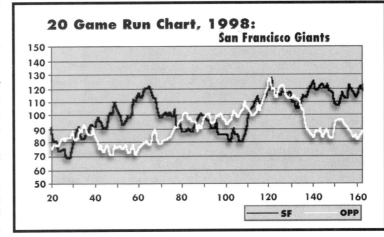

QMAX PRESENTS: "BAD" PITCHERS

COME AND GET IT!

In the manly world of baseball, the finesse pitcher's name is taken in vain by many a batter stomping back to the dugout after yet another 4-3 putout, muttering "challenge me, you (fork)!" in sneering reference to the pitcher's (lack of) stuff. Fortunately for his livelihood, most junkball pitchers turn the other cheek to this jab, knowing on what their daily bread depends. Until Terry Mulholland, that is.

As recently as 1993, Terry had been a stud lefthander for the pennant-winning, hairy-chested Phils, going 12-9 with a sparkling 3.25 ERA. By 1995, however, he had maybe lost a yard off a fastball that was never all that fast anyway, pushing him into the heart of QMAX's hostile "soldier of fortune" territory, where control pitch-

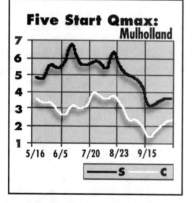

Five Start Qmax: Mulholland

ers go to die. It appears that Terry, like a lot of pitchers, wasn't ready to trade in his macho swagger for the nibbler's paintbrush. A look at Terry's 1995 QMAX bears this out; unlike most of the sad sack pitchers I've been writing about, this is not a pitcher trying to live in the inky blackness at the edge of the plate. This is a guy still full of bravado, saying "Here's my fastball. Just try and hit it."

Don't believe me? Take a look at that QMAX chart. Only once did Terry walk as many as four batters in a start, and only four times did he walk even three. Ah, but you say, I've read up on my QMAX and my Bill James, and you're talking vintage Tommy John pitching here! Throw strikes, get ground balls,

TERRY MULHOLLAND/SF 1995	1	2	3	4	5	6	7	5
1	2							2
2	1		2					3
3	1		1					2
4								0
5	1		1		1			3
6	1		2	2				5
7			2	5	2			9
C	6	0	8	7	3	0	0	24

let your defense do the work.

Now look a little closer. Your typical soldier of fortune nibbler (one who is not in denial, anyway) will always try to dance away from the sweet spot of the bat. If he gets hit hard one start, the next start will find him just a little farther off the plate, mugging for the ump and hoping his catcher can frame his pitches that much better. This means there will be spikes in his QMAX command line when neither ump nor catcher are cooperating. The absence of days like those in Terry's 1995 season point to the other conclusion: the man was still catching plenty of the plate and still challenging those hitters, just like when he was a young stallion, full of beer and vinegar. You'd think those 22 dingers he gave up in his 24 starts would have clued him in, but you know how it is: the poor sap is always the last guy to see it.

--Tom Austin

---

averting 100 losses with a 4-2 run in the last week of the year. Any team with 90 or more losses gets a nod in this l'amour peu category.

Those are the categories. Now for point values. Remember, this is subjective. You're free to disagree, but then again, I've got the pen and you don't. The higher the point value, the higher the "heartbreak quotient".

1) We will Rock You: +50 points. Winning a world championship, even five years back, is such a sweet memory that the next five years just don't hurt as bad.

2) So Close and Yet So Far: +10 points. You didn't win it all, but you got bragging rights on your real rivals, the teams in your league and your division.

3) Is That All There is? -5 points. It's starting to hurt now.

You reached the postseason, but the way you lost will stick with you all winter.

4) Hurts So Good: -20 points. This, I submit, is the most painful experience for a fan. For most of September, that AM-radio headpiece has been stuck into your ear like an implant, your boss is starting to grumble about "productivity", and your wife is doing more than grumbling. And when it's all over, you have bupkis to celebrate.

5) One Step Forward, Two Steps Back: 0 points . On average. -5 points if you declined from the year before, +5 if you rose from the cellar to mediocrity. We'll stick with zero for simplicity. There's not much heartbreak, generally, in the zone between .450 and .550.

6) Love Stinks: -10 points. It sucks following a lousy team. But your hopes never really get that high. You don't let yourself get vulnerable like almost winning lets you get.

OK, after I set up these categories, off I went into my tattered copy of Total Baseball 4 (and to Sean Lahman's site for 1995-98) and plunged ahead. For simplicity's sake, I set up my spreadsheet to give the standard values as outlined above and went in and manually made the following exceptions to the formula for historic, well-known heartbreaks:

1 1962 Dodgers, -5 for losing in the playoff to the Giants.

2 1964 Phillies, -10 for losing the way they did, with the nine-game losing streak, Chico stealing home to start it, while General Gene Mauch stewed away on the bench.

3 1969 Cubbies, -10 for coughing it up against the Amazin' Mets, even though they finished 9 games out at the end.

4 1978 Red Sox -10 for blowing a 14-game lead and losing on the Bucky *&%$# Dent homer.

5 1980 Dodgers, -5 for rallying to force a playoff with the Astros, then losing.

6 1981 Reds and Cardinals, -10 for having the best record in the division and staying home because the "Lords" of baseball wanted to hand it to the Yankees and the Dodgers with the bush-league "split-season" crap.

7 1984 Cubs -5 for gagging away the LCS to the Padres, and for actually believing they might win a pennant.

8 1986 Angels, -10 for Donnie Moore. Rest in Peace, Donnie.

9 1987 Blue Jays, -5 for earning the "Blow Jays" nickname

10 1993 Giants, -10 for winning 103 games and staying home.

11 1994 Expos, -20 for having the best record in baseball the day the "Lords" of Baseball killed the season. I could have given every team, and every fan, -100 heartbreak points for that year, but that would have just thrown the averages off.

12 1995 Angels, -10 for one of the all-time historic collapses.

13 1998 Giants, -5 for rallying to force a playoff for a wild card, then blowing a 7-0 lead to the Rockies and losing to the Cubs, and former Giant Rod Beck.

There are more I could award, I'm sure, but a lot of it does tend to come out in the wash, and the point values are arbitrary anyway. As I think you will see from the results, it kind of lines up with common sense already.

So what did I find? A treasure trove of stuff, worth an article in itself if you ask me. But since this is the Giants essay, I'll rein myself in. Let's go decade-by-decade (approximately) to see if Giants fans' delusions of heartbreak grandeur are justified.

Part one: What MMMight have been, 1958-68

The Giants had Mays, McCovey, and Marichal, plus Cepeda, Perry, the Alou boys, Jim Ray Hart, and scattered stardom from the likes of Mike McCormick and Don McMahon. Yet they only won one pennant, and even then there's the memory of Bobby Richardson gloving the smoking remains of McCovey's white-hot line drive with the tying and winning runs in scoring position. After that, the Giants finished in second

WPA BULLPEN BOX—SAN FRANCISCO GIANTS

	PI	WPA	P	PPPI
Starters	1011	-4.3	48.5	0.048
Relievers	645	3.4	44.2	0.068
Road	342	1.7	27.5	0.080
Home	303	1.8	16.7	0.055
Mar/Apr	105	2.3	7.2	0.069
May	116	0.7	8.6	0.074
June	107	1.9	7.9	0.074
July	97	0.6	5.6	0.057
August	111	-2.1	8.6	0.077
September	109	0.0	6.3	0.058
Non S/H Sit.	475	3.0	23.7	0.050
S/H Sit.	170	0.4	20.5	0.120
Low Pressure	243	0.5	3.3	0.014
Med. Pressure	209	-0.6	13.0	0.062
High Pressure	193	3.5	27.8	0.144
Entered behind	275	1.4	7.1	0.026
Entered tied	101	1.9	14.3	0.141
Entered ahead	269	0.0	22.8	0.085

Name	G	PI	WPA	P	PPPI	MI	ROB	T
Brock C	13	31	-.1	.4	.014	10	5	0
Darwin D	8	13	.1	.4	.034	4	0	1
Johnstone J	70	106	.5	5.7	.054	30	24	11
Mesa J	32	39	.0	3.0	.078	7	8	8
Morman A	9	10	-.8	.5	.045	1	4	1
Nen R	78	98	3.1	10.5	.107	19	13	19
Ortiz R	9	16	-.1	.3	.017	5	2	0
Poole J	26	43	.1	3.4	.079	11	13	5
Reed S	50	74	1.0	5.0	.067	23	23	5
Rodriguez R	68	96	1.3	7.8	.081	23	35	7
Tavarez J	60	105	-1.6	6.9	.066	35	27	7
Total		**645**	**3.4**	**44.2**	**.068**			

		------ Quality ----------					--- Pressure -------		
	Dis.	Poor	Fair	Good	Her.	Lo	Med	Hi
Brock C	0	0	13	0	0	10	3	0 (0)
Johnstone J	5	7	35	22	1	32	25	13 (10)
Mesa J	2	3	16	11	0	15	12	5 (1)
Nen R	10	2	23	34	9	22	23	33 (24)
Poole J	2	2	18	3	1	12	8	6 (3)
Reed S	3	5	22	19	1	20	17	13 (10)
Rodriguez R	2	10	33	21	2	21	26	21 (13)
Tavarez J	6	14	27	12	1	23	20	17 (8)
Others	2	4	29	1	0	26	7	3 (1)
TOTAL	**32**	**47**	**216**	**123**	**15**	**181**	**141**	**111 (70)**

	7th inning			8th inning			9th inning		
	0	+1	+2	0	+1	+2	0	+1	+2
Darwin D	0	0	0	1	0	0	1	0	0
Johnstone J	1	3	1	2	4	2	5	0	0
Mesa J	0	1	0	1	1	3	2	0	0
Nen R	0	0	0	1	0	1	10	12	18
Ortiz R	0	0	1	0	0	1	0	0	0
Poole J	0	1	0	0	1	1	1	0	0
Reed S	2	0	0	4	5	2	3	0	0
Rodriguez R	4	3	2	4	3	3	1	2	0
Tavarez J	1	1	5	4	3	4	1	0	0
Starters	15	3	11	3	1	3	1	0	0
TOTAL	**23**	**12**	**20**	**20**	**18**	**20**	**25**	**14**	**18**
Record	13-10	8-4	16-4	12-8	12-6	17-3	12-13	12-2	17-1

Sean Forman's

PROSPECT WATCH

NAME	AGE	POS	LEVEL	GR98	GR97	GR96	AVG
Edwards Guzman	21	3B	AAA	77	57	45	65
Jacob Cruz	25	OF	AAA	59	74	63	65
Wilson Delgado	22	SS	AAA	64	74	35	63
Dante Powell	24	OF	AAA	53	60	58	56
Michael Glendenning	21	OF	AA	50	57	55	53
Pedro Feliz	21	3B	AA	49	-	-	49
Yolvit Torrealba	19	C	AA	46	50	41	47
Jay Canizaro	24	2B	AAA	34	50	70	45
Ramon Martinez	25	2B	AAA	47	38	50	45

NAME	AGE	POS	LEVEL	GRADE
Chris Magruder	21	OF	High A	46
William Otero	21	SS	High A	44
Tony Torcato	18	3B	Rookie	43
Giuseppe Chiaramonte	22	C	High A	38

NAME	AGE	GS	S	C	T	W-L	ERA	K/H	LEVEL
Chris Brock	27	16	3.69	2.63	6.31	10-3	3.29	1.01	High
Steve Soderstrom	25	22	4.00	3.09	7.09	10-4	4.05	0.72	High
Jason Grilli	21	27	3.89	3.52	7.41	9-11	4.14	0.85	High
Randy Phillips	27	24	4.29	3.13	7.42	10-4	4.28	0.76	High
Joe Roa	26	27	4.67	2.78	7.44	12-9	5.17	0.51	High
Troy Brohawn	25	19	4.21	3.26	7.47	7-4	5.25	0.60	High
Scott Linebrink	21	21	3.62	4.10	7.71	10-8	5.02	1.27	High
Eddie Oropesa	26	20	4.10	3.85	7.95	7-9	3.78	0.73	High
Nathan Bump	21	13				6-1	1.75	1.65	Low

The Giants have been dealing away talent for the last few years, but some decent drafts may have turned the tide. Due to a mass exodus of free agents, the Giants had seven picks in the first 72 choices of the 1998 draft, and several of those draft picks had solid debuts. Jason Grilli, 1997 #1 pick, and Chiaramonte, also picked in 1997, have played well in their first pro action. The farm system won't be much help for a few years, but there is some talent in the lower levels.

COMMONWEALTH EDISON: Michael Glendenning

I'm grasping at straws here as the Giants don't have a lot of talent at the upper levels. Glendenning has hit fifty home runs in the last two years. His career batting average is just .255 in pro ball, which will not get him noticed. He's a big swinger who misses a lot, but he has some patience and could work in as a fourth outfielder/spot starter at some point. Comp: Sherman Obando with more strikeouts.

HANDY MAN: Dante Powell

Powell was dealt to the Diamondbacks for Alan Embree just after the end of the season. The Giants got sick of waiting for him to develop. Powell has speed coming out of his ears as he's stolen forty bases three of the last four years. However, he will be 25 next year and the Giants have complained that he doesn't have his head screwed on straight. Last year, he batted just .230 in the PCL with some power, but he drew a ton of walks and managed a .350 OBP. If the good Dante Powell (two years ago, he hit 21 home runs) shows up he is a potential 15-40 guy, with enough on-base ability to leadoff. If the bad one shows up, the Giants got a hard-throwing lefty for a fifth outfielder. Comp: Curtis Pride.

YOUNG 'UN: Tony Torcato

Torcato was the Giants' top pick in the 1998 draft. As an 18 year old third baseman, he won't be supplanting Bill Mueller anytime soon, but his debut was encouraging. He debuted in the Northwest League against mostly college talent with a .291/.333/.418 line. League managers voted him the third best prospect in the league behind a pair of collegians. He needs to improve his patience as he moves up the ladder, but there is plenty of time for that.

BACKSTOP: Giuseppe Chiaramonte

Baseball America named Chiaramonte the 10th best prospect in the California League. While batting .273, he showed some excellent power for a backstop with 58 extra base hits including 22 home runs. His plate coverage is lacking as he struck out 139 times in 502 at bats versus just 47 walks. He'll probably move up the Texas League next year and could be in PacBell Park at the China Basin by 2001.

ON THE MOUND: Jason Grilli

Grilli is a graduate of baseball power Seton Hall. You think I'm kidding? John Valentin, Mo Vaughn, Craig Biggio and Matt Morris are all recent Seton Hall alums. Grilli, a 6-4 right-hander, was the Giants' number one pick in 1997, but didn't pitch professionally until this year. Grilli began in AA and pitched quite well, with a 3.79 ERA and a 1.21 WHIP. He was banged around a bit in AAA, but I don't think it was anything of a serious problem. He made 29 starts, but the Giants didn't push him too hard as he averaged just 24 batters faced per start. He has over a hundred-point platoon differential. He will need to even that out before he will see extended success in the big leagues.

place about a hundred times in a row while the Dodgers and the Cardinals traded pennants. This is the decade in which the myth started.

If we look at the results of my scientific survey, however, the Giants are only the seventh most heartbreaking team for the period. Here's the list, listed by average heartbreak per year:

HEARTBREAK QUOTIENT (HQ), 1958-68

Let's take a closer look. The Astros and the Mets take the top two slots, courtesy of being just plain lousy the whole decade. Expansion clubs rank high here—three of the top four teams in HQ

Team	58	59	60	61	62	63	64	65	66	67	68	Avg.
Asros	0	0	0	0	-10	-10	-10	-10	-10	-10	-10	-10.00
Mets	0	0	0	0	-10	-10	-10	-10	-10	-10	0	-8.57
Senators	0	0	0	-10	-10	-10	-10	-10	0	0	-10	-7.50
A's	0	0	-10	-10	-10	0	-10	-10	0	-10	0	-5.45
Phillies	0	-10	-10	-10	0	0	-30	0	0	0	0	-5.45
Twins	-10	-5	0	-10	-20	0	0	10	0	-20	0	-5.00
Giants	0	0	0	0	10	0	-20	-20	-20	0	0	-4.55
Cubs	0	0	-10	-10	-10	0	0	-10	-10	0	0	-4.55
Angels	0	0	0	-10	0	-10	0	0	0	0	-10	-3.75
White Sox	0	10	0	0	0	0	-20	0	0	-20	-10	-3.64
Red Sox	0	0	0	0	0	0	-10	-10	10	0	0	-1.82
Reds	0	0	0	10	0	0	-20	0	0	0	0	-0.91
Indians	0	-5	0	0	0	0	0	0	0	0	0	-0.45
Braves	10	-5	0	0	0	0	0	0	0	0	0	0.45
Tigers	0	0	0	-5	0	0	0	0	0	-20	50	2.27
Pirates	0	0	50	0	0	0	0	0	-20	0	0	2.73
Orioles	0	0	0	0	0	0	-20	0	50	0	0	2.73
Cardinals	0	0	0	0	0	0	50	0	0	50	10	10.00
Dodgers	0	50	0	-20	-30	50	0	50	10	0	0	10.00
Yankees	50	0	10	50	50	10	10	0	-10	-10	0	14.55

for the period. The A's, transitioning from the Yankee farm team to Charlie's version of "Dynasty", are next, followed by the Phils and the Twins, who went from the third floor to a glimpse of the penthouse. The Giants earned their seventh-place finish due to heartbreaking second place finishes in '64, '65, and '66 (they finished second in '67 and '68 too, but by comfortable nine and ten-game margins).

Part Two: the MMorning after, 1969-79

The Giants sleepwalked through the 70s as Mays, McCovey and Marichal got old and the replacement talent (Bobby Bonds, Maddox, Mathews, Perry) got traded. The team won a division title in '71 but lost to the Pirates, and only finished as high as third twice more, 1973 and 1978, both times comfortably behind the winner. The Giants, however, still pulled off a seventh-place "heartbreak quotient" behind lousy expansion teams Seattle, Toronto, San Diego, Montreal, and Seattle/Milwaukee. Of the established teams, only St. Louis broke more hearts than the Giants with near-misses in 1973 and 74 and lousy teams in '76 and '78. Tied with the Giants were late-70s bridesmaids Philadelphia and Kansas City, who earned their "purple hearts" by each losing three straight LCS appearances from 1976-78.

Part Three: HuMMMM-baby, 1980-89

The 1980's saw an emergence from the doldrums, beginning with Joe Morgan's Dodger-killing homer in '82 (although the Giants still earned -20 that year by losing on the last weekend, the day before Morgan's shot, in fact) and continuing with the Roger Craig teams of the late '80's. In fact, the Giants slipped all the way down to 11th on the Trag-o-meter by winning a pennant in 1989 and a division title in 1987. The most heartbreaking teams of the '80's were the star-crossed Angels and Blue Jays (who lost titles most agonizingly from '85-'87), the Reds (with the 1981 fiasco, followed by lousy teams and Rosegate), Texas, Milwaukee, and Montreal (on the "hurts so good" list instead of "love stinks")

Part Four: "Bonds Gets MMillions, and He Still Sucks", 1990-98

In some ways, the 1990's Giants evoke the 60's Giants, with an underappreciated, moody superstar, at times a fine supporting cast, and no championships to support it. The Giants rode an all-time heartbreaker in 1993 , the 1996 dog-team, and near-misses in '97 and '98 to post their highest all-time disappointment score of -8.89 HQ's per year, a total higher than any non-expansion team had posted in previous decades. And yet the Giants only finished fifth. Sure, the D-Boys took the top two slots (all expansion teams do this, you will note), but two established teams have been more disappointing to follow than the Giants in the 90's. One is the near-miss Mets, who manage to miss the wild card by three games with frightening

regularity (this is one reason why HQ scores across the board are higher: more post-season slots mean more near-misses). The other? Hold on to your britches, bay area baseball fans: the second most heartbreaking (established) team in the 90's is none other than the Los Angeles Dodgers. That's right, the Dodgers. They were just plain crappy in '92, and in their contending years ('90, '91, '95-'97) they manage to take a pratfall at just the right time. Oh, how sweet it is.

Wrapup: It's Not a Sprint, it's a MMarathon, 1958-98

We'll toss out the D-boys for now. With their consistent, nay, true-blue ways of raising their hopes and dashing them, the Giants earned the third-place spot among established teams for the entire period, with a score of -5.37 HQ points per year. True, the Win and Place trophies both go to (former) expansion teams, but I feel both teams have more than earned their trophy in rent garments and spilled milk. The second-most disappointing team for the period 1958-98 is the other team I grew up following—the mirror-cracked, black-cat Angels (-6.18 HQ/yr), who as a team embody the term "tragic hero" better than anyone has a right to. Only the Red Sox (that same year, 1986) could manage to top the Grand Opera-style loss that the Angels managed, but at least they did it in the World Series.

TEAM BREAKOUT GIANTS 1998						
Category	RS	RA	W	L	Pct.	Rk
4- RUNS ALLOWED/HOME	268	114	41	10	.804	4
4- RUNS ALLOWED	477	220	71	20	.780	3
4- RUNS ALLOWED/ROAD	209	106	30	10	.750	3
RECORD IN BLOWOUTS/HOME	163	77	14	5	.737	4
5+ RUNS SCORED/ROAD	341	239	35	13	.729	11
5+ RUNS SCORED	677	447	67	25	.728	12
5+ RUNS SCORED/HOME	336	208	32	12	.727	12
CLOSE LOW SCORING GAMES/HOME	30	22	10	5	.667	4
RECORD IN BLOWOUTS	269	186	24	15	.615	3
RECORD IN CLOSE GAMES/HOME	166	154	24	16	.600	7
LOW SCORING GAMES/HOME	45	46	13	10	.565	11
SEASON TOTALS	845	739	89	74	.546	5
RECORD IN LOW SCORING GAMES	82	91	20	19	.513	8
RECORD IN CLOSE GAMES	351	345	40	39	.506	7
RECORD IN BLOWOUTS/ROAD	106	109	10	10	.500	8
SLUGFESTS/HOME	217	170	13	13	.500	11
4- RUNS SCORED/HOME	87	119	17	20	.459	3
RECORD IN SLUGFESTS	414	382	24	29	.453	13
LOW SCORING GAMES/ROAD	37	45	7	9	.438	7
RECORD IN CLOSE GAMES/ROAD	185	191	16	23	.410	12
SLUGFESTS/ROAD	197	212	11	16	.407	12
CLOSE LOW SCORING GAMES/ROAD	24	25	4	6	.400	11
CLOSE SLUGFESTS/HOME	75	79	4	7	.364	15
CLOSE SLUGFESTS/ROAD	87	92	4	8	.333	14
4- RUNS SCORED	168	292	22	49	.310	7
5+ RUNS ALLOWED/HOME	155	213	8	22	.267	7
5+ RUNS ALLOWED	368	519	18	54	.250	10
5+ RUNS ALLOWED/ROAD	213	306	10	32	.238	9
4- RUNS SCORED/ROAD	81	173	5	29	.147	16

The Most Heartbreaking Team award goes to: those French-Canadian heartthrobs, the Montreal Expos! (-6.83 HQ/yr). Sympathetic applause, please. From their Grande Orange days of Misery in Jarry Park to the present (M. Brochu and a "fallen" stadium), the Expos have broken the coeurs of their devout faithful year in and year out, either from bad play, bad players, bad owner, bad ballparks—and when they do get a great team together, wham! Le Strike.

So the Giants are bridesmaids even in heartbreak: the Heartbreak Quotient leaves their fans in exactly the same position they've been in for lo these many years by the Bay. And that's the fetal position. Not futile, not fatal, but awash in amniotic fluid and waiting for the pat on the butt that means it's OK to take that first breath. You know the title of the movie already, don't you? Sure you do—"Waiting to Inhale." Which is probably why Don Malcolm entitled this essay "Close, But No Cigar."

Rk	Team	Average
-	Diamondbacks	-10.00
-	Devil Rays	-10.00
1	Expos	-6.83
2	Angels	-6.18
3	Giants	-5.37
4	Mariners	-5.00
5	Brewers	-4.67
6	Rangers	-4.47
7	Mets	-4.19
8	Cubs	-3.90
9	Padres	-3.83
10	Astros	-3.51
11	Phillies	-3.29
12	White Sox	-3.17
13	Blue Jays	-2.73
14	Red Sox	-2.68
15	Rockies	-2.50
16	Royals	-2.50
17	Indians	-1.83
18	Twins	-1.59
19	Braves	-1.22
20	Tigers	-0.12
21	Pirates	0.12
22	Reds	0.24
23	Orioles	0.24
24	Dodgers	1.46
25	A's	1.46
26	Cardinals	1.83
27	Marlins	5.00

																Adj	Raw			
Name	AB	R	H	D	T	HR	RBI	BB	SO	SB	CS	BA	OBP	SLG	XR	XR/27	XR/27	OXW	DXW	TXW
Aurilia R	413	55	111	29	2	8	50	31	59	3	3	.269	.320	.407	53	4.56	4.53	1.51	2.01	3.52
Benard M	286	42	93	22	1	3	37	34	37	11	4	.326	.399	.440	49	6.47	6.35	2.47	0.17	2.64
Bonds B	554	123	167	46	7	34	125	128	88	27	11	.301	.435	.593	135	8.67	8.93	8.27	0.48	8.75
Burks E	147	22	45	6	1	5	22	19	30	8	1	.307	.388	.461	29	6.91	6.94	1.52	0.48	2.00
Carter J	105	15	31	7	0	6	30	6	12	1	0	.292	.318	.539	19	6.35	6.69	0.89	-0.08	0.81
Diaz A	62	5	8	2	0	0	5	0	14	1	1	.133	.133	.169	-1	-0.25	-0.33	-0.73	0.11	-0.62
Dunston S	51	10	9	2	0	3	8	0	9	0	2	.176	.222	.384	4	2.26	2.32	-0.19	0.08	-0.11
Hamilton D	368	66	109	20	2	1	27	58	51	9	8	.296	.393	.368	55	5.31	5.29	2.21	0.36	2.57
Hayes C	329	40	94	9	0	11	64	34	58	2	1	.285	.350	.411	48	5.35	5.48	1.90	0.47	2.37
Javier S	418	64	123	14	5	4	50	64	60	20	5	.293	.386	.379	64	5.40	5.33	2.59	0.38	2.97
Johnson B	308	35	73	9	1	12	35	28	63	0	2	.238	.310	.389	35	3.77	3.84	0.44	1.68	2.12
Jones C	90	14	17	2	1	2	10	8	27	2	1	.188	.249	.288	8	2.74	2.87	-0.16	0.06	-0.10
Kent J	526	96	156	39	3	28	131	48	106	9	4	.296	.359	.544	98	6.58	6.73	4.79	1.60	6.39
Mayne B	276	26	76	16	0	3	33	36	45	2	1	.276	.360	.367	36	4.62	4.54	1.11	0.87	1.98
Mueller B	535	95	159	29	0	9	60	78	79	3	3	.298	.385	.402	84	5.68	5.57	3.66	1.11	4.77
Sanchez R	316	45	91	15	2	2	31	16	45	0	0	.288	.328	.368	35	3.91	3.81	0.58	1.65	2.23
Snow J	436	67	109	31	1	14	81	57	80	1	2	.251	.333	.420	61	4.74	4.77	1.90	0.75	2.65
SF	5637	863	1553	310	27	148	820	669	991	98	47	.275	.354	.419	840	5.17	5.18	32.76	12.18	44.94

Pitcher	S	C	T	SS	ES	IC	HH	PP	TJ	S12	S35	S67	C1	C23	C45	C67	QWP
D Darwin	4.52	3.52	8.04	40%	8%	16%	32%	0%	0%	12%	56%	32%	4%	52%	36%	8%	.451
Estes	4.00	4.00	8.00	28%	16%	32%	24%	24%	4%	28%	48%	24%	12%	20%	56%	12%	.441
Gardner	3.67	2.97	6.64	55%	24%	52%	21%	9%	3%	45%	33%	21%	18%	45%	36%	0%	.566
Hershiser	3.97	3.59	7.56	44%	9%	35%	26%	6%	3%	29%	44%	26%	6%	50%	35%	9%	.498
Ortiz	6.00	4.00	10.00	0%	0%	0%	100%	0%	0%	0%	0%	100%	0%	0%	100%	0%	.163
R Ortiz	4.00	3.58	7.58	50%	0%	33%	25%	8%	8%	17%	58%	25%	0%	42%	58%	0%	.496
Rueter	4.13	3.38	7.50	47%	9%	34%	38%	3%	0%	28%	34%	38%	9%	59%	22%	9%	.493
SFG	4.04	3.48	7.52	44%	12%	35%	28%	8%	2%	28%	43%	28%	9%	46%	38%	7%	.493

LOS ANGELES DODGERS

DON MALCOLM

THE WORLD WE LEFT BEHIND

The flip side of any Golden Age, as historians often discover, turns up a gnarled set of skeletons in the closet. Yet nostalgia, both as inchoate longing and cottage industry, still casts a seductive shadow. It is precisely that shadow which adds a lustrous glow to memory, and makes the past seem somehow more desirable, even when cold facts provide evidence to the contrary.

Devotion to continuity will, in the end, lead to stagnation, and this is why most Golden Ages prove to be mythical. In the world of baseball, people speak of such an age as having existed during the 50s, when sixteen of twenty championships were won by teams from New York. What is usually overlooked in this rhapsody is the fact that shortly thereafter, two of those three teams left New York, paving the way for the game as we know it today. Also swept aside is the fact that baseball's post-war boom quickly turned sour in the fifties, and ushered in the era of franchise movement.

Walter O'Malley was the pioneer of Baseball as a Very Big Business. His bold pre-emptive move to Los Angeles shattered the myth of the Golden Age while simultaneously encasing it in amber. His actions forced baseball to expand, and made the game over in a new image, one that is now defined by market size.

Baseball's current myth is that teams cannot compete on a level playing field due to fatal disparities in market size. But as we've shown you (in "The Changing Face of Competition"), baseball has better competitive balance now than it had in the pre-expansion days. Back in those Golden fifties, two teams from the largest market in America—a market that even today could support three franchises—packed up and left.

In the nineties, baseball has learned its lesson. Expansion is a kind of self-regulating proposition: it precludes teams from seizing markets pre-emptively. By regulating expansion, baseball "grows the brand" more effectively, and ups its portfolio and revenue streams.

Those concepts were introduced into baseball by Walter O'Malley, but the irony of the Dodgers is that the franchise atrophied into "the last family business" in the hands of Walter's son. Peter O'Malley's desire for stability and tradition—that well-groomed patriarchal image—became increasingly at odds with a mutating economic milieu whose sweep is sufficient to materially alter America's social lexicon. Walter's attempt to seed a loosely strung empire with alliances of ex-Dodger executives during the second round of expansion ran aground against the first wave of this change in the early 70s; when his son assumed control, the Dodgers retreated from interventionism into a dowager-like isolation.

Within that ostensibly idyllic world, however, battles raged as legends aged. Al Campanis, the hand-picked heir to Buzzie Bavasi, dynamited a dynamic forty-year career in one ten-minute television appearance. His departure created discord within the organization, and set two combatants, Fred Claire (a "new breed" executive from the world of marketing and public relations) and Campanis disciple Tommy Lasorda, the long-time manager, who saw the leadership change as a slap to Dodger "tradition" and who was anxious to further consolidate his own power.

Amazingly, these two foes worked together for close to ten years, with Claire developing talent that Lasorda would often squander and misuse, with one major exception. An unheralded golden boy, the son of a childhood friend, turned out to be a singular hitting talent. His name: Mike Piazza. He became the Dodgers' brightest star, rescuing Lasorda from the

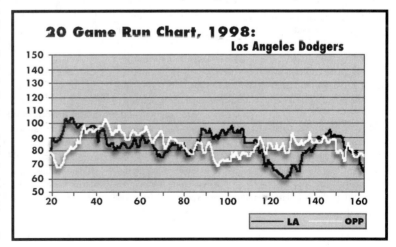

QMAX PRESENTS: "BAD" PITCHERS

THROW &#@% STRIKES, YOU BUSHER!

If you've been reading these boxes, by now you have probably noticed that most of the pitchers profiled have reasonable "command" ratings, but give up hits up the wazoo. Yearning for balance, the reader wonders where the Nuke Lalooshes are, the guys who hold the hits down, but walk so many that they give credence to the Maalox-swilling skipper's lament that "walks'll kill ya." The plain truth, however, is that managers usually pull the plug on these guys, either dumping them outright or banishing them to the bullpen until they are ready to be good boys.

We are fortunate, then, that wartime baseball, with its shortage of able-bodied men, gives us a laboratory to study marginal yet interesting players who might have been dumped in other years in favor of someone with more talent. One such case is Hal Gregg of the 1944 Brooklyn Bums. An examination of his QMAX totals for the year

reveals a severe and continuing control problem Despite giving up only about a hit per inning (much better than his mates-in-futility in this series), Gregg walked the ballpark. Only two of his 31 starts were in the desired 1,2 command region (leading to an execrable 4.61 "C" average for the year).

One can only imagine the torments young Hal suffered at the hands of his manager, the less-than-patient Leo Durocher, particularly during the hot summer months of June and July: from June 11 to July 29, Gregg lost nine starts in a row, completing six innings only twice in that span. Prince Hal sported a 9.40 ERA and walked 46 men in 44 innings in that span (5.61 "C"). It's not like he was a young Nolan Ryan, either; he also gave up 55 hits (5.0 "S").

But what of the QMAX dictum that wild men like Gregg often

HAL GREGG/BKN 1944							
1	2	3	4	5	6	7	S
		1	1				2
1	1	2		2		1	7
		2				1	3
					1		1
		1	2	4	1	2	10
	1		1	2	1	2	7
					1		1
1	2	6	5	8	3	6	31

improve in future years, once they harness their wildness a little? It's sort of true here, although Hal's full-season 4.13 "S" average is a bit high for inclusion in that category. In 1945, Hal cut his walks-per-nine down from 6 to 4.5, and his hits-per-nine down from 9 to 8, leading him to a quite-good 18-13, 3.47 season. In 1946, he was doing even better (6-4, 2.99 after 117 innings) he appeared to get hurt. At least I assume he got hurt; if he could stay in the rotation while walking a man an inning, I assume he'd stay in with a 2.99 ERA. At any rate, he was never the same after 1946, leading me to believe that he really did get hurt in 1946. Or maybe it was the 254 innings he pitched in 1945 that did it.

--Tom Austin

debacle of 1992, the team's worst season in eighty years. Benefiting further from divisional realignment, the Dodgers returned to the playoffs in 1995 and 1996, in large part due to Piazza.

The extra cachet that Lasorda had received due to Piazza's emergence was becoming insufferable for both Claire and Peter O'Malley, however, so when Tommy suffered a mild heart attack in June 1996, they wasted no time in announcing that Lasorda would be "retiring" to an executive's position. Lasorda fought this tenaciously, and it's rumored that his ongoing belligerence (abetted by his godson, Mike Piazza) was a leading factor in Peter O'Malley's decision to sell the club.

And with the takeover of Rupert Murdoch's team of Fox executives in 1998, Lasorda continued to stir the pot, helping to keep Piazza torqued up about his contract negotiations. But the old paternalism was gone, replaced by a group eager to flex its leadership muscle. When Piazza continued to press the issue, the new Dodger ownership bypassed both Claire and Lasorda and banished their Messiah to Miami, baseball's most hellish self-made wasteland. So eager were the new Dodger executives to rid themselves of Piazza that they permitted themselves to be extorted to the tune of $5 million by Gary Sheffield—a well-

traveled malcontent whose shoulder was meant to carry a designer chip, and who had a no-trade clause in his contract that needed waiving in order to complete the deal.

This didn't solve anything, of course, and created more of a siege mentality in the Dodger front office. Hideo Nomo, struggling on the mound, became unhinged at the swirl of events and demanded a trade. Fred Claire, bypassed during l'affair Piazza, took an uncharacteristically hard line, nuking Nomo instead of nurturing him, as had been his previous modus operandi. A month later, after having failed to work out a deal for Randy Johnson with the prickly Mariner front office, Fred was fired. In a gesture filled with grim irony, the Fox brain trust tapped Tommy Lasorda to replace him.

It took Tommy several weeks to wipe the cat-who-swallowed-the-canary grin from his face and begin to desecrate the Dodger farm system. By the end of July he had traded away six Dodger prospects, and even his shrill defender at the Los Angeles Times, Bill Plaschke, was reduced to uttering the journalistic equivalent of "no comment." Sensing the growing alarm, the Fox folks pressed their search for a new general manager and plucked Kevin Malone from the wreckage in Baltimore.

Malone surveyed the situation, and quickly hired Davey Johnson to manage the club. Like the proper procedure for mixing a martini, the Dodgers finally realized that they should be shaken, not stirred. But the key was acquiring a big-name pitcher. Big-name pitchers were the Dodgers' stock in trade, and there hadn't been one in LA since Fernando and Orel. As the free-agent skirmishes played out, the Dodgers looked like losers, having lost Randy Johnson to the the expansion Diamondbacks. Their "bold new direction" was going to consist of signing Devon White, and making two trades with the Mets in order to unload most of the detritus of the Piazza fiasco.

Finally, desperation reached its flashpoint. The Dodgers appealed to Rupert Murdoch for the combination to the safe, and Murdoch assented, knowing that extremism in the pursuit of ratings is no vice. Adding an appropriately Biblical note to the proceedings, the Dodgers agreed to a seventh year in their contract offer, and so made Kevin Brown into their newest Messiah.

Behind us is the old world, a relic, a phantasm, a carefully orchestrated montage that beckons to us with its flickering glow. Surrounding us is the jump cut world of fragments, of gerrymandered truths and corporate welfare and the sports-entertainment post-industrial complex. It's your world, but don't touch. It's the land of milk and honey, but the world has become a bee-hive, and that buzzing you hear may or may not be coming from inside your head.

THE DAN SCHMIDT MEMORIAL CULINARY DIGRESSION

And now, for something completely different. . .

First, a little explanation. Dan Schmidt is, to my knowledge, still very much alive. And I hope he stays that way, at least long enough to come face-to-face with another of my forays into the off-topic tropics.

Since Dan's an East Coast boy, he will doubtless find the following to be singularly useless, but readers who frequent the highways between Los Angeles and San Francisco may well find it to be the most valuable part of this entire book. (We just might run a poll on this at the BBBA web site, so watch out.)

What follows is a very personal list of the hidden culinary treasures one can find when driving from LAX to SFO (and avoiding the singularly horrible airline service between the two cities). It's a scenic drive to boot: lots to see while you're chowing down.

Leaving LA (and this is never a bad idea), by all means get ensnarled at Neptune's Net, at the very north edge of Malibu, just before a terrific twelve-mile stretch of old-style serpentine Highway 1 driving pleasure. Of course, with a name like that, you're surprised to discover that it's an Italian restaurant, right? Actually, it's a full-service joint, but the bar is the best spot to linger, with its fine ocean view.

Up the road about twenty miles, in the burgeoning town known as Oxnard (students of euphony, take note), we have Sal's

WPA BULLPEN BOX—LOS ANGELES DODGERS

	PI	WPA	P	PPPI
Starters	1083	4.3	54.0	0.050
Relievers	496	-2.2	32.2	0.065
Road	273	-1.1	20.0	0.073
Home	223	-1.1	12.2	0.055
Mar/Apr	107	1.2	6.9	0.064
May	96	-1.3	4.6	0.048
June	86	-0.9	7.2	0.083
July	86	0.0	4.7	0.054
August	76	-2.7	5.2	0.069
September	45	1.5	3.7	0.081
Non S/H Sit.	348	0.6	15.4	0.044
S/H Sit.	148	-2.8	16.9	0.114
Low Pressure	211	-0.3	2.5	0.012
Med. Pressure	158	-5.0	11.1	0.070
High Pressure	127	3.1	18.7	0.147
Entered behind	209	-0.1	4.2	0.020
Entered tied	91	0.7	10.6	0.116
Entered ahead	196	-2.8	17.4	0.089

Name	G	PI	WPA	P	PPPI	MI	ROB	T
Bruske J	35	56	-.2	3.1	.055	14	14	9
Clontz B	18	26	.0	1.4	.054	7	8	3
Guthrie M	53	73	.1	3.2	.044	18	18	7
Hall D	11	14	-1.0	.5	.034	3	3	2
Kubenka J	6	10	.6	1.2	.118	4	2	1
Lankford F	12	20	-.7	.3	.017	5	0	2
McMichael G	12	19	-.3	1.9	.099	7	8	5
Osuna A	54	80	1.3	6.2	.078	22	23	9
Radinsky S	62	80	-1.2	7.7	.097	17	23	9
Shaw J	34	38	-.1	3.4	.090	4	5	1
Total		496	-2.2	32.2	.065			

	Quality					Pressure			
	Dis.	Poor	Fair	Good	Her.	Lo	Med	Hi	
Bruske J	4	2	21	7	1	18	9	8	(4)
Clontz B	2	2	9	4	1	10	5	3	(2)
Guthrie M	1	7	35	10	0	31	18	4	(2)
Hall D	2	1	8	0	0	8	3	0	(0)
Lankford F	2	0	10	0	0	10	2	0	(0)
Maloney S	1	0	10	0	0	8	2	1	(0)
McMichael G	1	4	3	4	0	1	6	5	(3)
Osuna A	3	9	22	17	3	22	19	13	(9)
Radinsky S	8	8	24	21	1	21	22	19	(10)
Shaw J	4	1	9	20	0	9	16	9	(7)
Others	1	6	23	8	2	21	10	9	(6)
TOTAL	29	40	174	91	8	159	112	71	(43)

	7th inning			8th inning			9th inning		
	0	+1	+2	0	+1	+2	0	+1	+2
Brunson W	0	1	0	0	0	0	0	0	0
Bruske J	2	2	0	1	1	0	2	0	0
Clontz B	0	1	0	0	1	0	0	0	0
Dreifort D	0	0	0	0	0	0	1	0	0
Guthrie M	0	2	2	0	0	1	0	0	0
Hall D	0	1	0	0	0	0	0	0	0
Kubenka J	0	2	0	0	1	0	1	0	0
McMichael G	1	0	0	1	0	1	2	0	0
Osuna A	0	0	1	5	2	2	4	1	1
Radinsky S	0	0	0	6	4	4	6	5	4
Reyes D	1	0	0	0	0	0	0	0	0
Shaw J	0	0	0	0	0	1	1	8	11
Weaver E	0	0	0	1	0	0	1	0	0
Starters	16	16	13	4	12	11	0	2	4
TOTAL	20	25	16	18	21	20	18	16	20
Record	10-10	19-6	15-1	12-6	15-6	18-2	10-8	13-3	19-1

Sean Forman's
PROSPECT WATCH

NAME	AGE	POS	LEVEL	GR98	GR97	GR96	AVG
Adrian Beltre	20	3B	AA	102	90	76	94
Jon Tucker	21	1B	AA	71	56	64	65
Adam Riggs	25	2B	AAA	70	68	35	64
Hiram Bocachica	22		AAA	60	63	75	64
Wilfredo Romero	23	OF	AAA	61	65	57	62
Tony Mota	20	OF	AA	64	43	42	53
Alex Cora	22	SS	AAA	61	39	35	49
Angel Pena	23	C	AA	56	41	20	45
Juan Diaz	22	1B	AA	51	36	-	45

NAME	AGE	POS	LEVEL	GRADE
Tony Mota	20	OF	High A	68
Luke Allen	19	OF	High A	62
Jorge Piedra	19	OF	Rookie	55
Dane Tomaszewski	18		Rookie	51
Kimani Newton	19	OF	High A	50
Juan Diaz	22	1B	High A	46
Bernie Torres	18	SS	High A	45
Glenn Davis	22	OF	High A	41

NAME	AGE	GS	S	C	T	W-L	ERA	K/H	LEVEL
Ricky Stone	23	28	4.18	3.11	7.29	12-6	4.66	0.80	High
Toby Dollar	23	23	4.52	3.04	7.57	6-12	5.44	0.37	High
Gary Rath	24	24	4.42	3.25	7.67	8-7	4.52	0.65	High
Casey Deskins	26	15	4.80	3.13	7.93	3-8	4.63	0.56	High
Mike Judd	23	17	4.06	3.94	8.00	5-7	4.56	0.79	High
Onan Masaoka	20	20	4.15	4.15	8.30	6-6	5.32	0.82	High
Jeff Williams	26	27	4.89	3.52	8.41	11-8	4.37	0.63	High
Ignacio Flores	23	17	4.71	4.29	9.00	4-10	7.11	0.55	High
Jay O'Shaughnessy	23	17				4-9	5.01	1.32	Low

The Dodgers system is wobbling, but it appears to have survived the Attack of the Pasta Man. One of the ongoing debates I have with myself is the value of a deep farm system versus having just a couple of outstanding prospects. Of course, that assumes that depth doesn't beget quality, but I would take one outstanding prospect ahead of four good prospects on most days. Adrian Beltre is such a prospect.

TOP DOG: Adrian Beltre
Beltre is no longer a rookie, so he ineligible for the Rookie of the Year award. He has been handed the 1999 Dodgers' third base job and should hold it for sometime to come. Beltre is still extremely young and won't turn 21 until April, but he has the hitting skills of a more mature player. His 1998 performance (.321/.411/.581) was nearly a carbon copy of his 1997 season (.317/.407/.561). He has struck out less than he has walked and is plus base stealer with 45 steals in 58 attempts over the last two years. He is still learning defensively, but he'll do just fine if the Dodgers don't mess with him.

UP THE MIDDLE: Adam Riggs
If not for some bad luck on the injury front, Riggs might have been the starting second baseman for the Dodgers last year. Before he went down to injury in 1997, the Dodgers were willing to give him a shot. Once he was injured they picked up prodigal son Eric Young and signed him to a long-term deal. Riggs may not be better than Young. He has more pop and some patience, but he has been producing largely in great hitters' parks and is not considered a plus with the glove. Still he would be about $4 million a year less than Young would and that is the going rate for a middle of the rotation starter.

YOUNG 'UN: Luke Allen
Allen is a solid young hitter. In 1997, he surprised many people hitting .345 in the Pioneer League at the age of 18. This year he moved into the high-A California League, which is pretty unusual for a 19-year-old. He held his own batting .298/.347/.421, with 18 stolen bases. He was then called up to AA for 78 at bats and hit .333. He hasn't hit for much power yet, but he has been solid across the board. When looking at young players like this, I like to see a player who keeps his head above water and contributes. They don't have to dominate the league to be a good prospect, so long as they have can hold their own against the older competition.

TRADE BAIT: Hiram Bocachica
Bocachica was acquired in the Perez/Grudzielanek deal. The Expos weren't sad to see him go because of his maddening lack of development since his outstanding 1996 season. Since then he has been moved to the outfield because of defensive problems and his bat hasn't improved at all. With the perspective of two years, his 1996 season now looks like a big fluke. His current level of production isn't satisfactory for an outfielder, and the Dodgers aren't the most nurturing of organizations for prospects that might scuffle in the majors. Comp: Garey Ingram.

ON THE MOUND: Mike Judd
Judd is usually mentioned as the top Dodger pitching prospect now that Ted Lilly is gone, though Masaoka receives some mention as well. Judd split time between the big league squad and AAA Albuquerque. He was not outstanding in AAA as he allowed 1.5 baserunners per inning and 17 home runs in just 95 innings. Albuquerque is a tough park to pitch in and he did pitch much better on the road, so he should be all right once he makes it to the big leagues. I doubt he'll get much of a chance at starting next year, though if some pitchers go down to

Mexican Inn, a spacious, down-home dive with a wide range of authentic south-of-the-border cuisine. Sal's is our designated stop on the way to LA every Christmas Eve, but it's OK to go there any time.

After hooking back up with Highway 101 in Ventura, we slide on up to tony Santa Barbara, slip off at the Milpas Street exit, make a right past Madame Rosinka's Palm Reading emporium, and drive another nine blocks until the familiar light-blue panels of La Super Rica come into view. It's little more than an old-style Spanish shack with a tarpaulin-covered rear dining area, but the food is sublime, especially the delicate vegetarian tamales (topped with a decadent cream sauce). Also noteworthy are the unconscionably rich tacos de calibacita—zucchini, pork, and several layers of cheese blended together in an artery-clogging culinary apotheosis. It's worth the bypass operation.

About an hour later, we reconnect with the ocean at scenic, whimsically named Pismo Beach. There are actually five towns clustered in this general area, not counting San Luis Obispo ten miles inland. Your best bet for an unusual dining experience can be found at either the Speedy Gourmet in north Pismo, or at Alex's Bar-B-Q up the road in Shell Beach. Alex's has some unusual barbeque choices (including a variety of seafood) that are otherwise hard to find; the Speedy Gourmet, of course, is a drive-through burger joint.

Ten minutes away is the fantastically kitsch Madonna Inn, with its outrageous stone facades, a dining room ablaze in hot pink, and a series of rooms that beg you to leave your sunglasses on at night. (And, no, there's no affiliation with Ms. Ciccone—the proprietor's last name is actually Madonna.) What's great here, however, is the bakery, with an entire array of elaborate confections, topped by cakes and pies to die for. Pecan, Dutch apple, and apricot—Louise's favorite—are lying in wait. Bring a whole one home, or sit in the hysterically over-wrought hot-pink coffee shop and take it one slice at a time.

Up and over the prodigious Cuesta Grade we go, the car groaning due to all those extra pounds you've put on already, bypassing the In-and-Out Burger in Atascadero in favor of the Real Thing ten miles up the road. Get off at 24th Street in Paso Robles, turn left under the highway, and look for the smoky roof of Good Ol' Burgers, a shrine to the art of grilled ground beef. Ask for a bib—you'll need it. Afterwards, you guys in search of a cheap thrill can mosey up the street to the local A&W, where the carhop hiring policy remains gloriously sexist: the local talent on display is quite talented indeed.

It's all downhill from there—at least for the next sixty miles into Salinas, that is—and we veer off Highway 101 at Market St. in Steinbeck's hometown, heading toward the water again via Route 183 through Castroville, the self-proclaimed "artichoke capital of the world." Tucked away amidst all this overweening greenness you'll find the unassumingly pert Bing's Diner, where the cuisine is upscale Americana at its best. Be reassured as well that there is no relationship between this fine establishment and that overly arch crooner of yesteryear.

From Castroville, we rejoin Highway 1 and its infamous "safety corridor" en route to Santa Cruz. (Note that we are scrupulously avoiding the inland route through Gilroy and the ubersprawl of the Silicated Valley.) If you need something sweet to tide you over for the last eighty miles up the coast to San Francisco, try Donnelly's Handmade Chocolates, on the left side of Highway 1 in Santa Cruz as you drive north.

If you've timed it right, and it's late afternoon, the drive on the coastal side of the Peninsula is gloriously tinged with the waning rays of the sun, suffused over a seemingly endless parade of intimate, secluded beaches. Scott Creek, Ano Nuevo, Bean Hollow, Pescadero, Pomponio, San Gregorio, Tunitas Creek all sprawl out at your left as you drive the fifty-odd miles from Santa Cruz to Half Moon Bay. It's a glorious premonition of wilder ocean settings to be found north of San Francisco, and all that scenery can make you pretty hungry. North of Half Moon Bay, you'll find two adjacent restaurants where you can drink in the scenery and get a good meal: seafood at the Anchorage, and upscale American food at the aptly-named Highway One Diner.

Now we're almost within shouting distance of the City, but there are still more opportunities to don the old feedbag. In the cliffside community of Montara, stop in at Cafè Gibraltar for a splendid array of "Mediterranean food"—covering literally the entire region. Fortify yourself with some Greek coffee for the tricky five miles of high-wire driving ahead on a ribbon of road high above the crashing waves.

Having survived that, you'll need a snack, and thankfully you'll find it in picturesque Pacifica. Look for the restaurant called Vallemar Station, and turn right at the next street (Reina del Mar). Make a right into the first driveway, park, and walk up to a converted Spanish-style bungalow which houses Guerrero's Taqueria. (Unfortunately for those who are hoping against hope for some kind of baseball tie-in here, there is no truth to the rumor that Pedro Guerrero is the owner.) Guerrero's masterpiece is its taco al pastor (marinated pork), a savory blend of subtle spices. Those who go in for the really hot stuff should ante up for the chile verde, a first-rate scorcher. With or without Pedro, Guerrero's is a bonafide grand slam.

I've had suggestions that this eating tour be extended into San Francisco as well. My response: not on your life. The fine establishments above will benefit from whatever added business comes their way from those retracing these steps; a similar list of San Francisco eateries would only wind up with longer lines. You're gonna have to fend for yourself in the City, folks. OK, I'll give you one, just to be a mensch—and to make one last attempt

TEAM BREAKOUT DODGERS 1998						
Category	**RS**	**RA**	**W**	**L**	**Pct.**	**Rk**
5+ RUNS SCORED/HOME	183	99	23	3	.885	4
RECORD IN BLOWOUTS/HOME	75	34	8	2	.800	1
4- RUNS ALLOWED/HOME	219	122	43	12	.782	6
5+ RUNS SCORED	407	272	44	14	.759	9
4- RUNS ALLOWED	360	214	69	25	.734	6
SLUGFESTS/HOME	90	64	8	3	.727	3
CLOSE LOW SCORING GAMES/HOME	63	46	19	8	.704	2
LOW SCORING GAMES/HOME	83	60	23	11	.676	4
4- RUNS ALLOWED/ROAD	141	92	26	13	.667	6
5+ RUNS SCORED/ROAD	224	173	21	11	.656	13
RECORD IN CLOSE GAMES/HOME	164	152	29	19	.604	6
CLOSE SLUGFESTS/HOME	36	36	3	2	.600	4
RECORD IN LOW SCORING GAMES	132	116	34	25	.576	3
RECORD IN CLOSE GAMES	299	291	46	39	.541	5
RECORD IN SLUGFESTS	240	236	17	15	.531	7
SEASON TOTALS	669	678	83	79	.512	7
RECORD IN BLOWOUTS	170	177	15	15	.500	9
RECORD IN CLOSE GAMES/ROAD	135	139	17	20	.459	6
4- RUNS SCORED/ROAD	144	182	25	30	.455	4
LOW SCORING GAMES/ROAD	49	56	11	14	.440	4
CLOSE LOW SCORING GAMES/ROAD	24	26	6	8	.429	7
SLUGFESTS/ROAD	150	172	9	12	.429	11
CLOSE SLUGFESTS/ROAD	35	35	2	3	.400	12
4- RUNS SCORED	262	406	39	65	.375	3
RECORD IN BLOWOUTS/ROAD	95	143	7	13	.350	11
4- RUNS SCORED/ROAD	118	224	14	35	.286	5
5+ RUNS ALLOWED/ROAD	201	305	9	33	.214	10
5+ RUNS ALLOWED	309	464	14	54	.206	12
5+ RUNS ALLOWED/HOME	108	159	5	21	.192	13

to get even close to this book's ostensible subject matter.

Down on lower Haight, between Fillmore and Steiner, you'll find the superb Rosamunde Sausage Grill. At about half the price of what the Pac Bell mavens are going to extort for ye olde upscale ballpark frank, you get a choice of nearly a dozen top-notch wursten, with a full range of meats (beef, pork, veal, lamb, chicken). And given the impending corporatization of the Giants in their Coked-up new home, I suspect that my baseball experience is going to consist largely of a portable radio and a Rosamunde sausage, eating a great hot dog while listening to another (the orotund Jon Miller, of course).

AN ACTUARIAL POST-SCRIPT

With Kevin Brown and his portion of the GNP now in place at Dodger Stadium, we thought it would be wise to look ahead and see how likely it was that he'd still be pitching at age 40, when his Golden Age of Hollywood contract expires. Sean Forman did the research: here are the numbers.

From 1960 to the present, there are 96 pitches who had 15+ wins and 200+ IP at the age of 33. Flashing forward to the 38-40 age range, we find 54 are still pitching. Only nine of these pitchers are still generating 200+ IP per season at this age, however. Of the top five leaders in IP at this age, three were knuckleballers (Phil and Joe Niekro, Charlie Hough).

At age 40, there are 11 pitchers with 200+ IP—the three knuckleballers; Hall of Famers Warren Spahn, Early Wynn, Tom Seaver, Gaylord Perry and Don Sutton; soon-to-be HoFer Nolan Ryan; late bloomer Rick Rueschel; and the ageless Tommy John.

Using a crude measure (WPCT), Brown ranked eighth on a list of post-1960 age 31-33 pitchers (.662). Of the seven pitchers above him on that list, only one (Steve Carlton) was still pitching at the age of 40.

								<---	Park	Adjusted	Statistics								Adj	Raw			
Name	AB	R	H	D	T	HR	RBI	BB	SO	SB	CS	BA	OBP	SLG	XR	XR/27	XR/27	OXW	DXW	TXW
Beltre A	194	21	43	10	0	7	25	15	37	3	1	.223	.288	.384	22	3.69	3.39	0.24	0.30	0.54
Bonilla B	235	30	57	7	1	7	33	30	37	1	1	.244	.325	.374	29	4.09	3.79	0.62	-0.02	0.60
Castro J	220	27	44	7	0	2	16	15	37	0	0	.199	.249	.260	14	1.93	1.82	-1.04	1.02	-0.02
Cedeno R	239	36	59	12	1	2	18	28	57	8	2	.246	.324	.329	28	4.05	3.85	0.61	0.14	0.75
Eisenreich J	127	13	26	2	2	0	7	12	22	4	0	.202	.274	.256	9	2.45	2.23	-0.33	0.09	-0.24
Grudzielanek M	193	12	53	8	0	2	23	5	23	7	0	.275	.297	.346	20	3.47	3.12	0.10	0.64	0.74
Guerrero W	180	23	53	5	4	0	8	4	33	5	2	.293	.310	.359	19	3.82	3.46	0.29	-0.11	0.18
Hollandsworth T	175	24	48	6	4	3	22	9	42	4	3	.274	.314	.411	21	4.31	4.09	0.54	0.06	0.60
Howard T	76	10	15	5	0	2	4	3	15	1	0	.195	.227	.338	5	2.25	1.91	-0.27	0.18	-0.09
Hubbard T	208	32	63	10	1	7	19	18	46	9	4	.306	.366	.465	35	5.83	5.52	1.60	0.30	1.90
Johnson C	344	35	77	14	0	12	39	31	98	0	1	.224	.289	.372	35	3.44	3.16	0.16	0.66	0.82
Karros E	505	64	153	22	1	23	93	49	92	7	2	.303	.364	.489	90	6.57	6.24	4.76	0.51	5.27
Konerko P	144	15	31	1	0	4	17	10	30	0	1	.217	.275	.308	12	2.68	2.62	-0.30	-0.01	-0.31
Luke M	236	36	57	13	1	12	37	18	60	2	1	.241	.296	.458	32	4.61	4.39	0.95	0.54	1.49
Mondesi R	579	91	166	29	5	30	98	31	111	16	9	.287	.324	.511	92	5.74	5.41	4.10	0.35	4.45
Piazza M	149	22	42	5	0	9	33	11	27	0	0	.284	.333	.501	24	5.80	5.68	1.08	0.33	1.41
Prince T	81	8	16	6	1	0	6	7	24	0	0	.199	.280	.301	7	2.85	2.41	-0.10	0.20	0.10
Sheffield G	298	56	96	17	1	16	61	72	30	18	5	.323	.455	.550	78	9.62	9.13	5.45	0.72	6.17
Vizcaino J	237	32	63	10	0	3	31	17	35	7	3	.266	.316	.345	27	3.76	3.60	0.37	0.84	1.21
Young E	450	86	132	27	1	8	48	47	32	43	12	.295	.367	.413	73	5.71	5.27	3.32	1.22	4.54
Zeile T	158	24	41	7	1	7	28	10	24	1	1	.261	.309	.453	21	4.57	4.27	0.61	-0.04	0.57
LA	5440	726	1406	231	29	161	685	466	1049	139	48	.258	.319	.400	710	4.44	4.16	22.72	7.92	30.64

Pitcher	S	C	T	SS	ES	IC	HH	PP	TJ	S12	S35	S67	C1	C23	C45	C67	QWP
Bohanon	2.79	3.07	5.86	79%	14%	71%	7%	21%	14%	50%	43%	7%	0%	57%	43%	0%	.678
C Park	3.61	3.61	7.21	55%	18%	48%	30%	12%	0%	42%	27%	30%	6%	52%	27%	15%	.529
C Perez	3.36	3.27	6.64	64%	18%	45%	18%	9%	9%	36%	45%	18%	18%	45%	27%	9%	.599
D Reyes	4.00	4.67	8.67	0%	0%	33%	0%	33%	0%	33%	67%	0%	0%	0%	100%	0%	.433
Dreifort	3.96	3.19	7.15	38%	12%	46%	27%	19%	19%	27%	46%	27%	8%	54%	38%	0%	.550
I Valdes	3.96	3.41	7.37	44%	7%	33%	22%	4%	4%	26%	52%	22%	11%	56%	26%	7%	.514
Mlicki	3.80	3.05	6.85	55%	15%	40%	20%	10%	5%	30%	50%	20%	15%	45%	40%	0%	.558
Nomo	3.42	4.25	7.67	50%	25%	50%	25%	8%	0%	50%	25%	25%	8%	42%	17%	33%	.477
R Martinez	2.87	3.33	6.20	73%	13%	53%	13%	27%	7%	47%	40%	13%	20%	27%	47%	7%	.610
LAD	3.58	3.41	6.99	53%	14%	47%	22%	14%	7%	37%	42%	22%	10%	48%	34%	8%	.553

NATIONAL LEAGUE WEST

COLORADO ROCKIES

JIM FURTADO

There are times when a person must belabor a point in someone else's best interest. Take my two kids, for instance. I have two small boys, aged five and three. As all children should be at that age, they are very trusting and very friendly. They readily flash a smile at strangers.

In particular, my three year-old feels that it's his duty to say hello to everyone who comes within earshot. In response, most people smile back and comment about what a nice personality he has. This, of course, isn't necessarily the safest trait for my son can have. As a matter of fact, a perfect stranger recently felt compelled to advise me on this topic.

I had taken my little one to the dentist for a check-up. Being the friendly chap that he is, my son made his rounds in the waiting room saying hello to all the other children. One child, however, shied away from his advances. His mother commented how her little boy (also, three years-old) was very fearful around strangers. She remarked how nice it would be if her boy would be as friendly as my son. We exchanged small talk and a couple of minutes later my son and I were called for his check-up.

On our way out after the examination, the women with the shy little boy cautioned me about the dangers of my son's friendliness. She mentioned that she and her husband constantly warned her son of how dangerous it was to talk to strangers. She proudly stated that her son had taken to quickly locking their door as soon as they returned home. I thanked her for her advice and left the office with my smiling, happy boy in tow.

During my ride home, I thought about the experience. Although I was somewhat amused at the women's lack of understanding of the cause and effect of her son's shyness, I figured it wouldn't hurt to re-examine my own thoughts on the matter.

I came to the same conclusion that I had prior to the dentist visit. Right before my little one begins school, I will sit him down and talk to him about the dangers of talking with strangers. I will then re-visit the topic periodically to re-enforce the idea.

As much as I hate doing this, I must admit the importance of belaboring the danger to my kids. The world can be a dangerous place. So dangerous, in fact,

that absolute strangers feel they should admonish another parent, if they feel that the other parent's kids aren't sufficiently afraid of the world, even at such a tender age.

At this point, you may be thinking, "What the heck does this have to do with the Colorado Rockies?" Well, like my kids, the Rockies don't appear to be fully aware of one the dangers of the baseball world—the dangers of ignoring park effects.

Quite possibly, you may be tired of reading about this topic. As an informed Rockies fan (who has some pretty good knowledge about park effects), you may be thinking, "Enough with the park effects!" If that's true, I'm very sorry. I'll be belaboring the point again. In my defense, I'd like to point out that I'm doing this for your own good. That's because the Rockies management STILL doesn't appear to get it.

Remember this concept is not a new one. Many players, fan, analysts, and GMs understand the concept. Unfortunately, the Rockies hierarchy doesn't.

How do I know this? Well, I must admit I'm not privy to the inner workings of the Rockies front office. As a matter of fact, I don't appear to be on the Rolodex of Bob Gebhard because he has never called to fill me in on his thoughts on the team. Nevertheless, I believe my conclusions are valid since every Rockies action indicates they don't now what's wrong with their team.

What's do I think is wrong with the Rockies? Well, I keep hearing in the media that the Rockies are interested in picking up pitching. As a matter of fact, when I began my examina-

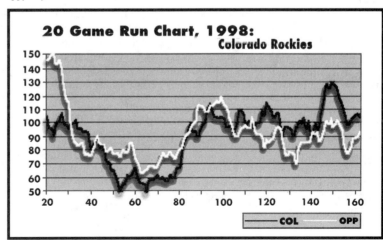

QMAX PRESENTS: "BAD" PITCHERS

MY BALLPARK DOESN'T UNDERSTAND ME

The aficionado of Bad Pitching must now be rubbing his hands together gleefully at the thought of the Rockies essay. Why, everyone knows the Rockies have the worst pitching around; surely there will be some juicy raw meat for the drooling, slavering jaws of the machine, some poor sap who will be anointed the worst of the worst. Well, as someone once said, it ain't necessarily so. We're going to give the poor Rocky pitchers a much-deserved break and examine, through the recent career of Kevin Ritz (1994-96), what spacious Coors does to a pitcher, through the QMAX lens darkly.

As you can see by the QMAX boxes, the overall distribution of Kevin Ritz' QMAX scores changes subtly as he goes from home to road. At home, Ritz is a classic "Grand Avenue" pitcher (studiously avoiding the Power Precipice and the Tommy John region), while on the road he shows a small but noticeable tendency toward the power precipice (12% of his starts there, vs. about 8%

league average). This makes sense, as one must prevent hits to get in the Power Precipice, and that's pretty damn hard to do at Coors, which inflates singles and doubles as well as home runs. While Ritz's road C score is only a quarter-point below his home score (3.98/3.73) , his home/road S differential is three times as large (4.73/3.98). That's bad enough, but even that dramatically understates the effect of Coors: Ritz' road ERA during the span was a semi-respectable 4.28, while his home ERA was a bloated 5.80, more than a run and a half higher.

What struck me the most about this study was how small the Coors effect is on everything except hits. A quarter-point difference in C between two forty-start is not that much above the noise level, and part of it is explainable by the correlation between short starts and high

KEVIN RITZ/COL 94-96 (home)

	1	2	3	4	5	6	7	S
1								0
2	1	1	1					3
3		1	3	2	1	1		8
4		1	3		1			5
5			1	3	2	1	2	9
6			2		1		1	4
7			4	2	1		1	8
C	1	3	14	7	6	2	4	37

KEVIN RITZ/COL 94-96 (road)

	1	2	3	4	5	6	7	S
1		1		1			1	3
2		1	4	1	1			7
3		1	4		1	1	1	8
4		2	1	2				5
5			3	3	1		1	8
6		1	2	5				8
7				2				2
C	0	6	14	13	4	1	3	41

C numbers. However, Ritz himself only averaged a tenth of an inning less (5.8/5.7) in his Coors starts than his road starts, and only four pitches more (96/92). The difference was almost entirely in the hits allowed, and within that the home runs. Ritz surrendered the long ball twice as often (0.8/start) in Coors as on the road (0.4/start).

We're going to have to keep looking at this one. A comparison of power vs. finesse pitchers at Coors should show some kind of a pattern, and QMAX is the tool to do that comparison.

--Tom Austin

tion I expected to find that they had a little trouble with their pitching staff. Unfortunately for Rockies fans, my objective examination of the team found just the opposite to be true. It's not the Rockies' pitching that needs upgrading; it's the Rockies' offense.

How did I come to this conclusion? Well, I have a few modified versions of James' Pythagorean formula (using 1.83 exponent) that I use to determine how good team offenses and defenses are. What they all basically do is park adjust the runs a team scores and gives up and relates them to league average. In that way, I come up with Winning Percentage for both a team's offense and its defense. The numbers they produce pretty much add up to the original Pythagorean WP. As you'll see, a lot of the time the numbers are dead on, although sometimes they are off by a few points. (That's due to the introduction of a linear step, to a non-linear formula.)

This is how the numbers matched up in 1998:

As you can see, the OFF+DEF numbers match up pretty good. The biggest difference between these numbers and the Pyth is the +/- .007 for LA, COL and SD. (In these three cases the OFF+DEF numbers are closer to the actual winning percentage than the regular Pyth projection is.)

Team	OFF	DEF	OFF+DEF	Pyth
ARI	.441	.468	.409	.410
ATL	.543	.617	.659	.656
CHI	.542	.478	.520	.522
CIN	.496	.498	.494	.494
COL	.440	.537	.477	.484
FLA	.472	.384	.356	.356
HOU	.576	.581	.657	.652
LA	.487	.514	.501	.494
MIL	.468	.472	.440	.437
MON	.481	.435	.416	.412
NY	.486	.555	.542	.541
PHI	.447	.494	.441	.443
PIT	.429	.525	.454	.455
SD	.558	.524	.582	.575
SF	.563	.497	.560	.561
STL	.540	.478	.517	.516

Anyway, here's the offensive and defensive winning percentage of all 1998 NL teams:

Rank	Team	OFF	Team	DEF
1	HOU	.576	ATL	.617
2	SF	.563	HOU	.581
3	SD	.558	NY	.555
4	ATL	.543	COL	.537
5	CHI	.542	PIT	.525
6	STL	.540	SD	.524
7	CIN	.496	LA	.514
8	LA	.487	CIN	.498
9	NY	.486	SF	.497
10	MON	.481	PHI	.494
11	FLA	.472	STL	.478
12	MIL	.468	CHI	.478
13	PHI	.447	MIL	.472
14	ARI	.441	ARI	468
15	COL	.440	MON	.435
16	PIT	.429	FLA	.384

As you can see, the Rockies offense ranked next to last, while their defense ranked near the top.

This directly contradicts the thinking of the Rockies. I say that because I keep reading about how they feel they need to upgrade their pitching. That's why the Rockies were so hot and heavy to acquire Kevin Brown and Roger Clemans during the off-season.

Unfortunately for all you Rockies fans, they are mistaken. That's why I feel the need to belabor the point about park effects: COORS FIELD RADICALLY INFLUENCES THE STATS OF THE PLAYERS WHO PLAY THERE. If this important fact isn't taken into account, it leads to improper conclusions (such as thinking your offense is OK, while you pitching need help, when in fact the opposite is true).

To further illustrate the point, here's a position-by-position comparison of the Colorado Rockies' Offensive Extrapolated Wins at each position and an average NL team in 1998.

Pos	AvgTmOXW	COL OXW	Diff
1B	4.86	4.55	-0.31
2B	2.83	-0.39	-3.22
SS	1.25	0.18	-1.06
3B	3.87	4.21	0.35
C	2.13	1.06	-1.08
CF	3.45	3.01	-0.44
LF	3.54	3.16	-0.38
RF	4.36	7.02	2.67

The only positions where the Rocks had above average results were 3B and RF. That's the positions manned by the Rockies two best offensive players: Vinny Castilla and Larry Walker. I suggest you take some time now to check out the Sabermetric Hitting Boxes of the different NL teams. If you compare the numbers of other teams to the Rockies you'll see that Rockies hitters don't look that good in comparison. This holds true even if you use raw numbers. The Rockies hitters in

WPA BULLPEN BOX—COLORADO ROCKIES

	PI	WPA	P	PPPI
Starters	1027	-0.3	57.1	0.056
Relievers	537	8.2	36.6	0.068
Road	221	1.4	13.4	0.061
Home	316	6.8	23.2	0.073
Mar/Apr	112	0.9	6.1	0.054
May	88	2.0	5.1	0.058
June	83	1.4	8.0	0.096
July	96	2.3	5.8	0.060
August	85	1.7	5.5	0.065
September	73	-0.0	6.1	0.084
Non S/H Sit.	401	3.1	19.4	0.048
S/H Sit.	136	5.1	17.2	0.126
Low Pressure	220	-0.0	3.4	0.015
Med. Pressure	201	1.5	14.8	0.074
High Pressure	116	6.7	18.3	0.158
Entered behind	288	2.5	9.9	0.034
Entered tied	54	0.2	8.1	0.150
Entered ahead	195	5.5	18.6	0.095

Name	G	PI	WPA	P	PPPI	MI	ROB	T
Astacio P	1	2	.1	.3	.125	1	1	0
DeJean M	58	83	2.2	4.7	.056	22	17	5
DiPoto J	68	78	1.2	6.8	.087	9	5	6
Jones B	15	25	.3	1.0	.039	6	10	0
Leskanic C	66	86	.8	5.7	.066	20	12	9
McElroy C	78	94	.7	8.3	.088	16	33	14
Munoz M	40	52	-.3	2.6	.051	9	15	2
Veres D	63	89	3.0	6.4	.072	23	21	5
Wainhouse D	10	13	.0	.7	.052	3	3	2
Total		537	8.2	36.6	.068			

		--------- Quality ----------					--- Pressure -------		
	Dis.	Poor	Fair	Good	Her.	Lo	Med	Hi
DeJean M	1	4	33	19	1	27	22	9 (9)
DiPoto J	5	9	26	26	2	27	25	16 (10)
Jones B	0	3	9	3	0	9	4	2 (2)
Leskanic C	4	9	29	22	2	22	35	9 (7)
McElroy C	6	9	29	32	2	30	30	18 (14)
Munoz M	2	7	20	11	0	20	16	4 (2)
Veres D	1	5	31	25	1	28	21	14 (11)
Others	0	2	14	3	0	11	5	3 (3)
TOTAL	19	48	191	141	8	174	158	75 (58)

	7th inning			8th inning			9th inning		
	0	+1	+2	0	+1	+2	0	+1	+2
Astacio P	0	0	0	0	1	0	0	0	0
DeJean M	1	3	3	0	5	1	0	0	1
DiPoto J	0	0	1	0	2	3	4	8	9
Jones B	0	1	0	0	0	1	0	0	0
Leskanic C	1	1	2	3	2	4	0	0	0
McElroy C	1	1	1	3	3	1	4	0	1
Munoz M	0	2	0	0	0	0	0	0	0
Veres D	2	0	2	0	1	2	1	2	4
Starters	15	11	6	8	2	3	3	1	0
TOTAL	20	19	15	14	16	15	12	11	15
Record	10-10	14-5	13-2	8-6	12-4	14-1	8-4	8-3	15-0

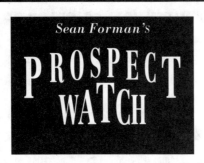

Sean Forman's
PROSPECT WATCH

NAME	AGE	POS	LEVEL	GR98	GR97	GR96	AVG
Ben Petrick	21	C	AA	72	61	59	66
Derrick Gibson	23	OF	AAA	57	71	60	62
Mike Rennhack	23	OF	AA	48	55	53	51
Wonderful Monds	25	OF	AA	34	72	56	50

NAME	AGE	POS	LEVEL	GRADE
Rene Reyes	20	1B	Rookie	59
Augustin Sanchez	19	OF	Rookie	56
Matt Holliday	18	3B	Rookie	55
Choo Freeman	18	OF	Rookie	51
Tomas Samuel	18	C	Rookie	49
Elvis Pena	21	2B	Low A	47
Miguel Vilorio	18	2B	Rookie	46
Juan Sosa	22	SS	High A	45

NAME	AGE	GS	S	C	T	W-L	ERA	K/H	LEVEL
Mike Kusiewicz	21	26	3.42	2.31	5.73	14-6	2.32	0.94	High
Scott Randall	22	28	4.07	2.82	6.89	9-14	3.83	0.64	High
Mark Brownson	23	21	4.05	3.29	7.33	6-8	5.34	0.63	High
Jason Brester	21	23	3.91	3.61	7.52	2-8	3.45	0.68	High
Joel Moore	25	24	4.17	3.58	7.75	6-11	5.15	0.71	High
Luther Hackman	23	22	4.55	3.41	7.95	2-9	5.12	0.54	High
Mike Saipe	24	23	4.65	3.39	8.04	5-11	5.16	0.74	High
George Glinatsis	28	16	4.75	3.75	8.50	2-9	5.86	0.86	High
Michael Farmer	29	22	5.14	3.77	8.91	6-7	5.61	0.43	High
Mike Vavrek	24	28	5.04	4.07	9.11	7-18	6.27	0.54	High
Stephen Shoemaker	25	27	3.81	5.33	9.15	5-12	6.66	0.95	High
Josh Kalinowski	21	28				12-10	3.92	1.35	Low

One of my joys each year is getting my STATS Minor League Handbook and checking out the MLE's for the Rockies' prospects. As most of you know, the premise of MLE's is that they are a representation of what a player would have done if he had played for the big league club rather than in the minor leagues. The Rockies' AA squad plays in a pitchers' park in a pitchers' league, so they often have some outrageous MLE's. Here are some MLE's around Dante Bichette's .866 OPS.

Name	Age	MLE OPS
Angel Echevarria	27	.868
Chris Kirgan	25	.877
Ben Petrick	21	.863
Jamie Taylor	27	.884
Derrick White	28	.911

TOP DOG: Ben Petrick

Petrick is another one of those testaments to the joys of secondary average. He has never hit over .250, but he still puts up respectable OPS's due to his good patience and decent power. His line in New Haven was .238/.343/.470 this year, which is pretty much in line with his past career except for improved power. His Coors-inflated MLE's read .259/.342/.521. I don't think he would do quite this well playing for the big league club, but he could outhit Kirt Manwaring fairly easily. He has historically been a good basestealer, but his percentage dropped dramatically this year, so he may be bulking up some for more power. He could steal 10 bases a year in the bigs. Comp: Eddie Taubensee.

YOUNG' UN: Choo Freeman

Freeman is a rare bird, indeed, a first round pick for the Rockies who isn't a pitcher. Freeman was drafted largely for his athletic ability, but he showed some good baseball skills as well in his Arizona League debut (.320/.391/.442). He was only caught once in fifteen steal attempts and didn't strike out an inordinate amount either. I'm guessing he'll end up in low A next year, but he needs to improve his defense before he can move through the system quickly.

HANDY MAN: Derrick Gibson

On the surface, Gibson's .292/.341/.429 line appears respectable, but it is a disappointment when you consider his previous performances. Gibson was a football athlete who was coaxed into baseball with a large signing bonus. He is currently listed at 6-2 and 244 pounds, and his fitness has been questioned in the past. The Rox don't really need another defensive liability given their outfield, so he's going to have to justify his presence with a big bat or improve in the outfield. I think he'll be able to play in the big leagues, but I'm not convinced he will be a plus player when considered through the lens of park effects. Comp: Brook Jacoby, with slightly less power and more speed.

JOHN DOE: Edgard Clemente

Edgard changed his surname prior to the start of the 1998 season from Velasquez to that of his uncle Roberto Clemente. Unfortunately, it didn't help his production at all. He repeated time in AAA and still his numbers dropped thirty points across the board to .251/.310/.456. He is a poor basestealer and has just once cracked the one walk per ten at bat threshold. He needs to hit for average and power to be an asset, and thus far he has done neither above AA. He will still be just 23 next year, so it isn't time to get anxious just yet. He needs to put together a monster year to get noticed in this organization. Comp: Steve Gibralter or Pedro Munoz.

ON THE MOUND: Mike Kusiewicz

The Rockies' pitching prospects tend to oscillate between good and bad. In 1997, Mike Vavrek and Steven Shoemaker appeared to be their best prospects, but as the chart above indicates, they struggled badly this year. I generally think it's a bad idea to have affiliates in severe hitters' parks, but with the Rockies playing in Coors, having a AAA team in Colorado Springs probably isn't a bad idea. Kusiewicz's pitched for AA New Haven, so he will face the Colorado Springs test next year. Kusiewicz has been outstanding for each of his four minor league seasons (2.75 ERA). His control has always been good, but he rose to another level this year (1.8 BB/9). He also is very good at keeping the ball in the park as he has allowed just eleven home runs the last two years. In my young pitcher's study, I'll probably pick some extra Rockies' prospects just to see what sorts of effects extreme parks have on players.

1998 just did not do a very good job.

(Keep in mind that this year's park adjusted data is calculated in a new manner. This is a direct result of the problem with Andres Galarraga's park adjusted numbers last season. That's why Jay came up with a different methodology. A methodology that all my studies indicate is better than any previous method. Anyway, I'll present a complete examination of the numbers either in next year's book and/or at the Baseball Think Factory web site.)

The pitching staff, on the other hand, had a pretty good season. One of the measures I like to use to compare pitchers is XR/G (or the number of Extrapolated Runs a pitcher is projected to allow per 27 outs). In 1998, the average XR/G in the NL was 4.65 runs.

How many Rockies pitchers finished with figures lower than that? To give you a perspective on where these guys stack up vs. the best starters in the NL last year, here's a list of the Top

15 qualifiers in XR/G:

Name	Team	XR/G
Maddux G	ATL	2.22
Glavine T	ATL	2.97
Smoltz J	ATL	2.97
Leiter A	NyN	2.99
Brown K	SD	3.01
Daal O	ARI	3.22
Schilling C	PHI	3.29
Wood K	ChN	3.46
Harnisch P	CIN	3.72
Neagle D	ATL	3.87
Hermanson D	MON	3.90
Cordova F	PIT	3.90
Lima J	HOU	4.13
Millwood K	ATL	4.21
Tomko B	CIN	4.25

It should come as no surprise to see Atlanta's staff well represented on this list. Although to find any Colorado pitcher we'd have to travel down to the number 28 position, just about all the Rockies' pitchers fared pretty well. In particular, the bullpen was quite impressive as every regular member posted above average numbers.

Will this hold true for the 1999 season?

In defense of Mr. Gebhard, the Rockies had a couple of young players in the lineup in 1998 who should improve in 1999, namely, Todd Helton and Neifi Perez. Additionally, 2B Mike Lansing and Larry Walker had, what appears to be, an off seasons. Therefore, we can expect some improvement next season. Unfortunately, I don't think they'll improve enough to get their offense up to a respectable level. This seems especially true when I consider the lack of any impact prospects in the Rockies' system.

So where do I think the Rockies will finish in 1999? Well, I don't have a crystal ball, but I'd guess that another second division finish appears likely.

No matter where they end up, however, the one thing I 100% certain of is that, once again, we'll be hearing a lot about the lack of pitching in Colorado with the inferiority of their offense going unnoticed. That's why next year in the Rockies' Team Esssay of the Y2K BBBA, someone will again belabor the point about how parks affect run scoring. That's, also, why you'll be reading a rehash of the main point of this essay: COORS FIELD RADICALLY INFLUENCES THE STATS OF THE PLAYERS WHO PLAY THERE.

But please keep in mind next year as you're forking out your dollars to buy this book that we won't be harping on the park effect topic to annoy Rockies fans, but to help them. Hopefully the result of all this repetition will bear fruit. Maybe, just maybe, someday Mr. Gebhard will get the message. That's assuming, of course, that he doesn't get annoyed at strangers who try to give him a little advice.

HERE COMES MR. HELTON

OK, so I stole this from one of my favorite movies. You know, the one where the angels in heaven (not the ones in Anaheim) make a mistake and knock off the prizefighter before his time, and have to find a new body for him. Still haven't got it? Here's a clue: Claude Rains plays the title character, who is not the hero.

Chew on that while we natter away on the subject of Todd Helton. Brock Hanke has a theory that hitters tend to exhibit a sort of ebb and flow as they develop, making advances on an every other year pattern while falling back the next. It's intriguing, but not well-quantified as yet. However, Brock's view is that such patterns probably don't operate much, if at all, in extreme hitter's parks. And so he surmises that Rockies' rookie first baseman Todd Helton, who had a pretty fair debut season in 1998, could skip the "adjustment phase" altogether.

Another clue on that old movie: the fussy angel who screws up and accidentally knocks off the prizefighter is played to perfection by Edward Everett Horton, which is kind of close to Helton, especially if you've had a few drinks.

Sean Forman, our man in Havana when it comes to

TEAM BREAKOUT ROCKIES 1998

Category	RS	RA	W	L	Pct.	Rk
5+ RUNS SCORED/ROAD	197	128	23	7	.767	7
4- RUNS ALLOWED/HOME	145	80	20	7	.741	9
5+ RUNS SCORED	660	504	61	26	.701	14
4- RUNS ALLOWED	328	195	51	25	.671	9
5+ RUNS SCORED/HOME	463	376	38	19	.667	15
4- RUNS ALLOWED/ROAD	183	115	31	18	.633	8
CLOSE LOW SCORING GAMES/HOME	15	16	4	3	.571	10
RECORD IN BLOWOUTS/HOME	165	152	11	9	.550	8
SLUGFESTS/HOME	407	391	26	24	.520	8
CLOSE SLUGFESTS/ROAD	41	41	3	3	.500	8
LOW SCORING GAMES/HOME	15	21	4	4	.500	13
RECORD IN BLOWOUTS	246	256	19	19	.500	8
RECORD IN CLOSE GAMES/ROAD	127	127	18	19	.486	3
RECORD IN SLUGFESTS	511	521	32	34	.485	10
SEASON TOTALS	826	855	77	85	.475	10
RECORD IN CLOSE GAMES	373	384	37	43	.463	11
RECORD IN BLOWOUTS/ROAD	81	104	8	10	.444	10
RECORD IN CLOSE GAMES/HOME	246	257	19	24	.442	14
CLOSE SLUGFESTS/HOME	175	183	10	13	.435	12
5+ RUNS ALLOWED/HOME	381	425	22	32	.407	3
RECORD IN LOW SCORING GAMES	81	105	17	25	.405	13
CLOSE LOW SCORING GAMES/ROAD	36	41	8	12	.400	10
LOW SCORING GAMES/ROAD	66	84	13	21	.382	8
SLUGFESTS/ROAD	104	130	6	10	.375	13
5+ RUNS ALLOWED	498	660	26	60	.302	6
4- RUNS SCORED/ROAD	103	222	12	39	.235	8
4- RUNS SCORED	166	351	16	59	.213	14
4- RUNS SCORED/HOME	63	129	4	20	.167	16
5+ RUNS ALLOWED/ROAD	117	235	4	28	.125	14

young players, thinks Helton could win the batting title this year, given that he's playing in Coors Field, and given that his second half numbers would have put him right in range for the 1998 crown: .359/.420/.579. Larry Walker, Todd's teammate in Colorado, won the batting title last year with a .363 BA.

I think it's possible that Brock's "adjustment" idea might also apply on an in-season level. In other words, the pitcher's grapevine may come into play even faster than a year one, year two type of beat. Todd Helton's numbers in the second half of 1998 might give us glimpse of such a process at work.

Of course, Mr. Helton won't have a guardian angel such as Claude Rains to look out for him, but if he has as much natural talent as Robert Montgomery (the hero of the movie) has rough-hewn charm, he'll be a cinch. Todd even has a crusty manager just like the one in the movie in Jim Leyland, who'd be a good choice to reprise the role played by James Gleason.

Month	AB	R	H	D	T	HR	RBI	BB	IBB	SO	BA	OBP	SLG
June	84	12	22	4	0	4	15	7	0	15	.262	.319	.452
July	84	13	27	5	0	6	15	3	0	6	.321	.359	.595
August	113	16	45	13	0	4	29	8	3	7	.398	.435	.619
September	77	12	24	3	0	4	13	15	2	10	.312	.430	.506

OK, let's look at the last four months of Mr. Helton's 1998. (The movie I keep teasing you with, by the way, was released in 1941.) Todd hit .394 and hit seven HRs in May after a slow, homerless April; the pitchers went to work and brought him back to earth. He rallied in July with six HRs, and was ultra-

aggressive at the plate, drawing only three walks. That's not abnormal for a young player, even one who's shown good plate discipline in the minors, as Todd has.

Todd exploded in August, hitting close to .400 and becoming the Rockies' RBI guy, plating 29 runs. Note that even though he's still being aggressive at the plate, the pitchers are getting leery, as the three intentional walks indicate.

In September, the pitchers are really getting leery of Todd, just as everyone is getting with Robert Montgomery when he claims he has a guardian angel. No one else can see him, you see. The pitchers could see what Todd Helton was doing, all right: they jumped his walk total from 6.7% in August to 16.6% in September. So that even though Todd's BA dropped, his OBP was still almost the same. Just as the prize-fighter in our movie is destined to be the champ, only he ends up being the champ as a different person than who he was at the beginning. By the end of 1998, Todd Helton had made a similar journey, and if he keeps walking like he did in September, he'll be a champ, too.

The name of that movie? Surely you've got it by now. It's the name of the Braves' new outfielder. It won't be but a few days into April before the Turner Classic Movie folks, sensing the perfect tie-in, will program this classic to coincide with his arrival. The banners will be hung in Turner Field, and they'll say: Here Comes Mr. Jordan.

But they'll have the right baseball name—and the bigger impact player over the next five years—up in Colorado. <DM>

						←	Park Adjusted Statistics						→			Adj	Raw			
Name	AB	R	H	D	T	HR	RBI	BB	SO	SB	CS	BA	OBP	SLG	XR	XR/27	XR/27	OXW	DXW	TXW
Abbott K	71	7	16	6	0	3	11	2	21	0	0	.231	.255	.418	8	3.57	4.38	0.05	0.03	0.08
Bates J	74	8	12	3	0	0	2	8	24	0	0	.160	.241	.202	2	0.79	1.37	-0.63	-0.05	-0.68
Bichette D	662	75	200	47	2	18	95	28	82	17	4	.302	.329	.458	90	4.96	6.03	3.11	0.49	3.60
Burks E	357	44	93	21	5	14	45	39	91	4	7	.260	.332	.465	53	4.97	5.85	1.82	0.33	2.15
Castilla V	645	86	186	27	4	40	114	40	99	6	9	.288	.332	.527	103	5.57	6.82	4.21	1.11	5.32
Colbrunn G	122	9	35	8	2	2	9	8	25	3	3	.286	.335	.426	16	4.81	5.60	0.53	0.02	0.55
Goodwin C	159	22	35	7	0	1	4	16	44	6	1	.221	.290	.277	14	2.73	3.31	-0.29	0.21	-0.08
Hamilton D	194	23	60	9	1	5	21	23	22	4	1	.310	.384	.437	34	6.42	7.30	1.73	0.49	2.22
Helton T	530	62	153	36	1	22	77	53	59	3	3	.289	.357	.485	86	5.80	6.80	3.86	0.89	4.75
Lansing M	584	57	147	37	2	10	52	39	97	12	3	.251	.302	.375	63	3.64	4.36	0.63	2.31	2.94
Manwaring K	291	26	65	11	3	2	21	38	54	1	5	.222	.317	.300	26	2.86	3.48	-0.38	1.53	1.15
Perez N	647	62	162	24	9	8	46	38	77	5	6	.251	.291	.350	66	3.38	4.03	0.18	3.24	3.42
Reed J	259	35	68	16	1	8	31	37	63	0	0	.263	.353	.422	39	5.21	6.17	1.52	1.25	2.77
Vander Wal J	104	15	28	9	1	4	14	16	32	0	0	.267	.361	.498	19	6.48	7.46	0.96	0.10	1.06
Walker L	454	90	149	44	3	19	52	64	68	18	4	.329	.414	.563	97	8.15	9.72	5.94	0.69	6.63
COL	5635	656	1491	321	34	156	622	466	1044	80	46	.265	.323	.417	733	4.42	5.30	23.24	12.64	35.88

Pitcher	S	C	T	SS	ES	IC	HH	PP	TJ	S12	S35	S67	C1	C23	C45	C67	QWP
Astacio	4.74	3.44	8.18	35%	9%	32%	41%	6%	9%	21%	38%	41%	9%	47%	38%	6%	.439
Bobby Jones	4.30	3.60	7.90	45%	10%	20%	40%	5%	5%	15%	45%	40%	10%	35%	50%	5%	.446
Dejean	4.00	5.00	9.00	0%	0%	0%	0%	0%	0%	0%	100%	0%	0%	0%	100%	0%	.240
J Thomson	4.08	3.08	7.15	50%	19%	38%	38%	0%	8%	31%	31%	38%	12%	54%	35%	0%	.515
Kile	4.43	3.29	7.71	40%	9%	37%	37%	6%	11%	23%	40%	37%	14%	46%	34%	6%	.485
M Brownson	4.00	2.50	6.50	50%	50%	50%	50%	0%	0%	50%	0%	50%	50%	0%	50%	0%	.498
Ma Thompson	5.67	4.50	10.17	0%	0%	0%	67%	0%	0%	0%	33%	67%	0%	0%	83%	17%	.207
Ritz	6.50	3.50	10.00	0%	0%	0%	100%	0%	0%	0%	0%	100%	0%	50%	50%	0%	.194
Saipe	6.50	2.50	9.00	0%	0%	50%	100%	0%	50%	0%	0%	100%	0%	100%	0%	0%	.367
Wright Jamey	4.53	3.88	8.41	38%	9%	29%	44%	9%	6%	21%	35%	44%	6%	35%	44%	15%	.404

NATIONAL LEAGUE WEST

ARIZONA DIAMONDBACKS

Doug Drinen

A RATIONAL CONVERSATION ABOUT IRRATIONAL SPENDING

Taking place at a ballpark near you. ..

Jonny: You get a look at some of these offseason signings? Totally ridiculous! Completely idio—

Catfish: No wait, don't tell me, lemme guess. It sickens you that these crybabies get paid obscene amounts of money to play a kid's game, right? Let 'em try workin' for a living for awhile. That'd fix their wagons, eh?

Jonny: No, that's not it. Our society's priorities do seem a bit out of whack from time to time, but that's exactly what it is: society's priorities. I learned about capitalism in civics class a long time ago, thank you very much. I understand that a person's worth is determined by—no, make that defined as—the amount that he can convince someone else to pay him. I can live with that. Beats all the alternatives that I'm aware of, anyway.

Catfish: Oh, then you must be one of those ticket price alarmists. You gonna quote the Fan Cost Index on me, tell me all about how a youngster in this day and age has to choose between college and an afternoon at the ol' ball game?

Jonny: Wrong again, smart guy, economics was the semester right after civics. Demand drives ticket prices. If salaries had anything to do with how much tickets cost, my Fiesta Bowl tickets would've been free. And another thing, baseball is damn cheap entertainment. The Diamondbacks are one of the toughest tickets in baseball, and with a week's worth of foresight you can get $5.50 or even $3.50 tickets to all but a handful of games. You can even park for free with a little ingenuity. Bring a couple of Dagwoods and you're set. Cheaper than a movie, hell, it's nearly cheaper than *renting* a movie.

Catfish: OK, I've got you figured. The salaries offend you because of the fact that the same few teams, the so-called 'large-market' teams, are the only ones that can afford to offer them. It's a cryin' shame that the Kansas Citys and Minnesotas and Montreals can't hope to compete, and all that.

Jonny: I really don't know if there actually are fundamental market-size problems in baseball today, but if there are, I think they're going to be tough to get rid of without eliminating a lot of the motivation to innovate and succeed. That's a price I'm hesitant to pay. The really funny thing about all this just-look-at-the-Marlins tripe Costas is always feeding us is that there have always been teams that couldn't, or at least didn't, compete. Criminy, Bob, wouldn't it just suck if the Yankees won 10 or 12 straight World Series or some damn thing like they did in the golden age of the 50s and 60s?

Catfish: Whew, didn't mean to get you st—

Jonny: And another thing, rooting for a team that barely has a snowball's chance can be a lot of fun. I grew up an Oklahoma State Cowboy football fan. They beat the Sooners when I was in kindergarten, and then again a coupla years after I graduated from college. They haven't beaten the Cornhuskers in my lifetime. Never even occurred to me to whine and moan that the Orange and Black weren't "on a level playing field."

Catfish: Alright, I'm stumped. What's the problem with the

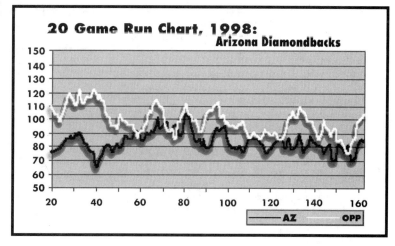

355

QMAX PRESENTS: "BAD" PITCHERS

COULDA BEEN A CONTENDAH

It wasn't supposed to end this way. Jeff Suppan was plucked off the Red Sox roster with the third overall pick by the Diamondbacks and promptly inserted in the rotation. After two months of inconsistent-to-poor results, however, he was dumped from the rotation and ultimately sold to the Kansas City Royals for the proverbial bag of broken bats and a pop-up toaster. What happened? Can QMAX shed any light on the subject?

Jeff's first four starts were mediocre at best, but that wouldn't have stood out much in the D-Backs' April, as the team was losing as expected. At the end of April, Jeff turned in a 3,3 start (six innings, five hits, five strikeouts, two walks) that looked like the guy they were hoping for. He turned in another strong start against the Mets (a 2,2 start this time, 6 1/3 innings, 4 hits, 2 walks), got bombed his next start (7,7) and turned in a complete-game four hit shutout against the Pirates on May 15. It seemed that Jeff was finding his groove.

His next three starts must have been very disappointing to the D-Backs, because that's pretty much all they gave him. He failed to reach the sixth inning in any of the three starts, although he threw over 100 pitches in two of them, going deep in the count regularly despite only walking two batters each time. He got two more starts at the cusp of Gemini and Cancer (a 6,3 and a 3,5 start) getting into, but not through, the sixth inning in both of those. Then, he disappeared and showed up with the Royals two months later.

This is a familiar story, although the suddenness of the D-Backs ' giving up on Suppan surprised a lot of baseball watchers. Suppan was considered a prize prospect in the Bosox' chain, and we were at BBBA had noticed an eerie similarity between Suppan's 95-97 QMAX numbers and the first two years of the career of a pitcher who's done, er, OK since then: Greg Maddux of the Braves.

So again, what happened? Suppan's 1998 was a far cry from Maddux' breakthrough 1988 season, but it was still better than his previous numbers, and he's only 23 years old. What are we missing here?

As it turns out, QMAX didn't pop with the answer this time. An examination of Suppan's 1998 numbers shows that right-handed batters hit an astounding .338/.384/.588 against him, and that this was not a new pattern: righties averaged .348/.401/.508 against him in 1995-97. The word is that Suppan had lost confidence in his breaking pitches after a 1996 injury. That's not a good sign.

--Tom Austin

---

offseason signings? Which offseason signings? Mike Piazza? Bernie Williams? Mo Vaughn?

Jonny: Don't really care about those signings. I'm a Diamondbacks' fan.

Catfish: So who, then? Reynoso? Colbrunn? Swindell?

Jonny: Don't play dumb, you know who I'm talking about: Stottlemyre and the Unit. Still smarting from Jay Bell and Matt Williams, too.

Catfish: Alright, Williams stunk up the joint last season, but he'll have a better year in 1999. And who else is Arizona going to play at 3rd, anyway? Don't you think Johnson and Stottlemyre will outpitch Amaury Telemaco and God-knows-who — Neil Weber? Chris Clemons? Willie Banks?

Jonny: Of course Todd Stottlemyre and Randy Johnson are better pitchers than Telemaco and Chris Clemons, but they're not 21 million dollars per year better. Stottlemyre, despite the fact that he "wants the ball" and "is a bulldog" simply isn't worth eight million a year. And the Unit, while a great pitcher, is 35 and has a history of back problems. 13 mil is way too high.

Catfish: Sheesh, how many more injury-free seasons does the guy have to have before people will quit acting like he's going to just break in half? And besides, I thought you said they were worth whatever they can get.

Jonny: I mean worth it to the Diamondbacks. Players generate wins. Wins generate revenue. Todd and Randy ain't gonna generate enough wins to generate enough revenue to cover their salaries.

Catfish: Whoa, I must have misunderstood. When you said you were a Diamondbacks fan, I took that to mean you were a fan of the baseball team, not the accounting team. One less ivory back-scratcher for Colangelo, what do you care?

Jonny: Colangelo's back can itch like billy-o, for all I care, but sooner or later these huge salaries are going to hurt the team on the field.

Catfish: Not following you. Runs per dollar don't win ball games, runs do. If Stottlemyre's a better pitcher than Neil Weber and I'm a Diamondback fan, I want Stottlemyre on the hill instead of Weber. Even Williams and Jay Bell are better than the current alternatives.

Jonny: OK, I'll give you that, but what about next year, or the next? These are all 4- or 5-year contracts. Will ay Bell be better than Danny Klassen in 2001? Will Matt Williams even be better than Danny Ainge? Tony Batista needs a place to play, too, and there's a kid named Jackie Rexrode on the farm that looks terrific. And it goes without saying, does it not, that

John Patterson, Brad Penny, and maybe Nick Bierbrodt will be preferable to Todd Stottlemyre. I'd go even money that one of those three will outpitch the Unit in 2001.

Catfish: I still don't see the problem. If the 2001 Diamondbacks can win more games with Klassen in the lineup than with Bell, then why can't they just play Klassen?

Jonny: You. think they're going to pay 5 million a year for a benchwarmer? Throw in Williams' 9 million and Stottlemyre's 8, and they'd be shelling out 22 million for a utility man, a bullpen scrub, and a second-rate interleague DH. Not gonna happen.

Catfish: They've gotta pony up the 22 million anyway. The choice is between paying the unholy trio 22 million to play and losing games, or paying them 22 million to sit — or play golf —and winning games. Which is the better business decision? Say, what do you do for a living, anyway?

Jonny: I'm in the widget game.

Catfish: Fantastic, I've read about guys like you. The way I hear it, you're always doing things in a theoretically sound manner. So let me lob this at you. Suppose your company lays out some unheard-of amount of money for a widget-manufacturing machine, which goes irreparably haywire after two years and starts producing bass-ackwards widgets. Whaddya do, shrug your shoulders and start packaging up those useless widgets? Doesn't make much sense, especially if you've got a perfectly adequate replacement machine in the back room.

Jonny: You're right that the economically sound decision, assuming you've already got them signed, is to eat their contracts and play the ones that give you the best shot to win, but that's not how most baseball teams act.

Catfish: Most baseball teams don't have Jerry Colangelo as a managing general partner. He takes pride in going against the grain and, whatever else you think of him, he is a good businessman. If Jay Bell's play deteriorates to an unacceptable level, which, by the way, was far from being the case in 1998, paying him not to play is exactly the type of stunt Jerry would pull. Not only would it be a good business decision, but it'd be a good PR move. The papers'd write it up as, "Colangelo makes statement: give 110% or you're gone, no matter how rich you are." The Arizona fans already appear to be fed up with Jay, they'd eat it up.

Jonny: Well, that remains to be seen, but I still have two complaints.

Catfish: Fire when ready.

Jonny: First, there's the draft picks that you give up when you sign these guys.

Catfish: No argument, the draft picks are definitely a cost. It's easy to forget about those dang draft picks. And second?

Jonny: Second, there's a danger that the team will refuse to address positions that are costing them games. In fact, it's already happening. Why do you think the DBacks don't have any better options at 3rd base

WPA BULLPEN BOX—AZ DIAMONDBACKS

	PI	WPA	P	PPPI
Starters	1043	-0.8	54.2	0.052
Relievers	517	-1.4	26.0	0.050
Road	250	-1.5	13.2	0.053
Home	267	0.1	12.8	0.048
Mar/Apr	89	-0.9	3.6	0.040
May	95	-0.5	4.4	0.046
June	80	-2.2	3.8	0.048
July	75	1.1	3.7	0.049
August	93	0.8	4.2	0.045
September	85	0.2	6.4	0.075
Non S/H Sit.	418	-2.6	15.8	0.038
S/H Sit.	99	1.2	10.2	0.103
Low Pressure	267	-1.0	3.7	0.014
Med. Pressure	146	-3.2	8.8	0.061
High Pressure	104	2.8	13.5	0.130
Entered behind	293	-0.4	6.0	0.021
Entered tied	66	-0.4	8.0	0.122
Entered ahead	158	-0.6	11.9	0.075

Name	G	PI	WPA	P	PPPI	MI	ROB	T
Banks W	33	52	.3	2.3	.044	17	12	3
Brow S	17	28	-.2	.6	.023	8	11	1
Chouinard B	24	39	-.2	2.3	.059	13	11	2
Corey B	3	4	.0	.0	.010	1	0	0
Daal O	10	13	-.2	.6	.048	2	1	3
Embree A	35	48	.3	3.3	.070	13	12	7
Ford B	8	12	-.4	.3	.028	3	2	0
Manuel B	13	19	.1	.6	.029	6	7	1
Michalak C	5	6	-.3	.1	.023	1	2	0
Nunez V	4	6	.0	.1	.013	2	0	0
Olson G	64	76	2.4	5.9	.078	10	9	8
Pickett R	2	2	.0	.0	.000	0	0	0
Rodriguez F	43	53	-2.3	2.2	.041	10	13	3
Small A	23	34	.4	1.9	.056	10	4	3
Sodowsky C	39	59	-.3	2.9	.049	17	13	6
Springer R	26	36	-1.0	2.0	.056	9	2	5
Telemaco A	9	18	.2	.5	.026	6	3	1
Valdez E	6	6	.0	.1	.013	0	2	0
Weber N	4	6	-.1	.2	.028	2	2	0
Total	517		-1.4	26.0	.050			

	|---------- Quality ----------|				|--- Pressure -------|		
	Dis.	Poor	Fair	Good	Her.	Lo	Med	Hi	
Banks W	2	5	14	12	0	16	11	6	(4)
Brow S	0	2	12	3	0	11	6	0	(0)
Chouinard B	1	5	14	3	1	11	7	6	(4)
Embree A	3	3	18	9	2	18	7	10	(8)
Manuel B	0	3	8	2	0	11	1	1	(1)
Olson G	5	2	31	23	3	31	19	14	(11)
Rodriguez F	5	5	29	4	0	30	9	4	(1)
Small A	1	2	12	6	2	13	6	4	(4)
Sodowsky C	2	7	23	4	3	23	10	6	(3)
Springer R	3	3	14	6	0	14	7	5	(2)
Others	1	9	36	5	0	37	13		(1)
TOTAL	23	46	211	77	11	215	96	57	(39)

	7th inning			8th inning			9th inning		
	0	1	2	0	1	2	0	1	2
Banks W	1	0	0	0	1	3	2	0	0
Chouinard B	1	1	1	1	0	5	0	0	0
Daal O	0	0	0	0	1	0	1	0	0
Embree A	1	1	0	0	2	2	1	0	1
Olson G	1	1	0	1	0	0	1	9	11
Rodriguez F	0	0	0	0	0	0	1	2	2
Small A	0	2	0	2	1	0	2	0	0
Sodowsky C	2	1	0	4	3	0	2	0	0
Springer R	0	0	1	3	1	1	1	0	0
Telemaco A	0	0	0	0	0	0	0	0	0
Starters	11	11	12	5	6	1	1	1	0
TOTAL	17	17	15	16	15	12	12	12	14
Record	4-13	10-7	10-5	5-11	11-4	11-1	4-8	10-2	13-1

Sean Forman's

PROSPECT WATCH

NAME	AGE	POS	LEVEL	GR98	GR97	GR96	AVG
Karim Garcia	22	OF	AAA	104	109	89	103
Danny Klassen	22	SS	AAA	79	71	36	69
Brent Brede	26	OF	AAA	49	61	75	57
Adam Hyzdu	26	OF	AAA	50	57	68	55
Hanley Frias	24	SS	AAA	47	60	33	49
Brent Cookson	28	OF	AAA	50	-	41	48
Edwin Diaz	23	2B	AAA	48	48	49	48
Garry Maddox	23	OF	AAA	51	44	-	48
Michael Stoner	25	1B	AAA	36	39	18	34

NAME	AGE	POS	LEVEL	GRADE
Jack Cust	19	OF	Rookie	75
Jackie Rexrode	19	2B	High A	74
Adolfo Joseph	17	OF	Rookie	68
J.D. Closser	18	C	Rookie	65
Carlos Urquiola	18	2B	Low A	64
Abraham Nunez	18	OF	Low A	63
Adam Neubart	20	OF	High A	56
John Adams	21		High A	51
Darryl Conyer	18	OF	Rookie	48
Jhensy Sandoval	19	OF	High A	48
Paul Weichard	18	OF	Rookie	48

NAME	AGE	GS	S	C	T	W-L	ERA	K/H	LEVEL
Bob Wolcott	24	21	4.71	2.95	7.67	8-6	5.18	0.64	High
Reid Cornelius	27	25	4.44	3.28	7.72	7-9	5.27	0.61	High
Nelson Figueroa	24	29	4.31	3.48	7.79	15-5	4.42	0.81	High
Brad Cornett	29	17	4.82	3.12	7.94	3-7	4.95	0.43	High
Chris Clemons	24	17	4.41	4.35	8.76	2-8	6.15	0.77	High
Brad Penny	20	28				14-5	2.96	1.50	Low

The Diamondbacks haven't had a AA affiliate until this year, so their older prospects have either had to play in Fast A or in AAA, which probably isn't ideal for their development, but I doubt it will make any difference in the long run. The Diamondbacks have some quality young prospects and some good middle of the infield prospects. The Diamondbacks minor league affiliates are largely in hitters' parks, so keep that in mind when evaluating their numbers.

MINOR LEAGUE ALL-STAR: Karim Garcia

Every year Garcia gets eighty or so at bats in the majors and every year he flops and is sent back to AAA. He then murders AAA pitching (to the tune of a .670 SLG% this year) and gets called back up. Frankly, I'm a bit skeptical if he will ever become a major league regular. He is still just 23 (maybe), and he hasn't reached 500 major league at bats yet. There is still hope for him, but one more year like this one, and he's going to have a tough time getting another shot.

PATIENCE, GRASSHOPPER: Jackie Rexrode

Of all the middle infielders that the Diamondbacks have percolating up through the system, Rexrode may be the best one. He is still very young, just 20 this year, but his leadoff skills are already remarkable. He has yet to post a sub .380 OBP in any league, and his basestealing is nothing short of phenomenal. Over the last two years has 63 steals in 75 attempts and he has drawn 175 walks vs. 137 strikeouts, all while batting over .300. He's mostly a doubles hitter thus far, but if you can get on base and steal, that's not a big deal.

UP THE MIDDLE: Danny Klassen

The Rattlers picked up Klassen in the expansion draft after the Brewers were kind enough to leave him unprotected. One of the problems with such an evenly distributed talent pool like the Brewers have is that you aren't entirely sure what baskets you should be putting your eggs into. Klassen swings a pretty good bat for a middle infielder and if Jay Bell and his model character weren't sitting in Phoenix he would probably be given a shot at a middle infield job. Bell is a fine player, but he is blocking many of the Diamondbacks' best prospects at a premium price tag, without premium play. Comp: Mark Lewis with more strikeouts.

Young 'un: Jack Cust

Cust was the D'Backs first round pick back in 1997 and he has been a great hitter since he first started swinging ash. He put a huge .344/.526/.598 line in

Lethbridge. However, that is a Pioneer League line, so you need to knock about 50 points off across the board to get a more realistic number. ust was a high school first baseman, but has been moved to the outfield for understandable reasons (Travis Lee). Despite some knocks on his speed he was 15 of 24 stealing bases, so he's not Hamelin-like on the basepaths. Still he might end up like Daryle Ward, stuck behind a star first baseman in the National League.

ON THE MOUND: Brad Penny

The Diamondbacks have been falling all over themselves to throw money at free agents. Despite that, they have the makings of a nice farm system and their pitching staff in High Desert was outstanding. They were second in the league in ERA despite playing in a severe hitters' park. Penny was the ace of that staff, though bonus baby John Patterson wasn't too far behind him. In three pro years, Penny has yet to post an ERA above 3.00. I couldn't get all of his starts, but in the 20 I do have his QMAX numbers were 3.30/2.90 vs. a 4.14/3.64 league average. Despite being a big-time strikeout pitcher (207 k's), he has tremendous control, just 35 walks. The Diamondbacks add an AA affiliate next year and I expect Penny will be anchoring that staff as well.

Catfish: than Matt Williams? It's because they've assumed all along that Williams is the man for the next 4 years. Maybe Williams' presence helps explain the current lack of 3rd-sackers in the system, buts it's not clear to me that they wouldn't upgrade the position if Williams' inadequacy were clearly holding the team back. Imagine the 2001 version of the Diamondbacks. Dellucci and Batista continue to develop, Lee is a monster, Johnson is still dom-inating, Benes, Omar Daal, and Stottlemyre are still above average, and a couple of the young pitchers are ready. If the Diamondbacks are convinced that signing a top-notch 3rd-baseman is the difference between mediocrity and contention, I

say they'll do it, Williams be damned.

Jonny: Ahhh, you've just gotten to the heart of the matter right there. The thing is, the Diamondback payroll will be so bloated by that time that there won't be any money left to sign that top-notch 3rd-baseman.

Catfish: Whaddya mean, won't be any money left? They've got the stuff in sackfuls.

Jonny: Look, every team has to have a budget. The Diamondbacks' is sure a lot higher than most teams', but it's not infinite. The 2001 Diamondbacks will be paying through the nose for Bell, Williams, Johnson Stottlemyre, and whatever other overpriced medioc-rities and one-season wonders they manage to throw money at between now and then. Eventually, there has to come a point where they just can't afford to spend anymore.

Catfish: No! The Diamondbacks do not have to have a budget. No team does. To the best of my knowledge, no other businesses operate like that—first set a budget and then maximize profit within that constraint. There's simply no reason for a business to restrict itself that way.

Jonny: So you're suggesting that the Diamondbacks can just spend as much as they want, and that's good business?

Catfish: Not at all. In fact, I'm not suggesting that they *spend* anything. You don't spend money on ballplayers, you invest money in them. You said it yourself, ballplayers generate wins and wins generate revenue. If the revenue generated by a top-notch 3rd-baseman exceeds his salary, then it's worth it for a team to sign that 3rd-baseman. That was true for teams in 1898, and it'll be true for teams in 2098. It's true for teams with 10 million dollar payrolls and it's true for teams with 100 million dollar payrolls. Since Bell, Williams, Stottlemyre, and Johnson don't affect the 3rd-base man's ability to put runs on the scoreboard, they don't affect his ability to generate rev-enue, and hence don't affect the price Arizona should be willing to pay for his services.

Jonny: Theoretically, no, but again, that's not the way baseball teams generally act.

Catfish: That's their problem. Once more, the guy calling the financial shots in Arizona has (a), a willingness to act in a way baseball teams don't generally act and (b), a solid understanding of the fact that the way to generate revenue is to win ballgames. Jerry's been around long enough to figure out that the good people of Phoenix will not support a loser, or even a mediocrity, for long, but will lite-rally dump their cash by the wheelbarrow full on the doorstep of a winning team.

Jonny: I wonder. Let's say the DBacks win about 75 games this year. Sound about right?

Catfish: 75 is precisely the figure I had in mind. At least 4 of the 5 starting pitchers should be above average, but all except Johnson will likely be barely above average. Meanwhile, the bullpen and the offense still look pretty dismal. .500 seems like a best-case scenario.

Jonny: And then in the winter of 99, they go on another spending spree similar to this one, picking up a few more over-the-hill 5-15 million dollar bores.

Catfish: That's the first time I've heard Randy Johnson referred to as a bore.

Jonny: I was thinking of Stottlemyre, Bell, and Matt Williams, actually. Willie Blair would be another example, although he was shipped out in favor of Bernard Gilkey, yet another.

And if those guys don't bore you, you're unborable. Anyway, do you deny that a couple more expensive lame-o's could be on the shopping list next year?

Catfish: No, I can't deny that.

Jonny: So in 2000, the payroll is up to, what, 70 or 80 million—right now I've got the '99 payroll figured at about 51 mill. Meanwhile, the team's getting older but not much better. Say 81-81.

Catfish: A not-unfathomable scenario.

Jonny: The Phoenix fans are going to be expressing displeasure in no uncertain terms about all the money being spent with no results. And your claim is that Colangelo is going to shell out *another* 10 or 20 or 30 million the following offseason to acquire whatever's necessary to get the DBacks into the playoffs?

Catfish: Again I ask, why not? If your scenario does indeed unfold, the DBacks will almost certainly be losing money. But regardless, if, say, Chipper Jones is the difference between losing 20 million and losing 5 million — and he may be, then he's still worth 15 million.

Jonny: But don't you think that, by that point, the Arizona brass will feel a little. . .well. . .snakebit?

Catfish: Cute.

Jonny: Thanks.

Catfish: This is a legitimate point. Let's assume for a moment that the Diamondbacks do in fact end up losing

TEAM BREAKOUT DIAMONDBACKS 1998

Category	RS	RA	W	L	Pct.	Rk
CLOSE SLUGFESTS/ROAD	16	13	2	0	1.000	1
5+ RUNS SCORED/ROAD	200	163	22	7	.759	8
5+ RUNS SCORED	435	309	46	15	.754	10
5+ RUNS SCORED/HOME	235	146	24	8	.750	11
CLOSE SLUGFESTS/HOME	51	46	5	2	.714	3
4- RUNS ALLOWED/HOME	174	90	26	11	.703	13
4- RUNS ALLOWED	324	197	51	27	.654	12
4- RUNS ALLOWED/ROAD	150	107	25	16	.610	10
SLUGFESTS/HOME	142	134	11	8	.579	4
RECORD IN SLUGFESTS	251	284	18	17	.514	8
CLOSE LOW SCORING GAMES/HOME	33	33	7	7	.500	14
LOW SCORING GAMES/HOME	46	57	10	12	.455	14
SLUGFESTS/ROAD	109	150	7	9	.438	10
RECORD IN CLOSE GAMES/ROAD	138	147	17	22	.436	9
RECORD IN CLOSE GAMES	289	306	32	44	.421	14
RECORD IN CLOSE GAMES/HOME	151	159	15	22	.405	15
SEASON TOTALS	665	812	65	97	.401	14
RECORD IN LOW SCORING GAMES	95	116	19	29	.396	14
RECORD IN BLOWOUTS/HOME	121	166	10	17	.370	13
LOW SCORING GAMES/ROAD	49	59	9	17	.346	12
RECORD IN BLOWOUTS	209	332	16	33	.327	13
RECORD IN BLOWOUTS/ROAD	88	166	6	16	.273	14
CLOSE LOW SCORING GAMES/ROAD	23	34	4	11	.267	15
4- RUNS SCORED/HOME	115	255	10	39	.204	15
4- RUNS SCORED	230	503	19	82	.188	16
5+ RUNS ALLOWED/HOME	176	311	8	36	.182	14
4- RUNS SCORED/ROAD	115	248	9	43	.173	13
5+ RUNS ALLOWED	341	615	14	70	.167	13
5+ RUNS ALLOWED/ROAD	165	304	6	34	.150	13

Jonny: Yup.

Catfish: There are two reasons why that might happen: either Colangelo miscalculated the amount of money each extra win would bring in, or he-or his baseball people—miscalculated the number of wins Stottlemyre would add. If it's the first, then he'll probably be less likely to make *bad* investments, but his willingness to make good ones shouldn't change. And that's really what we're talking about here. Neither of us really cares much if the Diamondbacks continue to sign Stottlemyres and Bells. We do care, however, whether or not they're willing to keep signing the Randy Johnsons.

Jonny: Well, OK, but I suspect it's the second reason.

Catfish: Alright then. It's obviously not clear how he's going to react, but my hunch is that he'll decide he wants a championship no matter what the cost. I think item #1 on Jerry's ego's to-do list is to solidify his standing as The Greatest Thing That Ever Happened To Phoenix Sports by bringing home its first major championship. Particularly if the Cardinals or Coyotes are near contention for their titles, then I think the answer to your question is yes, he will keep

money on many of these contracts—I think we both agree that that's likely.

throwing money at the problem.

Jonny: And if it doesn't work again? How long is this going to continue? How high can the payroll go?

Catfish: I have no way of knowing, but I suspect it may be high enough that Stottlemyre, Bell, and Williams won't even be significant.

Jonny: OK, bottom line. Was the Stottlemyre signing a good decision or not?

Catfish: From a financial standpoint for the Diamondbacks' ownership, almost certainly not. For us, lowly Diamondbacks' fans, it definitely means more wins in the short-term, and there's a strong possibility that it won't cost us wins in the long-term, no matter how much of a lemon he turns out to be at age 36 or 37. And the same goes for Jay Bell and Matt Williams, too. If, at some point in the future, management uses Stottlemyre's salary as an excuse not to sign someone else, then that's a far worse economic decision than the original Stottlemyre signing. That's when I'll start worrying about the DBacks' financial decisions. For now, though, I'm just gonna sit back, watch a lot of pitchers' duels, and enjoy 75-or-so wins.

Name	AB	R	H	D	T	HR	RBI	BB	SO	SB	CS	BA	OBP	SLG	XR	Adj XR/27	Raw XR/27	OXW	DXW	TXW
Batista T	291	45	78	16	1	18	40	20	57	1	1	.268	.318	.519	47	5.66	5.67	2.04	0.94	2.98
Bell J	541	78	133	28	5	20	65	89	140	3	6	.245	.357	.428	84	5.19	5.15	3.31	1.81	5.12
Benitez Y	205	17	40	7	1	9	29	15	48	2	2	.197	.265	.375	20	3.12	3.06	-0.14	0.27	0.13
Brede B	211	23	47	9	3	2	17	25	46	1	0	.221	.311	.321	21	3.31	3.33	0.04	0.16	0.20
Dellucci D	413	43	104	19	12	5	50	36	111	3	6	.253	.316	.392	49	4.10	4.22	1.05	0.58	1.63
Fabregas J	150	8	29	4	0	1	15	14	27	0	0	.195	.265	.242	10	2.14	2.15	-0.55	0.38	-0.17
Fox A	498	66	135	21	6	9	43	47	105	16	9	.270	.354	.391	72	5.22	5.29	2.92	0.66	3.58
Garcia K	331	38	72	10	8	9	42	20	84	5	4	.217	.260	.378	32	3.20	3.23	-0.14	0.65	0.51
Gilkey B	100	8	24	0	0	1	5	12	15	4	2	.242	.327	.273	9	2.81	2.84	-0.15	0.16	0.01
Klassen D	108	12	20	2	1	3	8	9	35	1	1	.189	.260	.312	8	2.18	2.21	-0.42	0.14	-0.28
Lee T	555	70	146	20	2	22	69	74	133	10	1	.262	.348	.426	83	5.26	5.24	3.35	0.78	4.13
Miller D	167	17	46	14	2	3	14	12	47	1	0	.277	.333	.437	23	4.97	5.14	0.84	0.56	1.40
Stankiewicz A	145	9	29	5	0	0	8	7	35	1	0	.202	.248	.236	8	1.73	1.81	-0.73	0.21	-0.52
Stinnett K	271	35	67	14	1	11	33	38	82	0	1	.249	.351	.431	40	5.04	5.17	1.52	0.49	2.01
White D	559	83	154	32	1	22	83	46	109	26	9	.275	.337	.456	88	5.44	5.38	3.64	0.90	4.54
Williams M	506	71	132	26	1	20	69	47	110	6	1	.261	.327	.437	67	4.61	4.61	2.05	1.11	3.16
ARI	**5445**	**657**	**1308**	**232**	**45**	**162**	**605**	**535**	**1338**	**85**	**43**	**.240**	**.314**	**.389**	**666**	**4.11**	**4.15**	**18.61**	**9.80**	**28.41**

(Park Adjusted Statistics)

Pitcher	S	C	T	SS	ES	IC	HH	PP	TJ	S12	S35	S67	C1	C23	C45	C67	QWP
Adamson	4.40	4.20	8.60	20%	0%	0%	20%	20%	0%	0%	80%	20%	0%	20%	80%	0%	.357
Andy Benes	3.91	2.91	6.82	47%	21%	41%	21%	3%	9%	29%	50%	21%	18%	53%	26%	3%	.566
B Anderson	4.25	2.22	6.47	53%	13%	56%	31%	0%	25%	19%	50%	31%	38%	53%	9%	0%	.597
Blair	4.48	3.22	7.70	43%	4%	26%	35%	0%	0%	22%	43%	35%	0%	74%	26%	0%	.480
Chouinard	4.50	4.00	8.50	0%	0%	0%	0%	0%	0%	0%	100%	0%	0%	0%	100%	0%	.416
Daal	3.50	2.95	6.45	55%	18%	55%	18%	9%	9%	45%	36%	18%	18%	45%	36%	0%	.582
Sodowsky	4.17	4.50	8.67	33%	0%	17%	33%	17%	0%	17%	50%	33%	0%	17%	67%	17%	.411
Suppan	4.77	3.69	8.46	23%	15%	15%	46%	8%	0%	15%	38%	46%	8%	38%	46%	8%	.397
Telemaco	4.22	3.17	7.39	50%	6%	33%	28%	11%	11%	17%	56%	28%	11%	50%	33%	6%	.528
Wolcott	4.00	3.67	7.67	50%	17%	17%	17%	0%	0%	17%	67%	17%	17%	50%	17%	17%	.466

PLAYER COMMENTS

AMERICAN LEAGUE

NATIONAL LEAGUE

**SECTION**FIVE

The (%) symbol appearing by some players' names in section five means that there is an entry in the "Hall of Fame Watch" in section three's "Percentiles: Past, Present, and Future."

PLAYER COMMENTS
American League

CATCHERS

SANDY ALOMAR, CLE

Sandy's seasons have been so inconsistent that it's difficult to say what this year's collapse "means" in any real sense. Turning 33, though, it's going to be harder and harder for him to recover that .300-hitting form that he's only shown twice.<BJH>

PAUL BAKO, DET

A decent prospect. He's already turning 27, but his minor league numbers do support an offense jump for the Career Year. He's going to be fighting Sophomore Slump for it, but he does have a real chance, either this year or 2000. The minor league skills he hasn't shown yet are some small line drive pop and the ability to take his walks. Those are frequently the last skills to come in the majors, which enhances the chances.

I don't mean to tout him too highly; in a better-manned position, a big jump would just put him near the starter/backup breakpoint. But in this current crowd, Paul has a chance to become a solid starter for the Tigers.<BJH>

PAT BORDERS, CLE

Pulled a couple of fluke campaigns out of his hat in 1996 and '97, but is too old to expect to come back again.<BJH>

KEVIN L. BROWN, TOR

A still-young catcher who is having trouble adjusting to AAA pitching. If I were Toronto, I'd have given him another year at Syracuse. In A and AA ball, he's hit for a decent average with good on-base.<BJH>

A few times this year I saw a cannon fire to second-base to nail a runner. I was surprised that Fletcher could make such a throw—then I realized it was a rare Kevin Brown appearance. The stats say he only caught 29% of runners (below league average) but that's better than Darrin Fletcher's 24%. The Jays think Brown should have spent the year at AAA but were forced to keep him on the roster by the Santiago injury. With Benito gone in '99, Brown probably will remain as the backup, though

Tim Johnson will probably play Fletcher most of the time again. Too bad: Brown deserves a chance. <ST>

MIKE DIFELICE, TB

One of the finest glove caddies in the game, though he can't hit at all.<BJH>

SAL FASANO, KC

Very similar in skill set and ability level to Joe Girardi, except that Sal is younger. In fact, he is turning 27, but he had a big jump in quality this time out, so I don't expect any great Career Year. He's going to struggle to hit .240, but what else is out there to bury him like decent competition should?<BJH>

JOHN FLAHERTY, TB

San Diego skimmed the cream off the top of his Career Peak. Now, he's toast.<BJH>

DARRIN FLETCHER, TB

The Blue Jays have done a lot of exceptional things lately with their roster. They identified Roger Clemens correctly as being anything but over the hill. They did the same with Jose Crankseco, although Jose isn't what he once was. And they did it again with Darrin Fletcher. Darrin has been a first-rate catcher for years, without anyone seeming to notice. As a consequence, he doesn't get paid first-rate wages. But there he is, turning in seasons like this one, campaign after campaign. And he hits lefty.

Can you still swipe him for next to nothing in fantasy ball, like you used to? Or have the guys who mechanically

American League Catcher			
PLAYER	OXW	DXW	TXW
Rodriguez I	3.46	3.37	6.83
Posada J	1.94	2.02	3.96
Hatteberg S	1.73	1.86	3.59
Fletcher D	0.98	1.47	2.45
Steinbach T	0.34	1.38	1.72
Hoiles C	2.02	-0.35	1.67
Girardi J	-0.02	1.53	1.51
Fasano S	0.27	1.23	1.50
Webster L	0.98	0.30	1.28
Walbeck M	0.59	0.68	1.27
Bako P	0.59	0.57	1.16
Wilson D	0.58	0.55	1.13
Sweeney M	0.42	0.58	1.00
Difelice M	-0.69	1.61	0.92
Varitek J	0.07	0.85	0.92
Haselman B	0.66	0.21	0.87
Macfarlane M	0.61	0.21	0.82
Hinch A	0.34	0.45	0.79
Marzano J	0.26	0.50	0.76
Brown K	0.40	0.28	0.68
Nevin P	0.20	0.42	0.62
Alomar S	-1.44	2.04	0.60
Flaherty J	-1.52	1.83	0.31
Kreuter C	0.17	0.14	0.31
O'Brien C	0.13	0.00	0.13
Machado R	-0.35	0.21	-0.14
Borders P	-0.71	0.49	-0.22
Oliver J	-0.47	0.21	-0.26
Valentin J	-0.87	0.19	-0.68

crank out the dollar values caught up to Darrin by now? If so, it's one of the very few instances of the true value of a player going unnoticed except by the Roti gang.<BJH>

JOE GIRARDI, NYY

All right. Let's get this straight right now. Joe Girardi never has been more than a good-field-no-hit platoon catcher, and he was 33 years old this time out, and he didn't even play half the time. For that player to rank sixth at catcher, behind a 36-year-old and a 31-year-old, means only one thing. That position is in big trouble in the American League. The Big Three of Ivan Rodriguez, Joe's teammate Jorge Posada, and Scott Hatteberg are basically all there is. They are the only three established top catchers in the American League. Everyone else doesn't really have a starting catcher.<BJH>

One of the goofiest looking players in all of baseball. His very small ears makes him look ape-like. Has only hit more than three homer in two seasons even though he played three years in Colorado (1994 - 4 HR, 1995 - 8 HR) <JF>

BILL HASELMAN, TEX

At his age and with his skills, we should probably regard Bill more as a pinch hitter than as a backup catcher. His bat is fine, but he plays poor defense. The Rangers count on not needing much backup catching, so their use of Bill makes perfect sense.<BJH>

SCOTT HATTEBERG, BOS

Well, Scott has had this season two years in a row, and this time, he wasn't Age 27. He also hits lefty. Is it possible that the two best players on the current Boston team are their catcher and their shortstop? Has that ever happened to the Bosox before? Usually, they bulk up on power-hitting first basemen and outfielders, like Mo Vaughn. But they don't have Mo now. What they have is this guy who only hits .275, with a dozen homers a year, but who plays a fine catcher in a league that, except for I-Rod (well, he's entitled to a nickname, isn't he?) doesn't have a lot of top talent. FINE FANTASY TOUT.<BJH>

A. J. HINCH, OAK

A young catching prospect that the A's are rushing. A. J. blew up A ball in 1997, which earned him a full jump to AAA. That didn't faze him at all. The A's made him their starting catcher on the

basis of that, and it was much more than he was up to. I say he's about two years away, if he gets a sane development program.<BJH>

He bunts well, which is unusual for a catcher. Twenty percent of his RBIs came on sacrifice flies. Neither of these are necessarily indicators of a bright future.**<SL>**

CHRIS HOILES, BAL

I, personally, am a fan of playing a man at the most valuable defensive spot he can handle, because having that extra bat in there usually helps the lineup more than the weak defense can possibly hurt it. I would, for example, play Mike Piazza at catcher and nowhere else. But there is a limit, and Chris Hoiles here has reached it. He simply cannot play catcher any more. His bat ranked him seventh here, but that's the result of working with a mathematical system.

Chris' defensive skills right now are so poor that it has to mess with the confidence of his pitchers. It has to mess with them to the extent that is hinders their pitching. And that has to be a factor in the well-documented lousy performance of his very expensive team. I don't know where to draw the mathematical line where the effect occurs, and I do believe that almost everyone else draws it too high, but it is higher than this, and it is higher at catcher than anywhere else, because the catcher interacts so much with the pitcher.<BJH>

CHAD KREUTER, CHW

Another aging backup catcher who isn't worn out because he's never had to play full time.<BJH>

MIKE MACFARLANE, OAK
(1998: KC-OAK)

He's 35 years old and collapsing rapidly. I'll be surprised, even in this climate, if he's in the major leagues at the turn of the millennium.<BJH>

ROBERT MACHADO, CHW

As he turns 26, he has some chance of putting up major league numbers that look at least something like his AAA ones. Unfortunately, even the AAA stats are lousy. Worse, he can't really play catcher. No Prospect. <BJH>

JOHN MARZANO, SEA

Do you realize that, at age 36 and having played ten years in the major

leagues, John Marzano, even if he's never been paid more than the minimum, is a millionaire twice over? Unless, of course, he's frittered it all away. <BJH>

PHIL NEVIN, ANA

Nevin has lost ground with the bat each of the last two years. This time, he was Age 27. I wouldn't have him on my team. <BJH>

CHARLIE O'BRIEN, ANA

Even the glove is gone. <BJH>

O'Brien started his career as a good glove, no hit catcher. Recently, he appears to have turned into a good hit, mediocre glove catcher. He's stuck with the good glove, no hit reputation, though, even if neither of those labels applies any more. <NL>

JOE OLIVER, FA
(1998: DET-SEA)

He's reaching that age when catchers start to go, and I think he's about gone.<BJH>

JORGE POSADA, NYY

Don't the Yankees have enough talent, without this kid coming up, too? I mean, isn't there some law against Boss Hogg getting free talent from the farm system alongside the people he buys? I mean, many times, when Der Poss Bresident has bought talent, he's had to make the deal as a trade, shipping off his organization's prospects in return for the proven stuff. Why didn't anyone loot Jorge Posada from him in one of those deals? I mean, if you've got Chuck Knoblauch to trade, don't you think you could get Jorge Posada in the deal? Well, Mr. Terry Ryan, why didn't you? Jeez.

By the way, although Jorge is an obvious fantasy tout, I don't expect him to make a big leap next year at age 27. He had that leap in power this time out, and should take a Sophomore Slump hit to counter the Career Year age.<BJH>

IVAN RODRIGUEZ, TEX (%)

It's rare for one player to lead a position in both OXW and DXW. Usually, some big hitter with a bad glove holds one honor and some hot glove who doesn't hit so well holds the other. On the other hand, it's also rare for one player to lead his position in At-Bats by over 150, and playing time will warp those XW values.

But Ivan Rodriguez doesn't just

lead the American League catchers in XW values. He leads in Defensive Winning Percentage (DW%), and would lead in Park Adjusted Runs Created per Game (PRC/27) as well except for Chris Hoiles. And Hoiles, as many have speculated, has lost the ability to actually play major league catcher any more.

When you're thinking about your own personal MVPs for the leagues, think about this. One very fair definition of the most valuable player in a league is the single player who most dominates his position. That is, the MVP, by this definition, would be the guy who has the most daylight between his TXW and the next TXW down at his position.

Ivan Rodriguez has close to three TXW over Jorge Posada. And Jorge couldn't catch Ivan, in either OXW or DXW, if he had played full time at full value, rather than platooning with Joe Girardi. **<BJH>**

BENITO SANTIAGO, CHC
(1998: TOR)

Benito's been a lousy player for so long that you may not remember he won he rookie of the year and his arm drew comparisons to Johnny Bench. He's till got the arm, more or less, but his other "skills" have gone ahead of Benito and are picking out retirement homes for him. I'll be stunned if he's still in the majors in three years. **<TA>**

TERRY STEINBACH, FA
(1998: MIN)

Tony LaRussa is trying to coax him out of retirement as Eli Marrero cancer insurance. Frankly, right now, Terry is still a better catcher than Eli is. On the other hand, if you're turning 37, and you've been a catcher all your career, and you've started hitting .250 instead of .280, I guess we can all forgive you if you decide to retire. **<BJH>**

—JEFF DRUMMOND WAXES ELO-QUENT ABOUT THE TWINS' POLICY OF BRING-ING HOME MINNESOTA NATIVES FOR A "SWAN SONG" TOUR WITH THE TEAM, AND IMPLORES TWINS' MANAGEMENT TO PUT AN END TO IT. AS WE SUSPECTED, THEY'RE NOT LISTENING, AND ARE ALSO TRYING TO BRING TERRY BACK, ALBEIT AT PENNIES ON THE DOL-LAR. <COJ>

MIKE SWEENEY, KC

Should rank with Posada and Hatteberg as the three hot young catchers in the league. He doesn't look like it in these XW rankings because he didn't hit as well and therefore didn't play nearly as much as the other two did. But Scott Hatteberg is turning 29, and Jorge Posada is turning 27, and Mike Sweeney is only turning 25, and has had as much major league experience as either of the others.

GOOD FANTASY BUY. He should get better this year, and no one else should. He could very easily end up as the #2 catcher in the league by 2000. In fact, he probably will. **<BJH>**

JAVIER VALENTIN, MIN

I know he's young, but so far, his entire career is one hot season with Fort Wayne in 1995. Fort Wayne is in low A ball. Still. You'd think that, with a name like that, he'd be able to play something like Stan Javier or John Valentin. Or Julian Javier. Or Jose Valentin. Or somebody. **<BJH>**

JASON VARITEK, BOS

Turning 27. Not a prospect, not on the same team as Scott Hatteberg. Unless Hatteberg gets hurt, Varitek figures to actually LOSE playing time at age 27, even if he does post a big gain year. He can't match Hatteberg's bat, and he can't match his glove, either.**<BJH>**

MATT WALBECK, ANA

Has been moving from team to team, as backup catchers will, except that the position is so weak right now that he really should rate a steady job.**<BJH>**

LENNY WEBSTER, BAL

A career backup who is gaining more and more playing time as he moves through his thirties. Yet another symptom that the position of catcher is unusually weak right now, aside from a very few top stars.**<BJH>**

DAN WILSON, SEA

Dan has played better than this, and a return to form would jump him several spots in the XW rankings. As a prediction, I would rank him about fifth in the league at this spot, right around Darrin Fletcher. A return to any of his seasons from 1995 through '97 would do that, so it's a good bet.**<BJH>**

Dan Wilson has been a decent offensive catcher for the past few years, but has been tailing off gradually since his heyday of 96. Last year was a low for Wilson in Seattle—he barely managed to scrape a .700 OPS. He had just hit a mini hot streak in July when he went down for two months with an ankle injury. He'll be the #1 catcher again in 1999, as he's a big favorite of Lou Piniella. He probably has another couple of years at his current production level before it dawns on Mariner management that they should be doing better. **<DJP>**

1ST BASE

TONY CLARK, DET

The Tigers keep expecting him to turn into God, but he remains mortal. This age-26 season saw a big jump in doubles and a good one in batting average. His last such jump was at age 24. Therefore, I don't expect another leap in 1999, at age 27.

The oddity of a 15-point jump in batting average accompanying a 18-point drop in On-Base Percentage is the result of Tony's walks dropping from 93 to 63, with an especial note of his drop in intentional walks from 13 to five. The combination causes me to believe that the managers of the league have figured out that Tony is, after all, just another solid starter, and not the All-Star the Tigers want him to be. The lower walks total is much more consistent with the rest of Tony's career.**<BJH>**

Impressive but streaky hitter. I've seen him look like the most powerful hitter I've ever seen one week, and, one week later, look like he didn't even know the purpose of swinging the bat was to hit the ball. If I had to make a guess about what to expect from him in 1999, I'd have to reply with two words-big things. Grab him while you can. <JF>

WILL CLARK, BAL (%)
(1998: TEX)

An old player, playing a top hitters' spot, down to about two TXW. That's the kind of guy who hurts your pennant chances. First, you think you have more player than you do, because you're remembering his seasons five years ago. Second, you're paying him as if he were still doing that. Third, you're putting him in the middle of your lineup, doing that. Fourth, you're not looking to replace him in spite of what he's doing. I don't want to imply that Will can't be a starter any more for some team, but the first thing that the Rangers, who are contenders, could do to improve themselves would be to cut Will loose and get themselves a championship-quality first baseman, rather than just another starter.**<BJH>**

I'm trying t-*o remember the last time that two teams essentially swapped players by signing the other one as a free agent. There is no doubt that the O's got the worst of this deal, even before you factor in the stalled development of prospect Cal Pickering. <DM>

Somebody finally helped him out with his uniform. Something just didn't look right to me. I can't quite put my finger on it, but I think he was wearing his pants too much like Ed Grimley. <SF>

American League FIRST BASE			
Player	OXW	DXW	TXW
Palmeiro R	6.61	0.77	7.38
Vaughn M	6.98	0.38	7.36
Delgado C	6.16	0.39	6.55
Thome J	5.29	0.40	5.69
Giambi J	5.31	0.23	5.54
Erstad D	4.30	0.57	4.87
Clark T	4.12	0.43	4.55
Clark W	4.25	0.24	4.49
Martinez T	3.91	0.42	4.33
Segui D	3.43	0.89	4.32
Mcgriff F	3.41	0.51	3.92
King J	1.98	0.57	2.55
Ortiz D	1.60	0.17	1.77
Morris H	1.45	0.24	1.69
Fielder C	1.41	0.11	1.52
Cordero W	1.14	0.32	1.46
Sexson R	1.24	0.13	1.37
Norton G	0.00	0.21	0.21

WIL CORDERO, FA
(1998: CHW)

Sabermetrics doesn't deal well with this type of guy. What we have here is a troublemaking, probably drug-addicted (according to rumor) ex-middle infielder with no real defensive value, whose last good year was 1994 with Montreal. He doesn't hit enough homers for a 1B, and he doesn't take walks, and he never will do either.

Against that is the lonesome hope that he'll turn his life around, combined with all that very young kid promise and the fact that only now is he turning age 27. If you believe in miracles, believe Wil will (heh) return to the keystone, run a BROCK2 projection from his 1994 out to 1999 and wow yourself with wonder. If you live in the real world, FORGET WIL CORDERO.<BJH>

CARLOS DELGADO, TOR

I'm still not convinced that moving Carlos to first base was a good move. His defense at catcher didn't seem all that awful

to me. But, then, I haven't interviewed the Toronto pitching staff lately, and they might think differently. I don't know.

I do know that there's a tendency to think that Carlos' big season with the bat was the result of the move. About that I am sure. It's baloney. Carlos Delgado, for all his years in the major leagues, is only now about to turn 27. He had a big breakout year at age 24, and an effective Sophomore Slump at age 25, and another step forward at age 26. That's where all the hitting came from. It's the age, not the position.

That being said, I don't expect another leap forward in 1999. As I've said elsewhere, most players have an on-year / off-year pattern to their growth. If they make big jumps at ages 24 and 26, they won't have another until age 28. If the first two were at 23 and 25, then Age 27 is the Career Year, most likely. Carlos is on the 24/26/28 pattern.<BJH>

Delgado is now truly an all-star-caliber 1st-baseman in the American League. His 2nd-half numbers project to 50 HR and 138 RBI for a full season. His defense looked better this year, though it showed up more in STATS' ZR than in BBBA's DXW. Next year his combination of offense and defense may make Carlos the best first-baseman in the league.. <ST>

DARIN ERSTAD, ANA

Darin had a jump season in 1997, at age 23, and so is due for another in 1999, and one more in 2001. On the other hand, the Angels are contenders and they now have Mo Vaughn. I assume they're going to DH one of the two. I sure as hell wouldn't want to unload Darin Erstad before I got a look at that age-25 campaign.<BJH>

JASON GIAMBI, OAK

Well, that was Age 27, and it was a disappointment as a Career Year, due mostly to the big drop in doubles. I can't explain the doubles drop, so, for the one year, I have to expect it to be a fluke, and the 40 doubles of '96 and '97 to return in '99. On the other hand, I think the jump to 27 homers was mostly the age effect, and should persist.

The projected season, with 40 doubles and 25 or so homers, would be more than most people expect. Also, most people don't think of Jason as being a veteran at his peak, but that's what he is. Therefore, in an unsophisticated fantasy league, YOU CAN PROBABLY GET HIM CHEAP. <BJH>

JEFF KING, KC

Hey! Royals! Yo! You in Kansas City! He's FINISHED! Toast! Dump Him Now! Rush a Rookie! Play Hal Morris! Anything! Those homers are all an illusion of the Offensive Surge! Really! There's Nothing Here! <BJH>

TINO MARTINEZ, NYY

His two worst years of the last four were the two when his Yankees won the World, and he was poised to be the Big Cleanup Hitter for the World Champions. Instead, the team gets touted for having no stars. That's silly, but it is true that their cleanup man has not dominated when they have won. <BJH>

Interesting idea for a study: how any teams who win the World Series have dominant offensive first basemen? It's a standard assumption, but the data isn't forthcoming. Let's use Tom Hull's percentile system to look at the first basemen for the 1990s World Champs:

YEAR	90	91	92	93	95	96	97	98
PCT	4	68	74	98	83	75	28	75

That's (in order): Todd Benzinger (Reds), Kent Hrbek (Twins), John Olerud (Jays, back-to-back in '92 and '93), Fred McGriff (his first off-year in '95), Tino, Jeff Conine (Marlins) and Tino. At least in the 90s, getting a stud at first is by no means mandatory for winning the World Series. <DM>

FRED MCGRIFF, TB (%)

Playing out the string with an expansion team, Fred didn't hit a lot for a first baseman. On the other hand, he gives Tampa a year or two to try to find a first baseman without totally lacking a cleanup man, and-in this instance at least-gives the fans a home-town hero to root for while they wait to develop a prospect.. <BJH>

Fred's decline over the past four years has killed his HoF chances, and now the question is will he hang on long enough to crack the 400 HR barrier. He is sinking fast. <DM>

HAL MORRIS, KC

Boy, did Hal get old fast. I like his basic type—the Ferris Fain style first baseman who beats you to death with OBP rather than SLG—but this is ridiculous. Hal has now hit exactly two home runs in his last 805 At Bats. Playing first base. <BJH>

GREG NORTON, CHW

With Big Crank playing DH and playing lousy, and Wil Cordero not really up to the task of playing first base every day, the Chisox had to find someone. It was either this kid or Ralph Kramden. <BJH>

Had a terrible time hitting late in the count (a miniscule .378 OPS-yes, OPS!). If he solves that not-so-little problem, he might yet make it to the level of a mid-pack starter. <DM>

DAVID ORTIZ, MIN

One of the symptoms of a poor team with little money is that their big hitting spots are usually undermanned. That's because people overpay for hitting without defense, and so the big guns go free agent or the equivalent. That often leaves the poverty-stricken teams with no option but to force a rookie a year or two early.

David Ortiz was 22 years old last season, with only 42 At-Bats at the AAA level. But he had been hot during his September call-up in 1997, so the Twins brought him up to stay after only 37 more AB at AAA. This time, the pitchers were ready, but now he's had that adjustment year.

Projection? His minor league numbers suggest .300+ with a .380+ OBP and mediocre pop, at least until he ages some. In 1999? Yep, I betcha. TOP FANTASY TOUT FOR LOW MONEY, especially if you're not power-starved. <BJH>

Showed the standard young hitter's splits in after 1-0/after 0-1 situations (.892/.612 OPS), but looks like a kid who may well walk 90-110 times. He's got a chance to be one of the top three players at this position in two to four years. <DM>

RAFAEL PALMEIRO, TEX (%)
(1998: BAL)

I still kick myself for being sure, back when they were kids, that Mark Grace would turn out to be at least the player Rafael has turned out to be. On the other hand, you've got a 33-year-old player here who bettered his career averages in batting average, slugging percentage, and on-base percentage, all three. How often does that hold up? <BJH>

Palmeiro will need to keep up his late-blooming power surge for another 2-3 years to get himself up to HoF levels in terms of raw numbers, but he has a shot at it. This is a much better career than most realize, and going to Texas should help his chances. <DM>

DAVID SEGUI, SEA

1999 in Seattle will be a mess at first base, as the team is sure that Jay Buhner won't be able to play the outfield, and are planning on having him play first. He may even DH, forcing Edgar Martinez to first. That leaves Segui without a position, except for a move to left field. That wouldn't be the end of the world, as his offense is fine for that spot, but his outfield days were generally considered to be behind him. His defense will be a big question, but if a team is willing to live with Glenallen Hill out there, as the Mariners were for the better part of last season, I don't see how Segui can be much of a dropoff.. <DJP>

RICHIE SEXSON, CLE

A very nice trial at the major league level. Richie represents injury insurance for the Indians against losing Jim Thome again, or their DH, or maybe an outfielder. The boy can hit. IF HE GETS AN INJURY REPLACEMENT JOB, PICK HIM UP FOR THE FANTASY SHORT TERM. He can help. <BJH>

I'm a little leery of his walk totals, and wonder whether pitchers will be able to adjust to a 6'6" guy with a big swing. He and Shane Spencer are two guys I want to see do it again before I'm convinced. <DM>

JIM THOME, CLE (%)

Not the Age-27 season we were looking for, but 1) he was hurt, and 2) that gave the Indians a chance to try Richie Sexson, and 3) Sexson is obviously ready.

What do I expect from Jim Thome in 1999? Something like his 1996 season, at age 25. That was a big jump year for Jim. Although he dropped an entire three batting average points, he picked up 12 points of OBP and 54 points of Slugging. That means that Age 27 was on pattern as the Career Year. Jim missed that, but it was due to injury, so I discard it when projecting the age 28 campaign. If Jim had had that career year in 1998, I would expect him to retreat a little in 1999, back to about the last big leap forward. That's the 1996, so that's what I expect. <BJH>

MO VAUGHN, ANA (%)
(1998: BOS)

He left Boston not with a whimper, but with a bang: A career-high .337 average (which brought him within a whisker of the batting championship), a career-high .591 slugging percentage, his second 40-homer season, his second 200-hit season. It was a year superior, in every regard, to his 1995 MVP campaign. He lost weight and was nimbler around first base than he'd been in years. He even erased the one black mark on his Red Sox ledger — his 0-fer in the 1995 divisional series — by hitting .412 with a pair of homers and seven RBI in the playoffs against Cleveland. He said repeatedly that he went out the way he wanted to go out, and he's certainly walking away with nothing to be ashamed of. It was the very definition of closure.

Why he walked—and why the Red Sox put as little effort as they did into stopping him—is a topic best suited for therapists and psychologists; the incomprehensible relationship between Vaughn and his former employer was beyond baffling to us baseball buffs. Focus instead on how, and not why, he left. As baseball legends go, it was something. <AM>

Brock Hanke thinks Mo is overpaid, and he's probably right. Still, he's a great hitter, and the numbers don't indicate that it's a park illusion. Disney is dead set on revisiting Gene Autry's I-can-buy-a-pennant approach, and who are we to stop them, anyway? If Mo has four more seasons like his last five, he'll have a helluva shot for the Hall. That's a big "if, " but Mo's no wraith, either. <DM>

2ND BASE

LUIS ALICEA, TEX

A reliable, consistent, middle-of-the-pack starting second baseman who cannot, for reasons that I do not understand, stay with one team, much less claim a job. Luis, at age 33, is still the best of the second basemen who are not really solid starting quality players. Since there are only seven of those currently available in the AL, Luis has value that no one seems willing to use. <BJH>

I, for one, blame the Republicans. <DM>

ROBERTO ALOMAR, CLE (%)
(1998: BAL)

As you long-time readers know, Roberto has been so good and so consistent for so long that I have trouble thinking anything up to say about him. Well, this year he had a big fat slump, at age 30, coming into a free agent year. As you no doubt know, players normally do tend to step up in those free agent years. And the drop from age 29 to age 30 isn't anything like THAT big. So, what happened?

Well, first the symptoms. Roberto's numbers dropped off big in 1) Batting Average, and 2) Home Runs. That'll mess with your OBP and SLG. The homers are easiest to explain. Since arriving in Baltimore, Roberto has had home/road homer splits of 14/8 and 10/4, for a total of

American League SECOND BASE			
Player	OXW	DXW	TXW
Offerman J	5.55	0.07	5.62
Easley D	2.79	2.44	5.23
Durham R	4.24	0.97	5.21
Knoblauch C	3.17	1.56	4.73
Alomar R	3.28	1.42	4.70
Fernandez T	3.55	0.15	3.70
Walker T	3.26	-0.26	3.00
Cairo M	0.44	2.03	2.47
Bell D	0.51	1.35	1.86
Mclemore M	1.05	0.73	1.78
Alicea L	1.53	0.11	1.64
Spiezio S	1.21	0.31	1.52
Cora J	2.14	-0.90	1.24
Benjamin M	-0.17	1.39	1.22
Velarde R	0.98	0.10	1.08
Grebeck C	0.28	0.51	0.79
Roberts B	0.52	0.00	0.52
Reboulet J	0.20	0.17	0.37
Lemke M	-0.54	0.54	0.00
Baughman J	-0.31	0.17	-0.14
Bournigal R	-0.63	0.24	-0.39
Martin N	-1.36	0.17	-1.19

24/12. That's a LOT of home ballpark effect, there. This year, the splits were a nice, even 7/7. That usually means that whatever quirk of the home park Roberto was exploiting went away, due to a park change or weather conditions or some such. In any case, the drop is usually a one-year fluke, so I expect Roberto to pick back up in taters.

Except, of course, that he won't be in Baltimore any more. Without that park, he may well stay put at the 15 level, especially as he has only exceeded 15 twice, once during his Career Year at age 28 (a one-year shift from the magic Age 27, either way, is hardly uncommon).

The Batting Average drop is harder to explain. My best guess - I haven't seen any monthly splits yet - would be a carry-over effect from the minor body troubles that led to the 112-game season of 1997.

But I don't know that. What I do know is that this .282 that Robbie hit was his lowest Batting Average since his rookie year in 1988, at age 20. Therefore, I expect him to step right back up in 1999.

Looking at the above, you can see that I expect, basically, a return to form, provided you don't think that those 22 homers in 1996 are "form" for Robbie. I expect a .300+ average, maybe 15 homers, a .350 OBP and a .450 SLG. That would be consistent with his age 25-27 seasons. <BJH>

One big difference was that Robbie didn't hit well in late-count situations during 1998 (.647 OPS, as opposed to .944 in 1997). That might have cut into his walk total, too. We'll have to see a bit more data before we can gauge how useful ByCount data is, but it's a working hypothesis. <SL>

JUSTIN BAUGHMAN, ANA

A Grade C shortstop prospect who the Angels rushed because they gave Luis Alicea away and Randy Velarde got hurt again. Since Velarde is turning 36, Justin might get to be overmatched some more in 1999. <BJH>

Someone called him a young Tony Womack. Certainly looked that way, until he broke his leg in winterball. Now, he'd be lucky to make it even to Womack's level. <NL>

DAVID BELL, SEA
(1998: CLE-SEA)

Miguel Cairo's older, weaker brother. David has clearly demonstrated that he is not a starting quality second baseman. Miguel has a couple of years left to establish that. That being said, there are only about seven starting quality second basemen in the American League, which may well mean that David Bell will start there all year for Seattle. <BJH>

The M's appear to have earmarked Carlos Guillen for their second base job, and David is going to have to catch on as a utility player. It's not always true that the son is a better player than the father. <DM>

MIKE BENJAMIN, PIT
(1998: BOS)

A serviceable backup shortstop who got pressed into service at the keystone when Boston's real plans there went awry. Mike is what Miguel Cairo will look like in eight years, if Miguel gets converted to shortstop, as he should. <BJH>

He's 33 years old. He entered last season with a career average of

.204. He got to play regularly only after three—count 'em, three —men ahead of him (Jeff Frye, Mark Lemke and Lou Merloni) suffered season-ending injuries. He hit .218 after the All-Star break, when he was in the lineup virtually every day. And the Pittsburgh Pirates signed him to a two-year contract to be their regular second baseman. P.T. Barnum was right.<AM>

Cam Bonifay, GM of the Pirates, must be a big fan of sideburns. That's because as far as I can tell, there is no logical reason for Mike Benjamin to get a two-year, $1.4-million deal. Now $1.4-million is chump change for major league players these days, so the cost isn't really too far out of whack. What's scary is that reports out of Pittsburgh indicate that the Pirates will be giving Mike some substantial playing time. As a matter of fact, Mr. Bonifay made the following comment at the time of the signing, "It depends on the flexibility of the moves we might make (this winter)," Bonifay said. "(Benjamin) could play shortstop as well. It's early, but we see him as a starting player candidate."

Maybe I'm missing something. Maybe the Pirate scouting reports indicate that Mike is something more than the 33 year-old, lifetime .224 hitter I watched play over 100 games last year. Either that or Mr. Bonifay doesn't really know what he's doing. <JF>

My, my, look at all this attention Mike Benjamin is getting from BBBA. You'd think the guy held some major league record or something. Actually, I doubt that the Bucs are going to make him their regular anything, and that Cam (like most GMs) is putting the best face on what is otherwise a ho-hum transaction. I mean, it's possible that we don't give GMs enough credit for having a sense of humor: they may well put out quotes like the ones above, go back in their offices, and laugh uproariously at those of us who take their statements at face value.

By the way, Mike holds the record for most consecutive hits, with 14. <DM>

RAFAEL BOURNIGAL, FA
(1998: OAK)

A glove caddy that the Dodgers fobbed off on the A's, who use him because they're desperate. At age 32, his glove wasn't even that good. <BJH>

MIGUEL CAIRO, TB

Good Field, No Hit. Everyone with 400 At-Bats who ranks below Miguel is really queasy as a starter. That does imply that there are only seven solid second base starters right now in the American League. Do you have problems with that? Well, take a look at the list. Who do you think is underrated or being treated unfairly? Is there anyone left who would be better than Luis Alicea if played for a full season? Is Luis your idea of a solid keystone starter at age 33? If so, how come he can't even stay with one team, much less hold a steady job? I use Alicea instead of Cairo because you all know about Luis. Miguel was a 24-year-old expansion rookie. But he played as well as Luis, and better than everyone who didn't. **<BJH>**

I, for one, blame the Republicans. But everyone else blames Chuck LaMar. **<DM>**

JOEY CORA, FA
(1998: SEA-CLE)

Had three hot seasons in Seattle, but isn't there any more, and so can't be expected to return to that level, especially at age 34. **<BJH>**

Cora is unlikely to get snapped up early on the free agent market, but he still has a pretty decent bat for a second baseman, and would be a useful pickup for a team that could pair him up with someone that can field. His career from here is probably more as a backup than a starter, unless somebody gets injured early next year and he gets to pull a Mark Lemke. **<DJP>**

RAY DURHAM, CHW

A surprise entry in the #3 slot at this spot. Toiling in obscurity behind the monster egos of Chicago (headed by the owner's own Ego of Godzilla), Ray improved on his previous best season of 1996, overcoming his slump of 1997.

This is normal. Most players, as they approach age 27, show an on-off pattern of growth. They'll establish some new level of offense one year, and then the pitchers of the league will adjust, and they'll have what amounts to a "Sophomore" slump, and then they'll counter-adjust, gaining more new ground.

Now, Ray Durham is turning age 27, and the pattern suggests an off year, while the age suggests a career year. In this situation, what often happens is that the two tendencies cancel out, so I do not expect Ray to improve much in 1999. But I do expect him to hold his own. The guys that make the big moves at age 27 are the ones whose "on" years were ages 23 and 25.

In general, though, I think the new

level of Batting Average and the new Home Run level will both hold for a few years. **<BJH>**

DAMION EASLEY, DET

An old favorite of Don Malcolm's, Damion has finally come into his own at age 28. Or maybe not. The first Big Gain in Damion's ability occurred in 1996 when, in a partial season, he moved to Detroit and picked up 50 Batting Average points. He has held those, and in 1997, he multiplied his expected Home Runs by five and made a huge jump in walks. This time out, he improved a small amount in homers, but dropped back down in taking free passes.

On balance, I think that the new 20-homer Easley is for real, but that the weak walk totals probably are the real thing, too. That is, I think this is Damion's real level of play. It's a good level, and should remain in the top five at this spot for the next few years, along with Offerman, Alomar, Knoblauch, and Durham. Of the five, Damion is possibly the weakest hitter, but he is also the best second baseman. **<BJH>**

TONY FERNANDEZ, TOR (%)

Tony is the only old guy among the league leaders at this position, and he did have a career year, and his defensive numbers are very poor, noticeably worse than Jose Offerman's, and he's a full XW worse than the guy right above him in the ranking list. On the other hand, he has always hit well in Toronto, and may know something special about Skydome. All in all, I think it's a fluke, and Tony will be back to the lower third among starters here by next season, declining rapidly. **<BJH>**

CRAIG GREBECK, TOR

Gets on base some, but that's about the end of his virtues, and he is turning 34. **<BJH>**

Played 2B full time after the Jays finally dumped Sprague (July 31). Had great clutch hitting stats, including a triple to cap a September sweep of the Red Sox. Overall, though, his low OBP/SLG makes 2B the Jays' biggest hole going into '99. **<ST>**

CARLOS GUILLEN, SEA

Obtained in the Randy Johnson trade, Guillen played a few games with the Mariners AAA team in Tacoma before being called up. At the tender age of 22, he was able to step in and contribute reasonably well. If he can maintain a .700 OPS and field second cleanly, he will be a very nice upgrade from Joey Cora.. **<DJP>**

CHUCK KNOBLAUCH, NYY (%)

Chuck has declined steadily from his Age-27 Career Year, and what we saw this time out is probably what we're going to continue to get, as that decline should level out. The one question is Home Runs. Chuck hit 12 of his 17 homers on the road, which probably means that he hasn't yet adjusted to the new ballpark. He might pick up some extra power when he does, converting some doubles to homers. But, on balance, I expect him to hold about this value for three or so years. **<BJH>**

Led the American League with 18 HBP. His 17 HRs were a career high in what was an otherwise disappointing year at the plate. Stolen bases were down 50% from 1997. **<SL>**

JOSE OFFERMAN, BOS
(1998: KC)

Is he worth it? That's the question, right? Is Jose Offerman worth the contract the Boston Red Sox extended him, especially given that Roberto Alomar wasn't really looking for that much himself, at least until Jose got his?

Well, the one-year numbers seem to say so. They say that Jose was the best hitting second baseman in the league, and that his defense wasn't all that awful. Of course, this was Jose's career year for hitting, and it was Roberto's worst year at the plate in many, and "everyone" knows that Jose Offerman can't field at all, and....

First, Jose with the bat. Yes, 1998 was his best year ever, but it was not really out of context for his last four years. So, he probably won't hit quite this well, but close. Maybe something like 1996, when he hit .303 with similar power stats to this time out. Of course, there is Fenway Park, so I guess we really should say that he probably will have batting numbers like 1998's, but they won't mean any more than the 1996 ones did. Still, that's a fine hitter for the position, very likely to be among the top two or three, and possibly the league leader.

Second, forget all that stuff about Jose's defense. Jose built his reputation as a stone glove while trying to play shortstop for Tommy Lasorda. He now plays second base, which is not as difficult. I don't mean to suggest that Jose has become a Gold Glove candidate—but he's not awful. He's adequate, and he'll probably turn the DP better than the merry-go-round of keystone kops the Sox slagged out there in 1998.

On balance, though, I'd rather have Roberto. He's proven more for longer.

But the Bosox may have good reasons to believe that Roberto is on his way down while Jose is just stabilizing at his real. Who knows what knowledge those insider guys might hoard? <BJH>

In any case, while the Bosox probably overpaid for Jose Offerman, they did not break any banks. They only overpaid a little. <BJH>

MARK MCLEMORE, TEX

When you figure out how the Rangers decided that this man must be their starting second baseman over Luis Alicea, who is even a year younger than Mark, please tell me. <BJH>

I, for one, blame the Republicans. <DM>

NORBERTO MARTIN, FA
(1998: ANA)

I assume that's "mar-TEEN", because "Norberto" is so obviously Spanish. No, wait. The rule is to accent the last syllable UNLESS it ends in a vowel, "n", or "s". Martin ends in "n", so it should be "MAR-teen", just like in English, except that the "i" sounds like a long "ee".

Oh, come on. YOU try to find something to say about this season. <BJH>

JEFF REBOULET, BAL

An elderly backup shortstop who got into 28 games as a second baseman because Roberto Alomar missed that many. He did take a bunch of walks and so got on base .351, which he's done twice before. He'd have been a minor hero if anyone else in Baltimore had done anything. <BJH>

BIP ROBERTS, FA
(1998: DET-OAK)

If you want to keep 12 pitchers on your roster, you need to condense some backup positions and a pinch-hit slot into one man. That, and that alone, is Bip Roberts' value to a team at age 35. <BJH>

SCOTT SPIEZIO, OAK

A Grade C- prospect that the A's are playing because they don't have anything else. Can't really hit, weak glove, only asset is youth. <BJH>

RANDY VELARDE, ANA

Turning 36 years old. Can't stay healthy. The Angels should have kept Luis Alicea, although Randy might be better if he could, like, you know, get into the line-up. <BJH>

TODD WALKER, MIN

This is the season that Jose Offerman is accused of having. Todd pounded American League pitching into the ground, but also waved at quite a few balls down there as well. He was just awful on defense, and I do have to suggest that his future may be at some less stressful position. His current hitting could certainly justify the outfield, if not first base, and he is only turning 26.

On the other hand, he did rank high at this position, and I don't know how many options the Twins think they have at the keystone. A lot will probably depend on managerial style. That is, we'll find out a lot about what Tom Kelly thinks regarding the middle of an infield by what he does with Todd Walker.

SECONDARY FIELDING STATISTICS
1998 AMERICAN LEAGUE
SECOND BASE

Name	G	GS	INN	TC	PO	A	E	DP	FPCT	RF	ZR	RZR	DP/G	DP/E	OOA	NRF	NDPR	NDPE
Damion Easley	140	136	1179	735	285	439	11	102	.985	5.53	.860	.679	0.78	9.3	70	111	119	141
David Bell	116	105	929	560	215	335	10	70	.982	5.33	.861	.721	0.68	7.0	35	107	104	107
Miguel Cairo	148	139	1233	724	279	429	16	110	.978	5.17	.965	.681	0.80	6.9	24	104	123	105
Norberto Martin	54	43	394	230	88	138	4	31	.983	5.16	.973	.863	0.71	7.8	8	103	109	118
Roberto Alomar	144	141	1236	710	250	449	11	86	.985	5.09	.915	.635	0.63	7.8	14	102	96	119
Mark McLemore	122	122	1056	595	249	331	15	71	.975	4.95	.887	.764	0.61	4.7	-5	99	93	72
Mike Benjamin	87	73	637	350	159	189	2	40	.994	4.92	.925	.810	0.57	20.0	-5	99	87	304
Justin Baughman	59	53	473	263	104	153	6	22	.977	4.89	.844	.844	0.42	3.7	-5	98	64	56
Craig Grebeck	91	77	723	403	144	249	10	38	.975	4.89	.908	.848	0.47	3.8	-8	98	73	58
Jose Offerman	152	152	1325	737	278	440	19	112	.974	4.88	.891	.447	0.76	5.9	-17	98	117	90
Lou Merloni	32	22	210	116	47	66	3	10	.974	4.84	.912	.943	0.43	3.3	-3	97	66	51
Scott Spiezio	112	110	956	524	195	316	13	71	.975	4.81	.861	.748	0.67	5.5	-19	96	103	83
Ray Durham	158	156	1357	738	282	438	18	129	.976	4.77	.898	.656	0.86	7.2	-32	96	131	109
Chuck Knoblauch	149	149	1293	695	274	408	13	85	.981	4.75	.876	.658	0.59	6.5	-35	95	91	100
Donnie Sadler	50	38	333	178	77	96	5	17	.972	4.68	.860	.900	0.46	3.4	-12	94	70	52
Tony Fernandez	82	81	693	360	129	222	9	43	.975	4.56	.861	.789	0.56	4.8	-33	91	86	73
Rafael Bournigal	48	26	270	136	55	81	0	20	1.000	4.54	.965	.867	0.67	—	-14	91	102	—
Randy Velarde	51	50	436	224	88	132	4	25	.982	4.54	.899	.808	0.52	6.3	-22	91	79	95
Todd Walker	140	139	1172	595	219	363	13	72	.978	4.47	.798	.654	0.55	5.5	-68	90	85	84
Bip Roberts	31	26	207	104	40	61	3	21	.971	4.40	.917	.848	0.91	7.0	-14	88	140	107
Joey Cora	151	147	1268	569	241	308	20	75	.965	3.90	.851	.713	0.53	3.8	-154	78	82	57

KEY: Inn-Innings; PO-Putouts; A-Assists; Er-Errors; DP-Double Plays; FPct-Fielding Pct.; RF-Range Factor; ZR-Zone Rating; DPR-Double Plays per RF(/9); DP/E-Double Plays per Error; OAA-Outs Above Average; NRF-Normalize; Range Factor (N=100); NDPR-Normalized DP per RF; NDPE-Normalized; DP/Error

Oh, yes. Since Todd had this huge jump at age 25, I expect a backslide at age 26, as the pitchers adjust to whatever it was that gave Todd 80 extra batting points. However, that also implies that I expect his next jump, and Career Year, to occur right on schedule at age 27 in the year 2000. BIG FAT YEAR 2000 FANTASY BALL TOUT THERE, especially in those leagues that don't count defense. <BJH>

ENRIQUE WILSON, CLE

What does he need to do to win a job? With the Indians having signed Roberto Alomar (which certainly isn't a bad signing), he doesn't have any place to play unless the Indians realize that Omar Vizquel is on the decline, which doesn't appear to be the case. <NL>

3RD BASE

GABE ALVAREZ, DET

A kid with good-looking minor league on-base numbers, but who struggled mightily at bat and in the field in 1998 and has been supplanted by Dean Palmer, of all people. He may be back on the underground railroad that runs between Detroit and San Diego.. <BJH>

See Troy Glaus, Ana. <NL>

MIKE BLOWERS, FA
(1998: OAK)

Skimmed a hot 150 AB off Seattle in 1997, which induced the A's to do something stupid (wasting possible development time for Mark Bellhorn, a kid they inexplicably seem to have given up on). <BJH>

WADE BOGGS, TB

Declining precipitously every year since 1994—which is worse than it seems in the face of the Offensive Surge that has dominated the game since that year—Wade no longer has any real value that would justify his star salary. That makes him perfect for teams like the Yankees, who don't worry about money, and expansion teams, who need the name. He needs only 78 hits to make 3000. That should happen with Tampa Bay, this year. Then, I presume, he will retire to make room for Bobby Smith. <BJH>

SCOTT BROSIUS, NYY

You've heard all about the Yankees and how they don't have any All-Stars and aren't, therefore, a typical George Steinbrenner dollar-sign champion. Well, let's skip whether we consider Derek Jeter or Bernie Williams or Chuck Knoblauch or David Cone or Andy Pettite or—get the point?—to be All-Stars, and let's concentrate of what all that New York Yankee money allows the team to do.

First, of course, it allows them to pick up All-Star free agents. That would include people like Knoblauch, who were, technically, gained in trade for players, but who were, in reality, free agents whose teams couldn't pay them, and who got what they could in anticipation of losing them to free agency. But, and more to the point of Scott Brosius, it allows the team to take gambles that other teams, that have to count their roster dollars, can't afford to take.

Consider the record of Scott Brosius. He was a poor part-timer for Oakland through his age-27 season. Then, at age 28, he made his very first big jump in ability, suspiciously coincident with the first full year of the Offensive Surge. Then, at age 29, he made another big jump forward, and was, for the very first time, an All-Star caliber player. He immediately collapse at age 30, at least partially due to injury.

So, how much would you gamble on this guy? He's turning 31. He's had one good season and one great one out of his entire career. He's injury-prone. You have both Wade Boggs and Charlie Hayes, although neither is happy because your manager can't make up his mind which one to play, which insults Boggs and puts unreachable expectation on Hayes. What would it take for you to jettison both Boggs and Hayes and gamble on this Scott Brosius character?

Well, George did it. I don't really know why, although the need for a one-year stopgap before Robin Ventura hit free agency does come to mind. It paid off in 1998, and it turned into quite a payday for Brosius. George, though, doesn't count the dollars.. And that is one big fat part of the recent Yankee success. That, and that the people he makes the ripoff trades with for those All-Star veterans never do seem to loot him for the Derek Jeters or the Andy Pettittes or even the Jorge Posadas while they're still minor league kids. <BJH>

I've never cared for the guy, but this is 3 good years in the last 4. Still, signing him for big bucks is silly. He's better than Mike Lowell, but Lowell is a pretty good player who will work cheap. I doubt the difference between the two players would amount to more than a game next year. Over the life of his contract, Lowell's fairly likely to be the better player. Ah well, it's only money. <RNJ>

ERIC CHAVEZ, OAK

The heir apparent at third for the A's. The next wave of Oakland bat prospects, despite the hype over the A's emphasis on OBP, doesn't appear to have anything like the plate discipline shown by Grieve, Christenson, McDonald, and Hinch. And with Gary Jones

American League THIRD BASE			
Player	OXW	DXW	TXW
Brosius S	3.88	1.14	5.02
Ventura R	2.99	1.08	4.07
Valentin J	2.68	1.20	3.88
Fryman T	2.65	0.24	2.89
Ripken C	2.11	0.67	2.78
Palmer D	3.07	-0.82	2.25
Smith B	1.50	0.64	2.14
Boggs W	1.38	0.42	1.80
Randa J	0.77	0.78	1.55
Hollins D	1.52	-0.05	1.47
Davis R	1.45	-0.44	1.01
Magadan D	0.64	0.10	0.74
Zeile T	1.08	-0.34	0.74
Coomer R	0.16	0.39	0.55
Blowers M	0.55	-0.35	0.20
Chavez E	0.21	-0.03	0.18
Shipley C	-0.11	0.26	0.15
Gates B	0.05	0.02	0.07
Alvarez G	0.01	-0.23	-0.22
Sprague E	0.09	-0.32	-0.23
Glaus T	-0.31	0.03	-0.28

out of the picture in Oakland with the departure of Sandy Alderson for greener pastures, this component of the A's may swiftly decline. Chavez may well be an excellent litmus test for this. <DM>

RON COOMER, MIN

A 32-year-old player who's only been in the majors for four years, Ron has declined for the last three of them. He is now in the position of being one desperate revival away from retirement. <BJH>

RUSS DAVIS, SEA

The Mariners need a new third baseman. <BJH>

Russ Davis completely lost the ability to field the ball at third. I lost track of the "low hops between the legs" and the side-saddle "ole's!". When he did manage to field the ball cleanly, it was always a nerve-wracking moment waiting for him to throw, especially if he had plenty of time. Definitely a case of the poor guy thinking too much when he was on the field. This follows the pattern of the previous couple of years, except that then, he was rescued from compiling really bad season error totals by a late season injury both times. Davis has pretty decent pop for a third baseman, but doesn't have particularly good strike zone judgment. Maybe he'd make a good umpire. When he was in his deepest fielding funks, his offense would disappear, too, and that's a bad combination.

What happens next season is very much open to question. Like many problem players, he may be traded for somebody else's problem, hoping a change of scenery will do them both good. Playing on grass to slow the ball down might help him a little. After three years of shaky defense, the Mariners will only keep him if they have no other option. <DJP>

TRAVIS FRYMAN, CLE

The defensive numbers at third base seem to be a little low this year, which sometimes happens, just as it sometimes happens that the wind blows so that Wrigley Field isn't a hitters' park. Still, This is not much defense for a man who is playing third base after starting out at shortstop. Doesn't it seem that his defensive ability should look more like John Valentin's?

That being said, the move to Cleveland seems to have helped Travis' bat struggles of the last few years.

Oh, yeah. How come all the good-fielding third basemen are at the top of the hitting rankings as well, while the lousy fielding third basemen are the same guys as the lousy hitters? Is this turning into an athlete's position or something? Has the search for the next Mike Schmidt gotten that obsessive? <BJH>

Moving Jim Thome to first in order to make room for (what ultimately turned out to be) Travis Fryman seems just a tad counter-intuitive, but John Hart seems maniacally determined to tear down his own handiwork. <DM>

BRENT GATES, MIN

Has done nothing to date to match his rookie campaign of 1993, in spite of the Offensive Surge. That's bad. The once-promising prospect is about through at age 29. Does anyone know what happened?. <BJH>

I WAS GONNA AGREE WITH DON MALCOLM THAT IT'S PROBABLY THE REPUBLICANS, BUT FROM WHAT I HEAR BRENT IS A REPUBLICAN. THE NEXT EXCUSE: INJURIES. THE REAL REASON? HE HAD A HOT TWO MONTHS EARLY IN HIS CAREER, AND EVERYONE GOT FOOLED BY IT. <COJ>

TROY GLAUS, ANA

WOW! Take a look at those minor league numbers. Don't be too concerned by his initial struggles in the bigs: Troy Glaus is turning all of 22. He blew up AA and AAA pitching this year for a combined .307 batting average with 35 home runs. Surely the Angels will give this kid some full-time major league job. Probably Dave Hollins'. TREMENDOUS FANTASY BUY unless you find out for sure that

SECONDARY FIELDING STATISTICS
1998 AMERICAN LEAGUE
THIRD BASE

Name	G	GS	INN	TC	PO	A	E	DP	FPCT	RF	ZR	DP/G	DP/E	OOA	NRF	NDPR	NDPE
Dave Magadan	30	26	204	73	15	52	6	7	.918	2.96	.833	0.31	1.2	7	112	182	90
Bobby Smith	97	81	740	244	70	165	9	11	.963	2.86	.783	0.13	1.2	18	108	79	94
Robin Ventura	161	158	1381	444	101	328	15	38	.966	2.80	.884	0.25	2.5	24	106	146	195
John Valentin	153	153	1326	425	121	289	15	26	.965	2.78	.836	0.18	1.7	21	105	104	133
Scott Brosius	150	147	1313	421	107	292	22	29	.948	2.74	.874	0.20	1.3	14	104	117	101
Joe Randa	118	105	950	291	72	212	7	18	.976	2.69	.826	0.17	2.6	5	102	100	198
Wade Boggs	78	75	639	187	52	130	5	12	.973	2.56	.803	0.17	2.4	-5	97	99	185
Brent Gates	77	66	608	179	59	113	7	5	.961	2.55	.772	0.07	0.7	-6	96	44	55
Gabe Alvarez	55	52	460	149	37	93	19	6	.872	2.54	.669	0.12	0.3	-5	96	69	24
Dave Hollins	91	91	746	224	63	145	16	13	.929	2.51	.707	0.16	0.8	-11	95	92	63
Troy Glaus	48	45	402	119	27	85	7	7	.941	2.51	.766	0.16	1.0	-6	95	92	77
Ed Sprague	128	126	1111	332	110	196	26	10	.922	2.48	.774	0.08	0.4	-20	94	48	30
Ron Coomer	76	75	628	177	56	116	5	9	.972	2.47	.845	0.13	1.8	-12	93	76	138
Todd Zeile	157	155	1365	392	104	265	23	19	.941	2.43	.753	0.13	0.8	-31	92	74	64
Cal Ripken	161	161	1365	375	101	266	8	23	.979	2.42	.815	0.15	2.9	-33	92	89	221
Mike Blowers	120	99	895	259	66	174	19	14	.927	2.41	.743	0.14	0.7	-23	91	83	57
Russ Davis	137	133	1144	338	56	250	32	26	.905	2.41	.715	0.20	0.8	-30	91	120	63
Travis Fryman	144	142	1266	349	100	236	13	21	.963	2.39	.775	0.15	1.6	-35	90	88	124
Tony Fernandez	54	52	453	109	32	73	4	3	.963	2.09	.770	0.06	0.8	-28	79	35	58
Dean Palmer	129	127	1102	276	69	185	22	16	.920	2.07	.696	0.13	0.7	-69	79	77	56

KEY: Inn-Innings; PO-Putouts; A-Assists; Er-Errors; DP-Double Plays; FPct-Fielding Pct.; RF-Range Factor; ZR-Zone Rating; DPR-Double Plays per RF(/9); DP/E-Double Plays per Error; OAA-Outs Above Average; NRF-Normalize; Range Factor (N=100); NDPR-Normalized DP per RF; NDPE-Normalized; DP/Error they're going to give him another year of "seasoning". <BJH>

See Adrian Beltre, LA. <NL>

DAVE HOLLINS, ANA

A completely different case from Dean Palmer. Dave isn't a good defensive third baseman, but he isn't awful, like Palmer is. He's right at Replacement Rate, which you can live with to get the bat. No, Dave's real problem is he can't stay healthy, and so you're rolling dice. The Angels, who could truly have used one of Dave's hot campaigns, got to play altogether too much of Craig Shipley and Troy Glaus while Dave didn't hit. <BJH>

DAVE MAGADAN, OAK

He's turning 36 years old, but he can still get on base, and he can still play a little third for you. That has value, but the world of major league ball has never been willing or able to understand that Dave Magadan had value. I can think of several contending teams that could really use him, but all of them are perfectly willing to let him while away the years in Oakland. <BJH>

DEAN PALMER, DET
(1998: KC)

This is so odd. Normally, major league teams won't play infielders who can hit but can't field. Dean Palmer, though, who plays third base as badly as anyone, has been an exception for years, and remains one even now that he is no longer with his original club. Is this some kind of bizarre tokenism, or what? <BJH>

Your prototype one-tool player. Palmer can still send it out of the yard, but everything else is short. No range, no glove, no strike zone judgment, no hitting for average. Still, he had a nice year, and Royals fans don't get to see home runs that often. Don't expect another year like it. <TA>

Especially given the fact that the Tigers pushed $35 mil in Dean's direction faster than Natasha Henstridge dropped her duds in Species. (No, Dean, imitation is not always the sincerest form of flattery.) Alien possession in the Tigers' front office may be a reality, though, since Tiger Stadium has been Palmer's second worst park performance-wise (.237/.271/.427). <DM>

JOE RANDA, KC
(1998: DET)

Joe Randa, for some reason, didn't deal well with Detroit's ballpark. Let's give it a year, and see whether he still has value or whether those two .300 seasons were just

his career peak playing itself out. <BJH>

For you numbers-hounds out there, Randa's home/road splits in 1998 were .628 home/.744 road. He slugged .566 in September, but the Tigers have replaced him with the man who replaced him in Kansas City (Dean Palmer). Traded to the Mets for Willie Blair, Randa will probably get moved again, since Robin Ventura is ahead of him on the Flushing Meadow depth chart. <SL>

Baseball is recursive, all right, and Joe Randa gets to replace the man who replaced him in Detroit, as part of Kansas City's ongoing self-schlub effort. Hold onto your hats, though, when you hear the name of the kid the Mets got in exchange for Joe.

Juan La Brawn

OK, it's acutally Le Bron, but I like my version better. (And so do all those guys in the Castro District, in their regulation indigo jeans and white T-shirts.) This is almost as good of an ethnic patty melt as the unforgettable Ross Moschitto, or the hokey stage name that Humphrey Bogart tried to palm off on an unsuspecting Warners contract player: Jose O'Toole.

Guy used to pitch for the Reds, right? No, no, wrong guy again. I always confuse ol' Jose with another ethnic cross-dresser—Zbigniew Gonzalez. <DM>

CAL RIPKEN, BAL (%)

Has grounded in to more double plays (312) than any other active player. Here's the 300 GIDP club:

GID	Player
328	Henry Aaron
323	Carl Yastrzemski
319	Dave Winfield
315	Eddie Murray
315	Jim Rice
312	Cal Ripken

If he plays in 1999, it's likely that he'll become the all-time leader. <SL>

BOBBY SMITH, TB

You know, if you just look at batting average, slugging percentage and on-base percentage—and what else should you be looking at, anyway —Bobby Smith had almost exactly the same offensive season as Wade Boggs. In the same ballpark. He's not going to take all those walks and get on base as much as Wade did when he was young, but he's only turning 25, and those major league numbers look just like all his minor league numbers. The D-Rays have something here. Yes, they do. <BJH>

ED SPRAGUE, PIT
(1998: TOR-OAK)

Hit 36 homers in his Career Year at age 28. Teams are still paying him for that season, I presume, as he has nothing left to offer at the major league level. <BJH>

ACTUALLY, THE ONLY THING ED HAS LEFT TO OFFER ON THE MAJOR LEAGUE LEVEL, AS DANDY DON HAS SO INDEFATIGABLY POINTED OUT FOR THE PAST FIVE YEARS, IS HIS WIFE-AND THAT'S STOOPING A LITTLE LOW EVEN FOR MLB, IF YOU ASK ME. STAY AT HOME, ED: YOU, YOUR MARRIAGE, AND BASE-BALL WILL ALL BE BETTER OFF. <COJ>

JOHN VALENTIN, BOS

The very best shortstop currently starting at third base for anyone. I thought for sure that the Sox would lose him years ago to some team that needed a shortstop of his caliber, which is to say to any of about 20 major league teams. But no, he re-signed with the Sox, and they moved him from second to third, and he just kept on ticking. <BJH>

ROBIN VENTURA, NYM
(1998: CHW)

The next time someone tries to tell you that college superstars never succeed in the major leagues, show them Robin Ventura's record. <BJH>

The Mets go for the pump, and the White Sox let all the air out of their balloon. Brock Hanke thinks Robin is a HoF caliber player if he could stay healthy; I think that's a bit of a stretch, but he's going to help the Mets make a serious run at the pennant in 1999. <DM>

TODD ZEILE, TEX
(1998: LA-FLA-TEX)

Does anyone else remember when Joe Torre wanted to call Zeile "inconsistent" because Todd hadn't hit like expected through the 1990 injury? Take a look. Todd has been one of the most consistent players in the game for the last decade. He was consistent in the minors before he came up, too. He drops off a little when injured, and loses some power when forced to change home ballparks in mid-season, but who doesn't? <BJH>

All true, but I can't help but wonder how many more times Todd is going to get traded in the middle of a season. Is anyone out there keeping tabs on all this? The Cards tossed Todd off to the Cubs mid-way through 1995; he went to Philly and Baltimore in 1996, then managed to spend a whole year in LA before being drop-kicked to Florida and, finally, to Texas in 1998. That's seven teams in four years, which has got be near the top of the list. If merely contemplating such movement makes you a bit dizzy, imagine what it must be like for Zeile, who's actually living it. He must jump every time the phone rings. <DM>

SHORTSTOPS

MIKE BORDICK, BAL

He's playing championship-quality shortstop. He can really help a team win a pennant. And still, the only thing I can really think to say is that he's no reason for moving Cal Ripken to third base. It was then and remains now a dumb, dumb move. You really can find a third baseman who hits better than this. <BJH>

It pains some people to admit it, but he had a good year. Average with the glove and above average for his position with the bat. Don't bet on it in 1999. <RNJ>

MIKE CARUSO, CHW

This is called "getting away with it for a year". The Chisox, apparently at a loss for what to do without Ozzie Guillen, promote this 21-year-old kid from - I am not kidding - Class A ball, where he was hitting a crisp .227. They get this fine season, with a lefty bat out of the middle infield to boot.

It won't last. Sophomore Slump is going to be a bitch. Still, just the fact that Mike could do this once, with that little preparation and at that tender age, indicates a fine major league career when all is said and done.

To be fair, Mike had hit .333 at a slightly-lesser Class A stop earlier in the year (and whatever did happen to Class B, C, and D, anyway?), and .292 in 1997 in low-grade Class A. <BJH>

DOMINGO CEDENO, FA
(1998: TEX)

"Domingo" means "Sunday" in Spanish. And even that's too often to play him. <BJH>

ROYCE CLAYTON, TEX
(1998: STL-TEX)

The problem, for those of you who don't live in St. Louis, is that Royce Clayton demanded to lead off the Cardinal batting order, and he can't get on base enough to do that. Tony LaRussa put up with the fiasco for a while, and then told Royce that he could only lead off if he'd

get his On-Base Percentage up to leadoff man levels. Royce never did, and began to complain, and wound up in Texas.

The last few years, Royce has been a Gold Glove contender at the position; this year, he was down. I presume that was the effects of throwing all his concentration into hitting, and that he will return to form with the glovewith the Rangers. Unless, of course, he has failed the reality check completely. <BJH>

DEIVI CRUZ, DET

Good field. No hit. Plays shortstop. What else do you want me to say? <BJH>

GARY DISARCINA, ANA

Consistent and fine on defense, Gary ranks like this when he hits well; not so high when he doesn't. Unfortunately, like the Ancient Mariner, Gary only hits well about one out of every three seasons. <BJH>

KEVIN ELSTER, FA
(1998: TEX)

Yes, we were all correct—1996 was a fluke. <BJH>

NOMAR GARCIAPARRA, BOS

Of the Big Three shortstops in the American League, Nomar has shown the least, yet he seems to have the best reputation. Nobody talks about Alex Rodriguez as being "the best" of anything, probably because he's on the same team as the older, more established Ken Griffey, Jr. But Griffey, hard as it is to imagine, is not in Alex' class. At Alex' age, Ken had led the league in no offensive categories at all, while Alex has led in several. And plays shortstop. And is two years younger than Nomar Garciaparra.

As for Derek Jeter: the New York press is determined, against all evidence, to make Joe Torre out to be a genius, and has promulgated the myth that the Yankees have no All-Stars. That's poppycock. Derek Jeter is obviously an All-Star. But the Joe Torre press suppresses his reputation, just like Ken Griffey suppresses Alex Rodriguez'.

That leaves Nomar. Now, Nomar has had one less full-time season than either Alex or Derek. He has never led the league in a major offensive category, while Derek Jeter has led in Runs Scored, and Alex Rodriguez has led in Runs and Batting Average. And all that is despite the fact that Nomar plays in Fenway Park, where it's easier to lead a league in a hitting

stat than in either Seattle or New York.

Please note that I'm not trying to knock Nomar. He's in the class of shortstops that includes people like Cal Ripken, Jr. And neither Alex Rodriguez nor Derek Jeter is out of Nomar's class. But the other two are just a bit better than Nomar, no matter what Peter Gammons says. <BJH>

It was the bottom of the ninth inning of the fourth and final playoff game against Cleveland. The Red Sox were trailing, 2-1, and the Fenway Park crowd was funereal, silently anticipating the end of what had been a brilliant baseball summer. Mo Vaughn—who had asked for extra batting-practice pitches before the game by pointing out, "It's my swan song, man"—was gone, having been pinch-run for in the eighth; he was in the clubhouse, physically and spiritually absent. The Sox who had ridden on his broad shoulders for so long were all alone.

And suddenly there was Nomar Garciaparra on the top step of the dugout, looking into the stands, waving his arms upward, imploring the fans not to lose faith, to keep cheering. They were stunned at first—in his two-plus seasons in Boston, Garciaparra had been the soul of reticence—and then delighted; they took the cue and began raising cain. Then, after Mike Jackson struck out Darren Bragg to end Boston's season, Garciaparra stepped onto the field and began theatrically applauding the customers, thanking and saluting them for their support. They returned his affection ten-fold.

There's a belief in Boston that Garciaparra is some sort of hothouse orchid, a natural introvert able to weave his magic only under Vaughn's protective shield. But there was a symbolic, and very public, passing of the torch last October 3. These are now Nomar Garciaparra's Red Sox. He's the new leader. Early returns are encouraging. <AM>

ALEX GONZALEZ, TOR

Not to be confused with the Alex Gonzalez who was a rookie for the Florida Marlins. This is the one who can play, but is also the one who is four years older than the other one. Note to Stats, Inc.: I don't care if they play in two different leagues, you need to start differentiating them by middle initial now, before confusion does set in. I found one list of AL shortstops that didn't even include this Alex Gonzalez, probably because the other one occupied the space in the database. <BJH>

I'm certain the Blue Jays' brass expected Alex Gonzalez to be jump, jive, and wailing on opposing pitchers by this point in his career, but it just hasn't happened yet. He has been stuck in a .240/.310/.390 rut the last four years. Though it didn't seem possible at the beginning of the year, his strike zone judgment has gotten worse. He won't keep you out of the playoffs, but he is not going to lead you there either. You don't have a thing, if you ain't got that swing. <SF>

SHANE HALTER, KC

Look. Kansas City has to play SOMEBODY. They can't just go out there without a shortstop at all. Shane was hitting .309 at AAA Omaha. I'm absolutely sure that the Royals' brain trust knew that wasn't real, but the alternatives was Mendy Lopez and Felix (the Thug) Martinez. Whaddaya gonna do? <BJH>

DEREK JETER, NYY

The idea that the Yankees have no All-Stars is silly. There are three big-time shortstops in the league, and this is one of them. This season, he ranked, in TXW, between Alex Rodriguez and Nomar Garciaparra, largely on the basis of being the best defensive shortstop of the three. But the contrapositive of that is that he is the worst hitter of the three. So what—he's clearly an All-Star. At shortstop. At age 24. That's not what you're looking for in a team of journeymen being dragged along by a brilliant genius of a manager. The New York press is full of it. <BJH>

I have a friend, who I'll call Gary, who thinks Derek Jeter is as good a player as Alex Rodriguez. Although Derek is a very good player, he's no Arod. Now, don't get me wrong, Derek Jeter isn't that far off from Alex, but he's far enough away to make my friend's opinion appear incorrect. The major difference between the two is that Jeter has a combination of skills that other top shortstops in major league history have had, while A-Rod has a combination of skills that no other shortstop has ever possessed.

I don't have to go back in history to find a pretty good comp for Jeter. Barry Larkin is pretty close. Just compare their numbers from 1998 to see what I mean. You could easily insert Jeter's first three seasons'

statistics into Larkin's record and nothing would look out of place. On the other hand, if you take A-Rod's first three years, and insert them into any other player's record, his stats really stand out. What makes A-Rod unique is that he's hit for average, he's hit a lot of homers AND he's stolen quite a few bases. Nobody else has done all three. The fact that Alex Rodriguez is two years younger than Derek Jeter (they'll be 23 and 25 in 1999) makes it unlikely that Jeter will be able to increase his offensive output to narrow the big gap in power.

Of course, we'll have to wait to ultimately find out who's right about this question. Things don't always work out the way you think they will. For confirmation, just ask the people who predicted a Hall of Fame plaque for Cesar Cedeno. <JF>

AARON LEDESMA, TB

According to Defensive Winning Percentage, Aaron here is the Gold Glove shortstop in the American League. True, it's only about 3/5 of a season, but still. What I want to know is why this guy wasn't in the majors before he turned 25. He was playing then for the Mets, who had - I can't remember who they had - playing shortstop. They traded him to the Orioles, who just had Cal Ripken, but moved him, but just had to bring in Mike Bordick instead of trying Aaron. Aaron hit .352 for them in the little chance they did give him, so they exposed him in the expansion draft and Tampa Bay snapped him up. But why weren't the Mets playing him when he was 24 or 25, if he had this glove and this bat?

Elsewhere, I suggest that the Devil Rays might move Bobby Smith, the heir apparent at third base, so that Wade Boggs can have that 3000-hit season. I noted that Bobby can play shortstop. Well, I do have to say that, as long as Aaron Ledesma can play like this, Bobby Smith ain't gonna play no shortstop for the Rays. He's gonna wait for Boggs to retire. <BJH>

MENDY LOPEZ, KC

A kid, one year older than Miguel Tejada, who hasn't even hit AA pitching with any consistency. And therefore, who is about one quarter the prospect that Tejada is. Don't be confused. <BJH>

PAT MEARES, MIN

Drifting down from his career peak the last couple of campaigns, but still a respectable starting shortstop on a team that aspires to no more than that. <BJH>

ALEX RODRIGUEZ, SEA (%)

I guess you can figure out that we've never seen this concentration of absolute top hitting talent at the shortstop position in one league. Garciaparra, Jeter, and A-Rod here would each stand up to Cal Ripken, who was the sensation of his decade. But even among these three, it's Alex Rodriguez who stands out, for two reasons.

First, he's the best of the three, albeit not by any huge margin. But he has more power than either of the others, and leads his league in more categories, and

American League SHORTSTOP			
Player	OXW	DXW	TXW
Rodriguez A	5.97	1.89	7.86
Jeter D	5.10	2.66	7.76
Garciaparra N	5.10	1.42	6.52
Bordick M	1.38	2.90	4.28
Vizquel O	1.41	2.78	4.19
Disarcina G	0.88	2.48	3.36
Caruso M	1.37	1.10	2.47
Ledesma A	0.72	1.71	2.43
Cruz D	-0.54	2.72	2.18
Gonzalez A	-0.30	2.32	2.02
Stocker K	-0.74	2.55	1.81
Clayton R	0.33	1.39	1.72
Tejada M	0.43	1.17	1.60
Meares P	-0.15	1.72	1.57
Elster K	-0.03	0.67	0.64
Lopez M	-0.48	1.08	0.60
Cedeno D	0.00	-0.04	-0.04
Halter S	-0.75	0.66	-0.09
Sojo L	-0.73	0.37	-0.36

more important categories. Nomar has led his league in At-Bats and Hits and Triples, which aren't the first water of stats to lead in. Derek Jeter has led the league in Runs Scored, which is a first-rate category, but there's only the one. A-Rod has led the league in At-Bats, Hits, Doubles, Total Bases, Runs Scored, and Batting Average. That's a tremendous set of league leads for a shortstop. Hell, it's a tremendous set of league leads for a first baseman.

To give you a comparison, Cal Ripken has led the league in the same categories, while not competing with the likes of Garciaparra and Jeter for most of his stay: Games Played almost every year, At-Bats twice, Hits, Doubles, Total Bases, Runs, and Sacrifice Flies. That is, except-

SECONDARY FIELDING STATISTICS
1998 AMERICAN LEAGUE
SHORTSTOPS

Name	G	GS	INN	TC	PO	A	E	DP	FPCT	RF	ZR	DP/G	DP/E	OOA	NRF	NDPR	NDPE
Aaron Ledesma	58	49	448	277	104	165	8	51	.971	5.40	.932	1.02	6.4	40	117	163	145
Chris Snopek	33	26	244	144	47	93	4	16	.972	5.17	.914	0.59	4.0	15	112	94	91
Mendy Lopez	72	66	563	337	101	221	15	53	.955	5.15	.959	0.85	3.5	34	112	134	80
Kevin Stocker	110	108	940	531	185	335	11	80	.979	4.98	.955	0.77	7.3	40	108	122	165
Deivi Cruz	135	132	1163	652	196	445	11	100	.983	4.96	.966	0.77	9.1	47	108	123	207
Mike Bordick	150	144	1238	688	236	445	7	90	.990	4.95	.956	0.65	12.9	48	108	104	292
Royce Clayton	141	138	1226	688	230	438	20	79	.971	4.91	.944	0.58	4.0	41	107	92	90
Miguel Tejada	104	104	915	524	173	325	26	74	.950	4.90	.894	0.73	2.8	30	106	116	65
Omar Vizquel	151	149	1316	718	271	442	5	94	.993	4.88	.965	0.64	18.8	40	106	102	427
Rafael Bournigal	38	29	266	143	54	89	0	18	1.000	4.84	.909	0.61	—	7	105	97	—
Pat Meares	149	145	1270	698	263	411	24	92	.966	4.78	.910	0.65	3.8	25	104	103	87
Mike Caruso	131	129	1121	629	217	377	35	91	.944	4.77	.923	0.73	2.6	21	104	116	59
Alex Rodriguez	160	160	1389	736	271	447	18	89	.976	4.65	.945	0.58	4.9	8	101	92	112
Gary DiSarcina	157	155	1371	705	253	438	14	103	.980	4.54	.938	0.68	7.4	-10	99	107	167
Nomar Garciaparra	143	143	1255	654	228	401	25	67	.962	4.51	.900	0.48	2.7	-12	98	76	61
Kevin Elster	84	84	735	371	107	255	9	49	.976	4.44	.921	0.60	5.4	-14	96	95	124
Alex Gonzalez	158	157	1398	703	260	426	17	98	.976	4.42	.942	0.63	5.8	-29	96	100	131
Derek Jeter	148	148	1305	625	225	391	9	81	.986	4.25	.933	0.56	9.0	-51	92	89	205

KEY: Inn-Innings; PO-Putouts; A-Assists; Er-Errors; DP-Double Plays; FPct-Fielding Pct.; RF-Range Factor; ZR-Zone Rating; DPR-Double Plays per RF(/9); DP/E-Double Plays per Error; OAA-Outs Above Average; NRF-Normalize; Range Factor (N=100); NDPR-Normalized DP per RF; NDPE-Normalized; DP/Error

ing Games Played, Cal has led the league in his entire career about as often, and in about the same categories, as Alex Rodriguez already has in his tiny three-season stay.

The second reason that Alex is the best of the Big Three is that he is two years younger than both Nomar and Derek. That's right. Alex is turning 23, while the other two are turning 25. I know that doesn't seem right, as Alex has been around for longer than the others, but he got started in the major leagues in 1994, at the age of 18. He's only had three full years out of his five, but Derek Jeter has only had three as well, and Nomar Garciaparra had only his second in 1998.

What all this sums up to is that Alex Rodriguez and no one else has the most Trade Value in the major leagues. There is no one else you'd rather have than this 23-year-old shortstop who is already an established hitting league leader. He's the best. Better than Cal. <BJH>

Third player to join the 40 HR/40 SB club. **<SL>**

Among 22 year olds all-time he leads in doubles, is second in hits, home runs, runs and RBI's (all behind Ott) and is in the top fifteen in stolen bases. At this rate he will reach 300-300 right around

his peak season. I you are the manager of a team with the two best players in the American League, to go along with the second best designated hitter, a top-five starter and you finish below .500, why aren't you canned almost immediately? Look at the Giants. If Dusty Baker can nearly ride a rotation containing Mark Gardner, Orel Hershiser, and Danny Darwin into the playoffs, why can't the Mariners make the playoffs on a regular basis? <SF>

LUIS SOJO, NYY

The Yankees' aging utility man. The Yankees, completely in contrast to the reputation the New York press gives out, have plenty of All-Stars, but no depth. <BJH>

KEVIN STOCKER, TB

Good field, no hit at all. <BJH>

I usually consider the influences of batting coaches on players to be minimal, but in this case, I wonder; granted, Stocker has never been that good ever since his fluke rookie season, but he, John Flaherty, and Dave Martinez, all of whom were merely mediocre before getting to Tampa Bay, fell into the horrible category once they got there. <NL>

MIGUEL TEJADA, OAK

A good-looking kid, just turning 23, who beat up AA pitching for a month and so became the A's shortstop. It was too much of a jump, but he did hit 11 homers in 365 at-bats, which implies that he's not completely overmatched. Therefore, GOOD FANTASY TOUT for 1999, if you can't get one of the Big Three. <BJH>

OMAR VIZQUEL, CLE

Has the highest ranking of any shortstop in the American League who is over the age of 25. That is, he was probably the #2 shortstop in the league, after Cal Ripken, until the Big Three Kids came along. And all that is not to mention that his defensive numbers, which are the anchor of his ranking, are actually down, as he passes thirty years of age.

Just a thought in defense of Seattle Mariner fans. If my team had had Ken Griffey, Jr. in center and Edgar Martinez to hit ahead of him and Omar Vizquel followed by Alex Rodriguez at shortstop, and still hadn't won anything, I'd be frustrated, too. <BJH>

LEFT FIELD

RICH AMARAL, SEA

A utility infielder who the Mariners put in left field for a while because, I presume, they didn't think they had anyone else. <BJH>

ALBERT BELLE, BAL (%)
(1998: CHW)

I don't know which is more amazing: that Albert Belle, after all he's put himself through, can still post up 8-XW seasons, or that no other AL left fielder is above three. The gap between Albert and everyone else is just unreal for an outfield spot, where hitters usually camp out.

Elsewhere, I comment that one of the possible tests for an MVP candidate is how much he dominates his position. That is, the player who has the highest margin above the rest of his immediate competitors has a real claim on the MVP. In that comment, I mention that this often happens at catcher or shortstop, but seldom at a hitters' spot. This is the exception. Albert Belle has as much claim to AL MVP or Player of the Year or whatever as anyone, at least, by that standard. <BJH>

Nobody noticed that Belle hit 16 HRs in July, and his .941 slugging percentage was the best monthly total for any major league regular in 1998. If people could just leave their enmity at the door, they'd see he's the best hitter in the American League. **<SL>**

RICH BUTLER, TB

His AAA numbers the last two years indicate that he's ready for prime time, but he didn't back that up when given the chance. He's only turning 26, and Tampa Bay will surely give him another chance, and so FINE FANTASY GAMBLE FOR 1999. I mean, this is the AL left fielders. Unless you've got Albert Belle, what have you got to lose? <BJH>

JEFF CONINE, KC

You know, this seems to happen an awful lot. Some team develops a guy and gets him to the point where he's worth something, but then lets him go. Some other team skims the cream off his career and then lets him go when he starts to decline. Eventually, the original team gets him back to play out the string. Kansas City has invested more in Jeff Conine, and received less, than seems at all fair. <BJH>

MARTY CORDOVA, MIN

Shouldn't players named "Cordova" be good with the leather? And shouldn't players who hit .309 at age 26, but have Sophomore Slump at age 27, recover to more than .253 at age 28? Yes, they should. And yes, I think the reason that Marty didn't was probably some sort of nagging injury. Therefore, I TOUT MARTY FOR 1999, glove or no glove. <BJH>

Collapse appears to be genuine, but still inexplicable. There is nothing in his minor league record that would suggest a collapse this quickly. Still not that old, so he may still rebound. <NL>

CHAD CURTIS, NYY

It's unusual to have your light-hitting-but-gets-on-base-some player stationed in left field, but the Yankees, rife with All-Stars in the normal light-hitting spots, can afford it. <BJH>

BRIAN GILES, PIT
(1998: CLE)

The reasons for platooning Brian Giles still escape me. If you look at his numbers and extrapolate them to a full year, you've got the #2 man at this position in the American League. True, the numbers would likely come down if he had to play full time, but the numbers do not suggest that he cannot hit lefty pitching, which would be the one real reason for platooning him. Platooning him with Mark Whiten makes no sense unless you're looking for glove value. <BJH>

Giles' numbers in "After 0-1" situations are intriguing. He draws walks ~13% of the time, but otherwise struggles (.190 BA). Only Mark McGwire walked more in that situation in 1998. If he can make some adjustments for that, we just might see a very big overall jump in his performance level. And this is the year to look for it, given that he's switching leagues and going to a better hitter's park. <DM>

LUIS GONZALEZ, AZ
(1998: DET)

A normal Luis Gonzalez season for age 30. It ought not be ranking this high, because the competition should be stronger. Now, one of the basic rules of baseball is that, when you see a position that is weakly manned right now, you're going to see an influx of hot new kids over the next three years or so, because that's where the job opportunities will be. Given that, Luis' future does not look good, as far as maintaining an above-average ranking is concerned. <BJH>

RUSTY GREER, TEX

A good, solid left field starter. Usually, though, there would be four or five people with TXWs above Rusty's mark here. Therefore, he wouldn't rank second, and no one would confuse him with an All-Star. In the current crop, though, he does stand out, and does get All-Star mention. <BJH>

American League LEFT FIELD			
Player	OXW	DXW	TXW
Belle A	8.29	0.64	8.93
Henderson R	4.05	0.63	4.68
Greer R	3.86	0.58	4.44
Stewart S	3.32	0.60	3.92
Surhoff B	3.06	0.76	3.82
Gonzalez L	2.85	0.56	3.41
Giles B	2.61	0.52	3.13
Curtis C	1.95	1.10	3.05
O'Leary T	1.69	0.99	2.68
Trammell B	1.33	0.27	1.60
Whiten M	0.81	0.40	1.21
Palmeiro O	0.89	0.30	1.19
Conine J	0.74	0.43	1.17
Cordova M	0.70	0.43	1.13
Mack S	0.93	0.05	0.98
Amaral R	0.45	0.24	0.69
Butler R	-0.16	0.60	0.44
Jefferies G	0.35	0.01	0.36
Ledee R	0.12	0.03	0.12
Monahan S	-0.27	0.31	0.04
Greene T	-0.02	-0.04	-0.06

Greer was the only major league player to drive in 100 or more runs without hitting twenty homers. **<SL>**

RICKEY HENDERSON, NYM (%)
(1998: OAK)

True, there is no excuse for a season of this few TXW ranking so high at a hitters' spot. But it's also true that Rickey Henderson is far too old to be posting up this kind of TXW. The reason that Rickey can do this is truly unique: Rickey Henderson can get the pitchers of the American League to walk him 118 league-leading times despite his posting a .236 batting average. Worse, the pitchers of the league know very well that Rickey can't hit for average any more. They know that his only weapons are the walk and the mediocre pop he still retains. And yet, knowing all that, they simply cannot get the ball over the plate against the man.

Bill James once wrote that one characteristic of the true Hall of Fame player is that he is unique; that there is no one else really like him. Rickey is the case in point. He has this unique ability to collect walks without any real threat to force pitchers to throw balls out of the zone. He also has retained enough speed at age 39 to lead his league in stolen bases, and with an 84% success rate on the attempts, to boot.

Simply put, Rickey Henderson is the acknowledged greatest leadoff man of all time, and his performance at this age is a road map for how you get to be a great leadoff man. That is, he is writing us a definition of what a great leadoff man is and does. We can read it all in these here numbers. <BJH>

SHANE MACK, SD
(1998:KC)

He's finally getting old enough that I don't want to tout him as a wasted starter any more. That he had to spend two of his finest seasons in Japan is silly, but that was life back then, and now is now, and right now, he's a backup outfielder / DH. At that job, he retains a lot of value. <BJH>

SHANE MONAHAN, SEA

A kid left fielder who the Mariners played because the alternative was more of Rich Amaral out there. Monahan, based on his AA numbers in 1997, might be ready in a couple of years, but might never be a serious contender for the majors. He's on the edge. <BJH>

With his highly touted hockey lineage, Monahan played a scrappy, flashy left field after Glenallen Hill was let go. He certainly energized the fans who had grown tired of Hill's antics in the field. Unfortunately, Monahan's offense is microscopic. He was hitting poorly in AAA, and continued that trend in the majors. But he managed to get some key hits to win games down the stretch, which will only add to his mystique. Hence he has all the hallmarks of a Lou Piniella favorite and a place in the fan's heart (as opposed to his head).

Next season, with any luck, Monahan will be a backup outfielder rather than a starter. Saints preserve us if he has a great spring. <DJP>

TROY O'LEARY, BOS

Now, THAT'S what I call a drop-off from the Age-27 Career Year. I doubt Troy has really dropped that far in ability; I have suspicions of an unusually strong adjustment by the pitchers of the league. As a consequence, I expect Troy to mount something of a comeback in 1999. That being said, it's at this level of play that you start looking for a hot kid to try out in left field. Troy and everyone who ranks below him are the people who are vulnerable to the replacements that will soon bring this position back to where it's no longer Albert Belle and the 13 dwarves. <BJH>

He did hit 23 home runs, and only Albert Belle hit more among regular American League left fielders. On the other hand, his .314 on-base percentage was the lowest of the regular left fielders and he hit an abysmal .238, with a just-as-awful .702 OPS (and only nine homers), after the All-Star break. Nor did he exactly salvage his year in the postseason, going 1-for-16 in four games against the Indians.

You get the feeling the clock has struck midnight on Troy O'Leary, one of the first and certainly the best of Dan Duquette's waiver reclamations. It's doubtful the Red Sox can win it all getting as little offense as they got last year from their outfield, and—considering their early offseason thrust was geared toward free-agent outfielders—it's just as doubtful they don't know it. Since O'Leary's defensive contributions are negligible and his speed is non-existent, he can only contribute with his bat. What he contributed in 1998 wasn't enough. <AM>

SECONDARY FIELDING STATISTICS
1998 AMERICAN LEAGUE
LEFT FIELD

Name	INN	TC	PO	A	E	DP	FPCT	RF	ZR
Mark Whiten	304	89	80	6	3	0	.966	2.55	.815
Marty Cordova	982	268	257	5	6	1	.978	2.40	.799
Orlando Palmeiro	304	81	81	0	0	0	1.000	2.40	.798
Rickey Henderson	1104	296	290	2	4	1	.986	2.38	.843
Chad Curtis	759	203	195	5	3	3	.985	2.37	.884
Brian S. Giles	792	211	199	7	5	1	.976	2.34	.818
Quinton McCracken	434	113	106	6	1	1	.991	2.32	.872
Ricky Ledee	190	48	43	4	1	0	.979	2.22	.808
Shannon Stewart	843	210	204	1	5	0	.976	2.19	.813
Mike Kelly	333	80	78	2	0	1	1.000	2.16	.814
Albert Belle	1365	334	315	11	8	3	.976	2.15	.787
Shane Monahan	492	117	113	3	1	1	.991	2.12	.873
Rusty Greer	1324	313	304	6	3	0	.990	2.11	.808
Jose Canseco	360	88	81	3	4	2	.955	2.10	.739
Troy O'Leary	1342	314	302	9	3	1	.990	2.09	.749
Jeff Conine	407	92	88	4	0	0	1.000	2.03	.810
Rich Butler	327	72	70	2	0	0	1.000	1.98	.791
Garret Anderson	303	66	64	2	0	1	1.000	1.96	.759
Shane Mack	252	54	52	1	1	0	.981	1.89	.781
Luis Gonzalez	1144	243	232	8	3	0	.988	1.89	.802
Larry Sutton	281	58	56	2	0	0	1.000	1.86	.757
B.J. Surhoff	1311	268	253	12	3	2	.989	1.82	.831
Darin Erstad	573	114	109	4	1	2	.991	1.77	.827
Tim Raines	353	64	60	3	1	2	.984	1.61	.847

KEY: Inn-Innings; PO-Putouts; A-Assists; Er-Errors; DP-Double Plays; FPct-Fielding Pct.; RF-Range Factor; ZR-Zone Rating

ORLANDO PALMEIRO, ANA

This season is consistent with — actually, a little better than—his minor league numbers. Still, this is no kid. He's turning 30, and you have to ask why, if he can hit .281 and rank in the top ten at his position, he hasn't had a job before now. Then, you look at the home run column, and you understand. **<BJH>**

With the arrival of Mo, Palmeiro is headed back to the recesses of the depth chart. He's a useful sub, but no more. <NL>

TIM RAINES, NYY (%)

Everyone who parroted the observation that the 1998 Yankees don't have a player headed to the Hall of Fame was forgetting about Rock. It's easy to overlook him because he's just a part-time player now. His stolen base numbers have been going down each year since 1991 (51, 45, 21, 13, 13, 10, 8, 8). With 801 career steals, he's pretty firmly entrenched in fifth place on the all-time list. Cobb is fourth with 892 which is clearly out of reach. **<SL>**

SHANE SPENCER, NYY

You are reading this book, so you probably know better than to expect Spencer to challenge Mark McGwire this year for the major league home run title. It's fairly rare for players to manage big careers when they debut at age 26. Here's my all-time team for post-war players debuting past their 26th birthday (enough parameters?)

C:	Roy Campanella (HR leader with 242 career dingers)
1B:	Dick Stuart
2B:	Jackie Robinson
3B:	Davey Lopes
SS:	Maury Wills (AB leader with 7588 AB)
OF:	Minnie Minoso (runs and rbi leader)
OF:	Gus Zernial
OF:	Monte Irvin

The list is nearly half early African-American players robbed of their early careers by segregation; without them, the team quality drops precipitously. **<SF>**

SHANNON STEWART, TOR

I though Shannon Stewart had a really good chance of posting a stronger rookie season than Ben Grieve, and touted him accordingly in the last BBBA. That didn't happen, of course, but Shannon was hurt early, too. I don't mean to imply that Stewart has more potential as a player than Grieve does. Ben is two years younger. But it still may be true that you can get Shannon Stewart in a fantasy league for a third or less of what it would take to pick up Ben Grieve. At that rate, Stewart is THE BEST FANTASY BARGAIN AT THIS POSITION. **<BJH>**

Some members of the Toronto media say the Jays need a "power-hitting outfielder". But the Jays already have three. Stewart hit 10 home runs after the All-Star Break (seven in September), and slugged .477 after the break. He could have a big year in the extra-base hit category in '99 to complement his fine on-base percentage. <ST>

B. J. SURHOFF, BAL

Surhoff may be the single player that the Offensive Surge of 1994 has helped the most. Before the Surge, his season high in home runs was seven (7). Since 1994, though, his totals have been 13, 21, 18, and 22. Since these seasons were his ages 30 through 33, he has shown no decline whatsoever in what is usually the beginning of the end for major league athletes. Instead, he has looked better in those four years than he ever did before.

Now, the question is, how much of that appearance is real and how much is Surge illusion. The answer is that most of it is real. Some is Surge Illusion, but B. J. Has gained much more ground than other players. That is, he has had an unusual ability to exploit the conditions of the Surge and make the new, enriched home run environment work for him.

What this means is two things. First, B. J. Surhoff, as long as the Offensive Surge lasts, is a quite valuable player, especially if he could move back to third base or catcher. Second, his value will collapse like a burst balloon if the Surge ever ends. That makes him an unusually-volatile gamble for a player his age with no extreme injury history. **<BJH>**

BUBBA TRAMMELL, TB

What an odd name. The image evoked by "Bubba" is almost exactly the opposite of that inspired, at least to baseball fans, by "Trammell". It's an odd career, too. He looked completely ready for prime time in 1996, but slid back hard in '97. This time, he looked completely ready again. But he's already turning 27, so this is about all you're going to get, unless he makes another jump at age 28. That is distinctly possible, and so I rate him a MILD

FANTASY TOUT FOR 2000. **<BJH>**

MARK WHITEN, CLE

When Mark had that big four-homer game, I did some research and decided that the players who had performed that feat had all held onto a serious level of power thereafter. Mark is the exception. His power dropped right off, rather than expanding to that of a 30-homer man, which is what I expected. He gets on base well, and fields well, and has some mediocre power, but Cleveland's use of him in a utility role is not a waste. **<BJH>**

CENTER FIELD

JEFF ABBOTT, CHW

A kid whose LOWEST minor league batting average was .320. He moved from .263 to .279 in the bigs this year, and I expect another 20 points in either 1999 (30% chance) or 2000(70%). Why the percentage chances? He made the big leap at age 25, so I expect the next one at age 27. However, he could go much higher than just .300, and that would take two jumps. **<BJH>**

BRADY ANDERSON, BAL (%)

Except for batting average, a season very much like 1997 and 1995, which are the years that surrounded the big 50-tater campaign. Right now, I have to rate the average as a fluke, and suggest that he still retains almost all of that value, and so will move up in the rankings next year. But I can't be sure. You never can with 35-year-olds. Some of them fade fast. Joe DiMaggio was a much better player, and he collapsed just as fast as this would suggest at its worst. **<BJH>**

Brady was hurt early, and spent at least a month playing hurt as well. He's probably going to permanently lose the BA, but his OBP was still around .400 in the second half of the year despite hitting just .253. As Brock points out, there are some warning signs here. <DM>

DAMON BUFORD, BOS

Let's see. It's a nice season, and it's consistent with his 1996 campaign. But both of those were very partial seasons. When the Rangers tried to use him more in 1997, he collapsed. Why? Ah, here it is, in the STATS, Inc. Player Profiles book.

Damon cannot hit right-handed pitching. He's a true platoon player. Unfortunately, platoon righties get the short end of the stick, because only about a quarter of the pitchers are lefties. That means that you can expect this level of play as long as you don't get more than this amount of playing time. If the Red Sox start asking him to start, he'll fail. **<BJH>**

MIKE CAMERON, CIN
(1998: CHW)
Traded to the Reds for Paul Konerko, Mike moves into an already crowded phone booth of outfielders in Cincinnati. A gifted CF who suffered through a brutal sophomore slump, Cameron needs a bit of nurturing, but has the talent to put up excellent secondary statistics; he'll need to keep the BA around .250 to keep the reductivist types who often wind up as GMs from getting too antsy. **<DM>**

RYAN CHRISTENSON, OAK
Some conflicting signals in his data. First, he didn't walk anywhere close to what he'd done in the minors. That is sometimes an artifact of the minors-to-majors transition, however, and so may reappear a bit later. He hit a lot better with men on base, which is at odds with his minor league profile as a OBP-driven hitter. Was downright lousy leading off an inning (.187/.238/.280). If his strike zone judgment returns, he might develop into a solid #2 hitter, which he'll need to do in order to keep a starting job in CF. **<DM>**

JOSE CRUZ, JR., TOR
Like Barry Bonds, Jose is a very similar player to his father. Jose Sr. Probably should have been a center fielder, and was a near-Hall of Fame hitter, whose stats were suppressed by the old Astrodome. Given that he even got a partial year of "seasoning" in AAA this time out, you have to regard Jose as established at this level of play, and very, very likely to make a big jump in 1999. All that it would take would be a return to his rookie season's power. **<BJH>**

The myth of the year in Toronto is that sending Cruz down to Syracuse was the key to turning around his disappointing start in '98. Cruz slumped early in the season and was often the odd man out after Delgado returned and Canseco was moved to the outfield. In his last 32 plate appearances before being sent down,

Cruz hit .296 with a .406 OBP and 2 stolen bases (no extra-base hits). He was working his way out of his slump, but the Jays sent him down in mid-June.

It was widely reported that Cruz struggled until sometime in July, when discussions with Lloyd Moseby brought him around. In fact, Jose hit 3 home runs in 47 at bats at Syracuse in June (.433 OBP,.553 SLG). During July, he hit 4 more home runs in 94 at bats (.425 OBP, .564 SLG).

Recalled July 30 after the Mike Stanley trade, Jose still found himself benched in favor of Tony Phillips. Phillips, however was shortly traded to the Mets, and Cruz broke through in August, (5 HR, .444 OBP, .644 SLG). He slowed down in September, but overall, Jose's season was a lot better than it was portrayed. One can seriously question whether the trip to Syracuse was really necessary. <ST>

JOHNNY DAMON, KC
Here's a surprise offering as the #5 center fielder in the league. The question is whether you want to upgrade his rating in your mind because of the high in-position finish, or whether you want to look at the fact that he's just the top of a mediocre group behind the Big Four at the spot. I vote for the second option. Johnny Damon didn't really have any great season; he just was at a position with only four big guns. His main value remains his young age.

Prediction here is hard. Johnny has never really had a big jump year. This time, his batting average and on-base percentage remained constant, but his power went way up, and across the board of extra base stats. Does that count as a Big Jump year, where you expect a countera-djustment slump the next time out? Or does that represent a flat year, where you'd normally expect a big jump in 1999 at age 25? I can't say, for sure. But the power is really nothing more than a repeat of his rookie half-season, rather than a jump up from anything previous. Therefore, I rate Johnny as a REAL GOOD FANTASY GAMBLE, as I think there's a real chance of his making that big leap in 1999. **<BJH>**

SECONDARY FIELDING STATISTICS
1998 AMERICAN LEAGUE
CENTER FIELD

NAME	INN	TC	PO	A	E	DP	FPCT	RF	ZR
Jason McDonald	248	92	83	5	4	1	.957	3.20	.920
Roberto Kelly	264	93	87	2	4	1	.957	3.03	.830
Darren Lewis	889	293	288	5	0	0	1.000	2.97	.834
Brian L. Hunter	1212	402	386	11	5	0	.988	2.95	.856
Tom Goodwin	1149	378	370	5	3	1	.992	2.94	.813
Mike Cameron	972	319	310	5	4	0	.987	2.92	.837
Ryan Christenson	891	286	275	6	5	2	.983	2.84	.821
Matt Lawton	365	116	113	2	1	2	.991	2.84	.764
Ken Griffey Jr	1345	423	407	11	5	2	.988	2.80	.792
Otis Nixon	923	285	278	4	3	0	.989	2.75	.782
Jim Edmonds	1313	404	389	10	5	1	.988	2.74	.788
Randy Winn	554	171	165	3	3	0	.982	2.73	.844
Shannon Stewart	317	94	91	2	1	1	.989	2.64	.789
Chad Curtis	349	104	98	4	2	0	.981	2.63	.855
Johnny Damon	1123	326	315	9	2	1	.994	2.60	.810
Jose Cruz Jr	872	254	243	7	4	1	.984	2.58	.776
Quinton McCracken	881	252	238	12	2	2	.992	2.56	.761
Shawn Green	276	79	77	1	1	0	.987	2.54	.725
Damon Buford	487	137	133	4	0	1	1.000	2.53	.833
Bernie Williams	1095	306	299	4	3	0	.990	2.49	.827
Kenny Lofton	1322	366	340	18	8	4	.978	2.44	.818
Jeff Abbott	264	74	71	0	3	0	.959	2.42	.787
Brady Anderson	1076	274	269	1	4	0	.985	2.26	.758

KEY: Inn-Innings; PO-Putouts; A-Assists; Er-Errors; DP-Double Plays; FPct-Fielding Pct.; RF-Range Factor; ZR-Zone Rating

JIM EDMONDS, ANA

This age 28 season is essentially identical to his Age-27 Career Year. The home run total is not down, but Jim had 97 more at-bats, so the rate is indeed off the 1997 pace. However, Jim made a huge jump in doubles to offset that. He did drive in and score more runs, but that was mostly the effects of the extra playing time, too. His batting average leapt too, by 16 points, but the lesser power kept any slugging increase down to six points, and Jim's OBP was the exact same as last year's, despite the extra hits. <BJH>

Strangely labeled a clubhouse cancer. Obviously, I'm not in their clubhouse, but it would seem to me that that should be hardly a reason to dump the team's top offensive player (after positional adjustment), as the Angels are rumored to be considering. <NL>

TOM GOODWIN, TEX

A poor starter in center field, Tom suddenly took 73 walks to get on base a handsome .378. He's never done that before, and he's already turning 30, and he played four full seasons, so I have to treat that as a fluke until he does it again. And, even if he does, he only ends up a respectable low-end starter, not any more. <BJH>

KEN GRIFFEY, JR., SEA (%)

A great player who is falling just short of the absolute top end of center fielders. Except for his Age-27 Career Year in 1997, Ken has never led his league in any stat that was not home-run related. Now that he's off that peak, even by just one year, and his league leadership is down to just home runs again. Ken's kid teammate, Alex Rodriguez, is littering the league leader boards with more than that.

And so, comparing Ken to Cobb or Speaker or Mantle or Mays just isn't going to work for the current star. Still, he's above that lesser class of greats that includes Duke Snider and Larry Doby. He's in between. Just off the pace set by the very top end, specializing in home runs. <BJH>

He's now at 350 career home runs, which puts him way ahead of the rest of the pack. Aaron had "just" 298 homers by his age 28 year, and the next highest to Griffey was Mel Ott (306), Jimmie Foxx (304), and Eddie Mathews (299). Of course, all the players ahead of Aaron faded at the end, while Aaron hammered away. Still, fifty home runs is a huge lead considering all the games that Griffey has missed due to the strike

and injuries. I'd say he's nearly even money to break the record. <SF>

2000 is the last year of Griffey's current contract. It would be a disaster of Titanic proportions to lose Griffey just as the team moves into its new ballpark. This shouldn't be a public relations disaster the way the Randy Johnson deal was, but I'm not sure I trust the front office to do it right. I'm not even sure if they realize just what a money making machine Griffey will be in the next decade as he makes his assault on Aaron's career home run record. <DJP>

BRIAN L. HUNTER, DET

OK, let's get this straight. Yes, this is the better of the two Brian Hunters. But still, he's a backup center fielder and pinch runner, not a serious starter. Never has been, never will be. <BJH>

ROBERTO KELLY, TEX

Right on the edge between starter quality and backup, Roberto has led the life you'd expect, moving from team to team to plug temporary holes. <BJH>

Johnny Oates seems to be a master of picking his spots for the bench. Both Kelly and Mike Simms were exceptionally productive in such roles for the Rangers in 1998. I'm wondering if an ability to create roles for part-time players is a managerial skill that is mutually exclusive with the ability to develop young talent. Anyone up for a research project? <DM>

DARREN LEWIS, BOS

The best defensive center fielder in the game. If he could actually hit, he'd be a star. As it is, he's no longer a joke, but a solid starting center fielder. I haven't been a fan of Darren's before, but this looks like a real establishment of a useful level of play. He'd be even more valuable in a ballpark with a larger outfield. <BJH>

Not since the days of Fred Lynn have the Red Sox gotten the kind of center-field defense they received from Darren Lewis and his sort-of platoon partner, Damon Buford, last year. (Lewis didn't actually leave the lineup when Buford entered it; he merely moved over to right field.) The Sox cut their runs allowed from 857 in 1997 to 729 in 1998, and while Pedro Martinez, Tom Gordon, Bret Saberhagen and friends had a lot to do with that, so, too, did Lewis and Buford, who spearheaded a defen-

sive upgrade that sparked the pitching improvement. Lewis chipped in with a career offensive year, as well, posting personal bests just about every category. His postseason reward was a three-year contract and the probable assurance that, no matter what the Sox might do in the free-agent/trade mart, his defense insures there'll be a spot for him somewhere in the Boston outfield in 1999.<AM>

American League CENTER FIELD			
PLAYER	OXW	DXW	TXW
Griffey K	6.40	1.44	7.84
Williams B	5.83	0.95	6.78
Edmonds J	4.57	1.35	5.92
Lofton K	3.39	0.92	4.31
Damon J	2.99	1.23	4.22
McCracken Q	2.07	1.76	3.83
Lewis D	1.64	1.63	3.27
Anderson B	3.18	0.04	3.22
Cruz J	2.12	0.76	2.88
Goodwin T	1.76	1.04	2.80
Kelly R	1.78	0.40	2.18
Buford D	1.31	0.74	2.05
Nixon O	1.25	0.61	1.86
Hunter B	0.22	1.50	1.72
Christenson R	0.89	0.65	1.54
Winn R	0.86	0.55	1.41
Abbott J	1.08	-0.01	1.07
McDonald J	0.67	0.33	1.00
Cameron M	-0.49	0.77	0.28

KENNY LOFTON, CLE (%)

Returned to Cleveland and had a sub-par campaign everywhere but in base stealing. I expect him to return to his previous Indian form next campaign. <BJH>

QUINTON McCRACKEN, TB

Played a real good defense and played all year. That's all it took to rise him out of the pack of journeyman and make him look like a top starter. I doubt that he is, although I don't really see anyone below Johnny Damon, except Jose Cruz, who leaps to mind as someone who will obviously surpass Quinton next year. LOUSY FANTASY BUY, as his value is mostly defense. <BJH>

JASON McDONALD, OAK

Jason has one big skill—he can take those walks and get on base. So far, he hasn't shown it at the big-league level in quantities that will get him a job. He's turning 27, though, and I'm giving him an 80% chance of breaking through with a .390+ OBP. He's exceeded that almost every year in the minors, with the one exception being the year they jumped him from A ball to AAA. <BJH>

The A's appear to have little confidence in Jason, and word is that they may sign Tony Phillips to be their leadoff hitter in 1999, thus leaving little or no room for McDonald in the outfield for a second straight year. Given the A's commitment to youth, it makes little sense to so assiduously block someone's path in this manner. <DM>

OTIS NIXON, ATL (%)
(1998: MIN)

Otis is down to only one skill, but at least you know what it is, and so you know exactly what to do with him in your lineup. <BJH>

BERNIE WILLIAMS, NYY (%)

Another one of the Yankee journeymen, I guess, if you listen to the New York press. I heard one New York writer say that the Yankees didn't have the league leader in any category. This was after the season, when the writer had to know that Bernie had won the Batting Average title. I guess you've figured out by reading all my Yankee player comments that I'm completely disgusted by this stuff.

I was also disgusted at Bernie's re-signing with the Yanks. I knew there had to be some chance that he was just using other bids to drive the price up and get as much out of George as he could. But I also felt that there was some chance that his early treatment at the hands of Steinbrenner would cause him to want to depart New York as soon as he could. Early in his career, you see, Bernie was a prime victim of "the Columbus Shuttle." If he had an off week for the Yanks, he was as likely as not going to find himself back in AAA ball, while Gerald Williams or some such journeyman got to play Bernie's position. I imagined that Bernie remembered that, and was not entirely enchanted with The Boss.

And let's give credit to Joe Torre for one thing. As noted earier, Joe has exactly two skills as a manager—he can handle the press and he can handle an owner. In New York, these are prime skills, which is why

Joe has presided over two World Champions. And one symptom of the second skill is that the Columbus Shuttle seems to be gone. <BJH>

Brock's from St. Louis, and as most of you know by now, has about as much love for the Yankees as Bill Clinton and Ken Starr have for each other. Unfortunately for him—and for millions of others who loathe the idea of another Yankee dynasty—Bernie Williams' decision to stay in New York was evidently based on just such an issue. All of which proves that none of us can truly escape the clutches of history; we can only come to terms with it in our individual ways. <DM>

RANDY WINN, TB

Hit .219 the last two months of the season, but Tampa seems to only recall the earlier portions of the year when he was hot. I'm not convinced that he's going to hold even this level. Not a good enough percentage base stealer to be turned loose on the basepaths. <DM>

RIGHT FIELD

GARRETT ANDERSON, ANA

Mixed signals. This season was a step forward for power but a step backwards for batting average and OBP. Garrett is turning 27. The rule of thumb is to assume that the average and OBP will jump at 27, while the power will hold constant. Therefore, I expect Anderson to make another gain in 1999. With luck, he might even get back to his rookie season. <BJH>

RICH BECKER, BAL
(1998: NYM-BAL)

No, no, no. Rich Becker is one of those low-power, good on-base center fielders that wander around the game. You don't put him out there in right field. He's turning 27. Give him a chance to play where he actually might be able to succeed. Don't waste all that foot speed. <BJH>

DARREN BRAGG, BOS

He was finally given the role his supporters thought he was born for: corner outfielder against right-handed pitching. And the results— .774 OPS, .495 offensive winning percentage—proved them wrong. He really doesn't contribute enough

offensively to be anything more than a backup, the first flycatcher off the bench. Too bad, because with his hustle and intensity he's impossible to dislike.<AM>

Darren Bragg reminds me of a friend of mine who I played with in the Little League. No matter what happened during the game, my friend always went home with a dirty uniform. Darren is the same way. He's always getting his uniform by dirty diving for balls or by sliding into bases. Unfortunately, like my friend, if he's playing everyday for your team, that means you don't have any better players at his position. That also usually means you don't have a very good team.

The Red Sox got away with playing a lot of guys just like Darren last season. Lightning will not strike twice. Although it pains me to say this, just as it pained me to tell my friend he really wasn't as good as the other kids whenever he complained about playing time, but, I hope Darren won't be playing quite so much next year for the Sox. <JF>

JAY BUHNER, SEA

Like Eric Davis, Jay's TXW are low because of playing time. Jay, unlike Eric, isn't that old, but, this time like Eric, he is injury-prone. And, turning age 34, it's going to be harder and harder to come back. Remember that Jay is walking the line already. His batting average is below .250 for the last couple of years. You and I know better, and look at the OBP and SLG. But I don't know about Mad Lou. Jay could get himself benched real soon if this keeps up. <BJH>

This could be the end of the line for Buhner, as he won't be ready for the beginning of the season, and isn't expected to be able to play the outfield. He's expected to play first base, but he'll be a lot less valuable there, even if he can perform at his pre-'98 level. Moving Buhner would also cause a whole chain reaction in the Mariner lineup that would hurt both offensively and defensively. <DJP>

FELIPE CRESPO, TOR

I guess it's sort of a Sophomore Slump, although Felipe didn't play all that much in 1997. Turning 26, Felipe had better make his move soon. <BJH>

ERIC DAVIS, STL (%)
(1998: BAL)

After ballpark and playing time adjustments, the best hitter at this position, by a respectable margin. And Eric played good defense, too. His TXW ranking is down solely because of playing time. But you know, that happens to 36-year-olds who still try to play like their 26. **<BJH>**

Nobody has ever taken such a long vacation from top form in the history of baseball. Using Tom Hull's percentile ranking system, I found only one player with a similar career drought between percentile rankings of 75 or higher:

Age	Rico Carty	Eric Davis
24	86	86
25	22	93
26	87	81
27	52	88
28	0	73
29	52	20
30	95	0
31	0	41
32	21	0
33	7	0
34	0	61
35	66	0
36	90	77

Eric's injuries sliced out seven years in the late prime of his career, which is two more than was the case for Rico Carty. Sheer talent is what permitted both of these guys to rebound when virtually all other players would have been distant memories.

That said, what are the prospects for Eric's future? The average percentile ranking for the players with a 75 or higher ranking at age 36 in the following year was 59. That's everyone, including the top guys (90+). For the players in the 75-80 range (where Eric falls due to issues of playing time), the age-37 percentile average is 50.

I expect Eric to exceed that average if he stays healthy. There's enough sheer talent here to produce at least a couple more highly productive seasons. **<DM>**

ROB DUCEY, SEA

Another of those late-80s Toronto outfield kids who looked like they were going to be stars, but never made it. I thought he'd break loose after the 1990 campaign, but he collapsed completely. Now, he's turning 34, and his career high in at-bats is this season's 217.

You know, now that I think about it, Bobby Cox left Toronto about the time that Rob Ducey collapsed. And there have been a couple of Atlanta kids, since Bobby arrived there, who have had similar disappointing careers once they left Atlanta and Bobby's care. Hmmm. **<BJH>**

JERMAINE DYE, KC

Did not make any counteradjustment to the Sophomore Slump of 1997. Now turning 25, Jermaine needs to make a move this year. Right now. But see the Rob Ducey comment above. . . **<BJH>**

JUAN ENCARNACION, DET

Juan Encarnacion has been steadily moving up the minor league ranks, adjusting to and then trashing pitchers at each level. His .329 average with .354 OBP and .561 SLG are completely in the context of his minor league run. If anything, the OBP is low; Juan took only seven (7) walks against 164 at-bats.

OK. Now guess how old Juan Encarnacion is. He's turning 23. FANTASY TOUT ALERT! **<BJH>**

JUAN GONZALEZ, TEX

How bad can AL MVP selections get? With Juan Gonzalez, there appears to be no limit. I have him ranked fourth at this position. Yes, he did hit better than any full-timer-but not by much. He was lousy in the outfield, though, and didn't play any extraordinary number of games. He made a lot of outs, because he won't take a walk.

Against that, there is a league lead in RBI, which is a phony result of taking no walks and having the entire Texas lineup configured to set him up. But it is a phony result that apparently hypnotizes sportswriters.

If you're talking about the best player in the league, it's either Alex Rodriguez or Ivan Rodriguez. If you're talking about the best player on the pennant winner, it's Derek Jeter or, maybe, Bernie Williams. In no case is it Juan Gonzalez. Hell, he isn't even the best player on his own team. Ivan is. And, at catcher, maybe three times as "valuable." **<BJH>**

MVP voting patterns deserve a book-length treatment, because everyone enjoys reading about someone else's opinion if the subject matter is surreal enough. I've been toying with exactly how you'd frame such a work for some time now, but one section of it would surely be entitled "Mass Hypnosis," a condition that Brock alludes to above.

I think players with tremendous secondary average performances generally pose

problems for the voters, and when you get a season like McGwire's, a lot of people's eyes just glaze over. It's so off the boards and so unusual, they can't get their arms around it. And it was compounded by a guy whose superficial stats were similar enough—and who played on a popular, underdog team who were in playoff contention—that they were swayed into a fallacious contextual argument concerning "value." If Sammy Sosa had hit 59 homers, or had the same stats for the Dodgers, I doubt he would have gotten the award.

Over in the AL, there were similar pitfalls for the voters. Griffey had just won, and

American League RIGHT FIELD		
PLAYER	**OXW**	**DXW**	**TXW**
Ramirez M	5.64	0.72	6.36
Gonzalez J	5.79	0.45	6.24
O'Neill P	4.86	1.29	6.15
Davis E	5.15	0.43	5.58
Lawton M	4.47	0.92	5.39
Green S	4.24	1.09	5.33
Grieve B	4.44	0.75	5.19
Higginson B	3.89	0.63	4.52
Anderson G	2.63	0.34	2.97
Hammonds J	1.46	1.24	2.70
Ordonez M	1.11	1.10	2.21
Bragg D	1.21	0.97	2.18
Simms M	2.02	0.15	2.17
Buhner J	1.49	0.41	1.90
Encarnacion J	1.37	0.20	1.57
Kelly M	0.08	1.22	1.30
Ducey R	0.61	0.30	0.91
Sutton L	0.26	0.43	0.69
Crespo F	0.36	0.24	0.60
Becker R	0.06	0.39	0.45
Dye J	-0.57	0.56	-0.01
Ochoa A	-0.42	0.28	-0.14

his team was a disappointment. The Yankees were too much of an ensemble to single out one outstanding player; Bernie Williams, their best player, missed 30+ games. There were three great shortstops, and you could throw a blanket over 'em, so there was no way to single one out. Albert Belle? Not in this lifetime. Manny Ramirez? A year too early, perhaps. Pitchers? Clemens was great, but not quite on a par with 1997: if he didn't win both MVP and the Cy Young then, this wasn't the year, either.

We're down to two guys: Juan and Ivan. If Ivan had hit .350, or won the batting title, I think he would have been MVP—catchers who win batting titles are as rare as virgins in a bordello—but he wore down in the second half. That left—Guess Who.

I'm not defending it, but I can see how it happened. Unlike many, I'm not convinced it would have happened without all of the specific circumstances that came into play as the season unfolded. If the Rangers had lost their division in the last week, the balloting may well have been completely different. There are times when context simply makes things more opaque; when that happens, the BBWAA, like most people, will be more vulnerable to false context. And that is what happened in the 1998 MVP voting. <DM>

SHAWN GREEN, TOR

Essentially, a return to his rookie season of 1995. That counteradjustment took a long time, didn't it? But now, the power is way up, and he's turning 26. You all know what that means, right? BIG FAT CAREER YEAR TOUT FOR 2000; a new Counteradjustment Slump in 1999. <BJH>

For those of you who write in asking for additional explication of Brock's terms "sophomore slump" and "counteradjustment", here's a very brief primer:

"Some hitters have big jumps at ages 23 and 25, peaking at 27. Some smaller number are a year off that pattern, leaping forward at ages 24, 26, and peaking at 28. Sometimes 26. The reason for the pattern is that each leap forward is met by an adjustment by the league's pitchers, which is the real reason for Sophomore Slump, which I call Counteradjustment Slump when it occurs in subsequent seasons . The reason for the one-year peak differential is, that we are dealing with human beings here, and they aren't, presumably, interchangeable."

I think it's an interesting theory, but I'd like to see that term "some" get quantified a bit more. A study that demonstrated the existence of this pattern in, say, upwards of 30% of all hitters would be a good illustration of a process that is part of baseball's conventional wisdom.

To look at Shawn Green for a moment, I wonder how many people would realize that Sean's 35-HR season here is really not much different from his 1995 data, as Brock points out. The average fan would think that this is a huge power surge, but Shawn's SLG and ISO in 1998 aren't much different than they were in 1995:

YEAR	AGE	SLG	ISO
1995	22	.509	.221
1998	25	.510	.232

Score one for Hanke, but dock him a notch for the fact that the pattern here, as described above, is off (as the ages above demonstrate). Shawn is not exhibiting a strict off-and-on pattern, as is posited by the theory, but another, more specific variation of it, which is carried in the idea that this "counteradjustment sure took a long time." In fact, it took all of an extra year:

YEAR	AGE	SLG	ISO
1995	22	.509	.221
1996	23	.448	.168
1997	24	.469	.182
1998	25	.510	.232

As you can see, the general idea of counteradjustment is supported by the data, but it's possible that the strict on-year/off-year

pattern being espoused is oversimplifying the concept too much. As Brock notes, players are human beings, and they don't always conform to any development theory. The age-27 theory itself, based on empirical evidence, is nothing more than a way to project a career peak; the arbitrariness in that method stems from the fact that it is using historical averages to model careers that have a complex set of forces operating on them.

The value in any projection method is in its ability to shape a credible view of what might happen. The theory of counteradjustment seems to do that, and if it is subjected to sufficient scrutiny so that the phrase "some hitters" can be replaced by a numerical value, then it will deserve to take its place as a refinement to the current projection methods available to us. <DM>

SECONDARY FIELDING STATISTICS
1998 AMERICAN LEAGUE
RIGHT FIELD

NAME	INN	TC	PO	A	E	DP	FPCT	RF	ZR
Matt Lawton	855	275	263	9	3	3	.989	2.86	.892
Jermaine Dye	513	159	153	4	2	3	.987	2.75	.879
Magglio Ordonez	1075	288	276	7	5	1	.983	2.37	.829
Karim Garcia	736	195	185	6	4	1	.979	2.34	.814
Garret Anderson	1050	277	262	9	6	2	.978	2.32	.818
Larry Sutton	365	95	91	2	2	1	.979	2.29	.843
Rich Becker	260	67	63	3	1	0	.985	2.29	.829
Bob Higginson	1196	298	277	16	5	3	.983	2.20	.814
Dave Martinez	700	168	158	9	1	1	.994	2.15	.842
Jeff Abbott	214	52	51	0	1	0	.981	2.15	.797
Rob Ducey	390	96	90	3	3	1	.969	2.14	.795
Johnny Damon	188	46	43	1	2	0	.957	2.11	.824
Alex Ochoa	394	95	88	4	3	0	.968	2.10	.736
Paul O'Neill	1299	307	292	11	4	5	.987	2.10	.846
Jay Buhner	572	134	127	5	2	2	.985	2.08	.733
Shawn Green	1071	253	234	13	6	4	.976	2.08	.782
Manny Ramirez	1319	309	292	10	7	1	.977	2.06	.834
Darren Lewis	408	93	89	1	3	0	.968	1.98	.874
Eric Davis	495	110	105	4	1	0	.991	1.98	.813
Willie Greene	228	51	49	1	1	0	.980	1.98	.873
Darren Bragg	881	194	188	5	1	2	.995	1.97	.877
Juan Gonzalez	1007	224	212	8	4	2	.982	1.97	.763
Ben Grieve	1281	272	262	8	2	0	.993	1.90	.803
Mike Kelly	295	60	58	2	0	0	1.000	1.83	.814
Jeff Conine	233	47	46	0	1	0	.979	1.77	.780
Mike Simms	224	44	43	1	0	0	1.000	1.77	.800
Jose Canseco	190	37	35	1	1	0	.973	1.70	.773

KEY: Inn-Innings; PO-Putouts; A-Assists; Er-Errors; DP-Double Plays; FPct-Fielding Pct.; RF-Range Factor; ZR-Zone Rating

BEN GRIEVE, OAK

I'd say he lived up to expectation, but let's not get too carried away. Ben is turning 23. Ken Griffey's age-22 season was a .300 average, with .366 OBP and .481 SLG. Ben's was .288, .386, and .458. Ah, but Ken Griffey was 22 years old in 1990, four years before the Offensive Surge. Ben is not really putting up that kind of numbers, and he's not playing center field, either. It's a fine rookie season, but it's a class down from Ken Griffey.. <BJH>

BOBBY HIGGINSON, DET

A brutal second half for Bobby (.238/.301/.399) after what looked like a return to his 1996 levels in the first half (.325/.401/.552). That's the sign of an injury being played through, or the sign of an accelerated decline from an early, flukish peak. <DM>

MIKE KELLY, TB

See Rob Ducey. That's as good an explanation for Mike's career as any other I can think of. <BJH>

MATT LAWTON, MIN

I am telling you. Right now. Matt Lawton will NOT have an Age-27 Career Year in 1999. He had it this time out. Big jump in batting average. Big jump in power. Yes, he's due for Counteradjustment Slump, but who cares? This season places him right smack in the pack of top right fielders. I did not see this coming. I had no idea Matt Lawton could do this. And I should have. It's completely consistent with him minor league numbers.

And he was among the Gold Glove defenders here, too. That, at least, makes sense. Matt plays several games a year in center. Um. Mr. Kelly, sir. Why don't you just put him out there and see what happens?<BJH>

When his plate appearances begin with a strike, Matt draws a walk 7.3% of the time. That's above average (MLB = 5.1%) but it's not up in the higher echelon (in case you were wondering, the 1998 leader in this category was Mark McGwire, at 17.9%). The hitters who are Matt's age and who have high walk rates in "After 0-1" situations are Brian Giles (13.0%), Rich Becker (10.8%), Jose Cruz Jr (9.3%). Those are the guys who probably have a shot at cracking 100 walks should they get full playing time. Matt could make it if he can turn just a few more 0-1 counts into walks; he's already won the playing time battle. <DM>

DAVE MARTINEZ, TB

A borderline starter/backup in his salad days, Dave is on an expansion club, which sounds like good news. But he didn't deal well with the ballpark, and the Rays have got kids, and I think Dave will be on his way soon, and out of the majors within three years. <BJH>

ALEX OCHOA, MIN

One of the worst touts I've ever made. I was completely convinced by those 1995 and '96 seasons with the Mets, but Alex has just completely fallen apart, and I do not know why. <BJH>

"Trades of Failed Prospects" would be a terrific article for BBBA, all right, and one that would have to be in such an essay would be last year's Ochoa-for-Becker deal. I'd still put my money on Richie. <DM>

PAUL O'NEILL, NYY (%)

Ah, yes. Another one of those Yankee journeymen who could not possibly be All- Stars. But this time, I'm not going to gripe about money. This one they got legit. The Yankees, several years ago, spotted Paul here having personality problems with Cincinnati management and convince the Cincy GM that he was about even with Roberto Kelly. Snicker. Paul has been one of the very best AL right fielders ever since the trade was made.

Note that I believe the details of the ranking numbers are correct. Paul is probably not as good a hitter as Manny Ramirez or Juan Gonzalez. However, he is a much better defensive right fielder than either one. This year, Paul's defensive edge was enough to carry him to the top of the TXW along with those guys.. <BJH>

MAGGLIO ORDONEZ, CHW

Doesn't that name just sound like a cross between the son of a Mafia Don and a Colombian Cocaine Lord?

I think he can probably play, albeit at a mid-pack starter level. He had a severe case of Sophomore Slump in 1998, but his minor league numbers suggest that aforementioned future. <BJH>

MANNY RAMIREZ, CLE

Your standard Manny Ramirez ranking. Not quite your standard Manny Ramirez season, however. Too much power, too few walks for the norm. Note that Manny, established veteran that he is, is about to turn 27. Note that his power took a big leap forward this year, but that his overall value was held back by drops in bat-

ting average and walks. So take that .328 average and the .415 OBP from 1997, and add in the .599 SLG from this year, and you get an idea of what to predict for 1999. IF CLEVELAND HITS BIG, MANNY IS PROBABLY THE 1999 MVP. <BJH>

MIKE SIMMS, TEX

Well, let's see. He's on the same team as the MVP, playing the same position, and our numbers say that he hit even better than the putative Valuable One. So, let's project Mike's 186 at-bats out to Juan Gonzalez' 606. That turns Mike's 16 homers into 52, and his 46 RBI into 150. Make any adjustment for the fact that Juan Gonzalez ALWAYS gets to bat in the prime RBI slot, and, well, yep, there it is.

Yes, I do know that this campaign is entirely out of the context of Mike Simms' previous career. In the Astrodome. He is only two years out of Death Valley, you know. And you know what else? If I were a General Manager, I might just try to see if I could steal this guy from the Rangers, even turning age 32, before they figure out what they've got here. I think this may well be real.

MVP, my ass. <BJH>

LARRY SUTTON, KC

What!? This guy has played six years in the minor leagues, and has four On-Base Percentages over .400, with a LOW of .357, and the Royals —the ROYALS —can't find a way to give him a cup of coffee before he turns 27? The Royals? Who the hell have the Royals got to keep this guy suppressed these last three seasons? So, fine. Now he's turning 29, and he had his Sophomore Slump. NOW will you guys give this on-base machine a real chance? <BJH>

DESIGNATED HITTER

BILLY ASHLEY, BOS

Someday someone will give this guy 500 AB and he'll put up 40+ HRs. Unfortunately for him, that someone will be coaching a few slow-pitch softball teams in his hometown. <JF>

HAROLD BAINES, BAL (%)

You know, mostly, there's not much to write about regarding the DH. They've done what their offensive numbers say they have, and nothing else. Furthermore, most of them are at least over 30, and playing out the string, having lost too much speed to function on defense. Harold here is a perfect example of this. What can I say about Harold Baines that you don't know? Nothing. He's playing out the string with Baltimore. They paid too much for his aging bat, but why suppress a kid's development by not allowing him to play in the field?

Several other DH comments will read "See Harold Baines". Now you know why. <BJH>

American League DESIGNATED HITTER			
PLAYER	OXW	DXW	TXW
Martinez E	6.79	0.03	6.82
Salmon T	6.23	0.10	6.33
Thomas F	5.12	0.00	5.12
Stairs M	4.90	0.16	5.06
Stanley M	3.82	0.14	3.96
Canseco J	3.50	0.17	3.67
Justice D	3.37	0.10	3.47
Strawberry D	2.80	-0.02	2.78
Stevens L	1.61	0.15	1.76
Baines H	1.55	0.00	1.55
Jefferson R	1.33	0.01	1.34
Sorrento P	0.81	0.31	1.12
Molitor P	0.84	0.01	0.85
Cummings M	0.85	-0.02	0.83
Davis C	0.44	0.00	0.44
Berroa G	0.13	0.13	0.26
Pendleton T	0.04	0.15	0.19
Mitchell Kev	-0.12	0.06	-0.06

GERONIMO BERROA, TOR
(1998: CLE)
See Harold Baines. <BJH>

JOSE CANSECO, TB
(1998: TOR)
See David Justice. <BJH>

Compared to an average American League hitter with the same number of plate appearances, Canseco hit 27 more home runs, stole 18 more bases, and drew 5 more walks, which is good for 46 more runs than average. But Canseco hit 40 fewer singles, 5 fewer doubles, 3 fewer triples, and took 27 more outs (including 12 extra caught stealing) from his teammates, which is about 33 runs worse than average. That's a net gain of about 13 runs over the average hit-

ter, which is what an average DH will do. The average DH will have less spectacular positives (less than 46 home runs) but less spectacular negatives (better than .237 average) and it will add up to the just about the same value. <ST>

MY THEORY, OF COURSE, IS THAT IT WASN'T JOSE AT ALL, BUT HIS TWIN BROTHER OZZIE WHO PLAYED FOR THE JAYS LAST YEAR. LIGHTER, LESS INJURY PRONE, AND A NOTCH OR TWO BELOW THE VINTAGE JOSE PERFORMANCE, THAT HR ZONE IS ENOUGH TO DEFLECT ATTENTION FROM ONE OF THE GREATEST CON JOBS IN THE HISTORY OF SPORT. THE ONLY QUESTION NOW IS WHICH ONE OF THEM IS GOING TO SHOW UP IN TAMPA. <COJ>

MIDRE CUMMINGS, BOS
A backup outfielder who got to play DH because the Boston outfielders weren't missing enough games, and Reggie Jefferson was hurt. <BJH>

CHILI DAVIS, NYY
See Harold Baines. <BJH>

CECIL FIELDER, FA (%)
(1998: ANA-CLE)
See Harold Baines. Oddly enough, Cecil had good numbers with the glove at first base. I assume that's a fluke. <BJH>

REGGIE JEFFERSON, BOS
See Harold Baines. Reggie isn't as good as Harold, but he's only 30. Therefore, he's reduced himself earlier to playing out the string. <BJH>

Here's an injury for the books: A lower back strain suffered when he twisted in an unsuccessful attempt to duck a beanball from Florida's Jesus Sanchez on June 27. He went 6-for-29 after the beaning, took himself out of a game in Tampa on July 14 and, despite two minor-league rehab attempts, missed the rest of the year. A similar ailment—though not incurred in similar fashion—wiped out a good chunk of his 1995 season.

When he's healthy, he hits—right-handers, at least, as his .325 average against them from 1993-98 attests. There was autumn talk of his being on the trade block, since his detractors see him as a 30-year-old, lead-footed, one-dimensional, platoon DH coming off a debilitating back injury. That's focusing on what he can't do. What he can do is hit right-handers. The Red Sox went

down in playoff flames for the lack of someone like him, and they'd be foolish to forget that.<AM>

DAVID JUSTICE, CLE
I've written ad nauseum about David, Darryl Strawberry, Jose Canseco, Eric Davis and body-building these last few years. The gist of the thing is that these guys don't really have the bone frames to handle the amount of muscle that modern body-building techniques can put on them. So they break easy, and end up hurt a lot. David will be back in the outfield as soon as he gets healthy. Of course, that might take five years, by which time, he'll be Harold Baines. <BJH>

EDGAR MARTINEZ, SEA (%)
Led the league in DH value. Played well on defense when the Mariners let him They ought to still be using him in the field. I've written this same comment for what, five years now?<BJH>

Thank you, Woody Woodward, for ruining what would have been a HOF career. Blocked by assorted stiffs at the start of his career. Now, he'll be remembered as a career DH, when he shouldn't have been. <NL>

Edgar is not entirely dead in the water re the HoF. There is one other player whose first full season didn't occur until age 27 who has been inducted: Earl Averill. Here is a comparison of Edgar and Earl using Tom Hull's percentile ranking system:

Age	Earl	Edgar
27	82	76
28	76	87
29	96	96
30	93	0
31	87	66
32	93	99
33	82	93
34	98	95
35	86	94
36	86	—
37	37	—
Pct	5345	4817

Averill trailed off a bit at 35, but Edgar stayed in the 90+ percentile range. Of the 42 previous players aged 35 who had a 90+ percentile, 11 of them had a 90+ percentile at age 36, a little better than one in four. A total of 20 had percentiles of 80+. Interestingly, age 37 is actually a bit rosier, thanks in part to the "last hurrah" phenomenon—14 of the 42, or one-third had percentile scores of 90+.

So if Edgar can stay in his groove for a couple more years, he'll pass Averill as the best player with a late debut, and gains a big lobbying point in the HoF discussion. With two batting titles, two doubles crowns, a .310+ lifetime BA, a .400+ OBP lifetime and in 7-8 seasons, he's a candidate——at least for the Veterans committee. <DM>

KEVIN MITCHELL, FA
(1998: OAK)

See Harold Baines. <BJH>

PAUL MOLITOR, MIL (%)

This reminds me of Stanley Frank Musial. In 1963, Musial, aged 42, hit .255, with 12 home runs and 58 RBI. It was in only 3/5 of a season, and the Cardinals were willing to have him back, but Musial said "No. That was not a Stan Musial season. I'm done. I retire." There was great weeping and wailing in St. Louis, some of it by the 16-year-old me, but Musial was absolutely correct. The Cardinals, suddenly in need of a left fielder, went out and traded a good starting pitcher for a kid named Lou Brock, and promptly won a pennant that they would not have won with Stan Musial in left field.

I don't mean to suggest that the Twins are one DH away from being World Champions, but Paul Molitor did the right thing. This was not a Paul Molitor season. So he retired. A class act to the last. A true Hall of Famer. Thanks, Paul, for all the good memories. And also for not putting us through two more seasons of bad ones. <BJH>

TERRY PENDELTON, KC

What!!? Somebody tried to DH Terry Pendelton? Terry Pendelton, the best third base glove I have ever seen, but a man whose power was strictly limited to hitters' ballparks? THAT Terry Pendelton is playing Designated Hitter in Kansas City's vast outfield prairie? <BJH>

TIM RAINES, NYY (%)

See Darryl Strawberry. Seriously, Tim is another guy with speed left who is DHing only because of age, injuries, and cocaine wear and tear. <BJH>

TIM SALMON, ANA

He was hurt, wasn't he? He'll be back in right field in 1999, right? Or did I miss something there? <BJH>

PAUL SORRENTO, TB

See Harold Baines AND Reggie Jefferson. Paul is somewhere in between. <BJH>

MATT STAIRS, OAK

See Harold Baines. Matt is a little young to have lost all defensive value, but still, here he is. <BJH>

MIKE STANLEY, BOS
(1998: TOR-BOS)

See Harold Baines. <BJH>

He hit .288 after returning to Boston from Toronto (via New York), and his batting skills and professionalism figure to make him an important part of the Red Sox mix in 1999. <AM>

LEE STEVENS, TEX

See Reggie Jefferson. <BJH>

It was about a million years ago that Lee Stevens was going to take over for Wally Joyner in Calfornia. Considering how bad Lee was at the time, it's a miracle that he's still in the league. Credit the restorative powers of the Japanese for plugging the Godzilla-sized holes in Lee's swing, because he's a legitimate major-league hitter now. He's a star like Brian Bosworth is an actor, though. While we're on that, his name and his all-American good looks tell me that, if he'd been born 40 years earlier, they'd have been talking about him as the next Gary Cooper. Probably with no more success.<TA>

DARRYL STRAWBERRY, NYY (%)

Probably hasn't lost enough speed to be reduced to Harold Baines. Might have lost it to injury and cocaine wear and tear, though. <BJH>

FRANK THOMAS, CHW (%)

Not Harold Baines. Season lost while playing through an injury. Expect him to be back. At first. <BJH>

I've not found any corroboration for the injury Brock references, but Frank's monthly rate stats do support such a possibility:

Month	BA	OBP	SLG
April	.273	.380	.500
May	.288	.397	.471
June	.240	.355	.404
July	.218	.367	.414
August	.250	.375	.538
September	.312	.411	.538

Frank has had a slow April or two in his career, but the next three months were seriously sub-par, and were accompanied by a precipitous drop against left-handed pitching. By August,

you can see that his power came back, and in September he had a month that would not be out of line in a normal Big Hurt season.

And then there's that odd DH/first base split, which persisted in 1998. Frank played 14 games at first base last year: six in April, once against the Royals on 6/2 to prepare for interleague play, and then seven away games in NL parks in June and July. His offensive numbers in those games: .302/.406/.547. It's uncanny, all right, and the evidence keeps mounting that it's a mental thing. <DM>

RELIEF PITCHERS

RICK AGUILERA, MIN

He illustrates how much a closer's potential value can change through no fault of his own or his manager's. Last year, I wrote that Rick's 1997 was the least eventful season of any closer, and his PPI was among the lowest of the relievers I kept track of. This season, he led the league in PPPI (.113). But his role did not change, the Twins just played a lot more tight games. As you know, he didn't take advantage. His 10 disastrous appearances were nearly as many as some entire teams had. A top-notch closer would've made a huge difference to the Twins last year. <DD>

SCOTT ALDRED, TB

He came on in May and provided what Ramon Tatis couldn't: spot lefty relief work that did not pose any safety risks to innocent bystanders. <DD>

MATT ANDERSON, DET

To me, the most aesthetically pleasing thing to watch on TV is a hard straight fastball from a righthanded pitcher. Anderson's is the best I've seen since Nolan Ryan, and I'm not sure Ryan's heater was any hotter.

The Tigers didn't just hand him Todd Jones' job, but they didn't waste much time exposing him to late-inning pressure either. His PPPI of .081 was 2nd on the squad, and he entered 13 tie games (Sean Runyan also entered 13, no other Tiger had more than 10) despite only being around for half a season. In fact, 31% of his appearances started with the game tied. That was the highest percentage in the AL by a wide margin (among relievers with 40 appearances, Paul Shuey was next at 23%). **<DD>**

PAUL ASSENMACHER, CLE

He was unique among lefty specialists on teams with well-defined closers in that he often stuck around to start the 9th innings of games with a 1- or 2-run lead. He started 4 9ths with a 1-run lead and 5 9ths with a 2-run lead.

A fairly low ERA masked the fact that he did not pitch particularly well in 98, allowing an OPS of .769. His RA of 4.21 was as high as it's been since 1989. **<DD>**

BOBBY AYALA, SEA

He wasn't half bad in low pressure situations. Here's the line for his games where the P was less than .05:

IP	H	R	ER	BB	K
37.2	36	15	15	9	38

His games with P > .20 were a different story:

IP	H	R	ER	BB	K
14.1	22	17	17	2	13

The AL's overall bottom 20 in WPA consist of Ayala (#1) and 19 starters. He was 2 and half games worse than the next worst reliever in the AL (Hernandez), and 1 and a half games worse than the next worst in the majors (Doug Jones). **<DD>**

SCOTT BAILES, TEX

Not a very exciting season for Scott. Only 6 of his 46 appearances were in save/hold situations. Only 3 were high-pressure (P > .15), and over half were classified as very low pressure (P < .01). As a result, nothing he did mattered much, which worked out well for him. 40 of his 46 appearances resulted in a WPA between -.05 and +.05, despite the fact that he had some real stinkeroos. **<DD>**

TRAVIS BAPTIST, MIN

A 27-year-old lefty who spent 3 years solving AAA. He finally did in 1997, and has

pretty solid minor league numbers over the last two years. He was rocked in his first exposure to the majors, 13 meaningless (PPPI: .030) late-season appearances. **<DD>**

ARMANDO BENITEZ, BAL

Armando Benitez: Incurable head-case or dominant reliever of the 00's? I don't have much to add to that debate, so I'll talk a bit about usage. His PPPI of .076 led the Orioles, but was 32nd in the AL. I don't have PPPI data for 1997, but my guess is the O's would have led the league, and that P was concentrated in two guys, Randy Myers and Benitez. In 98, they were middle of the pack in PPPI, and their distribution of P was very balanced, with 4 guys having P between 6.0 and 6.7. **<DD>**

DOUG BOCHTLER, DET

He was the Tiger's mopup man from day 1; only 3 of his 51 appearances were save/hold situations, and 4 were in tie games.

He looked like a solid reliever in 1995 and 96. In 97, his control left him. Last year, the hit prevention disappeared. He's on the ropes, at best. **<DD>**

DOUG BROCAIL, DET

File him under "we still don't know squat about pitchers, Exhibit #3195." He basically defined replacement level for 5 seasons in San Diego and Houston. Then he arrived in Detroit at age 30 in 1997 and posted a solid season. His 1998 wasn't solid, it was dynamite. Betcha didn't know Brocail had the 3rd-best OPS allowed in the AL last season. The Tigers evidently caught on around early June.

His PPPI in April and May was .038. After June 1st, it was .081. **<DD>**

HECTOR CARRASCO, MIN

Hector deviated from his norm and became extremely hittable last season; almost 11 hits per 9, and he allowed both righties and lefties to hit over .300 against him. He did a decent job of keeping extra-base hits to a minimum, though, as hitters had a .085 ISO against him. Maybe that's a sign that he just had an unlucky year, with more than his share of bloops and squibs falling in. Or maybe not. Hector isn't exactly known for being predictable. **<DD>**

JIM CORSI, BOS

A very steady, if unspectacular, season. He had only two disastrous (WPA <-.25) outings, the worst being a -.31, and one heroic (WPA > +.25) one. He ranked 3rd on the Bosox in P, so it's not like he was on mopup duty, he was just consistent. All his splits were very even as well. **<DD>**

TIM CRABTREE, TEX

A nice surprise for the Rangers. He was their long man and soaked up enough innings to rank 2nd on the team in P (to Wetteland). He also came up big in his high pressure (P > .15) situations.

	IP	H	R	ER	BB	K	ERA
Hi P	22.2	10	5	3	8	13	1.19
Other	62.2	76	35	31	27	27	4.45

Did a nice job of turning opposing hitters into Punches and/or Judies, as he allowed only 3 dingers and a SLG .347. I wouldn't be surprised to see a few more

**RELIEF PITCHER DATA,
AMERICAN LEAGUE 1998**

LEGEND: **SV**—Save; **SVOP**—Save Opportunity; **HLD**—Hold; **G/F**—Groundball/Flyball Ratio **IR**—Inherited Runners; **IS**—Inherited Runners Scored; **IRS%**—Inherited Runners Pct.

Name	TM	SV	SVOP	HLD	BA	OBP	SLG	OPS	SB	CS	GDP	G/F	IR	IS	IRS%
Mike James	Ana	0	0	2	.208	.309	.271	.580	0	2	1	1.29	5	2	40.0
Troy Percival	Ana	42	48	0	.186	.299	.314	.613	16	2	0	0.58	24	5	20.8
Pep Harris	Ana	0	1	14	.239	.307	.370	.677	3	1	4	1.73	57	13	22.8
Shigetoshi Hasegawa	Ana	5	7	10	.241	.302	.431	.733	3	1	10	0.93	55	18	32.7
Rich DeLucia	Ana	3	6	12	.221	.340	.399	.739	8	4	4	0.45	46	9	19.6
Mike Fetters	Ana	5	9	11	.267	.338	.427	.765	6	2	2	1.85	53	23	43.4
Trevor Wilson	Ana	0	2	2	.267	.378	.400	.778	0	0	1	1.14	15	5	33.3
Mike Holtz	Ana	1	2	13	.322	.397	.407	.804	1	3	6	1.72	56	18	32.1
Rich Robertson	Ana	0	0	1	.393	.419	.750	1.169	0	0	0	1.86	8	1	12.5
Alan Mills	Bal	2	5	19	.203	.326	.321	.647	11	2	6	1.29	42	8	19.0
Jesse Orosco	Bal	7	9	9	.221	.314	.341	.655	9	1	3	1.05	47	15	31.9
Armando Benitez	Bal	22	26	3	.199	.318	.361	.679	8	1	4	0.66	42	14	33.3
Arthur Rhodes	Bal	4	8	10	.233	.313	.369	.682	13	3	8	1.21	31	12	38.7
Rocky Coppinger	Bal	0	0	0	.246	.319	.446	.765	2	0	0	0.71	0	0	0.0
Terry Mathews	Bal	0	1	1	.342	.400	.645	1.045	3	0	3	1.13	22	11	50.0
Joel Bennett	Bal	0	0	0	.250	.455	.625	1.080	0	0	0	0.20	0	0	0.0
Radhames Dykhoff	Bal	0	0	0	.400	.500	.600	1.100	0	0	0	3.00	0	0	0.0

seasons like this one, but nothing better. **<DD>**

DEAN CROW, DET

A 26-year-old righthander who looks to be destined for mediocrity at best. He got hit pretty hard (.834 OPS allowed), but managed not to give up too many runs (3.94 ERA). **<DD>**

RICH DELUCIA, ANA

I think one of the reasons Anaheim's bullpen was a success last year was the fact that no one was overworked. In order to make this work, you've got to have several competent arms, which Anaheim did in Hasegawa, Harris, and Delucia. I don't see why Delucia doesn't have a few more good years in him with this kind of workload. **<DD>**

MIKE FETTERS, ANA

The back half of the AL West bullpens had something of a swap-meet feel to it with no less than three individuals (Fetters, Greg Cadaret, and Tony Fossas) stinking up the joint with two different AL West clubs. Tough year for Fetters, as he essentially did nothing right with either Oakland or Anaheim. **<DD>**

KEITH FOULKE, ChW

He was part of the infamous Alvarez/Darwin/Hernandez deal the Chisox made on deadline day 97. I might rather have him than Wilson Alvarez or Roberto Hernandez right now.

A very nice season, but I still think his future is in the starting rotation. He never did anything but start in the minors and did it relatively successfully. **<DD>**

TOM GORDON, BOS

He was discussed in detail in the WPA article.

An examination of the arm health of starters who moved to the bullpen mid-career would make an interesting study. Gordon got a pretty heavy workload (by closer standards), but it seems to have been spaced out well. He had 19 appearances on 0 days rest, but only pitched 3 straight days twice, and only had 2 layoffs of more than 4 days. He certainly finished the season as strong as he started it. My guess is he's as good a long-term roto investment as any closer in the AL right now. **<DD>**

BUDDY GROOM, OAK

Tied Eddie Guardado for 2nd in the AL with 49 appearances with runners on base. Despite that, his PPPI was relatively low (.059), so he didn't play a very crucial role in the fortunes of the A's pen (which is absolutely the highest compliment you can pay a member of that malodorous bunch). **<DD>**

EDDIE GUARDADO, MIN

A downright adequate second lefty, and even having him as the best southpaw in your pen doesn't necessarily doom you. He pitched 31 times on 0 days rest, and pitched on 3 straight days 11 times. He still managed to finish strong though.

He entered 49 games with runners aboard, 2nd in the AL to Dan Plesac. **<DD>**

SHIGETOSHI HASEGAWA, ANA

Obviously a very useful guy to have around, certainly the Angels' bullpen MVP. He came into every imaginable situation, and often stuck around for awhile, leading the Angels in multiple-inning appearances with 37 (3rd in the AL). He had a relatively low PPPI, but made up for it by pitching tons of innings, so his P turned out to be 13th in the AL at 7.2. **<DD>**

ROBERTO HERNANDEZ, TB

This was clearly not a successful season. The terrible WPA (-1.4, 2nd-worst in the AL) was due primarily to timing. In his 9 highest-pressure appearances, he was

IP	H	ER	R	BB	SO
11.2	14	10	10	9	7

I think there's a good chance he'll bounce back. He did prevent hits well, and allowed a SLG of only .296, 6th-best among AL relievers. **<DD>**

XAVIER HERNANDEZ, TEX

Another Texas reliever who pitched better in his high pressure (P > .15) situations.

	IP	H	R	ER	BB	K	ERA
Hi P	23.2	13	4	4	16	16	1.52
Other	34.1	30	23	19	14	25	6.03

It could now be argued that he has had a successful season outside the Astrodome. **<DD>**

DARREN HOLMES, NYY

There are worse ways for Steinbrenner to spend his money, I guess. Holmes' season was as meaningless (PPPI .038) as it was mediocre. **<DD>**

BOB HOWRY, ChW

He was tremendous in his high-pressure appearances and finished 5th in the AL in WPA despite only being around for a few months. Be that as it may, nothing in his track record suggests he's capable of sustaining a level anywhere near what he did in 98. **<DD>**

RELIEF PITCHER DATA, AMERICAN LEAGUE 1998

LEGEND: SV—Save; **SVOP**—Save Opportunity; **HLD**—Hold; **G/F**—Groundball/Flyball Ratio **IR**—Inherited Runners; **IS**—Inherited Runners Scored; **IRS%**—Inherited Runners Pct.

Name	TM	SV	SVOP	HLD	BA	OBP	SLG	OPS	SB	CS	GDP	G/F	IR	IS	IRS%
Bobby Munoz	Bal	0	0	0	.383	.439	.745	1.184	3	0	2	1.06	8	2	25.0
Carlos Valdez	Bos	0	0	0	.100	.375	.100	.475	0	0	1	2.00	4	1	25.0
Tom Gordon	Bos	46	47	0	.191	.254	.247	.501	7	0	4	1.50	38	8	21.1
Jim Corsi	Bos	0	3	18	.235	.301	.344	.645	4	5	10	1.90	37	9	24.3
Carlos Reyes	Bos	1	2	3	.242	.306	.358	.664	3	5	7	1.34	39	10	25.6
Derek Lowe	Bos	4	9	12	.267	.329	.352	.681	17	5	13	4.58	38	12	31.6
Rich Garces	Bos	1	3	6	.213	.327	.373	.700	5	1	1	1.12	16	4	25.0
Ron Mahay	Bos	1	2	7	.263	.358	.354	.712	6	0	2	0.61	27	11	40.7
Greg Swindell	Bos	2	5	24	.267	.331	.446	.777	3	3	7	0.89	48	5	10.4
Dennis Eckersley	Bos	1	4	9	.291	.331	.462	.793	12	1	4	1.20	24	8	33.3
John Wasdin	Bos	0	1	4	.288	.333	.479	.812	11	2	3	1.00	27	8	29.6
Brian Shouse	Bos	0	0	1	.281	.361	.500	.861	0	0	1	0.73	3	1	33.3
Dario Veras	Bos	0	0	0	.343	.465	.429	.894	0	0	0	1.09	3	0	0.0
Brian Barkley	Bos	0	0	0	.340	.441	.468	.909	5	0	1	0.62	4	1	25.0
David West	Bos	0	0	1	.538	.700	.769	1.469	0	0	0	1.00	2	1	50.0
Mike Heathcott	ChW	0	0	0	.182	.250	.273	.523	0	0	0	0.00	1	0	0.0
Chad Bradford	ChW	1	3	9	.229	.272	.280	.552	1	0	3	3.33	18	4	22.2
Bob Howry	ChW	9	11	19	.194	.270	.356	.626	3	2	4	0.70	23	2	8.7
Bill Simas	ChW	18	24	6	.206	.270	.389	.659	6	0	5	0.86	32	9	28.1

MIKE HOLTZ, ANA

The Angels' pen was about as balanced as a Cecil Fielder meal. Their overall bullpen WPA of +4.1 broke down as +5.9 for the righthanders and -1.8 for lefties. Holtz pitched reasonably well and in important situations in September (+.3 WPA and .098 PPPI), so there's hope that he could be part of the solution. **<DD>**

MIKE JACKSON, CLE

The man has not had a bad season in 13 tries. I'm glad to see him get some recognition. Hargrove's flip-flop of the roles of a proven (but bad) closer and a career setup man was, as far as I can tell, unprecedented. Nice job, Grover. **<DD>**

AL LEVINE, TEX

Another example of good (but obvious) bullpen resource allocation. Levine was obviously not Rangers' best option, so they pitched him in these situations:

	-5	-4	-3	-2	-1	0	+1	+2	+3	+4	+5	TOTAL
5	5	4	1	3	1	1						15
6		1	1			1				1		4
7	1											
8	1		2		1							4
9	1			1		1					2	5
10+						1						1
TOTAL	8	5	5	3	3	3	0	0	0	1	2	30

It resulted in a .031 PPPI, and Levine's .786 OPS allowed didn't hurt them a bit. **<DD>**

GRAEME LLOYD, NYY

For the second consecutive year, the Yanks placed absolutely no trust in him. His PPPI was .047, 6th of the 7 Yankee relievers with 20 appearances. A team-leading 44% of his appearances were classified as "very low P" (P < .01). A .528 OPS allowed is as impressive as it is unlikely to happen again. **<DD>**

ALBIE LOPEZ, TB

There were about 15 guys just like Albie Lopez taken in the expansion draft. Even with the benefit of full hindsight, I can't figure out how anyone could possibly have known that Lopez would pan out instead of, say, Clint Sodowsky or Chris Clemons or Bryan Rekar. In any event, a fine season by Lopez.

This probably doesn't mean anything, but Albie had a +2.2 WPA in his multiple-inning appearances and -1.1 in his single-inning appearances. **<DD>**

DEREK LOWE, BOS

He was the "other" player Seattle gave up in the Mariners' "other" trade on the eve of the trade deadline two years ago, but he may end up being the most valuable of the 6 players involved in those two deals. He was much better in relief than as a starter last season, but I expect him to succeed in the rotation eventually.

He had 5 heroic appearances (WPA > +.25) and only 3 disastrous (WPA < -.25) ones (leaguewide, the heroic-to-disastrous ratio was about 1-to-2). **<DD>**

T.J. MATHEWS, OAK

Every member of Oakland's bullpen was a disappointment last season, but Mathews was probably the most disturbing. His strikeouts were down, he allowed nearly 50% of his inherited runners to score, and lefties continued to pound him. He's not likely to get better than he is right now if he can't solve that last one. **<DD>**

JIM MECIR, TB

Quite simply, one of the best relievers in the American League last year. He ranked 9th in the league in WPA (+2.2), 9th in PWins (+1.5), and 14th in P. He had 7 heroic (WPA > +.25) appearances and only 3 disastrous (WPA < -.25) ones. I think the improvement is legit, and I expect more seasons like this one. **<DD>**

RAMIRO MENDOZA, NYY

Highly regarded by many, he's clearly useful, but not much more than that. His numbers look Julian Tavarezish to me, and I don't view that as a good thing. **<DD>**

ALAN MILLS, BAL

Mills really confuses me. Anyone who prevents hits as well as he does should be striking out more batters. He's the anti-Jon Lieber. Going into last season, he had a career H/9 of 8.0 and a K/9 of 6.5. He brought the hits down much further in 98 (6.4), but the K's didn't budge (6.7). What gives?

None of this takes anything away from his fine season. **<DD>**

MIKE MOHLER, OAK

Just what everyone wants — a lefty that can't get lefties out. In other news, he doesn't get righties out either. **<DD>**

JEFF MONTGOMERY, KC

He had 0 heroic (WPA > +.25) performances, and 6 disastrous (WPA < -.25) ones. But he had 27 good ones (between .05 and .025) and no poor ones (between -.05 and -.025). That, ladies and gentlemen, is a closer with an easy workload. His save situations were easy enough that when he blew one it cost the Royals bigtime, but he had enough of them that he was able to fatten up the 'good' column.

RELIEF PITCHER DATA,
AMERICAN LEAGUE 1998

LEGEND: **SV**—Save; **SVOP**—Save Opportunity; **HLD**—Hold; **G/F**—Groundball/Flyball Ratio **IR**—Inherited Runners; **IS**—Inherited Runners Scored; **IRS%**—Inherited Runners Pct.

Name	TM	SV	SVOP	HLD	BA	OBP	SLG	OPS	SB	CS	GDP	G/F	IR	IS	IRS%
Keith Foulke	ChW	1	2	13	.213	.283	.389	.672	3	1	3	0.79	40	10	25.0
Carlos Castillo	ChW	0	2	3	.246	.312	.440	.752	9	2	5	0.66	54	16	29.6
Bryan Ward	ChW	1	4	3	.278	.319	.463	.782	3	0	3	0.94	24	10	41.7
Tom Fordham	ChW	0	0	0	.279	.414	.443	.857	1	4	5	1.19	20	5	25.0
Todd Rizzo	ChW	0	0	0	.387	.474	.452	.926	0	0	2	2.29	7	4	57.1
Tony Castillo	ChW	0	0	1	.328	.395	.586	.981	2	2	5	1.64	19	8	42.1
Larry Casian	ChW	0	0	0	.400	.478	.600	1.078	0	0	0	3.00	0	0	0.0
Jason Rakers	Cle	0	0	0	.000	.500	.000	.500	0	0	0	1.00	0	0	0.0
Mike Jackson	Cle	40	45	1	.195	.252	.290	.542	1	4	7	1.00	26	4	15.4
Steve Reed	Cle	1	6	21	.194	.275	.316	.591	4	3	6	1.04	51	10	19.6
Paul Shuey	Cle	2	5	12	.229	.327	.370	.697	8	3	3	1.87	18	5	27.8
Paul Assenmacher	Cle	3	8	25	.286	.351	.418	.769	8	0	3	1.32	44	9	20.5
Doug Jones	Cle	13	22	5	.292	.328	.490	.818	2	1	3	1.00	30	9	30.0
Steve Karsay	Cle	0	0	2	.310	.355	.480	.835	0	2	0	1.09	11	5	45.5
Jim Poole	Cle	0	3	6	.301	.353	.494	.847	4	1	3	1.22	28	9	32.1
Ron Villone	Cle	0	0	1	.297	.425	.446	.871	2	2	4	1.73	13	5	38.5
Tom Martin	Cle	0	0	3	.408	.488	.676	1.164	1	0	0	1.39	12	4	33.3
Doug Brocail	Det	0	1	11	.211	.269	.296	.565	4	3	4	1.39	44	11	25.0
Roberto Duran	Det	0	0	0	.170	.389	.226	.615	0	0	0	0.36	8	0	0.0

He entered only 1 tie game. **<DD>**

JEFF NELSON, NYY

The Yankee starters were so good in 1998 that they did not even need a setup man. New York was tied or up 1 or 2 going into the 8th inning 41 times, and they stuck with the starter on 19 of those occasions, by far the highest ratio in the AL.

He's still one of my favorites to watch. That frisbee-style slider is downright Nintendoesque. **<DD>**

JESSE OROSCO, BAL

He did not have a single disastrous (WPA < -.25) appearance all year, which is very impressive considering how often he was in the thick of things. His splits were as even as you can get:

	G	PI	WPA	P	PPPI
Road	30	41	0.7	3.1	0.077
	B39	49	1.2	3.2	0.066
Low pressure	38	43	0.3	0.7	0.016
Med pressure	14	19	0.6	1.2	0.062
Hi pressure	17	28	1.1	4.5	0.161
Mar/Apr	10	11	0.1	0.6	0.059
May	11	16	-0	1.5	0.091
June	13	19	0.7	1.1	0.057
July	12	17	0.6	1.8	0.104
August	13	16	0.1	0.9	0.057
September	10	11	0.3	0.5	0.042
One-Inning Apps	49	49	0.5	3.2	0.066
Multiple-Inning Apps	20	41	1.5	3.1	0.076

<DD>

JOSE PANIAGUA, SEA

Came on late in the year and did a commendable job in middle relief, posting a +1.0 WPA in 18 appearances. He was perfect in his 4 high-pressure situations. Likely a fluke, but who the hell knows? **<DD>**

Acquired after the Devil Rays cut him in spring training, Paniagua has turned his career around. He pitched very well in Tacoma and turned it up a notch when he was called up to the Mariners in mid-August. Only 25, he appears to have found his feet, and could be a crucial part of the bullpen in 1999. If he continues to improve, he could be in line to take over as closer in a year or two in much the same way Mariano Rivera did for the Yankees. If I were a manager willing to give a young guy a shot at a key job, I'd consider him as the closer next year. Of course, in reality, Lou Piniella has the final say, so Paniagua may get a shot by about 2005. **<DJP>**

TROY PERCIVAL, ANA

His 1995 and 1996, which were carbon copies of each other, may have been the best two relief seasons in history, but inconsistency and injuries have made him a second-tier closer in my book. The K rate is still ungodly high, so I wouldn't be surprised to see him bounce back, but I also wouldn't be surprised if he never has another great season again.

His usage was fairly standard.

The high PPPI (.107 — 2nd in the AL) was because Anaheim was involved in a lot of close games. **<DD>**

DAN PLESAC, TOR

There was a lot of chaos in the Toronto pen last season, but he and Paul Quantrill were rocks. Those two combined for a +3.9 WPA and the rest of the Toronto bullpen was a -1.5. Plesac was 6th in the AL in P (first among lefties), and 7th in WPA. He led the AL in appearances in tie games and appearances with runners on base. He also pitched 31 times on 0 days rest. **<DD>**

PAUL QUANTRILL, TOR

Here's the usage matrix of a hard-working man:

	-5	-4	-3	-2	-1	0	+1	+2	+3	+4	+5	TOTAL
5												0
6												0
7				2	3		5	1	3			14
8	1		1	3	2	9	8	7	8	2	3	44
9			1	2	1	4	3	2		4	7	24
10+												
TOT	1		2	7	6	13	16	10	11	6	10	82

He led the AL in P and was 17th in WPA. He also started 10 tied 9th innings, more than any other AL pitcher.

Quantrill is the only reliever in the 90's to post an ERA below 3.00 while pitching more than 70 innings and allowing more than 9.5 hits per 9 innings, and he's done it two straight years. OK, so I tweaked the categories 'til Paul was the only guy left. Still, there's not much precedent for this kind of success with absolutely no ability to prevent hits. **<DD>**

STEVE REED, CLE
(1998: SF-CLE)

I'm sure you know by now that he's a terrific pitcher. One of the best in the business.

The right side of the Indians' bullpen is now about as strong as any bullpen has a right to be with Reed, Jackson, Shuey, and Spradlin. Rincon is a nice addition to the left side (although at a pretty steep price). If Assenmacher can bounce back, or even just stop his slide, this looks like far and away the best bullpen in baseball. **<DD>**

RELIEF PITCHER DATA, AMERICAN LEAGUE 1998

LEGEND: SV—Save; **SVOP**—Save Opportunity; **HLD**—Hold; **G/F**—Groundball/Flyball Ratio **IR**—Inherited Runners; **IS**—Inherited Runners Scored; **IRS%**—Inherited Runners Pct.

Name	TM	SV	SVOP	HLD	BA	OBP	SLG	OPS	SB	CS	GDP	G/F	IR	IS	IRS%
Will Brunson	Det	0	0	2	.263	.364	.316	.680	1	0	2	5.50	10	2	20.0
Todd Jones	Det	28	32	0	.249	.347	.382	.729	4	0	8	2.02	17	5	29.4
Matt Anderson	Det	0	4	6	.250	.378	.382	.760	1	2	6	0.98	30	15	50.0
Sean Runyan	Det	1	3	11	.255	.348	.413	.761	6	2	6	1.06	76	27	35.5
Bryce Florie	Det	0	0	4	.275	.354	.434	.788	8	6	17	2.88	32	14	43.8
Denny Harriger	Det	0	0	0	.327	.417	.404	.821	1	0	1	2.36	0	0	0.0
Dean Crow	Det	0	0	0	.313	.374	.460	.834	6	4	10	1.70	14	2	14.3
A.J. Sager	Det	2	3	1	.325	.383	.473	.856	11	3	9	3.42	28	14	50.0
Doug Bochtler	Det	0	2	2	.279	.381	.553	.934	7	3	5	0.80	50	21	42.0
Marino Santana	Det	0	0	0	.310	.474	.483	.957	0	0	1	1.75	7	3	42.9
Bart Evans	KC	0	0	0	.206	.206	.324	.530	0	0	0	1.75	3	2	66.7
Scott Service	KC	4	8	18	.231	.322	.363	.685	6	5	1	1.26	44	15	34.1
Ricky Bones	KC	1	2	3	.244	.327	.363	.690	4	1	5	1.70	28	9	32.1
Matt Whisenant	KC	2	5	16	.271	.365	.347	.712	2	1	9	1.86	64	20	31.3
Jeff Montgomery	KC	36	41	0	.264	.335	.418	.753	2	0	6	1.80	4	4	100.0
Brian Bevil	KC	0	2	5	.283	.373	.440	.813	1	0	0	0.81	23	10	43.5
Danny Rios	KC	0	0	0	.300	.421	.500	.921	1	0	2	1.86	5	3	60.0
Jim Pittsley	KC	0	0	1	.322	.401	.557	.958	6	2	10	1.46	15	8	53.3
Jose Santiago	KC	0	0	0	.444	.444	.556	1.000	0	0	0	3.00	0	0	0.0

ARTHUR RHODES, BAL

Another very good season, though not quite as good as his 1997. His high-pressure situations (P > .15 — he had 14 of them) were not the kind you usually think of when you think of high-pressure situations. They generally started in the middle innings and lasted 2 to 4 frames. In any event, he really boosted his WPA in those situations, by pitching as follows:

	IP	H	R	ER	BB	K	ERA
Hi Pressure	32.1	19	5	5	9	38	1.39
Other	44.2	46	25	25	25	45	5.04

Not so encouraging is the fact that his ERA was up and his Ks were down (although neither drastically so) when he returned from a DL stint. **<DD>**

BILL RISLEY, TOR

When I was researching 'elite' seasons for the WPA article an elite season is one in which your strikeout-to-hit ratio is above 1.5, and your WHIP is 1 or below), I was shocked to find that Risley posted one in 1994 (52.1 IP, 31 H, 19 BB, 61 K). A review of his complete record suggests that he is a damn fine pitcher when healthy. Unfortunately, that doesn't happen much.**<DD>**

MARIANO RIVERA, NYY

OK, just in case you haven't heard, Rivera's K rate is in the toilet. It went from 10.9 in 1996 to 8.5 in 97 to 5.3 last year. Let me put into perspective just how dire the situation is. Only 3 pitchers in the 90s have managed 30 saves or more while getting 6 Ks per 9 or fewer: Rivera last year, Doug Jones in 1990, and Jeff Russell in 1991. Only 22 relievers in the 90s (with more than 60 innings) have posted an ERA below 2.50 with a K rate below 6. One of the following things must happen next year:

1 Rivera will get the Ks back up and keep being the man,
2 Rivera will become the first closer since Dan Quisenberry to have consistent success despite a low K rate,
3 Rivera will go into the tank.

2 seems highly unlikely, and I'd say 1 or 3 is a tossup. Obviously, he is to be avoided. **<DD>**

SEAN RUNYAN, DET

Never a dull moment for this rookie. He led the AL in appearances (88), pitched 42 times on 0 days rest, and pitched on 3 straight days 16 times. He also entered with runners aboard 45 times, which is 4th in the AL. His usage matrix is bursting at the seams:

	-5	-4	-3	-2	-1	0	+1	+2	+3	+4	+5	TOTAL
5						1						1
6			1	7	2	1	2		1			14
7	2	1	4	5	3	4	3	1		1	2	26
8	3	1	1	2	6	3	4	3	1	4	2	30
9	3	1		3	3	2		1			1	14
10+						3						3
TOT	8	3	6	17	14	13	10	5	2	5	5	88

<DD>

SCOTT SERVICE, KC

He's the genuine article. Since being traded to Kansas City last year, he's fanned 119 in 99.2 innings. If he gets a closer job, he'll keep it. **<DD>**

PAUL SHUEY, CLE

It seems as though the working definition of setup man is "a reliever who pitches with a lead of 3 runs or less in the 8th, or in a tied 9th." Shuey fits that description. Young setup men, I'd suspect, tend to become closers, and Paul is reputed to have plenty of stuff. I expect him to be a good closer eventually, probably as soon as he gets the chance. **<DD>**

BILL SIMAS, CHW

A failure to get the job done in high-pressure situations really torpedoed his WPA, as he had 7 disastrous (WPA < -.25) outings and was only able to muster positive WPA in 6 of his 13 high-pressure appearances. **<DD>**

PAUL SPOLJARIC, PHI (1998: SEA)

A huge disappointment. I thought he had a chance to redeem the Jose Cruz trade to some extent, but he just became more of the replacement-level riffraff. Moved to the rotation late in the year, but didn't look good there either. The K rate is still high, so there may be hope. **<DD>**

MIKE STANTON, NYY

Very funky season. He allowed an OPS of 721, which isn't cause for celebration, but certainly doesn't suggest a 5.47 ERA. On the other hand, he had a 5.81 RA and -.7 PWins, but a WPA of 1.5.

He finished strong. My guess is he comes back with a strong all-around season next year. **<DD>**

DAVE STIEB, TOR

I'm a Dave Stieb fan. I think he was underappreciated in his prime, and he made a nice story. But let's not kid ourselves, he had about as much chance to contribute to Blue Jay victories in 1998 as Lloyd Moseby did. A PPPI of .022 is comically low. **<DD>**

**RELIEF PITCHER DATA,
AMERICAN LEAGUE 1998**

LEGEND: SV—Save; **SVOP**—Save Opportunity; **HLD**—Hold; **G/F**—Groundball/Flyball Ratio **IR**—Inherited Runners; **IS**—Inherited Runners Scored; **IRS%**—Inherited Runners Pct.

Name	TM	SV	SVOP	HLD	BA	OBP	SLG	OPS	SB	CS	GDP	G/F	IR	IS	IRS%
Allen McDill	KC	0	0	1	.333	.379	.741	1.120	0	0	0	0.90	9	2	22.2
Tim Byrdak	KC	0	0	0	.556	.556	1.000	1.556	0	0	1	0.67	2	2	100.0
Benj Sampson	Min	0	0	0	.172	.254	.207	.461	2	0	1	0.46	2	0	0.0
Travis Miller	Min	0	0	0	.272	.346	.348	.694	0	0	3	2.05	11	5	45.5
Rick Aguilera	Min	38	49	0	.262	.299	.416	.715	6	0	7	0.94	22	1	4.5
Hector Carrasco	Min	1	2	10	.304	.373	.389	.762	4	1	5	1.59	63	25	39.7
Mike Trombley	Min	1	4	23	.248	.332	.433	.765	2	4	8	0.83	58	14	24.1
Todd Ritchie	Min	0	0	0	.288	.345	.423	.768	0	0	1	1.26	7	3	42.9
Eddie Guardado	Min	0	4	16	.265	.332	.458	.790	3	0	4	0.73	77	31	40.3
Dan Naulty	Min	0	1	0	.269	.337	.484	.821	2	1	2	1.09	2	0	0.0
Dan Serafini	Min	0	0	2	.310	.365	.487	.852	6	1	4	0.86	18	3	16.7
Travis Baptist	Min	0	0	1	.321	.366	.566	.932	0	1	2	0.85	8	3	37.5
Graeme Lloyd	NYY	0	2	9	.191	.234	.294	.528	2	0	2	1.35	45	11	24.4
Jay Tessmer	NYY	0	0	1	.143	.242	.321	.563	0	1	0	0.46	2	0	0.0
Mariano Rivera	NYY	36	41	0	.215	.270	.309	.579	2	0	4	1.60	24	4	16.7
Ramiro Mendoza	NYY	1	4	5	.264	.314	.379	.693	2	4	17	2.12	24	10	41.7
Darren Holmes	NYY	2	3	2	.270	.321	.393	.714	5	1	4	1.13	22	12	54.5
Mike Stanton	NYY	6	10	18	.239	.307	.414	.721	0	2	8	1.12	48	11	22.9
Joe Borowski	NYY	0	0	0	.289	.357	.368	.725	0	0	2	1.67	0	0	0.0

GREG SWINDELL, BOS
(1998: MIN-BOS)

The Red Sox sorely needed a lefthander, as theirs was one of the most lopsided bullpens around. Swindell saw his share of action in his two months in Boston; 8 of his 29 appearances were in tie games. **<DD>**

RAMON TATIS, TB

Allowed an OPS of 1.156! Righthanders hit .500 off him (yes, that's a batting average), but he cooled lefties off to the tune of .333. Didn't cost the Rays much, though, because over half of his appearances were very low P (less than .01). His PPPI was 3rd-lowest in the AL among those with 20 relief appearances. WPA was -.4 despite -1.1 PWins. **<DD>**

BILLY TAYLOR, OAK

His PPPI was .106 in April and May, .083 in June and July, and .066 in August and September. He pitched very well in the first half. That, and Howe's liberal use of him, made him one of the AL's most valuable relievers over that span. He then had 5 disastrous appearances in a 25-day span immediately after the all-star break. Still finished with respectable numbers. His appearance matrix is a fun one.**<DD>**

	-5	-4	-3	-2	-1	0	+1	+2	+3	+4	+5	TOTAL
5												
6					1							1
7										1		1
8				2	2	3	5	4	5	1		22
9	1	1		2	3	6	6	8	5	7	2	41
10+						4			1			5
TOT	1	1		4	6	13	11	12	11	9	2	70

MIKE TIMLIN, BAL
(1998: SEA)

Posted a +2.4 WPA over the final three months of the season.

Timlin certainly falls into the at-risk category in terms of potential arm problems next year. He has a history of arm problems anyway, and this is the most innings he's thrown since his rookie year in 1991. Piniella has a reputation for overworking his relievers, but I'm not sure I see that. Here is the days rest chart for the M's:

RELIEF PITCHER DATA, AMERICAN LEAGUE 1998

LEGEND: **SV**—Save; **SVOP**—Save Opportunity; **HLD**—Hold; **G/F**—Groundball/Flyball Ratio **IR**—Inherited Runners; **IS**—Inherited Runners Scored; **IRS%**—Inherited Runners Pct.

Name	TM	SV	SVOP	HLD	BA	OBP	SLG	OPS	SB	CS	GDP	G/F	IR	IS	IRS%
Jeff Nelson	NYY	3	6	10	.278	.387	.392	.779	5	1	0	1.29	25	6	24.0
Jim Bruske	NYY	1	2	4	.277	.351	.429	.780	7	1	5	1.19	29	15	51.7
Mike Buddie	NYY	0	0	0	.286	.348	.441	.789	4	3	5	1.20	25	9	36.0
Ryan Bradley	NYY	0	0	0	.250	.373	.438	.811	2	0	1	0.55	2	2	100.0
Todd Erdos	NYY	0	0	0	.500	.545	.700	1.245	0	0	0	1.33	0	0	0.0
Billy Taylor	Oak	33	37	0	.255	.312	.388	.700	7	0	7	1.50	39	11	28.2
Buddy Groom	Oak	0	6	16	.274	.332	.385	.717	8	2	6	1.42	74	24	32.4
T.J. Mathews	Oak	1	4	19	.258	.328	.400	.728	7	1	4	0.86	45	16	35.6
Dave Telgheder	Oak	0	0	0	.235	.303	.444	.747	1	0	0	0.94	3	2	66.7
Tim Worrell	Oak	0	3	6	.262	.311	.452	.763	9	0	6	0.97	28	11	39.3
Mike Mohler	Oak	0	1	8	.289	.365	.413	.778	4	2	5	1.56	47	19	40.4
Mark Holzemer	Oak	0	0	2	.333	.386	.513	.899	1	0	2	4.00	13	6	46.2
Jim Dougherty	Oak	0	1	0	.340	.431	.520	.951	1	2	2	1.47	12	6	50.0
Steve Connelly	Oak	0	0	0	.435	.536	.435	.971	1	0	1	2.75	5	3	60.0
Jay Witasick	Oak	0	0	0	.310	.389	.621	1.010	1	1	2	1.18	3	1	33.3
Jose Paniagua	Sea	1	2	6	.200	.277	.347	.624	0	1	4	1.30	12	3	25.0
Mike Timlin	Sea	19	24	6	.264	.306	.358	.664	1	0	14	2.22	59	21	35.6
David Holdridge	Sea	0	0	0	.231	.323	.346	.669	0	0	0	2.20	6	0	0.0
Andrew Lorraine	Sea	0	0	1	.250	.438	.333	.771	0	0	2	1.25	5	1	20.0

—Days Rest—

Name	0	1	2	3	4	5+	3str
Ayala B	11	19	12	14	3	3	2
Fossas T	9	5	3	2	1	3	1
McCarthy G	6	6	8	0	2	7	1
Paniagua J	6	4	5	1	1	1	1
Slocumb H	9	13	15	10	6	4	1
Spoljaric P	11	13	5	6	11	7	2
Timlin M	18	18	18	11	2	3	4
Wells B	6	4	2	4	5	9	0

Only 3 guys in double-digits in the 0 column, and a total of 12 in the 3 straight column. Nothing here seems excessive. On the other hand, this chart may be a bit misleading because it doesn't tell you how bunched up those 3 straights and 0-days-rest appearances are. If you broke this down by month, you'd likely find that most of Ayala's 0-days-rest appearances were early in the year (during the brief period when he was pitching well) and most of Timlin's were later in the year. Looks to me like Timlin was right on the borderline of being overworked. **<DD>**

MIKE TROMBLEY, MIN

He earned his paycheck in 1998, the Twins would've been sunk without him. He was 10th in the AL in WPA (+2.0), 2nd in P (9.9), he led the league in multiple-inning appearances (40), was 8th in appearances which started with runners on base (38), and tied for 2nd in the league with 13 appearances in tie games. He would've been valuable even with an ERA a run higher than it was. **<DD>**

JOHN WASDIN, BOS

After taking a step forward in 1997, Wasdin lost that ground and then some in 98, as opposing hitters teed off to the tune of a .479 SLG. Time's running out on this former prospect. **<DD>**

JOHN WETTELAND, TEX

His season is discussed in the WPA article.

Oates does not appear to be concerned with getting him regular work. He appeared in only 63 games and pitched 62 innings, yet he worked on 0 days rest 19 times and worked on 3 straight days 8 times. **<DD>**

MATT WHISENANT, KC

His WPA (+1.7) exceeded his pitching wins (-.3) by 2 games because he really stunk up the joint in some less-than-meaningful situations. On August 7th in New York, for instance, he pitched one inning and gave up 5 runs. The Royals were down 8 when he entered and 13 when he left. WPA: 0. Here's the composite line from his worst 8 games:

IP	H	R	ER	BB	SO
5.1	22	25	22	6	0

That's about -2 PWins, but his WPA for those 8 games was -.5. It's tempting to want to call Matt fortunate that his hapless outings didn't cost the team much, but I don't think it's unreasonable to believe that he was working on new pitches or something. Whisenant doesn't have a real impres-

			TEAM RELIEF PITCHING DATA AMERICAN LEAGUE 1998									
Team	SV	BLSV	SVOP	IR	IS	Holds	Wins	ERA	Sv%	IRS%	NIRS	Holds/W
Bos	53	18	71	270	72	68	92	3.86	74.6	26.7	1.20	0.74
Tor	47	21	68	260	70	69	88	4.68	69.1	26.9	1.19	0.78
Ana	52	17	69	350	98	63	85	3.91	75.4	28.0	1.14	0.74
Cle	47	23	70	264	75	83	89	4.43	67.1	28.4	1.13	0.93
ChW	42	21	63	275	80	55	80	5.13	66.7	29.1	1.10	0.69
Min	42	22	64	301	90	70	70	4.47	65.6	29.9	1.07	1.00
NYY	48	18	66	217	65	46	114	3.76	72.7	30.0	1.07	0.40
TBD	28	20	48	278	87	38	63	3.84	58.3	31.3	1.02	0.60
Sea	31	21	52	266	89	36	76	5.44	59.6	33.5	0.96	0.47
Bal	37	18	55	275	98	52	79	4.45	67.3	35.6	0.90	0.66
Tex	46	13	59	339	121	52	88	4.04	78.0	35.7	0.90	0.59
Det	32	15	47	332	122	37	65	4.25	68.1	36.7	0.87	0.57
Oak	39	20	59	323	119	64	74	4.62	66.1	36.8	0.87	0.86
KCR	46	16	62	229	86	49	72	5.02	74.2	37.6	0.85	0.68

sive track record, so I'm not inclined to give him the benefit of the doubt, but you never know. <DD>

RICK WHITE, TB

Probably wouldn't have had a major league job if not for expansion, but he did have one (albeit not a very important one — PPPI .035), and made the most of it, posting a 3.80 ERA and holding opposing hitters to a .710 OPS. <DD>

TIM WORRELL, OAK

Since a very fine 1996 campaign with the Padres, Tim has been fighting to stay on the right side of replacement level. 98 was better than 97, and a K/BB ratio of 82 to 29 is commendable, but the longball continues to plague him (30 dingers in 209.1 innings over the past 2 years). <DD>

ESTEBAN YAN, TB

Started the season ablaze, both in WPA and traditional stats. He posted a WPA of -1.6 from May through August, before rebounding with a +.5 in September.

I see no reason not to like his future as much now as I did before last season started, which is quite a lot. <DD>

STARTING PITCHER

JIM ABBOTT, CHW

Given up for dead after a brutal year in 1996, Jim made one of those heartwarming comebacks that baseball is ravenously in search of. Even so, Jim

has pretty much just come back to league average, and there's little reason to think it will get much better. <DM>

YEAR	GS	S	C	T
1998	5	4.20	3.40	7.60
1996	23	4.87	4.17	9.04
1995	30	4.30	3.03	7.33
1994	24	4.21	3.25	7.46

PAUL ABBOTT, SEA

Journeyman righty who spent most of the 1990s at AAA, first with the Twins, and then for a procession of organizations who were uniformly off-put by his lack of control (80 BB in 118 major league innings). Finally wound up in the Mariners' organization in 1997, and got a September cup of coffee last year. Did OK, but he's strictly a #4-5 starter at best. <DM>

YEAR	GS	S	C	T
1998	4	4.00	3.75	7.75

WILSON ALVAREZ, TB

Fit right in as the ostensible "ace" of the Stingers' wild-ass starting staff, but posted his worst season since 1995, and had his worst command since his apprenticeship year in 1992 (right before the big 15-win year). Only 4% of his starts in 1998 were in the Elite Square, a steady five-yeas pattern of decline from his ES% high of 25% in 1994. If he regroups at all in 1999, you can safely bet the ranch on a late-July trade to a contender. <DM>

YEAR	GS	S	C	T
1998	25	3.68	4.12	7.80
1997	33	3.39	3.61	7.00
1996	35	3.91	3.60	7.51
1995	29	3.86	4.07	7.93
1994	24	3.50	3.25	6.75

KEVIN APPIER, KC

Until his injury last year, Kevin had been a very consistent, reliable #2 pitcher on a team that had no rotation anchor. His Elite Square and Hit Hard percentages for 1994-97 attest to this consistency:

YEAR	ES	HH	S12
1994	17%	22%	39%
1995	16%	23%	48%
1996	19%	22%	38%
1997	18%	18%	35%

As you can see, however, his percentage of top hit prevention games (S12) had been slipping; in his brief return last September he was clearly not 100%, and the prognosis for 1999 must, at this point at least, be considered as guarded. <DM>

				RELIEF PITCHER DATA, AMERICAN LEAGUE 1998										

LEGEND: SV—Save; SVOP—Save Opportunity; HLD—Hold; G/F—Groundball/Flyball Ratio IR—Inherited Runners; IS—Inherited Runners Scored; IRS%—Inherited Runners Pct.

Name	TM	SV	SVOP	HLD	BA	OBP	SLG	OPS	SB	CS	GDP	G/F	IR	IS	IRS%
Heathcliff Slocumb	Sea	3	4	2	.275	.379	.401	.780	7	4	5	1.10	39	12	30.8
Bob Wells	Sea	0	1	1	.261	.319	.502	.821	0	0	3	0.69	16	9	56.3
Greg McCarthy	Sea	0	1	3	.214	.365	.476	.841	5	1	1	0.81	22	8	36.4
Paul Spoljaric	Sea	0	2	9	.263	.369	.474	.843	10	1	9	1.07	38	9	23.7
Bobby Ayala	Sea	8	17	5	.323	.370	.484	.854	6	1	4	1.25	28	8	28.6
Felipe Lira	Sea	0	0	0	.319	.360	.623	.983	1	0	0	1.22	5	4	80.0
Steve Gajkowski	Sea	0	0	0	.389	.476	.694	1.170	0	0	2	1.78	11	8	72.7
Roberto Hernandez	TBD	26	35	0	.212	.330	.296	.626	5	2	7	1.73	18	3	16.7
Jim Mecir	TBD	0	3	14	.225	.306	.328	.634	5	3	11	2.03	46	11	23.9
Albie Lopez	TBD	1	5	4	.249	.326	.369	.695	4	4	4	1.26	43	19	44.2
Esteban Yan	TBD	1	5	8	.236	.326	.375	.701	12	3	7	1.38	41	18	43.9
Rick White	TBD	0	0	2	.253	.315	.395	.710	2	4	6	1.56	34	12	35.3
Scott Aldred	TBD	0	0	8	.280	.356	.364	.720	2	1	7	2.55	37	12	32.4
Eddie Gaillard	TBD	0	0	0	.148	.233	.519	.752	0	0	0	1.00	5	0	0.0
Mike Duvall	TBD	0	0	0	.267	.353	.533	.886	0	0	1	1.75	4	0	0.0
Matt Ruebel	TBD	0	0	1	.314	.385	.571	.956	1	1	1	1.50	6	2	33.3
Dan Carlson	TBD	0	0	0	.347	.429	.556	.985	0	2	1	1.04	13	3	23.1
Ramon Tatis	TBD	0	0	1	.418	.556	.600	1.156	0	1	2	1.00	15	2	13.3
Brad Pennington	TBD	0	0	0	1.000	1.000	1.000	2.000	0	0	0	—	1	1	100.0
John Wetteland	Tex	42	47	0	.203	.247	.320	.567	1	0	2	0.88	15	7	46.7
Xavier Hernandez	Tex	1	6	9	.207	.307	.322	.629	1	1	4	0.78	47	13	27.7
Tim Crabtree	Tex	0	1	10	.264	.335	.347	.682	6	5	11	2.01	64	26	40.6
Greg Cadaret	Tex	1	2	7	.274	.348	.430	.778	0	0	3	0.87	51	12	23.5
Al Levine	Tex	0	0	0	.294	.336	.450	.786	2	0	8	1.59	37	17	45.9

YEAR	GS	S	C	T
1998	3	5.33	3.67	9.00
1997	34	3.56	3.00	6.56
1996	32	3.66	3.13	6.78
1995	31	3.23	3.45	6.68
1994	23	3.65	3.26	6.91

ROLANDO ARROJO, TB

The veteran Cuban righty faded conspicuously in the second half, recording no games in the Elite Square after June. His month QWPs tell the story succinctly:

Month	QWP
April	.466
May	.598
June	.781
July	.489
August	.471
September	.393

While he clearly has the talent to be a "sub-six" pitcher based on his peak performance, Arrojo may be too old to develop much more than this. There's a 40% chance that we've already seen the best he has to offer. <DM>

YEAR	GS	S	C	T
1998	32	3.75	3.13	6.88

STEVE AVERY, FA
(1998: BOS)

Steve's command is still AWOL, even as his stuff has managed to re-manifest itself. Interestingly, though, Avery was never much of a control artist even in his top years with the Braves: our quick and dirty rule of thumb for that, the C13%, never got higher than 66% (in 1995), which is good, not great. In the past two seasons that percentage has been 38% and 35%, so you can see that Steve is really fighting his control.

Will he make it back to his earlier levels? Probably not in Boston, but that improvement in his "S" value is encouraging. He's still only 29, and one can envision a scenario where Steve has three or four seasons in his thirties that are similar to his early years with the Braves. <DM>

YEAR	GS	S	C	T
1998	23	3.78	4.26	8.04
1997	18	5.06	4.28	9.33
1996	23	4.13	3.26	7.39
1995	30	3.73	3.20	6.93
1994	24	3.21	3.21	6.42

JAMES BALDWIN, CHW

Baldwin is an example of someone whose seasonal average doesn't come close to telling the whole story. James began 1998 completely in the tank; he was banished to the bullpen in May with a QMAX "T" score hovering near ten. After a six-week "rest cure," he returned to the rotation and made some serious strides, as the breakout before and after reveals:

When	S	C	T
4/1-5/6	5.00	4.86	9.86
6/20-9/27	3.35	3.18	6.53

The data from June 20 on encompasses 17 starts, and it's the best sustained performance of Baldwin's career. He's someone to watch in 1999. <DM>

YEAR	GS	S	C	T
1998	24	3.83	3.67	7.50
1997	32	3.84	3.41	7.25
1996	28	4.00	3.25	7.25
1995	4	6.50	5.50	12.00

BRIAN BARBER, KC

A spectacular disappointment while on the banks of the Mississippi, Barber might yet redeem himself on the Kansas-Missouri border. I don't think we're looking at much more than a slightly above league average performer here, but that's a scenario that was all but unthinkable this time last year. Given the state of the Royals' rotation, one suspects that Brian will get a pretty good look in 1999. <DM>

YEAR	GS	S	C	T
1998	8	4.25	3.63	7.88
1996	1	5.00	7.00	12.00
1995	4	5.25	4.75	10.00

TIM BELCHER, FA
(1998: KC)

Tim took a big jump into the Tommy John region of the QMAX chart in 1998 (24%, as opposed to 10% in 1997). But just to make things problematic, he also showed a big gain in Power Precipice games (12%, compared with readings between 4-6% in past seasons). Perhaps the most important trend, however, is the fact that he had significantly more starts in the Hit Hard region of the chart (44%, as opposed to readings in the low-to-mid 30s in recent years). Teams looking for relatively inexpensive, semi-reliable #4-5 slot pitching to shore up their rotation (the Giants, Padres and Cubs come first to mind) might well give Tim a tumble in 1999. <DM>

YEAR	GS	S	C	T
1998	34	4.26	2.76	7.03
1997	31	4.35	3.10	7.45
1996	35	4.46	2.86	7.31
1995	28	4.25	3.79	8.04
1994	25	4.76	3.60	8.36

RICKY BONES, KC

Used exclusively in relief by the Royals in 1998, Bones might yet get a shot in the rotation, especially if Kevin Appier is still hurting. Ricky had one good year as a starter, but his QMAX progression (as you can see below) makes the shower scene in "Psycho" look like a nursery rhyme. I think the Royals won't move him from the bullpen unless they're forced to. <DM>

YEAR	GS	S	C	T
1997	13	5.46	3.92	9.38
1996	24	4.67	3.88	8.54
1995	31	4.42	3.55	7.97
1994	24	3.71	2.58	6.29

RELIEF PITCHER DATA, AMERICAN LEAGUE 1998

LEGEND: SV—Save; **SVOP**—Save Opportunity; **HLD**—Hold; **G/F**—Groundball/Flyball Ratio **IR**—Inherited Runners; **IS**—Inherited Runners Scored; **IRS%**—Inherited Runners Pct.

Name	TM	SV	SVOP	HLD	BA	OBP	SLG	OPS	SB	CS	GDP	G/F	IR	IS	IRS%
Julio Santana	Tex	0	0	0	.304	.407	.391	.798	1	0	0	1.14	2	0	0.0
Danny Patterson	Tex	2	2	19	.274	.332	.491	.823	1	3	10	1.75	32	9	28.1
Roger Pavlik	Tex	1	1	0	.286	.349	.500	.849	0	0	1	2.64	7	2	28.6
Tony Fossas	Tex	0	1	4	.330	.426	.429	.855	3	2	1	1.17	44	16	36.4
Eric Gunderson	Tex	0	2	9	.315	.358	.530	.888	0	1	7	1.14	68	21	30.9
Scott Bailes	Tex	0	0	5	.351	.385	.575	.960	1	2	6	1.95	42	20	47.6
Steve Sinclair	Tor	0	2	3	.232	.295	.286	.581	1	1	1	1.27	18	4	22.2
Dan Plesac	Tor	4	5	27	.224	.286	.372	.658	7	2	4	0.96	80	15	18.8
Paul Quantrill	Tor	7	14	27	.285	.334	.392	.726	5	0	12	2.45	70	26	37.1
Dave Stieb	Tor	2	2	1	.284	.351	.422	.773	5	3	2	0.88	3	1	33.3
Bill Risley	Tor	0	0	3	.259	.372	.438	.810	10	3	5	0.87	24	10	41.7
Carlos Almanzar	Tor	0	3	1	.286	.336	.479	.815	3	0	2	1.22	15	3	20.0
Shannon Withem	Tor	0	0	0	.250	.357	.500	.857	0	0	0	0.60	0	0	0.0
Ben VanRyn	Tor	0	1	3	.316	.444	.421	.865	2	1	1	1.06	20	4	20.0
Robert Person	Tor	6	8	0	.294	.379	.529	.908	3	1	1	0.80	9	2	22.2

MIKE BUDDIE, NYY

Mike Buddie *figured in one of the more memorable baseball nights in the Bay Area during 1998, when the Yankees tossed him out there as a sacrificial lamb in the second game of a double-header against the A's in early August. Buddie got hammered early, giving up five runs in the first three innings, but settled down and kept the Bronxters in the game. New York then pulled a preview of their World Series Game 1 performance by scoring nine runs in the ninth inning (led by two HRs by Darryl Strawberry) to pull out the second game and sweep the doubleheader.*

Oh, yes—Mike Buddie. An indifferent starter at AA for several years, he was converted to the pen in 1997 at Columbus and did rather well. His chances of cracking the Yankees' starting rotation in 1999 are roughly equal to the likelihood that the Pope will convert to Islam. <DM>

Year	GS	S	C	T
1998	2	6.00	3.50	9.50

DAVE BURBA, CLE

The QWP (Quality Winning Percentage, pronounced "quip") proclaims Burba as the Indians' best starter in 1998. That figure, however, was just .534, which argues for some additional face lifts to the Tribe's starting rotation. Dave got his command together in '98: our ratio of good vs. poor walk prevention starts ("C13"/"C47" on the QMAX chart) shows Burba at 61/39 last year, while in previous years he was never better than 44/56. He's become a pretty fair #3 starter, but Cleveland has enough of those to reignite Lake Erie. <DM>

Year	GS	S	C	T
1998	31	3.90	3.16	7.06
1997	27	3.93	3.93	7.85
1996	33	3.73	3.88	7.61
1995	9	3.78	3.67	7.44

JOHN BURKETT, TEX

I'd be willing to wager your house (as Joe Morgan said to Jon Miller during the World Series) that Burkett has been pitching through some kind of arm problem. He's always been an extreme finesse type pitcher, but that QMAX "S" of 4.90 in '97 is just a little too high to be taken otherwise. What kept John in the Rangers' rotation last year was: 1) a lack of viable options and 2) his ability to increase his Elite Square percentage from 10% to 19%. He also decreased his Tommy John percentage from 31% to 13%—another clue that his arm was less than 100% in 1997.

Burkett's ERA was up last year, primarily because he had a terrible record with runners in scoring position (a .353 BA and a

bone-chilling .965 OPS). Over the previous five years, his OOPS in RISP situations was a more sedate .773. Sometimes this stuff just catches up to a pitcher all at once; I suspect things will even out for John in '99 and his ERA will go down as a result. <DM>

Year	GS	S	C	T
1998	32	4.53	2.88	7.41
1997	29	4.90	2.38	7.28
1996	34	4.00	2.76	6.76
1995	30	4.43	3.10	7.53
1994	25	4.36	2.80	7.16

TOM CANDIOTTI, OAK

A really good pick-up by the A's, who—to steal a simile from Preston Sturges—needed an innings eater like the ax needs the turkey. One of C.O. Jones' most noxious fantasies (and believe it when I say that this covers a lot of ground. . .) is to have an entire starting rotation comprised of knuckleballers. I think we're getting close to being able to do it: Candiotti, Wakefield, Sparks, Springer, and Jeff Juden (oops! knuckleheads don't count, do they?). <DM>

Year	GS	S	C	T
1998	33	4.33	3.15	7.48
1997	18	3.83	3.33	7.17
1996	27	4.41	3.26	7.67
1995	30	3.93	3.03	6.97
1994	22	3.91	3.09	7.00

CHRIS CARPENTER, TOR

Another who bears watching in 1999: after July 1st, Chris posted a 6.40 QMAX "T" average. His QWP for the month of September was a rather impressive .716— even higher than the Rocket's. That being said, I don't expect him to jump up to any truly astonishing level of performance—he's too much of a finesse pitcher (21% TJ) to be a likely candidate for "sub-six" status. <DM>

Year	GS	S	C	T
1998	24	4.13	3.13	7.25
1997	13	5.15	3.92	9.08

FRANK CASTILLO, FA
(1998: DET)

Yikes! This is a job for Tom Austin, who might want to consider substituting Frankie Boom-Boom's season here for the "Bad Pitchers" feature for the Tigers. One of the odd things I discovered during QMAX research time this past year was Castillo's ability to pitch well in Coors Field. Maybe the Rockies will sign him on the cheap and give him a chance to rehabilitate himself. (Now there's a thought: a pitcher signing with Colorado in hopes of reviving his career. . .) <DM>

Year	GS	S	C	T
1998	19	5.58	4.05	9.63
1997	33	4.64	3.64	8.27
1996	33	4.42	3.18	7.61
1995	29	3.86	2.93	6.79
1994	4	4.25	3.00	7.25

ROBINSON CHECO, BOS

One barometer of the Red Sox' success in 1998 is that they were able to avoid turning to Checo as part of their major-league rotation. He's still not ready, and holding your breath is not advised. <DM>

Year	GS	S	C	T
1998	2	5.50	4.50	10.00
1997	2	4.50	3.00	7.50

JIN HO CHO, BOS

Jin Ho got rushed up to the majors in July when the Sox were hurting for starters, but his numbers at Trenton were impressive (5-2, 2.19 ERA). I doubt he'll stick with the big club out of spring training, but he could be back in Boston for a longer stretch sometime during 1999. <DM>

Year	GS	S	C	T
1998	4	5.50	3.50	9.00

ROGER CLEMENS, TOR

Though QMAX didn't rate him higher than #3 in the AL, Roger's second half was spectacular enough to notch him his fifth Cy Young Award. Over in the NL, Greg Maddux had a better year, but faded in the second half and was deprived of his fifth, which may drive him to serious drink. My only advice to you if you live near a city with an American League team is to get to the ballpark when Clemens is pitching; it's something that you should make sure you see in person. <DM>

Year	GS	S	C	T
1998	33	2.82	3.00	5.82
1997	34	2.82	2.29	5.12
1996	34	3.38	3.35	6.74
1995	23	3.87	3.74	7.61
1994	24	2.83	3.17	6.00

KEN CLOUDE, SEA

This is what's known as getting hit by a land mine. Cloude didn't have a five-start running "T" average below 7.60 in 1998; he just got hammered. We can't even blame this on the Kingdome: Ken's ERA splits are 5.11/8.27 (H/A). However, Cloude's minor league record didn't support the type of QMAX "S" value that he posted in 1997, and it was only nine starts. At this point, one can only throw up one's hands and say that he's probably a better pitcher than this; of course, one could have said the same thing about Ken

MISCELLANEOUS STARTING PITCHER DATA, AMERICAN LEAGUE 1998

LEGEND: NP—Number of Pitches thrown; **TW**—Team Wins in pitcher's starts; **TL**—Team Losses in pitcher's starts; **GS**—; **QS**—Quality Starts; **BS**—Blown Starts; **QmB**—Quality minus Blown pct.; **PPI**—Pitches thrown Per Inning; **IP**—Innings Pitched; **AdIP**—Adjusted Innings Pitched; **IP/S**—average Innings Pitched per Start

PITCHER NAME	TM	TW	TL	GS	QS	BS	QMB	IP	NP	STR	PPI	KPCT	ADJIP	IP/S
Jarrod Washburn	ANA	9	2	11	6	0	54.55	68.3	1103	675	16.14	61.2%	68	6.2
Steve Sparks	ANA	10	10	20	12	2	50.00	121.7	2121	1246	17.43	58.7%	130	6.1
Chuck Finley	ANA	18	16	34	18	3	44.12	223.3	3795	2263	16.99	59.6%	232	6.6
Omar Olivares	ANA	13	13	26	16	6	38.46	160.0	2682	1547	16.76	57.7%	164	6.2
Ken Hill	ANA	10	9	19	11	6	26.32	103.0	1729	1028	16.78	59.5%	106	5.4
Jack Mcdowell	ANA	9	5	14	6	4	14.29	76.0	1170	763	15.39	65.2%	72	5.4
Allen Watson	ANA	5	9	14	3	4	-7.14	71.3	1239	757	17.37	61.1%	76	5.1
Jason Dickson	ANA	8	10	18	4	8	-22.22	101.3	1638	1001	16.17	61.1%	100	5.6
Jeff Juden	ANA	3	3	6	1	3	-33.33	35.3	622	372	17.61	59.8%	38	5.9
Mike Mussina	BAL	16	13	29	18	2	55.17	206.3	3110	2062	15.07	66.3%	190	7.1
Scott Erickson	BAL	18	18	36	21	4	47.22	251.3	3896	2465	15.50	63.3%	239	7.0
Jimmy Key	BAL	6	5	11	7	3	36.36	65.0	1028	644	15.82	62.6%	63	5.9
Juan Guzman	BAL	6	5	11	5	2	27.27	66.0	1151	693	17.44	60.2%	70	6.0
Sidney Ponson	BAL	11	9	20	8	5	15.00	113.0	1876	1219	16.60	65.0%	115	5.7
Doug Johns	BAL	6	4	10	2	1	10.00	50.0	759	466	15.18	61.4%	46	5.0
Rocky Coppinger	BAL	1	0	1	0	0	0.00	5.0	92	58	18.40	63.0%	6	5.0
Scott Kamieniecki	BAL	2	9	11	3	4	-9.09	50.7	892	514	17.61	57.6%	55	4.6

Dixon, Ken Schrom, and Ken Howell as well. <DM>

YEAR	GS	S	C	T
1998	30	4.57	4.27	8.83
1997	9	2.78	3.89	6.67

BARTOLO COLON, CLE

When the name "Bartolo Colon" comes up, discussion rapidly turns to the issue of workload, and why not, when you have a 23-year old pitcher with a history of previous arm trouble throwing 100+ pitches in 21 of his 31 starts? There is a long, ignominious strain of pitcher arm abuse that can be traced throughout baseball history, but it wasn't until recently that we had so many people trying to quantify it.

Unfortunately, they're all trying to do so with one basic new measure—game-by-game pitch counts. (For example, 21 of 31 starts with 100+ pitches.) Problem is, we don't know exactly how bad that figure really is. Craig Wright's famous study didn't use pitch counts, it used an estimation of batters faced per start (BFS), and its primary grouping of pitchers came from the sixties—a decade where young pitchers were more numerous than at any point in baseball history. Its influence, though clearly warranted, has been distorted into a kind of stathead death cult which gathers together in its cave of woe around a cauldron with the distilled essence of Mark Fidrych boiling furiously to a speed metal soundtrack every time someone is allowed to throw 120+ pitches in a game.

Fact: we don't know exactly what the threshold is for arm abuse. Bartolo Colon was allowed to throw 135 pitches in his first start of 1998, and within hours the banshee wails and the bubbling cauldron (Macbeth for math geeks) had begun. The prevailing view was that Colon wouldn't even make it to the All-Star break.

What happened? Instead of breaking down, Colon had the "other thing" happen to him. He had 100+ pitches in sixteen of his first twenty starts, and he wore down. He got hammered in the second half of the season, as the monthly QMAX "T" scores indicate:

Month	S	C	T
Apr	4.00	3.60	7.60
May	3.00	2.83	5.83
Jun	1.80	2.00	3.80
Jul	5.00	3.33	8.33
Aug	5.20	4.60	9.80
Sep	6.00	3.75	9.75

Interestingly, however, Colon pitched well in the post-season; for now, we haven't got a real sense of whether he has been "ruined" by Indians manager Mike Hargrove. During the season I discovered that ten years earlier, a 22-year old pitcher was subjected to a similar workload while riding a first half hot streak. It struck me that if that ten-year-old tale could be transported to the present, we'd be hearing similar criticisms about how an idiotic manager was ruining the career of a potential all-time great. Sure enough, that young pitcher went into the tank for the rest of 1988.

Who was that pitcher? Greg Maddux.

The point is that pitchers do survive arm abuse. Even young pitchers. Craig Wright's study was not monolithic in this respect. And Craig's study did not identify a single career pattern that was followed by pitchers who were worked hard. More impor-

tantly, Craig never suggested that throwing more than 100 pitches in a single game was a point of no return. Starting pitchers threw 100+ pitches in 46.5% of their starts during 1997; that means that a pitcher with 31 starts in a season would, on average, have 14 100+ pitch games.

How far away from this average does a pitcher need to be before he is at risk? Is 21 out of 31, as in Colon's case, beyond the pale? Or are there other, more revealing patterns inside the data? And is looking at this on a game-by-game basis necessarily the right way? Let's look at a couple of alternatives.

First, let's consider the idea that arm strain may not come from throwing a simple quantity of pitches in a game, but the number of pitches in an inning. This number varies widely from inning to inning, from as few as three to as many as fifty or more. We can, however, focus on games where the average number of pitches per inning is significantly higher than the average (around 16 per inning).

Let's look at games where a pitcher throws at least five innings and averages at least 19 pitches per inning. These are games where there is more concentrated strain on a pitcher's arm in a shorter period of time. Let's call these game "trouble starts". That's a good name, because the pitcher is usually in a lot of trouble in these games, and the concentrated strain makes for a different kind of trouble.

We've included the full list of 1998's "trouble starts" in section seven; let's just look at the leaders in the American League for now.

Trouble Starts 1998 AL

Pitcher	TS
Tony Saunders	8
Jaret Wright	7
Juan Guzman	7
Chuck Finley	6
Tom Candiotti	6
Woody Williams	6

We can safely ignore the presence of Candiotti on this list; but note that several of these pitchers are either young, or have had arm trouble in the past, or both.

Despite his 21 100+ pitch games, Bartolo Colon had only 2 such "trouble starts" in 1998. The other young pitcher on the Indians, Jaret Wright, might well be at greater risk.

A different tack from the pitches-per-inning construct is the notion of three-game pitch counts. First, let's get a benchmark for this. In 1997, pitchers averaged 95 pitches per start. This means they averaged 285 pitches every three starts. Throwing 300 pitches in three starts, then, is only 5% higher than the league average. Thus the notion of the single-game threshold beginning at 100 pitches may be a bit low.

What we're looking for is a cumulative effect. Let's set the danger line at 350 pitches per three starts, or ~117 pitches per start, if it's easier for you to work with. Note that the pitcher has to average 117 pitches per start over three starts to get to the "danger line." We can then plot the running three-game pitch count for any starting pitcher, and see how often they approach or exceed this Arm Damage Limit (ADL).

And who better to look at than Bartolo Colon? Darn right. But to spice it up, and to look for additional patterns with respect to arm damage, we're going to also plot the 1997 season of Alan Benes, who was worked exceptionally hard by the Cardinals and suffered an arm injury in late July that kept him out for the rest of that season and all of 1998. Let's take a look at the chart:

3G PITCH COUNT COMPARISON

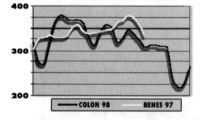

Both pitchers were worked very hard. But it appears that Benes' workload was unrelentingly close to the ADL. That looks like a recipe for disaster; and, as the suspended graph line indicates, Benes couldn't answer the bell in August.

Colon had several spikes where he was worked as hard (and maybe even a bit harder) than Benes, but he also had several dropoffs in workload. His wearing down after the All-Star break may have saved him from meeting a similar fate.

Was Colon's workload too high? Absolutely. It's way too close to the workload of a pitcher who has suffered a serious career interruption. We'll revisit the ADL with several other pitchers.

What will Colon be like in 1999

and beyond? My sense is that he may well survive and thrive. He averaged 2.94, 2.81/5.75 for sixteen starts with a big workload; that many starts is usually sufficient to establish a level of peak ability. Assuming no long-term affects from his heavy workload, I'd project Bartolo to come at around 6.60 on the QMAX "T" scale in 1999. **<DM>**

YEAR	GS	S	C	T
1998	31	4.10	3.32	7.42
1997	17	4.71	4.18	8.88

DAVID CONE, NYY

We looked at Cone's Hall of Fame chances in the Yankee essay; what's interesting to note here is that David has pretty much reversed his pitching style as measured by QMAX. His TJ% nearly doubled (13% in '98, 7% in '97). He's not quite the dominating pitcher that he once was, but his command snapped back to form, approaching his 1994 peak. 19% of his games were in the top command region (C1), up from 7% in '97 and 9% in '96. The big issue that QMAX raises in terms of his HoF chances has to do with how hittable he will get, and how fast. It looks as though there should be plenty of breathing room. **<DM>**

YEAR	GS	S	C	T
1998	31	3.48	2.84	6.32
1997	29	3.10	3.62	6.72
1996	11	2.73	3.64	6.36
1995	30	3.10	2.87	5.97
1994	23	2.96	2.57	5.52

ROCKY COPPINGER, BAL

He'll probably get a shot at cracking the Orioles' rotation in 1999, given how much disarray there is once you get past Mike Mussina. Rocky was 8-3, 3.50 at Rochester

last year, but he's still having command problems. **<DM>**

YEAR	GS	S	C	T
1998	1	4.00	4.00	8.00
1997	4	4.25	5.75	10.00
1996	22	4.05	3.86	7.91

JASON DICKSON, ANA

One measure of whether Terry Collins really has his wits about him will be whether or not he gets Dickson out of his rotation permanently. Jason has virtually no long-term prospects for big league success, and probably needs to get a head start on his post-baseball career. **<DM>**

YEAR	GS	S	C	T
1998	18	5.33	3.61	8.94
1997	32	4.66	3.03	7.69
1996	7	4.71	3.71	8.43

DOUG DRABEK, FA
(1998: BAL)

As the refrain of that old Paul Simon classic goes, "Slip slidin' away...". There's not much more left before the whole hillside will be down on the Coast Highway. **<DM>**

YEAR	GS	S	C	T
1998	21	4.81	3.48	8.29
1997	31	4.10	3.90	8.00
1996	30	4.57	3.33	7.90
1995	31	4.29	3.26	7.55
1994	23	3.09	2.48	5.57

SCOTT ERICKSON, BAL

Scott continues to refine his command little by little; his "C" value ranked *** in the AL in 1998. But his hit prevention experienced some serious decay. As a result, Erickson was in the Success Square only 42% of the time last

---

MISCELLANEOUS STARTING PITCHER DATA, AMERICAN LEAGUE 1998

LEGEND: NP—Number of Pitches thrown; **TW**—Team Wins in pitcher's starts; **TL**—Team Losses in pitcher's starts; **GS**—; **QS**—Quality Starts; **BS**—Blown Starts; **QmB**—Quality minus Blown pct.; **PPI**—Pitches thrown Per Inning; **IP**—Innings Pitched; **AdIP**—Adjusted Innings Pitched; **IP/S**—average Innings Pitched per Start

PITCHER NAME	TM	TW	TL	GS	QS	BS	QMB	IP	NP	STR	PPI	KPCT	ADJIP	IP/S
Nerio Rodriguez	BAL	1	3	4	1	2	-25.00	15.3	254	152	16.57	59.8%	16	3.8
Doug Drabek	BAL	10	11	21	5	11	-28.57	101.3	1632	1013	16.11	62.1%	100	4.8
Chris Fussell	BAL	0	2	2	0	1	-50.00	6.7	140	76	20.99	54.3%	9	3.3
Pete Smith	BAL	1	3	4	0	3	-75.00	18.0	336	209	18.67	62.2%	21	4.5
Richie Lewis	BAL	1	0	1	0	1	-100.00	4.3	84	45	19.40	53.6%	5	4.3
Bobby Munoz	BAL	0	1	1	0	1	-100.00	3.0	61	34	20.33	55.7%	4	3.0
Pedro Martinez	BOS	22	11	33	25	1	72.73	233.7	3765	2432	16.11	64.6%	231	7.1
Bret Saberhagen	BOS	19	12	31	18	5	41.94	175.0	2722	1776	15.55	65.2%	167	5.6
Tim Wakefield	BOS	22	11	33	16	5	33.33	210.0	3111	2026	14.81	65.1%	191	6.4
Pete Schourek	BOS	3	5	8	4	2	25.00	41.3	646	400	15.63	61.9%	40	5.2
Steve Avery	BOS	15	8	23	10	7	13.04	117.0	1870	1087	15.98	58.1%	115	5.1
Derek Lowe	BOS	2	8	10	4	3	10.00	48.0	785	476	16.35	60.6%	48	4.8
Butch Henry	BOS	2	0	2	0	0	0.00	9.0	150	97	16.67	64.7%	9	4.5
Brian Rose	BOS	4	4	8	2	2	0.00	37.7	653	405	17.34	62.0%	40	4.7
John Wasdin	BOS	2	6	8	2	2	0.00	39.7	653	421	16.46	64.5%	40	5.0
Jin Ho Cho	BOS	1	3	4	1	2	-25.00	18.7	294	200	15.76	68.0%	18	4.7
Robinson Checo	BOS	0	2	2	0	1	-50.00	7.7	140	77	18.28	55.0%	9	3.8

year, as opposed to 64% in '97. That was hardly the worst thing that happened to the Orioles' pitching staff in 1998, but it didn't help. And I don't expect that things will get any better in 1999. <DM>

YEAR	GS	S	C	T
1998	36	4.56	2.67	7.22
1997	33	3.82	2.79	6.61
1996	34	4.59	3.00	7.59
1995	31	4.35	3.35	7.71
1994	23	4.91	3.48	8.39

KELVIM ESCOBAR, TOR

Those two guys—devil and angel—at either side of my head:

"Careful, Don. Don't get too excited about ten starts. There's nothing in his minor league record to support this level of performance. Take a look at what happened to several other young pitchers who had a hot start. This guy might be the next Cisco Carlos."

"Come on, this guy's QWP was higher than the Rocket's (.682 to .654). Fifty percent of his games were in the S12 region. If you don't hype this guy, you're not standing behind the principles of your system."

The trouble I'm having isn't really with the message content of these two emissaries, but in distinguishing which one is the angel and which the devil. . . <DM>

YEAR	GS	S	C	T
1998	10	2.80	3.20	6.00

SCOTT EYRE, CHW

It's comforting to know that the White Sox had been grooming someone to take over when they finally pulled the plug on Jason Bere. <DM>

YEAR	GS	S	C	T
1998	17	3.94	4.59	8.53
1997	11	4.18	4.18	8.36

JEFF FASSERO, SEA

Slightly abashed plug for QMAX: what's very useful about it is that in many, many cases we see that a pitcher really is occupying a consistent level of performance despite the year-to-year perturbations of his ERA, league changes, etc. Jeff Fassero is a good example of this, a solid, dependable #3 starter in either Montreal or Seattle. <DM>

YEAR	GS	S	C	T
1998	32	4.06	2.63	6.69
1997	35	3.97	3.03	7.00
1996	34	3.85	2.59	6.44
1995	30	4.33	3.37	7.70
1994	21	3.57	2.86	6.43

CHUCK FINLEY, ANA

Now there's the irony of writing these comments in alphabetical order. After having used Jeff Fassero as the example of a steady, dependable pitcher, who comes along next but Chuck Finley, who is an even better example of that very principle.

That being said, I have a hunch that Chuck is about ready to have a performance drop-off. Why do I say this, aside from making me seem bold and assured? A couple of reasons: first, Chuck's performance in 1998 dropped off significantly after May. His Success Square percentage (SS%) was only 37% in his last 22 starts. Second, even though he's the same age as Jeff Fassero, he's thrown more than twice as many big league innings (roughly 2800 to 1300). The wear-and-tear factor does come into play at some point, and this just might be it. <DM>

YEAR	GS	S	C	T
1998	34	3.68	3.74	7.41
1997	25	3.72	3.28	7.00
1996	35	3.97	3.43	7.40
1995	32	3.91	3.53	7.44
1994	25	3.80	3.12	6.92

BRYCE FLORIE, DET

I still think Florie could become a decent #3-#4 starter if he were simply placed in the rotation and allowed to get his act together. Bryce was bounced around from the bullpen to the rotation and back, and it was clearly a detriment to his performance. I think some pitchers have a much tougher time adjusting to the move between the bullpen and the starting rotation, and there's probably no traceable pattern in terms of the type of pitcher, either; you just have to find out on a case by case basis. Bryce had a solid September, though, and it's possible that the Tigers will do as I suggest above. Note to Randy Smith and Larry Parrish: it's OK to blame me if it doesn't pan out. Really. No, I mean it—really. <DM>

YEAR	GS	S	C	T
1998	16	4.50	3.75	8.25
1997	8	3.25	4.38	7.63

TOM FORDHAM, CHW

Serious command problems have severely hampered this lefty—and you know they're serious when it's necessary to remove someone in the first inning because he has thrown only 3 of 16 pitches for strikes—against the Pirates, for Crissakes. There's an above-average arm here, but it's going to take an extremely capable and dedicated pitching coach to overcome the impediments to success. <DM>

YEAR	GS	S	C	T
1998	5	4.20	5.60	9.80
1997	1	4.00	4.00	8.00

CHRIS FUSSELL, BAL

A big-K, big-BB pitcher in the minors, Chris is very raw, and will probably need to get traded in order to find the necessary guidance to harness his stuff. It's odd what happens to pitching coaches who become managers—they seem to stop being able to develop young talent, and the number of arm injuries on the pitching staff seem to increase. It's called "The Ray Miller Story," and it's currently playing on cable station ABN (that's American Baseball Nightmares). <DM>

YEAR	GS	S	C	T
1998	2	4.00	6.00	10.00

DWIGHT GOODEN, CLE

Unlike his one-time counterpart Roger Clemens, Gooden has slipped badly and become at best a league-average pitcher. While 1998 didn't promise any kind of miraculous return to form, it was definitely an advance (52% of the Doc's games were in the Success Square, as opposed to readings in the 30's the past two years). I suspect he'll hang on for another 3-4 years in much the same manner that Fernando Valenzuela did, changing teams more than once, and having one more surprisingly good year somewhere. <DM>

YEAR	GS	S	C	T
1998	23	4.00	3.61	7.61
1997	19	4.26	4.05	8.32
1996	29	4.00	4.07	8.07
1994	7	4.29	3.43	7.71

RICK GORECKI, TB

Rick's one of those CAD guys with whom it's easy to sympathize. (What does CAD stand for, you ask? No, not Computer-Aided Dork; it's short for Chronic Arm Damage). Gorecki missed most of 1995, all of 1996, and a sizable chunk of 1997 due to arm miseries; he surprised many by making the Tampa Bay starting rotation out of spring training last year. His second start against the White Sox was a nice little 1,3 gem, but he came up lame in his next start and was on the shelf for the rest of the season.

There's some real potential here, but it may just not be possible to keep him healthy. Of course, in BBBA 1969, we could have said the same thing about Nolan Ryan or Jim Palmer. Gorecki is too old to be compared to those two, of course, but he has far more talent than most give him credit for. I hope it works out for you, Rick. <DM>

399

Year	GS	S	C	T
1998	3	3.33	4.00	7.33
1997	1	7.00	7.00	14.00

SETH GREISINGER, DET

After his first month (9.60 QMAX "T" and .338 QWP), Seth was above league average, and pitched better than 1997 staff ace Justin Thompson. When you compare Greisinger's supplemental QMAX data to the 1997 data for Brian Moehler, you see that he rates higher:

Pitcher	SS%	ES%	HH%	S12%
Greisinger 98	43	14	33	24
Moehler 97	35	10	35	16

Now I'm not saying that Seth is going to make the same jump that Moehler did, merely that there are a number of encouraging signs here. Seth got brought up to the majors quickly, and was successful in making the initial adjustments, which lends one to think that he may well be able to make more as he goes on. Don't be surprised if he moves into the high six region in 1999. <DM>

Year	GS	S	C	T
1998	21	4.24	3.38	7.62

JUAN GUZMAN, BAL
(1998: TOR-BAL)

The Human Ping-Pong Ball, as Ken Adams likes to call him, seems determined to bring QMAX to its knees—along with a procession of managers who have been trying to figure him out since he reached the big leagues. After all that bouncing around, however, Juan's 1998 season actually starts to look like what his average level of performance really is—a slightly above average pitcher who has mood swings that belong in a psychology textbook.

As for 1999, who knows? But if you want to win a deep discount on BBBA 2000, participate in our "What the Heck Will Juan Guzman's QMAX Score be in 1999" contest at the BBBA web site. It'll be running from March 1st through April 1st (a fitting day for a finale...), and the two persons with the closest answers will receive a BBBA Bucks certificate for $7 off the cover price of BBBA 2000. Yep, seven smackers, just like the carnival barkers used to say: "capture the ping-pong ball in mid-air and win a prize!!" <DM>

Year	GS	S	C	T
1998	33	3.61	3.67	7.28
1997	13	3.15	4.46	7.62
1996	27	3.19	2.70	5.89
1995	24	4.54	4.08	8.63
1994	25	4.36	4.08	8.44

JOHN HALAMA, SEA
(1998: HOU)

Destined to become known as the Replacement Unit, Halama was the shoe that dropped after the season ended and the Astros had to make good on their end of the Randy Johnson deal. Halama is what the pundits call a "stylish lefty"; at 6'5" and 195, he might try lifts and a fright wig to simulate his Unitness, but the smoothness of his delivery will be a dead giveaway. He's 25-6 at AAA over the past two seasons, and at 27, is a polished finesse pitcher. It remains to be seen if the Kingdome or Lou (the Master of Chaos) Piniella will turn him into a screaming lunatic first. The good news is he's guaranteed to have only a half-season of the former, and possibly the same of the latter. <DM>

Year	GS	S	C	T
1998	6	4.50	3.67	8.17

ROY HALLADAY, TOR

Halladay, you may remember, is the kid who threw 8 2/3 innings of no-hit ball against the Tigers on the final day of the season before Bobby Higginson broke it up with a homer. He's 22 this year, and has already spent two years at AAA, so it's quite possible that the Jays will hand him the #5 rotation slot this year. <DM>

Year	GS	S	C	T
1998	2	3.50	2.50	6.00

ERIK HANSON, FA
(1998: TOR)

"...Regard his hellish fall/Whose fiendful fortune may exhort the wise/Only to wonder at unlawful things/Whose deepness doth entice such forward wits/To practice more than heavenly power permits." <Marlowe, Dr. Faustus, Act V, Scene III>

Year	GS	S	C	T
1998	8	5.75	4.38	10.13
1997	2	3.50	3.50	7.00
1996	35	4.49	3.77	8.26
1995	29	4.00	3.00	7.00
1994	21	4.43	2.81	7.24

DENNY HARRIGER, DET

A soft-tossing minor league lifer who got brought up by the Tigers despite having what was clearly his worst season in five straight at AAA. He'll probably go to Japan, develop "wa," and single-handedly revitalize the Japanese economy. <DM>

Year	GS	S	C	T
1998	2	5.50	4.00	9.50

LATROY HAWKINS, MIN

One of the things that we like to do with QMAX is look at the running 15-game averages, just to see what the range looks like. Hawkins' best QMAX "T" for 15 consecutive starts: 7.60. His worst fifteen consecutive starts: 8.80. His QMAX "S" (hit prevention) range: 4.20 (best)/5.13 (worst). His QMAX "C" (walk prevention) range: 3.13 (best)/3.73 (worst).

Once we have that data, we then combine the best and worst range data and create a target range for the next season. In LaTroy's case, that range is: 7.33 to 8.86. We then take the average of the running fifteen game starts and fold those numbers in with the best and worst components and weight the individual measures according to trends in the ancillary data (changes in the Success Square percentage, Elite Square percentage, Hit Hard percentage, and "dominating game" (the S12 region on the QMAX chart) percentage. Those trends tell us how to weight each element, and then we run the calculations. For Hawkins, the ancillary stuff is better of late than in the past, and he grades out at a projected 7.91 QMAX "T" average for 1999.

Now the caveat here is that we're still working on validating this approach, and we may well have a lot more tweaking to do to make it really viable. We'll have a few other examples of this scattered around the pitcher comments to employ as an informal benchmark. Check back next year to see how close we came. <DM>

Year	GS	S	C	T
1998	33	4.64	3.42	8.06
1997	20	5.05	4.20	9.25
1996	6	5.00	3.67	8.67
1995	6	5.33	4.50	9.83

JIMMY HAYNES, OAK

All negative and backward trends for Haynes in 1998: HH% up markedly (to 45% from 23% last year). S12% (best hit prevention games) cut in half (15% in '98; 31% in '97). Replacing Bob Cluck with Rick Peterson did not help the A's young pitchers much at all. <DM>

Year	GS	S	C	T
1998	33	4.70	3.76	8.45
1997	13	4.00	4.23	8.23
1996	11	5.64	5.00	10.64
1995	3	1.33	3.67	5.00

RICK HELLING, TEX

Rick finally got it together in 1998 and became a solid, above-average starter. He also won 20 games pitching for a team that gave him nearly six runs a game of support. The popular impression is that Helling started fast and got a lot of wins early, but was poor down the stretch; when we look at his season in thirds with QMAX, however, we see a different pattern entirely:

	GS	S	C	T
1st 11		4.36	3.18	7.55
2nd 11		3.82	3.27	7.09
3rd 11		3.73	3.18	6.91

As this breakout makes clear, Rick actually pitched better as the season progressed. He looks as though he'll be a solid #3 type guy; on the Rangers, however, he's forced to impersonate a rotation anchor, which is clearly a stretch. <DM>

YEAR	GS	S	C	T
1998	33	3.97	3.21	7.18
1997	16	3.81	4.19	8.00
1996	6	2.67	3.00	5.67
1995	3	5.00	4.67	9.67
1994	9	4.33	3.56	7.89

BUTCH HENRY, SEA
(1998: BOS)

One of the poster boys for and prominent members of the CAD club (Chronic Arm Damage). Even though the Red Sox were extremely cautious with Butch in 1997, his arm may just not be salvageable. If he can pitch at all, however, he'll get several more chances. <DM>

YEAR	GS	S	C	T
1998	2	3.50	4.00	7.50
1997	5	3.40	3.00	6.40
1995	21	4.05	2.90	6.95
1994	15	3.67	3.07	6.73

PAT HENTGEN, TOR

Pat had an especially rough ten-start stretch from June 21st to August 14th, where his QMAX "S" average was 5.60. He'd been worked very hard in 1996-97, and had to be shut down in September, so what this looks like is someone trying to pitch through arm trouble. Hentgen's career, when we add in his 1993 QMAX data, shows a two-years on, one year off pattern, so barring any significant lingering effects from his injury, he should bounce back. <DM>

YEAR	GS	S	C	T
1998	29	4.66	3.45	8.10
1997	35	3.86	2.37	6.23
1996	35	3.43	2.83	6.26
1995	30	4.67	3.50	8.17
1994	24	3.54	2.88	6.42
1993	32	3.94	3.03	6.97

GIL HEREDIA, OAK

Back in the Bay Area after being traded by the Giants in 1992, Heredia surfaced from the minors in August and did a brilliant Tommy John impersonation for six starts. Given the A's desperation for anything in a jockstrap that can throw strikes, Gil may wind up as the #3 man in their rotation at the beginning of 1999. The odds aren't great that he'll be there at the end of 1999, however. <DM>

YEAR	GS	S	C	T
1998	6	4.17	1.83	6.00
1995	18	4.89	3.33	8.22
1994	3	3.33	2.33	5.67

ORLANDO HERNANDEZ, NYY

As was noted in the Yankees essay, this is the guy who put the Bombers over the top. The fact that El Duque was this good gave the Yanks the something extra to win 110+ games; he also was a pivotal factor in the postseason, pitching brilliantly in the absolutely crucial Game 4 against the Tribe. He did it again to the Padres in Game 2 of the Series, putting New York up 2-0.

In terms of dominating performances, Hernandez was right at the top of the league in 1998: his seven "1S" games (the very best hit prevention games) represented 33% of his total starts, tying Roger Clemens. He was a stalwart "big game" performer, with 29% of his starts in the Elite Square, a higher percentage than Clemens and Pedro Martinez and second in the AL only to teammate David Wells.

What will happen to El Duque in 1999? I'd expect some amount of retrenchment; the league will probably figure him out, at least to some extent. But a 3.05 QMAX "S" average should give him a pretty sizable amount of breathing room. <DM>

YEAR	GS	S	C	T
1998	21	3.05	3.24	6.29

KEN HILL, ANA

I don't think Ken's arm has been right for at least a couple of years, and his two-month stint on the DL may not have set it right, either. He was hit significantly harder this year than at any time in his career (47% HH as opposed to readings in the 20s and 30s in the past five years), and he looks to be pitching on little more than guile at this point. The Angels may have squeezed their coffers and wound up with a lemon. <DM>

YEAR	GS	S	C	T
1998	19	4.68	3.95	8.63
1997	31	4.03	4.06	8.10
1996	35	4.00	3.03	7.03
1995	29	4.31	3.59	7.90
1994	23	3.70	2.87	6.57

HIDEKI IRABU, NYY

This was a bit more like what the Yankees had in mind when they acquired the rights to Irabu from the Padres last year. (Odd how many connections between the two 1998 World Series teams you can find, isn't it? We covered that in the Padres' essay.) Irabu was hotter than over-endowed porno star Minka during April and May, but gave a lot of ground until recovering his form somewhat in September. Joe Torre, however, taking no chances, didn't use Irabu at all in the post-season. <DM>

YEAR	GS	S	C	T
1998	28	3.29	3.68	6.96
1997	9	5.22	4.00	9.22

JASON JACOME, CLE

The Tribe has a ton of lefty starters riding the Lake Erie Ferry from Buffalo to Cleveland (speaking of Buffalo, hello Ardyth Simmons, wherever you are...). In addition to Jacome, there's Huck Flener, Mike Matthews and Eddie Priest, and they're probably all going to be in Buffalo again next year. Jacome was 14-2, 3.26 there in 1998, however, and if he just

---

MISCELLANEOUS STARTING PITCHER DATA, AMERICAN LEAGUE 1998

LEGEND. NP—Number of Pitches thrown; TW—Team Wins in pitcher's starts; TL—Team Losses in pitcher's starts; GS—; QS—Quality Starts; BS—Blown Starts; QmB—Quality minus Blown pct.; PPI—Pitches thrown Per Inning; IP—Innings Pitched; AdIP—Adjusted Innings Pitched; IP/S—average Innings Pitched per Start

PITCHER NAME	TM	TW	TL	GS	QS	BS	QMB	IP	NP	STR	PPI	KPCT	ADJIP	IP/S
John Snyder	CHW	8	6	14	7	1	42.86	84.7	1343	840	15.86	62.5%	82	6.0
James Baldwin	CHW	15	8	24	11	5	25.00	137.3	2330	1405	16.97	60.3%	143	5.7
Mike Sirotka	CHW	17	16	33	16	8	24.24	211.7	3341	2113	15.78	63.2%	205	6.4
Jim Abbott	CHW	5	0	5	2	1	20.00	31.7	455	287	14.37	63.1%	28	6.3
Jim Parque	CHW	10	11	21	10	6	19.05	113.0	1955	1155	17.30	59.1%	120	5.4
Jaime Navarro	CHW	11	16	27	12	9	11.11	153.7	2553	1519	16.61	59.5%	156	5.7
Carlos Castillo	CHW	1	1	2	1	1	0.00	9.7	156	98	16.13	62.8%	10	4.8
Tom Fordham	CHW	3	2	5	1	1	0.00	17.3	323	169	18.64	52.3%	20	3.5
Scott Eyre	CHW	5	12	17	3	4	-5.88	87.0	1583	909	18.20	57.4%	97	5.1
Jason Bere	CHW	5	10	15	3	4	-6.67	76.7	1451	832	18.93	57.3%	89	5.1
Steve Karsay	CLE	0	1	1	1	0	100.00	6.7	97	58	14.54	59.8%	6	6.7
Bartolo Colon	CLE	18	13	31	17	2	48.39	204.0	3291	2038	16.13	61.9%	202	6.6
Dwight Gooden	CLE	10	13	23	13	0	43.48	134.0	2229	1314	16.63	59.0%	136	5.8
David Burba	CLE	16	15	31	18	5	41.94	200.0	3244	1959	16.22	60.4%	199	6.5
Jaret Wright	CLE	21	11	32	17	5	37.50	192.7	3362	2000	17.45	59.5%	206	6.0
Charles Nagy	CLE	19	14	33	17	7	30.30	210.3	3312	2031	15.75	61.3%	203	6.4
Chad Ogea	CLE	4	5	9	4	3	11.11	47.7	785	477	16.47	60.8%	48	5.3

had a little more stuff, might have been more than a cheap insurance policy. (And speaking of insurance, hello Carmen Ramos—you can sell me some insurance anytime...) <DM>

Year	GS	S	C	T
1998	1	7.00	4.00	11.00
1997	4	4.00	4.00	8.00
1996	2	6.50	6.00	12.50
1995	19	4.89	3.68	8.58
1994	8	4.13	2.88	7.00

DOUG JOHNS, BAL

When Jimmy Key and Scott Kamieniecki went down with injuries, the Orioles didn't turn to Rocky Coppinger, but instead to this man, whose arm has been doing a wet noodle impersonation for three years running. 'Twas ugly, very ugly (.284 QWP, 10% SS, 60% HH). I don't think even Ray Miller will try this again. <DM>

Year	GS	S	C	T
1998	10	5.50	3.80	9.30
1996	23	4.74	3.87	8.61
1995	9	3.33	3.89	7.22

JASON JOHNSON, TB

The Stingers rushed Jason to the majors, and pretty much got what you'd expect (23% SS). But I still think that Larry Rothschild has an interesting sense of the type of pitcher he wants to try to develop, and Johnson is not by any means a lost cause. Tampa and their young pitchers should be very, very interesting to watch over the next couple of years. <DM>

Year	GS	S	C	T
1998	13	4.62	4.23	8.85

JEFF JUDEN, FA
(1998: MIL-ANA)

It's hard to be considered a head case when you appear to possess only the reptilian portion of the brain, but this is Jeff Juden we're talking about, for Crissakes. I'm still convinced that he'll have one barnburner of a season somewhere, but it's beginning to look like it's going to be in the Moons of Jupiter League. <DM>

Year	GS	S	C	T
1998	30	4.17	3.80	7.97
1997	27	4.04	3.67	7.70
1995	10	3.20	4.00	7.20
1994	5	4.00	4.00	8.00

SCOTT KAMIENIECKI, BAL

Two points: 1) he can't stay healthy; 2) he's not that good anyway. <DM>

Year	GS	S	C	T
1998	11	4.55	4.36	8.91
1997	30	4.03	3.47	7.50
1996	5	6.00	5.60	11.60
1995	16	3.81	4.31	8.13
1994	16	3.75	3.69	7.44

STEVE KARSAY, CLE

Another member of the CAD club, Steve did manage to stay reasonably healthy in 1998, though he missed a few weeks while cavorting down in Buffalo. He's pretty much reduced to being a finesse pitcher, and he did show some excellent control in the minors this year. Still, I don't see a team with the Indians' profile giving him an extended chance in their rotation. <DM>

Year	GS	S	C	T
1998	1	5.00	3.00	8.00
1997	24	4.92	3.63	8.54
1994	4	3.50	2.50	6.00

GREG KEAGLE, DET

One more ex-Padre farmhand whom Randy Smith has inexplicably decided can pitch in the majors. The results speak for themselves. <DM>

Year	GS	S	C	T
1998	7	4.57	4.00	8.57
1997	10	4.80	4.10	8.90
1996	6	5.83	5.83	11.67

JIMMY KEY, FA
(1998: BAL)

Relegated to the bullpen after a disastrous July start after going on the DL seven weeks earlier, Jimmy might well have to hang it up. He hasn't quite had the career length or the flashy seasons necessary to be a serious candidate for the Hall of Fame, but his .614 lifetime winning percentage amd 3.51 ERA are close to that caliber. Ironically, he was pitching better in 1998 than he had for several previous years when he was forced to the sidelines. <DM>

Year	GS	S	C	T
1998	11	3.91	3.18	7.09
1997	34	3.97	3.47	7.44
1996	30	3.97	3.37	7.33
1995	5	5.40	2.80	8.20
1994	25	4.12	2.84	6.96

RICHIE LEWIS, BAL

The wild little righty, who's been around forever as a set-up man, spent 1998 in Rochester as a starter, and fanned more than a man an inning. His chances of making the Orioles' rotation in 1999, however, are about as good as Eddie Murphy playing Dr. Doolittle. Hey, wait a minute. . . <DM>

Year	GS	S	C	T
1998	1	5.00	7.00	12.00
1995	1	3.00	3.00	6.00

FELIPE LIRA, SEA

I'd say there's a 40% chance that Lira will surface somewhere (probably attired in scuba gear) and will get some more starts. I'd cut that percentage in half, however, for the chances that he'll get more than 10 in any given year, and cut it in half again (staying with me, math fans?) that he'll be as successful as he was in the past. <DM>

Year	GS	S	C	T
1997	18	4.56	4.06	8.61
1996	32	4.06	3.31	7.38
1995	22	4.05	3.68	7.73

MISCELLANEOUS STARTING PITCHER DATA, AMERICAN LEAGUE 1998

LEGEND: **NP**—Number of Pitches thrown; **TW**—Team Wins in pitcher's starts; **TL**—Team Losses in pitcher's starts; **GS**—; **QS**—Quality Starts; **BS**—Blown Starts; **QmB**—Quality minus Blown pct.; **PPI**—Pitches thrown Per Inning; **IP**—Innings Pitched; **AdIP**—Adjusted Innings Pitched; **IP/S**—average Innings Pitched per Start

Pitcher Name	Tm	TW	TL	GS	QS	BS	QMB	IP	NP	Str	PPI	Kpct	AdjIP	IP/S
Rick Krivda	CLE	1	0	1	0	0	0.00	5.0	93	53	18.60	57.0%	6	5.0
Jason Jacome	CLE	0	1	1	0	1	-100.00	5.0	93	58	18.60	62.4%	6	5.0
Brian Moehler	DET	17	16	33	21	4	51.52	221.3	3292	2075	14.87	63.0%	202	6.7
Justin Thompson	DET	13	21	34	21	5	47.06	222.0	3492	2178	15.73	62.4%	214	6.5
Seth Greisinger	DET	9	12	21	11	3	38.10	130.0	2103	1282	16.18	61.0%	129	6.2
Bryce Florie	DET	7	9	16	8	2	37.50	92.0	1505	873	16.36	58.0%	92	5.8
Denny Harriger	DET	0	2	2	0	0	0.00	10.0	183	118	18.30	64.5%	11	5.0
Greg Keagle	DET	2	5	7	1	1	0.00	35.3	627	380	17.74	60.6%	38	5.0
Tim Worrell	DET	3	6	9	4	4	0.00	47.7	803	512	16.84	63.8%	49	5.3
Brian Powell	DET	4	12	16	3	5	-12.50	82.7	1438	879	17.40	61.1%	88	5.2
Frank Castillo	DET	8	11	19	5	8	-15.79	92.0	1734	1060	18.85	61.1%	106	4.8
A.J. Sager	DET	2	1	3	0	2	-66.67	11.0	226	130	20.55	57.5%	14	3.7
Scott Sanders	DET	0	2	2	0	2	-100.00	8.7	202	116	23.30	57.4%	12	4.3
Jeff Suppan	KCR	0	1	1	1	0	100.00	6.0	92	59	15.33	64.1%	6	6.0
Tim Belcher	KCR	17	17	34	21	4	50.00	234.0	3590	2277	15.34	63.4%	220	6.9
Pat Rapp	KCR	16	16	32	17	6	34.38	188.3	3351	1911	17.79	57.0%	205	5.9
Jose Rosado	KCR	13	12	25	11	3	32.00	152.0	2527	1579	16.63	62.5%	155	6.1

ESTEBAN LOAIZA, TEX
(1998: PIT-TEX)

You know an organization has given up on you when they trade you for Todd Van Poppel. The odd thing about the trade, however, was that Loaiza had actually been pitching very well for the Pirates when they sent him to Texas. In the end, however, it wasn't of much account: "Good Ol' Steve," as the hitters in both leagues now call him with no small amount of fondness, is still getting tattooed for close to a .300 opposition BA and an OPS of .800+. In short, he's on a lot of hitters' Christmas card lists. . . <DM>

Year	GS	S	C	T
1998	28	4.68	3.29	7.96
1997	32	4.31	3.19	7.50
1996	10	4.70	3.60	8.30
1995	31	4.65	3.48	8.13

ALBIE LOPEZ, TB

The Stingers converted Albie into a set-up man, and he was pretty good, though he was rather poor at stranding runners. I don't see any room for Lopez in the Tampa rotation for the foreseeable future. <DM>

Year	GS	S	C	T
1997	6	4.67	4.67	9.33
1996	10	5.20	3.80	9.00
1995	2	2.00	2.50	4.50
1994	4	4.50	4.25	8.75

DEREK LOWE, BOS

Derek was not effective as a starter, but turned out to be quite useful in the bullpen for the Red Sox, where one suspects he will be found in 1999. <DM>

Year	GS	S	C	T
1998	11	4.70	4.00	8.70
1997	9	4.44	4.11	8.56

PEDRO MARTINEZ, BOS

A fine, fine follow-up to his stellar 1997, especially in adjusting to the change in league and home park. Very steady with his monthly QWP values, with only June (.584) coming in under .600. His .660 QWP was the highest in the league, just ahead of AL QMAX average leader David Wells and the man he replaced as the ace of Boston, Roger Clemens. All other QMAX vital signs (73% SS, 27% ES, 18% HH, 52% S12) are golden. <DM>

Year	GS	S	C	T
1998	33	3.09	2.58	5.67
1997	31	2.32	2.29	4.61
1996	33	3.48	3.03	6.52
1995	30	3.20	3.13	6.33
1994	23	3.30	3.17	6.48

BEN McDONALD, FA
(1998: injured)

Will Big Ben chime again? He seems to have disappeared into the Atchafalaya, but he might yet re-emerge from the bayou. To paraphrase one L. P. Berra, a wise yogi from further up the river, you ain't dead 'til you're dead. <DM>

Year	GS	S	C	T
1997	21	3.67	3.00	6.67
1996	35	4.03	3.00	7.03
1995	13	3.23	4.00	7.23
1994	24	3.83	3.21	7.04

JACK McDOWELL, ANA

After emerging from the DL in August, Jack's QMAX averages were 4.43,3.14/7.57, a tad better than league average. He didn't show anything like his old Big Game Percentage, however. (To compute BGPct., divide ES games by SS games; Jack's BGPct last year was 23%, as opposed to 43% in 1994-97.) <DM>

Year	GS	S	C	T
1998	14	4.86	3.07	7.93
1997	6	4.17	4.00	8.17
1996	30	4.30	3.27	7.57
1995	30	3.57	2.90	6.47
1994	25	4.16	2.32	6.48

RAMIRO MENDOZA, NYY

Joe Torre spotted Mendoza's starts brilliantly, putting him up against weakling hitting teams in 12 of his 14 outings. As a result, Ramiro probably shaved a good .60-.80 points off what his QMAX "T" average would have been had he faced average competition.

Don't get me wrong: a pitcher like Mendoza, who seems to be unaffected by slapdashing (that is, being moved back and forth from starting and relieving), is a valuable commodity, since few pitchers are able to be effective in both roles. But any thought that Ramiro is going to turn into the next Greg Maddux, or get much more than the number of starts in 1999 that he received for the Yanks in 1998, is simply misguided. <DM>

Year	GS	S	C	T
1998	14	3.71	2.93	6.64
1997	15	5.07	3.20	8.27
1996	11	5.82	3.64	9.45

ERIC MILTON, MIN

The Twins' booty from the Chuck Knoblauch fire sale, Eric had a couple of good months (June and July) but otherwise struggled. We ran our experimental 15-start QMAX analysis forecasting method on Eric and came up with a projected QMAX "T" average of 7.57 for him in 1999 (see the entry for LaTroy

Hawkins for more detail on that method). Most of the gain is expected to be in the "S" value; Milton had good hit prevention in his lone minor league season in 1997. Check back in next year's book to see how we did. <DM>

Year	GS	S	C	T
1998	32	4.41	3.78	8.19

BRIAN MOEHLER, DET

Across-the-board improvement from Moehler, who posted a 5.75 QMAX "T" value in 20 starts from April 19th through August 1st. While he's a big, beefy guy, he's not really overpowering, and so I think it will be hard for him to get much below the low sixes, but that's a solid #2-3 guy. Rick Reuschel looks like a reasonable analogue. <DM>

Year	GS	S	C	T
1998	33	3.85	2.76	6.61
1997	31	4.52	3.52	8.03
1996	2	4.50	5.00	9.50

JAMIE MOYER, SEA

In 1995, Jamie became a big-game pitcher, jumping his ES% from below 10 to just over 20, which is where it has remained ever since. Every year there's some analyst somewhere predicting that Jamie will collapse—in 1998 it was Rob Neyer, the doe-eyed doyen of ESPNet, whose home base is Seattle; evidently seeing is not believing. Moyer, however, has become a very reliable #2-3 guy who's had the good fortune to get runs scored for him and post a won-loss record that's pretty darned eye-popping. His QWP was .625 last year, which ain't chopped liver. I think it's time we gave him some credit for being an improbable (but nonetheless heartwarming) late bloomer. <DM>

Year	GS	S	C	T
1998	34	3.97	2.32	6.29
1997	29	3.93	2.83	6.76
1996	21	4.29	3.00	7.29
1995	18	4.00	3.17	7.17
1994	23	4.22	2.87	7.09

BOBBY MUNOZ, BAL

Big Daddy Munoz spent most of 1998 at Rochester, where he set the International League on its ear with a 1.06 ERA and 19 saves. He didn't show much with the O's (9.82 ERA in nine games), and so one figures that his mythic odyssey will continue throughout the second-tier cities of America, where his legend is as large (and as strangely ominous) as his looming, 6'8" shadow. <DM>

Year	GS	S	C	T
1998	1	5.00	5.00	10.00
1997	7	5.29	4.14	9.43
1996	6	5.83	3.67	9.50
1995	3	3.67	4.33	8.00
1994	14	3.79	2.79	6.57

MIKE MUSSINA, BAL

The QWP value for Moose in 1998 was .616, which works out to a projected team record of 18-11 in his 29 starts; the Orioles only went 16-13, however, which indicates that Mike pitched in some tough luck last year. Now 30, he's 118-59 in his career and has a good shot at a Hall of Fame career if he can keep the pace up for 3-4 more years. <DM>

YEAR	GS	S	C	T
1998	29	3.72	2.41	6.14
1997	33	3.55	2.58	6.12
1996	36	4.22	2.78	7.00
1995	32	3.34	2.50	5.84
1994	24	3.63	2.25	5.88

CHARLES NAGY, CLE

Charlie screwed up the on-off pattern that he'd been evidencing, and has pretty much slipped into being a league-average pitcher at best. His SS% has slipped to a dangerously low 33%; so far he's propped up by the fact that he's still reaching the Elite Square (ES%) about 15% of the time. This is not someone to pin your pennant hopes on. <DM>

YEAR	GS	S	C	T
1998	33	4.67	3.00	7.67
1997	33	4.64	3.06	7.70
1996	32	3.84	2.63	6.47
1995	29	4.31	3.24	7.55
1994	23	4.00	2.57	6.57

JAMIE NAVARRO, CHW

You've got to have a strong stomach to keep tossing a pitcher out there who's having as rough a stretch as Navarro had from May 19th to July 5th, but that's what Jerry Manuel did, and Jamie served up a 5.90 QMAX "S" average during that time.

Think about it. That's just a tenth of a point away from averaging being hit hard in every start. If the White Sox hadn't been paying Navarro all that cash, they wouldn't have kept on torturing themselves and their fans. Finally, in August, they'd seen enough and stuck him the bullpen.

Let's break out the QMAX matrix box for those starts and engage in some slack-jawed wonder:

JAIME NAVARRO 5/20 - 7/5/98								
	1	2	3	4	5	6	7	S
1								0
2								0
3	1			1				2
4								0
5								0
6	1		1	1				3
7		1	1		1	1	1	5
C	2	1	2	2	1	1	1	10

As you can see, the little girl with the curl has nothing on Navarro. Jamie was able to space things out so that every fourth start, he'd have a decent outing, which probably gave Manuel and the White Sox false hope.

The thing that's really scary is that this wasn't even his worst season—though, to be fair, he was hurt in 1994 and made only 10 starts. Never has anyone more richly deserved the shortest, sweetest palindrome in the English language: wow. <DM>

YEAR	GS	S	C	T
1998	27	5.07	3.85	8.93
1997	33	4.82	3.33	8.15
1996	35	4.03	2.86	6.89
1995	29	3.79	2.66	6.45
1994	10	5.50	3.60	9.10

CHAD OGEA, PHI
(1998: CLE)

Chad lost his ability to get into the Elite Square in 1997, and it doesn't look as though it's gonna come back. Without that, he's really unlikely to be able to hold even a #5 rotation slot with a team that has run through more pitchers than Ziegfield ran through chorus girls. Traded to the Phillies for Jerry Spradlin during the off-season—which may be a sufficiently galling insult to prove motivating. <DM>

YEAR	GS	S	C	T
1998	9	4.33	4.00	8.33
1997	21	4.43	3.48	7.90
1996	21	4.05	3.10	7.14
1995	14	3.86	3.29	7.14
1994	1	6.00	4.00	10.00

OMAR OLIVARES, ANA

He's stabilized at a performance level which is ultimately self-liquidating, but the Halos are so bereft of replacement possibilities that I suspect Omar will be around for at least another year or two. No Elite Square games whatsoever. <DM>

YEAR	GS	S	C	T
1998	26	4.23	4.00	8.23
1997	31	4.39	3.87	8.26
1996	25	4.28	3.68	7.96
1995	6	5.00	5.17	10.17
1994	12	4.92	4.08	9.00

MIKE OQUIST, OAK

Readers from last year may still be trying to recover from the description of QMAXX, the XBH-adjusted version of QMAX that we dust off when a pitcher has too much of a discrepancy from the league isolated power. It wasn't so much the description, but how it was presented—as part of an extended filagree that simultaneously celebrated and desecrated that ex-tra "X".

No, no, we won't go through that again. Mike Qquist is a good choice to revisit QMAXX, though, and how it works. QMAX measures only hits, and sometimes there are pitchers who give up far more total bases per hit than the league average. There aren't really a lot of pitchers who fall into this area—maybe 10-12%—but a few are far enough off that it keeps the QMAX "S" value lower than it really should be to show the real impact of the hits allowed.

The way we normalize for this (and get that ex-tra "X") is to calculate the individual pitcher's isolated power (ISO, which is opposition SLG minus opposition BA). We do the same for the league. In Qquist's case, his ISO is .184, while the AL in 1998 was at .161. The ISO factor for Oquist is thus 1.14, or fourteen percent above the league.

Next we look at those same two stats, opposition SLG and opposition BA, and divide SLG by BA for the pitcher and the league. This is the SLG/BA factor. Oquist has a SLG/BA of 1.62, while the league's is 1.59. That means the SLG/BA factor for Qquist is 1.02 (two percent).

We then add the two factors together, and divide by two. That gives us an QMAXX adjustment factor of 1.08. We multiply Oquist's QMAX "S" value (4.48) by 1.08, which works out to 4.83. We substitute this value for the old "S" value, add it to the "C" value, and the revised number is the QMAXX ranking.

So instead of Mike's QMAX values being 4.48, 3.34/7.83, his QMAXX values are 4.83, 3.34/8.18. We'll probably automate that function in time for next year's book, but in the meantime you'll see a few pitchers who've had their QMAX values augmented with a second 1998 average. These are pitchers whose ISO is at least 12% higher than league average.

And for guys like Oquist, it assists in seeing how their ERAs are so high. Ex-tra XBH relative to hits is a sure way to accelerate run scoring, and pitchers who are susceptible to this will often give up more runs than a pitcher with the same QMAX profile (or even H/9). QMAXX shows us how much more under the league Oquist really is, and that's an valuable adjustment. <DM>

YEAR	GS	S	C	T
1998	29	4.48	3.34	7.83
QMAXX	29	4.83	3.34	8.18
1997	16	3.94	3.56	7.50
1994	9	5.44	4.67	10.11

JIM PARQUE, CHW

A little lefty who had dominated high-A ball in 1997, Parque was rushed to the bigs after just nine starts at AAA, and struggled mightily. Like all the young White Sox hurlers, however, Jim actually had a reasonable September, and so there may be some hope for the future. I think someone should do a study to see if "force-feeding" young pitchers is as disastrous an approach as it appears to be. <DM>

Year	GS	S	C	T
1998	21	4.76	3.90	8.67

ROGER PAVLIK, FA
(1998: TEX)

I've got to remember to make a list of the CAD club. (You remember—Chronic Arm Damage). We're going to have to study all of those guys, and see if there is any thread that links them together. It's not going to be anything like physical size, or anything simple, but I'll bet there are several factors that can be identified if someone really can get the data laid out.

Anyway, Roger here was limited to just five relief appearances in 1998. Waiting for him to get healthy again is starting to resemble waiting for Godot, but the Rangers are pretty desperate: rumor is that they'll re-sign Roger as we lurch toward spring training. <DM>

Year	GS	S	C	T
1997	11	4.09	4.18	8.27
1996	34	4.32	3.65	7.97
1995	31	3.48	3.87	7.35
1994	11	4.55	4.91	9.45

MATT PERISHO, TEX

As I said, the Rangers are pretty damned desperate... <DM>

Year	GS	S	C	T
1998	2	6.50	7.00	13.50
1997	8	5.38	4.88	10.25

ROBERT PERSON, TOR

The Jays' new plan is to make Person into a closer. He was put into the role in September and was serviceable (6 SV, 4.09 ERA). Tim Johnson has an interesting way of blurring the lines between desperation and creativity. . . <DM>

Year	GS	S	C	T
1997	22	4.05	3.82	7.86
1996	13	3.54	3.62	7.15
1995	1	1.00	3.00	4.00

ANDY PETTITTE, NYY

Andy had it together only for a couple months in 1998—June and July. Oh, yeah, and October, too. As you can see, the big problem was command. Andy's C13% (the good to great control outings) fell from 83% to 57%. What kept Andy from falling over the edge was his ability to keep his ES% and HH% about the same as in the past. While he's not nearly as good a pitcher as

many consider him to be, he's better than just about anyone else's #4 starter. <DM>

Year	GS	S	C	T
1998	32	4.25	3.41	7.66
1997	35	3.83	2.71	6.54
1996	34	4.06	3.09	7.15
1995	26	4.00	3.23	7.23

HIPOLITO PICHARDO, KC

A quick note to the reader: keep in mind that if you want to use ERA as a benchmark for the pitchers discussed in this section, you'll need to consult a source that has ERA broken out by starts and relief appearances. In the case of Hipolito Pichardo, his 1998 ERA as a reliever was 13.05, while his ERA as a starter was 4.38. If you compare his QMAX score to his overall ERA (5.13), you'll be mixing apples and oranges. (And, as was briefly touched upon in the QMAX essay in Section Three, we've devised our own representation of a pitcher's ERA from the data, though we're going to test it a bit more before making it an official part of the QMAX toolkit. That QMAX ERA, or QERA, comes out as 4.15 for Pichardo.)

So what we've got here is a pitcher who's a bit better than league average, despite making the Success Square only 39% of the time, and without once setting foot in the Elite Square (in other words, 0%). How did he do it? He was much better than average in terms of being Hit Hard (just 17% compared to the AL average of 34%). While avoiding the Hit Hard region is not a guaranteed way to achieve success, it is the best way to avoid sure failure, because most games in the Hit Hard region have winning percentages below .300. <DM>

Year	GS	S	C	T
1998	18	4.00	3.56	7.56

JIM PITTSLEY, KC

Jimbo spent most of the year in the Royals' bullpen, where he was just plain dreadful. His 1995 arm injury has clearly had a lingering impact on his career, which was on the fast track three years ago, and now appears to be completely derailed. <DM>

Year	GS	S	C	T
1998	2	5.50	4.50	10.00
1997	21	4.24	4.29	8.52
1995	1	6.00	4.00	10.00

SIDNEY PONSON, BAL

Ponson was rushed into the Orioles' rotation when Key and Kamieniecki both went down, and it showed. There really needs to be a study of young pitches who get skipped leagues (either AA to the majors, or A to AAA) and the effects on their careers. Sidney is in the first category, and was very much overmatched in 1998. The question is: are there lingering effects from this, and can we quantify them? <DM>

Year	GS	S	C	T
1998	20	4.85	3.55	8.40

BRIAN POWELL, DET

Powell's second year at Lakeland (Florida State League) in 1997 was a big advance, and when he did pretty well at Jacksonville early last year, the Tigers rushed him to the big leagues. The results, mentioned as recently ago as the previous comment, were not particularly surprising. There are a lot of people who believe that the best pitching prospects can just skip AAA. I think that there's some truth to that, but I think it's a very individualistic thing; as with many other issues, we need a good study of the matter. As we've seen, there appears to be a lot of evidence

MISCELLANEOUS STARTING PITCHER DATA, AMERICAN LEAGUE 1998

LEGEND: **NP**—Number of Pitches thrown; **TW**—Team Wins in pitcher's starts; **TL**—Team Losses in pitcher's starts; **GS**—; **QS**—Quality Starts; **BS**—Blown Starts; **QmB**—Quality minus Blown pct.; **PPI**—Pitches thrown Per Inning; **IP**—Innings Pitched; **AdIP**—Adjusted Innings Pitched; **IP/S**—average Innings Pitched per Start

Pitcher Name	Tm	TW	TL	GS	QS	BS	QMB	IP	NP	Str	PPI	Kpct	AdIP	IP/S
Hipolito Pichardo	KCR	11	9	20	8	2	30.00	111.0	1807	1087	16.28	60.2%	111	5.5
Brian Barber	KCR	2	6	8	3	2	12.50	42.0	640	376	15.24	58.8%	39	5.3
Glendon Rusch	KCR	7	17	24	9	9	0.00	141.0	2401	1511	17.03	62.9%	147	5.9
Jamie Walker	KCR	0	2	2	1	1	0.00	10.3	159	102	15.39	64.2%	10	5.2
Chris Haney	KCR	5	7	12	3	6	-25.00	61.3	1065	654	17.37	61.4%	65	5.1
Kevin Appier	KCR	1	2	3	0	1	-33.33	15.0	271	174	18.07	64.2%	17	5.0
Benj Sampson	MIN	2	0	2	2	0	100.00	13.0	213	135	16.38	63.4%	13	6.5
Mike Morgan	MIN	9	8	17	10	3	41.18	95.0	1381	851	14.54	61.6%	85	5.6
Brad Radke	MIN	13	19	32	19	6	40.63	213.7	3390	2251	15.87	66.4%	208	6.7
Bob Tewksbury	MIN	11	15	26	11	5	23.08	152.0	2140	1405	14.08	65.7%	131	5.8
Dan Serafini	MIN	3	6	9	4	2	22.22	46.0	763	462	16.58	60.6%	47	5.1
LaTroy Hawkins	MIN	13	20	33	14	7	21.21	190.3	3144	1986	16.52	63.2%	193	5.8
Eric Milton	MIN	14	18	32	14	8	18.75	172.3	3012	1909	17.48	63.4%	184	5.4
Frank Rodriguez	MIN	5	6	11	5	4	9.09	60.3	1048	643	17.37	61.4%	64	5.5
David Wells	NYY	25	5	30	20	1	63.33	214.3	3172	2178	14.80	68.7%	194	7.1
Orlando Hernandez	NYY	16	5	21	14	3	52.38	141.0	2278	1379	16.15	60.5%	139	6.7
David Cone	NYY	24	7	31	19	3	51.61	207.7	3354	2120	16.15	63.2%	205	6.7

pointing in the other direction. <DM>

Year	GS	S	C	T
1998	16	4.81	4.00	8.81

EDDIE PRIEST, CLE
(1998: CIN)

Picked up by the Indians in a series of bizarre DFA moves in mid-June, Priest spent most of the summer in Buffalo, where he struggled. Someone in the Indians' organization may eventually get the idea to convert him into a reliever, because he does have very good control and pitching fewer innings per appearance might increase his effectiveness. <DM>

Year	GS	S	C	T
1998	2	6.00	4.00	10.00

ARIEL PRIETO, OAK

I happen to think that Prieto could still amount to something, but it's going to have to happen somewhere other than Oakland. Tampa looks like a good fit, what with the collection of Power Precipice types that have been stockpiled by Larry Rothschild. The A's may not recover from the effects of Bob Cluck for a long, long time. <DM>

Year	GS	S	C	T
1998	2	6.50	5.00	11.50
1997	22	4.95	4.36	9.32
1996	21	4.10	3.52	7.62
1995	9	4.33	4.22	8.56

BRAD RADKE, MIN

Last year, you may remember, we talked about the chances of Brad getting into the top echelon of pitchers. The suggestion was that he could become a "sub-six" pitcher, based on his nineteen-game string of "sub-five" pitching in 1997. The QMAX "T" value we named last year was 5.84; after fifteen starts in 1998, Radke's "T" value was indeed at 5.80. Then Brad—very possibly suffering from overwork (more starts than any other pitcher in baseball in 1996-97)—became exceptionally hittable for the balance of the season (4.94 QMAX "S"). The worst of it came on August 29th, when Brad was shelled for 10 hits and eight earned runs at the hands of the Blue Jays.

Looking more closely at the season, we can see that from the start, Brad wasn't reaching the Elite Square nearly as often, even though his Success Square ratio was actually higher in the first 14 starts than anyone else in the AL. Let's break down Brad's season into three periods: the first 14 starts, where his QMAX "T" score is 5.64, his next 13 starts, where he is simply racked, and the five September starts after the Blue Jay Blowout:

	GS	SS	ES	HH	S12	C1
1st 14		.79	.14	.07	.21	.29
Next 13		.15	.08	.62	.08	.00
Last 5		.60	.20	.40	.40	.20
1997		.51	.29	.31	.43	.34

We added in the pertinent Sector and Range data for some added perspective. Radke's 5.64 "T" score after 14 starts was "hollow" in the sense that it came from a lot of starts in the outer portion of the Success Square. We speak of the four "rings" of the Success Square: this is another way to see how good a pitcher's good starts really are. The inner rings, which encompass the Elite Square, account for 27% of the games in the entire Success Square, while the outer rings account for 73%. In 1997, Radke's ratio was 56/44. After 14 starts in 1998, that same ratio was 18/82. The chances of Brad continuing with a sub-six "T" value with a subpar "inner/outer ring ratio" (I/ORR, pronounced "eeyore" after the donkey in A.A. Milne) weren't very good—though the next 13 starts were a bit more catastrophic than anyone might have foreseen.

The good news is that Brad did come out of his deep, deep tailspin in September; his Sector and Range data for the last month of 1998 looks more like what he was doing in 1997. All of the vital signs (including the top hit and walk prevention categories, S12 and C1 respectively, came back into view along with Brad's pulse and blood pressure.) Our experimental 15-start QMAX forecasting method is a bit more cautious than we were last year, and tags Brad to come in with a 6.47 QMAX "T" score in 1999. (And, for those of you who like detail, that's a 4.03 QMAX "S" and a 2.43 QMAX "C".) As noted, we'll check to see how we did this time next year. <DM>

Year	GS	S	C	T
1998	32	4.28	2.63	6.91
1997	35	3.86	2.49	6.34
1996	35	3.91	2.71	6.63
1995	28	4.25	2.96	7.21

PATT RAPP, KC

Yes, that's how we spell it. And another way to trade on it is in hip-hop style: "If your pitchin' ain't as good as your own grandmother/Then it's time to step aside for your own little brother/When your stuff and command are this mediocre/The sad fact of the matter is that you are a joker."

With apologies to the late Jay Billington Bulworth and all those real "rappers" out there. <DM>

Year	GS	S	C	T
1998	32	4.25	4.25	8.50
1997	25	4.32	4.08	8.40
1996	29	4.55	4.31	8.86
1995	29	3.69	3.62	7.31
1994	23	4.04	4.00	8.04

BRYAN REKAR, TB

Coming back from a stint in the Rocky Horror of Coors Field and some probably not-unrelated arm injuries, Bryan had a good September (3.60,3.20/6.80) and might just become a solid #3 pitcher yet. <DM>

Year	GS	S	C	T
1998	15	4.47	3.13	7.60
1997	2	4.50	4.50	9.00
1996	11	5.18	4.09	9.27
1995	14	4.29	3.21	7.50

FRANK RODRIGUEZ, MIN

The Tom Kelly/Frank Rodriguez Dance of Death continues. In late August, after his first seven starts, Frankie actually had

---

MISCELLANEOUS STARTING PITCHER DATA,
AMERICAN LEAGUE 1998

LEGEND: NP—Number of Pitches thrown; **TW**—Team Wins in pitcher's starts; **TL**—Team Losses in pitcher's starts; **GS**—; **QS**—Quality Starts; **BS**—Blown Starts; **QmB**—Quality minus Blown pct.; **PPI**—Pitches thrown Per Inning; **IP**—Innings Pitched; **AdIP**—Adjusted Innings Pitched; **IP/S**—average Innings Pitched per Start

Pitcher Name	Tm	TW	TL	GS	QS	BS	QMB	IP	NP	Str	PPI	Kpct	AdjIP	IP/S
Hideki Irabu	NYY	16	12	28	17	5	42.86	171.0	2702	1623	15.80	60.1%	165	6.1
Andy Pettitte	NYY	20	12	32	16	3	40.63	213.4	3388	2064	15.88	60.9%	207	6.7
Ramiro Mendoza	NYY	10	4	14	7	2	35.71	88.3	1272	813	14.40	63.9%	78	6.3
Jim Bruske	NYY	1	0	1	0	0	0.00	5.0	71	52	14.20	73.2%	4	5.0
Mike Buddie	NYY	1	1	2	0	0	0.00	10.3	184	111	17.81	60.3%	11	5.2
Ryan Bradley	NYY	0	1	1	0	1	-100.00	5.0	104	67	20.80	64.4%	6	5.0
Mike Jerzembeck	NYY	1	1	2	0	2	-100.00	5.3	117	61	21.95	52.1%	7	2.7
Gil Heredia	OAK	3	3	6	4	0	66.67	40.0	536	363	13.40	67.7%	33	6.7
Kenny Rogers	OAK	19	15	34	21	1	58.82	238.7	3490	2119	14.62	60.7%	214	7.0
Jimmy Haynes	OAK	18	15	33	15	5	30.30	194.3	3369	2029	17.34	60.2%	206	5.9
Tom Candiotti	OAK	14	19	33	16	7	27.27	201.0	3259	1999	16.21	61.3%	200	6.1
Blake Stein	OAK	7	13	20	8	6	10.00	109.0	1967	1144	18.05	58.2%	120	5.4
Mike Oquist	OAK	12	17	29	11	9	6.90	170.0	2712	1700	15.95	62.7%	166	5.9
Dave Telgheder	OAK	1	1	2	0	0	0.00	9.3	144	91	15.43	63.2%	9	4.7
Jay Witasick	OAK	0	3	3	0	1	-33.33	15.7	321	189	20.49	58.9%	20	5.2
Ariel Prieto	OAK	0	2	2	0	2	-100.00	8.3	166	101	19.90	60.8%	10	4.2
Paul Abbott	SEA	3	1	4	2	0	50.00	24.7	386	247	15.65	64.0%	24	6.2

a 6.28 QMAX "T" score. He had a September not to remember (11.67 QMAX "T"). I think Frank's only hope is to get traded; another year of "Waltzing With Tom" might cause him to burst a blood vessel. **<DM>**

Year	GS	S	C	T
1998	11	4.27	3.82	8.09
1997	15	4.33	4.33	8.67
1996	33	4.42	3.61	8.03
1995	18	4.06	4.28	8.33

NERIO RODRIGUEZ, TOR
(1998: BAL)

Sent to the Blue Jays as part of the Juan Guzman trade, Nerio is another guy who was skipped a league (A-AAA) . He's a dark horse for the Jays' #5 slot, but I suspect that he might wind up in the bullpen if he sticks. He'd be a good candidate to audition for the closer role should Robert Person wind up doing a swan dive. **<DM>**

Year	GS	S	C	T
1998	4	4.50	4.75	9.25
1997	2	3.50	3.50	7.00
1996	1	2.00	3.00	5.00

KENNY ROGERS, OAK

A terrific comeback year for Kenny; it's clear, though, that a good bit of that is due to his new home park. Here is a selection of Rogers' QMAX data broken out by home/away:

Where	S	C	T	SS	ES	HH	S12
Home	2.76	2.71	5.47	.76	.18	.06	.65
Away	4.29	2.76	7.06	.41	.12	.35	.24

If I were in Billy Beane's shoes, I'd think seriously about trading Kenny while his value is probably at an all-time high. But Billy is the guy who kept Art Howe despite all of the indications that he has no real sense of how to develop a young team in general, and young pitchers in particular, and Billy is the guy who kept Art Howe because Kenny Rogers likes him and will stick around if Art's still around. The combination of young kids and good old boys seems antithetical to me, and I think we've just been given a glimpse of Billy's Achilles heel. **<DM>**

Year	GS	S	C	T
1998	34	3.53	2.74	6.26
1997	22	4.77	3.73	8.50
1996	30	3.97	3.83	7.80
1995	31	3.45	3.23	6.68
1994	24	4.21	2.92	7.13

JOSE ROSADO, KC

The good news is that Jose's arm doesn't seem to be nearly as ruined as many feared (Rob Neyer, for one, had already written off Rosado at the beginning of the 1998 season). The bad news is that he appears to be turning into a true Jekyll-Hyde type pitcher. While his dominating games went up (S12 of 34%), so did his Hit Hard games (up to 44%, which is much too high for any kind of real success).

And there's no trend in the smaller data samples for 1998 to indicate that this was simply an artifact of the arm problems: Jose's monthly HH% fluctuated only between 40% and 50% the entire year. With numbers like that, there really doesn't seem to be very much likelihood of the upside that we'd projected a couple of years ago. Our experimental 15-start QMAX projection system, in fact, figures that Jose has about reached his level, forecasting a 7.47 QMAX "T" in 1999. **<DM>**

Year	GS	S	C	T
1998	25	4.20	3.20	7.40
1997	33	4.36	3.45	7.82
1996	16	3.75	2.75	6.50

BRIAN ROSE, BOS

A big setback year for Rose, a kid who may have overachieved in 1997 at Pawtucket. He's shown that he's susceptible to the HR ball, and that may be a problem given his home park. While it's still far too soon to think of him as a washout, this year looms big. **<DM>**

Year	GS	S	C	T
1998	8	4.38	4.00	8.38
1997	1	6.00	5.00	11.00

MATT RUEBEL, TB

Retread lefty whose last good year was in AA ball in 1995. He got a look-see in Tampa, did poorly, and will very likely be discarded. **<DM>**

Year	GS	S	C	T
1998	1	5.00	5.00	10.00
1996	7	4.57	4.00	8.57

GLENDON RUSCH, KC

Another guy who skipped leagues (A-AAA) and has fallen victim to stalled development. Was pulled from the rotation in August and finished the year in the bullpen, where he pitched quite well. One wonders whether Tony Muser's light bulb might register a faint flicker... **<DM>**

Year	GS	S	C	T
1998	24	4.83	3.38	8.21
1997	27	4.67	3.26	7.93

BRET SABERHAGEN, BOS

A nice comeback for Bret, but he's well below his top form. In the past he was a big-game pitcher (20s and 30s in the Elite Square), but no more (down to 10%). His control is still excellent, but no longer laser-like

(a C1% of 16%, as opposed to a mind-bending 58% in 1994). Still, he righted himself impressively after a very poor May, had a vintage Sabes month in July (3.33, 1.83/5.17), and stayed healthy all year. He's now got 156 lifetime wins, and if justice prevails (and perhaps jurisprudence: there were rumors that Bret planned to retire because he didn't want to pay his ex-wife all that alimony), he just might make it to 200. **<DM>**

Year	GS	S	C	T
1998	31	4.06	2.81	6.87
1997	6	4.50	4.00	8.50
1995	25	4.28	2.80	7.08
1994	24	3.63	1.71	5.33

A.J. SAGER, DET

Tossed into the rotation on an emergency basis in May; might be well-advised to change those initials to "E.R." **<DM>**

Year	GS	S	C	T
1998	3	5.67	4.00	9.67
1997	1	3.00	3.00	6.00
1996	9	4.67	3.89	8.56
1994	3	5.67	3.33	9.00

BENJ SAMPSON, MIN

Middling lefty prospect came up after an ordinary season at Salt Lake City (try to imagine that Mormon town co-existing with a team named the Buzz. . .), and surprised everyone, including possibly himself, with a couple of very solid outings in September. Given the state of the Twins' rotation, you've got to figure that gives him the inside track on the #2 slot. . . **<DM>**

Year	GS	S	C	T
1998	2	2.00	3.00	5.00

JULIO SANTANA, TB

Larry Rothschild just loves these projects, and what's amazing is that he seems to be making a good bit of progress with most of them. On the other hand, Julio's best pitching came mostly against the league's weaker offenses, and his K/9 and K/BB ratios are still rather anemic. This might be about as good as Julio is going to get. **<DM>**

Year	GS	S	C	T
1998	19	4.11	3.58	7.68
1997	14	5.57	4.07	9.64

TONY SAUNDERS, TB

Of all the questions that one can fashion about Tony (and there are many of them), the most important may be whether he'll be able to stay healthy given how many pitches per inning he throws. Saunders had the most "trouble starts" in baseball last year with eight. (A "trouble start" is defined as a game where the pitcher throws at least five innings and averages 19 or more pitches per inning.)

Better news can be found in the small sample trends. After struggling for the first two months of the season, Tony got his QMAX score above league average over his last twenty starts (3.50,4.05/7.55). More encouraging were his last seven starts, where he got his "C" average down to near three (3.57 "S", 3.14 "C"/ 6.71 "T"). It's not quite large enough of a sample to tout, but there are some indications that Tony has turned a corner. Larry Rothschild couldn't be higher on Tony if he were his own son (that #1 pick in the expansion draft says it all), and we'll know soon enough if that affection is truly warranted. If he can stay healthy, of course—Tony's already had arthroscopic surgery this winter as I write this. **<DM>**

Year	GS	S	C	T
1998	31	3.90	4.13	8.03
1997	21	3.62	4.38	8.00

PETE SCHOUREK, PIT
(1998: HOU-BOS)

Pete hasn't fully recovered from his 1996 injuries, and while he's been able to make more starts, he's not making very much progress. The chances of him becoming a sub-seven pitcher again appear to be getting rather remote. **<DM>**

Year	GS	S	C	T
1998	23	4.09	3.65	7.74
1997	17	3.76	4.00	7.76
1996	12	4.75	3.58	8.33
1995	29	3.34	2.79	6.14
1994	10	4.30	3.60	7.90

AARON SELE, TEX

Now here's an 19-game winner built out of run support—6.27 runs worth, to be exact. Aaron improved his command, but the fact is he still didn't pitch as well as he did in 1994. **<DM>**

Year	GS	S	C	T
1998	33	4.42	3.55	7.97
1997	33	4.24	4.06	8.30
1996	29	4.69	3.79	8.48
1995	6	4.00	4.00	8.00
1994	22	4.05	3.41	7.45

DAN SERAFINI, MIN

1997's Benj Sampson: the major difference is that Serafini has less stuff. The Twins have a bushel's full of problematic prospects to choose from as they try to figure out what their #2-#5 slots behind Radke will look like. Memo to Tom (Mole) Kelly: when in doubt, pick 'em out of a hat. **<DM>**

Year	GS	S	C	T
1998	9	4.89	4.11	9.00
1997	4	4.25	3.25	7.50
1996	1	6.00	4.00	10.00

MIKE SIROTKA, CHW

A classic Jekyll/Hyde pitcher, Sirotka had 21% of his starts in the Elite Square, but was Hit Hard just under half the time. He's gotten his command in line with his minor league performance, but he's just too hittable to ever be more than a #4-5 guy. On the White Sox right now, however, he is their "ace." **<DM>**

Year	GS	S	C	T
1998	33	4.79	2.67	7.45
1997	4	4.50	2.25	6.75
1996	4	4.50	4.25	8.75
1995	6	4.83	3.83	8.67

JOHN SMILEY, CLE

He ought to be well-rested, that's for sure. But there's at least as much uncertainty about whether he'll pitch again as there is concerning Ben McDonald. Maybe the A's will wind up with both of 'em. Cleared waivers and was outrighted to the Indians' AAA farm club over the winter. **<DM>**

Year	GS	S	C	T
1997	26	4.65	2.92	7.58
1996	34	3.71	2.85	6.56
1995	27	3.89	2.63	6.52
1994	24	4.25	2.75	7.00

PETE SMITH, FA
(1998: SD-BAL)

Replacement filler at best. I really don't see him getting another shot anywhere in the big leagues at this point. **<DM>**

Year	GS	S	C	T
1998	12	4.75	4.08	8.83
1997	15	4.00	3.87	7.87
1995	2	6.00	4.50	10.50
1994	21	4.43	3.24	7.67

JOHN SNYDER, CHW

His monthly QWPs showed a steady progression after his July 4th debut against the Red Sox (.449, .526, .593). Even though his minor league record is completely bereft of any indication that he'd do even this well in the majors, stranger things have happened; he just might become a solid #3-4 starter for the Sox. Then again, he could be the next John Doherty. **<DM>**

Year	GS	S	C	T
1998	14	4.29	3.07	7.36

STEVE SPARKS, ANA

You gotta love these knuckleballers, especially the ones that drop completely out of sight for an entire year. Sparks fit in with the messiest pitching staff in the AL last season, and he stood out (like a sore thumb) as the Halos' second best starter. That revelation should make Terry Collins and the Edison Field faithful ready to simultaneously roll over and, er, knuckle under. **<DM>**

Year, GS		S	C	T
1998	20	3.90	3.85	7.75
1996	13	4.85	4.08	8.92
1995	27	4.22	3.33	7.56

PAUL SPOLJARIC, PHI
(1998: SEA)

Strictly an emergency, throw-in-the-towel starter after the Big Unit was shipped in that package crate to Houston. Not even Lou (the Master of Chaos) Piniella could seriously consider continuing such a charade, but Woody Woodward has made sure of that by trading Paul to the Phillies for Mark Leiter (of all people). **<DM>**

Year	GS	S	C	T
1998	6	4.33	4.67	9.00
1994	1	4.00	7.00	11.00

DENNIS SPRINGER, FA
(1998: TB)

The X-orcist wound up being excommunicated (as in sent to the minors) midway through the Stingers' inaugural season. He pitched a lot better in relief, and may soon embark on a new phase of his career as the next Hoyt Wilhelm. On second thought, better make that Bobby Tiefenauer. (That's Bobby "the X-orcist" Tiefenauer to you, Malcolm.) **<DM>**

Year	GS	S	C	T
1998	17	4.35	4.18	8.53
1997	28	4.04	3.18	7.21
1996	15	3.67	3.73	7.40
1995	4	3.75	4.00	7.75

BLAKE STEIN, OAK

One of the three amigos picked up by the A's in the Mark McGwire deal (no, the other two weren't named Moe and Curly. . .), Stein pitched well against Kansas City and the White Sox, and had a terrible time against just about everyone else, developing more and more control problems as the season wore on. It's just another indication that Bob Cluck's replacement, Rick Peterson, was no more effective in working with young pitchers, and it leaves the A's staff in a similar amount of disarray even as their young team of hitters gets closer to being ready for prime-time. There's a serious chance that the A's offense will be all dressed up with no place to go. <DM>

Year	GS	S	C	T
1998	20	4.05	4.20	8.25

TODD STOTTLEMYRE, AZ
(1998: STL-TEX)

Hey, you thought Brad Radke had a bad patch? Check this out. At the end of June, Todd Stottlemyre ranked fourth in the NL QMAX race, with a 5.50 "T" score. Over his next twelve starts, during which time he was traded to the Texas Rangers, Todd tossed out a really chewy 9.75 "T" average, including eight games (67%) in which he was Hit Hard. Thanks to the big bats of his teammates, Todd managed to win three times during this stretch (including back-to-back 6,6 and 7,4 outings), but he was doubtless relieved when the Rangers rolled into Tampa Bay to face the stinger-less Devil Rays. Stottlemyre promptly threw a five-hitter, and got back on track just in time to help boost Texas into their mercifully brief post-season. Todd has signed on with the D-backs for 1999. <DM>

Year	GS	S	C	T
1998	33	3.88	3.12	7.00
1997	28	3.29	3.21	6.50
1996	33	3.21	3.36	6.58
1995	31	4.39	3.16	7.55
1994	19	4.53	2.89	7.42

JEFF SUPPAN, KC
(1998: AZ-KC)

Run out of Phoenix by an angry cactus-wielding mob, Jeff landed in KC and promptly coughed up six innings of shutout ball against the White Sox, making him the new savior of the Royals. Jeff is one of those guys who looks so smooth on the mound that it's easy to forget that he's getting hammered. There were a few signs of marginal progress this year, but at this rate there will be another ice age before Jeff develops into Mike Maddux, much less Greg. <DM>

Year	GS	S	C	T
1998	14	4.57	3.64	8.21
1997	22	4.82	3.68	8.50
1996	4	4.75	4.75	9.50
1995	3	6.33	3.67	10.00

MAC SUZUKI, SEA

After all that hype about "Mac the Knife," the future closer of the Mariners, Seattle quietly turned Suzuki into a starter, and brought him up in September. The results weren't too encouraging, but considering some of their other choices, I think we'll probably see more of Mac in 1999 and possibly beyond. Hara-kiri, anyone?? <DM>

Year	GS	S	C	T
1998	5	4.80	4.40	9.20

BILL SWIFT, FA
(1998: SEA)

"Dear Roger: Thanks for pushing me to be the best I could be. Thanks to you and your slapdashing ways, I've become an old man before my time. I spend so much time in the whirlpool that my skin is permanently pickled. I've had to learn to write with my left hand My wife won't sleep in the same bed with me anymore. People have begun to mistake me for the Creature from the Black Lagoon. And I owe it all to you, the great Zen master of Humm Baby. The only solace I have is in joining CAD Anonymous, where people with Chronic Arm Damage can get together and curse you over cheese dip and soft drinks. If those cattle on your ranch trample you in a stampede, it will be too kind a way for you to go. Instead of the split finger, I salute you with the middle finger. Your pal, Billy" <DM>

Year	GS	S	C	T
1998	26	4.77	3.62	8.38
1997	13	4.77	3.77	8.54
1996	3	5.33	3.67	9.00
1995	19	4.53	3.74	8.26
1994	17	3.65	2.82	6.47

BOB TEWKSBURY, FA
(1998: MIN)

Oakland is the place where Bob should wind up in 1999, I think. The price will be right, thanks to that terrible September (0-4, 8.46 ERA) he turned in, and the A's need more aging innings-eaters while they try to nurse along another crop of undernourished pitching prospects. As the numbers below indicate, Tewk has been the quintessential poor man's Tommy John for five years in a row, and I'm beginning to think he

could do this blindfolded. <DM>

Year	GS	S	C	T
1998	25	4.40	2.60	7.00
1997	26	4.65	2.54	7.19
1996	33	4.21	2.79	7.00
1995	21	5.14	2.57	7.71
1994	24	4.75	2.38	7.13

JUSTIN THOMPSON, DET

The Tigers have pushed Justin very hard, especially considering his past history of arm trouble, and I have to wonder whether he's going to pay the price. As you would expect from such a sizable downturn in ERA and the basic QMAX data, Thompson also fell off across the board in the Sector and Range data as well: SS (65 to 47); ES (25 to 15); HH (up to 29 from 19); S12 (44 to 35); and C13 (75 to 59). He was a below league-average pitcher for the last two months of the season. Detroit doesn't have enough of a surplus of talent to be playing brinksmanship with one of their best players. <DM>

Year	GS	S	C	T
1998	34	4.03	3.24	7.26
1997	32	3.28	2.69	5.97
1996	11	4.27	4.09	8.36

TERRELL WADE, TB

Larry Rothschild's fascination with Power Precipice pitchers might well need to be upgraded to an obsession when we witness the return of Terrell Wade to the big leagues. There are very few pitchers who can strike fear in the hearts of their catchers when they go into their delivery; Wade is one of those. There is a perverse side of me (a big surprise to long-time readers, no doubt. . .) that wants to see 30+ starts of this. But I think Larry has more sense than that, and Tampa has more pitching than that, too. <DM>

MISCELLANEOUS STARTING PITCHER DATA, AMERICAN LEAGUE 1998

LEGEND: NP—Number of Pitches thrown; TW—Team Wins in pitcher's starts; TL—Team losses in pitcher's starts; GS ; QS Quality Starts; BS—Blown Starts; QmB—Quality minus Blown pct.; PPI—Pitches thrown Per Inning; IP—Innings Pitched; AdIP—Adjusted Innings Pitched; IP/S—average Innings Pitched per Start

Pitcher Name	Tm	TW	TL	GS	QS	BS	QMB	IP	NP	Str	PPI	Kpct	AdjIP	IP/S
Jamie Moyer	SEA	18	16	34	21	4	50.00	234.3	3559	2226	15.19	62.5%	218	6.9
Randy Johnson	SEA	11	12	23	13	2	47.83	160.0	2713	1709	16.96	63.0%	166	7.0
Jeff Fassero	SEA	16	16	32	15	2	40.63	224.7	3530	2196	15.71	62.2%	216	7.0
Makoto Suzuki	SEA	1	4	5	2	1	20.00	24.7	431	255	17.48	59.2%	26	4.9
Bill Swift	SEA	12	14	26	9	5	15.38	140.7	2268	1368	16.12	60.3%	139	5.4
Ken Cloude	SEA	13	17	30	11	10	3.33	155.3	2779	1692	17.89	60.9%	170	5.2
Paul Spoljaric	SEA	2	4	6	1	2	-16.67	26.7	498	299	18.67	60.0%	30	4.4
Jim Bullinger	SEA	0	1	1	0	0	-100.00	3.3	81	45	24.32	55.6%	5	3.3
Tony Saunders	TBD	10	21	31	20	5	48.39	192.3	3400	1995	17.68	58.7%	208	6.2
Julio Santana	TBD	9	10	19	10	2	42.11	116.7	1929	1156	16.53	59.9%	118	6.1
Rolando Arrojo	TBD	17	15	32	17	4	40.63	202.0	3153	1955	15.61	62.0%	193	6.3
Bryan Rekar	TBD	4	11	15	6	2	26.67	85.7	1420	905	16.58	63.7%	87	5.7
Wilson Alvarez	TBD	10	15	25	10	6	16.00	142.7	2479	1489	17.38	60.1%	152	5.7
Jason Johnson	TBD	6	7	13	4	2	15.38	60.0	1080	652	18.00	60.4%	66	4.6
Rick Gorecki	TBD	1	2	3	1	1	0.00	16.7	286	163	17.16	57.0%	18	5.6
Matt Ruebel	TBD	0	1	1	0	0	0.00	4.3	85	51	19.63	60.0%	5	4.3
Dennis Springer	TBD	5	12	17	3	3	0.00	93.0	1543	901	16.59	58.4%	94	5.5

MISCELLANEOUS STARTING PITCHER DATA, AMERICAN LEAGUE 1998

LEGEND: NP—Number of Pitches thrown; **TW**—Team Wins in pitcher's starts; **TL**—Team Losses in pitcher's starts; **GS**—; **QS**—Quality Starts; **BS**—Blown Starts; **QmB**—Quality minus Blown pct.; **PPI**—Pitches thrown Per Inning; **IP**—Innings Pitched; **AdIP**—Adjusted Innings Pitched; **IP/S**—average Innings Pitched per Start

PITCHER NAME	TM	TW	TL	GS	QS	BS	QMB	IP	NP	STR	PPI	KPCT	ADJIP	IP/S
Terrell Wade	TBD	1	1	2	0	0	0.00	10.7	151	96	14.15	63.6%	9	5.3
Rick White	TBD	0	3	3	1	1	0.00	14.3	253	153	17.66	60.5%	15	4.8
Dave Eiland	TBD	0	1	1	0	1	-100.00	2.7	66	32	24.72	48.5%	4	2.7
Rick Helling	TEX	25	8	33	17	3	42.42	216.3	3518	2181	16.26	62.0%	215	6.6
Aaron Sele	TEX	21	12	33	18	7	33.33	212.7	3516	2134	16.53	60.7%	215	6.4
Todd Stottlemyre	TEX	5	5	10	5	2	30.00	60.3	1058	641	17.54	60.6%	65	6.0
John Burkett	TEX	12	20	32	11	8	9.38	195.0	2995	1901	15.36	63.5%	183	6.1
Estaban Loaiza	TEX	6	8	14	5	4	7.14	79.3	1260	811	15.88	64.4%	77	5.7
Jonathan Johnson	TEX	1	0	1	0	0	0.00	4.3	93	48	21.48	51.6%	6	4.3
Darren Oliver	TEX	11	8	19	6	6	0.00	103.3	1777	1068	17.20	60.1%	109	5.4
Bobby Witt	TEX	6	7	13	3	4	-7.69	68.3	1132	676	16.57	59.7%	69	5.3
Todd Van Poppel	TEX	1	3	4	1	2	-25.00	19.3	340	200	17.62	58.8%	21	4.8
Eric Gunderson	TEX	0	1	1	0	1	-100.00	1.7	40	22	23.95	55.0%	2	1.7
Matt Perisho	TEX	0	2	2	0	2	-100.00	5.0	151	78	30.20	51.7%	9	2.5
Kelvim Escobar	TOR	7	3	10	8	0	80.00	69.0	1142	686	16.55	60.1%	70	6.9
Roger Clemens	TOR	24	9	33	25	1	72.73	234.7	3800	2279	16.19	60.0%	233	7.1
Roy Halladay	TOR	2	0	2	1	0	50.00	14.0	188	127	13.43	67.6%	12	7.0
Woody Williams	TOR	14	18	32	18	3	46.88	209.7	3540	2042	16.88	61.1%	217	6.6
Juan Guzman	TOR	9	13	22	13	3	45.45	145.0	2415	1450	16.66	60.0%	148	6.6
Pat Hentgen	TOR	14	15	29	14	5	31.03	177.7	2892	1781	16.28	61.6%	177	6.1
Chris Carpenter	TOR	14	10	24	12	5	29.17	152.3	2439	1508	16.01	61.8%	149	6.3
Erik Hanson	TOR	3	4	8	4	2	25.00	45.0	836	479	18.58	57.3%	51	5.6
Dave Stieb	TOR	1	2	3	0	1	-33.33	15.7	288	172	18.38	59.7%	18	5.2

YEAR	GS	S	C	T
1998	2	5.00	3.50	8.50
1997	9	5.44	4.11	9.56
1996	8	3.38	5.00	8.38

TIM WAKEFIELD, BOS

Basically, Tim is the perfect #4-5 starter for the Red Sox, a good, reliable innings-eater who can get hot for a couple of months. The stretch that Boston has been making over the past few seasons is trying to make Tim operate as the #3 guy. That's a job he's not really up to. Wakefield was much more of a middle-of-the-road pitcher in '98—he cut his HH% in half, but he had only 6% of his starts in the Elite Square, less than half of what he achieved in '97. <DM>

YEAR	GS	S	C	T
1998	33	3.91	3.33	7.24
1997	29	4.00	3.52	7.52
1996	32	4.31	3.41	7.72
1995	27	3.07	2.96	6.04

JAMIE WALKER, KC

An advanced-age prospect whom the Royals held in 1997 as a Rule V draftee, and who couldn't keep a slot on the big club when they were no longer forced to hold him. We have probably heard the last of him. <DM>

YEAR	GS	S	C	T
1998	2	5.50	3.00	8.50

JOHN WASDIN, BOS

May well get another shot at the #5 job, though he appears to have gotten a lot more hittable in the past year. He's more likely to wind up in middle relief, where his stuff might hold up better. <DM>

YEAR	GS	S	C	T
1998	8	5.25	3.25	8.50
1997	7	3.86	4.00	7.86
1996	21	4.29	3.57	7.86
1995	2	4.00	3.00	7.00

JARROD WASHBURN, ANA

I'm trying to recall the last time a starting pitcher got farmed out with a 5-2 record; that's what happened to Jarrod this year. At the time he was the second best pitcher on the Angels' staff. As Joe Garagiola used to say, baseball is a funny game. <DM>

YEAR	GS	S	C	T
1998	11	3.82	3.27	7.09

ALLEN WATSON, ANA

The Angels finally gave up and tossed Allen into the bullpen in August, where he pitched reasonably well. One presumes they'll keep him there until they are absolutely forced to do otherwise. <DM>

YEAR	GS	S	C	T
1998	14	5.00	3.93	8.93
1997	34	4.32	3.59	7.91
1996	29	4.03	3.34	7.38
1995	19	4.47	3.84	8.32
1994	22	4.23	4.00	8.23

DAVID WELLS, NYY

Boomer's pinnacle, and he didn't lose an inch in the post-season, either, posting a 4.75 QMAX "T" in his four starts. A really big big-game pitcher: in 1998, 37% of his starts were in the Elite Square. Only Greg Maddux and Pedro Martinez have done better than that in the past five years.

Will he keep it up? Probably not. This has career year written all over it. But he should be around 6.30-6.50 next year; for Yankee fans basking in the glow of 125 wins, that may be a big disappointment, however. <DM>

YEAR	GS	S	C	T
1998	30	3.60	2.00	5.60
1997	32	4.22	2.53	6.75
1996	33	4.33	2.73	7.06
1995	29	3.72	2.55	6.28
1994	16	4.19	2.31	6.50

RICK WHITE, TB

Sean Lahman can probably tell me for sure, but it sure looks like Larry Rothschild must have worked for Jim Leyland in Pittsburgh, too, as there were several former Pirates who wound up with the Stingers. Except in White's case, he was with them before they were in the AL: he pitched for Tampa's AA farm club in Orlando in 1997.

And was pretty darned mediocre then, too. <DM>

YEAR	GS	S	C	T
1998	3	4.33	5.00	9.33
1995	9	5.11	3.33	8.44
1994	5	4.00	2.60	6.60

WOODY WILLIAMS, SD
(1998:TOR)

The Wood-man is truly a bizarre and fascinating pitcher. Check out these two QMAX profiles:

S	C	T	SS	ES	PP	TJ	S12
2.17	2.83	5.00	83%	33%	17%	0%	67%
4.60	1.80	6.40	20%	20%	0%	60%	20%

Completely opposite pitching styles, right? This is Woody Williams in back-to-back months.

Needless to say, I'm entranced by this guy, and while I doubt that he's going to get much better, I have to admit that it would be appropriately astonishing if he could pull off either of these contrasting styles for an entire year.

But I think that, like the Big Lebowski, such consistency and oppressive orderliness would just bore the living bejesus out of the Wood-man. Waywardness is a way of life for Woody, and we should be grateful for witnessing his like. <DM>

YEAR	GS	S	C	T
1998	32	3.78	3.25	7.03
1997	31	4.19	3.29	7.48
1996	10	3.90	3.30	7.20
1995	3	2.67	4.33	7.00

JAY WITASICK, OAK

The archetypal "failed closer," Jay-boy has been converted back to a starter, which is how he began in the Cardinal organization. The results do not have TV mini-series written all over them. <DM>

Year	GS	S	C	T
1998	3	6.00	4.33	10.33

TIM WORRELL, OAK
(1998: DET-OAK)

The A's managed to avoid putting Worrell into their starting rotation after acquiring him from the Tigers, but the numbers say that he's just about at the same level as everyone they have behind Rogers and Candiotti. All of which tells you what the state of the A's rotation is, of course. More revealingly, the A's picked Tim up because of their leaky bullpen; it didn't occur to Art Howe that the best fix might have been to switch several pitchers' roles (e.g. Haynes and Stein) to see if their particular difficulties were lessened by pitching fewer innings per appearance. And conversely, no one has ever seen fit to give Worrell 20 consecutive starts to see if he can successfully adjust to the role. <DM>

Year	GS	S	C	T
1998	9	4.56	3.44	8.00
1997	10	4.20	4.10	8.30
1996	11	4.73	3.36	8.09
1994	3	2.67	3.67	6.33

JARET WRIGHT, CLE

Jaret lost ground in every ancillary QMAX category except for the ES% in 1998, which leaves only a faint flicker of hope for him to transform himself into something more than an enigmatic, hard-throwing #4 pitcher. Running a slightly more involved version of the 15-start QMAX projection method where 5-start and 10-start running averages are worked in, we get the following ranges of possibility for Jaret in 1999:

Scenario	S	C	T
Best	3.61	3.47.	7.08
Worst	4.34	3.90	8.24
Likely	4.01	3.63	7.64

As you can see, the "best" case scenario still leaves Jaret in the #4 starter range—though if he did manage that, it would be evidence for another possible level of evolution. If he winds up around the "likely" scenario, however, that would tend to confirm the tentative conclusion reached above.

Year	GS	S	C	T
1998	32	4.38	3.78	8.16
1997	16	3.69	3.75	7.44

PLAYER COMMENTS
National League

STARTING PITCHERS

JUAN ACEVEDO, STL

LaRussa-and-Duncan (we like to think of them as the Chang and Eng of baseball) got pretty desperate for a closer in late July and tossed Juan into the role, where he did quite well. He'd probably be a good #3-4 starter for the Cards, and it appears that he'll be in that role in 1999, since the Cards traded for Ricky Bottalico during the off-season. <DM>

Year	GS	S	C	T
1998	9	3.89	2.89	6.78
1997	2	2.50	4.50	7.00
1995	11	4.36	3.73	8.09

BRIAN ANDERSON, AZ

The Snakes' #1 pick had an interesting year of it, and showed himself to be a true member of the Tommy John school of grinning, charismatic finesse pitchers. (OK, maybe his smile is a bit too broad to be considered either charismatic or a grin; quibbling will only get you a left hook from Bunsey.)

As that stellar 2.22 "C" average below should indicate, Brian developed tremendous command this year. He also served up 39 homers, and batters' isolated power (ISO) against him was .199, a couple of standard deviations over the league average. That QMAX "S" value, as we've discussed earlier, needs to be adjusted in this case to reflect the added XBH power in those hits. When we do so, Brian's QMAX "S" is adjusted upward significantly (and that's not good). The revised "S" value goes all the way up to 4.95, which makes Brian into one of the harder hit pitchers around, and brings his 1998 performance more in line with the

league and with his past record.

That said, Brian still was a bit above league average in 1998, and if he can cut down on his ISO, could be close to what the conventional QMAX shows—a solid finesse pitcher with great control. While I don't think he'll necessarily hold that 2.22 "C" average, it's clear that he's going to be among the league leaders in that category for as long as he can survive the barrage of extra-base hits. <DM>

Year	GS	S	C	T
1998	32	4.25	2.22	6.47
QMAXX	32	4.95	2.22	7.17
1997	8	4.25	2.88	7.13
1996	9	4.44	3.22	7.67
1995	17	4.29	3.53	7.82
1994	18	4.44	3.28	7.72

ANDY ASHBY, SD

Until August, Andy Ashby was outpitching Kevin Brown and was the Padres' best starter. But Andy is a fragile pitcher, one who has spent some part of the last few seasons with arm problems, and he was clearly done in by the workload, posting QMAX "T" averages of over eight in both August and September. Those difficulties extended into the post-season, but thanks to the performances of Brown and Sterling Hitchcock, the Padres were able to work around it until the World Series, where Andy hit bottom.

He's still a fine pitcher, but the Padres really need to monitor his workload a lot more carefully. Bruce Bochy, a former wearer of the tools of ignorance, appears to be ignorant of this problem, as he's been handling Andy for four years now with similar results. <DM>

Year	GS	S	C	T
1998	33	3.76	2.67	6.42
1997	30	4.10	2.67	6.77
1996	24	3.88	2.75	6.63
1995	31	3.77	3.10	6.87
1994	24	3.46	2.75	6.21

PEDRO ASTACIO, COL

Welcome to Denver, Pedro. It's sure not like pitching a sea-level, is it? <DM>

Year	GS	S	C	T
1998	34	4.74	3.44	8.18
1997	31	3.94	3.06	7.00
1996	32	4.06	3.03	7.09
1995	11	4.09	3.73	7.82
1994	23	3.83	3.13	6.96

MANNY AYBAR, STL

Manny's S12% (best hit prevention games) fell below the life-support line this year (15%), and it's unlikely that the Cards will keep him on the respirator much longer. Still, the guy dominated in AAA last year (10-0, 2.60 ERA), so he'll get another chance somewhere. <DM>

Year	GS	S	C	T
1998	13	4.69	4.38	9.08
1997	12	3.92	3.67	7.58

ROGER BAILEY, COL

Roger didn't make it very far in his attempt to rebound from arm injuries in 1998, getting pummeled for an 8.71 ERA in Class A ball, with 11 walks in 10 1/3 IP. A finesse pitcher in Coors Field is a recipe for CAD (Chronic Arm Damage), and this looks to be no exception. <DM>

Year	GS	S	C	T
1997	29	4.45	3.28	7.72
1996	11	4.27	4.09	8.36
1995	6	4.33	3.33	7.67

MIGUEL BATISTA, MON

This is the guy the Expos got for Henry Rodriguez, and he's the type of pitcher Felipe Alou just loves—someone who can seemingly move from one role to another without apparent performance impact. He had two brief stretches in the Expo rotation in '98—one from late April to early June, and another in September. Here are the QMAX values for those two stretches:

When	S	C	T
4/29-5/31	4.14	4.29	8.43
9/1-9/25	3.20	4.20	7.40

It will be interesting to see, now that Felipe Alou is going to stay on in Montreal, whether Batista gets a more extended shot at the starting rotation. He clearly pitched better as a starter, and I doubt that Felipe has missed that point. <DM>

Year	GS	S	C	T
1998	13	3.77	4.31	8.08
1997	6	4.17	5.00	9.17

MATT BEECH, PHI

Matt goes into the minus column for QMAX, as his last ten starts of 1997 were not, in fact, an indication of impending improvement. As we refine the use of QMAX to project starter performance, though, we're beginning to see these small sample size snapshots as gradations of potential, and not as ironclad forecasts. I still think there's a scenario where Beech could reach the 6.70 "T" range, but it's just not very likely given what else we know. Running Matt's 1997 season through the more advanced version of the experimental 15-start QMAX projection method, we get the following forecast range for his 1998:

Scenario	S	C	T
Best	3.73	3.54	7.27
Worst	4.28	3.77	8.05
Likely	4.06	3.65	7.71

There just isn't anything in Matt's previous major or minor league numbers that will predict a big decline in his "C" average. But that's exactly what happened, and we'd be remiss if we didn't show it to you. Using more data (all of 1996-98), we get the following projection for Matt in 1999:

Scenario	S	C	T
Best	3.99	3.53	7.54
Worst	4.24	3.89	8.13
Likely	4.13	3.74	7.87

We're still not getting him up to the "C" value he had in 1998, but note that the "best" scenario has moved up a good bit (and up is not good in QMAX). And you can see that most of this change is actually in the "S"

value, because Matt hasn't been able to improve his hit prevention. Frankly, a lot of the trends we're applying to the forecast need more data points in order to be better validated; there's a lot more heavy-duty number-crunching required to get a handle on this. But it's interesting enough to preview, and who better to use it on than guys we didn't get right? Check back in next year's book to see how we do. <DM>

Year	GS	S	C	T
1998	21	4.29	4.10	8.38
1997	24	4.29	3.71	8.00
1996	8	4.63	3.38	8.00

ALAN BENES, STL

Alan missed the entire 1998 season due to the insane workload that LaRussa-and-Duncan imposed on him in 1997 (21 straight starts with 100+ pitches—for a look at that workload in context, check out the Bartolo Colon comment over in the AL). One only hopes that the extra time off will allow Alan to regain his 1997 form, and that the Mangler Brothers will have learned their lesson. (To their belated credit, it appears that they were a lot more cautious with Cardinal starters in 1998.) Good luck, Alan. <DM>

Year	GS	S	C	T
1997	23	3.04	3.17	6.22
1996	32	3.94	3.81	7.75
1995	3	5.67	3.33	9.00

ANDY BENES, AZ

Big Brother wound up in Phoenix and had a fairly typical year, starting slowly and then coming on like a house afire in the final months. (That's another great phrase, though not quite as evocative as "shit on a shingle," which is still served at Goody's Restaurant in Fort Bragg, CA., in case any of your army

---

MISCELLANEOUS STARTING PITCHER DATA, NATIONAL LEAGUE 1998

LEGEND: NP—Number of Pitches thrown; **TW**—Team Wins in pitcher's starts; **TL**—Team Losses in pitcher's starts; **GS**—; **QS**—Quality Starts; **BS**—Blown Starts; **QmB**—Quality minus Blown pct.; **PPI**—Pitches thrown Per Inning; **IP**—Innings Pitched; **AdIP**—Adjusted Innings Pitched; **IP/S**—average Innings Pitched per Start

Pitcher Name	Team	TW	TL	GS	QS	BS	QMB	IP	NP	Str	PPI	Kpct	AdIP	IP/S
Omar Daal	ARZ	10	12	22	13	1	54.55	145.3	2173	1372	14.95	63.1%	138	6.6
Brian Anderson	ARZ	16	16	32	19	5	43.75	208.0	2820	1893	13.56	67.1%	179	6.5
Andy Benes	ARZ	16	18	34	19	5	41.18	231.3	3684	2234	15.92	60.6%	234	6.8
Amaury Telemaco	ARZ	8	10	18	10	3	38.89	104.3	1597	1003	15.31	62.8%	102	5.8
Willie Blair	ARZ	5	18	23	10	4	26.09	146.7	2288	1378	15.60	60.2%	146	6.4
Bobby Chouinard	ARZ	0	2	2	0	0	0.00	6.0	86	51	14.33	59.3%	5	3.0
Clint Sodowsky	ARZ	3	3	6	1	1	0.00	28.7	491	283	17.13	57.6%	31	4.8
Jeff Suppan	ARZ	5	8	13	3	5	-15.38	66.0	1114	712	16.88	63.9%	71	5.1
Bob Wolcott	ARZ	1	5	6	1	2	-16.67	33.0	500	317	15.15	63.4%	32	5.5
Joel Adamson	ARZ	1	4	5	1	2	-20.00	23.0	354	205	15.39	57.9%	23	4.6
Greg Maddux	ATL	18	9	34	28	2	76.47	251.0	3311	2217	13.19	67.0%	211	7.4
Tom Glavine	ATL	24	9	33	26	2	72.73	229.3	3584	2165	15.63	60.4%	228	6.9
Denny Neagle	ATL	18	13	31	21	1	64.52	208.3	3199	2048	15.36	64.0%	203	6.7
John Smoltz	ATL	22	4	26	17	2	57.69	167.7	2461	1629	14.68	66.2%	157	6.4
Kevin Millwood	ATL	19	10	29	16	6	34.48	171.7	2884	1846	16.80	64.0%	183	5.9
Bruce Chen	ATL	3	1	4	2	1	25.00	20.3	352	212	17.31	60.2%	22	5.1
Dennis Martinez	ATL	1	4	5	2	1	20.00	26.3	401	271	15.22	67.6%	26	5.3

brats out there are interested.) Andy was particularly spectacular in September (an eye-popping 1.40 QMAX "S" and an .865 QWP for the month), and he was much more of a big-game pitcher (21% ES to just 47% SS) in 1998. He wasn't as dominating (S12 of only 29% instead of 46% in '97), but his command was sharper (18% of his games were C1, up from 8% the year before).

Needless to say, the Cardinals (who ran out of time in trying to re-sign Andy after the '97 season) would have loved to have had this year from him, even if it was a bit off the previous one. <DM>

Year	GS	S	C	T
1998	34	3.91	2.91	6.82
1997	26	3.08	3.00	6.08
1996	34	3.47	2.97	6.44
1995	31	4.13	3.74	7.87
1994	25	3.44	2.88	6.32

JASON BERE, CIN
(1998: CHW-CIN)

Jason pitched a lot better in his seven starts for the Reds than he did while going through pre-partum depression with the White Sox:

Team	S	C	T	SS%	S12%	C13/C47
CHW	4.67	4.93	9.60	13%	7%	13/87
CIN	3.29	3.71	7.00	70%	57%	57/43

Now, did the Reds discover something and correct it, or is this just part of Jason's mood swing thing that has been immortalized in all those slasher movies? (In sociology and film studies, they call it "random violence"; in statistics, we call it "random variation.") I'd chalk it up to a small sample and to the level of competition Jason faced (Expos, D-backs, and Pirates were among the teams), but we'll know soon enough—Jack is going to stick Jason into the Reds' rotation in 1999, trying to forget what he did in Chicago last summer. <DM>

Year	GS	S	C	T
1998	22	4.23	4.55	8.77
1997	6	2.67	4.67	7.33
1996	5	5.40	6.20	11.60
1995	27	4.48	4.93	9.41
1994	24	3.42	4.33	7.75

SEAN BERGMAN, HOU

Larry Dierker used a powerhouse offense to nurse through a mostly non-descript group of finesse pitching starters, and Bergman was one of those, a guy who stepped in when injuries to Chris Holt and Ramon Garcia (a couple of other non-descript finesse pitchers) left gaping holes in the rotation. Larry now has to decide if he wants to move Scott Elarton into the rotation, and he may also have Garcia and Holt back as well. It's looking crowded enough that Bergman will be the odd man out. <DM>

Year	GS	S	C	T
1998	27	4.48	2.93	7.41
1997	9	5.33	4.33	9.67
1996	14	4.29	3.36	7.64
1995	28	4.89	4.29	9.18
1994	3	5.00	3.67	8.67

WILLIE BLAIR, DET
(1998: AZ-NYM)

The vagaries of run support: Blair got more than five runs a game in Detroit during 1997, and won 16 games; he got just over three runs a game in 1998, and lost 16. He had two widely spaced starts during his two-month tenure with the Mets, and they were both "1S" games. One really wants to know why Bobby Valentine didn't see fit to turn to him again. In the right park, where his penchant for the gopher ball can be minimized, he's a serviceable #4-5 guy. Now back in Detroit, which isn't really the right park, but is the scene of Willie's lone success. <DM>

Year	GS	S	C	T
1998	25	4.20	3.12	7.32
1997	27	4.26	2.96	7.22
1995	12	3.58	3.58	7.17
1994	1	6.00	4.00	10.00

BRIAN BOHANON, COL
(1998: NYM-LA)

Bohanon came to the Dodgers in what us wags are now calling the Second Greg McMichael Trade (analogous, perhaps, to the Second Punic War), and it was a ridiculous ripoff, at least in 1998. Brian's "T" score with the Dodgers was 5.86, but LA could only go 5-9 in his starts due to putting up just over three runs a game when Brian was on the mound. That always seems to be the kind of thing that happens to a guy like Bohanon, who has been scuffling around the fringes of MLB for most of the decade. Brian was signed to a $9 million, three-year contract by the Rockies, as they continue to move away from their Coors southpaw phobia. <DM>

Year	GS	S	C	T
1998	18	2.89	3.28	6.17
1997	14	3.93	3.14	7.07
1995	10	4.90	4.50	9.40
1994	5	5.00	3.40	8.40

SHAWN BOSKIE, MON

As we've said umpteen times in these pages, there's just no reason for anyone to keep putting Shawn into the starting rotation. The guy is a relief pitcher, end of story. Don't these organizations read the STATS breakouts? From 1993-97, Shawn's ERA as a starter was 5.75; as a reliever, it was 3.68. It's about as plain as the nose on Jimmy Durante's face. <DM>

Year	GS	S	C	T
1998	5	6.00	4.00	10.00
1997	9	4.89	3.78	8.67
1996	28	4.71	3.36	8.07
1995	20	4.50	3.20	7.70
1994	15	4.07	3.60	7.67

KENT BOTTENFIELD, STL

Mister Adenoids himself, Ralph Barbieri of KNBR in San Francisco, was jeering the Giants for getting shut down by Bottenfield last July 23rd. It turned out that a lot of the NL had trouble with Kent after he was plucked from the Cardinal bullpen by LaRussa-and-Duncan. And once again, the umbilical cord tying together desperation and creativity got wrapped around Ralph's ungodly vocal cords; until he was shut down in September by an elbow problem, Bottenfield outpitched all but one of the Giants' starters, and became a very minor footnote in the 1998 Cardinal legacy. Ralph, of course, remains a major ear-sore for beleaguered Bay Area radio listeners. <DM>

Year	GS	S	C	T
1998	17	3.47	3.94	7.41
1994	1	6.00	6.00	12.00

KEVIN BROWN, LA
(1998: SD)

Should have done my homework with the start-by-start database last year. Brown had a great season for the Padres, and was a major reason why that talented but creaky franchise made it to the World Series. The major warning signal in 1997, a jump in Kevin's HH% from 9 to 27, didn't matter at all, especially given that Jimmy Qualls-com Stadium turned into a massive pitcher's park in 1998.

Which raises the question: did Brown take advantage of his home park? Here's the QMAX data:

Where	S	C	T
Home	3.05	1.73	4.78
Away	3.94	2.63	6.57

Why, yes, he did—though, interestingly, he actually won more games on the road because the Padres scored more for him there. In any event, I think it's a much safer prediction this time around that Brown will decline—though I expect him to have a couple more very good seasons in his next location. <DM>

Brown's amazing $105 million contract is an artifact of supply and demand, and the desperation of the Fox media hounds to DO something. Kevin's ERA from age 31-33 is the second best since 1946 behind Bob Gibson (but remember that Greg Maddux hasn't had his age-33 year yet).

All in all, we found 22 other pitchers who averaged 200+ IP from ages 31-33 with at least 45 wins (15 per year) and an aggregate ERA of 3.25 or better. Here's how those pitchers' careers play out over the next seven years:

age	No.	W	IP	ERA
31-33	23	18	264	2.88
34	22	15	241	3.20
35	22	13	201	3.41
36	22	11	172	3.28
37	19	10	154	3.41
38	16	7	116	3.70
39	11	8	152	3.62
40	8	10	155	3.70

The average pitcher in this group lost more than a half a run off his ERA by age 35, dipped under 200 innings at 36, and began losing serious ground to age and attrition by age 38. About a third of these pitchers were still active at age 40. The best of these were Nolan Ryan (2.76 ERA), Rick Reuschel (2.94) and Warren Spahn (3.01). So the odds of having a sub-3.00 ERA at age 40 if you were a top pitcher at age 31-33 are about one in ten. Those Fox guys will be paying $15 million in 2005 for a ten percent chance. **<SF>**

YEAR	GS	S	C	T
1998	35	3.46	2.14	5.60
1997	33	3.67	2.58	6.24
1996	32	2.88	1.91	4.78
1995	26	3.50	2.85	6.35
1994	25	5.16	2.84	8.00

MARK BROWNSON, COL

Brownson got called up from AAA in July, threw a four-hit shutout against the Astros in the Dome, came home and got popped by the Pirates, and then disappeared into the purple haze. Assuming he reappears, he's a middling prospect to throw in with a grab bag of youngsters and retreads trying to make the back end of the Rockies' rotation. **<DM>**

YEAR	GS	S	C	T
1998	2	4.00	2.50	6.50

MIKE BUSBY, STL

It seems like every other year or so LaRussa-and-Duncan get the hots for some young pitcher who isn't ready for the big leagues, trot him out there, watch him get hammered (either quickly, as with Busby here, or a bit more slowly, like Cliff Politte last year) and then send the kid back to the minors in a straitjacket. Busby hasn't been worth much in the minors over the past couple of years, but the Chang-and-Eng of St. Louis have faithfully kept bringing Busby back up to the big club every so often, possibly in search of something akin to instant karma.

Actually, of course, it was the injuries to the starting staff that prompted Busby's return; and, just to keep the bad karma of the Cardinal pitching mound intact, Mike came down with a medial strain in his pitching elbow during his second start. He didn't pitch again all season.

Yep, some years it just don't pay to get out of bed. . . **<DM>**

YEAR	GS	S	C	T
1998	2	4.50	3.50	8.00
1997	3	6.00	3.67	9.67
1996	1	7.00	6.00	13.00

PAUL BYRD, PHI

The ex-Brave and ex-Met made a big splash in Philly after he was picked up for about half a song (possibly sixteen or twenty measures, if memory serves) in mid-August. Yes, those numbers are way out of context with anything else he's done, and when we look at his eight starts, we see teams like the Expos, Dodgers, Pirates, Rockies (away from Coors), and the all-kid version of the Marlins. The one bonafide offense that he shut down was the Astros, but so did Mark (the Invisible Man) Brownson, for that matter. I don't think I'd bet Jon Miller's house (or even Joe Morgan's) on this continuing in 1999. **<DM>**

YEAR	GS	S	C	T
1998	8	2.63	2.88	5.50
1997	4	4.00	3.75	7.75

BRUCE CHEN, ATL

Just what the Braves need, a young pitcher whose top end looks as though it could be higher than #5 man Kevin Millwood. Just 22, Chen was 14-8 with a 3.05 ERA split between AA and AAA in 1998, then came up to the bigs and picked up a couple more wins in his first four starts. He's still raw, and has some tendency toward wildness, but the Braves have made room for him by dealing Neagle to the Reds for Bret Boone. **<DM>**

YEAR	GS	S	C	T
1998	4	4.25	4.00	8.25

BOBBY CHOUINARD, AZ

Ol' Four-Vowel Bobby, as dime-store linguists often call him, was pulled out of the Oakland wreckage in a mid-season trade, and put up some semi-credible numbers in the Arizona bullpen during the second half of the season. He'll never make the rotation, but he might hang around in middle relief for awhile.

(By the way, are there any dime-stores left??) **<DM>**

YEAR	GS	S	C	T
1998	2	4.50	4.00	8.50
1996	11	5.00	4.55	9.55

MARK CLARK, TEX
(1998: CHC)

"General" Mark Clark, as he's known to some of my family's long-time acquaintances who might charitably be described as "over-patriotic," might well cut a dashing figure in a uniform; under the microscope, however, he appears as nothing more or less than a garden-variety finesse pitcher whose basic QMAX Sector and Range values have been extremely consistent over the past three years:

Year	HH	S12
1996	34	28
1997	32	29
1998	36	27

The epitome of the #4 starter, Mark won ten less games than Kevin Tapani despite having better QMAX values and the same ERA. As they say, life is a crap shoot. . . **<DM>**

YEAR	GS	S	C	T
1998	33	4.48	2.67	7.15
1997	31	4.06	2.97	7.03
1996	32	4.09	2.56	6.66
1995	21	4.67	3.48	8.14
1994	20	4.15	3.25	7.40

MATT CLEMENT, SD

Matt is the Padres' Great Hope for their starting rotation, which is going to very likely have a big hole at the top when Kevin Brown goes elsewhere. He's been on a roll since learning a new pitch and getting his control together in 1997, and he might be one of those guys who transcends the early struggling he experienced in his career. His BB/9 rate was back up a bit in Las Vegas, however, and that could be a problem. **<DM>**

YEAR	GS	S	C	T
1998	2	4.00	4.50	8.50

STEVE COOKE, FA
(1998: CIN)

Tales of Woe, part 1998: Steve lasted all of one start for the Reds, coming up with an inflamed elbow after four-hitting the eventual NL champion Padres for six innings on April 2nd. He never pitched again, and was released by the Reds at the end of the year. Ah, well: the Reds will always have (Steve) Parris. . . **<DM>**

YEAR	GS	S	C	T
1998	1	2.00	2.00	4.00
1997	32	4.50	4.19	8.69
1994	23	4.74	3.39	8.13

FRANCISCO CORDOVA, PIT

Continuing to make slow but steady strides, Cordova had a very good year for those downtrodden Bucs. Gino Lamont is building a solid little blue-collar pitching staff that is as bereft of an offense as the Oakland A's hitters are bereft of a pitching staff. I think Cordova has a good shot to move up another notch, and become a solid #2-3 guy for a number of years. <DM>

YEAR	GS	S	C	T
1998	33	3.64	3.06	6.70
1997	29	4.03	3.07	7.10
1996	6	4.50	2.83	7.33

OMAR DAAL, AZ

QMAX says that Omar was the Snakes' best pitcher in 1998, and you've got to tip your cap to Buck Showalter, who got a pretty good rotation working for Arizona over the last couple of months of the year. I think Daal will give a little ground in 1999, but not a lot, and he should still be a solid #3-4 type pitcher for some time to come. <DM>

YEAR	GS	S	C	T
1998	22	3.50	2.95	6.45
1997	3	4.00	3.00	7.00
1996	6	4.17	4.00	8.17

JEFF D'AMICO, MIL

Could be another member of the CAD Club. Jeff missed the entire year, which was doubly unfortunate, since he was the Brewers' best starter in '97 and (at least pre-injury) the type of pitcher who might have really taken well to the NL. They just keep dropping like flies. . . <DM>

YEAR	GS	S	C	T
1997	23	4.04	3.22	7.26
1996	17	4.12	3.71	7.82

DANNY DARWIN, FA
(1998: SF)

The Ageless Wonder is no longer either, and frankly, he hasn't been so wonderful for quite some time now. Unless Brian Sabean plans to shamelessly bring him back for pesos on the dollar this time, I think that Ol' Grizzly may finally shamble off into the fog-drenched sunset. <DM>

YEAR	GS	S	C	T
1998	25	4.52	3.52	8.04
1997	24	4.63	3.08	7.71
1996	25	4.00	2.60	6.60
1995	15	5.07	3.27	8.33
1994	13	5.23	3.23	8.46

RYAN DEMPSTER, FLA

Just one year removed from a season in A-ball where he posted a 4.90 ERA, Dempster got brought up from AA to be the latest raw meat in the hands of Jim (Two All-Beef Patties) Leyland. Eleven most merciless starts later, Ryan was transported via Medevac to the Marlins' AAA club in Charlotte, where he managed to regroup (3-1, 3.27 ERA). In the kinder, gentler post-Fish fry administration of John Boles, there may yet be some small morsel of hope for a kid whose name is way to close to Dumpster for his own good. <DM>

YEAR	GS	S	C	T
1998	11	4.73	5.09	9.82

ELMER DESSENS, PIT

Elmer wasn't ready for his closeup, Mr. Lamont, even with the thoughtful assistance of scheduling his initial September start against Arizona. Dessens three-hit the Snakes for seven innings, but his next four outings were clinkers, and he's lucky not to be lying face down in the swimming pool narrating his tale of woe and wondering what it must have been like to have been Eric Von Stroheim, <DM>

YEAR	GS	S	C	T
1998	5	4.60	4.00	8.60
1996	3	6.67	4.33	11.00

DARREN DREIFORT, LA

Why We Are A Bit More Cautious About Applying Park Effects, Part 234: let's take a quick look at the home/road numbers for Darren Dreifort, who, as you know, pitches for a team (the Dodgers) who have what is known as a pitcher's park:

Where	S	C	T
Away	3.73	3.00	6.73
Home	4.13	3.33	7.46

Now if we applied a park factor to Darren without taking into consideration that his road performance was actually much better than his record at home (like some people we know), we'd end up telling you that he was a pretty lousy pitcher. Using just hits and walks as the benchmark, and not being in a big hurry to compensate for ballpark effects, we find that Darren pitched rather well—not great by any means, but better than league average.

Medical note: Darren missed most of the last month of the season with a "stiff arm." He's been through several arm injuries in the past, and there's some chance that he may yet wind up a member of the CAD Club. <DM>

YEAR	GS	S	C	T
1998	26	3.96	3.19	7.15

SCOTT ELARTON, HOU

Larry Dierker seems to like finesse pitching starters and power relievers; if so, Elarton is going to remain in the pen in 1999. With my personal bias right here on my sleeve, I sincerely hope that this won't be the case. Elarton has the makings of a #2 starter, and the Astros already have a flame-throwing closer in Billy Wagner. Despite Scott's effectiveness in the pen, I think his talents would be misplaced there. Let's see what Larry does about it. <DM>

If Larry Dierker helps Elarton improve at all this year, he could be a big story this year. In his fourteen minor league starts, Elarton posted a 2.93/3.36, 6.29 QMAX line, including being hit hard just once and reaching the elite square four times (29%). I love how the Astros broke him in pitching long relief, something that Earl Weaver was long known for. It makes me wonder if the Whiz

---

MISCELLANEOUS STARTING PITCHER DATA, NATIONAL LEAGUE 1998

LEGEND: NP—Number of Pitches thrown; **TW**—Team Wins in pitcher's starts; **TL**—Team Losses in pitcher's starts; **GS** = **QS**—Quality Starts; **BS**—Blown Starts; **QmB**—Quality minus Blown pct.; **PPI**—Pitches thrown Per Inning; **IP**—Innings Pitched; **AdIP**—Adjusted Innings Pitched; **IP/S**—average Innings Pitched per Start

Pitcher Name	Team	TW	TL	GS	QS	BS	QMB	IP	NP	Str	PPI	Kpct	AdjIP	IP/S
Terry Mulholland	CHC	4	2	6	4	0	66.67	39.7	597	373	15.05	62.5%	38	6.6
Kerry Wood	CHC	18	8	26	18	2	61.54	166.7	2836	1729	17.02	61.0%	180	6.4
Steve Trachsel	CHC	21	12	33	16	4	36.36	208.0	3390	2074	16.30	61.2%	216	6.3
Kevin Tapani	CHC	19	15	34	16	4	35.29	218.0	3427	2182	15.72	63.7%	218	6.4
Jeremi Gonzalez	CHC	11	9	20	10	3	35.00	110.0	1790	1099	16.27	61.4%	114	5.5
Mark Clark	CHC	12	21	33	14	6	24.24	213.7	3307	2144	15.48	64.8%	210	6.5
Mike Morgan	CHC	4	1	5	1	2	-20.00	22.7	385	221	16.98	57.4%	24	4.5
Don Wengert	CHC	1	5	6	0	2	-33.33	28.3	483	302	17.04	62.5%	31	4.7
Steve Cooke	CIN	1	0	1	1	0	100.00	6.0	72	45	12.00	62.5%	5	6.0
Pete Harnisch	CIN	19	13	32	22	1	65.63	209.0	3175	2043	15.19	64.3%	202	6.5
Jason Bere	CIN	4	3	7	5	2	42.86	39.7	604	375	15.23	62.1%	38	5.7
Brett Tomko	CIN	18	16	34	20	7	38.24	210.7	3357	2146	15.93	63.9%	214	6.2
Steve Parris	CIN	9	7	16	9	3	37.50	95.0	1535	955	16.16	62.5%	98	5.9
Mike Remlinger	CIN	11	17	28	11	5	21.43	155.7	2707	1610	17.39	59.5%	172	5.6
Scott Winchester	CIN	4	12	16	6	3	18.75	79.0	1187	747	15.03	62.9%	76	4.9
Dennis Reyes	CIN	5	2	7	4	3	14.29	37.0	644	363	17.41	56.4%	41	5.3
Dave Weathers	CIN	4	5	9	3	2	11.11	49.7	844	526	17.00	62.3%	54	5.5

Kids would be starting in New York now if they had been utilized in the same way. Keep this guy on your radar screen in fantasy leagues. <SF>

Year	GS	S	C	T
1998	2	4.50	3.00	7.50

CAL ELDRED, MIL

This is what is known as a Bad Trend. Phil Garner's overuse of Cal in 1992-93 has cost the Brewers a viable #2-3 man. Cal's now just barely holding on to a major-league job, and if the trend continues, he won't. <DM>

Year	GS	S	C	T
1998	23	4.57	3.74	8.30
1997	34	4.09	3.71	7.79
1996	15	3.80	3.73	7.53
1995	4	4.00	3.50	7.50
1994	25	3.52	3.36	6.88

SHAWN ESTES, SF

Shawn got worked hard in 1997, and since he's already had arm problems, it's perhaps not surprising that he went down for seven weeks in 1998 and was mostly ineffective upon his return.

In spite of this, there were some interesting patterns in Estes' season. For one, he actually had a higher percentage of starts in the Elite Square in 1998 (16% to 13%), and his Hit Hard percentage remained better than league average (24%) and close to the figure he'd posted in '97 (22%). Shawn is never going to have an especially low QMAX score, because he can get wild very fast and give up a flurry of walks. If his arm recovers, though, he'll probably have several more effective years like 1997 because he is capable of very solid hit prevention. Dusty Baker needs to be a little more careful with him over the next year or two, because he's a prime candidate for the CAD Club if he's pushed too hard. <DM>

Year	GS	S	C	T
1998	25	4.00	4.00	8.00
1997	32	3.31	3.88	7.19
1996	11	3.45	3.91	7.36
1995	3	3.67	3.00	6.67

ALEX FERNANDEZ, FLA

Alex is due back sometime in 1999, but the first question is whether or not he'll be pitching for the Marlins. The second question is whether the Marlins can get anyone to assume Alex's salary, or if they're going to have to eat a good bit of it in order to unload him. What's likely is that someone might take Alex sight unseen if the Fish pay 75% of his salary and agree to pay off the balance of the contract should the next team decide to release him. The Fish might get a

prospect or two out of the deal, and that might be better than what they'll get if they hold on to him. Decisions, decisions. <DM>

Year	GS	S	C	T
1997	32	3.50	2.88	6.38
1996	35	3.80	2.54	6.34
1995	30	3.83	3.03	6.87
1994	24	3.54	2.58	6.13

OSVALDO FERNANDEZ, FA
(1998: SF)

It's evidently a bad time to be a pitcher named Fernandez. Osvaldo was bought out of his deal with the Giants, who probably believed last year's ruse about some guy named Rey Pimentel being substituted by a Cuban government angry at all of the defections. It wasn't true, but it's probably a better story than the truth. The Giants just had the misfortune of signing someone whose shoulder wasn't far from going bad. They will be doing some shopping for pitchers this winter. <DM>

Year	GS	S	C	T
1997	11	4.91	3.36	8.27
1996	28	4.43	3.32	7.75

JOE FONTENOT, FLA

Florida's booty in the Robb Nen deal, Fontenot was highly regarded by many baseball analysis weenies, evidently on the (slender) fact that he had reached AA ball at the tender age of 20. There was also the fact that Joe hadn't pitched especially well at any level yet, but such often doesn't seem to matter to those who live to rail about prospects-for-veterans trades.

At any rate, Joe started quickly at AA in 1998, and was brought up to the Marlins in the midst of their Piazza Passover Daze. Like many of the young Fish fillets, he was hit hard (50% of his starts) and lasted eight starts before he was sent to AAA, where he made

one start before going on the DL for the rest of the year. This isn't a very unusual story in baseball, but it could be less usual, I think, if teams took a little more care with their young talent than they seem inclined to do. <DM>

Year	GS	S	C	T
1998	8	5.13	4.38	9.50

KEVIN FOSTER, FA
(1998: CHC)

Most everyone else in the Baseball Analysis Community (that's ABC, all mixed up) is gonna think I'm off my rocker for saying this (hell, a lot of 'em think that without me saying this. . .), but I still think that Kevin Foster could turn it around if he went to the right place. For example, St. Louis, or Oakland if someone there had a clue about pitchers. It's got to be a park that helps fly-ball pitchers, and there are only a few. Foster had a terrible year in AAA and he's probably about ready to pack it in, since he wasn't claimed on waivers when the Cubs took him off their 40-man roster, but the man still fanned more than a man an inning. There must be somebody in baseball who can figure out how to get him on track, and the Reds (who invited him to 1999 spring training) may be the first to try. <DM>

Year	GS	S	C	T
1997	25	3.80	3.92	7.72
1996	16	4.63	3.81	8.44
1995	28	3.50	3.46	6.96
1994	13	3.38	3.54	6.92

RAMON GARCIA, HOU

Out all year with arm problems, Ramon was an effective pitcher for the Astros in 1997, and might fit in as a swing man on next year's club if healthy. <DM>

MISCELLANEOUS STARTING PITCHER DATA, NATIONAL LEAGUE 1998

LEGEND: NP—Number of Pitches thrown; **TW**—Team Wins in pitcher's starts; **TL**—Team Losses in pitcher's starts; **GS**—; **QS**—Quality Starts; **BS**—Blown Starts; **QmB**—Quality minus Blown pct.; **PPI**—Pitches thrown Per Inning; **IP**—Innings Pitched; **AdIP**—Adjusted Innings Pitched; **IP/S**—average Innings Pitched per Start

Pitcher Name	Team	TW	TL	GS	QS	BS	QMB	IP	NP	Str	PPI	Kpct	AdjIP	IP/S
Scott Klingenbeck	CIN	1	3	4	1	1	0.00	22.7	362	235	15.97	64.9%	23	5.7
Gabe White	CIN	0	3	3	1	1	0.00	15.3	249	169	16.24	67.9%	16	5.1
Mark Hutton	CIN	0	2	2	0	1	-50.00	2.3	58	29	24.89	50.0%	4	1.2
Eddie Priest	CIN	1	1	2	0	1	-50.00	6.0	90	61	15.00	67.8%	6	3.0
Rick Krivda	CIN	0	1	1	0	1	-100.00	4.0	105	58	26.25	55.2%	7	4.0
Darry lKile	COL	14	21	35	21	5	45.71	228.3	3638	2195	15.93	60.3%	231	6.5
John Thomson	COL	10	16	26	14	3	42.31	161.0	2436	1554	15.13	63.8%	155	6.2
Jamey Wright	COL	17	17	34	14	7	20.59	206.3	3197	1890	15.49	59.1%	203	6.1
Bobby M Jones	COL	12	8	20	7	3	20.00	121.0	1965	1190	16.24	60.6%	125	6.1
Pedro Astacio	COL	18	16	34	13	10	8.82	208.0	3412	2093	16.40	61.3%	217	6.1
Mark Brownson	COL	2	0	2	1	1	0.00	13.3	185	118	13.88	63.8%	12	6.7
Mike Dejean	COL	1	0	1	0	0	0.00	3.0	47	28	15.67	59.6%	3	3.0
Mike Saipe	COL	1	1	2	1	1	0.00	10.0	184	112	18.40	60.9%	12	5.0
Mark Thompson	COL	2	4	6	0	3	0.00	23.3	422	247	18.09	58.5%	27	3.9
Kevin Ritz	COL	0	2	2	0	2	-100.00	9.0	165	106	18.33	64.2%	10	4.5
Livan Hernandez	FLA	14	19	33	18	4	42.42	234.3	3943	2358	16.83	59.8%	251	7.1
Jesus Sanchez	FLA	12	17	29	13	5	27.59	166.0	2733	1625	16.46	59.5%	174	5.7

YEAR	GS	S	C	T
1997	20	3.75	3.45	7.20
1996	2	5.00	3.50	8.50

MARK GARDNER, SF

The fate of the unfavored is epitomized in Mark Gardner's 1998 season. Having been the backbone of the Giants' drive for the WildCard with a 2.60,2,40/5.00 September, Gardner came up empty in the one-game playoff against the Cubs. It put a damper on what otherwise was easily his best year in the majors. Mark's jump in effectiveness is a little outsized for someone his age, but he's clearly in the category of late bloomer, and he might have another year or two at around the 6.80-7.20 level in him. <DM>

YEAR	GS	S	C	T
1998	33	3.67	2.97	6.64
1997	30	4.33	3.23	7.57
1996	28	4.43	3.29	7.71
1995	11	4.91	3.73	8.64
1994	14	4.29	3.57	7.86

TOM GLAVINE, ATL

If we've got Tom's pattern read properly, 1999 should be an off-year for him. He held most of his 1997 level quite well last year, however, and thanks to some generous run support from the Braves, was able to get back into the 20-win category for the first time since 1992. Two or three more seasons like this one and he'll start to look like a viable Hall of Fame candidate, even with the shadow of Greg Maddux hanging over him. <DM>

YEAR	GS	S	C	T
1998	33	3.45	2.82	6.27
1997	33	3.00	2.76	5.76
1996	36	3.72	3.25	6.97
1995	29	3.62	2.97	6.59
1994	25	4.08	3.44	7.52

JEREMI GONZALEZ, CHC

These young pitchers who come up and post QMAX shapes that are at odds with their minor league numbers are part of the ongoing puzzle. Many times, however, they'll revert toward that minor league profile in the next year, and that's what Gonzalez did, before he got hurt in late July. Jeremi looks to eventually be a reasonable #3-4 man, but that's probably the upper bounds of what can be expected from him. <DM>

YEAR	GS	S	C	T
1998	20	4.20	3.55	7.75
1997	23	3.48	3.87	7.35

MIKE GRACE, PHI

CAD Club, all the way. The Phillies have a raft full of these guys, all of whom are probably hindered more than helped by the Curt Schilling work ethic. The pattern is pretty grim, actually: good young arm who can't stay healthy, goes through several bouts of rehab, and finally doesn't have enough arm left to pitch the way he did, then tries to adjust to a new pitching style, usually with little success. The questions that are still almost impossible to answer are how much of it is workload, how much the type of pitches thrown, and how much is just the individualistic response to the trauma of throwing a baseball. When these results occur, those questions don't seem to matter; on the other hand, getting the answers to those questions seems even more important, so that what happens to pitchers like Mike Grace can be, at least, minimized. <DM>

YEAR	GS	S	C	T
1998	15	5.07	3.53	8.60
1997	6	3.17	2.67	5.83
1996	12	3.83	2.50	6.33
1995	2	3.50	3.50	7.00

TYLER GREEN, PHI

See above. Tyler appears to be holding his own against the CAD scenario, at least somewhat. He had six "1S" games last season, including one in his first start back after missing most of August due to bone chips. He eventually had surgery in the off-season. Green has more start-to-start extremes than anyone in MLB, going from untouchable to virtual batting practice quality in the space of five days. Despite everything, the arm still seems to be there, and if he's able to get through the next year or so without further problems, he might still put together a couple of big seasons somewhere in his early thirties. <DM>

YEAR	GS	S	C	T
1998	28	3.68	4.21	7.89
1997	14	3.79	4.36	8.14
1995	25	4.24	4.00	8.24

JOEY HAMILTON, TOR
(1998: SD)

In general, a Bad Trend is a-happenin' here. Over the course of five years, Joey's C13 percentages have nearly been halved (74% in 1995 to just 41% last season.) The Padres cashed in his reputation and sent him to Toronto for Woody Williams and two minor leaguers.. <DM>

YEAR	GS	S	C	T
1998	34	3.94	3.68	7.62
1997	29	4.17	3.24	7.41
1996	33	3.73	3.36	7.09
1995	30	3.83	2.80	6.63
1994	16	3.50	2.69	6.19

MIKE HAMPTON, HOU

We had guessed that Mike was going to take a step up into the mid-sixes in 1998, based on that performance level over the last fifteen starts of 1997. That didn't happen. Why? Well, primarily because we just haven't been able to gather anything remotely resembling enough trend data to be able to say for sure how reliable a 6.55 "T" value over fifteen starts is in terms of projecting future performance. There's a lot more to sift through, automate, and analyze before we'll be able to say that such a prediction is on track 25% of the time, 40%, or 60% of the time. (Our hunch is that it's in the middle, but we'll gather more data before sticking to that.)

In any event, we did run Hampton's 1997 season through the more elaborate version of the 15-start QMAX projection method, and we have a better idea about what happened, at least in terms of the forecast. Here are the three forecast figures:

Scenario	S	C	T
Best	3.57	3.15	6.72
Worst	3.98	3.47	7.45
Likely	3.72	3.27	6.99

The "best" value shows Mike within striking distance of his last-15 start performance in 1997; the "worst" value is just under the number that he, in fact, produced in 1998. The "likely" value came really close to the "C" score, but was too low on the "S" score, probably because we weren't able to take into account Mike's "S" score from 1996.

Retrofitting Mike's 1997 season was instructive, though, in that it did show that the forecasting method did in fact put him into a range that makes intuitive sense. Turning 26, Hampton could be expected to improve: a little over 60% of 25-year old pitchers improve their performance at 26. As you can see, that didn't happen; now, at least, we're getting a sense of what the larger picture looks like, and our future efforts in terms of forecasting will gradually become more robust.

What about 1999 for Mike? Mike's four year average is now 4.10,3.21/7.32; since he hasn't shown any significant upward direction since 1995, we're more inclined now to think that he's pretty much established his level. Somewhere in the low half of the sevens seems like the best bet. <DM>

YEAR	GS	S	C	T
1998	32	4.25	3.25	7.50
1997	34	3.91	3.32	7.24
1996	27	4.52	3.07	7.59
1995	24	3.79	3.08	6.88

PETE HARNISCH, CIN

Pete's best year since 1993, and one that has been seriously overlooked by those who are fixated on the Comeback Player of the Year award. Looking at the GS column below, however, it's pretty clear that Pete isn't a great bet to log as much work this year as he did in 1998. <DM>

YEAR	GS	S	C	T
1998	32	3.28	3.03	6.31
1997	8	4.63	4.75	9.38
1996	31	4.06	3.06	7.13
1995	18	3.89	2.61	6.50
1994	17	3.94	3.76	7.71

FELIX HEREDIA, CHC
(1998: FLA-CHC)

Felix' two starts came while he was still with the Fish, where even the ball boys seemingly got a couple of starts last season. He's strictly a bullpen guy in the Chicago scheme of things. <DM>

YEAR	GS	S	C	T
1998	2	6.00	4.00	10.00

DUSTIN HERMANSON, MON

Settling into his new role as starter quite well, Dustin upped his ES% ranking by a factor of almost four (27% as opposed to 7% in '97), and upped his C13 ratio from 50/50 to 66/34. The only negative: he was hit hard about twice as often (27%, up from just 14% the year earlier). Another stepwise progression in 1999 to match his 1998 progress, and he'll be hovering at the bottom edge of "ace" territory. <DM>

YEAR	GS	S	C	T
1998	30	3.47	3.10	6.57
1997	28	3.36	3.71	7.07

LIVAN HERNANDEZ, FLA

Another example of a young power pitcher going backwards in terms of stuff; Livan, though, had some "help" from his manager. Jim Leyland worked Livan very hard, and by the end of the year he was dragging (8.70 "T" score over the last two months of 1998). We've got a much better laboratory for observing what happens to these young pitchers now, and Livan's future fate will be one that is followed with intense scrutiny given the pitch counts he racked up during 1998. Livan threw 3926 pitches in 1998, third highest number in the MLB behind Curt Schilling and Randy Johnson, who both topped 4000. <DM>

YEAR	GS	S	C	T
1998	33	4.48	3.30	7.79
1997	17	3.29	3.65	6.94

OREL HERSHISER, FA
(1998: SF)

Orel has managed to keep a lid on his decline phase, but that continuing decay in his "C" value is just about ready to reach up and nab him, I think. The Giants bought out his option year partly to give themselves more room in the Kevin and Randy Bidding War, and partly because they recognized (in their own way, of course) that Orel's "S" value was over 5 for the last two months of 1998 and that anything more than a buyout could easily be throwing good money after bad results. <DM>

YEAR	GS	S	C	T
1998	34	3.97	3.59	7.56
1997	31	4.16	3.29	7.45
1996	33	4.55	3.09	7.64
1995	26	3.62	3.08	6.69
1994	21	4.10	2.90	7.00

STERLING HITCHCOCK, SD

A subtle key to the Padres' Big Success in 1998 was their 1996-97 trade with the Mariners, where they exchanged Scott Sanders for Sterling Hitchcock. (Ironically, Sanders—who blew up in Seattle and bombed in Detroit, is back with the Padres and just might be back in their rotation in the Post-Brown Era.)

Anyway, Hitch stepped up and recaptured something like the development trend that had looked likely after his 1995 season with the Yankees, a development that was interrupted by a year with the Lou (the Master of Chaos) Piniella in Seattle, and a period of rehabilitation with the Padres in 1997. Sterling gave the Padres a solid #3 starter (something they thought they had, but didn't, in Joey Hamilton) and, in concert with Brown, the first four months of Ashby and the incredible bullpen work of Trevor Hoffman, pushed San Diego to unprecedented heights—from which they will promptly fall like Humpty-Dumpty (a dead ringer for Padres' owner John Moores, except for the blue jeans, of course).

While Mr. Neyer of the ESPNet Neighborhood may have been astonished by Hitch's post-season performance, we weren't all that surprised. Sterling had a higher ES% score in 1995 (19%) than he did in 1998 (15%), so he's always had this capacity. What was also clear was that Sterling was pitching extremely well in his home park, especially in his last eight starts there (2.38,2.25/4.63). He merely continued that pattern in the post-season.

Now—will that pattern continue? Can he keep up such a level of performance at home (5.67 "T" score, vs. 8.00 on the road in 1998)? We're fresh out of tea leaves, but expect some backsliding from this, based on that home/road split. The Padres' string of rolling sevens is about to disappear in a puff of smoke. <DM>

YEAR	GS	S	C	T
1998	27	3.81	3.04	6.85
1997	28	4.36	3.46	7.82
1996	35	5.06	3.66	8.71
1995	27	3.56	3.52	7.07
1994	5	3.40	4.00	7.40

CHRIS HOLT, HOU

There's a good bit of reason to believe that Holt overachieved in 1997, and who knows but that his injuries were in some way related to that. He will fit in with the general tenor of the starting staff that Larry Dierker appears to favor—finesse and control. The fact that he missed an entire year can't be taken as a good sign, however. The CAD Club might want to get ready for another member. . . <DM>

YEAR	GS	S	C	T
1997	32	3.88	3.00	6.88

MARK HUTTON , CIN

Marky Mark was pretty much undressed by NL hitters in 1998, and got wild (though not in the "Boogie Nights" sense) to boot. He spent the summer in that hotbed of vice, Indianapolis (and I could tell you second-hand stories. . .), where he was able to emerge, alas, semi-clad. <DM>

YEAR	GS	S	C	T
1998	2	5.00	6.00	11.00
1997	1	7.00	3.00	10.00
1996	11	3.45	3.55	7.00

JASON ISRINGHAUSEN, NYM

And then there were two. . . <DM>

YEAR	GS	S	C	T
1997	6	4.67	5.17	9.83
1996	27	4.30	3.59	7.89
1995	14	3.64	3.00	6.64

JOSE JIMENEZ, STL

Amazing to think how ethnically insensitive that old 60s Bill Dana gag really was, isn't it? "My name. . . Jose Jimenez." Try that today, and there'd be more lawyers swarming around you than you could hope to slap with a fly-swatter. Anyway, this Jose Jimenez was 24 last year, and one year removed from A ball, and has shown little propensity for power pitching, which his first three starts in MLB last September rather conspicuously verified. <DM>

YEAR	GS	S	C	T
1998	3	4.67	3.33	8.00

MIKE JOHNSON, MON

A Rule Fiver who split time with Baltimore and Montreal in 1997, to little effect or consequence, and who had two widely-spaced starts, of the emergency nature, for the

Expos in 1998, each accompanied by the sound of breaking glass. <DM>

Year	GS	S	C	T
1998	2	6.50	4.00	10.50
1997	16	4.88	4.69	9.56

RANDY JOHNSON, AZ
(1998: SEA-HOU)

For you unabashed QMAX fans out there, here are Randy's numbers broken out by team:

Team	S	C	T
SEA	3.78	3.00	6.78
HOU	2.27	2.55	4.82

Of some note is the fact that Randy's July numbers while still in Seattle were 2.80,2.00/4.80, giving the sense that the change of scenery might have been more coincidental than has been otherwise assumed.

I had thought that the Dodgers were going to make sure that they got Randy after their midsummer meltdown (ultimately firing Fred Claire over the failure to close the deal), but the Unit opted for his home town, and will be the world's longest Snake for the next four years. <DM>

Year	GS	S	C	T
1998	34	3.29	2.85	6.15
1997	29	2.48	2.83	5.31
1996	8	3.00	3.75	6.75
1995	30	2.80	2.73	5.53
1994	23	2.91	3.13	6.04

BOBBY J. JONES, NYM

A reasonably dependable #3-4 starter who has a tendency to get a bit too hittable, but is otherwise unexceptionable. Actually, Bobby has cut down that Hit Hard tendency dramatically in the last four years (from 47% in 1995 to just 17% last year), and has had Elite Square percentages right at 17% for five years running. (Store in the QMAX Facts You Can't Get Anywhere Else section of your refrigerator.) <DM>

Year	GS	S	C	T
1998	30	3.70	2.83	6.53
1997	30	3.57	3.03	6.60
1996	31	4.48	2.84	7.32
1995	30	4.37	2.93	7.30
1994	24	4.00	3.08	7.08

BOBBY M. JONES, COL

Just for fun (though everyone knows that I've got a peculiar definition of that. . .), I thought we might want to break out Bobby Em's record by home (Coors Field) and road:

Where	S	C	T
Coors	4.64	3.91	8.75
Elsewhere	3.89	3.22	7.11

Turns out that Bobby Em is about average in Coors, where the overall QMAX "T" score over the past four years is 8.83. He's a bit better than average on the road, and that's probably the QMAX data to use when attempting to evaluate him. What I like the most about Bobby Em isn't that he's necessarily so great, but that as a lefty he is pioneering a counter-argument to the myth that southpaws get their lunch fed to them at Coors. Consequently (as an unrepentant lefty myself), I count myself as one of Bobby Em's biggest fans. <DM>

Year	GS	S	C	T
1998	20	4.30	3.60	7.90
1997	4	5.50	4.75	10.25

SCOTT KARL, MIL

The quintessence of league average, and impressively tenacious at it, to boot. <DM>

Year	GS	S	C	T
1998	33	4.27	3.52	7.79
1997	32	4.25	3.31	7.56
1996	32	4.31	3.16	7.47
1995	18	4.28	3.17	7.44

DARRYL KILE, COL

I do think it's possible that Kile might yet become the first Rockies' pitcher to get his QMAX "T" below seven pitching half his games in Coors Field. While not an event destined to be oversaturated with media coverage, it will (if it happens) be at least as historic. What are the odds? I'd say about 40-60. <DM>

Year	GS	S	C	T
1998	35	4.43	3.29	7.71
1997	33	3.03	2.85	5.88
1996	33	4.09	3.58	7.67
1995	21	3.43	4.14	7.57
1994	24	4.13	4.04	8.17

SCOTT KLINGENBECK, FA
(1998: CIN)

Scott "Static" Klingenbeck (I'll stop here so you can dive into the dirty clothes hamper. . .) is to Rick Reed what Reed is to Greg Maddux—meaning that he's turned into a decent major-league finesse pitcher who could help a number of teams (the A's just keep popping up at the top of this list). His career has definitely come to a halt, however, as a result of his decision to refuse waivers when the Reds tried to outright him back to AAA, where he had been 6-2, 2.86 earlier. No one picked him up, and he spent the rest of the summer perfecting his technique with Spray'n'Wash at the laundromat. <DM>

Year	GS	S	C	T
1998	4	4.25	3.50	7.75
1996	3	6.33	4.00	10.33
1995	9	5.44	4.89	10.33
1994	1	3.00	4.00	7.00

MARK LANGSTON, SD

The hammer came down on Mark and the Padres in the World Series (in the form of Tino Martinez' "gift" grand slam that iced the Yankees' seven-run seventh in Game 1), possibly as punishment for getting away with trotting Mark's nine-plus QMAX average out there so many times with so little penalty during the regular season. Langston was a darned good pitcher at his peak; it's a shame that his last moment in the limelight was so catastrophic. But the big question is: why on earth did Bruce Bochy leave him in so long? <DM>

Year	GS	S	C	T
1998	16	5.13	4.25	9.38
1997	9	5.22	4.56	9.78
1996	18	3.61	3.06	6.67
1995	31	4.23	3.16	7.39
1994	18	4.17	3.61	7.78

MISCELLANEOUS STARTING PITCHER DATA, NATIONAL LEAGUE 1998

LEGEND: NP—Number of Pitches thrown; TW—Team Wins in pitcher's starts; TL—Team Losses in pitcher's starts; GS—; QS—Quality Starts; BS—Blown Starts; QmB—Quality minus Blown pct.; PPI—Pitches thrown Per Inning; IP—Innings Pitched; AdjIP—Adjusted Innings Pitched; IP/S—average Innings Pitched per Start

Pitcher Name	Team	TW	TL	GS	QS	BS	QMB	IP	NP	Str	PPI	Kpct	AdjIP	IP/S
Joe Fontenot	FLA	0	8	8	4	2	25.00	42.7	743	429	17.41	57.7%	47	5.3
Kirt Ojala	FLA	3	10	13	7	4	23.08	73.0	1174	698	16.08	59.5%	75	5.6
Brian Meadows	FLA	13	18	31	11	8	9.68	174.3	2547	1635	14.61	64.2%	162	5.6
Ryan Dempster	FLA	5	6	11	3	3	0.00	48.7	863	481	17.74	55.7%	55	4.4
Chris Hammond	FLA	0	3	3	1	1	0.00	13.7	250	144	18.30	57.6%	16	4.6
Rafael Medina	FLA	2	11	13	4	4	0.00	71.7	1432	826	19.98	57.7%	91	5.5
Andy Larkin	FLA	3	11	14	5	7	-14.29	72.3	1305	758	18.04	58.1%	83	5.2
Eric Ludwick	FLA	2	4	6	1	3	-33.33	22.3	394	237	17.64	60.2%	25	3.7
Felix Heredia	FLA	2	0	2	0	1	-50.00	9.7	199	125	20.58	62.8%	13	4.8
Randy Johnson	HOU	10	1	11	10	0	90.91	84.3	1344	894	15.94	66.5%	85	7.7
Jose Lima	HOU	21	12	33	24	2	66.67	233.4	3373	2260	14.45	67.0%	215	7.1
Shane Reynolds	HOU	24	11	35	26	3	65.71	233.4	3517	2336	15.07	66.4%	224	6.7
Mike Hampton	HOU	20	12	32	22	1	65.63	211.7	3225	1958	15.24	60.7%	205	6.6
Sean Bergman	HOU	16	11	27	14	2	44.44	168.0	2377	1523	14.15	64.1%	151	6.2
Pete Schourek	HOU	8	7	15	5	2	20.00	80.0	1345	822	16.81	61.1%	86	5.3
Scott Elarton	HOU	1	1	2	0	0	0.00	12.3	211	135	17.11	64.0%	13	6.2
John Halama	HOU	2	4	6	2	2	0.00	32.3	538	341	16.64	63.4%	34	5.4

ANDY LARKIN, FLA

Think of these young Fish fillets as analogues to the young nymphets in all those teenage horror flicks. Just when you're getting comfortable with the character (which in the movies, at least, was proportional to how much young skin you'd just been shown), up pops that nasty slasher and leaves you with another nubile corpse. To slip back to the convenience food image (and, in truth, those young girls aren't really that hot unless they've been microwaved), if you take the Mrs. Paul's out of the deep freeze, you'll find that Andy here is the third one from the left. <DM>

Year	GS	S	C	T
1998	14	5.00	4.43	9.43
1996	1	2.00	5.00	7.00

AL LEITER, NYM

Signed by the Mets to a four-year deal worth $32 million after the season ended, and why not? Despite being 33, Al's thrown less than 1100 innings in his career, which means his arm is younger than any other veteran pitcher. His injuries have not been arm-related over the past three years. There aren't but a handful of pitchers who've gotten their QMAX "S" value under three in the past three seasons, and there are even fewer who've done it twice. And Al's command has even improved markedly. Others may quail, but I think that Al in hand beats any number of chips off the old bush. <DM>

Year	GS	S	C	T
1998	28	2.86	3.04	5.89
1997	27	3.52	4.33	7.85
1996	33	2.94	3.88	6.82
1995	28	3.64	4.14	7.79
1994	20	4.45	4.35	8.80

MARK LEITER, SEA
(1998: PHI)

Now a closer, and thanks to which, availed of a lease on life that would have seemed mightily improbable this time last year. I'm still rooting for a matchup between Mark and his brother Al, however—but the likelihood of this has gotten even more remote thanks to Mark's off-season trade to Seattle. <DM>

Year	GS	S	C	T
1997	31	4.65	3.45	8.10
1996	34	4.35	3.32	7.68
1995	29	3.76	2.90	6.66
1994	7	4.57	3.14	7.71

JON LIEBER, PIT

Mr. Finesse appears to have come full circle since his debut year, but there are a few subtle differences in the QMAX Sector and Range data that might be pertinent. Jon's ES% has risen up to 19%, and his S12% (top hit prevention games) is up to 33%, both single-season highs. He seems to have stabilized as a borderline #3-4 guy, but whether he can take another step is what's hard to figure. Most of the trends point to it being possible, but there's also the fact that Jon had only one start after August 20th. <DM>

Year	GS	S	C	T
1998	27	4.15	2.93	7.07
1997	32	4.16	3.09	7.25
1996	15	4.60	2.73	7.33
1995	12	5.33	3.17	8.50
1994	17	4.29	2.76	7.06

JOSE LIMA, HOU

Larry Dierker's biggest success yet, and easily the Astros' best pitcher until the arrival of the Unit. Notable in Jose's 1998 profile were the following: a high Big Game percentage (52% of his games in the Success Square were Elite games, about twice the average), a big Tommy John factor (30%, the highest in MLB in 1998), and command that was Maddux-like (91% of his games in the C13 range). All that said, I don't think he'll be this good in 1999: there are issues such as league adjustment, workload carry-over, etc. Keep in mind that his lifetime ERA prior to 1998 was 5.92. <DM>

Year	GS	S	C	T
1998	33	3.91	2.09	6.00
1997	1	2.00	5.00	7.00
1996	4	6.00	3.75	9.75
1995	15	4.27	3.67	7.93
1994	1	5.00	4.00	9.00

CARLTON LOEWER, PHI

Loewer tossed a 1,1 game in his major league debut on June 14th, and that was the only S12 game he had all year, giving him a frighteningly puny 5% for top hit prevention games. There's nothing in his minor league record to suggest that he's going to become anything other than a very hittable pitcher. <DM>

Year	GS	S	C	T
1998	21	5.14	3.38	8.52

SEAN LOWE, STL

Let's be succinct, and note that Sean's major league career will not take up very many lines in Total Baseball. <DM>

Year	GS	S	C	T
1998	1	7.00	7.00	14.00
1997	4	5.75	5.50	11.25

ERIC LUDWICK, TOR
(1998: FLA)

In the past two years, Ludwick has survived Bob Cluck and a line drive that broke his arm. It's hard to say which one did more damage, but the facts are that he's a 27-year old prospect who's a bit too old to be considered a Fish fillet. There is some talent here, however, and it's possible that his new team, the Blue Jays, may tap into it before Eric gets caught in an avalanche. <DM>

Year	GS	S	C	T
1998	6	4.83	4.67	9.50
1997	5	5.40	5.20	10.60
1996	1	6.00	3.00	9.00

GREG MADDUX, ATL

Another great Maddux year (yawn!), but one clouded over a bit by a noticeable loss of command in September:

Month	C13%
APR	100
MAY	100
JUN	100
JUL	100
AUG	80
SEP	20

MISCELLANEOUS STARTING PITCHER DATA, NATIONAL LEAGUE 1998

LEGEND: NP—Number of Pitches thrown; **TW**—Team Wins in pitcher's starts; **TL**—Team Losses in pitcher's starts; **GS**—; **QS**—Quality Starts; **BS**—Blown Starts; **QmB**—Quality minus Blown pct.; **PPI**—Pitches thrown Per Inning; **IP**—Innings Pitched; **AdIP**—Adjusted Innings Pitched; **IP/S**—average Innings Pitched per Start

Pitcher Name	Team	TW	TL	GS	QS	BS	QMB	IP	NP	Str	PPI	Kpct	AdIP	IP/S
Trever Miller	HOU	0	1	1	0	0	0.00	4.0	68	36	17.00	52.9%	4	4.0
Ramon Martinez	LAD	10	5	15	11	0	73.33	101.7	1667	1016	16.40	60.9%	106	6.8
Brian Bohanon	LAD	5	9	14	11	1	71.43	97.3	1425	839	14.64	58.9%	91	7.0
Carlos Perez	LAD	4	7	11	8	2	54.55	77.7	1117	717	14.38	64.2%	71	7.1
Ismeal Valdes	LAD	14	13	27	16	2	51.85	174.0	2767	1744	15.90	63.0%	176	6.4
Chan Ho Park	LAD	19	14	33	20	5	45.45	212.3	3403	2049	16.03	60.2%	216	6.4
Hideo Nomo	LAD	3	9	12	7	3	33.33	67.7	1114	645	16.46	57.9%	71	5.6
Dave Mlicki	LAD	12	8	20	10	4	30.00	124.3	1857	1179	14.93	63.5%	118	6.2
Darren Dreifort	LAD	14	12	26	11	4	26.92	165.0	2455	1544	14.88	62.9%	156	6.3
Dennis Reyes	LAD	1	2	3	0	0	0.00	15.3	265	146	17.28	55.1%	17	5.1
Brad Woodall	MIL	8	12	20	10	3	35.00	118.3	1821	1097	15.39	60.2%	116	5.9
Scott Karl	MIL	20	13	33	17	6	33.33	192.3	3105	1890	16.14	60.9%	198	5.8
Broswell Patrick	MIL	1	2	3	1	0	33.33	20.0	264	176	13.20	66.7%	17	6.7
Bill Pulsipher	MIL	5	5	10	5	2	30.00	56.0	904	548	16.14	60.6%	58	5.6
Rafael Roque	MIL	5	4	9	3	1	22.22	48.0	775	467	16.15	60.3%	49	5.3
Cal Eldred	MIL	11	12	23	9	4	21.74	133.0	2230	1343	16.77	60.2%	142	5.8
Jose Mercedes	MIL	3	2	5	2	1	20.00	27.7	436	271	15.76	62.2%	28	5.5

That's a pretty steep drop, even if we're talking about small sample sizes. Maddux' QMAX "T" in September was 7.00—not catastrophic, but not "Maddux" either. Is this a blip on the radar screen, or is it symptomatic of an oncoming decline? **<DM>**

Year	GS	S	C	T
1998	34	2.85	2.12	4.97
1997	33	3.39	1.79	5.18
1996	35	3.49	1.91	5.40
1995	28	2.57	1.86	4.43
1994	25	2.60	1.76	4.36

DENNIS MARTINEZ, RETIRED
(1998: ATL)

A stand-in for John Smoltz in the first month of the season, El Presidente managed to push his lifetime win total past Juan Marichal, and thus retire as the winningest Latin pitcher of all time. Tossed back into the bullpen, he actually pitched pretty well in September (2.83 ERA); despite that, I don't think we're going to see him on the mound again. **<DM>**

Year	GS	S	C	T
1998	5	5.60	3.40	9.00
1997	9	5.22	4.78	10.00
1996	20	4.30	3.65	7.95
1995	28	3.61	2.75	6.36
1994	24	4.04	2.42	6.46

RAMON MARTINEZ, FA
(1998: LA)

The Ramonster finally buckled after staving off serious career-interrupting injury for close to six years after being mangled by Tommy Lasorda. As is often the case, the irony was that Ramon was pitching as well as ever, if not better, when the injury (an additional tear to the rotator cuff) occurred. He's been bought out of his option year, and reports are that he won't be able to pitch again until at least the second half of 1999. **<DM>**

Year	GS	S	C	T
1998	15	2.87	3.33	6.20
1997	22	3.68	3.95	7.64
1996	27	3.56	3.89	7.44
1995	30	3.47	3.20	6.67
1994	24	3.50	2.88	6.38

BRIAN MEADOWS, FLA

Brian's monthly QWPs give you a very good sense of how things went for him in 1998:

Month	QWP
APR	.531
MAY	.399
JUN	.449
JUL	.354
AUG	.268
SEP	.365

As with several other young members of the Marlins' pitching corps (the ones we've

lovingly dubbed the Fish fillets), Brian's minor league record clearly shows that he is at best a second-tier prospect who was thrust into the majors well ahead of schedule due to Hurricane Wayne's enforced Fish Fry. The best that can be said for the unfortunate lad is that he has pretty good control. **<DM>**

Year	GS	S	C	T
1998	31	5.00	3.16	8.16

RAFAEL MEDINA, FLA

Part of the Kevin Brown trade, Rafael was airlifted to a "no-fry zone" after an especially grisly April. He returned in August, and didn't look a whole lot better. This may well be one Fish fillet who is better left uneaten. **<DM>**

Year	GS	S	C	T
1998	13	4.69	4.92	9.62

JOSE MERCEDES, MIL

Tough year for Jose: first he lost his way to the ballpark on a night he was supposed to pitch, and then he strained his rotator cuff and got lost in a more existential sense. His one rehab attempt later in the year, at AA El Paso, was a disaster. The Brewers seem to have more pitching injuries per capita than most teams; I think that's something that ought to be better quantified. And allow me to volunteer you, dear reader. . . **<DM>**

Year	GS	S	C	T
1998	5	4.40	3.40	7.80
1997	23	3.70	3.13	6.83

KEVIN MILLWOOD, ATL

Sorry, Rob Neyer, but Kevin Millwood wound up with a QWP of .504 in 1998, which means he was just about as average a pitcher as you'll find in the NL. Rob had waxed enthusiastic about Kevin after his one-hit, thirteen-K, no walk performance on April 14th. Basing his argument on Bill James' Game Score method, under which Kevin racked up a very high and very rare value, Neyer conferred greatness on Millwood. All of which has turned out to be a bit premature.

The Game Score is a fun tool for estimating dominance in a single game, but it's really just a glorified "freak show" stat in its current incarnation. Too much emphasis is placed on strikeouts in the calculational method: at the end of a season a two pitchers with identical H/9, BB/9 and ERA will always wind up with the man with more K's as the better pitcher. (You'll find a discussion of "1S" games and strikeout ratios in this year's QMAX essay, back in Section 3.)

The other thing that Rob neglected to consider, in part because it was early in the sea-

son and the pattern wasn't clearly established yet, was that Kevin threw his great game against the Pirates, who were not only one of the weakest offenses in the NL last year, but the least selective team in baseball, becoming the first non-expansion team in fifteen years to draw less than 400 walks in a season. Kevin had three other "1S" games in 1998: they came against two other weak offensive teams, the Expos and the Dodgers, and one mediocre offense (the Mets).

As it turns out Kevin's won-loss record (17-8) stems from judicious application of his only moderately above-average run support. In games where the QMAX "S" value was between 3 and 5 in 1998, starting pitchers had an aggregate winning percentage of .526 (726-655). Millwood's winning percentage in such contests? 9-2 (.818). Change that to 6-5—a closer match to the MLB average—and Kevin's won-loss record would have been 14-11 You're probably wondering what the 15-start projection method has in store for Kevin. (But just in case you're not, please fake it.) Kevin will be 24 next year, and there's about a 4% improvement rate that gets factored in; when we ran all the data, we got a little more of a spread in Kevin's numbers than for some of the others we've shown:

Scenario	S	C	T
Best	3.49	3.21	6.70
Worst	4.17	3.40	7.57
Likely	3.84	3.31	7.15

I'm hopeful that next year there will be a more complete method, one that can actually check for trends across pitchers with similar QMAX averages and similar Sector/Range data, which would add in the performance extreme probabilities and provide a more comprehensive comparison, but we're edging into jargon here and it's best to save that for a more detailed presentation (maybe as early as next year, if the Lord is willing and the creeks don't rise). Take with you the idea that Kevin Millwood, despite his won-loss record, was just about league-average in 1998, and isn't likely to be dramatically better in 1999. **<DM>**

Year	GS	S	C	T
1998	29	4.14	3.28	7.41
1997	8	4.25	3.63	7.88

DAVE MLICKI, LA
(1998: NYM-LA)

Dave's QMAX averages were 3.80,3.05/6.85 with the Dodgers; they're probably a bit better due to the park effect, but overall Dave has been right around a league-average pitcher ever since he first was put into the starting rotation. He's probably just as good as most teams' #5 men, and better than quite a few. **<DM>**

Year	GS	S	C	T
1998	30	4.17	3.27	7.43
1997	32	3.84	3.44	7.28
1996	2	5.00	2.50	7.50
1995	25	4.08	3.28	7.36

TREY MOORE, MON

Trey was part of the package of players who came to Montreal when Jeff Fassero was sent to Seattle, and he was jumped to the majors when Carl Pavano wasn't ready to answer the bell on Opening Day. He proved to be too hittable, but all in all he would appear to have an outside shot at become a league-average pitcher in the next couple of years. Left-handed, so he'll get an extra shot or two. <DM>

Year	GS	S	C	T
1998	11	5.09	3.45	8.55

MIKE MORGAN, FA
(1998: MIN-CHC)

Mike had one of the most amazing seasons in 1998 that I've ever seen. No, it wasn't because he was great, or terrible, and he didn't do something indelible or perverse (in other words, he didn't moon the fans from the pitching mound or anything). What he did was engage in the most non-decisions per start that I've ever seen. In 15 of his 22 starts, Mike left without getting a decision.

The teams he played for (Twins and Cubs) managed to go 13-9 in his starts, despite his below-average performance. The Cubs, who picked him up to sub for injured phenom Kerry Wood, somehow went 4-1 in his September starts, despite Mike being absolutely pathetic (9.40 QMAX "T" average) for them.

If anyone finds a pitcher with mor than 20 starts in a single season with a higher percentage of no-decisions in a single year (for the record, Mike's was 68.2% in 1998), please send it along. <DM>

Year	GS	S	C	T
1998	22	4.64	3.55	8.18
1997	30	3.97	3.43	7.40
1996	23	4.30	3.48	7.78
1995	21	4.24	2.90	7.14
1994	15	5.33	3.80	9.13

MATT MORRIS, STL

Matt seemed to rebound from his injuries without much difficulty, and sustained his performance level in a somewhat abbreviated sophomore campaign. He looks like a solid #3 guy, and he's got a chance to get even better. Both his ES and S12 numbers were up a bit, and he if he can add more hit prevention, he could move into the top ten starters in the league. <DM>

Year	GS	S	C	T
1998	17	3.47	3.24	6.71
1997	33	3.67	3.03	6.70

TERRY MULHOLLAND, CHC

Four of Terry's six starts came in September, and he came up with two especially timely gems during the last ten games of the season, when the Cubs needed them the most. It looks as though Terry might be ideally suited to a swingman role; there are some veteran pitchers who may be able to provide 130-150 innings over 50-odd games and 12-15 starts. Back in the old days, there were guys like Firpo Marberry who had even more innings, about this number of games, and upwards of 20 starts: someone is going to reintroduce this one of these days. <DM>

Year	GS	S	C	T
1998	6	3.17	2.67	5.83
1997	27	4.15	3.11	7.26
1996	33	4.61	3.03	7.64
1995	24	5.08	3.04	8.13
1994	19	5.16	3.32	8.47

DENNY NEAGLE, CIN
(1998: ATL)

Odd thing about Denny is that he always seems to win big at home, even if he doesn't pitch particularly well; he's 40-11 at home over the past six years, and was 9-3 there last year despite a 4.47 ERA; conversely, he was just 7-8 on the road in 1998 despite a fine 2.74 ERA. He basically slipped back a notch in 1998, and clearly became the Braves' #4 guy—though he'd still be a #2-3 guy on most other teams, and a #1-#2 guy on the Reds. <DM>

Year	GS	S	C	T
1998	31	3.68	2.87	6.55
1997	34	3.47	2.53	6.00
1996	33	4.03	2.58	6.61
1995	31	4.16	2.42	6.58
1994	24	3.75	3.54	7.29

HIDEO NOMO, NYM
(1998: LA-NYM)

It's not Nomo's stuff that has deserted him, it's his command. That's what got him into trouble in 1997, and it's gotten worse, as the QMAX Sector and Range data for the last four years indicates:

Year	SS	ES	HH	S12	C1	C23	C45	C67
1998	46%	18%	21%	54%	7%	32%	25%	36%
1997	45%	12%	24%	45%	6%	36%	48%	9%
1996	64%	21%	18%	48%	12%	61%	21%	6%
1995	68%	32%	18%	75%	14%	46%	29%	11%

Nomo actually had more S12 games in 1998 than in either 1996 or 1997, but his command was completely AWOL more than a third of the time. You can see that it was headed that way in 1997, with nearly half of his games in the C45 range, but he'd only had five games in his first three seasons where his control was in the Tommy Byrne category. That happened to him a total of eight times in 1998.

Conclusion: the league isn't really beating Nomo. Nomo is beating Nomo. <DM>

Year	GS	S	C	T
1998	28	3.36	4.46	7.82
1997	33	3.67	3.70	7.36
1996	33	3.21	3.12	6.33
1995	28	2.50	3.29	5.79

KIRT OJALA, FLA

I could certainly be swayed by an argument contending that if the Fish were determined to leap out of the aquarium and gasp around on the floor for the whole of 1998, they would have been better served by leaving their young prospects in the minors and giving more starts to someone like Ojala, who was pushing 30 and had five years at AAA under his belt. Instead, they leave Ojala in the bullpen for two-thirds of the season and let every Fish fillet in the immediate vicinity have a Warholian assignation with the starting rotation.

Kirt wasn't all that good, but that isn't the point. He could have eaten a lot more innings on the team and given a number of prospects more time to develop in the minors. There's a difference between playing the kids and force-feeding them. <DM>

Year	GS	S	C	T
1998	13	4.31	4.15	8.46
1997	5	3.80	4.60	8.40

DARREN OLIVER, STL
(1998: TEX-STL)

If you've been a careful reader of this section over the past several years, you'll instantly recall that this is the guy who first got me into a heap of trouble. It was easy to be seduced by a low "S" value in a small sample size: I know better now. (At least most of the time I do, anyway.)

The big lesson: wait until you get at least thirty starts before you start trying to generalize about a pitcher's career. Thirty starts into Darren Oliver's career would have prevented me from spending a couple of years expecting him to match those early handful of starts. Ah, well, confession is good for the soul: just ask Jimmy Swaggart.

Anyway, Darren did pitch a good bit better for the Cards (7.70 QMAX "T" vs. 9.05 in Texas), so we can expect him to break out this year and get his "S" average down to . . .

Just making sure that you're paying attention. <DM>

Year	GS	S	C	T
1998	29	4.90	3.69	8.59
1997	32	4.31	3.63	7.94
1996	30	4.47	3.73	8.20
1995	7	3.43	4.29	7.71

RUSS ORTIZ, SF

Russ showed enough to get a full shot as the #5 man in the Giants' rotation in 1999. He was a wild-ass closer in the minors through 1996, but was converted to starting in 1997 and has been slowly getting his command together as he learns the ropes of the rotation; he still has a tendency to lose the strike zone, often in the third or fourth inning of work. <DM>

Year	GS	S	C	T
1998	13	4.18	3.61	7.79

DONOVAN OSBORNE, STL

Definitely a card-carrying CAD. Donovan has been through more arm miseries than NBC has mini-series, and, despite all of that, still seems to come back as just about the same above-average pitcher that he's been since his debut. When you think about it, that's pretty darned amazing. <DM>

Year	GS	S	C	T
1998	14	4.00	3.00	7.00
1997	14	4.21	3.21	7.43
1996	30	3.70	2.73	6.43
1995	19	3.89	3.21	7.11

CHAN HO PARK, LA

I'm a little leery of that rising "S" value, but a good bit of this comes from a slow start caused by some lingering back problems. From July 1st to the end of the season, Chan Ho had 68% of his games in the Success Square, and 32% in the Elite Square. If his back problems are behind him, I envision him

getting back to his 1997 QMAX value, and maybe even improving on it. <DM>

Year	GS	S	C	T
1998	33	3.61	3.61	7.21
1997	29	3.14	3.28	6.41
1996	10	2.90	4.70	7.60
1995	1	2.00	4.00	6.00

STEVE PARRIS, CIN

Steve had just turned 30, and was thinking about giving up the wayward life of a baseball pitcher, one that had seen him scuffle through most of the eastern half of the United States since being assigned to Batavia, Pennsylvania by the Phillies (the first of four organizations he would belong to in the next nine years).

Finally, in Indianapolis, he met a wizened old metallurgist who dabbled in the mystical arts (when he wasn't eating hoagies); this crusty coot convinced him to undergo a mysterious procedure that would make his arm as young and resilient as a boy of eighteen. The only catch was that after every start he made, his arm would age faster than normal—about four months per start. The wrinkled wizard guaranteed him that he'd be back in the majors for sure in 1998, and he would have more success than he'd ever had.

When faced with this, Steve (whose lifetime major league ERA was 5.82) really had little choice, and put up even less resistance. He had the old man perform the procedure, and he began to pitch for Indianapolis. Lo and behold, he could suddenly blow the ball by the hitters! By early June he was leading the league in strikeouts and seemed like a completely different pitcher. The Reds, noticing his new-found heat, and desperate for pitching, called him up to the bigs, where—as the old man had promised—he pitched better than he ever had before.

In late August, he reached his peak,

tossing a three-hit shutout at Montreal. A couple of weeks later, he shut down Arizona. But in the last game of the season, he realized that the old man's description of the accelerated aging of his arm was all too true: for the first time in months when he went to warm up, he had nothing. He had made 26 starts, and—all too swiftly—his arm was approaching his real age again.

Ominously, the team that originally signed him ten years earlier, the Phillies, knocked him out in the third inning.

Right after the off-season, Steve went back to Indianapolis, looking for the old man. After many false starts, he found the building, but there was no trace of him.

It looks like Steve will be on his own in 1999. <DM>

Year	GS	S	C	T
1998	16	3.81	3.25	7.06
1996	4	5.00	3.75	8.75
1995	15	4.47	3.87	8.33

BRONSWELL PATRICK, SF
(1998: MIL)

After 1100+ innings in the minors, Bronswell Patrick finally made it to the big leagues (though it was Milwaukee, and there were some members of his family clever enough to tell him that it didn't really count). He didn't care about that, however; he just wanted to get that big-league meal money (as Lauren Bacall said to Bogart in Dark Passage, you're no featherweight. . .).

In pursuit of major-league eats all season long, Bronswell actually managed to do a little pitching, too, but discovered that he'd lost most of the slide from his slide step by mid-August. Before the Brewers could separate Bronswell from the braunschweiger, he was lunch meat. <DM>

Year	GS	S	C	T
1998	3	5.33	2.67	8.00

CARL PAVANO, MON

A promising but not electrifying debut by the kid Montreal received for Pedro Martínez. Pavano only had 9% of his games in the Elite Square, but 59% in the Success Square. That's the problematic ratio: sometimes the pitcher holds the SS% and adds to his ES%, and other times he holds the ES% and loses ground with his SS%. This year should tell us a good bit about how much upside Carl really has. <DM>

Year	GS	S	C	T
1998	22	3.82	3.32	7.14

MISCELLANEOUS STARTING PITCHER DATA, NATIONAL LEAGUE 1998

LEGEND: NP—Number of Pitches thrown; **TW**—Team Wins in pitcher's starts; **TL**—Team Losses in pitcher's starts; **GS**—; **QS**—Quality Starts; **BS**—Blown Starts; **QmB**—Quality minus Blown pct.; **PPI**—Pitches thrown Per Inning; **IP**—Innings Pitched; **AdIP**—Adjusted Innings Pitched; **IP/S**—average Innings Pitched per Start

Pitcher Name	Team	TW	TL	GS	QS	BS	QMB	IP	NP	Str	PPI	Kpct	AdjIP	IP/S
Steve Woodard	MIL	9	17	26	9	4	19.23	151.0	2333	1498	15.45	64.2%	148	5.8
Jeff Juden	MIL	10	14	24	10	7	12.50	138.4	2389	1481	17.27	62.0%	152	5.8
Paul Wagner	MIL	2	7	9	1	2	-11.11	50.0	884	517	17.68	58.5%	56	5.6
Carlos Perez	MON	11	12	23	16	1	65.22	163.3	2338	1567	14.31	67.0%	149	7.1
Dustin Hermanson	MON	17	13	30	17	2	50.00	184.0	2706	1756	14.71	64.9%	172	6.1
Carl Pavano	MON	11	11	22	11	3	36.36	126.7	2037	1266	16.08	62.2%	130	5.8
Miguel Batista	MON	4	9	13	5	1	30.77	71.4	1191	712	16.69	59.8%	76	5.5
Trey Moore	MON	3	8	11	5	2	27.27	56.0	868	547	15.50	63.0%	55	5.1
Mike Thurman	MON	7	6	13	4	2	15.38	66.0	1006	610	15.24	60.6%	64	5.1
Javier Vazquez	MON	10	22	32	8	7	3.13	171.3	2877	1751	16.79	60.9%	183	5.4
Marc Valdes	MON	0	4	4	1	2	-25.00	13.0	247	139	19.00	56.3%	16	3.3
Jeremy Powell	MON	1	5	6	2	4	-33.33	24.0	409	244	17.04	59.7%	26	4.0
Shawn Boskie	MON	1	4	5	1	3	-40.00	17.7	290	195	16.41	67.2%	18	3.5
Mike Johnson	MON	0	2	2	0	2	-100.00	7.3	152	89	20.74	58.6%	10	3.7
Willie Blair	NYM	1	1	2	2	0	100.00	14.3	170	107	11.86	62.9%	11	7.2
Al Leiter	NYM	20	8	28	21	0	75.00	193.0	3204	1891	16.60	59.0%	204	6.9
Rick Reed	NYM	17	14	31	24	3	67.74	212.3	3057	2030	14.40	66.4%	194	6.8

CARLOS PEREZ, LA
(1998: MON-LA)

The Dodgers ransomed their farm system to acquire Perez from the Expos, and Carlos eventually got it together with a big September (2.20,2.00/4.20); of course, it was way too late for LA by then. Perez had better hit prevention while with the Dodgers, but some of that could be due to the ballpark; all in all, he's established a very consistent level of performance—good, but nowhere near great. For the Dodgers to contend, they needed another, slightly taller, lefty. <DM>

YEAR	GS	S	C	T
1998	34	4.03	2.65	6.68
1997	32	3.88	2.78	6.66
1995	23	4.09	2.96	7.04

CHRIS PETERS, PIT

Moved into the rotation in June, Peters held his own and became part of a pretty fair blue collar group of Pirates starters. High BGPct (50%), low SS% (just 40%). <DM>

YEAR	GS	S	C	T
1998	20	3.90	3.20	7.10
1997	1	3.00	2.00	5.00
1996	10	4.30	3.80	8.10

MARK PETKOVSEK, STL

All or nothing for Mark when he was in the rotation in 1998—either in the success square (40%) or hit hard (60%). There was no in between. Mark began and ended his 1998 starts with games where he failed to make it out of the first inning. <DM>

YEAR	GS	S	C	T
1998	10	4.50	4.00	8.50
1997	2	6.00	3.50	9.50
1996	6	3.50	3.50	7.00
1995	21	4.14	3.00	7.14

CLIFF POLITTE, PHI
(1998: STL)

Six games in AA didn' translate into enough to get Cliff over the hump in his major league debut. The Cards were strapped for starters at the beginning of the year, what with Alan Benes, Donovan Osborne, and Matt Morris all out, so Cliff got stretched. There was a lot of that going on in baseball during 1998. And in 1999, Cliff will find out what it's like to pitch for the closest thing to a threshing machine in MLB. <DM>

YEAR	GS	S	C	T
1998	8	4.75	4.25	9.00

MARK PORTUGAL, BOS
(1998: PHI)

Mark's injuries seem to have swung him further into the finesse pitcher range; his C1 average was as high as his S12 in 1998 (27% for each). Despite a nice comeback, his contract was too rich for the Phillies and they bought out his option; . <DM>

YEAR	GS	S	C	T
1998	26	4.31	2.65	6.96
1997	3	4.67	4.67	9.33
1996	26	3.65	3.12	6.77
1995	31	3.87	3.23	7.10
1994	21	4.00	3.05	7.05

JEREMY POWELL, MON

In 1997, Jeremy was in the Florida State League, where he was not overpowering. He was brought up in late July, and his first two starts were very strong (including a two-hit, six inning performance against the Dodgers), but he was hit hard in three of his next four starts and did not pitch again after August 27th. <DM>

YEAR	GS	S	C	T
1998	6	4.17	4.33	8.50

BILL PULSIPHER, MIL
(1998: NYM-MIL)

And then there were two, as Kid Pulsipher was dropkicked out of New York. After all of that anguish and suffering over their Fizz Kids, you'd think they could have given Bill more than just one start once he'd made it back to the big leagues, but the Mets are in a hurry to upgrade their payroll. The Fizz Kids just don't fit in any more. Still very rusty from his two-year side trip, Pulse was inconsistent with the Brewers—who, frankly, don't seem like the kind of team that will be able to nurse Bill back into

something resembling his earlier form. <DM>

YEAR	GS	S	C	T
1998	11	4.36	3.91	8.27
1995	17	3.65	2.82	6.47

RICK REED, NYM

Score one for the good guys. A number of people wrote to inform me that they didn't think Rick Reed was going to hold his 1997 level. All I can say, folks, is that QMAX doesn't lie. (OK, only if absolutely necessary.)

Rick was pretty much spot on his fine 1997 effort last year: a little bit down on the SS and ES, but not much, and he was even more of a Tommy John pitcher in 1998 (23%, up from 16%). I do think that Rick is probably going to start to fade, but I suspect it will be slow and gradual. <DM>

YEAR	GS	S	C	T
1998	31	3.77	2.06	5.84
1997	31	3.52	2.32	5.84
1995	3	4.00	3.00	7.00
1994	3	3.67	4.33	8.00

MIKE REMLINGER, ATL
(1998: CIN)

Mike didn't quite pull it together in his big shot at the Reds' starting rotation, and it's likely that he'll end up back in the bullpen this year. It's been a long time since Mike was a phenom from Dartmouth drafted #1 by the Giants, and he has been tenacious in overcoming injuries and wildness to get to the big leagues long after most people had given him up for dead. But it appears that the success that looked to be within easy reach for Mike back in 1989 is going to elude him. Part of the Neagle-Boone trade, and it will be interesting to see if Leo Mazzone can work any miracles with him. <DM>

**MISCELLANEOUS STARTING PITCHER DATA,
NATIONAL LEAGUE 1998**

LEGEND: NP—Number of Pitches thrown; **TW**—Team Wins in pitcher's starts; **TL**—Team Losses in pitcher's starts; **GS**—; **QS**—Quality Starts; **BS**—Blown Starts; **QmB**—Quality minus Blown pct.; **PPI**—Pitches thrown Per Inning; **IP**—Innings Pitched; **AdIP**—Adjusted Innings Pitched; **IP/S**—average Innings Pitched per Start

Pitcher Name	Team	TW	TL	GS	QS	BS	QMB	IP	NP	Str	PPI	Kpct	AdjIP	IP/S
Bobby Jones	NYM	17	13	30	18	2	53.33	195.3	3017	1916	15.44	63.5%	192	6.5
Brian Bohanon	NYM	2	4	2	2	0	50.00	21.0	318	190	15.14	59.7%	20	5.3
Masato Yoshii	NYM	13	16	29	15	3	41.38	171.7	2571	1654	14.98	64.3%	164	5.9
Armando Reynoso	NYM	7	4	11	7	3	36.36	68.3	1104	643	16.15	58.2%	70	6.2
Hideo Nomo	NYM	6	10	16	6	4	12.50	85.7	1454	873	16.97	60.0%	92	5.4
Dave Mlicki	NYM	4	6	10	3	2	10.00	57.0	958	571	16.81	59.6%	61	5.7
Bill Pulsipher	NYM	1	0	1	0	1	-100.00	4.0	83	53	20.75	63.9%	5	4.0
Paul Byrd	PHI	5	3	8	6	0	75.00	55.0	830	542	15.09	65.3%	53	6.9
Curt Schilling	PHI	17	18	35	27	1	74.29	268.7	4213	2779	15.68	66.0%	268	7.7
Mark Portugal	PHI	15	11	26	13	5	30.77	166.3	2314	1543	13.91	66.7%	147	6.4
Carlton Loewer	PHI	10	11	21	10	4	28.57	122.7	1911	1192	15.58	62.4%	122	5.8
Tyler Green	PHI	9	18	27	10	5	18.52	159.3	2643	1492	16.59	56.5%	168	5.9
Mike Grace	PHI	7	8	15	5	3	13.33	82.7	1342	823	16.23	61.3%	85	5.5
Matt Beech	PHI	9	12	21	8	6	9.52	117.0	2105	1263	17.99	60.0%	134	5.6
Ken Ryan	PHI	0	1	1	0	0	0.00	3.0	55	28	18.33	50.9%	3	3.0
Garrett Stephenson	PHI	3	3	6	1	3	-33.33	23.0	465	258	20.22	55.5%	30	3.8
Mike Welch	PHI	0	2	2	0	2	-100.00	6.3	175	104	27.65	59.4%	11	3.2

YEAR	GS	S	C	T
1998	28	3.89	4.07	7.96
1997	12	3.75	3.50	7.25
1996	4	3.50	5.00	8.50
1994	9	3.67	4.33	8.00

DENNIS REYES, CIN
(1998: LA-CIN)

Reyes, aka Fernando Jr., was acquired by the Reds when Tommy Lasorda mortgaged the first part of the Dodger future in order to bring Jeff Shaw to LA. Dennis' first three starts upon joining the Reds were solid ones, but he didn't build on those, struggling in his next seven outings before having his season curtailed in early September. He may well get a longer look in 1999. <DM>

YEAR	GS	S	C	T
1998	10	3.90	4.50	8.40
1997	5	4.60	3.20	7.80

SHANE REYNOLDS, HOU

I think Reynolds' QMAX data shows both the value and the limitations of the method. Looking over the five-year pattern, we get a full sense of the recursive homogeneity that is apparent in close to half of the MLB starting pitcher population. If we look at just 1994-96, however, we'll probably decide that Reynolds is very possibly going to turn into an ace, which would have been the wrong forecast. Large-scale comparisons of pitchers, data, and patterns are just now becoming possible with QMAX, and next year's book might be the point when we can first synthesize some detailed and meaningful generalizations about starting pitcher performance. <DM>

YEAR	GS	S	C	T
1998	35	4.51	2.57	7.09
1997	30	4.03	3.03	7.07
1996	35	3.71	2.34	6.06
1995	30	4.20	2.53	6.73
1994	14	3.86	2.50	6.36

ARMANDO REYNOSO, AZ
(1998: NYM)

Staying with Reynoso instead of Nomo in the starting rotation proved to be the wrong hunch by Bobby Valentine. Armando coughed up 6,3 and 7,7 outings, losing both, as the Mets took their ignominious dive out of the Wild Card race in the last week. A classic Jekyll/Hyde type, Reynoso is the type of pitcher, as Sandy Koufax so astutely noted in his autobiography, who always seems better than he is because his good games look so good. His bad games, however, are something else entirely. I thought that it might be the Giants who would take a shot on Armando in 1999, but the Snakes dipped into the "Bargain Bin" for once and snagged him. <DM>

YEAR	GS	S	C	T
1998	11	3.64	3.82	7.45
1997	16	4.00	3.31	7.31
1996	30	4.60	3.30	7.90
1995	18	4.61	3.89	8.50
1994	9	4.11	3.67	7.78

KEVIN RITZ, COL

"Puttin' on the Ritz" is as outdated in Denver as it is in the world of show business. <DM>

YEAR	GS	S	C	T
1998	2	6.50	3.50	10.00
1997	18	5.22	3.78	9.00
1996	35	4.46	3.89	8.34
1995	28	4.00	3.61	7.61
1994	15	4.67	4.20	8.87

RAFAEL ROQUE, MIL

This guy could have been this year's Darren Oliver in terms of QMAX and predictions. We know better now, and there's the added fact that nothing in Roque's minor-league record indicates that he'll be able to sustain this kind of hit prevention over a large body of starts. Let's wait and see. <DM>

YEAR	GS	S	C	T
1998	9	3.56	4.11	7.67

KIRK RUETER, SF

You've got to credit Dusty Baker with managing to get to a Wild Card playoff game with the starting rotation that he possessed. Of course, you could say the same for Jim Riggleman—except that the Cubs had Kerry Wood. Speaking of which, "Woody" Rueter is a game little lefty who looks to have found his level at right around league average. That makes him the third #5 starter that the Giants have, which is why Dusty has to get that desperately creative with his bullpen. <DM>

YEAR	GS	S	C	T
1998	32	4.13	3.38	7.50
1997	32	3.91	3.13	7.03
1996	19	4.16	3.42	7.58
1995	9	3.56	3.22	6.78
1994	20	4.45	3.65	8.10

MIKE SAIPE, COL

The Rockies diddled with Saipe a bit in the minors in 1995-96, trying to figure out whether to make a starter or reliever out of him. He hasn't handled Colorado Springs very well at all, which has ominous analogies for what he might do in Denver. <DM>

YEAR	GS	S	C	T
1998	2	6.50	2.50	9.00

JESUS SANCHEZ, FLA

The booty in the Al Leiter trade, Jesus became a cause celebre in the early going due to the high pitch counts he received from Jim Leyland in several starts. The "cry wolf" contingent in pitcher workload has gotten more and more vocal, but they have done precious little analysis of whether isolated high pitch counts produce much arm damage in pitchers. Over in the AL comments, we discussed this issue in the Bartolo Colon comment; Sanchez, who had two 130+ pitch games in 1998, is a perfect place to revisit it.

To refresh your memory, we were wondering whether or not the matter of pitch counts might be better studied in terms of multiple games; we chose three games as the unit of measure, and posited that the effective limit was 350 pitches per three starts. Below that, you were probably all right; above that, you were asking for trouble. The corollary argument accompanying this model is that the closer one remains on a constant basis to that 350 pitch limit, the greater the risk of injury becomes.

We showed a chart with the three-game pitch counts for Colon's 1998 season and injured pitcher Alan Benes' 1997 season. Let's reprint that chart, and add in the running three-start counts of Jesus Sanchez:

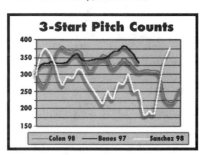

As we noted earlier, Benes remained perilously close to our "350 line" during almost the entire 1997 season (at least the portion that he pitched). Colon was also given a dangerously high workload, but it wasn't quite so consistently kept at the danger point; he suffered ineffectiveness rather than injury, which eventually brought his pitch counts down. While this is clearly not the preferred way to regulate pitch counts, it's certainly part of baseball's more primitive pitcher ecology.

Sanchez, on the other hand, had that early peak which got some people extremely lathered (you could almost hear their voices rise, as Jim Bouton put it so well in Ball Four, like a girl with a short skirt on a windy day). While those high-pitched guys might still want to contend that the early peak caused ineffectiveness which in turn produced the low pitch counts, the seasonal evidence doesn't point to this. Sanchez did not miss a turn, and his outings show no significant valleys caused by his pitch counts. And his pitch counts were extremely moderate for the rest of the year, until the very end, when Leyland let him go all the way to nail down his first complete-game shutout.

Therefore, I think it's at best false drama when analysts start squealing about single-game pitch counts; at worst, it's Bad Sabermetrics. Managers have become more conscious of single-game pitch counts; what we need to see happen next is that they become aware of consecutive-game pitch counts.

And as for Jesus Sanchez, he wound up having the highest SS%. ES%, and S12% on the Marlins. He wasn't too far off league average, despite the purported abuse and— probably far more important in terms of his development—the fact that he was jumped directly from AA into the big leagues.

Year	GS	S	C	T
1998	29	4.03	3.90	7.93

SCOTT SANDERS, CHC
(1998: SD)

Scott's roundabout journey home to San Diego was completed last July, when the Padres recalled him from Las Vegas. A dose of the Master of Chaos (Lou Piniella) produced a virulent reaction that became career-threatening, and he was unable to regroup even after being shipped to Detroit in a gunny sack. My suspicions that Scott might find himself in the San Diego rotation in 1999 were dashed when the Padres released him during the off-season; Wrigley doesn't seem like a good place for a fly-ball pitcher, though, as the Cubs may soon find out.. <DM>

Year	GS	S	C	T
1998	2	6.50	5.00	11.50
1997	20	4.65	4.05	8.70
1996	16	3.38	3.00	6.38
1995	15	3.47	3.33	6.80
1994	20	4.05	4.05	8.10

CURT SCHILLING, PHI

4,213 was Curt's magic number in 1998: that's the number of pitches that he threw last year. He is, of course, a great pitcher and an amazing workhorse (don't downplay those consecutive 300-K seasons; they're as rare as any achievement in the game). He's also probably the worst role model for other pitchers you can find, and even more so for his young teammates in the Phillies starting rotation. Probably the quintessential hurler, in that he really doesn't bother with much except for the high hard one; his other main pitch is the low hard one. <DM>

Year	GS	S	C	T
1998	35	3.46	2.06	5.51
1997	35	3.11	2.43	5.54
1996	26	3.00	2.69	5.69
1995	17	3.12	2.47	5.59
1994	13	4.31	3.15	7.46

JASON SCHMIDT, PIT

Jason made some progress with his command, but there's nothing in his performance that indicates he'll be making any startling leap forward in the near future. I think there's a better chance of that happening with either Cordova or Jose Silva (see below). <DM>

Year	GS	S	C	T
1998	33	4.21	3.09	7.30
1997	32	3.97	3.56	7.53
1996	17	4.18	4.41	8.59
1995	2	3.50	4.50	8.00

JOSE SILVA, PIT

We'll have to see how much Silva's broken arm affects his development. He had put together a very nice seven-start string prior to the injury (3.00,2.00/5.00) , but he wound up missing eleven weeks of the season and clearly wasn't close to his earlier form when he came back in September. If he's OK, I think he might have the biggest upside of any Pirate hurler, as he showed a high propensity for Elite Square games before he was hurt. <DM>

Year	GS	S	C	T
1998	18	4.06	3.28	7.33
1997	4	6.25	3.75	10.00

JOHN SMOLTZ, ATL

A little off in his command, as you might expect for a guy who was working through elbow problems, but otherwise John was right in the pocket, his usual #1-#2 type pitcher. The 1-2-3 combo of Maddux-Glavine-Smoltz is almost certainly going to rank up there as one of the greatest in baseball history, with 308 wins in six years (and one strike-shortened). <DM>

Year	GS	S	C	T
1998	26	3.35	2.81	6.15
1997	35	3.43	2.29	5.71
1996	35	3.09	2.23	5.31
1995	29	3.24	3.17	6.41
1994	21	3.33	3.24	6.57

CLINT SODOWSKY, AZ

Buck Showalter gave Clint a test drive in the starting rotation late in the year, but I don't think he liked what he saw; Sodowsky's future role, if any, with the D-backs looks to be confined exclusively to the bullpen. <DM>

Year	GS	S	C	T
1998	6	4.17	4.50	8.67
1996	7	5.71	5.43	11.14
1995	6	3.83	5.17	9.00

STAN SPENCER, SD

Stan is 30, and missed two years (1992 and 1996) with arm problems, but he's definitely got a chance to help the Padres next season, exactly when their rotation is going to

need it. As a matter of fact, if Kevin Towers is as gutsy as the media thinks he is, he'll try to unload the fading Joey Hamilton for one of the Reds' gazillion first base prospects and go with a rotation of Ashby, Hitchcock, Clement, Sanders and Spencer. But I tend to think that the ballyhooed fire in Kevin's belly is nothing more than a cigarette lighter. <DM>

Year	GS	S	C	T
1998	5	3.80	2.80	6.60

GARRETT STEPHENSON, STL
(1998: PHI)

Garrett and I took turns stepping on the banana peel last year, as he crashed and burned after a very nice partial season in 1997. Sometimes these guys just lose it all, and there's nothing that they nor I nor you nor even QMAX can do about it. <DM>

Year	GS	S	C	T
1998	6	4.83	5.33	10.17
1997	18	3.61	3.06	6.67

KEVIN TAPANI, CHC

See under Aaron Sele in the AL pitcher comments. <DM>

Year	GS	S	C	T
1998	34	4.44	2.91	7.35
1997	13	3.85	2.69	6.54
1996	34	4.03	3.09	7.12
1995	31	4.71	2.97	7.68
1994	24	4.54	2.67	7.21

AMAURY TELEMACO, AZ
(1998: CHC-AZ)

As with many younger pitchers, Telemaco probably needs to be given one role and permitted to fully adapt to it. He got into the doghouse in Chicago, and was waived to the Snakes late in May, who kept him in the pen for awhile and then moved him back into the rotation. He made some real progress, especially in terms of his command, and he might settle into being a useful #3-4 guy. What with the Great Starter Gold Rush in Phoneix over the off-season, though, it looks like Telemaco will be back in the pen in 1999. <DM>

Year	GS	S	C	T
1998	18	4.22	3.17	7.39
1997	5	4.80	3.60	8.40
1996	17	4.29	3.59	7.88

MARK THOMPSON, COL

I think Mark got blown out by Coors, and his arm appears to be toast at this point. His six starts in 1998 were almost all "nibblers," where he was building up big pitch per inning averages by trying to make perfect pitches. If he can't rear back and throw, he's in trouble, Interestingly, Mark is another one of those *pitchers who was skipped a league (A-AAA). We've got to do a study of that stuff.* <DM>

Year	GS	S	C	T
1998	6	5.67	4.50	10.17
1997	6	5.17	4.00	9.17
1996	28	4.14	3.68	7.82
1995	5	4.60	3.60	8.20
1994	2	6.00	6.00	12.00

JOHN THOMSON, COL

John doesn't seem to be as fazed by Coors as some of the other Rockies' pitchers, both present and past. Here are his 1998 home/road QMAX values:

Where	S	C	T
Coors	4.77	3.15	7.92
Away	3.38	3.00	6.38

You're probably saying, what does he mean, not fazed? Look at that S difference! All true, but consider that the league average for the past four years at Coors is 5.13, 3.70, 8.83, and the league average altogether is 4.04, 3.29, 7.33. That means that John is being hit harder at Coors, but he's not giving nearly as much away in terms of command; hence he's not trying to pitch differently there than he would on the road, which probably contributes to his success away from Coors.

Which is, of course, just as important as what he does at Coors. Those road numbers indicate that John is a fine pitcher, and if he keeps doing what he's doing, he could be one of the guys who helps to demonstrate how the discontinuity generated by playing in such an extreme park can be mitigated—a valuable and historic achievement, should it happen. <DM>

Year	GS	S	C	T
1998	26	4.08	3.08	7.15
1997	27	4.74	3.11	7.85

MIKE THURMAN, MON

Mike is another guy whose minor league numbers don't match the initial results he's posted in the big leagues. There is no indication that he's grown into his fastball or developed a new pitch to account for the additional hit prevention; his K/9 and K/BB ratio is at the bottom of the group of starters with a similar QMAX "S" score. Looking at his game logs shows the fanatical devotion to nursing his young pitchers that is the hallmark of Felipe Alou; Mike may have been given the gentlest workload of the past five years. <DM>

Year	GS	S	C	T
1998	13	3.62	3.92	7.54
1997	2	3.00	4.00	7.00

BRETT TOMKO, CIN

Odd voices in the noise: Brett's first six QMAX "S" scores in 1998 were 1, 5, 1, 5, 1, 5. After those six starts he was at 3.00,2,50/5.50; the distance between the quality level of his starts was very high, though, which usually signals trouble ahead. And in his next ten starts, Tomko was hit hard (4.80,3.60/8.40). At that point he settled down, and posted the following two nine-start units:

When	S	C	T
6/30-8/11	3.56	3.22	6.78
8/16-9/27	3.56	3.11	6.67

Looks as though Brett settled into his characteristic pitching pattern at about start thirty-five of his big league career, and suddenly became a hell of a lot more consistent.

I don't mean to suggest that Brett will now crank out endless seasons at this exact level (though he just might), but I do think this eighteen-start season segment is an interesting hypothesis for how pitchers "settle" at their performance level at any given point in their career.

If Brett stays in the 6.50-6.80 range in 1999, we'll have another glimmer of how that works. No giant beacon of light, but something out there to shoot for at the end of the tunnel. <DM>

Year	GS	S	C	T
1998	34	3.82	3.18	7.00
1997	19	3.32	3.47	6.79

STEVE TRACHSEL, CHC

One of the few reliable practitioners of the strict "on-off" seasonal pattern has now bit the dust, thanks to run support, El Nino, and Harry Caray's ascent into the empyrean, in roughly that order. <DM>

Year	GS	S	C	T
1998	33	4.03	3.48	7.52
1997	33	4.48	3.36	7.85
1996	31	3.45	2.90	6.35
1995	29	4.24	3.97	8.21
1994	22	3.27	3.09	6.36

ISMAEL VALDES, LA

Dodger pitchers really took it on the chin in 1998: it's almost as if they read Michael Wolverton's SNWL Report at the end of 1997 and said "he's right; we just ain't that good." But I think it was just some kind of bad patch that several Dodger starters just experienced as part of the evolution of their careers (Valdes and Park, for sure; Nomo is quite possibly another case entirely). Both Park and Valdes did turn things around in the second half, which bodes well for their future performance; let's take a look at Ismael's QMAX data broken into two roughly equal halves:

When	GS	S	C	T
4/11-6/5	13	4.77	3.62	8.39
6/11-9/25	14	3.21	3.21	6.42

Those last 14 games, interrupted by injury as they were, still look a hell of a lot more like representative Valdes numbers than what preceded them. Our studies of 15-game and 20-game QMAX running averages have identified that just about all pitchers, even very good ones, go through some bad patches and spikes in the course of their careers. I think early 1998 was precisely that for Valdes, and probably Park as well. I see no reason to think that Ismael won't post numbers similar to his past performance level in 1999. <DM>

Year	GS	S	C	T
1998	27	3.96	3.41	7.37
1997	30	3.30	2.70	6.00
1996	33	3.79	2.61	6.39
1995	27	3.00	2.63	5.63
1994	1	6.00	6.00	12.00

MISCELLANEOUS STARTING PITCHER DATA, NATIONAL LEAGUE 1998

LEGEND: NP—Number of Pitches thrown; **TW**—Team Wins in pitcher's starts; **TL**—Team Losses in pitcher's starts; **GS**—; **QS**—Quality Starts; **BS**—Blown Starts; **QmB**—Quality minus Blown pct.; **PPI**—Pitches thrown Per Inning; **IP**—Innings Pitched; **AdIP**—Adjusted Innings Pitched; **IP/S**—average Innings Pitched per Start

Pitcher Name	Team	TW	TL	GS	QS	BS	QMB	IP	NP	Str	PPI	Kpct	AdjIP	IP/S
Francisco Cordova	PIT	16	17	33	21	4	51.52	220.3	3227	2001	14.65	62.0%	205	6.7
Jason Schmidt	PIT	13	20	33	18	4	42.42	214.3	3483	2152	16.25	61.8%	222	6.5
Chris Peters	PIT	10	10	20	9	1	40.00	119.0	1784	1087	14.99	60.9%	113	5.9
Jon Lieber	PIT	10	17	27	15	5	37.04	168.7	2534	1638	15.02	64.6%	161	6.2
Jose Silva	PIT	8	10	18	9	5	22.22	100.3	1516	945	15.11	62.3%	96	5.6
Esteban Loaiza	PIT	6	8	14	5	2	21.43	78.3	1242	803	15.86	64.7%	79	5.6
Todd Van Poppel	PIT	3	3	7	3	2	14.29	37.0	590	356	15.95	60.3%	38	5.3
Elmer Dessens	PIT	0	5	5	1	1	0.00	26.7	414	237	15.52	57.2%	26	5.3
Mike Williams	PIT	1	0	1	0	0	0.00	5.0	71	47	14.20	61.9%	5	5.0
Sean Lawrence	PIT	1	2	3	0	2	-66.67	13.3	241	139	18.08	57.7%	15	4.4
Kevin Brown	SDP	22	13	35	29	2	77.14	256.0	3682	2397	14.38	65.1%	234	7.3
Andy Ashby	SDP	23	10	33	25	4	63.64	226.7	3164	2062	13.96	65.2%	201	6.9
Matt Clement	SDP	1	1	2	1	0	50.00	11.7	195	117	16.71	60.0%	12	5.8
Sterling Hitchcock	SDP	18	9	27	16	5	40.74	166.3	2571	1592	15.46	61.9%	164	6.2
Stan Spencer	SDP	3	2	5	3	1	40.00	28.7	435	285	15.17	65.5%	28	5.7
Joey Hamilton	SDP	18	16	34	19	7	35.29	217.3	3459	2090	15.92	60.4%	220	6.4
Donnie Wall	SDP	1	0	1	0	0	0.00	5.0	83	49	16.60	59.0%	5	5.0

JAVIER VAZQUEZ, MON

Another example of force-feeding: Vazquez is a 22-year old kid whose highest level of competition before last season was six starts at AA. Granted, he annihilated the Eastern League for a 1.07 ERA, but this was still a big stretch—and it showed.

Now I realize that over the course of baseball history there have been any number of young pitchers who were rushed up to the majors in similar circumstances, and some turned out to be fine major league pitchers—Nels Potter, Camilo Pascual, and Vern Law are three who immediately come to mind—but would any of these guys have been better off if they'd stayed in the minors for another year or two? 1998 was a year in which more young pitchers were rushed to the majors than any one I can identify—even 1969, when there were four expansion teams in a single year, didn't produce this volume of young pitchers in over their heads.

One could argue that Vazquez will be ready to make a big leap forward earlier than he might have. But from the experience of the three pitchers listed above—Potter, Pascual, and Law—their rise to proficiency took anywhere from four to seven years after they made their premature major league debuts. Will that also be the case for many of the class of 1998? <DM>

Year	GS	S	C	T
1998	32	4.59	3.91	8.50

PAUL WAGNER, MIL

Paul has his Sad Sack down to a science now, and he's even compressed the time it takes for him to go from a scattering of promising starts to injury to a game so unutterably bad that not even a manager with a cast-iron stomach will give him another start while he's in the organization. This year it took only nine starts, and here (though definitely not for the faint of heart) was the one that sent the camel into traction:

Date	IP	H	R	ER	BB	SO	HR
7/24	7	11	11	11	2	5	4

A lot of seven-eleven in there—but the convenience store kind, not the lucky kind for the star-crossed Wagner. <DM>

Year	GS	S	C	T
1998	9	4.56	4.22	8.78
1996	15	4.13	4.20	8.33
1995	25	4.08	3.64	7.72
1994	17	4.76	3.59	8.35

DONNE WALL, SD

In my "double dare" of Kevin Towers to ditch Joey Hamilton above, which looks like a send-up of those old Eveready battery commercials with Robert Conrad, I forgot to consider that the Padres could also, if need be, turn to Donne (Tear Down the) Wall to flesh out their rotation. I think that Kevin would probably sign Jack McDowell or Steve Avery or Armando Reynoso or Orel Hershiser or Bill Swift (I could go on, but this book can contractually be only 512 pages. . .) before doing so. <DM>

Year	GS	S	C	T
1998	1	3.00	3.00	6.00
1997	8	5.13	3.88	9.00
1996	23	4.39	2.87	7.26
1995	5	4.80	3.60	8.40

DAVID WEATHERS, CIN

We're getting toward the end of the section, and I readily admit to being a bit impatient to move on, so please forgive me if the following seems unnecessarily strident, even for me. But—

—Why on earth do GMs keep signing this guy, and why do managers keep putting him into ballgames? Next stop, Kansas City. <DM>

Year	GS	S	C	T
1998	9	5.11	3.89	9.00
1997	1	5.00	7.00	12.00
1996	12	5.08	4.17	9.25
1995	15	4.80	4.40	9.20
1994	24	4.75	3.96	8.71

MIKE WELCH, PHI

Mike was primarily a reliever when he was with the Mets organization, but the Phillies made him into a starter. That appears to have been their first mistake. Their second was giving him a start against the Giants on August 2nd, in which he gave up eight runs in three innings, and three homers. Their third mistake was giving him another start five days later in Houston, where he gave up another eight runs in three innings (but only two HRs).

As a reliever, though, Mike had a 1.88 ERA. Whatever the Phillies' brain trust is smoking, I'd like some—it evidently can make you follow Porky Pig all the way to Wackyland. <DM>

Year	GS	S	C	T
1998	2	6.50	6.00	12.50

DON WENGERT, CHC
(1998: SD-CHC)

Wengert got several emergency starts due to injuries to Jeremi Gonzalez and Kerry Wood. As you can see, the frequency of his games started over the last three years indicates that his managers have gotten wise to the risk involved. <DM>

Year	GS	S	C	T
1998	6	4.33	4.00	8.33
1997	12	4.67	3.58	8.25
1996	25	5.00	3.64	8.64

MISCELLANEOUS STARTING PITCHER DATA, NATIONAL LEAGUE 1998

LEGEND: NP—Number of Pitches thrown; **TW**—Team Wins in pitcher's starts; **TL**—Team Losses in pitcher's starts; **GS**—; **QS**—Quality Starts; **BS**—Blown Starts; **QmB**—Quality minus Blown pct.; **PPI**—Pitches thrown Per Inning; **IP**—Innings Pitched; **AdIP**—Adjusted Innings Pitched; **IP/S**—average Innings Pitched per Start

Pitcher Name	Team	TW	TL	GS	QS	BS	QmB	IP	NP	Str	PPI	Kpct	AdjIP	IP/S
Mark Langston	SDP	7	9	16	5	7	-12.50	78.3	1345	800	17.17	59.5%	86	4.9
Pete Smith	SDP	5	3	8	1	2	-12.50	39.7	667	409	16.82	61.3%	42	5.0
Brian Boehringer	SDP	0	1	1	0	1	-100.00	4.0	57	36	14.25	63.2%	4	4.0
Mark Gardner	SFG	17	16	33	21	5	48.48	212.0	3321	2057	15.67	61.9%	211	6.4
Orel Hershiser	SFG	20	14	34	17	4	38.24	202.0	3150	1902	15.59	60.4%	200	5.9
Kirk Rueter	SFG	18	14	32	14	6	25.00	181.7	2957	1733	16.28	58.6%	188	5.7
Danny Darwin	SFG	13	12	25	11	7	16.00	138.0	2151	1375	15.59	63.9%	137	5.5
Shawn Estes	SFG	11	14	25	11	7	16.00	149.3	2549	1521	17.07	59.7%	162	6.0
Russ Ortiz	SFG	9	4	13	5	4	7.69	75.7	1301	783	17.19	60.2%	83	5.8
Matt Morris	STL	11	6	17	13	0	76.47	113.7	1713	1066	15.07	62.2%	109	6.7
Jose Jimenez	STL	3	0	3	2	0	66.67	18.3	276	169	15.06	61.2%	18	6.1
Todd Stottlemyre	STL	10	13	23	17	2	65.22	161.3	2461	1523	15.25	61.9%	157	7.0
Mike Busby	STL	1	1	2	1	0	50.00	10.7	158	102	14.81	64.6%	10	5.3
Darren Oliver	STL	5	5	10	6	1	50.00	57.0	925	565	16.23	61.1%	59	5.7
Juan Acevedo	STL	6	3	9	4	0	44.44	50.0	735	472	14.70	64.2%	47	5.6
Kent Bottenfield	STL	5	11	17	9	3	35.29	99.3	1669	1006	16.80	60.3%	106	5.8
Donovan Osborne	STL	8	6	14	8	4	28.57	83.7	1274	814	15.23	63.9%	81	6.0
Kent Mercker	STL	19	11	30	11	6	16.67	160.7	2532	1557	15.76	61.5%	161	5.4
Manny Aybar	STL	6	7	13	3	4	-7.69	64.0	1124	684	17.57	60.9%	72	4.9
Mark Petkovsek	STL	4	6	10	4	5	-10.00	48.3	766	456	15.85	59.5%	49	4.8
Bobby Witt	STL	1	4	5	1	2	-20.00	24.3	432	258	17.75	59.7%	27	4.9
Cliff Politte	STL	4	4	8	1	4	-37.50	37.0	641	378	17.32	59.0%	41	4.6
Sean Lowe	STL	0	1	1	0	1	-100.00	1.7	51	28	30.54	54.9%	3	1.7
Brady Raggio	STL	0	1	1	0	1	-100.00	0.7	35	21	52.24	60.0%	2	0.7

GABE WHITE, CIN

Jack McKeon decided early on that White would be best used in the bullpen, and you can't argue with the results. Gabe might just be the Reds' closer in 1999. <DM>

YEAR	GS	S	C	T
1998	3	6.00	3.33	9.33
1997	6	3.67	2.83	6.50
1995	1	6.00	5.00	11.00
1994	5	4.00	4.80	8.80

MIKE WILLIAMS, PIT

Another bullpen success story. Mike fanned more than a man an inning and was particularly effective in the second half of the year. I don't think you'll be seeing him in the rotation any time soon, at least not in Pittsburgh. <DM>

YEAR	GS	S	C	T
1998	1	4.00	3.00	7.00
1996	29	4.41	3.76	8.17
1995	8	3.38	2.88	6.25
1994	8	4.63	3.38	8.00

SCOTT WINCHESTER, CIN

Way too hittable, and his control ain't great shakes, either. This was the "flop" part of Jack McKeon's flip-flop of roles performed on Winchester and Gabe White. Since Winchester had never started a single game in his professional career, this was a strange hunch to play. And it appears to have really messed Winchester up: when he went back to AAA in late July, he continued to start (as if to ratify Jack's decision), and continued to stink (6.67 ERA). <DM>

YEAR	GS	S	C	T
1998	16	4.94	3.81	8.75

BOBBY WITT, FA
(1998: TEX-STL)

See the David Weathers comment above. <DM>

YEAR	GS	S	C	T
1998	18	5.00	4.11	9.11
1997	32	4.69	3.19	7.88
1996	32	4.69	3.81	8.50
1995	29	4.28	3.66	7.93
1994	22	4.55	3.91	8.45

BOB WOLCOTT, BOS
(1998: AZ)

An escapee from Stalag Kingdome, where Lou (the Commandant of Chaos) Piniella has been doing a bizarre twist on Werner Klemperer's schtick for some time now, Wolcott was given the "rest cure" in Tucson this year. I think the odds are slim that Jimy Williams (his new team's manager) will be able to revive his career without intervention

from Bob Crane, Larry Hovis, Richard Dawson et al. <DM>

YEAR	GS	S	C	T
1998	6	4.00	3.67	7.67
1997	18	5.22	3.44	8.67
1996	28	4.68	3.75	8.43
1995	6	5.17	4.17	9.33

KERRY WOOD, CHC

There is a small (very small) faction out there who decided that Kerry was over-hyped after his 20-K day of glory (I saw the video tape, and it was something, let me tell you). After all, goes the argument, it was only one great game, even if it was the highest Game Score of all time. Or, to invoke QMAX (and why not?), it was only one 1,1 game.

And there is some truth to that. Wood had a fine season, and he definitely deserves to be the NL Rookie of the Year, but when you put his season against several other rookie pitching performances, for example Dwight Gooden in 1984 and Vida Blue in 1971, he comes up a little short.

On the other hand, Wood's QMAX "S" value of 2.69 was the best in baseball in 1998, and over the past five years it is sixth best. There are only four pitchers who have done better in the past five years: Pedro Martinez (2.32), Randy Johnson (2.48), Hideo Nomo (2.50), and Greg Maddux (twice, 2.57 and 2.60). Kerry is already in extremely select company, and he's only 21.

But then there's the question of the elbow problem. Wood missed all of September with it, and he'd been pitching through a good bit of August with what was reported in the press as a "dead arm." Here are Kerry's monthly QMAX numbers:

Month	S	C	T
Apr	3.25	4.75	8.00
May	2.00	3.40	5.40
Jun	3.00	4.40	7.40
Jul	2.00	3.67	5.67
Aug	3.33	3.33	6.67

There's not a huge amount of difference there, though Kerry was clearly more hittable in August. Will his arm hold up? Can hard throwers whose control is spotty enough that it forces them to throw a lot of pitches per inning make it through the formative years intact?

Based on our earlier discussions of young pitcher workload (see the Jesus Sanchez comment here in the NL starters, and the Bartolo Colon comment over in the AL), we can display graphically what Kerry's workload was like, and how it compares to the workload that cost Alan Benes at least a year and a half of his career. This is based on the idea that 350

pitches per three starts is the danger threshold, and that the greater amount of time a pitcher is kept above, at, or near that threshold, the more susceptible he is to injury. Let's look at the comparison between Kerry Wood and Alan Benes:

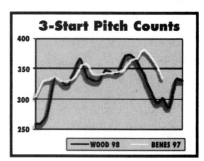

Sobering, isn't it? Wood was kept at a level very similar to Benes for almost as long. You can see where Riggleman started "baby-ing" him, by getting his three-start average down to 300—with a "dead arm"! When the three-start workload was increased toward the end of August, up popped the elbow injury.

The lesson is obvious: a young flame-thrower like Wood needs to be put on a strict pitch count for the first couple of years, just to be safe. A game like the 20-K game, which used 122 pitches in nine innings, is OK once in awhile, but there should be three to five games a year where the manager makes sure that Wood is out of there with no more than 90 pitches regardless of how well he's doing. From mid-June through late July, Riggleman let Kerry have ten consecutive starts with 100+ pitches. That's way too many for a young pitcher; the max should be four. The three-start total should only rarely approach the 350 danger zone.

That said, this is hard to do when you're a manager trying to win a division and your best pitcher is a 21-year old phenom who uses a lot of pitches per inning. The tendency is to ride that young stallion as far as he'll gallop. While professing to be cognizant of the need to control Wood's workload, Riggleman still pushed him to limits that clearly cause injury. He has to be a lot more vigilant in 1999 if he wants to make sure that Wood's career is not simply a meteor that blazed quickly across the sky, and was just as suddenly gone. <DM>

YEAR	GS	S	C	T
1998	26	2.69	3.85	6.54

BRAD WOODALL, MIL

After kicking around the Braves' system for a number of years, Woodall got a shot in the Brewers' rotation due to injuries that felled Jeff D'Amico and Jose Mercedes, and proved to be a couple of tads under league average. He pitched quite a bit better in relief, and I suspect that his future, such as it may be, is in the bullpen. <DM>

Year	GS	S	C	T
1998	20	4.35	3.50	7.85
1996	3	6.33	4.33	10.67
1994	1	3.00	3.00	6.00

STEVE WOODARD, MIL

Steve was the Brewers' best starter, and while he turned into a pretty fair little finesse pitcher, this fact is not one that bodes well for Milwaukee's future as a franchise. <DM>

Year	GS	S	C	T
1998	26	4.27	2.92	7.19
1997	7	4.43	2.86	7.29

JAMEY WRIGHT, COL

Let's look at Jamey's home/road QMAX numbers:

Where	S	C	T
Coors	4.94	3.94	8.88
Anywhere else	3.82	3.59	7.41

So he's pretty much a league average pitcher, since Coors has a "T" value of 8.83 from 1995-98 and the league is at 7.39 for that same period. That's a hard concept to digest when you see a set of traditional numbers as ugly as Jamey's, but there it is. <DM>

Year	GS	S	C	T
1998	34	4.38	3.76	8.25
1997	26	5.15	3.96	9.12
1996	15	4.80	3.60	8.40

MASATO YOSHII, NYM

Was very effective in the first two months of the year, but was under league average the rest of the way. Still, he'd be a cheap insurance policy for a number of teams who are short on a reliable guy to make into their #5 starter. His Elite Square presence is almost non-existent (3%), which may be one thing that explains his high number of no-decisions (53%; see the Mike Morgan comment).. <DM>

Year	GS	S	C	T
1998	29	3.76	3.24	7.00

RELIEF PITCHERS

JUAN ACEVEDO, STL

After floundering around for most of the season the Cardinals finally annointed Juan as their closer in late August. This was after three excellent starts in July which produced a 1.35 ERA, the last of which he shutdown the Dodgers on three hits over six innings. He was shutdown with an elbow problem on July 17th and missed the next month. When he came back he was placed in the bullpen and in the last month of the season Juan produced 10 saves and a 0.00 ERA in 14 and a third innings in which he gave up only five hits and four walks while striking out 11. <KA>

TERRY ADAMS, CHC

Still apparently feeling the afterburn from 1996, when he threw 101 relief innings at the age of 23, he really fell apart in the second half. Here's his WPA data by month:

	G	PI	WPA	P	PPPI
Mar/Apr	13	21	1	1.6	0.074
May	14	19	0	2.2	0.118
June	12	19	0	1.9	0.099
July	11	14	-0.6	0.8	0.058
August	8	13	-0.8	0.7	0.051
B5	8	-0	.5		0.062

His 16 appearances in tie games tied for 4th in the NL. <DD>

ANTONIO ALFONSECA, FLA

Poor season overall, but had a positive WPA (+.7) because of his performance in high pressure (P > .15) situations. This is one of the most drastic splits I've run across:

	IP	H	R	ER	BB	K	ERA
Hi Pressure	30.2	24	8	6	10	24	1.76
Other	40	51	28	26	23	22	5.85

It resulted in a high pressure WPA of +2.4 and a WPA of -1.7 in his other games. <DD>

WILLIE BANKS, AZ
(1998: NYY-AZ)

Willie has been disappointing teams in both leagues during this decade and at the age of 30 was approaching the point of no return to the majors. Luckily for Willie, it was an expansion year and he landed with the Diamondbacks after another early season failure with the Yankees. With the D-backs he produced a 3.09 ERA and only allowed 7.0 hits per 9. After the break his ERA was 2.18 with only 5.2 hits per nine, but we are looking at a small sample size of 33 IP. This should be enough to give Willie another chance. <KA>

ROD BECK, CHC

It goes without saying that he's a disaster waiting to happen, doesn't it? Many people, myself included, thought that going into last season, and really we weren't wrong. Beck got lucky in every way possible last season. His ERA was much better than his OPS would indicate,

---

RELIEF PITCHER DATA, NATIONAL LEAGUE 1998

LEGEND: **SV**—Save; **SVOP**—Save Opportunity; **HLD**—Hold; **G/F**—Groundball/Flyball Ratio **IR**—Inherited Runners; **IS**—Inherited Runners Scored; **IRS%**—Inherited Runners Pct.

Name	TM	SV	SVOP	HLD	BA	OBP	SLG	OPS	SB	CS	GDP	G/F	IR	IS	IRS%
Gregg Olson	Ari	30	34	0	.223	.295	.335	.630	7	2	7	1.56	16	0	0.0
Vladimir Nunez	Ari	0	0	0	.318	.360	.364	.724	0	0	0	1.57	0	0	0.0
Willie Banks	Ari	1	2	5	.247	.359	.388	.747	4	4	4	1.94	21	9	42.9
Felix Rodriguez	Ari	5	8	0	.259	.365	.400	.765	4	0	0	1.18	23	10	43.5
Clint Sodowsky	Ari	0	3	2	.283	.375	.391	.766	7	1	7	3.09	23	5	21.7
Alan Embree	Ari	1	3	12	.269	.343	.428	.771	1	3	2	1.10	31	13	41.9
Bobby Chouinard	Ari	0	1	6	.280	.322	.451	.773	4	1	2	0.96	19	9	47.4
Scott Brow	Ari	0	0	1	.272	.375	.432	.807	2	1	2	1.19	21	10	47.6
Aaron Small	Ari	0	2	4	.305	.365	.449	.814	2	2	11	1.35	27	11	40.7
Ben Ford	Ari	0	0	0	.295	.367	.455	.822	2	0	2	2.78	4	1	25.0
Neil Weber	Ari	0	0	0	.417	.533	.417	.950	0	0	0	2.50	2	1	50.0
Chris Michalak	Ari	0	0	0	.375	.448	.542	.990	1	0	0	0.88	3	3	100.0
Barry Manuel	Ari	0	0	0	.266	.405	.609	1.014	1	0	1	0.62	9	4	44.4
Bryan Corey	Ari	0	0	0	.375	.474	.563	1.037	0	0	0	1.75	0	0	0.0
Efrain Valdez	Ari	0	0	0	.368	.400	.737	1.137	0	0	1	0.86	3	1	33.3
Ricky Pickett	Ari	0	0	0	.600	.778	.800	1.578	0	0	0	—	0	0	0.0
Rudy Seanez	Atl	2	4	8	.195	.286	.266	.552	3	1	1	1.38	8	1	12.5
Kerry Ligtenberg	Atl	30	34	11	.193	.260	.295	.555	6	1	6	1.15	23	8	34.8
John Rocker	Atl	2	4	15	.172	.307	.297	.604	2	0	5	1.91	33	6	18.2
Odalis Perez	Atl	0	1	5	.244	.311	.341	.652	0	0	2	3.14	8	0	0.0
Russ Springer	Atl	0	4	7	.258	.357	.348	.705	7	2	3	0.84	14	7	50.0

TEAM RELIEF PITCHING DATA, NATIONAL LEAGUE 1998

TEAM	SV	BLSV	SVOP	IR	IS	HLDS	WINS	ERA	SV%	IRS%	NIRS	HOLDS/W
SDP	59	16	75	201	53	66	98	3.46	78.7	26.4	1.26	0.67
Hou	44	15	59	178	47	33	102	3.32	74.6	26.4	1.26	0.32
Atl	45	17	62	145	41	68	106	3.83	72.6	28.3	1.18	0.64
Pit	41	19	60	222	66	50	69	3.36	68.3	29.7	1.12	0.72
Mon	39	13	52	265	82	45	65	4.01	75.0	30.9	1.08	0.69
Cin	42	15	57	241	75	28	77	4.28	73.7	31.1	1.07	0.36
Mil	39	23	62	234	78	72	74	3.94	62.9	33.3	1.00	0.97
Phi	32	24	56	165	57	41	75	4.53	57.1	34.5	0.96	0.55
Fla	24	22	46	285	99	45	54	4.85	52.2	34.7	0.96	0.83
ChC	56	22	78	324	113	66	90	4.40	71.8	34.9	0.95	0.73
StL	44	31	75	243	85	70	83	4.23	58.7	35.0	0.95	0.84
SFG	44	23	67	268	94	70	89	3.16	65.7	35.1	0.95	0.79
NYM	46	26	72	193	71	51	88	3.85	63.9	36.8	0.91	0.58
Col	36	19	55	206	76	59	77	3.65	65.5	36.9	0.90	0.77
LAD	47	27	74	199	76	39	83	3.88	63.5	38.2	0.87	0.47
Ari	37	18	55	173	67	23	65	4.80	67.3	38.7	0.86	0.35

and his WPA was higher than his ERA would indicate.

Oh, by the way, he worked more innings than he's worked since 1992, and appeared 34 times on 0 days rest last year. He's the overwhelming favorite to have the worst WPA in the league this year. Run for your life. **<DD>**

STAN BELINDA, CIN

Stan had to be shut down due to an inflamed spinal cord and his career may be finished. He was in the midst of producing another workman like year with the Reds, putting in 60+ IP by mid August. He was effective against that important first batter, limiting them to a .194 batting average and a .636 OPS. **<KA>**

SHAYNE BENNETT, MON

I don't see a whole lot to like in Bennett, although he does have a few minor league seasons that suggest he has some promise. He was consistently subpar last season from start to finish, as were most of the non-Urbina Expo relievers. Fortunately, Montreal was not involved in many close games (team PPPI: .051), so Bennett et al didn't hurt them much. Among the many things on Montreal's list should be getting Urbina some support. **<DD>**

BRIAN BOEHRINGER, SD

Pitched much better in the second half vs. the first (5.27 ERA vs. 3.31 ERA), unfortunately, he had been relegated to mop-up duty by that time (PPPI: .063 in the first half, .029 in the second.) **<DD>**

RICKY BOTTALICO, STL
(1998: PHI)

Shortly after he was dealt to the Cardinals, I read a wire report that he "finished strong" after having midseason arm

problems. I thought that was odd, considering his ERA was 7.16 after his return, so I decided to check it out. Sure enough, in his last 7 appearances he sported a "strong" 1.50 ERA (1 ER in 6 IP). Of course, in his last 9, it was 7.04, and in his last 18 his ERA was 8.50. **<DD>**

JEFF BRANTLEY, PHI
(1998: STL)

I think trading him for Dmitri Young was a reasonable gamble for the Cards, but the thing with gambles is, sometimes they turn out like this.

Jeff was pretty solid in high-pressure (P > .15) situations, converting 10 of 12. But he really blew a lot of his easier chances, posting a 5.82 ERA in his medium- and low-pressure opportunities. His 9 disastrous (WPA < -.25) outings was a team high, on a team full of disastrous relievers. **<DD>**

NORM CHARLTON, FA
(1998: BAL-ATL)

I have no idea why so many people were so disgusted by Orioles giving him a shot last season. Sure, his 1997 was putrid, but it was really his first bad season, and he didn't cost the Orioles a damn thing. For the Braves to pick him up midseason was far more questionable. **<DD>**

JASON CHRISTIANSEN, PIT

His season and Ricardo Rincon's were remarkably similar, the primary difference being that Rincon allowed thrice as many homers as Christiansen did (6 to 2), so Jason's OPS allowed was 50 points lower (.592 to .642). Both pitched

in the roughly the same kinds of situations (Christiansen's PPPI was .078, Rincon's was .074), and their WPAs were +1.1 (Christiansen) and +1.2 (Rincon). I'm curious as to why Rincon was dealt rather than Christiansen. Did the Pirates like Jason more, or was Rincon's trade value higher? **<DD>**

BRAD CLONTZ, FA
(1998: LA-NYM)

To quote those SCTV Farm Film Critics, Big Jim McBob and Billy Sol Hurok, 'He blowd up reeeeal good!" **<KA>**

DENNIS COOK, NYM

Another good year, which should surprise no one. He was the one guy in the bullpen that the Mets could count on for the entire season.

He was 5th in the league in P, 2nd in most appearances with runners on base, and tied for 1st in appearances in tie games. His usage matrix is worth a look:

	-5	-4	-3	-2	-1	0	+1	+2	+3	+4	+5	TOTAL
5												
6	1			2		1	1	1				6
7	1		2	2	3	5	3	3	1			20
8		2	1	1	3	7	7	5	2	3	2	33
9				1	1	3	1	1	1	1	2	10
10+					1	3						4
TOT	2	2	3	6	8	19	12	9	4	4	4	73

<DD>

RICK CROUSHORE, STL

On July 26th, Croushore entered in the bottom of the 8th with 1 out and men on 2nd and 3rd of a Cardinals-Rockies game at Coors Field that the Cards led by 1. He shut the door to earn the save, and +.58 worth of WPA. That brought his WPA for the season up to +2.0, and lowered his ERA to 2.70. Two days later, he started the 9th inning at home against the Brewers with a 2-run lead. He surrendered 5 runs in a third of an inning. From that point on, Croushore put up a 9.68 ERA and a -2.1 WPA for the remainder of the season. **<DD>**

VIC DARENSBOURG, FLA

It was probably a good thing that the Marlins didn't have many options early in the season, or Vic would have found himself back in the minors with his

0-6 record and 6.33 ERA on June 1st. Thereafter he produced a 2.05 ERA while only allowing 5.5 hits per nine innings pitched and almost struck out 10 batters per nine. He stopped lefties with a .470 OPS and could prove to be a non-fried Fish. **<KA>**

VALERIO DE LOS SANTOS, MIL

This here is a hot prospect. Came up late in the year and pitched in 13 absolutely meaningless games (PPPI: .009). Meaningless or not, it's hard to argue with 21.2 innings, 15 baserunners allowed, and 18 whiffs. On the down side, 4 of the 11 hits he allowed were dingers. **<DD>**

MIKE DEJEAN, COL

His WPA of +2.2 was 9th in the NL. Of the 5 main Colorado relievers (DeJean, DiPoto, Leskanic, McElroy, and Veres), his innings were the least meaningful (PPPI of .056). However, he took advantage of the few opportunities he got, adding WP in 9 of 9 high pressure situations.

He's likely to drop off this year, possibly significantly. It's mighty tough to be successful while striking out 3.3 per 9. **<DD>**

JERRY DIPOTO, COL

His month-by-month WPA data is interesting:

	G	PI	WPA	P	PPPI
Mar/Apr	13	14	0	1.1	0.08
May	12	12	0.3	1.1	0.088
June	10	11	-0.8	1.2	0.111
July	12	16	0.4	0.7	0.043
August	11	13	0.7	1.5	0.117
September	10	12	0.6	1.1	0.096

He was looking OK until June, when the bottom fell out. His role was drastically scaled back in July (note the PPPI), he got his act back together and finished strong (2.16 ERA in 33.1 innings after the ASB). **<DD>**

BRIAN EDMONDSON, FLA

The Marlins apparently wanted to give him a large role (.084 PPPI in his first 22 appearances after joining the Fish), but then lost interest (.043 PPPI in his remaining 21 appearances). His ERA of 3.91 is not quite in line with an OPS allowed of .801 (in pitcher's parks, no less). My money says the OPS is telling the truth and the ERA is lying. K rate of 4.7 per 9 is not encouraging either. **<DD>**

SCOTT ELARTON, HOU

A very auspicious debut season for this much-heralded youngster. Dierker broke him slowly (.042 PPPI through August), and then gave him some big-game experience in September (PPPI .095). **<<DD>**

ALAN EMBREE, SF
(1998: AZ)

Everyone seems to like Embree, but I just don't see it. He has exactly one good season on his record (46 IP). In the rest of his career, he has allowed 22 dingers and 88 runs in 127.1 innings. He was traded for Dante Powell in the offseason, which is appropriate. Both will get more opportunities than they deserve for the rest of their careers. **<DD>**

CHAD FOX, MIL

Was damn near unhittable in April (WPA: +1.6, ERA: 0.52), then went on the shelf for awhile. When he returned, he was nothing special, finishing the season with a WPA of +1.5 and an ERA of 3.95. Even in the latter part of the year, he was still fanning hitters at a respectable clip, so I think he's likely to have some success in his future. **<DD>**

JOHN FRANCO, NYM

Quite an eventful season for John. He led the league in pressure per partial inning, and did a great job of converting those high-pressure (P > .15) situations:

	IP	H	R	ER	BB	K	ERA
Hi Pressure	33.2	21	7	7	15	30	1.87
Other	31	45	21	19	14	29	5.52

Included in there is a game in which Franco earned a P (and a WPA) of .73. He entered the Mets' June 21st game against Florida in the 8th inning with no one out, the bases full, and a 1-run lead. He stranded all three runners, and then worked a scoreless 9th.

Unfortunately, he had a habit of blowing the easier save opportunities, and ended up with 9 disastrous (WPA < -.25) appearances as well. **<DD>**

I have the good fortune of living in Cub territory, which means that I get to listen to Ron Santo and Pat Hughes on WGN radio. The Cubs were playing the Mets one day, and Bobby Valentine had made the call to the bullpen for John Franco. Hughes introduced Franco as a future Hall of Famer and Santo nearly gagged on his incredulity. I'm sure part of Santo's reaction was his own frustration at not yet taking his rightful place in the Hall of Fame, part of it was Franco's Metness, but another part of it is the belief that relievers just aren't all that important in the grand scheme of things.

Just what sort of chance does Franco have at making the Hall of Fame? Using some of the techniques Bill James used in his HOF book, Franco doesn't do all that well. He has led the league in saves 3 times, and he has never led in games. He is a five-time all-star and was

RELIEF PITCHER DATA, NATIONAL LEAGUE 1998														
LEGEND: **SV**—Save; **SVOP**—Save Opportunity; **HLD**—Hold; **G/F**—Groundball/Flyball Ratio **IR**—Inherited Runners; **IS**—Inherited Runners Scored; **IRS%**—Inherited Runners Pct.														
Name	**TM**	**SV**	**SVOP**	**HLD**	**BA**	**OBP**	**SLG**	**OPS**	**SB**	**CS**	**GDP**	**G/F**	**IR**	**IS**	**IRS%**
Dennis Martinez	Atl	2	4	12	.295	.332	.417	.749	7	2	9	1.89	17	3	17.6
Mike Cather	Atl	0	3	1	.255	.314	.451	.765	0	2	3	1.81	18	8	44.4
Norm Charlton	Atl	1	2	5	.275	.380	.409	.789	6	1	2	1.51	27	9	33.3
Mark Wohlers	Atl	8	8	0	.231	.464	.397	.861	3	0	0	1.63	2	0	0.0
Adam Butler	Atl	0	0	1	.278	.462	.500	.962	3	0	0	0.60	4	2	50.0
Kurt Miller	ChC	0	0	0	.200	.200	.200	.400	0	0	0	1.33	0	0	0.0
Terry Mulholland	ChC	3	5	19	.235	.304	.327	.631	0	0	10	2.09	55	15	27.3
Terry Adams	ChC	1	7	13	.255	.349	.369	.718	12	2	3	2.82	45	21	46.7
Felix Heredia	ChC	2	5	17	.252	.360	.367	.727	4	3	3	1.10	69	21	30.4
Matt Karchner	ChC	11	18	10	.253	.352	.390	.742	10	1	1	1.04	33	10	30.3
Rod Beck	ChC	51	58	1	.269	.311	.434	.745	8	1	3	1.19	32	9	28.1
Marc Pisciotta	ChC	0	0	7	.259	.380	.376	.756	4	0	5	1.20	35	10	28.6
Dave Stevens	ChC	0	0	0	.288	.364	.473	.837	8	4	2	0.85	27	8	29.6
Don Wengert	ChC	1	1	0	.297	.373	.484	.857	4	0	7	1.76	13	7	53.8
Rodney Myers	ChC	0	1	0	.342	.390	.513	.903	0	0	1	1.18	5	3	60.0
Bob Patterson	ChC	1	2	5	.391	.453	.576	1.029	4	1	1	0.59	32	10	31.3
Kennie Steenstra	ChC	0	0	0	.412	.444	.882	1.326	2	0	0	0.50	1	1	100.0
Kevin Foster	ChC	0	0	0	.500	.500	.875	1.375	1	0	0	0.25	2	1	50.0
Keith Glauber	Cin	0	0	0	.214	.226	.286	.512	1	0	0	0.47	9	2	22.2
Stan Belinda	Cin	1	2	4	.212	.304	.359	.663	7	3	4	0.90	11	4	36.4
Danny Graves	Cin	8	8	6	.252	.315	.354	.669	6	2	12	2.55	38	12	31.6

the fireman of the year, three times as well. Most of his chances hinge on how far up the all-time save list he is at his retirement. Currently, Lee Smith is the reigning leader at 478. Franco is the active leader with 397, just ahead of the retiring Dennis Eckersley with 390. If we use Favorite Toy to project some of the current top closers here is what we get for career marks.

Name	Age	Current	Projected
Rod Beck	29	250	538
Lee Smith	40	478	478
Trevor Hoffman	30	188	463
John Franco	37	397	461
John Wetteland	31	253	461
Randy Myers	35	347	450
Dennis Eckersley	43	390	390
Jeff Montgomery	36	292	356
Rick Aguilera	36	275	341
Doug Jones	41	291	320
Roberto Hernandez	33	191	316
Gregg Olson	31	203	293

Is Rod Beck the oldest-looking 29-year-old you have ever seen? Franco's 2.64 career ERA will work in his favor, but his lack of post-season experience will hurt his chances. Overall, if he can get by Smith and close out some World Series games, he will have a shot at enshrinement. The Mets have given him a fat extension, so they certainly think he can close for a few more years. **<SF>**

JOHN FRASCATORE, STL

John gobbled up a lot of innings in as average a manner as possible, and the Cardinals really needed that. After a surprisingly effective 1997, he returned to what now appears to be his true ability level. He'll likely be a non-embarrassing member of a bullpen for a few more years, but that's about it. **<DD>**

WAYNE GOMES, PHI

This 26-year-old appears to have a future. He soaked up a lot of innings of all descriptions and did not hurt the Phils. Here's his usage matrix:

	-5	-4	-3	-2	-1	0	+1	+2	+3	+4	+5	T
5			1	1								2
6			2	1		2	1	1				8
7	1		2		1	5	6	2		1	1	19
8	2	3	1		5	5	5	4	1	3	5	34
9	2	1										3
10+						5						5
TOT	5	4	6	2	6	17	12	7	2	4	6	71

Mark Leiter had 27 high-pressure appearances in 1998, Gomes had 22, and the next highest Phillie (Spradlin) had 8. With Leiter and Spradlin gone, he should be numero uno in the Philly bullpen this season. **<DD>**

DANNY GRAVES, CIN

Absolutely positively does not look like a closer to me, and apparently not to Trader Jack either, as his PPPI was a scrawny .046.

He was unhittable in his high-pressure (P > .15) appearances, as were almost all of the Reds' relievers:

	IP	H	R	ER	BB	K	ERA
Hi Pressure	23	12	2	2	10	12	0.78
Other	58.164	29	28	18	32	4.32	

<DD>

OSCAR HENRIQUEZ, NYM
(1998: FLA)

A discouraging debut, no doubt, as he allowed a .943 OPS and an 8.55 ERA in 20 early-season innings. After a particularly poor outing, Leyland threw a tantrum and had some choice words for Oscar. He was sent down not long after that (that's Henriquez, not Leyland, unfortunately for Fish fans) and pitched pretty well for the remainder of the season in AAA. He's about as good a prospect now as he was a year ago. It goes without saying that that's worth 10 Jorge Fabregases. **<DD>**

DOUG HENRY, HOU

Here is a pretty typical setup man's appearance matrix:

	-5	-4	-3	-2	-1	0	+1	+2	+3	+4	+5	T
5												
6		1					1					2
7				2	2	1	2	1	1	1		10
8	1	1		3	2	6	5	2	1	2	3	26
9				2	3	6		1	1	1	4	18
10+						3						3
TOT	1	2		7	7	16	7	5	3	4	7	59

Those 16 appearances in tie games were 4th-most in the NL, and he started 12 tied 9th innings, most in the league.

Henry unquestionably had a good season in 1998, his 2nd in his last 6 tries. The Astrodome seems to have that effect on pitchers. **<DD>**

FELIX HEREDIA, CHC
(1998: FLA-CHC)

His season and Matt Karchner's were very similar. At the start of the season, both were expected to be stabilizing forces in bad bullpens on bad teams, despite the fact that neither had a track record indicating that he could stabilize a damn thing. Both struggled early and were dealt to the Cubs in late July. Both then pitched in just about every game the Cubs played for the last two months of the season. Overall, both turned out to be fairly neutral.

Their paths will almost certainly diverge here. Heredia is only 23 and may well have a future, while Karchner will hang around for a few more years as a generic reliever before taking his position between Kappel, Joe and Kardow, Paul on a little-referenced page of TB. **<DD>**

TREVOR HOFFMAN, SD

I discussed his season in the WPA article.

I'm dying to know how this season ranks WPA-wise compared to other recent relief seasons like Eckersley 1990, Percival 1995 and 1996, Mesa 1995, Rivera 1996. That we may never know, but eventually, thanks to Retrosheet, we will be able to compare it to vintage Quisenberry, Gossage, Fingers, Hernandez and Mike Marshall seasons, among others.

Just for fun, here are Trevor's

	G	PI	WPA	P	PPPI
Road	33	41	3.9	4.8	0.118
Home	33	40	2.6	3.9	0.096
Low pressure	13	13	0.4	0.4	0.029
Med pressure	23	27	1.7	2.2	0.080
Hi pressure	30	41	4.4	6.2	0.151
Mar/Apr	11	15	1.2	1.6	0.110
May	9	12	1.3	1.3	0.112
June	13	15	0.7	1.2	0.077
July	12	13	1.3	1.6	0.125
August	11	14	0.9	1.3	0.095
September	10	12	1.2	1.6	0.134
One-Inning Apps	51	51	3.7	5.5	0.108
Multiple-Inning Apps	15	30	2.8	3.2	0.107

splits:**<DD>**

JOHN HUDEK, CIN

He pitched poorly and only in completely meaningless situations when he was in New York. Then, after being dealt to the Reds, he was more effective. Still prevents hits well. Still wild. **<DD>**

JOHN JOHNSTONE, SF

He was awesome in the first half, but came back down to earth in the second (Hits per 9: 6.5 in the first half vs. 8.3 in the second, Ks per 9: 10.3 vs. 7.0). He might've been overworked, as he tossed 47 innings before the break, or he might have just been returning to his actual level of performance after a particularly fortuitous first three months. I'm not sure anyone but John himself (and maybe not even him) knows which right now. **<DD>**

MATT KARCHNER, CHC
(1998: CHW-CHC)

He really pitched about as well last year as anyone has a right to expect him to.

The Cubs had no qualms about giving him the ball in important situations. Over a third of his appearances were high pressure (P > .15 - about 22% of all relief appearances fall into this category leaguewide). They also worked him hard: 12 of his 29 appearances were on 0 days rest. **<DD>**

CURTIS KING, STL

His -2.3 WPA was 3rd-worst in the NL. Here's how it happened:

	IP	H	R	ER	BB	K	ERA
Lo Pressure	19.1	14	2	2	7	12	0.93
Other	31.2	36	18	18	13	16	5.12

<DD>

STEVE KLINE, MON

1998 was the first time he exhibited any hit prevention at a level higher than A-ball. It's an even-money proposition whether he'll ever be an important contributor to anyone's bullpen. **<DD>**

JEFF KUBENKA, LA

Despite his otherworldly minor league numbers, Dodger fans are under strict orders from prospect gurus not to get too excited about this guy because he relies on guile rather than tools. Be that as it may, Kubenka has yet to find a league of hitters that he can't shut down. Radinsky is gone, leaving the Dodgers relatively thin from the left side, so I assume he'll get a full shot at the big

league level this season. I'll be watching with great interest. **<DD>**

MARK LEITER, SEA
(1998: PHI)

His career hits per 9 was 9.4 going into last season, when he posted a 6.8. Fluke or adjustment to new role? Well, lessee. He started the season hot, posting an ERA of 2.14 through the end of May, then limped home with a 4.42 ERA for the remainder of the year. The hit prevention, however, was there all along. His hits per 9 was 6.4 in April and May and 7.0 from June on. Given that, I'd say he's worth Spoljaric, though not much more. **<DD>**

CURT LESKANIC, COL

A pretty good hurler, but his inability to retire lefties will prevent him from getting any better. Had a very strong middle of the season: +1.9 WPA from May to August, -1.2 in April and September. **<DD>**

KERRY LIGTENBERG, ATL

His season would not look one bit out of line if you inserted it into the career record of Robb Nen or John Wetteland or Trevor Hoffman or any other great closer. His OPS allowed was 4th in the NL and his WPA was 5th. The Braves' bullpen as a whole posted positive WPA in 41 of their 52 high-pressure appearances, which is outstanding. Ligtenberg had 16 high-pressure appearances, twice as many as any other Brave, and converted 14 of them.

Possibly a small warning flag should be raised with respect to his

workload. 26 appearances on 0 days rest is quite a few. **<DD>**

RICH LOISELLE, PIT

Rich really mowed 'em down in his low pressure (P < .05) situations:

	IP	H	R	ER	BB	K	ERA
Lo Pressure	24	16	4	4	15	18	1.50
Other	31	40	22	17	21	30	4.94

That and $19.95 will get him a copy of BBBA 99. He only converted 12 of his 20 high-pressure appearances, and had 7 disastrous (WPA < -.25) ones. His WPA of -1.8 was 4th-worst in the NL. Listen up, Gene: Rich Loiselle might be a respectable middle reliever/spot starter, but nothing more. **<DD>**

MIKE MADDUX, MON

not-useless middle reliever, he became the 2nd-most important member of the Expos' bullpen late in the season, and did a decent job, allowing a paltry .638 OPS. **<DD>**

MIKE MAGNANTE, HOU

After a surprisingly adequate year in 1997, he reverted to form in last season. At .068, he had the 3rd-highest PPPI in the Astros' pen, and the highest among Astro lefties. Houston probably would have been better served letting Nitkowski pitch the tougher innings, as Magnante posted a -1.4 WPA, including -1.9 after April. **<DD>**

DENNIS MARTINEZ, ATL

There was a stretch there in May where he was pitching some big innings

---

RELIEF PITCHER DATA, NATIONAL LEAGUE 1998

LEGEND: **SV**—Save; **SVOP**—Save Opportunity; **HLD**—Hold; **G/F**—Groundball/Flyball Ratio **IR**—Inherited Runners; **IS**—Inherited Runners Scored; **IRS%**—Inherited Runners Pct.

Name	TM	SV	SVOP	HLD	BA	OBP	SLG	OPS	SB	CS	GDP	G/F	IR	IS	IRS%
Gabe White	Cin	9	13	6	.231	.284	.414	.698	4	5	2	0.60	52	16	30.8
Scott Sullivan	Cin	1	4	5	.253	.327	.420	.747	10	3	9	1.02	36	12	33.3
John Hudek	Cin	0	1	6	.219	.356	.399	.755	5	4	5	0.57	32	10	31.3
Marc Kroon	Cin	0	0	0	.250	.447	.357	.804	1	1	1	1.00	1	0	0.0
Todd Williams	Cin	0	0	0	.341	.420	.455	.875	0	0	6	2.10	6	3	50.0
Rick Krivda	Cin	0	1	1	.313	.417	.548	.965	3	2	4	1.39	15	0	0.0
Mark Hutton	Cin	0	0	0	.348	.483	.536	1.019	3	0	6	2.29	6	3	50.0
Ricardo Jordan	Cin	0	0	0	.308	.524	.846	1.370	0	0	0	0.50	7	3	42.9
Lariel Gonzalez	Col	0	0	0	.000	.000	.000	.000	0	0	0	2.00	0	0	0.0
Dave Veres	Col	8	13	8	.233	.301	.337	.638	5	3	6	1.29	42	12	28.6
Jerry Dipoto	Col	19	23	7	.232	.304	.384	.688	5	1	6	1.06	8	4	50.0
Chuck McElroy	Col	2	6	19	.268	.327	.378	.705	3	3	13	1.30	57	18	31.6
Mike DeJean	Col	2	3	11	.285	.340	.394	.734	5	6	11	1.59	32	15	46.9
Fred Rath	Col	0	0	0	.300	.348	.400	.748	0	0	1	3.67	2	1	50.0
Curt Leskanic	Col	2	5	12	.259	.350	.414	.764	1	3	7	1.33	20	6	30.0
Mike Munoz	Col	3	4	1	.312	.372	.459	.831	3	2	6	2.00	22	10	45.5
David Wainhouse	Col	0	1	0	.341	.431	.500	.931	0	0	4	2.09	5	4	80.0
Jim Stoops	Col	0	0	0	.385	.529	.769	1.298	0	3	1	0.50	0	0	0.0
Matt Mantei	Fla	9	12	2	.203	.308	.289	.597	1	2	4	0.55	31	10	32.3
Vic Darensbourg	Fla	1	2	13	.207	.289	.311	.600	8	3	2	0.76	33	4	12.1
Robby Stanifer	Fla	1	3	3	.277	.345	.410	.755	5	1	2	1.43	31	10	32.3

and pitching them well. For the rest of the season, he was pretty lousy, which should have surprised no one. **<DD>**

MATT MANTEI, FLA

This youngster clearly has something special growing out of his right shoulder, but his minor league career was plagued by injuries and wildness. He did a nice job of clearing up the wildness in 1998 (only 23 walks in 54.2 innings compared to 134 in 197.2 prior to last season), but health is still a major concern. **<DD>**

CHUCK MCELROY, COL

Obviously a good season without considering the park. It was otherworldly, Reedian even, after factoring in the Coors. WPA, however, was not particularly impressed, and I'm having a hard time figuring out why. Most of McElroy's really bad games were in low-pressure situations. Here's the breakdown:

	IP	H	R	ER	BB	K	ERA
Lo Pressure	27	34	16	16	11	24	5.33
Other	41.1	34	7	6	13	37	1.31

Seems very odd that someone who had a great overall season, and pitched better in the clutch than in garbage time, wouldn't have a massive WPA, but Chuck's WPA was merely +.7, compared to 1.7 PWins. This is a mystery to me at present. Possibly he bequeathed a lot of runners who were stranded by the other Rocky relievers. **<DD>**

GREG McMICHAEL, NYM
(1998: NYM-LA-NYM)

This was really Greg's first bad season, and it was pretty bad. He allowed 15.4 baserunners per 9. Prior to last season, his worst efforts in that category were 13.0 (in 94) and 11.5 (in 96), so this is a substantial drop. His PPPI with the Mets was .083 before the trade, and .044 after returning. **<DD>**

JOSE MESA, SEA
(1998: CLE-SF)

Let's see here. In 1997, Mesa loses the ability to prevent hits to the extent necessary to be a good closer. Then in 1998, he loses his control without regaining the hit prevention. Piniella's going to love this guy.

Did you catch Lou's comments after signing Mesa? Something to the effect of, "this guy's gonna be our closer. He's been in pressure situations before and blah blah blah." It was almost like he was lampooning himself. **<DD>**

DAN MICELI, SD

He was the 2nd-most valuable member of San Diego's bullpen last year, which is akin to being the 2nd-most popular Chumbawamba song. Seriously though, a very high-quality season, as his +1.6 WPA was good for 14th in the NL.

He also had a very eventful season. His 14 appearances in tie games was tied for 8th place in the league, and his total P of 7.7 was 13th. Around midseason, the Padres started shifting meaningful setup innings from Boehringer to Miceli. Miceli's PPPI from

April to June was .070, and from July on it was .102. **<DD>**

TREVER MILLER, HOU

Nothing he did mattered much. Only 3 of his 36 relief appearances were in save/hold situations, and 3 more were tie games. 16, on the other hand were classified as very low P (below .01). **<DD>**

TERRY MULHOLLAND, CHC

OK, I was wrong—he didn't end up in Minnesota last year as their number five starter, but he did work as a swingman. Other than May he pitched very well, and certainly helped the Cubs drive to the playoffs with his six late season starts, in which he went 3-0 with a 1.82 ERA. **<KA>**

MIKE MYERS, MIL

1997 may well turn out to be the best year Mike ever has, and it wasn't that great. 0.58 ERA before the break and 6.16 after. **<DD>**

ROBB NEN, SF

After pitching a lot of innings by closer standards, almost all of them high-stress innings, Nen was really very ordinary in the second half (by closer standards again). Combine this with the fact that consistency doesn't seem to be one of his strong points, and I'd put him on my roto Avoid list. **<DD>**

GREGG OLSON, AZ

It appears he made an adjustment around midseason. Check this out:

	IP	H	R	ER	BB	K	ERA
Pre-ASB	35	28	17	15	21	33	3.86
B3	3.2	28	8	8	4	22	2.14

The walk rate dropped from 5.4 per 9 to practically nothing, and the Ks came down a good bit too. His WPA after the break was +2.5, and he absolutely carried the DBacks' bullpen (non-Olson bullpen WPA for the season was -3.8).

Can he keep it up? Of course I don't know, but I wouldn't bet against it. I'd rather take him into the season as my closer than, say, Rod Beck. His workload was very light: only 10 times did he work two straight days and he never pitched three straight. **<DD>**

RELIEF PITCHER DATA, NATIONAL LEAGUE 1998

LEGEND: SV—Save; **SVOP**—Save Opportunity; **HLD**—Hold; **G/F**—Groundball/Flyball Ratio **IR**—Inherited Runners; **IS**—Inherited Runners Scored; **IRS%**—Inherited Runners Pct.

Name	TM	SV	SVOP	HLD	BA	OBP	SLG	OPS	SB	CS	GDP	G/F	IR	IS	IRS%
Kirt Ojala	Fla	0	0	1	.267	.351	.436	.787	10	6	14	0.99	11	4	36.4
Brian Edmondson	Fla	0	3	5	.266	.353	.448	.801	3	5	9	1.78	41	15	36.6
Antonio Alfonseca	Fla	8	14	9	.281	.359	.446	.805	3	1	6	1.44	38	18	47.4
Donn Pall	Fla	0	0	2	.326	.362	.504	.866	3	2	5	2.23	8	0	0.0
Gabe Gonzalez	Fla	0	0	0	.333	.600	.333	.933	0	0	0	2.00	6	3	50.0
Oscar Henriquez	Fla	0	0	0	.306	.390	.553	.943	1	0	0	0.85	5	3	60.0
Manuel Barrios	Fla	0	0	0	.308	.471	.538	1.009	0	0	2	2.00	5	3	60.0
Justin Speier	Fla	0	1	1	.325	.412	.651	1.063	3	1	1	0.65	11	5	45.5
Scott Elarton	Hou	2	3	2	.196	.270	.333	.603	1	0	2	0.82	9	3	33.3
Billy Wagner	Hou	30	35	1	.211	.292	.312	.604	2	0	5	1.10	9	0	0.0
C.J. Nitkowski	Hou	3	5	8	.228	.317	.340	.657	3	4	6	1.63	35	9	25.7
Doug Henry	Hou	2	5	11	.216	.307	.353	.660	9	0	6	0.78	41	11	26.8
Jay Powell	Hou	7	11	3	.225	.328	.360	.688	2	2	6	2.04	49	17	34.7
Trever Miller	Hou	1	2	1	.266	.332	.397	.729	3	2	3	1.82	22	4	18.2
Mike Magnante	Hou	2	4	3	.276	.368	.369	.737	3	1	4	1.83	23	7	30.4
Bob Scanlan	Hou	0	0	3	.245	.330	.429	.759	0	2	1	2.04	9	4	44.4
Reggie Harris	Hou	0	0	1	.261	.308	.478	.786	1	0	0	0.46	4	1	25.0
Mike Grzanich	Hou	0	0	0	.333	.500	.333	.833	0	0	0	0.00	0	0	0.0
Jose Cabrera	Hou	0	0	0	.389	.421	.611	1.032	0	0	1	0.63	2	2	100.0
Jeff Kubenka	LA	0	1	2	.138	.316	.138	.454	1	2	0	0.70	4	2	50.0
Eric Weaver	LA	0	0	0	.179	.324	.286	.610	0	3	3	2.00	7	2	28.6

ANTONIO OSUNA, LA

In last year's BBBA, I called Osuna the best mop-up man in baseball. Overall, his innings were a little more important in 1998 than they were in 1997, but his PPPI dipped when the Dodgers acquired Shaw. With Rojas and Mills in the mix now, it looks like Antonio's role will continue to be minimal. Fine job of pissing away 3 good years (probably 4 after this one) by the Dodgers. **<DD>**

LANCE PAINTER, STL

Despite mediocre surface numbers, Painter helped the Cardinals a lot last year because he got rocked when it didn't matter and turned it on when it did. Here are his low-pressure numbers

	IP	H	R	ER	BB	K	ERA
Lo Pressure	14	21	16	14	10	14	9.00
Other	33.1	21	8	7	18	25	1.89

(P < .05) vs. medium- and high-pressure: He started off slow, posting a -.6 WPA in April, but went +2.1 the rest of the way to finish at +1.6, 15th in the NL. Also 19th in the NL in P, despite the low number of innings (47.1). **<DD>**

JAY POWELL, HOU

He's been extremely consistent throughout his 3-year career, improving very slightly each year. He was relied upon heavily by both Florida and Houston in 1998, posting a P of 7.9 (9th in the NL) and a PPPI of .090. Also entered 17 tie games, tied for 3rd in the league. **<DD>**

SCOTT RADINSKY, FA
(1998: LA)

A good ERA obscures the fact that last year was pretty disastrous for Scott. He blew up in some key situations (resulting in a WPA of -1.2, 12th worst in the league), over half of his inherited runners scored, and he blew 11 saves. **<DD>**

ROBERTO RAMIREZ, SD

The Padres brought up the veteran Mexican League lefty to pitch to Barry Bonds in a critical series against the Giants. The strategy worked that night, but left-handed batters as a whole hit .321/.424/.786 against him. **<KA>**

RICARDO RINCON, PIT

One of the top relievers in the game for the first half of the season, but tailed off after the break. He also surrendered 10 unearned runs last season, resulting in an RA of 4.29 (his ERA was 2.91). Still, I'd say he's about as good a bet as anyone to turn in 60 or 70 innings of solid relief work this season. **<DD>**

JOHN ROCKER, ATL

His emergence as a left-handed setup man is apparently what made the Braves willing to part with Alan Embree. Wise choice, in my opinion. His minor league record indicates that he might be a good one, particularly in terms of hit-prevention. But he's still young, 24, and had just over 100 innings above A-ball prior to last season. I expect him to encounter some rougher times than he did last year, but he looks like a good prospect overall. **<DD>**

FELIX RODRIGUEZ, AZ

Nothing went right for Felix after about the first week of the season. He posted the 2nd-worst WPA in the NL (-2.3) despite pitching innings which were, on the whole, relatively meaningless (his PPPI of .041 was 2nd-lowest in the NL among those with 40 appearances). He's the only guy I've found so far for whom every split is negative: road, home, low pressure, medium pressure, high pressure, every month, 1-inning appearances and multi-inning appearances. He had a negative WPA in every one of those situations. He had more appearances (5) with WPA less than -.25 than appearances where his

WPA was over +.05 (he had only 4 of those).

No one else can come anywhere near this disastrous-to-decent ratio. **<DD>**

RICH RODRIGUEZ, SF

Another standard Rich Rodriguez season: solid, useful, very unexciting. I presume he's got a few more of those in him. **<DD>**

MEL ROJAS, NYM

I expected a big rebound season from Mel, and it didn't happen, as he was unquestionably much worse in 1998 than 97. The hits were way up and the Ks way down. Because the Dodgers can bury him in a meaningless relief role, he won't hurt them as much as Bonilla would have. And if he turns it around, so much the better. **<DD>**

RUDY SEANEZ, ATL

Had only one appearances with a WPA below -.05. It was a doozy, though, a -.55 against the Mets on September 5th.

Seanez was obviously a crucial part of the 'Brave New Bullpen' Atlanta put together after the Wohlers collapse. He shared setup duties with John Rocker for most of the second half, and did a tremendous job, posting a +1.7 WPA and a .087 PPPI in July and August, before slipping a bit in September. It's tough to take him too seriously at 30 years old with a career minor league ERA of 4.73, but a .547 OPS allowed is rather eye-popping. **<DD>**

RELIEF PITCHER DATA, NATIONAL LEAGUE 1998

LEGEND: **SV**—Save; **SVOP**—Save Opportunity; **HLD**—Hold; **G/F**—Groundball/Flyball Ratio **IR**—Inherited Runners; **IS**—Inherited Runners Scored; **IRS%**—Inherited Runners Pct.

Name	TM	SV	SVOP	HLD	BA	OBP	SLG	OPS	SB	CS	GDP	G/F	IR	IS	IRS%
Jeff Shaw	LA	48	57	0	.240	.284	.343	.627	7	0	10	1.64	34	11	32.4
Antonio Osuna	LA	6	11	12	.214	.311	.363	.674	1	3	4	0.89	37	7	18.9
Scott Radinsky	LA	13	24	8	.272	.337	.375	.712	1	4	3	1.42	41	20	48.8
Mark Guthrie	LA	0	1	8	.267	.347	.367	.714	6	3	2	1.42	30	7	23.3
Frank Lankford	LA	1	1	0	.288	.360	.400	.760	3	1	2	3.54	0	0	0.0
Sean Maloney	LA	0	0	1	.265	.357	.449	.806	1	0	1	2.20	7	3	42.9
Gary Rath	LA	0	0	0	.250	.357	.500	.857	0	0	0	1.33	0	0	0.0
Darren Hall	LA	0	1	0	.347	.411	.551	.962	4	0	0	1.43	4	2	50.0
Mike Judd	LA	0	0	0	.373	.475	.667	1.142	2	0	0	0.93	2	1	50.0
Travis Smith	Mil	0	0	0	.143	.143	.143	.286	1	0	0	1.00	1	1	100.0
Valerio De Los Santos	Mil	0	0	0	.151	.173	.356	.529	0	0	2	0.88	6	2	33.3
Greg Mullins	Mil	0	0	0	.250	.400	.250	.650	0	0	0	0.00	1	0	0.0
Bob Wickman	Mil	25	32	9	.262	.352	.346	.698	8	1	14	2.50	31	5	16.1
Chad Fox	Mil	0	2	20	.260	.326	.372	.698	3	0	5	1.07	24	6	25.0
Mike Myers	Mil	1	3	23	.249	.348	.379	.727	6	2	9	1.37	46	16	34.8
Dave Weathers	Mil	0	1	3	.295	.358	.409	.767	11	3	11	1.91	19	2	10.5
Eric Plunk	Mil	1	6	12	.277	.353	.428	.781	11	5	6	0.80	41	15	36.6
Al Reyes	Mil	0	1	10	.255	.352	.454	.806	3	3	6	0.70	40	16	40.0
Bronswell Patrick	Mil	0	0	0	.279	.339	.470	.809	3	1	10	1.42	32	12	37.5
Rodney Henderson	Mil	0	0	0	.313	.353	.750	1.103	0	0	0	0.50	0	0	0.0
Joe Hudson	Mil	0	0	0	1.000	.857	2.000	2.857	0	0	0	—	3	3	100.0

JEFF SHAW, LA

Not only did the Dodgers not really need to trade for Shaw (much less trade Konerko and Reyes for him), they did everything they could to ensure that he was adding as little value as possible. Compare Shaw's usage matrix in Cincy to his Dodger matrix:

CIN	-5	-4	-3	-2	-1	0	+1	+2	+3	+4	+5	T
5												
6												
7												
8				2		2	4	3	3			14
9	1			1		3	3	6	8		1	23
10+						1		1				2
TOT	1			3		6	7	10	11		1	39

LA	-5	-4	-3	-2	-1	0	+1	+2	+3	+4	+5	T
5												
6												
7												
8								2	2			4
9			1	1	1	9	8	5	1		1	27
10+						3						3
TOT			1	1	1	12	10	7	1		1	34

Shaw appeared in 6 tie games as a Red, 1 in LA. He came in in the 8th 14 times in Cincy, 4 times as a Dodger. His PPPI was .115 as a Red, and .090 as a Dodger. He also pitched 40% more partial innings in Cincinnati than he did in LA despite being traded right at midseason. Cripes, if you're going to pay through the nose for a guy, you may as well get your money's worth.**<DD>**

CLINT SODOWSKY, AZ

The court of talk radio declared Clint a lost cause sometime around mid-May, but Showalter remained committed to getting him regular work. There was-n't a whole lot of setup work to go around in Arizona last season, but Sodowsky did most of what there was of it for the first half of the season. Buck eventually gave up on him as an important part of the bullpen, and let him start a few games, which also weren't overly successful.

I don't know where Sodowsky's future is, but I think he can be salvaged. His SLG allowed was only .391, and his fastball does appear to be very 'heavy' when it's working. **<DD>>**

JERRY SPRADLIN, CLE
(1998: PHI)

Had a nice season pitching mostly mop-up innings for Philadelphia. The outstanding hit prevention (63 allowed in 81.2 innings, .216 BA allowed) came out of nowhere, so I don't expect it to stick, but he can be a useful innings-eater.Now with Cleveland. I'm not sure why they wanted him, but being the 4th best righthander there (which is no disgrace), he's in no danger of being thrust into a key role.**<DD>**

RUSS SPRINGER, ATL

He was a key member of the Diamondbacks' bullpen before being dealt to Atlanta, where he saw only garbage time.**<DD>**

ROBBY STANIFER, FLA

He's replacement level. Particularly got hammered in crucial situations, resulting in a -1.7 WPA, worst on the Marlins, 5th-worst in the NL. **<DD>**

SCOTT SULLIVAN, CIN

A disappointig sophomore campaign after looking great as a rookie in 1997. Didn't cost the Reds much though, as Sullivan, like almost all the Cincy relievers, pitched much better when something was on the line. His high-pressure (P > .15) vs. non-high-pressure breakdown:

	IP	H	R	ER	BB	K	ERA
Hi Pressure	29.1	18	14	12	12	29	3.68
Other	72.2	80	48	47	24	57	5.82

Including his minor league time, he pitched 343.1 innings, virtually all of it in relief, in the last three seasons.**<DD>**

JEFF TAM, NYM

This extreme control pitcher was called up for 10 relatively low-leverage appearances in June and July, and then was brought back for 5 more in September. He got hit pretty hard with the big club (.444 SLG allowed), but had a very nice-looking AAA season.**<DD>>**

JULIAN TAVAREZ, SF

Supposedly Julian has a "rubber arm," which is why he is so valuable in the bullpen. For the last four years the Indians and Giants have had Tavarez pitch over 80 innings in each season. The first time the Indians pulled this he melted down the next year going from a 2.44 to 5.36 ERA. This carried over to the first two months of the 1997 season when his ERA was over 7, but he rebounded and had an excellent season. Last season Tavarez pitched 62 innings before the break with a 2.60 ERA and then suffered an injury and finished the last two months with a 7+ ERA. Rubber arm or not, the Giants better take it easy on him. **<KA>**

ANTHONY TELFORD, MON

The summary stats indicate that Telford had a decent year, a .697 OPS allowed ain't

RELIEF PITCHER DATA, NATIONAL LEAGUE 1998

LEGEND: **SV**—Save; **SVOP**—Save Opportunity; **HLD**—Hold; **G/F**—Groundball/Flyball Ratio **IR**—Inherited Runners; **IS**—Inherited Runners Scored; **IRS%**—Inherited Runners Pct.

Name	TM	SV	SVOP	HLD	BA	OBP	SLG	OPS	SB	CS	GDP	G/F	IR	IS	IRS%
Ugueth Urbina	Mon	34	38	0	.157	.259	.229	.488	6	0	4	0.77	14	2	14.3
Mike Maddux	Mon	1	2	7	.243	.293	.345	.638	6	0	5	1.43	37	8	21.6
Steve Kline	Mon	1	2	18	.228	.333	.335	.668	6	3	1	1.89	53	14	26.4
Tim Young	Mon	0	0	3	.250	.357	.333	.690	0	0	0	0.44	9	1	11.1
Anthony Telford	Mon	1	5	8	.247	.322	.375	.697	1	3	4	1.77	35	14	40.0
Miguel Batista	Mon	0	0	3	.274	.359	.392	.751	10	7	13	2.08	33	10	30.3
Shayne Bennett	Mon	1	2	0	.276	.363	.410	.773	10	3	3	0.86	43	15	34.9
Rick DeHart	Mon	1	2	4	.291	.359	.453	.812	1	0	0	1.36	22	10	45.5
Marc Valdes	Mon	0	0	1	.285	.375	.444	.819	10	0	4	2.34	8	3	37.5
Kirk Bullinger	Mon	0	1	0	.400	.400	.543	.943	1	0	0	4.75	8	2	25.0
Turk Wendell	NYM	4	8	11	.221	.306	.349	.655	9	1	4	1.22	26	10	38.5
Dennis Cook	NYM	1	5	21	.240	.318	.348	.666	3	4	4	0.79	62	20	32.3
Rigo Beltran	NYM	0	0	0	.214	.303	.393	.696	0	0	0	0.43	4	1	25.0
John Franco	NYM	38	46	0	.267	.347	.364	.711	2	1	6	2.24	20	3	15.0
Brad Clontz	NYM	0	1	3	.218	.327	.402	.729	3	1	1	0.64	12	3	25.0
Masato Yoshii	NYM	0	0	0	.255	.316	.425	.741	15	3	15	1.17	0	0	0.0
Jeff Tam	NYM	0	1	1	.241	.317	.444	.761	1	0	2	2.08	4	1	25.0
Greg McMichael	NYM	2	7	10	.301	.386	.442	.828	8	4	4	2.14	36	19	52.8
Mel Rojas	NYM	2	6	7	.305	.391	.507	.898	13	4	8	1.17	17	9	52.9
Jerry Spradlin	Phi	1	4	5	.216	.270	.344	.614	7	3	4	1.50	27	6	22.2
Yorkis Perez	Phi	0	0	13	.209	.297	.340	.637	6	0	2	0.84	43	11	25.6

bad. He didn't fare well in high pressure (P > .15) situations though:

	IP	H	R	ER	BB	K	ERA
Hi Pressure	19.1	21	12	10	4	11	4.66
Other	71.2	64	33	29	32	48	3.64

Felipe drastically scaled back Telford's role early in the season: his PPPI was .085 in April and .042 from May onward, including .026 after July. **<DD>**

UGUETH URBINA, MON

The only thing that seperates Urbina from Hoffman is control. Ugueth walked 33 batters in 69 IP while Hoffman only walked 21 in 73 IP. Compare the two in opposition BAVG/OBP/SLG: Hoffman .165/.232/.229, Urbina-.157/.259/.229. With Felipe Alou he won't get overworked and should be able to hold up for many years to come. **<KA>**

Urbina has officially become my girlfriend's favorite ballplayer. Regrettably, however, Starting Line-up has not seen fit to recreate Ugueth doing a power glide off the mound after punching out yet another hapless batter. Come on get with the program, we want to see an Urbina doll! I saw a Marc Newfield in my local Hy-Vee for goodness sakes!

Urbina's "power glide" off the mound following an inning-ending strike-out has to rank up there with Carlos Perez's strikeout dance as my favorite mound antics. **<SF>**

DAVE VERES, COL

His was probably the best of the many outstanding performances from the Rocky bullpen in 1998. A .638 OPS allowed in Coors Field is impressive, to say the least. His WPA of +3.0 was 4th in the NL, trailing only Hoffman, Nen, and Urbina. **<DD>**

BILLY WAGNER, HOU

Dierker really eased back on Billy's workload in terms of the amount of pressure he was facing. He also had an unwelcome vacation in the middle of the season that limited him to a mere 60 innings. Yet he was still unable to finish strong.

His K rate continues to hover in the stratosphere (14.6), but he's not an elite closer just yet. **<DD>**

DONNE WALL, SD

Became a key member of the San Diego bullpen from June on. His PPPI in April and May was .046, after May it was .077.

Allowing 50 hits in 70.1 innings? Where did that come from? This is his first bullpen experience, so maybe he made an adjustment of some sort. Or maybe he just got lucky. I'd guess the latter. **<DD>**

TURK WENDELL, NYM

After a shaky first half of the season in which he posted a 4.40 ERA and pitched no meaningful innings to speak of (PPPI .053 before the break), he was a house afire in the second half (2.06 ERA), and the Mets eventually expanded his role (.089 PPPI after July). Turk was literally unscored-upon in his high-pressure (P > .15) appearances:

	IP	H	R	ER	BB	K	ERA
Hi Pressure	22.1	10	0	0	8	19	0.00
Other	54.1	52	25	25	25	39	4.14

All but 2 of his high pressure appearances were after July 27th. **<DD>**

DON WENGERT, CHC
(1998: SD-CHC)

This guy is simply horrendous. The A's go in for that sort of thing, so I can see how he stuck there for awhile. But how could not one but two non-Oakland teams give him a chance in 1998? **<DD>**

GABE WHITE, CIN

Very nice-looking K/BB ratio, but he has yet to display any sort of ability to keep the ball within the confines of the ballyard, and probably won't ever be of much use unless he does.

Another Red reliever who performed better in high-pressure situations. Here's a breakdown of his high-pressure appearances (P > .15) vs. the others:

	IP	H	R	ER	BB	K	ERA
Hi pressure	43.1	29	15	15	9	39	3.12
Other	53.1	57	31	29	18	44	4.89

<DD>

BOB WICKMAN, MIL

Stepped into the closer's role around the beginning of June and did a tremendous job. For awhile. He had only one imperfect appearance in June, and amassed a +1.9 WPA for that month. Then he did a pretty convincing Doug Jones imitation for the rest of the year, posting a 6.68 ERA and -1.1 WPA after the break. If he's numero uno in your pen, you've got problems, but he's a perfectly adequate setup man/innings eater. **<DD>**

MIKE WILLIAMS, PIT

After floundering around as a starter for five years, Mike was moved to the bullpen by the Pirates and produced his first sub 3 ERA with a 1.94 ERA. Not

RELIEF PITCHER DATA, NATIONAL LEAGUE 1998

LEGEND: **SV**—Save; **SVOP**—Save Opportunity; **HLD**—Hold; **G/F**—Groundball/Flyball Ratio **IR**—Inherited Runners; **IS**—Inherited Runners Scored; **IRS%**—Inherited Runners Pct.

Name	TM	SV	SVOP	HLD	BA	OBP	SLG	OPS	SB	CS	GDP	G/F	IR	IS	IRS%
Mark Leiter	Phi	23	35	1	.216	.331	.352	.683	2	2	6	1.15	17	9	52.9
Wayne Gomes	Phi	1	8	13	.258	.328	.374	.702	10	1	8	2.15	21	5	23.8
Toby Borland	Phi	0	0	0	.242	.342	.394	.736	1	1	1	1.71	9	5	55.6
Ken Ryan	Phi	0	0	0	.253	.396	.386	.782	1	0	1	0.96	5	3	60.0
Ricky Bottalico	Phi	6	7	3	.305	.390	.503	.893	1	0	4	0.81	5	4	80.0
Darrin Winston	Phi	1	2	5	.298	.348	.558	.906	1	0	1	1.06	15	8	53.3
Matt Whiteside	Phi	0	0	0	.338	.376	.600	.976	3	0	1	1.76	15	6	40.0
Robert Dodd	Phi	0	0	0	.333	.360	.667	1.027	0	0	0	1.29	0	0	0.0
Mike Welch	Phi	0	0	0	.310	.376	.679	1.055	2	0	2	0.96	8	0	0.0
Billy Brewer	Phi	0	0	0	.750	.833	.750	1.583	0	0	0	1.00	0	0	0.0
Ryan Nye	Phi	0	0	0	.500	.500	1.167	1.667	0	0	0	0.00	0	0	0.0
Mike Williams	Pit	0	1	7	.211	.271	.292	.563	4	5	6	1.85	30	8	26.7
Jason Christiansen	Pit	6	10	15	.216	.295	.297	.592	2	2	4	0.98	44	11	25.0
Ricardo Rincon	Pit	14	17	11	.208	.292	.350	.642	2	1	9	1.40	34	9	26.5
Jeff Tabaka	Pit	0	0	2	.204	.305	.354	.659	1	1	6	1.33	24	8	33.3
Marc Wilkins	Pit	0	1	4	.236	.358	.345	.703	1	0	2	1.64	9	3	33.3
Rich Loiselle	Pit	19	27	1	.262	.372	.332	.704	3	2	5	2.73	18	8	44.4
Javier Martinez	Pit	0	0	2	.248	.389	.401	.790	7	1	4	1.18	16	5	31.3
Elmer Dessens	Pit	0	1	6	.300	.351	.467	.818	4	1	8	1.91	17	7	41.2
Jeff McCurry	Pit	0	0	0	.324	.400	.581	.981	2	0	4	1.94	6	3	50.0
Trevor Hoffman	SD	53	54	0	.165	.232	.229	.461	7	0	7	0.92	26	4	15.4
Donne Wall	SD	1	4	16	.202	.293	.319	.612	3	2	5	1.26	14	3	21.4
Dan Miceli	SD	2	8	20	.238	.308	.346	.654	2	1	6	1.04	33	10	30.3
Randy Myers	SD	28	34	8	.267	.348	.412	.760	2	2	4	0.94	22	0	0.0
Brian Boehringer	SD	0	1	7	.257	.363	.418	.781	5	2	7	0.90	37	15	40.5
Roberto Ramirez	SD	0	0	6	.211	.348	.456	.804	0	0	0	1.21	17	2	11.8

only that but he was virtually unhittable against the first batter. <KA>

MARK WOHLERS, ATL

Based on the few interviews I've seen with Wohlers since his meltdown, and my vast store of psychological expertise (roughly enough to fill a medium-sized thimble), I think his career is over. I just hope he's able to get on with his life. He seems like a guy with more going for him than the 100-mph fastball. <DD>

TIM YOUNG, MON

Check out the minor league career of this 25-year-old lefthander:

IP	H	R	ER	BB	K	ERA
163.1	110	45	32	45	214	1.76

And yet I've never heard a peep out of any prospect-analyzer about him, possibly because he's only 5'9". He's worth keeping a close eye on. <DD>

CATCHERS

BRAD AUSMUS, HOU

I was a Brad Ausmus fan a few years ago, and touted him here, and he did nothing. Now, he comes up fourth in the XW rankings. Essentially, he still hasn't grown any with the bat; his power actually fell off badly. But he did take a few more walks than usual, which got the OBP up. The most important ingredient, though, is Brad's defense. His 2.46 DXW DXWf anyone ranked below him except Carlos Hernandez, and he hits enough, compared to normal catchers, to avoid dragging the defense ranking down.

Do remember two things. First, this is only possible at catcher and shortstop, where the defensive opportunity is large. Second, Brad still ranks five XW below the league leader at the spot. The real issue here is that there are only three true top catchers in the NL at this time. And that's normal for catchers. <BJH>

BOBBY ESTALLELA, PHI

A young prospect who will take his walks, but whose AAA numbers do not yet suggest that he is completely ready for prime time. Check back in 2000. <BJH>

TONY EUSEBIO, HOU

Tony entered the majors too old. His two .290 seasons, he was 27 and 28 years old. Since then, he has declined predictably. Right now, his glove is all he has left to offer. <BJH>

Judging by the Astros' addition of young switch-hitting catcher Mitch Meluskey to the playoff roster, I would be surprised if Eusebio was playing for Houston next year. He's not of much use to the Astros as Brad Ausmus is a good defensive catcher and Meluskey should be able to outhit Eusebio pretty easily next year. It may be back to AAA for Tony next year. <SF>

JORGE FABREGAS, FLA
(1998: AZ-NYM)

Had his Career Year at age 26, is now turning 29, and that age-26 season was just barely enough to keep him in the league. <BJH>

Chalk it up to photos of GMs in compromising positions, because otherwise it's not clear to me how he's still in the majors. First, Arizona tears up his contract after beating him at arbitration and gave him a big contract. Second, New York trades for him. Third, Florida trades a good prospect for him and cuts Gregg Zaun in favor of him. None of it makes sense. (And Steve Phillips was caught in a compromising position by someone, wasn't he?) <NL>

BROOK FORDYCE, CIN

Another peak-of-career season that strongly suggests that this is not a major league player. <BJH>

BOB HENLEY, MON

Turning 26, and he may still be a year away. He's hit this kind of .300 in the minors, but not in AAA ball. I'd expect one big fat Sophomore Slump this year, except that I don't really think he'll spend that much time in the major leagues. I think he'll be getting his AAA seasoning this year, pending a projected Age-27, Year 2000 arrival to stay. <BJH>

CARLOS HERNANDEZ, SD

Well, here's a surprise ranking out of nowhere. Carlos has been a career backup; this time, given a chance to start, he placed in the top half of NL starters. Still, before you get carried away, look at the component XWs. Essentially, we're out of catchers who can actually hit much; these rankings depend, essentially, on the players' DXW. Carlos has the highest, so he leads the list of this type of catcher. And, therefore, Carlos has NO VALUE IN FANTASY BALL, since defense doesn't count. <BJH>

I GOT THE IMPRESSION THAT THE PADRES GAVE CARLOS A THREE-YEAR CONTRACT BECAUSE THEY THOUGHT THAT KEVIN BROWN LIKED HIM, AND THAT THIS WOULD BE A SUBTLE INDUCEMENT FOR HIM TO RETURN. THIS WAS CERTAINLY MORE SUBTLE THAT THE EXTRA $45 MILLION THAT THE DODGERS HANDED

RELIEF PITCHER DATA, NATIONAL LEAGUE 1998

LEGEND: SV—Save; **SVOP**—Save Opportunity; **HLD**—Hold; **G/F**—Groundball/Flyball Ratio **IR**—Inherited Runners **IS**—Inherited Runners Scored; **IRS%**—Inherited Runners Pct.

Name	TM	SV	SVOP	HLD	BA	OBP	SLG	OPS	SB	CS	GDP	G/F	IR	IS	IRS%
Scott Sanders	SD	0	0	1	.329	.370	.497	.867	6	1	2	0.94	19	7	36.8
Will Cunnane	SD	0	0	0	.308	.357	.538	.895	0	0	0	3.00	2	0	0.0
Robb Nen	SF	40	45	0	.180	.239	.251	.490	10	0	2	1.17	21	5	23.8
Cory Bailey	SF	0	0	0	.167	.231	.417	.648	0	0	0	0.25	4	0	0.0
John Johnstone	SF	0	1	15	.224	.303	.394	.697	12	3	3	0.68	35	13	37.1
Rich Rodriguez	SF	2	6	22	.272	.322	.394	.716	3	1	7	1.85	57	25	43.9
Jose Mesa	SF	1	4	13	.273	.353	.390	.743	2	2	7	1.74	48	15	31.3
Julian Tavarez	SF	1	6	10	.298	.379	.410	.789	7	2	17	2.56	47	18	38.3
Chris Brock	SF	0	0	0	.279	.322	.468	.790	2	0	3	0.68	9	4	44.4
Alvin Morman	SF	0	2	9	.292	.367	.487	.854	4	2	4	1.29	40	15	37.5
Dean Hartgraves	SF	0	0	0	.385	.438	.577	1.015	1	0	0	0.46	5	2	40.0
Juan Acevedo	StL	15	16	3	.236	.301	.321	.622	2	5	9	1.15	10	4	40.0
Rich Croushore	StL	8	11	6	.213	.320	.362	.682	10	0	1	1.05	22	4	18.2
Mike Busby	StL	0	2	5	.256	.328	.381	.709	3	0	2	1.24	15	10	66.7
Kent Bottenfield	StL	4	5	6	.254	.333	.378	.711	6	3	9	1.05	6	4	66.7
Curtis King	StL	2	8	3	.262	.338	.387	.725	2	0	6	2.51	30	14	46.7
Jeff Brantley	StL	14	22	3	.220	.289	.445	.734	3	0	5	0.83	13	4	30.8
Lance Painter	StL	1	2	21	.249	.365	.373	.738	0	1	4	1.43	59	11	18.6
John Frascatore	StL	0	2	13	.256	.326	.415	.741	14	2	7	1.48	38	13	34.2
Mark Petkovsek	StL	0	5	6	.312	.375	.445	.820	3	4	13	2.56	29	15	51.7
Bryan Eversgerd	StL	0	0	4	.346	.387	.500	.887	0	0	0	1.71	9	1	11.1
Braden Looper	StL	0	2	0	.357	.375	.571	.946	0	0	0	2.00	2	2	100.0
Sean Lowe	StL	0	0	0	.440	.533	.720	1.253	0	0	1	4.67	2	0	0.0
Brady Raggio	StL	0	0	0	.579	.605	.737	1.342	0	0	1	2.25	3	2	66.7

BROWN, AND DOESN'T SEEM TO HAVE EVEN GRAZED KEVIN'S HEAD ON THE WAY BY. <COJ>

TYLER HOUSTON, CHC

Are the Cubs quite done with giving this obvious minor league player major league chances? This was the Age-27 Career Year, for crying out loud. <BJH>

BOBBY HUGHES, MIL

Had a hot Age-27 Career Year in AAA ball, so the Brewers thought they'd try to skim some cream, only to find there was none. <BJH>

BRIAN JOHNSON, SF

Essentially a journeyman, Brian surely has some play left in him after all those seasons of riding pine. I see no reason why he can't play this many games with essentially this result for the next five years. I'd be surprised to see him move up or much down from this. <BJH>

CHARLES JOHNSON, BAL
(1998: FLA-LA)

I'd suggest that the hitting collapse was caused by Dodger Stadium, except that Charles wasn't hitting in Florida, either. That causes me to suspect pitcher adjustment. You know what that means. One big fat expected return to form and —ooops —Charles is turning 27. HOT FANTASY TOUT, especially since he's out of LA. <BJH>

JASON KENDALL, PIT

This season was a surprise, because Jason had had no Sophomore Slump at all. Instead, his three year career has shown a steady growth that you simply don't expect out of a young player. Instead, what you do expect is a pattern of growth one year and then adjustment by the league's pitchers the next. But last year, Jason doubled his home run power and added half to his doubles power. then, this year, he made another 50% gain in homer power.

The result is what you have here. Jason still doesn't hit like Mike Pizza, but he's close enough so that his defensive edge causes him to outrank the man who should have been the 1996 and 1997 MVPs. The result is also that I can't really expect Jason to make many ore gains before his career should peak at age 27. It's got to stop somewhere, unless he's just going to turn into Mickey Cochrane. <BJH>

He is one of the rarest fantasy players, a catcher with speed and a very high average. Benito Santiago and John Wathan are the only non-dead ball era catchers I've found who hit .300 and stole 20 bases. Kendall should do that four or five times. Kendall is a bit of a throwback as he makes a lot of contact and loves to step into pitches. If the Pirates ever develop an alternate power source, Kendall should bat second (or perhaps leadoff), where he could score 110 runs. They should also tell him to get out of the way of some of those pitches, as you really don't want your best player getting plunked 30 times a season. <SF>

TOM LAMPKIN, STL

A lefty bat will keep a catcher in the league for a long time, as long as he's willing to ride the pine until someone gets hurt. <BJH>

JIM LEYRITZ, SD
(1998: BOS-SD)

A solid pinch hitter who can fill in a little at catcher. Retains enough with the bat to help a contending team. His catching glove skills are about gone. <BJH>

MIKE LIEBERTHAL, PHI

A fluke 20-homer campaign brought him full time work in 1997. This year was a very similar season, except that he didn't hit those taters. This cost him about 150 plate appearances, as the Phillies tried other options. I could be a lot more thrilled with the Phillies' other options, and therefore suggest that Mike might return to the 400-at-bat range next season. The 20 homers? Nope, I think that was all fluke. <BJH>

JAVY LOPEZ, ATL

Does this count as an Age-27 Career Year? Well, yes and no. Javy's slugging percentage didn't improve by any significant amount, and his OBP actually dropped, along with his batting average. But he did add 50% to his home run total, and a big jump in homers is the single most common distinguishing feature of the Career Year. Actually, the biggest oddity is the drop from ten intentional walks to only one. That accounts for all of Javy's total walks drop this year, and almost all of the drop in OBP.

My conclusion is to call this the peak season, but not dignify it with the capitalized title of Age-27 Career Year. That is, I don't think Javy has any more growing to do as a player. I think this is it if you bear in mind that "this" includes the 34-homer range, not the 23. Also note that, according to DW%, Javy is the Gold Glove catcher in the NL this year. That, too, represents a new career peak. <BJH>

KIRT MANWARING, FA
(1998: COL)

At one time, he couldn't hit, but was a Gold Glove candidate. Now, his glove skills are down to just good. He still can't hit. <BJH>

ELI MARRERO, STL

I don't think the thyroid cancer cost him that much, which is both good news and bad. The good news is that Eli probably will recover fully from the medical problem. The bad news is that he doesn't figure to get all that much better than this. I think a .270 batting average, with medium power and few walks, is about his limit. He's reputed to b a glove wizard, and posted good enough numbers this time out. I think that might improve, in which case, with the departure of Charles Johnson for the AL, Eli will become the leading candidate for the Gold Glove. <BJH>

MIKE MATHENY, MIL

Coming up on Age 27. Do you care? I don't care. Does anyone really care? <BJH>

BRENT MAYNE, SF

A journeyman platoon catcher with a lefty bat. That give him value, but apparently not enough to prevent him becoming a nomad. <BJH>

DAMIAN MILLER, AZ

Hit .285 in AAA ball four years ago, and has improved every season since. The expansion Arizona team figured that they might have some room to try such a player out. I call this experiment a success. If I were managing Arizona, I'd call Damian here my starter, and Kelly Stinnett would become a backup catcher/pinch hitter. <BJH>

GREG MYERS, FA
(1998: SD)

Another aging backup catcher with some glove value. <BJH>

MARK PARENT, PHI

Finished, finally, at age 37. <BJH>

EDDIE PEREZ, ATL

Javy Lopez' glove caddy when Greg Maddux pitches, if that makes any sense, which, given Javy's DW%, it doesn't. But I'm not going to argue with Greg Maddux' results. **<BJH>**

MIKE PIAZZA, NYM
(1998: LA-FLA-NYM)

This is the first year in quite few that Mike has not headed the Catcher TXW rankings for the National League. If you look at the component XWs, you can quickly see why. Mike does indeed outhit the other top catchers, but he is no more than an ordinary defender, while the others are better. Therefore, when one of them gets close to him as a hitter, like Jason Kendall did this year, he'll pass Mike up in total XW.

It may be important, in evaluating Mike, to realize that his defensive rankings are not really awful. He has a lousy reputation, because he lacks the flashiest of the catchers' defensive tools, but he's not awful, just ordinary.

I completely agree with the Mets' decision to play Mike at catcher, although it resulted in the silly positioning of Todd Hundley in left field. You should use a Mike Piazza, when you're lucky enough to get one, at the most demanding defensive spot that he an handle at all. Of course, you then do need to convert your Todd Hundleys into real usable trade value. The jury is still out on that gamble. **<BJH>**

I'm not in love with signing him for 7 years. The great catchers did not age particularly well as a group.

Seasonal averages by age for Dickey, Hartnett, Bench, Fisk, Lombardi, Campanella, Carter, Berra and Cochrane. (GC is games caught.)

Age	AB	H	2B	3B	HR	BA	OBP	SLG	GC
29	497	155	30	3	24	.311	.386	.533	132
30	489	144	28	2	21	.296	.381	.491	129
31	458	134	25	2	22	.293	.376	.499	119
32	440	121	20	2	19	.274	.358	.456	117
33	361	98	14	1	15	.272	.349	.439	92
34	373	104	17	2	12	.278	.354	.432	91
35	292	81	13	2	10	.276	.339	.431	68
36	219	62	10	1	9	.283	.353	.459	51
37	188	49	8	0	9	.259	.345	.450	46

Still if he stays fairly healthy he'll help whatever team he's with. He'll merely be overpaid. This isn't the case when you sign a mediocre player to a long-term deal. **<RNJ>**

MIKE REDMOND, FLA

This cup of coffee was Mike's Age-27 Career Year. His minor league numbers do not support this above AA level. **<BJH>**

JEFF REED, COL

A fine, underrated catcher,, Jeff would move up if only the Rockies would give him more playing time. On the other hand, asking a 36-year-old catcher to play full time is suicide, at least for the catcher. Therefore, I can't tout Jeff as likely to move up, as I can't imagine an increase in opportunity. **<BJH>**

SCOTT SERVAIS, FA
(1998: CHC)

The main reason why Tyler Houston keeps getting chances. The Cubs' most obvious need is for a major league catcher. **<BJH>**

Well on his way to early retirement. Hitting .222/.289/.338 in Wrigley Field generally spurs the need for retirement planning at an early age. This is especially true for catcher's with poor defensive skills. If you don't believe me, just ask Hector Villanueva for confirmation. **<JF>**

Amazingly, the Cubs agreed with our panel of experts and released Servais. Unfortunately, they promptly turned around and signed Benito Sanitago to replace him. As my wacky and wonderful Louise would say: Yikes!! **<DM>**

KELLY STINNETT, AZ

If the Diamondbacks had just used their heads a little bit during the expansion draft they would be in pretty good shape going into their sophomore season. They wasted a high pick on Jorge Fabregas when Bobby Abreu was available. They threw superstar money at merely good players. Stinnett, however, was a good pick, as he was in the top half of catchers in OPS. He will be 29 this year, but he has hit well each of the last three years, so he may have figured something out. **<SF>**

EDDIE TAUBENSEE, CIN

Has always been a platoon-player since he can't hit lefties. Plus, he's only adequate defensively. Since returning to the Reds, he's seen some playing time at 1B and in the outfield. But that's the last place that a guy can hope to find more playing time in Cincinnati. Taubensee signed an extension through 2000, but it's likely his playing time will start to dwindle. **<SL>**

CHRIS WIDGER, MON

That was age 27. it was not the season of a major league player. **<BJH>**

GREGG ZAUN, TEX
(1998: FLA)

Theoretically, he's on the age 24-26-28 track of good years, with the slumps being on the odd-numbered ages. But the age-26 season was so good, and this year's collapse so bad, that I can't imagine that we haven't seen the best he will ever have to offer. No, I have no idea whether he will

NATIONAL LEAGUE Catcher			
PLAYER	OXW	DXW	TXW
Kendall J	6.33	2.41	8.74
Piazza M	6.94	1.14	8.08
Lopez J	3.35	2.92	6.27
Taubensee E	2.97	0.61	3.58
Ausmus B	1.09	2.46	3.55
Reed J	1.52	1.25	2.77
Hernandez C	0.60	2.12	2.72
Perez E	1.58	0.85	2.43
Lieberthal M	0.73	1.45	2.18
Johnson B	0.44	1.68	2.12
Stinnett K	1.52	0.49	2.01
Mayne B	1.11	0.87	1.98
Marrero E	0.58	1.39	1.97
Johnson C	0.82	1.10	1.92
Leyritz J	1.46	0.38	1.84
Miller D	0.84	0.56	1.40
Henley B	1.08	0.13	1.21
Widger C	1.33	-0.14	1.19
Myers G	0.44	0.74	1.18
Manwaring K	-0.38	1.53	1.15
Eusebio T	0.02	1.01	1.03
Lampkin T	0.61	0.40	1.01
Redmond M	0.67	0.23	0.90
Hughes B	0.37	0.46	0.83
Fordyce B	0.27	0.45	0.72
Houston T	0.25	0.26	0.51
Servais S	-0.45	0.72	0.27
Parent M	-0.19	0.43	0.24
Matheny M	-0.29	0.49	0.20
Estalella B	-0.19	0.38	0.19
Pagnozzi T	-0.29	0.21	-0.08
Zaun G	-0.50	0.05	-0.45
Fabregas J	-0.74	0.19	-0.55

ever settle down in the middle of his huge hitting swings. **<BJH>**

Though I note that Brock has accidentally added an extra "G" at the end of Zaun's first name, this might be something for the Fish-who-was-fobbed-for-Fabregas to consider. After the season "Greg" had in 1998, anything "Gregg" does in 1999 can't help but be better. **<COJ>**

1ST BASE

JEFF BAGWELL, HOU

This is the first season in many that Jeff has not finished in the top two at NL first base. Is he aging? Well, yes, but not compared to McGwire and Olerud. So what is going on here? Well, first off, Jeff missed 13 games this year, which is very rare. Then, he didn't have a good - for him - campaign for home runs, and so his slugging percentage was down a bit.

Then John Olerud, who is not a consistent hitter, had a hot year. And Mark McGwire revealed his true level of ability in his first full season after moving out of Oakland's hitters' cemetery.

That is, until Mark gets old—in about three years —Bagwell here should not predict to lead the position in offense, although playing time might move him to the top spot in XW. But, except for Mark, Jeff is the best first baseman in the league. John Olerud won't hold this level of play. <BJH>

RICO BROGNA, PHI

Players like this end up on teams like this. That is the story, in a nutshell, of money in the major leagues. Note that I do not mean money since the evil days of free agency; this rule applied in the days of Ralph Kiner, too. <BJH>

Any time we get too cocky about the influence sabermetrics has had, we need only look at this guy. I honestly don't think he's among the top 50 players in organized baseball at his position, yet he's a firmly entrenched regular. There are still Mets fans who think the Mets were robbed. <RNJ>

SEAN CASEY, CIN

Started off slow and was slowed further by a close encounter with a batting practice ball. Once he got settled, he took off and hit .300/.394/.498 after the All-Star break. He's not going to be a big power guy, but some batting titles (with good patience) are a possibility. <SF>

Although some scouts thought he might not have a quick enough bat for the majors, he showed as the 1998 season wore on, that those opinions were unfounded. Todd Helton and Travis Lee got more press and more votes for the NL Rookie-of-the-Year, but this is the guy I think everybody

will be talking about the most three years from now. <JF>

GREG COLBRUNN, AZ
(1998: COL-ATL)

Well, let's see. Do you want to call this his Career Year, or opt for 1994, when he was 24 years old? The ones in between have been disappointments, haven't they? <BJH>

BRAD FULLMER, MON

Anyone who ranks below Brad, except for Roberto Petagine, is not really the sort of hitter you're looking for in your starting first baseman. That doesn't mean none of them count as starters - the league has to have 16, after all - but it means that the teams that have these guys are, or should be, still looking.

Fullmer, meanwhile, is only turning 24, and his minor league numbers suggest he can hit much better than this. Since he did have a cup of coffee in 1997, there is some chance that this season is his Sophomore Slump. Therefore, I predict a jump season for Brad, and possibly a huge one. NICE FANTASY GAMBLE. <BJH>

ANDRES GALARRAGA, ATL

All right. I admit it. I have no idea what makes Andres Galarraga tick. I was as sure as anyone that he would collapse at the age of 37, moving out of Colorado. There is some chance that this was a one-year fluke caused by a combination of advanced panic and Age-37 Last Hurrah season (which is fueled by the same panic), but I ain't guaranteeing anything. I'm cutting my losses and shutting up on this subject about which I obviously know far too little. And Bobby Cox obviously knows far, far more. <BJH>

I'm secretly pleased that the Big Cat confounded the stathead critics, myself included. If we were right all the time, the universe would seem dry and deterministic, like Physics in 1898. Also, Andres and I share a birthday, day and year. So when Galarraga hangs 'em up, I will become Old overnight. Until then, I'm in with a chance. <TA>

MARK GRACE, CHC

Still a quality first baseman, even though he is now old and never did have first base power. But he gets on and he plays good defense (down, due to age, from great defense), and he still is above average among starting first basemen. <BJH>

TODD HELTON, COL

His minor league numbers are better than this, and he's in Colorado, for crying out loud, so I expect a jump from Todd in 1999. That would put him on the age 25-27 track for growth, where he makes the big jumps at ages 25 and 27, with Counteradjustment Slump (he won't have a Sophomore Slump) at age 26.

Because 1999s jump will have to compete with the Sophomore Slump effect, I don't expect it to be all that big. However, that does set up age 27, in 2001, as one very likely very hot campaign. The only real question is whether he'll end up as a 30-homer man or a 20. <BJH>

I boldly predicted on my website that Helton's raw numbers would surpass Galarraga's, but a poor first half by Helton pretty much doomed that prediction. I'm going to guarantee it will happen this year. Helton got going in the second half and hit .359/.420/.579 compared to Galarraga's .305/.398/.553 after the All-Star break. Helton is my early favorite for next year's NL batting title. <SF>

JOHN JAHA, FA
(1998: MIL)

A very brief career, apparently lost to injuries. <BJH>

KEVIN JORDAN, PHI

Won't take a walk, doesn't have first base power. His main function seems to be to be bad enough that the Phillies can keep playing Rico Brogna. <BJH>

WALLY JOYNER, SD

His totals are down some, which was a red flag for me. Wally, you see, is turning 37 years old. Hitters who make it that far as starters have a remarkable tendency to post a big jump at age 37, which lasts only the one year. I call this the Age-37 Last Hurrah season, and I believe that it is fueled by the panic that comes from seeing your totals drop to the point where you're not proud of them any more and decide to work out all offseason to do something about it.

Wally is set up. I expect one last big year from him in 1999. HOT ONE-YEAR FANTASY TOUT. <BJH>

ERIC KARROS, LA

I wouldn't shove him up the middle of my lineup, like the Dodgers insist on doing, but at least he's consistent. This year, the batting average gain overpowered the home run drop, and it was his best campaign except for his Age-27 Career Year. **<BJH>**

DEREK LEE, FLA

The National League rookie first baseman crop was one of the deepest in recent history. Six National League teams had rookies starting for them at first base at some point in the season. Not surprisingly, these teams were out of contention. First base is so highly offensive in this day and age that it will be difficult for a rookie to put up enough offense to be even fair relative to the rest of the league. Without a good first baseman, the rest of the offense had better be running in high gear to make up for it.

Derrek Lee is in the middle of the pack with regards to this new group of first basemen. He has great power as his six-homer April will attest, but contact is a serious problem as his 120 K's and .233 batting average demonstrate. Lee is a very good athlete and should rebound next year. I suspect getting someone other than Leyland as his manager won't hurt either. **<SF>**

TRAVIS LEE, AZ

Read the Todd Helton comment first. Travis is turning 24, which is one year younger than Todd. His rookie year here is much less than his minor league numbers suggest, just like Todd's. Therefore, like Todd, I expect him to move up a little in 1999, with growth countering the Sophomore Slump effect. However, unlike Todd, that will put Travis on the age 24-26-28 track for growth. That's one more jump year than Todd should have. All of which means that I do expect Travis to become a better player than Todd. They're within reach of each other right now, but Travis predicts to get one more growth jump before he peaks. He also predicts clearly to become a 30-homer man. What a difference that one year makes. **<BJH>**

RYAN MCGUIRE, MON

I'm as much an admirer of walks as anyone, but when that's the only skill a player has, I really can't envision a major league career. **<BJH>**

MARK MCGWIRE, STL

If you think I'm going to add my puny couple of paragraphs of analysis to the roughly two trillion words that were written this season about Big Mac, you're crazy. All I do have to say is this: in the entire ten years I've been writing these comments for the various incarnations of the BBBA, plus, if I remember right, all the years Bill James printed XWs in his Baseball Abstracts, this is the very best offensive season that has occurred. By anyone. **<BJH>**

In July, McGwire had 10 intentional walks and 18 strikeouts. In August, he struck out 39 times and drew only 3 intentional walks. So you'd suspect he started slumping right? Wrong. Once they started pitching to him, he did strike out more, but his slugging percentage for August was 200 points higher than it was for July. McGwire set a National League record for walks in a season, and the only thing that surprises me is that he wasn't walked more. **<SL>**

McGwire may be the most extreme fly ball hitter in the history of baseball. In the last five years, McGwire has ground ball to fly ball ratios of .52, .53, .40, .46, and .50. Among active players only Joe Carter and Brian Hunter (the other one) have ever posted ratios below .50. **<SF>**

DAVE NILSSON, MIL

Nilsson started as a catcher, but suffered a serious back injury and hadn't been behind the plate at all since 1996 until September, when the Brewers tried to prepare him for possible part-time duty there in 1999. The experiment came to an end when Nilsson injured his leg—ironically, while playing first base. Despite these maladies, Nilsson had his best month at the plate in September, looking more like the hitter who managed a .900+ OPS in 1996. **<DM>**

JOHN OLERUD, NYM

At the end of the season, when the Mets were trying to finish up a run for the playoffs, their offense consisted entirely of John Olerud and Mike Piazza. Everyone else went into the tank, and the two of them, good as they are, proved not to be enough. The Mets' management is apparently aware of this, as they seem to regard every player on the team except these two to be expendable, and are trying to build their offense around the pair. As a die-hard New York hater, I find this depressingly scary. You Met fans, though, should rejoice.

Good management is the first big step towards the postseason. **<BJH>**

Blue Jay fans, including a talented satirist in the Toronto Usenet group named Spooky, may wish to contemplate what their lineup would look like if Gord Ash had not bundled up Johnny O and left him on the Mets' doorstep two years ago. (And, yes, this is definitely not the first time I've transparently attempted to foment mob violence. . .) **<DM>**

NATIONAL LEAGUE FIRST BASE		
Player	OXW	DXW	TXW
McGwire M	11.63	0.44	12.07
Olerud J	8.64	0.83	9.47
Bagwell J	7.34	0.84	8.18
Galarraga A	7.39	0.37	7.76
Grace M	5.26	0.72	5.98
Karros E	4.76	0.51	5.27
Helton T	3.86	0.89	4.75
Joyner W	4.00	0.42	4.42
Lee T	3.35	0.78	4.13
Young K	3.22	0.50	3.72
Fullmer B	2.75	0.16	2.91
Brogna R	1.94	0.94	2.88
Snow J	1.90	0.75	2.65
Lee D	1.85	0.60	2.45
Casey S	1.83	0.22	2.05
Nilsson D	1.42	0.07	1.49
Carter J	0.89	0.27	1.16
Jaha J	1.01	0.15	1.16
Colbrunn G	0.86	0.17	1.03
Petagine R	0.72	0.14	0.86
Jackson R	0.73	0.05	0.78
Perez E	0.48	0.16	0.64
Jordan K	0.00	0.35	0.35
Hamelin B	0.26	0.02	0.28
McGuire R	-0.64	0.10	-0.54
Cianfrocco A	-0.60	0.02	-0.58

EDUARDO PEREZ, FA
(1998: CIN)

Not even my idea of a good backup. **<BJH>**

ROBERTO PETAGINE, JAPAN
(1998: CIN)

Won the International League MVP for the second straight season. As Crash Davis would say, that's a dubious honor. For whatever reason, the word is out that this guy can't hit at the big league level. He's never been given a full season to disprove that theory, and I don't suppose he ever will. Jim Bowden tried to find a taker during the November GM meetings, but none of the other teams were willing to offer a player in exchange. The Reds sold his contract to the Yakult Swallows so Petagine can finally play everyday in Japan. **<SL>**

J. T. SNOW, SF

A fine glove man, which isn't worth that much here; J. T. has continued the iambic on-again off-again pattern of hitting far past the peak seasons of age 27 and 28. This was the off year, and it hurt the Giants considerably. 1999, though, predicts to be on, and each of his on years has been better than the last. **<BJH>**

KEVIN YOUNG, PIT

First base is so competitive that this really isn't good enough. He did manage 69 extra-base hits, but the plate discipline is so poor that he really needs to hit .310 or so. The Pirates desperately need an infusion of plate discipline, and picking up somebody like Ryan Klesko to play first base would be a good start—platooning Klesko and Young would be even better. By the way, Young outhit Jeff King again this year. **<SF>**

2ND BASE

CARLOS BAERGA, FA
(1998: NYM)

The biggest disappearing act in baseball in years. I mean, this wasn't a rookie fluke. Carlos was an established superstar who just fell down in 1996, when traded to New York, and never got up. I wonder if it isn't the ballpark. Look at Delino DeShields. Hit fine in Montreal. Got traded to Los Angeles. Stopped hitting. Moved to St. Louis. Started hitting again. Analysis? Can't hit in Los Angeles, where his marginal power disappears altogether into the ballpark effects.

Is Carlos the same? Can he simply not hit in New York? His splits the last few years don't suggest it. They suggest that he does all his hitting at home. But, still. You could get him for not much and you could win real, real big. . . **<BJH>**

TONY BATISTA, AZ

I thought Andy Stankiewicz would take the job, but Andy failed again, and I've about given up. It didn't take the Arizona management that long, and they tried their best available kid. To be fair, the kid had one hot half-year as a rookie with Oakland, and everyone else was probably a stopgap anyway. Tony figures to move up in the rankings over the next few years, especially as no one better than him is younger.

Good tout for the future, in fantasy or reality. **<BJH>**

18 HR in 293 AB for a middle infielder. Has been called the Mark McGwire of the Dominican Republic. Although he'll never hit over 60 in the big leagues, he could very well have a career much like Jeff Kent, and that's not bad. <JF>

DAVE BERG, FLA

Played pretty well. Although this was the Age-27 season, it was consistent with his minor league numbers. Dave's big problem is that he's behind Craig Counsell on the Florida roster, and his time window is limited. If he hasn't got a job within two years, he's gone the way of all 27 year old rookies. **<BJH>**

CRAIG BIGGIO, HOU

I still don't think it was a good idea. I'm talking, of course, about the Astros' decision, several years ago, to convert Craig Biggio to a second baseman from his original position of catcher. At the time, this was a disaster, although Biggio played just fine at the keystone. Converting Craig, though, left the Astros with no catcher, so they traded a center field prospect named Kenny Lofton to the Indians for a catcher named Eddie Taubensee. Taubensee is still playing, though not for the Astros. Lofton, you know about. For several years, the Astros struggled with the center field slot that Lofton would have easily filled, and the catching slot that Biggio would have manned, and they didn't win anything. That made my analysis of the move look good.

But I said at the time that the Astros would eventually get a payoff if Biggio remained a top keystone man after he would have declined at the more demanding catching spot. That has now happened. Biggio is still on another planet from the other second basemen in the league, and the Astros have been making the playoffs. Craig would not be a dominant force at catcher now, at age 32.

But think. This isn't 1956. You can't just assume that you're talking about the Astros keeping all of Biggio's career. They did, you know, come close to losing him last contract time. And they had to pay top dollar to keep him. It wasn't like they got a discount because they had moved him away from catcher or anything. Could they have gotten a top second baseman for the money if they had lost Biggio? Sure. Maybe not one as good as Craig is, but a top one. So they could still be winning those division titles, for the same money, if they had never converted Craig.

Would they have won anything earlier if they had kept Craig at catcher? We'll never know. But they would have had Biggio AND Lofton, and whatever second baseman they could pick up. Kenny Lofton. That can make a lot of difference there.

The theme here is this: take your profit now. That player whose knees you are saving won't be here in a few years, or if he is, you'll be paying him so much that you could have gotten another just as good. Take his value while you can. The Astros may be winning now, and they may be getting a lot out of Craig Biggio, but they've made no profit on the deal. Instead, they've lost about four years of Kenny Lofton play. It was still a bad move. **<BJH>**

BRET BOONE, ATL
(1998: CIN)

Still living off the hype of that one big year in 1994. Boone turned in 24 home runs and got everyone all hot and bothered again. But he still only hit .26, and he still doesn't take his walks, and so he still didn't play as well as Mickey Morandini or Delino DeShields, much less the big guns at the position. This season is an improvement over his lousy 1996 and '97 campaigns, but it only re-establishes him as a mid-pack starter, not an All-Star. **<BJH>**

It would be interesting to know just what it is about Bret that so fascinates the Braves, who have been trying to acquire him for several years and paid top dollar in the form of Denny Neagle in order to do so. It can't be his hitting in Turner Field (.301 OBP, .355 SLG, albeit in limited appearances). <DM>

LUIS CASTILLO, FLA

A very young good prospect fighting Craig Counsell and Dave Berg for

Florida playing time. I like Luis, but he's got to get out from behind those guys that are only a few years older but therefore a few years better. If you are a Major League general manager, will you please steal this kid from the Marlins before he gets discouraged? **<BJH>**

CRAIG COUNSELL, FLA

Did nothing with his Age-27 campaign. That's not to say he's worthless. He's a mid-pack starter at this level, and he's been in the majors for so little time that he could still be developing despite his age. He's about even in the rankings with Tony Womack, who got a similar late start. Womack has more speed; Counsell takes more walks. **<BJH>**

DELINO DESHIELDS, BAL
(1998: STL)

To my complete surprise, Delino turned in a respectable defensive season; hence the decent ranking. He's always had a good bat, except when Dodger Stadium robbed him of all semblance of power, but his glove has been just godawful before now. In particular, his range has been horrid, because he doesn't get to balls in the air. His usual results are about 50 Putouts less than they should be. This time, though, he turned in an above-average range result.

Is this real? I don't know. At this time, the Cardinals have not let him go, so I guess they may be the ones to find out. I'll say this: if Delino has finally solved his range problems, he moves into the strong starting ranks of second basemen, even as he turns 30. The bat is for real. **<BJH>**

ANDY FOX, AZ

A reasonably decent on-base year with the bat, but there's a problem. Andy has been moved around a lot in his career, which indicates that he can't really play the defensive positions his teams want him to. Why do they want him to play the positions they do want? Because he doesn't hit well enough to justify anywhere except the infield. This was his Age-27 career year, and his Slugging Percentage still wasn't .400. That's a problem.

In Arizona, I assume that Tony Batista will beat him out, and I assume that that was the Arizona plan all along. I think they really want Andy Fox to remain a utility player, sort of like Bip Roberts, although a little lower in quality. **<BJH>**

He hit about what you would have expected from his minor league numbers.

Apparently Buck Showalter has a fetish for ex-Yankee utility infielders named Andy, as he featured both Fox and Andy Stankiewicz on his roster and nearly wasted Tony Batista on the bench in an effort to play them. Fox is a valuable player for the right team. He isn't going to become much better than this as he's already 27, but for a contender he would fill a valuable role coming off the bench. The Braves could have used a guy like this instead of Marty Malloy coming off the bench. **<SF>**

TONY GRAFFANINO, ATL

Tony's going to have a tough time staying on the Braves' roster, what with Boone and Lockhart ahead of him. That eerily consistent OPS in both halves of the 1998 season (.593 BASB/.595 AASB) might have been the straw that put the camel on the DL. **<DM>**

WILTON GUERRERO, MON
(1998: LA-MON)

Young, but bad. He can't play second base on defense, and he doesn't have the power to move to the outfield. He also won't take a walk. I say, even turning only 24, Wilton is in trouble unless his arm can handle third base. I don't see where else he's going to play. **<BJH>**

I think Dev's assessment is on the money, but he could be overlooking several non-analytical elements herein. First, nepotism: as Vlad's brother, he might get to hang around a good bit longer than he would if his name were Basil Shabazz. Second, Felipe Alou: the Expos' manager has a weak spot for guys who "don't walk off the island." Third, versatility: while Wilton does not play any position particularly well, he can be stuck just about anywhere in a pinch. And the Expos are going to be pinched for some time to come. **<DM>**

PAT KELLY, STL

The Cardinals ran out of healthy infielders and got desperate and resurrected Pat from the minor leagues. I expect him to return to AAA in 1999. **<BJH>**

With DeShields going to the Orioles, Kelly may be re-resurrected as the Cards' second baseman. They've signed him to a minor-league deal just to cover their heinies. **<DM>**

JEFF KENT, SF

A fine, fine second baseman that the Mets never seemed to appreciate, and so the Indians looted him and then traded him to the Giants in the Matt Williams deal. Since the Indians don't have

Williams any more, I guess you can say that the Giants are the big winners in the Jeff Kent trades. **<BJH>**

The local press touts Jeff for the team MVP every year, and last year went to far as to push him for a dark, dark-horse league MVP candidate, banking heavily on those leadership, "gamer" intangible. I'd say the press guys have been snorting too many intangibles. He's nowhere near league MVP, and he's clearly the second-best hitter on the team. That's the problem, though: the best hitter on the team is Barry Bonds, and the local press would rather mainline drano than admit that Barry is by far the best player on the Giants.

That said, Kent had a hell of a year, almost in the Galarraga range of exceeding lowered expectations. The only flaw in a fine 1997 was a .316 OBP, and damned if Jeffrey didn't raise his OBP up to a decent .359, missing .300 in batting average by a hair in the process. His range is still short and he looks stiff out there, but he makes the routine plays. I'll take that for a second baseman who bats cleanup any day of the week. Be warned, though: last year was a career year. **<TA>**

MIKE LANSING, COL

Did not adjust well to the trade to Colorado, and stank op the joint, by his previous standards. When that happens in a big hitters' park, it's often a case of the hitter getting greedy and overswinging all year, looking for those taters. If so, then Mike will probably settle down and return to form in 1999. Of course, "return to form" would look like "career year" in the raw stats, before the Coors gas got adjusted out. Mike did play good defense, which helps in a park where your pitchers want to keep the ball out of the air and onto the ground. **<BJH>**

MARK LEWIS, CIN
(1998: PHI)

I've been waiting for mark to just break loose for years, ever since he was a very hot young kid in Cleveland. But it doesn't look like it's going to happen. This season was age 28, and the Phillies handed him a full-time job, and he fell down on it. He hasn't a quarter the future he did a year ago. Very disappointing. **<BJH>**

KEITH LOCKHART, ATL

Your basic Earl Weaver middle infielder. Hits a little, fields a lot. Since Bobby Cox is an Earl Weaver style manager, Lockhart is perfect in his current spot. <BJH>

Keith hit just .203 in the second half of 1998, and lost his starting job to Tony Graffanino, who didn't do much better. It will be mildly interesting to see which one Bobby Cox keeps to back up Boone; with the Ozzard of Whizz re-signed as "insurance" for Walt Weiss, Graffanino's ability to play SS may not matter as much as Lockhart's left-handed bat. <DM>

NATIONAL LEAGUE SECOND BASE			
Player	OXW	DXW	TXW
Biggio C	7.41	1.73	9.14
Vina F	4.61	3.26	7.87
Veras Q	4.19	2.53	6.72
Kent J	4.79	1.60	6.39
Young E	3.32	1.22	4.54
Boone B	2.38	2.01	4.39
Womack T	2.43	1.95	4.38
Morandini M	3.47	0.79	4.26
Deshields D	3.11	1.13	4.24
Counsell C	1.89	1.22	3.11
Fox A	2.92	0.07	2.99
Lansing M	0.63	2.31	2.94
Batista T	2.04	0.46	2.50
Baerga C	0.41	1.98	2.39
Lockhart K	0.98	1.24	2.22
Berg D	1.81	0.23	2.04
Lewis M	0.17	1.42	1.59
Guerrero W	1.33	-0.04	1.29
Castillo L	0.07	0.44	0.51
Lopez L	0.05	0.32	0.37
Graffanino T	-0.75	1.01	0.26
Kelly P	0.00	0.25	0.25
Vidro J	0.07	-0.02	0.05
Stankiewicz A	-0.73	0.21	-0.52

LUIS LOPEZ, NYM

This Age-27 season has completely established Luis Lopez as a backup middle infielder for the next ten years. At that job, he has value. <BJH>

Odd fact: in a bit less than 200 defensive innings, Luis averaged .91 double plays per nine innings while playing shortstop for da Metz. The ostensibly dazzling Rey Ordonez averaged .57 DPs per nine innings, which ranked third from the bottom amongst SS with 1000 or more defensive innings. I don't think that Luis can keep up such a pace if he played regularly, but I see no reason why the Mets shouldn't at least consider giving him a shot at the job. He's no world-beater, but he's got 100 points of OPS on Ordonez, a guy who makes Hal Lanier look like a slugger. <DM>

MICKEY MORANDINI, CHC

Mickey helped the Cubbies an awful lot in getting into the playoffs. He covered a position that has been a Cubbie problem since Ryne Sandberg retired the first time. He got on base, which is the skill that hitters' ballparks like Wrigley favor the most. The only thing he did not do well is play second base.

Better yet for the Cubs, this season is completely consistent with his previous three; it wasn't a fluke. At age 32, he figures to hold about this value for maybe three or four more seasons. I wasn't a Mickey Morandini fan his first few futile years in Philly, but he's aged reMarkably Gracefully. (Sorry.) <BJH>

ANDY STANKIEWICZ, AZ

I've touted Andy Stankiewicz for years, and for years he has let me down. I've kept this one bad pun ready for the season where I finally gave up on Andy. So, here it comes. Andy Stank. <BJH>

QUILVIO VERAS, SD

A favorite of mine from his rookie days. Quilvio got badly hurt in Florida, and took a while to recover. In 1997, though, he turned in a full campaign, and followed it with another this time out, for a career year to date. Now, part of that career year is that old magic Age 27, but part of it is simple bodily recovery. Quilvio has just, after all, caught up with his rookie season batting average; in fact, if he had played full time, his rookie season would still be his best. That means that I figure him to still have room for improvement. I would not be surprised to see him rank second at this spot in 1999, behind only Craig Biggio.

Reality top buy; rotisserie value discounted due to emphasis on defense and walks. <BJH>

JOSE VIDRO, MON

A kid only turning 24, who has struggled for at least one year at every new level of play. This would be partial year #3 in the Majors. His potential is to hit over .300 with some walks and a little pop. He did stink at the keystone this time out, but he's still a kid, and might even hit enough to play elsewhere. I rate him a fine prospect, but still too young to tout for fantasy play or anything. Give him a couple of campaigns. I'm sure he can beat out Wilton Guerrero. <BJH>

Vidro's power stats, which may have appeared as a benefit of the Harrisburg (Eastern League) ballpark, have pretty much vanished, even when he returned to Ottawa after the acquisition of Guerrero. He's going to need to get that back to unseat Guerrero any time soon—based on the predilections of Felipe Alou—and will likely be a utility player for the foreseeable future. <DM>

FERNANDO VINA, MIL

Apparently thrilled with whatever the difference is between NL pitching and AL, Vina turned in a career year featuring a big jump in doubles, which are his power stat. Since he is the Gold Glove keystone man in his new league, that was enough to rank him higher than any competitor other than the space alien Craig Biggio.

I am not sure that Vina will hold this ranking. For one thing, the NL pitchers will probably adjust some of that gas out of his hitting stats. For another, Quilvio Veras seems to be getting healthier. Veras is the other contender for the Gold Glove, and has about as little power as Vina, but gets on base more, if he hits for the same batting average. And, if he stays healthy, he will.

Vina, meanwhile, does not get on base much if he doesn't hit .300+. And he lacks power. And he isn't a good base stealer. That leaves a decent bat, plus the Gold Glove. Enough to keep him in the upper third at the position, but probably not enough to keep him Number Two. <BJH>

TONY WOMACK, PIT

His 1997 Age-27 season remains his Career Year, but this one wasn't much of a drop-off, and he should be able to hold this value for three or four more campaigns. Does anyone really know why the Pirates sat on him until 1997? His 1994 and '95 cups of coffee strongly indicated that he could hit major league pitching. <BJH>

Involved in a million rumors and being slagged across the Internet. Guys,

SECONDARY FIELDING STATISTICS
1998 NATIONAL LEAGUE
SECOND BASEMEN

Name	G	GS	INN	TC	PO	A	E	DP	FPCT	RF	ZR	DP/G	DP/E	OOA	NRN	NDPR	NDPE
Fernando Vina	158	158	1383	884	404	468	12	135	.986	5.68	.880	0.88	11.3	105	114	135	171
Luis Castillo	44	43	378	238	118	113	7	34	.971	5.50	.944	0.81	4.9	21	110	124	74
Pat Kelly	41	36	306	194	79	108	7	18	.964	5.49	.900	0.53	2.6	17	110	81	39
Mike Lansing	153	148	1275	781	346	425	10	118	.987	5.44	.912	0.83	11.8	64	109	128	180
Craig Counsell	104	101	893	539	237	297	5	72	.991	5.38	.957	0.73	14.4	39	108	111	219
Quilvio Veras	132	130	1126	670	255	406	9	88	.987	5.28	.925	0.70	9.8	37	106	108	149
Jeff Kent	134	134	1166	700	277	403	20	87	.971	5.25	.904	0.67	4.4	34	105	103	66
Delino DeShields	111	102	896	531	248	274	9	66	.983	5.24	.914	0.66	7.3	25	105	102	112
Mark Lewis	140	137	1229	729	276	437	16	73	.978	5.22	.928	0.53	4.6	32	105	82	69
Tony Graffanino	93	67	633	377	139	227	11	41	.971	5.21	.868	0.58	3.7	15	104	89	57
Manny Alexander	27	16	163	96	43	51	2	11	.979	5.18	.919	0.61	5.5	4	104	93	84
Tony Womack	152	149	1316	771	304	450	17	104	.978	5.16	.892	0.71	6.1	24	103	109	93
Luis Lopez	50	27	281	163	73	86	4	16	.975	5.09	.919	0.51	4.0	3	102	79	61
Tony Batista	41	31	281	156	72	83	1	23	.994	4.97	.940	0.74	23.0	-1	100	113	350
Eric Young	114	113	968	544	226	305	13	67	.976	4.94	.953	0.62	5.2	-6	99	96	78
Bret Boone	156	155	1358	753	329	415	9	100	.988	4.93	.876	0.66	11.1	-9	99	102	169
Craig Biggio	159	154	1368	763	318	430	15	91	.980	4.92	.909	0.60	6.1	-10	99	92	92
Carlos Baerga	144	135	1164	639	289	341	9	97	.986	4.87	.899	0.75	10.8	-15	98	115	164
Keith Lockhart	97	86	730	386	130	250	6	56	.984	4.68	.898	0.69	9.3	-25	94	106	142
Andy Stankiewicz	61	29	300	156	61	94	1	17	.994	4.65	.920	0.51	17.0	-11	93	78	259
Mickey Morandini	152	146	1304	674	265	404	5	70	.993	4.62	.893	0.48	14.0	-54	93	74	213
Wilton Guerrero	84	80	695	363	155	198	10	41	.972	4.57	.899	0.53	4.1	-32	92	81	62
Andy Fox	60	55	443	226	103	119	4	23	.982	4.51	.863	0.47	5.8	-24	90	72	88
F.P. Santangelo	35	29	237	120	47	71	2	7	.983	4.48	.892	0.27	3.5	-13	90	41	53
Jose Vidro	56	46	405	204	78	121	5	25	.975	4.43	.827	0.56	5.0	-26	89	85	76

KEY: Inn-Innings; **PO-**Putouts; **A-**Assists; **Er-**Errors; **DP-**Double Plays; **FPct-**Fielding Pct.; **RF-**Range Factor; **ZR-**Zone Rating
DPR-Double Plays per RF(/9); **DP/E-**Double Plays per Error; **OAA-**Outs Above Average;
NRF-Normalize; Range Factor (N=100); **NDPR-**Normalized DP per RF; **NDPE-**Normalized; DP/Error

he's not that bad. Wouldn't want him on my team, but he's almost certainly good enough to play. He's been roughly league average offensively at 2B in both of his years as a regular.

Normally stolen bases aren't too important. They can't be ignored when they're stolen at the rate and frequency that Womack steals them, however—60 a year at 89%. <RNJ>

ERIC YOUNG, LA

A fine hitting season, and a surprisingly good one with the glove. Eric did drop off after leaving Colorado, sure, but the drop wasn't anything like what his Rockie home/road splits suggested. And he apparently can play second base. The Dodgers did OK here. Right now, his biggest minus is that he's already turning 32. <BJH>

3RD BASE

EDGARDO ALFONZO, NYM

A fine player that the Mets can't seem to decide where to play. My rule? If you've got a guy you're shuttling all over the infield with the occasional game even at shortstop, drop the "occasional". See if he can play shortstop first. <BJH>

SHANE ANDREWS, MON

This is the other end of Scott Rolen. The Expos touted Shane Andrews, even though he was awfully old for a hot rookie, because they really didn't have anything else to tout. Well, Shane ain't much, either. He's turning 27, but I don't think I want to tout him to you fantasy guys. <BJH>

ADRIAN BELTRE, LA

What a great name for a home run hitter. And sure enough, he hit seven of them for the Dodgers in only 195 at-bats. What? You say that doesn't sound like-

much? Did I mention that Adrian will finally be able to vote this year? That'sright, he was 20 least year. BIG FAT FANTASY TOUT unless you find out that the Bums are going to give him another season of seasoning. <BJH>
See Paul Konerko, Cin. <NL>

SEAN BERRY, MIL
(1998: HOU)

The Astros are of the opinion that Sean Berry has failed, which seems to me to be a very odd interpretation of this season. That makes me wonder whether the problems they had were with his play or his personality. There's something funny going on here.

My rule of thumb when this happens is to assume that the man will be happier after he moves, and to predict a nice fat comeback when he arrives in a new ballpark. However, the only way Sean is going to "come back" from 1998 is to get more playing time. <BJH>

Berry slugged .520 as a third basemen, which was good enough for fourth among third baggers. Berry and his platoon mate, Bill Spiers, were a wonderful complement for the Astros this year. Berry hit .265 before the All-Star

SECONDARY FIELDING STATISTICS
1998 NATIONAL LEAGUE
THIRD BASEMEN

Name	G	GS	INN	TC	PO	A	E	DP	FPCT	RF	ZR	DP/G	DP/E	OOA	NRF	NDPR	NDPE
Shane Andrews	147	143	1232	437	95	322	20	28	.954	3.05	.830	0.20	1.4	56	115	120	108
Matt Williams	134	129	1127	391	99	281	11	18	.972	3.04	.819	0.14	1.6	49	115	85	126
Jeff Cirillo	149	147	1308	449	99	339	11	45	.976	3.02	.878	0.31	4.1	54	114	182	315
Kevin Orie	105	100	888	310	88	207	15	12	.952	2.99	.814	0.12	0.8	35	113	72	62
Freddy Garcia	47	46	397	137	28	102	7	9	.949	2.95	.793	0.20	1.3	14	112	120	99
Fernando Tatis	149	145	1282	442	109	306	27	22	.939	2.91	.794	0.15	0.8	39	110	91	63
Scott Rolen	159	159	1419	467	135	318	14	27	.970	2.87	.864	0.17	1.9	37	109	101	148
Aaron Boone	52	49	426	142	37	98	7	7	.951	2.85	.826	0.15	1.0	10	108	87	77
Jose Hernandez	72	54	508	167	45	115	7	4	.958	2.84	.820	0.07	0.6	11	107	42	44
Sean Berry	87	75	654	215	55	150	10	13	.953	2.82	.818	0.18	1.3	13	107	105	100
Bill Mueller	137	126	1137	374	83	273	18	32	.952	2.82	.849	0.25	1.8	22	107	149	137
Adrian Beltre	74	54	517	174	31	130	13	13	.925	2.81	.816	0.23	1.0	9	106	133	77
Pokey Reese	32	24	211	66	20	45	1	7	.985	2.78	.869	0.30	7.0	3	105	176	538
Bill Spiers	99	81	742	234	57	169	8	9	.966	2.74	.765	0.11	1.1	8	104	64	87
Gary Gaetti	119	112	971	296	71	220	5	17	.983	2.70	.834	0.16	3.4	6	102	93	262
Vinny Castilla	162	162	1423	438	110	315	13	39	.970	2.69	.829	0.25	3.0	8	102	145	231
Edgardo Alfonzo	144	136	1233	371	117	245	9	20	.976	2.64	.768	0.15	2.2	0	100	86	171
Willie Greene	76	69	618	188	48	128	12	20	.936	2.56	.833	0.29	1.7	-5	97	171	128
Chipper Jones	159	159	1400	408	105	291	12	28	.971	2.55	.836	0.18	2.3	-15	96	106	179
Ken Caminiti	127	126	1049	306	77	208	21	14	.931	2.45	.767	0.12	0.7	-23	93	71	51
Bobby Bonilla	85	82	687	200	59	124	17	14	.915	2.40	.736	0.18	0.8	-19	91	108	63
Charlie Hayes	46	37	340	90	22	67	1	6	.989	2.36	.817	0.16	6.0	-11	89	93	462
Aramis Ramirez	71	71	605	152	29	114	9	12	.941	2.13	.786	0.18	1.3	-34	81	105	103
John Mabry	38	31	272	70	18	46	6	1									

KEY: Inn-Innings; **PO**-Putouts; **A**-Assists; **Er**-Errors; **DP**-Double Plays; **FPct**-Fielding Pct.; **RF**-Range Factor; **ZR**-Zone Rating
DPR-Double Plays per RF(/9); **DP/E**-Double Plays per Error; **OAA**-Outs Above Average;
NRF-Normalize; Range Factor (N=100); **NDPR**-Normalized DP per RF; **NDPE**-Normalized; DP/Error

break and .368 after. Spiers before: .291, after: .241 after. Berry hit .383 vs. lefties and .276 vs. righties. Spiers vs. righties: .287, versus lefties: .143. As a unit they hit .305/.375/.466. Berry appears to have a maximum number of 300 at bats per season and anything above that doesn't work well for him. <SF>

BOBBY BONILLA, NYM
(1998: FLA-LA)

There are guys who wander as nomads through the league for years as gloves-for-hire to teams that lack infield defense. Bobby Bo is the opposite. He's a bat for hire. <BJH>

Bobby is slated to play right field for da Mets this year, with Robin Ventura in tow at third as the Mets beef up for a run at the Millennial Subway Series. And, of course, Bobby can beef with the best of 'em. <DM>

AARON BOONE, CIN

His career numbers, though age 25, are about as good as Bret's through age 30. That is, he's very likely a better hitter than Bret. And certainly a better fielder than Ike. <BJH>

KEN CAMINITI, HOU
(1998: SD)

His Defensive Winning Percentage is the worst of any of the starter-quality third basemen, which is contrary to his reputation and his previous performance. In addition, this season was an off year—his worst since the Offensive Surge began in 1994 - and he's turning 36. I don't mean to imply that he has no value or anything, but I'm not expecting a whole lot this time out. I expect him to be bad this season and then show a Last Hurrah year in 2000, and then fade away. LOUSY FANTASY BUY. <BJH>

VINNY CASTILLA, COL

I still think the only reason that he ranks even this well is that he is the exact type of hitter that Coors Field was built for—a righty fly ball hitter with some pop. Therefore, I think the ballpark effects of Coors are much greater for him than they compute out as for the whole team. His home/road splits the last few years just jump up and run around and scream and holler, "I Testify! I Testify!" <BJH>

Statheads like to suggest that if the Rox were smart they would let their players put up big Coors-assisted stats

and then dupe unsuspecting GM's out of their quality players. However, I think the other GM's are a bit brighter than we give them credit for. The Rockies have traded some of their positional players, and they haven't made out like bandits. Eric Young for Pedro Astacio and Ellis Burks for Darryl Hamilton are the trades that come to mind. I suspect that Major League general managers understand park effects better than we give them credit for. <SF>

JEFF CIRILLO, MIL

Except for his partial rookie season, Jeff has shown a classic even-age iambic growth pattern. That is, he has made strides forward when he was 26 and 28, and his age 25 and 27 seasons weren't as good. That usually implies that age 28 was the Career Year, and the age-29 campaign will show a drop-off. And, therefore, BEWARE JEFF CIRILLO IN FANTASY BALL, unless your league just doesn't have any idea that he's a real good player.

This is especially true since, of the true third basemen (Pokey Reese is a shortstop), Jeff is the clear Gold Glove winner, and that counts for nothing in most fantasy games. <BJH>

MATT FRANCO, NYM

Again, the Mets are skimming some cream off the top of a AAA ballplayer's career. <BJH>

GARY GAETTI, CHC
(1998: STL-CHC)

Finally, the Cubbies get lucky. They sign some old geezer who's having some struggle where he is (1/10 home/road homer split in St. Louis) and he just explodes for a month and drags them into the playoffs and thereby gets their popular star an MVP award. Of course, then they decide that he's found the Fountain of Youth and sign him to start when he's going to be 40 years old. Just says "Cubbies" all over, doesn't it? <BJH>

FREDDY GARCIA, PIT

Freddy's minor league numbers suggest that there's no more than five years of backup play at the major league level. <BJH>

CHARLIE HAYES, SF

If Charlie could play second or short, instead of just third and first, he'd have a lot more value as a utility man. As it is, he's become a nomad, moving year after year to whichever team feels a bit exposed at the hot corner. <BJH>

JOSE HERNANDEZ, CHC

The Cubbies have used Jose as a utility player for years now, and he wasn't all that good, even for that role. Take a look at his defense in the infield, for example. But right now, Jose has just had his age-27 and age-28 years and looks like he might be a starter. Don't be fooled. The Cubbies are just skimming a few hundred at-bats of cream off Jose's top. That's all. <BJH>

CHIPPER JONES, ATL

One of the themes running through this year's player comments is that young players tend to develop in an iambic pattern. That is, they'll have one year where they make a stride forward, and then they'll drop back the next year. When they reach 27 or 28 years of age, the gains stop overpowering the drops, and the players reach their peaks. Some players have a pattern where their jump years are ages 23, 25, and 27, while some lesser number have a 24, 26, and 28 pattern. The latter pattern - the even numbered one - produces a weaker Peak Year, and an age-27 year that is way

off prediction, if you simply predict the player to have his Career year at that magic age 27.

Now, bearing in mind that Chipper Jones hasn't really had any "off" years, take a look at his career numbers in some book like the STATS, Inc. Major League Handbook. See what's happening? His age 24 and 26 seasons, in 1996 and '98 are the jump years, while 1995 and '97 were comparatively weak.

Now, Chipper is turning 27, and so there's a tendency to take his 1998 campaign, add a little on to it, and make that the prediction for 1999. I ain't doin' that no more. Jones is on the even-numbered pattern. Age 27 should be an off year. It's the year 2000 that is the big one for prediction. And, even there, you have to make a decision. Some players, especially those whose birthdays are near to the major league "playing year" cutoff date of July 1, have career peaks that look like they were born in the "other" playing year. That means that some even-numbered pattern players have their Career Year at age 26 instead of age 28.

I do not yet know how to determine whether an even-numbered pattern player will peak at 26 or 28. Therefore, I can't really make a strong prediction for 2000. <BJH>

PAUL KONERKO, CHW
(1998: LA-CIN)

A fine, fine prospect who is only turning 23 years old. The good news for Paul occurred during the postseason, when he was traded to the Chisox for Mike Cameron, and then Robin Ventura left free agent. That sort of just hands the Sox hot corner to Paul, and he's no more than one year away. STRONG FANTASY TOUT (in the AL) for 1999, and even stronger in 2000 if he doesn't play so well that everyone knows about him. <BJH>

See Aramis Ramirez, Pit. Should be an excellent sidekick for Frank Thomas, though. <NL>

I was somewhat reassured of Konerko's ability when he hit well after being sent down to Indianapolis. He was moved to the White Sox, who gave up Mike Cameron for him. I like this trade for both teams. The Reds get a quality center fielder, who should be able to bounce back, and the White Sox get a great batting prospect. Konerko will probably be playing third base or perhaps some left field with Belle leaving. <SF>

BILL MUELLER, SF

One of my personal favorite players, He's form my home town, he has all the underrated skills, he got into the majors about two years after he should have, and he made the absolute best of his opportunity when it finally came. Because he has been in the league so few years, he doesn't really have a "growth pattern" to look at, and so I'm not completely sure whether last year, when he was Age 27, was his Career Year, or whether this one will be. His 1998 doesn't exactly LOOK like a Career Year, does it? <BJH>

NATIONAL LEAGUE THIRD BASE			
Player	OXW	DXW	TXW
Jones C	7.28	1.33	8.61
Rolen S	6.08	1.40	7.48
Cirillo J	4.63	1.77	6.40
Caminiti K	5.43	-0.09	5.34
Castilla V	4.21	1.11	5.32
Alfonzo E	3.83	1.01	4.84
Mueller B	3.66	1.11	4.77
Andrews S	3.37	1.06	4.43
Gaetti G	3.31	0.72	4.03
Berry S	2.94	0.51	3.45
Williams M	2.05	1.11	3.16
Hernandez J	1.80	1.05	2.85
Hayes C	1.90	0.47	2.37
Spiers B	1.83	0.47	2.30
Tatis F	1.60	0.42	2.02
Garcia F	1.03	0.33	1.36
Boone A	1.03	0.28	1.31
Bonilla B	1.15	-0.08	1.07
Orie K	0.21	0.55	0.76
Franco M	0.52	0.14	0.66
Beltre A	0.24	0.30	0.54
Reese P	0.22	0.29	0.51
Ramirez A	0.26	0.05	0.31
Konerko P	-0.10	0.28	0.18
Livingstone S	-0.45	0.01	-0.44
Strange D	-1.42	0.11	-1.31

KEVIN ORIE, FLA
(1998: CHC-FLA)

Had a good last half of the year for Florida and may finally be ready to support those minor league numbers he's been putting up. HOT FANTASY TOUT, unless your league already knows all about him. Most of the good ones do. <BJH>

ARAMIS RAMIREZ, PIT

See Gabe Alvarez, Det—oops, I guess I've led you full circle. It appears odd that so many highly regarded 3B *prospects (in this wild goose chase I led you, I listed Alvarez, Troy Glaus, Adrian Beltre, and Paul Konerko) came up the same year, and each of them, except for Eric Chavez, struggled once they got to the majors. Of course, we are not supposed to be disappointed yet, but it just seems odd. <NL>*

BROCK HANKE THINKS ARAMIS NEEDS A BIT MORE SEASONING IN THE MINORS, AND THE PIRATES AGREE WITH HIM, AS THEY HAVE SIGNED ED SPRAGUE TO A ONE-YEAR DEAL. THAT MEANS WE PROBABLY WON'T SEE RAMIREZ IN THE BIGS UNTIL AT LEAST LATE MAY. <COJ>

POKEY REESE, CIN

The best defensive third baseman in the league, which tells you that he's actually a shortstop. The Reds would tell you that, too, but they're not going to bench Barry Larkin for him. His bat doesn't really suggest starter status anywhere else. Some bright GM ought to trade them a Grade-C prospect for him and get some use out of that glove. <BJH>

SCOTT ROLEN, PHI

OK, he's as good as the Phillies touted him to be. Sometimes that happens; a bad team gets hold of a kid superstar. And sometimes it doesn't, and you get all this hype simply because the team has to talk about someone, and all their veterans are lousy, so they hype up a kid.

One other factor comes into play here. You can't just run a normal BROCK2 projection for Scott, precisely because he is so good already. If you try to run a normal projection for a player who has done all this by age 23, you get someone better than Mike Schmidt. That very seldom happens. Instead, what you've got to do is assume that Scott matured early and that the growth curve between now and age 27 in 2002 will be somewhat flatter than normal.

This especially happens to the guys who are just large human beings when they are young. That's a sign that the player matured early, physically. Scott Rolen is 6'4" tall and weighs 223 pounds, according to STATS. That's a big puppy. <BJH>

BILL SPIERS, HOU

A 33-year-old utility man who is finally fulfilling his younger promise after some very odd escapades with Milwaukee and New York. In my opinion, Bill is currently the very best established backup player in the National League.

Now, let's not get too worked up here. The best established backup player is usually some guy who would have clearly been a starter if he had been healthy when he was young. The question is which one of those guys do you think has gotten over the injury bug. I happen to think that Bill has done that. <BJH>

DOUG STRANGE, PIT

Why? <BJH>

FERNANDO TATIS, STL
(1998: TEX-STL)

I like Fernando a lot. He's only turning 24, he's beaten up minor league pitching everywhere he's gone, and this season looks pretty good when you realize that he was jumped from AA ball to the majors and then had to change teams when he couldn't immediately outplay Luis Alicea, who is awfully tough competition for a kid.

STRONG FANTASY TOUT. He doesn't even take many walks, so all his offense works for you. <BJH>

Tatis' plate discipline sky-rocketed upon his arrival with the Cardinals. I'm curious if the Cardinals worked with him on this or if as a young player he decided to emulate the players he saw on the field. He drew twice as many walks with the Cardinals in two-thirds the at bats than with the Rangers. Not surprisingly, his slugging jumped 140 points as he was laying off the bad pitches. The trade also came when he had reached 550 major league at bats, which as I've said before appears to be the point where young players take off. This could end up being a very good trade for the Cardinals. <SF>

MATT WILLIAMS, AZ

He's turning 33, and his defensive numbers still suggest he could probably play shortstop if he wanted to. The decision to convert him to a third baseman has cost him what? $20 million? More? The Hall of Fame? <BJH>

Remember when Matt Williams was considered the stiffest threat to Maris? The highlights could be sepia-toned as long ago as that seems. The D'Backs could have bided their time and waited a year before making a free agent splash. Then they could have tossed the twenty-six million per annum they threw at Benes, Blair, Bell and Williams at some real keepers like Bernie Williams and Mike Piazza. This would have allowed

them to play some of their strong middle infield prospects. Matt Williams' 1998 OPS: .766, Jeff Kent's OPS: .914. Brian Sabean is growing smarter by the minute. <SF>

SHORT-STOP

MANNY ALEXANDER, CHC

The Cubbie desperation plan if Jeff Blauser had one of his stinky years, which he did, but so did Manny. <BJH>

ALEX ARIAS, PHI

He's no glove wizard, but still. A player with those offensive numbers all those years should have gotten a lot more playing time at shortstop. And he just might get it, now that he's away from Edgar Renteria. HOT FANTASY GAMBLE. <BJH>

A good thought, to be sure, but those post-Lee Thomas Phillies, befuddled by Brogna, seem enraptured by Relaford for reasons known only to their local swami. Alex deserves a shot, but it may take gunfire in Philly to bring it about. <DM>

RICH AURILIA, SF

Turning 27, and on the odd-year iambic pattern. That is, Rich had an on year in 1997 and a drop-off in 1998, so he predicts to have a true Age-27 Career Year in 1999. HOT FANTASY TOUT, if you don't have Larkin. <BJH>

JAY BELL, AZ

For all the bitching, he still ranks high. I'll take him. Any shortstop who can get on base .353 and hit 20 homers and that's a BAD year, I'll take him. <BJH>

He's not worth a million more than Lee Majors in his prime. Jay can't run as fast as a speeding auto, can't leap ten feet into the air to snag line drives, can't punch more than twenty homers out of the park, and he doesn't make that cool mechanical sound when running around the bases. In fairness to Bell, his unadjusted OPS was the third-highest of his career, but I'm awfully glad my team isn't on the hook for twenty-eight million more to him. <SF>

JEFF BLAUSER, CHC
Unfortunately, the only consistency that Jeff Blauser has ever shown is with the glove. He's always lousy. <BJH>

TIM BOGAR, HOU
Very possibly the record-holder for most money per hit in the major leagues. In 1995, Tim Bogar hit .290, going 42 for 145. If he had hit .260, he would not be in the majors today, and probably would not have been in 1997. The difference between .290 and .260 in 145 AB is four (4) hits. Tim's entire major league salary between 1996 and whenever he leaves the league is entirely due to those four hits. <BJH>

ORLANDO CABRERA, MON
He played only half a year. If you doubled his TXW, he'd be about even with Neifi Perez. Is that real? Well, he has hit better than this in the minors, so I guess so. He's only turning 24, and what else do the Expos have to play? STRONG LOW-LEVEL FANTASY TOUT. <BJH>

JUAN CASTRO, LA
A Triple-A utility player who the Dodgers insist on keeping every year for no reason that I understand. <BJH>

CHRIS GOMEZ, SD
I have not been a Chris Gomez fan, but he made a huge across-the-board hitting leap at the magic Age 27, and he's always had the good glove. In a company where four and a half TXW can trail only Barry Larkin, having two and a half with the glove alone doesn't leave much to do with the bat. <BJH>

ALEX GONZALEZ, FLA
This is the "other" Alex Gonzalez, and just what we needed, another one. Alex is here in prime time because the Fish have tossed Edgar Renteria over the side, and have downgraded their accommodations from economy to the baggage section. Alex will also have to fight off the Return of Benji Gil, who was picked up in the Rule V Draft by the impossibly dapper Dave Dombrowksi. Be warned, Dave: I have pictures of you from your seventies "glam rock" phase. . . <DM>

OZZIE GUILLEN, ATL
The player who yielded the "most overrated" title to Rey Ordonez. <BJH>

RICKEY GUTIERREZ, HOU
I thought highly of Rickey when he was 26 in 1996. But that appears to have been his Career Year. This happens to no more than one in ten players, but it does happen. I wasn't aware then that that many players peaked that early. He's still valuable, but I clearly overtouted him two years ago. <BJH>

MARK GRUDZIELANEK, LA
(1998: MON-LA)
See Rickey Gutierrez. Mark also had a hot age-26 season, but has regressed. He is now one tenth the prospect he was in 1997. It doesn't help that he's a weak defensive shortstop. <BJH>

He's not a horrible player, he's just a poor-fielding shortstop who can't get on base. Those ten homers are nice, but no way in hell do they make up for his chunk-size flaws. As a Giant fan, I'm ecstatic that the Dodgers value a player like this. No improvement, when all is said and done, on Vizcaino. And Vizcaino's no bargain either. <TA>

BARRY LARKIN, CIN
Through the lens of the national League, we can see the real greatness of the American League's Big Three at shortstop: Alex Rodriguez, Derek Jeter, and Nomar Garciaparra. Just look at Barry Larkin. He's in the class of the Big Three. But he's 35 years old, and he still completely dominates this position in the NL. Yes, he's a great, great player, but that's ridiculous. <BJH>

MARK LORETTA, MIL
The Gold Glove winner, according to DW%. I like Mark a lot, and would certainly play him over Jose Valentin. The only warning I have to make is that he hasn't had a slump season yet, and I expect it to come this time, because he hit .300, and that gets the pitchers' attention even if you're a backup shortstop.

If you're a major league GM, steal this guy from the Brewers, will you? <BJH>

MIKE MORDECAI, SD
An incompetent backup shortstop. <BJH>

LUIS ORDAZ, STL
The AAA shortstop in the Cardinal organization, Luis got called up when injuries took every single big-league shortstop on the roster. He was only 22, and obviously not ready for prime time. Give him two years, and he's a serious prospect.. <BJH>

REY ORDONEZ, NYM
The least interesting Name ballplayer in the major leagues today. Ordonez has NEVER—not even once—been the Gold Glove shortstop in the National League. All he has is one flashy dive move. Oh, hell, I'm in a mean mood. Rey Ordonez is the most overrated ballplayer in the major leagues. Does that cover it? <BJH>

NATIONAL LEAGUE SHORTSTOP			
Player	OXW	DXW	TXW
Larkin B	5.90	1.68	7.58
Gomez C	2.53	2.61	5.14
Bell J	3.31	1.81	5.12
Aurilia R	1.51	2.01	3.52
Gutierrez R	0.66	2.77	3.43
Perez N	0.18	3.24	3.42
Weiss W	1.90	1.49	3.39
Loretta M	1.72	1.47	3.19
Grudzielanek M	1.53	1.41	2.94
Valentin J	1.73	1.12	2.85
Renteria E	1.54	1.19	2.73
Sanchez R	0.58	1.65	2.23
Sheets A	1.24	0.62	1.86
Cabrera O	1.21	0.63	1.84
Ordonez R	-1.16	2.63	1.47
Mordecai M	-0.02	1.47	1.45
Collier L	0.34	1.04	1.38
Guillen O	0.64	0.69	1.33
Vizcaino J	0.37	0.84	1.21
Arias A	0.57	0.27	0.84
Polanco P	0.13	0.68	0.81
Relaford D	-0.41	1.17	0.76
Blauser J	0.70	-0.13	0.57
Ordaz L	-0.63	0.67	0.04
Castro J	-1.04	1.02	-0.02
Alexander M	-0.38	0.35	-0.03
Polcovich K	-1.29	0.80	-0.49
Bogar T	-1.29	0.78	-0.51

He is a historically bad offensive player. Since 1955 only Hal Lanier has had a worse 3 year run of raw offensive stats and retained a full-time job. At least Lanier did this in a lower offensive climate. (Lanier more than any other factor kept the Giants from winning in a period when they had more top level players than anyone.)

Mark Belanger's name comes up a lot in discussions about Ordonez. However Earl Weaver handled Belanger very carefully. There's a clear correlation between Belanger's OPS and his plate appearances. When he didn't hit (which was often) he lost

SECONDARY FIELDING STATISTICS
1998 NATIONAL LEAGUE
SHORTSTOPS

Name	G	GS	INN	TC	PO	A	E	DP	FPCT	RF	ZR	DP/G	DP/E	OOA	NRF	NDPR	NDPE
Placido Polanco	28	21	196	126	38	82	6	18	.952	5.51	.944	0.83	3.0	20	120	131	68
Rey Sanchez	76	52	505	298	106	185	7	33	.977	5.19	1.005	0.59	4.7	33	113	93	107
Neifi Perez	162	156	1386	808	271	517	20	127	.975	5.12	.945	0.82	6.4	80	111	131	144
Luis Ordaz	54	46	394	235	68	154	13	34	.945	5.07	.977	0.78	2.6	21	110	123	59
Tony Batista	34	26	247	140	43	93	4	13	.971	4.96	.891	0.47	3.3	10	108	75	74
Mark Loretta	56	50	390	217	67	147	3	39	.986	4.93	.922	0.90	13.0	15	107	143	295
Tim Bogar	55	33	321	177	49	126	2	16	.989	4.91	.956	0.45	8.0	11	107	71	182
Ricky Gutierrez	141	129	1148	633	215	403	15	81	.976	4.85	.912	0.64	5.4	31	105	101	123
Rey Ordonez	151	147	1289	680	265	398	17	82	.975	4.63	.902	0.57	4.8	4	101	91	110
Mark Grudzielanek	156	156	1337	719	230	456	33	90	.954	4.62	.887	0.61	2.7	3	100	96	62
Jose Valentin	139	112	1061	564	173	370	21	69	.963	4.61	.888	0.59	3.3	1	100	93	75
Andy Sheets	39	26	262	139	41	93	5	18	.964	4.60	.959	0.62	3.6	0	100	98	82
Rich Aurilia	120	107	918	475	154	311	10	71	.979	4.56	.939	0.70	7.1	-4	99	110	161
Jay Bell	138	135	1176	612	197	397	18	77	.971	4.55	.926	0.59	4.3	-7	99	94	97
Lou Collier	107	98	862	453	148	287	18	56	.960	4.54	.902	0.58	3.1	-6	99	93	71
Edgar Renteria	130	129	1129	588	194	374	20	93	.966	4.53	.910	0.74	4.7	-9	98	118	106
Chris Gomez	143	136	1191	588	181	395	12	92	.980	4.35	.939	0.70	7.7	-33	95	110	174
Desi Relaford	137	135	1190	593	189	380	24	72	.960	4.30	.884	0.54	3.0	-39	94	86	68
Jose Vizcaino	66	65	556	262	89	169	4	32	.985	4.18	.940	0.52	8.0	-26	91	82	182
Ozzie Guillen	77	61	579	273	96	170	7	26	.974	4.14	.922	0.40	3.7	-30	90	64	84
Barry Larkin	145	142	1236	577	207	358	12	79	.979	4.11	.944	0.58	6.6	-67	89	91	150
Orlando Cabrera	52	48	411	190	64	123	3	20	.984	4.09	.950	0.44	6.7	-23	89	70	152
Walt Weiss	96	95	789	363	96	255	12	63	.967	4.00	.946	0.72	5.3	-52	87	114	119
Jeff Blauser	106	100	892	398	129	255	14	36	.965	3.87	.860	0.36	2.6	-72	84	58	58
Alex Gonzalez	25	23	209	89	29	58	2	17	.978	3.74	1.000	0.73	8.5	-20	81	116	193
Manny Alexander	50	26	267	112	37	71	4	15	.964	3.64	.895	0.51	3.8	-28	79	80	85

KEY: Inn-Innings; PO-Putouts; A-Assists; Er-Errors; DP-Double Plays; FPct-Fielding Pct.; RF-Range Factor; ZR-Zone Rating
DPR-Double Plays per RF(/9); DP/E-Double Plays per Error; OAA-Outs Above Average;
NRF-Normalize; Range Factor (N=100); NDPR-Normalized DP per RF; NDPE-Normalized; DP/Error

playing time. In addition Weaver pinch hit for him frequently in high leverage situations. Bobby Valentine let Ordonez hit in the 9th inning of some critical losses in the last week of the season. <RNJ>

What's the fascination with this guy? He's not among the top-three NL shortstops in any defensive category: 4th in range factor, chances per game, and double-plays last year, 6th in fielding percentage, and 12th in assists per game. Of all of the systems for measuring fielding, none of them indicate that Ordonez is anything special. And we already know the guy can't hit. No major league player with 450 PAs had a lower on-base percentage (.278) or slugging percentage (.299).**<SL>**

Every stathead's favorite whipping boy. I can't come up with the appropriate acid-etched witticism to properly dis St. Rey. Just let it be said that he's probably going to learn to hit, just to make statheads look like idiots. Then, during his Cooperstown acceptance speech, Rey will shake his finger. . .naah. Never happen. He'll always suck.<TA>

That is a fifteen yard penalty for piling on, gentlemen. Aw, what the hell, I can't resist: the best thing that could happen to the Mets' pennant chances this year would be for Rey Ordonez to pull a Judge Crater. <DM>

NEIFI PEREZ, COL

If he weren't only turning 24, I'd be saying nasty things here. He ranks in the middle of the pack of starters only because of his glove. His offensive weaknesses are magnified because the biggest one is that he won't take a walk, and therefore makes a lot of extra outs that hamstring the rest of the Colorado offense. And in Colorado, on-base long-sequence offense is the name of the game. I guess he's the class of the kids at this spot, but it's hard to get excited about a .313 OBP in Coors Field.

And those WEREN'T the nasty things. <BJH>

PLACIDO POLANCO, STL

A good-field no-hit second baseman who the Cardinals played at shortstop when they injured all the other options. If

Placido can just develop a little plate discipline and put on enough weight to show even a little pop, he can play major league shortstop. As a second baseman, he's a backup. So it's a good thing that his DW% at short is first-rate, and that he's only turning 23. <BJH>

DESI RELAFORD. PHI

In three seasons, his highest AAA batting average is .267. His Defensive Winning Percentage at shortstop was 48%. He's turning 25, but still, that's a AAA ballplayer and nothing more. <BJH>

EDGAR RENTERIA, STL
(1998: FLA)

What we have here is the iambic even-numbered pattern with a hot rookie year. That is, Edgar had better years with the bat at ages 20 and 22 than at age 21, and he'd like to get back to that age-20 campaign. I don't expect it this year, because he should regress a little from 1998 as the pitchers of the National League adjust. But look out in 2000. He'll be 24, which should give him a little extra pop. That's all he really needs to open up the defenses and jack the batting average up big time. I guess you know what I think of players who were competent rookies at age 20. <BJH>

Traded to the Cardinals in mid-December for two pitching prospects and a 20-year old shortstop, Pablo Ozuna, off a flashy year in A ball, Renteria may just be the glue in the middle that the Cards need, allowing them to try just about any of their other young infielders at 2B. What it also tells us that the Mayan fiscal policy in Florida is not over just because Hurricane Wayne has blown through. <DM>

REY SANCHEZ, KC
(1998: SF)
Another colorless mid-pack good glove shortstop. <BJH>

—I had the good fortune of visiting the Bay Area is summer and I was able to catch of couple of interleague games with the Mini Maestro. In one of the crazier games I've ever seen, we witnessed Rey Sanchez continue his march toward 10 career home runs, Kevin Mitchell leg out his first triple in four years, Ben Grieve steal his first base and Rafael Bournigal lead the A's with 3 RBI. <SF>

In case you haven't been to the BBBA web site, "Mini Maestro" is the colorful C.O. Jones' nickname for yours truly. Odd choice, considering that I tower over him by at least half an inch. I think Sanchez did what the Giants had hoped he would—provide Rich Aurilia with a foil and a competitor. He's now earned himself a starting job in Kansas City, where they'll doubtless need to play him every day. <DM>

ANDY SHEETS, SD
A competent backup shortstop. <BJH>

JOSE VALENTIN, MIL
Jeez. ANOTHER shortstop who peaked at age 26, with a bat season that wasn't good enough to be someone's peak. Like Rickey Gutierrez, his bat's on the verge of collapse. Like Mark Grudzielanek, he can't play shortstop well enough to really compensate. <BJH>

JOSE VIZCAINO, LA
Injured, and then allowed to heal very slowly while the Dodgers made a phantom run at the wild card slot with Mark Grudzielanek in his place. LA is suddenly awash in backup infielders, and it's up to Davey Johnson to read the tea leaves and decide which one of these guys he's going to play. If I know Davey, it will be the most complex platoon possible. <DM>

WALT WEISS, ATL
Your basic Walt Weiss season. The odd illusion that Walt keeps getting better and better with the bat as he passes through his 30s is entirely the result of Colorado and the Offensive Surge. Bobby Cox may be able to coax another year or two of this out of him, but no more. <BJH>

LEFT FIELD

MOISES ALOU, HOU
Like Bonds, Alou keeps finishing way up there in the rankings but gets no attention for it. I find this odd. I understand the Bonds problem. He has troubles with the press, and the press is who votes on the MVP awards and who builds reputations. But Moises Alou? Whatever has he done to those guys, except play consistent great baseball? <BJH>

Is it a coincidence that his two highest walk rates correspond with the years he got away from Dad? I don't think so. Much has been made here of Felipe Alou's free-swinging preferences and it looks now like he may have been stifling a fairly disciplined hitter. Alou has now drawn 70 and 84 walks after never cracking the 50-walk barrier with the Expos. In the minors, Moises was always walked more than once every ten at bats, but he never cracked that level in the majors until last year. What does this mean? It means don't hold your breath waiting for Vlad Guerrero, Brad Fullmer and Rondell White to draw 60 walks because you will just pass out. <SF>

DANNY BAUTISTA, ATL
A Triple-A outfielder with enough major league experience that a team will turn to him when they need an injury backup over a kid with much more potential. <BJH>

YAMIL BENITEZ, AZ
A glove caddy in the outfield. Such players don't tend to last, because you need a bat there. Yamil didn't even play any center. <BJH>

DANTE BICHETTE, COL
Yes, Rockie fans, this ranking is completely fair. Ballpark adjustments are really real. <BJH>

For those of you not scoring at home, here are Dante's road stats over the last three years .260/.290/.388, and at home: .370/.409/.633. The Coors gap appears to be widening here. The Rocks (as in head filled with) signed Dante to a three-year deal for way too much money. Now I'm not so sure that Dante is a strangely evolved batter capable of exploiting Coors better than most, and hence I'm not so sure that keeping him in a Rox uni is such a bad idea. However, if I'm Bob Gebhard, I ask my little Aunt Edna in Topeka to mail anonymous postcards to every other GM with the above stats on them. I then fax the above stats and a 3-year, $5 million (total, not per year) deal to Fonzie's agent rather than the $20 million they gave him. <SF>

BARRY BONDS, SF
Once again, Barry Bonds got no fanfare, no MVP comment, nothing except a mention that he might be aging - and is right at the top of all outfielders in Total XW. <BJH>

DAVID DELLUCCI, AZ
Turning 25, David has excellent minor league numbers, but only 17 games of AAA experience. Therefore, I expect him to move up in quality and quickly. He has a job with Arizona, and he has the potential and now he has the seasoning. He has league-leading triples speed and minor league home run power. All that adds up to ONE VERY HOT FANTASY TOUT FOR 1999. With good luck, David could actually finish fourth at this position next year. <BJH>

With Steve Finley's annuity in center and Gilkey's contract in left, Dave may have some problems getting playing time early in the year down in Arizona. Also, Dave lost a LOT of strike-zone judgment in the transition from AA to the majors. He's going to need to get that back to be a really good top of the lineup guy. His top end, I think, is as an ultimate #2 hitter with double figures in all XBH categories, 70-80 walks, and some steals. There are very few guys like that around these days, so here's hoping he gets it together. <DM>

J. D. DREW, STL
A tremendous cup of coffee with a truly weird track record. The Cards didn't know what level to start him out at, and guessed low. He was at least a AAA player, rather than a AA. This coming year, he'll be a major leaguer with a full time job opening spring training. I can't actually

tout him for you fantasy guys, because everyone knows about him already. How much did Ben Grieve go for in your league last spring?.<BJH>

CLIFF FLOYD, FLA

It's real rare for a player's on-base percentage to actually drop when his batting average jumps 48 points. But that's what happened to Cliff here. He doubled his 1997 walks total, but multiplied his at-bats by more than four (4). That is exceptionally odd, and I don't really know what to make of it.

What seems to be the case is that Cliff has had a big breakout year at the age of 25. That would put him on the 25-27 track for on years, so I expect a lot out of 2000 after a small Counteradjustment Slump in 1999. Since I don't know what caused the walks collapse, I don't know whether the plate discipline will come back. If it does, he'll move into the class of very good left fielders. If not, he'll remain here, with a mid-pack starter ranking but a low TXW. I'll know a lot more at the end of next season.<BJH>

The next Willie McCovey. At least that's what he was called on the way up. Although I doubt he'll live up to that comparison, I think he'll end up being a pretty good player. Next season he'll be two years removed from a career threatening wrist injury. That makes next season a pivotal one for his career. Good fantasy pick. <JF>

RON GANT, PHI
(1998: STL)

STATS Inc.'s John Dewan devised, several years ago, an approach to evaluating defense called "zone rankings". These involved inventing "zones" of field territory that the defenders are responsible for, and then counting up the percentage of the balls hit into the zone that the fielder turns into outs.

This all sounds good, and like an improvement over raw range factors. However, it doesn't test well when you actually run it for a league's worth of players. In 1997, for example, Ron Gant here was adjudged to have the best zone ranking of any left fielder. That is, STATS' official position was that Ron Gant had the best range at the position.

For those of us who watched Ron Gant play all year in St. Louis with a hurt ankle, the information was definitive proof that zone rankings don't work. Some refinement of them may work, and the

approach still seems plausible, but any method that gives the range nod to a man who played the whole year with obviously-diminished speed is obviously wrong.

Ron Gant's 38% Defensive Winning Percentage this year is much closer to the mark.<BJH>

For what it's worth, even Bill James has gone on record saying that he doesn't think zone ratings are any good. And one his closest friends is John Dewan. We have the germ of a revised system in the pipeline here at BBBA, and you can see a preview of it in Charlie Saeger's Context-Adjusted Defense rankings (CAD), which he's prototyped for the 1941 season in his essay "Ready for the Defense." Even with that, we still need a whole new method for defense, and the problem is that the work to get it is very labor intensive, even in the ever-accelerating thrust of the computer age. <DM>

BERNARD GILKEY, AZ
(1998: NYM-AZ)

Two poor seasons in a row is disturbing. He's had a couple before, but they've always been isolated, and he's come back strong. The Mets seemed to lose confidence in him very early last year, and I don't know why. This year is make it or break it for Bernard to be actually playing past age 35.<BJH>

GLENALLEN HILL, CHC
(1998: SEA-CHC)

A fine acquisition for the Cubbies. Glenallen hit very well his one partial season in Wrigley Field in 1993, and then had his best year to date in 1994. He's scary-looking in the field, but his rankings don't justify all of the bleating you hear about his defense. I have to say that, as long as he remains in Wrigley, I don't see why he can't continue to play until he's pushing 40.<BJH>

TODD HOLLANDSWORTH, LA

Only turning 26, but still has to match his rookie season. This year was up from 1997, but still below his career marks in batting average, SLG, and OBP. He needs to avoid the Counteradjustment Slump, and start making his run for glory now..<BJH>

No slot is currently available in the Dodger outfield for their most recent Rookie of the Year (and last for quite some time, thanks to Tommy Lasorda). LA had great success with Todd after Bill Russell took my adivce (via Ross Porter) to bat him leadoff in 1996; damned if he didn't hit .400 in the #1 slot in

1998. (Three games, but voodoo is more fun than science.) <DM>

TODD HUNDLEY, LA
(1998: NYM)

Not to be taken seriously as a left fielder. Todd is, with the departure of Charles Johnson, possibly the best defensive catcher among the established starters. He hits switch. Unless his arm is gone to injury, he should rank within the top three at the position of catcher, along with Jason Kendall and Mike Piazza.<BJH>

GEOFF JENKINS, MIL

Turning 24. His minor league numbers are good but not overpowering. He ought to be able to make a career as a backup. I have doubts about whether he can start for a decent team.<BJH>

RYAN KLESKO, ATL

The temptation here is to suggest that Ryan would rank higher if he got full playing time. But no, he's a real lefty platoon player, and this is about as much playing time as he should have. The disturbing item is that this is a power hitter; that's the strength of his game. And he's lost ground in slugging percentage every year he's played a hundred games. This, the putative Age-27 Career year, was actually below his career SLG, and about on the career mark in batting average and OBP.

I refuse to make predictions about players whose career movement defies all patterns.<BJH>

He hasn't put up that 40-homer season that many had expected by now. A variety of ailments slowed him down for his age 27 year including appendicitis. It appears that the new park has hurt him as well; his isolated power has fallen off markedly at home. <SF>

JOHN MABRY, STL

The experiment at third base having failed, Mabry remains the Cardinals' backup left and right fielder. That is, he's the injury backup for Eric Davis and the rookie failure backup for J. D. Drew. That gives him some value, but it's a gamble as to how much he'll play. He could probably start in right field for several teams.<BJH>

AL MARTIN, PIT

A lost year. Write it off. Pretend it never happened. His actual ability level will probably rank him about fourth at this position next season.<BJH>

Maybe so, but it doesn't seem likely to happen in Pittsburgh, where the Bucs have acquired Brian Giles to play left and Brant Brown to play center. Al has never matched his rookie season SLG, and he just seems to be one of those players who didn't progress. There's some chance he might get back to where he was, but where that was will be in some other place. <DM>

WILLIE MCGEE, STL

He's down to only one skill, and that's hitting for average, and he hit .253 last year. He'll play this year as a desperation backup while the Cardinals try to develop another prospect.<BJH>

MATT MIESKE, CHC

Played VERY well for the Cubs this year. Their outfield and first base slots are taken, so I don't expect him to start. But I do expect him to be one of the top bench outfielders of 1999.<BJH>

MARC NEWFIELD, MIL

Another one of these guys that sabermetrics doesn't deal with well. Marc just cremates minor league pitching, at all levels, but he can't seem to get going in the majors. He's still only turning 26, and could put it all together, but he's not a hundredth of the prospect he was four years ago, when I touted him so highly in Seattle. His one shining light is that 1996 season in Milwaukee. That showed his potential, but he's either been hurt or just unable to match it.<BJH>

TONY PHILLIPS, OAK
(1998: TOR-NYM)

Like Rickey Henderson, Tony has not lost all value, although he's not the player Rickey is. Also like Rickey, he's become a nomad; a leadoff man for hire to desperate teams. He hasn't had a public clubhouse incident since the drug thing, which might be a matter of understanding that, at this level of play, one more of those and he's retired, whether he wants to be or not.<BJH>

SIGNED BY THE A'S TO BAT LEADOFF AND CROWD OUT ONE OR BOTH OF OAKLAND'S YOUNG OBP-ORIENTED OUTFIELDERS (JASON MCDONALD AND RYAN CHRISTENSON), TONY MIGHT BE ABOUT READY TO HIT A BIG FAT .180 OVER THREE MONTHS AND STIR THINGS UP IN AMIABLE ART HOWE'S COMATOSE CLUBHOUSE. HE DIDN'T HIT MUCH BETTER THAN THAT IN HIS FINAL MONTH WITH THE METS, AND HIS OBP WENT DOWN EVERY MONTH AFTER HE GOT BACK TO THE MAJORS IN JULY. HE MAY BE OUT OF THE MAJORS BY JULY 1999. <COJ>

HENRY RODRIGUEZ, CHC

This ranking was a complete surprise. Or, rather, the small number of TXW was not a surprise, but the fact that only three outfielders beat it certainly was. I thought Henry was, to be honest, a lousy acquisition for the Cubbies. He was, essentially, a normal Sammy Sosa season. Lots of strikeouts, a low batting average, few walks, some homers, and a lot of Outs Consumed. That's exactly what he did; it's just that everyone else was no better.<BJH>

I just love these one-tool guys the Cubs seem to fall in love with. Henry carries on the proud tradition of Keith Moreland, Dave Kingman, and Hank Sauer. All I've got to say is, playing between Sosa and Oh Henry, Lance Johnson is going to be pretty sick of the phrase "it's all yours, One Dog!" by August. <TA>

AUGUST?? TRY EARLY JUNE, BIG BOY. <COJ>

You guys better look at the Secondary Fielding data below; you're in for quite a shock. Hank, as Ken Adams likes to call him, actually played well in left for the Cubs last year. He also slugged .563 after the All-Star Break, something that this notoriously first-half hitter had never done before. He also walked a lot more than he had in the past—the case of another guy getting away from Felipe Alou? Stay tuned. <DM>

F. P. SANTANGELO, SF
(1998: MON)

Started old, and is getting bad fast. The Giants seem to be aiming him at a utility role, where he will be fine for a couple of years, I imagine.<BJH>

CHRIS STYNES, CIN

Turning 26, and had a powerful down year. That implies two things. First, he's on the 24-26 iambic track for on years and off years. Second, he's due to come back big next season. His competition for playing time is not as strong as it seems. Yes, Dmitri Young will start for at least one more year in left field at Cincinnati. But Chris here showed good defense at second base, third, shortstop, left field, and right field. I'll bet he can get into his share of games if he hits like I think he will.

HOT FANTASY TOUT, especially if he moves around a lot and your league lets him qualify at second and short and third.<BJH>

GREG VAUGHN, SD

The numbers indicate that Greg Vaughn probably was a better player than Sammy Sosa this year, homers or no homers. But, then, Sammy didn't get the MVP for being the best player. The only Vaughn supporters were those guys who

NATIONAL LEAGUE LEFT FIELD		
PLAYER OXW	DXW	TXW
Vaughn G 8.16	0.68	8.84
Bonds B 8.27	0.48	8.75
Alou M 7.30	0.43	7.73
Floyd C 4.18	0.31	4.49
Rodriguez H 3.20	0.79	3.99
Young D 3.78	0.01	3.79
Bichette D 3.11	0.49	3.60
Klesko R 3.06	0.41	3.47
Gant R 2.87	0.07	2.94
Stynes C 1.14	0.80	1.94
Hill G 1.63	0.22	1.85
Dellucci D 1.05	0.58	1.63
Luke M 0.95	0.54	1.49
Santangelo F 0.82	0.52	1.34
Gilkey B 0.39	0.78	1.17
Phillips T 0.96	0.11	1.07
Martin A 0.52	0.43	0.95
Drew J 0.84	0.08	0.92
Mabry J 0.69	0.18	0.87
Cedeno R 0.61	0.14	0.75
Mieske M 0.65	0.02	0.67
Hollandsworth T 0.54	0.06	0.60
May D 0.19	0.13	0.32
Jenkins G 0.11	0.18	0.29
McGee W -0.03	0.19	0.16
Benitez Y -0.14	0.27	0.13
Newfield M -0.03	0.08	0.05
Bautista D 0.06	-0.09	-0.03
Hundley T -0.24	0.10	-0.14
Eisenreich J -0.33	0.09	-0.24

don't understand any stat except RBI. You know, the ones who keep electing Juan Gonzalez.<BJH>

Jay Walker would be the first to look at the TXW rankings in left field and tell you that a one-year park factor can do some screwy things, like lift Greg Vaughn over Barry Bonds.

SECONDARY FIELDING STATISTICS
1998 NATIONAL LEAGUE
LEFT FIELD

Name	G	GS	INN	TC	PO	A	E	DP	FPCT	RF	ZR
YAMIL BENITEZ	49	35	296	89	83	4	2	1	.978	2.64	.872
CHRIS STYNES	64	48	425	108	105	3	0	1	1.000	2.29	.871
HENRY RODRIGUEZ	114	112	876	223	215	7	1	1	.996	2.28	.807
DAVID DELLUCCI	95	80	714	169	164	3	2	3	.988	2.10	.879
MATT LUKE	50	41	347	81	76	4	1	0	.988	2.07	.817
F.P. SANTANGELO	72	53	471	111	103	5	3	0	.973	2.07	.787
DANTE BICHETTE	134	131	1104	260	237	14	9	6	.965	2.05	.761
BARRY BONDS	155	154	1337	308	301	2	5	5	.984	2.04	.804
BERNARD GILKEY	103	88	796	177	163	12	2	1	.989	1.98	.786
GLENALLEN HILL	99	95	723	162	153	4	5	1	.969	1.95	.800
AL MARTIN	114	110	922	201	192	6	3	1	.985	1.93	.796
GREG VAUGHN	151	150	1307	277	270	5	2	0	.993	1.89	.845
TONY PHILLIPS	54	44	397	86	81	2	3	0	.965	1.88	.788
CLIFF FLOYD	146	145	1267	268	251	10	7	1	.974	1.85	.739
MARC NEWFIELD	55	49	369	79	73	3	3	0	.962	1.85	.837
TODD HUNDLEY	34	34	215	49	42	2	5	0	.898	1.84	.672
GEOFF JENKINS	81	67	593	125	115	6	4	2	.968	1.84	.832
RON GANT	104	101	819	171	162	4	5	0	.971	1.82	.800
DMITRI YOUNG	91	85	725	154	142	3	9	0	.942	1.80	.778
TODD HOLLANDSWORTH	48	35	327	69	64	1	4	0	.942	1.79	.813
GREGG JEFFERIES	136	134	1055	201	193	7	1	0	.995	1.71	.756
MOISES ALOU	152	148	1330	242	227	11	4	2	.983	1.61	.741
RYAN KLESKO	120	119	917	156	146	9	1	1	.994	1.52	.777
DANNY BAUTISTA	53	27	292	47	45	0	2	0	.957	1.39	.778

KEY: Inn-Innings; PO-Putouts; A-Assists; Er-Errors; DP-Double Plays; FPct-Fielding Pct.; RF-Range Factor; ZR-Zone Rating

---

Odd one-year park effects have their pitfalls in that they can elevate a team's hitters beyond a reasonable context threshold. That happened in 1996 with Bernard Gilkey beating out Bonds. You all know what happened to Gilkey, right? Don't be surprised if something similar happens to Greg over the next couple of years. <DM>

DMITRI YOUNG, CIN

A big leap forward, but still one that exposes the man's weaknesses. He doesn't really have outfield power, and he runs poorly because - there's no way to gloss this over - he's fat. His DW% indicates strongly that his future, if any, is at first base. The Reds have better prospects there. <BJH>

He hasn't convinced me that he can play a passable left field, but I'm willing to withhold judgment for another season. His offensive numbers were good, not great (.310/.364/.481). He doesn't have home run power, but he did hit 48 doubles. As long as his bat outweighs his defensive liabilities, he's a cornerstone of the Reds offense.**<SL>**

CENTER FIELD

JERMAINE ALLENSWORTH, NYM
(1998: PIT-KC-NYM)

Turning 27. It would take so little to elevate him out of the crown he's currently in and make him a hot fantasy tout. Unfortunately, he had a jump year this time, and so is on the even-numbered iambic pattern. <BJH>

ADRIAN BROWN, PIT

Turning 25, but has had several outstanding years in the minor leagues. I think he can play and I think he'll hit it pretty big in 2000. This year, though, well, he gained too much ground in 1998 for me to tout him for 1999. <BJH>

BRANT BROWN, PIT
(1998: CHC)

Skim that cream, Cubbies. Skim that cream off the peak years of this AAA ballplayer. <BJH>

Looks like the Cubbies have skimmed a #3-4 rotation pitcher for Brant Brown in the

person of Jon Lieber. That's probably a good move for the Cubs, who can use another pitcher due to free-agent attrition and out-of-whack winning percentage/ERA combinations from several of their holdovers.

Addressing Brock's point—and his terminology ("skimming cream")—we can take it that he's referring to the fact that Brown has thus far exceeded his minor league projections, and that he's quite possibly due for a sudden, virtually irrevocable collapse. That is clearly a plausible hypothesis, but as noted in the Shawn Green comment, I think we need to make a better effort to quantify these matters.

A great deal of talk about performance projections goes on in sabermetric/stathead/fantarot circles (and they are somewhat concentric at that), but there is precious little large-scale analysis of the results, and what they might tell us. What we really need in the field is a distribution of how many players exceed, meet, or fail to meet the projections made for them. That would give us a much better sense of how likely it is that Brant Brown will either sustain his performance level or fall off toward his minor league performance level. While I'd be inclined to say that he will do the latter, that is based only on "feel" and an accession to the maxim of "regression to the mean." I'd like to see the numbers, as they will help evaluate the efficacy of what are some very compelling (but unquantified) theories being espoused herein. <DM>

ELLIS BURKS, SF
(1998: COL-SF)

Hit better in San Francisco than in Colorado this year. He's old, but he once had the potential to make a Hall of Fame run. He can easily hold this level of play. If he does, I think he'll move up in the rankings. <BJH>

JOHN CANGELOSI, FA
(1998: FLA)

One of the wasted talents of the last decade. John is an on-base machine, but teams just couldn't deal with his complete lack of power. What a shame. But, that being said, he's turning 36, and he played bad defense in center field this year, and that should be about all for John. <BJH>

ROGER CEDENO, NYM
(1998: LA)

Cedeno finally received something of an extended shot with the Dodgers after I'd been calling for such a move for about two years. He, of course, proceeded to fail badly. I'm not sure if he can ever become a good player in a Dodger uniform. Players who have run-ins with management at a young age are probably better off in another uniform. I still think he can become an above-average starter in CF, but it's going to have to be somewhere else. <SF>

SQUANDERED BY THE DODGERS, ROGER HAS BEEN PASSED OFF TO THE METS, WHERE HE FACES A SIMILAR SITUATION: A TEAM DESPERATE TO WIN, AND WHO HAS PLACED THREE OVER-30 VETERANS IN FRONT OF HIM. HE'S GOING TO NEED AN INJURY TO ONE OF THE THREE IN ORDER TO GET ANY SIGNIFICANT PLAYING TIME IN 1999. <COJ>

TODD DUNWOODY, FLA

Some sabermetricians really like this guy. I'm not sure why. He's turning 24, which is young but not Andruw Jones or anything, and this was first time he posted really good numbers in AAA ball. I think he can probably start for some seasons, but I don't see the All-Star team, much less the Hall of Fame. <BJH>

An interesting example of how the stathead community can lose its objectivity. There was nothing in his minor league record that said that Dunwoody could play and yet there were many normally thoughtful people claiming that he could replace Moises Alou with no substantial loss to the Marlins. (Most people expected Kotsay to be the CF with Dunwoody in LF)

Now I'm not going to claim I expected Alou to play as well as he did in Houston. I thought he was over his head in 1997. But Dunwoody didn't seem likely to post a .300 OBP.

He's got some chance. He looks to be pretty special in CF. He's got miles to go before he's an acceptable offensive player, however. <RNJ>

He was outhit by a rather wide margin by Moises Alou and Devon White whom he replaced in the Fish outfield. Dunwoody hit leadoff for most of the year and was a horrendously poor choice for the position. His strikeout rates were exceptionally high throughout the minors, though his walk rates were respectable. Not surprisingly, major league pitchers exploited his inability to make contact. He struck out 103 times and walked only 16 times as the leadoff batter sporting a .291 OBP. He can improve, but he clearly would be better suited to a position lower in the order. <SF>

CARL EVERETT, HOU

Carl had as much to do with the Astros' fine season as anyone. Houston has been hurting for center fielders ever since they traded away Kenny Lofton. Carl solved that problem, and it helped the team's defense and also the length of its offensive sequence. I do want to put out the Age-27 Career year warning on him;

he may never match this season again. But, for one year, he really put the finishing touches on his team. <BJH>

STEVE FINLEY, AZ
(1998: SD)

Had the two fine years in San Diego and then just fell apart. I'm afraid that this is the level of play I think he actually has now, turning age 34. But, then, I've underestimated Steve before. Still, this time I think I've got him nailed. <BJH>

Having gotten an impossibly good season out of Devon White, the Snakes decided to roll the dice and shake that moneymaker again, and they came up with Steverino here. I don' think he's got enough left to even give Arizona one big season to take the sting out of this one. <DM>

DOUG GLANVILLE, PHI

Turning 27. On the iambic pattern for a Career Year. I don't know if he's really good enough to help you in a fantasy league, but if all the better ones are tied up... <BJH>

CURTIS GOODWIN, COL

How did this guy ever get established as a major league backup center fielder? He doesn't hit and doesn't play center field well. He must be VERY easy to manage. <BJH>

MARQUIS GRISSOM, MIL

What happened here is very blunt. First, Marquis lost his speed early. Then his batting average, never a real strength, dropped off. Marquis responded by swinging at everything, refusing to take any walks, which dropped his OBP down to unacceptable levels. He can still play center, which will get him a prime bench role, but his days as a starter are probably over. The Brewers don't have much else, and that might keep Marquis out there for another year, but I'm afraid I don't expect any more out of that one than this one. <BJH>

DARRYL HAMILTON, COL
(1998: SF-COL)

Suddenly an aging player, Darryl has not lost the ability to play center field, and retains the ability to get on base. He, like every other hitter, loves Colorado, and he's the kind of guy who helps the team extra because he doesn't consume outs. <BJH>

RICHARD HIDALGO, HOU

First, the good stuff. He's only turning 23, he's had 273 at-bats in the major

---

SECONDARY FIELDING STATISTICS
1998 NATIONAL LEAGUE
CENTER FIELD

Name	G	GS	INN	TC	PO	A	E	DP	FPCT	RF	ZR
Rondell White	82	81	699	239	234	4	1	2	.996	3.06	.812
Terry Jones	60	57	493	168	162	4	2	3	.988	3.03	.845
Todd Dunwoody	111	96	875	284	272	9	3	4	.989	2.89	.798
Andruw Jones	159	156	1373	435	413	20	2	6	.995	2.84	.861
Devon White	144	141	1219	379	371	3	5	0	.987	2.76	.829
Carl Everett	121	111	1028	306	290	12	4	3	.987	2.64	.817
Richard Hidalgo	57	47	410	120	116	3	1	1	.992	2.61	.816
Ray Lankford	145	137	1216	349	337	7	5	2	.986	2.55	.783
Brant Brown	69	62	537	154	149	1	4	0	.974	2.51	.816
Jermaine Allensworth	94	82	747	212	204	4	4	2	.981	2.51	.807
Marquis Grissom	137	133	1169	328	317	8	3	3	.991	2.50	.761
Steve Finley	157	146	1335	369	350	12	7	5	.981	2.44	.831
Doug Glanville	158	155	1398	376	360	14	2	1	.995	2.41	.797
Reggie Sanders	88	79	658	177	169	3	5	0	.972	2.35	.818
Lance Johnson	78	68	636	163	154	5	4	2	.975	2.25	.806
Ellis Burks	114	109	892	224	213	8	3	0	.987	2.23	.723
Darryl Hamilton	144	136	1221	303	297	5	1	1	.997	2.23	.771
Brian McRae	154	144	1306	313	301	8	4	3	.987	2.13	.823
Raul Mondesi	94	94	803	187	178	5	4	1	.979	2.05	.771

KEY: Inn-Innings; **PO-**Putouts; **A-**Assists; **Er-**Errors; **DP-**Double Plays; **FPct-**Fielding Pct.; **RF-**Range Factor; **ZR-**Zone Rating leagues, and his career batting average there is .304. He gets on base; he has some pop.

Now the bad news. His career major league numbers would be the very best season he has ever had anywhere at any level. Something is amiss. Gamble if you want, but I trust seven years of minor league play more than two in the bigs. <BJH>

NATIONAL LEAGUE CENTER FIELD			
PLAYER	OXW	DXW	TXW
Lankford R	6.61	0.65	7.26
Jones A	4.02	2.77	6.79
McRae B	4.89	0.59	5.48
White R	4.06	1.15	5.21
Hamilton D	3.94	0.85	4.79
White D	3.64	0.90	4.54
Mondesi R	4.10	0.35	4.45
Everett C	2.89	1.25	4.14
Finley S	2.95	1.04	3.99
Burks E	3.34	0.48	3.82
Glanville D	1.71	1.73	3.44
Sanders R	2.40	0.46	2.86
Brown B	2.56	0.06	2.62
Ward T	1.37	0.70	2.07
Allensworth J	1.62	0.33	1.95
Hidalgo R	1.48	0.45	1.93
Dunwoody T	0.88	1.01	1.89
Frank M	-0.23	1.73	1.50
Grissom M	0.54	0.91	1.45
Johnson L	0.72	0.16	0.88
Cangelosi J	0.55	0.02	0.57
Brown A	0.24	0.26	0.50
Jones T	-0.15	0.61	0.46
Martinez M	0.38	0.08	0.46
Watkins P	0.24	0.18	0.42
Goodwin C	-0.29	0.21	-0.08

TRENIDAD HUBBARD, LA

He'd look like a prospect if he were turning 23 instead of 33. <BJH>

LANCE JOHNSON, CHC

One more season like this, and he's out of a job. He didn't hit, and he didn't play well in center field either. <BJH>

ANDRUW JONES, ATL

An astonishing defensive season; probably the best I've ever run numbers for in the outfield. When the person doing that is only turning 22, and hit 31 homers to go with the defense, you have to predict him to be at the top of the heap in a year or two.

Those of you who have been reading my comments on iambic pattern can probably see what's coming. Andruw made a huge leap forward this year, and so should suffer from some Counteradjustment Slumping next year, as the pitchers of the league figure him out. That puts him on the 21-23-25-27 pattern of growth, which leads to two comments.

First, it's in 2000, not 1999, that I expect Andruw to overtake Ray Lankford for the #1 slot at this spot. Second, with three growth years left to go, and no need to move to a lesser defensive position, Andruw Jones has as much chance as anyone to be the next huge Hall of Famer in baseball. <BJH>

Andruw has hit more home runs (54) by age 21 than anyone except Mel Ott (86) and Tony Conigliaro (84). He is also on the top twenty on the stolen base list, and is a Gold Glove centerfielder. He and Chipper should go a long way toward ensuring present and future Braves dominance. <SF>

A cautionary note should be sounded here, in that almost 40% of Andruw's value is based on defense, and in the historical scheme of 21-year old seasons, his offensive achievement was good, not great. On Tom Hull's percentile ranking system (based on raw RC), Andruw's year grades out at a 75. And that's not a 75 due to missing any playing time: he played in 159 games. Tom's method identifies eighteen players who had a percentile ranking of 90 or higher at the age of 21. Let's look at the list:

TOP 21-YEAR PERCENTILES

Name	Pct
Ty Cobb	98
Joe Jackson	98
Ted Williams	97
Al Kaline	97
Cesar Cedeno	97
Ken Griffey	96
Pete Browning	96
Tris Speaker	95
Rickey Henderson	95
Dave Eggler	95
Frank Robinson	94
Hank Aaron	92
Joe DiMaggio	92
Sherry Magee	92
Vada Pinson	92
Del Ennis	92
Sam Crawford	91
Tim Raines	90

The only bogey on this list is Dave Eggler, a washout from the old National Association in 1872. Almost all the rest of these guys are either already in the Hall of Fame, will be, or just missed.

The group from 80-89 also has some Hall of Famers, but its talent level is clearly lower. Here's the list:

Mel Ott, Joe Kelley, Mike Tiernan, Lloyd Waner, Stan Musial, Joe Medwick, Ross Youngs, Tony Conigliaro
Tom McCreery, Jose Canseco, Greg Luzinski, Buddy Lewis, Les Mann

We took a look at the players with the same 21-year old percentile ranking as Andruw in Tom's article "Percentiles: Past, Present and Future" (in Seciton Three). Mickey Mantle and Harry Heilmann had a 76 score at 21, but Mantle had already scored 98 at age 20 and Heilmann took an extra year to get in gear, having his first breakout season at age 24.

Andruw is clearly going to be an excellent player, but his top end as a hitter is still open to question. If his strike zone judgment returns this season, that would be a solid indication that he could indeed make the leap that many expect. Let's not jump the gun, guys. <DM>

TERRY JONES, MON

A good AAA player, not good enough to justify prime time, who got some work because of team need, nothing more. There isn't even any cream here to skim. Nice glovework. <BJH>

RAY LANKFORD, STL

Remains the best center fielder in the league, although Andruw Jones is certainly closing in. For fantasy play, note that Ray still outhits Andruw by quite a lot. Andruw's huge glove season is meaningless to most fantasy leagues. Actually, Ray usually is at or near the top of the defensive rankings here, due to his outstanding range. This year, though, the range is down and it took the ranking with it. Since Ray is turning 32, you have to take that seriously, even if it is only one year. Age takes speed first. <BJH>

MANNY MARTINEZ, FA
(1998: PIT)

Another fine AAA ballplayer who has some major league value as a backup right now, at his career peak. The Pirates are skimming cream. <BJH>

BRIAN MCRAE, NYM

Brian has transitioned over to "old player's skills," pushing his isolated power, secondary average and BBP up to career peaks. One suspects that he'll continue to exhibit these characteristics now that he's on the other side of 30. The question will be how long he's able to keep his batting average high enough to keep those in the dugout and front-office—who are still fixated on BA as a measure of value—satisfied with his overall performance. **<SL>**

RAUL MONDESI, LA

Not a center fielder. A right fielder. The Dodgers have him in center because Gary Sheffield sure can't play there. But you know, Gary could very easily play first base, and who is Eric Karros to be moving Raul Mondesi out of position?

Raul had the worst offensive season he's ever had, at age 27. How else do you explain that except to focus on the mental effort he had to put in to play a position he really hasn't the tools for? That's what Eric Karros cost the Dodgers. **<BJH>**

REGGIE SANDERS, CIN

A star youngster, Reggie has lost his career to injuries. The Reds would, according to rumor, like to unload him, but they keep asking for his value in 1993, rather than today. **<BJH>**

TURNER WARD, PIT

Another of the star kids in Toronto in the early 90s who didn't pan out. **<BJH>**

PAT WATKINS, CIN

Absolutely blew AAA pitching up this year, as he did to AA in 1997. I don't really think he'll be quite that good in the majors, but I think he's good to go. He made a huge leap this year over his 1997 major league play, but '97 was a statistically-insignificant cup of coffee, and even this year is not quite up to the expectations raised by his minor league numbers. So, let's say a 40% chance of another big jump this year, and almost no chance of a big drop. DECENT FANTASY GAMBLE if he comes out of spring training with a job. **<BJH>**

DEVON WHITE, LA
(1998: AZ)

The Offensive Surge keeps him going. It fills out his power, which should be declining, but instead remains strong for the position. It also keeps the ol' batting average up there above .260. Without those things, teams would start to wonder about him. Instead, he keeps a high ranking here, because he benefits more from the power help than most center fielders, who don't have any with or without help. **<BJH>**

That sound you heard was me and a million other Giant fans cackling with glee as the Dodger announced the solving of their center field problem by signing Devo for way too much money. It's comforting to know that other NL West clubs have the Proven Veteran fetish. Devon's 36, and about one pulled hamstring from losing enough speed to fall to fourth-outfielder status. He's a decent seventh-place hitter and still a smooth fielder, but that range is shrinking like week-old cheesecake. **<TA>**

RONDELL WHITE, MON

Turning 27, but made a big jump this year. I don't expect much of a drop-off, but some drop is what I do expect. I also expect Rondell to hold about this value for the next five or more years. This season is not much of an improvement over his 1994 and '95 campaigns, and he's been hurt, so you have to think that there is some value he has not yet tapped. The race is between recovering that value and losing ground to age. **<BJH>**

RIGHT FIELD

BOB ABREU, PHI

Abreu was a hot prospect in the minors who seemed about to fail to pan out. Now, this. He's only turning 25, and very other top right fielder is much older, so the future looks wide open. Give him a year, though. I can't imagine he'll post another growth year after this huge jump. And that means he's on the age 24-26-28 pattern of on years. And that means that his whole career depends on whether the pattern stops with a Career Year at age 26, or progresses on to age 28. I do not yet know how to make that prediction.**<BJH>**

He may be the best player to come out of the expansion draft, and all it took was Kevin Stocker to get him. He's not going to be the top bat in your lineup, but with Rolen and eventually Pat Burrell on the way, the Phillies should be very happy with him in RF. There will probably be some temptation to turn him into more of a home run threat, but the Phillies should resist that urge. He is plenty valuable the way he is. He'd be my #2 batter for about the next six years. **<SF>**

DEREK BELL, HOU

A very nice season, one of three that Derek has posted up in a most inconsistent career. I don't have any kind of good read on Derek any more, as I guess you've figured out.**<BJH>**

MARVIN BENARD, SF

Now, THIS is what I call a Career Year. No, I have no idea where it came from. No, I have no idea how much of it Marvin will retain in the long run, although I'd be astonished if he doesn't suffer some sort of Counteradjustment Slump in 1999.**<BJH>**

BRENT BREDE, JAPAN
(1998: AZ)

Brent's response to a poor year with an expansion club was to sign with a Japanese team. I don't know whether this counts as giving up or not. Brent did toast AAA pitching while he was down there, and I'd have regarded him as still a prospect. But he was about to turn 27, and perhaps he could see some writing on the wall.**<BJH>**

To me, Brede represents iron-clad proof that Buck Showalter is aware that minor league numbers are a more reliable indicator of major league hitting potential than tools and/or the endorsement of scouts are. To put it bluntly, Brede looked like a fool all year. He looked lost in the field, didn't cover much ground, and showed a weak arm. He seemed to struggle just to get one foot in front of the other on the basepaths. At the plate, he looked like a JVer against varsity pitching.

No self-respecting baseball man would put up with him for 3 games, especially with a well-chiseled alternative like Yamil Benitez twiddling his sinewy thumbs on the bench. Yet Brede's track record indicated that he'd be a better hitter than Benitez. That Buck gave Brent more than 200 PAs should be encouraging to Diamondback fans. **<DD>**

SECONDARY FIELDING STATISTICS
1998 NATIONAL LEAGUE
RIGHT FIELD

Name	POS	G	GS	INN	TC	PO	A	E	DP	FPCT	RF	ZR
Gerald Williams	RF	61	37	368	106	101	2	3	0	.972	2.52	.897
Jon Nunnally	RF	53	30	279	83	74	3	6	0	.928	2.48	.852
Mark Kotsay	RF	107	99	889	232	213	15	4	1	.983	2.31	.821
Reggie Sanders	RF	57	43	384	96	94	1	1	0	.990	2.23	.820
Vladimir Guerrero	RF	157	157	1360	348	321	10	17	3	.951	2.19	.834
Brian Jordan	RF	124	110	946	238	221	9	8	4	.966	2.19	.826
Larry Walker	RF	123	118	1011	248	236	8	4	2	.984	2.17	.790
Sammy Sosa	RF	156	153	1379	342	319	14	9	2	.974	2.17	.815
Dante Bichette	RF	29	25	213	53	51	0	2	0	.962	2.16	.718
Brent Brede	RF	39	26	239	60	55	2	3	1	.950	2.15	.821
Jose Guillen	RF	149	144	1254	305	279	16	10	4	.967	2.12	.823
Raul Mondesi	RF	54	53	457	109	106	1	2	0	.982	2.11	.814
Bob Abreu	RF	146	139	1260	296	271	17	8	0	.973	2.06	.756
Jeromy Burnitz	RF	161	158	1403	325	306	10	9	3	.972	2.03	.818
Butch Huskey	RF	103	94	795	179	167	8	4	1	.978	1.98	.826
Ruben Rivera	RF	73	24	317	71	68	1	2	0	.972	1.96	.829
Stan Javier	RF	95	78	720	158	156	0	2	1	.987	1.95	.825
Derek Bell	RF	154	149	1338	298	282	8	8	2	.973	1.95	.843
Marvin Benard	RF	64	48	444	95	92	1	2	1	.979	1.88	.871
Michael Tucker	RF	118	112	954	200	194	5	1	1	.995	1.88	.763
Gary Sheffield	RF	126	126	1099	227	216	9	2	4	.991	1.84	.762
Tony Gwynn	RF	116	115	902	149	143	5	1	0	.993	1.48	.774

KEY: Inn-Innings; **PO**-Putouts; **A**-Assists; **Er**-Errors; **DP**-Double Plays; **FPct**-Fielding Pct.; **RF**-Range Factor; **ZR**-Zone Rating

JEROMY BURNITZ, MIL

A drop from 1997, even though he turned ten doubles into homers and rid himself of the all-homers-at-home suspicion. But he dropped five walks despite picking up over a hundred at-bats, and he didn't steal bases, and he struck out an awful lot. I expect a comeback, although the patterns of development of young prospects don't apply, because he's already turning 30.<BJH>

MIKE FRANK, CIN

Of the Young, Frank, and Stynes OF combo. If for no other reason, I'll never forget his name. Fortunately for him, I may remember for another reason—he's a pretty good young player. Made his way to the big leagues in only two seasons after hitting .350 in 585 minor league AB. <JF>

When he's ready, he'll be the Reds starting RF. He emerged as the top hitting prospect in the organization after less than one year in the minors. He only played 28 games before a season-ending injury, but he played well enough to convince the Reds of his talent. Frank will play every day, which means Indianapolis if not Cincinnati.<SL>

KARIM GARCIA, AZ

Only turning 23, Karim has been murdering AAA pitching for four years now. And, for the same pour years, he has absolutely failed to transfer that to the major leagues. Well, 23 is only 23, but four is four. Karim has about one more year to avoid people like me putting out the Eric Anthony alert.<BJH>

Had the lowest on-base percentage (.260) of any major leaguer with 300 at-bats. **<SL>**

VLADIMIR GUERRERO, MON

Vladimir, at the age of 22, outhit the MVP winner, finishing second in the XW rankings only because he played poor defense. My, that is impressive. Still, I have to give a warning to those of you who expect him to show even more growth in 1999. Vlad's season had to have been a wakeup call to the pitchers of the National League. They are going to adjust. Guerrero's in for a Sophomore Slump, very, very likely. But then, watch out for the millennium.<BJH>

Mickey Mantle and Willie Mays were long before my time, so I never had much perspective on just what sort of talents they were. With players like Vlad Guerrero and Andruw Jones now in the league, I have a much better appreciation of just how talented those players were. Guerrero's ability is mind-boggling to me.

Once he adjusted to the majors after jumping all the way from AA, he wore out the opposing pitchers. Through the end of May, Guerrero had 557 career at bats, essentially one full year under his belt. From that point on he slugged .646 and batted .342.

He will swing at nearly anything, and against the Dodgers on Sunday Night Baseball he hit a pitch that bounced nearly out of the infield. His lack of patience hasn't seemed to hurt his production though. Most players need to draw some walks to be a great player, but Guerrero hits enough to be a star without great patience. I'm uncertain why teams would throw anything near the strike zone early in the count—he slugged .905 in first pitch situations. <SF>

JOSE GUILLEN, PIT

Sometimes consistency isn't all it's cracked up to be. Had AVG/OBA/SLG of .267/.300/.412 in 1997 and .267/.298/.414 in 1998. He'll only be 23 in 1999, so there is still a lot of room for improvement. He had better start learning to be a little more selective at the plate (only 38 BB in 1071 AB) or he'll never tap his full potential. <JF>

Don't be fooled. This is a fine, fine season for a 22-year-old who jumped from A ball to the majors only last season. And, since it was almost identical to the 1997 campaign, I'm going to go out on a limb and say HOT FANTASY TOUT. I think the seasoning process is over. I say 80% chance he explodes all over the league.<BJH>

TONY GWYNN, SD

Had the best K/W ratio (18/35) of any player with 350 or more ABs. With all due respect, Gwynn is fat. I have to wonder how much longer he can continue when he looks like he's playing with an inner-tube hidden under his shirt.**<SL>**

Be prepared for the 1999 replacement to the Big Mac Homer Watch, the Tony-and-Wade 3000 Hit Countdown. Gwynn passed Boggs last season, and now has a six-hit lead (2928 to 2922). If Tony wants a lot more than 3000 hits in his career, though, he may have to leave San Diego and become a DH. I think he'll retire rather than do that. <DM>

BUTCH HUSKEY, SEA
(1998: NYM)

One hell of a collapse season heading into age 27. Huskey's weakness is getting on base; his career high is still .319. The reason is that he still will not take a walk. Now, this season might just be a Counteradjustment Slump preceding a big jump season. But it also might be the death knell sounding in the form of pitchers the league over refusing to throw the man anything that even remotely resembles a strike.

Come to think about it, we may be talking about only one thing here. Learning to not throw Huskey strikes is certainly where I'd start adjusting to him if I were a pitcher. The jury has to be out regarding whether he'll adjust back, but this kind of player often does not and ends up a journeyman backup.**<BJH>**

All in all, I think the Mets could have gotten a bit more for Huskey in trade than they got from the Mariners. And given the ages of their new starters in the OF (Henderson is 40, Bonilla 35), and the fragility of Robin Ventura, it would have made sense to keep Butch around as insurance at what amounts to four positions (1B-3B-LF-RF). This looks like one of those "my way or the highway" Bobby Valentine edicts, and it might well burn the Mets, who will have no power threat on their bench as they go into 1999. **<DM>**

STAN JAVIER, SF

Stan has spent his entire career riding the boundary between starter quality and backup play. Actually, he's had several seasons, like this one, where he was certainly among the starters of the league (that is, he was among the 16 best right fielders in a 16-team league), but he can't sustain that. On the other hand, he has played 14 years in the major leagues, and shows no signs of being finished, and is a multimillionaire. The frustration of being borderline may be there, but I bet he doesn't complain much.**<BJH>**

You've got to give Dusty Baker credit in his ability to use personnel and get more out of marginal starters than just about anyone. Watching Dusty do this day in and day out during 1998, one was reminded that this is as much an art as a science, and that's a point that all of us erstwhile analysts should keep near the front of our fevered brows. **<DM>**

BRIAN JORDAN, ATL
(1998: STL)

A fine offensive season; the best Brian has ever had, in my opinion. It doesn't rank any higher than this because he just isn't any better than this. He doesn't

walk, and so the gap between his batting average and his on-base percentage is low. His TXW used to go higher in his good hitting years, because he used to be the Gold Glove right fielder. But much of his speed is gone to those injuries, and with it, the gold.**<BJH>**

MARK KOTSAY, FLA

An outstanding season for making the jump from AA ball at age 22. I see no reason for him not to improve, and become a star. I see no reason why that can't start in 1999. If you consider this to be his AAA seasoning year, you should expect improvement in the next campaign. GOOD FANTASY BUY. He's got a job, and he's got the goods.**<BJH>**

MEL NIEVES, FA
(1998: CIN)

Has everyone given up waiting for him to turn into Fred McGriff? He's turning 27, and I do expect some growth here, but his days as a super prospect are gone. He didn't even obliterate AAA pitching while he was down there.**<BJH>**

JON NUNNALLY, CIN

I thought Jon was poised to explode this year; instead, he had an amazing slump. This was one of the seasons that led me to start taking the even /odd thing seriously in development pattern analysis. When a player makes a huge jump like Jon did in 1997 at age 25, you should expect a dropoff season before the next growth spurt. I didn't know that last year; this year I do. And therefore, suicidal as it may seem, I'm going to tout Jon Nunnally again.**<BJH>**

CURTIS PRIDE, ATL

A nice rebound from 1997's collapse. Whether this is the result of Bobby Cox platooning or just a return to form, I don't know how to tell you. Curtis' career is simply too erratic to pattern out.**<BJH>**

RUBEN RIVERA, SD

His AAA numbers have not suggested the godlike stardom that the lower-level ones did. Actually, when you've put in parts of four seasons trying to master AAA, "stalled out" is not too harsh a term for your career.**<BJH>**

STALLED OR NOT, RUBEN WILL APPARENTLY MOVE TO CENTER AS THE PADRES ENTER THEIR INTERREGNUM DOLDRUMS BETWEEN FLUKE PENNANT AND BALLOT BOX PAYOFF. I'D

LAY AT LEAST EVEN MONEY THAT RUBEN ISN'T WITH THEM WHEN THEY MOVE INTO THEIR NEW DIGS. **<COJ>**

GARY SHEFFIELD, LA
(1998: FLA-LA)

Is it me, or does Gary seem to you to have settled down? I can't remember a clubhouse horror story in some years. Now, it's always been a given that the man could hit. He ranks as the best hitter at this position, according to Park-adjusted Runs Created per Game. He had a fine 60% Defensive Winning Percentage out there in the Dodger Stadium grass. He would

NATIONAL LEAGUE RIGHT FIELD			
Player	OXW	DXW	TXW
Sosa S	7.93	1.10	9.03
Guerrero V	8.38	0.51	8.89
Sheffield G	7.16	0.94	8.10
Walker L	5.94	0.69	6.63
Abreu B	4.92	1.12	6.04
Jordan B	5.27	0.70	5.97
Bell D	5.26	0.55	5.81
Burnitz J	4.94	0.63	5.57
Gwynn T	4.71	0.03	4.74
Kotsay M	1.89	1.55	3.44
Javier S	2.59	0.38	2.97
Benard M	2.47	0.17	2.64
Tucker M	1.74	0.79	2.53
Guillen J	1.28	0.97	2.25
Williams G	1.85	0.39	2.24
Rivera R	1.23	0.23	1.46
Huskey B	0.79	0.63	1.42
Vander Wal J	0.96	0.17	1.13
Nunnally J	0.54	0.50	1.04
Nieves M	0.73	0.16	0.89
Sweeney M	0.61	0.15	0.76
Pride C	0.46	0.18	0.64
Garcia K	-0.14	0.65	0.51
Brede B	0.04	0.16	0.20

have led this position in TXW had he played 20 more games. If anyone was worth Mike Piazza, he was. To get Charles Johnson as a bonus was, truly, a fine trade.**<BJH>**

Dev, your memory needs a bit more RAM on this one. Gary may be calmer, but that's because he has a large investment portfolio made possible by the folks at Fox, who handed him $5 million in chump change just to come to LA. That being said, he is the perfect poster *boy for the Fox Dodgers, a team that epitomizes their parent company's network persona of conflicted behavior, anorexic would-be sex kitten lawyers, and blue otherworldly cool. There is no doubt that Gary and Rupert completely understand one another.* <DM>

SAMMY SOSA, CHC

What an odd MVP award. The voters, early in September, just let us all know that there was really nothing Mark McGwire could do to get the accolade. It was going to Sammy Sosa, and that was that. At least Sammy didn't fall apart and end up with 20 fewer homers than Mark, or something. There are a couple of things to be said for Sammy. First, he did not exploit Wrigley Field for homers. His home/road splits are not obnoxious.

And second, he did lead the league in runs scored. It's not uncommon for a player of Sammy's type to lead the league in RBI. Sammy won't take a walk, and so he gets maximum RBI value out of his men on base. Juan Gonzalez is the same type of hitter. But this type of hitter seldom leads the league in runs scored, because he just doesn't get on base enough. But Sammy did that, courtesy of the people hitting behind him in the Cubbie batting order.

Even considering the men behind him, that's impressive. Mark McGwire got on base so many more times than Sammy. And therefore, unlike the joke award in the American League, Sammy's award has some credibility. If only the writers hadn't told us the fix was in, Sammy would get a lot more respect for what was a fine, fine season.<BJH>

MARK SWEENEY, SD

A collapse season after three pretty good ones. The most logical explanation I can think of is that he's finally given in to despair of ever getting a chance to establish himself as a starter.<BJH>

MICHAEL TUCKER, CIN
(1998: ATL)

Already turning 28, and he'd better hope his growth pattern extends to that age, rather than peaking at age 26. Otherwise, he's going to have trouble keeping a full-time job.<BJH>

JOHN VANDER WAL, SD
(1998: COL-SD)

Playing only part time, and in Colorado, John has this sort of nice season happen occasionally. Now out of Colorado, I doubt he can produce another one.<BJH>

LARRY WALKER, COL

Out with the bad overrating. In with the good ballpark adjustments. Yeah, I know. I'm still not over the silly MVP selection.<BJH>

I know we have to adjust Larry's numbers down for Coors, but it's still interesting to note that his 1.075 OPS last season was accompanied by only 67 RBI batting mostly in the #3 slot. That's the lowest RBI total ever generated by someone who had 130 games played and this level of production, and most of the blame can be placed on the hitters right in front of Larry in the batting order:

Team	BOP	OBP
COL	#1	.349
COL	#2	.309

Now it didn't help that Larry had a real barn-burner of a home/road split again this year, slugging .757 in Coors and just .488 on the road, while driving in just 23 runs away from Denver. But most of the problem in the Rox lineup is at the top of the order, and this might well be the key reason why Colorado didn't lead the league in runs scored for the first time in four years. <DM>

GERALD WILLIAMS, ATL

Astonishing. 31-year-old players don't do this sort of Career Year thing. Or is it the power of platooning? Stay tuned next year for another installment of The Bobby Cox Can Make A Star Out Of Anyone Show.<BJH>

CROSSING THE RUBICON

SECTION SIX

CROSSING THE RUBICON / *continued from page 6*

not moving from a Ptolemaic to a Copernican view of the universe here.

BJH: So how do you characterize BBBA's new method? Paradigm shift?

DM: No, I see it as an organic correction for one of the key flaws in the original formula, and preferable to Bill's modifications. And it doesn't hurt that it's more accurate than the new RC.

BJH: Wait a minute. How can it be more accurate than a method where RC has been set to equal team and league runs scored?

DM: Well, that's why we have Jim Furtado on board with us. He's gotten "inside" the new RC, and our readers will be able to follow his description of how it's computed, and what the base value of the measurement is before all of the adjustments are applied.

BJH: (pause) So that means that we're going to see all of the interim steps involved in calculating the new RC, right?

DM: Yep.

BJH: And so we'll be able to see what the original estimates are, before the final equalization takes place?

DM: Right. And while those results are an improvement over original RC, they still don't match up with BBBA's new XR method.

BJH: Well, bring it on!!

BBBA and XR/XW Join Forces

G. JAY WALKER

Section 6 of last year's BBBA featured two articles written by Brock Hanke and myself entitled WAR Redeclared and Beauty With A Blemish. In them, we talked about the problems we found with the Runs Created methodology and offered some solutions. At the time, we begged off from formal implementation of a new methodology, stating that "we were deliberating over these changes and their ramifications" (p. 11). Playing the hare proved to be prudent for two reasons.

First, Bill James came out with his revised Runs Created method in the STATS All-Time Major League Handbook. While the new RC method was more accurate than the previous ones, it was also more complex and more ambiguous. In many ways it was a definite improvement, but the more we looked it over, the more we had serious questions with some of Bill's techniques.

As for the second reason, while our articles last year were an important way station, we had to do a little "fine-tuning" ourselves (there was an overlooked glitch in the way the replacement level was represented). Looking at where we were at and where Bill seemed to be going, we used he extra time to go from there and develop an entire new system to measure offensive performance. We call the new system Extrapolated Runs/Extrapolated Wins (XR/XW).

The centerpiece of the system is our new measure of run production called Extrapolated Runs, and it is front-ended by our new park adjustment method and back-ended by our new measure of Offensive Wins Above Replacement, called Extrapolated Wins.

We do a more detailed critique of Bill James' new methods in (Jay's/Jim's) piece entitled _____, where we explain what those strange-looking team context formulas really do, describe (unambiguously) how he calculates his situational adjustments and look at how accurate his results are.

Once we figured out what Bill was doing with his method and looked at his results, we started to do a lot of thinking about whether a additive or multiplicative model was the best way to measure offensive performance. Is offense multiplicative? Absolutely. Is a multiplicative model the best way to measure offense? After much debate, we decided that it wasn't.

This decision was not made lightly. This publication traces a line back to the Bill James Baseball Abstracts, and we have always been big supporters of the Runs Created methodology. Even when we raised an issue with some parts of the methodology last year, we entitled the article Beauty With A Blemish. But we came to the conclusion that the multiplicative methods are like a classic car - when everything is running well, it's a thing of beauty, but it is also more subject to breakdowns.

Analysts like to use measures of standard error and other, more arcane formulations to make pronouncements about who's method is best. That's all well and good; we will keep one foot firmly in that tradition, as you will see. However, there is another criteria for judging the worth of a methodology, and that's how well it distributes the measure (runs produced) over the range of various outcomes. This has been a criticism of the Runs Created methodology in the past, that it rated the good players too high and the bad players too low. Because of the multiplicative process used in the formula, it had trouble "kicking in" for bad players, and be the time you got to the good players, the engine was revved up a too fast. It's the nature of the multiplicative models; they're just harder to control. The additive models are more robust.

While the new Runs Created method solved many of the problems the old one had, we found the solutions to be somewhat complex and contrived, and the results no better than some of the leading additive models. We decided to develop our own additive model. It wasn't that the multiplicative models and Runs Created are wrong: it's just a question of what works best in theory versus what works best in practice.

It was about this time we stumbled across Jim Furtado, or rather Jim Furtado's web page. We noticed that Jim had developed a park-adjustment method very similar to the one we had been developing, and—even better—that he had his own thoughts on additive vs. multiplicative debate that closely complemented our conclusions. And he was well on his way to developing an additive method which was, in general form, quite similar to what we were hoping to produce. Rather than re-invent the wheel, we contacted Jim and arranged for a rendezvous at a secret location (my sister's house). After five hours of intense negotiations, we agreed to join forces

I want to stress that this method was a collaborative effort between Jim Furtado and the BBBA staff, and that Jim was involved in not only with his new additive measure of run production, but with all components of the methodology. As mentioned above, we had independently developed similar ways to measure park effects, and BBBA wound up modifying our park effects method using some of Jim's ideas. The new measure of run production, Extrapolated Runs, is the method devised by Jim, and about all BBBA did there was to provide feedback to Jim in his final stages of development. The new Offensive Wins Above Replacement method, called Extrapolated Wins, began with some ideas that Jim sketched out, and we worked together to come up with the new methodology.

Each of the three main parts of the new system contain features which are, if not totally new, fairly innovative. The park-adjustment component uses the park factors over a multiple-year period to come up with park effects for the current year. The Extrapolated Runs component we feel is simply the most solid and accurate additive model yet devised. And the Extrapolated Wins component comes up with what I feel is the optimal solution to the outs vs. plate appearances debate.

For those of you who read the Beauty With A Blemish article last year, you may remember we were critical of the use of outs used by some methods to measure a player's offensive games (that is, his offensive playing time) and advocated using plate appearances instead as the markers to count playing time. As Brock Hanke observed, "teams consume outs, players consume plate appearances". Taking that idea along with some notions being kicked about in certain circles, Jim Furtado suggested keeping plate appearances as our method for counting

playing time, but placing the player in a team context and adjusting the team plate appearances according to the rate the player consumed outs. We worked it all out mathematically, and are satisfied with the results, hopefully you'll be too.

Finally, there seems to be a growing tendency in the baseball analysis community to keep methods "proprietary," not only the shielding the authors from a critique of their methods by other analysts, but putting you in a position where you have to pay to see the results of their methods, since you don't have the information to replicate them yourselves. At BBBA, not only do we fully explain our methods, but we encourage our readers to use them.

Now sometimes all you're interested in is a weekly update of offensive performance for your favorite team, or having a simple way of seeing what players are performing best; we acknowledge that this system might be a bit complex for "everyday" use. Therefore, we also developed what we call the Basic Version of the XR/XW method. Most of the differences between the basic and regular versions of XR/XW are in the complexity, but there is one key methodological difference. In the regular version, you first park-adjust, and then compute Extrapolated Runs using the park-adjusted raw stats. In the basic version, you first compute the Extrapolated Runs and then park-adjust the Extrapolated Runs. The basic version will give you 90% of the accuracy of the full-on XR/XW method with only 50% of the effort. It's the perfect solution for light, in-season use.

BBBA and Jim Furtado will regularly be posting analyses using the XR/XW method during the season at their web sites at www.backatcha.com and www.baseballstuff.com. One other person we'd like to express our thanks to is Stephen Tomlinson, who took the time to review our results from last year and provide some good food for thought in developing our new methodology. Stephen wrote our commentary on the Blue Jays this year (see p. xx) , and if you're interested in Blue Jays history from a sabermetric point of view, make sure to check out his website at www.stephent.com/jays.

WHY DO WE NEED ANOTHER PLAYER EVALUATION METHOD?

Jim Furtado

Recently, someone asked me this question. Why have I spent a good chunk of my limited free time researching and designing player analysis formulas? Without getting into my childhood and my psyche (my wife covers these areas sufficiently), the answer is simple-I don't feel that the available methods sufficiently answer my questions.

Now, don't get me wrong. I don't want to imply that all the available methods are useless, because they can be useful. However, they all fall short of the mark; they all lack something.

I'm not alone thinking this way, either. Just last year, in this very space, Jay Walker and Brock Hanke pointed out many of the problems with today's player evaluation systems. In particular, they wrote a very insightful examination of Bill James' Runs Created (RC) system.

Their critique was very interesting. Although I hadn't noticed the RC/27 outs issue, I had noticed RC's inaccuracies at the extremes. Because of this rather large problem I, too, had adopted Paul Johnson's Estimated Runs Produced (ERP) as my run model of choice.

What Jay and Brock missed in their examination was that ERP was essentially a linear formula dressed up in a convoluted package. Of course, this wasn't a big surprise. Many other analysts, including Bill James, had also missed it. As a matter of fact, I missed it myself for a long time. I only experienced my epiphany, regarding the matter, about a year before. Although I can't say the revelation changed my life, it did cause me to delve a little deeper into player statistics.

You see, when I made the realization, I was quite perplexed. Bill James long ago disparaged Pete Palmer's Linear Weight System (LWTS) because, in his words, "runs scoring is not a linear activity." I thought, "How could James, on the one hand, laud Johnson's linear formula as more accurate than his own, while knocking Palmer's linear formula?" These conflicting opinions couldn't both be true. The contradiction prodded me to study the matter myself.

During my investigation, I contacted Don to see if the guys at BBBA might be interested in checking out what I was up to. Luckily, they were. The ensuing collaboration produced something we are all proud of.

Read over the next few pages to find out more.

LOGIC AND METHODS IN BASEBALL ANALYSIS-REVISITED

In the 1984 Baseball Abstract, an article entitled "Logic and Methods in Baseball Analysis" appeared. In this article, Bill James not only demonstrated the Runs Created methodology, but also explained the philosophy behind it. Since the new methods presented in this chapter are as much a shift in philosophy at BBBA as a change in formulas, it's appropriate that I frame my part of the discussion similarly.

Bill James began the essay with the following statement, "Ultimately, what we are trying to do is to find answers to questions, baseball questions." Although it's best that I update his questions a little, his sentiment in the article remains true. We are trying to find answers to baseball questions. Who is the best player? Who is the Most Valuable Player? Should the Red Sox re-sign Mo Vaughn or let him go? Who should the Mets play at catcher? Baseball fans, including myself, ask these questions all the time. Consequently, we're constantly looking for the answers.

These questions can be answered many different ways. They can be answered subjectively or objectively; they can be answered based on feeling or scientific method. There is no right way or wrong way to find answers to our baseball questions, as long as we end up at truthful answers.

Bill James, also, used a road building analogy in the original essay on this subject. He stated, "The development of knowledge in any field waits upon two things: the development of methods and the availability of a compelling logic. Methods are the roads that one travels on in searching for the truth, and like all roads they can be constructed and abandoned as needed. The creation of a new method is basically a mental construction

project; if you need the road, if you know where you want to go, then there is no doubt about one's ability to develop a method to get there."

As is often the case, Bill James was on the mark with this idea. Once we properly frame the question, it is possible to develop methods that provide suitable answers. Certainly, our methods don't always provide perfect results, but as long as we constantly refine our questions and our methodology, we get closer and closer to our desired destination-the truth.

Of course, not everyone accepts the truth. Whether something is true or not is often very hard to determine. People disagree about "the truth" all the time. History is littered with examples, sometimes horrific, of the different ways "truth" has been defined or discussed. Fortunately, "the truth" baseball fans search for does not require bloodshed for resolution. Thankfully, the search for truth in baseball can be undertaken in more civilized fashion.

Like James, the way that I often search for baseball truth is sabermetrics. Sabermetrics, coined by Bill James, is defined as "the search for objective knowledge about baseball". Sabermetrics is a scientific process that tries to provide answers to questions based on fact and evidence, not feeling and intuition.

Since I'm a skeptic, sabermetrics greatly appeals to my sensibilities. However, although I definitely consider myself a fervid proponent of the discipline, I try to always keep in mind its limitations, namely, some components of play can't be quantified.

First, we can not properly account for the human element. Physical talent alone does not explain performance. If it did, only the best athletes would be the best players. "Tools" guys would be the only superstars. That's certainly not the case. Many players perform better than their athletic talent would indicate. Intelligence, diligence, and tenacity are some of the qualities that spark players to perform above their given talent.

Second, many results can not be appropriately apportioned among players. For example, say I tell you that a catcher allowed 30 stolen bases and threw out 6 other guys. Say I also tell you the only games he caught were with a particular pitcher on the mound. Can you tell me who was the weak link? You can't. Now, I know this is a rather extreme example, but many facets of play can't be broken down

These limitations do not mandate that all objective analysis be discarded. It just requires that questions and answers be framed in such a way that unmeasurable facets of play are either isolated from the question at hand, or, at the least, are recognized as shortcoming of the process. As long as these thoughts are kept in mind, sabermetric methods can be used in the quest for baseball truth.

Getting back to my friend, there are an abundance of systems which try to answer baseball questions. He's certainly right in this regard. There are plenty of methods vying for the attention of baseball fans. Some of the formulas work very well; some don't work too well; and some don't work at all. Unfortunately, it's not always readily apparent which is which. This is especially true for the statistically faint of heart.

I always hate to generalize but I think I'm on safe ground with the following statement: All baseball fans enjoy baseball stats. Now before you rush to correct me, let me add this hedge: To different degrees, all baseball fans enjoy baseball stats.

Every fan checks out the statistics they are most comfortable with. For some, the batting line on the television satiates the desire for information. Others (like you, otherwise, you wouldn't have purchased this book and wouldn't be reading this article) have a deeper thirst that can only be quenched by more in-depth analysis.

The differing statistical acumen leads to misconceptions. I can't begin to count the times I've heard a batter described as the "best batter in baseball" because he had the highest batting average. Certainly, batting average can be useful to determine a player's ability, but only when the question is properly framed. Unfortunately, in most cases, batting average is used to answer overly broad questions.

Batting average is not the only statistic that's used and abused. Others also get misused. At times, even intelligent baseball analysts choose the wrong statistics to answer the question at hand. I'm sure, at one time or another, I have done it myself. These analytical faux pas aren't the end of the world. People can enjoy baseball without being statistically adept. However, if the goal is a deeper understanding of the game with the help of statistical analysis, it's important that analysts carefully select and design methods to answer succinct questions. It's also important that those who have a deeper understanding pass along that knowledge. Hopefully, I can help do my part here.

AT THE FEET OF THE MASTERS

Back in the early 1970s, when I was a lad who spent most of my time playing baseball in the backyard with my brother, my father bought me a tabletop baseball game. I can't recall the exact name, but I do remember it had Sports Illustrated somewhere in the title.

Anyway, I spent hours and hours and hours playing that game. I mostly played with the Red Sox, but I remember playing other teams as well. I bring this up because this was the first time I ever really concerned myself with things like lineup building, the value of the bunt, pitching rotations, etc.

As my interest in baseball (and the tabletop game) grew, my father and I spent more and more time discussing baseball strategy. He passed on his considerable baseball knowledge, advised me to read books about the subject and recommended that I listen intently to radio and television broadcasters. Being a devoted son, I minded my father's words and consumed every baseball strategy tidbit that came my way. What I essentially learned, from all this, was the way of "The Book". As you know, "The Book" isn't really a book. It's just what everybody calls baseball's conventional wisdom.

As you might expect, it wasn't long before I could recite "The Book" backwards and forwards. I knew that Steve Garvey was the best fielding first baseman in baseball. Rod Carew was the best hitter. Tony Perez was a great clutch hitter. Pete Rose was the second best player. (Yaz was the best∅I'm from Red Sox country.) Bunting was a great play. Pitching was 75% of the game. Et cetera, et cetera, et cetera. The years passed and my confidence in my own baseball knowledge grew. That was until I discovered books by two knowledgeable gentlemen--Bill James and Pete Palmer.

In 1986, I walked into a bookstore and, as is my habit, I purchased some interesting looking baseball books. The two books, The Hidden Game of Baseball (HGB) and Bill James' Baseball Abstract (BJBA), were quite disconcerting. The ideas presented in the books clashed with the things I had learned to be true. The bunt wasn't really that good an idea. The Red Sox didn't necessarily have the best hitters. Pete Rose wasn't the best player in baseball. Clutch hitters didn't exist. Steve Garvey couldn't field. Batting average was overrated. Et cetera, et cetera, et cetera.

Don't get me wrong, I wasn't driven to the streets in turmoil. I didn't feel compelled to scream. "It's a maaad house! A maaaaaaad house!" like Charlton Heston did in the original Planet of the Apes movie. To be honest, at the time, baseball no longer consumed most of my waking thoughts. As often happens to young men, my primary focus had shifted to females. During this period of my life, baseball devolved into a secondary, but still substantial, interest.

Nevertheless, even with baseball's temporarily diminished importance, the books did have a profound effect. I started re-thinking everything I thought I knew about baseball. Of course, this was a very good thing. If it wasn't for these books, I wouldn't be writing this essay.

Unfortunately, I don't have the space to properly give everyone, who has contributed to our current baseball knowledge, credit. So what I'll do is give a very, very, very brief overview of the three most influential sabermetricians. Furthermore, I'll limit the scope of the overview to player evaluation systems.

I mention all this for one important reason: to pay homage to the people that laid the groundwork for the current state of sabermetrics. To go forward, we must look back.

Branch Rickey / Allan Roth

I'm sure you noticed two names here. No, they are not the same person. I include them together because it's impossible to separate their contributions. You've heard of Branch Rickey; you probably haven't heard of Allan Roth. That's unfortunate because Allan Roth probably was the first sabermetrician.

As far back as 1940, Mr. Roth was tabulating statistics that are now commonly known as situational stats. He, at one time or another, examined such things as batting by count, by situation, by lineup position. Additionally, he wrote many articles including an in depth examination of Hal Newhouser's 1945 season and including an examination of Bob Feller and strikeouts which appeared in The Sporting News in 1946.

Beginning in 1947, Mr. Roth began working with Branch Rickey. Their association culminated with the publishing of an article "Goodby to Some Old Baseball Ideas" in LIFE magazine August 2, 1954. Although the article lists Branch Rickey as its author, Roth appears to be the person responsible for its content.

In the article, Branch Rickey proposed a "device for measuring baseball which has compelled me to put different values on some of my oldest and most cherished theories. It reveals some new and startling truths about the nature of the game. It is a means of gauging with a high degree of accuracy important factors which contribute to winning and losing baseball games." The formula which he described as "a simple, additive equation" was the first system developed to compare run scoring difference to team wins. Its effect was revolutionary, though not instantly.

Rickey's thoughts remain controversial, "If the baseball world is to accept this new system of analyzing the game-and eventually it will-it must first give up preconceived ideas. I had to. The formula outrages certain standards that experienced baseball people have sworn by all their lives. Runs batted in? A misleading figure. Strikeouts? I always rated them highly as a determining force in pitching. I do now. But new facts convince me that I have overrated their importance in so far as game importance is concerned. Even batting average must be reexamined." Current sabermetricians are still trying to gain the widespread acceptance of these ideas.

As Palmer noted in HGB, "The first of the efforts to pare offensive statistics to their essence, runs, and then reconstruct them for individuals so as to reflect their run-producing ability, were Rickey's and Roth's." The truth of that statement is why the Rickey / Roth pairing warrants attention.

Pete Palmer

I can't give Pete Palmer's work the full credit it deserves since I can't possibly do so in such a short article. Besides his work in the HGB, Mr. Palmer also is the data wizard behind Total Baseball (TB). Along with John Thorn (his co-author for many projects), Pete Palmer is responsible for enlightening baseball fans, not only concerning sabermetrics, but baseball history in general. Mr. Palmer's work in verifying baseball records ensures that players, past and present, are properly credited for their performances.

Mr. Palmer has made many contributions to player evaluations. Although On Base Percentage is now commonly applied, it wasn't always so. Due directly to his championing of the stat, it is now available everywhere.

His work with park effects, including the development of park adjustments, was groundbreaking. Today's sabermetricians, including myself, often use the park effect system he developed for the HGB and TB.

His Linear Weights System (LWTS) of player analysis is the most widely used player evaluation method. In particular, the defensive assessment portion of LWTS is the standard for historical comparisons.

I could go on and on. This is just a tip of the Palmer statistical iceberg. If you want to find out more about Pete Palmer's handiwork, I suggest you borrow HGB from your local library, purchase a copy of TB, and/or visit the TB Internet web site at http://www.totalbaseball.com.

Bill James

Quite simply, Bill James is the "Father of Sabermetrics". Without him, who knows where baseball analysis would be today. Even though Pete Palmer's work was also groundbreaking, it was Mr. James' popularization of the genre that made the publication of sabermetric books possible.

Mr. James' style of analysis prodded a multitude of baseball analysts to dig deeper into data and think profoundly about various baseball questions. As with Pete Palmer's work, I could not possibly give Bill James' accomplishments proper credit here. Additionally, since BBBA is a direct descendent, you should be properly familiar with a good deal of his analysis. Instead, I'll re-visit a few elements from his aforementioned "Logic and Methods in Baseball" essay, since many of the points

remain true today, fourteen years later.

General Principles of Sabermetrics

In the essay from the 1984 Bill James Baseball Abstract, James defined several baseball axioms and sabermetric principles. I'll take the liberty of consolidating and slightly updating his list. This is done with great trepidation. I run the risk of offending the sensibilities of sabermetricians everywhere. To some, fiddling with anything done by Mr. James' amounts to sacrilege. Hopefully, these changes won't be met with the same contempt as Dr. Frankenstein's medical breakthroughs.

JIM FURTADO'S REVISED PRINCIPLES OF SABERMETRICS

1. The questions define the methods.

This one is pretty simple, really. In spite of that, it's constantly being violated. I don't know how many times I've seen people use the wrong method to answer a particular question. Using batting average to answer the "Who's the best hitter?" question is the most prevalent example. Another example is using pitcher wins to answer the "Who's the best pitcher?" question. Don't get me wrong, these stats can help us answer these questions, but, used as the sole criteria, they aren't useful.

This error isn't confined to statistical novices. People with substantial backgrounds in mathematics sometimes make the same error. Even prospective sabermetricians occasionally make this mistake. I recently came across such a case. This guy, who shall remain nameless, looked around at the available methods and decided the results didn't match his expectations. He then designed a system that produced results that matched his own subjective sensibilities.

In this instance, the designer didn't think defensive skill was properly credited. As a result, he created a method that placed a high value on players with strong defensive reputations. Unfortunately, he started with the answer and came up the question, rather than the other way around. Imagine his disappointment when his "objective" creation met with criticism. Too bad he didn't understand what "objective" means, or he could have saved himself a lot of time and effort.

2. Baseball is a team game; therefore, players should be evaluated in a team context.

In the original essay, James said. "A ballplayer's purpose in playing baseball is to do things which create wins for his team." He was certainly correct because, as he also said, a player is not in the game to rack up personal accomplishments but to help his team.

Many analysts don't factor in this important truism. Ignoring it is a mistake. The reason is simple: baseball is a complex game where player performances are heavily intertwined. The third baseman waves at a hard grounder; the pitcher is charged with a hit. The pitcher delivers slowly to the plate; a "SB Allowed" is added to the catcher's defensive record. The first baseman makes a great scoop; the shortstop makes the play. The outcome of games hinges on this interaction between players.

We can't possibly design an evaluation system that accounts for every interaction. Even the best simulations can't account for every possible permutation. However, rather than throw up our hands in defeat, we do the best we can with the available data. As long as we continue to incorporate as much information as we can, we inch our way toward our destination.

3. All offense and all defense occurs within a context of outs. (James)

In my mind, the important point to understand about this statement is that the opportunity for the team is not the same as the opportunity for players. For the team, opportunity is tied to outs--the team gets 27 outs. For players, opportunity is tied to plate appearances, times on the bases, and inning in the field. Certainly there is an interaction between the two. If a team's players consume outs at a high rate, the individual players get fewer opportunities to positively impact the team. What's also true is that this interaction isn't always readily apparent. Take the guy who gets on base in the sixth inning, which player(s) benefit? Directly, the other hitters who come up after him in the same inning. Indirectly, the player who gets an additional at bat in the ninth.

4. There are two essential elements of an offense: its ability to create opportunities and its ability to take advantage of those opportunities. (James modified)

In James' original description, getting on base (OBP) defined opportunity, while slugging defined the ability to take advantage of those opportunities. This is close, but slightly off the mark. A player lowers the number of opportunities for his team not only when he is at the plate, but also when he is on the bases. This must be accounted for to accurately assess a player's ability to create additional opportunities for this team.

Slugging Percentage defined the team's ability to take advantage of opportunities in the James' original principle. Again, this is close, but slightly off the mark. Every positive offensive play helps a team. A batter walks, steals second, advances to third on a wild pitch, and then scores on a soft grounder to the second baseman. The players in this example took advantage of the opportunity without a hit. The run they produced is just as valuable as a run driven in by a double.

5. There is a predictable relationship between the number of runs a team scores, the number they allow, and the number of games that they will win. (James)

This ties in with another of James' original axioms: "Wins result from runs scored. Losses result from runs allowed." The bigger the difference between the runs you score and runs you give up, the higher your winning percentage will be. This topic has been covered many times, so you should already be familiar with it.

6. Value is context driven: ability is context neutral.

The genesis for this item is the whole MVP debate. Every season people argue about who the Most Valuable Player is. The biggest point of contention is usually whether the player was on a contender or not. Another sore point is whether situationally dependent stats, such as RBI and Runs, should be factored in. To me, people meld together two different questions: "Who is the Most Valuable Player?" and "Who is the best play-

er?" Although sometimes the answer to both questions is the same, they ask two distinctly different things. While the MVP question is about value, the "best player" question is about ability. Value is context driven; ability is context neutral.

If I want to know who's most valuable, context is important because the value of a player's contribution changes with context. A home run has more value with the bases loaded than with the bases empty. A steal of second base has more value with nobody on than with two outs (you have more opportunities to drive the player in with less than two outs. A run in a 0-0 game has more value than a run in an 11-0 game.

With the changing value of events, it's very important to establish the context of the player's action to properly valuate his performance. Say a player batted with lots of runners on base and drove in an average number of those runners. What would the result be? You guessed it, a lot of RBIs. Say another player batted with relatively few runners on base, but drove in a high percentage of them. What would the result be? Again, a lot of RBIs. Which player's performance has more value? Well, that depends on the context of the production. We need to factor in team context to properly determine the value.

Wins are the currency of value for teams. Therefore, the team with the most wins has the most value. Since team wins are produced by the combined accomplishments of its players, the players' value equal the team's value. This means that two players who make exactly the same contribution do not necessarily have the same value. This greatly complicates answering the whole MVP question.

To illustrate, here's a word problem for you. Two gentlemen (let's call them Player A and Player B) play on two nearly identical teams. Each team scored 800 runs. Each team possessed fielders of exactly the same quality. The difference between the two ball clubs is the quality of the pitching staffs. Team A's pitchers allowed 650 runs, while Team B's pitchers allowed 700 runs. All this resulted in 96 wins for Team A and 91 wins for Team B. If I tell you both players generated 80 runs for their respective teams, does this mean they were equally valuable players?

Considering this is a baseball book rather than a math test, I'll just give you the answer: No, Player A was more valuable. Why? Because in the context he operated in, his runs were more valuableØthey bought more wins. Using a modified version of Pete Palmer's runs to wins formula, I determine it cost 9.97 runs per win in Team A's context $[(10/3)*SQRT((800+650)/162)]$ and 10.14 runs per win in Team B's context $[(10/3)*SQRT((800+700)/162)]$. Player A's 80 runs purchased 8.02 wins while Player B's 80 runs purchased 7.89 wins. Therefore, Player A was more valuable.

Ability, on the other hand, is context neutral. The ability to hit a ball 500 feet is the same whether a player is at Coors Field or at the Astrodome. The fact that the same ball might travel 540 feet at Coors is irrelevant. The change in conditions causes the ball to travel 40 feet farther, not a change in ability. (A non-baseball example of the same concept is weight. Take a 200 pound item on Earth and weigh it on the Moon. What does it weigh? About 32 pounds. The item doesn't change, the conditions do. The change in conditions, gravity in this example, accounts for the difference.)

Since the best player is the player with the most ability, ability is what we should measure to answer the "best player" question. To measure ability, we must first filter out context. Once that's done we can directly compare player in a neutral context-- we can compare their ability.

7. An accurate measure of performance is always to be preferred to a less accurate measure. (James)

This one shouldn't be needed, but it is. There are a lot of stats that aim to evaluate players. Many of them are developed using sound theoretical principles. I've included a few examples of them below. But how do we decide which one is best? Compare how well they correlate with actual run scoring.

8. All else being equal, opt for simplicity.

If two measures do essentially the same thing, choose the easier one to calculate.

O.K., that's enough with the philosophical stuff. Before Jay and I get into our reasons for creating a new evaluation system, I think it would be very useful to examine the design of some current statistics. I'll make the examination both rather broad and brief, since a complete examination would take an entire book.

LOOKING BACK TO GO FORWARD

Knowledge is not created in a vacuum, but, instead, expands on what comes before. With that in mind, it's probably a good idea to know a little about what other evaluation methods are out there. Here's a few of the better efforts. I include references, in case you want to check out what the inventor had to say at the statistic's unveiling.

Rate Stats

1. It's the base that counts

Some analysts look at the game and come to the conclusion that bases gained are what's important. If a player gains more bases than the number of outs he consumes the better he is. Although in the last twenty years many people have worked on developing such systems, the concept was applied to Major League Baseball as far back as the turn of the century. At that time, a man named Travis Hoke began compiling a base grounded system for Branch Rickey and the St. Louis Browns. Although the system stopped being used after two seasons due to the overwhelming burden of computation placed upon Mr. Hoke, it stands as the first time such as system was developed. (Read all about Mr. Hoke's system in Esquire magazine's October 1935 issue or at my web site at *http://www.baseball-stuff.com/btf/pages/essays/rickey/hoke.htm.*

Although I guess on some level the whole concept of evaluating players by comparing bases is true, I don't think it's the best way to go. The goal for an offense is to score runs, not to accumulate bases. Although base stats correlate with runs, the correlation is not as high as the correlation for the stats expressed in estimated runs.

Another problem with these statistics is that they are expressed as rate stats. The problem with rate stats is they don't tell you the aggregate value of a player's performance.

Additionally, the answer you end up with isn't really in a quantity that can be directly converted to wins (like runs). To express these stats in runs, a conversion step is required. Check out the "A Question of Accuracy" essay to see how they compare in this regard.

Anyway, any number of people have designed base counting statistics. Here's a sampling:

Thomas Boswell's Total Average (TA)

$TA = (((1B + (2B \times 2) + (3B \times 3) + (HR \times 4)) + HP + BB + SB) \neq CS) / ((AB - H) + CS + DP)$

Originally from Inside Sports, January 1981. Seasonal lists also appear each preseason in the same publication. Basically, it has total bases plus in the numerator and outs (without SF, SH) in the denominator.

Barry Codell's Base-Out Percentage (BOP)

$BOP = (TB+BB+HBP+SB+SH+SF)/(AB-H+CS+GIDP+SH+SF)$

Find it in the 1979 Baseball Research Journal. In the numerator, all the bases gained by the batter; in the denominator, all the outs accrued.

Mark Pankin's Offensive Performance Average (OPA)

$OPA = [1B + 2*2B + 2.5*3B + 3.5*HR + 0.8*(BB+HP) + 0.5*SB)] / (AB+BB+HB)$

Mark Pankin is a pretty inventive baseball analyst. OPA is one of his attempts to quantify offense. Although OPA was a good swing at player evaluation, the most interesting stuff he's worked on is his Markov chains and baseball line-up studies. Unfortunately for you, I cannot possibly give a brief overview about such complex subjects. If you're interested in learning more about it, you can read about Mark's Markov Models/Batting Order Optimization on the Internet at *http://www.retrosheet.org/mdp/baseball.htm.*

To read more about OPA read the July-August 1978 issue of Operations Research or visit my web site at *http://www.baseballstuff.com/btf/pages/essays/other/opa.htm.*

Bill Gilbert's Bases per Plate Appearance (BPA)

$BPA = (TB + BB + HB + SB - CS - GIDP) / (AB + BB + HB + SF)$

BPA = Bases per Plate Appearance

Find it on the Internet at *http://www.stathead.com/bbeng/gilbert/measoffperf.htm.*

Clay Davenport's Equivalent Average (EQA)

$EQA = 1/3 \times (H + TB + BB + SB) / (AB + CS + (1/3 \times SB) + (2/3 \times BB))$

Base of the Baseball Prospectus player evaluation system. Here's what the designer has to say about EQA, "It is, admittedly, an ugly function. This is partly because it is empirical; it is based not so much on theory but on what actually works. Another reason is due to its evolution: I added more information to the denominator to improve the correlation with run scoring. Placing stolen bases in the denominator is exceptionally odd, but it works to keep the ratings of player from non-caught stealing years in check."

I agree that it's an odd construct. EQA is designed to mirror the batting average range. That, I suppose, is what the 1/3 part is for. Other than that, it's easy to see that it's not really based on theory. Although it does work, it doesn't as well as they purport. But this isn't the place for that discussion.

Find it either in the Baseball Prospectus books or at *http://www.baseballprospectus.com.*

James Tuttle's Base Production (BP)

I can't really give you a description or formula because this statistic's design keeps changing. I correspond with BP's creator, James Tuttle, and promised him I'd include a mention of his work in this article. However, this isn't a "Hi mom!" mention. James is an intelligent guy who has some good thoughts about the process. Unfortunately he's a little unsure about what he wants his brainchild to measure. I include the reference here as a heads-up for the future.

You'll have to do a little detective work on the Internet to find information about this one. Go to *http://www.dejanews.com* and do a search using the following keywords: "James Tuttle", BP, baseball, "base production".

2. Get them on and drive them in

The next few stats are based on the premise that production should be measured by some combination of On Base Percentage (OBP) and Slugging Average (SLG). All the ones listed work pretty well on the team level. Unfortunately, when they are used on the player level, they don't. The reason is simple: a player's slugging does not interact with his ability to get on base. When the lead off hitter gets on base with a walk, it's not his slugging percentage that matters, it's the slugging percentage of the following hitters.

The limitations of the construct show up most when the formula is applied to individual players. Players like Frank Thomas, who usually have a high OBP and a high SLG, get overrated; players like Rey Ordonez, who usually have a low OBP and a low SLG, get underrated (if that's possible). Like I said previously, this limitation was the primary reason I began investigating alternatives. It's also the reason Bill James revised his own RC formula.

Rickey

*Rickey = [(H + BB + HP) / (AB + BB + HP) + 3/4 * (TB - H) / AB + R / (H + BB + HP)]*

*- [H / AB + (BB + HB) / (AB + BB + HP) + ER / (AB + BB + HP) - 1/8 * SO / (AB + BB + HP) - F]= G*

Here's a brief Rickey description, "It is a means of gauging with a high degree of accuracy important factors which contribute to winning and losing baseball games. It is most disconcerting and at the same time the most constructive thing to come into baseball in my memory." He also stated, "The formula is designed principally to gauge and analyze performance on a team basis. But certain elements in it provide a yardstick for measuring individual talent."

Although I include the full version of the formula here, I only evaluate the offensive component (the top half) in the accuracy essay. This part of the formula can be broken into three components:

On Base Average   (H+BB+HP)/(AB+BB+HP)
3/4 times Isolated Power   (TB-H)/AB
Scoring efficiency   R/(H+BB+HP)

This formula was the forebear of many of the equations

over the last thirty years.

Read all about it in Life magazine's August 2, 1954 issue or at the Baseball Stuff web site at: *http://www.baseballstuff.com/btf/pages/essays/rickey/goodby_to_old_idea.htm.*

Earnshaw Cook's Scoring Index (DX)

*DX = [(H+BB+HBP)/(AB+BB+HBP)] * [(TB+SB-CS)/(AB+BB+HBP)]*

One of the ancestors of Bill James' Runs Created. I'm not sure if James was aware of this or not when he created RC but if you compare them you'll see some similarities. Even though the reference I provide is from 1971, Mr. Cook published the first OBP*SLG model sometime in the early 1960's.

Earnshaw Cook fertile mind can examined by reading his two baseball books: Percentage Baseball (1966) and Percentage Baseball and the Computer (1971).

Dick Cramer's Batter Run Average (BRA or OTS)

*BRA = OBP*SLG*

A simple, yet, accurate measure for evaluating team offense. Like the other methods based on this concept. It doesn't work particularly well for individual players.

The original BRA article appeared in the 1972 Baseball Research Journal.

Pete Palmer's On Base Plus Slugging (OPS)

OPS = OBP + SLG

The Cliff Note version of player evaluation. Add together OBP+ SLG and you get a good approximation of player value. Of course, you only get a rate that doesn't include many facets of play. However, what you lose in accuracy is made up in simplicity. Nobody can calculate Extrapolated Wins in their head. Just about everybody can add together OBP+SLG easily. I use this stat quite often myself. If we could only get the networks to do the same, we'd actually get an accurate assessment of players' offensive skills over the television. Maybe, just maybe, we might even get Ray Knight to shut up once and a while.

Do yourself a favor and read The Hidden Game of Baseball(1984) and Total Baseball I-IV.

3. Power of the Run

The greatest advances in sabermetrics took place in the early 1980's through the work done by Bill James and Pete Palmer. I realize my praise of their work may be getting monotonous, but I make no apology for it. No matter how many times I mention them in this essay, I could not possibly give them enough credit.

By far the greatest contribution James and Palmer made to our understanding about the game is their work illustrating the relationship between runs and wins. Although the idea seems simple to grasp, its still not commonly accepted by mainstream baseball. That's unfortunate because James and Palmer clearly established the validity of the concept.

Even though Bill James and Pete Palmer agree on the value of estimated runs generated, they disagree on the process to get there. James based his RC on the OBP*SLG model, while Palmer based his Linear Runs on linear mathematics.

Which do I prefer? Keep reading.

471

4. Rate stat extensions

Essentially, the next few formulas are descendents of one of the rate stats that I noted above. Both RC formulas are descendents of the OBP*SLG model. EqR is an extension of EqA. They each inherit the limitations of their progenitors. They each try to work around their defects with a twist. This twist adds an additional level of complexity to the model without completely fixing the problem.

James' Runs Created (RC)

Basic RC = (H + W) * TB / (AB + BB)

RC-Tech1 = (H + HB - GIDP - CS) * [TB + ((W + HB - IBB)*.26) + ((SB+SH+SF)*.52)] / (AB + W + HB + SH + SF)

RC-HDG23 = A * B / C

A = (H + HB - GIDP - CS)

B = [TB + ((W + HB - IBB)*.29) + (SB*.64) + ((SH+SF)*.53)-(.03*K)]

C = (AB + W + HB + SH + SF)

I included only three versions of the formula: 1) the original Basic version, 2) the classic Tech-1 version, and 3) the new Historical Data Group-23 version (which is the used for 1955-1987). I could have included all 6,313,659 versions, but I doubt you would have paid $100 for this book. OK, I am being sarcastic. There aren't 6,313,659 versions; it just seems like it. In reality, there are just 24 new versions. The 14 old versions from the Historical Abstract are no longer needed.

Unfortunately, there is still another step needed to generate the new RC numbers. What you still need to do is apply what I call the fudge factor. I hope you have a sweet tooth.

To calculate individual player RC, you have to place the player stats into "a theoretical team context consisting of players with average skills and eight times as many plate appearances as the subject". I warn you it won't be easy.

Take the above A,B,C factors and place them into the following equation.

[((A + (2.4*C)) * (B + (3*C))] / 9 * C minus 0.9 * C

What does all this do for you? Well, it helps to minimize the errors caused by the inappropriate design of RC, namely, that the formula is designed to work on a team basis, not an individual player basis.

You may be wondering, "Does this work?" Well, yes and no. Yes, it does cut down on the error; no, it doesn't get rid of the error. But this isn't really the place for this discussion. If you want to read more about James' changes to RC, read Deciphering the New Runs Created where we tackle the discussion head on and in detail.

Oh yeah, I almost forgot. From 1988-1998 Bill James incorporates situational batting. You may want to know exactly how he does this. Join the club. Bill's keeping the details of this change under wraps.

Dick Cramer's RC (Runs Contributed)

R = [(H+BB+HBP) + (0.5 * SB) - CS - (1.5*GIDP)] * SLG

In the 1987 The Great American Baseball Stat Book, Dick Cramer presented his own RC formula. It's a twist on the OBP*SLG model. Unfortunately, the design flaws still are apparent. Mr. Cramer tried to get around the flaws by introducing a new twist. "Runs Contributed, computed as the difference in the number of runs the overall league would have scored if [the] player's batting totals had first been subtracted from the league totals."

Clay Davenport's Equivalent Runs (EQR)

EqR = (2 x RawEqA/LgEqA - 1) x (R/(AB+BB))league x (AB+BB)individual

Above I presented Davenport's EQA. I also stated that rate stats need an additional step to be expressed in runs. This is Davenport's step. I don't particularly care for the construct. The introduction of actual Runs into the equation is faulty. If the goal is to predict runs from the various events, you should not use actual Runs as part of the process. The problem is called circular reasoning--which essentially means using the answer to get the answer. Let me illustrate with an example.

Let's say the league EqA is .250 and the league scores 1000 runs in 6000 plate appearances. Say in 600 PA, the batter also produces an EqA of .250. How many EqR would he generate?

Since his EqA is the same as the league's, we can calculate it like this: 600/6000*1000 = 100. What this really means is that if you have a player with the same EqA as the league, all you have to do is figure what percentage of the league's PA he had, then multiply it by the league's runs. If a player has 10% of the league's PA, he gets credited with 10% of the league's runs. That doesn't feel quite right to me. Calculating player runs in this manner artificially increases the accuracy reading of EqA. In my Accuracy essay, I calculate EqR using Clay's method and also using the method I use to calculate runs for all the other rate stats. You can decide for yourself which one is correct.

5. Follow the linear brick road

People have tried to place a value on the various events since the year 1 A.B. (After Baseball). As time went on, the attempts evolved. Finally the light bulb went on and analysts realized that the value of events should be evaluated by how they relate to run scoring. Sabermetricians then employed different means to try and come up with the most accurate numbers. You'll soon be introduced to the result: Extrapolated Runs.

Lindsey Additive Formula

.41*1B+.82*2B+1.06*3B+1.42*HR

According to HGB and my own research, in 1963 an analyst named George Lindsey's became "the first to assign run values to the various offensive events which lead to runs. He based these values on recorded play-by-play data and basic probability theory." Although the values determined by Lindsey aren't quite right, as you'll see, they are in the ball park. All and all, though, an excellent effort and discovery.

From "An Investigation of Strategies in Baseball" in the July-August 1963 issue of Operations Research.

Pete Palmer's Batting Runs (BR)

Runs = 1B*.47 + 2B*.78 + 3B*1.09 + HR*1.40 + (BB+HB)*.33 -(AB-H)*?? - OOB*.50

OOB = H + BB + HB - Left On Base - R - CS

?? = Out coefficient determined so that the sum of the other events (for the league) equal zero.

Although I discuss Palmer's work below and in my Extrapolated Runs essay, I'd like to say a few things here about the foundation of his system.

First, using the out value to establish the baseline was a mistake. This decision restricts the usefulness of the formula. Instead of being expressed directly in runs, another step is required. That's not to say that this lessens the accuracy of the measure; it doesn't. However, the decision does limit BR use to the task it was designed for.

Second, the inclusion of the OOB only clouds the accuracy issue. Since OOB can't be used in the evaluation of individual players, it shouldn't be included. I didn't fully understand this idea myself until this fact was pointed out to me by one of the Internet's best baseball minds, David Grabiner. David was gracious enough to provide feedback on the design of XR.

During the process, I thought about including a similar term in my own formula. However, one of David's comments, "If you are trying to use a statistic to evaluate individual players, its reliability depends only on the reliability of that part of the team statistic which can be obtained from the individual statistics." helped change my mind. If sabermetricians wish to claim accuracy for a measure, they must keep this idea in mind.

Steve Mann's RPA

$RPA=(BB*.25+HBP*.29+1B*.51+2B*.82+3B*1.38+HR*2.63+SB*.15-CS*.28)*.52 + (BB+HBP+AB)*.008 + 3*((BB+HBP+AB)/6200)*1000*(OBP-.330)$

First version appeared in 1977. This updated version appeared in Baseball Superstats 1989 by Mann and Malling.

Paul Johnson's Estimated Runs Produced (ERP)

$ERP = (2*(TB+BB+HP)+H+SB- (.605*(AB+CS+GIDP-H)))*.16$

or

$ERP = (1B*.48) + (2B*.80) + (3B*1.12) + (HR*1.44) + ((HP+BB)*.32)+(SB*.16) - (OUTS*.10)$

$OUTS = AB+CS+GIDP-H$

New Estimated Runs Produced (NERP) = $(TB/3.15) + ((BB-IBB+HBP-CS-GDP)/3) + (H/4) + (SB/5) - (AB/11.75)$

or

$NERP = TB*.318 + ((BB-IBB+HBP-CS-GDP)*.333) + (H*.25) + (SB*.200) - (AB*.085)$

The original version first appeared in the 1985 Bill James Baseball Abstract. It was also used in last year's version of BBBA.

The revised version appeared in STATS 1991 Baseball Scoreboard. I didn't notice this when I originally read the book. Thankfully, around the time I started writing this article, a kindly visitor to my web site named David Smith passed along the updated formula.

6. Runs through Regression Analysis

Paraphrasing one of my math texts, I define regression as the process of estimating the value of a dependent variable, Runs, from one or more independent variables, 1B, 2B, 3B, etc.

Of course, the mathematical principles and methods required to generate the estimates are a lot more complex than can be described in one sentence. But rather than spend a bunch of space trying to describe the process, I explain it simply as the application of mathematical methods to generate the best possible run values for each offensive event.

Quite a few people have used the process to generate estimates. Although the values do fluctuate based on the events

and seasons used in the studies, you should notice that the numbers don't really vary much.

Jay Bennett and John Flueck's (ERP)

Expected Run Production = $(.499 \times 1B) + (.728 \times 2B) + (1.265 \times 3B) + (1.449 \times HR) + (.353 \times BB) + (.362 * HBP) + (.126 \times SB) + (.394 \times SF) - (.395 \times GIDP) - (.085 \times OUT) - 67$

$OUT = AB-HIT-GIDP$

Data from 1969-1997 seasons (192 teams).
From The American Statistician. February, 1983.

Alidad Tash

$RS = 1B*.507 + 2B*.658 + 3B*.906 + HR*1.447 + (BB+HBP)*.314 + SB*.145 - CS*.234 + LG*7.26 + SF*.594 + OUT*-.098 + GIDP*-.402 +SH*-.024 + SO*-.013$

$OUTS = AB - (H+SH+SF+CS+GIDP)$

Data from 1973-1997 seasons (652 teams).
From "Win and Run Prediction in Major League Baseball" at *http://www.baseballstuff.com/btf/pages/essays/other/tash.htm.*

Jefferson Glapski

$R = 1B*.50451 + 2B*.71574 +3B*0.99951 + HR*1.4228 + BB*.32052 - SO*.087327 + SB*.20291 - CS* 0.15383 -OUTS*0.098929 - LG*8.1139L$

$OUTS = AB - H - SO$

Lg = league (1=National League, 0 if American League)
Data from 1974-1990 seasons (460 teams).
Full text of study can be found at http://home.ican.net/~jng/sabr001.htm.

John Jarvis

$OUTS*-0.0971 + 1B*0.4222 + 2B*0.6369 + 3B*0.8816 + HR*1.49 + (BB+HP)*0.3098 + IBB*-0.0211 + SB*0.0737 + ROH*-0.0902 + GIDP*-0.3669 + ER\_BF*0.6662 + ER\_RA*0.4061 + RAO*0.0637 + RSO*0.7442 + K*-0.0916$

ROH = Runners Out on Hit (either base runners or the batter trying unsuccessfully for an additional base)
RAO = Runner Advance on Out (includes the traditional sacrifice)
RSO = Runs Scored on an Out

ER_BF and ER_RA are the number of times the batter is safe on first and the number of times a runner was able to advance on an error.

The OUT category includes outs that are not counted in other categories (CS, ROH, second out on a GDP, K).

Using play-by-play data, John included many new parameters in his equation. Consider this a look into the future. At some point, I'd like to incorporate some of John's ideas into a future super-advanced version of XR.

Data from 1967 AL and for both leagues in the 1980-1986, and 1992-1996 (360 teams).

From "A Survey of Baseball Player Performance Evaluation Measures" at *http://pacer1.usca.sc.edu/~jfj/runs_survey.html*

7. The Whole Enchilada
Offensive Wins Above Replacement (OWAR)

The system previously used in this book to evaluate players.

Palmer's Linear Weights System (LWTS)

The most popular player evaluation system. Due to its inclusion in Total Baseball and its all encompassing design, this method is a big hit with knowledgeable baseball fans. LWTS factors in batting, pitching, and fielding while adjusting for park, position, and era. Although the primary values are based on Palmer's Batting Runs, he also devised a method for incorporating defense and pitching. The end result is that anyone can pull out the book and compare Barry Bonds' 1996 performance with Ty Cobb's 1917 season. (They both accounted for 8.5 wins above average.) Anyone can also find out who the most valuable players of all time are. (No surprise, Babe Ruth is at the top with 107.7 wins. Nap Lajoie comes up a distant second with 94.2 wins. Sorry, you'll have to buy or borrow the book for the rest of the list.) All in all, the LWTS method is an intelligent look at baseball history.

Unfortunately, although I like LWTS and applaud the effort of Pete Palmer, I disagree with a few of his design decisions. First, the baseline is too high. From TB, "The Linear Weights measure of runs contributed beyond those of a league-average batter or team, such league average defined as zero."

Average is the baseline. That's too high. Average players have value. I won't get into the whole replacement level concept here, but average players help teams win pennants. No team can have a superstar at every position. But if it can put together a few stars with a bunch of average players they're in the hunt for a title. On the other hand, put those same stars on a team with a bunch of stiffs and they're an also-ran.

Although this isn't a very complicated concept, so many people still don't get it. To those people I ask this question: Who was more valuable during the 1986 season, Ray Knight or yours truly?

Ray played fairly well in '86. He wasn't a superstar or anything, but he put together a solid year hitting .298 with a .357 OBP and a .424 SLG in 486 AB. What does LWTS have to say about him? Ray Knight's Total Player Rating (TPR) for 1986 is -0.2 wins. This makes him pretty much an average player.

How did I fare in 1986? About average, I guess since I produced 0.0 wins. Now, before you start leafing through your copy of TB looking for my batting line, I'll tell you why I produced 0.0 wins--I didn't play in the majors that year. As a matter of fact, I never have played professional ball. Nevertheless, that didn't stop me from having a higher TPR in 1986 than Ray Knight did.

Of course, my argument is faulty. LWTS is designed to compare players who actually played. If we lowered the baseline, I'd still have a higher rating than a lot of players who, in reality, are a heck of a lot better than I am. So instead of comparing Ray to myself, let's compare Ray to someone who actually played-- Steve Kemp. What's Kemp's TPR rating? +0.1 wins. Since +0.1 > -0.2, a comparison of TPRs would indicate Kemp had a better season. Let's take a look at their numbers:

Name	AVG	OBP	SLG	AB	R	H	2B	3B	HR	RBI
Ray Knight	.298	.351	.424	486	51	145	24	2	11	76
Steve Kemp	.188	.350	.375	16	1	3	0	0	1	1

I think you'll agree with me that Knight was the more productive player in 1986. This points out the fatal flaw of using

average as the baseline. It greatly undervalues the contributions of average players. That's why Bill James invented the concept of the replacement player. That's also why Palmer's baseline is too high.

Another design decision I disagree with is the decision to incorporate positional adjustments in the batting component of the TPR. As Bill James said, players do not come to the plate as first baseman, second baseman or catchers, they come to the plate as hitters. All the runs they generate go into one pool. By comparing players position-by-position, what happens is the runs a shortstop produces end up looking better than the runs a first baseman produces. That's just not true. All the runs are equally valuable.

This problem is compounded further when defensive runs are added to Batting Runs. Skill position players, especially those who compete in eras with a low level of offense at their position, end up getting extra credit for their position. First, they get the benefit of being compared to a lower class of hitter. Second, they get extra fielding runs for playing a more active position. This doesn't make sense to me.

Keith Woolner's Value Over Replacement Player (VORP)/ David M. Tate's Marginal Lineup Value (MLV)

Here's Keith's own brief descriptions of VORP and MLV: "VORP measures how many runs a player would contribute to a league average team compared to a replacement level player at the same position who was given the same percentage of team plate appearances as the original player had. VORP, in its most advanced form, uses MLV to estimate the change in team run scoring attributable to the player's performance.

Marginal Lineup Value corrects the shortcomings of using RC for individual players by estimating how many additional runs an average team scores if you replace an average batter with the individual. This eliminates the 'batting yourself in' flaw in individual RC, and correctly estimates the impact of the extra team plate appearances a player creates with a high OBP. "

Although I don't agree with Keith's inclusion of offensive positional adjustments, I think his work deserves attention for some other ideas. First, his method of calculating replacement value is interesting. Second, his use of David M. Tate's MLV incorporates an element of play which has not been properly factored into to player evaluation formulas--if a player avoids making an out, other players (and the team) get more opportunities. David Tate was the first person to try factor in this component of run scoring. Unfortunately, although the MLV idea is a step in the right direction, I don't think it goes far enough.

A full description of VORP, MLV, and replacement value is available at the Stathead Baseball Engineering web site at *http://www.stathead.com.*

8. Lurking in the shadows

Not every sabermetrician's work can be fully enjoyed by the public. Many people with sabermetric knowledge are either current or past employees of professional baseball. Among others, the list includes Eddie Epstein, Mike Gimbel, and Craig Wright. Unfortunately, since their employers consider it in their best interests to keep the stuff proprietary, we all miss out.

DECIPHERING THE NEW RUNS CREATED

JIM FURTADO with G. JAY WALKER & DON MALCOLM

You attended the gala celebration at its release. You watched people fight over it on Jerry Springer. You watched the two-hour Dateline special discussing its impact. You participated in focus groups that discussed its construct. But you're still thinking, **"What does Bill James' new Runs Created (RC) formula actually do?"**

OK, maybe none of this is true. Maybe you didn't fork out the $79.95 to read a little about it in either of the new STATS, Inc. books The All-Time Baseball Sourcebook or The All-Time Baseball Handbook. Maybe, just maybe, you haven't seen anything at all about the new RC. In any case, you still may be wondering what changes Bill James made to his creation and how it works. If so, read on.

The new RC-a big improvement or a big disappointment?

While the RC method is one of the seminal developments in sabermetric history, it soon became apparent that there was a problem with the original RC construct. Bill James himself commented on its deficiencies in his 1985 Baseball Abstract: "I've known for a little over a year that the runs created formula had a problem with players who combined high on-base percentages and high slugging percentages ... The reasons that this happens is that the players' individual totals do not occur in an individual context". He went on to say, "I'll make some adjustments to the runs created formula within the next year or so. Right now, I don't know what they will be." That was fourteen years ago. If Bill intended to raise the level of anticipation for the changes, he certainly gave himself plenty of time.

Beyond the question of how much or little the new RC formula is an improvement over the old one, the work would have to be labeled a disappointment to many readers for the simple reason that Bill did not much explain his thought process behind the modifications, or for that matter even supply enough details so that others could easily replicate his work. He barely provided any justification for his changes themselves. Coming from the man who almost single-handedly broke the Elias monopoly on baseball information, it was disturbing to see him pitch his tent awfully close to those in the sabermetric community who fail to divulge the details of their methods or the thinking behind them in the name of propriety.

There is a rumor that Bill James will be releasing an update to his Historical Abstract sometime in 1999/2000. Maybe he figures he can explain the changes in more detail in the updated book. Without more information from Bill himself, we're left to speculate Speculate about how he came up with the changed formula. Speculate why he incorporated situational statistics. Speculate why—after criticizing Pete Palmer for using actual runs in Linear Weights—he now factors actual runs so much into the revised formula.

Rather than just make wild guesses, however, we undertook an involved examination of the new RC methodology, and then spent a lot of time discussing among ourselves the possible reasons behind the changes. Of course, we didn't always agree. That happens when people are put in the position to guess what someone else is thinking.

How is the new RC calculated?

I'll run through the new RC calculations using Ken Griffey's 1998 statistics as an example. This is appropriate because Bill James used Ken Griffey's 1997 stats for the descriptions in both of the new stats books. The big difference between James' description and this one is that we'll fully explain the parts he glossed over. We'll also comment on the changes.

Step 1   Calculate the A, B and C Factors

Figured just about the same way as James' classic tech version of the formula. The only difference is that James changes some of the terms depending on the availability of the data and the time period of the season in question. For the current time period (1988 to present), the Historical Data Group (HDG) 24 formula is used.

Calculate the A, B, and C terms as follows:

A = (H+ BB + HP - GIDP - CS)

B = [TB + ((BB + HB - IBB)*.24) + (SB*.62) + ((SH + SF)*.5)-(SO*.03)]

C = (AB + BB + HB + SH + SF)

For Ken Griffey Jr.:

A = (180 + 76 + 7 - 14 - 5) = 244

B = [387 + ((76 + 7 - 11) * .24) + (20 * .62) + ((0 + 4)*.5) + (121*-.03)) = 415.05

C = (633 + 76 + 7 + 0 + 4) = 720

If things were still calculated the classic way, we'd simply calculate Griffey's RC by A*B / C. This would give us what I call Griffey's "base H24". Putting the numbers together would give us 140.66 RC.

? **What Does this Do?** - This is the classic RC construct with a couple of minor changes. James slightly modified the "B" term. For comparison, the classic Tech-1 version's B factor looked like this: (TB+((BB+HBP-IBB)*.26)+((SF+SH+SB)*.52)). James also splintered SB off from SF+SH and then slightly changed the coefficient. The biggest change to this part of the calculation, however, was the addition of a term for strikeouts. This is an area of great debate among sabermetricians. My own research agrees with this adjustment. I found that although the difference between regular outs and strikeouts is rather small (-.008 for Extrapolated Runs), it is nonetheless something that should be included in run estimation formulas.

Step 2 - Calculate initial Runs Created (iRC) by inserting A, B, and C factors into theoretical team context and round off the result:

$$RC = [((A + (2.4*C)) * (B + (3*C)))/ (9*C)] - .9 * C$$

Griffey iRC = [((244+ (2.4*720)) * (415.05+(3*720)))/
(9*720)] - .9 * 720 = 135.64 or 136 iRC

Two additional things that happen here is **1)** iRC gets rounded into a whole number **2)** any negative results for individual players get changed to 0.

? **What Does this Do?** -This has been one of the most talked about changes to the new RC. Bill James describes this step as, "The runs created for each individual are now figured in a 'theoretical team' context, rather that assuming, as I did before, that an individual's offensive contributions interacted with one another. "

What do we think? Well, I had yet to hook up with the BBBA boys when the changes were made public, so while I was trying to decipher this step on the East Coast, Jay Walker was doing the same thing on the West Coast. In hindsight, that was a very good thing. Why? Because Jay and I took slightly different looks at this construct and came to different conclusions. Jay looked at the new construct and tried thinking along with Bill James. I looked at the construct and tried to see if I could separate the formula into two distinct parts 1) the original A*B/C construct and 2) a kludge factor. The interesting thing, though, is that both of our conclusions were correct.

What did Jay come up with? He came up with two expressions, Part 1 and Part 2.

Part 1 - ((A + 8*.300*C) * (B + 8*.375*C)) / (9*C)
Part 2 - ((8*.300*C) * (8*.375*C)) / (8*C)

Subtracting Part 2 from Part 1 not only gives the same results as James' calculation, but it can be shown algebraically that it is in fact James' equation, merely expressed in a different way.

With a bit of scrutiny of these two expressions, it becomes fairly obvious what Bill was trying to do. For simplicity, let's call Factor A, the on-base factor, which is similar to, but slightly different from the on-base average. In a similar manner, we'll call Factor B the slugging factor and Factor C the plate appearance factor. For his team context, Bill assumes you're on some sort of team with eight other players, and each of these eight players has an on-base factor of .300 and a slugging factor of .375. The Part 2 expression above is equal to the number of runs created that this team of eight players would produce, assuming each had the same number of plate appearances as you did. The Part 1 expression is the number of runs created that this team of eight players would produce with you added to the team. Subtract Part 2 from Part 1, and you get the number of runs created the team produces with you, minus the number they produce without you. The result is the runs that you create while in a team context.

While this is a fairly innovative technique, it also begs a number of questions. First, how were the .300 and .375 factors

derived? What kind of analysis went into deciding that these were the numbers to use? And given the preciseness of the coefficients in the various RC formulas, why are these numbers so rounded off? Might something like .302 and .374 be better choices? Or did .300 and .375 just happen to be the best? Second, what exactly do the .300 and .375 represent? Are the meant to be the numbers for an average team, a replacement team or something in between? Third, why are the .300 and .375 applied globally across all eras? Surely a representative on-base factor and slugging factor have varied over time? Or has this change over time already been factored into the coefficients of the RC formulas? Finally, why one could well imagine the Bill James of the 1980s presenting his formula in an understandable manner and explaining what it does and how it was derived, why does the Bill James of the late 90s camouflage his formula in such a way as to make his methods and purposes incomprehensible to most of his readers?

As I mentioned above I looked at the formula and came up with a different view of the calculation. My algebraic manipulations led to this:

$$[1/9* ((A*B)/C)] + [A/3 + 0.8*B/3 - 0.1*C]$$

Admittedly, this doesn't look that interesting at first glance. The bracketed part is the classic RC formula multiplied by 1/9. The second bracketed doesn't look like it makes much sense when I first examined it, but finally, it hit me. The second part is really just a linear formula dressed up in unfamiliar clothing. If you take the time to break it down like I did, you'll find that the second part equals (for Historical Data Group 24):

8/9 * [.5625*1B +.8625*2B +1.1625*3B + 1.4625*HR + .3345*(BB+HP-IBB) + .2625*IBB +.186*SB - .375*(CS+DP) +.0375*(SH+SF) -.1125*(AB-H-SO) - .1215*SO]

So the second part is really just 8/9th times a linear formula, which looks a lot like the Extrapolated Runs formula with different coefficients. What all this essentially means is that Bill James' new "team construct" is really just 1/9th of the classic Runs Created plus 8/9th of a linear formula. So in one sense you could say that since Bill is already up to his neck in the linear pool, he might as well get his hair wet. What's interesting is that he had previously stated when talking about Paul Johnson's Estimated Runs linear formula, "...there probably are compromises between the two methods that will prove to be yet more accurate than either method."

While I agree that the "West Coast" version accurately reflects Bill James' intentions in developing his team adjustment, my discovery is still very interesting. Bill James' work has led him to calculate player RC values that are 89% linear. This change has greatly increased the accuracy of RC on the player level. However, it still doesn't make them as accurate as Extrapolated Runs, a 100% American-made linear formula.

Step 3 Calculate the adjustment for home runs with runners on base

The first situational adjustment in the new RC method is made for how many home runs Griffey Jr. hits with runners on base. This is another adjustment that Bill James didn't fully explain. We need four bits of information for Griffey to do this adjustment:

1 Total AB = 633
2 AB with runners on base = 303
3 Total HR = 56
4 HR with runners on base = 26

Then calculate how many HRs Griffey would be expected to hit with runners on base, proportional to his AB.

Expected HRs = $(303/633*56) = 26.81$

Subtract Expected HR from actual HR with runners on base and round the result

$26 - 26.81 = -.81 \text{ or } -1$

This leaves Griffey with an adjustment for home runs with runners on base (HR-ROB) of -1.

Step 4   Calculate the adjustment for batting average
           with runners in scoring position
The information we need here is Griffey's regular batting average and his batting average with runners in scoring position. It's suggested you carry out this calculation to an extra decimal place.
Regular Batting = 180 hits / 633 at bats or .2844
Batting with runners in scoring position = 57 hits / 184 at
                                    bats or .3098
Subtract regular batting from batting with runners in scoring position, multiply the result times at bats with runners in scoring position, and round the result.

$(.3098-.2844)*184 = 4.674 \text{ or } 5$

This gives Griffey an adjustment for batting with runners in scoring position (AvgSP) or +5

?   What Does this Do? - whether or not to use
           situational stats is a point that has been debated by sabermetricians for years. Bill James' introduction of situational stats represents a major philosophical departure from anything he's previously done with his RC methods. The only justification he gives for now using situational stats is that their use "substantially reduces the standard error of team runs created estimates". This seems close to becoming his sole criteria for deciding what does and doesn't get included in the RC methodology.

This issue of whether to use situational stats really boils down to all the old arguments about clutch hitting. Does it exist? If it does, then why do some players hit better in the clutch? For those that do, does laziness or attitude cause them to perform less well in routine situations? And if so, how valuable are they really? There was a time when Bill expressed serious doubts about whether clutch hitters really existed, or if good and poor clutch hitting performances merely represented random fluctuations.

Regardless of his reasons for deciding to take his RC method down the situational path, James' choice of clutch-hitting stats, or in particular, his selection homers with runners on base, is curious. For any given player, that stat is highly dependent on the ability of the teammates who bat before him in the batting order to get on base. This introduces a whole subjective element to the RC method. If James chose not to use runs or

RBIs in previous versions of the RC methodology because of their subjective nature, why is he now bringing in these subjective stats?

There is no absolute truth about whether situational stats should be used in measuring offensive performance. However, there are certain questions to consider. They tie-in with the whole idea of framing a question properly and then choosing the proper methodology to answer that question. The original RC was the foundation of the answer to the "Who's best?" question. RC estimated the number of runs a player would create in a standard context. Although this context included park effects, James' later accounted for them by the Offensive Winning Percentage component of his evaluation method. The end result of his full method was a context free comparison of players.

Is James trying to answer a different question with his new RC methodology? If so, which one? It doesn't really answer the "Who's best?" question anymore with the inclusion of his situational stats plus a reconciliation step (discussed later), which introduce a subjective bias. Is he trying to answer the "Who's most valuable" question? Bill leaves us no clue as to what was behind this major philosophical switch, only that he wanted to "substantially reduce(s) the standard error of team runs created estimates". Maybe that's all there was - we don't know.

Step 5 - Calculate the Preliminary RC (PrelimRC)
Add together Griffey's initial Runs Created total with the situational adjustments to get his preliminary RC:
           PrelimRC $= iRC + HR\text{-}ROB + AvgSP$
           PrelimRC = $136 \ -1 + 5 = 140$

?   What Does this Do? - this step is rudimentary,
           other than to note that if you're in the camp that desires to have a context-free measure of offense, this contaminates it with situational adjustments.

Step 6   Calculate the team reconciliation factor
           After calculating PrelimRC for all players, sum all the rounded individual players' PrelimRC.
The 1998 Mariners PrelimRCs add up to 892 PrelimRC.
Divide the actual team runs (859) by the team PrelimRC (892) to calculate reconciliation factor (RF):
           1998 Mariners RF = $859 / 892 = .963$

?   What Does this Do? - if reducing the standard
           error of team runs created estimates is to your mind the only way to measure the worth of your offensive performance measure, then this becomes the perfect solution . Just reconcile the RC values of all the players on the team to the number of runs scored by the team and voila! - your standard error estimates are all reduced to zero. Can't do much better than that. If the glove don't fit, just plain force it.

This can be regarded as pretty much of a copout, an attempt to get all your numbers to balance, to reduce your error % and to try and skirt around the inadequacies of the model.

One of my sons once used a similar approach to solve a very different problem. Unable to find a pentagon-shaped hole on his toy, my son tried to use a toy hammer to force the pentagon-shaped peg into a round hole. When I saw him trying to do this, I spent a little time showing him why this wasn't a good idea. Of course, I can understand why he tried to fit it with his hammer. The shapes were pretty much the same. After looking over the other holes on the ball, he decided the circle hole was the only possible place to insert the ball. When it didn't fit quite right, he gave it a little help with his hammer. In his mind, this was the only available option.

Unfortunately, this appears to be the same conclusion Bill came up with. The BBBA crew and I prefer a different course. We'll keep looking for the right hole.

Step 7 Multiply team reconciliation factor times individual player's PrelimRC and round off to get the final RC result:
For Griffey, 140 PrelimRC * .963 = 134.82 or 135 Runs Created for 1998.

? What Does this Do? - beyond our criticism of
this method to force your run estimates to match the actual runs score, the application of the method introduces all kinds of subjective biases to your results. The 1998 Mariners had a 33-run shortfall between their runs scored and their summed up RC estimates. Who's to say how this shortfall should be distributed? Griffey absorbs 5 runs of the 33-run shortfall? Even if you believe you have to stick this shortfall on someone (and we don't) who's to say whether Griffey shouldn't instead absorb 10 runs of the shortfall? Or maybe Griffey should actually be credited with 2 additional RC and his teammates be left to absorb a 35-run shortfall instead of the 33 runs. It's all a guessing game. Read on...

Step 8 Reconciliation or incorporating the error for teams into player values.

Does new theoretical team context do what it's supposed to?
The team reconciliation process done in Steps 6 and 7 is the part of James' changes that we question the most. Here's what Bill James has to say about this part of the process:
"Finally, we reconciled runs created, after the fact, with the runs actually scored by the team. Suppose, for example, that the individual runs created estimates for the members of a team were to total up to 500, but the team actually scored 700 runs. This would be an extraordinary thing, and I don't think such a discrepancy has ever actually happened. We're ordinarily talking about an adjustment in the range of 20 runs per team, or two runs per player. But if it did happen, we would then increase the runs created for each individual on the team by 40%, since 700 divided by 500 is 1.4. We don't know who created these extra runs, but somebody on the team certainly did. The best we can do is distribute them among the hitters proportional to their accomplishments."
Is Bill correct about the error rate of the formula? Well, the average absolute error for all teams from 1984-1997 is about 20 runs. The range of errors is much broader however.

The biggest error for the formula during that time period is the +74 error for the 1987 Cubs. Since the Cubs scored 720 runs that season and the formula projects 794 runs, the formula overestimates by 10.2%. Who does the team reconciliation affect the most? Andre Dawson. Dawson loses 10 runs to "reconciliation". Instead of being credited with 110 runs, "The Hawk" gets credit for only 100.

Is this really fair? Did Andre's play generate less than the 110 runs the formula estimates? We don't know for sure, so it's not fair to penalize him. What's the point? Does subtracting the ten runs tell us something about Andre Dawson? No. The fact that the formula overestimates tells us that his team was less efficient than an average team, not that Andre was less efficient.

To further illustrate, let's look at the other extreme from the same season. The largest negative error for the 1987 National League belonged to the Cardinals. The Cardinals scored 798 runs enroute to the 1987 World Series title, while the Cardinal player's are estimated to have 755 RC, an error of -43 runs. To account for this discrepancy 43 runs must be added to the player totals.

Which player benefits the most from this largesse? Jack Clark. Clark gets credited with 124 runs instead of 117 runs. Again, is this fair? No. The fact that the formula underestimates tells us that Clark's team was more efficient than the average team, not that Jack was more efficient.

The end result of this "reconciliation" is that Jack Clark ends up with 24 more runs created than Andre Dawson. Compare this to the original difference of 7 runs (Dawson 110, Clark 117). The spread between the players is widened. Unfortunately this is due to the inaccuracy of the formula, not due to any quantifiable difference between them.

Remember we're looking for objective evidence. Is this so much different from looking at the numbers and fiddling with them? Another subjective method to divvy up the extra runs could be to guess who generated the runs. I could say, "Jack Clark is so awesome with all those slap-hitting single hitters around him, he must have created more runs than 117. Give him the extra 23 runs. He's the best!" Or I could base my reconciliation on the number of plate appearances. Is James' reconciliation really much different? Essentially what he says is that if a player accounts for 10% of the RC projection, then the player creates 10% of run overestimate or shortfall. It's just one of a number of subjective criteria that could be applied.

This problem is compounded when the situational adjustments are factored in. To illustrate, I present the data from the 1998 Seattle

SEATTLE	RC-H24	HR adj	Avg adj	PreRC	RC Book
RICH AMARAL	18	1	-4	15	14
DAVID BELL	11	0	-1	10	10
JAY BUHNER	40	2	2	44	42
JOEY CORA	79	-1	-10	68	65
RUSS DAVIS	66	0	4	70	67
ROB DUCEY	30	-1	0	29	28
CHARLES GIPSON	4	0	1	5	5
KEN GRIFFEY	136	-1	5	140	135
CARLOS GUILLEN	7	0	3	10	10
GLENALLEN HILL	40	-1	-5	34	33
RAUL IBANEZ	10	-1	0	9	9
EDGAR MARTINEZ	130	-1	-1	128	123
JOHN MARZANO	17	-1	-1	15	14
DAVID McCARTY	4	1	0	5	5
SHANE MONAHAN	19	0	1	20	19
JOE OLIVER	8	0	2	10	10
ROBERT PEREZ	2	0	1	3	3
RYAN RADMANOVICH	6	0	0	6	6
ALEX RODRIGUEZ	135	-4	5	136	131
RICO ROSSY	6	0	-1	5	5
DAVID SEGUI	89	-4	-3	82	79
RICK WILKINS	3	1	-2	2	2
DAN WILSON	40	2	-1	41	39
Totals	905	-8	-5	892	859

OAKLAND	RC-H24	HR adj	Avg adj	PreRC	RC Book
RICH AMARAL	18	1	-4	15	14
DAVID BELL	11	0	-1	10	10
JAY BUHNER	40	2	2	44	42
MARK BELLHORN	1	0	1	2	2
MIKE BLOWERS	46	1	7	54	57
RAFAEL BOURNIGAL	15	1	-1	15	16
ERIC CHAVEZ	7	0	2	9	9
RYAN CHRISTENSON	45	-2	2	45	47
JASON GIAMBI	103	1	2	106	111
BEN GRIEVE	101	1	0	102	107
RICKEY HENDERSON	89	0	6	95	99
A.J. HINCH	36	-2	-2	32	34
MIKE MACFARLANE	26	1	-3	24	25
DAVE MAGADAN	17	0	3	20	21
JASON MCDONALD	23	0	-2	21	22
KEVIN MITCHELL	11	0	4	15	16
BIP ROBERTS	23	1	0	24	25
SCOTT SPIEZIO	50	0	-2	48	50
MATT STAIRS	96	0	0	96	101
MIGUEL TEJADA	40	-1	-2	37	39
JACK VOIGT	3	1	2	6	6†
Totals	754	1	12	768	805

Mariners and the 1998 Oakland Athletics.

The reason I chose these two teams is simple, they are the teams who had the "actual run hammer" applied hardest. Seattle scored 859 runs in 1998, while team RC-H24 predicts 906 runs; Oakland scored 804 runs in 1998, while team RC-H24 predicts 752 runs.

Although the team RC is only slightly different than the summed individual player totals (Sea 906/905 and Oak 752/754), the difference between the PrelimRC totals and actual runs is still substantial. Seattle's team estimate over-projects by 32 runs, while Oakland's team estimate under-projects by 37 runs. The end result of the hammer application is that Ken Griffey loses 5 runs and Ben Grieve gains 5 runs due to nothing other than the inadequacies of the formula.

Moving on to inspecting the situational adjustments, notice that these adjustments can have considerable affect on player totals. Rickey Henderson gains 6 runs due the adjustment, while Joey Cora loses 11 runs. Is Rickey really a great clutch hitter? Is Joey Cora a bad one? How about Alex Rodriguez—what conclusion can we draw from his adjustments? Even though Alex's minus 4 HR adjustment would lead us to believe he doesn't hit so well in the clutch, his plus 5 Batting Average adjustment would lead us to believe he does. Without looking into the reasons a team's estimate over/under projects, it just becomes a guessing game as to who is responsible for an offense being more or less efficient. As Jay once commented to me: "When all is said and done, the situational adjustment and team reconciliation steps obfuscate more than clarify player analysis."

As Harry Chadwick was the premier baseball analyst of the 19th century, Bill James can probably lay as much claim as anyone to being the leading analyst of the 20th century. The BBBA staff and myself are admirers of a great deal of his work. Unfortunately, his New RC reminds us a lot of the New Coke. Although the New RC was supposed to be an improvement, like the New Coke, it's really just different. And like the New Coke, we don't like the way it tastes.

INTRODUCING XR (Extrapolated Runs)

Jim Furtado

Introduction

I have the best kids on the planet. My wife is the prettiest, most intelligent woman in the world. Nolan Ryan is my favorite player of all time. Ken Griffey Jr. has the prettiest swing I've ever seen. The Red Sox are my favorite team. Extrapolated Runs (or XR) is the simplest, most accurate run estimation formula currently available. What do all those statements have in common? They are my (admittedly biased) opinions.

Although many people spend a great deal of time and energy trying to convince others of the absolute validity of their opinions, I won't do so here. What would be the point? These are my opinions. Just because they are true for me, doesn't necessarily make them true for you. My needs and desires are most likely much different than your needs and desires. Because of that we might come to different conclusions regarding these questions.

So what am I going to do here? Well, rest easy, I'm not going to drone on and on about my family; you're not interested in hearing about them anyway. I also won't get into a discussion about my favorite players or my favorite team; this isn't the place for such a discussion. What I will do is explain my Extrapolated Run system to you. I figure that although you might not agree with me about who has the best family, you might agree with me about what makes a run estimation system useful.

A little background

A couple of years ago, while searching for sabermetric links to add to my Internet web site, I stumbled upon Stephen Tomlinson's homepage [http://www.stephent.com/jays/]. What caught my eye was an article Stephen wrote championing Paul Johnson's Estimated Runs Produced (ERP) formula. After reading his essay, I dug out my copy of The 1985 Bill James Baseball Abstract and re-read the original article about ERP.

I must admit when I first read the article back in 1986 it didn't make a lasting impression. Fortunately, that wasn't the case with my second look. In that pass, I noticed that besides Johnson's description of the method, the article also included a short comparison between ERP and RC.

James found that ERP was slightly more accurate on a team level than RC. He also found ERP didn't suffer from RC's problems with players with high OBA and high SLG. However, as interesting as those facts were it was another of James' comments that spurred me into to action. James said, "The excitement of finding Johnson's method is 1) it is so simple, and 2) it was developed entirely independently. These two things suggest that there probably are compromises between the two methods that will prove to be yet more accurate than either method."

His thoughts greatly excited me. You see, I had made my own discovery while reading Johnson's essay. If you take a look at the formula, I'll show you what I discovered.

Although the original equation
$$ERP = (2 \times (TB + BB + HP) + H + SB - (.605 \times (AB + CS + GIDP - H))) \times .16$$

looks a lot more complicated than it needs to, if you take the time to break it down, it is essentially a linear weighted formula—
$$ERP = (.48 \times 1B) + (.8 \times 2B) + (1.12 \times 3B) + (1.44 \times HR) + ((HP+BB) \times .32) + (.16 \times SB) - (.0968 \times (AB + CS + GIDP - H))$$

—a linear weighted formula, which, as opposed to Palmer's Batting Runs—
$$BR = (.47 \times 1B) + (.78 \times 2B) + (1.09 \times 3B) + (1.40 \times HR) + (.33 \times (BB+HB)) + (.30 \times SB) - (.60 \times CS) - (?? \times (AB-H)) - (.50 \times (OOB))$$

—uses a fixed value for an out.

Method	1B	2B	3B	HR	HP+BB	SB	CS	GIDP	Out
Johnson	.48	.80	1.12	1.44	.32	.16	.10	.10	.10
Palmer	.47	.78	1.09	1.40	.33	.30	.60	none	varies

This discovery was very fascinating for a couple of reasons. First, if you compare Johnson's values with Palmer's weights you can see that they came up with very similar values. The fact that they derived these values using different methodologies gives the values greater validity. Second, the fact that Bill James criticized Palmer's work in his 1985 Historical Abstract while lauding Johnson's work in his 1985 Baseball Abstract didn't make sense.

So what could this fledgling sabermetrician do? The only thing logical thing---I had to study the matter myself.

How was XR developed?
Could the linear formulas hold their own against RC in a larger study?

Before delving deeper into the matter, I had to determine if linear formulas could hold their own vs. RC in a larger study. To do that, I constructed an Excel spreadsheet and compared BR, RC, ERP and all the other formulas I knew about.

Of course, that wasn't quite as easy as you'd think. First I had to assemble team statistics for every club for the 1955-1997 period. This task, in itself, was difficult. Nevertheless, with the assistance of Sean Lahman and Tom Ruane, it was not an insurmountable problem.

I next had to make a decision about exactly how I would determine accuracy. As Brock Hanke pointed out in last year's BBBA, "The debate over the various Runs Created [he's using Runs Created as a generic term] methods is revealed as no debate over methods at all. It is a debate over standards. You tell me what standards you want to apply to Runs Created methods, and my computer can tell you which method best meets them."

Although Brock decided to adopt Bill James' standard, I made a different choice. Rather than choosing one or the other, I decided to use both Pete Palmer's accuracy standard and Bill James' accuracy standard. This way, I figured, people could use the standard they're most comfortable with.

(I won't go into the details here since I realize that some people will get bogged down by the math. Instead, I suggest that anyone interested read "A Question of Accuracy".and "Is Run Scoring Really Not a Linear Process?" both of which can be found elsewhere in this section.)

Anyway, what I found in my examination was that the linear formulas were comparable in accuracy to James' RC. Some years RC was better; some years ERP was better; and some years BR was better. Upon closer inspection, I theorized that the slight difference in accuracy between RC, ERP and BR could be the result of a few things the nature of the formulas 2) the data sets and 2) the time periods involved in the development and evaluation of the formulas. To check to see if these ideas could be correct, I decided to try and improve on Johnson's ERP by experimenting with different data sets and seasons.

Deciding on the data

The next step in the process was to decide which statistics to include in the formula. Since my initial accuracy study determined that the most accurate statistics were James' RC, Palmer's BR, and Johnson's ERP, I decided to mix and match from the various data sets. To save you some time, here's a comparison of their data sets:

RC	H	TB	BB	IBB	HP	AB	GIDP	SB	CS	SH
BR	1B	2B	3B	HR	HP	BB	AB	SB	CS	OOB
ERP	H	TB	BB	HP	AB	SB	CS	GIDP			

I also decided to experiment with strikeouts because I remembered that Bill James had estimated in his 1992 Bill James Baseball Book (pg.37) that for every additional 100 strikeouts a team would lose about 1 run.

Runs through regression

Using regression analysis, I determined which statistical ingredients should get throw into my run estimation pot. After literally running hundreds of regressions, and after comparing some of my own regressed numbers with those generated by others (again, see the "Runs through Regression Analysis" section in "Why Do We Need A New Player Evaluation Method?"), I generated some ball park numbers to start with.

Comparison to other models

I then spent some time comparing the regressed numbers to the values other people came up with using other techniques. Many analysts have generated run values of the various events using different techniques. George Lindsey, Steve Mann and Paul Johnson produced their numbers by examining play-by-play data. Pete Palmer generated his numbers with a simulation-based study. Others estimated values by building probability tables.

Since my goal was to generate numbers that would be mathematically accurate AND would be theoretically relevant, this part of the process was very important. I took a long, hard look at all this data to ensure that my numbers made sense.

Peer review

At this point of the process, I decided to get some input from other knowledgeable baseball analysts. I posted my preliminary figures on the rec.sport.baseball newgroup. I also contacted anyone who I thought could help in the process.

Luckily, I know some very knowledgeable baseball analysts. David Grabiner, Tom Ruane, John Jarvis, Alan Shank, Alidad Tash, Dan Szymborski, Greg Spira, James Tuttle, Arne Olson, and BBBA's own Don Malcolm and G. Jay Walker, all contributed something interesting or useful to the process. In particular, David, Tom, John, Jay and Don, each took time a bunch of time from their busy schedules to give me some very valuable input. I greatly appreciate their help.

Empirical analysis

As I said above, to ensure that the final numbers would be both accurate AND make sense, it was important that I properly balance theoretical and mathematical considerations to generate the final values of each event.

This required quite the juggling act. In particular, generating coefficients that would work during both relatively low scoring periods (1963-1968) and relatively high scoring periods (1994-1997) proved difficult. To get it right, I had to spend a great deal of time massaging the data.

Luckily through hard work, I was able to come up with numbers that accomplished this task.

What did I finally come up with? Read on.

Extrapolated Runs unveiled

Extrapolated Runs was developed for use with seasons from 1955 to the present. I came up with three versions of the formula. The three formulas are:

XR - Extrapolated Runs

$$= (.50 \times 1B) + (.72 \times 2B) + (1.04 \times 3B) + (1.44 \times HR) + (.34 \times (HP+TBB-IBB)) + (.25 \times IBB) + (.18 \times SB) + (-.32 \times CS) + ((-.090 \times (AB - H - K)) + (-.098 \times K)) + (-.37 \times GIDP) + (.37 \times SF) + (.04 \times SH)$$

XRR - Extrapolated Runs Reduced

$$= (.50 \times 1B) + (.72 \times 2B) + (1.04 \times 3B) + (1.44 \times HR) + (.33 \times (HP+TBB)) + (.18 \times SB) + (-.32 \times CS) + ((-.098 \times (AB - H))$$

XRB Extrapolated Runs Basic

$$= (.50 \times 1B) + (.72 \times 2B) + (1.04 \times 3B) + (1.44 \times HR) + (.34 \times (TBB)) + (.18 \times SB) + (-.32 \times CS) + (-.096 \times (AB - H))$$

As you can see, calculating XR requires only addition and multiplication. Its simplicity of design is one of its greatest attributes. Unlike a lot of the other methods, you don't need to know team totals, actual runs, league figures or anything else. You just plug the stats into the formula and you are all set.

Another of XR attributes is that the formula is pretty much context neutral. Other than park effects, the only remaining residue of context is due to the inclusion of IBB, GIDP and SF. Although I could have removed them from the full version, I felt that the inclusion of these terms was important since my research showed there was a strong correlation between the IBB, SF and GIDP opportunities that players face. I also felt, like Bill James, that these statistics do tell us something valuable about players. Of course, I knew some people might not agree with me. For them, I created two other versions.

XR also accounts for just about every out. James correctly understands that the more outs an individual player consumes the less valuable his positive contributions are. Since XR will be used as the base of the Extrapolated Win method, I thought it was important to include as many outs as possible in the formula.

Another nice thing about XR is that if you add up all the players' Extrapolated Runs, you'll have the team totals. That's a benefit of using a linear equation.

You may now be wondering how well these stats compare to other statistics in accuracy? Well although I go into more detail in the <A Question of Accuracy> article, I do want to give you some idea about how these three methods compare to each other and, of course, to a few of the other methods.

A player example

To illustrate how to calculate a player's XR, I'll use Mark McGwire's 1998 statistics.

$$XR = (.50 \times 61) + (.72 \times 21) + (1.04 \times 0) + (1.44 \times 70) + (.34 \times (6+162-28)) + (.25 \times 28) + (.18 \times 1) + (-.32 \times 0) + ((-.090 \times (509 - 152 - 155)) + (-.098 \times 155) + (-.37 \times 8) + (.37 \times 4) + (.04 \times 0) = 166.35$$

If I had used the other versions of XR, I'd generate slightly different numbers. For example: XRR = 167.05 and XRB = 169.03. The differences stem from the excluded data. In McGwire's case, the discrepancy stems from this SF/GIDP difference and the large number of walks he had in 1998.

For the time period of 1984-1998, I found that players' values differ, on average, by about 0.7 runs. Of course, some players' values change much more. Players with extremely high totals of GIDP, HP, SO, BB can have their values change quite a bit. For XRR, Howard Johnson gained the most runs (+6, in 1991) due to the great disparity between his 15 SF and his 4 GIDP. At the other extreme, Jim Rice lost the most runs (-8, 1984) mainly due to 36 GIDP and only 6 SF.

A league example

To give you an idea how XR works on a team level, here's some numbers from the 1998 season. Since both XR and James' new RC were designed before the 1998 season data became available, this is the first comparison where the methods are flying solo.

1998 AMERICAN LEAGUE

Team	R	XR	XRR	XRB	RC-H24	RC-T1	ERP	NERP
ANA	787	771	772	769	777	787	785	784
BAL	817	849	852	847	849	863	865	858
BOS	876	871	877	867	878	894	893	884
CHI	861	843	835	834	840	850	849	848
CLE	850	873	868	869	874	887	887	883
DET	722	754	749	742	753	760	767	770
KC	714	732	722	715	724	730	735	737
MIN	734	708	716	715	706	713	730	717
NY	965	933	936	931	937	957	948	937
OAK	804	758	755	751	752	762	766	771
SEA	859	902	894	889	906	923	908	916
TB	620	671	676	676	670	678	693	687
TEX	940	906	907	908	914	935	921	915
TOR	816	856	849	834	851	862	870	866

1998 NATIONAL LEAGUE

Team	R	XR	XRR	XRB	RC-H24	RC-T1	ERP	NERP
ARI	665	672	680	672	666	675	691	690
ATL	826	847	839	833	848	862	852	855
CHI	831	817	821	823	815	827	831	823
CIN	750	749	750	752	747	757	762	756
COL	826	849	858	858	867	878	874	862
FLA	667	655	659	658	653	662	675	674
HOU	874	866	874	865	877	889	887	873
LA	669	673	664	665	662	666	672	678
MIL	707	713	721	713	711	719	734	724
MON	644	661	659	651	657	662	674	675
NY	706	714	714	716	712	720	727	716
PHI	713	734	722	721	729	737	735	734
PIT	650	660	647	629	653	658	660	669
SD	749	753	748	747	748	757	761	763
SF	845	843	839	840	845	857	851	843
STL	810	850	853	854	852	862	865	859

One interesting thing you should notice is how, generally speaking, all the methods make similar errors. For example, if one method is off by about +30 runs, the other methods are all pretty close to the +30 figure. That leads me to believe that typical error is due to either things which the method doesn't take into account and/or are the result a non-standard distribution of events. These are things that mostly cancel out, but as you can see they don't even out completely.

Comparing accuracy

This is the point where there is disagreement. Bill James uses standard deviation and average absolute errors to score methods. Pete Palmer uses regression equations to determine error. None of these methods is inherently superior. They just measure the error in slightly different ways.

How do the methods compare in 1998? Here's the summary data.

1998 AMERICAN LEAGUE

Tm	XR	XRR	XRB	RC-H24	RC-T1	ERP	NERP
ANA	-16	-15	-18	-10	0	-2	-3
BAL	32	35	30	32	46	48	41
BOS	-5	1	-9	2	18	17	8
CHI	-18	-26	-27	-21	-11	-12	-13
CLE	23	18	19	24	37	37	33
DET	32	27	20	31	38	45	48
KC	18	8	1	10	16	21	23
MIN	-26	-18	-19	-28	-21	-4	-17
NY	-32	-29	-34	-28	-8	-17	-28
OAK	-46	-49	-53	-52	-42	-38	-33
SEA	43	35	30	47	64	49	57
TB	51	56	56	50	58	73	67
TEX	-34	-33	-32	-26	-5	-19	-25
TOR	40	33	18	35	46	54	50

1998 NATIONAL LEAGUE

Tm	XR	XRR	XRB	RC-H24	RC-T1	ERP	NERP
ARI	7	15	7	1	10	26	25
ATL	21	13	7	22	36	26	29
CHI	-14	-10	-8	-16	-4	0	-8
CIN	-1	0	2	-3	7	12	6
COL	23	32	32	41	52	48	36
FLA	-12	-8	-9	-14	-5	8	7
HOU	-8	0	-9	3	15	13	-1
LA	4	-5	-4	-7	-3	3	9
MIL	6	14	6	4	12	27	17
MON	17	15	7	13	18	30	31
NY	8	8	10	6	14	21	10
PHI	21	9	8	16	24	22	21
PIT	10	-3	-21	3	8	10	19
SD	4	-1	-2	-1	8	12	14
SF	-2	-6	-5	0	12	6	-2
STL	40	43	44	42	52	55	49

To make the comparison easier, here's a table with error data broken down.

	Measure	XR	XRR	XRB	RC-H24	RC-T1	ERP	NERP
AL	STD	32.2	30.9	29.9	31.7	35.4	37.2	36.7
	AvgErr	29.7	27.4	26.1	28.3	29.3	31.1	31.9
	SE Regr	34.1	32.8	31.7	33.8	33.3	34.8	35.9
NL	STD	15.8	15.9	15.9	17.6	23.2	24.9	22.0
	AvgErr	12.4	11.4	11.3	12.0	17.5	19.9	17.8
	SE Regr	14.5	14.4	15.1	15.4	14.7	15.1	15.7
MLB	STD	24.8	24.1	23.5	25.2	29.5	31.2	29.8
	AvgErr	20.5	18.8	18.2	19.6	23.0	25.2	24.3
	SE Regr	24.9	24.3	24.3	25.2	24.5	25.6	26.1

Using standard deviation (STD, root mean square error), XRB comes out on top for the AL and MLB, while XR tops the NL.

Using Average absolute Error (AvgErr, or the sum of the absolute errors), XRB makes a clean sweep.

Using the Standard Error of Regression (SE Regr, or Palmer's choice, which he calls linear curve fitting), XRB tops the AL, XRR tops the NL, and they both tie for the lead for MLB.

One thing I'd like to point out is that 1998 was an off year for all the evaluation methods. Every evaluation method scored worse than it normally does. Since XRB, is less accurate over the 1955-1997 time period, the fact that it comes out on top this year is very suspect. I consider its win this year as a fluke.

Another factor to keep in mind is that these values are generated from team totals. As Jay and I showed in our <RC article>, the summed individual player totals for RC does not equal the team total. This means that the RC totals presented here are for RC on the team level only. It also means that RC is slightly more inaccurate than these numbers imply.

To get a better idea of how these measure compare, read the essay <A Question of Accuracy>.

Top Players in 1998

Who were the top players in 1998? Here's their ranking by XR:

	1998 National League		1998 American League	
	Name	**XR**	**Name**	**XR**
1	Mark McGwire	166.35	Albert Belle	146.26
	Sammy Sosa	142.73	Ken Griffey	135.31
	Barry Bonds	138.57	Alex Rodriguez	132.82
	Craig Biggio	129.26	Mo Vaughn	129.08
5	Chipper Jones	127.69	Edgar Martinez	127.06
	Moises Alou	127.35	Juan Gonzalez	126.28
	John Olerud	126.09	Rafael Palmeiro	124.97
	Jeff Bagwell	123.77	Manny Ramirez	122.16
	Andres Galarraga	123.59	Carlos Delgado	115.55
10	Greg Vaughn	122.43	Nomar Garciaparra	114.83
	Scott Rolen	122.26	Frank Thomas	113.51
	Vladimir Guerrero	120.88	Jose Offerman	112.89
	Vinny Castilla	120.71	Derek Jeter	111.05
	Ray Lankford	113.57	Ray Durham	108.37
15	Mike Piazza	112.03	Paul O'Neill	108.32
	Larry Walker	110.21	Shawn Green	107.64
	Derek Bell	108.49	Bernie Williams	106.85
	Mark Grace	107.35	Tony Clark	106.02
	Jason Kendall	107.02	Jason Giambi	103.82
20	Dante Bichette	105.60	Tim Salmon	103.75
	Barry Larkin	105.47	Matt Lawton	103.61
	Jeromy Burnitz	104.56	Kenny Lofton	102.85
	Gary Sheffield	102.28	Rusty Greer	102.56
	Fernando Vina	101.56	Will Clark	102.52
25	Brian Jordan	101.34	Jim Thome	102.11

It should come as no surprise that Mark McGwire generated the most runs of any player. However, having said that, I like you to keep one thought in mind. These runs are only a tip of the iceberg. XR only measures the DIRECT runs that a player produces.

Since baseball is a team game, a player's ability to avoid making outs affects other players. That means that besides the runs a player produces while he is at the plate, he is also partially responsible for the runs his teammates produce later on in the game. I won't go into any more detail about it here. I just mention this because although XR doesn't deal with this part of the run scoring process, the Extrapolated Win method does. To find out more, you'll have to read on.

MEASURING ACCURACY IN RUN ESTIMATION METHODS

JIM FURTADO

How do all the offensive statistics measure up in an accuracy comparison? To answer that question, I put together a study to examine how well each statistic relates to run scoring. Unfortunately, setting up the study wasn't a straightforward proposition. That's because there isn't a general agreement among sabermetricians about how accuracy is best calculated.

As a matter of fact, the two greatest minds in sabermetrics disagree about this. Bill James uses standard deviation (really Root Mean Square Error or RMSE) and absolute errors to compare accuracy. Pete Palmer uses regression equations to answer the question.

How did I decide to answer the question? Rather than restrict my study to either Mr. James' or Mr. Palmer's accuracy standard, I decided to study the matter employing both of their standards. By doing so, I figured, anyone looking it over could chose whichever standard they preferred.

Because this is a baseball book and not a math book, I won't take up a bunch of time explaining the entire process in detail. If you don't already have an understanding of standard deviations, regression equations, correlation and the like, I regret to tell you that you won't find an explanation of them here.

The reasons are simple. First, there aren't an infinite number of pages that this book can hold. If I had to explain every math term and concept here, it would have to be at the expense of other material. Other material that is a heck of a lot more interesting to read than mathematical techniques.

Second, I'm not properly qualified to teach them to you. I'm a baseball analyst, not a math professor. Rather than trying to learn it from me, you'd be better off taking a good introductory college statistics class. Of course, you might not have the time or desire to do that. If that's true, but you'd still like to get a basic understanding of the methodology, I suggest you pick up a copy of Baseball by the NUMBERS—How Statistics Are Collected, What They Mean, and How They Reveal the Game by Willie Runquist. In this book the author examines many baseball statistics with a focus on the underlying mathematics. Reading it won't replace a good stats class; but if you are comfortable with math, it will help you understand the methods used in this essay.

How did I generate run totals for the different stats?

As noted in "Why Do We Need a New Player Evaluation Method?", rate statistics need an additional step to express the measure in runs. How did I do this? I divided the team measure by the league average and then multiplied the result by the league runs per out and by the number of team outs (which I calculated as AB-H+SH+SF+CS+GIDP).

Here's an example using batting average and the 1955 Boston Red Sox. In 1955, the Red Sox hit .264 that season and consumed 4145 outs. The league averaged a .258 batting average and scored .170 runs per out. To generate the Red Sox run total, I put all the numbers together: .264/.258 x .170 x 4145 = 721.037 Runs. Using this method, I produced run estimates for every stat included in the study. This was done for every team from 1955-1997 (1002 team seasons).

For the statistics that are already expressed in runs, things were much simpler to calculate. I directly compared estimated runs with actual runs.

What numbers did I calculate?

I calculated figures that correspond to the methodology used by Bill James and Pete Palmer.

Bill James Methodology

I applied the standard that Bill James used in his Baseball Abstracts.

RSME - Root Mean Square Error or Standard Deviation between projected and actual runs

Gross E - Gross Error or the sum of absolute difference between the projected and actual runs

AAE - Average Absolute Error - the average of the absolute difference between the projected and actual runs

% Off - Gross E divided by the sum of actual runs

MAE - Median Absolute Error or the error located at the halfway point of all errors

Pete Palmer Methodology

In The Hidden Game of Baseball, Pete Palmer ranked a few stats using what he called "linear curve fitting". Linear curve fitting, in this context, is nothing other than the use of a regression equation to measure the linear relationship between estimated runs and actual runs.

SE regr - Standard Error of the Regression using the standard formula $y=mx+b$ where y = actual runs, m=slope of the regression line, x=estimated runs, and b=intercept point of the regression line

R - correlation coefficient or how closely the estimated runs and actual runs conform to a linear relationship (If there is a perfect correlation between the two, this number would equal 1.)

R^2- Coefficient of determination or the proportion of the variation in runs that can be explained by relating actual runs to estimated runs

What are the numbers?

Rate Stat Scorecard

1955-1997	Rank	RMSE	Ranked by Standard Deviation Gross E	AAE	% Off	MAE	Rank	SE regr	Ranked by Regression Equation slope	intercept	R	R^2
OTS	1	24.9	19946.4	19.9	2.9%	16.5	1	24.0	1.033	-28.7	96.7%	93.6%
TA	2	29.0	23427.1	23.4	3.5%	19.3	3	27.4	1.118	-80.1	95.7%	91.6%
BOP	3	30.9	24874.9	24.8	3.7%	21.3	4	29.1	1.129	-87.3	95.2%	90.6%
DX	4	31.2	25055.6	25.0	3.7%	21.6	2	24.6	.930	30.7	96.6%	93.3%
Rickey	5	35.3	28262.2	28.2	4.2%	24.3	5	32.5	1.166	-118.2	93.9%	88.3%
BPA	6	37.0	29806.5	29.7	4.4%	25.7	6	35.5	1.123	-78.8	92.7%	86.0%
SLG	7	38.0	30693.6	30.6	4.5%	26.2	7	36.5	1.114	-83.1	92.3%	85.2%
OPA	8	39.7	31968.6	31.9	4.7%	26.4	8	37.5	1.158	-113.3	91.9%	84.4%
EQA	9	41.3	33267.6	33.2	4.9%	28.2	11	39.1	1.163	-116.9	91.1%	83.0%
Grab	10	41.3	33307.2	33.2	4.9%	27.4	10	39.1	1.163	-116.4	91.1%	83.0%
OPS	11	41.4	33298.0	33.2	4.9%	27.7	9	38.6	1.160	-118.9	91.4%	83.5%
OBP	12	48.7	38854.3	38.8	5.7%	31.1	12	47.5	1.131	-94.7	86.6%	75.0%
AVG	13	49.4	39603.5	39.5	5.9%	33.6	13	48.5	1.108	-79.8	85.9%	73.8%

Run Stat Scorecard

1955-1997	Rank	RMSE	Ranked by Standard Deviation Gross E	AAE	% Off	MAE	Rank	SE regr	Ranked by Regression Equation slope	intercept	R	R^2
XR	1	20.9	16424.6	16.4	2.4%	13.5	1	20.9	1.000	0.2	97.5%	95.2%
EqR	2	21.8	17307.8	17.3	2.6%	14.5	3	21.7	.971	19.7	97.4%	94.8%
NERP	3	21.9	17241.4	17.2	2.5%	14.2	5	21.9	.996	2.2	97.3%	94.7%
XRR	4	22.0	17293.3	17.3	2.6%	14.2	10	22.1	1.001	-0.2	97.3%	94.6%
BR(.081fixed)	5	22.1	17537.4	17.5	2.6%	14.5	9	22.0	1.010	-5.3	97.3%	94.6%
RC-H23-24-Player	6	22.2	17422.5	17.4	2.6%	13.8	4	21.9	.963	25.6	97.3%	94.7%
RC-HDG23-24	7	22.2	17479.6	17.4	2.6%	14.2	8	22.0	.968	22.5	97.3%	94.6%
RCt1	8	22.3	17555.7	17.5	2.6%	14.8	7	22.0	.962	24.2	97.3%	94.6%
LinearRC	9	22.3	17599.8	17.6	2.6%	14.4	6	21.9	.963	27.0	97.3%	94.6%
XRB	10	22.6	17710.2	17.7	2.6%	14.2	12	22.5	1.004	-4.5	97.1%	94.3%
BR	11	23.7	18925.0	18.9	2.8%	15.4	14	23.1	.964	28.3	97.0%	94.1%
ERP	12	24.3	19317.6	19.3	2.9%	15.9	11	22.2	.992	-4.0	97.2%	94.5%
B&F	13	24.5	19855.9	19.8	2.9%	17.2	2	21.5	.971	31.0	97.4%	94.9%
Cramer's RC	14	24.9	19721.1	19.7	2.9%	16.0	13	22.8	.904	62.5	97.1%	94.2%
RCsb	15	25.4	20290.2	20.2	3.0%	16.8	16	24.4	.965	29.6	96.6%	93.4%
RC	16	25.9	20598.3	20.6	3.0%	16.9	17	25.2	.969	26.4	96.4%	93.0%
Mann's RPA	17	28.2	22478.3	22.4	3.3%	19.1	15	24.4	.869	91.5	96.6%	93.4%
Lindsey	18	144.4	139963.3	139.7	20.7%	142.4	18	36.6	.996	-136.5	92.2%	85.1%

Although most of the statistics' abbreviations are defined elsewhere, a few aren't. Included are a couple of RC spin-offs: LinearRC is the linear component of the new RC calculation that I explained in <RC article>. RC-H23-24-Player is the number of runs that the player context formula generates if team stats are placed into the formula. BR(.081fixed) is Palmer's BR using a set value (-.081) for outs for the entire period. Grab is David Grabiner's suggested modification to OPS (1.2*OBP+SLG).

What should you make of these numbers?

I'd prefer that you draw your own conclusions but since I realize that you may want my opinion, here's a few things to keep in mind. (Feel free to stop reading here, if my opinion doesn't really interest you.)

XR was developed with the same data used in the validation study. This means XR gets something of a helping hand. Because of that I also supply a few other comparisons. The first is a decade-by-decade comparison (with only RMSE and SE regr). The numbers indicates that XR holds its accuracy advantage across different periods.

Decade Match-up

On the team level, there really isn't that much of a difference between most of the run estimation methods. Although XR comes out on top, the gap isn't earth shattering. Of course, as Jay and I pointed out in the <RC article>, the numbers generated on the team level don't necessarily equal the numbers used for player comparisons. This means that for most methods, the accuracy on the player level is different than the accuracy on the team level. This is true even for Palmer's Batting Runs. Since BR contains a term for Outs On Base for team calculations, but excludes the term for player calculations, accuracy for individual players is worse than this study indicates.

EQA's accuracy lies in the eye of the beholder. If you figure things out the way Clay Davenport tells you to, it looks pret-

Period	Measure	#Teams	B&F	BR	BR(.081)	EqR	ERP	LinearRC	Mann's RPA	NERP	RC-H23-24	RCt1	XR	XRB	XRR
1955-1959	RMSE	80	26.1	22.7	22.1	22.4	25.6	23.6	27.6	22.5	23.7	23.7	22.1	25.1	23.9
	SE regr		22.7	22.6	21.8	22.6	24.3	23.5	23.8	22.5	23.5	23.6	22.3	24.8	24.0
1960-1969	RMSE	198	27.2	23.7	21.0	21.6	21.7	22.8	31.2	22.2	21.5	21.3	20.9	22.5	22.4
	SE regr		20.3	22.7	20.7	21.6	21.7	20.4	22.5	21.5	20.3	20.5	20.0	22.2	21.7
1970-1979	RMSE	246	21.3	23.2	21.1	20.1	22.8	20.2	24.9	20.1	20.3	20.2	19.3	21.0	20.2
	SE regr		19.5	22.1	21.1	19.9	19.9	19.7	21.7	20.1	20.0	20.1	19.3	20.6	20.2
1980-1989	RMSE	260	25.2	23.7	22.7	22.8	25.4	23.3	27.7	22.1	23.2	22.6	21.4	22.9	22.2
	SE regr		22.6	23.0	22.8	22.8	22.5	23.1	25.2	22.1	23.1	22.4	21.5	22.7	22.3
1990-1998	RMSE	258	23.9	24.7	23.5	22.9	26.7	22.7	30.2	23.7	23.1	24.8	21.6	23.0	22.9
	SE regr		22.1	24.5	23.5	22.7	22.9	22.5	25.6	22.9	22.8	22.9	21.5	23.1	22.9

ty good; if you don't, it doesn't look very good. As a matter of fact, if you compare EQA to Grab, you won't find much difference. This indicates to me that EQA isn't really much different than OPS.

OPS doesn't possess the accuracy that Pete Palmer's study implies. David Grabiner pointed out a possible explanation. David explained that the reason OPS is considered to have better accuracy than my study shows is that Palmer's OPS accuracy claims are based on OPS's correlation with OTS. What this means is that if OPS had a perfect linear relationship with OTS, the accuracy of OPS would be the same as the accuracy of OTS. I investigated this and found OPS's correlation with OTS was indeed very high (.998556). I then took a look at David's suggested modification 1.2*OBP+SLG (GRAB). GRAB had a correlation coefficient (R) figure of .999173. Although this correlation figure is pretty high, it's still not a perfect correlation. To generate a better correlation figure, a much more involved formula is required. David sent me a formula [OTS = .333*.400 + (OBP-.333)*.400 + .333*(SLG-.400) + (OBP-.333)*(SLG-.400) -.333*.400 + (1.2*OBP+SLG)/3 + (OBP-.333)*(SLG-.400)] which produces an almost perfect correlation figure (1.00000000).

You might be thinking, "OK, what does this really mean?" Well, what it means is that although OPS is a very good quick and dirty method, it's not as accurate as some of its proponents claim. So if you want to get a good quick estimate, OPS works fine; if you want a more accurate assessment, you're better off using one of the other methods.

My study shows that with the proper selection of event values, a linear formula is more accurate for the different run scoring periods.

Linear vs. non-Linear Match-up

1963-1968	Rank	RMSE	SE regr	1994-1997	Rank	RMSE	SE regr
DX	1	24.5	23.8	OTS	1	20.8	21.0
OTS	2	26.3	22.4	TA	2	26.4	25.9
TA	3	30.7	26.0	BOP	3	27.2	26.6
BOP	4	32.9	27.6	Rickey	4	33.9	33.1
Rickey	5	36.1	27.8	SLG	5	34.5	34.2
SLG	6	37.0	32.2	BPA	6	35.5	35.1
BPA	7	38.6	31.8	OPA	7	36.0	35.5
OPA	8	41.4	34.4	OPS	8	36.6	35.9
Grab	9	43.3	36.2	Grab	9	37.0	36.4
EQA	10	43.5	36.6	EQA	10	37.4	36.9
OPS	11	43.6	35.4	DX	11	39.0	23.1
AVG	12	52.2	48.7	OBP	12	44.1	44.0
OBP	13	53.2	49.0	AVG	13	45.0	45.

1963-1968	Rank	RMSE	SE regr	1994-1997	Rank	RMSE	SE regr
BR(.081fixed)	1	20.4	20.5	XR	1	19.9	19.9
XR	2	21.3	20.4	LinearRC	2	20.8	20.9
ERP	3	21.7	21.7	RC-H23-24-Player	3	21.0	21.0
RCt1	4	22.3	21.3	XRR	4	21.1	21.1
EqR	5	22.3	22.1	XRB	5	21.6	21.8
NERP	6	22.4	21.8	RC-HDG23-24	6	21.8	21.4
RC-HDG23-24	7	22.7	21.3	EqR	7	22.2	21.9
XRR	8	22.9	22.2	NERP	8	22.3	21.3
XRB	9	23.0	22.5	BR(.081fixed)	9	22.8	22.9
RC-H23-24-Player	10	23.5	21.1	RCsb	10	24.3	24.0
Cramer's RC	11	24.2	21.0	B&F	11	24.6	20.4
BR	12	24.4	22.5	RCt1	12	24.8	21.3
LinearRC	13	24.5	21.0	RC	13	24.9	24.6
RC	14	26.7	24.0	ERP	14	25.2	21.0
B&F	15	26.8	20.4	BR	15	25.2	25.3
RCsb	16	28.0	24.0	Mann's RPA	16	30.5	23.3
Mann's RPA	17	35.6	22.5	Cramer's RC	17	32.6	22.1
Lindsey	18	164.5	29.5	Lindsey	18	121.4	34.6

Although the other formulas move around in ranking, XR stays near the top for both run scoring environments. This finding directly contradicts James' assertion in the Historical Baseball Abstract that linear formulas cannot accurately estimate runs because "run scoring is not linear." Although I agree with Mr. James that run scoring is not linear, I don't believe that this fact prevents the use of a non-linear formula to estimate runs created. That's because as long as the frequency and distribution of events is pretty stable (and it has been) run scoring can be looked at as linear—the more positive events that a team packs into a game, the more runs it scores. My numbers confirm this assertion.

XR is designed for use from 1955 onward. Although you can use the formula for seasons prior to 1955, I haven't confirmed its validity for that period. Having said that, I've already begun work on creating other versions for seasons prior to 1955.

Closing thoughts

As I mentioned at the top of the article, I'm a baseball analyst, not a math professor. With that in mind, I'd like to encourage any and all input from all the math experts reading this article. Although I'm confident that I've got a good handle on the topic, I'm open to other ideas about how to examine the accuracy question.

Also, if any of you math experts have written (or can write) something that explains all the underlying math in a simple, easy to understand manner, and if you're willing to share your knowledge, please contact me. I'd really like to include a nice explanation in the web version of this article.

Speaking of the web, I encourage everyone with Internet access to check out the web version of this article. Since my web site does not suffer from the space constraints that the printed word does, I'm free to include more, more, more data. You can find the webified version at http://www.baseballstuff.com/btf/scholars/furtado/accuracy.htm.

In closing, I suggest that anyone interested in other looks at the same question, read John Jarvis' "A Survey of Baseball Player Performance Evaluation Measures" at *http://pacer1.usca.sc.edu/~jfj/runs_survey.html* and Alidad Tash's "Win and Run Prediction in Major League Baseball" at *http://www.baseballstuff.com/btf/pages/essays/other/tash.html.*

CREATING WELL-ADJUSTED STATISTICS:

PARK FACTORS FOR TODAY AND TOMORROW

G. JAY WALKER

PARK EFFECTS TODAY

WHAT COMES FIRST, THE PARK EFFECT OR THE RUN PRODUCTION METHOD?

There are two ways that you can apply park effects. The first is to compute your measure of offensive value, that is some runs created or runs produced type of number, and then apply your park factor to that number. The second is to compute and apply park factors to a player's raw statistics, and then use these park-adjusted raw statistics in computing your offensive value measure. The second method is to be preferred unless a key criteria is ease of use. Then the first method might be preferable.

The second method (first park adjust your raw stats and then compute your statistic) is preferred because different types of parks effect different types of offense. Some might favor line drive gap hitters, while others might favor medium-range fly-ball hitters. A park which is favorable to home run hitters may be detrimental to singles hitters, or vice-versa.

The principle would also apply to the strikeout and walk rates. Visibility and the ways curveballs break all effect strikeouts, while a small park can increase walk totals as pitchers become cautions to put the ball over too much of the plate. Not examining the individual components of a player's raw stats in terms of park effects will result in rewarding or penalizing certain players more than they should.

When we start looking at the individual components, we need to concern ourselves with how these relate to each other. Parks that have a high strikeout factor will impact the number of home runs hit since the placement of your outfield fences is immaterial if the batter can't get wood on the ball. Moreover, just comparing, say, the numbers of homers that are hit in the home park and on the road is not going to yield the optimal value for a home run factor. Everything should be computed in terms of rates since many other things can effect the raw totals (these would include how many games go to extra innings, how often the home team bats in the bottom of the 9th as well as how often batters get on base and the overall level of run scoring).

We used five rate statistics that will be used to convert a player's raw stats into park-adjusted stats:

a   Strikeouts per plate appearances
b   Bases on balls per plate appearances
c   singles per balls put in play (balls put in play = PA - BB - K - HBP - SH - SF)
d   Extra-base hits (doubles and triples) per ball put in play
e   Home runs per balls put in play

In theory, separate factors should be calculated for doubles and triples, however the number of triples hit is often too small to produce reliable rates.

For example, to compute the strikeout factor for Fenway Park, you would calculate the total strikeouts and plate appearances for the Sox and their opponents at Fenway. You'd do the same for the Sox and their opponents for the Red Sox road games. Then the strikeout factor for Fenway would equal:

$$\frac{(K/PA) \text{ for Red Sox games (both teams)}}{(K/PA) \text{ for Red Sox road games (both teams)}}$$

Actually that's not quite true. You could probably get away with using that calculation in the days when schedules were relatively balanced and there was no interleague play. These days, that's no longer the case. The simple solution of assuming every team has road park factors of 1.00 is tenuous with each team now playing a varied number of games at each road park and inter-divisional teams playing different sets of opponents in interleague games. A more complex solution is required, and I think we'll stick that in the Appendix where the more sabermetrically-inclined among you can pursue it. In the meantime, before we move on to the centerpiece of our new measures of offensive performance, Extrapolated Runs, here's an example of how a player's raw stats would be park-adjusted, featuring the Colorado Rockies and Larry Walker.

THE PARK-ADJUSTMENT CALCULATION USING COUSIN LARRY

Here are the park factors (expressed in decimals) for the Colorado Rockies for 1998:

Factor	Home	Road
Strikeouts (K/PA)	.800	1.024
Bases on Balls (BB/PA)	1.011	1.000
Singles (Singles/BIP)	1.179	.990
Extra-base Hits ((Doubles+Triples)/BIP)	1.036	.995
Home Runs (HR/BIP)	1.352	.968

Coors Field unsurprisingly has high park factors for offense, particularly homers. The road factors will be near one, but deviate from 1.00 due to the unbalanced schedule and interleague play. For road games, the Rockies played in parks which were skewed slightly in favor of strikeouts and against homers.

Here's Larry Walker's relevant home and road stats for 1998:

	AB	H	2B	3B	HR	BB	HBP	K	GDP	SH	SF
Home	239	100	26	2	17	30	1	32	7	0	1
Away	215	65	20	1	6	34	3	29	4	0	1

Walker had an 271 plate appearance at home and 253 on the road, with an on-base average of .483 at home and .403 on the road, with a slugging average of .757 at home and .488 on the road.

To get Walker's park-adjusted stats, perform the following steps:

Step 1 -   calculate the balls put in play at home = PA - BB - K - HBP - SH - SF =
271 - 30 - 32 - 1 - 0 - 1 = 207 balls put in play

Step 2 -   calculate the adjusted home strikeouts and home bases on balls

adjusted home strikeouts = home strikeouts/home strikeout factor = 32/.800 = 40.00
adjusted home bases on balls = home bases on balls/home bases on balls factor = 30/.977 = 29.67

Step 3 -   calculate the adjusted balls put in play at home = PA - adj. BB - adj. K - HBP - SH - SF =
271 - 29.67 - 40.00 - 1 - 0 - 1 = 199.33 adjusted balls put in play

Step 4 - calculate the balls put in play home adjustment factor = adjusted balls put in play at home/initial balls put in play at home = 199.33/207 = .9629

Step 5 - find the adjusted number of home singles =
(home singles x balls put in play at home adjustment factor) / home singles park factor =
(55 x .9629) / 1.179 = 44.92

Step 6 - repeat Step 5 for extra base hits (doubles and triples) and home runs
adjusted number of home extra base hits = ((26 + 2) x .9629) / 1.036 = 26.02
adjusted number of home home runs = (17 x .9629) / 1.352 = 12.11

The adjusted number of home doubles = (26/28) x 26.02 = 24.16
The adjusted number of home triples = (2/28) x 26.02 = 1.86

Step 7 - repeat Steps 1 to 6, only using the away data and the road park factors

Walker has 253 - 34 - 29 - 3 - 0 - 1 = 186 balls put in play on the road.
He has 29/1.024 or 28.32 adjusted road strikeouts and 34/1.000 or 34 adjusted road walks.
His adjusted balls put in play on the road is 253 - 34 - 28.32 - 3 - 0 - 1 = 186.68
His balls put in play road adjustment factor = 186.68/186 = 1.0037
Walker has 38.53 adjusted road singles (38 x 1.0037)/.990
He has 21.18 adjusted road extra-base hits (21 x 1.0037)/.995,
which breaks down into 20.17 adjusted road doubles and 1.01 adjusted road triples.
He has 6.23 adjusted road home runs (6 x 1.0037)/.967

Step 8 - create new lines of park-adjusted home and road stats, and add them up

Here's Larry Walker's park-adjusted home and road stats for 1998. (Note - the adjusted at-bats equals the adjusted balls put in play plus the adjusted strikeouts)

	AB	H	2B	3B	HR	BB	HBP	K	GDP	SH	SF
Home	239.33	83.05	24.16	1.86	12.11	29.67	1	40.00	7	0	1
Away	215.00	65.94	20.17	1.01	6.23	34.00	3	28.32.	4	0	1
Totals	454.33	148.99	44.33	2.87	18.34	63.67	4	68.32	11	0	2

And here's a comparison of Walker's raw stats and park-adjusted stats (park-adjusted numbers rounded to the nearest integer).

	AB	H	2B	3B	HR	BB	HBP	K	GDP	SH	SF
Raw	454	165	46	3	23	64	4	61	11	0	2
Adjust.	454	149	44	3	18	64	4	68	11	0	2

Walker had a .445 on-base average and a .630 slugging percentage. His park-adjusted figures were .413 and .559.

Step 9 - plug the park-adjusted stats into the runs produced vehicle of your choice

The runs produced vehicle of our choice is our new Extrapolated Runs (XR) method, but that really leads into our next article. By the way, Larry Walker produced 110.2 Extrapolated Runs, but only 95.7 park-adjusted Extrapolated Runs.

PARK FACTORS FOR TOMORROW

What exactly makes up a park effect?

Lately I've taken to questioning if the common methods used to compute park effects (ours included) are doing just that. I define a park effect as the influence a ballpark has on the events and outcome of a game (perhaps you have some other definition?), yet I wonder if the current methods carry some hidden assumptions that produce park effects with some baggage attached.

If I was to compare the bushels of beet production on my lower forty to Farmer John's down the road, how would I go about it? Measure it in the first year and say mine produces 10% more? Then measure it in the second year and say no, my field actually produces 5% more? What if we measure in Year 3 and it turns out that my field produces 15% more? And suppose if in Year 4, Farmer John's field produces 3% more? Would we constantly be switching the estimates of how better or worse my field is, going back and forth with "hey it's this, no it's really that" statements every year? Yet this is the present state-of-the-art in measuring park effects.

Or would we instead measure the yields and make our estimate for the first year and then adjust that estimate with the results from the second year? Isn't this the way most statistical sampling is done - take a series of samples or measures and find some kind of average to derive your estimate?. Where else but with park effects is the last measurement regarded as the only one that should be used to make your estimate Granted, if Farmer John and I decided to farm new fields, we would likely ignore the prior results from the old fields. Baring that, there would be no good reason not to use multiple year results to compare our beet production.

The park effect methods are purported to measure precisely that, park effects, but I would maintain that they actually measure three things:

1. the park effect
2. the interaction between the players and the park
3. random fluctuations (or what we might call sampling error)

For all three of these, a case can be made that we'd be better served to compute park effects using data for multiple years rather than just for a single year. Since any data outside of the most tightly controlled experiments will have random fluctuations, sometimes these fluctuations will be on the low end of whatever the true value is, often they'll be near the middle and sometimes they'll be on the high end. Using data for multiple years ensures that these fluctuations have a much greater chance of balancing out, while with a single year's results, you have no guarantee what you are getting - you risk the chance that these fluctuations could be closer to a high or low extreme. Similarly, if we want to isolate the park effect, examining data for multiple years gives a much better chance of coming up with a value closer to whatever the true park effect value is than if we rely on a single value for a single year.

Finally, we have the interaction between the players and the park. For example, a park might have a short right-field porch that a lefty slugger might be able to take advantage of, leading to increased home run production. The question is who gets the credit - the player or the park? If the advantage can be easily and repeatedly duplicated, then give credit to the park. However, if the advantage proves somewhat difficult to replicate, then shouldn't the player receive credit? Isn't this the mark of a great strategist - to be able to exploit your situation in a manner superior to ordinary men? If the particulars of a ballpark provide the opening you need to best take advantage of your abilities, I say more power to you.

What does this have to do with single vs. multiple year park effects? Under the single season measurement of park effects, the park always gets the credit. Any occurrence in the home park which can't be replicated on the road is labeled as part of the park effect, with the stats of those who play there diminished accordingly. In this case, all the lefty slugger with the short right field porch is doing is feeding the park effect.

However, with multiple-year measurements, the question becomes one of difficulty of replication. The player is given credit unless the results can be routinely replicated by those who play in the park over time. Since multiple year park effects involve some kind of averaging, if a situation repeats itself consistently, it will become part of the average and folded into the park effect.

One might argue that out lefty slugger shouldn't reap the benefit of playing in a park that plays to this strength. But isn't much of baseball strategy involved with putting players in situations they can take advantage of? What is behind the whole idea of platooning but to place players in situations which are most favorable to them? Yet we don't hear cries of adjusting a player's stats for a "platooning effect". If the nature of a given park can be exploited commonly by many players, then it is indeed a park effect. Yet if only select players can take advantage of opportunities that a park offers, then give credit to those players who successfully manage to exploit them.

Can we talk about the Rockies?

Exhibit A when looking at multiple years is, of course, the Colorado Rockies and Coors Field. Here is the Coors Field park factors listed by Stats, Inc. in their annual Major League Handbook:

1995 - 164
1996 - 172
1997 - 133
1998 - 160

If I played for the Rockies and annually produced the exact same stats which resulted in 150 runs produced or created, here are approximations for the number of park-adjusted runs created I might be given credit for each year (assuming an equal number of plate appearances at home and on the road):

1995 - 114
1996 - 110
1997 - 129
1998 - 115

I played in the same park and produced the same stats in 1997 as the other years, yet are we to believe that I suddenly got better, only to fall back to my previous level in 1998?

The problem isn't limited to the Rockies. Here are Stats, Inc. park factors for the Padres and Jack Murphy/Qualcomm Stadium:

1995 - 88
1996 - 87
1997 - 92
1998 - 75

So did something happen to the park causing the Padre batters to take a dive at home last year? Or did something happen with their pitchers on the road? I lean a bit towards the pitchers theory, but I think the main reason for the clubs low park effect in 1998 is that the Padres had a veteran, harmonious club that got off to a good start, and all those contributed to their playing exceptionally well as a club on the road. So because of that do we cut the production of Padre batters at home by 17% from 1997?

So you prefer your poison in nice, discrete, self-contained units?

Why have analysts been reluctant to tackle using multiple years to compute park factors? For one thing, single years are a lot easier to deal with. With multiple years, you encounter questions of how much weight to I give each year's data or what if a team moves to a new ballpark. Also you run into a problem with what I call current vs. historical comparisons. Suppose I wanted to look at data over a 5-year period to compute park factors. If I was interested in looking at park-adjusted performance for the 1940 season, I might look at data for the 5 years from 1938 to 1942. What do I do if I want to look at park-adjusted performance for the 1998 season? Ten years from now, I would probably look at the 1996 to 2000 seasons. But for the moment in time, I'd have to settle for using data from 1994 to 1998.

Another possible reason analysts have avoided multiple-year park effects is because it's simply easier to treat each year as a nice, discrete unit. You never have to consider why things are different from last year, it can all be passed off as due to the effect of the park. You just happen to have a set of fleet fielders this year who run down everything in your spacey outfield. Park effect. Your guys are hitting great in the clutch this year because of that fine home cooking (or stinking in the clutch because they're constantly fighting with the wife). Park effect. Either that or the cosmic fickle finger of fate just wills it to be so. If that's how you view things, limiting park effect calculations to a single year makes perfect sense. Moreover, start getting into multiple year park effects and you have to begin making some subjective judgments. Things can get start getting messy and your methods are open to criticism. In ways it can seem a lot easier to treat each year as a nice little self-contained package.

I should remark that our colleague Jim Furtado prefers computing single-year park effects, and he cites a reason we haven't discussed yet - weather, or what we might call park-environment interaction. Jim has a good point, and the first situation that comes to mind is the Cubs and Wrigley Field with the question of how much in any given year does the wind blow in or out. Indeed in 1997, the Cubs showed a pronounced spike in their park effect for home runs. Was the wind blowing out more in 1997 than in a normal year. I don't know, but I do know that in two places where the weather should be a minimal consideration, San Diego and Los Angeles, the Padres had a home run spike in 1994 even more pronounced than the Cubs spike, while the Dodgers showed a home run factor depression in 1995 and 1996 which was about equal in magnitude to the Cubs spike. I'm not adverse to changing the methodology if it can be demonstrated that the weather has a greater effect on park factors than the other issues raised in this article. While it is likely weather has some effect, I'm not convinced that it is by any means the dominant one.

Part of my job involves developing casualty forecasts for combat scenarios, and it's one of the best examples of what I call reality-based modeling. The theoretical purity of your methods isn't going to amount to squat if tax money is being squandered on unneeded personnel and supplies, or even worse, men and women wind up dying because of lack of these resources. The task is to "make the best estimates you can with the information you have available", and simple, nice solutions be damned.

So with park factors, are you going to settle for what is theoretically nice and clean or are you going to try and make the best estimate you can with the information is available? There is no true way of putting forth a value and saying definitively that it's a team's park factor for a given year. Park factors are always guesses - but some guesses are better than others.

APPENDIX

Computing Park Effects With An Unbalanced Schedule And Interleague Play

Much as we like interleague play, unfortunately it's not much fun when it comes to computing park effects. We'll use the Red Sox strikeout factor for illustrative purposes:

Step 1 - compute the total strikeouts and plate appearances for the Sox and their opponents at Fenway. Do the same for the Sox and their opponents for the Red Sox road games, and divide:

$$\frac{(K/PA) \text{ for Red Sox games (both teams)}}{(K/PA) \text{ for Red Sox road games (both teams)}}$$

Call this the Preliminary Home Park Strikeout Factor.

Step 2 - this is the hard one. Compute a Preliminary Opposition Park Factor which is the summation of the base home factor you already computed for each opponent times the percent of road games you play against them. For example, suppose the Red Sox during the course of the season played 3 games in Anaheim, 2 in Atlanta, 6 in Baltimore and so forth out of a total of 81 games on the road. For the Red Sox Preliminary Opposition Park Strikeout Factor, you would have something like:

(Angels home strikeout factor * 3/81) + (Braves home strikeout factor * 2/81) + (Orioles home strikeout factor * 6/81) + ...

A lot of work, but it's probably the price you have to pay if you're going to do things right in these days of unbalanced schedules.

Step 3 - your Preliminary Home Park Strikeout Factor was calculated under the assumption of a balanced schedule. We need to correct for this. So we have:

$$\text{Semi-Final Home Park Strikeout Factor} = \frac{\text{Preliminary Home Park Strikeout Factor}}{\text{Preliminary Opposition Park Strikeout Factor}}$$

Step 4 - the other hard one. Compute the Semi-Final Opposition Park Strikeout Factor the same way you did the Preliminary Opposition Park Strikeout Factor in Step 2, the only difference being you use the Semi-Final Home Park Factors computed in Step 3 instead of the Preliminary computed in Step 1.

Step 5 - Just a mopping up operation from here. Compute the Yearly Home Park Strikeout Factors by adjusting the Semi-Final Home Park Strikeouts Factors so that the average for all teams is 1.000 (you would multiply each Semi-Final Factor by the number of teams and divide by the sum of all Semi-Final Factors).

Step 6 - compute the Yearly Opposition Park Strikeout Factors by adjusting the Semi-Final Opposition Park Strikeouts Factors so that the average for all teams is 1.000

By the way, the Opposition Park Factors should be near 1.00, and will only fall outside of the 0.95 to 1.05 range infrequently.

EXTRAPOLATED AVERAGE

G. JAY WALKER

Extrapolated Runs and the soon to be discussed Extrapolated Wins are the two pillars of the new offensive production system. Extrapolated Runs **(XR)** is your production stat and Extrapolated Wins **(XW)** is the new measure for estimating how many extra wins your team can expect to gain from having your offensive production in the line-up instead of that of a replacement player.

Both **XR** *and* **XW** *are a function of playing time. The more you play, the more* **XR** *you produce and the more* **XW** *you pile up (assuming you're better than a replacement player). However, at times it's useful to have a simple rate stat, a measure of how well you perform regardless of your playing time, which is the same as a measure of how much you produce given your playing time. Our simple rate stat is called Extrapolated Average, and it's equal to your Extrapolated Runs divided by your Plate Appearances* **(XR/PA)**. *We call it* **XAVG** *for short.*

XAVG is it's own stat; it's not rescaled to resemble batting average or anything else. If you're "hitting" .200 with **XAVG**, it's nothing to be ashamed of - only three players had an **XAVG** over .200 in 1998. (One's named McGwire and one's named Walker, but none of the three are named Sosa or Furtado). An **XAVG** of .100 is not particular good, but is still above the atrocious range. An average **XAVG** seems to be around the .125 range. The American League had an **XAVG** of .128 in 1997 and .129 in 1998. For the National League, the figures are .121 in 1997 and .120 in 1998. Let's run through a few examples to get an idea what might some typical **XAVG** values for different levels of play. All these figures here are derived from raw stats which are not park-adjusted: Here are some **XAVG** summary figures for 1998, looking at all players with 400+ plate appearances:

	AL			NL		
80th Percentile	Jason Giambi	Oak	.158	Brian Jordan	StL	.164
50th Percentile	Jose Cruz	Tor	.136	Eric Young	LA	.133
20th Percentile	Mike Bordick	Bal	.113	Wilton Guerrero	LA-Mtl	.108
Bottom	Sandy Alomar	Clev	.077	Rey Ordonez	NY	.068

Here are the **XAVG** numbers for the starters on the World Series participants:

Yankees		Padres	
Bernie Williams	.185	Greg Vaughn	.185
Paul O'Neill	.161	Ken Caminiti	.160
Derek Jeter	.160	Tony Gwynn	.155
Tino Martinez	.153	Wally Joyner	.140
Scott Brosius	.150	Quilvio Veras	.126
Jorge Posada	.137	Steve Finley	.112
Chuck Knoblauch	.134	Chris Gomez	.110
Chad Curtis	.122	Carlos Hernandez	.092

Finally, here are the non-park adjusted top tens in **XAVG** for each league in 1998:

AL			NL		
Albert Belle	Chi	.207	Mark McGwire	StL	.244
Jim Thome	Cle	.190	Larry Walker	Col	.210
Mo Vaughn	Bos	.190	Barry Bonds	SF	.199
Edgar Martinez	Sea	.189	Sammy Sosa	Chi	.198
Juan Gonzalez	Tex	.189	Andres Galarraga	Atl	.191
Ken Griffey Jr	Sea	.188	John Olerud	NY	.190
Carlos Delgado	Tor	.186	Moises Alou	Hou	.188
Bernie Williams	NY	.185	Jeff Bagwell	Hou	.187
Manny Ramirez	Cle	.184	Gary Sheffield	Flo-LA	.186
Tim Salmon	Ana	.183	Greg Vaughn	SD	.185

By the way, Larry Walker's park-adjusted **XAVG** was .183.

XAVG answers the question of how many Extrapolated Runs does a player produces every time he steps to the plate. Just as **XR** measures quantity, **XAVG** measures quality. It's the basic rate stat used to link Extrapolated Runs to the new measure of offensive wins above replacement, Extrapolated Wins.

EXTRAPOLATED WINS

G. JAY WALKER and JIM FURTADO

INTRODUCTION

On November 19, 1998, Major League Baseball posted the following on its web site:

Sammy Sosa may have fallen short in his epic home run chase with Mark McGwire, but the Chicago Cubs outfielder had a season that carried more clout with the baseball writers. Sosa today was named National League Most Valuable Player by the Baseball Writers Association of America, easily defeating McGwire, the St. Louis Cardinals first baseman who hit a major-league record 70 homers, four more than his rival and close friend. The 30-year-old Sosa received 30 of the 32 first-place votes and was second on the two other ballots for 438 points.

Was Sammy Sosa or Mark McGwire the best offensive player in 1998? Both players are decent but non-stellar fielders playing a lesser-skill position, so one would assume defense didn't play much of a role in deciding the final vote. One would also like to assume that for a group as astute as the baseball writers, the "supporting cast" argument (Sosa's team making the playoffs while McGwire's didn't) wasn't the deciding criteria in this one-on-one matchup of history's most prolific single-season home run hitters (actually a big if). So were the writers correct in their near unanimous preference for Sosa as MVP? Bonus question—how many more wins did the real winner add to his team compared to the runner-up? One? Two? Do I hear three? We'll reveal the answer at the end of this article.

Many of you are familiar with the Offensive Wins Above Replacement (**OWAR**) methods used in previous editions of this book. The basic idea was to measure how many offensive wins a player was worth to his team over a replacement-level player. The general method to calculate **OWAR** would be to compute a player's run production rate and subtract that from the run production rate of a replacement level player. You would then multiply the result by the number of offensive games a player was credited with (basically a measure of playing time) to get his **OWAR**.

Extrapolated Wins (**XW**) is the second pillar of our new **XR/XW** methodology and it replaces the **OWAR** methodology. The concept is the same—to measure value over a replacement player—but the entire methodology has been revamped.

In last year's BBBA, we made our case that the way of measuring **OWAR** had some underlying problems. We're not going to run through the whole argument again, but the gist of it centered around measuring the games a player was credited with in terms of the outs he recorded. So if a player is perfect and records no outs, then under that system, the player would be credited with zero offensive games and his **OWAR** would be zero. So if a perfect player is worth nothing, at what point did the system start breaking down and do something other than what it was intended to do?

We outlined some possible solutions, including using plate appearances as the way to measure how many offensive games to credit a player with. While plate appearances are better than outs, it is still not the optimal solution. That's because 1) it doesn't take into account the different contexts players operate in, and 2) it ignores the indirect effect a player has on his team's run scoring.

Of course, these two limitations are intertwined. Context is not only driven by outside influences like park effects, but is also dependent on the interaction between players and the decisions the manager makes about whom to play and where to place those players in the lineup.

These two notions of placing a player in a team context and measuring his indirect effect on team run scoring are at the heart of the new Extrapolated Wins methodology.

HOW SHOULD RUN PRODUCTION BE MODELED?

Bill James and many others have long postulated that run scoring could be represented by:

$$\frac{(On\ Base) * (Advancement)}{Opportunity}$$

With a small loss of accuracy, this can be re-written as **OBA*TB** (which, of course, is the foundation of James' Runs Created). Although this is close, we think it's slightly off the mark. A better representation would be:

*Run Scoring = Opportunities * Run Production Ability*

This is a very simple concept. The more opportunities you have and the better you are at taking advantage of those opportunities, the more runs you'll score. Of course the trick is how to best represent this basic concept.

MEASURING OPPORTUNITY

The first concern in setting up a system to measure players is how could we properly represent the interaction between players on a team. We centered on the idea that "players consume plate appearances, teams consume outs". In particular, we wondered what would be the best way to properly account for the difference between the opportunity for the team (measured in outs) and the opportunity for the team's players (measured in plate appearances).

We start with the 27 outs that a team gets to work with each game. At this point of the process, the number of opportunities for the team (27) is the same as the opportunities for players (27). Of course, when the game starts, the clock starts ticking and things change.

Outs are the minutes on baseball's clock. When a team runs out of outs, it can't score any more runs. However, unlike a regular clock, baseball's timing mechanism nudges along sporadically. That's because whenever a player avoids making an out, time stands still.

We can account for that piece of the picture by defining opportunity as follows:

$$\textbf{\textit{Opportunities}} = \textit{TeamOuts / (Outs Consumed / Plate Appearances)}$$

In the numerator are the outs a team gets in a season. (In a normal season this would equate to 4374 outs or 162 games times 27 outs.) This figure equates to the team's opportunity.

In the denominator is the rate that the players on the team consume outs. The faster players consume outs, the faster the baseball clock ticks and as a result, the fewer opportunities (in plate appearances) the players on the team will get. This step represents the conversion process from the team's opportunities to the players' opportunities. The result is the number of opportunities the team's players have to generate runs-the team's total plate appearances.

The denominator, (Outs Consumed/Plate Appearances), we call the OUT% and is defined as:

$$\textit{OUT\%} = \textit{(AB-H+CS+GIDP+SF+SH) / PA}$$

Then we have *Opportunities* = *(TeamOuts/OUT%)* and

$$\textbf{\textit{Run Scoring}} = \textit{(TeamOuts/OUT\%)} * \textit{Run Production Ability}$$

MEASURING RUN PRODUCTION ABILITY

To generate the number of runs a team will score, we must come up with a measure of the ability of players to generate runs or, more specifically, the rate that players produce runs given a certain opportunity. Since we've already developed a run production method, Extrapolated Runs **(XR)**, this process is easy. All we have to do is divide **XR** by the plate appearances. If you've been reading the other articles in this section, you already know that we refer to this as Extrapolated Average or **XAVG**.

The formula can now be written as:

$$\textbf{\textit{Run Scoring}} = \textit{(TeamOuts/OUT\%)} * \textit{XAVG}$$

Note that for a team at the end of a season, all the extra terms cancel out leaving only **XR**:

$$\textbf{Run Scoring} = \textit{(TeamOuts/OUT\%)} * \textit{XAVG} = \textit{TeamOuts/(TeamOuts/TeamPA)} * \textit{XR/TeamPA},$$
and the TeamOuts and TeamPA terms cancel, leaving XR.

ADDING THE PLAYER INTO THE MIX

Of course, if we only wanted to measure teams, we wouldn't have to go through all these steps, **XR** would suffice. However, to properly assess players we need these extra measures.

This leads us to the next few steps which measure how an individual player affects a team's run scoring, or more specifically, how a player affects the team's Opportunities and Run Production Ability.

To do that, we first place each player into a standard team context. This step is important. As Jim said in the historical piece on offensive production measures, "Baseball is a team game; therefore, players should be evaluated in a team context." That's what the XW methodology does. It places players into a standard team context. The standard context we chose is an average team. Now, you may be shaking your head because Jim questioned Pete Palmer's choice of an average baseline for his Linear Weights method. Don't worry; we're not being inconsistent, because we're talking about two different things.

Pete's baseline was the comparison of a player to an average player. We don't do that. This is what we do:
- **a.** Place a player in an average team context
- **b.** Compute his effect on the team's run production
- **c.** Replace the player with a replacement player
- **d.** Compute his effect on the team's run production
- **e.** Compare the difference

In effect, we use an average team's context and a replacement player's baseline.

Returning to our formula from above, we have:

$$\textbf{\textit{Run Scoring}} = \textit{(TeamOuts/OUT\%)*XAVG}$$

To evaluate a player's effect on the team, we must calculate the effect his play has on both the team's Opportunity **(TeamOuts/OUT%)** and its Run Production Ability **(XAVG)**. To accomplish this task we factor in playing time.

Bill James used outs to represent the player's part of this process, but as Jay pointed out last year in his Beauty With A Blemish article, there are problems with using outs in this way. Instead, we factor this part of the puzzle by using something we call Play Percentage **(PLAY%)**. **PLAY%** is simply the player's total plate appearances (AB+TBB+HP+SF+SH) divided by his team's total plate appearances.

For example, say a player had 600 PA, while his team had 6000 PA. That player would then have a **PLAY%** of 10.0%. This method takes into account not only a player's playing time, but also, his line-up placement. Additionally, it filters out the run scoring ability of his original team. Players who play on high scoring teams get to the plate more often because their team's offense is very efficient. That's one of the reasons Derek Jeter got to the plate 694 times in 1998 even though he missed 13 games. Of course in Jeter's case, he was helped because he also batted either first or second in the lineup all year.

THE BIG HURT EXAMPLE

We'll now illustrate how we incorporate these factors with an example. We'll use the 1998 American League and Frank Thomas.

Let's start off with some league figures:

Here are some basic numbers...

$$\text{\textbf{LXR}} = \text{League Extrapolated Runs} = 11426.3$$
$$\text{\textbf{LPA}} = \text{League Plate Appearances} = 88165$$
$$\text{\textbf{LOuts}} = \text{League Outs} = AB - H + CS + SH + SF + GDP = 60915$$

which are used to compute the three stats we'll need:

$$\text{\textbf{LOUT\%}} = \text{League Out \%} = LOuts/LPA = 60915 / 88165 = .6909$$
$$\text{\textbf{LXAVG}} = \text{League XAVG} = LXR/LPA = 11426.3/88165 = .1296$$
$$\text{TeamOuts} = \text{\# of Outs for an average team} = 60915/14 = 4350.9$$

With these stats we can calculate the expected number of Extrapolated Runs an average team would score using the **(TeamOuts/OUT%)*XAVG** formula.

For the 1998 AL: $(4350.9/.6909)*.1296 = 816.1$ Extrapolated Runs

What would an average team score with Frank Thomas in the lineup? First, his basic numbers:

Extrapolated Runs	=	113.51
Plate Appearances	=	712
Outs	=	455
White Sox Plate Appearances	=	Team PA = 6280

Important note - to keep this first example straight-forward, we're going to use Thomas' actual numbers instead of his park-adjusted ones. The results we derive from this example for Thomas will vary a bit from results you see elsewhere in the book, because those other results use park-adjusted figures.

The stats we'll use are:

$$\text{OUT\%} = Outs/PA = 455 / 712 = .6390$$
$$\text{XAVG} = \text{Extrapolated Average} = XR/PA = 113.51 / 712 = .1594$$
$$\text{PLAY\%} = \text{Playing Time Percent} = PA/Team\ PA = 712 / 6280 = .1134$$

Using these three stats, in addition to the league average stats, we can calculate how many runs an average team would score with Frank Thomas. To illustrate, we'll break the formula into its two components: Opportunity and Run Production Ability.

OPPORTUNITIES: FRANK THOMAS IN THE LINEUP

Plate appearances represent the number of opportunities for a team, and we saw above that this can be expressed as **(TeamOuts/OUT%)**. To adjust this figure for Thomas, we use Thomas' **OUT%** for the amount of playing time he had, and use the league **OUT%** (**LOUT%**) for the balance. Since Thomas' **OUT%** is less than the league average, he will generate additional plate appearances for his team.

$$\text{\textit{NewTmPA}} = (TeamOuts / ((OUT\%*PLAY\%) + (LOUT\%*(1-PLAY\%)))$$

For Thomas the calculation is: $4350.9/((.6390*.1134) + (.6909*(1-.1134))) = 6351.5$ PA

Without Thomas, an average team would be estimated to have 6297.4 PA, so with the outs Thomas avoids over an average player, he gives his team another 54 plate appearances.

Before we move on, a brief digression. Note that to calculate the plate appearances gained by Thomas, we couldn't use the formula:

$$\text{\textit{(Thomas plate appearances)*(LOUT\% - Thomas' OUT\%)}} = (712)*(.6909 - .6390) = 36.95.$$

While Thomas directly saves 37 outs, to assume the team gains only 37 plate appearances makes the assumption that all those additional plate appearances resulted in outs. In fact, on average about 25 or 26 will result in outs, while the remaining 11 or 12 will result in men getting on base, generating still more plate appearances. Once all is said and done, the team should have about 54 additional plate appearances resulting from the outs Thomas avoided.

RUN PRODUCTION ABILITY: FRANK THOMAS IN THE LINEUP

Next, we calculate how Thomas would affect the team's Run Production Ability. The basic idea is the same as in the previous step, we use Thomas' Extrapolated Average (**XAVG**) for the amount of playing time he had, and use the **LXAVG** for the balance:

$$NewTmXAVG = (XAVG*PLAY\%) + (LXAVG*(1-PLAY\%))$$

For Thomas the calculation is: $(.1594*.1134) + (.1296*(1-.1134)) = .1330$
Putting it all together:

$$Run\ Scoring = Opportunities * Run\ Production\ Ability = NewTmPA * NewTmXAVG.$$

For Thomas this equals $(6351.5) * (.1330)$ or 844.7 runs.
An average team with Thomas playing in place of an average player will score 844.7 - 816.1 or 28.6 additional runs.

THE REPLACEMENT EXAMPLE

Now we give a replacement player the same treatment Thomas got. We need three figures for the replacement player, the replacement **PLAY% (RPLAY%)**, the replacement **OUT% (ROUT%)** and the replacement **XAVG (RXAVG)**.

For the replacement:
RPLAY% = .1134
ROUT% = .7484
RXAVG = .1001

Since the replacement player is taking the place of Thomas, his PLAY% is the same as Thomas'. Appendix A and Appendix B show how the values for **ROUT%** and **RXAVG** are derived.

Appendix A is actually a discussion of what is meant by the replacement rate and replacement level. In it, we talk about the concept of the Runs Deflator. We strongly suggest you read it. Appendix B gets into the actual calculations for **ROUT%** and **RXAVG**. That one we leave up to you.

While there is general agreement as to what a good "ballpark" replacement rate should be, the actual replacement value is a subjective call. For Extrapolated Wins purposes, we define the replacement rate as a .350 offense (with an average defense).

OPPORTUNITIES - REPLACEMENT PLAYER IN THE LINEUP

We use the exact same idea here that we did for Frank Thomas. To adjust the team's opportunities or plate appearances because of the replacement player, we use his **OUT%** for the amount of playing time he had, and use the **LOUT%** for the balance.

$$NewTmPA = (TeamOuts / ((ROUT\%*RPLAY\%) + (LOUT\%*(1-RPLAY\%)))$$

For the replacement player this equals: $4350.9/((.7484*.1134) + (.6909*(1-.1134))) = 6238.6$ PA
It is estimated that the average team would have 6297.4 PA, so with the outs that the replacement player incurs over an average player (given Thomas' playing time), an average team would lose 6297.4-6238.6 or about 59 plate appearances for the season.

RUN PRODUCTION ABILITY - REPLACEMENT PLAYER IN THE LINEUP

This calculation also parallels the one for Frank Thomas. Again, the basic idea to use the replacement's XAVG for the amount of playing time he had, and use the **LXAVG** for the balance:

$$NewTmXAVG = (RXAVG*PLAY\%) + (LXAVG*(1-PLAY\%))$$

For the replacement player this value is: $(.1001*.1134) + (.1296*(1-.1134)) = .1263$
Finally for the replacement player:

$$Run\ Scoring = Opportunities * Run\ Production\ Ability = NewTmPA * NewTmXAVG, which\ equals\ (6238.6) * (.1263)\ or\ 787.9\ runs.$$

An average team with a replacement player in place of an average player will cost the team 816.1 - 787.9 or about 28 runs (given Thomas' playing time).

BRINGING IT HOME

Now that we know how many runs an average team would score with Frank Thomas in their lineup compared to a replacement player, the rest if just a mopping up operation using some familiar tools. We place these runs into the Pythagorean Projection formula to estimate the winning percentage for a team with Thomas versus a team with a replacement player:

$$= \frac{AverTRuns(Thomas)^{1.83}}{AverTRuns(Thomas)^{1.83} + AverTRuns(Rpl)^{1.83}}$$

$$= \frac{(844.7)^{1.83}}{(844.7)^{1.83} + (787.9)^{1.83}} = .5318$$

This is the estimated winning % for a team with Thomas against a team with a replacement player. If we were to compute winning % for an average team against the team with a replacement player, the result would be .5161. Computing the winning percent for a team with a replacement player against itself gives a trivial result of .500.

The final step in computing the Extrapolated Wins for Thomas is to plug this number into a variation of the old Offensive Wins Above Replacement (**OWAR**) formula. The original **OWAR** formula was of the form:

OWAR = (Player Games) x (Player Winning % - Replacement Player Winning %)

One problem with this formula is trying to define Player Games, especially when the measuring unit is in terms of outs. But now, everything is defined in a team context:

Extrapolated Wins = (Team Games) x (Thomas Team Winning % - Replacement Team Winning %)
= (162) X (.5318 - .5000) = 5.15 Extrapolated Wins

Frank Thomas has 5.15 Extrapolated Wins for 1998. This is the estimated number of games an average team would win with Thomas in their lineup in place of a replacement player. Keep in mind that this is the number of Extrapolated Wins (XW) for Thomas using non-park-adjusted numbers.

The number of XW that an average player would have, given Thomas 712 plate appearances, is 162 * (.5161 - .5000) = 2.61. At least for 1998, Thomas produced about two and a half more offensive wins than an average player.

Okay, now that the math is out of the way, who were the best offensive players in 1998?

	American League					National League		
Rank	**Pos**	**Name**	**OXW**		**Rank**	**Pos**	**Name**	**OXW**
1	LF	Albert Belle	8.29		1	1B	Mark McGwire	11.63
	1B	Mo Vaughn	6.98			1B	John Olerud	8.64
	DH	Edgar Martinez	6.79			RF	Vladimir Guerrero	8.38
	1B	Rafael Palmeiro	6.61			LF	Barry Bonds	8.27
5	CF	Ken Griffey	6.40		5	LF	Greg Vaughn	8.16
	DH	Tim Salmon	6.23			RF	Sammy Sosa	7.93
	1B	Carlos Delgado	6.16			2B	Craig Biggio	7.41
	SS	Alex Rodriguez	5.97			1B	Andres Galarraga	7.39
	CF	Bernie Williams	5.83			1B	Jeff Bagwell	7.34
10	RF	Juan Gonzalez	5.79		10	LF	Moises Alou	7.30
	RF	Manny Ramirez	5.64			3B	Chipper Jones	7.28
	2B	Jose Offerman	5.55			RF	Gary Sheffield	7.16
	1B	Jason Giambi	5.31			C	Mike Piazza	6.94
	1B	Jim Thome	5.29			CF	Ray Lankford	6.61
15	RF	Eric Davis	5.15		15	C	Jason Kendall	6.33
	DH	Frank Thomas	5.12			3B	Scott Rolen	6.08
	SS	Nomar Garciaparra	5.10			RF	Larry Walker	5.94
	SS	Derek Jeter	5.10			SS	Barry Larkin	5.90
	DH	Matt Stairs	4.90			3B	Ken Caminiti	5.43
20	RF	Paul O'Neill	4.86		20	RF	Brian Jordan	5.27

You may be wondering how McGwire could possibly be 3.70 **XR** better than Sosa.

A COMPARISON USING BASIC STATISTICS

To compare McGwire and Sosa, let's begin with a comparison of some of their raw numbers:

	BA	OBP	SLG	XR
McGwire	.299	.470	.752	166
Sosa	.308	.377	.647	143

Sosa topped McGwire in Batting Average by nine points or 3%.
McGwire bested Sosa in **OBP** (25%), **SLG** (16%), and **XR** (16%).
Of course these are the "raw" numbers. Let's take a look at their park adjusted ones:

	aBA	aOBP	aSLG	aXR
McGwire	.298	.467	0742	164
Sosa	.304	.372	.637	140

Notice that both players appear to have played in slight hitter's parks in 1998. Also notice that adjusting for park doesn't radically change either's production figures.

Taking these statistics in isolation doesn't paint a complete picture. Each individual stat can be thought of as an individual color on our player evaluation palette. To capture the subtle nuances of the game and to create a realistic depiction, we must capably utilize our statistical brush. That's what the **XW** methodology was designed to do-to better capture the interaction between player and team.

A COMPARISON USING SOME OF THE XW STATISTICS

Let's take a look at how Sosa and McGwire compare using the **XW** methodology. Here's the park-adjusted stats needed to calculate their **XW**:

	aXAVG	aOUT%	PLAY%
Mark McGwire	0.241	0.545	10.62%
Sammy Sosa	0.194	0.668	11.29%

Both McGwire's and Sosa's park-adjusted **XAVG (aXAVG)** are very impressive. They both rank at the top of the NL in 1998.

502 Plate Appearances needed to qualify.

Rank	Name	aXAVG
1	Mark McGwire	.241
	Greg Vaughn	.200
	Vladimir Guerrero	.198
	John Olerud	.196
5	Sammy Sosa	.194
	Gary Sheffield	.194
	Barry Bonds	.194
	Andres Galarraga	.188
	Jeff Bagwell	.186
10	Larry Walker	.185
	Moises Alou	.185
	Mike Piazza	.184
	Ray Lankford	.181
	Chipper Jones	.177
15	Ken Caminiti	.177

McGwire's **aXAVG,** however, is .047 better than Sosa's. That means that, on average, McGwire produced .047 more runs each PA than Sosa did, or an additional run for about every 21 plate appearances.

Looking at the Top 15 in **aOUT%**, we see that McGwire again tops the list, while Sosa's name is conspicuously absent.

502 Plate Appearances needed to qualify.

Rank	Name	aOUT%
1	Mark McGwire	.545
	John Olerud	.573
	Gary Sheffield	.586
	Barry Bonds	.604
5	Jason Kendall	.610
	Jeff Bagwell	.610
	Larry Walker	.614
	Craig Biggio	.620
	Ray Lankford	.622
10	Moises Alou	.628
	Mike Piazza	.629
	Barry Larkin	.630
	Andres Galarraga	.630
	Quilvio Veras	.631
15	Bob Abreu	.633

As a matter of fact, we'd have to include twenty more names on the list before Sosa would appear. In 1998, his .668 **OUT%** ranked 35th behind such notable players as Andy Fox (30th with .662) and Chris Gomez (32nd with .664). This indicates that Mark McGwire used up far less outs in producing runs than Sammy Sosa did. This is the key reason why McGwire had so many more Extrapolated Wins than Sosa.

Regarding the last piece of the **XW** "stats pack", Sosa's **PLAY%**. is slightly higher than McGwire's **PLAY%**. This means that over the course of the season, Sosa had more opportunities to affect his team's offense (not by a radical difference, though).

THE STATS TRANSLATED TO THE XW METHODOLOGY

If these numbers are inserted into the **XW** system, we can generate some other figures for comparison. We take a slightly different approach here by starting with the final **XW** result and working our way back through the numbers.

The final **XW** numbers indicate that McGwire (11.63) would be 3.70 wins better than Sosa (7.93) when both are compared to a replacement player.

If Mark McGwire and Sammy Sosa were placed on a team completely comprised of average players in 1998, and if each were given the same amount of their Plate Appearances as in real life, how many runs would their respective teams score?

McGwire's team would score 853.8 runs while Sosa's would score 809.9. That's a difference of 43.9 runs. Where does that stem from?

Step 1

Because of the high rate of runs per PA **(XAVG)** that McGwire and Sosa produced, each would generate more runs than an average player would. Given the same percentage of PA as each player had in 1998, McGwire would generate 80.15 additional runs, while Sosa would generate 52.17 additional runs.

For this part of the equation, McGwire adds 27.98 more runs than Sosa because of his higher **XAVG**.

Step 2

Because McGwire and Sosa make outs at a lower rate than average player, they give their team more opportunities (more PA) to produce runs. McGwire presented 150.12 more PA to the Cards, while Sosa gave the Cubs an additional 31.96 PA. This is the part of run scoring that other methods ignore. That's why other methods don't properly evaluate a player's

ability to get on base and avoid making outs.

Part of the additional plate appearances that McGwire and Sosa generate come full around to directly give them more plate appearances at their higher production rates. McGwire's ability to avoid outs directly gave him the additional plate appearances to produce another 3.84 more runs for his team, while Sosa produced 0.70 more runs with his additional opportunities.

After Step 2, McGwire is now up to 83.99 runs. Sosa is up to 52.87. Big Mac now has a 31.12 run lead over Sosa.

Step 3

Most of McGwire's and Sosa's ability to avoid outs and generate additional opportunities goes to the benefit of their teammates in the form of additional plate appearances. Because of these additional opportunities, McGwire's teammates would generate 16.16 more runs; Sosa's teammates would generate 3.42 more runs.

Adding these runs to the totals from Step 2 gives McGwire 100.15 runs produced and Sosa 56.29 runs produced.

Since McGwire has more runs produced, we'll subtract Sosa's totals to generate the difference in their run production ability: 100.15-56.29 = 43.86 or 43.9 runs.

McGwire was the better offensive player in 1998 because he was better in the two areas that are most important for run scoring: the ability to get on base and avoid making outs, and the ability to directly produce runs.

WRAPPING IT UP

Like the old **OWAR** method, the new Extrapolated Wins method attempts to measure offensive wins above replacement. The key differences is that **XW** places the player in a team context and measures not only a player's direct contribution to the team but also his indirect contribution of (hopefully) avoiding outs and giving more opportunities to his teammates. Look for updates on the **XR/XW** methodology during the season at our web sites at *www.backatcha.com and www.baseball-stuff.com.*

Appendix A- Replacement Rates, Replacement Levels

There's been a lot of recent confusion about replacement rates, and I suppose BBBA isn't totally innocent in this matter. In last year's book when we were sketching out some proposed ideas and methods that evolved into the more rigorous **XR/XW** methodology, we inadvertently left off a replacement level-related term in one formula which caused our run estimates to be too conservative. Admittedly, our terminology was imprecise last year. Let's see in we can clear up any problems we may have caused last year as well as some of the general confusion out there.

To get a better handle on this replacement rate business, this year we've introduced the use of the Runs Deflator (our thanks to Stephen Tomlinson for this recommendation). You can combine the Runs Deflator with the Pythagorean formula to answer questions like how many fewer wins can I expect my team to have if they score 10% fewer runs. Or how many fewer wins will they have if they allow 20% more runs. Or you can combine the two - if my batters score 10% less runs AND my pitchers allow 20% more runs how many wins will it cost me? **This leads us to a few other premises:**

There are separate offensive and defensive replacement rates

The two are independent of each other (at least to the extent offense and defense are independent of each other in a real baseball game)

If the offensive and defensive replacement rates are the same, the team replacement rate will be something different, except for the value of .500. (This isn't so much of a premise but something that will be shown with the Pythagorean formula. We just thought we'd mention it here.)

Let's illustrate an example of using the Pythagorean formula to compute the Runs Deflator: How many fewer runs would my offense have to score and how many more runs would my defense have to give up so that my team can expect to play at a .350 level? Let's define terms first:

AvgRS - average runs scored (this would usually imply a league average)
AvgRA - average runs allowed (also usually a league average)
RD - Runs Deflator

Using the Pythagorean formula, we get an equation:

$$\frac{(AvgRS * RD)^{1.83}}{(AvgRS * RD)^{1.83} + (AvgRA / RD)^{1.83}} = .350$$

Make sure to note the differences in the two terms in the denominator. **(AvgRS * RD)** is the percent of runs you would expect to score compared to the average, and **(AvgRA / RD)** is the percent of runs you would give up compared to average.

If we solve for **RD,** we get RD = .8444. If my offense scores runs at 84.44% of an average offense and my defense gives up runs at (1/RD) = (1/.8444) = 118.42% of an average defense, we can expect that team's winning percentage to be around .350.

If you're assuming this is what BBBA means by a replacement level of .350, you're wrong. What we talk about is an offensive replacement level of .350. We don't make any assumptions about the defense other than to assume the player is on an average defensive team. The equation to solve for the Runs Deflator using the BBBA definition of replacement rates is:

$$\frac{(AvgRS * RD)^{1.83}}{(AvgRS * RD)^{1.83} + (AvgRA)^{1.83}} = .350$$

Make sure to note the difference in this equation and the one above it, namely the second part of the denominator is now **(AvgRA)** instead of **(AvgRA/RD)**. We're assuming a defense that gives up only an average number of runs. If we solve this equation for RD, we get RD = .713 as a Runs Deflator. In other words, if our offense scored only 71.3% of the runs of average offense, we would expect the team to play at the .350 level, given that the defense allowed an average number of runs. The .713 value is the amount of run reduction necessary to reach a replacement level as we define it.

The other point to note is that our .350 replacement rate is the offensive replacement rate given an average defense. What too many have been guilty of, including ourselves in the past, is to throw around the term "replacement rate", not clarifying as to whether it's the replacement rate for the entire team or just for the offense, and not specifying if the assumption is that the offense plays with an average defense or with a replacement defense.

So if our .350 replacement rate represents a .350 offense with an average defense, what would be the expected winning percentage for a replacement team, that is one with both a replacement offense and defense? We know that at the .350 replacement level the Run Deflator value is .713, we just have to apply that now to both the offense and defense. Our Pythagorean equation would look like this:

$$\frac{(.713)^{1.83}}{(.713)^{1.83} + (1 / .713)^{1.83}}$$

which equals .225, the expected winning percentage for a replacement team, that is, replacement players on both offense and defense. Over a 162 game schedule, this replacement team would expect to go 36-126. In last year's book, when we spoke of a replacement team going 57-105, we were imprecise. The 57-105 record is what would be expected of a replacement offense (with an average defense). A complete replacement team, both offense and defense, would be expected to have the 36-126 record.

Finally, why does BBBA set their replacement level at .350? There is no absolutely true replacement level, it is all a matter of conjecture. It's set at whatever level you feel most comfortable with. Some argue that the replacement rate should be set at the value of a utility player, some say it should be at the value of a Triple-A level player, some think you should look at lousy teams to get a sense of what is a proper replacement rate. All these are interesting arguments, but they're also theoretical arguments. If the replacement rate is part of a broader methodology like our **XR/XW** methodology, the replacement rate in practice becomes the point where you feel quantity and quality are in balance.

What do we mean by that? If you set you replacement rate too high, quality is going to trump quantity. Put it high enough and at some point guys with 50 Extrapolated Runs in 200 plate appearances are going to be rated higher than someone with 150 Extrapolated Runs in 700 plate appearances. Set the replacement rate too low, and quantity becomes foremost at the expense of quality. At some point guys with 90 Extrapolated Runs in 700 plate appearances will be rated ahead of players with 80 Extrapolated Runs in 500 plate appearances.

A general consensus has developed that a replacement level around .350 is the proper point where quantity and quality come into balance, and that is the value BBBA has used. In most seasons, only a handful of regular and semi-regular players have offensive seasons where they finish below this replacement level. The .350 level is a best guess, and theoretical arguments aside, replacement rates are always a best guess. There is no one right answer. It's the place where you feel comfortable that quantity and quality are in balance.

Appendix B - calculating the Out % (ROUT%) and the Extrapolated Average (RXAVG) for replacement players

If you've already read Appendix A, you've read about the Runs Deflator and how it's equal to 71.3% or .713 as we define it. It represents the percent of runs a team would score compared to an average team if they were at the "replacement level", which we define the as having a .350 offense accompanied by an average defense.

To get the **RXOUT%** and **RXAVG** for the replacement player, we first need to compute the amount of direct runs lost by the team because of the replacement player. From that, we can then compute **ROUT%** and **RXAVG**. We then apply these figures to a team context in a manner similar to what we did for Frank Thomas to get the total runs the replacement player costs the team, both direct and indirect.

The amount of direct runs the replacement player costs his team is:

$$(PA) * (LXAVG) - (PA) * (LXAVG) * (Runs\ Deflator) = (712)*(.1296) - (712)*(.1296)*(.713) = 26.48\ runs$$

How are these runs lost? Basically, the replacement player records outs in situations where the average player would get on base. If we had a way of measuring the expected runs gained for an offensive event where the batter reached base, and the expected runs lost for an offensive event where the batter made an out, we could estimate how much it would cost in runs each time a player made an out instead of getting on base. From there it would be a straightforward calculation to estimate the expected number of outs the replacement player makes over an average player to cost the average team the 26.48 runs.

How do we find the expected number of runs gained from each positive (on base) event and the number of runs lost from each negative (out) event? Actually, we already have this with our Extrapolated Runs formula. We only need to multiply the frequency of occurrence of the offensive events by the worth in runs for each of the events according to Extrapolated Runs coefficients.

On-Base Events	XR Coefficient	Frequency (1998 AL)
1B	0.5	14121
2B	0.72	4248
3B	1.04	408
HR	1.44	2499
HBP	0.34	762
IBB	0.25	420
UBB	0.34	7318
SB	0.18	1675
Total		**31451**

If we take a weighted average of the coefficients, we get a value of .5499. That is, each on-base event represents on average of a little over half a run gained.

Out Events	XR Coefficient	Frequency (1998 AL)
CS	-0.32	754
GIDP	-0.37	1772
SH	0.04	538
SF	0.37	711
K	-0.098	14438
Non-K Out	-0.09	42702
Total		**60915**

If we take a weighted average of the coefficients, we get a value of -.0964. That is, each negative event represents on average of about a tenth of a run lost.

So each time a Replacement player makes an out in a situation when an average player would get on base, he figures to cost his team .5499 + .0964 or .6463 runs. (For the NL in 1998, the value was .6411 runs).

Therefore, if a replacement player costs an average team 26.48 direct runs, it would be expected that he would record 26.48/.6463 or 40.97 additional outs more than an average player, given Thomas' plate appearances.

We've already calculated the **LOUT%**, or the **OUT%** for an average team at .6909, and we estimate that a replacement player would record 40.97 additional outs over an average player (given Thomas' plate appearances). Therefore **ROUT%**, the **OUT%** for a replacement player equals:

$$ROUT\% = LOUT\% + 40.97/PA = .6909 + 40.97/712 = .7484$$

To calculate our other value, **RXAVG,** we need to take the league Extrapolated Average, **LXAVG**, and multiply that by the Run Rate Deflator. Note that we are dealing with run rates here rather than runs themselves, so we need to adjust by the Run Rate Deflator as opposed to the Run Deflator.

What is the Run Rate Deflator? Well, we had earlier used this equation:

Run Scoring = (TeamOuts/OUT%) * Run Production Ability

We can use a similar type of structure to express the relationship between the production deflators for a replacement player:

Runs Deflator = (Out Rate Deflator) * (Run Rate Deflator)

The Runs Deflator was discussed in Appendix A and equal to .713. For the Out Rate Deflator:

Out Rate Deflator = (League OUT% / Replacement OUT%) = .6909 / .7484 = .9232

The Runs Deflator formula above can be re-expressed in terms of the Runs Rate Deflator:

Runs Rate Deflator = (Runs Deflator) / (Out Rate Deflator) = .713 / .9232 = .7723

Finally, for the Replacement XAVG or RXAVG:

RXAVG = LXAVG * (Runs Rate Deflator) = (.1296) * (.7723) = .1001

With values now for both **ROUT%** and **RXAVG**, we can calculate how many runs, both direct and indirect, the replacement player costs his team.

From this point, you'd proceed to the formulas under the heading "Opportunities - Replacement Player in the lineup".

XR OVER EASY

G. JAY WALKER

Rather than keep our methods proprietary, at BBBA we not only lay out our methods in detail, but we encourage our readers to use them in the privacy of their own homes, hopefully free of government regulation or intervention. Most of the time, we look for methods that will give the best results for the available data. However, this can lead to somewhat complex solutions, as you may have noticed if you checked out our park-adjustment methodology or read Extrapolated Wins article.

If you're anything like me, there are times when a rough approximation will do. There are times when I don't really care if a particular method is a half or quarter of a percent better. In fact, sometimes I might not even care if a method is 4% or 5% better, I just want something that will give me some kind of decent answer in a simple, non-time consuming manner.

Hence the XR Over Easy method. It's designed to take advantage of some of the key parts of the XR methodology in

the simplest possible way. Maybe you want to do weekly updates of the local nine without a lot of hassle, or maybe you're even sitting in candlelight during a blackout with, heaven forbid, nothing but pen and paper in hand. What better time to break out the XR Over Easy method.

Step 1 - calculate Extrapolated Runs using the basic version of the formula:

XR Basic = (.50 x 1B) + (.72 x 2B) + (1.04 x 3B) + (1.44 x HR) + (.34 x TBB) + (.18 x SB) + (-.32 x CS) + (-.096 x (AB - H))

This allows you to calculate a basic run production figure even if you don't have data available on hit batters, intentional walks, grounded into double plays or sacrifices.

Step 2 - if you want to park-adjust the results, multiply the

XR Basic found in Step 1 by the park factor found below:

Ari - 0.99	Chi - 0.97	Atl - 1.01	Ana - 1.01	Chi - 1.04
Bal - 1.03	Col - 0.79	Cin - 0.99	Flo - 1.05	Oak - 1.05
Cle - 0.98	Bos- 0.98	LA - 1.08	Hou - 1.06	Mtl - 1.03
Sea - 1.01	Det - 0.99	NYY-1.02	SD - 1.06	Mil - 0.97
NY - 1.03	Tex - 0.95	KC - 0.98	TB - 0.96	SF - 1.03
Pit - 0.97	Phi - 0.98	Min - 0.99	Tor - 1.01	StL - 1.00

You can skip this step if you want to calculate figures that aren't park adjusted. These park factors are overall factors dervied from 1995 to 1998 data. They're intended more as a guess to what the 1999 season might produce for park factors, rather than to be used for a particular season. The more formal park-adjustment method individually at the components that make up offense rather than work with an overall figure.

Step 3 - Calculate the Extrapolated Average (XAVG)using XR Basic (either park-adjusted or otherwise):

$$XAVG = (XR\ Basic)\ /\ (Plate\ Appearances)$$

This gives you a basic XR Over Easy rate stat.

Step 4 - Estimate offensive wins over replacement using XR Basic (again, either park-adjusted or otherwise):

$$Owar\ (Est.) = 0.1\ x\ (XR\ Basic) - 0.0085\ x\ (Plate\ Appearance)$$

For example, if a player has 100 XR in 500 PA, it is estiamted he produces 0.1 x 100 - 0.0085 x 500 or 5.75 offensive wins above a replacement level player.

I'm not even going to pretend this is like Extrapolated Wins, since Extrapolated Wins uses a much richer context to estimate the value of a player to his team. Nevertheless, this will provide a quick and dirty estimate of how well a batter is performing above the replacement level.

XR Over Easy will produce good results for many players; for a handful it will give distorted results. For all players you will lose the kind of precision that the complete XR/XW system gives. This isn't the system I would want to use to evaluate players at season's end or to do a historical analysis. You lose information on secondary stats like hit batsman, sacrifices and double plays, park effects are guesstimates and the accuracy is simply not as good. On the other hand, as an on-the-run method or an in-season weekly update tool, it suits the purpose just fine.

OTHER EARTHLY DELIGHTS

SECTION SEVEN

THE BBBA WEB PAGE

DON MALCOLM

As you might be able to tell, there just isn't enough room in BBBA the book for all of the material we generate. Please join us at our web site (http://www.backatcha.com) for additional data, features, and our premium service called BBBA Plus. Space limitations have forced us to make BBBA's Annotated Opinionated Glossary available at the web site, and not here in the book. Here's a look at some of the data you'll find at the site that you won't find anywhere else.

PRO+ BY POSITION

Thanks to Tom Ruane for developing a PRO+ value for 1990-1998 that applies to each of the teams and their defensive positions. We've reprinted ten of these

KC	1990	1991	1992	1993	1994	1995	1996	1997	1998	AVG
P		-100			283	-100		-59	-42	-3
C	88	105	92	111	95	76	102	75	80	91
1B	136	96	114	126	126	129	100	103	95	113
2B	69	69	102	55	88	80	98	101	114	86
3B	101	96	106	80	78	119	102	79	90	94
SS	80	82	62	91	82	74	58	111	49	76
LF	103	107	121	101	61	91	98	85	84	94
CF	124	91	79	99	91	87	78	74	93	90
RF	111	163	68	84	110	99	86	92	75	98
DH	105	104	107	92	128	79	89	127	89	102
PH	44	96	76	89	96	82	91	70	27	74
TOTAL	102	102	95	94	95	93	90	93	85	94

SEA	1990	1991	1992	1993	1994	1995	1996	1997	1998	AVG
P	-100							14	-73	-53
C	78	62	80	100	41	81	82	86	80	76
1B	97	82	91	109	113	131	115	126	117	108
2B	94	89	70	95	80	80	76	99	96	86
3B	124	131	123	106	98	104	74	87	78	102
SS	69	71	84	67	78	66	144	105	134	90
LF	109	99	94	61	79	80	88	93	94	88
CF	139	154	130	158	157	90	143	152	152	141
RF	89	106	98	124	133	121	122	122	78	110
DH	110	77	114	97	95	182	146	145	147	123
PH	58	80	67	90	128	81	77	72	53	78
TOTAL	101	98	98	102	99	104	109	112	108	103

CLE	1990	1991	1992	1993	1994	1995	1996	1997	1998	AVG
P								-54	38	-8
C	98	64	69	63	105	89	59	121	50	79
1B	89	75	105	109	96	119	112	148	137	110
2B	100	68	120	117	103	112	70	93	71	94
3B	99	105	66	104	109	148	150	103	104	109
SS	77	86	81	68	62	78	95	82	84	79
LF	109	129	103	138	180	178	158	132	100	136
CF	92	103	95	114	137	94	105	87	99	102
RF	88	88	94	88	116	147	139	138	136	114
DH	116	81	99	93	83	116	109	114	98	101
PH	106	75	78	66	80	25	126	49	78	75
TOTAL	97	89	93	100	110	118	111	112	97	103

NYY	1990	1991	1992	1993	1994	1995	1996	1997	1998	AVG
P		-100					-100	-100	-55	-88
C	87	103	106	127	133	119	86	81	102	104
1B	107	106	102	119	111	93	112	151	113	112
2B	81	107	94	88	83	80	76	84	107	88
3B	79	66	105	106	132	112	87	95	111	99
SS	47	65	79	89	74	75	100	105	117	83
LF	74	114	103	121	113	87	100	94	101	100
CF	101	93	114	102	112	126	128	148	139	118
RF	128	85	112	123	175	123	126	131	135	126
DH	97	89	101	124	102	91	109	109	128	105
PH	64	112	72	113	95	113	54	61	80	84
TOTAL	89	93	102	111	116	101	102	110	116	104

charts here; you'll find all 30 at the BBBA web site.

Tom's PRO+ numbers are park-adjusted just like the ones in Total Baseball, but instead of measuring the performance level of individual players, these values give you the offensive performance turned in by the players who played 1B for the Indians in 1990-98, or RF for the Yankees over the same period.

One of the most interesting breakouts that Tom provides is in the Indians' data, where the PRO+ figures indicate that Cleveland's offense took a serious nosedive in 1998. The decline of the Tribes' production in left field since the departure of Albert Belle is noteworthy: 178 and 158 with Belle through 1996, but 132 and 100 in the past two years.

We should mention that the PRO+ numbers are normalized to a league average baseline which is set at

100. That means that the adjusted PRO+ (park-adjusted on-base plus slugging) for Cleveland left fielders in 1995 was 78% above league average; in 1998, the Indians were at dead average. That's quite a drop.

You can also see how the Yankees' offense worked so well in 1998: every single position wound up with a PRO+ above league average.

The nine-year snapshots give you a sense of the ebb and flow for teams at various positions over the seasons. For example, the loss of Jay Bell's offense at SS was keenly felt by the Royals, whose PRO+ at SS fell from 111 in 1997 to just 49 in 1998. You can also see at a glance that left field has been an offensive sinkhole for the Mariners for vitually the entire decade.

Over in the NL, the park-adjusted data shows us that the Rockies' offense is really about at league average. The Dodgers lost a tremendous amount of firepower at catcher, going from a 175 to just 84 with the departure of Mike Piazza. Park-adjusting for Dodger Stadium, however, shows us that the LA offense had

ATL	1990	1991	1992	1993	1994	1995	1996	1997	1998	AVG
P	8	10	15	10	11	14	41	21	23	17
C	65	87	91	87	103	123	111	121	134	102
1B	92	92	121	131	171	128	130	114	156	126
2B	95	116	85	89	100	77	73	95	71	89
3B	75	139	133	102	91	112	130	130	149	117
SS	78	77	96	133	87	75	92	134	87	95
LF	127	105	115	130	124	143	139	118	95	121
CF	131	132	123	97	111	86	123	133	114	116
RF	137	135	124	139	144	120	108	108	119	126
DH								73	94	83
PH	101	74	104	100	77	74	88	65	79	84
TOTAL	95	103	105	107	108	100	109	111	109	105

SD	1990	1991	1992	1993	1994	1995	1996	1997	1998	AVG
P	9	-22	1	-24	-4	3	-8	-9	3	-5
C	92	100	89	73	82	93	87	88	104	89
1B	147	154	164	114	93	113	106	125	125	126
2B	108	110	74	98	109	97	68	89	117	96
3B	115	71	159	121	98	140	172	125	128	125
SS	87	103	95	79	75	61	84	78	116	86
LF	102	88	66	125	113	92	109	95	163	105
CF	86	102	89	89	111	115	138	105	105	104
RF	117	125	122	127	164	135	122	152	142	134
DH								95	164	129
PH	66	54	46	63	95	99	62	90	51	69
TOTAL	99	97	99	95	100	100	103	101	115	101

COL	1990	1991	1992	1993	1994	1995	1996	1997	1998	AVG
P				-10	-21	1	17	-3	4	-2
C				78	67	62	85	77	84	75
1B				137	128	100	127	130	122	124
2B				71	86	99	88	89	74	84
3B				116	103	114	107	117	132	114
SS				79	73	89	82	88	74	80
LF				86	97	121	129	106	113	108
CF				85	144	97	118	108	105	109
RF				118	116	135	104	174	152	133
DH								76	1	38
PH				55	95	125	42	84	76	79
TOTAL				89	95	99	98	104	99	97

LA	1990	1991	1992	1993	1994	1995	1996	1997	1998	AVG
P	2	2	1	28	8	-19	-26	-3	10	0
C	109	116	83	151	139	146	175	175	84	130
1B	157	105	107	95	109	153	126	117	124	121
2B	109	117	104	95	83	106	64	94	98	96
3B	111	102	86	78	137	110	89	127	86	102
SS	55	73	99	90	72	101	91	79	68	80
LF	147	118	88	88	89	94	114	89	100	103
CF	110	121	136	117	146	110	90	98	111	115
RF	112	139	92	109	117	109	133	141	139	121
DH								156	34	95
PH	60	53	118	73	112	62	92	55	71	77
TOTAL	105	102	95	97	106	106	101	107	95	101

actually been better than league average from 1994-97. That wasn't the case in 1998.

The brilliant year-in year-out performance of Barry Bonds can be seen in the Giants' LF numbers over the last six seasons--not a single year with a PRO+ value under 170. According to positional PRO+, the Giants' offense in 1998 was almost as good as the star-crossed 1993 team.

Pittsburgh and Atlanta continued their streaks of above and below-average offensive performance, with the Bucs taking an especially sharp nosedive in '98.

And note that the only other team in the past nine years to have all of its defensive positions post a PRO+ higher than 100 was the team the Yankees polished off in the 1998 World Series--the San Diego Padres. Odds are overwhelming that San Diego will not repeat this feat in 1999.

Take a look at the BBBA web page for the complete listing of 1990-98 PRO+ data.

SF	1990	1991	1992	1993	1994	1995	1996	1997	1998	AVG
P	-29	10	-29	13	3	-14	-1	-16	12	-5
C	104	68	83	98	62	86	91	79	92	84
1B	120	146	155	131	71	116	88	131	110	118
2B	87	126	106	121	73	80	69	120	135	101
3B	118	131	97	143	146	137	121	105	114	123
SS	81	60	79	90	78	78	76	88	89	79
LF	141	131	104	209	175	171	186	174	176	163
CF	120	112	91	74	88	90	87	97	106	96
RF	93	88	94	119	112	102	103	95	115	102
DH								51	5	28
PH	108	66	88	49	84	54	53	99	86	76
TOTAL	100	101	94	113	95	98	94	103	110	100

PIT	1990	1991	1992	1993	1994	1995	1996	1997	1998	AVG
P		12	-15	-1	12	5	-2	-27	-7	-2
C	103	118	115	96	90	83	108	117	132	106
1B	127	121	91	83	94	100	118	109	112	106
2B	84	77	67	90	78	91	93	91	75	82
3B	110	124	98	105	85	98	88	108	72	98
SS	98	117	101	119	117	105	96	109	70	103
LF	167	159	200	122	109	95	110	111	77	127
CF	129	115	150	112	94	92	85	86	96	106
RF	138	133	85	111	97	109	108	101	92	108
DH								145	102	123
PH	64	98	86	107	76	85	117	87	56	86
TOTAL	109	112	104	99	90	91	96	96	84	97

Sean Forman's

PROSPECT WATCH

Prospectwatch: Top picks for 1999

Here are the top prospects in all the land, from sea to shining sea. The list is based on past performance, defensive position, and future potential. Note: all the values (2B, HR, etc.) are projected out to 600 plate appearances.

AL ROY: JEREMY GIAMBI
NL ROY: J.D. DREW

HIGH MINORS (STILL ROY ELIGIBLE)

Name	Age	POS	Affil	League	PA	Grade	BA / OBP/ SLG	2B	3B	HR	BB	SO	SB
Eric Chavez	20	3B	OAK	AAA-PCL	206	110	.325/.364/.588	52	0	32	35	93	6
				AA-SL	368	99	.324/.399/.606	44	2	34	67	99	18
J.D. Drew	22	OF	STL	AA-TL	101	97	.316/.465/.519	48	6	12	131	107	6
Russ Branyan	22	3B	CLE	AA-EL	198	93	.294/.419/.693	33	9	48	106	176	3
Chad Hermansen	20	OF	PIT	AAA-PCL	508	103	.258/.331/.520	31	6	33	59	180	25
Jeremy Giambi	23	OF	KCR	AAA-PCL	382	95	.372/.466/.634	33	3	31	90	101	13
Calvin Pickering	21	1B	BAL	AA-EL	586	86	.303/.418/.556	28	2	32	99	123	4
Ruben Mateo	20	OF	TEX	AA-TL	463	83	.309/.354/.522	41	4	23	39	73	23
Ron Belliard	23	2B	MIL	AAA-PCL	576	81	.321/.403/.503	38	7	15	72	80	33
Lance Berkman	22	OF	HOU	AA-TL	510	74	.306/.422/.555	40	0	28	100	96	7
Mitch Meluskey	24	C	HOU	AAA-PCL	478	83	.356/.471/.590	51	0	21	107	72	3
Dernell Stenson	20	OF	BOS	AA-EL	585	76	.255/.361/.436	21	1	24	85	138	5
Michael Barrett	21	C	MON	AA-EL	476	75	.318/.357/.526	40	3	24	34	54	9
Carlos Febles	22	2B	KCR	AA-TL	502	82	.326/.428/.531	32	11	17	91	81	61
George Lombard	22	OF	ATL	AA-SL	493	79	.308/.408/.543	30	5	27	86	170	43
Mario Encarnacion	20	OF	OAK	AA-SL	407	78	.270/.376/.454	22	3	22	87	177	16
Gabe Kapler	22	OF	DET	AA-SL	613	74	.322/.395/.583	46	6	27	65	91	6
Ben Petrick	21	C	COL	AA-EL	405	72	.238/.343/.470	31	4	27	83	132	10
Alex Gonzalez	21	SS	FLA	AAA-IL	450	76	.277/.322/.443	27	13	13	37	107	5
Ben Davis	21	C	SDP	AA-SL	475	63	.286/.349/.460	37	3	18	53	76	5
Ricky Ledee	24	OF	NYY	AAA-IL	414	64	.283/.377/.506	30	1	28	78	157	10